LSAT®

PrepTests 52–61

Unlocked

Exclusive Data, Analysis, & Explanations for
10 New Actual, Official LSAT PrepTests with
Comparative Reading

KAPLAN

PUBLISHING

New York

LSAT® is a registered mark of the Law School Admission Council, Inc.

© 2018 by Kaplan, Inc.

Published by Kaplan Publishing, a division of Kaplan, Inc.
750 Third Avenue
New York, NY 10017

ISBN: 978-1-5062-3706-0
10 9 8 7 6 5 4 3 2 1

Kaplan Publishing print books are available at special quantity discounts to use for sales promotions, employee premiums, or educational purposes. For more information or to purchase books, please call the Simon & Schuster special sales department at 866-506-1949.

Table of Contents

Introduction

About This Book

This book contains complete explanations to every question from officially released LSAT PrepTests 52 through 61, along with exclusive data and analysis of test taker performance and question difficulty on each one of these LSAT exams. It is the perfect companion to these tests individually, or to the LSAC's bundle of these tests released under the title *10 New Actual, Official LSAT PrepTests With Comparative Reading*.

Whether you are taking a prep course or studying on your own, taking officially released LSATs is an essential component of successful preparation. LSAT students are fortunate that LSAC (the organization that develops and administers the test) has historically released three LSATs—the test forms given in June, in the Fall, and in December—each year. Practice with recent LSATs is especially valuable, and the tests covered by this book range from the test administration in September 2007 through the one in October 2010. Although some of those tests are over 10 years old at this point, they are still largely representative of today's test structure because they all contain the last major test change—the introduction of Comparative Reading, which debuted in June 2007.

While practice tests are necessary, LSAT experts will tell you that simply taking and scoring tests isn't sufficient to maximize your score improvement. You need to know why you missed questions, and how to get to the right answers even more efficiently. That's where this companion comes in. For each of the 10 tests explained and analyzed here, Kaplan provides exclusive data about how test takers perceived the tests' difficulty. We then compare that to actual student performance on the test, and we identify each test's 10 most difficult questions and categorize the difficulty of all of the test's questions. You'll also see how representative each test is of the LSAT's most recent trends and learn about anything that makes a particular test administration unique or unusual. Finally, you get complete explanations for every question, game, and passage in the test, including explanations for every wrong answer.

Start by reading the section called "Introduction: How to Use Kaplan LSAT Explanations," so that you get familiar with Kaplan's methods, strategies, and terminology. Then, after taking any of the practice tests covered by this volume, put your practice experience in context by reading the test's "Inside Story" page. Finally, review your performance on any question, game, or passage from the test. Kaplan's LSAT experts encourage you to review every question—even those you got right—to learn how top LSAT scorers use patterns to approach the exam effectively and efficiently.

No matter how you choose to use the information and explanations included in this book, Kaplan is here to encourage and support your study and practice. For over 70 years, our commitment has been to raise scores for every test taker. So, here's to good luck, and, more importantly, good preparation!

How to Review a PrepTest

Taking full-length practice LSAT tests is an essential part of comprehensive preparation for this important exam. Not only do practice tests contain examples of all the questions, games, and passages used by the testmaker, but by taking practice LSATs, you also get a feel for the timing restrictions that make each section of the LSAT so challenging. Moreover, when you take full-length exams, you approximate the endurance and stamina demands of Test Day.

The LSAT is unique among the major post-graduate admissions exams in that the LSAC (the organization that creates and administers the LSAT) releases three previously administered, official LSAT tests each year. To help our students get the most out of these valuable practice resources, Kaplan has a team of LSAT experts who evaluate each test, and write comprehensive explanations for every question (indeed, for every answer choice) immediately after the exam's release. Now, for the first time, we are making these explanations available to everyone who is serious about his or her LSAT preparation.

Here are a few tips for the best way to use the explanations.

1. Learn the Kaplan Methods for Each Section

Every official LSAT contains two sections of Logical Reasoning, and one section each of Logic Games (or Analytical Reasoning, as the LSAC calls it) and Reading Comprehension. Test takers who train with Kaplan learn simple but highly effective methods for the questions, games, and passages in these sections. Thus, our explanations are written so that they follow the steps of those methods consistently. As you review the questions in the test, the explanations here will not only explain why a particular answer is correct, it will show you how an LSAT expert efficiently untangles the question, and how she can demonstrate that all four other answers are incorrect.

The Kaplan Methods for each type of scored section are outlined for each section later in this chapter. The methods are somewhat intuitive, so you'll get the gist of each one pretty quickly. In addition, you'll learn about some of the specific strategies Kaplan students learn in class. Keep an eye out for those strategies again as you review the questions in your test.

Terminology and Definitions

In our comprehensive LSAT prep courses, Kaplan students learn a sweeping vocabulary of terms, categories, and distinctions for the question types, patterns of reasoning, flaws, conclusions, and rhetorical devices employed by the testmaker. If you are not currently in a Kaplan LSAT prep course, you may come across terms with which you're unfamiliar, or unsure how to understand in the context of the test. For such terms, we've created a glossary that you can find at the back of this book.

2. Evaluate Timed Practice Differently than Untimed Practice

We'll stipulate that you have already completed the test. Why else would you be looking at the explanations? Now, a couple of questions: First, did you take the LSAT under strict, timed conditions? If you did, review questions in context. Were you running out of time near the end of the section? Did you have to guess? Did you spend far too long to get one or two questions correct, thus costing yourself the opportunity to try other questions? Many of the explanations in this book will give you strategies for answering questions more efficiently and effectively, as well as always explaining how to answer them correctly. Speed and confidence can be important to your score on Test Day—in some cases, as important as expertise.

If you did not time yourself, or if you gave yourself extra time to complete the LSAT, review the questions to assess your mastery of LSAT skills. There is nothing wrong with untimed practice. Indeed, Kaplan's expert LSAT instructors encourage their students to engage in untimed, mastery practice whenever the students learn a new question type. When you are reviewing a test on which you took extra time, your focus should be on assessing how you did on each step of each question, and especially on how well you executed the skills rewarded by the LSAT.

3. Note the Question Difficulty

At the beginning of each section of explanations, you will see a list of the questions in that section of the test. For each question, we provide the question type and a difficulty rating of between 1 star (easiest) and 4 stars (hardest). Pay attention to the difficulty level of the questions you got right and those you missed.

Because our students take official, released LSAT tests for practice during their courses, we at Kaplan have hundreds of thousands of data points on the questions in these released tests. We can accurately determine the difficulty of every question on each exam, and even determine which incorrect answers gave students the most trouble, and which ones they dismissed easily.

Here's how the star ratings work. Four-star questions are the 10 most difficult questions on the test. Typically these are answered correctly by one-third of students or less. The next 20 questions in difficulty are assigned a 3-star rating. The next 30 get a 2-star rating. And, the rest (the easiest 40 or 41 questions on the exam) are given a 1-star rating. On most LSATs, the 1-star questions are answered correctly by 70 percent or more of students.

The difficulty ratings help you assess your performance in two important ways. First, when you miss a 4-star or 3-star question, you're in good company. These questions are difficult for most students. Study the explanation to a 4- or 3-star question carefully, and note the strategic approaches that allows LSAT experts to solve these tough verbal and reasoning puzzles. On the other hand, when you miss a 1- or 2-star question, focus on where you may have misinterpreted the instructions or some key piece of information. While these questions are not too hard for most students, even top scorers occasionally miss 1- and 2-star questions, usually because of same kinds of oversights you'll see cleared up in the explanations in this book.

The second way difficulty ratings can help you is by providing insight into your score. Here is a chart showing how raw score (the number of correct answers a test taker generates) translates into scaled score (the 120 to 180 score law schools see on your score report) and into percentile (the percentage of test takers who scored below you on a given exam).

Raw Score (#correct)	Scaled Score	Percentile
92	172	99th
85	167	95th
81	164	90th
74	160	80th
67	156	70th
63	154	60th
58	151	50th
55	149	40th
50	146	30th
45	143	10th
39	139	10th

How raw score (number of questions correct)
translates into scaled score and percentile ranking

PrepTest 77 (December 2015)

Because the LSAC score report is comparing you to all those who took your test, and to the cohort of applicants likely to apply to law school at the same time you do, the translation from raw score to scaled score and percentile change slightly from test to test. This chart, however, provides a good estimate of scoring on most recent LSATs. As you can see, on most tests, you could miss nine of the ten 4-star questions and still score a 172, placing you in the 99th percentile, and giving you a score competitive at any law school in the country. Were you to miss all of the 4- and 3-star questions, you would still get 71 correct answers, producing a scaled score around 158, better than 75 percent of test takers. To place above the 50th percentile (or, to score over 151, if you like), you'll need to get about 58 correct answers, that's all of the 1-star and not quite a majority of the 2-star questions. Now, most test takers get a mixture of easier and harder questions right, and even top scorers occasionally mess up and miss a 1-star question. But, take note of what happens once you are scoring over the 50th percentile: adding between five and ten correct answers to your performance can move your percentile score up 10 points or more, making your application stronger than those of thousands of other test takers.

4. Recognize Patterns in the LSAT and in Your Performance

As a standardized test, the LSAT is nothing if not predictable. You won't know the content of the questions or passages you'll see on your official exam, of course, but repeated practice can reveal patterns that will help you improve your performance. As you review multiple tests, you will begin to see that certain question types recur with greater or lesser frequency. Moreover, each question type is amenable to a handful of expert strategies, which are often outlined in the explanations in this book. Beyond the patterns associated with question strategies and correct answers, you'll see that even the incorrect answers regularly fall into a handful of definite types as well. Whenever this is the case, the Kaplan explanations will highlight and articulate the incorrect answer pattern.

Use these patterns and categories to help assess your own performance. Ask yourself the following questions, and answer honestly. Do you regularly struggle with a particular Logic Reasoning question type? Is a certain pattern in Logic Games easier for you? Does another game type trip you up? Do some topics or question types in Reading Comprehension give you more trouble than others? Throughout the test, are there incorrect answer types to which you are routinely susceptible?

In our comprehensive Kaplan LSAT prep courses, we provide tools that help all of our students identify their individual strengths and weaknesses, and then we provide personalized instruction to help them maximize their potential on the test. If you are preparing on your own, identifying the patterns that impact your performance (for better or worse) will require more time and attention, but don't skip this important part of review. Determine your areas of greatest opportunities for improvement, and focus on them as you continue your practice. That leads directly to the next tip.

5. Apply What You Learn

This is the most significant tip of all. Taking a practice LSAT is important. If you complete your practice test under timed, test-like conditions, it will give you a great snapshot of your performance as it stands now. But, to get a genuine understanding of your strengths and opportunities—and, more importantly, to improve your performance—you need to take and review multiple tests.

The greatest value of these explanations is that you can use each practice test to evaluate your performance. That will point you in the right direction the next time you practice. Don't be content with getting a question right. Review the explanation until you are satisfied that you can get a similar question right the next time you see one, and that you can get it right as quickly and efficiently as you'll need to under the time constraints of the test. When you get a question wrong, don't simply read the correct answer and think, "Oh, I get it now." Make sure you know how you misread or misunderstood the question, and why the particular incorrect answer you chose was tempting.

Practice and review the LSAT consistently with the help of expert explanations, and you will improve.

Logical Reasoning Method and Strategies

The Kaplan Method for Logical Reasoning has four steps. The order of Steps 1 and 2 may surprise you a little bit.

LOGICAL REASONING METHOD

1. Identify the Question Type
2. Untangle the Stimulus
3. Predict the Correct Answer
4. Evaluate the Answer Choices

Every Logical Reasoning question has three easily identifiable parts: the stimulus, the question stem, and five answer choices. The **stimulus** is the paragraph or short dialogue at the top of the question; it may contain an argument or a set of statements. Beneath the stimulus is the **question stem**; it gives the test taker her task, e.g., identify an assumption in the argument, pick the answer that makes the argument stronger or weaker, describe a flaw in the author's reasoning, or choose the answer that follows from the statements in the stimulus. Underneath the question stem, there are five **answer choices**, exactly one of which fulfills the task called for by the question stem; the other four answer choices are demonstrably incorrect.

The Kaplan Method for Logical Reasoning takes the most efficient and strategic route through the questions. You will see this Method reflected in the explanations to every Logical Reasoning question.

Step 1: Identify the Question Type

Begin with the question stem. Find out what your task is. That way, you'll know what to look for as you are analyzing the stimulus. The explanations will show you how an expert approaches the stimulus differently depending on the question type found in the question stem.

LOGICAL REASONING STRATEGY

Identify the Question Type

As you review your test, take note of the task, or question type, for every Logical Reasoning question. You'll soon notice that certain question types are more prevalent. Moreover, you'll begin to see how LSAT experts approach the same question types consistently to maximize their accuracy and speed. Note: Every question type is defined in the glossary.

Step 2: Untangle the Stimulus

Once you understand your task, read the stimulus actively, focusing on the sentences or statements that will help you choose the correct answer.

LOGICAL REASONING STRATEGY

Effectively Analyze Arguments

In questions that ask you to analyze an **argument**, you will want to first locate and paraphrase the author's **conclusion**, meaning the assertion or opinion about which the author is trying to convince the reader. After identifying the conclusion, focus on the author's **evidence**, the statements or premises the author offers in support of the conclusion. Many questions require that you then determine the author's **assumption**(s), the unstated premise(s) that logically connect the evidence to the conclusion.

The explanations will outline expert argument analysis whenever it is relevant, but here's a simple demonstration. Imagine a stimulus with this simple argument:

This raspberry lemonade is a very sour drink. Therefore, it will not pair well with the pasta dish.

Here, the author's conclusion is that the raspberry lemonade will not pair well with the pasta dish. His evidence is that the raspberry lemonade is quite sour. From this, you can determine that the author assumes that very sour drinks will not pair well with the pasta dish. You may agree or disagree with the author; the LSAT doesn't care about that. The test will reward you for being able to untangle and analyze the explicit (conclusion and evidence) and implicit (assumption) parts of the author's argument. You'll see argument analysis demonstrated in a majority of the Logical Reasoning explanations.

LOGICAL REASONING STRATEGY

Effectively Catalog Statements

In cases where the stimulus does *not* contain an argument, the LSAT typically rewards you either for making a valid inference based on the stimulus, or for resolving an apparent paradox described in the stimulus. Because there is usually no argument in these stimuli, LSAT experts approach them differently, but no less strategically.

In non-argument-based questions, experts note five patterns:

Concrete statements/assertions: The statement "All students at State U must complete Composition 102" is far stronger, and thus more likely to lead to valid deductions, than a statement such as "Some students at State U have taken Professor Manning's archaeology seminar."

Shared terms: When two statements share a term, they often combine to produce valid deductions. For example, if the author tells you that "Project X receives government funding," and then tells you that "projects which receive government funding are subject to annual review," you can infer that Project X is subject to annual review.

Keywords: Words that highlight how an author thinks two statements relate to one another can be helpful in making inferences. Consider what you can infer about a fictional politician named Carson in the following sentence: "The population of Crow County is quite conservative, *but* Carson is likely to be elected Commissioner." That's quite different than what we could infer were the author to say: "The population of Crow County is quite conservative, *and so* Carson is likely to be elected Commissioner."

By the way, every Paradox question stimulus will contain a contrast Keyword, highlighting the two seemingly contradictory statements at issue.

Conditional statements: Also known as Formal Logic, conditional (or "If-then") statements are powerful tools for making valid inferences. Consider a statement such as "If Rebecca auditions for the role of Desdemona, then Jonas will audition for the role of Hamlet." This makes Jonas's audition necessary for Rebecca's. If this stimulus went on to say, "Jonas will not audition for the role of Hamlet," then you can deduce that Rebecca will not audition for the role of Desdemona. Note: Formal Logic is discussed further at the end of this chapter.

Uncertain statements: Statements containing terms such as *some, several,* and *most* are less concrete than those containing *all, every,* or *none.* LSAT experts, however, learn to recognize patterns to produce valid deductions. One of these patterns, fairly common on the LSAT, is a pair of "most" statements. For example, if a stimulus states that "Most members of the water polo team are in-state students," and tells you that "Most members of the water polo team are scholarship athletes," an LSAT expert will deduce that "At least one in-state student is a scholarship athlete."

Untrained test takers instinctively read the stimulus first, after all, it is at the top of the question. When they next read the question stem, however, they often have to reread the stimulus now that they know their task. The Kaplan Method for Logical Reasoning eliminates this redundancy. The strategies outlined here help the well-trained test taker zero in on the relevant, helpful statements in the stimulus.

Step 3: Predict the Correct Answer

After untangling the stimulus, an LSAT expert will pause very briefly to paraphrase what the correct answer must say. This allows the expert to evaluate the answer choices more efficiently and effectively.

Without pausing to "pre-phrase" the correct answer, a test taker is likely to read answer choice (A), and then to reread the stimulus. If still unsure whether choice (A) is correct, this untrained test taker will do the same thing with choices (B), and (C), and so on. This reading, rereading, and comparing of answer choices is far too time consuming, and can make you more confused about the question than you were to begin with.

An LSAT expert, armed with a strong prediction, evaluates the answer choices by asking, "Does this answer choice match my prediction?" If the answer is "No," she crosses it out. If the answer is "Yes," she can confidently circle it and move on to the next question.

LOGICAL REASONING STRATEGY

Accurately Predict Correct Answers

Different Logical Reasoning question types (e.g., Assumption, Strengthen/Weaken, Flaw, Inference) reward different skills. LSAT experts learn to predict correct answers accurately and in the ways that best fit the different question stem tasks.

Here are some of the ways LSAT experts treat the prediction step differently in the most common Logical Reasoning questions.

Assumption questions: In the simplest arguments, it's easy to spot (and to state) the author's assumption. For example, if an author concludes that "Socrates is mortal" because of evidence that "Socrates is human," then this author is assuming (correctly, in fact) that "Humans are mortal." On the LSAT, however, arguments are usually a bit more complex than that. Moreover, the LSAT may ask for an assumption *necessary* to the author's argument, or for an assumption *sufficient* to establish the author's conclusion. In the explanations, you'll see how LSAT experts predict the correct answer differently depending on the Assumption question stem.

Strengthen/Weaken questions: In these questions, the correct answer states a fact that makes the author's conclusion more or less likely to follow from the author's evidence. That's different than saying that the answer will prove or disprove the argument. For example, if an author argues that "The new public tennis courts will not be built because MegaCorp has withdrawn its offer to fund the new public tennis courts," the author assumes that *only* MegaCorp's funding would make the construction of new courts possible. To weaken that argument, the test will provide a correct answer that names a potential alternate source of funding. That is the LSAT expert's prediction: "The correct answer here will point out another way to pay for the construction." The LSAT expert does not try to guess which source the test will choose (a tax levy, a bond issue, a wealthy philanthropist, a private tennis club), but he knows with confidence that the one correct answer will provide an alternative source and that the four incorrect answers will not.

Flaw questions: It is common for some Flaw questions to be among the toughest questions on a given LSAT. That's because they ask you to describe an error in the author's reasoning. The answer choices often contain abstract wording and avoid reference to the subject matter of the stimulus. For a Kaplan-trained LSAT expert, however, Flaw questions can be among the easiest for predicting what the correct answer will contain. That's because there are a handful of Flaw types that the testmaker uses again and again. Some of them will sound familiar (ad hominem, circular reasoning, correlation versus causation, unrepresentative samples, equivocation) even if you can't easily define them at this point. Of course, the explanations will always point out these common flaw types when they appear in questions or in answer choices, and definitions of every flaw type appear in the glossary.

Inference questions: These are often the hardest questions in which to accurately predict the correct answer. After all, there are sometimes dozens of things you could infer from a series of three or four statements. When you are preparing to evaluate the answer choices in Inference questions, pay careful attention to the question stem. Does it ask for a correct answer that "must be true" given the statements in the stimulus, or does it ask for the one that is "most strongly suggested" by the statements in the stimulus? Beyond that, keep an eye out for the patterns discussed above in the strategy labeled "Effectively Catalog Statements." If you are given two statements that share a common term, or if you spot conditional statements, you can be fairly certain that the testmaker wants you to use those tools to reach the correct answer.

Step 4: Evaluate the Answer Choices

In the discussion of Step 3, you saw how an LSAT expert uses a solid prediction of the correct answer to confidently evaluate each answer choice. Test takers who truly master the Logical Reasoning Method become so confident that, if choice (C) is clearly the correct answer, they may not check choices (D) and (E) at all, or if they do, they do so quickly, just to confirm that they are clearly incorrect. In the explanations in this book, we always present the correct answer first to reinforce the strategies of predicting and evaluating. In addition, we discuss each wrong answer thoroughly, even though you (if you follow the Method) may not need such thorough analysis on Test Day.

LOGICAL REASONING STRATEGY

Spot Common Wrong Answer Patterns

The LSAT is so standardized, that particular types of incorrect answers appear over and over throughout the test. Spotting these common wrong answer types will make you more efficient throughout the Logical Reasoning section.

The most common wrong answer type is Outside the Scope, an answer that introduces a fact or consideration irrelevant to the argument or statements in the stimulus. Other important wrong answer types include 180 and Extreme. A 180 incorrect answer states exactly the opposite of what the correct answer must say. These 180 answers can be effective "traps" for an inattentive test taker. If the correct answer must weaken an argument, for example, it's not uncommon for one or more of the wrong answers to effectively strengthen the argument. Extreme wrong answers stay within the scope of the stimulus, but overstate what the correct must say. If you can infer, for example, that at least one in-state student is a scholarship athlete, one of the wrong answers might state that "most in-state students are scholarship athletes."

NOTE: There are a handful of other incorrect answer patterns. Whenever an answer choice fits one of the these patterns, the explanations will make note of the pattern, and the term describing the incorrect answer type will be defined in the glossary.

In our comprehensive LSAT prep courses, Kaplan students learn and practice the Logical Reasoning Method over several class sessions, and in dozens of additional *LSAT Channel* lessons and homework assignments. If you are not in a Kaplan course, we still want you to improve your LSAT score as much as possible. That's why we make the Logical Reasoning Method the foundation of every question's explanation, and why we always highlight and explain the strategies outlined here.

Logic Games Method and Strategies

Every Logic Games section contains four games, each with five to seven questions. To finish the section within the allotted 35 minutes, you need to average around 8 and 1/2 minutes per game. That's a tall order, one most test takers are not able to fill. The Kaplan Method for Logic Games is designed to attain the maximum combination of speed and accuracy within this section.

LOGIC GAMES METHOD

    1. Overview
    2. Sketch
    3. Rules
    4. Deductions
    5. Questions

You may find it striking that the LSAT expert completes four steps in this Method before turning her attention to the questions. That seems counter-intuitive. Don't we want to get to the questions as quickly as possible? As you study the logic games explanations in this book, however, you'll see that the expert's approach, which involves organizing the game's information first, allows her to answer the questions much more efficiently, sometimes in a matter of seconds. These explanations will demonstrate the enormous power of patience in logic games, and will convince you of the value of consistently applying the Method to every game you encounter.

To understand what each step involves, let's first define the parts of a logic game as they appear in the test booklet. To conduct your overview of the game, you'll examine the game's **setup**, the short description of the game's situation, entities (the people or things you're asked to arrange in the game), and action (the game's task). Beneath the setup, the testmaker always includes some **rules**, which are listed in indented text. These rules provide restrictions on how the entities may behave within the game's action and framework. After that, you'll see the game's **questions**. In most games, one or more of the questions will begin with a hypothetical "If" condition. Such a condition acts like an additional rule, but it applies *only* to that individual question. Keep your Master Sketch with the rules that apply throughout the game separate from your scratchwork on individual questions containing New-"If"s that are unique to that question.

Step 1: Overview

The goal here is to have a clear mental picture of your task. Ideally, you could describe your job within the game in a single sentence, e.g., "I will be dividing eight students into two teams of four with no overlap," or "From among seven books, I will select four and reject three." Be as precise as you can without overstating the limitations imposed by the setup. Make sure, for example, that the game asks you to choose "exactly four books" and not "at least four books." In logic games, every word is important.

LOGIC GAMES STRATEGY

Ask the SEAL Questions to Conduct Your Overview

To make sure that they have a strong grasp of the game's layout and task, LSAT experts ask four questions, known to Kaplan students by the acronym SEAL, from the first letter of each word.

What is/are the...

Situation—What is the real-world scenario being described? What is the deliverable information—an ordered list, a calendar, a chart showing what's matched up?

Entities—Who or what are the "moving parts," the people or things I'm distributing, selecting, sequencing, or matching?

Action—What is the specific action—distribution, selection, sequencing, matching, or a combination of those—that I'm performing on the entities?

Limitations—Does the game state parameters (e.g., select exactly four of the seven, sequence the entities one per day) that determine or restrict how I'll set up and sketch the game?

Throughout Kaplan Logic Games explanations, the LSAT experts will often break down their Overviews just like this. Be sure you see what they see before you move into the complicated rules and deductions.

Step 2: Sketch

Based on your Overview, create a simple framework in which you record and organize the game's information, rules, and limitations. The testmaker uses just a handful of game types, so as you review your work and study the expert's sketches in the explanations, learn to identify the most common actions and the sketches typically associated with them. Here are two good rules of thumb: 1) Always list out the entities in abbreviation (e.g., M O P T W Y) above your sketch framework, and 2) make your framework as simple and easy to copy as possible (since you will want to repeat it when a question offers you a New-"If" condition).

LOGIC GAMES STRATEGY

Learn the Standard Sketch for Each Game Type

Every game needs a Master Sketch. It provides a framework into which you can build the rules and restrictions that will allow you to answer the questions. Fortunately, the LSAT uses the same game types test after test, and you can learn some standard patterns that will save you time and frustration on Test Day. Here's how LSAT experts typically set up the most common game actions.

Strict Sequencing—These games ask you to arrange or schedule entities in numbered positions, or on specific days or times. A series of numbered slots (either horizontal or vertical) usually suits this task.

$$\text{A B C D E F}$$

$$\underline{} \quad \underline{} \quad \underline{} \quad \underline{} \quad \underline{} \quad \underline{}$$
$$\ \ 1 \quad\ \ 2 \quad\ \ 3 \quad\ \ 4 \quad\ \ 5 \quad\ \ 6$$

Loose Sequencing—These games are similar to Strict Sequencing, but here, the setup does not provide numbered slots or days of the week. Instead, all of the rules describe the relative position of two or more entities. The rules can be combined to show all of the known relationships among the entities.

Selection—These games ask you to choose or select a smaller group of entities out of a longer list. All you really need here is a roster of all the entities. Then, you can circle those selected and cross out those rejected.

A B C D E F G

Matching—These games ask you to match up members of one group with those of another, or to assign certain attributes to some members and different attributes to others. A list or grid fits the bill here.

x y z

A	B	C	D	E	F

or

	A	B	C	D	E	F
x						
y						
z						

Distribution—These games give you a group of entities and ask you to break it up into smaller groups (two or three smaller groups is most common, but you will see four on occasion).

L M N O P R S

1	2	3

For every game, the Kaplan explanations will show the LSAT expert's initial sketch framework and explain how she chose it. Then, you'll see how the expert develops the sketch to accommodate the rules and deductions provided by the game. Study the sketches carefully and make sure you see why the expert chose the one she did.

Now, some games may have twists or special requirements that require you to vary or add to these standard sketches, and Hybrid games combine two or three of the standard actions together. Don't let these exceptions deter you from learning the standard sketches. Once you know the common patterns, it will be easier to see how LSAT experts can account for the unique features of any game within them.

Step 3: Rules

Once you have created a sketch framework, you will then analyze and sketch each rule. Make sure to consider what each rule does and does not determine. Again, every word in Logic Games is important. A rule stating that "A gives his presentation on a day earlier than the day on which B gives his presentation" is different than one stating that "A gives his presentation on

KAPLAN

the day immediately before the day on which B gives his presentation," and both are distinct from the rule "A gives his presentation on the day immediately before or the day immediately after the day on which B give his presentation." As you review the explanations, pay careful attention to how the LSAT expert sketched out each rule to make sure you didn't over- or under-determine the rule's scope.

LOGIC GAMES STRATEGY

Build Rules Directly into the Sketch Framework

Always seek to depict rules in the most concrete, helpful way possible. If you can, build them right into the sketch, so that you can see their impact on the setup and the entities.

When you encounter a rule that establishes exactly where an entity should go, your instinct will rightly be to place that entity right into your sketch framework. Consider, for example, a game that asks you to sequence six entities—A, B, C, D, E, and F—into six numbered positions—1 through 6. If you get a rule that says "D will be placed in Position 4," you'll just jot down "D" on top of that slot in your framework. Perfect! The entity can't move, and you'll always see where it is.

With other types of rules, however, many test takers do not add them to the sketch in the most helpful way. When analyzing Logic Games rules, LSAT experts always consider what the rules does and does not restrict. Sometimes, the negative implications of a rule are stronger than its affirmative ones. For example, consider a game that asks you to sequence six entities—A, B, C, D, E, and F—into six numbered positions—1 through 6. A typical rule for that game might say: C must be placed before A. You could jot down something like "C ... A," but that doesn't tell you anything concrete. You cannot easily place that into your sketch framework. The negative implications of that rule, however, are very strict: C absolutely cannot go in position 6, and A absolutely cannot go in position 1. If you write something like "~C" directly underneath slot 6 and "~A" underneath slot 1 in your sketch, you will have a very clear visual depiction of this rule.

Throughout the Kaplan explanations, take time to study how LSAT experts draw and depict the rules. It's okay if your drawings don't look identical to those in the explanations, but you're sure to encounter a few instances in which the expert's sketch makes a lot of sense, and teaches you a few new tactics for handling games and their rules.

Step 4: Deductions

This is the step that most untrained test takers miss, but it is also the step that can transform your performance on a game. Deductions arise when you are able to combine rules and restrictions to determine additional information. Logic games reward test takers for being able to quickly and accurately determine what must, can, and cannot be true about the entities in the game, and deductions can increase your brain's processing power enormously. Take the simplest kind of deduction, accounting for "Duplications," in other words, entities mentioned in more than one rule. Here's the scenario:

In a game that asks you to arrange six entities (call them A, B, C, D, E, and F) into six hour long spots from 1 PM through 6 PM, you have two rules:

  B gets an earlier spot than C.
  D gets a later spot than C.

Combining those two rules (B ... C and C ... D) produces a three-entity list (B ... C ... D). That's pretty routine, but consider the implications. You now know that D will never take 1 PM or 2 PM, that C will never take 1 PM or 6 PM, and that B will never take 5 PM or 6 PM.

Most deductions are more elusive than that, and some are even more powerful in their effects on the entities within the game. As you review your work and study the explanations, pay attention to the deductions made by the LSAT experts.

Especially in games where you feel that you really struggled, discovering that there was an available deduction that you missed can make the entire game clearer and more comprehensible.

LOGIC GAMES STRATEGY

Use the BLEND Checklist to Make All Available Deductions

One of the hardest things to learn to do in logic games is to make all of the deductions quickly, and then to be confident enough that there are no more deductions that you can move on to tackle the question set. To help with this difficult task, Kaplan's LSAT experts have created a mnemonic of the five most common deduction-producing patterns seen in the rules and restrictions. We call it BLEND, for the first letter of each item in the list. Check for these patterns, and you'll be sure you don't overlook an available deduction, and you'll know when there are no more deductions to be found.

Blocks of Entities: When a rule forces two or more entities to occupy adjacent spaces in a list, or to be placed together in a group, check to see where space is available for them, and where they may prevent other entities from appearing.

Limited Options: When a rule (or combination of rules) restricts the entire game to just two or three patterns, LSAT experts will often create dual sketches to depict the game. Pay careful attention to Limited Options in the explanations. They aren't always easy to spot, but when they occur, they make the questions much, much easier to answer.

Established Entities: When a rule (or combination of rules) restricts an entity to just one space in a list, or forces the entity to be placed into a particular group, note it. This is powerful not only because you have firmly placed one entity, but also because that entity's placement may prevent others from being assigned to the same position or group.

Number Restrictions: When rules and limitations within a game restrict the number of entities that may be placed into a particular group, it makes the game much easier to solve. Being asked to split up seven students into two teams doesn't tell you much, but deducing that Team A must have three students and Team B must have four tells you a lot.

Duplications: When an entity appears in two rules, it allows the rules to be combined. We just described the simple B ... C + C ... D = B ... C ... D type of duplication, but duplications can be far more sophisticated, and may appear in any type of logic game.

In the explanations to every game, the expert will note when one or more of these patterns appears, and the term will appear in the glossary in case you've forgotten how it's defined.

Step 5: Questions

We alluded to the fact that logic games reward you for being able to determine what must, can, and cannot be true about the placement of the entities within the game. Scan the questions from any logic games section, and you'll see multiple variations asking "Which one of the following is an acceptable arrangement/could be true/must be false/etc.?" Throughout the explanations, you'll see how an LSAT expert uses the Master Sketch (including the additional deductions he's made) to make short work of these questions.

Quite often, the question stem opens with a New-"If" condition, but then asks one of these same questions given the new constraint or limitation. In most cases, LSAT experts tackle these with new "mini-sketches" so that they can make the new condition concrete. This strategy is discussed briefly here.

LOGIC GAMES STRATEGY

Use "Mini-sketches" to Take Control of New-"If" Questions

One "rookie mistake" that untrained test takers will make in Logic Games is to create a Master Sketch for a game and then try to use it for all of the game's New-"If" questions. Let's say a game has five questions, and when our untrained test taker comes to Question 2, he sees that it begins with a New-"If" condition. He then adds the new restrictions into his overall Master Sketch and works out the implications. That's great for that one question, but here are a few reasons why it's a bad strategy for the rest of the game:

Subsequent questions will either have different New-"If" conditions, or they will have no new conditions at all. That means that to use his Master Sketch again, the untrained test taker will have to erase all of the work he did on Question 2. At a minimum, that will be messy and will take up some time. The bigger risk is that the test taker will forget exactly which of the deductions he made at the beginning of the game, and which he made specifically for Question 2. He could wind up inadvertently leaving some of Question 2's work in the sketch, or erasing some of the initial deductions he'd made. Either way, he's now in danger of missing all the subsequent questions associated with the game.

Additionally, if our untrained test taker effectively erases the work in the sketch that was unique to Question 2, he will no longer have that work to refer to. In the next strategy note, you'll learn how LSAT experts sometimes consult their work on earlier questions to help answer later ones. If you are building-erasing-rebuilding your sketch as you go, you won't have a record of the work you've done throughout the question set.

LSAT experts avoid these pitfalls by creating a Master Sketch containing the setup, rules, and deductions for the overall game. And, then, they leave it alone. They can consult the Master Sketch for questions without New-"If" conditions. For each New-"If" question, however, they quickly copy the Master Sketch and label it with the question number of the New-"If" question. They add the question's New-"If" condition to this copy, and work out the question's implications there. When they move on, they leave that question's work as a reference, just in case it helps them on a subsequent question.

As you review, study the new "mini-sketches" that experts make for New-"If" questions. You'll learn not only how they got a particular question right, but also how they effectively manage an entire game.

There are a handful of relatively rare Logic Games question types, but well-trained test takers can use the same sketches and techniques to answer them, as well. At times, test takers who have truly mastered the Logic Games Method will even use their work on one or two questions to help them quickly answer another. That's why it is valuable to review an entire game, from Step 1 all the way through the last question, even when you only missed one or two of the questions along the way. Your review will not only reveal where you went off track on the questions you missed, it also will likely show you how you could have handled the entire game more quickly and confidently.

LOGIC GAMES STRATEGY

Use Previous Work to Determine What Could Be True

The LSAT always provides enough information to answer every question. That's comforting to know, but open-ended questions that ask you what could be true or must be false in a game without giving you any new conditions or constraints can be very time consuming. For most students, their instincts tell them to try out every answer choice one by one.

LSAT experts know to keep track of the work they do on every question, and when they can use it to help them solve these open-ended questions. If they see that an open-ended question will be very time consuming, or will require them to test every answer choice, they often skip that question temporarily. After working through the other questions in the set, they'll come back to the open-ended question.

Here's how it works. Let's say a question asks "Which one of the following must be false?" You check your Master Sketch, but you don't see anything there that definitively rules out one of the answer choices. Work through the rest of the questions for the game. Along the way, you'll likely encounter one question that asks for an "acceptable arrangement" of entities. You'll probably also have two or three questions with New-"If" conditions, and you'll solve those by creating "mini-sketches" that reveal some additional "acceptable arrangements." Now, the expert test taker uses critical thinking: "Since the correct answer to the open-ended question must be false, all four of its wrong answers could be true." Then, he can check any acceptable arrangement he has discovered or created along the way. Any answer choice for the "must be false" question that appears in an acceptable arrangement is an incorrect answer, and he can cross it out. Sometimes, you may be able to eliminate all four wrong answers in this way.

Students in Kaplan's comprehensive LSAT prep courses drill with the Logic Games Method in class and throughout their homework. They are assigned chapters in Kaplan's LSAT treatise "The LSAT Unlocked" that go over the strategies, tactics, and techniques associated with each step of the Method. They practice it on dozens of real LSAC-released logic games in Mastery Assignments, a library of over 3,000 official LSAT questions arranged by question/game/passage type and by level of difficulty. As you review your work in these explanations, follow along with the LSAT experts who make the Logic Games Method their template for accuracy and speed in this section.

Reading Comprehension Method and Strategies

For many students, Reading Comprehension is the section of the LSAT in which they find it most difficult to improve their scores. This is due, in part, to how familiar Reading Comprehension feels. In one way or another, you have been tested from grade school through college on how well you understood or remembered something that you had read. Learning to read actively and strategically, in the way rewarded by the LSAT, takes some getting used to. Kaplan's Reading Comprehension Method is designed to make your performance on this section of the test just as efficient and effective as our Logic Games Method can on that section.

READING COMPREHENSION METHOD
1. Read the Passage Strategically 2. Analyze the Question Stem 3. Research the Relevant Text 4. Predict the Correct Answer 5. Evaluate the Answer Choices

Given that you have four passages (and their accompanying questions) to complete in 35 minutes, time is precious in Reading Comprehension. LSAT experts will usually complete Step 1 for a passage in around 3 to 4 minutes. That leaves between 4 to 5 minutes to tackle the questions, using Steps 2 through 5 for each one. Here's what each step accomplishes.

Step 1: Read the Passage Strategically

LSAT Reading Comprehension passages are excerpts of around 450 to 500 words, typically from academic writing in fields covered by social science, natural science, humanities, and law. The writing is dense, and the topics are rarely, if ever, familiar to the casual reader. This content is pretty intimidating, and students often compound the problem by trying to read and remember the details and facts in these arcane passages.

But, here's what LSAT experts know: The LSAT is far more interested in *how* and *why* the author wrote the passage than it is in *what* the author said about the details. Here's why. Imagine if you saw this question on the LSAT.

> In which of the following years did George Washington lead Continental Army troops across the Delaware River?

This is a question that rewards knowledge, not reading comprehension. If you happen to know the answer, you could get this question right even without the passage. Law schools need to evaluate your skill level in comprehension and analysis. So, the LSAT asks questions more like these.

> The author of the passage would most likely agree with which one of the following statements about Washington's military leadership?

> The author includes a reference to Washington's crossing of the Delaware in order to

> The primary purpose of the fourth paragraph of the passage is

To answer LSAT questions, you need to read for the passage's structure, and the author's opinions, and not just for names or dates or facts. Anticipating the kinds of questions that the test asks, LSAT experts read actively, interrogating the author as they proceed. When the author offers an opinion, the expert looks for where and how the author supports it. If the author describes two theories, the expert looks for the author's evaluation of them, or for language in which the author prefers one theory over the other. An LSAT expert's reading is never passive or wayward.

READING COMPREHENSION STRATEGY

Use Keywords to Read Effectively

Given the LSAT's emphasis on opinion and purpose, Kaplan has compiled a list of Keywords that indicate text that is likely to be relevant in answering LSAT questions. These include terms that indicate an author's point of view, her reason for including a detail or illustration, and words that show contrast or correspondence between two things or ideas. LSAT experts circle or underline these Keywords when they encounter them in the passage, and they use Keywords to effectively paraphrase or summarize chunks of text.

To see why Keywords are so helpful, try to answer the following question:

Type X coffee beans grow at very high altitudes. Type X coffee beans produce a dark, mellow coffee when brewed.

With which one of the following statements would the author most likely agree?

1. Coffee beans that grow at high altitudes typically produce dark, mellow coffee when brewed.
2. Coffee beans that grow at high altitudes typically produce light, acidic coffee when brewed.

You cannot answer that question from the text alone. It contains only facts. To understand the author's point of view, and thus to answer the LSAT question about it, you need for the author to supply Keywords that logically connect the facts in a specific way. Observe:

> Type X coffee beans grow at very high altitudes, *but* produce a *surprisingly* dark, mellow coffee when brewed.

Now, choice (2) is the correct answer on the LSAT. Choice (1) is clearly incorrect. But, what if the author had written the following?

> Type X coffee beans grow at very high altitudes, *and so* produce a dark, mellow coffee when brewed.

Now, it's choice (1) that is supported by the passage. Notice that the facts did not change at all, but when the author changes the Keyword, the correct answer on the LSAT changes. Keywords indicating a passage's structure or an author's point of view are not the kinds of words you typically pay attention to when you are reading for school, so you need to train yourself to spot them, and use them, on the LSAT.

Throughout the Kaplan LSAT explanations for Reading Comprehension, LSAT experts will show you the Keywords and phrases that they circled or underlined in the passage text. Then, as they explain individual questions associated with a passage, they will demonstrate how they refer back to those Keywords to research the passage, predict correct answers, and evaluate the answer choices. The categories of Keywords are defined in the glossary.

By circling or underlining Keywords, and then jotting down succinct notes in the margin next to the passage, an LSAT expert creates a "Roadmap" of the passage. This helps the expert quickly research the text when one of the questions refers to a detail, illustration, or argument in the passage.

While a Roadmap of Keywords and margin notes is helpful on most questions, there are typically a few questions accompanying each passage that call for broader answers, such as the author's "primary purpose" or the passage's "main idea." To prepare for these questions, an LSAT expert also summarizes the "big picture" of the passage as she reads. Keeping in mind the kinds of questions that the LSAT asks, these summaries must go beyond mere subject matter to encompass how and why the author wrote the passage. Big-picture summaries are described in the following strategy note.

READING COMPREHENSION STRATEGY

Summarize the Passage's Big Picture

In addition to circling Keywords and jotting down notes in the margins next to the passage, LSAT experts also mentally summarize passages as they strategically read LSAT Reading Comprehension passages. To do this efficiently, experts will usually break down the passage's big picture into Topic, Scope, Purpose, and Main Idea. You'll see these "big picture" terms referenced throughout Kaplan's LSAT explanations, and for most passages, the discussion following the Sample Roadmap will paraphrase the expert's summaries for you.

The Topic means the overall subject matter. It almost always appears in the first paragraph. At this high level, the subject matter is likely to be familiar to you, even if you don't know much about it.

The Scope refers to the aspect of the Topic that interests this author. For example, if the Topic is George Washington, the Scope could be Washington's economic policies, Washington's education, or Washington's service as a general in the Continental Army. Usually, you will have some idea of the Scope from the passage's first paragraph, although occasionally, it may not be entirely clear until the second (or even third) paragraph. The Scope must be narrower than the Topic, and it is important that you recognize *the author's* Scope and avoid imposing your thoughts about a Topic onto the passage.

Identifying the author's purpose is central to your LSAT success. To put your finger on why the author is writing the passage, look to the passage's structure. Does the author begin by describing someone else's idea or theory about the subject? If so, the author's purpose may be to *rebut* the other thinker's idea. On the other hand, the author might go on to *explain* how this other person's theory influenced subsequent ideas on the subject. In another passage structure common on the LSAT, the author opens with a description of an event or phenomenon. She might go on to *evaluate* the importance of the phenomenon, or she might *advocate* for a particular kind of response to it. Notice that all of the italicized words here are verbs, and learn to paraphrase the author's Purpose as a verb in your own summaries. Remember, you want to capture *why* and *how* the author examines a subject, and not only *what* she says about it.

If you have summarized the Topic, Scope, and Purpose accurately, you can usually combine them into a fairly clear statement of the passage's Main Idea. For example, if the Topic is George Washington, the Scope is Washington's time as commander of the Continental Army, and the author's Purpose is to *illustrate* how his military career influenced his political career, then the Main Idea might be something like: "Washington's generalship trained him to be consultative and decisive in political battles with Congress." In the most academic passages on the LSAT, you may encounter a one-sentence thesis statement or summary that makes the Main Idea explicit, but more often, you will need to paraphrase the Main Idea by combining the Topic, Scope, and Purpose you have identified from the passage structure and the author's point of view.

As you review Reading Comprehension sections using these explanations, you'll see how LSAT experts handle "main idea" and "primary purpose" questions using the kinds of big picture strategies we've just discussed.

In Reading Comprehension, Step 1 should take you around 3–4 minutes. Think of your passage Roadmap much as you would your Master Sketch in a logic game. It highlights and organizes the most important information in the passage, and it gets you ready to answer the questions.

Step 2: Analyze the Question Stem

Reading Comprehension passages are usually accompanied by 5–8 questions. Start your analysis of each question by identifying two things: the question type and any clues that will help you research the passage text. Kaplan always identifies the question type at the start of every question's explanation. The question types are defined in the glossary, as well.

As we've already alluded to, some Reading Comprehension questions ask about the "big picture." Kaplan calls these Global questions, and if you've summarized the Topic, Scope, Purpose, and Main Idea of the passage, you won't need do any further research. Just use your summaries to predict the correct answer.

Other question types focus on the specifics of what the author said. Occasionally, you'll encounter a Detail question. These usually begin with a phrase such as "According to the passage …" making it clear that the correct answer is something stated in the passage. The LSAT also often tests details through Logic Function questions. These question stems cite the detail from the passage and then ask *why* the author included the detail or *how* he used it. A common phrasing for this question type is: "The author refers to *xxx* (lines 24–26) in order to." Use the detail, and any line or paragraph reference to research the text. Keywords before or after the detail ("*but* xxx is different" or "xxx is *especially important because*") will often demonstrate the author's reason for including it, and will help you predict the correct answer.

By far, the most common question type in Reading Comprehension is the Inference question. These ask you for something that the passage implies, but does not state explicitly. Inference question stems can be open-ended ("With which one of the following statements would the author of the passage most likely agree?") or they may include references to a detail in the passage ("Based on the information presented in the passage, which one of the following economic policies would Washington have been most likely to endorse?"). Whenever a research clue is present, use it to pinpoint the relevant text in the passage. For example, the "economic policies" mentioned in the second Inference question stem would likely take you to a particular paragraph, and maybe even to a particular line in the passage about Washington.

A handful of questions in the Reading Comprehension section will mimic the skills tested in the Logical Reasoning section. A Reading Comprehension question could, for example, ask you to strengthen an argument made by the author, or to identify a method of argument parallel to one in the passage. To manage these questions, LSAT experts employ the skills they've learned for the comparable question types in the Logical Reasoning section. This is a good reminder that you should review complete tests, even when you're primarily concerned with just one or two sections.

Step 3: Research the Relevant Text

Don't answer LSAT Reading Comprehension questions on a whim. Whenever you are able to research the passage, do so. But, be careful. Don't passively re-read the passage, or go on a "fishing expedition" for details you don't remember.

An LSAT expert uses the research clues that he finds in question stems in conjunction with his strategic reading Roadmap to put his finger right on the relevant text in the passage. Moreover, the expert always seeks out Keywords that indicate *why* the author included a detail, or *how* the author used it in the passage. In some questions, the LSAT testmaker will include wrong answers that use words or phrases directly from the passage, but that distort what the author had to say about those words or phrases. The following strategy examines how LSAT experts use research effectively and efficiently.

READING COMPREHENSION STRATEGY

Use Research Clues to Answer Questions Efficiently

Most LSAT test takers are pretty good readers. Given unlimited time, a lot of test takers could probably get all of the Reading Comprehension questions correct. Of course, the LSAT does not give you unlimited time. Indeed, the 35-minute time limit may be your biggest obstacle to Reading Comprehension success.

LSAT experts combat the test's time constraints by very effectively avoiding pointless re-reading. There are five kinds of research clues they recognize in question stems that help them zero in on the relevant text and predict the correct answer.

Line References—Experts research around the referenced detail, looking for Keywords that indicate why the referenced text has been included and how it is used.

Paragraph References—Experts consult their Roadmaps to check the paragraph's scope, and its function in the passage.

Quoted Text (sometimes accompanied by a line reference)—Experts check the context of the quoted term or phrase, and they consider what the author meant by it.

Proper Nouns—Experts check for the context of the person, place, or thing in the passage; they check for whether the author made a positive, negative, or neutral evaluation of it; and they consider why the author included it.

Content Clues—Experts take note when question stems mention terms, concepts, or ideas highlighted in the passage, knowing that these almost always refer to something that the author emphasized, or about which the author expressed an opinion.

If you struggle to maintain your accuracy while trying to complete the Reading Comprehension in time, pay attention to how Kaplan's LSAT experts explain their work in Step 3. It could really change the way you take the test.

Step 4: Predict the Correct Answer

Once you have researched the passage (or, for Global questions, once you have paused to consider your big picture summaries of the passage), take a moment to paraphrase (or "pre-phrase," if you like that term) what the correct answer must contain. Taking a few seconds to predict the correct answer can save you a lot of time as you move through the answer choices. Just as they do in Logical Reasoning explanations, the Kaplan experts who write the Reading Comprehension explanations will always share their predictions with you in their analysis of Step 4. Pay careful attention to this step if you want to improve your speed and accuracy in Reading Comprehension.

Step 5: Evaluate the Answer Choices

Every question on the LSAT has one correct answer and four demonstrably incorrect ones. This is especially important to remember in Reading Comprehension because comparing answer choices back to the text can lead to endless re-reading and wasted time. Armed with a solid prediction (or, at a minimum, with a clear idea of the author's purpose and point of view), evaluate the choices boldly. If (A) does not contain what the correct answer must say, cross it out and move on. Those who master the Reading Comprehension Method often become so confident that once they spot the correct answer, they do not even need to read the rest of the answer choices. In the Kaplan explanations, we always explain why every wrong answer is wrong, even when the correct answer is (A). On Test Day, however, you will be well served by the ability to predict and evaluate consistently.

READING COMPREHENSION STRATEGY

Spot Common Wrong-Answer Patterns

LSAT experts use the standardized nature of the LSAT to their advantage in Reading Comprehension (just as they do in Logical Reasoning) by anticipating certain types of wrong answers that occur over and over again.

Many of the wrong answer types in this section are the same ones associated with Logical Reasoning questions. You will see a fair share of Outside the Scope wrong answers, and in Reading Comprehension Global questions particularly, you will see incorrect answers that go beyond the scope, encompassing more than what the author included in her Purpose or Main Idea. You will also see Extreme and 180 incorrect answers similar to those in Logical Reasoning.

Two incorrect answers types that are more common in Reading Comprehension than they are in Logical Reasoning are the Distortion and Half-Right/Half-Wrong answer choices. Distortion incorrect answers are those that stay within the scope of the passage, but then twist what the author has said in a way that misstates the author's position or point of view. Half-Right/Half-Wrong answer choices are those that start off well, matching the passage up to a point, but then incorrectly characterize or contradict the passage in their second half.

Whenever an answer choice fits into one of the common wrong answer categories, the Reading Comprehension explanations will point it out. If there is an incorrect answer type that doesn't make sense to you, check out its description in the glossary.

Students in Kaplan's comprehensive LSAT prep courses make Reading Comprehension a regular part of their practice. They understand that they have to. After all, improvement in Reading Comprehension requires diligent practice. Kaplan instructors encourage both un-timed and timed practice so that students can learn the skills and strategies rewarded by the Reading Comprehension section, and then evaluate them under test-like conditions. In addition to having access to hundreds of released LSAT Reading Comprehension passages, Kaplan students also hone their skill set with *LSAT Channel* lessons covering the full range of ability levels, from Fundamentals to Advanced. Even if Reading Comprehension is your strongest section initially, practice and review it throughout your LSAT prep. Steady improvement in this tough section will lead to a higher score on the exam.

A Note About Formal Logic on the LSAT

In college and university Philosophy departments, Formal Logic is an enormous topic that may cover several semesters and hours and hours of difficult reading. Its reputation as a formidable and intimidating subject is well deserved. The LSAT, however, tests only a small sliver of Formal Logic, a sliver that can be mastered with a few hours of expert instruction and diligent practice.

The aspect of Formal Logic tested on the LSAT is restricted to **conditional statements** (also called "If-then" statements). You'll see them from time to time in Logic Games, and multiple times in Logical Reasoning on every test. Here's a brief introduction to how you will see Formal Logic described and discussed in these explanations.

Conditional Statements: Sufficiency and Necessity

A conditional statement is defined by having a **sufficient** clause and a **necessary** clause. That's a hifalutin' way of saying it has an "If" clause and a "then" clause. Here's a simple example:

If this car is running, then it has gasoline in its gas tank.

That means that gasoline in the gas tank is necessary for this car to run. So, the necessary clause follows "then." That's always the case. Now, notice that the clause "this car is running" is sufficient to establish that the car has gasoline in its gas tank. The "If" clause is always sufficient (that is, it is enough by itself) to establish the truth of the necessary (or "then") clause.

In the explanations, the LSAT expert will often abbreviate Formal Logic by using an arrow for the "then" clause, like this:

$$\textbf{If} \quad \textbf{car running} \quad \rightarrow \quad \textbf{has gas}$$

Translating Conditional Statements

There are many ways to express conditional logic in the English language, and the LSAT uses them all. For example, on the test, the previous conditional statement might be expressed in any of the following ways:

> This car will run only if it has gasoline in its gas tank.
> This car will not run unless it has gasoline in its gas tank.
> Only if this car has gasoline in its gas tank will this car run.
> If this car does not have gasoline in its gas tank, then this car will not run.

From the perspective of Formal Logic these are all equivalent statements. They all present exactly the same relationship of a sufficient term to a necessary term. LSAT experts learn to recognize conditional statements and to quickly and accurately translate them into the "If-then" format. You'll see this skill demonstrated several times in the explanations to any LSAT test.

The final version of our statement about the car ("If this car does not have gasoline in its gas tank, then this car will not run") is also known as the contrapositive of the original statement. Being able to formulate the contrapositive of any conditional statement is a crucial skill for LSAT success.

Contrapositives

The logic underlying contrapositives is simple. Since the term that follows "then" is necessary for the term that follows "If," when you negate the necessary term, you must also negate the sufficient term. In other words, when you remove something that is necessary, you can't have the thing it's necessary for. So, to abbreviate our previous example:

$$\textit{If \quad NO gas \quad} \rightarrow \textit{\quad car NOT running}$$

If our original statement is true, then this one must be true as well. And, that's it. To form the contrapositive of a conditional statement, reverse *and* negate its sufficient and necessary terms.

Be careful, though, because if you reverse without negating, or if you negate without reversing, you will create illogical statements (and the LSAT will punish illogical statements with wrong answers). For example, here's what we would get by negating our original statement's terms without reversing them too:

$$\textit{If \quad car NOT running \quad} \rightarrow \textit{\quad NO gas}$$

But that could be wrong, couldn't it? If the car is not running, it might have a dead battery, or a broken transmission, or it might even be turned off. In any of those cases, it might have gasoline in its gas tank.

Similarly, here's what we'd get by reversing without negating:

$$\textit{If \quad has gas \quad} \rightarrow \textit{\quad car running}$$

Again, the mistake is obvious in our simple example. Having gasoline is necessary for the car to run, not sufficient for it to run. It could have a full tank of gas, but if its battery is dead, it would not be running.

To see why contrapositives are important on the LSAT, consider a Logic Games rule: "If Katherine is selected, then Malik will be selected." It's easy to translate and jot down:

$$\textit{If \quad K \quad} \rightarrow \textit{\quad M}$$

That will be helpful any time you know that Katherine is selected in the game. But, here's what the test is likely to ask: "If Malik is not selected, then which one of the following must be true?" An LSAT expert may even anticipate a question like this one because as soon as he sees the original conditional statement among the rules, he will also note its contrapositive by reversing and negating the original terms:

$$\textit{If \quad NOT M \quad} \rightarrow \textit{\quad NOT K}$$

There's no doubt that if Malik is not selected, then it must be true that Katherine is not selected either.

Conditional Statements with Multiple Terms

From time to time, the LSAT will include conditional statements that have more than one term in the sufficient clause, in the necessary clause, or in both. For the most part, these work just the same as the previous example, but there is one important additional note we need to make about contrapositives in conditional statements with multiple terms. To see this, let's add a term to the necessary clause of our original statement:

$$\textit{If \quad car running \quad} \rightarrow \textit{\quad has gas AND has charged battery}$$

This statement now has two terms in the necessary clause, and *both* are necessary: If this car is running, then it has gasoline in its gas tank AND it has a charged battery. Because both conditions are necessary, the negation of either one will cause the car not to run. Thus, the contrapostive would read:

$$\textit{If \quad NO gas OR NO charged battery \quad} \rightarrow \textit{\quad car NOT running}$$

When we reverse and negate to form the contrapositive, we must also change the "and" linking the two necessary terms to "or." This will always work, regardless of whether the "and" or the "or" are found initially in the sufficient clause or in the necessary clause. We can illustrate this with another Logic Games rule. Imagine that the test tells you the following: "If Juliana and Nestor attend the dance, then Patricia will not attend the dance." That is, if J and N are *both* there, P will not be. Here's that rule in Formal Logic shorthand:

$$If \quad J\ AND\ N \quad \rightarrow \quad NOT\ P$$

Now, to form the contrapositive, reverse and negate the terms, and change the "and" to an "or":

$$If \quad P \quad \rightarrow \quad NOT\ J\ OR\ NOT\ N$$

That might look funny initially, but it is absolutely true based on the original statement. Patricia will not go to the dance if both Juliana and Nestor go. So, knowing that Patricia *is* at the dance is sufficient to establish that at least one of the other two is absent.

Any time you see a conditional statement, you can form its contrapositive correctly by reversing and negating the terms, and changing "and" to "or" or vice versa.

Combining Conditional Statements

The LSAT often rewards your ability to combine conditional statements to reach valid deductions that may not be apparent at first. The most obvious example is when they give you two statements like these:

$$If \quad A \quad \rightarrow \quad B$$

$$If \quad B \quad \rightarrow \quad C$$

From this, we can pretty easily deduce the following:

$$If \quad A \quad \rightarrow \quad B \quad \rightarrow \quad C$$

And, thus:

$$If \quad A \quad \rightarrow \quad C$$

When the example is that straightforward, the deduction is pretty easy to see. However, on the LSAT, the testmaker will sometimes add a step or two. Imagine that you see these rules in a logic game:

Danny will audition for any play that Carla directs.

Danny will not audition for a play unless Rebekkah also auditions for that play.

First, you will need to translate those sentences into Formal Logic abbreviations:

$$If \quad C_{dir} \quad \rightarrow \quad D_{aud}$$

$$If \quad \sim R_{aud} \quad \rightarrow \quad \sim D_{aud}$$

Now, the result of the first statement (its necessary clause) is that Danny auditions. The trigger (or sufficient clause) of the second sentence is that Rebekkah does *not* audition. Right now, you can't combine those statements. But look what happens when you formulate the contrapositive of the second sentence:

$$If \quad D_{aud} \quad \rightarrow \quad R_{aud}$$

Now, the trigger (the sufficient clause) of the second statement is that Danny auditions. Thus:

$$If \quad C_{dir} \quad \rightarrow \quad D_{aud} \quad \rightarrow \quad R_{aud}$$

So, when combined, those statements allow you to deduce that Rebekkah also auditions for any play that Carla directs.

The skill of combining conditional statements doesn't only appear in Logic Games. In fact, it's far more common in Logical Reasoning questions. Wherever they encounter Formal Logic on the test, LSAT experts are adept at spotting conditional statements, translating them into the "If-then" format, formulating their contrapositives, and combining them to reach deductions.

For students in a comprehensive LSAT prep program, they regularly practice Formal Logic in and out of class, in their books, and their homework assignments, and they hone their skills watching Formal Logic *LSAT Channel* sessions. Whenever you encounter Formal Logic in these explanations, the LSAT expert will explain the analysis thoroughly, using abbreviations like those you've seen here. Always give Formal Logic an extra careful review.

Taking a Kaplan LSAT Course: A Personalized Experience

Preparation for the LSAT is a combination of two things: instruction and practice—lots of it. And every student is different, with different strengths, weaknesses, goal scores, and dream schools. That means every student has different needs. So Kaplan customizes the LSAT preparation experience for you. You get the right instruction and the right practice at the right time for you. Here's how we do it:

Personalized Instruction: Core Curriculum + The LSAT Channel

First, Kaplan customizes instruction. There's not one long "one-size-fits all" course for you to sit through. There is a core curriculum—10 sessions in our In Person or Live Online classes, including three full-length, proctored practice tests—that everyone attends. The core sessions cover the key concepts for each and every question type. If you are enrolled in our Self-Paced program, this material is presented in short, digestible chapters.

But how do we personalize it? We recently introduced a new innovation called *The LSAT Channel*. It's nightly, live-streamed, live online instruction with Kaplan's best teachers, and it features over 100 unique one-hour episodes on every LSAT topic imaginable. If you're rocking Logical Reasoning, you can attend advanced episodes tailored for you. If you're struggling in, let's say, Hybrid Logic Games, you can attend foundations episodes to go deeper into the basics. *The LSAT Channel* provides unique, customizable, niche live instruction (lots and lots of it), and all of the *LSAT Channel* lessons are also available in an On Demand archive for viewing whenever you want.

Personalized Practice: Practice Library, Explanations, and Smart Reports

Second, Kaplan customizes practice. The LSAT has not changed substantially since 1991, and you'll have access to every officially released LSAT PrepTest. That's over 85 exams and 8,500 questions. Plus, you'll have detailed answers and explanations to each. But additionally, we give you Mastery Assignments where you can drill specific question, game, and passage types. These Mastery Assignments are offered at three levels of difficulty—Foundations, Mid-Level, and Advanced—that way you can practice questions in the specific areas and levels of difficulty where you need the most help. These assignments can either be done online or printed out.

How will you know what to do? Kaplan's scoring analytics tool, Smart Reports, evaluates your performance on practice tests to tell you exactly where you need help and where you need to focus your time.

Personalized Promise: Kaplan's Higher Score Guarantee

And finally, you can be confident in your decision to prep with Kaplan, as our courses feature the industry-leading Higher Score Guarantee. If you are not ready to take the LSAT for any reason or are unhappy with your score, you can repeat your course and have continued access to your resources for free—no questions asked. And if for whatever reason your score does not improve, even though you've done the required work, you'll receive a full tuition refund. You'll have the confidence to rock the LSAT on Test Day.

Kaplan LSAT Course Options

All of the benefits of a Kaplan comprehensive course are available in four different ways:

> Private Tutoring – Get the attention you need from a personal tutor
> In Person – Learn in a real classroom taught by an expert, Kaplan-trained instructor.
> Live Online – Get the convenience of a live classroom in the comfort of your home.

Self-Paced – Study at your own pace in a location that's convenient for you.

Free LSAT Events

Kaplan regularly hosts free, live online LSAT events for prospective law students to learn more about the test and the admissions process. Find LSAT Practice Tests, Preview Classes, Free *LSAT Channel* Previews, Admissions Seminars, and more.

PrepTest 52

The Inside Story

PrepTest 52 was administered in September 2007. It challenged 49,785 test takers. The following chart shows the average number of students to miss each question in each of PrepTest 52's different sections.

Percentage Incorrect by PrepTest 52 Section Type

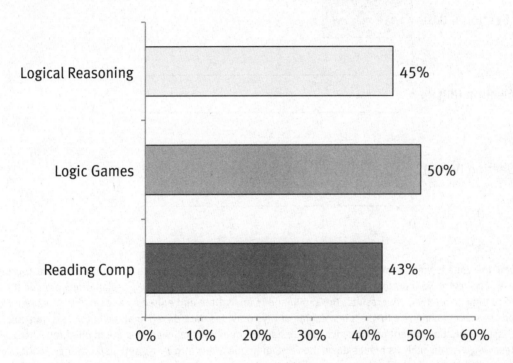

On average, students were most likely to miss questions in Logic Games. Although Logic Games was somewhat higher in actual difficulty than Logical Reasoning and Reading Comprehension, the percentages are not that disparate, so students were missing about 11–12 questions in each individual section.

Additionally, although Logic Games was the hardest section, only one of the test's 10 hardest questions came from that section. Here were the locations of the 10 hardest (most missed) questions in the exam.

Location of 10 Most Difficult Questions in PrepTest 52

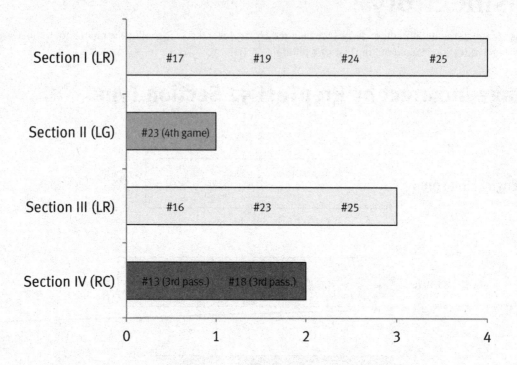

The takeaway from this data is that, to maximize your potential on the LSAT, you need to take a comprehensive approach. Test yourself rigorously, and review your performance on every section of the test. Kaplan's LSAT explanations provide the expertise and insight you need to fully understand your results. The explanations are written and edited by a team of LSAT experts, who have helped thousands of students improve their scores. Kaplan always provides data-driven analysis of the test, ranking the difficulty of every question based on actual student performance. The 10 hardest questions on every test are highlighted with a 4-star difficulty rating, the highest we give. The analysis breaks down the remaining questions into 1-, 2-, and 3-star ratings so that you can compare your performance to thousands of other test takers on all LSAC material.

Don't settle for wondering whether a question was really as hard as it seemed to you. Analyze the test with real data, and learn the secrets and strategies that help top scorers master the LSAT.

7 Can't-Miss Features of PrepTest 52

- At the time of its release, PrepTest 52 contained the fewest number of pure Argument-Based questions on any test ever. There were only six total—two Main Point and one each of Role of a Statement, Point at Issue, Method of Argument, and Parallel Reasoning. To date, there have only been three PrepTests with that few: PrepTest 52 and PrepTest 76 (October 2015), which each had six and PrepTest 58 (September 2009), which had only five.
- The halcyon era of Loose Sequencing was brief, but grand. PrepTest 52—along with PrepTest 51 (December 2006)—are the only two tests ever to have a Logic Games section with two Loose Sequencing Games.
- PrepTest 52 was just the second test ever to feature Comparative Reading. And for the second time in a row, it appeared second in the section and contained six questions. However, this time it was a Social Sciences set of passages.
- For just the second time ever, a question was removed from the Reading Comprehension section. So, when you take this test, you'll have an extra three seconds per question in that section than did the original test takers.
- With 23 questions, you'd expect each answer—(A) to (E)—to show up four or five times in the Logic Games section. However, PrepTest 52 was the first test ever when two answer choices—(A) and (D)—each only showed up twice. That means (B), (C), and (E) accounted for the other 19 answers.

- Usually EXCEPT questions are not the norm, except on the first logic game of PrepTest 52. Four of the seven questions contained the word *EXCEPT*—a record for the most EXCEPT questions in a single game.
- PrepTest 52 (September 2007) was the first test proctors may have needed to tell some test takers to shut off their iPhones, which were first released in late June 2007.

PrepTest 52 in Context

As much fun as it is to find out what makes a PrepTest unique or noteworthy, it's even more important to know just how representative it is of other LSAT administrations (and, thus, how likely it is to be representative of the exam you will face on Test Day). The following charts compare the numbers of each kind of question and game on PrepTest 52 to the average numbers seen on all officially released LSATs administered over the past five years (from 2013 through 2017).

Number of LR Questions by Type: PrepTest 52 vs. 2013–2017 Average

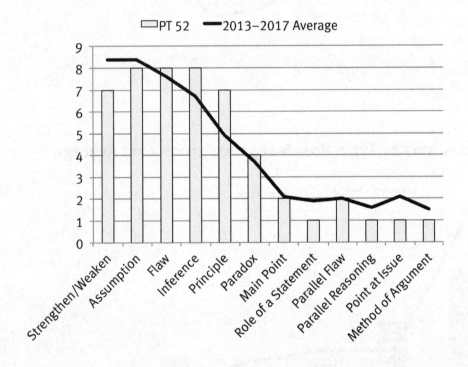

Number of LG Games by Type: PrepTest 52 vs. 2013–2017 Average

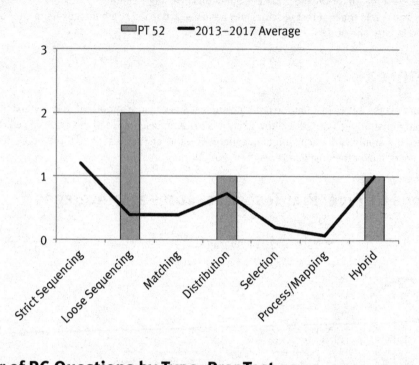

Number of RC Questions by Type: PrepTest 52 vs. 2013–2017 Average

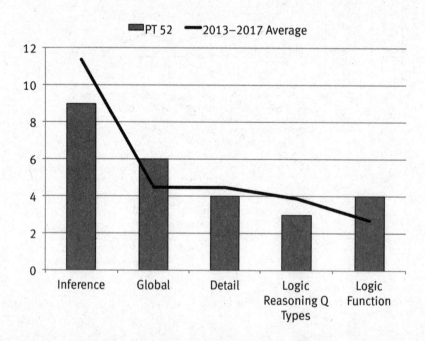

There isn't usually a huge difference in the distribution of questions from LSAT to LSAT, but if this test seems harder (or easier) to you than another you've taken, compare the number of questions of the types on which you, personally, are strongest and weakest. Then, explore within each section to see if your best or worst question types came earlier or later.

KAPLAN

Students in Kaplan's comprehensive LSAT courses have access to every released LSAT and to a library of thousands of officially released questions arranged by question, game, and passage type. If you are studying on your own, you have to do a bit more work to identify your strengths and your areas of opportunity. Quantitative analysis (like that in the charts shown here) is an important tool for understanding how the test is constructed, and how you are performing on it.

Section I: Logical Reasoning

Q#	Question Type	Correct	Difficulty
1	Main Point	C	★
2	Flaw	D	★
3	Parallel Reasoning	A	★
4	Strengthen	C	★
5	Inference	B	★
6	Flaw	E	★
7	Inference	A	★★
8	Principle (Identify/Strengthen)	C	★
9	Weaken	D	★
10	Assumption (Necessary)	A	★★
11	Paradox (EXCEPT)	C	★
12	Weaken	E	★★
13	Inference	E	★
14	Paradox	C	★★★
15	Inference	B	★★
16	Parallel Flaw	A	★★★
17	Assumption (Sufficient)	E	★★★★
18	Inference	B	★★
19	Principle (Identify/Strengthen)	E	★★★★
20	Assumption (Sufficient)	E	★★★
21	Weaken	C	★★
22	Principle (Apply/Inference)	D	★★★
23	Flaw	D	★★★
24	Inference	E	★★★★
25	Assumption (Necessary)	E	★★★★

1. (C) Main Point

Step 1: Identify the Question Type
Because the question stem asks you to identify the conclusion, this is a Main Point question.

Step 2: Untangle the Stimulus
Because this is a Main Point question, expect that the conclusion will not be marked with a Conclusion Keyword. Instead look for Contrast Keywords. In this stimulus, [b]ut in the sixth line seems to indicate the author shifting from background to conclusion. Apply the One Sentence Test to verify that statement is the conclusion. What is the author really trying to say about this system? It's not fair. Does the rest of the argument support that? Yes, the first half describes the system, and the second half illustrates why it might yield unfair results.

Step 3: Make a Prediction
The correct answer will say that the system described in the stimulus is unfair.

Step 4: Evaluate the Answer Choices
(C) closely matches the prediction and is the right answer.

(A) gives a detail about the system in question, rather than the author's evaluation of the system.

(B) also merely describes the system.

(D) includes *unfairness* but is too narrow because the author's conclusion isn't limited to just those workers in "exceptionally strong work groups."

(E) is the stimulus's last sentence, but the Keyword [f]urthermore in the stimulus indicates that it is the continuation of what precedes it, which is evidence for the author's argument, not the conclusion.

2. (D) Flaw

Step 1: Identify the Question Type
The phrase "most vulnerable to criticism" is common language for a Flaw question. Look for the unwarranted assumption or the common LSAT flaw.

Step 2: Untangle the Stimulus
Signaled by the Keyword [s]o, the conclusion comes at the end of the stimulus. Napping likely causes insomnia. The evidence is based on two pieces of data, both showing that people who nap have insomnia.

Step 3: Make a Prediction
Because the conclusion makes a claim of causation (i.e., that naps cause insomnia) based on evidence of a correlation (between nappers and insomniacs), the classic flaw present here is causation vs. correlation. In other words, the author is improperly assuming that just because two things happen together, that one causes the other. The author is overlooking

the possibility that something else causes both naps and insomnia or that insomnia is the cause of the naps.

Step 4: Evaluate the Answer Choices
(D) matches the prediction by pointing out that the author has overlooked the possibility that insomnia actually leads to naps, rather than naps leading to insomnia.

(A) makes an Irrelevant Comparison between frequency of insomnia in university students and the general population. Note that in the first study, university students with insomnia are compared to university students without insomnia, not against the general population.

(B) is Extreme because the author never claims there is only one cause to *all* cases of insomnia, just that napping is among the causes.

(C) accurately describes the stimulus but not a logical flaw in the argument. Whatever definition of *napping* the author uses, it appears to stay constant between the evidence and the conclusion.

(E) goes Outside the Scope by focusing on one piece of evidence, rather than on how that evidence connects to the conclusion.

3. (A) Parallel Reasoning

Step 1: Identify the Question Type
The phrase "pattern of reasoning … most similar to" indicates that this is a Parallel Reasoning question. Analyze the argument into evidence and conclusion, as you would for any other argument-based question.

Step 2: Untangle the Stimulus
The conclusion, marked by [t]herefore, is that Joe took his car to K & L to get it fixed.

The evidence describes a chain of Formal Logic: if Joe's car was vacuumed, K & L employees did it; if K & L employees did it, Joe took his car to K & L for service. Finally, the author also informs us that Joe's car was indeed vacuumed.

Step 3: Make a Prediction
The conclusion can be characterized as an assertion of fact: something definitely happened. Eliminate answers when possible by comparing the conclusions of each answer choice to the conclusion in the stimulus. The entire argument can be rewritten in Formal Logic algebra to help reveal its underlying structure: if X → Y → X; X, therefore Z. The conclusion type and overall argument structure of the stimulus and correct answer will be the same.

Step 4: Evaluate the Answer Choices
(A) matches both the type of conclusion and overall argument structure of the stimulus. Correct.

(B) fails on the conclusion test—its conclusion asserts that something did not happen rather than that something did happen.

(C) matches in terms of its conclusion, but its evidence is very different, as it lacks the chain of Formal Logic statements found in the stimulus.

(D) fails on the conclusion test because it adds a qualifier (i.e., only on certain days).

(E) matches in terms of its conclusion, but the evidence goes Outside the Scope by introducing an either/or choice rather than giving a chain of Formal Logic statements.

4. (C) Strengthen

Step 1: Identify the Question Type
The question asks for something that "would most strengthen," so this is a Strengthen question.

Step 2: Untangle the Stimulus
The editorialist concludes that the president has a duty to keep the corporation's profits high. The author's evidence is that one of the responsibilities of the president of a large corporation is to "promote the key interests of the shareholders."

Step 3: Make a Prediction
Start by finding the assumption. In the conclusion, the editorialist says the president must keep profits high. In the evidence, the editorialist says corporation presidents must promote key interests of shareholders. Therefore, the editorialist assumes that the key interests of shareholders and high profits are connected. The right answer will reinforce the connection between the interests of shareholders and high profits.

Step 4: Evaluate the Answer Choices
(C) directly matches the prediction by suggesting that high profits help shareholder interests.

(A) goes Outside the Scope by focusing on shareholder satisfaction, rather than shareholder interests.

(B) goes Outside the Scope by introducing the board of directors; both the evidence and conclusion are about what the president does.

(D) goes Outside the Scope by focusing on potential shareholders, whereas the argument is about the existing shareholders.

(E) goes Outside the Scope by bringing up other responsibilities of the president, rather than the responsibility to keep profits high.

5. (B) Inference

Step 1: Identify the Question Type
Whenever the correct answer is a statement that "must be true" based on the statements in the stimulus, that is an Inference question.

Step 2: Untangle the Stimulus
The [e]veryone, [n]o, and only should tip you off that this is Formal Logic, so translate as you inventory the stimulus. The first sentence translates to "if in the neighborhood, then permitted to swim at some time during each day pool is open." The second sentence translates to "if under age 6, then not permitted to swim between noon and 5." The final sentence translates to "if between 5 and close, then reserved for adults."

Step 3: Make a Prediction
Given that everyone in the neighborhood is allowed to swim at some time, but that kids under age 6 aren't allowed to swim in the afternoon or evening, it looks like these kids (if there are any in the neighborhood) will have to be allowed into the pool in the morning.

Step 4: Evaluate the Answer Choices
(B) must be true because if there is a kid under 6, that kid will need to be allowed into the pool in the morning.

(A) could be false because the stimulus provides no information about how many children of any age are in the neighborhood.

(C) could be false because the stimulus provides no information about how many adults swim in the pool.

(D) could be false because the stimulus provides no information about whether or not children actually swim in the pool when it is open.

(E) could be false because the stimulus informs us that children over age 6 are allowed to swim in the afternoon. Therefore, these children could swim without necessarily breaking the rules that the stimulus provided information about. Also, no information is given about the rules prior to 12 P.M., so it still remains possible children could swim then without breaking the rules.

6. (E) Flaw

Step 1: Identify the Question Type
Because the question stem indicates that the right answer is the flaw in Beck's argument, this is a Flaw question.

Step 2: Untangle the Stimulus
Beck concludes that the computer program is accurate. The evidence is that the program provides consistent figures.

Step 3: Make a Prediction
Start by finding Beck's assumption. The conclusion is about accuracy, but the evidence is about consistency. Thus, Beck is assuming that consistency is indicative of accuracy. Beck is overlooking the possibility that the program could be consistent but inaccurate. For example, if your watch is off by 5 minutes, it may be consistent all day, but it's not accurate.

Step 4: Evaluate the Answer Choices
(E) matches the prediction by suggesting that consistency may not always lead to accuracy.

(A) makes an Irrelevant Comparison between the importance of consistency and accuracy. The argument is about how consistency might suggest accuracy, not about which one is more important.

(B) goes Outside the Scope by introducing "other tasks" that the argument is not about.

(C) is a Distortion between consistency and accuracy in the argument. The argument isn't about how the accuracy of the estimates would affect their consistency, but about how the consistency of estimates affects their accuracy.

(D) is Extreme by suggesting that the *sole* value of the program is its accuracy. The author is only interested in judging the program's accuracy, but that does mean that the accuracy is the only thing that contributes to the program's value.

7. (A) Inference
Step 1: Identify the Question Type
Because the information in the stimulus "provides the most support" for the right answer, this is an Inference question.

Step 2: Untangle the Stimulus
Don't get caught up in the scientific language. As with any other Inference question, take inventory of the information given in the stimulus. Inertia affects the flow of water. When the pump is switched on, it takes time to get the water up to speed; when the pump is switched off, it takes time for the water to slow down and stop. The last sentence introduces a new element, but all it does is tell us that inductance in electrical circuits works like water in pipes.

Step 3: Make a Prediction
If inductance in electrical circuits works like water in pipes, it must be true that electrical circuits take time to get up to speed and then again to taper off.

Step 4: Evaluate the Answer Choices
(A) is vaguer than the prediction but a solid match. For inductance to be like inertia, it must affect the rate of flow.

(B) is a Distortion of the stimulus. While the stimulus does indicate that inductance is similar to inertia, it does not support the statement that electrical circuits require inertia.

(C) is another Distortion between the connection between inertia and inductance. The stimulus says that they are similar, not that one causes the other.

(D) goes Outside the Scope by introducing electrical engineers.

(E) goes Outside the Scope by introducing very specific details about exactly how long it takes a water pump to taper

off. **(E)** is possible, but it is not something that must be true based on the stimulus.

8. (C) Principle (Identify/Strengthen)
Step 1: Identify the Question Type
The phrase "most helps to justify the ... reasoning" indicates that the correct answer will identify a principle that strengthens the argument.

Step 2: Untangle the Stimulus
The journalist's conclusion is that the practice of pricing drugs lower in poorer countries is unjustified. The evidence is that the overall wealth of a country doesn't necessarily reflect the ability of individual citizens to pay.

Step 3: Make a Prediction
As in a regular Strengthen question, start by finding the assumption. Here, the conclusion is about what should happen to entire countries, whereas the evidence is about the ability of some individual citizens to pay. Thus, the assumption is that companies should make their decisions about entire countries on the basis of some individual citizens of those countries. The correct answer will reinforce this assumption in general terms.

Step 4: Evaluate the Answer Choices
(C) matches the prediction in general terms. The characteristics of individuals are more important than the characteristics of the societies.

(A) makes an Irrelevant Comparison regarding ill people. The stimulus is about ability to pay, not how much somebody needs the drugs.

(B) is a Distortion of the stimulus. The pharmaceutical companies are already expending some resources to help the less fortunate by making the drugs available at a much lower price in poor nations. However, the journalist disagrees with the fairness of the effects of that practice, not the original intent of it.

(D) goes Outside the Scope. The author does not discuss a disparity in the quality of care available in wealthy or poor nations. The same drugs are available in both types of nations; the respective price points of those drugs in the two types of countries is what the author thinks is currently unjustified. The author is concerned about giving middle class people in poor nations breaks on drug prices, when poor people in wealthy nations do not receive the same breaks.

(E) makes an Irrelevant Comparison by introducing distribution of wealth in comparison to access to health care.

9. (D) Weaken

Step 1: Identify the Question Type

The correct answer is something that would go against Samantha's argument, so this is a Weaken question. The stimulus is in dialogue format, so even though you'll read both parts, focus on Samantha's argument.

Step 2: Untangle the Stimulus

Samantha concludes that a year-round schedule won't allow teachers to cover more new material. Her evidence is that the number of school days will be roughly the same.

Step 3: Make a Prediction

Start by finding Samantha's assumption. Here, Samantha is assuming that if the number of school days is roughly the same, no other factor might give the teachers more opportunity to teach new material on the proposed schedule. So, look for the answer choice that weakens the argument by pointing out some factor that could allow teachers to cover more material in the year-round schedule.

Step 4: Evaluate the Answer Choices

(D) matches the prediction, suggesting that the year-round schedule would cut back on review time, thus allowing teachers to cover more new material.

(A) goes Outside the Scope by focusing on what teachers would accept rather than on how much new material they would be able to cover.

(B) also goes Outside the Scope by focusing on child supervision. The supervision schedule does not affect whether or not more material can be covered by the teachers.

(C) goes Outside the Scope by discussing school districts where the year-round schedule increases the total number of school days. As Samantha's evidence points out, the proposed schedule does not increase the total number of school days.

(E) is another Outside the Scope wrong answer. Focusing on student preferences is immaterial to whether or not the proposed schedule will allow more material to be taught.

10. (A) Assumption (Necessary)

Step 1: Identify the Question Type

Because the question stem directly asks for the assumption that the argument depends on, this is a Necessary Assumption question.

Step 2: Untangle the Stimulus

The conclusion, marked by [t]*herefore*, is that, at first, the mayor won't be able to collect the money that he plans to charge drivers for being downtown. The evidence is that the mayor's plan requires the sophisticated camera system for enforcement, and that system will not be ready until the end of next year.

Step 3: Make a Prediction

If the mayor's plan won't work without the camera system, and the author's conclusion is that the mayor's plan won't work, then we know that the author is assuming that the mayor will implement his plan before the camera system is ready. That means that the mayor will implement his plan sometime before the end of next year, when the system will be ready.

Step 4: Evaluate the Answer Choices

(A) matches the prediction.

(B) goes Outside the Scope by introducing the idea of a budget deficit and neglecting the idea of whether or not the mayor's plan will be effectively enforced.

(C) contradicts the argument rather than providing its missing piece. The author is suggesting that at first the plan will not be effectively enforced. **(C)** goes against this, suggesting that the plan should not be implemented until it can be effectively enforced.

(D) makes an Irrelevant Comparison between the importance of raising revenue and reducing congestion.

(E) is both Outside the Scope and Extreme. It does not matter whether or not the mayor's plan is the most effective; it does matter whether or not the plan will be implemented before it can be fully enforced. Furthermore, referring to the plan as the "most effective way" is a red flag that the answer will fail the Denial Test.

11. (C) Paradox (EXCEPT)

Step 1: Identify the Question Type

The phrase "contributes to an explanation" indicates that this is a Paradox question. In this question, the four wrong answers will explain the difference in recover rates; the one right answer will not.

Step 2: Untangle the Stimulus

The stimulus tells us that people at smaller, rural hospitals are more likely to recover from their illnesses than those at large, urban hospitals.

Step 3: Make a Prediction

The four wrong answers will each suggest either some fact about rural hospitals that makes them a better place for recovery or some fact about urban hospitals that makes them a worse place for recovery. The right answer will either make the paradox less explainable (perhaps by suggesting that rural hospital should be terrible places to recover or urban hospitals should be great places to recover), or it will be outside the scope.

Step 4: Evaluate the Answer Choices

(C) is correct because it fails to affect the paradox. If there is no correlation between prestige of a doctor's school and patients' recovery rate, then one possible explanation of the paradox can be ruled out.

(A) explains the paradox because it suggests that patients at rural hospitals get better care.

(B) explains the paradox because it suggests that large, urban hospitals stress patients out, which could hurt their recovery.

(D) explains the paradox because it suggests that patients at large hospitals could get sent home before they properly recover.

(E) explains the paradox because it suggests that staff members at large hospitals aren't properly informed how to care for patients by the busy doctors there.

12. (E) Weaken

Step 1: Identify the Question Type

Because the stem directly asks for the answer choice that *weakens* Perry's argument, this is a Weaken question.

Step 2: Untangle the Stimulus

Perry concludes that lenders who want to minimize risks shouldn't loan money to worker-owned businesses. His evidence is that inefficiencies in worker-owned businesses can lead to low profitability and increase the risk for lenders.

Step 3: Make a Prediction

Start by finding Perry's assumption. Perry's evidence cites just one factor against worker-owned businesses: operational inefficiency. On the basis of that one factor, Perry broadly concludes that worker-owned businesses are risky to lend money to. For this to be true, Perry must assume that there are no other relevant factors that might make worker-owned businesses a safe borrower. The correct answer will suggest some new factor about worker-owned businesses that makes them likely to be safe borrowers.

Step 4: Evaluate the Answer Choices

(E) weakens the argument because if workers at worker-owned businesses compensate for their inefficiencies, then worker-owned businesses are less likely to be a risky investment.

(A) goes Outside the Scope by focusing on "[b]usinesses with the most extensive divisions of labor," rather than on worker-owned businesses.

(B) goes Outside the Scope by focusing narrowly on "[l]enders who specialize in high-risk loans," while the stimulus is about whether lenders in general should loan to worker-owned businesses.

(C) makes an Irrelevant Comparison between investor-owned businesses and worker-owned businesses; the stimulus is just about worker-owned businesses.

(D) goes Outside the Scope by discussing where the loans come from; the argument is just about how risky the loans would be, not where the loans have traditionally originated.

13. (E) Inference

Step 1: Identify the Question Type

Because the right answer "logically completes the argument," it is a statement that must be true on the basis of the stimulus. Thus, this is an Inference question.

Step 2: Untangle the Stimulus

Make an inventory of the statements. Some paleontologists thought that dinosaurs guarded their young for a long time after they hatched because of fossils discovered in special nests. However, crocodiles build special nests, too, but do not guard their young for long.

Step 3: Make a Prediction

Whenever a stimulus on the LSAT starts by telling you what "some [people] believe," look for a Contrast Keyword. Typically authors discuss what "some [people] believe" in order to disagree with it. Here, that seems to be the case. Although the evidence about dinosaur fossils might seem to support the paleontologists' hypothesis, the evidence about crocodiles seems to go against it. Therefore, the author would logically conclude the stimulus by saying that the paleontologists haven't yet proved their case.

Step 4: Evaluate the Answer Choices

(E) matches the prediction.

(A) is a 180. It directly contradicts the stimulus because we know the paleontologists in question have some evidence; the author just happens to think that evidence is not convincing.

(B) is Extreme. The author only suggests that the one piece of evidence offered by paleontologists is insufficient. That does not mean they will *never* know.

(C) is also Extreme. Just because the evidence about crocodiles seems to go against the paleontologists' belief, it isn't enough prove what hadrosaurs did or didn't do. It could be true that hadrosaurs built similar nests to those of crocodiles but still watched their young for a long time.

(D) goes Outside the Scope by introducing other dinosaurs. The point is not whether the hadrosaur fossils are evidence for conclusions about other dinosaurs but whether or not the nests containing hadrosaur fossils are actually good evidence for a conclusion about hadrosaurs.

14. (C) Paradox

Step 1: Identify the Question Type

Because the right answer "most helps to explain," this is a Paradox question.

Step 2: Untangle the Stimulus

The researchers concluded that studying more increased a student's chances of earning a higher grade, even though the students who studied the most didn't get the highest grades.

Step 3: Make a Prediction

Although it seems like the study's findings don't fit with its conclusions, a closer look reveals that the author has shifted scope. The conclusion is about earning a higher grade (in one class), while the evidence is about all of a student's grades. The correct answer will provide additional data suggesting that in a given class, when a student studies more, that grade improves.

Step 4: Evaluate the Answer Choices

(C) resolves the paradox by specifying that in a given course, when students study more their grades improve.

(A) makes an Irrelevant Comparison. "Some students who studied for less time than the average" could be as few as one student, so this new piece of information isn't strong enough to resolve the paradox.

(B) goes Outside the Scope by correlating grade change with time of year, rather than with increased study time.

(D) goes Outside the Scope by focusing on just the students who spent the least time studying, rather than a representative group of students.

(E) goes Outside the Scope by shifting the scope from grades to understanding. Understanding doesn't necessarily correlate to better grades.

15. (B) Inference

Step 1: Identify the Question Type

Because the correct answer is "most strongly supported" by the stimulus, it is a statement that follows from the stimulus. This is an Inference question.

Step 2: Untangle the Stimulus

Make an inventory of the statements. Three groups of professional cyclists cycled for an hour, one at each of three levels of intensity. The lowest-intensity group reported the most benefits related to anger and depression, the middle group less, and the highest-intensity group reported some negative effects.

Step 3: Make a Prediction

Because the stimulus gives information about "[m]ost members" of each of the three groups, the right answer will need to be phrased cautiously. Comparing the three studies, it looks like the level of intensity could have some effect on the emotions of the cyclists.

Step 4: Evaluate the Answer Choices

(B) is cautious enough ("tends to depend at least in part") and is in scope, focusing on how intensity affected mood. It must be true.

(A) goes Outside the Scope by being too broad, referring to "sustained exercise" in general. The stimulus covered only a small range of pulse rates and one specific type of exercise. Additionally, be cautious of an answer indicating two things are indefinitely directly proportional. Perhaps the trend of the three studies would not hold at higher or lower intensities.

(C) is Extreme. Just because one form of exercise is better than two others for improving mood doesn't mean that it must be the absolute best form of exercise for improving mood.

(D) makes an Irrelevant Comparison between psychological factors and physical factors that contribute to depression. The stimulus does not support that those factors equally contribute to depression.

(E) goes Outside the Scope by focusing on physical benefits, rather than on benefits for mood. Further, the stimulus doesn't define [m]oderate or intense cycling, so it cannot support a comparison of those two things.

16. (A) Parallel Flaw

Step 1: Identify the Question Type

The phrase "flawed reasoning most similar to" indicates that the right answer will have the same logical flaw as the stimulus. This is a Parallel Flaw question.

Step 2: Untangle the Stimulus

Because the stimulus is brief and includes some Formal Logic, starting with its first word, [a]nyone, attack by taking its entire structure into account. The author's argument boils down to this:

- If you believe in ETs, then you believe in UFOs.
- There are no UFOs.
- Therefore, there are no ETs.

Step 3: Make a Prediction

Whenever Formal Logic comes up in a Flaw or Parallel Flaw question, think carefully about contrapositives. Here, it looks like the second and third statements simply form the contrapositive of the first—but there's an element in the first sentence that doesn't reappear: belief. The initial statement in this argument isn't about whether or not ETs or UFOs exist—it's about believing in them. Thus, the true contrapositive of the first sentence would simply be this:

$$ \text{If} \quad \sim \textbf{believe in UFOs} \quad \rightarrow \quad \sim \textbf{believe in ETs} $$

We have no information that ties the actual existence of ETs to the actual existence of UFOs. The correct answer will make the same error by starting from a Formal Logic statement about belief and improperly shifting to evidence and conclusion about existence. In other words, the correct answer needs to have this overall structure:

If   believe in X   →   believe in Y

No Y; therefore, no X.

Step 4: Evaluate the Answer Choices
(A) has the exact same structure as the stimulus and thus contains the same flaw. Correct.

(B) is actually logical, not flawed. Here, the second statement is a valid contrapositive of the first.

(C) makes a contrapositive error but doesn't shift scopes like the stimulus. In **(C)**, both statements are about belief, rather than one being about belief and the other about existence.

(D) is much less definite than the stimulus. "[N]o good reason to believe" is much weaker than "conclusively refuted."

(E) switches the order of the elements. The sufficient term from the initial Formal Logic statement (unicorns) "has been conclusively proven" not to exist, rather than the necessary term (centaurs). In the stimulus, the necessary term (UFOs) from the initial Formal Logic statement is the one that was proven not to exist.

17. (E) Assumption (Sufficient)

Step 1: Identify the Question Type
The phrase "if assumed, enables the argument's conclusion to be properly drawn," indicates that this is a Sufficient Assumption question.

Step 2: Untangle the Stimulus
The author concludes that it is "imprudent to appear prudent." The reason is that people are generally resented when they wait for evidence in order to judge others.

Step 3: Make a Prediction
As in many arguments, the conclusion introduces an element that wasn't anywhere to be found in the evidence. Here that element is *imprudent*. The element of prudence is in the evidence because prudence is doing things cautiously, like waiting for evidence to make a judgment about someone. The evidence also includes an element not found in the conclusion—here it is being resented by others. The correct answer will connect imprudence to inspiring resentment in others.

Step 4: Evaluate the Answer Choices
(E) strongly connects inspiring resentment to imprudence.

(A) fails to include anything about the mismatched term of imprudence.

(B) fails to include anything about the mismatched term of resentment.

(C) is a Distortion. People resent those who appear prudent, not people who appear less prudent.

(D) goes Outside the Scope by focusing on people who are intuitive, rather than on the connection between imprudence and resentment.

18. (B) Inference

Step 1: Identify the Question Type
This is an Inference question, but with a twist. The question stem indicates that the four wrong answers could be true based on the statements in the stimulus. That means that the one right answer must be false based on the statements in the stimulus.

Step 2: Untangle the Stimulus
Make an inventory of the statements. Regular smokers do better on certain memory tests than non-smokers, so long as the smoker has either just smoked or smoked within eight hours.

Step 3: Make a Prediction
The stimulus seems to suggest that smokers who smoke generally do better on the memory test than nonsmokers. The correct answer will contradict this, perhaps by saying that nonsmokers do better than smokers.

Step 4: Evaluate the Answer Choices
(B) contradicts the stimulus by saying that a nonsmoker who has just smoked does better on the memory test. This directly goes against the last clause of the first sentence in the stimulus: "whether or not the nonsmoker has also just smoked a cigarette ..."

(A) could be true because it compares two different groups of nonsmokers, something the stimulus gives no information about.

(C) could be true because it compares nonsmokers to smokers who haven't smoked for more than eight hours. The stimulus gives information about smokers who have smoked within eight hours, but not those who haven't.

(D) could be true because it brings in a lot of information not in the stimulus. For example, the stimulus does not specifically cover those smokers who do no better on the memory test even after just smoking. The stimulus also does not discuss the effect of heavy smoking on memory.

(E) could be true because it compares two groups of smokers. The stimulus only provides information for comparing smokers and nonsmokers.

19. (E) Principle (Identify/Strengthen)

Step 1: Identify the Question Type
The phrase "most help to justify the educator's reasoning" indicates that the correct answer will identify a principle that strengthens the educator's argument.

Step 2: Untangle the Stimulus

Attack the stimulus like a Strengthen question. The educator's conclusion is that the organization should not make decisions by direct vote but should continue to elect officers to make decisions. The evidence is that by electing officers, individual voters will likely have more influence on policy.

Step 3: Make a Prediction

Start by identifying the assumption. In the conclusion, the author recommends against organizations making decisions in a certain way. In the evidence, the author talks about giving individuals more influence on policy. Thus, the author assumes that the organization should do things that would give individuals more influence on policy. The correct answer will reinforce this assumption, likely in general terms.

Step 4: Evaluate the Answer Choices

(E) matches the prediction. The reason to choose one decision-making procedure over another is maximizing the influence of individuals.

(A) goes Outside the Scope by focusing on the weight of each individual's vote. It fails to address the educator's recommendation that decision making should be done by elected officials.

(B) goes Outside the Scope by including organizational "benefits" and "fairness," neither of which figure into the educator's argument.

(C) is Outside the Scope. It might match the educator's conclusion about having elected officials make decisions, but it completely neglects the educator's evidence and instead adds the element of mastering information.

(D) goes Outside the Scope by focusing on what individual officers should do. The stimulus is about whether or not officers should be the decision makers, not about how they should make particular decisions.

20. (E) Assumption (Sufficient)

Step 1: Identify the Question Type

The phrase "if which one of the following is assumed" indicates that this is a Sufficient Assumption question.

Step 2: Untangle the Stimulus

The author concludes that the amygdala has more influence over the cortex than the cortex has over the amygdala. The evidence is that the neural connections carrying signals from the amygdala to the cortex are better developed.

Step 3: Make a Prediction

This is a classic Mismatched Concepts argument. Because both the evidence and conclusion mention the amygdala and the cortex, these are not the mismatched terms. Looking past the amygdala and the cortex, the conclusion is about exerting influence. The evidence is about the development of neural

connections. The assumption will connect these two ideas. The author must be assuming that the more development there is in a set of neural connections, the more influence it has.

Step 4: Evaluate the Answer Choices

(E) matches the prediction. "[D]irectly proportional" just means that as one thing goes up, so too does another. That would be Extreme if this was a Necessary Assumption question, but here it is acceptable because this is a Sufficient Assumption question.

(A) goes Outside the Scope by introducing the rest of the brain, rather than just the amygdala and cortex.

(B) also goes Outside the Scope. Other brain regions are irrelevant to whether the development of neural connections is an indication of influence.

(C) goes Outside the Scope by discussing the region "that has the most influence on the cortex." The stimulus is only about the amygdala and the cortex. **(C)** would strengthen the argument, but by itself, it is not sufficient to reach the conclusion that the amygdala exerts a greater influence on the cortex than vice versa.

(D) also goes Outside the Scope, much like **(A)** and **(B)**, by introducing areas of the brain besides the amygdala and the cortex.

21. (C) Weaken

Step 1: Identify the Question Type

Because the right answer is the one statement that "weakens the reasoning" in the stimulus, this is a Weaken question.

Step 2: Untangle the Stimulus

The author concludes that the *Iliad* and the *Odyssey* were almost certainly not the work of the same author. His evidence is that there are significant differences in tone, vocabulary, and details.

Step 3: Make a Prediction

Start by finding the assumption. Here, the author is assuming that significant differences between two works means that the two works must not have the same author. In other words, he's overlooking the possibility that an author could change his tone and vocabulary between works. The correct answer will attack the author's assumption, perhaps by pointing out that an author could change his writing style significantly in two different works.

Step 4: Evaluate the Answer Choices

(C) matches the prediction by giving a modern example that shows an author can use different styles in different works.

(A) might indicate that the attributions of the hymns are also wrong, but because we have no evidence that these varied works were indeed created by the same author, it doesn't affect the likelihood that Homer wrote both the *Iliad* and *Odyssey*.

(B) might explain how two works by the same author came to differ, but the errors and corruptions described here are "minor" and don't account for the "great" discrepancies the author describes in Homer.

(D) goes Outside the Scope by focusing on internal consistency in a work rather than on the consistency between two different works. Similar to **(B)**, a book can fail to have "complete consistency" without having the kind of large differences discussed in the stimulus.

(E) is a 180 because it directly supports the author's conclusion. It gives another reason why the two works would not have had the same author.

22. (D) Principle (Apply/Inference)

Step 1: Identify the Question Type

The phrase "conforms to the principles stated by" indicates that the one right answer must be true based on the principles in the stimulus. This is an Apply the Principle question.

Step 2: Untangle the Stimulus

Start by summarizing the principle in the stimulus. This stimulus is full of Formal Logic, so translate and contrapose the statements. The first statement translates to:

If	*wholly truthful*	→	*true AND made without intended deception*

Contraposed, it states:

If	*~ true OR made with some intention to deceive*	→	*~ wholly truthful*

The second statement translates to:

If	*intended to deceive OR the speaker knows it has been misunderstood but doesn't clarify*	→	*lie*

Contraposed:

If	*~ lie*	→	*~ intended to deceive AND the speaker would clarify it upon learning that it had been misunderstood*

Step 3: Make a Prediction

Because the answer choices are filled with specific scenarios, it will be hard to make a precise prediction. Instead, use the Formal Logic translations to evaluate each answer choice as you go.

Step 4: Evaluate the Answer Choices

(D) is the match. The answer choice is about whether or not something was a lie, so check the second Formal Logic statement. Based on this statement, because Walter's statement was intended to deceive, it does follow that it was a lie.

(A) is about whether or not something was wholly truthful, so compare it to the first Formal Logic statement. In the first Formal Logic statement's contrapositive, if something is not true, then it is not wholly truthful. Ted's statement was not true, therefore it cannot be wholly truthful. Thus, **(A)** does not match the principle in the stimulus.

(B) is about whether or not something was a lie, so use the second Formal Logic statement. If a speaker intends to deceive, it is a lie. Tony intended to deceive his granddaughter; therefore his statement was a lie. Thus, because **(B)** suggests that Tony was not lying, it fails to match the principle in the stimulus.

(C) fails to match either Formal Logic statement because it seeks to connect not telling a lie with not wholly truthful. The stimulus made no such connection. Note that the one idea that does come up in both of the stimulus's statements, deception, is not mentioned in **(C)**.

(E) is about whether or not something was a lie, so use the second Formal Logic statement. In the second Formal Logic statement, if a speaker intends to deceive, it is a lie. The tour guide intended to deceive the tourists, so his statement was a lie. Thus, because **(E)** suggests that the tour guide did not lie, it fails to match the principle in the stimulus.

23. (D) Flaw

Step 1: Identify the Question Type
The phrase "most vulnerable to criticism" indicates that this is a Flaw question. The correct answer will describe the flaw in the application of the principle.

Step 2: Untangle the Stimulus
Simply put, the principle states that if an activity is healthy for a kid's intellectual development, then it does not take away from the child's social development. Contraposed, it states that if something does take away from a kid's social development, then it is not healthy for the kid. The application seems to fit with the contrapositive. Because Megan's reading decreases the amount of time she spends with others, the author concludes that reading is unhealthy for her.

Step 3: Make a Prediction
Find the assumption that the application makes. Because the application concludes that Megan's reading is unhealthy, the author must assume that Megan's reading takes away from her social development. Note, the application only suggests that it reduces the amount of time she spends with others, not that it actually takes away from her social development. The correct answer will suggest that the author assumes that just because something reduces the amount of social time, that it actually gets in the way of social development.

Step 4: Evaluate the Answer Choices
(D) matches the prediction by calling out the author's assumption.

(A) goes against the language of both the principle and the application. The language in the principle is categorical, and the application takes it that way.

(B) is a Distortion of the conclusion of the application. The application is about whether or not the activity is healthy, not about whether or not some other benefit to the activity is more important than its healthiness.

(C) almost describes the application accurately—the application does interpret the principle to be about what is unhealthy. This is perfectly logical, though, and not a misinterpretation. By contraposing the principle's Formal Logic, we deduced a logical statement about one sufficient explanation for something to be unhealthy.

(E) suggests that the application confuses sufficiency and necessity or, in other words, misforms the contrapositive. But, the application gets the logical structure of the contrapositive correct. The problem with the application is that it makes an unwarranted assumption about what would satisfy the sufficient condition of the contrapositive.

24. (E) Inference

Step 1: Identify the Question Type
The phrase "provide the most support for which one of the following claims" indicates that the right answer is supported by the information in the stimulus. Thus, this is an Inference question.

Step 2: Untangle the Stimulus
Make an inventory of the information in the stimulus. McElligott flash pasteurizes its apple juice because of past bacterial infections traced to the juice. Intensive pasteurization would kill more bacteria, but it also kills the taste. Citrus juices seem to be safe, so they're not pasteurized.

Step 3: Make a Prediction
Because McElligott now does some pasteurizing of its apple juice, it is likely that its apple juice has fewer bacteria than it used to. At the same time, both its citrus and apple juices could still have some bacteria because the company aren't using the most effective method for eliminating bacteria in either of them.

Step 4: Evaluate the Answer Choices
(E) must be true based on the stimulus because intensive pasteurization does eliminate more bacteria than the flash process that McElligott's uses.

(A) goes Outside the Scope because the stimulus provides absolutely no information about other companies' citrus juices.

(B) could be true, but it need not be. There is no support for a comparison between McElligott's apple and citrus juices. Just because the citrus juice isn't pasteurized doesn't say anything about how much bacteria there is in it.

(C) goes Outside the Scope by comparing McElligott's citrus juices with pasteurized citrus juices in general. The stimulus doesn't tell us whether or not there are some pasteurization processes (perhaps even flash pasteurization) that do not affect flavor.

(D) is Extreme because it talks about "[t]he most effective method." The stimulus compared two specific methods, but there could be other methods out there that are more effective at eliminating bacteria but don't destroy flavor.

25. (E) Assumption (Necessary)

Step 1: Identify the Question Type
Because the "argument requires the assumption," this is a Necessary Assumption question.

Step 2: Untangle the Stimulus
The conclusion is that legislators who value democracy shouldn't propose laws barring behavior that only hurts the person engaging in the behavior. The evidence is that general acceptance of the idea that individuals can't look out for

themselves hurts society, and the assumptions imputed to our legislators tend to spread to the rest of society.

Step 3: Make a Prediction

Start by identifying the mismatched terms. Both the evidence and conclusion discuss protecting democracy, so that idea doesn't need to be in the assumption. The idea of widely spread ideas comes up in both pieces of the evidence, so that doesn't need to be in the assumption either. What's left over in the conclusion is laws barring self-destructive behaviors. What's left over in the evidence is individuals not being able to look out for themselves. The assumption will connect the ideas of laws barring self-destructive behaviors and of individuals not being able to look out for themselves.

Step 4: Evaluate the Answer Choices

(E) connects legislators banning self-destructive behaviors and individuals being seen as incapable of looking out for themselves.

(A) goes Outside the Scope by focusing on what legislators value, rather than on what they should not do. Additionally the word "invariably" is Extreme to be needed by the argument.

(B) is a Faulty Use of Detail. It repeats an idea from the evidence in more general terms. The evidence states that people accept the assumptions of legislators, so it is irrelevant whether people accept the beliefs of other prominent and powerful people as well.

(C) goes Outside the Scope by discussing what legislators already do, rather than what they should do in the future. The author may believe that legislators may currently be undertaking an action injurious to democracy, despite valuing it.

(D) goes Outside the Scope by focusing just on the likelihood that behavior that is harmful to the person who does it is also harmful to others. The stimulus focuses on whether or not to propose legislation barring such behavior, not its frequency.

Section II: Logic Games

Game 1: Water Valves

Q#	Question Type	Correct	Difficulty
1	Acceptability	E	★
2	Could Be True EXCEPT	C	★★
3	"If" / Could Be True EXCEPT	B	★★
4	"If" / Could Be True EXCEPT	B	★★
5	Must Be True	E	★★★
6	"If" / Could Be True	B	★
7	"If" / Must Be True EXCEPT	B	★

Game 2: Field Trip Chaperones

Q#	Question Type	Correct	Difficulty
8	Acceptability	B	★
9	"If" / Must Be True	E	★★★
10	"If" / Could Be True	A	★★★
11	Must Be False (CANNOT Be True)	D	★★★
12	Must Be False (CANNOT Be True)	C	★★★

Game 3: Sales Conference Seminars

Q#	Question Type	Correct	Difficulty
13	Acceptability	B	★
14	"If" / Could Be True	E	★★★
15	"If" / Must Be True	C	★★
16	Must Be False (CANNOT Be True)	B	★★★
17	"If" / Could Be True	D	★★★

Game 4: Bread Truck Deliveries

Q#	Question Type	Correct	Difficulty
18	Acceptability	C	★★
19	"If" / Must Be True	A	★
20	"If" / Must Be True	E	★★★
21	Must Be True	C	★
22	"If" / Could Be True	C	★★★
23	Must Be False	E	★★★★

Game 1: Water Valves

Step 1: Overview
Situation: Workers opening valves at a water plant

Entities: The valves—G, H, I, K, L, N, O, P

Action: Loose Sequencing. A quick glance at the rules indicates there are no Established Entities or Blocks of Entities, so this will be Loose Sequencing.

Limitations: Each valve is opened exactly once, and no two valves are opened at the same time. So all entities will be sequenced, one at a time.

Step 2: Sketch
Because this is a Loose Sequencing game, simply jot down a list of entities. If you started by drawing slots, don't worry; they may be useful later.

GHIKLNOP

Step 3: Rules
Rule 1 presents a loose relationship: K and P are both opened before H. Because the order of K and P isn't given, just align them both before H horizontally:

K
 ＼
  H
 ／
P

Rule 2 states O is opened before L but after H. Build this on to what you've already drawn out for Rule 1.

K
 ＼
  H — O — L
 ／
P

Rules 3, 4, and 5 give three additional relationships: L after G (G — L), N before H (N — H), and I after K (K — I). Add each of these relationships to the Master Sketch.

    I
   ／
  K
N — H — O — L
P ／   ／
      G

Step 4: Deductions
As is usual with Loose Sequencing games, most (if not all) of the deductions will come from the D in BLEND: Duplications. The Master Sketch already reflects all of those Duplications, so there's nothing left to draw in.

As always with Loose Sequencing, take a moment to determine which entities could be first and which could be last. Because K, N, P, and G have no valves that need to be opened before them, any one of them could be first. Similarly,

because I and L have no valves that need to be opened after them, either one of them could be last.

With no Established Entities, this is as far as Deductions will take you.

Step 5: Questions

1. (E) Acceptability
For Acceptability questions, go through the rules one at a time, eliminating answers that violate the rules.

None of the answers violate the first rule, but don't panic. There are still four more rules to go. O comes after L in **(B)**, so that answer violates Rule 2. With L before G, **(D)** violates Rule 3. With H before N, **(C)** violates Rule 4. And finally, with I before K, **(A)** violates Rule 5. That leaves **(E)** as the only acceptable answer.

2. (C) Could Be True EXCEPT
The "EXCEPT" indicates that the correct answer will be a valve that cannot be opened fifth. The remaining four answers will list valves that can be.

In order for a valve to be opened fifth, it must have no more than four valves opened before it and no more than three valves opened after it. Because K has to have I, H, O, and L opened after it, the latest it could be opened is fourth. Therefore, it can't be fifth, making **(C)** the correct answer.

H has only three valves that need to be opened before it (K, N, P) and only two valves that need to be opened after it (O, L). So it could be opened at any time from fourth to sixth. You can eliminate **(A)**.

(B) is wrong as well. I only has to have K opened before it, so it could be opened any time from second to eighth.

As for **(D)**, N could be opened first (as we already determined) and has to have only H, O, and L opened after it. So it could be opened any time from first to fifth.

Finally **(E)** is also incorrect. Valve O has to have H, K, N, and P opened before it. That means the earliest O can be opened is fifth, which is enough information to eliminate this answer.

3. (B) "If" / Could Be True EXCEPT
K has to come before I, so if I is opened second, K will be opened first. Plus, because only I or L could be the final valve opened, L must be last.

K	I						L
1	2	3	4	5	6	7	8

As for the rest of the valves, N and P still need to be opened before H, so H can't be opened any earlier than fifth. That means **(B)** can't be true, making it the right answer.

Because G has to be opened before L only, it can be opened in any of the free spaces in the sketch—from third to seventh—which means **(A)** and **(E)** are incorrect.

In **(C)**, if P is fifth, G and N could fill in spots 3 and 4. That would leave H in sixth and O in seventh. This is an acceptable sketch.

K	I	G/N	G/N	P	H	O	L
1	2	3	4	5	6	7	8

In **(D)**, if O is opened sixth, it must to be followed by G in the seventh spot. N and P, which must come before H, would be opened third or fourth, while H would be opened fifth.

K	I	N/P	N/P	H	O	G	L
1	2	3	4	5	6	7	8

4. (B) "If" / Could Be True EXCEPT

If L is the seventh valve opened, that means it can't be last. Once again, knowing that the last valve opened can only be I or L lets you determine that I must be in spot 8. Because I is last, it can't possibly be opened second. That means **(B)** is the correct answer.

						L	I
1	2	3	4	5	6	7	8

For **(A)**, G only has to be opened before L. Because L is opened seventh, G is free to be opened any time before that, including second.

Meanwhile, K, N, and P have to be opened before H, but in no particular order. They can be opened first, second, and third, with any one of them being opened second. That makes **(C)**, **(D)**, and **(E)** incorrect.

5. (E) Must Be True

The correct answer is something that must be true at all times. The remaining four answers are either certainly false or could be false. Look at **(E)**, the correct answer. If five or more valves are opened before N, only two or fewer valves can be opened after it. That doesn't leave enough room for H, O, and L, all of which must be opened after N. Therefore, it must be true that four or fewer valves are opened before N.

Nothing has to be opened before P or G, so that knocks out **(A)** and **(B)**. O can be fifth because it has to come after only K, N, P, and H. That means it can certainly have more than two valves opened after it, which eliminates **(C)**. H can be fourth because it has to come after only K, N, and P. That means it

can certainly have more than three valves opened after it, which eliminates **(D)**.

6. (B) "If" / Could Be True

If K is opened fourth, three valves must be opened before it and four valves after it. Based on the Master Sketch, the four valves that must be opened after K are I, H, O, and L. That leaves G, N, and P to be opened before it. Given that G, N, and P can be in any order, N can certainly be opened third, making **(B)** the correct answer.

			K				
1	2	3	4	5	6	7	8

P/N/G   H — O — L
                              I

Valve I can't be opened second because it must come after K, thus eliminating **(A)**.

Because G, N, and P must be opened before K, **(C)** and **(E)** are eliminated.

Finally, because O has to be opened after H, which in turn must be opened after K, O can't be opened fifth. This eliminates **(D)**.

7. (B) "If" / Must Be True EXCEPT

Start out by drawing a Strict Sequencing sketch, putting G first and I third. For the third time this game, knowing which entities could be opened last is important: I being third makes L the only valve that can be opened last. Then, because I must be opened after K, K must be second (because G has already been placed first). That leaves N, P, H, and O. N and P will be fourth and fifth (in any order), followed by H sixth and O seventh.

G	K	I	N/P	P/N	H	O	L
1	2	3	4	5	6	7	8

Because N and P are not definitively determined, **(B)** is the only answer that could be false. **(A)**, **(C)**, **(D)**, and **(E)** all must occur in the question's sketch.

Game 2: Field Trip Chaperones

Step 1: Overview

Situation: Nine people taking a field trip to a museum

Entities: Six children—j, k, l, s, t, v—and three adults—M, O, P

Action: Distribution. The six children must be divided up among the three accompanying adults.

Limitations: Each adult accompanies exactly two children.

Step 2: Sketch

This is a standard Distribution game with a strictly defined numeric setup. Set up three columns, one for each adult, and put two slots under each column to fill in the children.

$$j, k, l, s, t, v$$

$$\underline{\quad M \quad} \mid \underline{\quad O \quad} \mid \underline{\quad P \quad}$$

$$\underline{\quad}\ \underline{\quad} \mid \underline{\quad}\ \underline{\quad} \mid \underline{\quad}\ \underline{\quad}$$

Step 3: Rules

Rule 1 is pure Formal Logic: if Juana is with Margoles, Lucita is with Podorski. As with all Formal Logic, be sure to write the original rule and its contrapositive:

$$\frac{M}{j} \rightarrow \frac{P}{l}$$

$$\sim\frac{P}{l} \rightarrow \sim\frac{M}{j}$$

Rule 2 is more Formal Logic. Once again, jot down the rule and its contrapositive:

$$\sim\frac{M}{k} \rightarrow \frac{O}{v}$$

$$\sim\frac{O}{v} \rightarrow \frac{M}{k}$$

Rule 3 limits who can accompany Thanh. Because Thanh must go with either Margoles or O'Connell, he can't be accompanied by Podorski. So add "no t" under Podorski in the sketch. Also, in order to keep the rule positive, rather than just negative, put "t" with an arrow toward Margoles and O'Connell.

Rule 4 may be long, but it simply lists three pairs of children who can never be together. Jot down these restricted pairs:

Never jk
Never ls
Never tv

Step 4: Deductions

Because half the rules are conditional, it's hard to come up with any absolute deductions. Moreover, none of the children are duplicated in the Formal Logic, so you can't even combine those rules.

Because Thanh can be accompanied by only two of the three adults, using Limited Options is a possibility. However, if Thanh goes with Margoles, all you know is Veronica doesn't. Having Thanh accompanied by O'Connell prevents Veronica from being with O'Connell, which mean Kyle visits the museum with Margoles (Rule 2). Still, that's likely not enough to warrant drawing two sketches.

Instead, in the questions, look for information that triggers the Formal Logic and be mindful of the children who can't be together. Entering the questions, the Master Sketch should look something like this:

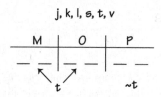

Step 5: Questions

8. (B) Acceptability

For Acceptability questions, go through the rules one at a time, eliminating answers that violate any of them. Because Formal Logic is more complicated to test, it's easier to start with the more concrete rules.

By Rule 3, Thanh can't be accompanied by Podorski, which eliminates **(E)**. **(D)** puts Lucita and Salim together, violating Rule 4. To test Rule 1, look for any remaining answer that has Juana accompanied by Margoles. **(A)** does, but Lucita is not with Podorski as Rule 1's Formal Logic requires. So **(A)** is eliminated. Finally, **(C)** has Kyle accompanied by Podorski, not Margoles, thereby triggering Rule 2. But in that case, Veronica should be with O'Connell. Because she's not, **(C)** is no good, leaving **(B)** as the right answer.

9. (E) "If" / Must Be True

Putting Lucita and Thanh with Margoles means Margoles is complete. Because of that, Kyle can't be accompanied by Margoles. Due to Rule 2, Victoria must then be with O'Connell. That leaves Juana, Kyle, and Salim for the remaining three slots.

Because Juana and Kyle can't be together (Rule 4), one of them must be with O'Connell and the other with Podorski. Putting j/k in each column, that leaves one space left in

Podorski's group, which goes to the last child, Salim. And that makes **(E)** the correct answer.

M		O		P	
l	t	v	j/k	j/k	s

Because both Juana and Kyle could go with either O'Connell or Podorski, they are the only children not definitively placed. That lets you knock out **(A)**, **(B)**, **(C)**, and **(D)**.

10. (A) "If" / Could Be True

Once again, one adult is completely assigned: Podorski accompanies Juana and Veronica. Because Veronica is not with O'Connell, this triggers the contrapositive of Rule 2. That puts Kyle with Margoles. That leaves Lucita, Salim, and Thanh. Because Lucita and Salim cannot be together (Rule 4), they will be split between the remaining two adults: Margoles and O'Connell. That leaves one open space under O'Connell for Thanh.

M		O		P	
k	l/s	t	l/s	j	v

Margoles will thus accompany either Kyle and Lucita or Kyle and Salim. The latter option is the correct answer, as shown in **(A)**.

(B), **(D)**, and **(E)** are all incorrect because Thanh must go with O'Connell. Finally, **(C)** can't be true because while Margoles must accompany either Lucita or Salim, she can't accompany both (Rule 4).

11. (D) Must Be False (CANNOT Be True)

The question asks for a pair of children Podorski CANNOT accompany. By Rule 3, Podorski can't accompany Thanh. That immediately makes **(D)** the correct answer!

Your previous work from the second question of the set shows Podorski could accompany either Juana and Salim or Kyle and Salim, which means both **(B)** and **(C)** are possible.

For **(A)**, if Podorski accompanied Juana and Lucita, then Thanh, Kyle, Veronica, and Salim must be divided between Margoles and O'Connell. If Kyle goes with O'Connell, then, according to Rule 2, Veronica will as well. That leaves Thanh and Salim with Margoles. That's an acceptable sketch.

M		O		P	
t	s	k	v	j	l

Finally, for **(E)**, if Salim and Veronica go with Podorski, Margoles must accompany Kyle (Rule 2's contrapositive), and Juana must be with O'Connell (Rule 1's contrapositive). Thanh and Lucita can go with either Margoles or O'Connell.

M		O		P	
k	t/l	j	l/t	s	v

12. (C) Must Be False (CANNOT Be True)

This question asks for a pair of children O'Connell CANNOT accompany. Because any child can be accompanied by O'Connell, it helps to consider what triggers the Formal Logic involving O'Connell. According to Rule 2, if Kyle is not with Margoles, then Veronica must be with O'Connell. However, in **(C)**, Kyle is with O'Connell (i.e., not with Margoles) but Veronica is not. Therefore, **(C)** violates Rule 2, making it the right answer.

Your previous sketches can help eliminate some of the wrong answers. In the second question of the set, O'Connell can accompany Juana and Victoria, eliminating **(B)**. In the third question of the set, O'Connell can accompany Lucita and Thanh, eliminating **(D)**.

If O'Connell accompanies Juana and Lucita, then according to Rule 3, Thanh must go with Margoles. Kyle must also be with Margoles (Rule 2's contrapositive). That leaves Salim and Victoria with Podorski. This is acceptable, so **(A)** is incorrect.

M		O		P	
t	k	j	l	s	v

If both Salim and Veronica visit the museum with O'Connell, then Thanh must go with Margoles (Rule 3). Juana and Kyle can't go together, so they must be split between Margoles and Podorski. That leaves Lucita to fill the final space with Podorski. This is valid, so **(E)** is incorrect.

M		O		P	
t	j/k	s	v	l	k/j

Game 3: Sales Conference Seminars

Step 1: Overview

Situation: A three-day sales training conference featuring several seminars

Entities: Six seminars (three long: H, N, T; three short: g, o, p) and three days

Action: Distribution/Sequencing Hybrid. At first glance, this seems like a standard Distribution game: determine which seminars will be held each day. However, the overview states that the seminars are given consecutively, suggesting a Sequencing component, making this game a combination of both actions.

Limitations: Each seminar will be given exactly once with exactly two seminars each day.

Step 2: Sketch

Start by setting up a Distribution chart. Then, line up slots within each column to account for the Sequencing. When you list the entities, use lowercase and uppercase letters to differentiate between short and long seminars.

Short: g o p   Long: H N T

	1	2	3
—	—	—	—

Step 3: Rules

Rule 1 states that each day must have one short and one long seminar. However, it doesn't say which one has to come first. Because of the Sequencing component of this game, you can't simply label one slot "short" and one slot "long" in each column, so just write this rule in shorthand off to the side.

Rule 2 provides a sequencing element: Goals and Objections (both short) have to be given before Telemarketing. The shorthand for this rule will be just like in any other Sequencing game:

Note that Goals and Objections cannot be on the same day (because of Rule 1). However, nothing in the rule prevents Goals or Objections from being on the same day as Telemarketing, as long as Telemarketing is the second seminar of the day.

Rule 3 provides more sequencing:

p —— N

Again, these two seminars do not have to be on different days. They can be given on the same day with Persuasion first and Negotiating second.

Step 4: Deductions

The first rule greatly limits the placement of Telemarketing. Because it has to be preceded by two short seminars, it can be placed only on either the second or third day of the conference. The placement of Telemarketing affects not only Goals and Objections but also the other two long seminars, Humor and Negotiating. This makes it worth drawing out Limited Options.

In Option I, if Telemarketing is on the second day, Goals and Objections must be the short seminars for days one and two, in either order. Whichever one is on the second day must precede Telemarketing that day. Furthermore, that leaves the last short seminar, Persuasion, for the third day. By Rule 3, Negotiating will also have to be on the third day, with Persuasion coming before it. That leaves Humor as the long seminar for the first day, although the order of the seminars that day cannot be determined.

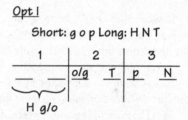

For Option II, Telemarketing goes on the third day. If Telemarketing is on the third day, that leaves Humor and Negotiating as the long seminars for the first and second days. Because Persuasion cannot come after Negotiating (by Rule 3), the short seminar for the third day must be either Goals or Objections. Whichever one is there must precede Telemarketing on that day (by Rule 1).

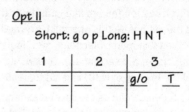

Step 5: Questions

13. (B) Acceptability

For Acceptability questions, go through the rules one at a time, eliminating answers that violate the rules. **(D)** puts two short seminars, Goals and Objections, on the first day, violating Rule 1. **(A)** puts Goals after Telemarketing, and **(E)** puts Objections after Telemarketing. Both answers violate Rule 2. **(C)** has Persuasion after Negotiating, violating Rule 3. That leaves **(B)** as the right answer.

14. (E) "If" / Could Be True

Option I shows Goals is a possible seminar for day one. That sketch shows Telemarketing is an acceptable seminar for day two, which matches **(E)**, the correct answer.

Even without Limited Options, you could have gotten this answer. If Goals is on the first day, the other seminar that day will be a long seminar. It can't be Negotiating because that has to come after Persuasion. And it can't be Telemarketing because Telemarketing still needs Objections before it. So, the only long seminar left is Humor. Knowing that Goals and Humor are the two seminars for the first day eliminates **(A)**, **(B)**, **(C)**, and **(D)**.

15. (C) "If" / Must Be True

Putting Negotiating before Objections allows you to combine the two sequencing rules to create a long string:

$$p—N—o—T$$
$$g$$

With five of the six entities lined up, the sequencing is very limited. However, based on the answer choices, you don't have to worry about distributing them into the three days. All of the answers refer to the relative sequencing. A quick scan reveals **(C)**, which is definitely supported by the sketch. **(A)** and **(B)** could be true based on the sketch but don't have to be true. **(D)** and **(E)** both include Humor, which isn't included in the sequence and therefore has a large amount of freedom.

16. (B) Must Be False (CANNOT Be True)

This question asks for a seminar that cannot be the second seminar on day two. The Limited Options show only Telemarketing as a seminar that could definitely be the second seminar on the second day (Option I), but Telemarketing isn't even listed as a possible answer. Anyone who skips this question though and completes the last question of the set before this one will be rewarded with a sketch that shows Humor, Objections, and Goals as possible second seminars for the second day. That would eliminate **(A)**, **(C)**, and **(E)**, leaving only **(B)** and **(D)** for testing.

To test **(B)**, put Persuasion as the second seminar of the second day. This is only possible in Option II. However, in that case, there would be no room for Negotiating after Persuasion because the third day is filled. That would violate Rule 3. Therefore, **(B)** cannot be true, making it the correct answer.

For practice, test **(D)**. If Negotiating is the second spot on the second day, you must still be in Option II. Persuasion could then go on the morning of the second day, while Humor and

either Objections or Goals could fill the spots in the first day. This would be an acceptable sketch, so **(D)** is incorrect.

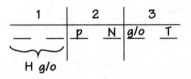

17. (D) "If" / Could Be True

Humor could only be scheduled for the second day in the Option II. That would leave Negotiating as the long seminar for the first day. Because Persuasion has to come before Negotiating, it must be the first seminar. That leaves either Goals or Objectives as the short seminar for the second day. The order for the second day doesn't matter.

	1		2		3
p	N	H	o/g	g/o	T

Or

	1		2		3
p	N	o/g	H	g/o	T

With that, only **(D)** is possible.

(A) and **(C)** both contradict Option II by putting Telemarketing on a day other than the third day. The New-"If" in this question puts Humor, a long seminar, on the second day, so **(B)** cannot be true because Negotiating is also a long seminar, and Rule 1 requires only one long seminar per day. **(E)** also contradicts Option II by putting Persuasion on the already full third day.

Game 4: Bread Truck Deliveries

Step 1: Overview
Situation: A bread truck making deliveries to six restaurants on its route

Entities: The six restaurants: F, G, H, K, L, M

Action: Loose Sequencing. Determine the order in which the truck delivers bread to the restaurants. A quick glance at the rules reveals that there are no Established Entities or Blocks of Entities, so this will be Loose Sequencing.

Limitations: Exactly one delivery to each restaurant in succession. So, all entities are sequenced, one at a time.

Step 2: Sketch
Because this is a Loose Sequencing game, simply jot down a list of entities. You'll build a Loose Sequencing tree after going through the rules.

F G H K L M

Step 3: Rules
Rule 1 gives a typical Loose Sequencing relationship. G will come before K and after F:

F —— G —— K

Rule 2 gives another, even simpler relationship (**H — G**). Build it onto the information so far:

F⟍
   G —— K
H⟋

Rule 3 introduces some Formal Logic. Although not common in Loose Sequencing, it's still handled as any other Formal Logic rule:

If F —— M → L —— H

The basic contrapositive would normally look like this:

If Not L —— H → Not F —— M

However, when forming the contrapositive, try to turn negatives into positives. Because the truck delivers to each restaurant one at a time, another way of saying "The truck doesn't deliver to L before H," is "The truck delivers to H before L." Same goes for F and M. Having positive triggers and results will make dealing with the Formal Logic much easier. So the contrapositive would be easier to work with if it looked like this:

If H —— L → M —— F

Rule 4 gives a lot of information, so it's important to analyze it piece by piece. First, start out with the two possibilities:

M —— H or K —— M

Then, the final part of the rule says that you can't have both. That means if the truck delivers to M before H, it can't deliver to K before M. In that case, the truck would deliver to M before K.

Similarly, if the truck delivers to K before M, it can't deliver to M before H. So in that case, it would have to deliver to H before M.

Finally, because one of these two scenarios must happen, you get two possible outcomes:

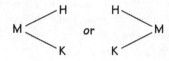

This means that the truck will deliver to M either before both H and K or after them both.

Step 4: Deductions
Because Rule 4 provides two possible outcomes that use half the entities, and some of those entities are duplicated in the other rules, this is an ideal situation for Limited Options.

Start with the two sketches set up by Rule 4. Add G to both options such that G comes after H (Rule 2) and before K (Rule 1). This will likely require some redrawing.

Opt I
M —— H —— G —— K

Opt II
H —— G —— K —— M

Once that's set up, add F before G (by Rule 1) in both options.

Opt I
M —— H —— G —— K
           F⟋

Opt II
H —— G —— K —— M
  F⟋

The last thing to consider is the Formal Logic of Rule 3. In the first option, the relationship between M and F is undetermined: either of them could come before the other. Therefore, L cannot be placed. However, in the second option, the truck delivers to F before M. This triggers the Formal Logic, requiring L to be delivered before H. So, the Master Sketch of the two options looks like this:

Opt I

M —— H —— G —— K
　　　　F

(L is a floater)

Opt II

L —— H —— G —— K —— M
　　　　F

Finally, with Loose Sequencing, always take a moment to determine what could be first and what could be last.

In the first option, no restaurants need to be delivered to before M and F, so they can be first. Also, because L is a Floater in this option, it can also be first. Then, because no restaurants have to be delivered to after K, K could be last. However, so could the Floater, L.

In the second option, no restaurants need to be delivered to before L or F, so either one of those could be first. However, M is the only restaurant that doesn't have another restaurant delivery following it, so M must be sixth. Before that must come K, making K fifth. Before that comes G, making G fourth. That's where the deductions end because you don't know whether F or H comes third.

Step 5: Questions

18. (C) Acceptability
For Acceptability questions, go through the rules one at a time, eliminating answers that violate the rules.

(D) violates Rule 1 by making Ginsberg's delivery after Kanzaki's. **(E)** violates Rule 2 by making Harris's delivery after Ginsberg's. Both **(A)** and **(B)** have Figueroa's delivery before Malpighi's, but **(A)** then has Harris's delivery before Leacock's, which violates the Formal Logic of Rule 3. Finally, **(B)** violates Rule 4 by having Malpighi's delivery after Harris's and before Kanzaki's, satisfying neither rule's criteria. Therefore, the only answer to follow the rules is **(C)**.

19. (A) "If" / Must Be True
Figueroa's delivery can only be fourth in the first option. In the second option, the latest the truck can deliver to Figueroa's is third.

So, looking using the first option, if Figueroa's delivery is fourth, there are two restaurants that must be delivered to later: Ginsberg's, then Kanzaki's. Therefore, Kanzaki's delivery is sixth, and Ginsberg's must be fifth. That makes **(A)** correct.

$$\frac{}{1} \quad \frac{}{2} \quad \frac{}{3} \quad \frac{F}{4} \quad \frac{G}{5} \quad \frac{K}{6}$$

Meanwhile, the first, second, and third deliveries are undetermined. Because Malpighi's must come before Harris's, the truck must deliver to Malpighi's either first or second. Harris's, then, could be second or third. Leacock's, however, could come first, second, or third. That flexibility means **(B)** through **(E)** all could be true, but none of them must be.

20. (E) "If" / Must Be True
Because this question establishes two entities, start by drawing a Strict Sequencing sketch and placing M and L in the first and third spaces, respectively.

Malpighi's delivery can only be first in the first option. With Leacock's established, the only restaurant that can be delivered to last in that option is Kanzaki's, so Kanzaki's is sixth, and Ginsberg's is right before it at fifth. The only uncertainty is the order of Figueroa's and Harris's deliveries.

$$\frac{M}{1} \quad \frac{F/H}{2} \quad \frac{L}{3} \quad \frac{F/H}{4} \quad \frac{G}{5} \quad \frac{K}{6}$$

With that, **(E)** must be true. **(A)**, **(B)**, and **(C)** all could be true because Figueroa's and Harris's order is undetermined. **(D)**, however, must be false because the truck delivers to Kanzaki's last.

21. (C) Must Be True
Remember that with Limited Options, a Must Be True answer has to be true in *both* options, not just one.

(C) is confirmed in both options, making this the right answer. For the record:

Because Leacock's is a Floater in the first option, its delivery doesn't have to be earlier or later than any other restaurant's. That eliminates **(A)**, **(B)**, and **(D)**.

(E) is definitely false in the second option.

22. (C) "If" / Could Be True
Kanzaki's delivery can only be before Leacock's in the first option. Because these two restaurants were the only possibilities for the last delivery, that means Leacock's delivery is sixth. Working backward, Kanzaki's must be fifth, which eliminates **(D)**, and Ginsberg's must be fourth, which eliminates **(B)**.

$$\frac{}{1} \quad \frac{}{2} \quad \frac{}{3} \quad \frac{G}{4} \quad \frac{K}{5} \quad \frac{L}{6}$$

That leaves Malphigi's, Harris's, and Figueroa's deliveries to fill the first three spots, with Malphigi's delivery coming before Harris's.

With no other deductions standing out, it's time to go back to the Formal Logic. Because Leacock's delivery is last, Harris's delivery must come before it. This triggers the contrapositive of the Formal Logic in Rule 3, which means the truck must deliver to Malpighi's before Figueroa's. Now, because Malpighi's must come before both Figueroa's and Harris's, that means Malpighi's delivery is first, eliminating **(A)** and **(E)** and leaving **(C)** as the correct answer.

23. (E) Must Be False
Again, with Limited Options, the correct answer to a "must be" question needs to be confirmed by both options.

Checking **(E)** in the first option, there are three restaurants that must be delivered to after Malpighi's. That's too many for Malpighi's to be the fourth delivery. In the second option, Malpighi's delivery must be last, so this answer must be false, making it the right answer. For the record:

(A) could be true in either option, so this is a quick elimination.

In the first option, Ginsberg's delivery only has to come before Kanzaki's. Therefore, its delivery certainly could be fifth, which eliminates **(B)**. (Furthermore, this is confirmed by the sketches for the second and third questions of the set.)

In the second option, only three restaurants have to be delivered to after Harris's, meaning that it can be delivered to third. That eliminates **(C)**.

Because Leacock's is a Floater in the first option, it can be delivered to at any time, eliminating **(D)**.

Section III: Logical Reasoning

Q#	Question Type	Correct	Difficulty
1	Principle (Identify/Assumption)	D	★
2	Main Point	D	★
3	Strengthen	B	★
4	Flaw	B	★
5	Method of Argument	D	★
6	Weaken	C	★★
7	Assumption (Necessary)	A	★
8	Flaw	A	★★
9	Assumption (Necessary)	C	★
10	Point at Issue	E	★★
11	Principle (Identify/Assumption)	B	★
12	Flaw	E	★
13	Assumption (Necessary)	D	★★
14	Inference	C	★
15	Assumption (Sufficient)	D	★★
16	Flaw	C	★★★★
17	Role of a Statement	B	★★★
18	Principle (Identify/Inference)	D	★★★
19	Weaken	A	★★
20	Paradox	E	★★
21	Flaw	E	★
22	Paradox	E	★★★
23	Inference	A	★★★★
24	Parallel Flaw	C	★★
25	Principle (Parallel)	A	★★★★

1. (D) Principle (Identify/Assumption)

Step 1: Identify the Question Type

The question stem directly asks for a principle. The stimulus will provide a specific argument, and the correct answer will present the reasoning underlying that argument in more general terms.

Step 2: Untangle the Stimulus

The stimulus opens with the author's conclusion: a recommendation that no museum should display the upside-down airplane stamp. The next two sentences provide the author's evidence. The stamp will be damaged if it is displayed because ultraviolet light will cause its red ink to fade. The final sentence basically reiterates the author's conclusion. The stamp should be locked up, despite the disadvantage to the public.

Step 3: Make a Prediction

The author suggests that because displaying the airplane stamp would cause it harm, it should not be put on view. Any time an author makes a negative recommendation, he assumes the costs outweigh any possible benefits: in this case, the stamp's safety outweighs the public's curiosity. The correct answer will be more general but will follow that same reasoning.

Step 4: Evaluate the Answer Choices

(D) fits the argument's reasoning—if displaying an item would damage it, it shouldn't be displayed.

(A) is Outside the Scope by including a criterion for public judgment of museums' quality. The stimulus is about how museums should behave in a particular circumstance, not about how the public should rate museums.

(B) also is Outside the Scope. While protective display cases would solve the problem, that isn't the author's argument. The author thinks museums should protect their items by not displaying them at all, not by displaying them in special cases.

(C) goes Outside the Scope by discussing when red ink should not be used. The argument is about what museums should do with items that can be damaged, not about what printers (or other ink users) should do. Even further, the stimulus mentions items that will be exposed to ultraviolet light, whereas this answer choice discusses items that won't be.

(E) argues against the author, suggesting a possible reason why a museum would display an item, even if damage is possible.

2. (D) Main Point

Step 1: Identify the Question Type

Because this question asks for the conclusion of the argument, it is a Main Point question.

Step 2: Untangle the Stimulus

The dietitian opens by describing some consumers' high expectations for "fake fat"—they think they'll get all the positives and none of the negatives of real fat. However, if these consumers are trying to drop a few pounds, the dietitian says, fake fat may be a disappointment. After all, research shows eating fake fat leads to an increase in overall calorie consumption.

Step 3: Make a Prediction

Looking for Contrast Keywords can often help you find the conclusion in Main Point questions. Here, "however," indicates the dietitian's point of view. The dietitian warns consumers that their weight-loss hopes for fake fat are unsupported and then backs up the conclusion with research results. You want an answer that says "fake fat" consumers won't see the positive results they anticipate.

Step 4: Evaluate the Answer Choices

(D) is the author's main point.

(A) is too general. The stimulus is about how "fake fat" affects the number of calories people eat, not about what is generally true "no matter what types of food" people eat.

(B) makes an Irrelevant Comparison about nutrition. The dietitian says people who eat "fake fat" foods take in at least as many calories as are saved, but while the number of calories doesn't decrease, it's unclear whether those calories are more or less nutritional than those in fatty foods.

(C) is an Irrelevant Comparison and Extreme. The dietitian suggests fake fat won't help dieters, not that it will hurt them or become a significant cause of obesity. No mention is made of which foods are more or less likely to cause obesity.

(E) is Outside the Scope. It may be true because that is the reason why so many diet-conscious consumers are excited, but this is not the dietitian's main point. "Fake fat's" taste is discussed in the first sentence, which is simply the setup for the dietitian's argument. Furthermore, the word *indistinguishable* is Extreme based on the information in the first sentence.

3. (B) Strengthen

Step 1: Identify the Question Type

Because the question asks for something that will strengthen the banking analyst's argument, this is a Strengthen question.

Step 2: Untangle the Stimulus

The Contrast Keyword [*b*]*ut* indicates the banking analyst's conclusion: it's "not an ideal business practice" to offer free services only to new customers. Her evidence, indicated by the Keyword *since*, is that this practice excludes long-term customers, who make up most of a bank's business.

Step 3: Make a Prediction

The banking analyst argues against excluding long-term customers. Thus, the banking analyst assumes any undesirable or negative consequences that result from excluding long-term customers would outweigh any possible benefits. You want an answer choice that increases the likelihood that neglecting regular customers is detrimental to banks.

Step 4: Evaluate the Answer Choices

(B) suggests banks greatly benefit by giving special deals only to long-term customers. This supports the bank analyst's argument because it provides evidence why excluding longtime customers from special deals is a bad idea. While this answer choice doesn't completely prove the bank analyst's argument, it does make the argument more likely to be true, which is exactly what a strengthener needs to do.

(A) goes Outside the Scope because it only compares banks to each other. It doesn't address the main comparison at issue: the advantages of offering promotions to new versus long-term customers.

(C) is a 180. It weakens the banking analyst's argument by suggesting a reason why banks shouldn't extend special deals to their long-term customers.

(D) is another 180. It weakens the argument because it makes it unlikely that banks will lose their long-term customers by failing to offer them free services.

(E) is yet another 180. It weakens the argument by showing that at least one bank that doesn't follow the analyst's advice is very successful.

4. (B) Flaw

Step 1: Identify the Question Type

"[V]ulnerable to criticism" is classic language used to indicate that the argument is inherently flawed, making this a Flaw question.

Step 2: Untangle the Stimulus

The panelist concludes that publicity influences the judgment of medical researchers when they're determining the importance of prior research. His evidence is that research that has received a lot of mainstream press coverage is more likely to be cited in later medical research.

Step 3: Make a Prediction

This argument follows the classic causation pattern: the panelist assumes the mainstream press coverage causes the subsequent citations in medical research. The panelist overlooks the three alternatives to causation: Is it just a coincidence? Is causation reversed? Is there another factor that caused both? In this case, that last possibility seems most likely; maybe there's a reason everyone is citing the same medical research.

Step 4: Evaluate the Answer Choices

(B) gives a plausible reason why everyone is citing the same medical research: it actually is important, and the press is doing a good job covering it.

(A) goes Outside the Scope; the stimulus includes no "counterarguments."

(C) goes Outside the Scope by discussing how the "eminence of the scientists" affects the press, rather than how mainstream press coverage affects subsequent medical research. The panelist never mentions scientists' eminence.

(D) goes Outside the Scope because the panelist isn't concerned that the mainstream press isn't reviewing more medical research articles but simply with the fact that when they do, the same articles tend to pop up again later in medical research. In fact, if the media only covers a small amount, then that would make the panelist's worry even more valid because the likelihood of coincidental overlap would diminish.

(E) incorrectly suggests that the panelist uses circular reasoning. As seen in Step 2, though, the evidence and conclusion are not logical equivalents because the conclusion introduces a claim of causation.

5. (D) Method of Argument

Step 1: Identify the Question Type

The "argument does which of the following" language lets us know that the correct answer will describe the Method of Argument. Use Keywords to determine structure and focus on how the author makes the argument, rather than what the argument is about.

Step 2: Untangle the Stimulus

Lahar lays out three possible options for how to decide on meeting agendas, then proceeds to explain why two of them won't work. Finally, with the Conclusion Keyword [c]learly, he concludes by recommending the remaining option.

Step 3: Make a Prediction

Lahar's method is to argue for one option, not by offering evidence for it, but by instead rejecting other possibilities.

Step 4: Evaluate the Answer Choices

(D) matches nicely because Lahar's recommendation is based on eliminating the alternatives.

(A) is Outside the Scope because no constitutional grounds are offered for the options Lahar advocates rejecting; he says all three are allowed by the club's constitution.

(B) is Extreme. It partly matches the conclusion because Lahar does say one procedure is appropriate. However, Lahar recommends that procedure for one specific task: setting an agenda. This choice goes beyond Lahar's recommendation by suggesting that one procedure would work for "every" decision.

(C) is a Distortion. It misses the mark because Lahar never recommends changing the constitution; he draws on the constitution to find the three options he evaluates.

(E) is also a Distortion because Lahar doesn't introduce an ad hominem attack; he argues against alternatives, not their supporters.

6. (C) Weaken

Step 1: Identify the Question Type
The question asks for something that *undermines* the mayor's reasoning, so this is a Weaken question.

Step 2: Untangle the Stimulus
The mayor concludes, in the second sentence, that taxes alone would reduce smoking in his city. He supports his conclusion with "strong evidence" from surveys that cigarette sales drop in cities that significantly increase cigarette taxes.

Step 3: Make a Prediction
The mayor's conclusion is about people smoking less, but the evidence discusses cigarette sales. The mayor assumes that fewer sales mean less smoking. The mayor's argument can be weakened by attacking that assumption. The correct answer will suggest that people in the city will smoke as much as ever, even though cigarette sales there may decrease.

Step 4: Evaluate the Answer Choices
(C) exploits the gap in the mayor's argument by introducing an alternate reason why sales fell in cities with high cigarette taxes. Smoking didn't decrease; buyers just went elsewhere to purchase cigarettes.

(A) is a 180 because it strengthens the mayor's argument by reinforcing the connection between increased taxes on cigarettes and a reduction in smoking.

(B) makes an Irrelevant Comparison between the effects of different types of price increases. The stimulus is only about prices increasing due to higher taxes.

(D) goes outside the scope because the mayor's argument focuses on reducing smoking by increasing taxes, not on the effects of education. This would weaken his offhand comment that the effectiveness of education programs is debatable, but neither his conclusion nor his provided evidence is about those programs.

(E) is Outside the Scope. It may be the logical result of such funding, but it doesn't address the mayor's argument that smoking will diminish. Like **(D)** it improperly focuses on the education programs.

7. (A) Assumption (Necessary)

Step 1: Identify the Question Type
The question asks for the argument's assumption. Because the assumption is *required*, the question is looking for a

necessary assumption, and you can, if need be, use the Denial Test to confirm or eliminate answers.

Step 2: Untangle the Stimulus
Gotera's conclusion, indicated by "[w]e can conclude," is categorical: speech acquisition is entirely a motor control process and not an abstract or mental one. His evidence is that babies are physically unable to produce particular sounds but babble randomly, and that it takes years for children to develop the ability to produce all of the required sounds for language.

Step 3: Make a Prediction
The categorical language in the conclusion is a tip-off that Gotera is overlooking an alternative possibility, namely that speech acquisition could be a function of more than one thing, like motor control and something else (perhaps cognitive ability). The correct answer will fill the hole in Gotera's argument by ruling out anything besides motor control as a factor in speech acquisition.

Step 4: Evaluate the Answer Choices
(A) gets it exactly right by eliminating any other possible factor in speech acquisition—it is only the ability to produce the sounds that matters.

(B) is Outside the Scope. Gotera is concerned with whether infants can intentionally produce particular sounds, which is different from intentionally moving their tongues.

(C) is also Outside the Scope. It incorrectly focuses on the babbling stage. Gotera isn't concerned with when the babbling stage ends but about when the voluntary production of sounds starts.

(D) is Outside the Scope. It's possible there is another stage before babbling, but that doesn't affect Gotera's conclusion that speech acquisition is a motor control process. Note that the detail about babbling in the first sentence is mentioned in three tempting wrong answers, but it is not an essential piece of evidence for Gotera's conclusion.

(E) is a 180 because it actually contradicts Gotera's argument by saying that speech acquisition has a mental aspect.

8. (A) Flaw

Step 1: Identify the Question Type
The phrase "most vulnerable to criticism" is common language for a Flaw question. Look for the unwarranted assumption or the common LSAT flaw.

Step 2: Untangle the Stimulus
Caldwell's conclusion comes at the end of the stimulus, with the Keyword *clearly*: the government's demolition of the naval base was inefficient and immoral. His evidence is that using the facilities for the good of the community would have "benefited everybody."

Step 3: Make a Prediction

Caldwell assumes that not doing something to benefit the community is behaving immorally. This is quite a strong claim though, especially considering Caldwell also mentions that the government's actions were perfectly legal.

Step 4: Evaluate the Answer Choices

(A) matches by attacking Caldwell's assumption that failing to act for everyone's benefit is immoral. Maybe, as **(A)** suggests, an action can be moral even if the alternative is to everyone's advantage. In other words, deciding against that alternative is not, in itself, immoral.

(B) is a 180. Caldwell's argument hinges on the belief that the consequences of the action (the benefit or lack thereof to "everyone") decide an action's morality.

(C) is Extreme. Caldwell mentions only one specific instance when the government was inefficient. To say that the government "never acts in the most efficient manner" goes beyond that one instance.

(D) is both Out of Scope and Extreme. Caldwell simply claims the government's demolition of the naval base is both inefficient and immoral; it doesn't mention actions that are efficient, and it certainly doesn't go so far as to say "any" actions that are efficient are moral.

(E) is a Distortion of the argument. Caldwell doesn't suggest there were no other alternatives, only that using the facilities for the good of the community would have been a better use, from both an efficient and moral standpoint, than the action chosen by the government.

9. (C) Assumption (Necessary)

Step 1: Identify the Question Type

The question asks for the argument's assumption. Because the argument *depends* on the assumption, it's a Necessary Assumption question, and you can use the Denial Test to confirm or eliminate answers.

Step 2: Untangle the Stimulus

The conclusion comes in the first sentence: less stress = less pain sensitivity. The evidence is based on a study. People who listened to music before and after surgery seemed to have less pain than did those who listened to talking.

Step 3: Make a Prediction

The conclusion is about stress, but the evidence is about music. The assumption must connect these two different ideas. For the argument to make any sense, the author must be assuming that listening to the music tape diminished stress.

Step 4: Evaluate the Answer Choices

(C) directly matches the prediction by providing the crucial connection between music and stress.

(A) is a Distortion. It's possible that some patients listened to a mix of the two tapes, but the author is only concerned with those who listened to only music or only conversation.

(B) makes an Irrelevant Comparison between the stress of pre- and post-surgery. Meanwhile, the evidence is about the calming effects of music versus conversation.

(D) is Outside the Scope because the argument addresses stress only, not any psychological effects. Further, the argument is about how listening to music affects the need for anesthesia or painkillers, not about how drugs might change the effect listening to music has.

(E) is a Distortion. That anesthesia and painkillers reduce stress may be true, but it doesn't affect the researchers' argument that reducing stress reduces the need for the two in the first place.

10. (E) Point at Issue

Step 1: Identify the Question Type

When a question asks for something two people are "committed to disagreeing about," it's a Point at Issue question. Summarize both speakers' arguments, and then look for an answer with which one speaker would agree and the other would disagree. You can use the Decision Tree to confirm your choice.

Step 2: Untangle the Stimulus

Samuel's argument is that computer communication causes lasting communal bonds to deteriorate because computer communication is private and anonymous. Tova points out Samuel's underlying assumption—that computer communication is taking the place of better forms of communication—and then suggests an alternative conclusion. Tova says computer communication can actually be a substitute for asocial or antisocial behavior.

Step 3: Make a Prediction

Tova's alternative conclusion—that computer communication replaces antisocial behavior—seems to contradict Samuel's conclusion—that computer communication replaces creating lasting communal bonds. Look for the answer choice that discusses what people would be doing if they didn't communicate via computer.

If that prediction does not come to mind, use the Decision Tree to find the correct answer choice. Once you find the answer choice that contains something discussed by both Samuel and Tova, as well as a point of disagreement, then you have the answer.

Step 4: Evaluate the Answer Choices

(E) is the match because Samuel thinks computer interactions keep people from other interactions, while Tova thinks some people wouldn't be interacting at all without the computer.

(A) goes Outside the Scope because it discusses "a general trend of modern life." Neither Samuel nor Tova holds an opinion about general trends.

(B) is Extreme because it discusses "all purely private behavior." Neither Samuel nor Tova discusses an opinion about all private behavior.

(C) matches Samuel's opinion. However, Tova never states an opinion about the connection between face-to-face communication and social bonds. Tova might even agree with Samuel. Tova merely says that face-to-face communication isn't what computer communication replaces.

(D) goes Outside the Scope because it discusses replacing old social bonds. Neither Samuel nor Tova holds an opinion about replacing old social bonds.

11. (B) Principle (Identify/Assumption)

Step 1: Identify the Question Type

The question stem asks for a principle. The stimulus will provide a specific argument, and the correct answer will present the reasoning underlying that argument in more general terms.

Step 2: Untangle the Stimulus

The author's conclusion is that we should not yet spread iron particles over the surface of the oceans. His evidence is that the side effects of iron seeding have not been tested and the oceans are very important.

Step 3: Make a Prediction

Start by finding the author's assumption. The conclusion is about avoiding a course of action for now. The evidence says the action has both a known benefit to the atmosphere and unknown side effects for the ocean, an important resource. So, the author assumes the possible negative side effects outweigh the known positives when an important resource is at stake. The assumption will lead us to the matching principle. Remember that the principle may be in more general terms than the assumption.

Step 4: Evaluate the Answer Choices

(B) is the match. The "problem-solving strategy" is iron seeding, and it should not be done because its side effects on the oceans are unknown.

(A) is Out of Scope. The stimulus only discusses a situation in which the side effects are unknown. The author doesn't give any direction as to what should happen were the side effects known.

(C) goes Out of Scope by introducing an idea not in the stimulus—"consequences ... more serious than the problem itself." The author's evidence is that the consequences are unknown. Granted, they might be more serious than the problem, but currently that's unclear.

(D) is more Extreme than the author. The author hasn't said the resource (oceans) shouldn't be altered, only that first he recommends having a solid understanding of the consequences of such an action.

(E) is a Distortion of the stimulus by suggesting that the risk would be exacerbating the original problem. The author, however, was concerned with the unknown side effects creating a new problem in the oceans, not that spreading the iron particles would "exacerbate" the greenhouse effect.

12. (E) Flaw

Step 1: Identify the Question Type

The phrase "most vulnerable to criticism" is common language for a Flaw question. Additionally, the question stem specifically asks for the possibility the argument has overlooked, so keep that in mind as you approach the stimulus.

Step 2: Untangle the Stimulus

The author's conclusion is a recommendation for historians. They should interpret the perceptions of people who actually participated in historical events rather than the events themselves. The author's evidence is that even the best of historians have biases that affect their work.

Step 3: Make a Prediction

Based on the question stem, we know the author has overlooked something important. Finding the assumption will reveal it. The author offers a solution (focus on past people's thoughts) to a problem (historian bias). The author must be assuming that the suggestion will actually solve the problem. However, if all historians have biases, it could be true that those biases will affect the way historians interpret past people's perceptions just as much as the biases affect the way historians interpret past events.

Step 4: Evaluate the Answer Choices

(E) is the match because it suggests the historian's solution may not actually solve the problem that bias poses.

(A) goes Outside the Scope by providing an additional detail about historians. Even if historians with different biases sometimes agree, the problem of bias in historical interpretations still remains.

(B) goes Outside the Scope by discussing scholars besides historians. Whether or not other scholars also have bias does not affect whether the author's recommendation will serve its purpose.

(C) is Outside the Scope because the author wants to remove bias totally, not simply identify how it affects historian's work. Ignoring the fact that some effects of bias have been identified is not a flaw in the author's argument because doing so doesn't undermine his conclusion.

(D) is a Faulty Use of Detail. The author does consider this, so it's not something he fails to consider. In fact, his knowledge of that lack of awareness is why the author is trying to shift historians' focus.

13. (D) Assumption (Necessary)

Step 1: Identify the Question Type
The question asks for the argument's assumption. Because the argument *depends* on the necessary assumption, you can use the Denial Test to confirm or eliminate answers.

Step 2: Untangle the Stimulus
The conclusion is in the first sentence: country X should institute a nationwide system for transporting seriously injured people to specialized trauma centers. The evidence is that getting injured people to medical care faster could save lives, and the people saved would end up contributing a lot to the nation's economy.

Step 3: Make a Prediction
The author says saving lives would boost country X's gross national product. To complete his argument, the author must assume that the people whose lives are saved would actually get jobs and earn money.

Step 4: Evaluate the Answer Choices
(D) is the author's Necessary Assumption. Use the Denial Test to prove it. When **(D)** is denied, it says if more persons survived serious injury, there would be no change in total employment. If there were no change in total employment, then there would be no change in earnings. Without the change in earnings, there would be no increase in taxes paid to the government. Thus, denying **(D)** destroys the author's reasoning.

(A) makes an Irrelevant Comparison. The author doesn't rely on any financial information from country Y in formulating his argument; he only mentions that the other country has implemented such a transportation system.

(B) goes Outside the Scope; the issue is transportation to trauma centers, not their existence.

(C) is another Irrelevant Comparison; you don't know (or care) anything about the cost anywhere else. The author isn't concerned with the cost of the treatment, just the future income of the patient. Even if the cost at trauma centers is more expensive than elsewhere, the author's argument may still be valid.

(E) is a Distortion. The author indicates improved transportation to specialized trauma centers makes long-term financial sense. Whether or not most people seriously injured in auto accidents currently use those facilities does not impact that financial question. Perhaps the improved transportation network would increase the use of the facilities

in the future. Furthermore, the word "most" should always be a red flag in Necessary Assumption questions.

14. (C) Inference

Step 1: Identify the Question Type
In typical Inference question style, you're asked to identify the choice that is supported by the statements above. Accept each statement as true, seek out Formal Logic, and pay careful attention to the level of certainty exhibited by the language in the stimulus. The correct answer choice is the one that is supported by information in the stimulus.

Step 2: Untangle the Stimulus
Early urban societies needed to be close to big farming areas because large-scale farming is the only way to support the dense populations of urban societies. Until recently, big farming areas needed to be near rivers or lakes.

Step 3: Make a Prediction
Connect the chain of information given in the stimulus to predict the right answer. Early urban societies needed to be close to large-scale farming, which needed to be close to rivers or lakes. Therefore, it must be true that early urban societies were close to rivers or lakes.

Step 4: Evaluate the Answer Choices
(C) might look slightly different from the prediction, but it is the exact same idea, just in negative terms. If early urban societies had to be near rivers or lakes, then it must also be true that there were no urban societies far from rivers of lakes.

(A) is Extreme. The stimulus indicated urban societies needed to be close to rivers or lakes, but it did not indicate whether "[m]ost" people lived in those types of societies.

(B) is too broad by covering "societies" in general, rather than just "urban societies." It is a subtle difference, but one that affects whether the answer follows from the stimulus.

(D) is a 180. It contradicts the stimulus because according to the stimulus, "[l]arge-scale farming requires irrigation."

(E) goes Outside the Scope by focusing on rural societies rather than urban ones.

15. (D) Assumption (Sufficient)

Step 1: Identify the Question Type
The word *assumed* identifies this as an Assumption question. Furthermore, the *if* indicates that you are looking for a sufficient assumption. While there may be several assumptions that would be sufficient to ensure that the conclusion follows logically from the evidence, only one answer choice will state such an assumption.

Step 2: Untangle the Stimulus
The economist concludes that countries that put collective goals first can't emerge quickly from a recession. The

economist's evidence is that rapid emergence requires investment, and investment only happens when citizens have confidence. The Formal Logic would look like this:

Evidence:

$$\text{If } \begin{array}{c} \textit{emerge} \\ \textit{from} \\ \textit{recession} \end{array} \rightarrow \begin{array}{c} \textit{new} \\ \textit{infrastructure} \end{array} \rightarrow \textit{confidence}$$

Conclusion:

$$\text{If } \begin{array}{c} \textit{collective} > \\ \textit{individual} \end{array} \rightarrow \begin{array}{c} \sim \textit{emerge from} \\ \textit{recession} \end{array}$$

Step 3: Make a Prediction
There's a big gap between evidence and conclusion—the evidence is about confidence, and the conclusion is about putting collective goals ahead of individuals' goals. The author assumes a connection between putting collective goals first and lack of confidence.

Argument:

$$\text{If } \begin{array}{c} \textit{collective} > \\ \textit{individ.} \end{array} \rightarrow \sim \textit{conf.} \rightarrow \begin{array}{c} \sim \textit{new} \\ \textit{infra.} \end{array} \rightarrow \begin{array}{c} \sim \textit{emerge} \\ \textit{from rec.} \end{array}$$

Step 4: Evaluate the Answer Choices
(D) explicitly connects putting collective goals first and lack of confidence. In fact, it is the only answer choice of the five that mentions confidence.

(A) goes Outside the Scope by discussing countries that do not emerge quickly from recessions. The economist says if a country will rapidly emerge, then investment is needed. She presents no information about what happens investment-wise if a country does not quickly emerge from a recession. This answer goes backward on the Formal Logic.

(B) is a Distortion. The author never argues that recessions do or do not affect people's support for government policies. Rather, people's confidence in government policies affects their investment, which affects the quick emergence or lack thereof from the recession.

(C) goes Outside the Scope by discussing the wrong countries: those that put individuals first. The argument provides information only about countries that put collective goals first. This answer choice, like **(A)**, also goes backward on the Formal Logic.

(E) goes Outside the Scope by focusing on what would cause a country to experience, not get out of, a recession. The argument is about what kind of policies would keep a country in recession rather than how the country's recession started in the first place.

16. (C) Flaw

Step 1: Identify the Question Type
The phrase "most vulnerable to criticism" is common language for a Flaw question. Look for the unwarranted assumption or the common LSAT flaw.

Step 2: Untangle the Stimulus
The author concludes that University Hospital could discharge people sooner without affecting quality of care. The evidence is that Edgewater Hospital has a shorter average stay, even though people treated for similar illnesses recover at similar rates in the two hospitals.

Step 3: Make a Prediction
The conclusion is about the average length of stay for all patients at University Hospital, but the evidence is about a particular subset of patients, those with similar illnesses in the two hospitals. What the author doesn't explicitly demonstrate is whether the patients with the illnesses described in the evidence are actually representative of all the patients at University. The author overlooks the fact that, in general, the patients at University might be much more seriously ill than those at Edgewater. It could be true, for example, that the patients with minor colds at both hospitals recover in the same amount of time. However, if minor colds account for a large proportion of the patients at Edgewater but only a small proportion of the patients at University, then the average length of stay at both hospitals should not, in fact, be equal.

Step 4: Evaluate the Answer Choices
(C) correctly exposes the overlooked possibility that the patient populations at each hospital could be different.

(A) directly contradicts the conclusion, where the author suggests that the average length of stay could be decreased without affecting the quality of care.

(B) inappropriately suggests that the author has confused necessity and sufficiency in the argument. The argument, however, is not stated in terms of Formal Logic. For example, the author never states that length of stay is necessary to quality of care.

(D) is Extreme because the author never states that length of stay "never" affects recovery.

(E) goes Outside the Scope by focusing on patient preferences.

17. (B) Role of a Statement

Step 1: Identify the Question Type
The phrase "the role played … by the claim" indicates this is a Role of a Statement question. Using Keywords, determine whether the statement in question is evidence or conclusion, and then go back and refine your categorization as necessary.

Step 2: Untangle the Stimulus

The philosopher opens by giving Graham's argument (evidence and conclusion). The Contrast Keyword [*b*]*ut* signals the philosopher's disagreement and the philosopher's conclusion: Graham is wrong. To support this point, the philosopher introduces sleep as a counterexample that suggests people can be truly happy without doing things.

Step 3: Make a Prediction

Because the question asks about the role played by the last statement of the stimulus, research that statement. The statement in question was neither Graham's nor the philosopher's conclusion, so it must be evidence. Because the statement goes against Graham's argument, the statement must be evidence for the philosopher's conclusion that Graham is wrong. More specifically, the statement goes against Graham's evidence that people need to be doing something in order to be truly happy.

Step 4: Evaluate the Answer Choices

(B) correctly describes the role of the statement in question. The philosopher uses the statement against Graham by introducing a counterexample to his evidence.

(A) is wrong because the statement is not part of Graham's argument.

(C) is wrong because the statement is neither part of Graham's argument nor an analogy.

(D) wrongly targets Graham's conclusion, rather than Graham's evidence.

(E) assigns the statement the wrong role in the philosopher's argument. The philosopher's conclusion is "we should not be persuaded by Graham's argument." The statement in question is the evidence for that conclusion.

18. (D) Principle (Identify/Inference)

Step 1: Identify the Question Type

You're asked to identify the *proposition* that is supported by the statements in the stimulus. That makes this an Identify the Principle question. Accept each statement as true and seek out an answer choice that is broader than the stimulus. The correct answer is the only one supported by information in the stimulus.

Step 2: Untangle the Stimulus

The historian starts by giving us the opinion of "some people." These people have disputed the historian's claim that West influenced Stuart. In other words, they think that West did not influence Stuart. Their evidence is that Stuart's diaries seldom mention West's work. The Contrast Keyword [*b*]*ut* suggests that the historian disagrees with these people. After [*b*]*ut*, he lists a series of facts connecting Stuart and West.

Step 3: Make a Prediction

The Contrast Keyword [*b*]*ut* indicates the historian wants to counter those who think the single mention of West's work in Stuart's diaries prove West didn't influence Stuart. In response, the historian presents a list of connections between Stuart and West. He must be trying to prove West likely had some sort of influence on Stuart.

Step 4: Evaluate the Answer Choices

(D) cautiously suggests that Stuart's work was influenced, at least a little bit, by West. That must be true based on the historian's evidence of the connections between the two. Additionally, even the historian's opponents agree Stuart's diaries mention West's work once.

(A) could be true but also could be false. The historian cites Stuart's discussions with Abella as a possible way that West influenced Stuart, but that is not the only way provided. Thus, even if Stuart's discussions with Abella did nothing to spread West's influence to Stuart, it could still be true that West influenced Stuart at one of their several meetings.

(B) makes an Irrelevant Comparison. This could be true, but the stimulus gives us no information about Stuart influencing West. Therefore, the stimulus provides no grounds for weighing that likelihood.

(C) is a Distortion. The only thing we know about Stuart's contemporaries is that they didn't use West's terminology. It's possible they were influenced by West in some other way.

(E) is another Distortion. While it is true West's terminology is now commonplace, the stimulus says nothing about how it got that way. It may or may not have been Stuart's influence on other people.

19. (A) Weaken

Step 1: Identify the Question Type

The question asks for something that *undermines* the theory in the stimulus, so this is a Weaken question.

Step 2: Untangle the Stimulus

The theory is introduced in the first sentence: drug overdose caused the dinosaur extinction. Push past the scientific language in the middle of the stimulus and notice the Emphasis and Evidence Keywords, "strongest support," in the last sentence. So, the author's central evidence is that the theory explains why dinosaur fossils are found in contorted positions.

Step 3: Make a Prediction

The conclusion is that dinosaurs overdosed. The evidence is that overdoses would explain contorted fossil positions. That's a somewhat flimsy piece of evidence, and this argument is left with a gaping hole. The author's assumption will fill that hole. Thus, the author assumes that nothing besides overdoses would explain why dinosaur fossils are in contorted positions. The weakener will suggest some other explanation that could better explain why dinosaur fossils are in contorted positions.

Step 4: Evaluate the Answer Choices

(A) says mammals are also found in contorted positions, which would strengthen the argument if mammals are also overdosing and weaken it if they are not. If "large mammals" appear to be Outside the Scope, go back and research the science details in the middle of the stimulus. There, the author mentions that mammals both avoid the plants dinosaurs theoretically overdosed on and have livers that can detoxify the drugs. If mammals aren't overdosing and they're still contorted, then something besides overdoses must be the cause of the contortions. The extinction theory's main support is now no longer pertinent. This makes **(A)** correct.

(B) may be true but doesn't hurt the idea that the "drugs" caused the dinosaurs to die off.

(C) might appear to undermine the idea that all dinosaurs were overdosing, but if the carnivorous dinosaurs ate the dinosaurs who had consumed the angiosperms, they might still have suffered the effects. Or, if vegetarian dinosaurs died off, then carnivorous dinosaurs would have been left without a food source.

(D) goes Outside the Scope by talking about other plants. The argument is about only those plants that do produce amino acid–based alkaloids.

(E) is a 180. It actually strengthens the argument, confirming that angiosperms cause fatal drug overdoses in other animals.

20. (E) Paradox

Step 1: Identify the Question Type

The phrase "contributes to an explanation" indicates that this is a Paradox question. The paradox in question is why the first alternative mentioned is almost never adopted.

Step 2: Untangle the Stimulus

Given that not adopting the first alternative, continuous maintenance, is the paradox that needs to be explained, there must be some important benefit to continuous maintenance. The third sentence informs us that the benefit to continuous maintenance is that it costs much less in the long run than radical reconstruction.

Step 3: Make a Prediction

The prediction doesn't need to be specific because there could be many different ways to resolve the paradox. Instead, predict more generally. The correct answer will give some reason why continuous maintenance is not done, even though it is more cost-effective.

Step 4: Evaluate the Answer Choices

(E) shows that continuous maintenance is not done because there's no urgency spurring people to do it. If problems show up very gradually, people might very well put off fixing them until it's too late and radical reconstruction is needed.

(A) is a 180 because it makes the paradox deeper by suggesting that radical reconstruction has severe drawbacks. Given that, we would expect continuous maintenance to be used more frequently.

(B) goes Outside the Scope by introducing specifics about how funds are distributed when money is tight. That information has nothing to do with the method generally used to repair transportation infrastructure.

(C) is another 180 because it gives another reason why continuous maintenance is good, and thus it deepens the paradox.

(D) also is a 180. It gives another reason why radical reconstruction is bad, making continuous maintenance even more attractive and thus deepening the paradox.

21. (E) Flaw

Step 1: Identify the Question Type

The phrase "most vulnerable to criticism" is common language for a Flaw question. Look for the unwarranted assumption or the common LSAT flaw.

Step 2: Untangle the Stimulus

The author concludes that repeating an activity is a good way to get past fear of that activity. Her evidence is simply an example: people who have parachuted 10 times or more are less fearful of parachuting than first-timers.

Step 3: Make a Prediction

The author assumes that the increased experience of the people in the evidence is the only reason they're less fearful. In classic flaw terms, she's overlooking alternative possible explanations. Maybe there is some other reason why the people who parachuted many times report being less fearful.

Step 4: Evaluate the Answer Choices

(E) correctly suggests that the author overlooks the possibility that the people who parachuted many times were people who were not frightened of parachuting in the first place. This is a case of reverse causation. Instead of repeat parachuting resulting in less fear, less fear led to repeat parachuting.

(A) goes Outside the Scope by including the idea of participating in lots of different dangerous activities. The argument is only about repeating one particular dangerous activity that inspires fear.

(B) is true but has no effect on the argument—the author has simply compared two distinct groups. It is not a logical flaw for the author to not include a third group in the comparison.

(C) is Outside the Scope. The stimulus does not weigh in on whether people's fear of an activity is accurate before trying it, just that they should do it repeatedly to get over that fear.

(D) is also Outside the Scope. The argument isn't about what's good or bad for people to do but about whether a particular method is effective for reducing fear.

22. (E) Paradox

Step 1: Identify the Question Type

The phrase "most helps to reconcile" indicates that this is a Paradox question. Something about the beliefs of economists will not seem to fit with the consequences observed by most wine merchants. The correct answer will show how they do fit together.

Step 2: Untangle the Stimulus

The belief of most economists is in the first sentence— reducing price should result in increased demand. The Contrast Keyword, [h]owever, introduces the other side of the paradox: when wine merchants reduce the price of domestic wine, sales of more expensive imported wine that costs more than the newly priced domestic wine increase.

Step 3: Make a Prediction

The economists' reasoning indicates that decreasing the price of domestic wine should lead to an increased demand for that wine. While the wine merchants report that sales of imported wine actually goes up, they say nothing about what happens to domestic wine. Perhaps demand for all wine, including the domestic wine, increases.

Step 4: Evaluate the Answer Choices

(E) puts together the observed increase in demand for imported wine with the economists' prediction that domestic sales should increase. According to (E), when one goes up, they both should.

(A) provides a reason that the wine merchants' experience might deviate from the economists' theory, but it doesn't reconcile the two.

(B) is Outside the Scope. The economic phenomenon should occur whether or not the wine sellers understand or anticipate it.

(C) goes Outside the Scope by introducing the element of superiority. We have no information about one wine or the other being superior.

(D) is a 180. It deepens the paradox by suggesting another reason why imported wines should not sell more than domestic wines. Not only are the imported wines more expensive, they are also no better in quality.

23. (A) Inference

Step 1: Identify the Question Type

In typical Inference question style, you're asked to identify the choice that is supported by the statements in the stimulus. Accept each statement as true, seek out Formal Logic, and pay careful attention to the level of certainty exhibited by the language in the stimulus. The correct answer choice is the one that is supported by information in the stimulus.

Step 2: Untangle the Stimulus

Take inventory: certain bacteria produce hydrogen sulfide. Oxygen would kill these bacteria, but the hydrogen sulfide removes it. The hydrogen sulfide also kills other organisms, which the bacteria can use as a food source. So a dense colony of this bacteria can "continue to thrive indefinitely."

Step 3: Make a Prediction

If the dense colony is thriving indefinitely, then it must be able keep making enough hydrogen sulfide to take care of the potential oxygen problem and to kill the other organisms for food.

Step 4: Evaluate the Answer Choices

(A) explains that the colony is able to produce hydrogen sulfide indefinitely. That's exactly what it would take for the colony to thrive indefinitely.

(B) is a Distortion, blurring two concepts in the stimulus. The author says hydrogen sulfide both removes oxygen and kills other organisms. However, the author doesn't say that hydrogen sulfide kills other organisms by removing oxygen.

(C) is Extreme because of "[m]ost." The stimulus tells us that hydrogen sulfide kills other organisms, thus producing food, but it doesn't say how many of those organisms can function as a food source.

(D) is Extreme because of "only." The stimulus never says that this is the only way this bacterium can thrive, just that it's one way.

(E) is Extreme because it includes all types of bacteria that produce hydrogen sulfide. The stimulus tells us only about certain bacteria.

24. (C) Parallel Flaw

Step 1: Identify the Question Type

The phrase "questionable pattern of reasoning" coupled with "most similar to" indicates this is a Parallel Flaw question. Approach the argument as you would a Flaw question. As you identify the conclusion and evidence and pinpoint the gap between the two, keep common flaw types in mind. The correct answer choice will exhibit the same pattern of reasoning and the same flaw as the stimulus.

Step 2: Untangle the Stimulus

The opening piece of evidence, the first sentence, suggests that if a book presents a utopian future, then it will be popular. The next statement, after "[s]ince," suggests that books that predict a gloomy future aren't utopian. Based on that, the author concludes that such gloomy books will not likely be popular.

Step 3: Make a Prediction

The author has made a classic LSAT flaw in this argument by incorrectly contraposing a Formal Logic statement. The first statement, "If utopian future, then popular," should be contraposed as "If not popular, then not utopian future." The author's conclusion is based on an incorrect contrapositive that negates both sides of the Formal Logic but fails to reverse them. Basically, the author's conclusion is "If not utopian, then not popular." The correct answer will make the same Formal Logic error—negating both sides of a statement without reversing them.

Step 4: Evaluate the Answer Choices

(C) makes the same mistake as the stimulus because it starts from this statement—"If complicated with special effects, then expensive"—and ends by incorrectly contraposing it as "If not complicated and no special effects, then not expensive."

(A) is different from the stimulus in two important ways. First, its opening statement has an extra piece in its Formal Logic chain: if art portrays people as happy, then it tranquilizes, and then it appeals to certain people. Second, the conclusion to **(A)** starts by negating the final result of the evidence rather than by negating the evidence's sufficient condition. In other words, **(A)** does not make the same contrapositive error that the stimulus does.

(B) fails to match the stimulus by not using Formal Logic statements. The first sentence of **(B)** is much more tempered and cautious than the evidence in the stimulus, suggesting only that something "may" happen, not that it "will always" happen.

(D) also fails to match the stimulus by not using Formal Logic statements. The first sentence of **(D)** describes what "usually" and "often" happens rather than what "will always" happen.

(E) has Formal Logic, but the structure doesn't match the stimulus. **(E)** starts with the Formal Logic statement "If self-employed, then fluctuating salaries." Then, it describes government bureaucrats as not self-employed. For **(E)** to be parallel with the stimulus, its conclusion would have to be that government bureaucrats do not have fluctuating salaries. Instead, it concludes that not everyone with a fluctuating salary is a government bureaucrat.

25. (A) Principle (Parallel)

Step 1: Identify the Question Type

The word *principle* makes it clear that this is a Principle question. This particular Principle question mimics a Parallel Reasoning question, as evidenced by the phrase "most closely conforms ... illustrates." First, identify the principle behind the argument in the stimulus. Then, search for the answer choice that follows the same reasoning and correctly applies that same principle.

Step 2: Untangle the Stimulus

Historians can find clues about a region's distant history by studying the present, but the further distant the period is, the less useful study of the present becomes. In other words, the further removed we are from the period, the less we can learn about it by looking at the present.

Step 3: Make a Prediction

While the correct answer could introduce many different specific situations, it must still conform to the principle that the further in the past something is, the less one can learn about it by looking at current data.

Step 4: Evaluate the Answer Choices

(A) conforms to the principle illustrated by the stimulus. While astronomers can make some inferences about the past of the solar system, they know less about the very earliest era of the solar system's history, its origin.

(B) goes Outside the Scope by suggesting the amount of studying makes learning new things harder. The stimulus suggests the passage of time makes it harder to learn about things.

(C) goes Outside the Scope. It introduces the element of "world view," rather than focusing on the passage of time.

(D) also goes Outside the Scope. It discusses things beyond ordinary sensory experience and fails to include anything about the passage of time.

(E) goes Outside the Scope by introducing the element of being impressed. Like **(C)** and **(D)**, it also fails to mention the passage of time as an obstacle to knowledge.

Section IV: Reading Comprehension

Passage 1: Ousmane Sembène's Films

Q#	Question Type	Correct	Difficulty
1	Global	E	★
2	Detail	E	★
3	Logic Reasoning (Strengthen)	A	★
4	Inference	D	★★
5	Inference	C	★
6	Detail (NOT)	A	★

Passage 2: Professional Writing

Q#	Question Type	Correct	Difficulty
7	Global	D	★
8	Inference	B	★
9	Detail	A	★★
10	Logic Reasoning (Method of Argument)	C	★★
11	Logic Function	B	★
12	Inference	D	★

Passage 3: Animal Conflict Behavior

Q#	Question Type	Correct	Difficulty
13	Global	C	★★★★
14	Logic Function	E	★★
15	Item Removed from Scoring		
16	Inference (LEAST)	D	★★
17	Logic Function	E	★★
18	Inference	B	★★★★
19	Global	A	★★

Passage 4: Philosophical Anarchism

Q#	Question Type	Correct	Difficulty
20	Global	C	★★★
21	Detail	A	★
22	Inference	B	★★
23	Inference	A	★★★
24	Logic Reasoning (Principle)	B	★
25	Inference	C	★★
26	Logic Function	D	★★
27	Global	D	★★

Passage 1: Ousmane Sembène's Films

Step 1: Read the Passage Strategically
Sample Roadmap

line #	Keyword/phrase	¶ Margin notes
1	agree; primary	Critics - focus on Semb is sociopol
5	asserts; not meant	
6	but rather	Semb - raise awareness
8	But	
9	strikingly; successfully	Auth - originality is using film in W Afr culture
18	for instance	Semb - draws from W Afr storytelling
24	In fact	
28–29	for example	
33	Moreover	
37	reveals	Semb - uses dilemma tales with open endings
39	for example	
44	Finally	
48	hopes; denounce	Semb - type of narrative
55	seems likely	Auth: W Afr infl > Marxist infl
57	more than	

Discussion

Paragraph 1 starts off with something "many critics" agree about: the sociopolitical commitment by filmmaker Ousmane Sembène. But that's not all, according to the author. What really makes Sembène's films stand out ("strikingly," line 9) is how Sembène used West African oral culture techniques in order to convey his sociopolitical messages to Senegalese audiences. In fact, by the end of the last sentence, this first paragraph has given you everything you're looking for: the **Topic** is Sembène's films, and the **Scope** is their use of African oral culture techniques. The **Purpose** of the passage is to discuss Sembène's use of African techniques in his films, and the author's **Main Idea** is a paraphrase of the last sentence: what makes Sembène's films so notable is that they use West African oral culture techniques to express Sembène's sociopolitical messages.

From there, the rest of the passage goes into detail about the specific techniques Sembène uses in his films. You don't have to memorize the multiple examples, but you should be aware that the answer to a Detail question will likely come from here. Paragraph 2 discusses the use of symbolic characters with multiple examples: tree, trickster, street merchant. "Moreover," (line 33) paragraph 3 discusses another connection to West African storytelling: the open-ended plot structure, which comes from the West African tradition of letting the audiences decide stories' endings. "Finally," (lines 44) paragraph 4 continues the list of links between Sembène's films and West African oral tales by showing how Sembène uses traditional "journey" narratives to make his sociopolitical commentary and to bring about change in the viewer (lines 46–48). The author goes even further, arguing that the binary oppositions found in Sembène's films stem not from his Marxist ideology but rather from techniques of African oral storytelling (lines 55–58).

1. (E) Global

Step 2: Identify the Question Type

The phrase "main point" indicates that this is a Global question.

Step 3: Research the Relevant Text

For a Global question, Step 3 is less about finding specific information in the passage and more about consulting the Topic, Scope, Purpose, and Main Idea you determined during Step 1.

Step 4: Make a Prediction

Reviewing what you learned from paragraph 1, the author's main point was that Sembène's films are notable for their use of West African oral storytelling techniques to convey sociopolitical messages.

Step 5: Evaluate the Answer Choices

(E) says exactly the same as the prediction did.

(A) is too narrow because it focuses too much on the details of paragraphs 2 and 3 without mentioning paragraph 4 and how these techniques are used to convey sociopolitical messages.

(B) is even narrower than **(A)**, only discussing information from paragraph 2.

(C) is a Distortion. Nowhere does the author suggest that these techniques were previously considered unsuitable for film.

(D), in addition to leaving out the entire discussion about traditional techniques, also attributes Sembène's sociopolitical beliefs to "most of the Senegalese people," which is an Extreme suggestion at best.

2. (E) Detail

Step 2: Identify the Question Type

Any question that directly asks about what "[t]he author says" is a Detail question.

Step 3: Research the Relevant Text

Here, the question stem doesn't give you a lot of help finding a specific place to research because every single paragraph contains info about what Sembène does in his films.

Step 4: Make a Prediction

However, your Roadmap definitely comes in handy. A quick glance tells you that paragraph 2 talks about symbolic characters, paragraph 3 talks about open-ended plots, and paragraph 4 talks about characters experiencing journeys.

Step 5: Evaluate the Answer Choices

(E) sounds like the "open-ended plots" of paragraph 3. Sure enough, lines 36–38 say that, by using such plots, Sembène "leaves it to his viewers to complete his narratives." That's a perfect match, so **(E)** is correct.

(A)'s mention of symbols would take you to paragraph 2. However, the symbols mentioned there are a tree, a trickster, and a street merchant. No animals.

(B) doesn't look familiar. Paragraph 3 discusses freeze-frames but not slow motion. Plus, the passage is concerned with Sembène's use of traditional West African techniques, not his artistic ones, so **(B)** is Outside the Scope.

(C) uses the term "oral," which pops up several times within the passage. However, Sembène uses traditional West African oral techniques, not oral narration—a film technique as Outside the Scope as the "slow motion" of answer **(B)**.

(D) is another answer that takes a term from the passage ("juxtaposition" in paragraph 4) and distorts it. The paragraph says this juxtaposition is more a feature of African oral storytelling than it is of Marxist ideology. Plus, **(D)** talks about Marxist symbols, which the author never discusses.

3. (A) Logic Reasoning (Strengthen)

Step 2: Identify the Question Type

This question asks you to strengthen a claim made by the author in the passage. This resembles a Strengthen question in the Logical Reasoning section.

Step 3: Research the Relevant Text

The question stem directs you to lines 54–58, in which the author claims that the binary oppositions used by Sembène are more closely related to African storytelling than Marxist ideology.

Step 4: Make a Prediction

As with any other Strengthen question, examine the evidence given to support a claim and determine any relevant assumptions. The author provides evidence that Sembène's binary oppositions are also used in West African tales. The author assumes that this correlation is probably causal and more likely a reason than is Marxism for Sembène's use of binaries. You need an answer that strengthens this assumption.

Step 5: Evaluate the Answer Choices

(A) does that nicely, claiming several African novelists who are known to draw upon oral traditions and use binary oppositions, yet have never read Marxist theory. That indicates binary oppositions are a common component of West African oral traditions, which increases the likelihood that Sembène is pulling from there.

(B) is irrelevant. That binary oppositions are—or are not—found elsewhere in the world doesn't affect the author's claim: that binary oppositions specifically found in West African oral traditions have influenced Sembène's films. If anything, **(B)** is a weakener because if binary oppositions are common to narratives across the world, then the possible influences on Sembène's work are multiplied.

(C) would actually weaken the author's claim since it suggests Marxist theory actually has more of a role in Sembène's films than the author claims.

(D), like **(B)**, is irrelevant. Just because few European or North American filmmakers use binary oppositions does not make it more likely that Sembène was influenced by African oral storytelling.

(E) is tempting but not good enough. While the filmmakers mentioned in this answer may subscribe to Marxist principles, that doesn't necessarily mean their films represent these principles. Furthermore, though binary oppositions don't play an "essential" role in those films, they might play a secondary role. If so, that would undermine the author's

suggestion that Marxist ideology isn't the influence behind the binary oppositions found in Sembène's films.

4. (D) Inference

Step 2: Identify the Question Type

In addition to the word "inferences" in the question stem, you also have the phrase "most strongly supported by the passage," which also indicates an Inference question.

Step 3: Research the Relevant Text

As in the second question from the set, the stem doesn't give you anything to help you research because the entire passage is about Sembène.

Step 4: Make a Prediction

Because your research isn't limited to a specific part of the passage, the answer is tough to predict. You'll have to go into the answer choices prepared to select the one choice that *must* be true.

Step 5: Evaluate the Answer Choices

(D) must be true. Your Roadmap tells you that the author discusses characters in paragraph 2. Starting on line 20, the author mentions the example of "the trickster," who appears in various films as a thief, a civil servant, and a member of the elite. That's certainly a broad range of social strata. **(D)** is therefore the correct answer.

(A) is Outside the Scope. You only know that Sembène is trying to reach African viewers with his message. Whether his films are popular (in Africa or elsewhere) isn't mentioned.

(B) mentions government support, which is definitely Outside the Scope. The passage discusses the techniques of Sembène's films, not their production.

(C) is a Distortion. The critics mentioned at the very beginning do not misunderstand Sembène's films. Their only mistake, according to the author, is not recognizing the primary importance of Sembène's use of West African oral tradition in his work. Additionally, the critics mentioned are not necessarily in Senegal, as this answer choice states.

(E) introduces government censorship, which is Outside the Scope. The author never discusses government responses to Sembène's films.

5. (C) Inference

Step 2: Identify the Question Type

The question stem asks you about the meaning of a specific word used by the author in context. This type of vocabulary question is classified as an Inference question, but you could also view it as a Logic Function question focused on *how* the author uses the word.

Step 3: Research the Relevant Text

The line reference takes you back to the beginning of paragraph 4. Since this question tests the meaning of vocabulary in context, read the entire sentence from lines 44 to 48.

Step 4: Make a Prediction
The "initiatory" journey is described as one that brings about a change in a person's worldview. You want an answer that suggests the idea of change.

Step 5: Evaluate the Answer Choices
(C) fits the bill perfectly.

(A) is tempting if you try to answer the question without going back to the passage. This is a good basic definition of the word *initiatory*, but it's not how the author uses it. This is the most common wrong answer trap for these kinds of questions. Always go back to the passage for context.

(B) is off because there's nothing experimental about the journey—it actually happens.

(D) may also be tempting because of a possible connection between "initial" and "unprecedented." But again, this is not correct in context.

(E) has the prefix "*pre-*," which suggests the beginning or "initial" position, but given the definition of prefatory ("located at the beginning") and the context of "initiatory" in the passage, the two terms don't match up.

6. (A) Detail (NOT)

Step 2: Identify the Question Type
Because this question stem asks you to identify the answer choice NOT supported or mentioned by the passage, this is a Detail EXCEPT question. You'll have to do some careful research to eliminate the wrong answers.

Step 3: Research the Relevant Text
In a Detail EXCEPT question, your research will be guided by the answer choices themselves.

Step 4: Make a Prediction
You won't be able to predict the answer because there's a whole universe of things the passage *doesn't* mention. Instead, be prepared to find lines in the passage to justify any answer choice you want to eliminate.

Step 5: Evaluate the Answer Choices
(A) turns out to be correct. You know Sembène has a message to convey, but the passage never talks about his feelings toward other reformation attempts.

(B) appears in lines 12–15. Sembène uses the traditional techniques and strategies of West African oral culture to express his thoughts and reach contemporary viewers. In paragraph 2, the author further elaborates on those motifs.

(C) is mentioned in lines 48–49, which clearly states Sembène's films denounce social injustice.

(D) is discussed in lines 27–32. The beleaguered street merchant of *Borom Sarret* illustrates Sembène's interest in ordinary people's problems.

(E) can be found in lines 5–7, which claim Sembène is not trying to entertain his audience but rather to raise awareness.

Passage 2: Professional Writing

Step 1: Read the Passage Strategically
Sample Roadmap

line #	Keyword/phrase	¶ Margin notes
Passage A		
2	but	
4	perniciousness	
7	sap	Historical academic writing too abstract
11	unfathomable	
12	cannot	
25	But	Despite fad of 'narrative' still not enough stories stirring emotion
27	very few	
Passage B		
30	inevitably	
32	to a greater extent	Legal writing + conformity – creativity, humor, voice
34	because	
35	necessarily ruled	
37	virtue; suspect	
38	forbidden; mute	
41	too often	
42	badly	
44	not yet exactly clear	
45	but; nonetheless	Narrative?
48	But	Legal analysis strips narrative of its story
52	may well turn out	
53	potentially subversive	Narrative could have + or – effects
55	but	
58	even	
59	important	

Discussion

The author of passage A is unhappy. The author claims reading should both surprise and engage the imagination "but" (line 2) finds that the academic writings of historians are formulaic and unimaginative. As a teacher, the author is upset because the "perniciousness of the historiographic approach" prevents students from connecting to history emotionally. There seems to be a glimmer of hope in the second paragraph, when the author suggests that historians have started to discover the art of storytelling. However, a history conference supposedly devoted to "narratives" finds those stodgy historians adding "Narrative" to their titles but resorting to their usual dry, scholarly papers, interesting only to other historians. The **Topic** of this passage is academic historian writing; the **Scope** is its major shortcoming. The author's **Purpose** is to state dissatisfaction with the lack of interesting writing in the field of history. The **Main Idea** is that history writing is bland and uninspiring and, with a lack of narrative, it keeps students from connecting to history emotionally or intellectually.

Like the author of passage A, the author of passage B is also unhappy. And again, it's because of bad writing. In this passage, the author is concerned with legal writing. The first paragraph introduces the first concern: legal writing is too linear; there are no surprises and voice is constrained. But in the second paragraph, the author goes a step further by suggesting that legal writing has become just plain bad. Like the author of passage A, this author sees a glimmer of hope in the current movement for attention to narrative in legal education. But that hope has a lot to overcome; current practice in legal analysis is to remove the story, or the human narrative content, from the abstract, legal aspect of the case. In the final paragraph, the author acknowledges that it's possible the current fashion might infiltrate education without changing how legal writing is taught—or written—but argues that even awareness of narrative could be an important adjustment. Here the **Topic** is legal writing, and the **Scope** is its major shortcoming. Again, that shortcoming is the lack of narrative. This author's **Purpose** is also to show concern about the lack of interesting writing, only this time in the field of legal writing. However, the last line offers a somewhat more optimistic outlook. The **Main Idea** is that legal writing is generally uninteresting and poorly written, but incorporating narrative could correct some of this.

Before going to the questions, you should always consider the relationship between the two passages. Both have writings in their respective profession as a Topic, and the Scope of both passages is the lack of quality of that writing. They both feel that their professions' writings are uninteresting, and they both feel that the use of narrative (or storytelling) could potentially add value to the writings.

7. (D) Global

Step 2: Identify the Question Type

This question stem is vaguely worded, but the beginnings of each answer choice discuss a broad view of both authors. Most questions that ask about the broad views of an author are Global questions. If you had perceived this as an Inference question about the author's attitude though, that would have led you to the same line of thinking for Steps 3 and 4.

Step 3: Research the Relevant Text

There's no specific place in either passage to consult for your answer, so you may have to let your knowledge of the shared Topic and Scope, as well as the answer choices, guide your research.

Step 4: Make a Prediction

Simply knowing the relationship between the passages can save time. Reexamining the relationship between the two, you know both passages talk disparagingly about the lack of narrative in their respective profession's writings.

Step 5: Evaluate the Answer Choices

(D) turns that prediction into a positive. If the authors are upset by the lack of narrative, it's likely they would find more storytelling a welcome addition.

(A) is a Distortion. While both authors are teachers, neither discusses effective methodology.

(B) is Outside the Scope. Both passages are concerned with points of view well within the normal realm of their respective disciplines.

(C) is Extreme. While both authors believe writing in their disciplines is not currently creative, neither states that such a goal is impossible. In the last sentence of passage B, the author sees some potential for the future of legal writing.

(E) is Outside the Scope. Neither author is happy with the current state of writing in their field, but they don't discuss eliminating elements from other fields. Instead, they do discuss bringing in new elements of narrative.

8. (B) Inference

Step 2: Identify the Question Type

Both the word "inferences" and the phrase "passages most strongly support" indicate an Inference question. Instead of asking about how passage A relates to passage B, this question wants to know how the author of passage A relates to the profession mentioned in passage A, and the same for the author of passage B.

Step 3: Research the Relevant Text

Look for clues in each passage that point to the identities of the authors—personal pronouns such as "I" or "we." Line 5 suggests the author of passage A is a history teacher. "[W]e who teach the law" in line 30 indicates the author of passage B is a law professor.

Step 4: Make a Prediction
Passage A's history teacher discusses academic history writing, while passage B's law professor critiques legal writing. Both appear to be professionals within the worlds they are scrutinizing.

Step 5: Evaluate the Answer Choices
(B) is the only answer that says that both authors are members of the discussed professions.

(A) is a 180. Both authors are definitively involved in the discussed professions.

(C) mischaracterizes passage B, whose author is definitively involved in the law profession.

(D) is a Distortion. Both authors are active members, but of their respectively discussed professions. They're not both in the field of law.

(E) is also off because the author of passage B is not an active member of the history field.

9. (A) Detail

Step 2: Identify the Question Type
The question stem asks not about what the passage implies but what it indicates. That makes this a Detail question.

Step 3: Research the Relevant Text
The word "typical" in the question stem tells you to look for what each author identifies as the status quo in his or her respective field's writing. This leads you to paragraph 1 in passage A and paragraphs 1 and 2 in passage B.

Step 4: Make a Prediction
A scan of these lines yields several adjectives that are consistent with these authors' viewpoints: "sap the vitality" (line 7); "formulaic" (line 9); "abstract" (line 10); and "aimed ... at the head" (lines 11–12) from passage A are in line with "ruled by linear logic" (line 35); "without diversions, surprises, or reversals" (line 36); and "abstract" (line 49) from passage B. The correct answer will agree with these words and phrases.

Step 5: Evaluate the Answer Choices
(A) is a great match. The impersonal implication of "abstraction" fits both authors' criticism that current historical or legal writing turns human situations into intellectual situations. Plus, passage A uses the word "abstract" in line 10, and passage B uses it in line 49. **(A)** is therefore correct.

(B) goes against both passages because the authors describe the writings as "formulaic" (line 9) or "without diversions" (line 36). Hyperbole (or exaggeration) is out of the question.

(C) is not used to describe typical legal writing. Passage B uses the word *subversive* to describe the recent movement toward using narrative (line 53). And subversion isn't mentioned by passage A at all.

(D) should be eliminated because while both authors discuss "narrative," each time it is in the context of discussing recent, possibly corrective trends. Neither uses "narrative" to describe typical, or status quo, writing.

(E) is a 180. Passage A says that historiography "leave[s] little to the imagination" (line 3), and passage B says that in legal writing, "creativity [is] suspect" (line 37).

10. (C) Logic Reasoning (Method of Argument)

Step 2: Identify the Question Type
The question stem is vague, and again it helps to glance at the answer choices. All of them discuss how the authors present their arguments. That makes this a LR–Method of Argument question.

Step 3: Research the Relevant Text
The Keywords "not parallel" mean that you'll have to determine what passage A does that's different from what passage B does. There's no specific text to research, so consult your global understanding of the passages' differences from Step 1 of the Kaplan Method.

Step 4: Make a Prediction
You might have found this answer tough to predict. When two passages are as similar as these two, you'll often have to go through the answer choices to find out what they don't have in common.

Step 5: Evaluate the Answer Choices
(C) is the correct answer. Passage A mentions the American Historical Association conference—a particular example—while passage B has no such specificity. So this choice is correct.

(A) is out because passage A presents an argument for the author's own position but never for the opposition. Plus, the passage doesn't reject any arguments.

(B) is Half-Right/Half-Wrong because passage A certainly makes evaluative claims (calling the historiographic approach "pernicious" in line 4), but so does B (saying in lines 41–42 that lawyers too often write badly).

(D) is also Half-Right/Half-Wrong because passage B certainly offers criticism, but so does passage A (lines 6–7 say that some scholarly monographs "sap the vitality of history").

(E) is wrong because neither passage discusses any theories.

11. (B) Logic Function

Step 2: Identify the Question Type
Some questions will require you to combine multiple LR skills. In this case, "the phrase … plays a role in" and "most analogous to the role played" sound like two LR question types: Role of a Statement and Parallel Reasoning. You will need to find the role or function of the statement from passage A and then find another statement that has the same function in passage B. So, this is a Logic Function question, although it could be classified other ways as well.

Step 3: Research the Relevant Text
As with any question containing a line reference, it's not just the lines themselves that you need to read. You also need to read the surrounding lines for context.

Step 4: Make a Prediction
First, you need to figure out what role the phrase from passage A serves. Reading back for context, that phrase is part of the discussion about how unimaginative historical writing is. By saying that it "saps the vitality of history," the author emphasizes the writing's lack of appeal. Knowing that, you need to find a phrase in passage B that does the same thing.

Step 5: Evaluate the Answer Choices
(B) highlights what the author sees as an attack on imagination within legal writing. This is certainly the correct answer.

(A) explains writing is important to law but doesn't critique that writing for being unimaginative.

(C) explains *why* the writing is so bad, but it doesn't emphasize what's bad about it.

(D) tells you why narrative should be used but doesn't explain that the lack of narrative is what makes current writing so unappealing.

(E) suggests that the author has hope for the future of legal writing but doesn't criticize the lifelessness of its current state.

12. (D) Inference

Step 2: Identify the Question Type
The phrase "the author … would be most likely to expect" indicates an Inference question. You'll have to combine the question stem's hypothetical with the information from passage B to determine what *must* be true.

Step 3: Research the Relevant Text
To determine what passage B's author would expect from a legal document describing the facts of a case, go back to your Roadmap. The author assesses the state of legal writing in paragraphs 1 and 2 of passage B.

Step 4: Make a Prediction
According to lines 35–38, the author would expect a legal document to be linear, unsurprising, and without creative voice. Furthermore, at line 42, the author argues current legal writing is often bad. Finally, at lines 48–49, the author says that legal analysis strips away the case's human narrative content. So, the correct answer will be consistent with those ideas.

Step 5: Evaluate the Answer Choices
(D) is entirely consistent with lines 48–49, making it the correct answer.

(A) starts off well—the author would expect it to be poorly written, according to line 42. However, if you re-read that section of the passage, you see legal writing is bad primarily because lawyers mimic other lawyers, not because they missed out on advice from law professors. In fact, this answer choice is actually a 180. The author says poor writers are "influenced by education," which means law professors' advice is likely detrimental to legal writing's quality.

(B) is a 180. The author says at lines 48–49 that legal analysis strips away the personal narrative, meaning that it will not be "crafted to function like a piece of fiction."

(C) also conflicts with the author's characterization of legal writing. In lines 41–42, the passage says lawyers "too often write badly." As a result, the author certainly wouldn't expect the document to be "a well-crafted piece of writing."

(E) falls Outside the Scope. The author thinks legal writers neglect emotional details (e.g., concerns, conflicts, and feelings). However, the author never says those writers neglect to reference relevant legal doctrines.

Passage 3: Animal Conflict Behavior

Step 1: Read the Passage Strategically
Sample Roadmap

line #	Keyword/phrase	¶ Margin notes
1	Traditional; assert	
3	does not	Trad. animal conflict theory - ritualized; no variation - prevents injury
8	for instance	Ex - Gal. tortoise
14	however; varies greatly	Spider exception
15	In addition	
17	argues; recently developed	
18	provides a closer fit	Riechert - evolutionary game theory better exp.
20	because it explains	
24	adapted from	
26	In both	Similarities with classic game theory
30	For example	
31	only if	
33–34	however, two major differences	2 differences
35	First, whereas	Instinct over rational thought
40	The other difference	Payoffs - reproductive success
47	predicts	
50	will all affect	Richert predictions
51	In addition; predicts	
56	predicts	More willing to fight when good habitat scarce

Discussion

Paragraph 1 introduces the "[t]raditional theories" of animal conflicts within species—visual and vocal displays evolved to reduce injuries during contests. The Galápagos tortoises are provided as an example. So you have the **Topic**: conflict behavior in animals. Of course, rarely does an LSAT passage provide a "traditional" theory without contrasting it with a newfangled theory.

As anticipated, paragraph 2 introduces a counterexample of the spider *A. aperta*, which is sometimes willing to violently fight. Susan Riechert believes this behavior can be explained by evolutionary game theory, which states that animals' fighting may escalate if the prize is sufficiently important. This gives you your **Scope**: differing theories for animal conflict. The second half of paragraph 2 discusses the two differences between evolutionary game theory (for animals) and its predecessor, classical game theory (for humans). First, in classical theory, the level of fighting is decided based on rational thought, while in evolutionary theory the decision is based on instinct. Second, classical theory says the value of the payoff is based on personal judgment, but evolutionary theory says it's based on what's better for reproduction.

The author's opinion on this theory still hasn't appeared, and paragraph 3 doesn't introduce one. Instead, the paragraph discusses how Riechert uses the new theory to predict how *A. aperta* spiders would behave in two different habitats: grassland and riparian. In fact, paragraph 3 has three sentences and the verb in each of them is "predict." [So, when you come across the inevitable question about Paragraph 3, you can already bet that its predictions will be involved in the answers.] Based on the evolutionary game theory, Riechert believes spiders will be more willing to engage in escalated fighting in the grassland because a smaller percentage of land is suitable for occupation and thus territory is more valuable.

Without an author's opinion, the **Purpose** of this passage is purely to introduce the new theory, and the **Main Idea** is that the new theory may explain the fighting behavior of certain animals, notably the *A. aperta*.

13. (C) Global

Step 2: Identify the Question Type

Any question seeking the "main idea" of the passage is definitely a Global question.

Step 3: Research the Relevant Text

Instead of looking for lines to re-read in the passage, go back to your assessment of the big picture: Topic, Scope, Purpose, and Main Idea.

Step 4: Make a Prediction

As stated before, the Main Idea is that there's a new theory (evolutionary game theory) that may better explain some

animals' conflict behavior (namely, that of the spider *A. aperta*) than the traditional species-specific theory.

Step 5: Evaluate the Answer Choices

(C) matches well, even though it doesn't specifically mention *A. aperta*. Notice the tentative language: "may be useful." While this passage discusses Susan Riechert's theory, it never says evolutionary game theory is a proven model.

(A) is a Distortion. While these theories are both mentioned in the passage, classical game theory is included simply to explain the origins of evolutionary game theory; it's not part of the main point. Furthermore, this answer ignores the passage's spider example.

(B) is too narrow. It leaves out evolutionary game theory and instead focuses solely on details from paragraph 3.

(D) is Extreme. The traditional theory doesn't quite fit the behavior of *A. aperta*, but that's hardly enough to say it can't explain behavior of *most* species.

(E) is a Distortion. Evolutionary game theory doesn't explain *how* spiders choose web sites, just how they will act in conflict situations (which can be triggered by territorial disputes). Additionally, though Riechert believes evolutionary game theory can be used, the rest of the scientific community is not necessarily on board.

14. (E) Logic Function

Step 2: Identify the Question Type

The phrase "most likely in order to" indicates a Logic Function question. The focus is not on what the author says about the Galápagos tortoises but *why* the author introduces them in the first place.

Step 3: Research the Relevant Text

Examples usually come *after* the point they support, so be sure to check your Roadmap above the example for context.

Step 4: Make a Prediction

Paragraph 1 introduces the traditional theory of animal conflict: animals' fighting behavior has evolved so that conflicts don't result in injury. The Galápagos tortoise is an example of an animal whose behavior fits this theory.

Step 5: Evaluate the Answer Choices

(E) is exactly like the prediction. The Galápagos tortoise acts as evidentiary support of the statements that immediately precede it: that animals use displays to settle disputes.

(A) is a Distortion. According to the traditional species-specific theory, this kind of behavior is the norm for all animals. Even if the new theory is valid, you still don't know how many species may still fit the old theory—it could be a lot more than "only a few."

(B) is also a Distortion. The author does not mention the tortoise as an exceptional example of "some but not all" species. The author includes the tortoise as an excellent example of a species whose conflict behavior fits the classical model.

(C) is another Distortion. The description of the tortoise extending its neck illustrates a *type* of contest and what it takes to win, not the consistency of that contest. Also, the traditional theory is just that: a theory. The example of one animal does not support that theory's application to "most species."

(D) is unsupported by the passage. The tortoise provides one example of a nonaggressive fighting style, but nothing suggests this display style is unique.

15. Item Removed from Scoring

This question was removed from scoring and was not published when the test was released.

16. (D) Inference (LEAST)

Step 2: Identify the Question Type
The question stem asks you to find the answer choice that *doesn't* agree with a theory in the passage. Always characterize the answer choices so you don't accidentally choose a wrong answer.

Step 3: Research the Relevant Text
Riechert is introduced in paragraph 2, but a quick glance at the answers tells you that you want to check out her paragraph 3 predictions regarding grassland versus riparian habitats. Lines 51–59 say Riechert predicts spiders are more willing to engage in escalated fighting in the grassland (where only 12 percent of land can be occupied) than in the riparian habitat (where 90 percent of land can be occupied).

Step 4: Make a Prediction
It's impossible to know what the *least* consistent answer will say. However, you do know that four answers will fit this theory and one will not.

Step 5: Evaluate the Answer Choices
(D) sticks out as inconsistent right away. Riechert doesn't predict spiders in both habitats are equally prone to escalated fighting. **(D)** is the correct answer.

(A) fits the passage. Escalated fighting for desirable territory in the grassland agrees with Riechert.

(B) also fits. No escalated fighting for imperfect territory in the riparian habitat? Riechert would give that the thumbs-up.

(C) is consistent. Because territory in riparian areas is more plentiful, riparian spiders would be less prone to escalated fighting (i.e., more prone to displays) than grassland spiders.

(E) is consistent because it follows that if riparian spiders are less willing to engage in escalated fighting, they would be more willing to withdraw.

17. (E) Logic Function

Step 2: Identify the Question Type
Any question asking you to determine the function of a detail, quote, reference, or entire paragraph is a Logic Function question. Focus on the "why" or the "how," not the "what."

Step 3: Research the Relevant Text
The entirety of paragraph 3 has to be assessed. It could take a long time to re-read the entire paragraph, so this is where your Roadmap—especially any margin notes—will come in handy.

Step 4: Make a Prediction
Looking at your Roadmap should tell you paragraph 3 is all about Riechert's predictions—based on the recently introduced evolutionary game theory—for *A. aperta* in riparian and grassland habitats.

Step 5: Evaluate the Answer Choices
(E) is the only answer to mention these predictions and is therefore correct.

(A) is a Distortion. While evolutionary game theory was introduced in the preceding paragraph, the species-specific theory was introduced in paragraph 1. Additionally, paragraph 3 doesn't compare the two theories; it describes behavior that could be expected if the new theory is true.

(B) is Extreme. The author never states that evolutionary game theory (which, incidentally, was only described in paragraph 2, not the first two paragraphs) is controversial.

(C) is a Distortion. Paragraph 3 describes predictions, not an actual experiment.

(D) makes the same mistake. Paragraph 3 does not describe actual observed behavior. It's all predictions. Granted, paragraph 2 actually presents behavior that the theory in paragraph 1 can't account for, but this question is concerned with paragraph 3.

18. (B) Inference

Step 2: Identify the Question Type
Because this question asks for what the passage "suggests" rather than what it states, this is an Inference question.

Step 3: Research the Relevant Text
Be sure not to confuse anticipated results with actual observations. Remember that paragraph 3 refers to what Riechert *predicts* these spiders would do. That doesn't tell you what the passage suggests about their actual behavior. For that, you have to check paragraph 2—specifically, lines 13–23 and lines 30–33.

Step 4: Make a Prediction
Lines 13–23 say *A. aperta* spiders' fighting behavior is violent and varies from contest to contest, possibly because of differences in size, age, and experience. Lines 30–33 explain

spiders may escalate their fighting only when the prize in dispute is sufficiently valuable. The correct answer choice will be consistent with this information.

Step 5: Evaluate the Answer Choices
(B) matches. If *A. aperta* fights will escalate only if a resource is valuable, then you can infer the contrapositive: if a resource isn't valuable, fights won't escalate.

(A) is Extreme and a Distortion. Riechert *predicts* that site availability factors into spiders' fights, but the passage doesn't give any evidence to show it is an actual factor, let alone the primary one.

(C) is Extreme. While the *A. aperta* spider exhibits variations in fighting behavior, traditional theories assert that conflict within a species does *not* vary from contest to contest. The spiders, then, are not necessarily similar to "most" other species.

(D) is a Distortion. The passage says that the level of fighting varies from contest to contest, but nothing in the passage suggests which is more frequent: aggressive or nonaggressive.

(E) is Extreme. You don't know which species, or how many species, are similar or dissimilar to *A. aperta*. So, saying *A. aperta* is more willing to fight than "most" other species is extreme.

19. (A) Global

Step 2: Identify the Question Type
The words "primary purpose" indicate this is a Global question.

Step 3: Research the Relevant Text
You can't research a specific part of the passage for a Global question. Instead, revisit the Topic, Scope, Purpose, and Main Idea to form the basis of your prediction. Keep an eye on the author's tone.

Step 4: Make a Prediction
This author introduced the new theory but never really had a strong opinion one way or the other.

Step 5: Evaluate the Answer Choices
(A) is an exact match. The verb "present" is consistent with the author's neutral tone.

(B) is a Distortion. While examples of a phenomenon are provided, this is not the author's Purpose. Those examples are provided to illustrate the new theory.

(C) mischaracterizes the author's tone. The author does no evaluation. This is simply a descriptive passage.

(D) is Extreme. While the *A. aperta* doesn't quite fit the traditional theory, the passage never suggests that the traditional theory is entirely refuted or is "controversial."

(E) is also a Distortion. The author doesn't suggest that the new theory may be inadequately supported. No critique is evident.

Passage 4: Philosophical Anarchism

Step 1: Read the Passage Strategically
Sample Roadmap

line #	Keyword/phrase	¶ Margin notes
1	Most; acknowledge	
6	commonly supposed	Common beliefs
11	But	
12–13	denies this view, arguing instead	Phil Anarchism disagrees - no moral duty to obey laws
15	Some	
16	have rejected; because	
17	highly counterintuitive implications: (1)	Some reject due to 2 implications
20	(2)	
22	In fact, however; does not	Author disagrees with rejectors
24	First	Author rejects reason #1 - can still evaluate morality
27	Even if	
34	In short; perfectly	
35	consistent	
37	Second	
40	Even if	
44	Moreover	Author rejects reason #2 - still moral duties even without laws
49	And	
52	Thus	

Discussion

Paragraph 1 starts out with what "[m]ost people" acknowledge: while it may be morally legitimate to disobey the law in exceptional cases, people generally are morally bound to follow the law. Then, with the "[b]ut" in line 11, the author introduces the **Topic**: the theory of philosophical anarchism. According to this theory, society has no moral duty to obey government laws.

This is immediately followed by the opinion of commentators, who feel philosophical anarchism has two counterintuitive implications. The implications serve as the **Scope** of the passage. According to commentators, the first implication of philosophical anarchism is that because all governments are equally illegitimate, they are then all morally equal. The second is that people can do whatever they please. With the Contrast Keyword *however* at line 22, the author's point of view appears. The author defends philosophical anarchism, saying these implications are not justified by the theory's tenets. You now know the **Purpose** of this passage, which is to defend philosophical anarchism against critics.

You can expect the author to back up his viewpoint, and he does. Paragraph 2 explains why the first implication doesn't logically follow from philosophical anarchism. Even if people are not morally bound to follow government laws, governments can still be evaluated on a moral scale. Some governments can have better moral policies and actions than others. Paragraph 3 lays out why the second implication doesn't hold water. According to philosophical anarchism, even without laws, people have a moral obligation to not only refrain from harming others but also to actively help others.

While the author argues that philosophical anarchism is unfairly criticized, he never actually gives full-fledged support for the theory. That means the **Main Idea** will be more neutral than an endorsement of philosophical anarchism. The author believes philosophical anarchism, though under fire, doesn't imply all governments are morally equal, and neither does it imply people can just do whatever they want.

20. (C) Global

Step 2: Identify the Question Type
Because this question asks for the "main point" of the entire passage, it's a Global question.

Step 3: Research the Relevant Text
Instead of researching a specific part of the passage, use your broader understanding of Topic, Scope, Purpose, and Main Idea to make your prediction.

Step 4: Make a Prediction
In a passage with multiple opinions, it's important to keep those opinions separate—especially the author's. According to the Main Idea from Step 1, the passage isn't necessarily saying philosophical anarchism is the way to go, just that the philosophy doesn't imply what critics suggest.

Step 5: Evaluate the Answer Choices
(C) is consistent with the prediction. The author introduces commentators' two common (incorrect) conclusions in paragraph 1 and then dismisses each in paragraphs 2 and 3.

(A) distorts the point of view. While commentators believe the implications of philosophical anarchism are highly counterintuitive, the author does not call those commentators' beliefs "highly counterintuitive." Instead, he just says philosophical anarchism "does not entail these claims."

(B) distorts points of view again. As the author points out, neither of these two points is actually contrary to what philosophical anarchists claim. Commentators simply think they are.

(D) is too narrow because it focuses entirely on the author's rebuttal of the second assumed implication but completely ignores the rebuttal of the first.

(E) is a classic Half-Right/Half-Wrong answer. It starts off perfectly (as a contrast to the commentators). However, philosophical anarchism *does* conflict with the ordinary view of obeying the law because it is the law. This is not the point the author contests.

21. (A) Detail

Step 2: Identify the Question Type
This is a Detail question because it asks you to find what the author states or, in this case, "identifies."

Step 3: Research the Relevant Text
The phrase "commonly held belief" directs you to the first paragraph, where the author details what "[m]ost people acknowledge" (line 1) and what's "commonly supposed" (line 6).

Step 4: Make a Prediction
Lines 9–11 summarize the commonly held view perfectly: "we generally have a moral duty to obey a law simply because it is the law." Look for the answer choice that states or paraphrases this idea.

Step 5: Evaluate the Answer Choices
(A) is practically identical to the author's statement in the passage.

(B) is a Faulty Use of Detail. This is what commentators feel philosophical anarchism implies.

(C) falls Outside the Scope. The generally held opinion does not differentiate between laws you participate in establishing and other laws.

(D) is a 180. The general opinion is that you are morally obligated to follow the law, so breaking the law would generally be considered immoral, not morally neutral.

(E) misuses a detail from the passage. In paragraph 3, the author states that philosophical anarchists believe people have a moral duty to not harm others, but that's not necessarily a commonly held belief. Moreover, it's unknown how many existing laws do protect others from harm, so it is extreme to say a "majority" do.

22. (B) Inference

Step 2: Identify the Question Type

The question stem asks you to characterize the author's "stance," which makes this a specific type of Inference question: one focusing on the author's attitude.

Step 3: Research the Relevant Text

There isn't one specific area where the author boldly declares his viewpoint. However, based on the Purpose and Main Idea, you can put together a prediction.

Step 4: Make a Prediction

Always begin predicting an author's attitude by first broadly determining whether it's positive, negative, or neutral. Because the author spends the majority of the passage defending philosophical anarchism, you're definitely looking for something positive. However, you should also note that the author doesn't necessarily endorse the theory; the author just says commentators' objections are invalid.

Step 5: Evaluate the Answer Choices

(B) is just moderate enough to be the right answer.

(A) is Extreme. The author finds two of the commentators' implications unjustified, but that doesn't mean he strongly approves of *most* of philosophical anarchism's ideas.

(C) is a 180. It is in line with the commentators' two assumed implications, which the author flatly denies.

(D) is also a 180. The author is defending the theory, not rejecting it, so **(D)** is out.

(E) is another 180. The author shows no displeasure with the theory or its logical consequences, so that eliminates **(E)**.

23. (A) Inference

Step 2: Identify the Question Type

When a question stem asks you what an author "most likely means" with a certain quote or reference, you're being asked to make an Inference.

Step 3: Research the Relevant Text

Going back to paragraph 1, you'll recall that the two implications are that all governments are morally equal or equally illegitimate and that people may do whatever they please.

Step 4: Make a Prediction

These implications seem to be completely against the majority opinion presented earlier in the paragraph. This would be what the commentators mean by "counterintuitive."

Step 5: Evaluate the Answer Choices

(A) is a perfect match.

(B) is a 180, as it is in line with the author's opinion, not the commentators'. Be careful of wrong answers that conflate the points of view in the passage.

(C) is a Distortion. The commentators *do* believe that philosophical anarchism has these implications. The implications just conflict with common sense. Meanwhile, the author says that logic indicates philosophical anarchism doesn't have such implications. Like **(B)**, this answer mixes opinions in the passage.

(D) also distorts the commentators' view. The implications are actually unrelated to one another. They just both are incompatible with common beliefs according to the commentators.

(E) is tempting, but the implications are not *internally* inconsistent, just inconsistent with common sense. At best, the author may feel this way, not the commentators themselves.

24. (B) Logic Reasoning (Principle)

Step 2: Identify the Question Type

This is an LR-Principle question because the stem asks you to take information in the passage—in this case, the broad views of the anarchists—and select the answer choice that has a specific similar scenario consistent with it. This question mimics an Apply the Principle Logical Reasoning question because the referenced lines present a "view," or principle, and the correct answer will be a specific situation that conforms to that principle.

Step 3: Research the Relevant Text

In the referenced lines, philosophical anarchists say that all people have moral duties to one another—duties not to harm others. In addition, people have a moral responsibility to avoid actions most governments consider illegal, such as murder and theft.

Step 4: Make a Prediction

You don't know exactly what the correct answer will say. However, you want to find a situation that illustrates a situation in which someone makes a moral choice to prevent causing others harm without committing widely forbidden crimes.

Step 5: Evaluate the Answer Choices

(B) is an exact match. The executive chooses to stop dumping because doing so contaminates the water supply, something that would invariably cause harm to others. **(B)** is correct.

(A) isn't a match. In this scenario, the party member is acting for her own benefit, not to prevent the harm of others. In fact, exposing other party members would likely cause them harm.

(C) doesn't match. While the person may be protecting his coworker from the harm that would result from being fired, he's still allowing the coworker to steal funds, a no-no according to philosophical anarchists.

(D) references yet another person acting in her own self-interest.

(E) is Outside the Scope of lines 37–44. While philosophical anarchists may be okay with this, this has nothing to do with the views in question, which deal with acting morally with respect to others' well-being. This answer actually relates to the discussion about conventional laws in lines 49–57.

25. (C) Inference

Step 2: Identify the Question Type
Even without the word "inferred," this would still be an Inference question because it asks you to find the answer choice with which "the author would be most likely to agree."

Step 3: Research the Relevant Text
The only clue from the question stem is the mention of the author. You'll need to stick closely to where the author's point of view is most clearly outlined. This probably means the last sentence of paragraph 1, or paragraphs 2 and 3 will provide support for the correct answer.

Step 4: Make a Prediction
With a vaguely worded Inference question, the best you can do is to compare the answer choices to what you know of the overall Scope, Purpose, and Main Idea. Fortunately, this author has a clear point of view throughout the passage, so you can quickly eliminate answer choices inconsistent with that view. Here, the author argues philosophical anarchism does not imply what some commentators believe; in fact, the theory says governments may be unequal morally, and people have a moral duty to not harm others.

Step 5: Evaluate the Answer Choices
(C) has evidence that can be found in lines 46–49, which says people may decide to support governmental efforts because of their moral duty to care for one another. That makes **(C)** the correct answer.

(A) is unsupported. You know that obeying the law is generally held to be moral, but you're not told know how much else is generally considered moral, so you can't say whether the author thinks philosophical anarchism subjects one to more or less obligations than do commonly held beliefs.

(B) is likewise unsupported. Paragraph 2 talks about governments with different levels of morality, but the author never suggests that morally superior governments recognize

that citizens can disobey the laws. Essentially, that would be saying morally superior governments are those that recognize philosophical anarchism, and while the author defends the theory, he never actually endorses it.

(D) isn't a valid inference. It's generally believed that people have a moral duty to obey the law because it is the law, but the author doesn't discuss or evaluate the arguments supporting that view. Moreover, the number of governments that have that moral right is unspecified, so "most" is Extreme.

(E) introduces the issue of enforcement. Philosophical anarchism wouldn't have any principles regarding the creation and enforcement of laws because the theory argues no one has a moral duty to obey such laws anyway.

26. (D) Logic Function

Step 2: Identify the Question Type
The words at the end of the question stem ("functions primarily to") mean that you're being asked to determine what the author does with these lines, not what the author means. That makes this a Logic Function question.

Step 3: Research the Relevant Text
The text in question refers to the philosophical anarchists' belief that people have a moral duty to care for one another. The Keyword "[m]oreover" at the beginning of the sentence suggests the author is continuing a previous thought. Reading back, you can see this is all part of the author's defense against what commentators' believe is philosophical anarchism's second implication: that people can do whatever they want.

Step 4: Make a Prediction
The text in question is part of the author's defense, which says that while philosophical anarchists believe people are not morally obligated to follow the law, they still have basic, as well as positive, moral obligations to one another.

Step 5: Evaluate the Answer Choices
(D) is a great match. Not only are people required to not harm others, they actually have a moral obligation to help.

(A) is a 180. The passage says philosophical anarchists would support such efforts.

(B) falls Outside the Scope. The author implies such laws exist but doesn't mention what philosophical anarchists think about their rarity or frequency.

(C) is a Distortion. The text in question suggests philosophical anarchism actually has a solid moral foundation, which isn't inconsistent with widely held beliefs. **(C)** reflects what the commentators believe: that the theory is inconsistent with generally held beliefs. That opinion appears much earlier in the first paragraph. The text in question is used to support the author's defense of the theory, which appears in paragraphs 2 and 3.

(E) is the right idea with the wrong reference. This answer refers to the previous sentence (lines 40–44). And even though the two ideas are related, the text in question is not an example of an obligation to refrain from common crimes. Looking at Keywords could help you here. "Moreover" indicates the text introduces an additional idea; it doesn't illustrate the idea just presented.

27. (D) Global

Step 2: Identify the Question Type
The word "primarily" indicates a Global question. Specifically, you're asked to identify the author's primary purpose.

Step 3: Research the Relevant Text
For a Global question, there isn't a specific place in the passage to research. Instead, you'll consult your broader understanding of Topic, Scope, Purpose, and Main Idea.

Step 4: Make a Prediction
By the end of the first paragraph (lines 22–23, specifically), you can recognize that the author's Purpose is to defend political anarchism against the criticisms made by the commentators mentioned in line 15.

Step 5: Evaluate the Answer Choices
(D) comes straight from the prediction.

(A) is wrong because the author is defending the theory, not describing its origins.

(B) is a Distortion. The author defends the theory by showing how it doesn't go against common sense in the ways critics think. However, the idea of not having a moral obligation to follow the law is still against the grain. So the author doesn't quite establish all-around conformity.

(C) is a 180. The author argues the implications are fallacious, not "necessary."

(E) misses the mark because the author doesn't admit to the alleged defects of philosophical anarchism. The commentators do, but the author defends the theory against those criticisms.

PrepTest 53

The Inside Story

PrepTest 53 was administered in December 2007. It challenged 42,250 test takers. The following chart shows the average number of students to miss each question in each of PrepTest 53's different sections.

Percentage Incorrect by PrepTest 53 Section Type

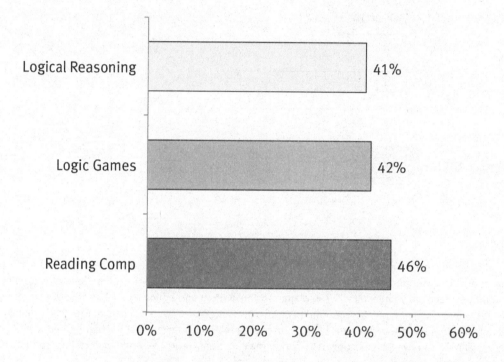

On average, students were most likely to miss questions in Reading Comprehension. Although Reading Comprehension was somewhat higher in actual difficulty than Logical Reasoning and Logic Games, the percentages are not that disparate, so students were missing about 10–12 questions in each individual section.

Additionally, although Reading Comprehension was the hardest section, only three of the test's 10 hardest questions came from that section. Here were the locations of the 10 hardest (most missed) questions in the exam.

Location of 10 Most Difficult Questions in PrepTest 53

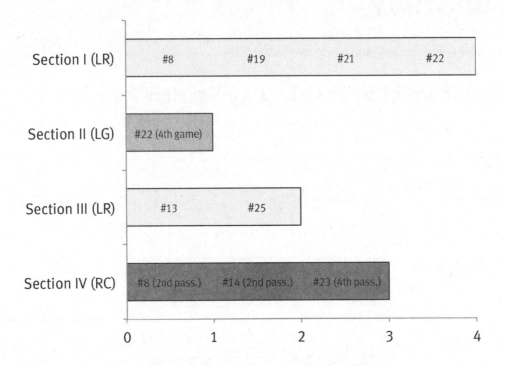

The takeaway from this data is that, to maximize your potential on the LSAT, you need to take a comprehensive approach. Test yourself rigorously, and review your performance on every section of the test. Kaplan's LSAT explanations provide the expertise and insight you need to fully understand your results. The explanations are written and edited by a team of LSAT experts, who have helped thousands of students improve their scores. Kaplan always provides data-driven analysis of the test, ranking the difficulty of every question based on actual student performance. The 10 hardest questions on every test are highlighted with a 4-star difficulty rating, the highest we give. The analysis breaks down the remaining questions into 1-, 2-, and 3-star ratings so that you can compare your performance to thousands of other test takers on all LSAC material.

Don't settle for wondering whether a question was really as hard as it seemed to you. Analyze the test with real data, and learn the secrets and strategies that help top scorers master the LSAT.

7 Can't-Miss Features of PrepTest 53

- With 12 Strengthen/Weaken questions, PrepTest 53 was only the third test ever with 12 or more on a single LSAT. The two other times this happened were in 1999 (PrepTests 28 and 30), which had 13 and 14 Strengthen/Weaken questions, respectively.
- This was the first PrepTest since December 2001 (PT 36) with two Hybrid games. It's also happened four times since PrepTest 53's administration.
- This was just the third appearance ever for Comparative Reading, but for the first time, it had just five questions. In hindsight that's pretty rare, it only happens about 15% of the time.
- PrepTest 53 had some interesting distribution of its answer choices. (D) was only correct in Logic Games twice—tied for the fewest times (D) was ever correct in that section. However, (D) was correct in Reading Comprehension nine times—tied for the most ever in that section.
- The most times a single answer choice has ever occurred as the correct answer in the two Logical Reasoning sections is 15 times. PrepTest 53 is the only test ever, though, when that answer has been (A)—otherwise it's always been (B), (C), or (D)—but still never (E).

- The first question of the first LR section on this test was a Strengthen/Weaken EXCEPT question. An EXCEPT question has only led off a Logical Reasoning section four times. This was the first time it happened since October, 2001 (PT 35), and it hasn't happened since PrepTest 53.
- The week leading up to Test Day the #1 song on the Billboard Hot 100 was "No One" by Alicia Keys. Undoubtedly, some well-trained test takers instinctively translated the Formal Logic of "No one can get in the way of what I feel for you" into If/Then format.

PrepTest 53 in Context

As much fun as it is to find out what makes a PrepTest unique or noteworthy, it's even more important to know just how representative it is of other LSAT administrations (and, thus, how likely it is to be representative of the exam you will face on Test Day). The following charts compare the numbers of each kind of question and game on PrepTest 53 to the average numbers seen on all officially released LSATs administered over the past five years (from 2013 through 2017).

Number of LR Questions by Type: PrepTest 53 vs. 2013–2017 Average

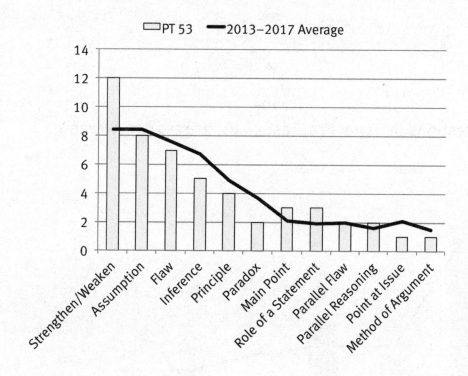

Number of LG Games by Type: PrepTest 53 vs. 2013–2017 Average

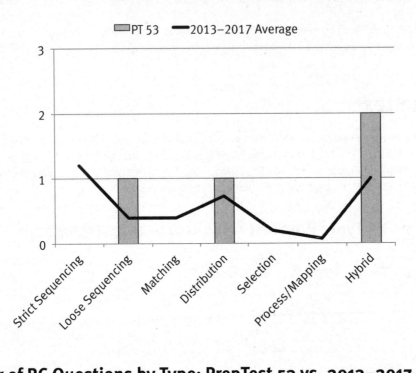

Number of RC Questions by Type: PrepTest 53 vs. 2013–2017 Average

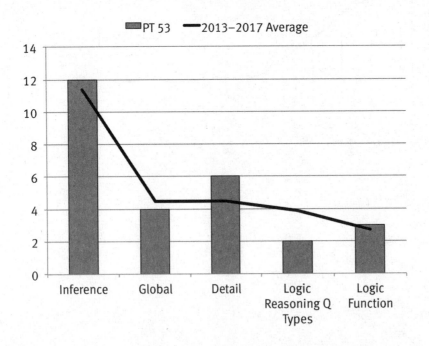

There isn't usually a huge difference in the distribution of questions from LSAT to LSAT, but if this test seems harder (or easier) to you than another you've taken, compare the number of questions of the types on which you, personally, are strongest and weakest. Then, explore within each section to see if your best or worst question types came earlier or later.

Students in Kaplan's comprehensive LSAT courses have access to every released LSAT and to a library of thousands of officially released questions arranged by question, game, and passage type. If you are studying on your own, you have to do a bit more work to identify your strengths and your areas of opportunity. Quantitative analysis (like that in the charts shown here) is an important tool for understanding how the test is constructed, and how you are performing on it.

Section I: Logical Reasoning

Q#	Question Type	Correct	Difficulty
1	Strengthen (EXCEPT)	C	★
2	Point at Issue	B	★★
3	Weaken	B	★
4	Main Point	A	★
5	Principle (Identify/Inference)	E	★
6	Strengthen	A	★
7	Inference	A	★★★
8	Weaken	D	★★★★
9	Assumption (Necessary)	A	★
10	Strengthen	D	★
11	Role of a Statement	D	★
12	Flaw	C	★★
13	Assumption (Necessary)	A	★
14	Role of a Statement	D	★★
15	Assumption (Necessary)	B	★
16	Inference	E	★★
17	Principle (Apply/Inference)	B	★★
18	Flaw	B	★★
19	Parallel Reasoning	A	★★★★
20	Assumption (Sufficient)	C	★★★
21	Parallel Flaw	A	★★★★
22	Flaw	E	★★★★
23	Assumption (Necessary)	D	★
24	Paradox (EXCEPT)	D	★★
25	Flaw	B	★★

1. (C) Strengthen (EXCEPT)

Step 1: Identify the Question Type
The question stem indicates that four answer choices will strengthen the argument. The correct answer is the exception that will *not* strengthen it, but instead will either weaken it or be irrelevant.

Step 2: Untangle the Stimulus
The conclusion is the judgmental recommendation that "consumers should be skeptical of the claims made in advertisements." The evidence is that accuracy in advertising is not necessary for advertising to assist businesses in maximizing profits.

Step 3: Make a Prediction
The assumption is that if something (i.e., accuracy in advertising) is not necessary to maximizing profits, then businesses will not do it. Information firming up that assumption will strengthen the argument, as will any reason to doubt advertisements. The correct answer will be either a strengthener or irrelevant. So, any reason to believe in the accuracy of advertisements or any information that does not affect whether advertisements should or should not be believed would be a correct answer.

Step 4: Evaluate the Answer Choices
(C) is correct because it does not provide a tangible reason to be skeptical of advertisements. This choice indicates that at least one person is skeptical of advertisements, but does not provide any reason for the skepticism. It is circular reasoning to argue that people should be skeptical of advertisements because some people are skeptical of advertisements.

(A) provides a motive for using inaccurate information in advertisements and, thus, strengthens the recommendation to be skeptical of the ads.

(B) provides a reason to be skeptical of advertisements, so it strengthens the argument.

(D) at least to some degree increases the likelihood of inaccuracies in advertisements and, thus, strengthens the recommendation to be skeptical of the ads.

(E), like **(D)**, at least to some degree increases the likelihood of inaccuracies in advertisements and, thus, strengthens the recommendation to be skeptical of the ads.

2. (B) Point at Issue

Step 1: Identify the Question Type
A question stem that asks what two speakers *disagree* about is a Point at Issue question. Select the answer that identifies an issue that both speakers have expressed an opinion on and about which they disagree.

Step 2: Untangle the Stimulus
According to Elaine, museum displays should reflect the best examples of each artistic period and genre, not just recognized masterpieces, because the purpose of art museums is to preserve artworks and make them available to the public.

According to Frederick, museums should devote their limited resources to buying works of recognized masters in order to preserve the greatest works of art.

Step 3: Make a Prediction
It is typically not necessary for a Point at Issue question to identify the assumptions of each speaker's argument. Try to recognize an explicit point of disagreement. If you do not see it, assess each answer choice by asking if both speakers have an opinion on this issue and whether they disagree with each other.

Elaine and Frederick most apparently disagree on whether to limit acquisitions to recognized masters (Frederick) or to expand the scope of purchases to examples of non-masters (Elaine). However, remain open to less obvious possibilities.

Step 4: Evaluate the Answer Choices
(B) meets the criteria of an issue that both at least implicitly have an opinion on and about which they disagree. Elaine explicitly identifies a goal of representing *each* genre of art in a museum's collection. While Frederick does not explicitly address this goal, he does state that the limited funds should be devoted to the singular pursuit of recognized masters, which excludes other goals. That is not to say that Frederick believes that efforts should be made to avoid certain genres, but merely that Frederick does not agree that it should be a goal to purposefully seek to include *all* genres.

(A) is something that neither speaker expresses an opinion on. At the end of her argument, Elaine merely accepts implicitly that it is possible that some artistic masterpieces are not recognized as masterpieces by experts. Frederick does not discuss "artistic masterpieces."

(C) is a 180. It is something that both speakers agree on.

(D) is not a point of disagreement. Frederick would not recommend this course of action, because he limits the use of museum funding to the greatest works of recognized masters. However, Elaine's opinion on this is not discernible. Elaine does state that museums should *seek* to display the best examples, but does not indicate what should be done if it is impossible to acquire the best examples, let alone whether an *unusual* example should be sought.

(E) is Out of Scope. Frederick does not discuss what qualifies as a *masterpiece,* and Elaine, too, does not address this specific issue, even though she does imply that some of the best examples of artistic genres might not be recognized as masterpieces.

3. (B) Weaken

Step 1: Identify the Question Type

The question stem explicitly indicates that the task is to weaken the argument. As with many Strengthen or Weaken questions, the stem identifies what to use as the conclusion: the *explanation* for the claim that humans have so many diseases in common with cats. That the conclusion is described as an *explanation* also indicates the argumentation pattern found in the stimulus.

Step 2: Untangle the Stimulus

The scientist focuses on the interesting phenomenon that humans have many diseases in common with cats and provides a genetic explanation for that phenomenon.

Step 3: Make a Prediction

The stimulus contains an important pattern in which an interesting phenomenon can be observed and concludes by providing a causal explanation for that phenomenon. The standard assumption is that there is no other explanation, and most commonly the correct Weaken answer choice will provide an alternative explanation. For this question, the correct answer choice most likely will provide an alternative explanation, besides genetics, for the number of diseases shared by humans and cats.

Step 4: Evaluate the Answer Choices

(B) is correct. Rather than providing an alternative explanation for the commonality of diseases in humans and cats, as predicted, this choice more directly indicates that genetics cannot be the explanation for this commonality. This is a great example of the value of being very clear about the conclusion of an argument and selecting the answer that stays on point with that conclusion. The conclusion of this argument is that the explanation is *genetics*. Weaken that with an answer that indicates that it is *not genetics*.

(A) is Out of Scope. The issue is whether genetics is the explanation for the commonality of diseases in humans and cats. The subsequent development in cats of resistance to some of those diseases cannot affect the cause of the overlap of diseases in humans and cats.

(C) is an Irrelevant Comparison. It provides no insight as to why humans and cats do have some diseases in common, which is the sole point of the argument.

(D) is Out of Scope because the severity of the disease is irrelevant. **(D)** provides no insight as to why humans and cats do have some diseases in common, which is the sole point of the argument.

(E) is an Irrelevant Comparison. Even if humans have more genes in common with nonhuman primates than with cats, that doesn't affect whether genetics is the proper explanation for why humans and cats have so many diseases in common. Humans may also have diseases in common with nonhuman primates. The question is simply whether the explanation for

any common diseases is genetic, regardless of how closely related the animals are.

4. (A) Main Point

Step 1: Identify the Question Type

The question stem directly asks for the main conclusion of the argument. Select the answer that specifically matches the meaning of the conclusion. Resist answers that drift into the evidence, paraphrase the entire argument, or speculate beyond the conclusion.

Step 2: Untangle the Stimulus

The conclusion is the judgment that there is a need to find new ways to help business grow. The phrase "after all" signals the transition to the evidence. While *so* is a Conclusion Keyword, in this argument it signals a subsidiary conclusion helping to support the recommendation to find new ways to grow business.

Step 3: Make a Prediction

The correct answer should match the first sentence in meaning: the "region must find new ways to help business grow."

Step 4: Evaluate the Answer Choices

(A) is correct because it is just a rewording of the first sentence, which is the conclusion of the argument.

(B) is implied by the evidence, but is not the conclusion of the argument.

(C) is a piece of evidence stated in support of the conclusion.

(D) is a subsidiary conclusion, but not the main conclusion. The author's statement that new manufacturing areas are needed helps support the main conclusion that the "region must find new ways to help business growth"—not vice versa.

(E) is also a piece of evidence.

5. (E) Principle (Identify/Inference)

Step 1: Identify the Question Type

The term *proposition* typically indicates a Principle question. Also, the phrase "exemplified by the situation" indicates a Principle question, because an example is a specific situation that illustrates a general rule or principle. Also, because this Principle question stem refers to the "situation presented above,", without reference to an argument or reasoning, it is not necessary to break the stimulus down to evidence and conclusion. This is an Identify the Principle question that acts like an Inference question. Paraphrase the situation in the stimulus in broad terms.

Step 2: Untangle the Stimulus

According to the information, modern medicine is increasing life spans, resulting in a higher percentage of older people. This increased proportion of older people is potentially devastating financially for some social welfare programs.

Step 3: Make a Prediction

Contrast Keywords, such as [*b*]*ut*, highlight distinctions on which it is vital to focus. The correct answer will likely focus on modern medicine's positive effect on healthy life spans and its negative effect on the financing of social welfare programs. Also, the correct answer may well be stated in broader terms. Wrong answers will contain distortions of, or deviations from, the stimulus, rather than just paraphrases of the stimulus.

Step 4: Evaluate the Answer Choices

(E) is correct, broadly paraphrasing the positive and negative effects of modern medicine, without any deviations. This choice properly indicates what *can* happen, using a single example.

(A) is a Distortion because the stimulus only discusses the effects of modern medicine in two specific arenas, rather than a sweeping rule that technology cannot solve all problems. Modern medicine was not a failed *solution* at fixing financial problems in social welfare programs—those problems are just an unintended consequence. Perhaps a different innovation or technology may be able to solve those financial problems, too. It cannot be inferred that the author agrees with the broad statement of **(A)**.

(B) is Out of Scope because the stimulus does not recommend delaying the implementation of any technologies.

(C) is Extreme. A single example does not support a general rule covering *every* enhancement of the quality of life.

(D) is also Extreme. A single example does not support a general rule covering *all* social institutions.

6. (A) Strengthen

Step 1: Identify the Question Type

The question stem explicitly asks for a strengthener. Identify the assumption, and firm up the bridge between the evidence and conclusion.

Step 2: Untangle the Stimulus

The author concludes that Jackie will probably like The Cruel Herd's new album. The primary reason is that Jackie is a big fan of Moral Vacuum's music, and some of The Cruel Herd's music on their new album contains lyrical styling similar to some of Moral Vacuum's.

Step 3: Make a Prediction

The argument is based on an analogy between The Cruel Herd's new album and Moral Vacuum's music. Strengthen by identifying a further similarity between the music on The Cruel Herd's new album and Moral Vacuum's music or by eliminating a potential difference.

Step 4: Evaluate the Answer Choices

(A) is correct because it bolsters the likelihood that The Cruel Herd's new album is similar musically to Moral Vacuum's music. The portion of this choice that indicates that Jackie has not previously cared for The Cruel Herd is not a problem because the author's conclusion is limited to The Cruel Herd's current album.

(B) does not strengthen the argument because it would need to speculate that Jackie would be more likely to appreciate music produced by a successful mainstream popular music producer, despite the indications in the stimulus that Jackie has more eclectic tastes in music.

(C) is incorrect. While it does provide a similarity between Moral Vacuum and The Cruel Herd, it does not relate to The Cruel Herd's new album, which is the sole focus of the conclusion.

(D) is incorrect because it indicates that for Jackie to listen to something on a regular basis, it must be rock music. However, that does not mean that Jackie likes all rock music or even a significant proportion of rock music, and The Cruel Herd's new album, while rock music, is pretty eclectic.

(E) is a 180 because it provides a difference between Jackie's favorite Moral Vacuum songs, which have somber and political lyrics, and the new Herd album, which has witty and humorous lyrics.

7. (A) Inference

Step 1: Identify the Question Type

The phrase "must be true" indicates an Inference question and articulates the test for an Inference question answer. Formal Logic is generally common in Inference stimuli, but particularly if the question stem asks for what "must be true."

Step 2: Untangle the Stimulus

The stimulus defines what a superconductor is and asserts that its economic feasibility depends on finding a substance that superconducts at a temperature above minus 148 degrees Celsius. The only potential substance would be an alloy of niobium and germanium, but such alloys superconduct at temperatures no higher than minus 160 degrees Celsius.

Step 3: Make a Prediction

Focusing on the Formal Logic and the Opinion Keyword *unfortunately* yields a concrete, predictable deduction.

If	economically feasible	→	superconduct above minus 148

$$\text{If } \begin{array}{c} \sim \textbf{superconduct} \\ \textbf{above minus} \\ \textbf{148} \end{array} \rightarrow \begin{array}{c} \sim \textbf{economically} \\ \textbf{feasible} \end{array}$$

$$\text{If superconduction} \rightarrow \begin{array}{c} \textbf{alloy} \\ \textbf{of} \\ \textbf{N} \\ \textbf{and} \\ \textbf{G} \end{array} \rightarrow \begin{array}{c} \textbf{superconduct} \\ \textbf{minus 160} \\ \textbf{max} \end{array}$$

Deduction:

$$\text{If superconduction} \rightarrow \begin{array}{c} \textbf{alloy} \\ \textbf{of N} \\ \textbf{and} \\ \textbf{G} \end{array} \rightarrow \begin{array}{c} \textbf{superconduct} \\ \textbf{minus 160} \\ \textbf{max} \end{array} \rightarrow \begin{array}{c} \sim \textbf{econ.} \\ \textbf{feasible} \end{array}$$

Using the endpoints of the Formal Logic chain yields the *unfortunate* deduction that superconduction is not economically feasible.

Step 4: Evaluate the Answer Choices

(A) matches the Formal Logic deduction described in Step 3. While extreme, this choice is supported by the definite statements in the stimulus.

(B) is a 180 because it contradicts the stimulus. According to the stimulus, the only feasible superconductor would be an alloy of niobium and germanium ("must be an alloy …").

(C) is a Distortion on two fronts. According to the stimulus, superconduction at temperatures *above* (not *below*) minus 148 Celsius is necessary (not sufficient).

(D) is a 180 because it contradicts the stimulus. According to the stimulus, alloys of niobium and germanium can superconduct at minus 160 Celsius and below ("no higher than minus 160 degrees …").

(E) is Out of Scope and Extreme, as other uses of alloys of niobium and germanium—beyond superconductors—are not discussed and could well be economically feasible.

8. (D) Weaken

Step 1: Identify the Question Type

The question stem explicitly asks for a weakener. Identify the assumption and attack it.

Step 2: Untangle the Stimulus

The phrase "this suggests that" indicates that the preceding evidence supports the conclusion that follows. Thus, the conclusion is that "if night-lights cause nearsightedness, the effect disappears with age." The evidence is from studies that found a correlation between the use of night-lights and

nearsightedness in a study group of younger children but not in study groups of older children.

Step 3: Make a Prediction

There are two important patterns to notice: 1) this is a causal argument, and 2) this is a Weaken question with technical or scientific evidence. Regarding the causal pattern, take notice of the limitation on the doctor's conclusion. The doctor does not conclude or assume that night-lights cause nearsighted-ness because the doctor limits her conclusion to the hypothetical of "*if* night-lights cause nearsightedness." However, the doctor does assume that nothing besides the aging process and the passage of time accounted for the reduction in nearsightedness in the studies of the older children. Thus, the sufficiency of the studies to accurately measure the level of correlation between night-light use and nearsightedness is still significant. Additionally, while premises should be accepted as true and, thus, you should not normally seek to weaken an argument by attacking the validity of the evidence, it is possible to attack the adequacy and accuracy of an experiment. Any time the doctor relies on a study or other scientific evidence, the doctor assumes that the study was sufficiently adequate and accurate to accept the results. The argument can be weakened by a choice that attacks the adequacy of the study in some relevant way.

Step 4: Evaluate the Answer Choices

(D) is correct. This choice weakens the argument by attacking the adequacy of the two studies finding diminished rates of nearsightedness in the older children. The conclusion is qualified by the hypothetical condition that night-lights do cause nearsightedness. But it is still necessary to the argument's assertion of a disappearance of those effects with age that the studies discern changes in the correlation between night-light use and nearsightedness in the different age groups.

(A) is irrelevant to the doctor's conclusion that the effects of night-lights on nearsightedness in children disappear as the children age, because the argument does not assume that the nearsightedness will develop immediately during infancy. This study is conducted too early to determine if "the effect disappears with age."

(B) is superficially a 180 because it eliminates the possibility of reverse causation. However, it really has no effect on the argument, because the conclusion is limited by the hypothetical condition that night-lights do cause nearsightedness.

(C) is Out of Scope because the focus of the argument is limited to whether the effects on those who were subjected to night-lights disappear with age. This choice is only relevant to whether the night-lights actually caused the nearsightedness, as the doctor limits her conclusion by beginning with the condition "*if* night-lights cause nearsightedness." Such limitation in the scope of a conclusion restricts the potential avenues of attack on an argument. Also, as to the question of whether the night-lights caused the nearsightedness, **(C)** says that *most* of the children in this study were not nearsighted. However, the stimulus only indicated that use of a night-light made them more likely to be nearsighted. It didn't claim that the majority of those who used night-lights would develop nearsightedness. So, the results of this study do not weaken the doctor's argument for multiple reasons.

(E) does not weaken the argument because the doctor does not assume that no older children will have nearsightedness, but only that any increase in the levels of nearsightedness caused by night-lights will disappear with age. Let's illustrate that by making up numbers. Let's say the normal level of nearsightedness would be 10 in 100, but night-light use increases that to 20 in 100. If the doctor is correct, then as children age the level of nearsightedness should fall back to the normal level of 10 in 100, not fall to zero. The doctor concludes that "the *effect*" of night-light use disappears, not that nearsightedness disappears altogether. The word *several* should merely be interpreted as "at least one." So, the presence of one or more older children with nearsightedness out of a group of 100 is completely consistent with the doctor's argument.

9. (A) Assumption (Necessary)

Step 1: Identify the Question Type
A question that asks for an assumption required by the argument is a Necessary Assumption question. Build the core bridge between the evidence and conclusion, without which the argument cannot stand.

Step 2: Untangle the Stimulus
The author concludes that the leatherback turtle is clearly in danger of extinction based on the principle that any species whose population declines by more than two-thirds in 15 years is in grave danger of extinction. Also, it is known that the population of "nesting female leatherback turtles" has declined by that amount.

Step 3: Make a Prediction
An important category of scope shift to recognize is when a limitation or qualification in the evidence is not carried over to the conclusion. Note that the evidence on the decline in leatherback turtles is specific to "nesting females." However, the general principle that the author applies to the turtles is stated in terms of the entire population. Thus, the author must assume that the decline in the nesting females is representative of the overall decline in the species.

Step 4: Evaluate the Answer Choices
(A) matches the prediction described in Step 3.

(B) is Extreme. An Assumption answer may be in the form of a conditional statement, as in this choice. To be correct, it must

be in the form of "If evidence, then conclusion" (or its contrapositive). This answer is in that form, but states the conclusion too forcefully: "species *will* eventually become extinct." The argument less forcefully indicates that they will be in "danger of extinction."

(C) is a Distortion of the necessary assumption. The argument assumes that the *decline* in nesting females is representative of the *decline* in the species overall, not that there needs to be equal numbers of females and males in the global population.

(D) is essentially an Irrelevant Comparison between wild and captive populations. The surveys utilized include the entire "earth's population," and the principle relied on makes no distinction between wild and captive populations. This answer does not work as an ignored possibility assumption because by its terms, the argument encompasses all turtles, wild and captive.

(E) is Out of Scope and Extreme. The argument does not even mention captive breeding, and the word *only* is an indicator that a Necessary Assumption answer choice is likely Extreme. It is not required by the author that there is *only* one way to ensure the survival of the species.

10. (D) Strengthen

Step 1: Identify the Question Type
The question stem explicitly asks you to strengthen the argument. Identify the assumption, and firm up the connection between the evidence and conclusion.

Step 2: Untangle the Stimulus
The paraphrase of the author's conclusion should include a definition of the vague term "the campaign": the campaign to increase vegetable consumption would be more effective if it included tips for making vegetables more appetizing. The evidence is that the campaign to date has had little effect on people's diets.

Step 3: Make a Prediction
There really is no specific evidence to support the idea of giving tips to make vegetables more appetizing. The author only says that the current campaign is not working, and basically just throws out an idea. The assumption is that this idea is likely better than something that's not working. Strengthen that assumption with an answer that links such tips to increased vegetable consumption.

Step 4: Evaluate the Answer Choices
(D) is correct, indicating that giving tips on making vegetables more appetizing will get more people to eat vegetables. This answer essentially states that the conclusion is correct. Do not pass over an answer because it seems too obvious or on point with the author's conclusion.

(A) is Out of Scope. The evidence is about people who dislike vegetables, whereas this answer is about those that love the taste of vegetables. Whether the previous campaign—which focused on health— impacted those that love vegetables is irrelevant to whether a new campaign—which focuses on making vegetables more appetizing to those that dislike them—will work.

(B) is a 180 because it merely provides something negative about ways of making vegetables more appetizing. More importantly, it does not provide any reason to believe that tips for making vegetables more appetizing will be effective in convincing people to consume more vegetables.

(C) makes an Irrelevant Comparison between those who don't like the taste of most vegetables and those who like a few. If anything, this is a 180 because it suggests that making vegetables more appetizing does not increase consumption.

(E) is in one sense a 180 because all it does is set a really high bar for what should be considered an effective campaign. By the terms of the argument, the campaign could be considered effective if it makes any significant impact on people's diet. A rule making it necessary that everyone learn to find vegetables appealing is very unlikely to be effective.

11. (D) Role of a Statement

Step 1: Identify the Question Type
A question stem that asks for the *function* of a claim is a Role of a Statement question. It identifies a specific piece of the stimulus and asks you to identify how the author uses it. Underline the statement in the stimulus, and then focus on the structure of the argument and how the relevant claim fits in that structure.

Step 2: Untangle the Stimulus
The claim about private corporations follows the Evidence Keyword *since* and precedes the author's main conclusion that public funds should be used to support pure scientific research.

Step 3: Make a Prediction
From the structure and Keyword, it is definite that the relevant claim is a piece of evidence supporting the conclusion. You should eliminate answers that assign the evidence a different role. To make an even stronger prediction, ask how the claim about private corporations supports the recommendation to use public funds. Essentially, it says that private corporations will not provide the money. So, the statement supports the recommendation by eliminating a different option.

Step 4: Evaluate the Answer Choices
(D) matches the prediction described in Step 3.

(A) incorrectly identifies the statement as the conclusion of the argument, rather than supporting evidence.

(B) incorrectly asserts that the statement provides a definition of the term "pure science," which it does not. The claim about private corporations follows the word [s]*ince* in the third sentence. That is the only part of the argument being asked about. The definition of "pure science" is instead in the first sentence.

(C) incorrectly asserts that the statement *distracts* from the conclusion rather than supporting it.

(E), while it does assign a supporting evidentiary role to the statement, inaccurately describes the statement as an example of a single case. Instead the claim is a broad rule about private corporations. Furthermore, there are no examples of "unfortunate consequences" from failing to follow the recommendation.

12. (C) Flaw

Step 1: Identify the Question Type
Typically this type of a Flaw question would ask how the second speaker specifically *misinterprets* the remarks of the first. In this case the word *ambiguity* means there is an equivocation flaw present, it's just your task to determine on which word or phrase Jack equivocates.

Step 2: Untangle the Stimulus
Melinda concludes that hazard insurance decreases an individual's risk because insurance spreads that risk among all of the company's policyholders.

Jack concludes that he *disagrees*. Any instance in which one speaker simply asserts a disagreement with the other speaker should be taken to mean that they have come to different conclusions. So, Jack concludes that hazard insurance does *not* decrease an individual's risk because having insurance does not lessen the chances that his house will burn down.

Step 3: Make a Prediction
The answer choices list words or phrases that at least one of the speakers uses. The correct answer must be a word or phrase that is susceptible to multiple interpretations, and Jack must employ a different meaning than Melinda intended.

Keeping in mind the general rule that the conclusion is the most important component of any argument, it is likely that the correct answer must be "hazard insurance," *decreases*, or *risk* (the three terms in Melinda's conclusion, with which Jack disagrees). Are any of those used to connote different things? Yes, risk. Melinda is describing the role of insurance in decreasing financial risk, i.e., the level of financial liability incurred by being the victim of some catastrophe. Jack incorrectly believes or pretends that Melinda is talking about the statistical odds or risk of being the victim of a disaster.

Step 4: Evaluate the Answer Choices
(C) is correct, as described in Step 3.

(A) is incorrect because *judiciously*, while a fancy word, is not subject to multiple interpretations in this context, especially because Jack agrees that it would be judicious (wise) to buy fire insurance.

(B) is incorrect. [*M*]*any* is a very ambiguous word meaning anywhere from just 1 to 100 percent. However, whether the financial risk is spread among a small number of policyholders or a large number of policyholders does not affect Jack's argument that buying insurance does not decrease the statistical odds of being the victim of a fire.

(D) is incorrect because both Melinda and Jack interpret the term *decrease* to mean to lessen or make lower.

(E) is incorrect because Jack does not trade on an ambiguity in the term "hazard insurance." He uses a specific type of hazard insurance ("fire insurance") as an example to make his point. Both Jack and Melinda interpret hazard insurance as a type of insurance that covers events such as fires and floods. Jack's point would be the same if considering floods or some other hazard instead of fires.

13. (A) Assumption (Necessary)

Step 1: Identify the Question Type

A question that asks for an assumption *required* by the argument is a Necessary Assumption question. Build the core bridge between the evidence and conclusion, without which the argument cannot stand.

Step 2: Untangle the Stimulus

The author concludes that a certain drug has no effect on the duration of vertigo. The evidence is that a three-month shortage of the drug did not have a significant effect on the duration of vertigo.

Step 3: Make a Prediction

The author jumps from the lack of an effect on the duration of vertigo during a three-month shortage to a broad conclusion that the drug has no effect on the duration of vertigo. This assumes that if the drug does have an effect on the duration of vertigo, it would wear off in three months with diminished use.

Step 4: Evaluate the Answer Choices

(A) is correct. One way to think of the assumption of an argument is: "If this evidence, then this conclusion." The correct answer can be in that form or in its contrapositive. In this case, the author assumes that if evidence (that a three-month shortage of a drug does not affect duration of vertigo), then conclusion (that the drug does not affect the duration of vertigo). Or, in contrapositive form, if a drug does affect the duration of vertigo, then a three-month shortage of the drug would produce a significant change in the average duration of vertigo. This matches **(A)**.

(B) is a Distortion and a 180. There is at least a belief by some doctors that there has been a decrease in the average duration of vertigo since the introduction of this drug. Contrary to this choice, the author asserts, based on other evidence, that the drug has no effect on the duration of vertigo.

(C) may be a tempting answer because a major issue in this argument is whether a three-month period is sufficient to gauge the effects of the drug. The author does assume that three months is sufficient, but does not necessarily assume that a longer period would not be better.

(D) appears to be a potential Overlooked Possibility. The Denial Test should be used to confirm whether an Assumption answer choice with the word *not* in it is a necessary assumption in the form of an ignored possibility. Taking the word *not* out of the answer choice should yield a statement that, if true, would cause the argument to fall apart. In this case, removing the word *not* would mean that changes in diet and smoking habits *are* responsible for the change in average duration of vertigo observed by some doctors since the introduction of the drug. That would actually support the author's conclusion that the drug was *not* responsible for the change in the average duration of vertigo. The denied form of **(D)** does not cause the argument to fall apart, so this choice is not a necessary assumption of the argument.

(E) strengthens the argument that the drug does not affect the duration of vertigo by providing an alternative explanation for the decrease in the duration of vertigo that some doctors believe has occurred since the introduction of the drug. However, it is not *necessary* to the author's argument that this specific explanation be the correct explanation for the doctors' reports of decreased vertigo duration. For example, the doctors simply being mistaken in their belief that the average duration of vertigo has decreased would also suffice.

14. (D) Role of a Statement

Step 1: Identify the Question Type

The question stem repeats a statement from the stimulus and asks you what *role* it plays in the argument. Underline the statement in the stimulus, and then focus on the structure of the argument and how the relevant claim fits in that structure.

Step 2: Untangle the Stimulus

The statement that "television is so important politically and culturally" follows the Evidence Keyword *since*. The conclusion of the argument that "some government control is needed" immediately precedes it. Following the statement about television's importance are reasons why it is so important.

Step 3: Make a Prediction

The statement about television's importance is the primary support for the assertion that some government control of television is needed. So, the correct answer might describe it as a premise or evidence. The argument also provides many reasons why television is important. So, it is more likely that the correct answer will describe the statement as a subsidiary conclusion. This is a statement supported by evidence that in turn supports the ultimate conclusion.

Four of the answer choices indicate that the statement about the importance of television is either a premise or an intermediate conclusion in support of a claim. The wrong answers will inaccurately describe the conclusion of the argument that is being supported by this statement.

Step 4: Evaluate the Answer Choices
(D) is correct because it accurately describes the statement as a subsidiary or intermediate conclusion, as well as accurately describing the conclusion of the argument. The conclusion is that there is a need for government control, based on evidence that television is important politically and culturally.

(A) is a 180 because much of the argument is designed to *support*, rather than *discredit*, the claim that television is important politically and culturally.

(B) is incorrect because it inaccurately describes the conclusion of the argument as television should be thought of as nothing more than a toaster with pictures. This is actually a claim that the author refutes.

(C) is incorrect because it inaccurately describes the conclusion as the idea that we let market forces determine the design of kitchen appliances.

(E) is a reversal. It inaccurately indicates that because television is important politically, it is the primary medium through which many voters obtain information. To the contrary, the fact that television is the primary medium through which many voters obtain information supports the claim that television is important politically.

15. (B) Assumption (Necessary)

Step 1: Identify the Question Type
An assumption on which the argument *depends* is a necessary assumption. Build the core bridge between the evidence and conclusion, without which the argument cannot stand.

Step 2: Untangle the Stimulus
The conclusion is that application of alkaline limestone should make soil more attractive to earthworms. The evidence is that decomposition of dead plants makes the top layer of soil acidic, and earthworms prefer soil that is neutral.

Step 3: Make a Prediction
The assumption is that alkaline limestone applied to soil in conjunction with acidic plant decomposition byproducts means neutral soil. The author concludes that the soil will be attractive to earthworms, and this soil is defined in the

background as neutral. So, the scope shift is evidence of adding alkaline limestone to a conclusion of neutral soil.

Step 4: Evaluate the Answer Choices
(B) is correct. It is the only answer that gets to the necessary result of the argument that the acidity will be neutralized. Applying the Denial Test, if the limestone does *not* stay in the soil long enough to neutralize the acid, then it no longer makes sense to claim that applying limestone will make the soil more attractive to earthworms.

(A) is Out of Scope because what earthworms actually *do* is irrelevant to the conclusion that the limestone will make the soil more attractive to earthworms.

(C) is Out of Scope because it is not necessary to know the exact contents of the limestone. This is irrelevant to the argument's general conclusion that the limestone will make the soil more attractive to earthworms.

(D) is a Distortion. Acidity and decomposition are both discussed in the stimulus, but their relationship is not necessary to the argument's conclusion that the limestone will make the soil more attractive to earthworms.

(E) is Out of Scope because the benefits to the soil are irrelevant. The argument is focused on what can be done to make the soil hospitable for the worms, not how the worms can benefit the soil.

16. (E) Inference

Step 1: Identify the Question Type
The question stem explicitly asks what can be inferred from the statements. Accept all statements as true, and focus on the most concrete facts to make a deduction as to what else must be true.

Step 2: Untangle the Stimulus
According to the jurist, a nation's laws are expressions of a moral code that transcends those laws. So, the jurist concludes that any moral prohibition against the violation of statutes must leave room for exceptions.

Step 3: Make a Prediction
While Inference questions are typically not argument-based, this stimulus is in the form of an argument. In such cases, the inferences (what must be true based on the information provided) can be similar to the necessary assumptions (what must be true in order for the argument to stand). The jurist believes that a moral code transcends laws, so concludes that there must be exceptions to prohibitions against violations of the laws. Thus, the jurist must assume that the laws and moral code will occasionally conflict, because otherwise there would not be a need for exceptions.

Step 4: Evaluate the Answer Choices
(E) matches the prediction explained in Step 3.

(A) is Extreme. The word *primarily* is a red flag that is rarely, if ever, found in a correct Inference answer choice. There is no concrete deduction that can be made regarding what lawmakers are primarily concerned with.

(B) is Out of Scope. There is no suggestion of other criteria that should be used in choosing one set of laws over another, besides the moral code.

(C) is a 180. If moral behavior and compliance with laws were indistinguishable, then there would be no need to leave room for exceptions to prohibitions against violations of the law. Furthermore, **(C)** is a Distortion because it introduces concerns about the *legality* of breaking the *moral* code, whereas the stimulus is concerned with the *morality* of breaking the *legal* code.

(D) is another 180. The jurist says that laws are extensions of a preexisting moral code. Therefore, it can be inferred that there are probably many statutes that citizens have a moral obligation to obey.

17. (B) Principle (Apply/Inference)

Step 1: Identify the Question Type
The question stem describes the stimulus as containing a principle and asks you to conform that general rule to one of the specific judgments in the answer choices. Thus, this is an Apply the Principle question.

Step 2: Untangle the Stimulus
The principle stated is that association of two conditions does not establish that one condition caused the other, because both could be the result of another cause.

Step 3: Make a Prediction
The principle in this stimulus is commonly tested on the LSAT: correlation does not mean causation. The correct answer should contain a situation in which two things are correlated (appear together or seem to be related), but are actually both caused by a third thing.

Step 4: Evaluate the Answer Choices
(B) is correct. There is a correlation between high blood pressure and being overweight, but rather than concluding that obesity causes high blood pressure, it could be that both are the result of an unhealthy lifestyle.

(A) is not an accurate match. Rather than identifying an alternative cause of two things (rapid growth of the money supply and inflation), the two things are judged to be really the same thing.

(C) is not an accurate match. The judgment that the occurrence of two things (ice cream consumption and crime) may be purely *coincidental* is not the same as believing that a third factor is the cause of them both.

(D) is not an accurate match. Rather than an alternative cause for both moods and clothing color, this choice raises the possibility of reverse causation.

(E) is a 180. Rather than discounting a causal relationship between two things because of a potential alternative cause of them both, this choice refutes the claim of an outside cause (an earlier language). It favors a direct causal relationship (Greek and Latin borrowed from each other, as did Marathi and Telegu).

18. (B) Flaw

Step 1: Identify the Question Type
The phrase "vulnerable to criticism" indicates a Flaw question. The question stem further indicates that the flaw is an ignored possibility.

Step 2: Untangle the Stimulus
The salesperson concludes that success as a salesperson requires being in sales for at least three years. The evidence is that success as a salesperson requires establishing a strong client base, and studies have shown that three years is sufficient to develop that client base.

Step 3: Make a Prediction
The salesperson concludes that success requires at least three years in sales, and the question stem tells you that this is flawed because it ignores a possibility. Therefore, you know that it is possible that a salesperson could be successful in less than three years. There is only one choice, **(B)**, that indicates that a salesperson could achieve some measure of success in less than three years, so it must be correct.

To more fully understand the flaw at issue here, notice that the argument indicates that establishing a strong client base is a prerequisite to success as a salesperson.

| *If* | *successful* | → | *strong client base* |

The evidence indicates that three years is a sufficient time period to develop that client base, but does not indicate that three years is necessary.

| *If* | *3+ years* | → | *strong client base* |

However, in concluding that success requires three years ...

| *If* | *successful* | → | *3+ years* |

... the salesperson confuses three years being sufficient to it being necessary. This ignores the possibility that some salespeople could develop their client base in less than three years.

Step 4: Evaluate the Answer Choices

(B) matches the prediction described in Step 3.

(A) is incorrect because the salesperson concludes three years is necessary for success, but does not assume that three years is sufficient. If the salesperson concluded that three years as a salesperson was a guarantee of success, then this would fail to consider that some people who have been in sales for more than three years are not yet successful.

(C) cannot be an ignored possibility flaw because this hypothetical (an unsuccessful person who has spent less than three years in sales) strengthens the salesperson's argument. A Flaw answer choice in the form of an ignored possibility—in order to be correct—must, if true, weaken the argument.

(D) cannot be an ignored possibility flaw because this hypothetical (a salesperson that needs more than three years to develop a strong client base) is completely consistent with the salesperson's argument. A Flaw answer choice in the form of an ignored possibility—in order to be correct—must, if true, weaken the argument.

(E) is irrelevant. Whether or not salespeople can afford to develop a client base is irrelevant to whether it is necessary to do so to be successful. The salesperson does not claim that there are a large number of successful salespeople.

19. (A) Parallel Reasoning

Step 1: Identify the Question Type

The phrase "argument most similar to" indicates a Parallel Reasoning question. Find the answer that has an argument with the same *type* of evidence and the same *type* of conclusion as the argument in the stimulus.

Step 2: Untangle the Stimulus

The conclusion is that *most* people who sleep less than six hours can *probably* cause their anxiety levels to fall by sleeping eight hours. The evidence is that people who slept less than six hours *typically* felt less anxious if they began to sleep eight hours.

Step 3: Make a Prediction

Basically, the argument is that if something has been *typically* shown to produce a certain effect, then it can be concluded that *most* who try it will *probably* produce that result as well. The words in italics are the level-of-certainty words, and answers that don't match those levels of certainty can be eliminated.

Step 4: Evaluate the Answer Choices

(A) is correct. Based on evidence that companies that start advertising on the Internet *generally* improve financially, the argument concludes that *most* companies that do so can *probably* improve financially as well.

(B) is not a match because the evidence is only that *certain* companies have improved financially after advertising on the Internet. This does not rise to the level of *typically* or *generally*. Those *certain* companies may be only a small overall percentage.

(C) is Extreme. It is not a match because its conclusion is far too definite in claiming that *any* company *will* improve its financial situation.

(D) is not a match because the evidence includes a necessary condition indicated by the phrase "only if," which does not have a counterpart in the evidence of the stimulus.

(E) is a near perfect match with one deviation at the end. This choice has all the correct levels-of-certainty qualifiers in the evidence and conclusion: *usually, most,* and *probably.* However, the conclusion in the stimulus and the correct answer are that a condition will probably be *improved* (a relative state). This choice indicates that the company will probably become "financially strong" (an absolute state).

20. (C) Assumption (Sufficient)

Step 1: Identify the Question Type

A Sufficient Assumption question is indicated by the phrasing: "if assumed … conclusion is properly drawn/follows logically/is properly inferred." Build a forceful bridge between the evidence and conclusion that guarantees the conclusion is true.

Step 2: Untangle the Stimulus

The biologist concludes that skeletal anatomy alone cannot be used to infer whether extinct predatory animals hunted in packs. The reason is that lions and tigers have indistinguishable skeletal anatomies, yet one hunts in packs and the other does not.

Step 3: Make a Prediction

The biologist makes a leap from evidence of two specific animals to a broad conclusion regarding all predators. On the basis of lions and tigers having similar skeletal anatomies, yet different hunting strategies, the biologist makes the sweeping generalization that no reasonable inference about whether an animal hunted in packs can be made based on skeletal anatomies. Lions, for example, might be a rare anomaly (the only animal with a particular skeletal anatomy that does not hunt in packs) among dozens of other species with that anatomy that all hunt in packs. Then would it not be reasonable to infer that extinct animals with that anatomy also hunted in packs? Potentially, but you need an answer that makes sure that the biologist is right: based on this single contradictory result, skeletal anatomy cannot be used to infer whether an animal hunted in packs.

Step 4: Evaluate the Answer Choices

(C) is correct. Notice that this choice and two other choices are in If/Then form. An Assumption answer choice in If/Then form should more specifically be in the form of "if this evidence, then this conclusion," or its contrapositive. This choice indicates that if skeletal anatomy alone is ever inadequate to infer hunting behavior, which is what the evidence indicates based on the example of lions and tigers, then it is never reasonable to infer from skeletal anatomy that a species hunted in packs. So, this answer essentially confirms that the biologist was absolutely correct to reach this conclusion.

(A) is a Distortion. Lions and tigers themselves don't have to be skeletally similar to any extinct predatory animals. The biologist is just using the case of lions and tigers to extrapolate to extinct predatory animals. Even if this was true, it would not guarantee the conclusion.

(B) is not enough to draw the conclusion. The mere existence of two anatomically indistinguishable extinct dinosaurs would not guarantee that the biologist is correct that anatomy alone cannot be used to infer hunting behavior. If they did exist and it was known that they also had different hunting behaviors, then it would strengthen the argument, though not be enough to prove the conclusion true. But this choice does not even indicate that they had different hunting behaviors.

(D), like **(C)**, is in If/Then form. This choice correctly describes the evidence in the trigger, or "if" clause, of this Formal Logic statement, but flips the conclusion around in the result, or "then" clause. The argument concludes that skeletal anatomy cannot be used to infer hunting behavior. This choice concludes that hunting behavior cannot be used to infer skeletal anatomy.

(E), like **(C)** and **(D)**, is in If/Then form. However, rather than putting the assumption in "if evidence, then conclusion" form, this choice puts the assumption in "if conclusion, then evidence" form.

21. (A) Parallel Flaw

Step 1: Identify the Question Type
The phrase "flawed pattern of reasoning most similar" indicates a Parallel Flaw question.

Step 2: Untangle the Stimulus
The Formal Logic maps out as follows:

Evidence:

If	April rain exceeds 5 cm	→	trees blossom in May

If	April rain exceeds 5 cm	→	reservoirs are always full on May 1

Conclusion:

If	reservoirs ~ full on May 1	→	trees ~ blossom in May

Step 3: Make a Prediction
Based on the evidence, it does not follow that just because the reservoirs are not full on May 1 that the trees will not blossom in May. Yes, one potential cause for the reservoirs not being full on May 1 would be that April rains failed to exceed 5 cm. And, yes, if April rains failed to exceed 5 cm, then there would not be a guarantee that the trees would blossom in May. But the author misinterprets both Formal Logic statements. April rain exceeding 5 cm is a guarantee that the reservoirs will be full on May 1, but is not necessary for the reservoirs to be full. So, there could be some other reason besides insufficient April rain for the reservoirs not being full. Moreover, even if it is the case that April rains failed to exceed 5 cm, it does not follow from the first statement that the trees will not blossom in May. Again, April rains in excess of 5 cm guarantee that the trees will blossom in May, but are not necessary for that to happen.

But you don't need to work through all that to get the right answer. More broadly, this relates to the classic flaw of assuming correlation equals causation, when in actuality there is a separate cause of both results. Here, April rain independently causes two results: full reservoirs and trees blossoming. The author should not infer a direct causal relationship between those two results, as this argument does. So, the prediction is an answer that has evidence of one thing causing two different results and a conclusion that in the absence of one of those results, you can't have the other result.

Alternatively, the easiest way may be to just map out the Formal Logic and find the answer that maps the same way.

Evidence:

If	X	→	Y

If	X	→	Z

Conclusion:

If	~Z	→	~Y

Step 4: Evaluate the Answer Choices

(A) maps out the same way and commits the same flaw in assuming a direct causal relationship between two independent results of a separate causal factor.

Evidence:

If	**garlic in pantry (X)**	→	**garlic fresh (Y)**

If	**garlic in pantry (X)**	→	**potatoes on basement stairs (Z)**

Conclusion:

If	**potatoes not on basement stairs (~Z)**	→	**garlic not fresh (~Y)**

(B) does not map out the same way. Its evidence consists of two different triggers leading to two different results, which can be chained together.

If	**over the burner for 2 minutes**	→	**optimal temperature**	→	**contents liquefy immediately**

To be parallel, it needed to have one trigger pointing to two different results. Furthermore, the conclusion says:

If	**over the burner for 2 minutes**	→	**contents liquefy immediately**

So, **(B)** is also not parallel because it is an unflawed argument that follows the format of If X → Y → Z, therefore, If X → Z.

(C), like **(B)**, contains valid logic and thus cannot match the flaw in the stimulus. The evidence lines up as If X → Y → Z, and from that the author correctly concludes that If ~Z → ~X:

If	**set with wooden type**	→	**200+ years old**	→	**special**

If	**~ special**	→	**~ set with wooden type**

(D) does not map out the same way. Its evidence does not consist of a single trigger leading to two different results. Instead, the evidence has two different triggers:

If	**mower operates (X)**	→	**~ flooded (~Y)**

If	**foot pedal depressed (Z)**	→	**flooded (Y)**

Conclusion:

If	**foot pedal ~ depressed (~Z)**	→	**mower operates (X)**

The logic is certainly flawed here because, based on the evidence, ~Z is not a trigger for anything. However, this flaw isn't structured the same way as the one in the stimulus.

(E) is in the same format as **(C)**. It contains valid logic and thus cannot match the flaw in the stimulus. The evidence lines up as If X → Y → Z, and from that the author correctly concludes that If ~Z → ~X:

If	**kiln too hot**	→	**plates crack**	→	**redo the order**

If	**~ redo the order**	→	**kiln ~ too hot**

22. (E) Flaw

Step 1: Identify the Question Type
The question stem explicitly asks for the flaw in the argument. Notice any disconnect between the evidence and conclusion, and keep the common LSAT flaws in mind.

Step 2: Untangle the Stimulus
The doctor concludes that being slightly overweight is sufficient to be healthy because slightly overweight people are healthier than those who are considerably underweight.

Step 3: Make a Prediction
There is a distinction between a relative state (healthier) and an absolute state (healthy). Just because one is healthier than another does not mean an absolute state of healthy has been achieved.

Step 4: Evaluate the Answer Choices

(E) is correct because the doctor mistakes the relative condition of being *healthier* with the absolute condition of being *healthy*.

(A) is not correct because, rather than ignore them, the doctor explicitly mentions the contrary opinions and relies on other evidence, however improperly, to reach a different conclusion.

(B) is not correct because it is not a logical flaw to fail to define a term.

(C) is not correct because the doctor neither states nor necessarily assumes that everybody's appropriate weight is the same.

(D) is not correct because, according to this choice, the doctor uses evidence of a lack of a property that would suffice to make a person unhealthy to reach a conclusion that the person must be healthy. Essentially:

If   X   →   unhealthy

Therefore:

If   ~X   →   healthy

That would indeed be a flaw, but the doctor's evidence does not mention any property that is sufficient to make a person unhealthy. The doctor does not argue that being overweight guarantees being unhealthy (in fact the doctor concludes that some overweight people are healthy). And the doctor does not argue that being underweight guarantees being unhealthy (the doctor only says that those that are considerably underweight are not as healthy as those that are slightly overweight).

23. (D) Assumption (Necessary)

Step 1: Identify the Question Type

An assumption on which the argument *depends* is a necessary assumption. Build the core bridge between the evidence and conclusion, without which the argument cannot stand.

Step 2: Untangle the Stimulus

The author concludes that growing crops in good soil is a better way of reducing vulnerability to insects than killing insects. The evidence is that robust crops are less likely to be attacked by insects and can better withstand insect attacks, while killing insects does not address the underlying vulnerability to insect attack.

Step 3: Make a Prediction

The mismatched concepts are from evidence of the reduced vulnerability of robust crops to a conclusion about the

reduced vulnerability of crops grown in good soil. So, the author equates crops grown in good soil with robust crops. Strategically, notice that growing crops in good soil is the concept that is unique to the conclusion and, thus, must be included in any correct scope shift–based answer. There are only two answer choices that reference growing crops in good soil, and one is Extreme.

Step 4: Evaluate the Answer Choices

(D) matches the prediction explained in Step 3 and is modestly phrased.

(A) is a Distortion. It is certainly within the scope of the information in the stimulus, but it is not necessary to the author's argument that the application of nutrients and organic matter causes improvements in the soil's microbial activity. The argument merely defines good soil as having those three elements, but it is not concerned with how good soil is created.

(B) does relate to crops grown in good soil, but it is Extreme. For the author to conclude that good soil *reduces* insect vulnerability does not require that insects *never* attack crops grown in good soil.

(C) strengthens the argument, but is not necessary to it. The author could still properly conclude that growing crops in good soil is a *better* way to reduce insect vulnerability even if the application of pesticides to weak crops does reduce insect damage to some degree. Such an application of the Denial Test is a good way to distinguish between something that supports the conclusion and something that is necessary for the conclusion.

(E) is a 180 because it favors the use of pesticides, and the point of the argument is that growing crops in good soil is better than killing insects.

24. (D) Paradox (EXCEPT)

Step 1: Identify the Question Type

A question stem that asks you to resolve or explain a conflict, discrepancy, or even a plain result, as is the case here, is a Paradox question. The correct answer to a Paradox EXCEPT question will either have no effect or deepen the mystery.

Step 2: Untangle the Stimulus

On the one hand, color-blind people cannot distinguish red from green due to an absence of certain photopigments. On the other hand, among people who were not color-blind, a significant percentage failed to report distinctions between many shades of red that most of the people in a study were able to distinguish.

Step 3: Make a Prediction

The paradox is that people who are not color-blind (they can distinguish red from green and are not lacking in photopigments) did not distinguish between different shades of red. One thing to notice is that the stimulus states that these people did not report distinctions, not that they were incapable of seeing the distinct shades. On Paradox questions, you should not necessarily try to make specific predictions. There can be many different ways of resolving a paradox. This is especially true on a Paradox EXCEPT question because there will be four choices that have ways to resolve the paradox. So, you are looking for an answer that provides a reason people did not report differences in shades of red despite not having a complete deficiency in the photopigments that would cause color blindness.

Step 4: Evaluate the Answer Choices
(D) is correct because it is irrelevant to the question of why people who are able to distinguish red from green did not report distinctions between shades of red. This choice merely provides some further clarification about what photopigments are lacking in some color-blind people.

(A) helps to resolve the mystery by clarifying that it is not simply a matter of either not having the pigments and being color-blind or having the pigments and having perfect color sight. Among those who have sufficient pigments to discern red from green, a low level of those pigments can result in not being able to discern shades of those colors.

(B) provides an explanation as to why some might not have reported distinctions between shades of red. The subjects could see the distinct shades, but the study's questions about shades were not well crafted, or at the very least ambiguous.

(C) provides an explanation as to why some might not have reported distinctions between shades of red. The subjects simply weren't interested in the subtle differences and, as a result, didn't notice or speak up about them, even if they were capable of seeing those distinct shades.

(E) also provides an explanation as to why some might not have reported distinctions between shades of red. Even if they were capable of seeing those distinct shades, they had no names for certain shades, so they could not accurately report differences among them.

25. (B) Flaw

Step 1: Identify the Question Type
The phrase "vulnerable to criticism" indicates a Flaw question. Notice any disconnect between the evidence and conclusion, and keep common flaws in mind.

Step 2: Untangle the Stimulus
The occultist concludes astrology is both an art and a science. As evidence, the occultist points to "scientific components" of astrology as well as the artistic aspects.

Step 3: Make a Prediction
The occultist assumes that if something has artistic aspects, then it is an art, and that if something has "scientific components," then it is a science. However, it might be possible that something can contain "scientific components" without being a science (or artistic components without being an art). The occultist overlooks this possibility.

Step 4: Evaluate the Answer Choices
(B) describes the scope shift from evidence of having "scientific components" to a conclusion that astrology is a science, as predicted in Step 3.

(A) is incorrect because it is in the form of an unwarranted assumption and, thus, to be correct must be a necessary assumption of the argument. The occultist does state that complicated mathematics is an example of a "scientific component," but the argument does not depend on *all* sciences having that component.

(C) is incorrect because it fails to pass the baseline test of "does the author do that?" No, the occultist does not exclude the possibility that astrology involves components that are neither artistic nor scientific just because she does not mention them.

(D) may be a pesky answer to grasp because it plays off the similar-sounding, but different, fields of astronomy and astrology. The occultist does not infer that *astronomy* is a science, but rather her conclusion is that astrology is a science. The evidence directly states that astronomical knowledge is scientific, so that is not incorrectly inferred by the occultist.

(E) is functionally identical to **(A)**, except that it deals with the assumption about art instead of science. Thus, it is incorrect for the same reason as **(A)**. The occultist does state that the synthesis of a multitude of factors and symbols is an artistic aspect, but the argument does not depend on *all* art having that characteristic.

Section II: Logic Games

Game 1: Talent Agency Performers

Q#	Question Type	Correct	Difficulty
1	Acceptability	B	★
2	Could Be True	A	★★
3	Must Be True	B	★★
4	Completely Determine	B	★
5	"If" / Must Be False	C	★

Game 2: Architects' Designs

Q#	Question Type	Correct	Difficulty
6	Acceptability	C	★
7	Must Be False (CANNOT Be True)	A	★
8	"If" / Must Be True	A	★
9	"If" / Could Be True EXCEPT	D	★★
10	Must Be False (CANNOT Be True)	C	★
11	Partial Acceptability	B	★★

Game 3: Burglary Suspects

Q#	Question Type	Correct	Difficulty
12	Could Be True	B	★★
13	"If" / Could Be True EXCEPT	E	★★★
14	"If" / Could Be True	A	★★★
15	Must Be True	E	★★
16	"If" / Could Be True EXCEPT	A	★★★
17	"If" / Must Be True	D	★★

Game 4: Debate Team Tournament

Q#	Question Type	Correct	Difficulty
18	Partial Acceptability	E	★
19	"If" / Could Be True	A	★★
20	"If" / Could Be True	B	★★★
21	"If" / How Many	C	★★
22	"If" / Could Be True	E	★★★★
23	Could Be True EXCEPT	B	★★★

Game 1: Talent Agency Performers

Step 1: Overview

Situation: Recruiting performers at talent agencies

Entities: Five performers (Traugott, West, Xavier, Young, Zinser) and three talent agencies (Fame, Premier, Star)

Action: Distribution. Distribute the five performers among the three agencies.

Limitations: Each performer signs with exactly one agency, and each agency signs at least one performer. That means at least one agency has to sign multiple performers.

Step 2: Sketch

This calls for a standard Distribution game sketch, with one column for each agency and one slot to start with under each column. Two more slots will be added as the game proceeds:

```
      TWXYZ
Fame  Prem  Star
 —     —     —
```

Step 3: Rules

Rule 1 places Xavier with Fame Agency. Draw an X in the slot under Fame, and leave the column open for other possible performers.

Rule 2 states that Xavier and Young will sign with different agencies. Because Rule 1 places Xavier with Fame, this simply means that Young will *not* sign with Fame. Draw "~Y" under Fame, or draw "Y" with arrows to Premier and Star.

Rule 3 creates a Block of Entities with Zinser and Young:

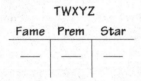

Rule 4 introduces some Formal Logic. Shorthand the original Formal Logic (if Traugott is with Star, West is also with Star) and its contrapositive:

$$\frac{Star}{T} \longrightarrow \frac{Star}{W}$$

$$\sim\frac{Star}{W} \longrightarrow \sim\frac{Star}{T}$$

Because each performer must be assigned to one of the agencies, you could also turn the negatives of the contrapositive into positives. That is, if an entity is *not* with Star, it must be with Fame or Premier. This is not necessary to do, but some test takers may find it helpful.

$$\frac{Fame}{W} \text{ OR } \frac{Prem}{W} \longrightarrow \frac{Fame}{T} \text{ OR } \frac{Prem}{T}$$

Step 4: Deductions

By Rule 3, Young and Zinser must be in the same agency, but it cannot be Fame because Xavier is there (Rule 1), and Young cannot be in the same agency as Xavier (Rule 2). That leaves only two possible agencies for Young and Zinser: Premier or Star. Knowing which one would establish three performers in the sketch (Xavier, Young, and Zinser). That's certainly worth setting up Limited Options:

	Fame	Prem	Star
I)	X	Y	—
		Z	

	Fame	Prem	Star
II)	X	—	Y
			Z

In both options, the only performers yet to be placed are Traugott and West.

In the first option, either Traugott or West (or both) must sign with Star Agency. However, by the contrapositive of Rule 4, if West isn't signed by Star, then neither is Traugott. That would mean *nobody* is signed by Star. That can't happen. So, West *must* be signed by Star. However, that does not confirm which agency signs Traugott. It could be Star, but it could be any of the others, too:

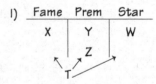

In the second option, either Traugott or West (or both) must sign with Premier Agency. However, by Rule 4, if Traugott is signed by Star, then so is West. That would mean *nobody* is signed by Premier. That can't happen. So, Traugott cannot be signed by Star (although West still could):

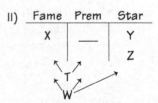

Step 5: Questions

1. (B) Acceptability

For Acceptability questions, just go through the rules one at a time, and eliminate answers that violate the rules.

Rule 1 says Xavier signs with Fame; that eliminates **(D)**. Rule 2 says Xavier and Young must be signed by different agencies; that eliminates **(E)**. Rule 3 says Zinser and Young must sign with the same agency; that eliminates **(C)**. Finally, according to the Formal Logic of Rule 4, if Traugott is signed by Star, then so is West. In **(A)**, Traugott is signed by Star, but West is signed by Premier. That answer can be eliminated, leaving **(B)** as the correct answer.

2. (A) Could Be True

The correct answer here will be the only one that could be true. The four wrong answers will be definitely false.

If Young and Zinser are signed by Premier (as seen in the first option), then West could be signed by Star Agency. That does not trigger the Formal Logic of Rule 4, so Traugott could be signed elsewhere, leaving West as the only performer signed by Star Agency. That means **(A)** is possible, and thus the correct answer. For the record:

If West was signed by Premier Agency with Young and Zinser, Xavier would be signed by Fame Agency, leaving Traugott as the only performer signed by Star Agency. But that would violate Rule 4, eliminating **(B)**.

Zinser and Young must be placed together (Rule 3), which eliminates **(D)**. And they cannot be signed by the same agency as Xavier (Rule 2), which eliminates **(C)**. Xavier signs with Fame Agency, so Zinser and Young must sign with a second agency together. If Fame signed three performers, it would have to be Xavier along with Traugott and West because Rule 2 prohibits Xavier from being placed along with the Young-Zinser block. However, if Xavier, Traugott, and West all signed with Fame, one agency would be left with no performers because the Young-Zinser block would still need to stay together. That eliminates **(E)**.

3. (B) Must Be True

The correct answer here must be true no matter what. The four wrong answers may be possible, but could also be false.

West and Zinser could sign with different agencies (as seen in the first option). However, West could sign with the same agency as Zinser if Zinser signs with Star (as seen in the second option). Then Traugott could sign with Premier, and everyone would be placed:

Fame	Prem	Star
X	T	W
		Y
		Z

So, **(A)** does not have to be true and can be eliminated. This same outcome also shows that Fame and Star do not have to sign the same number of performers, and that Traugott does not have to sign with the same agency as West. That eliminates **(C)** and **(D)**.

Young and Zinser, who must be placed together, cannot sign with Fame because Xavier does (Rule 1), and Young cannot sign with the same agency as Xavier (Rule 2). That leaves only West and Traugott to sign with Fame alongside Xavier. However, if Fame signed all three, then one agency would be left with no performers. So, the most Fame could sign is two performers, making **(B)** the correct answer. For the record:

West *could* sign with Fame Agency, along with Xavier. Then Traugott would sign with Premier, leaving Young and Zinser to sign with Star Agency. That eliminates **(E)**.

Fame	Prem	Star
X	T	Y
W		Z

4. (B) Completely Determine

The correct answer to this question will make it possible to determine, with certainty, which agency each performer signs with.

If Traugott signs with Fame Agency, then West is not restricted to a particular agency. Young and Zinser could still sign with either Premier or Star (as seen in either option), so **(A)** does not help and can be eliminated.

If Traugott signs with Star Agency (which can only happen in Option I), then so does West (Rule 4). Xavier signs with Fame (Rule 1). That leaves Young and Zinser, who must sign with the same agency (Rule 3). They must be sign with Premier, determining the placement of everyone:

Fame	Prem	Star
X	Y	T
	Z	W

That makes **(B)** the correct answer. For the record:

If West signs with Premier, Traugott can't sign with Star (Rule 4). That means Young and Zinser would sign with Star, but Traugott could still sign with either Fame or Premier. That eliminates **(C)**.

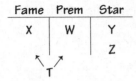

Xavier always signs with Fame (Rule 1), so that adds nothing new and certainly does not lead to one complete outcome. That eliminates **(D)**.

If Zinser signs with Premier (as seen in Option I), then Young would sign with Premier (Rule 3). However, Traugott could still sign with any agency. That eliminates **(E)**.

5. (C) "If" / Must Be False

For this question, Zinser signs with Star Agency, which means so does Young (by Rule 3). As determined in the second option, Traugott cannot sign with Star, otherwise so would West (Rule 4). That would leave nobody for Premier Agency. That means **(C)** must be false and is thus the correct answer. For the record:

West could sign with Star alongside Zinser and Young. Then Traugott would sign with Premier:

Fame	Prem	Star
X	T	Y
		Z
		W

In this outcome, nobody other than Xavier signs with Fame, one performer signs with Premier, and three performers (including West) sign with Star. That shows that all of the remaining choices are possible.

Game 2: Architects' Designs

Step 1: Overview
Situation: Design competition for a student union building

Entities: Six architects (Green, Jackson, Liu, Mertz, Peete, Valdez)

Action: Loose Sequencing. Determine the order in which the architects submitted their designs.

Limitations: Each architect presents exactly one design, each presented one at a time.

Step 2: Sketch
List the entities by initial. You could set up six slots to determine the order, but a quick glance ahead reveals that every rule involves relative sequencing ("some time before" and "some time after"). Therefore, this is a Loose Sequencing game, so a tree diagram will most likely be more useful.

Step 3: Rules
Rule 1 is a typical Loose Sequencing relationship. Peete will present a design before Mertz, who in turn will present a design before Liu:

$$P—M—L$$

Rule 2 offers two possible outcomes: Green will present either before Jackson or after Liu:

$$G—J \quad or \quad L—G$$

However, the last part of the rule says that both cannot happen. So, if Green presents before Jackson, Green cannot also present after Liu. In other words, if Green presents before Jackson, Green will also present before Liu. Similarly, if Green presents after Liu, Green cannot present before Jackson, so Green would present after both Liu and Jackson. Add this information to both possibilities:

That means Green will present before both Liu and Jackson or after both Liu and Jackson—never in between.

Rule 3 is exactly the same as Rule 2, only with different architects. Using the same logic, Valdez can present before Green (thus having to present before Peete) or after Peete (thus having to present after Green):

Again, this means that Valdez presents either before or after both Green and Peete—never in between.

Step 4: Deductions
Deductions in Loose Sequencing typically come from combining rules with Duplications. In this case, that would involve combining Rule 1 four times into the various options of Rules 2 and 3. That would take up a lot of room and make the Master Sketch a little bulky for quick reference.

Furthermore, the last two rules each seem to indicate Limited Options. However, if the two outcomes of Rule 2 were used to set up Limited Options, each sketch would have to be broken into two more sketches to accommodate Rule 3. The same would happen if the two outcomes of Rule 3 were used. Again, that would create four sketches.

Time is a factor to consider. While it may be comforting to have all four possibilities drawn out ahead of time, it also means having to check answers against all four sketches at once. That can get confusing. It's more likely that questions will be easily answered by properly interpreting the rules and only drawing out full sketches when necessary.

Step 5: Questions

6. (C) Acceptability
A typical Acceptability question is best managed by testing the rules one at a time against the answer choices.

By Rule 1, Peete, Mertz, and Liu should present in that order. That eliminates **(B)** and **(E)**, both of which have Liu before Mertz. By Rule 2, Green must present before Jackson or after Liu. That eliminates **(A)**, in which neither of those options occurs. By Rule 3, Valdez must present before Green or after Peete—but *not both*. That eliminates **(D)**, in which Valdez does both. That leaves **(C)** as the correct answer.

7. (A) Must Be False (CANNOT Be True)
The correct answer to this question will be a position in which Mertz *cannot* present. The remaining answers will all be possible positions.

By Rule 1, Mertz has to present a design after Peete (so Mertz cannot present first) and before Liu (so Mertz cannot present last—i.e., sixth). Because Mertz cannot present sixth, **(A)** is the correct answer.

8. (A) "If" / Must Be True
For this question, Liu presents sixth. That means everyone, including Green, will present before Liu. Because Green does not present after Liu, Green must present before Jackson (Rule 2), making **(A)** the correct answer.

___ ___ ___ ___ ___ L
 1   2   3   4   5   6

P—M—L

G
  J

9. (D) "If" / Could Be True EXCEPT

For this question, Jackson will present before Mertz. This does not help determine which options from Rules 2 or 3 will be used. However, Rule 1 shows that at least *two* architects present before Mertz:

P
  >M—L
J

Even with that, any of the four outcomes listed in Rules 2 and 3 are possible. So, the answers need to be tested to find the one that must be false.

Jackson needs to present before Mertz, who needs to perform before Liu. That means Jackson cannot be one of the last two presenters (fifth or sixth), but there are no other definite restrictions. So, Jackson could be any of the first four presenters, including second. That eliminates **(A)**. However, because Jackson cannot be fifth, that immediately makes **(D)** false and thus the correct answer. For the record:

Like Jackson, Peete needs to present before Mertz and Liu, but there are no other definite restrictions on Peete. So, Peete cannot be fifth or sixth, but can be any of the first four presenters—including third or fourth. That eliminates **(B)** and **(C)**.

Liu has to present after Jackson, Peete, and Mertz, so Liu cannot be one of the first three presenters. However, with no further definite restrictions, Liu could be any of the last three presenters—including fifth. That eliminates **(E)**.

10. (C) Must Be False (CANNOT Be True)

The correct answer to this question will be an architect that cannot present first. The remaining four answers will be architects who could.

By Rule 1, both Mertz and Liu have to present after Peete, so neither one of them can be first. Because Liu cannot present first, **(C)** is the correct answer.

11. (B) Partial Acceptability

While the answers do not list the order of all six architects, it is still most efficient to start testing the rules one at a time, eliminating answers that violate. Be sure to consider positions not listed when testing.

By Rule 1, Peete has to present before Mertz, who has to present before Liu. If Mertz is first, there would be no place in the sequence for Peete. That eliminates **(A)**. Also, **(D)** has

Peete fourth and Liu fifth. That leaves no room for Mertz in between, so that can be eliminated.

By Rule 2, Green has to present before Jackson or after Liu—but not both. **(C)** has Green before Jackson in fifth and sixth, respectively. However, that would force Green to also be after Liu, so **(C)** can be eliminated.

Finally, by Rule 3, Valdez has to present before Green or after Peete—but not both. **(E)** has Valdez fourth, Green fifth, and Liu sixth. That means Valdez is before Green. However, with the last three spaces filled, Valdez would also have to be after Peete, so **(E)** can be eliminated.

The only answer that doesn't violate the rules is the correct answer, **(B)**.

Game 3: Burglary Suspects

Step 1: Overview

Situation: Detectives questioning burglary suspects

Entities: Seven suspects (S, T, V, W, X, Y, Z)

Action: Sequencing/Matching Hybrid. Primarily, determine the order in which the suspects were questioned (Sequencing). The overview also suggests that some suspects will confess and others will not (Matching).

Limitations: For the Sequencing, each suspect is questioned on a different day, and each suspect is questioned only once. The Matching is not limited, as the overview provides no information about how many suspects will confess.

Step 2: Sketch

The primary action is Sequencing, so list the entities and set up seven slots to place them in order. You can note below each slot whether a suspect confesses ("c") or not ("n"):

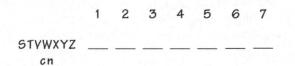

Step 3: Rules

Rule 1 establishes T as the suspect questioned on day 3. Add "T" to slot 3 and move on.

Rule 2 establishes that the suspect on day 4 does not confess. Add "n" below slot 4.

Rule 3 states that S is questioned some time after W:

$$W \ldots S$$

Rule 4 is more standard sequencing: X and V will be questioned at some time after Z:

Rule 5 states that no suspects confessed after W. Jot this in shorthand for now:

NEVER

$$\underline{\quad W \quad} \ldots \underline{\quad}_{c}$$

Rule 6 provides some concrete numbers. Exactly two suspects confess after T:

$$\underline{\quad T \quad} \ldots \underline{\quad}_{c} \ldots \underline{\quad}_{c}$$

(Exactly 2 confess)

Step 4: Deductions

The last rule leads to a lot of important deductions. T is questioned third (Rule 1). That leaves four suspects after T, two of whom must confess (Rule 6). However, the fourth suspect questioned does not confess (Rule 2). So, that means two of the last three suspects will confess.

Those suspects cannot be questioned after W (Rule 5), so W cannot be one of the first four suspects questioned. Also, because S is questioned after W (Rule 3), W cannot be last. That means W is questioned fifth or sixth. However, if W was questioned fifth, the last two suspects cannot confess—which would mean only one suspect after T could confess. That would violate Rule 6, so W cannot be questioned fifth.

That means W must be questioned sixth. By Rule 3, that means S must be questioned seventh. And because no suspect can confess after W, that means S does not confess. That leaves the fifth and sixth suspects to be the two that confess after T:

1	2	3	4	5	6	7
—	—	T	—	—	W	S
			n	c	c	n

With the third, sixth, and seventh suspects determined, the only rule left to consider is Rule 4. Z has to be questioned before at least two suspects: X and V. So, Z cannot be either of the last two positions remaining (fourth or fifth). So, Z will be one of the first two suspects questioned. Furthermore, neither X nor V could be questioned first. That means the first suspect must be either Z or Y (the Floater—which has been marked with an asterisk):

	1	2	3	4	5	6	7
STVWXŶZ	Z/Y	—	T	—	—	W	S
c n					n	c	c	n
				~Z	~Z		

Step 5: Questions

12. (B) Could Be True

The correct answer will be the only one possible. The four wrong answers must be false.

By Rule 4, X has to be questioned after Z, so X cannot be questioned on day 1. That eliminates **(A)**. V merely has to be questioned after Z. If Z is questioned on day 1, then V can certainly be questioned on day 2. That makes **(B)** the correct answer. For the record:

Based on the final deductions, W must be sixth with S seventh—otherwise, everyone after W would not confess (Rule 5), which wouldn't leave enough confessions after T to satisfy Rule 6. That eliminates **(D)** and **(E)**. Then with the sixth and seventh suspects determined, Z couldn't be fourth. Otherwise, there would not be enough room for both V and X to be questioned after. That eliminates **(C)**.

13. (E) "If" / Could Be True EXCEPT

For this question, Z will be the second suspect to *confess*, not necessarily the second suspect questioned. However, Z can only be one of the first two suspects questioned. After all, T is questioned third (Rule 1). W and S must be sixth and seventh, respectively, so that two suspects confess after T (Rule 6) and none confess after W (Rule 5). And Z still has to be questioned before both V and X.

If Z is the second suspect to confess, Z must be questioned on day 2. That means the suspect on day 1 also confesses. V and X would have to be questioned on days 4 and 5, in either order. That leaves Y as the only suspect who can be questioned on day 1:

1	2	3	4	5	6	7
Y	Z	T	V/X	X/V	W	S
c	c		n	c	c	n

In that case, T could confess or not, so either **(A)** or **(B)** could be true. And if V and X were fourth and fifth, in that order, then V could not confess when X does. So, **(C)** and **(D)** could be true. However, Y is questioned on day 1 and *does* confess, so **(E)** is false, making it the correct answer.

14. (A) "If" / Could Be True

For this question, Y will be questioned some time in between V and X, in that order. Because Z has to be questioned before V and X (Rule 4), an order of Z, V, Y, X is created. T is already questioned on day 3 (Rule 1), and W and S must be questioned on days 6 and 7, respectively, so that two suspects confess after T (Rule 6) and none confess after W (Rule 5). That means Z, V, Y, and X will be questioned on days 1, 2, 4, and 5, respectively:

1	2	3	4	5	6	7
Z	V	T	Y	X	W	S
			n	c	c	n

$$Z - V - Y - X$$

Based on that, only **(A)** is possible, making it the correct answer. **(B)**, **(C)**, **(D)**, and **(E)** all must be false.

15. (E) Must Be True

The correct answer is a suspect who must be questioned before T. The remaining four could all be questioned at some time after T.

T is questioned third (Rule 1). As deduced from the beginning, Z must be questioned before that. Again, W and S must be sixth and seventh, respectively, so that two suspects confess after T (Rule 6) and none confess after W (Rule 5); and Z still has to be questioned before both V and X. That makes **(E)** the correct answer.

Even without those deductions, V, W, X, and Y can all be questioned after T, as seen in sketches from previous questions.

16. (A) "If" / Could Be True EXCEPT

For this question, X and Y will confess. Earlier rules and deductions place T third (Rule 1) and W and S sixth and seventh so that two suspects confess after T (Rule 6) and none confess after W (Rule 5). With no confession on day 4 (Rule 2), three days are still left for X and Y to confess: days 1, 2, and 5.

However, that leaves only V and Z to be questioned on day 4. Because Z has to be questioned before V and X (Rule 4), Z cannot be questioned on day 4. So, V is questioned on day 4:

1	2	3	4	5	6	7
		T	V		W	S
			n	c	c	n

X	Y
c	c

Because of that, V cannot confess, making **(A)** false and thus the correct answer. All of the remaining answers are possible without violating any rules.

17. (D) "If" / Must Be True

For this question, neither X nor V confesses. With T on day 3 (Rule 1), W and S are on days 6 and 7 so that two suspects confess after T (Rule 6) with no suspect confessing after W. Because the suspect on day 4 does not confess (Rule 2), the two suspects that confess after T are on days 5 and 6. That means neither X nor V will be questioned on day 5, and Z cannot be questioned on day 5, because Z has to be questioned before V and X (Rule 4). That leaves Y as the only suspect that can be questioned on day 5. So, that leaves Z, V, and X on the remaining three days. V and X can be questioned in either order, but Z has to be questioned before them both. So, Z has to be questioned on day 1. X and V will be on days 2 and 4 (in either order), but both will not confess as seen in the New-"If" of the question stem:

1	2	3	4	5	6	7
Z	V/X	T	X/V	Y	W	S
	n		n	c	c	n

With Y confessing on day 5, **(D)** must be true and is thus the correct answer. All the remaining answers *could* be true, but none of them *have* to be.

Game 4: Debate Team Tournament

Step 1: Overview
Situation: High school debate tournament

Entities: Three school teams (Fairview, Gillom, Hilltop) and six members (Mei, Navarro, O'Rourke, Pavlovich, Sethna, Tsudama)

Action: Distribution/Sequencing Hybrid. Determine the ranking for each team, and distribute the six members among the teams.

Limitations: Each team has exactly two members. The teams will take the highest three places in the tournament: first, second, and third.

Step 2: Sketch
Because the rules describe rankings as "higher" than one another, set up three columns, one for each place (first, second, third). Do not label each column with the schools (Fairview, Gillom, Hilltop) because they may appear out of order. Instead, have a blank slot in each column to determine the order of the schools, and add two separate slots to determine the team members:

```
                  1   2   3
  Fa  Gi  Hi     ___ ___ ___
                 _____
  MNOPST         ___ ___ ___
                 ___ ___ ___
```

Step 3: Rules
Rule 1 provides a Block of Entities. There's no indication about what place this team finishes in, so jot the rule down in shorthand:

Rule 2 can be built right into the sketch, putting a "T" in one of the second-place slots.

Rule 3 states that Mei and Pavlovich will be on different teams. It could be any two teams, so just make a note for now:

Rule 4 sets up some relative sequencing: Pavlovich will place higher than Navarro:

$$P \ldots N$$

Because of this, Pavlovich cannot be at the bottom (third place), and Navarro cannot be at the top (first place). Add "~P" and "~N" next to the appropriate columns in the sketch.

Rule 5 sets up more relative sequencing, but with teams instead of members: Gillom will place higher than Hilltop:

$$Gi \ldots Hi$$

This means Gillom cannot be at the bottom (third place), and Hilltop cannot be at the top (first place). You could add "~G" and "~H" next to the appropriate columns in the Master Sketch, but this rule also provides a great opportunity for Limited Options.

Step 4: Deductions
Gillom is duplicated in Rules 1 and 5. Rule 1 puts Gillom in a Block of Entities with Sethna, and Rule 5 limits Gillom to one of two places: first or second. A block with only two possible placements is grounds for setting up Limited Options.

In the first option, Gillom will get first place, with Sethna on the team. Unfortunately, there are no other concrete deductions in this option. The remaining two schools (Fairview and Hilltop) could place in either order. Furthermore, the rules about Mei, Navarro, and Pavlovich do not allow any of them to be placed with certainty:

I)	1	2	3
	Gi	Hi/Fa	Fa/Hi
	S	T	___
	___	___	___

However, the second option allows for a lot more. In that option, Gillom will get second place, with Sethna on the team. With Tsudama also on the second-place team (Rule 2), that team is complete. By Rule 5, Hilltop has to place lower than Gillom. So, Hilltop will be the third-place team, leaving Fairview to be the first-place team. As for the team members, Pavlovich still has to rank higher than Navarro (Rule 4). With the second-place team filled up, Pavlovich will be on the first-place team, and Navarro will be on the third-place team. Finally, Mei cannot be on the same team as Pavlovich (Rule 3), so Mei must be the other person on the third-place team, leaving O'Rourke as the other person on the first-place team:

II)	1	2	3
	Fa	Gi	Hi
	P	S	N
	O	T	M

Note that Limited Options are not necessary here. However, with one option completely filled, it can be extremely helpful.

Step 5: Questions

18. (E) Partial Acceptability

Four answers will violate the rules, leaving one that is acceptable. Eliminate the violators by testing the rules one at a time.

By itself, Rule 1 cannot be tested because the schools are not listed in the answers. By Rule 2, Tsudama must be on the second-place team. That eliminates **(A)**. By Rule 3, Mei and Pavlovich must be on different teams. That eliminates **(B)**. By Rule 4, Pavlovich must place higher than Navarro. That eliminates **(C)**.

By Rule 5, Gillom must place higher than Hilltop, but the schools are not listed in the answers. However, combined with Rule 1, Sethna (who must be on the team from Gillom High) must place higher than Hilltop. So, Sethna cannot place third, which eliminates **(D)**. That leaves **(E)** as the correct answer.

19. (A) "If" / Could Be True

For this question, Pavlovich will be on the team from Hilltop. Gillom places higher than Hilltop (Rule 5), and Pavlovich places higher than Navarro (Rule 4). So, to accommodate all of this, Gillom must place first (as it does in Option I), with Hilltop (including Pavlovich) second and Fairview (including Navarro) third.

Tsudama is on the second-place team (Rule 2), so Tsudama is on the team from Hilltop along with Pavlovich. Sethna is on the team from Gillom (Rule 1) in first place. That leaves Mei and O'Rourke. One of them will take the final spot at Gillom, and the other will take the final spot at Fairview:

1	2	3
Gi	Hi	Fa
S	T	N
M/O	P	O/M

With that, only **(A)** is possible, making it the correct answer. **(B)**, **(C)**, **(D)**, and **(E)** all must be false.

20. (B) "If" / Could Be True

For this question, O'Rourke is on the second-place team (which can only happen in Option I), along with Tsudama (Rule 2). That fills up the second-place team. Pavlovich must place higher than Navarro, so Pavlovich will have to be on the first-place team, with Navarro on the third-place team. Sethna must be on the team from Gillom (Rule 1), which cannot place third (Rule 5). So, Pavlovich, with Sethna, must be on the first-place team (Gillom). That leaves Mei to take the other

place on the third-place team. Although all of the team members are placed, the last two teams (Fairview and Hilltop) cannot be determined for certain:

1	2	3
Gi	Hi/Fa	Fa/Hi
S	T	N
P	O	M

With that, only **(B)** is possible, making it the correct answer. The other answers all must be false.

21. (C) "If" / How Many

If Pavlovich and Tsudama are teammates (which can only happen in Option I), then they must be on the second-place team together (Rule 2). Because Pavlovich has to place higher than Navarro (Rule 4), Navarro will then be on the third-place team. Sethna must be on the team from Gillom (Rule 1), which cannot place third (Rule 5). With the second-place team filled, Gillom must be the first-place team, and it will include Sethna and exactly one of either Mei or O'Rourke. That leaves the other one of Mei and O'Rourke to be on the third-place team:

1	2	3
Gi	Hi/Fa	Fa/Hi
S	T	N
M/O	P	O/M

That means only four teammates (Pavlovich, Navarro, Sethna, and Tsudama) can be determined exactly. That makes **(C)** the correct answer.

22. (E) "If" / Could Be True

For this question, Mei will place higher than Hilltop (which can only happen in Option I). That means Mei must be on the first- or second-place team. Because it cannot be determined for certain, draw out both possibilities (both of which are based on Option I).

If Mei is on the first-place team, Pavlovich must be on another team (Rule 4). However, Pavlovich must still place higher than Navarro, so Pavlovich must be on the second-place team along with Tsudama (Rule 2), placing Navarro on the third-place team. Sethna must be on the team from Gillom (Rule 1), which cannot place third (Rule 5). With the second-place team filled, Gillom, with Sethna, must be on the first-place team. That leaves O'Rourke to take the last spot on the third-place team. The second- and third-place teams will be from Fairview and Hilltop, in either order:

	1	2	3
	Gi	Hi/Fa	Fa/Hi
	S	T	N
	M	P	O

For this question, if Mei is on the second-place team, Hilltop must be the third-place team. Tsudama will be on the second-place team with Mei (Rule 2). That fills up the second-place team. Gillom's team has to include Sethna (Rule 1), so it cannot place second. That means Gillom will place first (with Sethna), and Fairview will place second. Pavlovich has to place higher than Navarro. With the second-place team filled, Pavlovich will have to be on the first-place team, and Navarro will be on the third-place team. That leaves O'Rourke to take the remaining spot on the third-place team:

	1	2	3
	Gi	Fa	Hi
	S	T	N
	P	M	O

In either variation, Gillom always places first, which eliminates **(A)** and **(B)**. And Navarro and O'Rourke are always on the third-place team, which eliminates **(C)** and **(D)**. Pavlovich could be on the first-place team (in the second sketch for this question). That means **(E)** is the only answer that could be true, making it the correct answer.

23. (B) Could Be True EXCEPT

The correct answer to this question will be someone who *cannot* be on a team with Sethna. The four wrong answers list people who *could* be on a team with Sethna.

Sketches for the previous four questions show how Sethna could team with Mei, O'Rourke, or Pavlovich. That eliminates **(A)**, **(C)**, and **(D)**. If you drew out Limited Options from the start, the option with Gillom High placing second puts Sethna on a team with Tsudama. Because that's possible, **(E)** is eliminated, making **(B)** the correct answer. For the record, here is why Navarro cannot be on a team with Sethna:

If Sethna were on a team with Navarro, it would be the team from Gillom High (Rule 1). However, they would then have to place higher than the team from Hilltop (Rule 5) and lower than the team with Pavlovich (Rule 4). That would make it the second-place team—but then there would be no room for Tsudama (Rule 2). Thus, Sethna cannot be teammates with Navarro.

Section III: Logical Reasoning

Q#	Question Type	Correct	Difficulty
1	Strengthen	A	★
2	Flaw	C	★
3	Main Point	E	★
4	Weaken	A	★
5	Main Point	E	★
6	Flaw	D	★
7	Inference	A	★
8	Assumption (Necessary)	A	★★
9	Weaken	E	★★
10	Role of a Statement	B	★
11	Strengthen	C	★★★
12	Principle (Identify/Strengthen)	B	★★
13	Parallel Flaw (EXCEPT)	B	★★★★
14	Weaken	A	★★
15	Assumption (Necessary)	E	★
16	Weaken	B	★
17	Flaw	A	★★
18	Principle (Identify/Assumption)	E	★★
19	Inference	A	★
20	Assumption (Necessary)	D	★★★
21	Inference	C	★★★
22	Paradox (EXCEPT)	B	★★★
23	Parallel Reasoning	D	★★★
24	Method of Argument	A	★★★
25	Strengthen	C	★★★★

1. (A) Strengthen

Step 1: Identify the Question Type

This is a Strengthen question, because the correct answer "strengthens the argument" in the stimulus.

Step 2: Untangle the Stimulus

Break down the argument into evidence and conclusion. The conclusion follows ([*h*]*owever*) in the second sentence. Basically, the author's main point is that extended warranties on electronics are usually not good for customers. The evidence, which follows the conclusion, is that most problems with electronics happen during the regular warranty period.

Step 3: Make a Prediction

Based on the evidence, we know that most problems happen during the regular warranty period. But we do not know what kinds of problems happen after the regular warranty period or how expensive they are to fix. What if those problems that typically happen after the regular warranty period are predictably severe and expensive to fix? If that is the case, then it might be a good idea for customers to buy the extended warranty. Thus, the author has overlooked the possibility that the extended warranty is actually a good idea because the problems that happen after the regular warranty period are severe and expensive to fix. The correct answer will strengthen the argument by ruling out the overlooked possibility. So, the correct answer will state that the problems that typically happen after the regular warranty period are not severe or expensive to fix. If that is the case, then it is more likely to be true that buying the extended warranty is not a good idea.

Step 4: Evaluate the Answer Choices

(A) matches the prediction because it describes the extended warranty as more expensive than the problems it would fix. Thus, buying an extended warranty is more likely a bad idea.

(B) goes Outside the Scope and is a potential weakener. If the price of extended warranties is low, that may be a potential reason to get one. However, if extended warranties are unlikely to help with anything, it does not matter how cheap they are. Something that is cheap but useless is still a waste of money. What is still unknown is the cost of potential problems absent a warranty.

(C) goes Outside the Scope by not specifying when the "special circumstances" would make the items in question more likely to break. If the items are more likely to break during the time frame covered by the regular warranty, then **(C)** strengthens the argument because the regular warranty would already cover those problems. If the items are more likely to break after the time frame covered by the regular warranty, then **(C)** weakens the argument because the extended warranty would cover the time frame the problems tend to occur. Because you need additional information

(when the items would break) to decide if **(C)** is a strengthener or a weakener, it is neither.

(D) goes Outside the Scope by focusing on certain extended warranties that cover the regular warranty period as well. **(D)** fails to say anything about whether these warranties would actually be used or how much they cost.

(E) goes Outside the Scope by focusing on how the extended warranties benefit the stores that offer them. Just because the extended warranties are good for the stores does not mean they are bad for the customer. In fact, **(E)** says nothing about how the customer would or would not use the extended warranty.

2. (C) Flaw

Step 1: Identify the Question Type

Because the correct answer describes how the "argument's reasoning is flawed," this is a Flaw question.

Step 2: Untangle the Stimulus

Break down the argument into evidence and conclusion. Following [*c*]*learly*, the conclusion ends the stimulus. Basically, the author's main point is that environmental regulations will not solve environmental problems. The author's evidence is that there are more environmental regulations than there used to be, but also more environmental problems.

Step 3: Make a Prediction

Start by finding the assumption. The evidence correlates rising environmental regulations with rising environmental problems. The conclusion suggests that environmental regulations are bad (or at best, neutral). Thus, the author assumes that environmental regulations have no benefit or actually make environmental problems worse. This argument overlooks the possibility that if the environmental regulations had not been there, then the environmental problems could be much worse than they are now.

Step 4: Evaluate the Answer Choices

(C) matches the prediction.

(A) is a Distortion of the conclusion. The author attacks the regulations proposed by environmentalists, not the environmentalists themselves.

(B) is Extreme. While the author does suggest that more regulations will not fix the problem, **(B)** goes much further by suggesting that the *only* way to stop environmental problems is to have no regulations whatsoever.

(D) is an Irrelevant Comparison. It suggests that the author is more concerned with reducing excess regulations than with preserving the environment. In contrast, the author seems interested in preserving the environment, but thinks that regulations may actually be contributing to environmental problems.

(E) accurately describes the stimulus in that it does not include a consideration of the environmentalists' opponents. While the author's style for not including opposing points of view might be criticized, this is not a logical flaw. Even without mentioning the environmentalists' opponents, the author has included evidence and a conclusion. The flaw has to do with how the author connects the evidence and conclusion, rather than with some other point of view that the author has not mentioned.

3. (E) Main Point

Step 1: Identify the Question Type
This is a Main Point question because the correct answer "accurately expresses the main conclusion of the argument" in the stimulus.

Step 2: Untangle the Stimulus
Read the entire stimulus, paraphrasing as you go. In the first sentence, the author acknowledges that there are advantages to looking at music history in a particular way (i.e., musical knowledge grows over time). In the second sentence, the author describes advances in knowledge about music over time. In the third sentence, the author gives an example of advances in knowledge about music over time.

Step 3: Make a Prediction
Both the second and third sentences provide factual information that supports the claim made in the first sentence. Thus, the first sentence must be the author's conclusion. The correct answer will suggest that music knowledge does grow over time.

Step 4: Evaluate the Answer Choices
(E) matches the prediction.

(A) describes an idea from the first piece of evidence given in the second sentence.

(B) describes an idea from the second piece of evidence given in the third sentence.

(C) describes the idea given in the first sentence, which the author ultimately dismisses by finding specific examples where it *is* wise to take a developmental view of music.

(D) is a Distortion because the stimulus never suggests that one composer is "better than another." When the stimulus does compare composers, it is to suggest that one was a developmental advance over another. Just because something is a developmental advance does not necessarily mean that it is better. For example, it would not make sense to say that elementary school age children are better than toddlers, even though they are more developmentally advanced.

4. (A) Weaken

Step 1: Identify the Question Type
Because the correct answer "seriously weakens the argument" in the stimulus, this is a Weaken question.

Step 2: Untangle the Stimulus
Break down the argument into evidence and conclusion. Following *thus* in the last sentence, the conclusion is that the electric device will kill lots of bugs, but will not do much to help control the mosquito population. The evidence is that the electric device killed more than 300 bugs, but only 12 mosquitoes.

Step 3: Make a Prediction
Start by finding the assumption. The author concludes that the device will not help much with mosquitoes, but the evidence shows that the device did kill 12 mosquitoes. Thus, the author must be assuming that there are many more than 12 mosquitoes to be killed. If, on the other hand, the mosquito population only consisted of 12 mosquitoes, and now they are all dead, then the electric device would have helped control the mosquito population. Thus, the correct answer will suggest that the device actually did kill a large proportion of the mosquitoes in the area, helping to control the mosquito population.

Step 4: Evaluate the Answer Choices
(A) matches the prediction. If the electric device killed all the mosquitoes, then the electric device is likely to have helped to control the mosquito population.

(B) is Out of Scope and a potential strengthener. What proportion of the bugs attracted to the device were non-mosquitoes is irrelevant as long as it's attracting and killing enough mosquitoes to control the population. However, **(B)** suggests that the electric device may be ineffective at attracting (much less killing) mosquitoes.

(C) is an Irrelevant Comparison about *beneficial* and *harmful* insects. It makes the electric device look bad, but does not weaken the conclusion. It is immaterial to whether the device controls the mosquito population.

(D) strengthens the argument. If the electric device kills mosquito-eaters, then the electric device is acting in at least one way to *not* help keep the mosquito population down.

(E) goes Outside the Scope. It fails to provide information about the effect that the electric device has on the mosquito population. Even if it doesn't kill *all* the insects it attracts, if it still attracts and kills enough mosquitoes to control the population, then it is effective. However, if it doesn't, it isn't.

5. (E) Main Point

Step 1: Identify the Question Type
The correct answer "most accurately expresses the main conclusion of the argument" in the stimulus. Therefore, this is a Main Point question.

Step 2: Untangle the Stimulus
Read the entire stimulus, paraphrasing as you go. The first sentence describes what brain-scanning technology is. The second sentence gives a condition of what is required of brain-scanning technology for it to help brain researchers. In other words, the second sentence can be translated into Formal Logic:

$$\text{If} \quad \begin{array}{c} \textbf{\textit{brain scans}} \\ \textbf{\textit{help}} \end{array} \quad \rightarrow \quad \begin{array}{c} \textbf{\textit{subjects give}} \\ \textbf{\textit{accurate}} \\ \textbf{\textit{verbal reports}} \end{array}$$

The third sentence describes how brain-scanning technology is not useful when the condition described in the second sentence is not satisfied.

Step 3: Make a Prediction
The first sentence gives background context, so it cannot be the main point. The third sentence refers back to information given in the second sentence, so it is subordinate to the second sentence. Thus, the second sentence, which states a necessary condition, is the main point. The correct answer will suggest that brain-scanning technology is useful to researchers *only* when the researchers can rely on the accuracy of verbal reports given by subjects while their brains are being scanned.

Step 4: Evaluate the Answer Choices
(E) matches the prediction.

(A) is Extreme. It describes what would be true if researchers could not rely on the accuracy of verbal reports given by subjects having their brains scanned.

(B) is also Extreme. Although researchers do need accurate verbal reports, that does not mean there is no way to get them. The correct answer to a Main Point question adds no information to the stimulus, nor does it make an inference based on the stimulus.

(C) is a Distortion. The author never suggests how the results of brain-scanning research should be evaluated. Although it is necessary to have accurate verbal reports, the author does not indicate that they should be viewed with "great skepticism."

(D) is another Distortion. If researchers can trust the accuracy of verbal reports of brain-scan subjects, then researchers can get useful information from brain scans. Brain scans, however, do not give useful information about the accuracy of verbal reports given by subjects.

6. (D) Flaw

Step 1: Identify the Question Type
This is a Flaw question because the correct answer describes the grounds on which the argument in the stimulus is "vulnerable to criticism."

Step 2: Untangle the Stimulus
Break down the argument into evidence and conclusion. The conclusion comes in the first sentence, marked by the phrase "my research shows that." Basically, the main point is that the bird species in question does not primarily eat vegetation. The ornithologist's evidence is that he's been watching the birds in the morning for a long time, and more than half of what he sees them eat is insects and other animal foods.

Step 3: Make a Prediction
The ornithologist has been watching the birds in the mornings, but not at other times. But the ornithologist's conclusion is about the total diet of the birds (in other words, not just about what they eat in the mornings). Thus, the ornithologist is shifting scope from morning food in the evidence to all food in the conclusion. The ornithologist must be assuming that what the birds eat in the morning is representative of their total diet. The ornithologist overlooks the possibility that the birds eat one way in the morning, but a different way in the afternoon and evening.

Step 4: Evaluate the Answer Choices
(D) matches the prediction.

(A) disputes the ornithologist's evidence. The ornithologist suggests that he was "concealed in a well-camouflaged blind," and we have no reason to doubt this. Therefore, it would seem unlikely that the birds knew they were being observed. In Flaw questions, look for errors in reasoning, not potential issues with the evidence.

(B) accurately describes a piece of the ornithologist's evidence, but not a flaw in the stimulus. If something is an "animal food source," then it is not "vegetation." There is no logical reason why the ornithologist would have to specify what the other animal food sources are in order to support the conclusion about the portion of the bird's diet that is vegetation.

(C) is a Distortion because the ornithologist does *not* adopt the widespread belief about the birds' feeding habits. In contrast, the ornithologist's conclusion refutes the widespread belief about the birds' feeding habits.

(E) goes Outside the Scope by introducing the idea of diet change over time. The argument just looks at what the diet of the birds is at the present time.

7. (A) Inference

Step 1: Identify the Question Type

This is an Inference question because the correct answer "logically completes" the argument in the stimulus. Whenever a stimulus ends with a fill-in-the-blank, accompanied by a Conclusion Keyword, it is an Inference question.

Step 2: Untangle the Stimulus

Read the entire stimulus, paraphrasing as you go. The first statement includes the necessity Keyword *only*, so translate it into Formal Logic:

$$\text{If} \quad \begin{array}{c} \text{successfully} \\ \text{learn about a} \\ \text{topic} \end{array} \quad \rightarrow \quad \begin{array}{c} \text{genuine} \\ \text{curiosity} \end{array}$$

The second statement suggests that genuinely curious students enjoy learning for the sake of learning. The third statement contrasts this idea, suggesting that very few students come to the classroom with enough of their own curiosity to learn everything that will be taught.

Step 3: Make a Prediction

The correct answer will suggest what a teacher's job is. Figure this out by connecting the other statements in the stimulus together. You know that curiosity is crucial for students to learn, but that students don't have enough of their own curiosity to learn everything. Thus, it must be that a teacher's job is to help students become more curious so that they can successfully learn everything.

Step 4: Evaluate the Answer Choices

(A) sounds complicated, but matches the prediction. Paraphrased in simpler terms, **(A)** suggests that teachers both need to help students become more curious in order for those students to learn, as well as to provide topics that the students enjoy learning.

(B) goes Outside the Scope by introducing "rewards that are not inherent in the learning process itself." The students that the stimulus discusses find learning itself to be rewarding. Nothing must be true about using *rewards*.

(C) goes Outside the Scope by failing to mention curiosity. The teacher could focus on any topic, so long as the teacher inspires enough curiosity in students.

(D) goes Outside the Scope by focusing on students taking responsibility for their own learning. By contrast, the stimulus is about how teachers can kick-start students' learning processes by helping the students generate curiosity.

(E) goes Outside the Scope by introducing learning that is "not necessarily enjoyable." The stimulus discusses learning that is enjoyable, or at the very least learning that produces genuine curiosity.

8. (A) Assumption (Necessary)

Step 1: Identify the Question Type

Because the correct answer is the *assumption* the argument in the stimulus *requires*, this is a Necessary Assumption question.

Step 2: Untangle the Stimulus

Break down the argument into evidence and conclusion. Following [*t*]*hus* in the last sentence, the conclusion is that turning landfills into parks is bad for human health. The evidence comes in two pieces. First, cleaning products go into landfills. Second, when bacteria degrade, the toxic vapors from cleaning products are released.

Step 3: Make a Prediction

Use the mismatched concepts to find the assumption. First, both the evidence and the conclusion discuss landfills, so that is a matched concept. Additionally, the evidence discusses toxic vapors, and the conclusion discusses damage to human health. This is based on the idea that it is in the very nature of toxic vapors to damage human health; that's just what it means to be a toxic vapor. Next, the evidence presents the idea of bacteria degrading cleaning products. The conclusion presents the idea of public parks. The assumption will connect these final two ideas together. Thus, the assumption is that there are bacteria degrading cleaning products in the public parks.

Step 4: Evaluate the Answer Choices

(A) matches the prediction. Test it with the Denial Test to prove that it is correct. The denied version of **(A)** is: "None of the landfills that have been converted into public parks have bacteria that degrade household cleaning products." If there are no bacteria that degrade household cleaning products, then there would be no toxic vapors and no damage to human health. Thus, when you deny **(A)**, it absolutely destroys the argument.

(B) is Extreme. It suggests that the *only* thing that could damage human health is toxic vapors. The environmentalist is arguing that because of the toxic vapors, human health will be damaged. The environmentalist is not, like **(B)** proposes, arguing that the *only* thing that could be damaging is the toxic vapors.

(C) is a Distortion. It addresses "vapors from household cleaning products" in general, rather than the toxic vapors from household cleaning products that are a result of bacteria degrading the products.

(D) is a 180. It goes against the conclusion by suggesting an additional measure that could avoid damage to human health, and this undermines the definitive nature of the conclusion. Other measures in general are Out of Scope.

(E) is another Distortion. It does talk about landfills and cleaning products, but fails to mention landfills converted into parks. The conclusion does not require that some degradation in landfills is harming humans—only that landfills converted to public parks are harming humans. Subjected to the Denial Test, **(E)** would say, "If vapors are produced in a landfill … then *no* humans suffer." That would not destroy the environmentalist's argument, which is limited to harm done by converted land.

9. (E) Weaken

Step 1: Identify the Question Type
This is a Weaken question because the correct answer "weakens the argument" in the stimulus.

Step 2: Untangle the Stimulus
Break down the argument into evidence and conclusion. Marked by the Keyword *therefore*, the conclusion comes at the end of the stimulus. Basically, the author's main point is that regularly drinking camellia tea can lead to an increased risk of kidney damage. The evidence, following [*f*]*urthermore*, is that regular camellia tea drinkers are more likely than the average person to develop kidney damage.

Step 3: Make a Prediction
We know that regular tea drinkers are more likely to have kidney damage than the average person, and based on that the author concludes that tea is what's causing the kidney damage. Therefore, the author is assuming that because the tea is causing the increased risk of kidney damage, there is nothing else that is causing this increased risk. The correct answer will likely point out the overlooked possibility that something else is causing the increased risk of kidney damage in regular tea drinkers.

Step 4: Evaluate the Answer Choices
(E) matches the prediction. If there are other beverages that tea drinkers consume that cause kidney damage, it is less likely to be true that the tea is the cause of tea drinkers' increased risk of kidney damage.

(A) goes Outside the Scope by focusing on the addictive nature of tea. The part of the stimulus before [*f*]*urthermore* (including the part about withdrawal) is not the important part of the main evidence and conclusion. Even if other beverages have the same addictive chemical, the camellia tea drinkers are still more likely to develop kidney damage.

(B) goes Outside the Scope in the same way as **(A)**. The author never connects tea's addictive properties to the kidney damage it may cause. It's immaterial to the author what specific aspect of tea is leading to heightened risk of kidney damage, as long as it's some property of the tea.

(C) goes Outside the Scope by introducing what "some people claim" about drinking tea. **(C)** makes no mention of what does or does not cause kidney damage. Even if the tea has a potential benefit of stress reduction, it may still cause kidney damage.

(D) goes Outside the Scope by focusing on what proportion of tea drinkers actually develop kidney damage. Even if they never develop kidney damage, they could still have an increased risk of developing kidney damage. So, the author's argument still holds even if the tea causes kidney damage in a minority of those that drink it. If that's challenging to wrap your head around, imagine this example: whether or not it actually does break, a mug that I drop on the floor has an increased risk of breaking compared to a mug that rests peacefully on the table. Breaking and the risk of breaking are two separate ideas.

10. (B) Role of a Statement

Step 1: Identify the Question Type
This is a Role of a Statement question because the correct answer describes the role played in the stimulus by "the reference to the claim of certain art collectors."

Step 2: Untangle the Stimulus
First, identify the statement in question. "The reference to the claim of certain art collectors" is the second sentence. Next, read the entire stimulus, paraphrasing as you go. The first sentence puts forward the intentions of avant-garde artists. The second sentence puts forward the point of view of some art collectors. The third sentence, introduced with the Contrast Keyword [*h*]*owever*, adds the information that change in a society's beliefs happens slowly. Finally, the last sentence, marked with the Conclusion Keyword [*t*]*herefore*, describes a paradox: the very thing that would make avant-garde art successful proves that it is not successful.

Step 3: Make a Prediction
The statement in question (the second sentence) is one of two points of view that the artist ultimately shows leads to a paradoxical outcome. It is neither the evidence (which follows *since* in the last sentence) nor the conclusion (which is the rest of the last sentence).

Step 4: Evaluate the Answer Choices
(B) matches the prediction.

(A) describes the evidence, but the statement in question is not the evidence.

(C) is a Distortion because the position of the avant-garde artists ("the initial premise in the argument") does not support the position of the art collectors. The two positions are simply different and, as the artist later hopes to demonstrate, incompatible.

(D) is like **(C)**. Neither of the two premises that open the stimulus (the positions of the artists and art collectors) supports the other one.

(E) is a Distortion because the artist never gives a counterargument to the initial premise (the artists' point of view). In contrast, the entire argument is designed to argue against the art collectors' point of view—not the artists'.

11. (C) Strengthen

Step 1: Identify the Question Type
This is a Strengthen question because the correct answer "strengthen[s] the reasoning" of the argument in the stimulus.

Step 2: Untangle the Stimulus
Break down the argument into evidence and conclusion. The conclusion follows [*t*]*hus* at the end of the stimulus. The author's main point is that travel-related stress causes insomnia in traveling businesspeople. The evidence is that traveling businesspeople are unlike non-traveling businesspeople in two ways. First, traveling businesspeople have travel-related stresses. Second, traveling businesspeople are more likely to have insomnia.

Step 3: Make a Prediction
Because the author is making a causal argument, there is a built-in assumption. The author's claim is that travel stresses cause insomnia in traveling businesspeople. Therefore, the author is assuming that there is no other cause of insomnia in traveling businesspeople. The correct answer will support this assumption, likely by ruling out some other possible cause of insomnia in traveling businesspeople.

Step 4: Evaluate the Answer Choices
(C) matches the prediction. If businesspeople were insomniacs before they accepted a traveling assignment, then it would be very likely that their insomnia had a cause other than travel-related stress. Thus, by suggesting that the traveling businesspeople did not have increased rates of insomnia before they started traveling, **(C)** makes it more likely to be true that traveling is what caused their insomnia.

(A) goes Outside the Scope by providing details about which countries international businesspeople travel between, but it says nothing about insomnia. If anything, **(A)** may weaken the argument by indicating that most international travel may not have as much travel-related stress given that contiguous borders may mean less change in climate and time zones.

(B) goes Outside the Scope by focusing on the preferences of some businesspeople, rather than on the effect that travel-related stress has on their sleeping. If anything, **(B)** may weaken the argument because it indicates that at least some people do not experience stress, but actually enjoy their travel-related changes.

(D) is a potential 180. It suggests that some of the travel-related stresses mentioned in the stimulus actually help people with insomnia, and, therefore, it would weaken—not strengthen—the argument.

(E) is incorrect on two accounts. First, it goes Outside the Scope by introducing "various sleep-related ailments." The stimulus is just about insomnia. If these other ailments are related to other sleep problems, then this has no effect on whether travel-related stress causes insomnia. Second, even if those ailments do refer to insomnia, if there are salespeople still experiencing insomnia long after any international travel, then it's possible that their insomnia predated their international travel. As such, it would be a preexisting condition that wasn't caused by the travel-related stress. Alternatively, the insomnia could have also arisen along with or after the international travel, which may make for a correlative relationship but not a causal one. As stated, **(E)** does not strengthen a causal link between travel-related stress and insomnia.

12. (B) Principle (Identify/Strengthen)

Step 1: Identify the Question Type
This Principle question resembles a Strengthen question, because the correct answer is the principle that "helps to justify the reasoning" in the argument in the stimulus.

Step 2: Untangle the Stimulus
Treat the stimulus like you would a Strengthen question. So, break down the argument into evidence and conclusion. The conclusion is between [*b*]*ut* and *since* in the second sentence. Basically, the author recommends against climbing Mount Everest. The author gives two pieces of evidence. First, in the same sentence as the conclusion, the author suggests that there is a big risk in attempting to climb Mount Everest. Second, following [*m*]*oreover*, the author suggests that successfully ascending Mount Everest has given climbers some negative feelings (exhaustion and fear), but not any spiritual enlightenment.

Step 3: Make a Prediction
Find the author's assumption using the mismatched concepts. The evidence shows that a high-risk activity leads to disappointment rather than enlightenment. The conclusion recommends against doing some activity. Therefore, the author assumes that if a risky activity will not lead to enlightenment, then you should not do it. The correct answer will support this assumption, likely restating it in general terms.

Step 4: Evaluate the Answer Choices
(B) matches the prediction.

(A) is a Distortion because the stimulus never suggests that spirituality is the *primary* motivation for the risky project (climbing Mount Everest). The first sentence indicates that it is the "ultimate achievement," but "spiritual discovery" is only added as a secondary piece of evidence. As written, **(A)** would not strengthen the argument because it may not even refer to anyone that attempts the climb. The author would dissuade all people from making the climb, not just those that do it *primarily* for spiritual reasons.

(C) goes Outside the Scope by introducing legal prohibitions, which the author never mentions in the stimulus.

(D) is a Distortion because the author never suggests that there *are* ways of achieving profound spiritual experiences. The author only shows that one activity will *not* lead to profound spiritual experiences.

(E) is another Distortion. The conclusion of the argument is a recommendation *against* doing an activity (i.e., climbing Mount Everest). In contrast, **(E)** makes it seem like the conclusion of the argument is a recommendation to do some activity (i.e., examine underlying reasons). Furthermore, **(E)** fails to mention risk and spiritual disappointment altogether. The author says that "climbers should not attempt this climb." So, there's no need to recommend that climbers consider their underlying reasons, because the author doesn't cite any justifiable circumstances to climb the mountain.

13. (B) Parallel Flaw (EXCEPT)

Step 1: Identify the Question Type
This is a Parallel Flaw EXCEPT question because the four wrong answers will exhibit "flawed reasoning similar to" the flawed reasoning in the stimulus. The one correct answer will either contain a different flaw or it will be logically sound.

Step 2: Untangle the Stimulus
Analyze the argument by separating it into evidence and conclusion. Ending the stimulus, the conclusion is that the universe has a structure that is so simple it is elegant. The evidence is that each of the smallest pieces of the universe has a structure that is so simple it is elegant.

Step 3: Make a Prediction
Because this is a short stimulus, it will be more efficient to predict the flaw than it will be to try to simply match up conclusion types. To find the flaw, find the assumption. The evidence in the stimulus is about parts of the universe. The conclusion is about the whole universe. Therefore, the author is assuming that what is true of the parts of the universe must also be true of the whole universe. This is a classic flaw. Just because each part of something has a given characteristic does not prove that the whole thing has that characteristic. Eliminate the four wrong answers that assume that what is true of the parts must be true of the whole.

Step 4: Evaluate the Answer Choices
(B) is the correct answer. While **(B)** is structurally parallel to the stimulus, it is logically sound. If each part of a desk is made of metal, it must be true that the desk is indeed made of metal.

(A) makes the same error as the stimulus. Just because each part of the car is nearly perfectly engineered does not prove that the whole thing is. For example, it could have been assembled poorly.

(C) makes the same error as the stimulus. Just because each brick is rectangular does not prove that the wall is. For example, you could build many differently shaped walls out of rectangular bricks.

(D) makes the same error as the stimulus. Like **(A)**, the pieces of the chair could be assembled in such a way that the whole chair is not sturdy.

(E) makes the same error as the stimulus. Like **(A)** and **(E)**, the sentences of the novel could be assembled in such a way that the whole novel is poorly constructed.

14. (A) Weaken

Step 1: Identify the Question Type
Because the correct answer will "most seriously weaken" the argument in the stimulus, this is a Weaken question.

Step 2: Untangle the Stimulus
Break down the argument into evidence and conclusion. The conclusion is the first sentence. Basically, the criminologist's main point is that if a court system punishes criminals quickly, then that helps reduce violent crime. The criminologist's evidence comes in two pieces. First, slow trials lead to criminals feeling like they can get away with crimes. Second, when criminals know that punishment quickly follows being caught, they think twice before committing crimes.

Step 3: Make a Prediction
The overall premise of the argument is that the behavior of the court system affects the behavior of criminals. In order for this to be true, the criminologist must be assuming that criminals think about the court system before they commit crimes. This assumption overlooks the possibility that some criminals do not think about their crimes in advance. Maybe violent criminals act in the heat of the moment. The correct answer will likely point out this overlooked possibility.

Step 4: Evaluate the Answer Choices
(A) matches the prediction. If violent crime is not premeditated, then violent criminals would not be thinking about how the court system will affect their punishment before they commit violent crimes. Thus, an efficient court system would not be likely to deter violent crime.

(B) goes Outside the Scope by focusing on suspected criminals who are actually innocent. Additionally, **(B)** fails to say anything about how the efficiency of a court system could affect violent criminals.

(C) goes Outside the Scope by focusing on the criminal history of violent criminals, rather than on how the efficiency of a court system could affect violent criminals.

(D) goes Outside the Scope by introducing the rights of the accused. The argument in the stimulus looks at a possible benefit of quick trials, but never discusses who does or does not have a right to a trial.

(E) is a 180. It strengthens the argument in the stimulus by providing additional evidence that quick trials do indeed lead to fewer violent crimes.

15. (E) Assumption (Necessary)

Step 1: Identify the Question Type
Because the argument in the stimulus "depends on assuming" the correct answer, this is a Necessary Assumption question.

Step 2: Untangle the Stimulus
Break down the argument into evidence and conclusion. The conclusion follows [*t*]*herefore* at the end of the stimulus. The journalist's main point is that we should keep mandatory retirement at age 65. The journalist's evidence is that there would be bad consequences if mandatory retirement was stopped. If mandatory retirement was stopped, young people would be unfairly prevented from getting jobs, and they would be upset about it.

Step 3: Make a Prediction
The basic structure of this argument is that if doing something (stopping mandatory retirement) has bad consequences (frustrated, jobless youngsters), then we should not do that thing. Such an argument depends on the assumption that doing the thing (stopping mandatory retirement) actually does lead to the bad consequences (frustrated, jobless youngsters). In this argument, the journalist has overlooked the possibility that even without mandatory retirement, people still might retire by or before age 65. If everyone did retire by or before age 65, then taking away mandatory retirement would not keep youngsters out of jobs. Thus, the journalist must be assuming that if mandatory retirement was stopped, then some people would keep working past age 65.

Step 4: Evaluate the Answer Choices
(E) matches the prediction. The Denial Test confirms this as the right answer: "If retirement ceases to be mandatory at age 65, *no one* will choose to work past 65." In that case, there'd be no reason for the journalist's recommendation.

(A) goes Outside the Scope by merely correlating someone's age with the number of years they have worked. **(A)** has nothing to do with the effect that ending mandatory retirement would have on young people. Even if there is a small minority of people that, for example, started working at

age 20 and worked 40 years until age 60, the journalist's argument still holds.

(B) is Extreme because it focuses on "all young people." In the evidence, when the journalist discusses young people, the focus is specifically on those young people who have trained for a profession. This need not be "all young people."

(C) is a Distortion of the evidence. The argument doesn't require this. Even if it *is* fair for a young person not to get a job in the profession in which he or she was trained, he or she will probably still be dissatisfied, which is something the journalist cites as an "unacceptable outcome."

(D) goes Outside the Scope by introducing a bad consequence of *keeping* mandatory retirement. In contrast, the argument is about bad consequences of stopping mandatory retirement.

16. (B) Weaken

Step 1: Identify the Question Type
This is a Weaken question because the correct answer "most seriously weakens" the argument in the stimulus.

Step 2: Untangle the Stimulus
Break down the argument into evidence and conclusion. The conclusion opens the stimulus. The editorial's main point is that it is not so hard to teach preschoolers. The evidence, following the word *for*, comes in two pieces. First, preschoolers have strict systems that are good for learning. Second, preschoolers are very curious about new things.

Step 3: Make a Prediction
The editorial explicitly declares that preschoolers' strict systems are good for learning. But the editorial never says that their curiosity is good for learning. Thus, the editorial must be assuming that curiosity is good for learning and that this makes it easier to teach preschoolers. This overlooks the possibility that their curiosity might make preschoolers difficult students. The correct answer will weaken the argument by suggesting that something about preschoolers' curiosity actually makes it difficult to teach them.

Step 4: Evaluate the Answer Choices
(B) matches the prediction by suggesting that preschoolers' curiosity might make it difficult to teach them. A weakener need not disprove the conclusion, only make it less likely.

(A) explains why preschoolers develop strict routines, but says nothing about how difficult it is to teach preschoolers.

(C) goes Outside the Scope by discussing older children rather than preschoolers.

(D) is an Irrelevant Comparison of preschoolers to older children. Because the stimulus does not describe how easy it is to teach older children, comparing preschoolers to them says nothing about how easy it is to teach preschoolers.

(E) could be seen as an Irrelevant Comparison (because it compares preschool teachers to other teachers), Outside the Scope (because it focuses on stress levels rather than difficulty of teaching), or a strengthener (because, if anything, lower stress levels would seem to suggest easier teaching).

17. (A) Flaw

Step 1: Identify the Question Type

Because the correct answer describes the grounds on which the argument in the stimulus is "most vulnerable to criticism," this is a Flaw question.

Step 2: Untangle the Stimulus

Break down the argument into evidence and conclusion. The conclusion follows [*t*]*hus* at the end of the stimulus. The lawyer's main point is that an overall collection of circumstantial evidence is still valid, even if a few of its pieces are discredited. The evidence draws an analogy between rope and the overall collection of evidence.

Step 3: Make a Prediction

Because the evidence is an analogy, the lawyer's assumption is that the rope and the collection of evidence really are similar (because they both can be strengthened by adding extra strands). This assumption overlooks a crucial distinction between rope and evidence though. In rope, each strand that makes up the rope is equally as important as the others. In a collection of evidence, however, some pieces are much more important than others. For example, a piece of evidence that helps put the accused criminal's DNA at the scene of the crime could be much more important than a piece of evidence that merely demonstrates something about the accused criminal's phone record.

Step 4: Evaluate the Answer Choices

(A) matches the prediction.

(B) is a 180. In contrast to (B), the lawyer is trying to show that the overall strength of the collection of evidence is *more*—not *less*—than the sum of its parts.

(C) is a Distortion. The lawyer refers to a situation where "a few items" of evidence are discredited, not where "many items" are discredited. Although no definite values can be placed on those terms, the lawyer does not necessarily fail to consider that a body of circumstantial evidence can eventually be weakened if *enough* pieces of evidence are discredited. Given the analogy, the lawyer argued that "if one strand breaks," the rope is not broken. Sticking to that analogy, at some point if too many strands break, then the rope is indeed broken.

(D) is another Distortion. The lawyer demonstrates that a collection of evidence and a rope have at least one thing in common: they both get stronger as you add more pieces. Although arguments by analogy tend to be weak, the lawyer

in this instance did at least point out one shared characteristic.

(E) is Outside the Scope. It accuses the lawyer of circular reasoning. Circular reasoning occurs when the evidence is the same as the conclusion. Here, the evidence provides different information (the rope analogy) than the conclusion.

18. (E) Principle (Identify/Assumption)

Step 1: Identify the Question Type

This is an Identify the Principle question because the correct answer is the principle to which the reasoning in the stimulus *conforms*. Because the question stem mentions the ethicist's *reasoning*, the principle will act like an assumption that underlies the argument.

Step 2: Untangle the Stimulus

Break down the argument into evidence and conclusion. The ethicist's conclusion is the last part of the last sentence of the stimulus. Basically, the ethicist's main point is that an argument to preserve nature based on its beauty is logically stronger than an argument to preserve nature based on its moral value. The ethicist gives two pieces of evidence. First, the fact that people find nature beautiful is a reason to preserve nature. Second, it is philosophically undeniable that nature is beautiful, whereas it is disputable whether nature is morally valuable.

Step 3: Make a Prediction

The correct answer will state the argument's assumption in general terms. Generalized, the conclusion suggests that one kind of argument (preserving nature on the basis of beauty) is logically stronger than another (preserving nature on the basis of morals). Generalized, the evidence suggests that the stronger kind of argument is a reason in itself (people find nature beautiful) and is philosophically undeniable. Therefore, the correct answer will state that an argument for preserving nature is stronger when it is based on something that is a reason in itself and is philosophically undeniable.

Step 4: Evaluate the Answer Choices

(E) matches the prediction.

(A) is a Distortion because the ethicist thinks that the stronger argument for preserving nature is based on what makes nature worth preserving (i.e., its beauty). So, the ethicist does not seek to *avoid* the issue of what makes nature worth preserving.

(B) is another Distortion. Just because the ethicist suggests that an argument based on beauty is *stronger* than an argument based on morals does not mean that an argument based on morals "does not provide a sufficient reason for preserving nature." The ethicist may believe an argument based on morals is still convincing, just not *as* convincing as one based on beauty.

(C) fails to address the issue of what kind of argument for preserving nature is logically stronger. The principle in **(C)** applies to the stimulus by saying that if it is disputable that nature has moral value, then nature would be more worth preserving if it did not have moral value. It would be Extreme to say that just because the ethicist says an argument emphasizing beauty is *stronger* that the ethicist would say that nature has *no* moral value.

(D) is Extreme and possibly a 180. According to the ethicist, beauty, *not* moral value, is the better argument for preserving nature. Although it's possible that the ethicist believes **(D)**, the argument definitely doesn't conform to the idea that *anything* morally valuable is worth preserving.

19. (A) Inference

Step 1: Identify the Question Type
This is an Inference question because the correct answer "must be true" on the basis of the statements in the stimulus.

Step 2: Untangle the Stimulus
Make an inventory of statements, paraphrasing as you read. First, there will be a textbook with essays from different authors. At least one of three authors (Lind, Knight, or Jones) will be included. At most two of the three authors will be included. If Knight is included, then Jones is, too.

Step 3: Make a Prediction
This stimulus resembles a Selection game from Logic Games. To predict the right answer, combine the statements about number requirements with the Formal Logic statement. The Formal Logic statement and its contrapositive are as follows:

If	Knight	→	Jones

If	~ Jones	→	~ Knight

So, if Knight is selected, then Jones is, too. That means the maximum number has been reached and Lind must be rejected.

If	Knight	→	~ Lind

And the contrapositive of that statement must also be true (otherwise, all three would be selected):

If	Lind	→	~ Knight

While there could be other statements that must be true based on this stimulus, the stimulus seems designed to lead to the prediction that if Lind is selected, then Knight must be rejected. Scan the answer choices looking for that statement,

knowing that if it isn't there, you can eliminate wrong answers by checking them against the information in the stimulus.

Step 4: Evaluate the Answer Choices
(A) matches the prediction. If the textbook includes Lind, it can't also include Jones because an appearance by Jones would also mean an appearance by Knight. Then all three authors would be there in violation of the prohibition that the textbook cannot contain all three authors.

(B) is possible, but does not have to be true. It could be false because the textbook could contain two essays, one each by Jones and Knight. It could also include two essays, one each by Lind and Jones. Although the stimulus says the textbook contains essays by "several different authors," it does not say that Jones, Knight, and Lind are the *only* possibilities, so it's possible that just one of them appears in the textbook.

(C) could be false. Knight's essay could be included along with Jones's, or Knight could also be the only one of the three authors in the textbook.

(D) could be false. It is possible to select Lind and reject Jones (which would lead to rejecting Knight), leaving Lind as the only one of the three authors in the textbook. Although the stimulus says the textbook contains essays by "several different authors," it does not say that Jones, Knight, and Lind are the *only* possibilities. If they were the only three possibilities, then **(D)** would definitely be true because Lind and Knight were deduced to be mutually exclusive, so including Lind would also mean including Jones to reach "several authors." However, the stimulus does not limit the textbook to just those three, so **(D)** need not be true.

(E) could be false. It is possible to reject Lind and select either both Knight and Jones or just Jones.

20. (D) Assumption (Necessary)

Step 1: Identify the Question Type
This is a Necessary Assumption question, because the correct answer is "an assumption on which the argument depends."

Step 2: Untangle the Stimulus
Identify the argument's evidence and conclusion. The conclusion opens the stimulus. The author's main point is that the development of intelligent brains in mammals is related to mammals' ability to control their body temperature. The evidence comes in a logical chain. The brain is a chemical machine in which reactions must occur at proper temperatures. Because mammals have internal thermostats, the chemical reactions in mammal brains occur at the proper temperatures.

Step 3: Make a Prediction
Predict the assumption using the mismatched concepts. Both the evidence and conclusion discuss body temperature. However, only the conclusion discusses intelligence, and only

the evidence discusses chemical reactions. Therefore, the author must be assuming that chemical reactions factor into the development of intelligence.

Step 4: Evaluate the Answer Choices

(D) matches the prediction. Applying the Denial Test would give a denied answer of "the development of intelligence *is* independent of chemical reactions taking place at the proper temperature." If that was the case, the author's conclusion that intelligence is related to the ability to control body temperature would fall apart.

(A) goes Outside the Scope by discussing animals that *cannot* control their internal temperatures. Nothing would *need* to be true about such animals for the author's conclusion to be properly drawn.

(B) is Extreme by ruling out the possibility that animals besides mammals might control their internal temperature. The argument is only about mammals, and even if there were some other animals with the capacity, the author's argument would not be ruined, so **(B)** is not necessary.

(C) is Extreme. We know that chemical reactions at the proper temperature are a *factor* in the development of intelligence in mammals, but we do not know that mammal intelligence absolutely depends on chemical reactions at the proper temperature. Said another way, chemical reactions may be part of a sufficient group of factors for intelligence, but they are not a prerequisite.

(E), like **(A)**, goes Outside the Scope by discussing animals that cannot control their internal temperatures. Furthermore, although those animals' internal temperatures may not be controlled, it is a Distortion to say that they have *unpredictable* chemical processes.

21. (C) Inference

Step 1: Identify the Question Type

Because the statements in the stimulus "strongly support" the correct answer, this is an Inference question.

Step 2: Untangle the Stimulus

Make an inventory of statements, paraphrasing as you read. First, a hazardous waste storage site has been proposed. Some people object to it, saying that it could fail to contain the waste. The author thinks that it is very unlikely that the site will fail to contain the waste. The author also thinks that it is risky to delay moving the site from its current unsafe location. Next, the author suggests that waiting for a different, new location would result in the site remaining in its current location for many years. Finally, keeping the site in its current location for many years is unacceptably dangerous.

Step 3: Make a Prediction

The stimulus focuses on the question of where to store the hazardous waste, and there appear to be three possibilities.

First, the waste can stay where it is, but the author thinks that is unacceptably dangerous. Second, an entirely new location for the waste could possibly be located, but that would lead to keeping the waste where it currently is, and that would be unacceptably dangerous. Finally, the waste could be moved to the proposed site, which appears to be the safest of the three alternatives because the risk of the new site failing is low.

Step 4: Evaluate the Answer Choices

(C) matches the prediction. Of the three possible options for the site's location, moving the waste to the proposed site appears to be the safest.

(A) goes Outside the Scope by focusing on what should have happened in the past. The stimulus gives us no information about what the options for storing the waste were when the current location was started. By contrast, the stimulus is about what should happen to the waste now and in the future.

(B) contradicts the stimulus because looking for the "most secure location that can ever be found" would possibly take a long time, and that would mean keeping the waste in its current unsafe location for a long time.

(D) is Extreme by proposing a general principle for moving waste, rather than addressing the specific question of where the waste discussed in the stimulus should go.

(E) is also Extreme. While the author thinks that the proposed site would be safer than the present site, the stimulus does not suggest that *any* site would be safer.

22. (B) Paradox (EXCEPT)

Step 1: Identify the Question Type

Because the four incorrect answers will "resolve the survey's apparently paradoxical results," this is a Paradox EXCEPT question. The correct answer will either deepen the apparent paradox or go outside the scope of the paradox.

Step 2: Untangle the Stimulus

First, read to understand why the survey's results seem to be paradoxical. On the one hand, it appears that people are reading fewer books each year. On the other hand, bookstores are profiting more over the same period of time. How can these facts both be true at the same time?

Step 3: Make a Prediction

In Logical Reasoning EXCEPT questions, predict the four incorrect answers. In this question, the incorrect answers will each provide new information about book purchasers or bookstores that will explain how it is that bookstores profit more even though people read fewer books. For example, it could be that increased profits of bookstores are due to the sales of products besides books (magazines, games, beverages, etc.). Alternatively, it could be that bookstores have marked up the prices on books so that they profit more even though they sell fewer books. Remember that there will be four answers that resolve the paradox, so there must be many different ideas that would show how bookstores profit more even though fewer books are read.

Step 4: Evaluate the Answer Choices

(B) is irrelevant and therefore correct. **(B)** suggests that shoplifting from bookstores has remained stable. This idea goes Outside the Scope of the paradox because it provides no way in which the profits of bookstores could actually increase (it "has left bookstores largely unaffected"). There is also no explanation for a decrease in the average number of books read.

(A) resolves the paradox by suggesting that people who used to get books at public libraries might now have to buy them from bookstores. This would lead to an increase in bookstores' profits even though people are reading fewer books. Alternatively, even if people aren't buying them at bookstores, the change at libraries may just explain the decrease in the number of books read if library-goers are reading less because new contemporary novels are unavailable there. Either way, one side of the paradox is affected.

(C) resolves the paradox by suggesting that bookstores' increased profits are due to coffee sales.

(D) resolves the paradox by suggesting that bookstores' increased profits are due to selling more lucrative books.

(E) resolves the paradox by suggesting that bookstores' increased profits are due to people purchasing individual magazine issues at bookstores instead of subscribing to magazines.

23. (D) Parallel Reasoning

Step 1: Identify the Question Type

Because the correct answer has *reasoning* that is "similar to" the reasoning of the argument in the stimulus, this is a Parallel Reasoning question.

Step 2: Untangle the Stimulus

Identify the argument's evidence and conclusion. The conclusion follows [t]*herefore* in the last sentence. The evidence is in the first sentence.

Step 3: Make a Prediction

In order to find the parallel argument, characterize the naturalist's conclusion and then compare it to the conclusion of each of the answer choices, eliminating answer choices with conclusions that do not match the naturalist's. The naturalist's conclusion is an explanation that an action (cutting down trees) is not causing some consequence (threatening the species) but that the way in which the action is being performed (rapidly cutting down trees) is causing the consequence. If necessary, compare the evidence of an

answer choice against the evidence of the conclusion. The naturalist's evidence is a general principle about what really leads to a given outcome (rapid environmental change is what really leads to species loss).

Step 4: Evaluate the Answer Choices

(D) matches the reasoning structure of the stimulus. An action (change) is not causing some consequence (fear), but the way in which the action is being performed (without fully informing the employees) is causing the consequence.

(A) fails to match the naturalist's conclusion. It does not reject one potential cause in favor of another. **(A)**'s conclusion could be rewritten to match the naturalist's conclusion as follows: the problem is not that we are using fossil fuels, but rather that we are using them too quickly. However, the evidence still differs because in the stimulus the species can continue to survive indefinitely, but in **(A)** it says that the fossil fuel supply is limited.

(B) fails to match the naturalist's conclusion. **(B)**'s conclusion is a recommendation, whereas the naturalist's is an explanation. There is also no parallel in the stimulus to the *well* versus *adequate* distinction in **(B)**.

(C) arguably matches parts of the conclusion. An action (studying) is not causing some consequence (doing well in school), but the way in which the action is being performed (thoroughly) is causing the consequence. However, certain aspects of **(C)** are not parallel. First, its evidence begins with "[s]ome students," whereas the stimulus presents a principle about species in general, not just *some* species. Second, **(C)** states what is "most important," whereas the stimulus does not make such an extreme assertion. Finally, **(C)**'s evidence fails to match the naturalist's evidence because it merely presents a correlation between two things (studying thoroughly and doing well in school), but the evidence in the stimulus suggests a causal relationship (rapid change causes species extinction).

(E) fails to match the naturalist's conclusion. **(E)** explains that two factors (soil rapidly eroding and no replacement for good soil) cause a consequence (decline of agriculture).

24. (A) Method of Argument

Step 1: Identify the Question Type

This is a Method of Argument question because the correct answer will describe how the argument in the stimulus *proceeds*.

Step 2: Untangle the Stimulus

Start by paraphrasing the stimulus. First, the professor compares two different people and considers one to be more free than the other. Based on the comparison, the professor suggests that real freedom cannot be determined quantitatively because another factor ("the extent of differences among the alternatives") matters.

Step 3: Make a Prediction

As indicated by the phrase "[i]t is clear, then," the conclusion is the second sentence of the stimulus. The evidence is the first sentence. The evidence is a very specific example (about two particular people and their choices of beverage), but the conclusion is a general principle (about how to measure meaningful freedom). Thus, the correct answer will suggest that the argument proceeds by using a specific example as evidence for a general principle.

Step 4: Evaluate the Answer Choices

(A) matches the prediction.

(B) is a Distortion of the argument's structure. It confuses evidence for conclusion and vice versa. It should be that the professor draws a conclusion that is a general principle on the basis of a particular case, rather than the reverse.

(C) goes Outside the Scope because there is no analogy in the stimulus. An analogy is a statement that one thing is similar to (or "analogous to") another thing. The professor does not compare beverage selection to the principle about freedom. Instead, the beverage selection is an example of quantitative versus qualitative choice. Consider that the stimulus could be reorganized with the conclusion first, and then the evidence preceded by the phrase "for example." However, it would not make sense to reorganize the stimulus with the conclusion first, and then the evidence preceded by the phrase "A similar case would be that ..."

(D) goes Outside the Scope because the conclusion is not about a "whole group." In fact, a "whole group" is never mentioned in the stimulus.

(E) is a Distortion of the evidence. It suggests that it is a principle that is more general than the conclusion, when the evidence is actually a very specific example about beverages.

25. (C) Strengthen

Step 1: Identify the Question Type

Although the stimulus contains a principle, this is a Strengthen question because the principle has already been identified and applied within the stimulus. The correct answer just "justifies the stated application of the principle." However, even if you did technically characterize the question as a Principle question, it shouldn't have changed how to approach Step 2.

Step 2: Untangle the Stimulus

Conveniently, the stimulus is divided into principle and application. Paraphrase them both. The principle has two components. First, a meeting should be kept short, and it should be relevant to most of the people attending. Second, if a meeting is altogether irrelevant to a person, then that person should not be required to attend the meeting. The application states that Terry should not be required to attend a meeting.

Step 3: Make a Prediction

The correct answer will support the judgment that Terry should not be required to attend the meeting. The second piece of the principle gives a situation when somebody should not be required to attend a meeting. So, if the meeting will address no issues that are relevant to Terry, then Terry should not be required to attend the meeting. The correct answer could follow just that piece of logic, but doing so would leave out the first piece of the principle, and that seems unlikely. However, the two pieces of the principle can be combined. The first piece indicates that a meeting should address those issues that are relevant to a majority of those attending. Thus, the correct answer will state that none of the issues that the meeting should address (i.e., those that are relevant to a majority of those attending) are relevant to Terry.

Step 4: Evaluate the Answer Choices

(C) matches the prediction.

(A) goes Outside the Scope by introducing the idea of making a presentation.

(B), like **(A)**, goes Outside the Scope by introducing the idea of making a presentation.

(D) addresses the first piece of the principle, but not the second. According to **(D)**, Terry's attendance will alter what should be discussed in the meeting. However, **(D)** fails to show that Terry should not be required to attend the meeting because it never connects what will be discussed at the meeting (whether he attends or not) and what is relevant to Terry.

(E) is a Distortion. It fails to match the second piece of the principle, which would support Terry not going to the meeting if *none* of the issues to be discussed are relevant to him. But if the issues relevant to Terry are simply less than a majority of the issues, there may still be many issues relevant to Terry. Even if there's just a single issue that is relevant to Terry, the principle does not recommend Terry not attend. **(E)** distorts the use of "the majority" to refer to the majority of issues, rather than the majority of those in attendance.

Section IV: Reading Comprehension

Passage 1: Wing Tek Lum's Poetry

Q#	Question Type	Correct	Difficulty
1	Global	A	★
2	Inference	C	★★
3	Logic Function	D	★★
4	Detail	C	★★
5	Logic Function	D	★
6	Inference	D	★

Passage 2: The Study of Common Law

Q#	Question Type	Correct	Difficulty
7	Global	D	★★
8	Inference	A	★★★★
9	Inference	C	★★
10	Inference	E	★★
11	Inference	D	★★★
12	Detail	B	★
13	Inference	B	★★★
14	Global	A	★★★★

Passage 3: University Research and Business Interests

Q#	Question Type	Correct	Difficulty
15	Detail	A	★
16	Detail	C	★
17	Detail	D	★
18	Inference	C	★
19	Inference	D	★★★★

Passage 4: Controlling Crop Pests by Predation

Q#	Question Type	Correct	Difficulty
20	Global	C	★
21	Logic Reasoning (Principle)	D	★★★
22	Detail	E	★
23	Inference	A	★★★★
24	Inference	C	★★★
25	Logic Function	D	★★★
26	Logic Reasoning (Strengthen)	E	★★
27	Inference	A	★★★

Passage 1: Wing Tek Lum's Poetry

Step 1: Read the Passage Strategically
Sample Roadmap

line #	Keyword/phrase	¶ Margin notes
2	generally	
3	one of two ways : either	2 characteristics of Asian Amer poems
4	or	
6	such as	
8	striking	Lum's poems transcend
9	no	
10	while	
12	does not do so at the expense	explore traditional themes, but tie to local lifestyle
14	informed by	
19	different	
21	In one	Ex. celebration
23	both	
25	while	
27	equally important	old ties
28	hence	new identity
30	significant	
32–33	as well as	
37	refuses	Ex. Chinese poet praise some traditions
38	instead	
39	elitist	criticize others
42	complex	Ex. relation between heritage and local culture
44–45	vastly disparate	
47	avoids; excessively	
48	while	
50	central	
53	hopeful; however	to form new identity, balance individual success with homeland tradition
54	caution; strong	
55	emphasis	
57	difficult should be	

Discussion

Paragraph 1 begins by describing two ways in which Asian American poetry from Hawaii is generally characterized: as portraying a multicultural paradise or as exploring familiar Asian American literary themes. Then the author introduces someone whose work transcends the general rule. In this case, that's poet Wing Tek Lum. By introducing Lum in this way, we get a sense of the **Topic** (Lum's poems), **Scope** (Lum's individual style of writing), and **Purpose** (to discuss how Lum's poems differ from typical Asian American poetry).

In the second half of the paragraph, the author explains what makes Lum's poetry so striking, thus setting up the **Main Idea** of the passage: Lum's voice is distinctive because he explores traditional Asian American literary themes, but relates them to the local Hawaiian lifestyle and population. The remaining paragraphs offer three examples of Lum's poetry that support this idea.

Paragraph 2 includes details about two of Lum's poems. In the first, he attends a traditional Chinese celebration that lets him distinguish between homeland life and Hawaiian life and how important it is to have ties to both. In the second, he praises a famous Chinese poet, yet refuses to give in entirely to tradition by criticizing some celebrated Chinese poets.

Paragraph 3 discusses a poem that expresses the dreams of Asian immigrants for a communal local society, but also stresses the importance of retaining ties to the homeland in order to develop a healthy sense of identity.

1. (A) Global

Step 2: Identify the Question Type

This is a Global question because it asks for the "main point" of the entire passage.

Step 3: Research the Relevant Text

No need to go back into passage. Just use the Main Idea that was determined in Step 1.

Step 4: Make a Prediction

The multiple examples in the last two paragraphs support the main point discussed in paragraph 1: Lum's poems differ from typical Asian American poetry in that they explore traditional themes, but relate them to local Hawaiian life.

Step 5: Evaluate the Answer Choices

(A) matches the author's assessment of Lum's poetry.

(B) is too narrow, focusing too much on the details of the poem mentioned in paragraph 3. Also, the phrase "in part" suggests that this answer only focuses on one aspect of the passage as opposed to the overall main idea.

(C) is a Distortion. Lum does reject the romanticized notion of multicultural life (a popular literary tradition of Hawaiian writers), but he actually accepts some traditional literary

features (lines 10–12). More importantly, this answer ignores the scope of the passage: Lum's individual style and unique voice.

(D) is a Distortion. Lum's perspective is only described as his own, not as illustrative of others poets' perspectives. He may use his own perspective to illustrate other Asian American Hawaiians in general, but not the narrow scope of just Asian American *writers*.

(E) is Out of Scope. The author never judges the value of Lum's poems, let alone suggests they're *unsuccessful*. In fact, the author's reference to the poems as *striking* (line 8) suggests a more positive assessment, if anything.

2. (C) Inference

Step 2: Identify the Question Type

This is an Inference question because it asks for something that Lum is "most likely to believe."

Step 3: Research the Relevant Text

Lum's opinions are certainly not restricted to one section of the passage. They are exemplified in the three poems discussed in the last two paragraphs.

Step 4: Make a Prediction

There are many opinions ascribed to Lum throughout the last two paragraphs. Predicting the right opinion won't be possible, so test the answer choices individually, making sure to stay within the scope of the passage.

Step 5: Evaluate the Answer Choices

(C) is supported by the last sentence (lines 53–59), in which Lum's poem suggests that people should identify the struggle between individual success and retaining homeland traditions.

(A) is Out of Scope. Images are brought up in paragraph 3, but it's never suggested that these images be explained to assist a reader's comprehension.

(B) is Extreme. While Lum's situation has allowed for a unique perspective on cultural traditions, it's never suggested that living away from home is *necessary* for developing a healthy perspective.

(D) is a Distortion. Lum's poems do recognize an identity "flux within Hawaiian society" (line 33). However, poetry is meant to reflect that, not make it static.

(E) is a 180. As the last sentence says, it's difficult, but that struggle should be identified and can be responded to in ways that allow for both a new identity and a connection to cultural traditions.

3. (D) Logic Function

Step 2: Identify the Question Type

The phrase "in order to" indicates that this is asking *why* the author uses the cited phrase. That makes this a Logic Function question.

Step 3: Research the Relevant Text

The question references line 33, but it's important to consider the surrounding text for context.

Step 4: Make a Prediction

This "flux within Hawaiian society" is described as "integral to [Hawaii's] heterogeneity" (line 34), and this diversity comes from the immigrants mentioned in Lum's poems (lines 30–31). So, the flux refers to Hawaii's diverse society, which undergoes changes due to the introduction of immigrants.

Step 5: Evaluate the Answer Choices

(D) matches the author's references to change and diversity (i.e., heterogeneity).

(A) is a Distortion. The flux is described as integral to heterogeneity, not to any unmentioned tension among Hawaiian citizens.

(B) is a Faulty Use of Detail. The distinction between Hawaiian and continental Asian Americans is discussed in lines 15–20. Furthermore, those lines suggest that the societies are distinct.

(C) is Out of Scope. The author never actually identifies the actual process by which immigrants adapt.

(E) is a Distortion. The flux describes a change to "Hawaiian society," not to immigrants' attitudes toward traditional culture. Lines 31–34 refer to traditional culture "as well as" the flux, so Lum's references to traditional culture and this flux are two separate things.

4. (C) Detail

Step 2: Identify the Question Type

The question asks how some literature has been characterized "[a]ccording to the passage," which means this will be a Detail lifted straight from the passage.

Step 3: Research the Relevant Text

Asian American literature from Hawaii (particularly poems) is characterized at the very beginning of the passage (lines 1–6).

Step 4: Make a Prediction

The opening lines provide two characterizations: 1) they describe a multicultural paradise, and 2) they explore Asian American themes, such as generational conflict. The correct answer will describe one of these.

Step 5: Evaluate the Answer Choices

(C) refers to the "generational conflict" (conflict between different age groups).

(A) is Out of Scope. No literature in the passage is described as preventing the formation of a local identity.

(B) is a Faulty Use of Detail. "Individual drive" is mentioned in line 55 as something emphasized in U.S. culture, not in Asian American literature.

(D) is a Distortion. Only Lum is said to focus on retaining such ties, but this is not part of how Asian American literature is *characterized* in general. Furthermore, the word *primarily* is Extreme because even Lum does not treat retaining ties to the homeland as the primary focus.

(E) is another Distortion. This matches something Lum focuses on, but it is not part of the general characterization of Asian American literature.

5. (D) Logic Function

Step 2: Identify the Question Type

The phrase "in order to" indicates this question is asking *why* the author calls Lum's work *striking*. That makes this a Logic Function question.

Step 3: Research the Relevant Text

The question refers to lines 7–8, but be sure to use surrounding lines for context.

Step 4: Make a Prediction

The author calls the work *striking* because it "demands to be understood on its own terms." The words "[i]n this light" at the beginning of the sentence also suggest that calling it *striking* is a response to the previous sentence, which describes typical Hawaiian Asian American poetry. So, the author calls it *striking* because it has its own style that is different from typical Asian American poetry.

Step 5: Evaluate the Answer Choices

(D) matches the author's comparison of Lum's work to other Asian American works.

(A) is not supported. The author doesn't directly describe the work as forceful or contentious, especially not in the context of this sentence.

(B) is Out of Scope. There's no discussion of literary critics in this passage.

(C) is an Irrelevant Comparison. The passage discusses the difference between Lum's work and typical Asian American poetry, not between Lum's earlier and later work.

(E) is Out of Scope. This passage is not concerned with poetic form.

6. (D) Inference

Step 2: Identify the Question Type

The question asks for something with which the author is "most likely to agree." That makes this an Inference question.

Step 3: Research the Relevant Text
The entire passage is about Lum's poetry, so it is all relevant.

Step 4: Make a Prediction
It will be inefficient to predict a specific inference, so test the answers one at a time, and stay focused on the author's Scope and Purpose.

Step 5: Evaluate the Answer Choices
(D) is supported throughout the passage. There are frequent references to Lum assessing both homeland traditions and building a new identity (lines 10–13, lines 25–29, lines 54–59).

(A) is unsupported. The author never indicates any negative reaction to Lum's work and never mentions political ideology.

(B) is a Distortion. While Lum does appreciate *one* poet in his ode to Li Po (lines 34–40), he makes no mention of showing appreciation for "stylistic contributions."

(C) is Extreme. There is no mention of the "most fruitful" way to understand his works. Moreover, Lum's poems (which don't refer to people making a "choice between new and old") are distinctly Hawaiian; they don't necessarily apply to *any* human in *any* culture.

(E) is a 180. In lines 25–26, Lum identifies ties to his homeland as "comforting and necessary," which hardly conveys antipathy.

Passage 2: The Study of Common Law

Step 1: Read the Passage Strategically
Sample Roadmap

line #	Keyword/phrase	¶ Margin notes
1	weighs heavily	Common law
5	frequently required	British law students study ...
7	based solely on	
10	basis both	
12–13	not only; but also	Need history to understand common law
14	cannot properly be understood without	
16	Yet	
17	seldom	Yet modern study ignores evolution
20	ignore	
21	significance; reasons	2 reasons:
22	partly; partly	
23		1. Theoretical
27	deemphasizes	laws seen as static
28	in favor of	
29	no more than	
31		2. Political
32	necessary	
33	far from	
34	seldom	
35	requires	retain appearance of fairness
37–38	To suggest otherwise; dispiriting	
39	demoralizing	
40	argued	Goodrich opinion:
41	however; most fruitfully	
42	rather than	common law should be seen as evolutionary
48	as influential as	
49–50	as significant as; as strong as	
51	not only	common law adapts to contemporary circumstances
52–53	but also	

Discussion

The first sentence of paragraph 1 introduces the **Topic** of the passage: common law. The paragraph discusses how contemporary students study the history of common law and ends with the sentiment that taking a historic look at common law is necessary to understanding it.

Paragraph 2 opens with [*y*]*et*, which signals a sudden shift in tone. Despite the importance of studying the history of common law, academics rarely treat it as historically evolving. That leads to the **Scope** of the passage: the contradiction within the study of common law—academics focus on the history of common law but don't treat it as evolving throughout history.

The second half of paragraph 2 offers two reasons for this: First is a theoretical reason: academics consider common law to be a static set of rules that can be studied consistently at any given time. Second is a political reason: people need to believe the law is based on pure logic, otherwise it could be seen as unfair and people would feel dispirited.

Paragraph 3 finally brings in an opinion about the current academic approach to common law. Historian Peter Goodrich argues against the reasoning in paragraph 2 by suggesting that common law should be studied as a continually developing system, not a set of purely logical rules. According to Goodrich, the history of common law serves to illustrate how it has developed over time to adapt to contemporary circumstances.

Lacking a strong authorial opinion, the **Purpose** of the passage is to merely describe the unusual thinking behind common law study and introduce an opinion suggesting a new line of thinking. The **Main Idea** is that the study of common law focuses on its history, but it is rarely treated as historically evolutionary, which one historian suggests it should be.

7. (D) Global

Step 2: Identify the Question Type
This question asks for the "main idea" of the whole passage, making it a Global question.

Step 3: Research the Relevant Text
Because it's a Global question, the whole passage is relevant. Use the Main Idea from Step 1 as a prediction.

Step 4: Make a Prediction
The correct answer will discuss the unusual concept of studying the history of common law while rarely considering its historical evolution. The answer will also incorporate Goodrich's opinion that common law *should* be studied as a developing phenomenon.

Step 5: Evaluate the Answer Choices
(D) matches the theme of the passage piece by piece.

(A) is too narrow, focusing on minor details from paragraph 1 while completely ignoring the rest of the passage.

(B) is a Distortion. The second paragraph discusses both theoretical and political reasoning for how common law is studied. But the interpretations are not presented as "at odds with" each other.

(C) is a Distortion. While the first paragraph calls common law *unwritten*, it's not exactly described as an "oral history." Also, in the last paragraph (lines 42–43), Goodrich says that common law should *not* be studied as a set of rules.

(E) is Half-Right/Half-Wrong. Yes, common law is studied as unitary and logical. However, nothing in the passage suggests that common law shows the body of law to be inconsistent and unfair.

8. (A) Inference

Step 2: Identify the Question Type
The question asks for something the author would believe that can be *inferred* from the passage. That makes this an Inference question.

Step 3: Research the Relevant Text
The question asks about how the "history of law" (seen at the end of paragraph 1) relates to "modern jurisprudence" (which shows up in paragraph 2).

Step 4: Make a Prediction
At the end of paragraph 1, the author mentions how understanding common law requires "a long historical view" (line 15). However, in lines 16–21, the author complains that modern jurisprudence *seldom* does this and can even "ignore the practical contemporary significance of its historical forms." That means modern jurisprudence fails to allow people to properly understand legal history.

Step 5: Evaluate the Answer Choices
(A) matches the idea of the misguided nature of modern jurisprudence.

(B) is a 180. The author directly says that historical forms of common law *are* relevant to modern jurisprudence—some current studies just ignore that (lines 18–21).

(C) expresses the exact opposite of what Goodrich says in paragraph 3 (lines 41–43). The author never disputes Goodrich. If anything, the use of Goodrich as an example suggests that the author agrees with him, making this a 180.

(D) is a 180. In the author's view, contemporary jurisprudence overemphasizes order and coherence at the expense of history (lines 26–28).

(E) is a Distortion. The author does accuse the mainstream theories of ignoring history, but admits that they do so in an attempt to *avoid* dispiriting people (lines 37–39).

9. (C) Inference

Step 2: Identify the Question Type
The question asks for something that would "best exemplify" the theory described. An example won't be provided in the passage, but it will directly follow from the language used. That makes this an Inference question.

Step 3: Research the Relevant Text
The question makes reference to the first sentence of paragraph 2 (lines 16–21).

Step 4: Make a Prediction
The theories mentioned start in line 18, and are said to "acknowledge the antiquity of common law" but "ignore the practical contemporary significance." The correct answer will describe a theory that looks at history but fails to see how it relates to the present.

Step 5: Evaluate the Answer Choices
(C) matches the logic, looking at history (medieval laws) but ignoring the present (modern laws).

(A) is a 180. This *does* connect modern customs to historical practices.

(B) is also a 180. This compares historic elements of theater to modern courtroom elements.

(D) is an Irrelevant Comparison. The passage focuses solely on English laws. There's no support for a comparison to German laws.

(E) is also an Irrelevant Comparison. There's no support for comparing civil courts to criminal courts.

10. (E) Inference

Step 2: Identify the Question Type
The question directly asks for something that can be *inferred* and that Goodrich is "mostly likely to agree with." That makes this an Inference question.

Step 3: Research the Relevant Text
Goodrich's opinions on common law are laid out in paragraph 3.

Step 4: Make a Prediction
Goodrich starts out by arguing that common law should be studied as "a continually developing tradition rather than as a set of rules" (lines 41–43). He mentions how common law is like a *text* that develops throughout history (lines 45–46) and states that common law will continuously adapt to contemporary legal circumstances (lines 52–54). The correct answer will be consistent with these views.

Step 5: Evaluate the Answer Choices
(E) matches Goodrich's sentiments. Goodrich refers to common law as a sort of text (lines 44–45), one that will continuously be rewritten and adapted (lines 52–54). This suggests that things will look different in the future.

(A) is a Distortion. Goodrich suggests that common law is continually developing, but that's not to say it's a *relic*—as if it were no longer relevant. In lines 53–54, Goodrich suggests continuous rewriting of the common law to adapt to modern times, so he wouldn't argue against its use as a legal code. It's just a legal code that needs to continually evolve.

(B) is a Distortion. Again, Goodrich never takes the negative tone that common law has *degenerated*, but rather says that it has adapted to contemporary circumstances.

(C) is a 180. This is the political reason for ignoring the common law's historical evolution (lines 30–32), reasoning that Goodrich does not agree with.

(D) is another 180. Goodrich uses a literary model in his analysis, but feels that common law *does* adapt and *is* applicable to modern life.

11. (D) Inference

Step 2: Identify the Question Type
The question asks for the definition of a term used in the passage. The definition won't be provided directly, but it can be inferred based on context. That makes this an Inference question.

Step 3: Research the Relevant Text
The author uses *political* to label the line of reasoning described in lines 30–39.

Step 4: Make a Prediction
The *political* reasoning described in lines 30–39 is all about ensuring *fairness* in the law and preserving the "prestige of the legal institution." The correct answer will match this concept of upholding the reputation of the legal system.

Step 5: Evaluate the Answer Choices
(D) fits the concept of the legal institution retaining its reputation as fair so that it can remain effective.

(A) is a Distortion. This may be how *political* is used in an office environment, but not in context of the legal institution as described in the passage.

(B) is Out of Scope. There's no mention of "covert and unethical methods."

(C) is a Distortion. The political reasoning is more about maintaining prestige than it is about remaining ethical. Ethical concerns are Out of Scope.

(E) is a Distortion. Perception is a part of the concept, but it is the perception of the public, not radical theorists.

12. (B) Detail

Step 2: Identify the Question Type
The question asks for something the passage outright *states*, which makes this a Detail question.

Step 3: Research the Relevant Text
What students of British law are required to do is mentioned in lines 4–9.

Step 4: Make a Prediction
Lines 4–9 explicitly list three things students are required to do. And the only one that mentions what they *study* is the first: "medieval cases."

Step 5: Evaluate the Answer Choices
(B) matches the text.

(A) is a Distortion. Students are said to "confront doctrinal principles," but not directly study political history.

(C) is Out of Scope. The author never mentions treatises.

(D) is Out of Scope. The author never mentions Roman law, just Latin phrases.

(E) is Out of Scope. The author never mentions essays, let alone ones on "narrative development."

13. (B) Inference

Step 2: Identify the Question Type
The question asks for something that "best describes the author's opinion." That's an Inference question.

Step 3: Research the Relevant Text
The author's view on modern theories is addressed in paragraph 2.

Step 4: Make a Prediction
The author's chief complaint about modern academics is that it seldom treats common law as constantly evolving and can even ignore common law's contemporary significance.

Step 5: Evaluate the Answer Choices
(B) is correct. The "essential dimension that would increase their accuracy" is treating common law as a "constantly evolving phenomenon" (lines 17–18).

(A) is Out of Scope. The author doesn't address the level of detail in the theories.

(C) is a 180. The author mentions theories that *ignore*—rather than overemphasize—practical aspects (lines 18–21) and talks about theoretical reasons for the omissions in modern theories (lines 23–30).

(D) is a 180. According to the first paragraph, contemporary students do study historic legal cases.

(E) is either Out of Scope or a 180. The author does not explicitly attribute the terms *art* or *science* to the modern academic characterization of common law, making this Out of Scope. It could also be argued that the author suggests that modern academics treat the common law as a coherent system of rules (as a *science*), rather than as an evolving institution (as an *art*). In this case, **(E)** reverses the order of the author's characterization.

14. (A) Global

Step 2: Identify the Question Type
The question asks for the "primary purpose" of the entire passage, making this a Global question.

Step 3: Research the Relevant Text
The entire text is relevant here, so use the Purpose from Step 1.

Step 4: Make a Prediction
As predicted from the beginning, the author simply introduced the odd way in which common law is studied and offered one historian's opinion on how to better study it.

Step 5: Evaluate the Answer Choices
(A) is a match. The paradoxical structure can be seen as the author ends the first paragraph, indicating that common law "cannot be properly understood without taking a long historical view." Then the second paragraph, with the Contrast Keyword [*y*]*et*, introduces the paradox. Goodrich's view in the third paragraph is the new view of the situation.

(B) is Out of Scope. The passage references the history of common law, but offers no "chronological summary."

(C) is Out of Scope. The only theorist mentioned is Goodrich. However, he's never described as *influential*, and the author never evaluates his work—ongoing or otherwise.

(D) is Out of Scope. The passage is entirely concerned with modern academic study, not past theories. Additionally, it's only one thing—common law—that the author suggests should be studied differently; there are no other theories discussed.

(E) is a Distortion. Only Goodrich advocates a school of thought, and it's hardly considered *traditional*. Furthermore, Goodrich's theory is just a suggestion, not necessarily a new *trend*.

Passage 3: University Research and Business Interests

Step 1: Read the Passage Strategically
Sample Roadmap

line #	Keyword/phrase	¶ Margin notes
Passage A		
3	long been	Research as commodity threatens role as a public good
4	recent tendency	
5	threatens	
7	traditionally	
8–9	uniquely suited	
10	Unfortunately	Market wants results
11	ill suited	
13	impatient	
14	averse; And	discourage long-term experimentation
15	even more important; few	
16	needed	
17	shattered	
18–19	Further; since; little affinity	Results kept hidden
22	for example	
24	high price to pay	no more sharing
25	undoubted	
26	Important	
28	instead	Auth: worried about future
30	worry	
Passage B		
32	once	
33	primarily	Past: science good for public
36	thus	
38	Today; however; critical role	
40	transformed	Today: science is commodity
41	For example; exploiting	Affects legal claims re: intellectual property
47	not just; but in	
48	crucial	
49	Previously	Desire for profits affects patents
52	Today	
53	however	
55	have led to	
56	blurring; both	discovery vs. invention
57	and	
59	argues	Industry claims right to profit from discovery
61	entitled	

Discussion

The first paragraph sets up the **Topic** (treating research findings as commodities) and the **Scope** (effect on scientific research). The author of passage A is concerned that treating findings as commodities is a threat to using research for public good.

Paragraph 2 offers some detail, discussing how businesses are looking for quick results and returns on their investments. They aren't interested in thorough, long-term testing that could cultivate new ideas. Paragraph 3 offers *more* detail, per the Continuation Keyword [*f*]*urther*: with entrepreneurs buying the results, researchers no longer share ideas as often as they did in the past.

By the last paragraph, the author once again expresses concern and provides a succinct summary of the passage. The **Purpose** is to show concern about treating research as a marketable commodity. The **Main Idea** is that when investors are concerned with using research for business gains, the research is less likely to lead to discoveries that could benefit the public as a whole.

The author of passage B also discusses a shift in research from a public service to a market commodity (**Topic**), as support comes more from industries looking to make profits. However, by the end of paragraph 2, passage B starts looking at the legal side of the issue (**Scope**) and how industries look to assert legal claims to "intellectual property." The author discusses the industry's desire for profits and patents, which is causing the legal distinction between discoveries and inventions to be blurred.

This author's **Purpose** is to discuss the legal implications of industry's use of scientific research for profits and patents. The **Main Idea** is that, for industries, an important aspect of scientific research is the legal ownership of the results for use in turning out profitable products.

There is a clear relationship between both passages in that they both address the Topic of research shifting from a public good to a marketable commodity. However, more important is the distinction between passage A's concern with the ramifications for science and passage B's interest in the legal implications. This difference in Scope will be helpful in working with some of the questions.

15. (A) Detail

Step 2: Identify the Question Type
The question asks for something *discussed* in one passage, making this a Detail question about something explicitly mentioned.

Step 3: Research the Relevant Text
The detail is said to appear in passage B but not in passage A. So, the entire text of both passages is relevant.

Step 4: Make a Prediction
While there's no way to predict the exact detail the correct answer will raise, it helps to consider the key difference between the two passages. Unlike passage A, passage B contains information about the legal implications of treating research as a commodity. Anticipate that the correct answer will refer to some legal aspect of the issue.

Step 5: Evaluate the Answer Choices
(A) is correct. Passage B brings up this blurring in lines 56–57, while passage A never discusses legal issues.

(B) is a 180. Passage A discusses effects of the market throughout the second paragraph.

(C) is a 180. Passage A discusses research as a public good in the first paragraph.

(D) is a 180. Passage A brings up new pharmaceuticals (drugs and therapies) in line 25.

(E) is a 180. Passage A directly talks about "bury[ing] research" and "hiding knowledge" (lines 19–21).

16. (C) Detail

Step 2: Identify the Question Type
The question asks for something both authors explicitly state in their passages, making this a Detail question.

Step 3: Research the Relevant Text
A conflict involving a transition from one concept to another is the central Topic of both passages, so look at the opening paragraphs.

Step 4: Make a Prediction
Passage A starts off lamenting research findings switching from "a public good" to "commodities" (lines 3–6). Passage B discusses the same switch (lines 39–41). So, both passages draw a distinction between public goods and commodities.

Step 5: Evaluate the Answer Choices
(C) is a match.

(A) is Out of Scope. Neither passage discusses unsuccessful research.

(B) is a Distortion. Passage A mentions methods and results in line 24, but never puts them in opposition. Furthermore, passage B never discusses methods.

(D) is only brought up in passage B. Passage A never brings up this distinction.

(E) is Out of Scope. Both passages are concerned solely with scientific research, not any other types of inquiry.

17. (D) Detail

Step 2: Identify the Question Type
The question asks for something both passages explicitly "refer to," making this a Detail question.

Step 3: Research the Relevant Text
Without any content clues, the entire text of both passages is relevant.

Step 4: Make a Prediction
Both passages share a number of ideas, so it will be inefficient to predict all of them. Use the answer choices to guide your research, and make sure the correct answer is directly mentioned in both passages.

Step 5: Evaluate the Answer Choices
(D) is brought up in both passages. Passage A mentions biotechnology in line 22, and passage B mentions it in line 44.

(A) is mentioned in passage A (line 17), but never in passage B.

(B) is mentioned in passage A (line 29), but never in passage B.

(C) is Out of Scope. While both passages discuss science in general, neither passage explicitly refers to physics or chemistry.

(E) is mentioned in passage A (line 13), but never in passage B.

18. (C) Inference

Step 2: Identify the Question Type
The question asks for something *inferred* that both authors would *believe*, making this an Inference question.

Step 3: Research the Relevant Text
The question asks for the source of "constraint on access to scientific information." This is brought up in paragraph 3 of passage A and in the last paragraph of passage B.

Step 4: Make a Prediction
Passage A mentions how entrepreneurs "bury research" so that they can hide knowledge from their competitors (lines 19–21). Similarly, passage B mentions how the industry will keep research for its own use for the sake of a "return on its investment" (lines 61–64). Thus, both authors see the source of increased constraints as basically arising from greed: the desire to push away the competition and make money.

Step 5: Evaluate the Answer Choices
(C) matches both authors' attitudes.

(A) is Out of Scope. Neither author cites an "increase in the volume of scientific knowledge."

(B) is a Distortion. Both passages cite the desire for returns and money, but by industry as a whole, not by individual researchers. Furthermore, the lack of shared access is due to financial reasons; it's not about who gets *credit* for the work.

(D) is Out of Scope. Neither passage discusses "moral reservations."

(E) discusses "government funding," which is only discussed by the author of passage B, and no mention is made of a "drastic reduction" in such funding.

19. (D) Inference

Step 2: Identify the Question Type
The question asks for something "supported by" both passages, which means this is an Inference question.

Step 3: Research the Relevant Text
The question offers no content clues, so the entire text is relevant.

Step 4: Make a Prediction
A prediction here will be inefficient, so start by eliminating answers that focus on just one passage or go outside the scope of either passage.

Step 5: Evaluate the Answer Choices
(D) is supported by both passages. The author of passage A mentions a "reduction in the free sharing of research methods and results" (lines 23–24), indicating more access in the past. And the author of passage B mentions how, in the past, "no individual was entitled to restrict access to [the benefits of research]" (lines 36–37).

(A) is a Distortion. Both passages discuss the increase in research funded by the biotech industry, but nothing in either passage suggests that researchers are leaving universities to work in private labs. In fact, the passages imply that the biotech industry is funding the universities.

(B) is another Distortion. Passage A mentions patents only in passing in the last paragraph. And, while the author of passage B discusses the legal implications for patents, there's nothing to suggest that the industry's patents are *invalid*.

(C) is a Faulty Use of Detail. It mentions a distinction between discoveries and inventions, which is only discussed in passage B, whereas the question stem calls for a statement supported by *both* passages.

(E) is a 180. The author of passage B states in the first paragraph that government-funded research was originally perceived as being motivated by what was in the public good.

Passage 4: Controlling Crop Pests by Predation

Step 1: Read the Passage Strategically
Sample Roadmap

line #	Keyword/phrase	¶ Margin notes
1	no more effective	Pests can be controlled by predators
3	case in point	Ex. cycl mites controlled by Typh
5	effectively	
8	but	
9	significantly damaging	
13	keep them from	
14	significantly damaging	
15	owes its effectiveness	Why Typh effective
16	several factors	
17		1. match reproduction rate
24		2. synch reproduction cyles
26	also	
32	except when	3. eat other food when cycl population low
34	well-suited	
38	verified	
39	importance	Experiment verifies cycl mites controlled with Typh
44	but	
47	but	reached dangerous levels w/o Typh
48	significantly damaging	
50	clear case	
51–52	far more harm than good	
54	damaging	Results duplicated in agricultural fields
55	but	
60	more abundant	
61	than	

Discussion

The first sentence starts off with an interesting claim: sometimes the most effective way to control crop pests is to let its predators roam free. Right away, this provides a sense of both the **Topic** (crop pests) and **Scope** (methods for controlling them). The very next sentence opens with "[a] case in point …" and provides an example of cyclamen mites that infest strawberry fields. They are controlled when their predators, *Typhlodromus* mites, show up in the fields.

This example is described in great detail throughout the rest of the passage, establishing the **Purpose**: to provide support for the initial claim. That makes the initial claim the **Main Idea**: predators are an effective way of controlling crop pests, as illustrated by *Typhlodromus* mites controlling cyclamen mites.

Paragraph 2 addresses why *Typhlodromus* is so successful at controlling cyclamen mites. The paragraph offers three details: 1) *Typhlodromus* can reproduce as fast as cyclamen, 2) *Typhlodromus*'s population waxes and wanes at the same time of year as cyclamen's, and 3) when there aren't many cyclamen, *Typhlodromus* can survive on other food. The last sentence mentions that other predator-prey relationships work like this, emphasizing that *Typhlodromus* is a prime example of the initial claim.

Paragraph 3 brings up experimental support for the claim about controlling pests using predators. In a greenhouse, a control group of strawberry plants had both sets of mites, while the test group was treated with a pesticide that killed the predator, the *Typhlodromus* mites. The cyclamen mite population was controlled in the test group, but reached damaging levels in the predator-free group. Paragraph 4 further supports the claim by observing similar results in working agricultural fields.

20. (C) Global

Step 2: Identify the Question Type
The question asks for the "main point" of the entire passage, making this a Global question.

Step 3: Research the Relevant Text
Because this is a Global question, the entire passage is relevant. Use the Main Idea from Step 1 as a prediction.

Step 4: Make a Prediction
As determined from the very beginning, the main point is that predators are an effective way to control agricultural pests, as exemplified by how *Typhlodromus* effectively controls cyclamen mites.

Step 5: Evaluate the Answer Choices
(C) is a perfect summary.

(A) is a Distortion and Out of Scope. This focuses too much on the pesticides used in the experiments in paragraph 3. The author spends far more time on the benefits of predators than the downsides of pesticides. Furthermore, there is no discussion of pesticides that can both kill the predators and control the pests.

(B) is Extreme. The experimental results in paragraph 3 are useful to the author in illustrating the effectiveness of predators, but the purpose of the passage is not to demonstrate the *need* for such experiments.

(D) is Extreme. While the predator may be the most effective way to control the cyclamen mites, that doesn't mean it's the *only* way.

(E) is way too narrow, focusing on two scientific details from paragraph 2 and ignoring paragraph 3 (as well as the rest of the passage).

21. (D) Logic Reasoning (Principle)

Step 2: Identify the Question Type
The question asks for a principle the author would "probably hold" "[b]ased on the passage." That makes this a Principle question that is a broad inference from the passage.

Step 3: Research the Relevant Text
The question asks for something fundamental to long-term predatory control. That suggests using paragraph 2, which discusses what makes *Typhlodromus* so effective.

Step 4: Make a Prediction
At the end of paragraph 2, the author argues that the same factors that make *Typhlodromus* so effective are "common among predators that control prey populations." Those factors are described earlier in the paragraph: *Typhlodromus* reproduces as fast as cyclamen, varies its population seasonally (matching its prey), and can survive when its prey is scarce. So, a good general principle would entail a predator being able to adjust in one of these ways.

Step 5: Evaluate the Answer Choices
(D) matches the behavior of *Typhlodromus*, which can effectively control cyclamen mites in part by responding to and matching the cyclamen population size.

(A) is a Distortion. Synchronized rates are great, but the *Typhlodromus* is described as adjusting *in response* to population changes, not "just prior" to them.

(B) is a Distortion. While the experiments provide great support for the author's point, there's no suggestion that such experiments are "fundamental to long-term predatory control."

(C) is a Distortion. The idea of predatory control is to reduce the *prey* population. There's no suggestion that the prey should be able to survive low crop productivity. It seems unlikely that the author would object to the prey being entirely eliminated provided it doesn't return.

(E) is Out of Scope. The author's recommendation is merely to control pests with predators. The author offers no information about what type of pesticides (if any) the predators can tolerate.

22. (E) Detail

Step 2: Identify the Question Type
The question asks for something directly "mentioned in the passage," which makes this a Detail question.

Step 3: Research the Relevant Text
The author lists three factors in paragraph 2 that contribute to the effectiveness of *Typhlodromus*.

Step 4: Make a Prediction
According to paragraph 2, what makes *Typhlodromus* effective is its ability to adjust the size of its population to the cyclamen's population (lines 17–18), its ability to synchronize its reproductive cycle to match the cyclamen's (lines 23–27), and its ability to find other food sources when cyclamen levels are low (lines 27–32). The correct answer will mention one of these three factors.

Step 5: Evaluate the Answer Choices
(E) matches the third factor.

(A) is a Distortion. The passage says that *Typhlodromus* can't withstand parathion, but it never tells us about any other insecticides, let alone "most insecticides."

(B) is Out of Scope. There's no mention of predators of *Typhlodromus* mites.

(C) is Out of Scope. There's no mention of different climates or regions.

(D) is a Distortion. While *Typhlodromus* is said to be able to find food when cyclamen are scarce, the author never outright describes a "constant food supply" as a contributing factor to its effectiveness as a predator.

23. (A) Inference

Step 2: Identify the Question Type
The question poses a hypothetical situation and asks for something that would "most likely" occur, "[b]ased on the information in the passage." That makes this an Inference question.

Step 3: Research the Relevant Text
The question makes reference to the experiments from paragraph 3, so that seems like a likely source for information. But the pesticide mentioned here slows reproduction of cyclamen mites, not *Typhlodromus*. The effect of slow cyclamen reproduction is actually mentioned in paragraph 2, starting at line 27.

Step 4: Make a Prediction
This change would only affect the test plot of paragraph 3. The control group (the plots with no pesticide) would stay the same: cyclamen populations kept in check by *Typhlodromus*. The new test group (with the new pesticide) would reduce cyclamen levels. In that case, by lines 27–32, *Typhlodromus* would find a way to stick around, allowing it to effectively keep cyclamen mites in check in case they come back. So, this new pesticide would create a win-win scenario.

Step 5: Evaluate the Answer Choices
(A) matches the expected results. Cyclamen mites would be controlled in both treated and untreated plots.

(B) is unsupported. If the *Typhlodromus* mites were absent, there would be no predators to eat the cyclamen mites. So, even if pesticide slowed cyclamen reproduction, there would still be no predators to keep the population in check. In that case, it is likely that the cyclamen population would ultimately be higher, not lower.

(C) is a 180. The details of paragraph 2 suggest that *Typhlodromus* is able to maintain synchrony, even during seasonal dips in population.

(D) is Half-Right/Half-Wrong. With a slower reproduction rate for cyclamen, it might make sense that *Typhlodromus* populations would decrease initially. But *Typhlodromus* is said to match cyclamen rates. If the pesticide keeps cyclamen rates low, there's no reason to expect *Typhlodromus* to increase again.

(E) is a 180. Because the *Typhlodromus* population would still be present to keep the cyclamen mites in check, the cyclamen mite population would never reach "significantly damaging" levels. Pesticide X would just mean there was slower growth of cyclamen mites, and *Typhlodromus* would still be able to adjust for its prey's slower population growth.

24. (C) Inference

Step 2: Identify the Question Type
The question asks for something that can be *inferred* that the author is "most likely to agree with," making this an Inference question.

Step 3: Research the Relevant Text
The author's general opinion about using predators is expressed in the very first sentence. However, the entire passage is filled with details supporting that opinion, so everything is relevant.

Step 4: Make a Prediction
With this vague sort of question, there are too many possible details to choose from. Instead, test the answers individually, eliminating answers that are clearly outside the scope. The correct answer is likely to be consistent with the author's

assertion that predators are often most effective in controlling pests.

Step 5: Evaluate the Answer Choices

(C) matches the author's tone. In lines 50–52, the author argues that the experiments in paragraph 3 illustrate how pesticides can be a bad idea. If, as the author claims in lines 1–3, there is "no more effective means" than predators, then the author would certainly agree that predators should be chosen over insecticides when possible.

(A) is a Distortion. According to paragraph 3, parathion has no effect on cyclamen mites. So, if the predators don't control the cyclamen mites, the parathion won't do anything either.

(B) is Out of Scope. The author never discusses the effects of predators on beneficial insects, only the effects of predators on pests.

(D) is a 180. Based on that first sentence, the natural predators can be the most effective means of controlling pests. This goes against the idea of insecticides being a better alternative if both are effective.

(E) is Out of Scope and Extreme. The author certainly favors the use of predators, but never mentions that they don't harm crops. Furthermore, the first sentence says that [s]*ometimes* predators are the most effective way to control pests, but that does mean, as **(E)** says, that they are *generally* more effective. Predators may be the best way in only a minority of instances.

25. (D) Logic Function

Step 2: Identify the Question Type

The phrase "in order to" indicates the question is asking *why* the author mentions egg-laying abilities. That makes this a Logic Function question.

Step 3: Research the Relevant Text

The question refers to lines 20–23, but be sure to read surrounding lines for context.

Step 4: Make a Prediction

The lines referenced describe the number of eggs each mite can lay over a period of time. This provides details for the first reason why *Typhlodromus* is an effective predator: its population can increase as rapidly as that of the cyclamen mites (lines 17–18).

Step 5: Evaluate the Answer Choices

(D) matches the prediction.

(A) is a Distortion. Doing the math, cyclamen lay about 12–15 eggs (3 eggs daily for 4–5 days). *Typhlodromus* lay about 16–30 eggs (2–3 eggs daily for 8–10 days). Those rates are not equal.

(B) is a Distortion. The details only refer to *Typhlodromus*, not predatory mites in general.

(C) is a Faulty Use of Detail. Synchrony is a different factor that is not described until later in the paragraph (lines 23–27).

(E) is another Faulty Use of Detail. Slower reproduction in the absence of cyclamen mites is a different factor that doesn't come up until later in the paragraph (lines 27–32).

26. (E) Logic Reasoning (Strengthen)

Step 2: Identify the Question Type

The question asks for something that would *strengthen* the author's position, making this akin to a Strengthen question from the Logical Reasoning section.

Step 3: Research the Relevant Text

The author's conclusion is in the first sentence, with the entire example of cyclamen mites and *Typhlodromus* as evidence to support it.

Step 4: Make a Prediction

The author concludes that predatory control can be effective because of the predator's ability to adapt its population to its prey's population. However, for this argument to work, the author has to assume that there's no overlooked factor that would negate this ability. To strengthen this argument, the correct answer will provide another effective factor or show that nothing negatively affects the *Typhlodromus* mite's ability to survive and control cyclamen mites.

Step 5: Evaluate the Answer Choices

(E) would certainly help, allowing the *Typhlodromus* to survive in the environment where cyclamen mites live. If it couldn't tolerate that environment, *Typhlodromus* would die and wouldn't be able to keep cyclamen in check. So, **(E)** rules out a potential weakener.

(A) is irrelevant. A correlation between lifespan and number of eggs has no effect on connecting *Typhlodromus* to controlling cyclamen mites.

(B) is a 180. If the insecticides also killed the prey, then there would be no need for the predators to keep prey in check.

(C) is irrelevant. According to the passage, winter is when cyclamen numbers dwindle and the *Typhlodromus* mites subsist on honeydew. The passage says nothing to indicate whether the winters in question are short and mild or long and frigid. So, **(C)** adds no value to the author's argument.

(D) is irrelevant. The author's recommendation involves *not* using parathion, so the existence of predators of *Typhlodromus* and their susceptibility to parathion has no bearing on the author's claims.

27. (A) Inference

Step 2: Identify the Question Type
This question requires taking the information provided and using it to support the correct answer. That means the correct answer will be an inference.

Step 3: Research the Relevant Text
The question offers no specific clues, so the entire text is relevant.

Step 4: Make a Prediction
With nothing to work with, the only approach is to test the answers individually, making sure to stick to the Scope and Purpose of the passage.

Step 5: Evaluate the Answer Choices
(A) is supported by results in paragraph 4. That paragraph describes a strawberry field in which both mites existed in untreated plots, and cyclamen mites were kept in check. The passage suggests that allowing *Typhlodromus* to thrive can be an effective solution to strawberry pests. No agricultural technique that destroyed the crop would be much of a solution.

(B) is Extreme. Cyclamen and *Typhlodromus* mites happen to have the same mode of reproduction, but the author does not go so far as to say that this is a reason for (let alone "crucial to") the effectiveness of the control.

(C) is Out of Scope. The author makes no mention of how *Typhlodromus* affects other strawberry plant pests.

(D) is a 180. According to paragraph 1, cyclamen mites don't reach damaging levels until the second year (lines 8–10).

(E) is Out of Scope. The author never implies any such causality. The passage doesn't state what actual strawberry growers have tried; there's only information about the data from the greenhouse and field experiments.

PrepTest 54

The Inside Story

PrepTest 54 was administered in June 2008. It challenged 28,939 test takers. The following chart shows the average number of students to miss each question in each of PrepTest 54's different sections.

Percentage Incorrect by PrepTest 54 Section Type

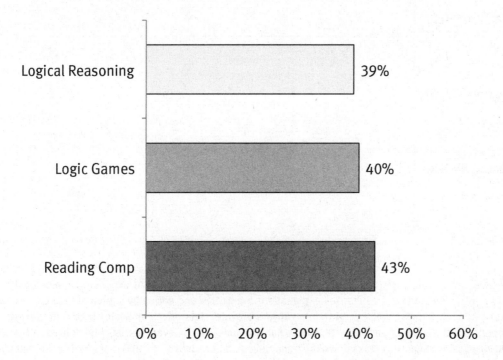

On average, students were most likely to miss questions in Reading Comprehension. Although Reading Comprehension was somewhat higher in actual difficulty than Logical Reasoning and Logic Games, the percentages are not that disparate, so students were missing about 9–12 questions in each individual section.

Additionally, although Reading Comprehension was the hardest section, only three of the test's 10 hardest questions came from that section. Here were the locations of the 10 hardest (most missed) questions in the exam.

Location of 10 Most Difficult Questions in PrepTest 54

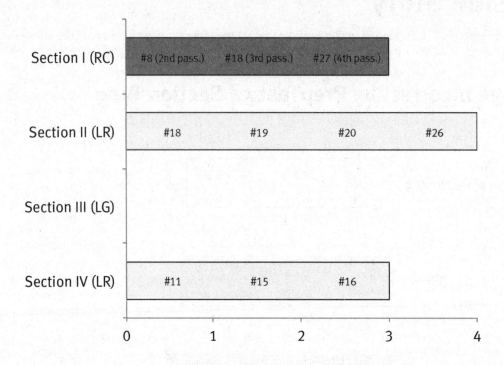

The takeaway from this data is that, to maximize your potential on the LSAT, you need to take a comprehensive approach. Test yourself rigorously, and review your performance on every section of the test. Kaplan's LSAT explanations provide the expertise and insight you need to fully understand your results. The explanations are written and edited by a team of LSAT experts, who have helped thousands of students improve their scores. Kaplan always provides data-driven analysis of the test, ranking the difficulty of every question based on actual student performance. The 10 hardest questions on every test are highlighted with a 4-star difficulty rating, the highest we give. The analysis breaks down the remaining questions into 1-, 2-, and 3-star ratings so that you can compare your performance to thousands of other test takers on all LSAC material.

Don't settle for wondering whether a question was really as hard as it seemed to you. Analyze the test with real data, and learn the secrets and strategies that help top scorers master the LSAT.

8 Can't-Miss Features of PrepTest 54

- Although PrepTest 53 had 12 Strengthen/Weaken questions, PrepTest 54 only had six. That ties the record for the fewest on a single PrepTest. The three times it's happened are PrepTest 32 (October 2000), PrepTest 54, and PrepTest 58 (September 2009).
- PrepTest 54 had no Point at Issue questions. Recently, that's not all that uncommon. However, in the 10 years (1998–2007) leading up to PrepTest 54, it had only happened two times.
- A harbinger of things to come? There were three Strict Sequencing games on PrepTest 54. As of its release it was just the second time that had ever happened—the other was PrepTest 50 (September 2006). However, it happened four times from December 2009 to June 2013 (PT 59–69).
- PrepTest 54 featured the only Selection game from 2007–2008.
- This was just the fourth test featuring Comparative Reading. However, for the first time, the Comparative Reading question set contained seven questions.
- Although it was prefaced with the warning "[t]his passage was adapted from an article published in 1996," some test takers may have chuckled when reading the first paragraph of the first passage, which explained what the Internet was.

- But not all topics are dated. Question 16 of the second Logical Reasoning section talked about "growing economic incentive" to build colonies on the moon. Then, just over three months later, Elon Musk's SpaceX's Falcon 1 became the first non-governmental vehicle to orbit the Earth.
- *The Incredible Hulk* was the #1 film the weekend PrepTest 54 was administered. It's good to take the test when you're feeling strong, but you don't want to take it when you're angry.

PrepTest 54 in Context

As much fun as it is to find out what makes a PrepTest unique or noteworthy, it's even more important to know just how representative it is of other LSAT administrations (and, thus, how likely it is to be representative of the exam you will face on Test Day). The following charts compare the numbers of each kind of question and game on PrepTest 54 to the average numbers seen on all officially released LSATs administered over the past five years (from 2013 through 2017).

Number of LR Questions by Type: PrepTest 54 vs. 2013–2017 Average

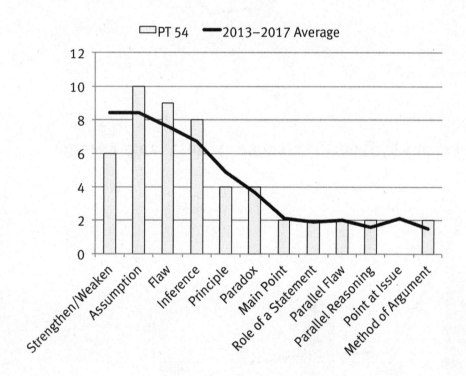

Number of LG Games by Type: PrepTest 54 vs. 2013–2017 Average

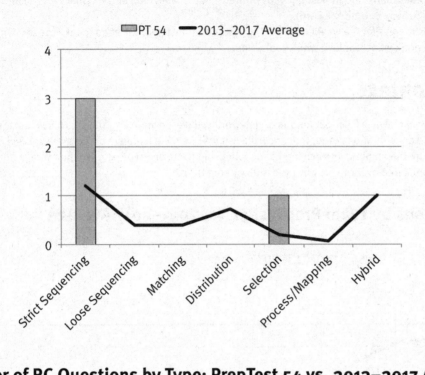

Number of RC Questions by Type: PrepTest 54 vs. 2013–2017 Average

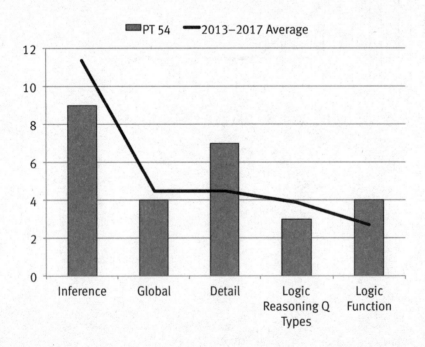

There isn't usually a huge difference in the distribution of questions from LSAT to LSAT, but if this test seems harder (or easier) to you than another you've taken, compare the number of questions of the types on which you, personally, are strongest and weakest. Then, explore within each section to see if your best or worst question types came earlier or later.

Students in Kaplan's comprehensive LSAT courses have access to every released LSAT and to a library of thousands of officially released questions arranged by question, game, and passage type. If you are studying on your own, you have to do a bit more work to identify your strengths and your areas of opportunity. Quantitative analysis (like that in the charts shown here) is an important tool for understanding how the test is constructed, and how you are performing on it.

Section I: Reading Comprehension

Passage 1: Internet Regulation

Q#	Question Type	Correct	Difficulty
1	Global	A	★
2	Logic Function	C	★
3	Detail	D	★
4	Inference	D	★
5	Logic Function	E	★★

Passage 2: Drilling Muds

Q#	Question Type	Correct	Difficulty
6	Global	B	★★
7	Detail	E	★
8	Inference (EXCEPT)	E	★★★★
9	Inference	B	★★★
10	Inference (EXCEPT)	B	★★
11	Logic Reasoning (Strengthen)	C	★
12	Detail	A	★

Passage 3: Aida Overton Walker's Cakewalk

Q#	Question Type	Correct	Difficulty
13	Global	C	★★
14	Logic Function	D	★★
15	Logic Reasoning (Parallel Reasoning)	C	★★
16	Detail	E	★
17	Inference	E	★★★
18	Inference	A	★★★★
19	Detail	A	★★

Passage 4: Group Cohesion and the "Groupthink" Problem

Q#	Question Type	Correct	Difficulty
20	Global	A	★
21	Inference	C	★★
22	Logic Reasoning (Strengthen)	C	★★★
23	Detail	B	★
24	Inference	E	★★★
25	Detail	E	★★★
26	Logic Function	A	★★★
27	Inference	B	★★★★

Passage 1: Internet Regulation

Step 1: Read the Passage Strategically
Sample Roadmap

line #	Keyword/phrase	¶ Margin notes
1		Internet defined
4	As a result; astonishing	
5	unimpeded	
7	serious difficulties; traditional	Challenges for lawmaking/enforcement
9	crucial	
11	defining attribute	Assumptions of lawmaking
12	presupposes	
13	But	sovereignty, ability to control hampered
16	For example	
19	But	
20	too great	
23	thus	gov't would have to deny internet access
24	draconian	
25	almost certainly; extremely	
26	unpopular; since	unpopular w/ citizens
28	decidely outweigh	
29	especially sensitive	Geog. issue: trademarks
32	requires	TM's registered by each country
33	Moreover	
39	But	Internet allows TM's to cross borders
45	?	Can one country control TM's in another?
46–47	or should	
48	Otherwise	
51	also	Addt'l issue: no way to regulate some situations
52	needed; but cannot	
53	For example	
55	perplexing	Ex: privacy
59	?	
60	challenge	

Discussion

Paragraph 1 defines the Internet and introduces a new problem it creates for lawmakers. The ability of the Internet to allow information to flow freely across borders creates new legal concerns about legislation and law enforcement. By the end of the paragraph, you get a sense of the **Topic** (the Internet), the **Scope** (the many novel issues concerning legal regulation that the Internet raises), and perhaps even the author's **Purpose** (to outline the new challenges lawmakers face in regulating the Internet in light of traditional approaches).

In paragraph 2, the author explains how lawmakers traditionally determine the extent of regulation among objects and things—by physical borders. The author goes on to identify the first issue created by the Internet for lawmakers: It's just too big. Finally, the author does away with the *draconian* solution of banning use of the Internet altogether.

The final two paragraphs each present two more issues for lawmakers to consider in determining how best to regulate the Internet: trademark and privacy. In paragraph 3, there is the issue of trademarks. Currently, trademarks are regulated within a country, not globally. In addition, the same name can be used for different companies or trades within that country. But the open question is: Who has jurisdiction over the content of the Internet, which crosses all borders? In paragraph 4, the author offers up the privacy concerns of regulating transmissions between countries. Again, the author leaves this question of privacy open. The **Main Idea** of the passage should reflect this neutrality—the Internet's ability to transcend geographic boundaries raises new issues in legal regulation of trademark, information, and privacy.

1. (A) Global

Step 2: Identify the Question Type
This is a Global question because it asks you to identify the "main point" of the passage.

Step 3: Research the Relevant Text
Instead of researching a specific part of the passage to predict your answer, base your prediction on the Main Idea you determined during Step 1.

Step 4: Make a Prediction
The multiple examples in the last two paragraphs support the main point hinted at in paragraph 1: The Internet presents new issues in legal regulation of trademark, information, and privacy in light of its ability to transmit a broad array of information across borders.

Step 5: Evaluate the Answer Choices
(A) is a match.

(B) is Outside the Scope. The passage isn't about the effect of the Internet on governments' ability to control the speech and financial activities of their citizens. Also, nothing in the passage suggests that the Internet *promotes* governmental control.

(C) is Extreme. The author does say in paragraph 3 that government regulation of Internet activity would likely be unpopular, but that's in the hypothetical situation of people being banned from using the Internet altogether. Nothing indicates people would oppose *any* government efforts.

(D) is Outside the Scope and Extreme. The author never blames the Internet for an increase in crime, let alone a substantial increase.

(E) is also Extreme. While the author does discuss law enforcement and regulatory challenges posed by the Internet, that's a far cry from saying that governments around the world are in danger of melting down as more people gain access to the Internet.

2. (C) Logic Function

Step 2: Identify the Question Type
The words "mentions … primarily to" indicate a Logic Function question. Here, your job is not to determine what the author says, but why the author says it.

Step 3: Research the Relevant Text
Lines 57–59 are relevant, but it's also important to read the surrounding lines, including the beginning of the paragraph that contains lines 57–59.

Step 4: Make a Prediction
In paragraph 4, the author discusses another issue regarding the legal regulation of the Internet, namely who should retain jurisdiction over certain Internet communications given their global accessibility. Note the Keywords "for example" in line 53. These Keywords indicate that the author is using the French officials as a hypothetical example to bolster the main point of the paragraph.

Step 5: Evaluate the Answer Choices
(C) matches this prediction.

(A) echoes other parts of the passage, and while the author does discuss the global nature of information available on the Internet, the context of lines 57–59 show that these lines aren't being used to make that point.

(B) is Outside the Scope. The author never makes a point about the number of languages used on the Internet.

(D) is not only a Distortion of a point the author raises about trademarks, but it also involves details from paragraph 3, which isn't relevant to the lines in question.

(E) is Outside the Scope. The author never discusses the origins of the Internet.

3. (D) Detail

Step 2: Identify the Question Type

The phrase "[a]ccording to the passage" is a clear sign of a Detail question.

Step 3: Research the Relevant Text

The words "essential property of political sovereignty" are a content clue leading you to the beginning of paragraph 2.

Step 4: Make a Prediction

Lines 10–11 say that a "defining attribute" (or, essential property) of sovereignty is the control over the objects located within a physical space.

Step 5: Evaluate the Answer Choices

(D) is therefore correct.

(A) is a Distortion. According to the beginning of paragraph 2, the control must be *within* a physical space, not across territorial boundaries.

(B) is Outside the Scope. The author identifies control over physical space and the objects located in it. Communicative exchanges are not explicitly referenced.

(C) introduces a detail from a different part of the passage. Trademarks are mentioned in paragraph 3 as another issue to consider in light of the jurisdictional concerns the Internet poses, but this question is only concerned about the issue of sovereignty presented in paragraph 2.

(E) is Extreme. The key attribute of a country's sovereignty is control over territories and objects therein, not over commercial matters involving *any* of its citizens. Sovereignty would not extend necessarily to wherever in the world a country's citizens might travel.

4. (D) Inference

Step 2: Identify the Question Type

This is an Inference question because it asks you to find the author's attitude toward a particular part of the passage.

Step 3: Research the Relevant Text

Hypothetical measures a government might take to deny its citizens Internet access are discussed at the end of paragraph 2.

Step 4: Make a Prediction

In line 24, the author characterizes a government's decision to deny its citizens access to the Internet as *draconian*, or unusually severe. This is the only time the author weighs in with an opinion on this measure.

Step 5: Evaluate the Answer Choices

(D) is therefore correct.

(A) is used by the author as a reason why citizens affected by the measure would likely oppose it.

(B) isn't a word that could convey the author's attitude toward anything; *decidedly* just means "absolutely" or "definitely."

(C) is the likely attitude of the citizens toward the government's measure, but the author goes farther than that in judging complete Internet censorship by a government. It's not just that people wouldn't like it (*unpopular*), it's that it is unnecessarily harsh (*draconian*).

(E), like **(A)**, is part of the author's reasoning for why citizens would oppose an effort by their government to take away their Internet access.

5. (E) Logic Function

Step 2: Identify the Question Type

Any question asking for the purpose of a particular paragraph is a Logic Function question.

Step 3: Research the Relevant Text

The fourth paragraph is relevant, of course, but remember also that you wrote margin notes for a reason. Use them to help you predict your answer.

Step 4: Make a Prediction

In paragraph 4, the author presents one last legal issue raised by the global accessibility of the Internet. The entire paragraph, as well as the two paragraphs prior, are written to support the author's original claim that the Internet poses new issues for lawmakers deciding how best to regulate the Internet.

Step 5: Evaluate the Answer Choices

(E) is a perfect match.

(A) is a 180. The argument made in the second paragraph is that of the author. The author would not then turn around and weaken his or her own argument later in the passage.

(B) is a 180 because the last paragraph supports and illustrates the claim made in the first paragraph rather than questioning it.

(C) is a Distortion. Paragraph 4 introduces a new issue in order to support the claim from paragraph 1. It doesn't summarize arguments made earlier.

(D) is a Distortion. The third paragraph is all about trademarks, while paragraph 4 moves on to a different jurisdictional challenge posed by expansion of Internet usage.

Passage 2: Drilling Muds

Step 1: Read the Passage Strategically
Sample Roadmap

line #	Keyword/phrase	¶ Margin notes
Passage A		
2	essential	Drilling muds play role in oil wells
5		Five functions of muds
12		Composition of muds
14	By far	Barite important ingredient
17		Other uses of barite
21		Individual recipes developed
23	One problem	Hard to study effects of discharges
Passage B		
33	main	Tight regs on discharge of muds (environmental concern)
34	concern	
38	One type	Properties of WBMs
41	not particularly	
42	current	
48	typical difference	Comparison to OBMs
50		More barite, other chemicals
52	greater potential; negative	
53	impact; because	More environmentally dangerous
54	may	
56	may; Currently	

Discussion

In paragraph 1, the author of passage A introduces the **Topic** (drilling muds) and examines the roles drilling muds play in drilling. In paragraph 2, the author introduces barite (a key ingredient of drilling muds) and discusses its other uses. Finally, in paragraph 3, the author introduces a problem associated with studies of drilling waste byproducts. Because drillers have devised so many different recipes and a variety of names for proper drilling fluids, there's no clear way to identify which ingredients are contained in a drilling fluid.

This author's **Purpose** is to provide information on the composition as well as the roles of drilling muds. The **Main Idea** is that drilling muds are used in drilling in five ways, contain barite, and are hard to analyze in detail due to variation in recipes.

The author of passage B also discusses the composition of drilling muds. But passage B's focus on the environmental impact of drilling muds and the current environmental practices of drilling companies becomes clear right away. In paragraph 2, the author discusses WBMs—water-based muds—to show how some drilling muds may be better environmentally speaking. Finally, the author discusses OBMs—oil-based muds that contain more barite—to show that they may have a more negative environmental impact than WBMs do.

This author's **Purpose** is to explain current regulations and practices for the use of drilling muds. The **Main Idea** is that, currently, WBMs can be dumped and OBMs, which pose more of a threat, must be controlled.

Both passages have the same **Topic** of drilling muds—this is common in Comparative Reading. However, the passages diverge when it comes to **Scope**, which is also common in Comparative Reading. Passage A is more concerned with discussing the functions and composition of drilling muds, while passage B focuses not just on the composition of muds, but also on their environmental impact. This difference in Scope will be helpful as you answer the questions.

6. (B) Global

Step 2: Identify the Question Type
This is a Global question because it asks you to find the "primary purpose" of both passages.

Step 3: Research the Relevant Text
In Step 1 of Comparative Reading, it's always important to determine areas of overlap between the passages when it comes to the Big Picture—Topic, Scope, Purpose, and Main Idea. This will help you predict answers to questions like these.

Step 4: Make a Prediction
Your Roadmap tells you that each passage spends at least two paragraphs describing the functions, features, and composition of various drilling muds.

Step 5: Evaluate the Answer Choices
(B) matches this prediction perfectly.

(A) is hinted at in the beginning of passage B, but isn't discussed in passage A at all.

(C) is discussed in paragraph 3 of passage B, but not in passage A.

(D) is only discussed at the beginning of passage A.

(E) is Outside the Scope of both passages. Regulation is mentioned in passage B, and difficulties in studying the environmental impact of drilling wastes is mentioned in passage A, but neither passage discusses difficulties in regulation.

7. (E) Detail

Step 2: Identify the Question Type
This is a Detail question because it asks what both passages explicitly mention.

Step 3: Research the Relevant Text
The mention of barite in the question stem is a content clue leading you to lines 14–19 in passage A and lines 50–56 in passage B.

Step 4: Make a Prediction
Passage A says barite is the largest ingredient in drilling muds and is a "very heavy mineral" (line 15). Passage B discusses how OBMs contain a greater concentration of barite—a "heavy mineral." Both passages mention barite as a key ingredient of drilling muds that is particularly heavy.

Step 5: Evaluate the Answer Choices
(E) is therefore correct.

(A) is only mentioned in passage B.

(B) is a Distortion. While passage B mentions that barite is found in OBMs in *greater* concentrations than in WBMs (which contain bentonite), the author never suggests that barite is *not found* in WBMs or any other drilling muds that contain bentonite.

(C) is a Distortion. Passage B mentions that the drilling mud discharges are tightly regulated, but the author never explicitly states that barite is tightly regulated.

(D) is also a Distortion. Neither author explicitly states that barite is the most *commonly* used ingredient in drilling muds. Passage A only mentions that it is the largest by *weight*.

8. (E) Inference (EXCEPT)

Step 2: Identify the Question Type
The phrase "supported by one or both of the passages" indicates an Inference question. But in this case, you'll need to find the answer choice that is *not* directly supported by the information in the passages.

Step 3: Research the Relevant Text
The question stem doesn't give research clues to direct your research, so you'll have to research each answer choice as you evaluate it.

Step 4: Make a Prediction
In the absence of research clues in the question stem, go straight to the answer choices. Keep in mind that four of the answer choices will have direct textual support and will therefore need to be eliminated.

Step 5: Evaluate the Answer Choices
(E) is the odd man out. It's never implied by passage A and contradicts parts of passage B. In the last sentence of paragraph 2 of passage B, it states that OBMs are recycled "until their properties are no longer suitable," and then they are dumped. And in paragraph 3, it says residues are dumped "after the cuttings are sieved from the drilling fluids." So, in both cases, fluids are not *continuously* discharged throughout the entire process.

(A) is supported by passage A, which states that drilling muds are made of bentonite and other clays and polymers (lines 12–14).

(B) is supported by passage B, which states that WBM is not particularly toxic to marine organisms and disperses readily (lines 40–42).

(C) is supported by passage A, which refers to a problem associated with studies of the effects of drilling waste discharges that can be made from toxic ingredients (lines 23–30).

(D) is supported by passage B. Lines 48–49 say that OBMs contain 30 percent more mineral oil than WBMs. This fact coupled with the earlier statement that OBM discharges, which contain cuttings, are tightly regulated (lines 31–35) establishes support for (D).

9. (B) Inference

Step 2: Identify the Question Type
The phrase "can be most reasonably inferred" indicates an Inference question.

Step 3: Research the Relevant Text
Always read question stems carefully. Here, the correct answer needs to have textual support from *both* passages and not just one individually.

Step 4: Make a Prediction
The scope of the question stem is broad, and this is an Inference question, so prediction may be tough. Take each choice in turn, and eliminate any choice that is either supported by only one of the two passages or unsupported by either passage.

Step 5: Evaluate the Answer Choices
(B) can only be inferred by combining both passages. Lines 16–19 in passage A support the idea that barite can be consumed safely by humans, and lines 54–56 in passage B suggest that barite can harm scallops, which are a marine organism.

(A) is Extreme. While passage A does state that barite is the largest ingredient of drilling muds by weight (lines 14–15), passage B doesn't go as far as saying that barite is the *most* environmentally damaging of all drilling mud ingredients.

(C) is an Irrelevant Comparison. Neither passage lays out any differences between land-based and offshore oil drilling.

(D) is unsupported. Passage B does say that the use of drilling mud discharges is tightly regulated (line 35), but neither author expresses an opinion on how effective those regulations are.

(E) is hinted at by the end of passage B, which says that the residues adhering to cuttings are the only ones discharged overboard (lines 56–59). However, passage A doesn't address the environmental impact of cuttings at all.

10. (B) Inference (EXCEPT)

Step 2: Identify the Question Type
This is an Inference question because it asks about what is and is not "supported by" the information in the passages. Be careful—the word *EXCEPT* means that the correct answer to this question will *not* be supported by the passages.

Step 3: Research the Relevant Text
You don't have any research clues from the question stem to help you do your research. So, save your research for the answer choices.

Step 4: Make a Prediction
It's next to impossible to predict what *isn't* implied by the passages. So, instead of predicting, go straight to the answer choices and eliminate any choice for which you can find direct support in the text.

Step 5: Evaluate the Answer Choices
(B) is not supported by either passage. Passage B says that the use of drilling muds is tightly regulated, but that doesn't necessarily mean that one of the specific regulations involves disclosure of *all* of the ingredients in the muds.

(A) is supported by lines 7–10 in passage A and lines 43–46 in passage B. It would appear from these lines that oil drillers are keeping a close eye on their muds and will discontinue their use once they stop being suitable.

(C) is supported by lines 16–19 in passage A, which say that barite is added to food and also has a medical purpose.

(D) is supported by lines 1–11, which detail the different functions of drilling muds as relates to cutting into rock during the oil-drilling process.

(E) is supported by lines 20–23, which mention that drillers have devised recipes for different drilling jobs. Passage B also hints at this by distinguishing between different types of muds that are used for wells of different depths.

11. (C) Logic Reasoning (Strengthen)

Step 2: Identify the Question Type
This is a Strengthen question because it asks for the answer choice that, if true, would support a prediction that OBMs will be used more often in oil-well drilling operations.

Step 3: Research the Relevant Text
The mention of OBMs in the question stem sends you to paragraph 3 of passage B.

Step 4: Make a Prediction
From lines 47–48, you know that OBMs are used to drill deeper wells. Thus, anything requiring drillers to drill deeper and deeper wells in the future would increase the likelihood that they'd need to use OBMs in their operations.

Step 5: Evaluate the Answer Choices
(C), therefore, strengthens the prediction in the question stem by suggesting that drillers will drill fewer shallow wells and more deep wells.

(A) is an Irrelevant Comparison. The author doesn't say that cost factors into drillers' decision to use OBMs over WBMs.

(B) might explain why barite is in greater concentrations in OBMs, but it provides no reason to believe that the use of OBMs will increase in the future.

(D) is a 180. If the efficiency of OBMs is in doubt, then it might be less likely that the proportion of OBMs used will increase.

(E) is Outside the Scope. Even if barite is limitless, its availability doesn't provide an inducement for drillers to *increase* the proportion of OBMs used. All **(E)** does is make it more likely that OBMs can continue to be manufactured in the future.

12. (A) Detail

Step 2: Identify the Question Type
The phrase "[a]ccording to passage B" identifies this as a Detail question.

Step 3: Research the Relevant Text
The author of passage B differentiates OBMs from WBMs in lines 48–54. The content clue "potentially more

environmentally damaging" narrows your research to lines 52–54.

Step 4: Make a Prediction
Lines 52–54 say that OBMs impact the environment more strongly because they don't disperse as readily as WBMs.

Step 5: Evaluate the Answer Choices
(A) is therefore correct.

(B) is a Distortion. Passage B mentions that WBMs contain bentonite, but doesn't say whether OBMs contain it, too.

(C) is another Distortion. OBMs are said to contain additives (line 51), but not necessarily a greater number of them than WBMs contain. Furthermore, the additive content of OBMs isn't given as a reason for their greater environmental impact.

(D) is a difference cited by the author in lines 47–48. But this isn't given as a reason why OBMs are potentially more harmful to the environment.

(E) is not mentioned in passage B. Although recycling WBMs is discussed in paragraph 2, it cannot be inferred that OBMs *cannot* be recycled. Furthermore, even if they can't be recycled, nothing in passage B indicates that's *why* OBMs are "potentially more environmentally damaging."

Passage 3: Aida Overton Walker's Cakewalk

Step 1: Read the Passage Strategically
Sample Roadmap

line #	Keyword/phrase	¶ Margin notes
2	most widely acclaimed	Walker popularized cakewalk
3	known largely	
6	originally	Origin of cakewalk
13	such as	African influence
16	added	Cakewalk blends Afr/Euro features
20	Ironically; while	
22	one of the first	
24–25	satiric intent	Euro elements added for satire
28	To add a further irony	Cakewalk was itself parodied by Eur Amer performers
33	While; complex	Cakewalk's complexity → popularity
37	in fact; enabled	
42	had to be	Why: culture required versatility for appeal
43	in order to appeal	
45	remarkable success	Walker able to appeal to multiple groups
47	rested on	
50	for example	1) Middle-class African Americans
51	denounced; disreputable; complaint	
53	won over	
55	Meanwhile; because	
56	threatened	2) Middle- and upper-class European Americans
57	tremendous; flux; prized	
59	success	
60	derived from	
61	widely acclaimed; most	
62	Finally; admiration	3) Nouveau riche
65	fitting	

Discussion

In paragraph 1, the author introduces the **Topic**, a dance form referred to as the *cakewalk*. First, Aida Overton Walker is accredited with popularizing the cakewalk in the early 20th century. Then, the pre–Civil War origins of the cakewalk dance form are discussed. After reading the first paragraph, the **Scope** of the passage will be the history of the cakewalk and how Walker popularized it.

In paragraph 2, the African American modifications to the dance are discussed, resulting in two ironies. Originally meant to parody slave owners, the cakewalk became one of the first cultural forms to transcend the racial divide in the United States. In addition, European American performers were themselves parodying the dance by the end of the 19th century.

In paragraph 3, the author gives the social and cultural context that laid the groundwork for Walker's success. The cakewalk's constant state of flux along with its characteristic layering by the beginning of the 20th century enabled it to mean different things to different people; this led to the cakewalk's universal appeal.

In paragraph 4, the author emphasizes the various ways in which Walker popularized the cakewalk. For middle-class African Americans, the cakewalk came to be more refined and graceful; for upper-class European Americans, the cakewalk was regarded as an authentic form of stability in such culturally tumultuous times; and for the nouveau riche in the United States, the cakewalk represented the grandeur of celebrating their newfound role in society.

The author's **Purpose** is to explain how Walker was able to successfully popularize the cakewalk. The **Main Idea** is that Walker was successful in popularizing the cakewalk because she could seize on the varying cultural demands placed on the dance from its complex evolution.

13. (C) Global

Step 2: Identify the Question Type
This is a Global question because it asks you for the "main point of the passage."

Step 3: Research the Relevant Text
Instead of researching a specific part of the passage, use your understanding of the Topic, Scope, Purpose, and especially the Main Idea to predict your answer.

Step 4: Make a Prediction
The author's Main Idea is that Walker popularized the cakewalk in America by focusing on the varied demands placed on the dance by its complicated cultural development.

Step 5: Evaluate the Answer Choices
(C) is therefore correct.

(A) is a Distortion. The opening lines of the passage do mention that Walker was an acclaimed African American performer, but that's hardly the main point of the passage. **(A)** deemphasizes the centrality of the cakewalk to the author's discussion.

(B) focuses too much on the reason Walker was able to popularize the cakewalk with European Americans (lines 55–61), but European Americans were only one group Walker won over by her interpretation of the cakewalk.

(D) is Outside the Scope. The author never compares Walker's version of the cakewalk to other versions that existed at the time she was performing and choreographing it.

(E) is Extreme. The passage says that the cakewalk was "one of the first cultural forms to cross the racial divide" (lines 22–24), but that doesn't mean that it was the very first. Furthermore, the groundbreaking nature of the cakewalk isn't attributed to the elements that African Americans *originally* included in its performance.

14. (D) Logic Function

Step 2: Identify the Question Type
The phrase "in order to" indicates a Logic Function question. The focus here is why the author discussed the socioeconomic flux, not what was said about it.

Step 3: Research the Relevant Text
The question stem directs you to paragraph 3. The socioeconomic flux is discussed specifically in lines 38–44. Be prepared, however, to consult the lines before and after it to form your prediction.

Step 4: Make a Prediction
Lines 33–38 establish that the author is using paragraph 3 to point to a phenomenon that aided the cakewalk in gaining broader appeal and popularity.

Step 5: Evaluate the Answer Choices
(D) is a match for this prediction.

(A) is a Distortion. Just because the socioeconomic flux aided the cakewalk in gaining broader appeal doesn't mean that such flux was *necessary* to bring about that popularity.

(B) is a Distortion. The fusion of African and European dance forms is discussed much earlier, in paragraph 2.

(C) attempts to conflate two parts of the passage. The parody within the cakewalk was meant to convey the intent of the people who developed the dance. Whether that had anything to do with the socioeconomic flux is an unrelated issue that isn't supported by the author.

(E) is not in line with the purpose of paragraph 3. While paragraph 2 mentions that parodies helped to shape subsequent versions of the cakewalk, the author does not go so far as to claim that the socioeconomic flux was the reason why the cakewalk was able to reach wide audiences.

15. (C) Logic Reasoning (Parallel Reasoning)

Step 2: Identify the Question Type
The phrase "most analogous to" signals a Parallel Reasoning question.

Step 3: Research the Relevant Text
The question stem directs you to the second paragraph. Summarize the author's account of how Europeans came to enjoy the cakewalk.

Step 4: Make a Prediction
According to lines 20–25, the modifications added to the cakewalk helped it appeal to Europeans, but the original intent of the modifications was to parody other processional dances. The correct answer may not have to do with dance, but it will contain this same ironic situation.

Step 5: Evaluate the Answer Choices
(C) is a one-to-one match.

(A) would be correct if the author said that the cakewalk became more popular than the types of dances it parodied. But the author gives no such indication.

(B) introduces a generational element that wasn't part of the cakewalk's development.

(D) doesn't match because nothing in the passage suggests that the cakewalk had lost its audience before it began to incorporate elements of European dances.

(E) doesn't match because the author never suggests that the introduction of the cakewalk ignited interest in African dance forms.

16. (E) Detail

Step 2: Identify the Question Type
The direct language of the question stem ("the passage asserts") makes this a Detail question.

Step 3: Research the Relevant Text
Unfortunately, the word *cakewalk* isn't much of a research clue; the entire passage discusses the cakewalk. This means you'll save your research for Step 5.

Step 4: Make a Prediction
Because the author says innumerable things about the cakewalk, it's impossible to predict the correct answer. In cases like this, check each choice against the passage, seeking the one that's stated or paraphrased in the text.

Step 5: Evaluate the Answer Choices
(E) is stated almost directly in lines 22–24.

(A) is contradicted by the passage. Lines 28–32 say that by the end of the 19th century (that is, before Walker came along), European Americans were already familiar with the cakewalk.

(B) is Outside the Scope. While Walker may be credited with popularizing the cakewalk, it remains unknown how many others performed the cakewalk professionally.

(C) is a Distortion. Walker did tone down the parodic nature of the cakewalk in her interpretation (lines 59–61), but Walker could have been unique in this regard. Other performers may have continued to perform it satirically.

(D) isn't mentioned. Nothing in the passage suggests that Walker's interpretation of the cakewalk led to an increased awareness of the dance's West African origins.

17. (E) Inference

Step 2: Identify the Question Type
The phrase "author would be most likely to agree with" indicates an Inference question.

Step 3: Research the Relevant Text
This stem doesn't give you any research clues to help you research the passage, so save your research for the answer choices.

Step 4: Make a Prediction
It's tough to predict in a general sense what the author will or will not agree with, so instead of predicting, check each choice against the passage. Don't select an answer until you can find direct textual support for it.

Step 5: Evaluate the Answer Choices
(E) is directly supported by lines 62–66. If the newly rich were attracted to the cakewalk because they considered it a "fitting vehicle for celebrating their newfound social rank," then it must be true that they were seeking to bolster their social identities.

(A) is too broad. Yes, the cakewalk was one of the first cultural forms to cross America's racial divide (lines 22–24), but this may not necessarily be true of satiric art forms in general.

(B) is a Distortion. The "mimetic vertigo" discussed in paragraph 3 was a result of the layers of parody that characterized the cakewalk by the end of the 19th century, not of cross-racial interactions.

(C) is unsupported. Nothing in the passage suggests that the middle-class European Americans that Walker won over with her authentic cakewalk went on to enjoy other African American dances.

(D) is Outside the Scope. "Popular dances that later emerged in the United States" aren't discussed in the passage.

18. (A) Inference

Step 2: Identify the Question Type
This is an Inference question because it asks for the answer choice that the author "would be likely to agree with."

Step 3: Research the Relevant Text

Walker's significance in the history of the cakewalk is discussed primarily in paragraph 4.

Step 4: Make a Prediction

According to paragraph 4, Walker's success at gaining a broad audience for the cakewalk rested on her ability to reshape her interpretation based on varying demands from different social groups. The correct answer will be consistent with this idea.

Step 5: Evaluate the Answer Choices

(A) is consistent with paragraph 4. Line 54 says that Walker won over middle-class African Americans by emphasizing the cakewalk's *fundamental* grace. Lines 59–61 say that Walker won over middle-class European Americans with her authentic version.

(B) isn't supported by the passage. Walker didn't accentuate the satiric dimensions of the cakewalk in any part of paragraph 4.

(C) is a subtle Distortion. Walker didn't have multiple interpretations of the cakewalk. The author only credits her with a single interpretation that contained elements appealing to various groups.

(D) credits Walker with the "mimetic vertigo" from paragraph 3, but that vertigo evolved from the different parodic layerings from paragraph 2 and not through any of Walker's work.

(E) gives a reason for Walker's success that, like **(B)**, is not discussed in the passage.

19. (A) Detail

Step 2: Identify the Question Type

The question stem focuses solely on the factual information provided in the passage, so this is a Detail question.

Step 3: Research the Relevant Text

The question stem doesn't give you any clues, so your research will have to happen during Step 5.

Step 4: Make a Prediction

Without a clear place to research, prediction is impossible; the passage provides information sufficient to answer a whole host of questions. Instead of trying to predict, research each answer choice and select the one that can be answered with lines from the passage.

Step 5: Evaluate the Answer Choices

(A) can be answered from lines 11–14. The Illustration Keywords "such as" indicate that gliding steps and an emphasis on improvisation are two examples of elements of African dance forms that the cakewalk incorporated.

(B) isn't answered. Walker became known for popularizing the cakewalk, but as far as you know from the passage, there could have been professional dancers who practiced the dance before Walker.

(C) is Outside the Scope. Other North American dance forms aren't discussed.

(D) can't be answered by the passage. The stage parodies of the late 19th century (discussed in lines 29–32) aren't said to have added elements to the cakewalk.

(E) also can't be answered. The author doesn't mention how long into the 20th century the cakewalk retained its popularity.

Passage 4: Group Cohesion and the "Groupthink" Problem

Step 1: Read the Passage Strategically
Sample Roadmap

line #	Keyword/phrase	¶ Margin notes
3–4	much better job	*Cohesive groups make better decisions*
7	To overcome	*How to promote cohesion*
8	need	
13		*Advantages of cohesion*
17	Typically	
21	But; pitfalls; :	*Danger of high cohesion*
22	while	
26	danger	
29	but	*How cohesion can lead to groupthink*
30	without; critical scrutiny	
31	strong objections	
32–33	misgivings; not worth pursuing; should	
35	fall victim	
37	defined as	*Groupthink defined*
40	major fiascoes	*Factors in groupthink*
43	:	
44		*1)*
45	for example	
47		*2)*
48		*3)*
53	essential	*Cohesion nec but not suffCohesion nec but not suff*
54	but not; so; important	
56	deteriorate	*More research needed*
57	or allow	

Discussion

Paragraph 1 starts off with the author touting the benefits of having a cohesive group when faced with group decision making. Right away, you get a sense of the **Topic** (group decision making). The author lists some of the advantages of high group cohesion and contrasts those with the psychological disadvantages of low group cohesion.

In paragraph 2, though, the author switches gears and focuses on the pitfalls of cohesion. Now you know the **Scope** (the advantages *and disadvantages* of cohesion). For the remainder of the paragraph, the author lays the groundwork for a *syndrome* of cohesion known as groupthink.

The author ends paragraph 2 by defining a key term, so you can predict that the next paragraph will expand on that term—and that's exactly what happens. After the author lists factors involved in groupthink, the passage ends by noting that cohesion is a necessary condition for groupthink but not a sufficient one. (Formal Logic can even appear in Reading Comp!)

The author's **Purpose** is to advocate high group cohesion and warn against a potential pitfall. The **Main Idea** is that cohesive groups make better decisions, but that same helpful cohesion has the potential to cause detrimental groupthink.

20. (A) Global

Step 2: Identify the Question Type
Any question asking you for the "main point" of a passage is a Global question.

Step 3: Research the Relevant Text
The entire passage is relevant to a Global question. Instead of researching a specific part, use your work from Step 1 to form your prediction.

Step 4: Make a Prediction
The author's main point is that high group cohesion is helpful in decision making, but under certain circumstances can promote groupthink.

Step 5: Evaluate the Answer Choices
(A) is a good match for this prediction.

(B) is a Distortion. The author's purpose is not to suggest possible safeguards against groupthink.

(C) focuses too much on details from paragraph 3 and ignores the preceding paragraphs in which the author touts the value of high group cohesion.

(D) is Extreme. While high cohesion can lead to groupthink, the author never suggests that low cohesion is ever preferable.

(E) is a trap for test-takers who mistake the last sentence of a passage for the Main Idea, but this answer concentrates too

much on that sentence and not enough on the role high group cohesion plays in groupthink.

21. (C) Inference

Step 2: Identify the Question Type
This is an Inference question because it asks you to infer the author's opinion (what he "would be most likely to say") about a hypothetical situation.

Step 3: Research the Relevant Text
The phrase "marked by disagreement over conflicting alternatives" is a content clue suggesting that the group in question has low cohesiveness. Therefore, paragraph 1 is relevant for your research.

Step 4: Make a Prediction
Groupthink can only happen in groups with high cohesion—that is, groups that are so in sync that they put the group consensus above all else. That doesn't sound like the group in question. This group sounds like they have little or no cohesion.

Step 5: Evaluate the Answer Choices
(C) is therefore correct. Groupthink can't occur in groups with low cohesion.

(A) is Outside the Scope. The author doesn't suggest any conditions under which "chronic indecision" occurs.

(B) is unsupported by the passage. Nothing in the text indicates that groupthink can develop from the level of disagreement exhibited by the group in the question stem.

(D) assumes that groupthink occurs in situations other than the ones the author discusses, which makes **(D)** Outside the Scope.

(E) is unsupported. More research may be a way to guard against reluctant acceptance in a group setting, but nothing in the passage definitively supports this idea.

22. (C) Logic Reasoning (Strengthen)

Step 2: Identify the Question Type
This is a Strengthen question because it asks for the answer choice that will *support* the author's argument.

Step 3: Research the Relevant Text
The conditions under which groupthink takes place are discussed primarily in paragraphs 2 and 3.

Step 4: Make a Prediction
Groupthink is characterized by overestimation of the group's power and morality, closed-mindedness to warnings of problems and alternative viewpoints, and unwarranted pressures toward uniformity. These all lead to the conclusion that cohesive groups are most susceptible to groupthink when they rely on or trust the group as a whole. The correct answer will make this conclusion more likely to be true.

Step 5: Evaluate the Answer Choices

(C) supports the author's argument by suggesting that groupthink doesn't occur when groups aren't cohesive enough to trust each other's judgments.

(A) doesn't help the author's contentions. The frequency with which groupthink occurs has no bearing on the argument about how it occurs.

(B) might support the author's claims about the features of groups with a healthy level of cohesion, but it doesn't do anything to help the author's groupthink argument.

(D) is a 180. The author claims that groupthink happens when group members defer to group consensus above all else. The development of factions suggests that the group wouldn't be cohesive, which is a prerequisite for groupthink.

(E) is a 180. Voluntary deference to the group opinion is a condition that helps promote groupthink (lines 31–34). So, if it's not necessary—as (E) says—that wouldn't help strengthen the author's case about what contributes to groupthink.

23. (B) Detail

Step 2: Identify the Question Type

The phrase "the passage mentions" indicates a Detail question.

Step 3: Research the Relevant Text

The components of groupthink are discussed in lines 42–52.

Step 4: Make a Prediction

The author asserts in these lines that the members of a group engaged in groupthink overestimate the group's power, close their minds to problems or alternate viewpoints, and censor themselves even when they doubt the validity of the group's reasoning.

Step 5: Evaluate the Answer Choices

(B) is therefore correct.

(A) is a Distortion. A group engaged in groupthink is less likely to entertain alternate viewpoints, but this doesn't mean that the group has "unjustified suspicions" of their adversaries.

(C) is Half-Right/Half-Wrong. Illusions of the group's invulnerability are mentioned in lines 45–46 as a feature of groupthink, but the passage doesn't say that these illusions develop out of high stress levels.

(D) is mentioned as something groups can avoid when they become more cohesive (lines 14–17), but that in and of itself doesn't cause a cohesive group to slide into groupthink.

(E) is a component of healthy cohesion in groups, but in groupthink, objections to majority positions *aren't* considered (lines 25–31).

24. (E) Inference

Step 2: Identify the Question Type

Two clues make this an Inference question: the word *inferred* and the phrase "author … and researchers … would be most likely to agree."

Step 3: Research the Relevant Text

The researchers are mentioned in paragraph 3, where the author discusses the factors of groupthink.

Step 4: Make a Prediction

Any part of paragraph 3 can form the basis of a valid inference. Instead of predicting all the statements that must be true based on this paragraph, check the text against the answer choices.

Step 5: Evaluate the Answer Choices

(E) is supported by the passage. The author and the researchers characterize groupthink as a *pitfall* of high cohesion. Also, the author's negative tone toward groupthink suggests that it's not considered a good thing for groups. For example, the author says groups can *deteriorate* (line 56) into groupthink and contrasts it with *effective* decision making.

(A) contradicts lines 52–54, which say that high group cohesion is not a sufficient condition for groupthink. Remember that the word *all* signals sufficiency.

(B) is unsupported. The author and the researchers characterize groupthink as a "recurring pattern" (line 43), so it's likely that the causal factors are not unique to each case.

(C) contradicts lines 54–58, which say that further research into group cohesiveness can help illuminate our understanding of groupthink.

(D) is Extreme. Although groups suffering from groupthink may exhibit closed-mindedness to outside viewpoints, that doesn't mean they *cannot* be influenced—it may just make them harder to influence. Also, the passage doesn't rule out the possibility that "outside information" may actually *support* the group's decision, so the information can be influential by cementing the group's belief that it is always right.

25. (E) Detail

Step 2: Identify the Question Type

This is a Detail question because it asks for what "the author says" as opposed to what the author implies, suggests, or would likely agree with.

Step 3: Research the Relevant Text

"Conformity in decision-making groups" is a content clue leading you to paragraph 1.

Step 4: Make a Prediction
Lines 5–7 say that when a group has little or no cohesion, people are likely to comply with the dominant idea out of a fear of reproach.

Step 5: Evaluate the Answer Choices
(E) is a match for this prediction.

(A) isn't mentioned in the passage. While groupthink and low cohesion can give rise to reluctant acceptance of group ideas, the author doesn't state that some group members actively *enforce* conformity on other members. And no situations describing when that would be *appropriate* are mentioned.

(B) distorts the author's brief mention of military decision making in paragraph 3. The only thing the author says about these military decision makers is that some of them helped researchers gain an understanding of the factors relevant to groupthink.

(C) is a Distortion. Inappropriate group conformity is shown to occur when members of the group don't want to upset the status quo or raise a fuss. Nothing is said about such inappropriate conformity coming from a lack of information.

(D) makes an Irrelevant Comparison between voluntary and involuntary conformity, which isn't raised in the passage.

26. (A) Logic Function
Step 2: Identify the Question Type
The phrase "in order to" signals a Logic Function question. Your job is to determine *why* the author mentions low group cohesiveness.

Step 3: Research the Relevant Text
The question stem points you to line 5. But the surrounding lines will also be important as you determine how the mention of low group cohesiveness fits into the overall argument.

Step 4: Make a Prediction
Lines 5–7 describe what can happen when group cohesion is low. The preceding sentence makes the point that a highly cohesive group is better at decision making than one that is less cohesive. So, this mention of low group cohesiveness is intended to support that point.

Step 5: Evaluate the Answer Choices
(A) is therefore correct.

(B) is an Irrelevant Comparison. Groupthink isn't even introduced as a concept until the end of paragraph 2.

(C) is unsupported by paragraph 1, which isn't arguing for dissent in groups of decision makers.

(D) also mentions groupthink, which the author hasn't discussed yet. Furthermore, the passage says that *only* highly cohesive groups are in danger of groupthink (lines 52–54).

(E) might be tempting because lines 7–12 discuss necessary conditions to overcome the fear that can result from low group cohesiveness. That's not the same as saying that the author is making a *proposal* for overcoming the effects of low cohesion. The passage as a whole is set up to argue for high cohesion and caution against groupthink—not to fix the "debilitating effects of low cohesion."

27. (B) Inference
Step 2: Identify the Question Type
Two clues make this an Inference question: the phrases "can be inferred" and "author would be most likely to agree with."

Step 3: Research the Relevant Text
The author's view is expressed throughout the passage. You'll likely do the bulk of your research in Step 5.

Step 4: Make a Prediction
Instead of trying to make a prediction, go straight to the answer choices. Don't select one as correct, however, until you can find support for it in the passage.

Step 5: Evaluate the Answer Choices
(B) is a valid inference. In paragraph 1, the author says that more cohesiveness means less censoring of ideas (lines 17–20). Also, in paragraph 2, the author points out that high-cohesion groups are much freer to deviate from the majority (lines 22–23) than low-cohesion groups. Then, the author goes on to discuss the pitfall of that freedom is that blind allegiance to the group, a characteristic of groupthink, prevents members from voicing objections and thinking through the issues thoughtfully.

(A) discusses negotiating styles, which aren't part of the author's analysis.

(C) is unsupported. If anything, a group that is too cohesive might not reach as sound a decision as a group with varied viewpoints that can be properly discussed and evaluated.

(D) is also unsupported. Groupthink does involve pressures toward group uniformity (lines 48–52), but that doesn't necessarily translate to "intense stress and high expectations."

(E) goes against the author's main contention that groupthink develops *only* in groups with high cohesion (lines 52–54).

Section II: Logical Reasoning

Q#	Question Type	Correct	Difficulty
1	Flaw	D	★
2	Assumption (Necessary)	E	★
3	Weaken	A	★
4	Paradox	E	★
5	Flaw	B	★
6	Assumption (Necessary)	C	★
7	Inference	C	★
8	Principle (Identify/Inference)	A	★
9	Assumption (Necessary)	A	★
10	Method of Argument	B	★
11	Main Point	B	★
12	Inference	D	★★
13	Assumption (Sufficient)	B	★
14	Weaken	C	★★
15	Flaw	E	★★
16	Inference	D	★
17	Role of a Statement	D	★★★
18	Principle (Identify/Assumption)	C	★★★★
19	Flaw	D	★★★★
20	Inference	E	★★★★
21	Parallel Flaw	A	★★
22	Flaw	E	★★
23	Parallel Reasoning	C	★★★
24	Strengthen	A	★★★
25	Inference	D	★★★
26	Assumption (Sufficient)	D	★★★★

1. (D) Flaw

Step 1: Identify the Question Type
The question stem explicitly asks for the flaw in the argument. Notice the disconnect between the evidence and the conclusion, and keep the common LSAT flaws in mind.

Step 2: Untangle the Stimulus
The executive concludes that a recent survey of retirees proves the company treats its employees fairly. The evidence is that 95 percent of respondents reported they had been treated fairly.

Step 3: Make a Prediction
A classic flaw is to improperly assume that a survey sample is representative of a larger population. Consider if any factor might make the survey group biased or skewed toward the executive's claim. In this case, the fact that the sample is of the company's retirees, but does not include current employees or past employees who quit or were fired, raises the possibility of a non-representative sample. Additionally, it could be true that mainly retirees who felt favorable toward the company bothered to answer the survey.

Step 4: Evaluate the Answer Choices
(D) describes representativeness, the common flaw implicated by the argument. The survey results are from retirees who chose to respond to the survey, so the results might not accurately reflect the views of retirees who chose not to respond, current employees, or past employees who quit or were fired.

(A) does not fit the argument, which does not employ circular reasoning. Indeed, the truth of the premise (a 95-percent approval rating among the respondents) is not dependent on already believing the conclusion. The logical issue is how to interpret that data.

(B) is incorrect. There is no reason to believe that the results of such a survey could not be verified by independent questioning of the respondents.

(C) does not apply to this argument. While there are multiple definitions of *fairly*, the executive uses the word consistently. In both instances, the word *fairly* is used to mean "equitably."

(E) is a 180. Because the respondents to the survey are retirees, to use their responses to conclude that the company has a long, ongoing history of good relations with its employees, the executive must assume that the company's more recent interactions with employees are at least as good as its older interactions. This answer would be correct if "presumes, without providing justification" were replaced with "fails to consider." It is vital to distinguish between Flaw answer choices that mention what the author assumes versus what the author ignores.

2. (E) Assumption (Necessary)

Step 1: Identify the Question Type
Even without clear language of necessity, a question stem that simply asks for the "assumption made by the argument" is a Necessary Assumption question.

Step 2: Untangle the Stimulus
The conclusion is that animal lovers actually contribute to cruelty to animals. The evidence is that they likely feed meat to their dogs and cats.

Step 3: Make a Prediction
The assumption needs to link the act of feeding animals meat to somehow being cruel to animals.

Step 4: Evaluate the Answer Choices
(E) directly bridges the gap between the evidence and conclusion.

(A) does not connect the evidence to the charge of animal cruelty. Additionally, saying *all* forms of animal life is Extreme.

(B) is Out of Scope. This stimulus is limited to those animal lovers who *do* keep domestic pets. Additionally, as with the prior choice, this answer fails to make a connection to the charge of animal cruelty.

(C) is quite possibly true, but does not need to be true for the argument to stand. It's irrelevant where some animal lovers are employed. And, as with the two prior choices, this answer doesn't explain why feeding pets meat means owners are contributing to animal cruelty.

(D) is Out of Scope. The stimulus is concerned with pets that *do* eat meat, not those that eat other foods.

3. (A) Weaken

Step 1: Identify the Question Type
The question stem directly asks you to weaken the argument. Identify the assumption and attack it.

Step 2: Untangle the Stimulus
The conclusion is that "these reading campaigns" are largely unsuccessful. But you need to define vague terms when paraphrasing the conclusion. So, paraphrase the conclusion as follows: Campaigns to encourage people to read fiction have been largely unsuccessful. The evidence is that revenues from sales of fiction have declined in most bookstores over the past five years.

Step 3: Make a Prediction
This argument makes two mistakes. First, this argument uses specific evidence to reach a more general conclusion. The evidence is limited to bookstore sales, but the conclusion suggests that fiction reading in general has gone down. The author overlooks the possibility that people have been buying books elsewhere (e.g., online), increasing their use of libraries, borrowing books from friends, etc. Second, the

author claims the reading campaigns have been unsuccessful, but it's possible the decline in fiction sales would be even more pronounced if the campaigns had not occurred. Therefore, they may still have been significantly successful. The correct weakener will introduce one of these overlooked possibilities.

Step 4: Evaluate the Answer Choices

(A) weakens by providing an alternate source of fiction books. This answer breaks the connection between bookstore sales and readership levels.

(B) veers off track by focusing on profitability versus revenue. Additionally, it introduces an Irrelevant Comparison. Novels may have been less profitable than newspapers and periodicals over the past five years, but that doesn't tell you anything about the amount of people reading fiction. Perhaps newspapers and periodicals have always been more profitable than novels.

(C) is Out of Scope. Biographies are not fiction, so this answer choice is irrelevant to a claim about fiction readership. It's possible that low prices would encourage people to read biographies instead of fiction, thus *explaining* the decline, but this isn't a Paradox question. This information doesn't affect the validity of the conclusion that fiction readership has declined.

(D) starts off well, because a predictable counterbalance to book stores' declining fiction sales would be increased library traffic. However, this answer is Out of Scope because it focuses only on a very specific category of *non*fiction books. You cannot infer from this that fiction readers are also frequenting libraries more often.

(E) is Out of Scope because the argument is limited to the success of *national* campaigns to increase fiction reading. It is irrelevant if fiction readership is stable or increasing in other countries.

4. (E) Paradox

Step 1: Identify the Question Type

A question stem that asks you to resolve or explain a conflict, discrepancy, dispute, or paradox is a Paradox question. Identify the two most apparently contradictory facts, and find the alternative explanation or factor that allows both to be true.

Step 2: Untangle the Stimulus

On the one hand, due to its high sugar content, you would expect honey to cause tooth decay. However, people who consume a lot of honey tend to have fewer cavities.

Step 3: Make a Prediction

Many Paradox questions depend on identifying an alternative factor that would make sense of the situation. Considering sugar levels alone, it's nonsensical that honey would cause

fewer cavities. Thus, there must be some other factor involved—either something in honey that's beneficial for teeth or something about the habits of people who consume honey that would explain the low cavity count.

Step 4: Evaluate the Answer Choices

(E) provides the additional factor that makes sense of the situation: Bacteria in honey inhibit tooth decay.

(A) may be tempting at first, because it limits *additional* sugar sources. But, regardless, honey eaters are still ingesting a lot of sugar. In order to be correct, this choice would have to indicate that the *overall* sugar intake of honey eaters is less than the rest of the population. However, this answer choice does not include that vital comparison.

(B) is both too modest and irrelevant. First, *many* merely means "at least one," which is not enough to affect the paradox. Second, the issue is not the preferred *way* people consume honey, but rather the *amount* of honey they are consuming. This answer choice doesn't provide any indication that dissolving honey in drinks would mitigate its effects.

(C) is probably true, but both *people* and "vary greatly" are so unspecific that this choice doesn't affect the paradox. Variation in dental hygiene habits would only resolve this paradox if better dental hygiene habitats were positively correlated with high honey consumption.

(D) is an Irrelevant Comparison. First, the paradox is about honey and sugar in general, not refined and unrefined sugar. Second, the paradox only discusses cavities, not health problems overall. Even if the stimulus had clearly defined honey as unrefined, and other sugars that tend to cause more cavities as refined, that still does not mean that dental health is one of the "more health problems" linked to refined sugars. This paradox would be resolved by a more explicit relationship between refined sugars and greater harm to dental health than unrefined sugars, but this choice does not make that connection.

5. (B) Flaw

Step 1: Identify the Question Type

The question asks you to identify a flaw in the argument. Notice any disconnect between the evidence and conclusion, and keep the common flaws in mind.

Step 2: Untangle the Stimulus

Byrne concludes that Thibodeaux failed to appear on time for a quarterly board meeting. The evidence is that two things guarantee suspension: 1) failure to appear on time for a quarterly board meeting or 2) missing two monthly general meetings. Thibodeaux was suspended but has never missed a general meeting.

Step 3: Make a Prediction

Byrne mentions two reasons for suspension, but the evidence does not explicitly dictate that those are the *only* reasons for suspension. This flaw could be described in different ways. First, the correct answer could be phrased as an unwarranted assumption that nothing else could have caused the suspension. Second, this flaw could be described as confusing a sufficient condition for a necessary condition, because either of these reasons is sufficient to result in a suspension. But Byrne treats them as the *only* reasons for suspension, i.e., *necessary* for suspension.

Step 4: Evaluate the Answer Choices

(B) describes the flaw in the form of an unwarranted assumption. If you are unsure, translate the vague terms in the answer into the more concrete terms in the stimulus: Byrne presumes, without providing justification, that if missing two monthly meetings or being late to a quarterly meeting each result in a suspension, then no other event is sufficient to result in suspension. In other words, Byrne assumes that Thibodeaux's suspension must be because of one of those two events.

(A) is an attractive answer because Byrne does fail to consider in general that other actions might be cause for suspension. However, because the stimulus doesn't indicate that being late for two or more monthly meetings necessarily results in suspension, failing to consider this *specific* possibility is not a flaw.

(C) uses Formal Logic words—*required* and *sufficient*— and may initially seem to match the prediction, but it subtly goes astray. Byrne's flaw is that he assumes sufficient reasons for suspension are also necessary ones. In other words, he makes an assumption about evidence. He does not, however, make an assumption about an *assumption*, as this answer suggests.

(D) is irrelevant. It is acceptable for Byrne to discuss tardiness without specifying the exact point at which someone would be late. Because both the evidence and conclusion correctly use the same terminology ("fails to appear on time"), this choice doesn't point out a flaw.

(E) is also irrelevant. Byrne's conclusion would not be affected by the amount of time Thibodeaux was an officer, and thus it is not a flaw for him to ignore it.

6. (C) Assumption (Necessary)

Step 1: Identify the Question Type

The assumption on which an argument depends is a necessary assumption. Look to bridge the gap between the evidence and conclusion. You can use the Denial Test to check your answer.

Step 2: Untangle the Stimulus

The author concludes that in the future, if recycled paper becomes the norm, paper manufacturers will have to use more filler. The evidence is that to make recycled paper look white, rather than gray, filler is required. Additionally, recycled paper requires more filler than non-recycled paper. Also important, notice that the author removes two possibilities: that whiteness can be achieved in ways other than filler and that filler use will become more efficient.

Step 3: Make a Prediction

The author is careful in the phrasing of his argument, but not careful enough. While he doesn't overlook the possibility that paper manufacturing could improve or that alternate whitening sources could be found, he does ignore the possibility that people may be fine with grayish paper. The argument can be boiled down to two Formal Logic statements:

Evidence:

| If | recycled paper looks white | → | extra filler |

Conclusion:

| If | recycled paper becomes the norm | → | extra filler |

The mismatched concepts are "the norm" and *white*. The author assumes that if recycled paper replaces other types of paper, current brightness standards will remain the same.

Step 4: Evaluate the Answer Choices

(C) matches the prediction. Assuming that the norm must be white is the same as ignoring the possibility that gray could become the norm. Answers describing ignored possibilities typically contain the word *not* and indicate what the author is *not* considering. The Denial Test is a great way to confirm whether this answer is Out of Scope or an ignored possibility. Just remove the word *not* and see if the negated version of the answer destroys the argument. If grayish writing paper *will* be a universally accepted alternative to white writing paper, then it no longer makes sense to claim more filler will be needed.

(A) is Out of Scope. The argument is limited to writing paper and what will need to be done to produce it.

(B) is also Out of Scope. Harm to the environment is unmentioned and irrelevant to whether more filler will be needed. It would be relevant to whether using filler is on balance a good idea, but that is not within the scope of this argument.

(D) is not necessary to the argument. The point at which filler becomes superfluous is irrelevant. If anything, this is a 180 because placing a ceiling on how much filler can be utilized effectively actually weakens the author's argument that more filler will be needed.

(E) strengthens the argument, because more paper would mean more filler. However, it is not *necessary* to the argument because more paper means more filler *only* if paper has to be white. If grey paper becomes the norm, it does not matter how much paper is produced.

7. (C) Inference

Step 1: Identify the Question Type
A question that asks you to fill in the blank to complete the argument (essentially provide a conclusion) should be treated as an Inference question. Fill in the blank with something that must be true based on the information in the stimulus. Do not select an answer choice that speculates beyond the scope of the evidence.

Step 2: Untangle the Stimulus
The stimulus is full of words that indicate Formal Logic: *only, any, no,* and *unless.* Translate each sentence into Formal Logic:

Sentence 1:

If	***stop carbon dioxide buildup***	→	***reduce burning of fossil fuels***

Sentence 2:

If	***a country reduces burning of fossil fuels***	→	***country reduces gross national product***

The third sentence requires you to equate "the costs of an action" with "reduce its gross national product." It translates to:

If	***a country is willing to bear costs***	→	***won't bear costs single handedly***

In other words:

If	***a country reduces its gross national product***	→	***a country won't do it alone***

Finally, the conclusion says, if we are to stop the catastrophic consequences of atmospheric carbon dioxide—or, in other words:

If	***we are to stop carbon dioxide buildup***	→	_____

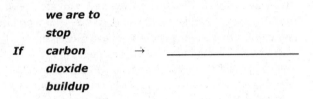

Step 3: Make a Prediction
A classic inference results from stringing together Formal Logic statements or a causal chain of events and then focusing on the endpoints: A leads to Z. All three of the pieces of evidence can be linked together to create:

If	***we are to stop carbon dioxide buildup***	→	***a country won't do it alone***

Thus, the blank in the conclusion should be filled with an answer that indicates that the countries reducing their emissions will not single-handedly bear the costs of doing so. In other words, the answer should indicate that there will be a global push to stop carbon dioxide buildup.

You can go through all the steps of translating the Formal Logic, but if the stimulus makes sense to you in plain English, then you don't need to bother. This stimulus could be summarized pretty simply: to stop carbon dioxide buildup, the world has to reduce the burning of fossil fuels. Doing so, however, would reduce a nation's gross national product, and a nation wouldn't be willing to be the only one to do that. Therefore, if there is any hope of fixing the problem, all nations must participate.

Step 4: Evaluate the Answer Choices
(C) indicates that multiple nations would have to participate. An international agreement on emissions standards would put countries on equal footing and prevent one country from bearing the costs single-handedly.

(A) is a 180 because avoiding the consequences of excessive carbon dioxide requires that nations become *more* concerned with pollution than economic burdens.

(B) may be initially temping because it includes an international scope. However, the stimulus discusses countries, not corporations, so this choice is Out of Scope. It's not clear whether a reduction in emissions by multinational corporations would be sufficient.

(D) is both Out of Scope and Extreme. While trust might impact whether countries are willing to enter into some sort of agreement to share the burden, trust is not mentioned anywhere in the stimulus. Additionally, distrust might not need to be completely *eliminated* for countries to work together voluntarily (or to be forced to by an international body).

(E) is Extreme. The stimulus merely indicates countries have to work together, not that they need to be merged into a world government.

8. (A) Principle (Identify/Inference)

Step 1: Identify the Question Type

The term *generalization* indicates a Principle question. Additionally, an illustration or an example is a specific situation. Thus, according to the question stem, the stimulus will contain a specific example from which you need to identify the principle, which will be in the answer choices. Paraphrase the stimulus in general terms, and watch out for answers that deviate from the stimulus rather than just broaden it.

Step 2: Untangle the Stimulus

The stimulus begins with a "clear advantage" of digital technology: Digital documents don't create waste. On the other hand, the Contrast Keyword [*h*]*owever* highlights a disadvantage: Digital documents are easily destroyed.

Step 3: Make a Prediction

Contrasts are of vital significance on the LSAT, both in Logical Reasoning and Reading Comprehension. Always note Contrast Keywords and understand the contrast being made. Here, it is likely the correct answer will generalize that a technology can both have a clear advantage and still have some disadvantages.

Step 4: Evaluate the Answer Choices

(A) looks great. You may have wondered about the phrase "a *property* of a technology" in this choice. What property do the statements refer to? That digital documents are "patterns of electronic signals," and that property is what causes both the advantage and disadvantage mentioned.

(B) is Extreme. It touches on the contrast but deviates from the stimulus, which mentions only one problem. Also, there is no suggestion that the disadvantage outweighs the advantage.

(C) is an Irrelevant Comparison. First, the stimulus introduces a *contrast*, not a *comparison of importance*. Second, while the stimulus mentions information preservation (or lack thereof), it does not discuss easy accessibility. While, based on your experience, you probably know that digital technology can increase accessibility, the positive *actually* mentioned in the stimulus is that it doesn't create waste.

(D) does not accurately describe the contrast made in the stimulus between an advantage and a disadvantage. Also, the statements describe only an advancement that causes

the risk of lost information, not any innovations that decrease that risk.

(E) incorrectly adds in the idea of convenience, while leaving out the mentioned disadvantage of ease in destruction.

9. (A) Assumption (Necessary)

Step 1: Identify the Question Type

A question asking for an assumption *required* by the argument is a Necessary Assumption question. Bridge the gap between the evidence and the conclusion. You can use the Denial Test to check your answer.

Step 2: Untangle the Stimulus

The museum visitor concludes that the mandated increase in the minimum wage will adversely affect the museum-going public. The evidence is that the museum does not have surplus revenue. This evidence supports the subsidiary conclusion that the museum will have to either raise admission fees or decrease services.

Step 3: Make a Prediction

A couple of assumptions come to mind. First, the museum visitor assumes there are no other ways, such as improving efficiencies, to deal with the minimum wage increase. Second, the argument presumes that at least some museum workers are paid either the minimum wage or within 5 percent of the minimum wage, so they will get a pay increase.

Step 4: Evaluate the Answer Choices

(A) is correct. The Denial Test is useful here to distinguish between this answer and some of the incorrect answers. "Some ... not" negates to "All ... are." If all of the museum's employees are paid significantly more than minimum wage, then the mandated raise in the minimum wage would not have any effect on the museum. The argument falls apart. So, it is *necessary* to the argument that at least some workers make minimum wage or within 5 percent of the minimum wage.

(B) strengthens the argument by eliminating a possible weakener. If the museum's revenue is on an upward trend, then it could provide for the increased wages. However, this exact scenario is far too specific to be *necessary* to the argument. For example, even if this were the primary issue, would it be necessary that wages had remained constant for exactly five years, rather than three or six? No.

(C) is a 180 because it indicates that workers make more than minimum wage, which minimizes the impact of a minimum wage raise. Also, stating that *some* make more does not necessarily imply that some do *not* make more.

(D) is also a 180 because it indicates a trend of increasing revenue that might result in revenue exceeding expenses in the near future, which could pay for any increase in the payroll costs.

(E) is not necessary to the argument. Whether all visitors have to pay a fee or not, the fact, as stated, is that current revenues do not exceed current expenses.

10. (B) Method of Argument

Step 1: Identify the Question Type
A question stem that asks you to identify an author's or a speaker's argumentative technique, method, or strategy is a Method of Argument question. This is a Dialogue/Response Method of Argument question, asking how the second speaker responds to the first. Focus on the structure of the second argument.

Step 2: Untangle the Stimulus
Helen analogizes reading a book to investing money.

Randi asserts that the analogy applies only to vocational books. As far as reading fiction is concerned, Randi believes the accurate analogy would be watching a sitcom.

Step 3: Make a Prediction
After the Contrast Keyword [b]ut, Randi narrows Helen's analogy. Randi accepts that the analogy applies to vocational books, but only vocational books. Then Randi asserts that reading fiction is analogous to watching a sitcom, i.e., wasting time. So, the correct answer will indicate that Randi partially refutes one analogy by using a different analogy.

Step 4: Evaluate the Answer Choices
(B) is an accurate description of how Randi makes her point. This answer has two components: 1) disputing the scope of Helen's analogy and 2) presenting another analogy. The second part is the easier to confirm. Yes, Randi explicitly presents her own analogy: reading fiction is like watching a sitcom. What about "disputing the scope of Helen's analogy"? Yes. Helen applies her analogy to all reading, but Randi disputes its applicability to all but vocational books.

(A) does not describe Randi's argument. She does not even mention how the evidence was gathered, let alone challenge the method.

(C) is Extreme. Randi does not go so far as to accuse Helen of reaching an absurd conclusion, especially because she partially accepts Helen's analogy as it applies to vocational books.

(D) is a Distortion. Randi does use an analogy, but she draws an analogy to sitcoms, which Helen doesn't mention.

(E) is Extreme. Randi does not deny the relevance of Helen's example because she accepts it in reference to vocational books.

11. (B) Main Point

Step 1: Identify the Question Type
The question explicitly asks for the argument's conclusion, so this is a Main Point question.

Step 2: Untangle the Stimulus
The author refutes recent speculation by predicting that no hardware store will open in the shopping plaza. The remainder of the stimulus provides the reasons why the author believes there will not be a new hardware store: If there were going to be a new store, then there would be publicity. But there hasn't been any publicity.

Step 3: Make a Prediction
The correct answer to a Main Point question should match the conclusion of the argument, without drifting into the evidence or speculating beyond the scope of the argument. The correct answer will match the author's prediction that a hardware store will not open in the shopping plaza.

Step 4: Evaluate the Answer Choices
(B) is correct.

(A) is background information about the view of others that the author refutes.

(C) is one of two premises supporting the author's conclusion. It is the Formal Logic statement the author presents.

(D) is Out of Scope. The author predicts that it will not happen, but does not give any opinion as to whether it is *unwise* to open a hardware store in the shopping plaza.

(E) is one of two premises supporting the author's conclusion. It is the negation of the necessary condition of the author's Formal Logic statement.

12. (D) Inference

Step 1: Identify the Question Type
A question stem that asks you to use the statements above to support one of the following answers (direction of support flowing downward) is an Inference question. Inventory the facts, focusing on the most concrete and emphasized facts, as well as any deductions that can be made by combining statements.

Step 2: Untangle the Stimulus
Contrast Keywords frequently highlight the most important information in the stimulus or passage. This stimulus contains several Keywords. *Although* points out that science has its own value system. *Yet* indicates that this value system does not require that possible negative consequences of theoretical research be considered. Finally, "[i]n contrast" calls attention to the idea that ordinary morality requires the consideration of foreseeable consequences.

Step 3: Make a Prediction
It is likely that the correct answer will relate to the contrast between ordinary morality and science's traditional value system. However, the correct answer to an Inference question can come from anywhere in the stimulus, no matter how

seemingly unimportant, so for each answer ask yourself if it is supported by the stimulus.

Step 4: Evaluate the Answer Choices

(D) is a modestly phrased deduction from the contrast between ordinary morality and science's traditional value system. It is possible for a scientist who ignores foreseeable consequences of her research to be in compliance with science's traditional value system but fail to meet standards of ordinary morality.

(A) is Out of Scope. The ethicist identifies the distinction between ordinary morality and scientific values but does not make a judgment as to which is correct.

(B) may be tempting, but it is a Distortion. According to the stimulus, ordinary morality requires only the consideration of *foreseeable* consequences. The harmful applications of some research may not have been foreseeable.

(C) is a 180 and a Distortion. The first sentence contradicts the view that science is morally neutral, indicating instead that it has a traditional value system of its own. Additionally, while the stimulus says both that science is thought to be morally neutral and that it does not consider consequences, the stimulus does not suggest that science is considered morally neutral *because* it ignores those consequences.

(E) is a 180 and Extreme. The stimulus explicitly says scientists can *sometimes* foresee future applications of their research. So, *never* is much too strong a word.

13. (B) Assumption (Sufficient)

Step 1: Identify the Question Type

The phrasing "conclusion ... follows logically if ... assumed" indicates a Sufficient Assumption question. Bridge the gap between the evidence and conclusion to prove the conclusion true. Keep an eye out for Formal Logic, which often appears in Sufficient Assumption questions.

Step 2: Untangle the Stimulus

The author concludes that companies that fail to offer the best quality *and* fail to offer the lowest prices will eventually go bankrupt (remember that "neither ... nor" means "not *and* not"; it does not translate to "not *or* not"). The evidence is that consumers want the highest quality at the lowest prices, and companies that fail to offer products attractive to consumers eventually go bankrupt.

Step 3: Make a Prediction

A sufficient assumption must prove the conclusion true by building a concrete bridge from the evidence. Look at the two pieces of the argument that contain a common term: go bankrupt. The assumption will link up the two mismatched concepts in those statements.

Evidence:

If	~ attract consumers	→	go bankrupt

Conclusion:

If	~ best quality AND ~ lowest price	→	go bankrupt

In order for the conclusion to be true, the author must be assuming that companies won't attract consumers if they don't offer the best quality and they don't offer the lowest prices.

If	~ best quality AND ~ lowest price	→	~ attract consumers

By contrapositive, the assumption is this:

If	attract consumers	→	best quality OR lowest price

In other words, one of those two things is necessary; nothing else would attract consumers.

Step 4: Evaluate the Answer Choices

(B) matches the prediction. If you want confirmation, link the answer choice to the evidence. If the deduction equals the conclusion, then the choice is correct. Here, the assumption links up to the evidence like this:

If	~ highest quality AND ~ lowest price	→	~ attract consumers	→	go bankrupt

The first and last terms in the chain match the conclusion, so this is the right answer.

(A) is Extreme. If a consumer is attracted to a company, then the company offered the lowest price or the highest quality. Perhaps no single company offers both, as **(A)** says. However, that wouldn't guarantee the conclusion that those that offer neither the best quality nor best price go bankrupt.

(C) is an incorrect contrapositive of the conclusion and thus would not prove the conclusion true. This choice negates without reversing. Also, an easier way to knock out this answer is to recognize that it includes the term *bankruptcy*, which is common to both the evidence and conclusion. Common terms will not bridge the gap in an argument.

(D) may be tempting because it eliminates another possible way to attract consumers (brand loyalty), but it's too tentative to be correct for a Sufficient Assumption question. If just *some* consumers won't patronize a company out of brand loyalty, then that doesn't guarantee the conclusion. As a necessary assumption, the author may assume that not *all* consumers will continue to patronize a company out of brand loyalty, but that's not what this choice says anyway. Additionally, this choice doesn't link up the two mismatched terms.

(E) is Out of Scope. The author merely points out one thing that will lead to bankruptcy. The author never says—nor assumes—that failing to attract consumers is the *only* way for a company to end up bankrupt. Additionally, this choice doesn't link the two mismatched terms in the argument.

14. (C) Weaken

Step 1: Identify the Question Type
The question stem explicitly asks you to weaken the argument. Identify the assumption and attack it.

Step 2: Untangle the Stimulus
The author concludes that the reduced speed limit caused the decrease in serious traffic accidents. The evidence is that the amount of serious accidents in the four years after the speed limit decreased was lower than the number of serious accidents in the four previous years.

Step 3: Make a Prediction
This is a classic causal argument. Evidence of a correlation (the reductions in both the speed limit and the number of serious accidents occurring at the same time) is used to support a conclusion of causation (the reduction in the speed limit *caused* the reduction in the number of accidents). The built-in assumption is that nothing else caused the lower number of serious accidents. You can weaken this argument by pointing out an alternative cause of the reduction in accidents. Factually, it is not possible that the subsequent reduction in the accident rate caused the earlier reduction in the speed limit, so reverse causation is not an issue. Watch out for 180 answers that strengthen the argument.

Step 4: Evaluate the Answer Choices
(C), as predicted, provides an alternative cause of the reduction in serious accidents. Fewer vehicles using that road over that timeframe could explain why there were fewer serious accidents.

(A) is a 180. To conclude that the lowered speed limit caused the reduction in accidents requires assuming that everything else that could affect the number of accidents was constant

between the two time periods. This answer strengthens the argument by indicating that traffic enforcement was constant. In other words, this choice eliminates a possible weakener.

(B) is also a 180. Increased police patrols would be a potential weakener, i.e., an alternative cause of the reduced accidents. This choice eliminates that potential weakener, thereby strengthening the author's case.

(D) is Out of Scope because the argument is limited to serious accidents.

(E) is a 180 because the implication is that after 1986, more accidents would be classified as serious. A potential weakener would have been a *stricter* definition of a *serious* accident starting in 1986, not a *looser* definition. Thus, this choice strengthens the argument by eliminating a weaken possibility.

15. (E) Flaw

Step 1: Identify the Question Type
The question stem specifically asks you to identify a flaw in the argument. Notice the disconnect between the evidence and the conclusion, and keep in mind common flaws.

Step 2: Untangle the Stimulus
The author reaches the subsidiary conclusion that humans are not rational and in turn ultimately concludes that humans are not superior to animals. The evidence, highlighted by the Contrast Keyword [*b*]*ut*, is that humans despoil the air, water, and soil through pollution and bad farming practices, which does not seem to satisfy the definition of *rational*: to have a capacity for well-considered thinking and behavior.

Step 3: Make a Prediction
The author makes assumptions both in going from the evidence to the subsidiary conclusion and from the subsidiary conclusion to the ultimate conclusion. First, the author assumes that acting *irrationally* in the care of natural resources means that humans are not rational. There is a scope shift between having a capacity and acting in accordance with it, as well as an assumption that how humans act in the areas mentioned is representative of human capabilities overall. Second, the author assumes that if humans are not rational, then humans are not superior to animals. This ignores the possibility that some other characteristic could still make humans superior to animals. Be open to an answer relating to either of these gaps in the argument.

Step 4: Evaluate the Answer Choices
(E) is correct. You can substitute the specifics from the stimulus for the broad terms in the answer and see if it is an accurate description of the argument: "fails to recognize that humans may *possess a capacity* (be rational) without displaying *it* (rationality) in *a given activity* (stewardship of natural resources)."

(A) is a Distortion. The argument's definition of rationality as having "a capacity for well-considered thinking and behavior" is not internally contradictory.

(B) is not an assumption of the author. The author clearly states that humans knowingly pollute, but the argument does not imply or depend on humans being aware that it is arguably irrational to do so.

(C) is Out of Scope. The author's conclusion is limited to the charge that *humans* are neither rational nor superior to animals. The author neither concludes that animals are rational nor that animals are superior to humans, so the author has no burden to provide evidence supporting such claims.

(D) is a Distortion. The author concludes that humans are not superior to other animals, but neither asserts nor assumes that humans are no worse than other animals.

16. (D) Inference

Step 1: Identify the Question Type
The question stem asks for an inference that must be true. Inventory the facts, focusing on the most concrete and emphasized facts, as well as any deductions that can be made by combining statements or Formal Logic.

Step 2: Untangle the Stimulus
The stimulus introduces two types of cats: good hunters and bad hunters. Then it provides some characteristics of good hunters:

> **If   good hunter   →   can kill up to half body weight AND has a high muscle-to-fat ratio**

The last two statements are less concrete. Most wild cats are good hunters, as are some domestic cats.

Step 3: Make a Prediction
First, notice that nothing in the stimulus provides information about bad hunters; therefore, the correct answer choice cannot be about bad hunters. (Remember that the negation of "good hunter" is "not good hunter," it's not "bad hunter.") Because most wild cats are good hunters, it can be deduced that *most* wild cats can kill prey weighing up to half their body weight and have a high muscle-to-fat ratio. The same can be said for *some* domestic cats. The correct answer will likely involve one of those deductions. Be wary of any answer choices that talk about *all* cats; those choices will likely be Extreme.

Step 4: Evaluate the Answer Choices
(D) may not be mind-blowing, but it must be true based on combining the fact that some domestic cats are good hunters with the absolute statement that all good hunters have a high muscle-to-fat ratio.

(A) could be true but does not have to be. While all good hunters must have a high muscle-to-fat ratio, the stimulus does not tell you anything about what *must* occur if a cat has a high muscle-to-fat ratio. Those cats may all be good hunters or a mix of good and bad.

(B) may be tempting because it compares *most* (more than 50 percent) to *some* (at least one). However, there are three problems here. First, this choice commits the logical flaw of confusing proportions and numbers. Just because *most* wild cats, compared to *some* domestic cats, are good hunters and thus have a high muscle-to-fat ratio, you cannot conclude that a greater *number* of wild cats are lean. There may be so many domestic cats in the world that even a small percentage would outnumber the wild cats. Second, *some* could mean anything from "at least one" to *all*. Therefore, based on the evidence, it's possible that the majority—or entirety—of domestic cats have a high muscle-to-fat ratio, thus completely disrupting the comparison. Third, this stimulus says only that *most* wild cats and *some* domestic cats are *good hunters*. But the answer choice compares how many have a high muscle-to-fat ratio. But just because all good hunters have a high muscle-to-fat ratio does not mean that *only* good hunters have a high muscle-to-fat ratio. It is possible many domestic cats are bad or mediocre hunters, yet have a high muscle-to-fat ratio, which would again skew the comparison.

(C) is Extreme. The stimulus does not provide *any* information about bad hunters; therefore, it is impossible to conclude anything about *all* of them. This choice isn't even simply an incorrect contrapositive of the Formal Logic rule, because the negation of *good* is "not good" and the negation of *high* is "not high" (not *bad* and *low*, which this answer includes).

(E) is Extreme. It improperly implies that all cats that meet one necessary condition of being a good hunter also meet the other. However, you cannot infer anything based on a necessary condition being met. Some cats might have a high muscle-to-fat ratio yet not be good hunters, so those cats do not necessarily have the ability to kill heavy prey.

17. (D) Role of a Statement

Step 1: Identify the Question Type
A question stem that reiterates a claim from the stimulus and asks what role it plays in the argument is a Role of a Statement question. Underline the claim in the stimulus before breaking down the argument into its component parts.

Focus on the *structure* of the argument and how the relevant claim fits in that structure.

Step 2: Untangle the Stimulus

The claim quoted in the question stem is the first sentence in the stimulus, an observation about the varying severity of drunk driving penalties. The next sentence provides a rule or principle about moral responsibility—that it depends solely on intentions and not results. The argument then concludes, indicated by the Keyword [*t*]*herefore*, that legal responsibility, at least in some cases, differs from moral responsibility.

Step 3: Make a Prediction

The first sentence is an example of a specific situation that, in combination with the principle articulated in the next sentence, supports the conclusion. The principle indicates that intentions are what matters for moral responsibility, whereas the example of drunk-driving penalties shows a situation in which results affect legal responsibility. This evidence supports the conclusion that moral and legal responsibility can differ.

Glancing at the answers reveals that each properly describes the statement as a piece of evidence in support of a claim or conclusion, but each of the answers describes the conclusion differently. Thus, this is a Role of a Statement question that at heart is really a Main Point question; the key is to find the answer that accurately describes the conclusion.

Step 4: Evaluate the Answer Choices

(D) is correct because it properly describes the relevant statement as evidence supporting a claim or conclusion. It also properly describes the conclusion that legal responsibility depends, in at least some cases, on factors other than intentions. This choice does not mention the conclusion's assertion that moral and legal responsibility differ, which may cause some test takers to reject it, but it is the only choice that is not explicitly wrong.

(A) is Extreme. It correctly identifies the relevant statement as evidence supporting a claim but does not accurately describe the conclusion. The actual conclusion is tentative, saying legal responsibility depends "in at least some cases" on factors other than intentions; it does not say legal responsibility depends *solely* on unintended results.

(B) is a Distortion. It correctly identifies the relevant statement as evidence (an *illustration* is evidence) supporting a claim but does not accurately describe the conclusion. The argument does not say that the criteria for legal responsibility *always* includes intent (the sole determinant of moral responsibility). If this were the case, then drunk-driving penalties would have to revolve around intent in addition to results.

(C) correctly identifies the relevant statement as evidence but goes wrong when describing the claim. The idea that people can be held morally responsible but not legally responsible is

an inference one could make, but this is not the argument's stated conclusion.

(E) correctly identifies the relevant statement as evidence but mistakes which claim it supports. The specific situation is only about legal responsibility (legal penalties) and thus cannot support a claim about moral responsibility. The claim about moral responsibility is another piece of evidence that, when combined with the specific situation about drunk driving, leads to the conclusion about legal responsibility.

18. (C) Principle (Identify/Assumption)

Step 1: Identify the Question Type

The phrase "conforms to which one of the following principles" indicates an Identify the Principle question. Additionally, because the question stem cites *reasoning*, the stimulus will contain an argument and the correct answer choice will be an assumption that underlies that reasoning.

Step 2: Untangle the Stimulus

The conclusion recommends against taking a strong position on an issue unless all conflicting evidence has been considered. The evidence is that understanding an issue fully requires considering such conflicting evidence impartially.

Evidence:

	If	understand an issue fully	→	consider conflicting evidence impartially

Conclusion:

	If	taking a strong position	→	all conflicting evidence has been considered

Step 3: Make a Prediction

There is a scope shift from evidence about understanding an issue fully to a conclusion about what is required for taking a strong position. So, the columnist assumes that taking a strong position requires understanding the issue fully. The stimulus is already stated in broad terms, so the correct answer should sound a lot like the assumption.

Step 4: Evaluate the Answer Choices

(C) is correct as it is the contrapositive of the prediction described in Step 3.

(A) confuses the stimulus's dictate regarding what is *necessary* to take a strong position and turns it into something *sufficient* to take a strong position.

(B) flips the chronology. Rather than taking necessary steps *before* taking a strong position, this choice describes what should be done regarding an issue on which one has *already* taken a strong position.

(D) is a Distortion of the evidence. According to the argument, understanding an issue fully *requires* impartially considering all evidence (i.e., not misinterpreting or ignoring evidence), not that impartially considering all evidence is *why* one should try to understand an issue fully. Additionally, this choice fails to address the conclusion of the argument, which must be included in a Principle question.

(E) is a Distortion. This choice properly identifies a necessary condition for taking a strong position. However, it incorrectly describes that necessary condition as the *existence* of conflicting evidence, rather than the impartial consideration of any conflicting evidence.

19. (D) Flaw

Step 1: Identify the Question Type
The phrase "vulnerable to criticism" indicates a Flaw question. Notice any disconnect between the evidence and conclusion, and keep common flaws in mind.

Step 2: Untangle the Stimulus
The author concludes that Jennifer's presence in the game will ensure the Eagles' victory. The evidence is that the Eagles have lost only when Jennifer was not playing. In other words, the Eagles have won every game in which she has played.

Step 3: Make a Prediction
This is a classic causal flaw. The author takes a correlation (when Jennifer has played, the team has won) and assumes a causal relationship (Jennifer's playing *causes* the team to win). When an author makes a causal flaw, the author is automatically overlooking three possibilities: alternative causation, reverse causation, and mere coincidence. The answer choice will likely suggest either that the argument makes a causal flaw or that the argument ignores one of the three possibilities.

Step 4: Evaluate the Answer Choices
(D) is correct. It is stated abstractly, but this choice suggests the author assumes that because Jennifer's playing and the Eagles' winning have coincided in the past, those events will continue to coincide in the future. In other words, it suggests that every time Jennifer plays the Eagles will win. In other words, the author ignores the chance that the past was just a fluke.

(A) is a very convoluted. Substitute in terms from the argument to see if it makes sense. This choice says the author concludes that, because Jennifer's participation is *sufficient* to result in a team win, Jennifer's absence is *necessary* for a team loss. There are a few problems here. First, this choice doesn't match the actual argument, which asserts what "will

ensure," i.e., is *sufficient* for, a certain result, not what is necessary. Second, the evidence does not actually indicate that Jennifer is sufficient for a win, it only indicates that the team has not lost when she played. Finally, this choice describes an accurate contraposition of logic, so it can't be the answer to a flaw. The issue is with the author treating a correlation as though it was Formal Logic; the issue is not that the author mishandled any Formal Logic.

(B) is a Distortion. Rather than relying on a computer analysis, the author acknowledges that "no computer was needed" to discover the information that led to the conclusion.

(C) describes a representativeness flaw, which is not at play here. The author does not extrapolate from the use of computer analysis in the case of Jennifer and the Eagles to the use of computers in sports generally. The argument stays within the scope of Jennifer and the Eagles.

(E) is a Distortion. While the stimulus does indicate that computer analysis provided no facts beyond what was already known, the conclusion is not about the value of computer analysis.

20. (E) Inference

Step 1: Identify the Question Type
A question stem that asks you to use the information above to support one of the following answers (direction of support flowing downward) is an Inference question. Inventory the facts and make any deductions possible. Beware of answer choices that are worded more strongly than the stimulus merits.

Step 2: Untangle the Stimulus
The stimulus discusses food containers made of recycled Styrofoam. Egg cartons are among the easiest to make because the used Styrofoam does not need to be as thoroughly cleaned as it does for other food containers. The reason for this is that the egg shells keep the actual food from touching the Styrofoam.

Step 3: Make a Prediction
The correct answer will likely focus on the contrast between egg cartons and other food containers. If egg containers don't need to be as thoroughly cleaned because the food does not come into contact with the container, it can be deduced that other containers need to be more thoroughly cleaned because the food *does* come into contact with the container. Still, evaluate each answer based on whether it receives direct support from the stimulus.

Step 4: Evaluate the Answer Choices
(E) is a modestly phrased answer that can be properly inferred from the stimulus. The fact that egg cartons do not have to be as thoroughly cleaned because the food does not touch the carton implies that at least some other Styrofoam

containers—those that have to be more thoroughly cleaned—come in contact with the food they contain.

(A) is Extreme. It is quite possible that other food containers can also be safely made from less thoroughly cleaned Styrofoam. The stimulus says Styrofoam for egg cartons does not need to be as thoroughly cleaned as that used for *other* food containers, but *other* does not necessarily mean "*all* other." Indeed, the stimulus only refers to egg cartons as *among* the easiest to make, indicating that some others are approximately as easy to make (likely because they also don't need to be thoroughly cleaned).

(B) is both Out of Scope and Extreme. There is no discussion of a food that cannot be packaged in recycled Styrofoam, nor is there an indication that such a restraint might exist.

(C) is a Distortion and Extreme. The only reason mentioned for cleaning the Styrofoam is to protect the future food that will come into contact with the container, not to remove residual food. Additionally, though the stimulus mentions *a* reason to clean Styrofoam, you cannot necessarily infer that is the *main* reason.

(D) could be true, but it is unsupported by the stimulus. Though egg cartons are among the easiest containers to make from recycled Styrofoam, that does not imply that the majority are actually made from recycled Styrofoam. It may be easier, or cheaper, to make egg cartons from other materials.

21. (A) Parallel Flaw

Step 1: Identify the Question Type
The question stem asks for the pattern of reasoning that is both parallel and flawed. Therefore, this is a Parallel Flaw question. Understand the type of flaw in the stimulus, and find its match in one of the answers.

Step 2: Untangle the Stimulus
The argument concludes that a child prone to depression is likely to become an adult who suffers from migraines. The evidence is that most adults who suffer from migraines were prone to depression as children.

Step 3: Make a Prediction
This is an overlapping sets issue. The argument assumes there are relatively equal numbers of the two groups in order to reach its overly simplistic conclusion.

Consider a more extreme example. Hypothetically, there are 10 chess prodigies in the world. Eight of them grew up in Russia. Would it be reasonable to then conclude that Russian children will likely grow up to be chess prodigies? No, there are millions of Russian children and only a handful of people will become chess prodigies. Similarly, just because most migraine sufferers were prone to depression as children does not dictate that children who are prone to depression will likely suffer from migraines as adults.

If you do not conceptually understand the flaw, you can get the right answer by generally mapping out the logic and looking for a match. In this stimulus, you see the following structure:

Most X's used to be Y. Hence, Y's are likely to become X.

Mapped out, the conclusion looks like an improper contrapositive, though the statements are less concrete than those used in Formal Logic.

Step 4: Evaluate the Answer Choices
(A) is correct. It shares the flaw described and maps out the same way: Most X's (good tempered dogs) were Y (vaccinated against rabies as puppies); hence, Y's (puppies vaccinated against rabies) are likely to become X (good tempered dogs).

(B) is incorrect for two reasons. First, it adds another variable: pet owners. Second, it doesn't make a prediction about what will likely happen to ill-treated young dogs in the future; instead, it makes an assertion of fact about what happened in the past.

(C) has an Extreme conclusion. The stimulus describes what will *likely* happen, while this choice indicates what will *definitely* happen.

(D) is incorrect because, like **(B)**, it adds another variable, and thereby has a conclusion that is an Irrelevant Comparison between dogs and other pets. In order to be correct, it would need to conclude that most dogs are likely to go to the vet.

(E) is incorrect because it is not logically flawed. Additionally, like **(B)**, it makes a conclusion about what happened in the past, while the stimulus draws a conclusion about what will occur in the future.

22. (E) Flaw

Step 1: Identify the Question Type
The phrase "error in reasoning" indicates a Flaw question. Notice the disconnect between the evidence and conclusion, and keep in mind common flaws.

Step 2: Untangle the Stimulus
The student's conclusion is that glassblowing must have originated somewhere other than Egypt. The student's reason is that there is insufficient evidence to claim glassblowing originated in Egypt.

Step 3: Make a Prediction
If the student is going to dismiss Egypt based on a lack of evidence, then theoretically the student should also dismiss every location for which there is insufficient evidence that it was the birthplace of glassblowing. That logic could very well lead to the conclusion that glassblowing did not originate anywhere.

The classic, though rare, flaw at issue here is the assumption that a lack of evidence *for* a conclusion is evidence *against* it.

Step 4: Evaluate the Answer Choices

(C) describes the predicted flaw.

(A) is incorrect because it is not a logical flaw to disagree with the majority opinion of experts; logic is not a democracy.

(B) is not an accurate description of the argument. The student cautiously limits her argument by using the conditional phrase "[i]f Professor Vallejo is correct."

(C) is incorrect, as it does not describe a logical flaw. While the student does not provide such criteria, that lack doesn't hurt her conclusion, and therefore is not a flaw. Do not critique an author for failing to define a term in the argument. (Although do be wary when an author *uses* a term two different ways, which indicates an equivocation flaw.)

(D) is incorrect because the evidence clearly states that the majority view is the traditional view. Remember, on the LSAT you must accept the evidence as true. You can merely critique the conclusion reached from that evidence.

23. (C) Parallel Reasoning

Step 1: Identify the Question Type

The phrase "similar … reasoning" indicates a Parallel Reasoning question. Characterize the conclusion in the stimulus, and compare it to those in the answer choices. If needed, compare the argument as a whole.

Step 2: Untangle the Stimulus

The author concludes that every mattress at Southgate Mall is on sale for 20 percent off. The evidence is that at Southgate Mall only Mattress Madness sells mattresses and all its mattresses are on sale for 20 percent off.

Step 3: Make a Prediction

Because this argument strings together two Formal Logic statements to reach a *valid* deduction, it will be best to compare the stimulus as a whole to the answer choices. Map it out, turning terms into variables:

Evidence:

If	mattress for sale at Southgate Mall (X)	→	Mattress Madness selling mattress (Y)
If	Mattress Madness selling mattress (Y)	→	20% off (Z)

Conclusion:

If	mattress for sale at Southgate Mall (X)	→	20% off (Z)

Step 4: Evaluate the Answer Choices

(C) is correct and maps out the same way.

Evidence:

If	food in Diane's apartment (X)	→	food in Diane's fridge (Y)
If	food in Diane's fridge (Y)	→	purchased in past week (Z)

Conclusion:

If	food in Diane's apartment (X)	→	purchased in past week (Z)

(A) is incorrect because the evidence does not link together into a chain.

Evidence:

If	food in Diane's apartment (X)	→	food in Diane's fridge (Y)
If	food purchased in past week (Z)	→	food in Diane's fridge (Y)

Additionally, the conclusion drawn is flawed. All of Diane's food, including the food she purchased in the past week, is in the fridge. But that doesn't mean all the food in her apartment (i.e., all the food in the fridge) was purchased in the past week.

(B) is incorrect and maps out as follows.

Evidence:

If	Diane's fridge AND food in fridge (V and W)	→	in Diane's apartment (X)

If   **food in Diane's fridge (W)**   →   **purchased in past week (Y)**

Conclusion:

If   **food in Diane's apartment (Z)**   →   **purchased in past week (Y)**

This choice probably would have been safe to eliminate after mapping the first line of evidence. Additionally, the conclusion is flawed. The evidence only discusses the food in Diane's *fridge*. It's impossible to conclude that all the food in her *apartment* (including possibly the food in the freezer and pantry) was bought in the past week.

(D) is close, but it fails in its conclusion. It maps out as follows.

Evidence:

If   **food in Diane's apartment (X)**   →   **food in Diane's fridge (Y)**

If   **food in Diane's fridge (Y)**   →   **purchased in past week (Z)**

Conclusion:

If   **purchased in past week (Z)**   →   **food in Diane's apartment (X)**

The conclusion flips the direction of the arrow between the X and Z terms. This conclusion could be true, but also could be false. It's possible Diane has eaten or donated some of the food she bought in the past week, and therefore it is no longer in her apartment.

(E) is incorrect and maps out as follows.

Evidence:

If   **food purchased in past week (X)**   →   **food in Diane's fridge (Y)**

If   **food purchased in past week (X)**   →   **food in Diane's apartment (Z)**

You can stop mapping here because the evidence does not link up into a chain of X to Y to Z. Additionally, the conclusion is flawed. The evidence doesn't tell you anything about food Diane purchased prior to last week. That food might not be in her refrigerator.

24. (A) Strengthen

Step 1: Identify the Question Type
A question stem that asks you to use an answer choice to support the argument above (direction of support flowing upward) is a Strengthen question. Identify the assumption and firm it up.

Step 2: Untangle the Stimulus
The author concludes that giving cows a better-quality diet could limit the total amount of methane produced by cows. The evidence is that individual cows produce less methane when on better-quality diets.

Step 3: Make a Prediction
Initially, there does not seem to be much of a logic gap to firm up. The conclusion stays within scope of the argument. Additionally, it does not make the usual mistakes: suggesting such a route should be taken, is practical, or would secure the buy-in of farmers. However, because this argument is on the LSAT, the author has to be overlooking something. The clue actually comes from the first sentence. The number of cows is growing, and this growth is due to demand for meat and milk. This leads to two overlooked possibilities. First, because the cow population is increasing at an unknown rate, lessening the amount of methane gas each *individual* cow emits might not be enough to keep the *total* amount of methane from cows in check. Second, there is a certain amount of demand for meat and milk. If bettering cows' diets leads them to produce less milk and meat, then more cows would be needed, which could negatively affect the *total* amount of methane produced by cows. The correct answer will indicate that one of these overlooked possibilities will not occur.

If those overlooked possibilities didn't jump out at you, look for an answer choice that, if added to the evidence, somehow indicates a change in diet would limit methane production. Or, look for a choice that eliminates a possible weakener.

Step 4: Evaluate the Answer Choices
(A) matches the second prediction. Initially, this choice might seem irrelevant because the conclusion is limited to methane production, not the overall utility of a better-quality diet. Yet, it eliminates a potential weakener. If a better-quality diet produced leaner cows that yielded less milk, then more cows would be needed to produce the same amount of food. Therefore, even with less methane produced per cow, the overall amount of methane emissions could go up. On the other hand, if each cow is producing less methane

individually while also yielding more meat and milk, then the number of cows required by the dairy and meat industries might go down, further decreasing the total methane emissions.

(B) challenges the author's contention that higher-quality feed will lead to lower methane production by cows. Because it calls one of the argument's premises into question, it certainly doesn't support the author's conclusion. Also, remember that on the LSAT, all evidence must be accepted as true.

(C) is Out of Scope. It introduces the unrelated topic of cost, which would influence farmers' decisions. However, the conclusion concerns only what would happen if cows were given higher-quality feed, not whether such a plan is feasible or likely, or whether farmers would participate.

(D) is an Irrelevant Comparison. The argument is concerned about overall methane production from cows and does not attempt to split apart the gas coming from dairy cows versus meat cows.

(E) is another Irrelevant Comparison. The argument does not mention carbon dioxide or compare relative impacts on global warming. The argument is focused only on whether a better-quality diet will reduce methane production by cows.

25. (D) Inference

Step 1: Identify the Question Type
The question stem explicitly asks for what can be "properly inferred" from the statements above. Inventory the statements and make any possible deductions. Keep an eye out for words that indicate Formal Logic.

Step 2: Untangle the Stimulus
According to the stimulus, facing danger only for pleasure is not courageous. The word *only* in the second sentence signals a necessary condition for real courage. Courage requires both acting to attain a goal and persevering through fear of danger.

If	real courage	→	acting to attain a goal AND facing a fear

Step 3: Make a Prediction
The correct answer will likely follow from the Formal Logic in the second sentence, potentially indicating that in the absence of one of the necessary conditions, an action is not courageous.

Step 4: Evaluate the Answer Choices
(D) is correct. It is a restatement of the second sentence of the stimulus. Someone who is working to attain a goal (benefiting others) must also persevere in the face of fear (i.e., that

person must also be afraid) in order to actually exhibit courage. In other words, someone must display both necessary conditions. Remember that "only if" indicates a necessary condition.

(A) is incorrect because it is incomplete. Although avoiding future pain is "acting to attain a goal," this choice doesn't indicate whether the person also perseveres in the face of fear. If so, *then* that person *could* be called courageous. **(A)** does not specify if the person is acting out of fear, so it can't be inferred that they're *not* exhibiting courage.

(B) is a 180. Rather than precluding a determination of courageousness, experiencing fear is a necessary condition for courageousness.

(C) is incorrect. Even if one *happens* to derive pleasure from a dangerous situation, it is possible to meet the necessary conditions for courage as well. A person is not courageous only if pleasure is the *sole* reason for facing danger.

(E) is Extreme. The person might experience fear in situations that not everyone else would fear. In those situations, therefore, the person might be considered courageous.

26. (D) Assumption (Sufficient)

Step 1: Identify the Question Type
The phrasing "conclusion follows logically ... if ... assumed" indicates a Sufficient Assumption question. Bridge the gap between the evidence and conclusion to prove the conclusion true. Keep an eye out for Formal Logic, which often appears in Sufficient Assumption questions.

Step 2: Untangle the Stimulus
The author concludes that if the newspaper is correct (new sirens will enhance public safety), then the public will be safer during severe weather in the future. In other words, the author concludes that if the newspaper is correct, new sirens will be installed. The evidence consists of a factual piece of evidence (the local replacement parts company has gone out of business) and a Formal Logic chain:

If	replacement parts are difficult to come by	→	government will install new sirens	→	public safety enhanced

Step 3: Make a Prediction
The author's conclusion matches the necessary condition of the evidence. Therefore, the author must think that the sufficient condition will occur, i.e., replacement parts will be difficult to come by. However, you might recognize the scope shifts from the closing of the local replacement parts company to the condition that replacement parts will be difficult to come by. The author incorrectly assumes the two

are one and the same: The demise of the local replacement parts company means replacement parts will be difficult to get. If that is actually the case, it would logically follow that new sirens will be installed and thus the public will be safer.

Step 4: Evaluate the Answer Choices

(D) matches the prediction described in Step 3. It ensures that the closing of the local company will result in replacement parts being hard to find.

(A) is incorrect, as it is merely an improper contrapositive of the newspaper's claim.

(B) takes a sufficient condition in the conclusion and says it has been satisfied; i.e., this choice makes the conclusion concrete instead of conditional. However, that doesn't actually bridge the gap between the *evidence* and the conclusion. This would be an assumption only if the conclusion was not qualified by the phrase "if the newspaper is correct."

(C) does not by itself guarantee that the conclusion will follow. The argument still requires the further assumption that if replacement parts cannot be purchased locally, then it will be difficult to obtain them. If parts could easily be bought online or outside the local area, which this choice doesn't preclude, then the conclusion would not logically follow. This answer would strengthen the argument, but it is not sufficient to prove the conclusion true.

(E) may be tempting, but like **(C)**, does not by itself guarantee that the conclusion will follow. The argument would still require the further assumption that the government wouldn't go ahead and purchase inferior replacement parts. This answer would strengthen the argument, but it's not sufficient to prove the conclusion true.

Games

age

on Type	Correct	Difficulty
	C	★
Be True)	D	★★
urate List	E	★
	C	★
	C	★★

gs

on Type	Correct	Difficulty
	A	★
7	"If" / Must Be True	A	★★
8	"If" / Must Be True	D	★★
9	"If" / Could Be True	E	★★
10	Must Be False (CANNOT Be True)	D	★★★
11	"If" / Could Be True	E	★★
12	Must Be False (CANNOT Be True)	B	★★

Game 3: Cake Layers

Q#	Question Type	Correct	Difficulty
13	Acceptability	A	★
14	"If" / Could Be True	B	★★
15	"If" / Complete and Accurate List	E	★★★
16	"If" / Could Be True	B	★
17	Partial Acceptability	B	★

Game 4: Contract Bid Review

Q#	Question Type	Correct	Difficulty
18	Acceptability	B	★★
19	Must Be False (CANNOT Be True)	A	★★★
20	Must Be False (CANNOT Be True)	B	★★
21	"If" / Must Be True	D	★★
22	Must Be True	C	★★★
23	"If" / Could Be False	A	★★★

Game 1: Dancers on Stage

Step 1: Overview

Situation: A choreographed dance on a stage

Entities: Six dancers—three male (Felipe, Grant, Hassan) and three female (Jaclyn, Keiko, Lorena)

Action: Selection. Determine which of the six dancers will be on stage at any given time.

Limitations: None. There's no minimum or maximum number of dancers at any time. This game's limits will be entirely determined by the rules.

Step 2: Sketch

Because there's no fixed number of dancers to be selected, there's definitely no need to set up slots. Simply list the entities for now. As you go through the rules, circle the dancers selected to be on stage and cross out entities left off stage.

Men	Women
FGH	jkl

Step 3: Rules

Rule 1 is a basic conditional: If Jaclyn is on stage, Lorena is off stage. By the contrapositive, if Lorena is *not* off stage (i.e., on stage), then Jaclyn is off stage. So, if one of them is on stage, the other one is off. In short, Jaclyn and Lorena can't both be on stage together. You can write out the Formal Logic like this:

$$j \rightarrow \sim l$$
$$l \rightarrow \sim j$$

Or you can use a different notation—which may be simpler and more direct than drawing out a full rule and its contrapositive—to indicate Jaclyn and Lorena cannot be on stage together:

Never ⓙ ⓛ

Rule 2 is similar to the first rule, but it has significant differences. This time, if Lorena is off stage, Jaclyn has to be on stage. By contrapositive, if Jaclyn is off stage, Lorena is on stage:

$$\sim j \rightarrow l$$
$$\sim l \rightarrow j$$

In short, if one of them is off stage, the other one is on stage. So, in lieu of writing out the Formal Logic, you could also simply note that at least one of Jaclyn or Lorena must be on stage at any given time:

ⓙ/ⓛ   At least 1

Rule 3 states that if Felipe is off stage, then Jaclyn is off stage. By the contrapositive, if Jaclyn is on stage, then Felipe is on stage. It's best to write that rule in Formal Logic form:

$$\sim F \rightarrow \sim j$$
$$j \rightarrow F$$

Rule 4 is less specific. If any woman (Jaclyn, Keiko, or Lorena) is on stage, then so is Grant. So, by the contrapositive, if Grant is not on stage, then none of the women are on stage:

$$j \text{ or } k \text{ or } l \rightarrow G$$
$$\sim G \rightarrow \sim j \ \& \sim k \ \& \sim l$$

Step 4: Deductions

Most games that hinge entirely on Formal Logic lack major deductions. However, because of the Duplication of Jaclyn and Lorena in the first two rules, there's important information to consider—if you didn't in Step 3 already—before going to the questions.

Combining the results from the first and second rules: 1) At least Jaclyn or Lorena must be on stage, but 2) they can't both be on stage. So, *exactly* one of them must be on stage. Furthermore, since Jaclyn and Lorena are both women, then at least one woman must be on stage at any given time. That sets off the Formal Logic of Rule 4: Grant must be on stage no matter what.

So, at a minimum, at least two dancers will be on stage: Grant and Jaclyn or Grant and Lorena. Plus, if the woman is Jaclyn, Rule 3 requires that Felipe is also on stage. Therefore, it's possible to set up Limited Options:

	Men	Women
I)	Ⓕ Ⓖ H	ⓙ k l̸
II)	F Ⓖ H	j̸ k Ⓛ

Keep in mind that Hassan and Keiko are Floaters. They can be on stage or off stage without directly affecting any of the other dancers.

Step 5: Questions

1. (C) Acceptability

As with any Acceptability question, go through the rules one at a time, and eliminate answers that violate those rules.

By Rule 1, if Jaclyn is on stage, then Lorena cannot be. That eliminates **(E)**. By Rule 2, if Lorena is *not* on stage, then Jaclyn should be. However, Lorena is not on stage in **(A)**, and Jaclyn is also not on stage. That can be eliminated. Felipe is not listed (i.e., off stage) in any of the remaining choices. According to Rule 3, that means Jaclyn should be off stage, too. That eliminates **(D)**. Finally, there are women on stage in both **(B)** and **(C)**, which means Grant should be there, too. That eliminates **(B)**, leaving **(C)** as the correct answer.

2. (D) Must Be False (CANNOT Be True)

The correct answer will be false no matter what. The four wrong answers will all be possible, if not definitely true.

Properly translating Rule 2 leads to the Numbers deduction: at least Jaclyn or Lorena must be on stage at any given time. Therefore, Keiko cannot be the only woman on stage, making **(D)** the correct answer.

For the record, Hassan is a Floater, so Hassan never has to be on stage. Therefore, as **(A)** says, Felipe and Grant can be the only men on stage. Similarly, as long as Jaclyn is not on stage, Grant and Hassan can be on stage without Felipe. So, **(B)** can be true. Finally, if Jaclyn is selected, Lorena is off stage. And Keiko is a Floater, so she can be on stage with Jaclyn (making **(E)** possible) or off stage (making **(C)** possible).

3. (E) "If" / Complete and Accurate List

If Jaclyn is on stage, then Lorena must be off stage (Rule 1), and Felipe must be on stage (Rule 3). Furthermore, because Jaclyn is a woman, Grant must be on stage (Rule 4). If you drew out Limited Options, this would have already been drawn out as Option I.

I) (F)(G)H   (J)k/L

The question asks for a list of all dancers that could be off stage. Lorena must be included, since she has to be off stage. Hassan and Keiko are Floaters, which means either one (or both) could also be off stage. So, the complete list is Lorena, Hassan, and Keiko, making **(E)** the correct answer.

4. (C) "If" / How Many

For this question, there must be more women on stage than men. Because at least one woman must be on stage, Grant must also be on stage (Rule 4). That means at least two women must also be on stage. However, Jaclyn and Lorena cannot be on stage together (Rule 1), so all three women cannot be on stage. Therefore, exactly two women must be on stage—either Jaclyn and Keiko or Lorena and Keiko. That means there can only be one man on stage—and that has to be Grant.

With Grant as the only man on stage, Felipe and Hassan must be off stage. With Felipe off stage, Jaclyn must also be off stage (Rule 3). Therefore, the two women on stage must be Lorena and Keiko:

F (G)H   J(k)(L)

So, the final tally is two women and one man, for a total of three dancers on stage. That makes **(C)** the correct answer.

If you had set up the Limited Options, a quick glance at Option I reveals that with two men already circled (Felipe and Grant), there is no way to circle *more* women (Lorena is already crossed off), so that meant the New-"If" for this question puts you in Option II. At that point, to keep the number of men less than the number of women, both Felipe and Hassan would get crossed off. Then, per Rule 3, Jaclyn would also get crossed off, leaving Keiko to be circled so there are more women on stage. That results in **(C)** as well.

5. (C) Minimum

This question asks for the smallest number of people on stage at any given time. By Rule 2, either Jaclyn or Lorena must be on stage. And because they're both women, there will always be at least one woman on stage, which means Grant will always be on stage (Rule 4). That's already a minimum of two dancers.

If Jaclyn were on stage, that would automatically put Felipe on stage (Rule 3), raising the number of dancers to three. However, if Lorena is on stage—Option II—then there is no need for Felipe to be on stage. Further, because Hassan and Keiko are not affected by any rules, neither one of them has to be on stage:

F (G)H   J/k(L)

So, two is the absolute minimum. That makes **(C)** the correct answer.

Game 2: CD Star Ratings

Step 1: Overview
Situation: A critic reviewing and rating CDs

Entities: Six CDs (*Headstrong*, *In Flight*, *Nice*, *Quasi*, *Reunion*, *Sounds Good*) and four possible star ratings (1, 2, 3, 4)

Action: Strict Sequencing. On the surface, this seems like a Matching or Distribution game (more similar to Distribution, because each CD will only get one rating, so the CDs can be distributed into four columns). However, a glance ahead at the rules shows a couple of rules that place CDs based on which has *more* stars than others. So, this can be classified as a Strict Sequencing game because the order of the columns matters and multiple rules deal with creating blocks that will straddle multiple columns. However, if you perceived this as a Distribution game, your setup would likely be identical. The exact game type label is less important than creating a proper Master Sketch that allows you to build in the information from the rules and then make deductions.

Limitations: Each CD gets only one rating, but there is nothing in the overview about how many CDs can get each rating—or whether each rating will be used.

Step 2: Sketch
The sketch should be one column for each rating (1–4 stars). It's understandable to originally consider setting this up with CDs at the top of a chart, with one space to assign the rating. However, ordering the columns by star ratings makes it easier to visualize which CDs receive more stars than others. With six CDs and only four ratings, there will be some ties in the sequence. Each CD will be sequenced once into one of the four star ratings.

Step 3: Rules
Rule 1 defines the limitations for the four star ratings. Each rating will be given out at least once, but no more than twice. Start by adding one slot to each column of the sketch and making a note about the maximum (e.g., "Max 2/rating").

Rule 2 provides some sequencing. *Headstrong* has to receive exactly one more star than *Nice*, which means *Headstrong* will be in the column directly to the right of *Nice*:

This means that *Headstrong* cannot receive a rating of just 1 star, and *Nice* cannot receive a rating of 4 stars. If you find it

helpful, add "~H" and "~N" under the appropriate columns in the Master Sketch.

Rule 3 establishes two options for a Block of Entities. *In Flight* will receive the same number of stars as either *Headstrong* or *Reunion*:

Rule 4 places a limitation on CDs rated higher than *Quasi*. There cannot be more than one CD with a higher rating than *Quasi*. However, it's important to realize that there doesn't *have* to be a CD rated higher than *Quasi*. Also, this restriction has no effect on CDs receiving the *same* rating as *Quasi*:

Max 1 CD > Q

Step 4: Deductions
The Numbers of this game are crucial. Based on the first rule, each star rating must be given to at least one and no more than two CDs. Figuring out the Numbers, that means that two ratings will be given to a single CD and two ratings will be given to exactly two CDs.

By Rule 4, *Quasi* can only have one CD rated higher than it. Thus, *Quasi* cannot receive a rating of just 1 or 2 stars. It is possible to set up Limited Options based on whether *Quasi* gets 3 or 4 stars, but neither outcome allows for any concrete deductions to be made. Therefore, it's not worth the effort.

Beyond that, there is very little that can be determined. Rules 2 and 3 set up some blocks, but only one offers some helpful information. By Rule 3, *In Flight* will receive the same rating as either *Headstrong* or *Reunion*. This could be any rating except for 4 stars. After all, that would mean two CDs get a 4-star rating, neither of which is *Quasi*. Thus, there would be at least two CDs better rated than *Quasi*, which would violate Rule 4.

The block of *Nice* and *Headstrong* (Rule 2) can occupy any consecutive pair of ratings. No entities are established for certain, and *Headstrong* is the only Duplication in the rules. Even that doesn't help because those two rules can only be combined if *In Flight* is paired with *Headstrong* as opposed to *Reunion*. The one final thing to consider is that *Sounds Good* is the Floater of the game, so it can be starred in the entity list.

So, the final Master Sketch should look akin to this:

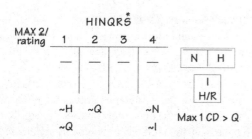

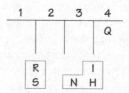

The 4-star rating can't go to two CDs for this question, because *Quasi* (by itself) would then get a lower rating than two CDs. So, the 4-star CD is either *Quasi* or *Nice*. However, *Nice* has to get a rating exactly one lower than *Headstrong*, so *Quasi* must be the 4-star CD, making **(D)** the correct answer.

	1	2	3	4
				Q
	R		I	
	S		N H	

For the record: With *Quasi* getting a 4-star rating by itself, there are two pairs of ratings that can be assigned to the block of *Nice* and *Headstrong*: 1- and 2-star, or 2- and 3-star. Then, the block of *Reunion* and *Sounds Good* will go to the empty rating. **(A)**, **(B)**, **(C)**, and **(E)** are all possible depending on the order of the blocks. However, none of them *must* be true.

9. (E) "If" / Could Be True

Here, *Nice* and *Reunion* will get the same rating—one star. To satisfy Rule 3, *In Flight* must get the same rating as *Headstrong*. Plus, by Rule 2, *Headstrong* (along with *In Flight*) will have to get a 2-star rating. That leaves *Quasi* and *Sounds Good* for the 3- and 4-star ratings, in either order:

1	2	3	4
N	H	Q/S	S/Q
R	I		

With that, only **(E)** is possible, making it the correct answer. **(A)**, **(B)**, **(C)**, and **(D)** all must be false. Unsurprisingly, an answer about the Floater—*Sounds Good*—is the credited answer choice to a Could Be True question.

10. (D) Must Be False (CANNOT Be True)

The correct answer to this question will be definitely false. The remaining four answers will all be possible, if not definitely true.

The most effective way to handle this question is to skip it temporarily and return after all sketches have been drawn for other questions. In that case, **(A)** and **(B)** would be eliminated immediately as possible by referring to the sketches for the previous question. **(C)** would be eliminated as possible after looking at the question stem of the question after this one! That would leave only two answers to test. Testing **(D)** shows that it is impossible (as described in detail later in this explanation), making it the correct answer.

Step 5: Questions

6. (A) Acceptability

Even with few deductions, Acceptability questions can be managed by going through the rules and eliminating answers that violate them.

By Rule 1, each star rating must be assigned to one or two CDs. No answers violate that. By Rule 2, *Headstrong* has to receive *exactly* one star more than *Nice*. It receives three more stars than *Nice* in **(D)**, so eliminate that. By Rule 3, *In Flight* has to receive the same rating as *Headstrong* or *Reunion*. That eliminates **(C)**. Finally, Rule 4 sets a maximum of one CD rated higher than *Quasi*. That eliminates **(B)** and **(E)**, both of which give *two* CDs higher ratings than *Quasi*. That leaves **(A)** as the only acceptable answer.

7. (A) "If" / Must Be True

For this question, *Headstrong* will get a 2-star rating. By Rule 2, *Nice* must get a 1-star rating. The question also states that *Headstrong* is the *only* CD to receive a 2-star rating. That means *In Flight* must get the same rating as *Reunion* (Rule 3). Only two CDs can receive any given rating, so *In Flight* and *Reunion* cannot receive a 1- or 2-star rating. Also, they cannot get a 4-star rating (otherwise *Quasi* would have to be rated below both of them, violating Rule 4). That means they get a rating of 3 stars. *Quasi* must then get a rating of 4 stars. There are no restrictions to the Floater—*Sounds Good*—so it can get a 1-star rating along with *Nice* or a 4-star rating along with *Quasi*.

1	2	3	4
N	H̲	I	Q
		R	

In that case, **(A)** must be true, making it correct. **(B)**, **(C)**, and **(D)** all must be false, and **(E)** is merely possible, but not definitely true.

8. (D) "If" / Must Be True

For this question, *Reunion* and *Sounds Good* will get the same rating. That means, to satisfy Rule 3, *In Flight* must get the same rating as *Headstrong*. With those four CDs paired up, the remaining two (*Nice* and *Quasi*) must each receive a different rating so that each star rating is assigned (Rule 1).

Alternatively, the question can be managed efficiently by grouping answers together to test more than one at a time. First, consider **(A)** and **(B)**, each of which gives *Quasi* a rating by itself. The only rule that affects *Quasi* is Rule 4, but that merely affects how many CDs can get a *higher* rating. *Quasi* can receive either a 3- or 4-star rating by itself. That means both answers are possible, and thus can be eliminated.

The remaining answers state that *Reunion* is the only CD to get a given rating. In that case, *In Flight* would get the same rating as *Headstrong* (Rule 3), both of which must then get a rating one star higher than *Nice* (Rule 2). *Headstrong* and *In Flight* could not both get a rating of 4 stars, otherwise they would both be better rated than *Quasi*, violating Rule 4. So, they must get a rating of either 2 or 3 stars. If they received 2 stars, *Nice* would get 1 star. *Reunion* could then get a rating by itself of either 3 or 4 stars. *Quasi* would get the other rating:

1	2	3	4
N	H	Q/R	R/Q
		I	

If *Headstrong* and *In Flight* get a rating of 3 stars, *Nice* would get 2 stars. *Quasi* would have to get a 4-star rating, leaving *Reunion* to get a 1-star rating:

1	2	3	4
R	N	H	Q
		I	

So, *Reunion* could get a rating of 1 or 3 stars by itself, eliminating **(C)** and **(E)**. However, it could not get a rating of 2 stars by itself, making **(D)** the correct answer.

11. (E) "If" / Could Be True

Here, *Reunion* will be the only 1-star CD. That means (by Rule 3) that *In Flight* will get the same rating as *Headstrong*. Combining that with Rule 2, those two CDs will get a rating of one star more than *Nice*. With *Reunion* being the only 1-star CD, that means *Nice* and *Headstrong*/*In Flight* will either receive 2 and 3 stars, respectively, or 3 and 4 stars.

However, *Headstrong* and *In Flight* can't both be 4 stars; otherwise, they would both get a higher rating than *Quasi*, violating Rule 4. Therefore, *Headstrong* and *In Flight* receive 3 stars, and *Nice* receives 2. Already having two 3-star CDs, *Quasi* must receive 4 stars. *Sounds Good* can be paired up with the 4-star *Quasi* or 2-star *Nice*:

1	2	3	4
R	N	H	Q
		I	

With that, only **(E)** is possible, making it the right answer.

12. (B) Must Be False (CANNOT Be True)

The correct answer to this question will be a CD that cannot get a rating of 4 stars. The remaining answers all could get a 4-star rating. If *In Flight* was a 4-star CD, *Headstrong* or *Reunion* would be, too. That would cause two CDs to get a higher rating than *Quasi*, violating Rule 4. So, *In Flight* can't get 4 stars, making **(B)** the correct answer. This question could have been immediately answered by looking at the Master Sketch if the relevant deduction from Step 4 was made.

For the record, this question can also be managed by looking at sketches for previous questions. *Quasi* has received 4-stars in several setups, eliminating **(C)**. It was possible to rate *Reunion* 4-stars in the trial-and-error sketches for the fifth question of the set, eliminating **(D)**. And it was possible to rate *Sounds Good* 4-stars based on the new sketch for the fourth question of the set, eliminating **(E)**. Finally, **(A)** could be eliminated because *Headstrong* could get 4 stars, too, like this:

1	2	3	4
I	S	N	H
R			Q

Game 3: Cake Layers

Step 1: Overview

Situation: Creating a layer cake

Entities: Six flavored layers (lemon, marzipan, orange, raspberry, strawberry, vanilla)

Action: Strict Sequencing. Place the flavored layers in order from bottom to top. Sequencing—turned upside-down.

Limitations: Each layer completely covers the layer below it, so there will be no overlapping layers. It's one-to-one sequencing: each layer used, one at a time.

Step 2: Sketch

Because the cake is described as being built bottom (layer one) to top (layer six), the sketch should be vertical to reflect that visual:

```
      L M O R S V

    6  ___
    5  ___
    4  ___
    3  ___
    2  ___
    1  ___
```

Step 3: Rules

Rule 1 prohibits the raspberry and strawberry layers from being consecutive—in either order:

Rule 2 creates a block, setting marzipan directly on top of lemon:

Rule 3 provides the relative sequencing of three layers. The orange layer will be somewhere between the marzipan and strawberry layers, with the strawberry above the orange and marzipan below:

Step 4: Deductions

One Duplication is marzipan, which is in Rules 2 and 3, and these rules can be combined to form one complete string:

Strawberry is also duplicated in the rules, but those rules cannot be combined to form any concrete deductions. The marzipan/lemon block can be layers 1 & 2, 2 & 3, or 3 & 4. However, only one of those outcomes (3 & 4) leads to anything significant. With only five questions in this game (including three "Ifs"), it's not worth setting up three Limited Options.

Just note that the order of four entities is already determined. As for the remaining two: raspberry merely needs at least one layer between it and the strawberry layer. And there are no restrictions on the vanilla layer—it is a Floater—so, it can potentially be any layer.

Step 5: Questions

13. (A) Acceptability

The four wrong answers will violate the rules, so test each rule individually, eliminating answers to find the one that's acceptable. Just be careful to note that the answers are listed from bottom layer to top layer. By Rule 1, raspberry and strawberry cannot be consecutive. That eliminates **(B)**. By Rule 2, from bottom to top, lemon should be directly below marzipan. That eliminates **(C)**, which puts marzipan on the bottom. Finally, by Rule 3, the orange layer must be between the marzipan and strawberry layers. That eliminates **(D)** and **(E)**, leaving **(A)** as the right answer.

14. (B) "If" / Could Be True

For this question, strawberry cannot be immediately above orange. The strawberry layer must be above the orange and marzipan layers (Rule 3), with the lemon immediately below that (Rule 2). So, strawberry cannot be one of the bottom three layers. It also cannot be fourth, because that would place orange directly below it (with marzipan and lemon in the bottom two layers). That means the strawberry layer can only be fifth or sixth.

If the strawberry were fifth, the orange layer could not be fourth here. So, orange would be third, with marzipan second, and lemon first. That leaves raspberry and vanilla to be the fourth and sixth layers. However, either way, raspberry and strawberry would be consecutive—a clear violation of Rule 1.

```
6   R/V
5    S
4   V/R
3    O
2    M
1    L
```

```
6    V
5    S
4   ___
3   ___
2   ___
1   ___
```

That means strawberry must be the sixth layer. Now, the fifth layer can't be orange and it can't be raspberry (Rule 1). It can't be marzipan or lemon, which have to be below orange. That leaves vanilla to be fifth. The marzipan/lemon block could be either layers 1 & 2 or 2 & 3. If the block were 1 & 2, raspberry and orange would be the remaining layers in either order. If the block were 2 & 3, then orange would be layer 4, with raspberry on the bottom:

```
6    S          S
5    V          V
4   O/R   or    O
3   R/O         M
2    M          L
1    L          R
```

With that, only **(B)** is possible, making it the correct answer.

15. (E) "If" / Complete and Accurate List
For this question, strawberry is not the top layer. It still has to be above the orange and marzipan layers (Rule 3), which must be immediately above the lemon layer (Rule 2). So, strawberry will be either layer 4 or 5.

If strawberry is the fourth layer, then the three layers below it will be (in order from top to bottom) orange, marzipan, lemon. The remaining layers will be vanilla and raspberry. Because raspberry and strawberry cannot be consecutive (Rule 1), that makes vanilla fifth and raspberry sixth:

```
6    R
5    V
4    S
3    O
2    M
1    L
```

If strawberry is the fifth layer, the sixth layer cannot be orange, marzipan, or lemon (all of which must be below strawberry). And it can't be raspberry, which cannot be consecutive with strawberry. That leaves vanilla for layer 6:

Although more can be deduced in the previous sketch, the question asks for all possible layers that could be vanilla and that information has already been determined. Depending on which layer is strawberry, vanilla can be either the fifth or sixth layer—and that's it. That makes **(E)** the correct answer.

16. (B) "If" / Could Be True
For this question, lemon is the third layer. That means marzipan is the fourth layer (Rule 2), which means the fifth and sixth layers must be orange and strawberry, respectively (Rule 3). The first and second layer will be raspberry and vanilla, in either order:

```
6    S
5    O
4    M
3    L
2   R/V
1   V/R
```

With that, only answer **(B)** is possible, making it the correct answer. **(A)**, **(C)**, **(D)**, and **(E)** all must be false.

17. (B) Partial Acceptability
The correct answer will be the one pair of layers that could be layers 1 and 2, in that order. Even though all layers are not listed, start by testing the rules one at a time and eliminating answers that violate them.

By Rule 1, raspberry cannot be consecutive with strawberry. That eliminates **(E)**. By Rule 2, lemon must be immediately topped by marzipan. That eliminates **(A)**, which puts raspberry, not marzipan, directly on top of lemon. It also eliminates **(C)**, which puts marzipan on the bottom, leaving no room for lemon underneath. And it also eliminates **(D)**, which puts raspberry, not lemon, immediately below marzipan. That leaves **(B)** as the only possibility, and thus the correct answer.

Alternatively, this question could be approached by consulting previous work. In the new sketch for the previous question, the bottom two layers are raspberry and vanilla in either order—so that quickly shows that **(B)** is possible.

Game 4: Contract Bid Review

Step 1: Overview
Situation: A panel reviewing contract bids

Entities: Six bids (H, J, K, R, S, T)

Action: Strict Sequencing. The note that no two bids have the same cost suggests Sequencing. A quick glance at the rules (with terms such as *lower* and *higher*) confirms that. The twist about choosing exactly one bid as accepted hints at Selection. However, the first rule confirms that the choice is limited between just two bids, so it is a pretty miniscule part of the game's overall action. That said, if you alternatively classified the game as a Hybrid of Sequencing and Selection, you'd be justified in labeling the game as such.

Limitations: For the Sequencing, no two bids have the same cost. For the Selection twist, exactly one bid gets accepted.

Step 2: Sketch
The game primarily revolves around sequencing the bids in order of cost, and because the rules use the terms *higher* and *lower*, a vertical sketch would be ideal:

HJKRST

Highest 6	___
5	___
4	___
3	___
2	___
Lowest 1	___

As for the Selection component, the accepted bid should be distinguished in some way. Either circling it or marking it with an asterisk in the sketch or list of entities would suffice.

Step 3: Rules
Rule 1 provides a lot of information about the accepted bid: it must be K or R, and it will be second or third lowest in cost. Make a note in shorthand next to the sketch, using arrows to indicate it will be in the second or third lowest slot.

Rule 2 provides some relative sequencing. J and K will both be higher in cost than H, with no defined relationship between J and K:

$$J \quad K$$
$$\diagdown \diagup$$
$$H$$

Rules 3 and 4 both involve Formal Logic. What's more significant, through, is that both rules revolve around the placement of J. One indicates what will happen if J is fourth lowest in cost, the other if J is *not* fourth lowest. Because there are no other options (either J is fourth lowest or it's not) and J is also mentioned in Rule 2, these Formal Logic rules

will be used to set up Limited Options. Draw two sketches out, one with J in the fourth slot from the bottom, the other with "~J" next to the fourth slot. Save the rest of the information for making deductions.

Rule 5 limits the fifth lowest bid to R or S. Place "R/S" in the fifth spot from the bottom in each sketch.

Step 4: Deductions
With two options drawn, it's time to add the information from Rules 3 and 4 into the appropriate sketches.

The first option is based on Rule 3, with J as the fourth lowest bid. By Rule 3, S and T will have a higher cost, putting them in the top two spots. However, according to Rule 5, the fifth lowest can only be R or S. So, S will be the fifth lowest and T will be the sixth lowest (i.e., the highest). The remaining bids (H, K, and R) will be the lowest three bids. With H having a lower cost than K (Rule 2), H cannot be third lowest, and K cannot be the absolute lowest:

I)			
Highest	6	T	
	5	S	
	4	J	~H
	3	___	(K/R)
	2	___	
Lowest	1	___	~K

The second option is based on Rule 4, with J *not* the fourth lowest bid. By Rule 4, J will have a higher cost than S and T. And, by Rule 2, J must have a higher cost than H. That means J cannot be one of the three lowest bids. It won't be fourth lowest for this option, and it can't be fifth lowest (Rule 5), so it must be sixth lowest (i.e., highest). R or S will be fifth lowest (Rule 5). By Rule 2, K must still be higher in cost than H. So, H will not be fourth lowest, and K will not be the lowest:

II)			
Highest	6	J	
	5	R/S	
	4	___	~H
	3	___	(K/R)
	2	___	
Lowest	1	___	~K

For both options, J always has a higher cost than H, satisfying Rule 2. So, for that rule, the one thing to remember is that K will also have a higher cost than H. So, make sure that information from Rule 2 is noted to the side of one or both Limited Options.

$$K$$
$$|$$
$$H$$

Step 5: Questions

18. (B) Acceptability

As with any Acceptability question, go through the rules one at a time, knocking out violating answers. Be careful, noting that the answers are listed from lowest to highest.

By Rule 1, the second or third lowest bid has to be K or R. That eliminates **(C)**. By Rule 2, J and K must both be ranked higher than H. That eliminates **(A)**, which ranks K *lower* than H. J is fourth lowest in **(D)**, but is ranked higher than S. That violates Rule 3, so it can be eliminated. By Rule 4, if J is not fourth, it must be higher in cost than S and T. However, J is not fourth in **(E)** and is *lower* than S and T. That can be eliminated, leaving **(B)** as the correct answer. Rule 5 would have also knocked out **(A)** had it not already been eliminated by Rule 2.

19. (A) Must Be False (CANNOT Be True)

The correct answer will be a bid that can never be fourth lowest. The remaining four answers list bids that could be fourth lowest. J is fourth lowest in the first option, so that eliminates **(B)**. If J is not fourth (as in Option II), it can only be sixth lowest. In that case, R or S will be fifth highest. The only other restriction is that H has to be lower in cost than K. That means H cannot be fourth lowest, because there would be no spot left for K. H cannot be fourth lowest in either option, making **(A)** the correct answer.

20. (B) Must Be False (CANNOT Be True)

The correct answer will be a bid that can never be second lowest. The remaining four answers list bids that could be second lowest. The Limited Options do not provide clear information on which bids *can* and *cannot* be the second lowest. K and R appear to be able to go there, but need not be placed there. So, in order to avoid significant trial and error, it is important to consider if there are already Established Entities that would not be second lowest simply because they've already been otherwise placed.

J is fourth lowest in Option I. If J was not fourth lowest—Option II—it would have to higher in cost than S and T (Rule 4), as well as H (Rule 2), placing it definitely sixth lowest. Thus, J could never be second lowest, making **(B)** the correct answer.

21. (D) "If" / Must Be True

For this question, R is the accepted bid, which means it must have the second or third lowest cost (Rule 1). Unfortunately, that does not limit the information to a single option. However, it does guarantee that S is the fifth lowest bid (Rule 5):

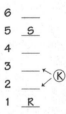

That makes **(D)** the correct answer. All of the remaining answers are possible, but none of them must be true.

22. (C) Must Be True

The correct answer to this question must be true no matter what. The remaining answers could all be false.

If J was not fourth lowest in cost (Option II), S and T could be anywhere lower in cost (Rule 4). That means either one could be the lowest in cost, so H does not *have* to be lower in cost than either one. That eliminates **(A)** and **(B)**.

If J was fourth lowest (Option I), S and T would have the highest two costs (Rule 3). S would then be higher, not lower, in cost than both J and K. That eliminates **(D)** and **(E)**.

That leaves **(C)** as the correct answer. After all, if J was fourth lowest in cost (Option I), the costliest bids would be S and T. K would have to have a lower cost than J in that case. And if J was *not* fourth lowest in cost (Option II), it would have to be the sixth lowest (i.e., highest) in cost. K would have to be lower in cost there, too.

23. (A) "If" / Could Be False

For this question, R will be the lowest in cost. That doesn't point to a specific option, but it does lead to two pieces of information: K will be the accepted bid (Rule 1), and S will have to be fifth lowest in cost (Rule 5):

6 _____
5 _S_
4 _____
3 _____↘
2 _____↗Ⓚ
1 _R_

With K as the accepted bid, it must be second or third lowest in cost, but it still has to be higher in cost than H (don't forget about that part of Rule 2). So, K must be third lowest, with H second lowest. That leaves J and T to be the fourth and sixth lowest bids. Either order is acceptable without violating the rules:

```
6   J/T
5    S
4   T/J
3   (K)
2    H
1    R
```

So, J does not have to be highest in cost. That means **(A)** could be false, making it the correct answer. All the remaining answers must be true.

Section IV: Logical Reasoning

Q#	Question Type	Correct	Difficulty
1	Strengthen	E	★
2	Method of Argument	D	★
3	Assumption (Necessary)	A	★
4	Flaw	D	★
5	Inference	E	★
6	Paradox	C	★
7	Assumption (Necessary)	D	★
8	Parallel Flaw	C	★
9	Principle (Identify/Strengthen)	A	★★★
10	Weaken	D	★★★
11	Main Point	C	★★★★
12	Inference	D	★
13	Paradox	A	★★
14	Flaw	D	★★
15	Role of a Statement	B	★★★★
16	Flaw	A	★★★★
17	Principle (Apply/Inference)	E	★★
18	Assumption (Necessary)	C	★★
19	Flaw	B	★
20	Strengthen	A	★★★
21	Paradox	C	★★
22	Assumption (Sufficient)	B	★★★
23	Inference	B	★★★
24	Assumption (Necessary)	E	★
25	Parallel Reasoning	C	★★

1. (E) Strengthen

Step 1: Identify the Question Type
Because the correct answer "most strengthens" the editorialist's argument, this is a Strengthen question. The correct answer will reinforce the editorialist's assumption or fill a hole in the argument.

Step 2: Untangle the Stimulus
Break down the argument into evidence and conclusion. The conclusion follows [*t*]*hus* at the end of the stimulus. The editorialist's main point is that election results do not necessarily reflect the pure opinion of the people. The editorialist's evidence is that political strategists use advertising techniques designed to sway public opinion.

Step 3: Make a Prediction
The strengthener can be found by analyzing overlooked possibilities. By assuming that the use of political advertising means election results are not representative of the people's true opinions, the editorialist overlooks the possibility that advertisements fail to influence voters. The correct strengthener will rule out this possibility.

Step 4: Evaluate the Answer Choices
(E) matches the prediction. Political ads have a tangible effect.

(A) is an Irrelevant Comparison. The editorialist's argument is solely about democratic countries.

(B) doesn't address whether political advertisements influence voters. If anything, this choice would be a weakener, because people would be more able to resist obvious manipulation.

(C) is Out of Scope. It discusses the amount *spent* on political advertising, rather than focusing on the *effect* of political advertising.

(D) is a 180, because it weakens the argument. This choice suggests that the political ads are less likely to change the results of the election, because people who don't view the advertisements are more likely to vote.

2. (D) Method of Argument

Step 1: Identify the Question Type
Because the correct answer describes the way in which Terry "responds to" Kris, this is a Method of Argument question. Read Kris's argument, but focus your attention on Terry's rebuttal. Expect Terry to point out a flaw in Kris's logic. Knowing common flaw types can help.

Step 2: Untangle the Stimulus
Start by paraphrasing Kris's argument. Kris's conclusion is that the cell phone industry should be regulated. Kris compares the pollution of the cell phone industry to that of the chemical industry, which is currently regulated. Next, paraphrase Terry's response. Terry strongly disagrees with

Kris, pointing out that chemical pollution can be more harmful than cellular pollution.

Step 3: Make a Prediction
Kris's argument uses evidence of how two things share a characteristic (both industries pollute) in order to draw the conclusion that they should be treated similarly (both should be regulated). Thus, Kris's argument draws an analogy between the two industries. Terry refutes the faulty analogy by pointing out a relevant difference between chemicals and cell phones (namely, that chemicals are harmful, while cell phones are at worst just annoying).

Step 4: Evaluate the Answer Choices
(D) matches the prediction.

(A) is Out of Scope. Terry never mentions the source of Kris's information.

(B) is also Out of Scope. Terry doesn't question the accuracy of Kris's evidence, just its relevance.

(C) is a Distortion. Terry does talk about cause-and-effect, but only to point out that the effects of cell phone pollution and chemical pollution aren't sufficiently similar for Kris's conclusion to follow. Terry doesn't suggest that a causal relationship in Kris's argument is reversed.

(E) is a Distortion. Terry does not question Kris's interpretation of "technological progress." Rather, Terry's response is based on the crucial difference between the two types of *pollution*.

3. (A) Assumption (Necessary)

Step 1: Identify the Question Type
This is a Necessary Assumption question because the correct answer is the assumption *required* by the argument in the stimulus. You can use the Denial Test to check your answer.

Step 2: Untangle the Stimulus
Break down the argument into the evidence and conclusion. The researcher's main point is the first sentence: A country can determine the best type of public school system for it by looking at other countries' school systems. The researcher suggests how this could work: Nationwide tests could be given, and the school system of the highest scoring country could be co-opted.

Step 3: Make a Prediction
This argument is based on a giant scope shift. The conclusion is about finding the best type of school system for a *particular* country. The evidence suggests looking at the test results of *foreign* school systems. Therefore, the researcher must be assuming that what gets good results in one country would work just as well in another. Said differently, this argument overlooks the possibility that there are important differences between countries that could prevent a school system from being successfully adopted.

Step 4: Evaluate the Answer Choices

(A) matches the prediction. If a school system that works well in one country would *not* work well in any other country, then the researcher's argument falls apart.

(B) goes Out of Scope by introducing private schools. This argument is just about public school systems.

(C) takes the argument further than necessary. The researcher's argument is about finding the best school system, not figuring out *why* that system is the best.

(D) might make the researcher's job easier, but it isn't necessary to the argument. Even if they *aren't* currently administering nationwide tests, the researcher's plan might still be valid.

(E) describes a control that could make the various tests more representative and easier to compare, but it isn't required by the argument. Even if the testing *doesn't* target similar grade levels, the researcher might still be able to find the best school system (maybe by comparing percentage correct, for example).

4. (D) Flaw

Step 1: Identify the Question Type

Because the correct answer describes why the argument "is most vulnerable to criticism," this is a Flaw question.

Step 2: Untangle the Stimulus

Analyze the argument's evidence and conclusion. The conclusion follows [*t*]*herefore* in the last sentence. Ray's main point is that hitting a pothole is not what caused the trunk of Cynthia's car to open. Ray's evidence is that her car's trunk has opened at other times when there was no pothole involved.

Step 3: Make a Prediction

Ray bases his argument on past evidence: Several times previously, the trunk of Cynthia's car opened without her hitting a pothole. Therefore, Ray says, hitting a pothole was *not* the cause this time. This question is testing your understanding of causal relationships. Here, Ray is overlooking the possibility that even though the trunk popped open for some other reason the first few times, a pothole might still have been at fault this time.

Step 4: Evaluate the Answer Choices

(D) matches the prediction. Ray does not consider that the trunk could pop open for many different reasons, sometimes because of a pothole, sometimes not.

(A) is Out of Scope. Ray's argument is just about Cynthia and her car.

(B) goes Out of Scope by introducing the effect a pothole could have on a car's engine. Ray's argument is just about the trunk of Cynthia's car, not her car's engine. While he does fail to consider this possibility, any effects on the engine wouldn't affect his argument about the trunk, so ignoring this is not a flaw.

(C) is a Distortion. While it does address causal relationships, **(C)** doesn't match the stimulus. Ray basically argues that a single event (the trunk popping open) cannot have two different causes (something besides a pothole and a pothole), whereas this choice suggests he says a single event cannot cause two results.

(E) describes circular reasoning, which is when the evidence is essentially the same as the conclusion. Ray, however, offers evidence that differs from the conclusion, however questionable that evidence may be.

5. (E) Inference

Step 1: Identify the Question Type

This is an Inference question because the correct answer is "supported by the information" in the stimulus. The correct answer will follow directly from the stimulus.

Step 2: Untangle the Stimulus

Make an inventory of the statements in the stimulus, paraphrasing as you read. First, journalists all agree lying is wrong. However, that's where the agreement ends. In the first case, some reporters think a quote should be reported word-for-word, while others think it is acceptable to change the words to make the quote more concise. In the second case, some reporters think that not identifying oneself as a reporter is allowed in order to expose wrongdoing, but others think that it is not.

Step 3: Make a Prediction

Connect ideas that come up more than once in the stimulus. You know that reporters all think lying is wrong. But they do not all agree on what exactly constitutes *lying*. For example, is changing a quote lying? Is failing to identify oneself lying? Reporters disagree about the answer to these questions.

Step 4: Evaluate the Answer Choices

(E) matches the prediction.

(A) is both Out of Scope and a 180. It addresses ethical behavior in general, rather than just lying. Additionally, the stimulus is about journalists trying to define ethical behavior. While it's possible journalists don't actually *behave* ethically, it's unlikely given the amount of thought put into the definition of lying.

(B) contradicts the stimulus. Although reporters disagree on what counts as lying, the first sentence says they all agree that lying is always wrong.

(C) matches what some reporters think regarding identifying oneself as a reporter, but contradicts what others think. Therefore, **(C)** is not a statement that is supported by the passage.

(D) goes Out of Scope. The stimulus does not indicate that lying is permissible in some situations, nor does it judge reporters on their belief that it is not.

6. (C) Paradox

Step 1: Identify the Question Type
The correct answer "helps to explain" something from the stimulus, so this is a Paradox question. Something about "the results of the earthquake" will appear contradictory, but the correct answer will explain how the situation actually makes sense.

Step 2: Untangle the Stimulus
Follow the clue from the question stem and read for what seems odd about the results of the earthquake. After the earthquake, a wood-frame house was destroyed but the masonry house next to it was undamaged. This is strange because wood-frame houses generally withstand earthquakes better than masonry houses.

Step 3: Make a Prediction
Based on the generality in the stimulus, one would expect that the recent earthquake would have caused more damage to the masonry house. However, because this is not the case, there must either be something about this particular wood-frame house that made it especially vulnerable to earthquake damage, or there must be something about this particular masonry house that made it especially resistant to damage.

Step 4: Evaluate the Answer Choices
(C) matches the prediction. If the wood-frame house has already been damaged in a flood, then it could be especially vulnerable to an earthquake. This would explain why the wood-frame house suffered more damage than did the masonry house.

(A) is an Irrelevant Comparison between the number of masonry versus wood-frame houses in earthquake-prone areas. It doesn't address why the earthquake left this particular wood-frame house destroyed while the masonry house next door was untouched.

(B) makes the exact same error as **(A)**, merely reversing which type of house is more prevalent.

(D) is another Irrelevant Comparison. You cannot infer any particular relationship between the expense of a house and its ability to resist earthquake damage.

(E) may be a true statement, but it is too general to resolve the paradox. The fact that structures in general are always vulnerable doesn't address the difference between masonry houses and wood-frame houses, or, more importantly, what was special about this particular masonry house and wood-frame house.

7. (D) Assumption (Necessary)

Step 1: Identify the Question Type
Because the correct answer is the assumption *required* for the argument, this is a Necessary Assumption question. You can use the Denial Test to check your answer.

Step 2: Untangle the Stimulus
Break down the argument into the evidence and conclusion. The conclusion comes after the Keyword [*t*]*herefore* in the last sentence. The author attests that the snail learned to associate the shaking of the tank with the bright light. The evidence is based on an experiment performed by biologists. Initially, biologists simultaneously shook the snail's tank and shined a bright light on the snail. When both actions were done, the snail tensed its foot. Later, when biologists only shone the light into the tank, the snail continued to tense its foot.

Step 3: Make a Prediction
The evidence presents two causal relationships. The first is that movement and light together caused the snail to tense its foot. The second is that light alone caused the snail to tense its foot. Based on this, the author concludes that the snail must have been conditioned to associate the bright light with the shaking tank. In other words, movement, though indirectly, is still the cause of the snail's tensing. The flaw in this argument is that the author overlooks the possibility that the bright light, not the movement, might have always been the actual trigger causing the snail to tense its foot. The assumption will likely rule out this overlooked possibility.

Step 4: Evaluate the Answer Choices
(D) matches the prediction. This proves that the snail's reaction was a result of the experiment, not just a natural response to light.

(A) is Out of Scope, focusing on all snails in the ocean, rather than just on the snail in the experiment. Additionally, this choice only addresses turbulence, not light. It may be that all sea snails in the ocean also tense when faced with light.

(B) goes Out of Scope by discussing snails' normal exposure to bright light. To be relevant, this choice would need to discuss how snails ordinarily *react* to bright lights. Just because snails are not ordinarily exposed to bright lights does not determine whether or not snails would normally tense their foot when exposed to bright lights.

(C) is Out of Scope for the same reason that **(A)** is. This choice links the snail in the experiment to other members of its species, which is irrelevant because the stimulus does not indicate how other members of the species ordinarily respond to bright lights.

(E), if anything, weakens the argument. If tensing is an *instinctual* reaction to turbulence, then it becomes less likely that tensing would be a *learned* reaction to light. Additionally, this choice only addresses turbulence, and not light.

8. (C) Parallel Flaw

Step 1: Identify the Question Type

The stimulus asks you to compare two arguments—one in the stimulus and one in the answer choices—both of which are flawed. Therefore, this is a Parallel Flaw question. Keep common flaws in mind.

Step 2: Untangle the Stimulus

For Parallel Flaw questions, it is usually better to look for the flaw type rather than compare conclusions. So, start by analyzing the argument. The conclusion says each of the twelve members in the purchasing department is efficient. The evidence is that the overall department is efficient.

Step 3: Make a Prediction

The evidence is about the department as a whole, but the conclusion is about each individual member of the department. Thus, the author assumes that what is true about the whole must be true about each member. In other words, the author shifts scope from the whole group to the group's individual members. This is called a parts-versus-whole flaw. The argument overlooks the possibility that some members of the group might be less than highly efficient, but that other members in the group might balance them out. The correct answer will contain an analogous argument suggesting that if a group has a characteristic, its members do, too.

Step 4: Evaluate the Answer Choices

(C) matches the prediction. The evidence is that the supercomputer as a whole has a certain characteristic (most sophisticated and most expensive) while the conclusion is that each of the computer's individual pieces must share those same characteristics, too.

(A) starts with evidence about individuals, rather than about a group. You could reject this answer choice even without looking at the conclusion. The conclusion, however, also does not match. It discusses a likely result of the characteristic.

(B) is nearly the same flaw as the stimulus, but reverses it. This choice starts with evidence about the individual members of the group (each member of the public relations department), yet draws a conclusion about the group as a whole.

(D) fails to match the stimulus in the same way as (B). It presents evidence about the individual members (chapters) in order to draw a conclusion about the whole group (the book).

(E) isn't flawed at all, even though its evidence discusses a department and the conclusion mentions the department's members. This choice presents evidence about a necessary condition for membership in a department, and then rightly concludes that all members must have fulfilled that condition.

9. (A) Principle (Identify/Strengthen)

Step 1: Identify the Question Type

Because the correct answer is a principle, this is an Identify the Principle question. Additionally, because that principle will *justify* the reasoning in the argument, this is a Principle question that resembles a Strengthen question. Therefore, break down the argument into conclusion and evidence, pinpoint the gap, and predict what broad rule would close that gap.

Step 2: Untangle the Stimulus

The conclusion follows [*thus* at the end of the stimulus. The author believes that simply telling callers that they have the wrong number would not be wrong, but that passing on Sara's real number would be admirable. The evidence comes in two pieces. First, the Jacksons did not give Sara the impression that they would pass on the correct number. Second, passing out the number would be helpful and easy.

Step 3: Make a Prediction

Both the evidence and the conclusion are complex, so the principle connecting the two will likely be as well. There is a slight scope shift between the two parts of the evidence and the two parts of the conclusion. The correct principle will address those two scope shifts, indicating that the terms in the evidence and the conclusion are essentially the same. In other words, if help was not assured then not helping is not wrong, while being helpful is laudable.

Step 4: Evaluate the Answer Choices

(A) matches the prediction. Note that (A) is an extreme statement and is therefore stronger than what the assumption would need to be. But that makes it a perfect strengthener. If it is always laudable to do something helpful, then it is much more likely to be true that the Jacksons would be doing something laudable by passing on Sara's number. Similarly, if leading someone on is *required* for an action to be wrong, then the Jacksons are not wrong to not pass on Sara's number.

(B) distorts the conclusion. The conclusion says the Jacksons can either do something laudable or something not wrong. Unlike in (B), there is no suggestion that helping someone could ever be wrong.

(C) distorts the author's conception of right and wrong. The author says it wouldn't be wrong for the Jacksons to *ignore* Sara's request, but (C) suggests that it wouldn't be wrong for them to *help*. The conclusion distinguishes between two courses of action, both with a single quality, whereas this choice indicates that a single course of action would have two qualities (laudable *and* not wrong).

(D) contradicts the stimulus in two ways. First, the stimulus suggests that passing on Sara's number would be laudable even though it is "of no difficulty for them." This choice, however, says high difficulty is a necessary requirement of any laudable action. Second, the stimulus never suggests that something is laudable only when it is wrong *not to do it*. On the contrary, the author says it would *not* be wrong for the Jacksons to ignore Sara's request, yet still maintains that passing on her number would be laudable.

(E) would translate to the following:

If	laudable	→	~ wrong to refrain from doing

While the stimulus discusses actions that are both laudable and not wrong to refrain from doing, it doesn't draw a relationship between the two and say that one is required for the other. Rather, the stimulus suggests that passing on Sara's number is laudable because it is *helpful*, *not* because the Jacksons could ethically ignore her request. Additionally, the author specifically points out that the action would be "of no difficulty," whereas this choice removes difficulty from the equation.

10. (D) Weaken

Step 1: Identify the Question Type
Because the correct answer is the rebuttal that Albert can make to Erin, this is a Weaken question. Notice that Erin's opinion comes second in the stimulus and should be where you focus your attention. However, because Erin's argument is a response to Albert's, you must still read the entire stimulus.

Step 2: Untangle the Stimulus
Start by paraphrasing Albert's argument. Albert questions the need for the proposed regulations on automobile exhaust that aim to reduce the amount of PAHs released into the air. His evidence is that it is not proven that those emissions cause cancer. Next, analyze Erin's argument. Erin's conclusion follows the Keyword [*s*]*o* in the last sentence. Erin points out that the regulations on automobile exhaust would save many lives. Her evidence is that scientists blame PAHs for many deaths from lung and heart disease.

Step 3: Make a Prediction
Find Erin's assumption. Erin says, according to experts, PAHs cause lung and heart disease. She concludes that the regulations *will* save lives. Her assumption is simple but easily overlooked: She's assuming the regulations will work and will have the desired effect. The correct weakener will provide some reason why the regulations won't have the result Erin expects.

Step 4: Evaluate the Answer Choices
(D) matches the prediction. If most of the PAHs in the atmosphere come from automobile tires, then reducing the

PAHs released by automobile exhaust is not likely to save thousands of lives.

(A) goes Out of Scope by introducing the preferences of automobile manufacturers. The argument is whether the regulations would save lives, not whether automobile manufacturers support them.

(B) is also Out of Scope. The role of PAHs in other diseases wouldn't affect Erin's argument, which is limited to lung and heart disease.

(C) presents an alternative way PAHs may be reduced—lowered automobile usage—but doesn't address whether the regulations would be successful at saving lives.

(E) veers Out of Scope by focusing both on cancer and on components of automobile exhaust beside PAHs. Erin's argument is about lung and heart disease and their connection to PAHs only.

11. (C) Main Point

Step 1: Identify the Question Type
Because the correct answer "most accurately expresses the main conclusion of the argument," this is a Main Point question. Be wary of Conclusion Keywords and analyze which part of the argument is supported by the rest.

Step 2: Untangle the Stimulus
Read the entire stimulus, paraphrasing as you go. The first sentence presents an interesting phenomenon: Australia has fewer carnivorous mammals than do other continents, but approximately an equal number of carnivorous reptiles. Then the author provides a possible explanation for this disparity: a sparse ecosystem. Finally, you learn that carnivorous mammals must eat more than carnivorous reptiles, which puts mammals at a disadvantage in sparse ecosystems.

Step 3: Make a Prediction
The second sentence introduces the author's opinion, indicated by the word *probably*. The author presents a possible cause for an observed phenomenon. The first and third sentences, on the other hand, both provide accepted facts. The last sentence does include the Conclusion Keyword *thus*, but the fact that mammals are at a disadvantage in sparse ecosystems *supports* the author's suggestion that Australia's sparse ecosystem is the reason for the continent's small amount of carnivorous mammalian species. Expect the statement following *thus* to show up as a wrong answer choice. The correct answer will state that the likely reason why Australia has comparatively fewer carnivorous mammalian species is that the ecosystem is unusually sparse.

Step 4: Evaluate the Answer Choices
(C) matches the prediction.

(A) states the situation that the conclusion attempts to explain.

(B) is the expected trap answer. It restates the final piece of evidence, which follows a Conclusion Keyword.

(D) summarizes both pieces of evidence given in the third sentence of the stimulus.

(E) is both Extreme and a Distortion. The main point in the stimulus has a lower level of certainty than does **(E)**, because the stimulus includes the tentative word "probably." Additionally, this choice indicates that Australia's sparse ecosystem is the reason why carnivorous mammals are at a *disadvantage*, not that it is the reason why there are *fewer species* of carnivorous mammals.

12. (D) Inference

Step 1: Identify the Question Type
This is an Inference question because the correct answer is "supported by" the stimulus. Inventory the stimulus and make any possible links between statements.

Step 2: Untangle the Stimulus
This is an unusual Inference stimulus because it actually contains an argument. First, the linguist presents the Sapir-Whorf hypothesis: Language influences a society's worldview. Second, the linguist presents his concern: The hypothesis cannot be verified like a hypothesis of physical science could be. Third, the linguist states his evidence: There does not seem to be an obvious way to test the hypothesis.

Step 3: Make a Prediction
Attempt to connect ideas, focusing on the linguist's conclusion and evidence. If the Sapir-Whorf hypothesis might not be able to be tested, then it might not be able to be verified. Test the answer choices against the stimulus, asking yourself whether each must be true.

Step 4: Evaluate the Answer Choices
(D) must be true based on the information in the stimulus. If the Sapir-Whorf hypothesis cannot be verified because it cannot be tested, then it cannot be determined whether the hypothesis is true or false. If this choice did not jump out at you, work to eliminate the other possibilities.

(A) is Extreme. Just because it's unclear if the hypothesis can be tested does not mean that the hypothesis is "probably false." Rather, it means that such a determination is impossible.

(B) is Extreme. The stimulus suggests that the hypotheses of physical science are verifiable, but that does not mean *only* the hypothesis of physical science are verifiable. You cannot make inferences about other hypotheses based off information about hypotheses of physical science and a single additional example.

(C) is Out of Scope and Extreme. The stimulus does not mention anything about what is and is not deserving of serious consideration. Additionally, *only* is an extreme word, which is unsupported by the stimulus.

(E) makes the same errors as **(C)**. The stimulus never provides information about what should be taken seriously, nor do you know what would be restricted to *only* the hypotheses of physical science. Be careful not to make the additional assumption that if something cannot be verified, then it should not be taken seriously.

13. (A) Paradox

Step 1: Identify the Question Type
Because the correct answer "helps to reconcile the apparent conflict" in the stimulus, this is a Paradox question. The correct answer will resolve the apparent paradox in the stimulus.

Step 2: Untangle the Stimulus
The two seemingly conflicting parts of the stimulus will often be indicated by a Contrast Keyword. Here, it's [y]et. On one hand, wind and precipitation wear down mountains. On the other hand, the tallest mountains are in places where there is the most wind and precipitation. This does not seem to make sense because one would expect that erosive forces would have worn down a greater part of the mountains.

Step 3: Make a Prediction
The correct answer will introduce a new fact that explains why the tallest mountains are in the places with the most wind and precipitation.

Step 4: Evaluate the Answer Choices
(A) resolves the paradox. If the tallest mountains *cause* extreme weather conditions, then it makes perfect sense that the two are found together.

(B) is a 180 because it deepens the paradox. If the tallest mountains have less erosion-reducing vegetation, then one would expect them to erode more, ultimately becoming less tall.

(C) is Out of Scope because it focuses both on lower mountain ranges, rather than on the highest mountain ranges, and on the formation of mountains, rather than their erosion. Additionally, information about only *some* ranges—meaning at least one range— would not be enough to resolve a paradox.

(D) is not strong enough to resolve the paradox. Even if precipitation varies over time, that still doesn't explain why it's more prevalent near the highest mountain ranges. It may be that the precipitation has only recently become stronger near taller ranges and thus has not had time to wear down the mountains, but such an explanation requires too many unwarranted inferences on your part

(E) is Out of Scope and potentially a 180. If something about the highest mountains causes them to sink over time, then it's a mystery why they remain the highest. Additionally, this choice is Out of Scope because it offers no explanation about the effects of wind and precipitation.

14. (D) Flaw

Step 1: Identify the Question Type
This is a Flaw question because the correct answer describes how "the reasoning in the expert's argument is flawed." Keep common flaw types in mind.

Step 2: Untangle the Stimulus
Analyze the argument's evidence and conclusion. The conclusion follows [*h*]*ence* in the last sentence of the stimulus. When the conclusion states that a position is incorrect or wrong, as this one does, make sure your paraphrase includes the position being discussed. Here, the expert's main point is that an antenna does not need to be symmetrical in shape and have a fractal structure in order to work equally well at all frequencies. The expert's evidence is that the new antenna, which is symmetrical and has a fractal structure, does not work equally well at all frequencies.

Step 3: Make a Prediction
This question doesn't have a classic "if/then" structure, but it still involves Formal Logic. If you recognized that fact, you probably noticed that it contains one of the most classic Formal Logic flaws: a confusion of sufficiency versus necessity. The scientists have found a necessary condition:

If **antenna works equally well at all frequencies** → **symmetrical AND fractal**

According to the expert, the new antenna has both the necessary conditions, but it doesn't satisfy the sufficient one. According to Formal Logic, those two statements aren't actually contradictory. Even if being symmetrical and fractal is not *sufficient* for an antenna to work equally well at all frequencies, those two conditions may still be *necessary*. Therefore, the scientists may be correct. In other words, an antenna that is not symmetrical or not fractal can't work equally well at different frequencies, while an antenna that is symmetrical and fractal may or may not work equally well at different frequencies.

Step 4: Evaluate the Answer Choices
(D) matches the prediction.

(A) is not a logical flaw. It might be poor style not to define every technical word in an argument, but it is not an issue of logic. Arguments don't need to define every word in them.

(B) is a Distortion. The expert *does* deny in the conclusion the claim of scientific authorities, but *doesn't* rely on the truth of that claim as evidence. Instead, the expert presents alternative evidence: the antenna the researchers developed.

(C) describes an argumentative strategy that shows up occasionally on the LSAT, but is not at play here. The expert suggests that the researchers' evidence is contradictory, not insufficient.

(E) is Out of Scope. The fact that the antenna works better at frequencies below 250 megahertz is enough for the expert to claim that the researcher's antenna does not work equally well at all frequencies. The expert does not need to discuss how the antenna performs at exactly 250 megahertz.

15. (B) Role of a Statement

Step 1: Identify the Question Type
This is a Role of a Statement question. The correct answer describes "the role played in Singletary's argument" by the information about driver education. Identify whether the statement in question is evidence or conclusion, and then refine as necessary.

Step 2: Untangle the Stimulus
Start by underlining the statement mentioned in the question stem. Driver education appears in the third sentence. Next, find the conclusion. It follows the Conclusion Keyword [*t*]*hus* in the last sentence. Singletary thinks the ordinance shows the city cares more about the appearance of safety than actual safety. Singletary's evidence is that if the city cared about safety, it wouldn't require helmets but would instead add bicycle lanes and educate drivers.

Step 3: Make a Prediction
The statement in question appears in the evidence. It is one part of a two-step plan that the city would enact if, according to Singletary, it cared about bicyclists' safety. The correct answer choice will say this statement is evidence, but it may also describe what this statement supports. Make sure the answer indicates that the statement supports the claim that the city doesn't really care about bicyclists' safety.

Step 4: Evaluate the Answer Choices
(B) matches the prediction.

(A) is a Distortion. Though this choice rightly says the statement in question is evidence, Singletary's conclusion is that the city doesn't care, not that it *misunderstands*.

(C) is Extreme and a Distortion. While Singletary may insinuate that the ordinance will not be as effective as possible, he doesn't explicitly weigh in on the effectiveness of requiring helmets. Instead, he indicates preferable actions the city could or should have taken to support his actual conclusion that the city is more concerned with appearance than with actual safety.

(D) is also a Distortion. Singletary mentions driver education as an alternative plan that the city *would* do *if* it really cared about bike safety. Singletary does not actually think the city *will* educate drivers. Rather, driver education is an action the city *isn't* taking.

(E) is a Distortion of the statement's role. While Singletary does think—at least when it comes to bike safety—that the city is more concerned with public image than with actual safety, driver education isn't an *example* of the city's superficial interest. Rather, it's presented as an action the city would take were it more concerned with safety.

16. (A) Flaw

Step 1: Identify the Question Type
This is a Flaw question because the correct answer will explain why the argument in the stimulus is "vulnerable to criticism." Keep common flaw types in mind as you approach the argument.

Step 2: Untangle the Stimulus
Analyze the argument's evidence and conclusion. The conclusion follows [*t*]*hus* in the last sentence. Max predicts that, despite their great expense, Moon colonies will almost definitely be built in the future. Max's evidence is that as the amount of unoccupied space on Earth declines, the economic incentive to provide housing on the Moon will grow.

Step 3: Make a Prediction
Start by finding Max's assumption. Max's evidence merely suggests that the economic incentive to build Moon colonies will increase. Yet his conclusion is stronger: Colonies *will almost certainly* be built. Max must be assuming that the economic incentive will increase enough to make Moon colonies worth the expense. This flaw would be categorized as a "possibility versus certainty" scope shift. The correct answer will point out this assumption.

Step 4: Evaluate the Answer Choices
(A) matches the prediction. Max assumes that economic incentive would increase enough to make it worth it to take on the expense of building colonies on the Moon.

(B) is Extreme. Max suggests that colonies on the Moon would relieve overcrowding on Earth, but doesn't argue other strategies for relieving overcrowding would *not* work. This choice confuses sufficiency and necessity. Max says Moon colonies would be sufficient to relieve overcrowding, while this choice says he thinks they are necessary.

(C) is Out of Scope. The building of Moon colonies without economic incentive is outside of Max's argument. Overlooking this possibility is not a flaw in his argument.

(D) is also Out of Scope. Max's argument focuses exclusively on whether or not there will be enough of an economic

incentive to build the Moon colonies. What happens afterward to them is irrelevant to his argument.

(E) veers Out of Scope by focusing on people's preferences during a time when Earth is not overcrowded. Max's argument is about what will happen once Earth *is* overcrowded.

17. (E) Principle (Apply/Inference)

Step 1: Identify the Question Type
This is a Principle question because the correct answer is the situation that "conforms to the principle cited" in the ethicist's argument. Because the principle is found in the stimulus, this is an Apply the Principle question. The principle will often contain Formal Logic in these types of questions, so keep an eye out.

Step 2: Untangle the Stimulus
Read the stimulus and make sure you understand the principle. This principle provides two Formal Logic statements outlining when an action is wrong or right. Translate both statements into shorthand:

If	an action violates a rule AND the rule promotes general welfare	→	an action violates a rule AND the rule promotes general welfare
If	an action is required by a rule AND the rule promotes general welfare	→	right

Step 3: Make a Prediction
If you glance at the answer choices, you may notice that the conclusions (which act as the necessary condition) are all whether the individual's action is right or wrong while the evidence (which acts as the sufficient condition) describes the action. Therefore, you won't need to contrapose the Formal Logic in the stimulus, because both statements follow that same pattern. Additionally, you can knock out any choices whose conclusions are not either "the action is right" or "the action is wrong," because the Formal Logic in the stimulus provides information on those two scenarios only. Otherwise, find the choice whose logic follows that in the stimulus. Notice that, based on either statement, both sufficient conditions will need to be fulfilled.

Step 4: Evaluate the Answer Choices

(E) matches the prediction. The conclusion is that Edward's action is right, so check the evidence against the second Formal Logic statement. Edward's action satisfies both sufficient conditions because his action is required by a rule of society, and that rule promotes the general welfare.

(A) is a Distortion and a 180. It includes the judgment that Amelia's lie is not wrong. Neither of the Formal Logic statements in the stimulus leads to "not wrong" as a necessary consequence. Amelia's action violates a rule of her society that promotes the general welfare, so the proper judgment would be that Amelia's action *is* wrong.

(B) is Out of Scope. It includes a rule that is "not detrimental to the general welfare," but this type of rule is never mentioned in the stimulus. Rather, the stimulus includes the term "the rule promotes the general welfare." Even contraposed, this would become "the rule does not promote the general welfare." "Not promoting" the general welfare is different than "not being detrimental" to it.

(C) is also Out of Scope. The conclusion is that Elgin's action is wrong, which means only the first Formal Logic statement would be relevant. However, Elgin has *obeyed* a rule of his society, rather than *violated* a rule, so the first sufficient condition is not met. Additionally, rules that are "detrimental to the general welfare" never appear in the stimulus.

(D) is Out of Scope. Dahlia doesn't follow a rule, nor does she violate one. Therefore, neither Formal Logic statement applies.

18. (C) Assumption (Necessary)

Step 1: Identify the Question Type

This is a Necessary Assumption question because the correct answer is the assumption *required* by the argument in the stimulus. You can use the Denial Test to check your answer.

Step 2: Untangle the Stimulus

Start by breaking down the argument into the evidence and conclusion. The conclusion opens the stimulus. Teresa's main point is that the best way for movie studios to make a profit is not to produce small-budget films, but rather to produce big-budget films. Teresa's main evidence follows the Evidence Keyword [*f*]*or* and continues the comparison between small-budget and big-budget films. Small-budget films cannot attract a mass audience, but big-budget films can.

Step 3: Make a Prediction

Identify the mismatched concepts between the evidence and conclusion. First, both the evidence and the conclusion compare small-budget and big-budget films. However, the evidence discusses attracting a mass audience, while the conclusion mentions maximizing profits. Teresa's argument is missing the bridge from "mass audiences" to "maximizing

profits." In other words, she must be assuming that the *only* way to garner maximum profits is to attract mass audiences.

Step 4: Evaluate the Answer Choices

(C) matches the prediction, although it is phrased in "not … unless" form. Translated into simple "if/then" form, **(C)** reads: "If a film studio will maximize its profits → at least some of its films attract mass audiences." Or in other words, attracting mass audiences is *required*. The denied version of this choice (attracting mass audiences is *not* required for maximum profits) would make the conclusion—that studios should only focus on big-budget films—fall apart.

(A) is Extreme. Just because small-budget films *never* attract mass audiences does not mean that *every* big-budget film is guaranteed to attract a mass audience. Further, **(A)** fails to include the idea of maximizing profits, which is the mismatched concept from the conclusion.

(B) is Out of Scope. Nothing in the stimulus suggests that studios can make only one type of film. Rather, Teresa merely suggests that film studios should "concentrate on" big-budget films, not that they must eliminate small-budget films entirely.

(D) is Extreme and a Distortion of Teresa's evidence. Just because big-budget films carry a higher risk of unprofitability does not mean that such films can *never* be produced in a financially efficient manner. Further, **(D)** fails to include the idea of maximizing profits, which is the mismatched concept from the conclusion.

(E) is Out of Scope. Teresa never indicates that studios *should* maximize profits, nor that doing so should be their *primary* goal; she just makes a claim about what they should do *if* they want to aim for maximum profits.

19. (B) Flaw

Step 1: Identify the Question Type

This is a Flaw question because the argument in the stimulus is "vulnerable to criticism." Additionally, the question stem points out that the correct answer will involve an overlooked possibility. Pay attention to what the author ignores.

Step 2: Untangle the Stimulus

The conclusion, marked by *therefore*, ends the stimulus. The author's main point is that last year's winner of the Tour de France must have had exceptional lung capacity. The author's evidence comes in three pieces. First, all winners of the Tour de France have had some kind of physiological abnormality. Second, the typical abnormalities are exceptional lung capacity and exceptionally powerful hearts. Third, last year's winner did not have an exceptionally powerful heart.

Step 3: Make a Prediction

The question stem announced that the argument's problem lies in an overlooked possibility. The conclusion makes an extreme claim, saying last year's winner "must have" exceptional lung capacity. The author is overlooking the possibility that the winner did *not* have exceptional lung capacity. Or, in other words, the author is overlooking the possibility that last year's winner has some sort of physiological abnormality, but one that is atypical for Tour de France winners.

Step 4: Evaluate the Answer Choices

(B) matches the prediction in more general terms. Last year's winner may be one of those winners who have neither exceptional lung capacity nor exceptionally powerful hearts—but rather some different abnormal physiological constitution.

(A) is not overlooked by the argument. The author's evidence suggests that both those physiological abnormalities may be beneficial in cycling, because they are typical of the Tour de France winners.

(C) veers Out of Scope by addressing cyclists in general, rather than Tour de France winners.

(D) is Out of Scope because it focuses on *how* typical Tour de France winners get their exceptional lung capacity and powerful hearts, which is irrelevant. Additionally, **(D)** fails to affect the author's extreme conclusion about last year's winner.

(E) is not overlooked by the argument. The notion of *exceptional* capacities is inherently relative. The typical Tour de France winner's lungs and heart are exceptional relative to the average cyclist. This doesn't affect the author's conclusion about last year's winner.

20. (A) Strengthen

Step 1: Identify the Question Type

Because the correct answer *strengthens* the argument in the stimulus, this is a Strengthen question. Find the answer choice that makes the meteorologist's conclusion more likely to be true.

Step 2: Untangle the Stimulus

Analyze the argument's evidence and conclusion. The conclusion comes in the stimulus's opening sentence. The meteorologist says her station's weather forecasts are more useful and reliable than those of the area's most popular news station. The meteorologist's evidence, signaled by the Evidence Keywords "[a]fter all," comes in two pieces. First, viewers care most about whether it will rain. Second, when her station predicts rain for the next day, the prediction is right most of the time.

Step 3: Make a Prediction

Although it might seem at first like the TV meteorologist has made a solid argument, she has left out a crucial piece of information, creating a numbers problem. Her evidence is

partial: Her station's affirmative predictions for rain are at least more than 50% accurate, whereas those of the competing stations are not. But how often does the meteorologist's station actually predict rain versus how often does it not predict rain? Suppose over the past year, the meteorologist's station predicted rain on just five days, and on three of those it actually rained. The station's positive predictions would thus be *mostly* correct—60%. But what if it actually rained every day of the year? That means when they predicted it wouldn't rain they were wrong every time. A competing station that predicted rain more often, even if such forecasts were accurate less than 60% of the time, might actually be more useful for viewers because they may have also had a high level of accuracy about days it wouldn't rain. The correct answer will likely point out that the meteorologist's station predicted rain at least as often as did the competing stations, or that other stations were less accurate at predictions about days with no rain, too.

Step 4: Evaluate the Answer Choices

(A) matches the prediction. If the meteorologist's station predicted rain more often than the popular station *and* was more accurate with such predictions, then it is more likely that her station's forecasts are more useful and reliable.

(B) is Out of Scope. Whether the competing meteorologists work full-time or not does not affect the reliability of their reports.

(C) explains *why* the most popular news station is popular, but investigative news reports are Out of Scope of the argument.

(D) is Out of Scope. It introduces an irrelevant policy of the meteorologist's station. The evidence presented by the meteorologist is about next-day forecasts, not about forecasts that are more than three days in advance. If anything, this choice weakens the argument that the meteorologist's station's forecasts are more *useful*, because the station doesn't give viewers a far-reaching view of the upcoming weather.

(E) does not strengthen the argument. It introduces evidence about the number forecasts of *no* rain, but not about the accuracy of those forecasts. So, it can't support the meteorologist's assertion that her station is more reliable. This answer choice also shows a similarity between the meteorologist's station and other stations, whereas the meteorologist is trying to point out that they are different. Finally, **(E)** links the meteorologist's station with "at least one of its competitors," rather than with the most popular news station. The conclusion of the stimulus compares the meteorologist's station only with the most popular news station.

21. (C) Paradox

Step 1: Identify the Question Type
Because the correct answer "helps to resolve the apparent conflict" in the stimulus, this is a Paradox question. Additionally, the question stem reveals that the paradox will revolve around the responses of the witnesses.

Step 2: Untangle the Stimulus
First, find the information about the "witnesses who gave testimony containing fewer inaccurate details during the first lawyer's questioning." When questioned by a lawyer who was trying to elicit inaccurate testimony, the testimony of these particular witnesses tended to be accurate; however, when questioned by a lawyer whose goal was to get them to correct their earlier errors, they tended to be less accurate than other witnesses.

Step 3: Make a Prediction
These witnesses behaved in a manner that was opposite of what one would expect. Despite what the questioning lawyer intended, the witnesses seemed to do the opposite. The only way this could be explained is if the manner of questioning didn't affect these particular witnesses (or for some reason affected them differently than everyone else).

Step 4: Evaluate the Answer Choices
(C) matches the prediction.

(A) does not resolve the paradox. Better observation skills may explain why this group of witnesses was more accurate when questioned by the first lawyer, but it would not explain why they were less accurate when questioned by the second lawyer. If anything, this choice deepens the paradox.

(B), like **(A)**, doesn't resolve the paradox. Better memory would explain the witnesses' responses to the first lawyer but not the second.

(D) contradicts the stimulus. This choice indicates that the witnesses' memories became more accurate as they were questioned, when in fact the opposite occurred.

(E) is an Irrelevant Comparison. The *number* of details that the witnesses included is not important; rather, the *accuracy* of those details is pertinent.

22. (B) Assumption (Sufficient)

Step 1: Identify the Question Type
This is a Sufficient Assumption question because the correct answer is the assumption that *if* assumed "enables the conclusion" to follow.

Step 2: Untangle the Stimulus
Start by isolating the conclusion. The conclusion follows "[b]ecause of this" in the last sentence. The author says businesses often have good reason to choose the moral course of action. The evidence is that the moral course of action usually serves a business's long-term interest.

Step 3: Make a Prediction
Both the evidence and the conclusion talk about businesses pursuing the moral course of action, but the presented reasons differ. The evidence indicates that businesses may act morally because it serves their long-term interests, while the conclusion merely says they are motivated by "compelling reasons." The correct answer choice will indicate that serving a long-term interest is a compelling reason for businesses to act morally.

Step 4: Evaluate the Answer Choices
(B) matches the prediction.

(A) is a Distortion. The stimulus discusses moral acts and long-term interests, but never the "moral interests" of a business. Even if moral interests were relevant, you need an answer discussing what *does* cause business to act, not what doesn't.

(C) is likely true, based on the logic of the stimulus (although the stimulus says only that *when long-term and short-term interests conflict*, long-term interests tend to align with the morally preferable choice; in other words, you don't know anything about when long-term and short-term interests *don't* conflict). In any case, **(C)** is not the sufficient assumption because it fails to connect the evidence to the conclusion. In particular, **(C)** fails to mention "compelling reasons," which is the mismatched concept from the conclusion.

(D) is a Distortion. The stimulus presents one scenario in which short-term interests tend to conflict with the morally preferable act (when short-term and long-term interests conflict). It's unclear if short-term interests *usually* conflict with morally preferable acts. Nor is this information enough to prove that businesses have "compelling reasons" to act morally.

(E) doesn't connect the evidence to the conclusion. Whether morality is the sole consideration or one of many doesn't affect the assertion that businesses often have compelling reasons to act morally.

23. (B) Inference

Step 1: Identify the Question Type
This is an Inference question because the correct answer "follows logically from" the statements in the stimulus. Inventory the statements, keeping an eye out for Formal Logic and any possible connections.

Step 2: Untangle the Stimulus
The words *must, if, requires,* and *no* should have alerted you that this stimulus contains Formal Logic. Translate each statement and try to link them together. The first statement includes the necessity Keyword *must* and the sufficiency Keyword *if.* It translates to:

If	remain competitive in global economy	→	overcome current math education crisis

The second statement contains the necessity Keyword *requires*. It translates to:

If	overcome current math education crisis	→	use successful teaching methods

The third statement could be rephrased as "no method of teaching can succeed if it doesn't get students to spend a significant amount of time studying outside of class." The contrapositive translates to:

If	use successful teaching method	→	significant amount of time studying outside of class

Step 3: Make a Prediction

Connect the Formal Logic statements together to create the following chain:

If	remain competitive (W)	→	overcome crisis (X)	→	successful teaching (Y)	→	significant outside of class studying (Z)

While any link that follows the logic of that chain must be true, the correct answer is likely to use both ends of the chain. Thus, the correct answer will likely state one of the following: if we are to remain competitive, students must study significantly outside of class ("If W → Z") or if students are not studying significantly outside of class, then we won't remain competitive ("If ~Z → ~W").

Step 4: Evaluate the Answer Choices

(B) doesn't exactly match the prediction, but it does follow the logical chain of evidence. Remember, "not A unless B" always translates to "if A → B." Therefore, **(B)** translates to "if the crisis is overcome → students study significantly outside of class." That matches the chain by going from "If X → Z."

(A) reverses the Formal Logic of the stimulus without negating. It indicates "If Z → X."

(C) is an Irrelevant Comparison. The relative importance of mathematics to other subjects is Out of Scope. The stimulus just discusses the connection between math education and staying competitive in the global economy.

(D), like **(A)**, reverses the Formal Logic of the stimulus, without negating. Remember that "only if" means *then*, so translated into if/then form, **(D)** becomes: If students spend a significant amount of time outside of class studying mathematics → we succeed in remaining competitive in the global economy. That's "If Z → W."

(E) is like **(A)** and **(D)** in that it treats students studying outside of class as a sufficient idea, whereas it is a necessary term in the stimulus. Additionally, this choice is too tentative, saying studying "would help," whereas the argument speaks in concrete terms.

24. (E) Assumption (Necessary)

Step 1: Identify the Question Type

Because the correct answer is the assumption *required* by the argument in the stimulus, this is a Necessary Assumption question. You can use the Denial Test to check your answer.

Step 2: Untangle the Stimulus

Break down the argument into the evidence and conclusion. The conclusion follows "it is clear that," in the last sentence. The author says Petropolis's downtown is going through a big economic downturn. The author's evidence comes in two pieces. First, some large buildings have been demolished downtown. Second, the number of large buildings is an indicator of economic health.

Step 3: Make a Prediction

The author bases the conclusion that the downtown is in economic decline on the number of *demolished* buildings. Yet, the evidence also says economic health is reflected by the *total* number of large buildings. The author is assuming that the demolishing of 60 large buildings has caused the total number of large buildings to decline. In other words, the author overlooks the possibility that while 60 buildings have been demolished, 60 or more new buildings may have been built. The correct answer will remove the argument's overlooked possibility, stating that fewer than 60 large buildings have been newly built.

Step 4: Evaluate the Answer Choices

(E) matches the prediction.

(A) goes Out of Scope by focusing on the timing of the demolitions over the five-year period. The author compares (however questionably) the downtown's current economic health to its economic health five years ago; how the economic health may have varied during that five-year period is irrelevant.

(B) is both Extreme and Out of Scope. For the conclusion to be true, it doesn't need to be true that there were *never* significantly more than 100 large buildings downtown. Additionally, the scope of the stimulus is the past five years, not its entire history.

(C) is Out of Scope because it introduces the reason *why* the buildings were torn down. The author cares about numbers, not reasons.

(D) may be tempting because it shows the demolished buildings were replaced. However, the replacements were *small* buildings, not large ones, so this choice is Out of Scope.

25. (C) Parallel Reasoning

Step 1: Identify the Question Type

This is a Parallel Reasoning question because the correct answer has reasoning that is "similar to" the reasoning in the stimulus.

Step 2: Untangle the Stimulus

Because this argument is built out of Formal Logic statements, it will be more efficient to work with the stimulus as a whole, rather than to compare conclusions. So, translate the evidence and conclusion into if/then Formal Logic statements. Following [*t*]*hus* in the last sentence, the conclusion translates into:

If	~ eligible for a free soft drink	→	~ eligible for a free dessert

The evidence translates into two Formal Logic statements:

If	eligible for a free dessert (W)	→	order an entrée (X) AND a salad (Y)
If	order an entrée (X) OR a salad (Y)	→	eligible for a free soft drink (Z)

Step 3: Make a Prediction

Notice that the two evidence statements can't be combined into a chain because one includes an *or* while the other contains an *and*. You can generalize the argument as so:

Evidence 1:

If	W	→	X and Y

Contrapositive:

If	~X or ~Y	→	~W

Evidence 2:

If	X or Y	→	Z

Contrapositive:

If	~Z	→	~X and ~Y

Conclusion:

If	~Z	→	~W

The correct answer will match that Formal Logic structure.

Step 4: Evaluate the Answer Choices

(C) matches the prediction. In **(C)**, "grow azaleas" becomes "W," "rich in humus" becomes "X," "low in acidity" becomes "Y," and "grow blueberries" becomes "Z."

(A) starts out well and ends well, with a first sentence and a conclusion that matches. However, the second sentence is distorted in a few ways. First, it adds the new "Z" term (worked at Teltech for more than six months) to the sufficient clause rather than the necessary, and it adds the "X" term (university diploma) to the necessary rather than the sufficient. It also says "does *not* have sales experience," rather than keeping sales experience positive like it is in the first sentence. So, the second sentence translates to: If Z AND ~Y → X, which doesn't match.

(B) has evidence that matches. However, the conclusion does not. This choice doesn't negate the sufficient condition. Rather, the conclusion translates to: If Z → ~W, when—to be parallel—it should translate to ~Z → ~W.

(D) immediately goes wrong by using *or* instead of *and* in the necessary condition of the first piece of evidence. Additionally, the second piece of evidence does not contain an *or* in the sufficient condition.

(E) has evidence that matches, but goes astray in the conclusion. The conclusion translates to: If ~W (no discount) → ~Z (no coupon). This reverses the order of the conclusion of the stimulus, without negating. In fact, because you *can* get a coupon without buying ice cream (and therefore *could* get a coupon without getting the discount), this choice contains faulty logic.

PrepTest 55

The Inside Story

PrepTest 55 was administered in October 2008. It challenged 50,721 test takers. What made this test so hard? Here's a breakdown of what Kaplan students who were surveyed after taking the official exam considered PrepTest 55's most difficult section.

Hardest PrepTest 55 Section as Reported by Test Takers

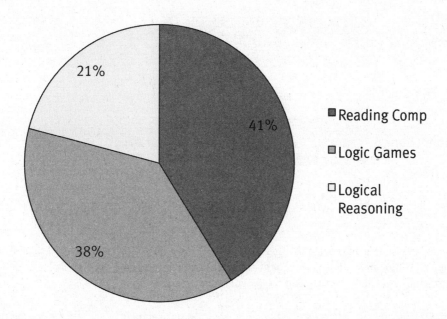

Based on these results, you might think that studying Reading Comprehension and Logic Games are the key to LSAT success. Well, those sections are important, but test takers' perceptions don't tell the whole story. For that, you need to consider students' actual performance. The following chart shows the average number of students to miss each question in each of PrepTest 55's different sections.

Percentage Incorrect by PrepTest 55 Section Type

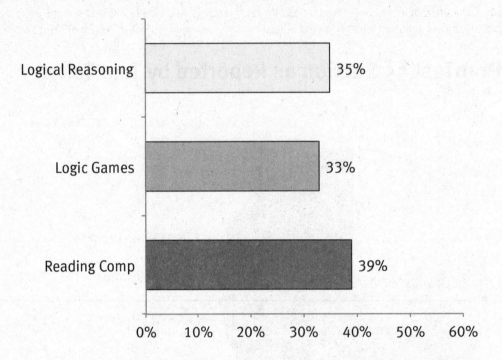

Actual student performance tells quite a different story. On average, students were almost equally likely to miss questions in all three of the different section types. Although test takers were right about Reading Comprehension being the most difficult section, Logic Games was somewhat lower in actual difficulty than Logical Reasoning.

Maybe students overestimate the difficulty of the Reading Comp or Logic Games sections because a really hard passage or Logic Game is so easy to remember after the test. But the truth is that the testmaker places hard questions throughout the test. Here were the locations of the 10 hardest (most missed) questions in the exam.

Location of 10 Most Difficult Questions in PrepTest 55

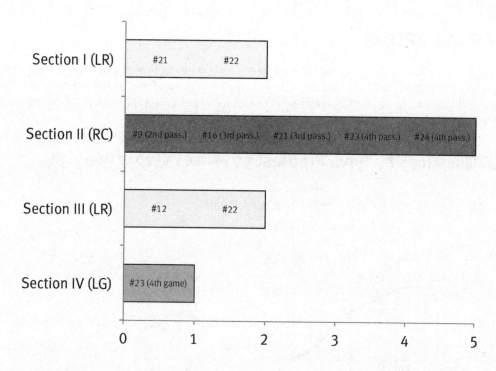

The takeaway from this data is that, to maximize your potential on the LSAT, you need to take a comprehensive approach. Test yourself rigorously, and review your performance on every section of the test. Kaplan's LSAT explanations provide the expertise and insight you need to fully understand your results. The explanations are written and edited by a team of LSAT experts, who have helped thousands of students improve their scores. Kaplan always provides data-driven analysis of the test, ranking the difficulty of every question based on actual student performance. The 10 hardest questions on every test are highlighted with a 4-star difficulty rating, the highest we give. The analysis breaks down the remaining questions into 1-, 2-, and 3-star ratings so that you can compare your performance to thousands of other test takers on all LSAC material.

Don't settle for wondering whether a question was really as hard as it seemed to you. Analyze the test with real data, and learn the secrets and strategies that help top scorers master the LSAT.

7 Can't-Miss Features of PrepTest 55

- PrepTest 55's first Logical Reasoning question was a Parallel Flaw question. That's only the second time that's ever happened, and the first since October 1993 (PrepTest 9).
- For the second test in a row the LSAT contained no Point at Issue questions.
- There have only been four Distribution/Matching Hybrid games ever. PrepTest 55 was the third test to ever feature one—the others were on PrepTest A (February 1996), PrepTest 25 (June 1998), and PrepTest 60 (June 2010). However, this was the only test to ever have one leading off the Logic Games section.
- PrepTest 55 was the fifth test with Comparative Reading and some trends started to emerge. This was the fourth time it appeared as the second passage and the third time it was a set of Natural Science passages.
- Don't just guess the first thing you see in Logic Games—(A) was only correct two times in that section. The record still remains PrepTest 17 (December 1995) when (A) was correct only once.
- Section I, Question 14 mentions financial irresposibility. Speaking of—the week leading up to PrepTest 55 Lehman Brothers and Washington Mutual declared bankruptcy and President George W. Bush signed off on the 700 billion financial system bailout.

- In August before PrepTest 55, hopefully some test takers were inspired to work hard when Michael Phelps set the record for most gold medals at a single Olympic games with eight in Beijing, China.

PrepTest 55 in Context

As much fun as it is to find out what makes a PrepTest unique or noteworthy, it's even more important to know just how representative it is of other LSAT administrations (and, thus, how likely it is to be representative of the exam you will face on Test Day). The following charts compare the numbers of each kind of question and game on PrepTest 55 to the average numbers seen on all officially released LSATs administered over the past five years (from 2013 through 2017).

Number of LR Questions by Type: PrepTest 55 vs. 2013–2017 Average

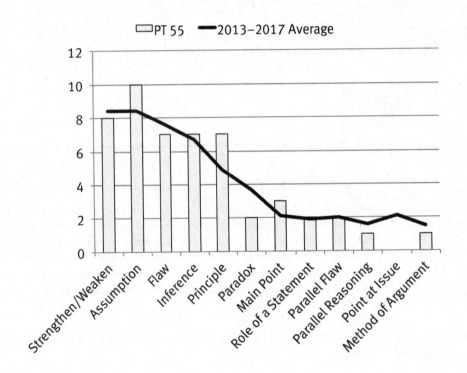

Number of LG Games by Type: PrepTest 55 vs. 2013–2017 Average

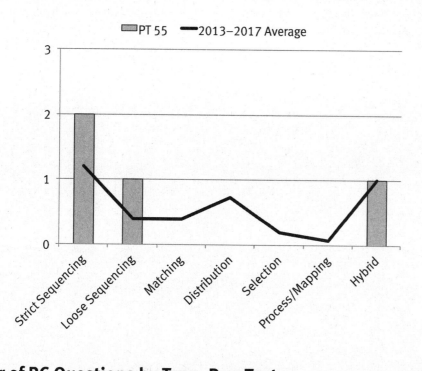

Number of RC Questions by Type: PrepTest 55 vs. 2013–2017 Average

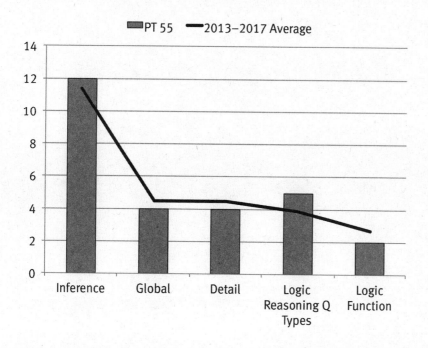

There isn't usually a huge difference in the distribution of questions from LSAT to LSAT, but if this test seems harder (or easier) to you than another you've taken, compare the number of questions of the types on which you, personally, are strongest and weakest. Then, explore within each section to see if your best or worst question types came earlier or later.

Students in Kaplan's comprehensive LSAT courses have access to every released LSAT and to a library of thousands of officially released questions arranged by question, game, and passage type. If you are studying on your own, you have to do a bit more work to identify your strengths and your areas of opportunity. Quantitative analysis (like that in the charts shown here) is an important tool for understanding how the test is constructed, and how you are performing on it.

Section I: Logical Reasoning

Q#	Question Type	Correct	Difficulty
1	Parallel Flaw	B	★
2	Assumption (Necessary)	A	★
3	Method of Argument	C	★
4	Assumption (Sufficient)	A	★
5	Inference	B	★
6	Principle (Identify/Strengthen)	A	★
7	Weaken	A	★★★
8	Inference	D	★★
9	Weaken	D	★
10	Principle (Identify/Inference)	B	★★
11	Principle (Parallel)	E	★
12	Assumption (Necessary)	C	★
13	Paradox	D	★★
14	Flaw	E	★★
15	Inference	D	★★★
16	Principle (Apply/Inference)	B	★★
17	Assumption (Necessary)	D	★★★
18	Main Point	E	★★★
19	Role of a Statement	C	★★★
20	Flaw	A	★★
21	Principle (Identify/Assumption)	B	★★★★
22	Weaken	E	★★★★
23	Strengthen	B	★★
24	Flaw	D	★★★
25	Inference (EXCEPT)	C	★★★

1. (B) Parallel Flaw

Step 1: Identify the Question Type

A question stem that asks you to match the similar flawed reasoning is a Parallel Flaw question. Understand the flaw in the stimulus before looking for the same flaw in the choices.

Step 2: Untangle the Stimulus

The author concludes that a magazine editor's criticism of spelling and grammar errors on a TV program should not be trusted because her magazine has contained similar errors.

Step 3: Make a Prediction

This is an *ad hominem* attack. Logically, the author should evaluate the merits of the editor's criticism rather than the editor's past history of errors in her magazine. Whatever the reason for the errors in her magazine, the current criticisms are either right or wrong based on their merits alone. So the correct answer should contain an *ad hominem* flaw, as well as likely retain the close relationship between evidence of mistakes or inadequacies in a specific area and a conclusion that the maker of those mistakes should not be trusted to judge others in that same area.

Step 4: Evaluate the Answer Choices

(B) is correct. It has both evidence of the news program's improper hiring practices and a conclusion that this past behavior disqualifies the news program from judging others' hiring practices.

(A) has a similar conclusion that a newspaper's criticism (of ethics) should not be trusted. However, the evidence is not a match. Rather than evidence of the newspaper's own past ethical misdeeds, the reason is an unrelated spelling error.

(C) has a somewhat similar conclusion that a criticism (regarding lack of safety) should not be trusted. However, the evidence is entirely different. Instead of evidence of the agency's safety lapses, there is reference to a regulatory provision. This choice actually includes an unwarranted assumption; just because selling a product is allowed doesn't mean the product is necessarily safe.

(D) has a similar conclusion that a criticism (of swimming practices) should not be trusted. However, the evidence is not of the coach's own past bad swimming practices but of an irrelevant promotional deal.

(E) has a conclusion that doesn't match. It is a recommendation rather than a value judgment about trustworthiness. Additionally, the evidence doesn't attack the magazine's past practices, and thus doesn't match.

2. (A) Assumption (Necessary)

Step 1: Identify the Question Type

A question that asks for an assumption "required by" an argument indicates a Necessary Assumption question. You can use the Denial Test to check your answer.

Step 2: Untangle the Stimulus

The author recommends not presoaking beans if one wants a quality, rather than a quick, dish. The reason is that not presoaking beans results in plumper beans.

Step 3: Make a Prediction

The unique term or concept in the conclusion is *quality*. The assumption must link "plumper beans" (evidence) to *quality* (conclusion).

Step 4: Evaluate the Answer Choices

(A) is correct as it links plumper beans to a higher quality dish. Negated, this choice says plumper beans don't enhance quality. If that's the case, then the author's recommendation to not soak beans doesn't make any sense.

(B) is both Extreme (*no* dishes) and Out of Scope for an argument limited to bean dishes.

(C) is an Irrelevant Comparison between taste and appearance. The argument does not define quality as either.

(D) is Out of Scope. The argument does not reference other ingredients.

(E) has two problems. First, the author does not assume quality keeps improving with ever greater plumpness. There may be a point at which increased plumpness is no longer desirable. Second, the argument does not define quality as taste, either explicitly or implicitly. Perhaps quality is related to multiple factors, such as visual appeal, texture, taste, and so on.

3. (C) Method of Argument

Step 1: Identify the Question Type

The question stem phrase "method of reasoning" clearly indicates a Method of Argument question. Focus on the structure or, in other words, *how* the author presents the argument.

Step 2: Untangle the Stimulus

Break down the argument sentence by sentence. Durth indicates that an increasingly common practice of businesses is to use direct mail advertising. Durth judges this practice to be both annoying and immoral. He alleges it is wasteful and that if others caused that much waste, it would be considered immoral.

Step 3: Make a Prediction

Essentially, Durth concludes something is immoral based on analogous situation in which it would be considered immoral. Find an answer that matches, and make sure it does not contain any deviations from what Durth does.

Step 4: Evaluate the Answer Choices

(C) is a match for the prediction. The phrase "one of its results" might not have made it into your prediction, so go back to the stimulus and see if it matches anything in the argument. Sure enough, it matches with the result of wasting paper.

(A) deviates from the argument, which does not contain any contrary contention that "direct mail advertising is *not* immoral."

(B) is a Distortion. Durth is concerned about the current waste, not just the amount of waste if direct mail advertising increases in the future.

(D) is also a Distortion. The claim that direct mail is annoying is half of the conclusion itself, not the evidence on which the conclusion is based.

(E) is implicit in the background introduction, but it is not directly asserted. Additionally, this choice ignores the conclusion and primary pieces of evidence.

4. (A) Assumption (Sufficient)

Step 1: Identify the Question Type
The phrasing "conclusion is properly drawn if ... assumed" indicates a Sufficient Assumption question, which requires you to pick an answer choice that, if added to the evidence, proves the conclusion true.

Step 2: Untangle the Stimulus
The author concludes that motor power alone does not indicate a vacuum model's cleaning effectiveness. The evidence is that motor power does not necessarily correlate with dust filtration efficiency.

Step 3: Make a Prediction
The link you need to make is from dust filtration efficiency to cleaning effectiveness. In other words, you need to show that the evidence is relevant to the conclusion, that dust filtration efficiency affects cleaning effectiveness. The power of the motor is the common concept that shows up in both the evidence and the conclusion, and thus is not part of the assumption. Wrong answers will likely improperly reference the power of the motor.

Step 4: Evaluate the Answer Choices
(A) matches the prediction.

(B) is a 180 and a Distortion. It contradicts the evidence, which indicates that vacuums with identically powerful motors can have different dust filtration efficiencies. Additionally, this choice does not link to the conclusion, which discusses cleaning effectiveness.

(C) is a 180, contradicting the conclusion that motor power does not indicate cleaning effectiveness. Additionally, this does not contain the concept "dust filtration efficiency" from the evidence.

(D) contains both unique concepts from the evidence and conclusion—dust filtration efficiency and cleaning effectiveness—but it doesn't connect the two. If added to the evidence, this answer choice doesn't prove the conclusion

true because it still links motor power to cleaning efficiency (albeit only when dust filtration systems are the same). An answer, like **(D)**, that says power is the determining factor for cleaning efficiency doesn't guarantee a conclusion that says power alone can't be used to determine cleaning efficiency because it still leaves open the possibility that power *is* all that is needed to determine cleaning effectiveness.

(E), like **(C)**, fails to link the conclusion to "dust filtration efficiency" from the evidence. Maybe power is an additional factor in determining cleaning effectiveness or maybe it isn't. Either way, **(E)** doesn't guarantee the conclusion because it is contrary to the conclusion that power does not alone indicate cleaning effectiveness.

5. (B) Inference

Step 1: Identify the Question Type
A question stem that directs you to use the information above to support one of the following answers (direction of support flowing down) is an Inference question. Inventory the facts and focus on any Formal Logic, concrete statements, and emphasized statements.

Step 2: Untangle the Stimulus
The stimulus indicates that many scientists believe bipedal locomotion evolved as hominids moved to grasslands because of the advantages it would confer. However, the author acknowledges that because standing upright would also have been advantageous in the forest, the exact evolutionary origins remain disputed. Finally, the author provides another evolutionary reason for standing upright: attracting a mate.

Step 3: Make a Prediction
While the origins of bipedal locomotion seem hazy, the advantages of standing upright are not. The correct answer will likely have something to do with these advantages. Critical information in Inference questions is often emphasized by a Contrast Keyword, such as *however*. For example, the third sentence beginning with [*h*]*owever* is also the most emphatic: "bipedalism also would have conferred substantial advantages upon early hominids who never left the forest—in gathering food."

It is likely that the correct answer will relate to this emphasized fact. You don't necessarily need to predict in Inference questions, but for each answer in "most supported" questions, make sure to ask yourself, "Does this receive direct support in the passage?" Go back to the stimulus to find support for your choice.

Step 4: Evaluate the Answer Choices
(B) is correct. It is supported in both the second and third sentences. In the grasslands, standing upright would let hominids see over tall grasses to locate food, and in the

forest, it would help them gather food found within standing height of the ground.

(A) is not supported by the stimulus. Indeed, because hominids moved from life in the forests to life in the grasslands, it may be that the grasslands were more hospitable.

(C) is a 180, contradicting a statement in the stimulus. In the second sentence, the author says bipedalism would allow hominids to see over the tall grasses of the grasslands. Doing so would help hominids both find food and avoid predators.

(D) is too strong for the stimulus. While bipedal locomotion *may* have evolved in forests, the author also says many scientists believe it actually evolved in the grasslands. Because the "debate continues," it cannot be inferred that one or the other is *probably* where standing upright originated.

(E) is an Irrelevant Comparison. The author doesn't mention which of the advantages resulting from bipedal locomotion is more important.

6. (A) Principle (Identify/Strengthen)

Step 1: Identify the Question Type
A question stem that asks for a principle to justify an argument indicates an Identify the Principle question that mimics a Strengthen question. Approach it like a typical Strengthen question, but be open to a more generalized answer.

Step 2: Untangle the Stimulus
The conclusion can be paraphrased as this: only teach pre-university students calculus if they can handle the abstraction. The reason is that if calculus is taught before students are ready, the level of abstraction can make them give up on math altogether.

Step 3: Make a Prediction
This argument contains a typical pattern: a recommendation conclusion with an implicit balancing of pros and cons. Any recommendation conclusion (for or against) assumes that the benefits that would result from following the recommendation would outweigh any downsides.

This stimulus here includes a recommendation to make sure students are ready for abstraction before teaching calculus. The benefit of following that advice would be that some students might be less likely to give up on math. The assumption is that any possible cons resulting from waiting to teach calculus would not outweigh the pro. Strengthen the conclusion by choosing an answer that provides any additional pro or eliminates a potential con.

However, for a Principle question that mimics a Strengthen question, the correct answer will often just paraphrase the evidence and conclusion in broader terms than the specific situation in the stimulus. If the broader principle is true, then the specific situation is more likely to be true. In this case, the strengthening principle might indicate only students who are ready for something should be taught it.

Step 4: Evaluate the Answer Choices
(A) matches the prediction. The word *only* indicates Formal Logic that can be diagrammed:

	introduce new intellectual work	→	handle challenge without losing motivation
If			

The contrapositive is:

	~ handle challenge without losing motivation	→	~ introduce new intellectual work
If			

The contrapositive is a generalization of the evidence and conclusion in the stimulus, and thus is correct.

(B) is a Distortion. The stimulus suggests that students need to be ready for abstraction before calculus is taught at all. The math teacher doesn't suggest that only concrete parts of calculus be taught. Additionally, this answer leaves out the critical concept of students abandoning a subject.

(C) is a significant Distortion in that the argument focuses on the level of abstraction, not the amount of effort required. The correct answer to a Principle question can be phrased more broadly, but it cannot contain a shift in meaning (a rose may be called a flower but not called a carnation). Additionally, this answer choice doesn't indicate whether such tasks should be taught or not, or when.

(D) also veers off track. The concern is not about how to get students to learn effectively but how to not scare off students.

(E) is a 180. The argument *advocates* considering the level of abstraction.

7. (A) Weaken

Step 1: Identify the Question Type
The question stem directly asks you to weaken the argument.

Step 2: Untangle the Stimulus
The author concludes (indicated by *therefore*) that certain legislation increased overall worker safety in high-risk industries. The evidence is that since the passage of the legislation, the likelihood that a worker in a high-risk industry will suffer a serious injury has decreased.

Step 3: Make a Prediction

This is a classic causal argument. The evidence is a correlation (two things occurring over the same time period), and the author jumps to a conclusion that one thing caused the other. The inherent assumption is that it is the legislation and nothing else that caused the lowered risk of injury. The most common way to weaken a causal argument is with evidence of an alternative cause (or reverse causation). Thus, your general prediction is that something else could have caused the reduction in the risk of injury.

Step 4: Evaluate the Answer Choices

(A) meets the needs of the general prediction. It provides another potential cause (technological innovations) of the reduction in injuries.

(B) is Out of Scope because it doesn't provide enough information. It relates only to injuries prior to the passage of the law. It may be that most work-related injuries after 1955 were also caused by worker carelessness.

(C) may be tempting, but it doesn't actually weaken the conclusion for two reasons. First, the stimulus is about high-risk industries only, while the answer choice discusses *all* industries, which would be Out of Scope. Second, this answer choice is a Distortion because it discusses total *number*, while the evidence mentions *likelihood*. If industry grew, the total number of injuries might go up while the likelihood of injury would go down.

(D) is Out of Scope. The number of injuries occurring in industries that are not high-risk is irrelevant to this argument's conclusion, which is explicitly limited to the effect of the legislation on high-risk industries.

(E) is a 180. It corroborates the effectiveness of the legislation passed in 1955 because improvements in safety also occurred in industries other than high-risk industries.

8. (D) Inference

Step 1: Identify the Question Type

A question stem that directs you to use the information above to support one of the following answers (direction of support flowing down) is an Inference question. Inventory the facts and focus on any Formal Logic, concrete statements, and emphasized statements.

Step 2: Untangle the Stimulus

Inventorying the statements provides:

1) Sunflower seed used to be a large production crop in Kalotopia.

2) Sunflower seed brings in money for other countries.

3) Renewed sunflower seed production in Kalotopia would relieve the farming industry and provide a variety of products with little cost to the environment.

Step 3: Make a Prediction

There is nothing in the stimulus that is particularly emphasized, and there are no clear deductions to be made. It seems likely the correct answer will deal with how great sunflower seed production can be, but assess each answer to make sure it does indeed receive support from the stimulus.

Step 4: Evaluate the Answer Choices

(D) is correct. The statements very much support the idea that renewed farming of sunflower seeds, a crop historically grown in Kalotopia, would provide a range of significant benefits for the country. While the choice does not specifically refer to sunflower seeds, it is not too broad of an answer. The choice merely indicates that there is one crop that used to be farmed in Kalotopia that would be beneficial to farm again. This choice is different from **(C)**, which applies to *every* crop historically grown in Kalotopia.

(A) is Extreme. The statements clearly assert substantial benefits of renewed farming of sunflower seeds and that the farming industry is currently unstable, but asserting that the farming industry *definitely* will deteriorate in the absence of renewed sunflower production is too strong.

(B) is both Extreme and does not have to be true. First, this answer choice isn't limited only to sunflower seed production. Sunflower seed production is one way to "provide relief" to the unstable farming industry (note that the stimulus does not indicate that it will *stabilize* it), but there may be other ways to stabilize Kalotopia's farming industry that *would* damage the environment. Second, even if this choice mentioned sunflower seed production, the stimulus says sunflower oil would provide products at *little* cost to the environment, not at *no* cost. Based on the information provided, it is impossible to know if this choice is true.

(C) is also Extreme because it extrapolates to *any* of the crops that historically were large production crops. Perhaps eliminating production of one of the other cash crops was a good move for the Kalotopians.

(E) is an Irrelevant Comparison. If an author only discusses one thing, you cannot compare it to others. You cannot infer that just because the economist extols the virtues of sunflower seed, and only sunflower seed, that it is a better crop than those left unmentioned.

9. (D) Weaken

Step 1: Identify the Question Type

The question stem directly asks you to weaken the argument.

Step 2: Untangle the Stimulus

The Contrast Keyword [*b*]*ut* highlights the conclusion: a new earthquake prediction method will be useful in deciding when to evacuate a town. The supporting evidence is that scientists detected changes in the electric current in the earth's crust before every major quake in a region over the past 10 years.

Step 3: Make a Prediction

The discovery initially sounds great. Detect the change in electric current and evacuate the town. However, that assumes that not only do the electric current changes occur before every major earthquake but also *only* before major earthquakes. What if the electric current changes also occur before every minor earthquake as well? Or just randomly? People would quickly tire of evacuating for minor earthquakes, and eventually may resist evacuating at all. Essentially, the author assumes that the changes in the electric current will accurately predict major earthquakes and make evacuating effective. You need to find an answer choice that decreases the connection between changes in current and major earthquakes or undermines the utility of the prediction method.

Step 4: Evaluate the Answer Choices

(D) makes the prediction method less useful for guiding evacuation decisions. "Considerable variation" in the length of time between the changes in the electric current and the subsequent earthquake could mean that once the current change is detected, a major earthquake might follow within an hour or within a year or more. People will be resistant to evacuate their homes for an indeterminate time that might extend to months or years. Additionally, the reference in this choice to the variation in the length of time should focus your attention on the conclusion's confident assertion that the method will enable scientists to decide "exactly when" to evacuate.

(A) does not weaken the argument. Its incomplete explanation of what causes the changes in current might nag at the scientists' intellectual curiosity, but that does not undermine the utility of the warning. Even if you do not understand completely how a clock functions, the alarm is just as effective in waking you up in the morning.

(B) is a 180. Taking the time to turn negative phrasing into positive indicates that the new method in this choice is more predictive of earthquakes than most other existing predictors.

(C) is irrelevant to the utility of the prediction method for determining when to evacuate towns. It merely highlights the increasing value of having some means of accurately predicting earthquakes.

(E) isn't enough to weaken the argument. While the fact that only one station exists in the region *might* place some limitation on the geographic range for which predictions can be made, it does not undermine the claim that the method will be of *some* aid. The conclusion is very modest in claiming the method will be of some aid, but is extreme in claiming that it will be helpful in determining *exactly when* to evacuate—that is what is vulnerable to attack.

10. (B) Principle (Identify/Inference)

Step 1: Identify the Question Type

The term *proposition* indicates a Principle question, requiring you to match specific information in the stimulus with a more broadly stated answer choice. This question stem is also formatted as an Inference question, with information in the stimulus supporting an answer. Thus, as you assess these answer choices, keep in mind that Inference questions merit modest, *knowable* answers.

Step 2: Untangle the Stimulus

The stimulus essentially says that due to a large number of competing manufacturers, fax machines were incompatible and limited in their usefulness until the manufacturers agreed on a common format.

Step 3: Make a Prediction

The answer to a Principle question will describe the situation more broadly, not focusing specifically on fax machines. Additionally, because this question mimics an Inference question, the correct answer should be stated modestly. Maybe, in this case, collaboration in business is sometimes useful.

Step 4: Evaluate the Answer Choices

(B) is correct. It applies the example of the fax machine industry more broadly to other industries, but does so very modestly ("some industries … to some extent"), meeting the needs of both a Principle and an Inference answer.

(A) is Extreme. It accurately describes the situation in the fax industry, but with the word [w]*henever*, it asserts that competition is damaging in *every* industry in which machines are interdependent.

(C) is too broad. The stimulus is limited to competition in a high-tech industry where products are interconnected. This answer choice discusses *all* high-tech industries. Additionally, the stimulus does not provide a direct relationship between the number of competitors and the amount of cooperation.

(D) is an Irrelevant Comparison. While in the stimulus some cooperation did remedy a particular problem, there is no comparison to pure competition, which could also remedy the problem (if one manufacturer drove the others out of business and cornered the market). It's impossible to know which would be more beneficial.

(E) is also Extreme. While the stimulus is limited to one type of industry, nothing in the stimulus indicates other types of industries would not benefit from cooperation as well.

11. (E) Principle (Parallel)

Step 1: Identify the Question Type

The question stem explicitly identifies this as a Principle question. However, notice that according to the question stem, the principle itself is never explicitly stated in the stimulus or in the answers, both of which are situations *illustrating* a principle. Thus, this is a Parallel Principle question, asking you to match different specific situations on different subjects that share an underlying principle. Paraphrase the situation in the stimulus in general terms, and then find the answer choice that can be generalized the same way.

Step 2: Untangle the Stimulus
The information indicates that in the specific context of improving education, critiques of teachers lead to improved educational outcomes if presented as one of several factors influencing educational outcomes.

Step 3: Make a Prediction
The correct answer will analogize that specific example to another circumstance in which a critique of some sort is more effective if presented not just as a personal evaluation, but also as part of a broader plan to improve an overall outcome. Watch out for deviations or parts of an answer that do not match with the stimulus.

Step 4: Evaluate the Answer Choices
(E) is correct because the criticism of the athlete was part of an overarching strategy to improve the entire team, which is wholly analogous to the situation in the stimulus.

(A) is Out of Scope. It concerns peer pressure rather than focusing on an individual evaluation made as part of an effort to improve a larger situation.

(B) is Out of Scope. It concerns how people feel about criticisms of others rather than themselves, and it is also not a component of a broader strategy. In the stimulus, the teacher's performance *is* part of the group of factors affecting educational outcomes.

(C) is a deviation because it concerns self-criticism rather than outside criticism. Additionally, it does not concern a component of a broader strategy.

(D) is a deviation because there is no reference to a critique or a component of a broader strategy to improve something. Also, like **(B)**, this answer goes askew by making the individual *not* part of the group, rather than a member of the group like the teacher is in the stimulus.

12. (C) Assumption (Necessary)

Step 1: Identify the Question Type
Even though the stem includes some phrasing common in Sufficient Assumption questions ("conclusion to be properly drawn"), the question explicitly asks for the assumption necessary to the argument and thus is a Necessary Assumption question.

Step 2: Untangle the Stimulus
The conclusion, highlighted by [*t*]*hus,* asserts that shifts of narrative point of view detract from the merit of novels. The evidence, highlighted by *since,* indicates that such shifts focus reader attention on the author.

Typically, you would work initially with the conclusion and a single key reason. However, the first sentence, rather than background, consists of a Formal Logic statement. Such absolute information will almost always be important. So, according to the first sentence:

If	novel of highest quality	$\rightarrow$	most readers are emotionally engaged

Step 3: Make a Prediction
Ignoring for a moment the Formal Logic rule in the first sentence, the disconnect between the evidence following *since* and the conclusion is a change in scope from "focus on the author" to "detract from the merit of the work." Thus, the critic implicitly equates a focus on the author with lesser quality work.

However, anticipate that you will need to tie in the Formal Logic; it indicates that a lack of reader emotional engagement detracts from the quality of the work. Thus, the critic *also* assumes a connection between a focus on the author and a loss of readers' emotional engagement. Therefore, the critic makes two necessary assumptions in this stimulus; the answer choices will only include one of those, likely the one tied to the Formal Logic.

Step 4: Evaluate the Answer Choices
(C) matches the prediction. It bridges the gap between a focus on the author and a reduction in readers' emotional engagement.

(A) is a Distortion. It is an incorrect contrapositive of the Formal Logic in the first sentence. Additionally, it does not link to the focus on the author.

(B) is Out of Scope. It discusses readers' imagination rather than their emotional engagement. Furthermore, it distorts the Formal Logic of the first sentence and fails to link to the focus on the author.

(D) is a possible way to explain why the shift in narrative would focus attention on the author, but explaining *why* readers focus on the author is not necessary to the argument. Indeed, because you must accept the evidence as true, it is not your task in an Assumption question to explain a piece of evidence. You are not explaining why narrative shifts tend to make readers focus on the author, but rather why that focus would lead to a lesser quality work.

(E) is Extreme and not necessary to the argument. A shift in narrative could serve some literary purpose and yet still detract from the overall merit of the work.

13. (D) Paradox

Step 1: Identify the Question Type
A question stem that asks you to resolve or *explain* a discrepancy of some sort ("puzzling facts") is a Paradox question. Start by identifying the two apparently contradictory facts.

Step 2: Untangle the Stimulus
On the one hand, people aged 46 to 55 spend more money on average than any other age group. On the other hand, television advertising is geared heavily toward people aged 25 and under.

Step 3: Make a Prediction
A general prediction is typically sufficient and preferred for a Paradox question. The correct answer should provide a reason for gearing advertisements toward young people even though older people are spending the most money (or, looked at from the other direction, a reason not to gear ads toward older people despite their greater buying power). A specific explanation might be that older people spend money on items not advertised on television, such as houses, while younger people spend money on items that are advertised. Or, if older people spend the most money on their children, it might make sense to gear ads toward the younger groups. Generally understand how to resolve this paradox; if a specific explanation jumps to mind, great, but remain open to another.

Step 4: Evaluate the Answer Choices
(D) might not have specifically jumped to mind, but ask yourself, "Is this a reason to not advertise to the older people despite their greater buying power?" Yes! There's no point in advertising to people who are not open to changing their brand preferences.

(A) does not resolve the unexpected comparison between older and younger consumers. Although a comparative answer choice is necessary for a Paradox question that focuses on an unexpected comparison, as this one does, the correct answer must explain why one group is targeted over the other. This answer choice just mentions "people who are most likely to purchase" but doesn't give any indication which group that is.

(B) is an Irrelevant Comparison. While it is a comparative answer, it compares costs of ad slots, not the two groups of people discussed in the stimulus. Even if one were to make the unwarranted assumption that older people are more likely to watch the news and younger people are more likely to watch sitcoms whose leading characters are young adults, this would not resolve the mystery. The issue is not how much

is spent on advertising aimed at the two groups, but why the focus is almost exclusively on people under age 25.

(C) is Out of Scope. It has nothing to do with advertising, but only decisions on which shows to renew. Even if the aired shows are most popular amongst the under 25 demographic, that's not to say that there's still not a considerable number of people from the 46 to 55 demographic that also watch the shows. There's nothing in (C) that explains why it's still not worth advertising to the 46 to 55 group based on their higher spending habits.

(E) is Out of Scope and possibly a 180. One might speculate that advertisers balance their ad efforts between television and print, assuming that older people are more likely to read and younger people more likely to watch television. However, one also might speculate that this information deepens the mystery. If print media ad campaigns recognize older people's buying power, why don't television ad campaigns? Unlike the correct answer, this choice does not provide an unequivocal distinction between the two age groups that is directly relevant to the discrepancy in television ad campaigns. Always choose the answer that is directly relevant rather than the off-topic answer that you might want to build a clever case for.

14. (E) Flaw

Step 1: Identify the Question Type
The phrase "vulnerable to criticism" indicates a Flaw question. Notice any disconnect between the evidence and conclusion, and keep in mind common flaws.

Step 2: Untangle the Stimulus
The moralist's conclusion is a recommendation against trying to acquire expensive new tastes. The evidence consists of negative aspects of acquiring and maintaining those expensive tastes.

Step 3: Make a Prediction
A very common argument pattern is a recommendation, which is based on a balancing of pros and cons. In recommending against something because of a few downsides, an author assumes that those cons outweigh the pros, if any. In this question, the correct answer will point out that the moralist overlooked possible benefits, or mistakenly assumed that the cons would outweigh the pros.

Step 4: Evaluate the Answer Choices
(E) precisely fits the pattern described in Step 3, describing the flaw of making a recommendation without adequately balancing the costs and benefits.

(A) describes a circular reasoning flaw, which is not at play. The conclusion is a recommendation against acquiring new tastes, which does not simply restate the negative results listed in the evidence.

(B) is phrased as an assumption, as Flaw answer choices often are. In order to be correct, the choice must accurately state the argument's necessary assumption, and this one does not. The moralist says expensive tastes are a "drain on your purse," but that is evidence, not an assumption. Additionally, a "drain on your purse" doesn't necessarily equal "financial irresponsibility."

(C) is incorrect because the precise definition of the term *sensations* is not critical to the logic of the argument. A failure to define a term is not a logical flaw on the LSAT, though using a word in a way that confuses two different potential meanings is (known as equivocation).

(D) is incorrect. Although causation is a critical concept on the LSAT, this argument does not address what causes people to attempt to acquire expensive new tastes. Rather it speaks to whether or not it is advisable to do so.

15. (D) Inference

Step 1: Identify the Question Type
The question stem explicitly asks you what can be inferred from the passage. Focus on the most concrete and emphasized information and look for potential deductions, especially from any Formal Logic statements.

Step 2: Untangle the Stimulus
The stimulus indicates that on most Wednesdays, Zack's will have free poetry readings. Also, on every day with a poetry reading, Zack's provides half-priced coffee all day.

Step 3: Make a Prediction
The statements can be linked as follows:

$$\text{If} \quad \text{(most) Wednesdays} \rightarrow \text{free poetry} \rightarrow \text{all day half-priced coffee}$$

This yields the deduction that on most Wednesdays, Zack's will offer half-priced coffee. Beware of answer choices that mention days other than Wednesday. The stimulus provides no information on either of those.

Step 4: Evaluate the Answer Choices
(D) matches the prediction. It is acceptable to say "if not all Wednesdays" because even those Wednesdays when Zack's doesn't have free poetry readings, they may still offer half-priced coffee for some other reason.

(A) cannot be inferred from the information in the stimulus. Though *most* Wednesdays have half-priced coffee, maybe Zack's offers half-price coffee *every* Saturday. You have no information about other days or other events that might yield half-priced coffee, so you cannot make this comparison.

(B) is wrong for the same reason as the prior choice: the stimulus offers no information about what happens on other days. Maybe free poetry readings are also held every Monday and Friday, which would mean most readings are *not* on Wednesdays. On the LSAT, you can never infer anything from omission (from what is not mentioned).

(C) distorts the logic of the stimulus. The stimulus says that if there is a poetry reading, then half-priced coffee is offered. That does not necessarily mean that most days with half-priced coffee also have poetry readings. Any time the stimulus contains Formal Logic, watch out for answer choices that distort and/or reverse the logic rather than properly contraposing or combining statements.

(E) may be tempting, but does not actually have to be true. Zack's might offer half-priced coffee every Wednesday, even if a poetry reading isn't held.

16. (B) Principle (Apply/Inference)

Step 1: Identify the Question Type
The phrase "conforms to" is typically used in a Principle question, and *position* often indicates a general policy or viewpoint. Thus, you are asked to match the general position in the stimulus with a specific situation in the answers. This is an Apply the Principle question that functions as an Inference question because the question stem explicitly states that the correct answer is a valid inference. In other words, the answer choice is an example that must be true based on the philosopher's statements.

Step 2: Untangle the Stimulus
The stimulus contains two general Formal Logic rules that you can translate as follows:

Statement 1:

$$\text{If} \quad \text{action based on specific motivation} \rightarrow \text{intentional}$$

$$\text{If} \quad \sim \text{intentional} \rightarrow \sim \text{action based on specific motivation}$$

Statement 2:

$$\text{If} \quad \begin{array}{l} \text{action} \sim \text{based on specific motivation} \\ \text{AND} \\ \sim \text{explained by physical processes} \end{array} \rightarrow \text{random}$$

$$\text{If} \quad \sim \text{random} \quad \rightarrow \quad \textit{action based on specific motivation OR explained by physical processes}$$

Step 3: Make a Prediction

Though the result in the contraposed Statement 1 (~ action based on specific motivation) also shows up in the trigger of Statement 2, it's only half of the complex trigger. Therefore, these Formal Logic statements will not link up.

When a Principle stimulus contains a Formal Logic statement that will be applied to situations in the answer choices, the sufficient condition will match the correct answer's evidence and the necessary condition will match the conclusion. This would apply to the contrapositive as well. In this case, all the answers have conclusions of *intentional* or *random*. Therefore, you need to compare the choices only to the original translations of the two Formal Logic statements, not their contrapositives.

Finally, while the correct answer must be true based on the stimulus, it does not need to incorporate both rules.

Step 4: Evaluate the Answer Choices

(B) matches the first Formal Logic statement. The evidence (trigger) is that Ellis acted on the basis of specific motivation (to read the contents), and the conclusion (result) is that this act was intentional.

(A) isn't enough to trigger the second Formal Logic statement. Though Tarik's action was not based on a specific motivation, there's no evidence that the action was not explainable by normal physical processes. Therefore, both parts of the sufficient condition are not present, so it is improper to draw the conclusion that the event was random.

(C) is a Distortion that fails to distinguish between an action and the consequences of that action. Based on the philosopher's position, Judith's act of hailing the cab should be considered intentional, but any subsequent results of that action are not covered by the principle.

(D) is incorrect for the same reason as **(A)**. The lack of specific motivation by itself is not enough to trigger the second Formal Logic statement. The trigger consists of two conditions, both of which must be satisfied in order for the necessary condition to follow. Because no information is given about whether Yasuko's breathing was explainable by normal physical processes, it cannot be concluded that her action was random.

(E) improperly combines and distorts the two rules. Based on the first Formal Logic statement, in order to know an action is

intentional (conclusion), you must know for sure that it was based on a specific motivation. It's unlikely Henry dropped the wrench on purpose.

17. (D) Assumption (Necessary)

Step 1: Identify the Question Type

That the assumption is *required* by the argument makes this a Necessary Assumption question. You can use the Denial Test to check your answer.

Step 2: Untangle the Stimulus

The author concludes that somebody else's claim is mistaken. Paraphrase the author's conclusion by negating the other claim. Others claim that ancient people did not know what moral rights were simply because their language did not contain an appropriate term for a "moral right." So, the author concludes that people who lack a term for "moral right" *can* still know what a moral right is. (Beware of going too far and saying the author argues ancient people *knew* what moral rights were; the author merely thinks it's possible.) The author's evidence is an analogy to knowing what a fruit is without knowing its name.

Step 3: Make a Prediction

The author makes two assumptions here. First, that the analogy is a valid comparison and, second, that the analogy is sufficient to prove his point (and doesn't include its own gap). The author essentially says it would be ridiculous to say someone who harvests and studies a wild fruit doesn't have any idea what it is until it is named. If that's the case, then the author must be assuming that it is possible to know what something is from using and studying it, even if it there is no specific term for it. If you weren't able to predict this, remember that the Denial Test can help you out with the answer choices.

Step 4: Evaluate the Answer Choices

(D) is correct. Using the Denial Test, if a person who harvests and studies a fruit has *no* idea of what it is before knowing the name, then the analogy would be completely irrelevant.

(A) is incorrect. The Formal Logic can be laid out like this:

$$\text{If} \quad \textbf{know the name} \quad \rightarrow \quad \textbf{know what it is}$$

$$\text{If} \quad \sim \textbf{know what it is} \quad \rightarrow \quad \sim \textbf{know the name}$$

The author argued that if someone doesn't know the name (only a necessary term in the Formal Logic of this choice), then they *could* still know what something is. So, the Formal Logic of this choice is not necessary for the author's argument. The author's argument still holds even if someone could name an obscure fruit (e.g., a cherimoya or a persimmon) but has no idea how that fruit looks or tastes. To the author, knowing a name is irrelevant.

(B) is an Irrelevant Comparison. The argument does not compare who knows something better than another.

(C) is Extreme. The author diminishes the importance of a name, but this choice goes too far in assuming that a name cannot provide *any* useful information. A blueberry is indeed both blue and a berry.

(E) flips the reasoning around. The author does not address whether or not knowing something is necessary to name it, but whether or not knowing the name is necessary to know what it is. If denied, this choice would still be consistent with the author's argument.

18. (E) Main Point

Step 1: Identify the Question Type

The question stem explicitly asks you to identify the conclusion of the argument, so this is a Main Point question.

Step 2: Untangle the Stimulus

The author begins by identifying a claim made by others (that it is wrong to criticize anyone for being critical) and asserts there is little plausibility to that claim. The author provides evidence, saying that assessments are necessary and can't all be positive. The first sentence initially seems like it will be the conclusion (it's opinionated and supported by evidence).

But the Contrast Keyword [*h*]*owever* highlights the author's transition to the primary point of this argument: "there is wisdom behind the injunction against being judgmental." The final sentence supports this viewpoint, introducing a negative: being judgmental means not trying to understand before judging.

Step 3: Make a Prediction

The correct answer should match the claim that "there is wisdom behind the injunction against being judgmental." The answer to a Main Point question is not a summary of the entire argument and should not speculate beyond the stated conclusion.

Step 4: Evaluate the Answer Choices

(E) is an exact verbatim match of the conclusion. So, the key to getting this point is recognizing the third sentence as the author's big idea. Contrast Keywords, such as *however*, almost always signal that what follows is important (either the author's conclusion or a key piece of evidence). In this argument, [*h*]*owever* signals the transition from an idea that the author does not regard highly to a somewhat related idea that the author supports.

(A) matches the last sentence in the argument, which is the sole evidence supporting the author's conclusion in the prior sentence. There is no Keyword connecting these two

sentences to assist in determining which is the evidence and which is the conclusion. So, if you were torn between these last two sentences, you could have asked which provides support for the other.

(B) is a 180. It is found in the background introduction to the argument and is the opposite of what the author believes. The author finds "little plausibility" in the claim that it is "absurd to criticize anyone for being critical."

(C) incorrectly identifies the first sentence as the conclusion and distorts the meaning of the implication. To assert that there is "little plausibility" to a claim is to attack it. Although this attack does tacitly accept that there may be *some* plausibility, that is not the point. To state there is "some plausibility" to a claim is to positively attest that the claim is not implausible. While the statistical upshot is similar, the connotation of the two versions of this statement are very different. More importantly, this choice addresses a claim that is only raised by the author as a segue to the argument's actual focus. Even a verbatim restatement of the first sentence would not suffice as the correct answer.

(D) incorrectly identifies the second sentence as the conclusion. While it does begin with an Emphasis Keyword, it is not the conclusion for a couple of reasons. First, [*o*]*bviously* is not a great candidate for a Keyword leading into the conclusion of an argument. That which is obvious, or accepted by all, does not make for an interesting opinion or claim to be put forward by an author and supported by evidence. Why support with evidence that which is obvious? Indeed, this premise is support for the more subjective opinion in the first sentence.

19. (C) Role of a Statement

Step 1: Identify the Question Type

The question stem reiterates a claim from the stimulus and asks you what role it plays in the argument. Thus, this is a Role of a Statement question, requiring you to understand the structure of the argument and how a particular piece fits into that structure. First, underline the relevant claim in the stimulus. Then, break down the argument as normal.

Step 2: Untangle the Stimulus

The claim that "some painters are superior to others in the execution of their artistic vision" is found at the end of the first sentence.

The first sentence introduces what the author believes to be an irrefutable point: that some painters are superior to others in their artistic execution. The Contrast Keyword [*b*]*ut* signals the transition to the author's main idea regarding how this superiority must be measured: against the artist's purposes. Subsequently, the author provides an example of an artist to support that claim.

Step 3: Make a Prediction

The identified claim in the first sentence is thus neither the conclusion of the argument nor a piece of evidence supporting that conclusion. It is an idea related to the author's conclusion in that the conclusion is an assertion of how this idea should be measured. Look for an answer that describes that type of connection to the conclusion. Eliminate any answer that suggests that the statement is itself the conclusion or evidence supporting the conclusion.

Step 4: Evaluate the Answer Choices

(C) is an accurate description of the role the identified statement plays in the argument. The phrase "a claim ... to be understood" fits because the conclusion directs that a painter's superiority "must be measured" in a certain way.

(A) incorrectly indicates that the argument attempts to refute the claim that some painters are superior. Rather, the point of the argument is how that irrefutable superiority should be measured.

(B) may be initially tempting because the argument does utilize an example. However, this choice goes wrong in the same manner as **(A)** because the author does not object or attempt to refute the claim that some painters are superior.

(D) may be a little tough to follow, but it describes a subsidiary conclusion. It clearly goes astray at the end by asserting that the statement in question is used to support the argument's conclusion. The only support for the conclusion is found at the end of the last sentence after the Evidence Keyword *since*. The mere existence of some painters' superiority is not evidentiary support for *how* such superiority should be measured.

(E) is likely the most tempting wrong answer because it incorporates the specific example used in the argument and avoids directly referring to the claim as evidence or conclusion. However, the existence of some painters' superiority is only a starting point for the argument regarding how superiority should be measured. The statement plays no further role in the argument, not even justifying the relevance of the example.

20. (A) Flaw

Step 1: Identify the Question Type

The question stem explicitly asks you to identify the flaw. Notice the disconnect between the evidence and conclusion, and keep common flaws in mind.

Step 2: Untangle the Stimulus

The author concludes that something in mammalian chromosomes precludes the possibility of parthenogenesis. Two important pieces of evidence are highlighted by the Contrast Keyword [*h*]*owever* and the Evidence Keyword *since*: 1) no studies have demonstrated parthenogenesis in

mammals, and 2) parthenogenesis is known to occur in a wide variety of nonmammals.

Step 3: Make a Prediction

Notice that the evidence merely indicates that nobody has yet found parthenogenesis in mammals. One relatively common flaw is to assume that the lack of evidence for something proves it doesn't exist or is impossible.

Additionally, this argument makes the assumption that the reason parthenogenesis is absent in mammals is due to mammalian chromosomes and no other explanation. This is another common pattern: the author identifies an interesting phenomenon and then provides an explanation for the phenomenon, with the built-in assumption that no other possibilities exist.

Be open to an answer touching on either of these LSAT patterns.

Step 4: Evaluate the Answer Choices

(A) matches the first LSAT flaw type described in Step 3.

(B) incorrectly describes a representativeness flaw. While this choice accurately indicates that the evidence states that parthenogenesis is found in some nonmammalian species, it misstates that conclusion. The argument neither concludes nor assumes that *all* nonmammalian species undergo parthenogenesis. The conclusion is only about mammals.

(C) is also not an accurate description of the argument. The conclusion puts forward an explanation (mammalian chromosomes preclude parthenogenesis), but doesn't rule out another. Also, the phrase "on the grounds that" indicates that the *evidence* provides the explanation of the phenomenon, but in actuality, only the conclusion does. Many Flaw answers provide a description of the argument's evidence and conclusion. In order to be correct, the pieces in the answer must accurately reflect the evidence and conclusion as stated by the author.

(D) describes a necessary versus sufficient flaw, which is not involved here. To be correct, the evidence in the stimulus would have to say that parthenogenesis requires some condition, and the conclusion would need to say that condition guarantees parthenogenesis. This argument does not identify any condition (necessary or sufficient) for parthenogenesis to occur in the evidence.

(E) is a Distortion of the stimulus. The author does not presume *anything* about why the rabbit study was flawed. The author merely states that it was.

21. (B) Principle (Identify/Assumption)

Step 1: Identify the Question Type

The question stem explicitly identifies this as Principle question. Note that the question stem further directs that the general principle will be found in the answers, so this is an

Identify the Principle question. Furthermore, the stimulus consists of an argument (*reasoning*) regarding a specific situation. This question looks for a principle that underlies that reasoning, and therefore it mimics an Assumption question.

Step 2: Untangle the Stimulus

The advertiser concludes that anyone wanting to keep a television show on the air should buy the products advertised during the show. The evidence is that if people generally fail to do so, then the show will be cancelled.

Step 3: Make a Prediction

Notice the scope shift between the evidence and the conclusion. The evidence focuses on what will happen if people *generally* fail to buy the advertised products, while the conclusion recommends that *everyone* should thus buy the advertised products. The generalized descriptions of this specific situation should retain that scope shift.

Also, notice that every answer choice is in "if/then" form. Thus, the correct answer should paraphrase the argument as "if evidence, then conclusion."

Step 4: Evaluate the Answer Choices

(B) properly paraphrases the argument. Its evidence is that a show will be cancelled unless many people take certain actions (i.e., buy advertised products), and its conclusion is that everyone wanting to keep the show on the air ought to take those actions (i.e., buy those products).

(A) is a Distortion because it places too much emphasis on *one* individual. The argument does not assert that the continued existence of the show depends on the action of one individual, but that it depends on whether people *generally* buy the advertised products.

(C) is also a Distortion. First, the argument does not depend on an objective determination that a show *is* worth preserving. Second, it doesn't require that *everyone* should take action, just those who feel the show is worth preserving. Third, this answer choice encompasses *all* possible actions in order to stop cancellation, while the stimulus focuses only on those actions that, if not done, would trigger cancellation.

(D) does not retain the connection between the actions that, if not done, would trigger the show's cancellation and the recommendation to take those actions. Also, this answer choice is more tentatively phrased than the stimulus: "take at least some actions" versus "buy the products."

(E) also contains a Distortion because the argument does not recommend that only those "who feel the most strongly" take action, but that *anyone* who feels the show is worth preserving take action.

22. (E) Weaken

Step 1: Identify the Question Type

The question stem explicitly asks you to weaken the psychologist's argument.

Step 2: Untangle the Stimulus

The psychologist concludes that heart disease can result from psychological factors. The evidence states:

1) Fits of anger cause temporary incidents of high blood pressure.

2) A study has shown a correlation between people who are easily angered and permanently high blood pressure.

3) There is a correlation between permanently high blood pressure and heart disease.

Step 3: Make a Prediction

The psychologist connects a predisposition to anger, which is a psychological factor, to high blood pressure and, in turn, to heart disease. This is a classic correlation to causation argument. The most likely way to weaken a causal argument is to identify an alternative cause of both the anger and the high blood pressure and heart disease. Another way to weaken the argument would be to suggest reverse causation, i.e., high blood pressure or heart disease can cause a person to be susceptible to anger.

Step 4: Evaluate the Answer Choices

(E) is correct. It suggests that alternative physiological factors are actually the cause of both anger and high blood pressure, rather than anger causing high blood pressure.

(A) is irrelevant to this argument regarding whether or not anger causes heart disease. The likelihood of recovery is Out of Scope of the conclusion.

(B) is an ambivalent answer that could arguably weaken *or* strengthen the argument, and thus it would not suffice as the correct answer to either question type. While a Weaken or Strengthen answer need not disprove or prove an argument, it must unambiguously take the argument in one direction. This choice just mentions *moods* in general; whether this choice weakens or strengthens the argument depends on whether this medication makes one more angry (correlated with higher blood pressure) or more tranquil (correlated with lower blood pressure).

(C) is a 180. It provides more evidence of a connection between anger and heart disease, independent of high blood pressure.

(D) may be tempting because it appears to be a reverse causation answer. However, selecting this answer requires equating becoming easily frustrated with being easily angered.

23. (B) Strengthen

Step 1: Identify the Question Type

The question stem explicitly asks you to strengthen the argument.

Step 2: Untangle the Stimulus

The author concludes that online books will not make printed books obsolete. The evidence is that a majority of students assigned to read an online case study printed the study out on paper.

Step 3: Make a Prediction

The argument makes a couple of assumptions. First, the argument assumes that printing the online case study out on paper somehow indicates a continuing use of mass printed books, rather than a trend for individuals to print out texts as needed. Additionally, the author assumes that this group of students is representative of other readers.

Step 4: Evaluate the Answer Choices

(B) is correct. This choice bolsters the assumption that this group of students is representative of a broader population.

(A) does not bolster the assumption that the group discussed in the stimulus is representative of the broader population. If anything, this choice expands the group to non-business students, but even that is tenuous. The answer choice merely says *several*; it's not clear what percentage (majority or no) of the non-business students printed out the assignments. *Several* might just mean three more students, for example. Furthermore, although this may expand the overall number of people that prefer printed material, it still makes a generalization related to *all* book users on the limited information about students in courses.

(C) indicates a potential impediment to moving books fully online, but it has a similar problem to **(A)**. Just because at least one person (the definition of *some*) will develop vision problems from reading online, this isn't enough to strengthen an argument already based on a strong majority.

(D) also raises a potential impediment to full conversion to online books, but it also provides a ready remedy. So, this choice is ambiguous as to whether it strengthens or weakens.

(E) is incorrect. Its relevance is suspect from the beginning with its analogy to books on tape, but really veers off into irrelevance with its discussion of sales of movies adapted from books. Whether people want to buy movies adapted from books does not indicate whether people will choose to read a printed book or an online version of a book.

24. (D) Flaw

Step 1: Identify the Question Type

The phrase "vulnerable to criticism" indicates a Flaw question. Moreover, the question stem specifies the flaw is an overlooked possibility. By definition, it is a logical flaw to

overlook a possibility that, if true, would weaken the argument.

Step 2: Untangle the Stimulus

The advertisement's author concludes that anyone following the diet, which includes more protein than any other nutrient and makes breakfast the biggest meal of the day, is guaranteed to lose weight.

The evidence is a study showing a correlation between those who got more calories from protein than carbohydrates and ate a large early meal and those who lost the most weight.

Step 3: Make a Prediction

There are two assumptions or argument patterns to focus on within this stimulus. First, this is a common pattern in which an author uses a correlation to support an assertion of a causal relationship. Such an argument assumes that nothing else was responsible for the observed result. So, in this case, the advertisement's author assumes that nothing else was special about the study participants who lost the most weight.

Second, notice how absolute the conclusion is: *anyone* who follows this diet is *sure* to lose weight. While the unspecified number of people who lost the most weight all had a similar diet, many people might have followed this diet without losing any weight. Even the existence of a single person who followed this diet but did not lose any weight would undermine this absolute conclusion.

Step 4: Evaluate the Answer Choices

(D) is correct. While the existence of a few anomalous counterexamples would not weaken a conclusion that such a diet *generally* causes significant weight loss, in this case, the existence of even a single counterexample would weaken the conclusion's absolute guarantee.

(A) is not mentioned by the argument and thus might have been overlooked by the advertisement's author; however, this would not make it a logical flaw. If this choice were true, it could still be consistent with the argument. It indicates that the recommended diet might be difficult to follow, yet the diet could still be effective.

(B) also would not weaken the argument, and thus it is not a logical flaw for the advertisement's author to fail to consider this possibility. Asserting that this diet is a guaranteed way to lose weight (i.e., sufficient to lose weight) does not depend on it being the *only* way to lose weight (i.e., necessary to lose weight) or even the best or most assured way to lose weight. The existence of a few people who lose weight some other way does not undermine a claim that the high protein, big breakfast diet is a sure thing.

(C) is a tempting answer because it presents an alternative cause for the weight loss. However, this choice would weaken the argument only if it was clear that the people who exercised all also belonged to the group that got more calories from protein and ate a large breakfast. Then this choice would offer an alternate reason (other than diet) why that group saw results. However, as it stands, this choice merely introduces another way people lost weight. As discussed for **(B)**, the conclusion is a guarantee that anyone who uses the particular advertised diet will lose some weight, not that the diet is the best or only way to lose weight. Therefore, pointing out another successful option doesn't weaken the conclusion.

(E), like **(A)**, is not mentioned by the argument, and thus is technically overlooked by the advertisement's author. However it would not be a logical flaw to fail to consider this possibility because, if true, it is fully consistent with the argument. This answer simply provides an explanation for *why* a big breakfast is beneficial. If anything, this choice strengthens the argument that this diet is effective.

25. (C) Inference (EXCEPT)

Step 1: Identify the Question Type
A question stem that asks what follows logically from the statements or information above (direction of support flowing downward from the stimulus to the answers) is an Inference question. For an Inference EXCEPT question, eliminate any answers that must be true and find the answer that does not have to be true (either contradicts the stimulus or is Out of Scope). Inventory the facts and combine statements to make any potential deductions.

Step 2: Untangle the Stimulus
The stimulus provides three facts. First, some 20th-century art is great art. Then, two Formal Logic statements:

If	great art	→	original ideas

If	~ influential	→	~ great art

Step 3: Make a Prediction
Work first with the absolute information in the last sentence. Contraposing the last idea yields the deduction that great art must be influential as well as involve original ideas. So, if art is not influential or does not involve original ideas, then it cannot be great art.

If	great art	→	original ideas AND influential

If	~ original ideas OR ~ influential	→	~ great art

Also, recall that some 20th-century art is great art. This type of *some* statement does not yield a contrapositive, but it can be interpreted two ways. It means that out of all the 20th-century art, there is at least one piece of great art, and also that out of all the great art, there is at least one piece of 20th-century art.

Finally, remember that any modestly phrased answers are more likely to be true and thus are candidates for elimination on this EXCEPT question, while forceful answers are more likely to be the correct answer.

Step 4: Evaluate the Answer Choices
(C) does not have to be true and so is correct. This choice indicates that for art to be influential, it must involve original ideas. This would diagram as:

If	influential	→	original ideas

The statements in the stimulus cannot be contraposed or combined to yield such a deduction. You know that great art is both influential and original, but the stimulus doesn't say what *influential* would trigger. Because you cannot know for sure if this answer choice is true, it does not follow logically from the statements and thus is the correct exception.

(A) is a modestly phrased statement that must be true. Because all great art involves both original ideas and is influential and because some great art exists (as some 20th-century art is great), it must be true that some influential art involves original ideas.

(B) is another modestly phrased statement that must be true because some 20th-century art is great, and great art must also involve original ideas.

(D), while forceful, is a valid logical deduction from the statements. It states the main deduction made in Step 3:

If	great art	→	influential AND original ideas

(E) is a modestly phrased statement that must be true because some 20th-century art is great, and thus it must also involve original ideas and be influential.

Section II: Reading Comprehension

Passage 1: Injunctions Against the Disclosure of Trade Secrets

Q#	Question Type	Correct	Difficulty
1	Global	D	★
2	Inference	A	★
3	Global	A	★
4	Inference	B	★
5	Inference	E	★
6	Detail	E	★★★

Passage 2: Purple Loosestrife

Q#	Question Type	Correct	Difficulty
7	Detail	A	★★
8	Detail	E	★
9	Logic Reasoning (Point at Issue)	B	★★★★
10	Inference	E	★★
11	Inference	A	★★★
12	Logic Reasoning (Method of Argument)	C	★
13	Logic Reasoning (Weaken and Strengthen)	A	★★★

Passage 3: Maxine Hong Kingston and "Talk-Story"

Q#	Question Type	Correct	Difficulty
14	Global	A	★
15	Inference	D	★★★
16	Inference	C	★★★★
17	Logic Reasoning (Parallel Reasoning)	B	★★★
18	Inference	C	★★
19	Logic Reasoning (Weaken)	D	★★
20	Logic Function	B	★
21	Inference	A	★★★★

Passage 4: Dutch Tulips—A Speculative Bubble?

Q#	Question Type	Correct	Difficulty
22	Global	D	★★
23	Logic Reasoning (Parallel Reasoning)	D	★★★★
24	Inference	B	★★★★
25	Detail	B	★★
26	Logic Function	C	★
27	Inference	D	★★

Passage 1: Injunctions Against the Disclosure of Trade Secrets

Step 1: Read the Passage Strategically
Sample Roadmap

line #	Keyword/phrase	¶ Margin notes
5	irreconcilable:	dilemma non-disclose vs. right to work
9	Nevertheless	courts try to balance
12	but	
14	argued; because	both sides criticized
17	hardly effective	
19	But; doubtful	
21	obviously impossible	can't forget expertise
23	Nor	
26	Nevertheless	can't un-learn
27	legimately	
28	:	but knowledge is corp. property
36	But	courts can ban obvious use but subtle? intuitive?
37–38	for example	
41	Theoretically	in theory—yes
42	However	hard to distinguish
46	And even if	
47–48	appear suspicious; further problem	
51–52	major stumbling block	so—injunctions against disclosure don't work, except concrete works
53	since	
55	therefore unlikely	
56	actually prevents	
57	except	

Discussion

Paragraph 1 starts by introducing the **Topic**, corporate intellectual property, and a dilemma within that Topic. When an employee leaves her old company, she has a right to seek new employment, but at the same time, her former employer has a right to protect its trade secrets. These two goals, says the author, "appear irreconcilable." The author goes on to refine the **Scope** of the passage: how courts get caught up in the dilemma. Courts want to allow employees to work for their new employers, but will restrain employees from disclosing secrets learned in their old jobs. Finally, the author contrasts those who criticize the courts' moves as bad for employees—how can they really seek new work if they can't talk about their old jobs—with those who claim that the courts' injunctions don't really protect employers. Note that the author hasn't weighed in yet, but look for language suggesting a point of view.

Paragraph 2, anchored by the Keyword *nevertheless* in line 26, illustrates the dilemma in a little more detail. Employees can't just forget what they learned at their old jobs, but employers have a proprietary interest in almost all data and information not publicly available.

After two expository paragraphs, you should expect the author to give an opinion, and you get it in paragraph 3. First, the author gives further dimension to the problem by telling us that the "leakage" of trade secrets may be subtle or even subconscious. This becomes a "major stumbling block" to the former employer's attempt to assert that the employee is disclosing proprietary information. All of this leads to a succinct statement of the author's **Main Idea** in the passage's final sentence (signaled by the Conclusion Keyword *therefore* in line 55): Except in the most concrete cases, injunctions against disclosure are unlikely to protect former employers. That Main Idea sheds light on the author's **Purpose**, which is to evaluate the courts' approach.

1. (D) Global

Step 2: Identify the Question Type
This is a Global question because it asks you to identify the "main point" of the passage.

Step 3: Research the Relevant Text
Instead of researching a specific part of the passage to predict your answer, base your prediction on the Main Idea you determined during Step 1.

Step 4: Make a Prediction
The Keyword *therefore* in line 55 signals the author's Main Idea during Step 1: Court injunctions intended to protect a company's trade secrets from unauthorized disclosure probably aren't effective.

Step 5: Evaluate the Answer Choices
(D) is a close match.

(A) is Outside the Scope. You may be tempted to think that because injunctions aren't likely to work, something else must be better. However, the author never addresses the possibility of what would work. It's possible that there is just no way to solve this problem.

(B) speculates beyond what the passage addresses. The author offers no solutions or recommendations for fixing the shortcomings of injunctions.

(C) is Extreme due to its use of the word *impossible*. The author mentions some cases—"the passage of documents or other concrete embodiments of the secrets" (lines 57–59)—in which injunctions would be effective.

(E) is a 180. According to the author, the interests of the former employers are at a greater risk of being violated than are the rights of the former employees.

2. (A) Inference

Step 2: Identify the Question Type
This is an Inference question because it asks you to find the answer choice that isn't stated directly in the passage, but is nonetheless consistent with its tone and content.

Step 3: Research the Relevant Text
You don't have any content clues in the question stem to guide your research. Therefore, any part of the passage is fair game.

Step 4: Make a Prediction
When you're answering an Inference question without a clear reference to specific parts of the passage, predicting the answer can be tough. Instead, go straight to the answer choices and select the one that *must* be true based on the passage.

Step 5: Evaluate the Answer Choices
(A) follows naturally from the passage. The key phrase in **(A)** is the opening caveat—"given the law as it stands." In lines 19–20, the author says that current law probably can't keep a company's former employees from divulging its trade secrets. So, if you're operating under the current law and you want to preserve your trade secrets, you'd benefit from retaining your employees.

(B) is not in keeping with the author's point of view on injunctions. It's also Outside the Scope; the author does not address alternatives and so doesn't opine as to which method of handling this dilemma is "most effective."

(C) is unsupported. The author doesn't give suggestions on how to improve the law; he stops at just criticizing it. For all we know, he might think that giving more enforcement power to former employers would be too restrictive on employees' rights.

(D) does too much outside speculation. Moreover, the phrase "waste of time" runs counter to the author's assertion that the current law may be useful in concrete cases (lines 57–59).

(E) distorts what the author said in paragraph 3 about the subtle nature of information "leakage" and mixes it up with the criticism in paragraph 1 that suspicion of wrongdoing can create psychological barriers to an employee's full use and expression of her skills and knowledge. Furthermore, the word *inevitably* is more Extreme than the tone of the passage.

3. (A) Global

Step 2: Identify the Question Type
Any question asking you to identify the author's "primary purpose" for writing the passage is a Global question.

Step 3: Research the Relevant Text
You already researched this answer when you came up with the author's Purpose during Step 1.

Step 4: Make a Prediction
The author's Purpose is to evaluate the effectiveness of disclosure injunctions when it comes to protecting trade secrets and employee rights.

Step 5: Evaluate the Answer Choices
(A) says it somewhat differently but is nonetheless correct. It accurately describes both sides of the dilemma that the author wrestled with throughout the passage.

(B) is not only too narrow and detail focused to be the correct answer to a Global question, but also contradicts what the author had to say about documents and concrete disclosures.

(C) is Outside the Scope. The author neither addresses what could be done to resolve the dilemma, nor makes any plea for us to find solutions.

(D) is Outside the Scope. The author stays focused on his critique of the current law; he doesn't say we should abandon the *concept* of protection.

(E) is a Distortion. The author says that injunctions aren't effective at protecting all trade secrets as currently constituted, but that doesn't mean that injunctions are not necessary at all. Lines 57–59 give an instance of injunctions protecting against the transfer of concrete trade secrets.

4. (B) Inference

Step 2: Identify the Question Type
The phrase "passage provides the most support" indicates an Inference question.

Step 3: Research the Relevant Text
Just as in the second question of the set, this question doesn't give you any content clues to guide your research. The right answer can be supported by any part of the passage.

Step 4: Make a Prediction
Even though prediction is tough on this question, you can still evaluate the answer choices strategically. You know that the right answer will be consistent with the content of the passage, and it will also be in keeping with the author's Purpose and Main Idea.

Step 5: Evaluate the Answer Choices
(B) is supported by the author's Main Idea. It's further supported by lines 4–9, which say that protecting both the intellectual property of employees and the rights of employees appear at cross-purposes. The word *apparently* in **(B)** matches the tone of these lines and keeps this answer from being Extreme.

(A) is Extreme and Outside the Scope of the passage. The author doesn't offer any opinion that injunctions should be used *only* under one set of circumstances.

(C) is unsupported. The author doesn't comment on courts' decisions not to prohibit employees from working for competitors of their former employers, but even if he did comment, the passage suggests that he'd agree with the courts.

(D) is a Distortion. According to the author, the multiple ways of transmitting information make injunctions of questionable efficacy. The author is silent on the question of whether it increases the need for injunctions.

(E) is Outside the Scope. The author never hints that injunctions are used as retribution by companies.

5. (E) Inference

Step 2: Identify the Question Type
This is an Inference question because it asks you to find the statement with which the author would be "most likely to agree." You'll, therefore, have to infer the answer; it won't be directly stated.

Step 3: Research the Relevant Text
You're given a content clue ("documents and other concrete embodiments") and a line reference, so reading that entire sentence for context is a good start.

Step 4: Make a Prediction
Checking lines 54–59, you see that "documents and other concrete embodiments" are mentioned as exceptions to the author's conclusion that injunctions won't prevent the transfer of sensitive information. To phrase that affirmatively, the author believes that injunctions are more likely to work in cases involving "documents and other concrete embodiments." The right answer will be consistent with this view.

Step 5: Evaluate the Answer Choices
(E) is a perfect match.

(A) is unsupported. For the author, the mode of transferring the information is irrelevant to the amount of harm the disclosure causes to the former employer.

(B) is an Irrelevant Comparison. The author never provides a hierarchy of which sources are likely to be more or less informative.

(C) is Outside the Scope. The author doesn't indicate that injunctions should *specify* which materials are included. Even more telling, the tone of policy recommendation (what injunctions *should* do) doesn't follow from the author's discussion of documents and concrete materials.

(D) is a 180. Documents are the source of information most likely controlled by injunctions. The author doesn't qualify this statement based on the size of the document transfer.

6. (E) Detail

Step 2: Identify the Question Type

The categorical wording of the question stem ("author makes which one of the following claims") indicates a Detail question.

Step 3: Research the Relevant Text

This Detail question doesn't provide any content clues to help you research effectively. You'll have to save your research for the answer choices.

Step 4: Make a Prediction

Predicting the correct answer is next to impossible, so as you evaluate the answer choices, make sure you can locate reference to the right answer before you select it.

Step 5: Evaluate the Answer Choices

(E) is mentioned in lines 47–51, where the author details the difficulties with distinguishing independent invention from protected trade secrets.

(A) is not mentioned as an impediment created by injunctions when it comes to employees' rights.

(B) distorts the author's claim that injunctions are more likely to work when applied to cases involving documents and concrete materials (lines 57–59), but the author doesn't say that those are the only cases in which injunctions are necessary.

(C) distorts the author's claim that when trade secrets are disclosed, it's more likely to be unintentional than conscious on the part of the employee (lines 36–37), which is a far cry from this answer's claim that whenever someone goes to work for a competitor, they'll probably wind up breaking the law.

(D) is Outside the Scope. The author never discusses what the new employer may or may not do to persuade their new employee to divulge their old employer's secrets.

Passage 2: Purple Loosestrife

Step 1: Read the Passage Strategically
Sample Roadmap

line #	Keyword/phrase	¶ Margin notes
Passage A		
1		Purple loosestrife
6	disastrous	big impact on native species
11	but; serious	
12–13	In addition	animals too
15	Although	
17	greatly	
18	While	
19	little	long-term control difficult
21	successfully; but	
26	needed	need integrated control
27	hinges on	
Passage B		
30	apparently	
33	Indeed	
36	rather than; Accordingly	people like author A say they're trying to help environ.
37	dutifully	
41		but—just oldstyle nature control
43	Regardless	
46	Consequently	
48	failed	
52	bulk of the justification	Evid. of harm from loosestrife small esp'ly on animals
53	However; other than	
57	though none	
59	What is threatened	Actually econ. is problem

Discussion

The strategic reader can get a jump start on these paired passages by taking note of the italicized introductory blurb. Passage A is more likely to take an ecological or environmental angle, while passage B, written by a sociologist, is more likely to focus on human issues of some kind.

Passage A introduces the **Topic**—an invasive plant species called purple loosestrife—right away. The **Scope**—the plant's impact and control—begins to take shape in the remainder of the long first paragraph. The author considers purple loosestrife's impact on native vegetation *disastrous* (line 6) and its impact on birds and animals *serious* (line 11), with several examples. The author goes on to emphasize that the spread of purple loosestrife is "greatly accelerated" (line 17) in disturbed habitats. Finally, the author summarizes what is known about controlling the species. Not much is known about long-term control of purple loosestrife, nor do we know much about the ecological impact of the one herbicide used against the species.

Paragraph 2 sounds a call to action. The author reasserts the immediacy of the problem and stresses "integrated control" (line 25) as the solution. Currently, says the author, we rely on early detection. So, in this paragraph, you get the author's **Purpose** (to discuss loosestrife's impact and advocate control) and **Main Idea**—purple loosestrife seriously impacts native ecosystems and we need integrated control to stop it.

As you learn from the pointed tone of lines 30–33, the author of passage B has a different **Scope**: the motives of those who—like passage A's author—are calling for a "war on purple loosestrife." Passage B's author is skeptical of their claimed concern for nature—note the Emphasis/Opinion Keywords *apparently* (line 30) and *dutifully* (line 38)—and he sums up the ecologists' view as "purple loosestrife is a pollution."

In paragraph 2, passage B's author details the implications of the ecologists' view, which he characterizes as ideological and a justification for human control of nature (lines 43–50). As a result, the ecologists overstate the impact of purple loosestrife on birds and animals, very few of which are actually threatened. Note the examples in lines 53–58, not unlike the examples in passage A at lines 10–15.

Finally, passage B's author tells you that the real issue is the economic impact. As we would expect from a sociologist, passage B's author's tone is scholarly. This passage's **Purpose** is to refute the overestimation of the impact of loosestrife. The **Main Idea** is that the ecologists' philosophy distorts the ecological impact of purple loosestrife and ignores the economic impact. In fact, passage B could very well have been written in response to passage A. It attempts to cool the rhetoric of passage A and refocus the discussion of the purple loosestrife's impact.

7. (A) Detail

Step 2: Identify the Question Type
This is a Detail question because it asks what both passages "explicitly mention."

Step 3: Research the Relevant Text
Without a clear reference to a specific part of the text, any of the passages' 65 lines could contain the correct answer.

Step 4: Make a Prediction
Instead of scouring both passages looking for common subjects, attack the answer choices with targeted research. Don't select an answer choice until you can locate references to it in each passage.

Step 5: Evaluate the Answer Choices
(A) is correct. Furbearing animals are mentioned in lines 11–12 in passage A and lines 56–58 in passage B.

(B), glyphosate, is mentioned only in passage A, in line 21.

(C), economic impacts, are mentioned only in passage B, in lines 60–65.

(D) is mentioned only in passage B, in lines 44–46.

(E) is mentioned only in passage B, in lines 36–37.

8. (E) Detail

Step 2: Identify the Question Type
Don't be thrown by the wording of this question stem. It asks about the information contained in the passage, so it's a Detail question.

Step 3: Research the Relevant Text
Once again, you don't have content clues to point you to a specific part of the passages.

Step 4: Make a Prediction
In the absence of content clues in the question stem, go straight to the answer choices. They will provide the information needed to help you verify or eliminate them.

Step 5: Evaluate the Answer Choices
(E) is a question answered by both passages. Both passages tell us that wetlands are impacted: passage A in line 7, and passage B in lines 46 and 64.

(A) is answered only by passage A in line 4. Passage B doesn't mention the arrival of purple loosestrife at all.

(B) is answered only by passage B in line 36, and even then, it doesn't mention hunters in connection with that literature. Hunting is mentioned much later in the passage, in line 63.

(C) is Outside the Scope because farmers are nowhere to be found in either passage.

(D) might be tempting, but although passage A mentions impact on water fowl (in line 11), only passage B mentions the canvasback specifically (in line 53).

9. (B) Logic Reasoning (Point at Issue)

Step 2: Identify the Question Type

This is like a Point at Issue question from the Logical Reasoning section because it asks what the authors of the passages "would most likely disagree about."

Step 3: Research the Relevant Text

Without clear content clues, any part of the passages can form the basis of the correct answer. But in a question asking about opinions, use Emphasis/Opinion Keywords, as well as your understanding of the authors' Main Ideas, to form your prediction.

Step 4: Make a Prediction

You know from analyzing the relationship between the passages that the author of passage A considers the ecological threat of loosestrife quite serious, but that the author of passage B considers that threat not as serious as its economic impact.

Step 5: Evaluate the Answer Choices

(B) is therefore correct.

(A) is something that the author of passage A would agree with (lines 17–18), but the author of passage B offers no opinion on this.

(C) is a Distortion. Neither author actually expresses an opinion on the motives of most people who want to control purple loosestrife (and the "most people" in **(C)** sends this choice into Extreme territory).

(D) is another Distortion. The author of passage A does point to the amount of biomass displaced in wetland communities, but you still don't know whether he thinks this amount exceeded general opinion. Moreover, passage B doesn't weigh in on this at all.

(E) is Outside the Scope of both passages. The only non-native plant species discussed throughout is purple loosestrife.

10. (E) Inference

Step 2: Identify the Question Type

This is an Inference question because it asks about one author's attitude toward something discussed in the passages.

Step 3: Research the Relevant Text

Pay attention to the Emphasis/Opinion Keywords in passage B— these will help you make an inference. The author of passage B indicates his opinion of the argument represented in passage A in lines 30–42. Noting Keywords like *apparently* (line 30) and the sarcastic *dutifully* (line 38), you can characterize the tone here as acerbic and her attitude toward the kinds of ecologists represented in passage A as doubtful.

Step 4: Make a Prediction

You now know you're looking for an answer choice consistent with being doubtful or unconvinced. Eliminate any answer choices that are too positive or neutral.

Step 5: Evaluate the Answer Choices

(E) is a great match.

(A) is a 180. The author doesn't agree at all—much less enthusiastically—with passage A's take on purple loosestrife's effects.

(B) also characterizes passage B's tone as one of agreement, which doesn't match the Opinion Keywords from passage B.

(C) is too detached. If **(C)** were correct, passage B wouldn't contain any Opinion Keywords.

(D) would be correct if the author of passage B hedged her opinion at all. However, passage B isn't torn between two opinions concerning the views of the ecologists.

11. (A) Inference

Step 2: Identify the Question Type

This is an Inference question because it asks what the two authors "would be most likely to agree with." Make sure your answer is consistent with the statements of *both* authors.

Step 3: Research the Relevant Text

Because the scope of this question is both passages, the entire text is relevant. Nevertheless, you can use your understanding of the relationship between the passages to predict a general area of agreement (or some likely wrong answers).

Step 4: Make a Prediction

When two passages disagree on opinions, a likely area of agreement will surround something factual. Given that the main point of passage B is that folks like the author of passage A have distorted and exaggerated the ecological impact of purple loosestrife and aren't admitting to its real costs. As in a Point at Issue question in the Logical Reasoning section, avoid any answer choices that are discussed in only one of the two passages.

Step 5: Evaluate the Answer Choices

(A) is the only acceptable answer. Passage A's author thinks the reduction in wildlife populations has been *serious* (line 11) but passage B's author would admit to *some* decreases—at the very least, the canvasback (lines 53–54).

(B) uses the strong phrase "disastrous effect" concerning vegetation, which marks this answer as something only passage A would agree with.

(C) was only mentioned in passage A, and even there, it was mentioned as having been used successfully (line 21).

(D) has strong language that the authors of the two passages would likely disagree over. Passage A's author might be on board with it, but it would likely strike passage B's author as Extreme.

(E) is Outside the Scope. Neither author addresses the question of how quickly purple loosestrife returns after removal.

12. (C) Logic Reasoning (Method of Argument)

Step 2: Identify the Question Type

This is a Method of Argument question because it asks about the relationship between the two passages. In other words, it asks what the authors *do* in relation to each other.

Step 3: Research the Relevant Text

There's no specific place to do research for a question like this, but if you've properly characterized the relationship between the passages during Step 1, you have everything you need for your prediction.

Step 4: Make a Prediction

Questions about the relationship between the passages are incredibly common in Comparative Reading, so be prepared to answer them efficiently. Passage A charged out with a strong argument and called for action; passage B took a scholarly look at the philosophy underpinning the kinds of arguments made in passage A and criticized the results.

Step 5: Evaluate the Answer Choices

(C) is a match for this prediction. The author of passage B must be aware of the kinds of arguments made in passage A (the whole Purpose of passage B is to respond to those arguments), but nothing in passage A suggests an awareness that sociologists are studying and critiquing ecologists' arguments.

(A) is a 180. Passage B is responsive to the evidence presented in passage A, but not the other way around.

(B) is also a 180. Passage B explicitly critiques the way in which those like passage A's author make their arguments; passage B's author could hardly be said to take passage A's arguments for granted.

(D) is a Distortion. Passage B makes no policy recommendations. Furthermore, passage A cannot be said to reject any policy, except perhaps for indirectly rejecting a policy of inaction.

(E) is a 180. It's passage B that downplays the seriousness of the ecological claims made in passage A, not vice versa.

13. (A) Logic Reasoning (Weaken and Strengthen)

Step 2: Identify the Question Type

This is a Weaken question because it asks for the answer that "would cast doubt on" passage B's argument, but it's also a Strengthen question because it asks for what would *bolster* passage A's.

Step 3: Research the Relevant Text

Because both passages are primarily concerned with making arguments, use the Main Ideas of the passages to help pre-phrase your answer.

Step 4: Make a Prediction

You're seeking a fact that would help passage A's argument but harm passage B's argument. The authors disagree on the severity of the ecological damage caused by purple loosestrife, so the correct answer will likely say that the impact caused by the spread of purple loosestrife is as bad as passage A argues.

Step 5: Evaluate the Answer Choices

(A) is exactly the kind of fact you're looking for. Passage B attempts to weaken arguments like that in passage A with evidence indicating that few species impacted by purple loosestrife are threatened or endangered. But if local population reductions forecast widespread endangerment, passage A's slippery-slope argument would be properly defended against passage B.

(B) is Outside the Scope. Neither side's argument relies on the date of discovery of purple loosestrife's problematic spread.

(C) is a 180. This would strengthen passage B's contention that the real impacts of purple loosestrife are economic in nature.

(D) is also a 180. This is consistent with passage B's characterization of those who advance arguments like the one found in passage A.

(E) is Outside the Scope. Both authors address loosestrife only as it appears in North America, as an invasive species. Its native habitat isn't discussed.

Passage 3: Maxine Hong Kingston and "Talk-Story"

Step 1: Read the Passage Strategically
Sample Roadmap

line #	Keyword/phrase	¶ Margin notes
2	suggested	Critics say MHK not in Chinese-Am tradition
4	lack	
6	But	
7	only	Auth = critics overlook "talk-story"
9	overlooked	
13	Traditionally	
15	rarely	talk-story typically in family, not print
20	Thus	immigrants brought to U.S.
24	simply embraced	new subject matter
25–26	as in the case	
27	believes	MHK identifies w/talkstory tradition
30	distinguishes	
32	from	
35	Nor	
36	substantially change	
41	but	extended to print
44	evidenced in	Ex. "China Men" has talk-story features
46	:	
52	also succeeds	China Men uses Eng. in Chinese way

Discussion

Paragraph 1 of this passage demonstrates a classic LSAT structure, introducing the Topic through some critics' view and the Scope through the author's contentious response. The **Topic** is Maxine Hong Kingston's work. The critics' view is that it shows no influence from Chinese American heritage. As soon as you read "some critics have suggested" in line 2, you can expect the author or someone else to weigh in. The author's response (and the introduction of the **Scope**) is introduced with the Contrast Keyword *but* (line 6). The author argues that the critics have *overlooked* (line 9) the influence of talk-story, a traditional Chinese oral literature style. The long, final sentence of the first paragraph actually hints at the author's **Purpose**: to argue against critics who deny Kingston's inheritance of Chinese American heritage by showing how she used "talk-story." You can anticipate that the remainder of the passage offers support for this contention.

Paragraph 2 describes talk-story. The author gives details of the genre's origins to establish (as indicated by the Conclusion Keyword *thus* in line 20) that Chinese immigrants to the United States would have been familiar and comfortable with talk-story. Immigrants applied the events of their new lives to this oral narrative style, and Maxine Hong Kingston shows this process applied in writing.

In paragraph 3, you learn that Kingston identifies herself as an inheritor of talk-story. This paragraph is anchored by Kingston's contrast between the personal nature of memory in the oral tradition and the linear, sequential nature of memory in print cultures. The author supports this idea by pointing out that Kingston continues to think of "writer" as a synonym of "singer" or "performer."

In paragraph 4, the author details how one of Kingston's books exemplifies the passage's thesis. The author cites four similarities between *China Men* and talk-story: fixed themes, stock characters, symmetrical structures, and repetition. It is all but inevitable that at least one question will focus on this extended example. The **Main Idea** is therefore that contrary to the critics' view, Kingston's work is strongly steeped in Chinese American traditions, as exemplified by the use of "talk-story" in works such as *China Men*.

14. (A) Global

Step 2: Identify the Question Type
This is a Global question because it asks you for the "main point of the passage."

Step 3: Research the Relevant Text
Instead of researching a specific part of the passage, use your understanding of Topic, Scope, Purpose, and especially Main Idea to predict your answer.

Step 4: Make a Prediction
The author's Main Idea is that the critics who say Kingston's work shows no Chinese heritage are wrong because her work shows the influence of talk-story. Yes, this is a paraphrase of lines 6–12, but the author's Main Idea is not always so explicitly stated in one part of the passage.

Step 5: Evaluate the Answer Choices
(A) is therefore correct.

(B) focuses too much on Kingston's beliefs as they're laid out in paragraph 3. Those beliefs are only given to support the author's contention that she has, despite what critics say, inherited a Chinese literary tradition.

(C) distorts the main point of the passage. The author might agree that a new kind of literary analysis is needed for ethnic literatures, but that goes beyond the scope of the main point.

(D) misses the author's dispute with the critics mentioned in paragraph 1. Furthermore, the word *especially* distorts the author's reference to the retention of the texture and qualities of Chinese speech in *China Men*. This retention was one of several features that demonstrated the book's affinity with talk-story, not necessarily the most noteworthy feature.

(E) also misses the author's overall Purpose, which was to refute the critics. Also, the idea that Kingston's work has rekindled an interest in talk-story is Outside the Scope.

15. (D) Inference

Step 2: Identify the Question Type
The phrase "can be most reasonably inferred" indicates an Inference question.

Step 3: Research the Relevant Text
This question stem provides no content clues to focus your research, so any part of the passage is fair game.

Step 4: Make a Prediction
Without clear guidance for research, prediction can be very difficult. That means you'll have to evaluate the answer choices one by one and do your research then, which can makes these vaguely worded Inference questions time-consuming. Keep in mind as you evaluate the choices, though, that the correct one *must* be true based on direct textual evidence.

Step 5: Evaluate the Answer Choices
(D) is a valid inference and is therefore correct. **(D)** paraphrases lines 30–35, in which Kingston distinguishes between the personal nature of memory in oral cultures and the linear, sequential memory of print-oriented cultures.

(A) is an Irrelevant Comparison. The only written talk-story forms that are discussed are those written in English by Kingston.

(B) is a Distortion. Chinese ethnic enclaves are mentioned in paragraph 2 as the location of talk-story's origin (lines 13–14), not to support any claim about talk-story's uniqueness. Distortions like this can be avoided by conducting careful research rather than relying on a hunch or memory.

(C) is a Distortion. Paragraph 2 discusses how talk-story made it to the United States, but nothing in the paragraph indicates that it was developed through a combination of other storytelling forms. Rather, the passage suggests that it arrived in America fully formed and ready to be used by writers like Kingston.

(E) is also a Distortion. The critics mentioned in paragraph 1 presumably don't even recognize Kingston as a writer who uses talk-story. The author indicates the critics have *overlooked* (line 9) this connection.

16. (C) Inference

Step 2: Identify the Question Type
The phrase "can be inferred from the passage" makes this an Inference question. The other clue that this is an Inference question is the question stem's focus on what an author means by using a particular phrase.

Step 3: Research the Relevant Text
The question stem points you to line 32, but check the surrounding lines and your Roadmap to infer meaning.

Step 4: Make a Prediction
Lines 29–35 tell you that Kingston associated personal memory with oral traditions and distinguished it from the precise, sequential memory favored in print-oriented cultures. The correct answer must reflect this distinction as well.

Step 5: Evaluate the Answer Choices
(C) is therefore correct. Even if you didn't predict the exact words "partially idiosyncratic," these words are a nice contrast to the "precise sequences of words" Kingston resists in lines 34–35.

(A) is a Distortion. Nothing in the passage defines talk-story as a first-person narrative. All of Kingston's stories may very well be told in second or third person.

(B) is also a Distortion. Kingston's notion of personal memory isn't necessarily limited to one's own past. In fact, the context of the passage implies that memories of others' stories are possible.

(D) is a 180. This is the exact opposite of the kinds of narratives Kingston constructs.

(E) is Outside the Scope. The ease or difficulty with which literary themes can be identified is not discussed.

17. (B) Logic Reasoning (Parallel Reasoning)

Step 2. Identify the Question Type
This is a Parallel Reasoning question because it asks for the answer choice "most analogous to" something described in the passage.

Step 3: Research the Relevant Text
The question stem directs you to lines 51–55. Read these carefully and paraphrase Kingston's process with English.

Step 4: Make a Prediction
In *China Men*, Kingston used written English in a special way to make it sound like a spoken Chinese talk-story. So, we must be looking for an answer that has cotton fabric being used in a special way to feel or appear like some other kind of cloth or fabric.

Step 5: Evaluate the Answer Choices
(B) is a direct match for lines 51–55. The "investing idiomatic English with ... the Chinese language" parallels the use of the word *weaving* in **(B)**.

(A) misses the idea of making the original work appear to be like something else. The scraps of cotton cloth in **(A)** presumably retain the appearance of cotton cloth.

(C) is Outside the Scope. To be analogous, lines 51–55 would have to describe how Kingston used the English language at times when spoken Chinese was *inappropriate*.

(D) is a Distortion. Kingston doesn't use English instead of Chinese because they're so similar. In fact, lines 51–55 stress the fact that Kingston uses English in a special way to make it appear like spoken Chinese.

(E) is also Outside the Scope. There is nothing parallel to a "savings in price" in the passage. **(E)** would be correct if lines 51–55 described Kingston switching back and forth between English and Chinese or using both languages together because doing so was more economically viable than simply writing in Chinese.

18. (C) Inference

Step 2: Identify the Question Type
The phrase "most clearly suggests" indicates an Inference question.

Step 3: Research the Relevant Text
Read all question stems carefully. Here, you're asked to make an inference based not on the author's beliefs, but on Kingston's. This leads you to paragraph 3.

Step 4: Make a Prediction
The focus of Kingston's self-evaluation is that she's part of the talk-story tradition, elaborating the past (lines 28–29), creating work in the present (lines 39–40), and setting the stage for those who will build on the work she's done

(lines 41–42). The correct answer will be consistent with these views.

Step 5: Evaluate the Answer Choices

(C) corresponds to Kingston's last point, which is that other stories will "grow both around and from" her current work (lines 41–42).

(A) is unsupported. Kingston never expresses frustration about being unable to adequately perpetuate the traditionally Chinese talk-story genre in written English. English is simply the language in which she's writing.

(B) is a Distortion. Kingston identifies herself within the talk-story tradition, but doesn't go as far as to suggest that critics view her work through any specific ethnic lens.

(D) is Extreme. The word *best* doesn't fit with Kingston's self-analysis, which imposes no hierarchy on the ways to present Chinese history.

(E) is a 180 because Kingston works in written texts.

19. (D) Logic Reasoning (Weaken)

Step 2: Identify the Question Type

This is a Weaken question because it clearly asks for the answer choice that would most weaken the author's argument.

Step 3: Research the Relevant Text

In order to predict a valid weakener, you need to revisit the author's conclusion (summarized neatly in lines 6–12) and evidence (primarily the discussion of *China Men* in paragraph 4).

Step 4: Make a Prediction

To be an effective weakener, the correct answer must either attack Kingston's own self-evaluation from paragraph 3 (which doesn't seem likely) or make *China Men* a poor example of her writing. If an answer choice does the latter, then it impairs the author's ability to establish the Conclusion based on the Evidence. As you know from Logical Reasoning, this would make it hard for the argument to hold together.

Step 5: Evaluate the Answer Choices

(D) is a valid weakener because it attacks the value of *China Men* as an exemplar of Kingston's work.

(A) is Outside the Scope. Finding out that other writers inherited oral traditions wouldn't make Kingston any less an inheritor of the Chinese literary tradition.

(B) is also Outside the Scope. The author is trying to make an argument about the work of Kingston only, not about any other writers. There could be many Chinese Americans who don't work within Chinese literary traditions, even though Kingston does.

(C) is also irrelevant. Similarities between two different literary traditions in no way undermine the claim that a particular writer (Kingston) is working within one of them.

(E) is another Outside the Scope answer. It introduces the idea of *authenticity*, but without directly connecting that idea to being steeped in Chinese literary tradition, it doesn't affect the author's argument.

20. (B) Logic Function

Step 2: Identify the Question Type

This is a Logic Function question because it asks the author's purpose not for writing the whole passage, but for including a particular detail or reference.

Step 3: Research the Relevant Text

To know why the author detailed typical talk-story forms, you need to read not just lines 43–51, but also the surrounding lines. Your Roadmap can also provide guidance.

Step 4: Make a Prediction

In this part of the passage, the author lists similarities between *China Men* and the talk-story genre. This list in intended to show how *China Men*, and Kingston's work by extension, has heritage within the talk-story tradition.

Step 5: Evaluate the Answer Choices

(B) is therefore correct.

(A) is a Distortion. The first two lines of the passage establish Kingston as a major literary figure. The author doesn't need to do this within the passage.

(C) is a Distortion. The critics don't doubt the existence of literary antecedents for Chinese American literature; they doubt that Kingston's work shows adherence to those antecedents.

(D) is a Faulty Use of Detail. Kingston does, indeed, characterize writers as "privileged keeper[s]" (line 39), but proving that is not the author's reason for listing the similarities between Kingston's work and talk-story in lines 43–51.

(E) distorts the passage. As far as you know, everyone considers Kingston's work literature and no one is making recommendations for how it should be judged. The debate in the passage is over whether Kingston's work is recognizably influenced by the Chinese American literary tradition.

21. (A) Inference

Step 2: Identify the Question Type

Any question asking about the author's attitude toward something discussed in the passage is an Inference question.

Step 3: Research the Relevant Text

The content clue in the question stem means that any place where the author discusses talk-story is relevant.

Step 4: Make a Prediction

The author uses few Emphasis/Opinion Keywords to describe talk-story (or anything else, for that matter). Near the end of the first paragraph, the author describes talk-story as a "highly developed genre" with a "long ... tradition" (lines 10–11). Beyond this, almost everything we learn about talk-story is dryly factual. The correct answer needs to reflect this tone.

Step 5: Evaluate the Answer Choices

(A)'s use of "scholarly appreciation" makes it a good match.

(B) is too negative. The author never points out any faults in talk-story.

(C) is a Distortion. The author doesn't defend talk-story against any attack from critics. The author is the only one in the passage who discusses talk-story.

(D) is tempting, but is a Half-Right/Half-Wrong answer. The author does seem to respect talk-story, but nothing in the passage indicates that this is because talk-story is diverse and ancient in its derivation.

(E) is too strongly positive to match the author's tone." Lines 11–12 define talk-story as a "genre of song and spoken narrative," but the author uses no Keywords regarding that defining characteristic of talk-story that match an attitude of "open admiration."

Passage 4: Dutch Tulips—A Speculative Bubble?

Step 1: Read the Passage Strategically
Sample Roadmap

line #	Keyword/phrase	¶ Margin notes
3	not by	speculative bubble def. doesn't use earnings
4	but rather by	
9	According to	Mackay—19th C. tulip mkt <u>was</u> bubble
12	example; But	
13	challenges	Garber—no evid
14	arguing; no evidence	
19–20	For example	
22	on the other hand	
23	According to	MacKay's thesis
25	surged	
26	further states	
27	collapsed	
32	acknowledges	Garber admits high prices
34	But; argues	
35	should not	
37	can be explained	but says invest was rational
38	argues	
41	Thus	
44	However	
47	But	
48	does not mean	could sell "offspring" of bulbs for big $
49	irrational; for	
51	even if	
52	Given that	
54	even if	
56	need not	

Discussion

Paragraph 1 opens with a definition of the **Topic**, "speculative bubbles." These are large increases in an asset's price driven not by its fundamentals, but by speculation on further price increases. When the bubble *bursts*, the price falls dramatically. Next, the author narrows this to the **Scope**—whether the Dutch tulip market of the 17th-century constituted a speculative bubble. True to LSAT form, the author introduces two contrasting points of view. Mackay argues that the Dutch tulip market was a speculative bubble, but Garber argues that Mackay's view isn't supported by the evidence.

Paragraph 2 opens with a description of the tulip bulb market in 17th-century Holland, highlighting the Semper Augustus, a bulb that sold for a particularly high price. Then the author gives Mackay's account of the rise and fall of tulip bulb prices. Presumably this is Mackay's evidence that a speculative bubble existed.

As you could have anticipated, the author outlines Garber's counter-argument in paragraph 3. Garber acknowledges the dramatic price increases, but believes that they can be explained by the commodity's fundamentals and, therefore, do not indicate a speculative bubble. The author describes Garber's thinking in detail, so use the Keywords in the passage *[t]hus* in line 41; *[h]owever* in line 44; *[b]ut* in line 47; *for* in line 49) to get a handle on the gist of Garber's argument. The high price of new prized bulbs is not irrational because the buyer will make so much money from the bulbs' descendants (although the individual reproduced bulbs will be cheap).

Whenever an author discusses competing points of view, check to see whether the author weighs in. In this passage, the author does not evaluate Mackay's and Garber's claims and takes no side in the debate. The **Purpose** is therefore neutral—to explain or outline the debate over the Dutch tulip market as a bubble. The **Main Idea** is straightforward: Mackay says the tulip prices indicate a speculative bubble; Garber says they reflect economic fundamentals.

22. (D) Global

Step 2: Identify the Question Type
This is a Global question because it asks for the "main point" of the passage.

Step 3: Research the Relevant Text
For a Global question, the entire text is relevant. So instead of researching a specific part of the passage, use the Main Idea you came up with during Step 1 to form your prediction.

Step 4: Make a Prediction
The author's Main Idea was that Garber disagrees with Mackay's interpretation of tulip bulb prices in Holland during the 17th-century as a speculative bubble.

Step 5: Evaluate the Answer Choices
(D) is therefore correct.

(A) is a Distortion. You don't know from the passage how widely held Mackay's view is, and the word *mistakenly* imputes a view to the author that doesn't exist. For all you know, the author could agree with Mackay.

(B) is Outside the Scope. The author doesn't weigh in on Mackay's analysis of the earnings that came from Dutch tulip bulbs. As with **(A)**, this answer choice doesn't reflect the author's neutral tone.

(C) would be correct if the author's purpose were merely to define a speculative bubble. But this answer leaves out the vast majority of the passage, in which the author describes Mackay's and Garber's views.

(E) is too narrow. This is one piece of Garber's analysis as described in paragraph 3, but this is hardly the author's overall Main Idea.

23. (D) Logic Reasoning (Parallel Reasoning)

Step 2: Identify the Question Type
When a question stem asks for an answer choice "most analogous to" something discussed in the passage, it's a Parallel Reasoning question.

Step 3: Research the Relevant Text
You're asked to find an answer that treats another commodity the way Garber analyzed Dutch tulip bulbs. Therefore, the relevant text here is paragraph 3.

Step 4: Make a Prediction
Garber said the new bulbs were priced so high because the buyer will make so much money from the bulbs' descendants (although the reproduced bulbs themselves will be cheap). So evaluate the answers and choose the one that has an original item purchased for a high price so that its offshoots can be sold more cheaply.

Step 5: Evaluate the Answer Choices
(D) is a match. The publisher pays a high price for the original so that he can sell many cheap copies.

(A) misses the mark by making no reference to anything that could be considered original or descendant the way that the novel and its copies are in correct answer **(D)**. Nothing in Garber's analysis implies a withdrawal and reapplication.

(B) is a Distortion because the same original painting is being resold, not its descendants or copies.

(C) is also a Distortion. What is resold in **(C)** is the original high-priced item, rather than descendants or copies made from that item. And the "substitute parts" have no analog in the passage.

(E) contains nothing about buying an original with the intention of selling copies made from it.

24. (B) Inference

Step 2: Identify the Question Type
The words "strongly support" and *inference* indicate that this is an Inference question.

Step 3: Research the Relevant Text
This question asks specifically about what Garber would agree with, so focus on paragraph 3 to get Garber's argument.

Step 4: Make a Prediction
Paragraph 3 says that Garber does not believe that the tulip prices indicated a speculative bubble. He thinks, rather, that the buyers rationally calculated the fundamentals, concluding that they could make money by selling descendants of the original bulbs. That's why Garber says the original was expensive and the descendants were cheap. The correct answer will be consistent with this.

Step 5: Evaluate the Answer Choices
(B) is consistent with lines 47–55.

(A) is Outside the Scope. Garber's general opinion on the frequency of speculative bubbles isn't indicated in the passage; rather, the author gives Garber's view on the Dutch tulip market in particular.

(C) gets the sufficiency-necessity relationship backward. (Yes, this concept can even appear in Reading Comprehension.) Garber would argue that if the prices are not irrational, then there is not a speculative bubble in the market.

(D) is Outside the Scope. Nothing in the passage implies what Garber would think about the Dutch investors' activities outside the tulip market.

(E) is a Distortion. Mackay claimed that the original high prices were irrational, and that the later low prices showed this. This idea is what Garber thought was mistaken.

25. (B) Detail

Step 2: Identify the Question Type
Any direct, categorical language such as "the passage states" indicates a Detail question.

Step 3: Research the Relevant Text
This question stem asks about Mackay's claims, so research paragraph 2.

Step 4: Make a Prediction
Your Roadmap should point you to "[a]ccording to Mackay" in line 23 and "Mackay further states" in line 26. Mackay claims that speculation drove prices high over several months, and that those prices suddenly collapsed, bottoming out over a century later.

Step 5: Evaluate the Answer Choices
(B) matches lines 23–26.

(A), if anything, is a 180. Mackay may well *agree* that the tulips' popularity attracted investors, triggering the

speculation that led to what he sees as a speculative bubble. So there is nowhere in the passage that Mackay indicates the rapid rise in price was "not due" to the popularity of the tulips.

(C) contradicts lines 16–17, which say that the Netherlands was *a* center of tulip cultivation. Furthermore, this isn't one of Mackay's claims.

(D) is a 180. Mackay claimed that the price of tulip bulbs was evidence of a speculative bubble, so he believes that the price fluctuations were irrational and not based on rational market fundamentals.

(E) is a Faulty Use of Detail. It repeats a detail from paragraph 3, which is where Garber's view is discussed. Mackay is silent on this idea.

26. (C) Logic Function

Step 2: Identify the Question Type
Any question that asks for the purpose of a detail, quote, reference, or paragraph is a Logic Function question.

Step 3: Research the Relevant Text
Whenever a question asks for the purpose of an entire paragraph, consult your Roadmap to make your prediction.

Step 4: Make a Prediction
Paragraph 2 gives the author's description of the tulip market as background for Mackay's thesis and interpretation of the data.

Step 5: Evaluate the Answer Choices
(C) is therefore correct.

(A) only accounts for the beginning of paragraph 2. Mackay's view as presented in the latter half of the paragraph is certainly not "accepted by all experts in the field."

(B) is Outside the Scope of paragraph 2. Garber does allege that Mackay makes a mistaken inference, but that isn't introduced until paragraph 3.

(D) goes wrong with its first word, *undermine*. This verb doesn't match the author's neutral tone. It's Garber, and not the author, who hopes to undermine Mackay.

(E) is a Distortion. The author presents facts common to both Mackay's and Garber's inferences. Not even Garber accuses Mackay of factual errors; rather, Garber thinks Mackay interpreted the facts incorrectly.

27. (D) Inference

Step 2: Identify the Question Type
This is an Inference question because it asks you to infer what a word or phrase "most nearly means" from its context.

Step 3: Research the Relevant Text

Line 38 is relevant, of course, but you must read the surrounding lines for context to see how the author uses the phrase.

Step 4: Make a Prediction

With the phrase "standard pricing pattern" in line 38, the author is explaining Garber's criticism of Mackay, in which Garber says that the investors were rationally paying high prices for the original bulbs thinking they could make their money back selling cheap descendants. That's *standard* stuff for new flower varieties, Garber says; it happens that way over and over.

Step 5: Evaluate the Answer Choices

(D) is a match.

(A) is Outside the Scope. Nothing indicates that the prices of any other commodities would be measured against the one that recurs for new flower varieties.

(B) is a subtle Distortion. Investors may conform to the pricing patterns whenever a new flower variety comes out, but that doesn't mean that they do so because they've all agreed cooperatively.

(C) is Outside the Scope. The fact that the pricing pattern was standard doesn't have anything to do with whether or not people found it acceptable.

(E) is unsupported. Nothing in the passage indicates that the author or Garber would consider the flower pricing pattern an example of anything or a pattern on which other pricing patterns should be based.

Section III: Logical Reasoning

Q#	Question Type	Correct	Difficulty
1	Paradox	B	★
2	Flaw	C	★
3	Assumption (Sufficient)	B	★
4	Weaken	A	★
5	Inference	A	★
6	Principle (Identify/Inference EXCEPT)	D	★
7	Role of a Statement	E	★
8	Assumption (Necessary)	E	★
9	Weaken	D	★★
10	Assumption (Sufficient)	D	★★
11	Flaw	B	★
12	Inference	D	★★★★
13	Main Point	D	★★
14	Strengthen	B	★
15	Parallel Reasoning	E	★★★
16	Inference	C	★
17	Principle (Identify/Strengthen)	A	★★
18	Flaw	E	★★
19	Assumption (Necessary)	C	★★★
20	Main Point	B	★★
21	Assumption (Sufficient)	A	★★★
22	Weaken	A	★★★★
23	Parallel Flaw	C	★★
24	Assumption (Necessary)	D	★★★
25	Flaw	B	★★★

1. (B) Paradox

Step 1: Identify the Question Type
This is a Paradox question because the correct answer will "resolve the apparent discrepancy" in the stimulus. Additionally, the question stem provides the paradox: the difference between Aristophanes's portrayal of Socrates and others' portrayals of the philosopher.

Step 2: Untangle the Stimulus
Follow the hint in the question stem and search for the difference between Aristophanes's portrayal of Socrates and others' portrayals of Socrates. Apparently, Aristophanes portrayed Socrates as an atheist philosopher interested in natural science, but others portrayed Socrates as a religious philosopher intrigued by ethics.

Step 3: Make a Prediction
The correct answer will provide a reason why it makes sense that Socrates was portrayed both as atheistic and interested in natural science, and yet also religious and focused on ethics. The stimulus hints at a crucial difference between Aristophanes's portrayal and the portrayals of others. Aristophanes's play was written when Socrates was in his mid-40s, at least 20 years earlier than when other surviving portrayals were written. So, if Socrates himself changed, then it would make sense that portrayals of him did as well.

Step 4: Evaluate the Answer Choices
(B) matches the prediction.

(A) goes Out of Scope by introducing the idea of flattery. Even if flattery were relevant, this choice still doesn't explain *why* the portrayals differ.

(C) focuses on philosophers before Socrates, who are Out of Scope. Nothing in the stimulus indicates that portrayals of Socrates would somehow be influenced by other philosophers' interests, rather than by a change in Socrates's own views during the course of his life.

(D) indicates a change either in Socrates himself or the environment in which he lived, but it isn't sufficient to explain the discrepancy. An increase in controversy doesn't necessarily correlate with a move from atheism to religion or from natural science to ethics, so this choice wouldn't explain the difference between the portrayals.

(E) goes Out of Scope by focusing on philosophers after Socrates, rather than on a change in portrayals of Socrates. Additionally, if the philosophers who came along after Socrates's death were concerned with natural science, then the depictions of Socrates as a religious, ethical philosopher seem even more anomalous.

2. (C) Flaw

Step 1: Identify the Question Type
Because the correct answer will describe "the grounds" on which the argument in the stimulus is "vulnerable to criticism," this is a Flaw question. Identify what's wrong with the gap between the evidence and conclusion, and keep common flaw types in mind.

Step 2: Untangle the Stimulus
Break down the argument into evidence and conclusion. The conclusion follows [*h*]*ence*, at the end of the stimulus. The board member's point is that the work done because of the grant violated the conditions of the grant. The first sentence describes those conditions. So, in other words, the board member concludes that the work done contained material detrimental to the J Foundation's reputation. The evidence, following [*b*]*ut*, is that the work does not mention any of the J Foundation's accomplishments.

Step 3: Make a Prediction
Start by finding the board member's assumption. The board member makes a rather large scope shift, presenting evidence that the work did not mention achievements as evidence that the work was detrimental. Thus, the board member must be assuming that when good stuff is left out, it's actually bad for someone's reputation. The correct answer will describe this assumption.

Step 4: Evaluate the Answer Choices
(C) matches the prediction. Remember that *presumes* is a synonym for *assumes*.

(A) is Out of Scope. It mischaracterizes the conclusion, which is not about the "intellectual value" of the work, but about whether the work was detrimental to the J Foundation's reputation.

(B) describes a necessary versus sufficient flaw, which is not at play here. While it is true that the board member describes a necessary condition for receipt of the grant (not harming the reputation of the J Foundation), the board member never treats the necessary condition as if it were sufficient (i.e., non-detrimental work is enough to merit a grant). Rather, the board member tries to argue that the necessary condition was, in fact, never satisfied.

(D) is Out of Scope. Whether or not grant recipients normally strive to meet a foundation's conditions isn't at issue in this argument. The board member argues that one recipient in particular failed to meet the conditions; this conclusion could still be logically drawn regardless of the effort put forth by that recipient, or by recipients in general.

(E) does introduce something the board member fails to consider, but its omission does not actually harm the argument. The board member's main point is that a particular condition was not met; other conditions, whether satisfied or not, are Out of Scope.

3. (B) Assumption (Sufficient)

Step 1: Identify the Question Type

By providing the Evidence Keyword *since* and then a blank, this question asks you to identify an unstated piece of evidence that would allow the preceding conclusion to follow. That makes this an Assumption question. Look for the existing gap between the psychiatrist's conclusion and the rest of the stimulus.

Step 2: Untangle the Stimulus

The psychiatrist's conclusion, marked by [*t*]*herefore* in the middle of the stimulus, is that addicted smokers who quit smoking are more likely to be motivated by social pressure than by health concerns. The psychiatrist describes social pressure as an "immediate concern." This is notable because in the first sentence, the psychiatrist says immediate concerns act as better motivation for breaking habits than do long-term concerns.

Step 3: Make a Prediction

The psychiatrist says immediate concerns are better motivators than long-term concerns. Additionally, the psychiatrist concludes social pressure is a better motivator than health. Based on the hierarchy the psychiatrist sets up, the conclusion will follow logically only if it's true that health is a long-term concern and not an immediate one.

Step 4: Evaluate the Answer Choices

(B) matches the prediction.

(A) presents an Irrelevant Comparison. The psychiatrist's conclusion focuses exclusively on breaking an addiction to cigarettes.

(C) misses the point of the argument, which is to establish that health is less of a motivator than is social pressure. This answer doesn't affect that conclusion. Additionally, while this choice may or may not be true, it's irrelevant: the psychiatrist discusses quitting smoking, which would relieve social pressure but would *not* exacerbate health concerns.

(D) is Out of Scope. The argument weighs the strength of motivators for people who successfully break their addiction, regardless of how many tries it takes them to accomplish their goal.

(E) is Extreme because it's too limited. There may be other reasons why people quit smoking. Additionally, **(E)** fails to point out a difference in power between social pressure and health concerns.

4. (A) Weaken

Step 1: Identify the Question Type

This question asks for "the logically strongest counter that Cassie can make to Melvin's argument," or, in other words, the statement that will hurt Melvin's argument the most. That makes this a Weaken question.

Step 2: Untangle the Stimulus

Because the correct answer will weaken Melvin's argument, give more attention to Melvin than to Cassie, though you must read both arguments. Cassie's main point is that the real estate agency should decrease the number of clients each agent serves at a time. In response, Melvin argues that it will not be possible for the agency to decrease the number of clients each agent serves, because the agency will not be able to recruit the additional qualified agents that are necessary to spread out the current number of clients.

Step 3: Make a Prediction

Start by finding Melvin's assumption. Melvin argues that qualified agents can't be recruited and so client load cannot be reduced. Melvin overlooks the possibility that rather than add extra agents, the real estate agency could decrease its number of clients. In order to keep the current number of clients though, Cassie could also take advantage of another possibility that Melvin has overlooked: that the chain of events may work better in reverse. If the agency reduced the number of clients each agent served, then the agency might be better able to recruit additional qualified agents. The correct answer will likely point to one of these overlooked possibilities.

Step 4: Evaluate the Answer Choices

(A) matches the second overlooked possibility.

(B) provides an additional reason why the agency might want to reduce client loads, but it fails to counter Melvin's argument that it would be impossible to recruit new agents. So, although **(B)** strengthens Cassie's recommendation, it fails to weaken Melvin's argument.

(C) is like **(B)** in that it strengthens Cassie's recommendation but fails to weaken Melvin's argument. It does not address the feasibility of actually changing the current client loads.

(D) is Out of Scope and perhaps even a 180. It provides an alternative to Cassie's suggestion that client loads should be reduced. Because the speakers are focused on Cassie's plan and the likelihood of implementing it, an alternative course of action is Out of Scope. The prospect of hiring additional support staff also doesn't weaken Melvin's argument because it doesn't address his contention that reducing client loads is unfeasible.

(E) is a 180. It strengthens Melvin's argument by reinforcing the idea that it would be difficult to hire more agents.

5. (A) Inference

Step 1: Identify the Question Type

This is an Inference question because the correct answer is "most strongly supported by the information" in the stimulus (direction of support flowing downward). Beware of answers that are Extreme or Out of Scope.

Step 2: Untangle the Stimulus

Paraphrase each statement as you read the stimulus. There is a type of mole that does not see well, but whose nose ends in tentacles. The tentacles help the moles hunt by detecting the electric fields of other animals, such as worms and insects.

Step 3: Make a Prediction

Look for ideas that come up more than once in the stimulus. Tentacles are mentioned a couple of times. The tentacles help the moles hunt by detecting animals' electrical fields. Suitable prey for the moles include worms and insects. Thus, it is strongly supported that worms and insects have electric fields so that the moles' tentacles can detect them.

Step 4: Evaluate the Answer Choices

(A) may not be mind-blowing, but it follows from the stimulus. It makes sense that worms and insects produce electric fields because the mole finds prey by detecting electric fields, and worms and insects are examples of *suitable* prey.

(B) is Extreme. Although the moles do not see well, it cannot be inferred that moles do not use their eyesight "at all" for survival. It could be true that moles use their eyesight for something important for survival besides hunting.

(C) is both Extreme and Out of Scope. Just because the mole uses its tentacles to hunt does not mean that it "does not rely at all" on its smell. Additionally, because the stimulus never actually mentions smell, nothing can be inferred about it. You can only use the information provided to draw inferences; you cannot use an author's omissions.

(D) is Extreme. Just because the star-nosed mole is one example of a hunting animal with tentacles that detect electric fields does not mean there is no non-hunting animal that has tentacles that detect electric fields. It could be true that some other animal uses such a nose for another purpose (e.g., in order to evade predators or attract mates, rather than to hunt prey).

(E) is Out of Scope. The stimulus makes no mention of whether or not the mole has an electric field of its own.

6. (D) Principle (Identify/Inference EXCEPT)

Step 1: Identify the Question Type

In an EXCEPT question, the words before EXCEPT define the four wrong answers. Thus, the four wrong answers to this question will each be principles that come from the cases described by the psychologist in the stimulus. Therefore, the one correct answer will *not* be a principle coming from the cases described by the psychologist. The correct answer will be either contradictory to the pattern described by the psychologist or unrelated, i.e., Out of Scope.

Step 2: Untangle the Stimulus

Paraphrase the cases described by the psychologist. Basically, the psychologist describes a pattern: a child wants something and is denied, so the child misbehaves until the parent gives in. Once the child gets what it wanted, it stops misbehaving for the time being. The end result is that the problem escalates; the cycle continues with the child misbehaving more and more when it wants other things.

Step 3: Make a Prediction

In Logical Reasoning EXCEPT questions, the four wrong answers can be predicted with greater specificity than the correct answer can be. Here, the four wrong answers will each describe, in general terms, the pattern, or a part of the pattern, described in the stimulus. So, the four wrong answers will paraphrase the idea that giving in to kids' misbehavior can actually increase the problem in the long run. The one correct answer will *not* match this prediction.

Step 4: Evaluate the Answer Choices

(D) goes against the pattern described by the psychologist. The parents' behavior is consistent with the child's intended goals because the final result is the parent giving in to the child's demands. Additionally, because success causes the child's misbehavior to escalate, it's likely the child eventually *intentionally* influences the parent.

(A) matches the stimulus, which says that when parents yield to a child's demands, the child's misbehavior will be reinforced, increasing the chances that such misbehavior will occur.

(B) matches the stimulus. A child's problematic behavior can escalate until a parent gives in, while a parent's acquiescence encourages a child to continue to misbehave in the future. Each party is influencing the other.

(C) matches the stimulus. Parents yield because they are exasperated, and doing so solves the immediate problem. But this actually reinforces and increases a child's misbehavior in the long term.

(E) matches the stimulus. According to the psychologist, a child will initiate problematic behavior (something the parent doesn't want the child to do) until the parent gives in to the child's demand.

7. (E) Role of a Statement

Step 1: Identify the Question Type

Because the correct answer "describes the role played in the scientist's argument" by a specific statement, this is a Role of a Statement question. Decide if the statement is part of the evidence, part of the conclusion, or if it functions in a different capacity.

Step 2: Untangle the Stimulus

First, locate and underline the statement in the stimulus. The statement about chemical R not causing cancer in laboratory rats is the first sentence of the stimulus. Next, break down the argument into the evidence and conclusion. The conclusion, that chemical R is not necessarily safe for humans, is the second sentence. The evidence, following the Evidence Keywords "[a]fter all," explains why many substances that cause cancer in humans do not do so in rats.

Step 3: Make a Prediction
The statement in question is neither the scientist's evidence nor conclusion. Rather, it is a preliminary premise that the scientist suggests will not support a conclusion that chemical R is safe for humans.

Step 4: Evaluate the Answer Choices
(E) matches the prediction.

(A) is Extreme. The scientist doesn't actually conclude chemical R is safe, nor is the statement used as evidence *against* a conclusion. It's merely insufficient evidence *for* a conclusion.

(B) incorrectly describes the conclusion. The scientist says the particular finding isn't enough to conclude that chemical R is safe for humans, but the scientist does not make the much more Extreme assertion that test results from lab rats can't be extrapolated to humans in general. Additionally, while the last sentence in the stimulus does explain why a conclusion about humans can't be drawn from *these* particular results, that's not the statement in question. So, if **(B)** had said "it is advanced to support the contention that *these* test results …" then it would have described the role of the *last* sentence of the stimulus.

(C) is a Distortion and Extreme. First, the scientist doesn't assert that rats are unsuitable test subjects; the fact that the scientist is performing tests on rats indicates that she thinks they sometimes *are* suitable test subjects. Second, even if this answer choice accurately represented the scientist's thoughts about rats as test subjects, it's not a claim that the statement in question supports. Rather, the statement in question plus the scientist's evidence about rats as test subjects join together to support a separate claim: that chemical R is not necessarily safe for humans.

(D) is like **(A)** in that it mischaracterizes the scientist's conclusion. The scientist concludes that chemical R is not necessarily safe for humans, not that it *definitely causes* cancer in humans. Additionally, the statement isn't used to support any conclusion; the scientist specifically says, "we cannot conclude from this."

8. (E) Assumption (Necessary)

Step 1: Identify the Question Type
This is a Necessary Assumption question because the correct answer is "an assumption *required* by" the argument in the stimulus. You can use the Denial Test to check your answer.

Step 2: Untangle the Stimulus
Analyze the argument's evidence and conclusion. The conclusion opens the stimulus. The department store manager concludes that the store should not offer free gift wrapping. The evidence comes in two pieces. First, if most customers use the free gift wrapping, then the store will spend lots of time and money. Second, if few customers use the free gift wrapping, then there's no advantage in it.

Step 3: Make a Prediction
The manager's evidence covers two situations: few customers wanting gift wrapping or most customers wanting gift wrapping. Both of those situations would lead to negative outcomes for the store, so the manager makes a relatively extreme conclusion that there is "no reason" for the store to offer free gift wrapping. However, both those situations are on the far ends of the spectrum. The manager overlooks the possibility that the number of customers who want free gift wrapping may be more than a few but less than most, in which case it may be beneficial for the store to offer free gift wrapping. In order for the manager's conclusion to follow, the manager must assume that the intermediate possibility does not exist or, in other words, that only a few or a majority of shoppers will want the free gift wrapping.

Step 4: Evaluate the Answer Choices
(E) matches the prediction. Check **(E)** using the Denial Test. The denied version would be something like this: more than few but fewer than most of the customers would want free gift wrapping. If that were true, then the department store manager's evidence would be completely irrelevant to the conclusion and the argument would fall apart. Thus, **(E)** is the argument's necessary assumption.

(A) is an Irrelevant Comparison. The argument is not about the relative expense of gift wrapping (although cost could be one drawback to offering the service), but about how there is *no* advantage in offering the service. Even if gift wrapping would cost *less* this holiday season, the manager might still be correct in stating that the service has no advantage.

(B) is both Out of Scope and Extreme. The argument says gift wrapping will be time-consuming for the store, but does not indicate that it would necessarily slow down shoppers; therefore, this answer choice isn't clearly relevant. Additionally, even if customer speed were relevant, the manager doesn't need to make an assumption about *anything* that slows down shoppers in order for a conclusion about gift wrapping to follow.

(C) is Out of Scope because it introduces charging for the service. The argument is limited to free gift wrapping.

(D) is also Out of Scope. While the manager does say gift wrapping will be expensive, she doesn't mention why. Marketing may or may not be the reason. Regardless, a single reason not to offer gift wrapping (expensive customer outreach) is not enough to prove there is *no* reason to offer the service. If you were to deny this choice (informing customers is cheap), the manager's argument doesn't necessarily fall apart.

9. (D) Weaken

Step 1: Identify the Question Type
Because the correct answer "weakens the argument" in the stimulus, this is a Weaken question.

Step 2: Untangle the Stimulus
Break down the argument into evidence and conclusion. The conclusion is at the end of the stimulus, marked by *so*. The author's main point is that behavior modification works better than sleeping pills for helping people go to sleep. The main piece of evidence comes in the same sentence: people who use only behavior modification fall asleep faster than do people who use only sleeping pills.

Step 3: Make a Prediction
Start by finding the author's assumption. Here, the evidence distinguishes between two groups of people: those who use only behavior modification and those who use only sleeping pills. The conclusion asserts the superiority of behavior modification over sleeping pills. Therefore, the author must be assuming that the evidence is adequate for such a determination. In other words, the author is assuming that the two groups of people are similar in all other relevant respects. The author overlooks the possibility that something about the makeup of these groups affects the efficacy of the pills or behavior modification techniques. The correct answer will likely point out some reason why the groups are dissimilar.

Step 4: Evaluate the Answer Choices
(D) matches the prediction. If the people who use sleeping pills initially had more trouble falling asleep than those in the other group, then it may not be true that sleeping pills are less effective. The two groups did not start out on equal footing.

(A) is Out of Scope. It focuses on the total hours asleep each night, rather than on difficulty falling asleep. Additionally, this choice doesn't necessarily address the two groups in question: "[p]eople who do not take sleeping pills" could include those who don't have any trouble falling asleep.

(B) goes Out of Scope by comparing people who use behavioral modification with people who have no trouble falling asleep. By contrast, the stimulus compares two groups of people who *both* have trouble falling asleep.

(C) fails to introduce information relevant to the comparison between the sleep strategies or the comparison between the two groups of people. If anything, **(C)** seems to be a mild strengthener. If the people who use only behavior modification have never used sleeping pills, then this choice

removes the possibility that previous use of sleeping pills could influence the effectiveness of behavior modification.

(E) *does* introduce something distinctive about the group who uses behavior modification. Unfortunately, the aversion to using drugs isn't a factor that would influence the speed with which those people would fall asleep.

10. (D) Assumption (Sufficient)

Step 1: Identify the Question Type
Because the correct answer is the assumption that makes the conclusion follow logically, this is a Sufficient Assumption question. The correct answer should, if inserted as a piece of evidence, make the argument seamless.

Step 2: Untangle the Stimulus
Analyze the argument's evidence and conclusion. The conclusion follows [*t*]*herefore* in the last sentence. The lawyer's main point is that the witness's testimony should be excluded. The lawyer's evidence is the sentence beginning with [*y*]*et*. The witness claims to recognize the assailant, but not the lawyer's client (who was the victim of the assault).

Step 3: Make a Prediction
Sometimes an assumption is as easy as: "If this evidence is true, then the conclusion must be true." In other words, the author assumes that the evidence is relevant. In this case, the lawyer must be assuming this:

If	~ recognize both parties in an assault case	→	exclude the witness's testimony

Contrapositive:

If	~ exclude the witness's testimony	→	recognize both parties in an assault case

Step 4: Evaluate the Answer Choices
(D) matches the contrapositive of the predicted assumption.

(A) reverses the assumption without negating. While the lawyer thinks the witness must recognize both parties in order for the testimony to be valid, nothing indicates that the lawyer thinks recognition is *enough* for a witness's testimony to be included.

(B) is Out of Scope. The lawyer's argument concerns only the one specific witness. Additional witnesses are irrelevant.

(C) veers Out of Scope by focusing on whether the witness *actually* recognized the assailant, rather than on what the witness claims. The lawyer's evidence is limited to what the witness merely claims. The feasibility of proving those claims is not at issue.

(E) might increase the likelihood that the witness is unreliable, but it's not enough to decisively establish the conclusion that the testimony should be excluded. It's possible that the *unlikely* chance occurred.

11. (B) Flaw

Step 1: Identify the Question Type

Because the correct answer describes the grounds on which the argument in the stimulus is "vulnerable to criticism," this is a Flaw question. Identify what's wrong with the gap between the evidence and conclusion, and keep common flaws in mind.

Step 2: Untangle the Stimulus

Break down the argument into its evidence and conclusion. The conclusion follows the Contrast Keyword [*b*]*ut* in the last sentence. The biologist's main point is that the evolution of the human brain was *not* caused by the difficulty of adapting to ice ages. The biologist's evidence follows the Evidence Keyword *for*. The reason behind the biologist's conclusion is that other species adapted to ice ages without their brains evolving.

Step 3: Make a Prediction

The biologist makes a pretty blatant scope shift. The biologist's evidence is about most other species, but her conclusion is about humans. Thus, the biologist assumes that humans and other species are sufficiently alike. The biologist overlooks the possibility that humans and animals are different enough that the same condition might not produce the same result in the two groups.

Step 4: Evaluate the Answer Choices

(B) matches the prediction.

(A) fails to address the biologist's scope shift from most other animal species to humans. Instead, **(A)** is written as if both the evidence and conclusion were about the same species.

(C) is worded similarly to **(B)** but, unlike **(B)**, incorrectly confuses sufficiency and necessity. The opening sentence includes the phrase "is responsible for," which indicates that adapting to ice ages is *sufficient* to cause human brains to evolve. So, there could be other sufficient events that would *also* result in the evolution of the brain. The biologist points out that the adaptation to ice ages wasn't *sufficient* to produce the change in other animal species. This answer choice, however, says the biologist ignores that a *necessary* condition for one species might not be *necessary* for others. The biologist doesn't indicate what is *needed* for any species to evolve, so omission of this information is irrelevant.

(D) is actually a 180. In order to use other species as evidence for a conclusion about humans, the biologist must assume

that their experiences were similar. If humans and other species had actually experienced different levels of difficulty, then the biologist's evidence would become irrelevant.

(E) describes a causal flaw. However, that isn't at play here because the biologist actually says adapting to ice ages did *not* cause the human brain to evolve. Additionally, the stimulus doesn't indicate that the two events occurred at the same time, as this answer choice suggests.

12. (D) Inference

Step 1: Identify the Question Type

Because the correct answer is "strongly supported by the information" in the stimulus, this is an Inference question.

Step 2: Untangle the Stimulus

Make an inventory of the information in the stimulus, paraphrasing as you read. First, the number of book titles published in North America each year has quadrupled in the time since TV started. Second, in the early days of TV, the sale of new book titles went up quickly. However, recently the sale rate of new book titles has slowed down from that point (though it is still increasing). Finally, library circulation has stayed the same or decreased in recent years.

Step 3: Make a Prediction

Find ideas that come up more than once in the stimulus, and try to connect them. In this stimulus, all the information is about what has happened since the advent of TV. Based on the stimulus, TV coincided with an increase in both the number of books published and sold. Be cautious here that the stimulus only suggests a correlation, not a causal relationship. Additionally, the idea of "recent years" also comes up in both the second and third sentences. By connecting these sentences, we can infer that recently both the increasing sales of new book titles slowed and library circulation stayed the same or decreased. The correct answer will likely correspond with one of these connections between ideas in the stimulus.

Step 4: Evaluate the Answer Choices

(D) matches the prediction. The stimulus says that in the early years of TV, both the publishing and sales of new book titles increased. Therefore, TV does not always cause a decline in the number of book titles published or sold.

(A) commits a causal flaw, shifts scope, and distorts the evidence. First, it's not proven in the stimulus that television has "brought about" anything. It merely coincides with an increase in books published and sold. Second, the stimulus discusses book publishing and sales, but not reading. We cannot necessarily connect book sales and the amount of per capita reading. For example, books may not be the only type of published material people are reading. Third, the stimulus says that the "rate of increase has slowed." That means sales are still actually increasing, just at a slower pace. There hasn't been a "reduction" in sales, and thus it's unlikely there would be a reduction in reading (assuming sales and reading are equivalent, which they aren't).

(B) is Extreme. That library circulation has stagnated or declined in recent years does not mean TV *usually* leads to the decrease in library use. Additionally, the stimulus merely suggests a correlation, while this choice indicates that TV *caused* a change in library use. Finally, library *circulation* and *use* are not necessarily the same thing.

(C) is a Distortion. The rate of increase in retail sales has slowed, but it hasn't reversed. Additionally, the stimulus only mentions new titles whereas this answer choice encompasses all titles. It may be that classics are selling far better than they used to.

(E) is Extreme. It suggests TV is responsible for expanding the book market in North America. While the introduction of TV happened at the same time as an increase in publishing and sales of new book titles, the stimulus does not support the idea that TV *caused* that increase.

13. (D) Main Point

Step 1: Identify the Question Type
Because the correct answer "accurately expresses the conclusion" made by the botanist, this is a Main Point question. Keep an eye out for Contrast Keywords, and be wary of any Conclusion Keywords.

Step 2: Untangle the Stimulus
Paraphrase the stimulus as you read. First, the botanist puts forward a common belief: people with pets or children should not have poinsettias at home. Next, the botanist sets up a contradiction, using the Contrast Keyword [*a*]*lthough*. The botanist mentions that although many child-rearing books have encouraged this belief, the belief is mistaken. In the final sentence, the botanist presents evidence: research that shows poinsettias are safe for children and pets.

Step 3: Make a Prediction
This stimulus follows a pattern common in both Logical Reasoning and Reading Comprehension. The author introduces a commonly held belief in order to refute it. Here, the main point is the botanist's refutation of the commonly held belief that poinsettias should not be in homes with children or pets. The last sentence of the stimulus is the botanist's evidence for that refutation.

Step 4: Evaluate the Answer Choices
(D) matches the prediction.

(A) is a Distortion. The correct answer to a Main Point question directly paraphrases the author's conclusion. Nowhere in the stimulus does the botanist suggest that people should be *encouraged* (by child-rearing books or other sources) to have poinsettias in their homes. The botanist is

merely interested in refuting an incorrect but commonly held belief about the potential danger of poinsettias to pets and children.

(B) is another Distortion. While the idea that poinsettias are poisonous has supported the belief that the plants should be kept out of homes with children or pets, the biologist's main point is a challenge to the belief itself, not the reason for it. After all, it could be true that even though poinsettias are poisonous, they are nonetheless not a risk to pets or children (perhaps because pets and children do not seek to ingest poinsettias).

(C) is a 180. It cites the evidence that has encouraged the belief that poinsettias should be kept out of homes with pets or kids. The botanist's conclusion is that belief is mistaken.

(E) cites the botanist's evidence rather than the botanist's conclusion. Using the One Sentence Test, the fact that poinsettias pose no risk helps support the notion that it's acceptable to have them in the house with children. It's not the case that the acceptability of having poinsettias around pets and children helps support that poinsettias are not dangerous.

14. (B) Strengthen

Step 1: Identify the Question Type
The correct answer will "strengthen the ... reasoning" in the stimulus, so this is a Strengthen question.

Step 2: Untangle the Stimulus
Break down the archaeologist's argument into evidence and conclusion. The conclusion is the final sentence of the stimulus, introduced by [*t*]*herefore*. The archaeologist says the ancient stone building they are studying was likely not a dwelling. The evidence comes in three pieces. First, the building was made of quartz, granite, and limestone. Second, limestone is the only one of those materials that comes from the area where the building is. Third, most of the other buildings at the site from the same time period were dwellings and were composed solely of limestone.

Step 3: Make a Prediction
Start by finding the archaeologist's assumption. The archaeologist's conclusion is about a specific building. The evidence mentions a property of most dwellings that the building in question does not share. Therefore, the archaeologist assumes that the type of stone used in construction is somehow connected to a building's use. The archaeologist overlooks the possibility that this could merely be coincidence. The correct answer will strengthen the connection between building materials and a building's use, either by increasing the likelihood that limestone-only buildings were dwellings or that buildings composed of several types of rock were usually used for something else.

Step 4: Evaluate the Answer Choices

(B) matches the prediction by strengthening the tie between buildings made of imported stone and buildings that weren't dwellings.

(A) is a 180 because it expands the types of buildings that were used as dwellings. The building in question was in part made of limestone, so if **(A)** is true, then that building would fit the description of most dwellings.

(C) indicates that the building excavated at the site has a unique composition, but doesn't give any clue as to the building's use.

(D) is Out of Scope or potentially a 180. It expands the evidence, which says only that most buildings *from the same time period* were dwellings. Here that scope grows to encompass most buildings regardless of era. If anything, this choice weakens the argument by decreasing the likelihood that the building would be something other than a dwelling.

(E) shows that the building in question is unique, but doesn't in any way tie uniqueness to use. A unique building could still be a dwelling. Therefore, this choice doesn't affect the argument.

15. (E) Parallel Reasoning

Step 1: Identify the Question Type

Because the correct answer is the one whose "pattern of reasoning … most closely parallels the pattern of reasoning in the argument," this is a Parallel Reasoning question.

Step 2: Untangle the Stimulus

A quick glance at the stimulus reveals that it is mostly built of Formal Logic statements. Thus, the key task for untangling the stimulus is to translate the statements into Formal Logic. The important word in the first sentence is *only*, which indicates necessity. Therefore, the first sentence translates to:

If	files return on time	→	accountant prepares AND ~ ask for additional documents

The second sentence translates to:

If	accountant prepares	→	ask for additional documents

The third sentence, which is the argument's conclusion, is not Formal Logic. It asserts that Theodore will not be able to file on time.

Step 3: Make a Prediction

The first part of the evidence presents two necessary conditions that both need to occur in order for Theodore to file on time. The second sentence indicates that the conditions are mutually exclusive. In other words, there is no way for them both to occur. Therefore, the author concludes that the sufficient condition will not happen. You can abstract this further by using variables. The argument is structured as follows:

If	X	→	Y and ~Z

If	Y	→	Z

So, no X.

Step 4: Evaluate the Answer Choices

(E) matches the prediction. The first sentence translates to:

If	relaxing vacation (X)	→	children behave (Y) AND ~ suspicious (~Z)

The second sentence shows those two necessary conditions cannot both occur:

If	children behave (Y)	→	suspicious (Z)

Therefore, the sufficient condition (that she has a relaxing vacation) cannot occur (so, no X). Perhaps even easier to notice, **(E)** is the only answer choice that includes a Formal Logic statement with a conjunction (*and*) in its necessary term. So, the other answers can be quickly eliminated even without translating their entire structures.

(A) fails to match the structure of the stimulus. It doesn't easily translate into Formal Logic, and it has a different level of certainly than the stimulus due to the qualifier *probably*.

(B) creates a Formal Logic chain that the stimulus does not. The first two sentences translate to:

If	away on business (X)	→	~ attend concert (~Y)	→	~ another opportunity (~Z)

Therefore, since Tovah will be away on business (X), she will not have another opportunity this month (~Z). This answer lacks a Formal Logic statement with two necessary terms, so it can be immediately discarded as unparallel.

(C), like **(B)**, also creates a Formal Logic chain in the evidence:

$$\text{If } \begin{array}{c} \text{children} \\ \text{are} \\ \text{content} \\ (X) \end{array} \rightarrow \begin{array}{c} \text{play} \\ \text{video} \\ \text{games} \\ (Y) \end{array} \rightarrow \begin{array}{c} \sim \text{ other} \\ \text{activities} \\ \text{planned} \\ (\sim Z) \end{array}$$

So, because it has no Formal Logic statement with two necessary terms, **(C)** can be eliminated. Additionally, the conclusion itself is a Formal Logic statement, whereas the conclusion in the stimulus is merely a statement of fact.

(D) presents a Formal Logic statement and then says that the trigger will occur, so the result will as well:

$$\text{If } \begin{array}{c} \sim \textit{first class} \\ (\sim X) \end{array} \rightarrow \begin{array}{c} \textit{business class} \\ (Y) \end{array}$$

Therefore, because Teresa is not sitting in first class (~X), she must be sitting in business class (Y). There are only two terms presented; **(D)** does not contain a third Formal Logic term—a (Z) term. That is just one of the ways its structure doesn't match the structure of the stimulus.

16. (C) Inference

Step 1: Identify the Question Type
Because the correct answer is "strongly supported on the basis of" the stimulus, this is an Inference question. The correct answer will be follow from the information in the stimulus.

Step 2: Untangle the Stimulus
Make an inventory of the information in the stimulus, paraphrasing as you read. First, the stimulus says the news media tends to report only unusual cases when dealing with something that is commonly life threatening, such as automobile or industrial accidents. Conversely, when it comes to a "rare threat," occurrences are universally reported. Finally, in general, people estimate the risk of threats based on how often those threats are brought to their attention.

Step 3: Make a Prediction
Identify ideas that come up in more than one statement, and try to connect them. Here, the final statement connects with each of the first two. If people estimate the riskiness of threats based on how often they hear about them, then, due to reporting practices, people might overestimate the risk of rare threats while underestimating the risk of common threats.

Step 4: Evaluate the Answer Choices
(C) matches the prediction. Due to what gets featured in the news, people's assessment of threats may be skewed.

(A) is Out of Scope. Governmental action is not included in the stimulus.

(B) veers Out of Scope by introducing both "particularly dreadful" threats and the idea of control.

(D) is also Out of Scope. It introduces the aspect of time (long-range future threats versus immediate threats), which isn't covered by the stimulus.

(E) makes an Irrelevant Comparison about resources spent on avoiding certain threats. However, neither resources nor weather threats are discussed in the stimulus.

17. (A) Principle (Identify/Strengthen)

Step 1: Identify the Question Type
The correct answer is the principle that "helps to justify" the argument in the stimulus, so this is an Identify the Principle question that resembles a Strengthen question. Treat the question as if it were a Strengthen question, but expect the answer to be phrased generally.

Step 2: Untangle the Stimulus
Break down the argument into the evidence and conclusion, just as you would with a Strengthen stimulus. The conclusion, indicated by the Contrast Keyword [*h*]*owever*—and after the *since* clause—ends the stimulus. The real estate agent argues that sellers who plan to keep their large appliances are morally obligated to either take them away before showing the house or find some other way to inform prospective buyers that the appliances are not included in the purchase. The agent's evidence is that prospective buyers would likely expect the large appliances to be included in the purchase of a home, even though their inclusion is not a legal requirement.

Step 3: Make a Prediction
Start by finding the real estate agent's assumption. Here, the conclusion is about a moral obligation of sellers. The evidence is about the expectations of prospective buyers. Thus, the agent assumes that buyers' expectations are enough to create a moral obligation for sellers. The correct answer will support this assumption, thereby making the real estate agent's conclusion more likely to be true.

Step 4: Evaluate the Answer Choices
(A) matches the prediction. It connects the evidence (about buyers' assumptions) to the conclusion (about moral obligations). In fact, **(A)** expands the real estate agent's argument by indicating the obligation applies to all *belongings*.

(B) is a Distortion. The real estate agent isn't worried that buyers will assume large appliances are *permanent fixtures,* but that buyers will assume appliances will be *included*. Sellers don't have to fix buyers' misconceptions about legal terms, but they do have to protect against any misconceptions concerning the sale, *if* they plan to keep major appliances.

(C) is also a Distortion. The real estate agent's conclusion is about what sellers need to communicate to buyers, not what they actually have to *include* in the sale. The background information says that "the sellers are legally entitled to remove any items that are not permanent fixtures," which would include large appliances. Sellers can also keep large appliances, even if they were in the home when it was shown to buyers, as long as they inform buyers that the appliances aren't included.

(D) is Extreme. The sellers in the real estate agent's argument are not trying to "deliberately mislead" buyers, and therefore this principle wouldn't apply to them.

(E) is Out of Scope. It focuses on sellers who have indicated that appliances *will* remain (and what they therefore need to include in the sale), whereas the real estate agent's argument is that sellers must indicate which items will *not* be included in the sale. Also, like **(C)**, this choice discusses what sellers must do *after* a showing rather than what they must communicate or do *before* a showing.

18. (E) Flaw

Step 1: Identify the Question Type
Because the correct answer describes the grounds on which the argument in the stimulus is "vulnerable to criticism," this is a Flaw question.

Step 2: Untangle the Stimulus
Break down the argument into its evidence and conclusion. The conclusion comes after the Contrast Keyword [*b*]*ut* in the second sentence. The author disagrees with the belief held by many parents. So, the author's main point is that rigorously organizing a child's activities during playtime does not actually enhance the child's cognitive development. The evidence is the last sentence, in which the author suggests, based on an analogy to writing a novel, that organizing a child's playtime would not lead to a creative and resourceful child.

Step 3: Make a Prediction
The author presents two scope shifts. First, the author presents the analogy of novel writing. Any time an author includes an analogy, you should ask if the two things being compared are sufficiently similar for the analogy to be valid. Structured novel writing may not be like structured playtime. Second, the author draws a conclusion about cognitive development, but the evidence is that organizing a child's playtime will not lead to a creative, resourceful child. Thus, the author assumes cognitive development is equivalent to

creativity and resourcefulness. Yet, there could be many varieties of cognitive development that do not involve creativity and resourcefulness. The correct answer will likely focus on one of these gaps.

Step 4: Evaluate the Answer Choices
(E) matches the prediction, pointing out that cognitive development and creativity and resourcefulness are not necessarily linked.

(A) is a Distortion. The author actually argues that organizing a child's playtime is *neither* conducive to enhancing a child's cognitive development *nor* to producing creativity and resourcefulness.

(B) is Out of Scope because it focuses on what children enjoy, rather than on the effect organizing playtime does or does not have on cognitive development. While the author does overlook this possibly, enjoyment doesn't figure into the argument and therefore is not a possibility that needs to be considered.

(C) describes a sufficiency versus necessity flaw, which is not at play. This argument was not built on Formal Logic statements, and there is no mention of sufficient or necessary conditions.

(D) focuses on the analogy to novel writing but ignores the conclusion. Whether novel writing requires anything other than creativity and resourcefulness doesn't affect the author's assertion that structured playtime won't enhance a child's cognitive development. Therefore, while the author may ignore this possibility, doing so is not a flaw.

19. (C) Assumption (Necessary)

Step 1: Identify the Question Type
Because the correct answer is an assumption that the argument *requires*, this is a Necessary Assumption question. You can use the Denial Test to check your answer.

Step 2: Untangle the Stimulus
Analyze the argument's evidence and conclusion. The conclusion comes at the end of the stimulus, following the Conclusion Keywords "for this reason." The bureaucrat's main point is that an ideal bureaucracy will have a constantly increasing system of regulations. The reasoning is that new regulations will be created whenever a complaint reveals an unanticipated problem.

Step 3: Make a Prediction
Use the mismatched concepts to find the assumption. The evidence shows complaints that reveal unanticipated problems spur additional regulations. The conclusion says that the system of regulations is therefore ever-expanding. But in order for the ideal bureaucracy to perpetually expand, complaints that fall outside the purview of current regulations would have to continue to spring up. Otherwise, the

bureaucracy would have no reason to continue expanding its system of regulations. Therefore, the bureaucrat must be assuming that new complaints that reveal unanticipated problems will always exist.

Step 4: Evaluate the Answer Choices

(C) is phrased negatively, but it matches the prediction. **(C)** can be rephrased in positive terms: an ideal bureaucracy will always have some complaint about problems that are not covered by that bureaucracy's regulations. The Denial Test confirms **(C)**—it would say, "an ideal bureaucracy could be permanently without complaints …" In that case, the bureaucrat's prediction would fall apart.

(A) merely combines two points made by the bureaucrat in the evidence. However, nothing in **(A)** suggests that the system of regulations will keep expanding. The appeal *process* can exist without any actual complaints that would yield new regulations.

(B) is Out of Scope because it focuses on the past, rather than the future. The conclusion, conversely, is a prediction. Additionally, it's entirely possible that the bureaucracy has anticipated, defined, and classified problems without complaints first being lodged.

(D) is a Distortion. The argument provides a goal and what the bureaucrat sees as the logical result of *pursuing* that goal. This choice focuses on what is both sufficient and necessary for *achieving* that goal. Additionally, **(D)** makes no mention of complaints revealing unanticipated problems, which is the crucial evidence for the bureaucrat's prediction that the system will be forever expanding.

(E) is Extreme. The evidence in the stimulus is only about complaints that happen to reveal unanticipated problems. It is not necessary for the conclusion that *every* complaint reveals unanticipated problems. Some people may bring complaints that they are unaware are already covered by the existing regulations.

20. (B) Main Point

Step 1: Identify the Question Type

The correct answer "accurately expresses the overall conclusion" in the stimulus, so this is a Main Point question. Keep an eye open for Contrast Keywords, which will often signal the author's opinion.

Step 2: Untangle the Stimulus

Paraphrase each statement of the stimulus. First, scientists have made a finding about common bacteria. Second, some microbiologists have drawn a general conclusion from the specific finding of the scientists. Third, the author concedes that the microbiologists' conclusion would be valid if bacteria were all generally quite similar. Fourth, bacteria are very different, so most types of bacteria probably do not hibernate regularly.

Step 3: Make a Prediction

There are three distinct groups in this stimulus: 1) the scientists, who have been researching a common type of bacteria, 2) *some* microbiologists, who have drawn a conclusion based on the scientists' research, and 3) the author. As commonly happens in a Main Point question, the author disagrees with another opinion. Here, the author disagrees with the microbiologists. Notice that the author's disagreement, and hence the conclusion, is indicated by the Contrast Keyword [*b*]*ut*. So, while some microbiologists think bacteria in general are usually in hibernation, the author argues it is unlikely that most types of bacteria are regularly hibernating. The author's evidence, signaled by the Evidence Keyword *since*, is that bacteria are extremely diverse.

Step 4: Evaluate the Answer Choices

(B) matches the prediction.

(A) is a 180. It matches the microbiologists' conclusion, which is the point of view the author refutes.

(C) is a Distortion. First, it seems to include both the author's evidence and conclusion, whereas most correct answers to Main Point questions exclude the evidence. Secondly, the word [*i*]*f* makes the evidence conditional, whereas the author says bacteria are diverse as a statement of fact.

(D) is the author's conditional concession. However, the author then goes on to say the condition isn't met, i.e., bacteria *aren't* similar, and therefore the microbiologists' conclusion is unlikely.

(E) is Extreme. While the author essentially points out that a conclusion about all bacteria can't be made based on evidence about one type, the author does not go so far as to say it's likely that "only one type" hibernates regularly. Rather, the author argues it's "unlikely that most types" hibernate regularly.

21. (A) Assumption (Sufficient)

Step 1: Identify the Question Type

Because the correct answer is the assumption that makes the argument in the stimulus "follow logically," this is a Sufficient Assumption question. Keep an eye out for Formal Logic, which often appears in Sufficient Assumption questions.

Step 2: Untangle the Stimulus

The first word of the stimulus should immediately make you think of Formal Logic, as should the following two instances of *if*. Start by translating the conclusion, found following [*t*]*herefore* at the end of the stimulus. It can be written as:

	reading assignments AND ~ written assignments		~ student will get a high grade
If		→	

The evidence is two sentences long but basically repeats itself. It translates to:

$$\textbf{If} \quad \begin{array}{c} \textbf{\textasciitilde{} written} \\ \textbf{assignments} \end{array} \rightarrow \begin{array}{c} \textbf{\textasciitilde{} do all reading} \\ \textbf{assignments} \end{array}$$

Step 3: Make a Prediction

Both the evidence and the conclusion include the same sufficient term "~ written assignments." The correct answer will connect the mismatched term in the evidence (its necessary term) to the mismatched term in the conclusion (its necessary term). The author must be assuming that if students do not do all the reading assignments, then they cannot get a high grade. Alternately, the correct answer could state the contrapositive:

$$\textbf{If} \quad \begin{array}{c} \textbf{student gets} \\ \textbf{a high grade} \end{array} \rightarrow \begin{array}{c} \textbf{did all the reading} \\ \textbf{assignments} \end{array}$$

Step 4: Evaluate the Answer Choices

(A) matches the prediction. **(A)** is phrased as "No X is Y," which translates to "If X → ~Y." Therefore, this choice translates to:

$$\textbf{If} \quad \begin{array}{c} \textbf{a student completes} \\ \textbf{less than all} \\ \textbf{(i.e., not all) of} \\ \textbf{the reading} \\ \textbf{assignments} \end{array} \rightarrow \begin{array}{c} \textbf{student will} \\ \textbf{\textasciitilde{} get a high} \\ \textbf{grade} \end{array}$$

(B) negates the assumption without reversing. The argument assumes that completing the required reading is necessary to earn a high grade, whereas this choice says doing so is sufficient.

(C) makes the same error as **(B)**, only adding in the qualifier "highly motivated." The argument's conclusion was about all students, regardless of motivation.

(D) incorrectly contraposes one of the pieces of evidence. Additionally, this choice fails to include the mismatched term from the conclusion: "no student in that course will receive a high grade." To link the evidence to the conclusion, the correct answer needs to include either "students do *not* get a high grade" as a necessary term or "students *do* get a high grade" as a sufficient term. **(D)** includes neither of these.

(E) is too narrow to guarantee the conclusion to follow, because it discusses only "some highly motivated" students. Even if it were broad enough, this choice incorrectly has "earn high grades" as the necessary condition, rather than "will not earn high grades." It also doesn't contain the unmatched

term from the evidence ("do not do all the reading assignments").

22. (A) Weaken

Step 1: Identify the Question Type

Because the correct answer "weakens the argument," this is a Weaken question. Identify the gap between the evidence and conclusion, and pick the answer choice that would widen it.

Step 2: Untangle the Stimulus

First, find the argument's conclusion. The conclusion is indicated by the Conclusion Keyword [*t*]*hus* at the beginning of the last sentence. The author contends that the best way to lose body fat is to eat lots of protein and avoid carbohydrates. The author's evidence describes the results of a study involving two groups of people. The first group ate a high-protein, low-carb diet, and its members lost more weight than did those in the second group, who ate a high-carb, low-protein diet.

Step 3: Make a Prediction

Start by finding the author's assumption. The conclusion discusses body fat, but the evidence concerns weight. Therefore, the author must be assuming that the two are at least proportional, if not equivalent. This overlooks the possibility that the people in the study who ate the high-protein, low-carb diet retained their body fat but lost muscle or water-weight. Conversely, the argument also overlooks the possibility that those on the high-carb, low-protein diet lost body fat but gained muscle or retained water. The correct answer will likely point out that something other than body fat may have accounted for the difference in weight loss.

Step 4: Evaluate the Answer Choices

(A) matches the prediction. If the low-protein group is retaining more water than the high-protein group, then water rather than body fat may be the reason for the disparate weight loss.

(B) is Out of Scope because it introduces "many people who consume large quantities of protein." In contrast, the stimulus is about people on diets with a high protein-to-carb ratio and a limited amount of total calories. **(B)** provides no information about the carb or overall calorie consumption of these "many people." Furthermore, [*m*]*any* only guarantees at least one person, and a single exception would not be sufficient to weaken the author's general conclusion about the "most effective way to lose body fat."

(C) strengthens the argument, suggesting that regardless of what happens with weight loss, the high-protein, low-carb diet is useful for reducing body fat.

(D) may strengthen the argument, because the high-carb dieters are engaging in extra exercise yet still losing less weight than those on the low-carb diet. However, it also may weaken the argument because it may be the case that those on the high-carb diet are converting all their body fat to muscle (which is heavier). The problem is that this choice doesn't make a direct connection to body fat, which is the conclusion's concern, and therefore could move the argument in either direction.

(E) veers Out of Scope by presenting information about the effects of returning to a *normal* diet. The argument is concerned with the results of the study, which compared a high-protein, low-carb diet and a low-protein, high-carb diet, not about what occurred to participants after they stopped following the restrictions.

23. (C) Parallel Flaw

Step 1: Identify the Question Type
Because the correct answer is an argument with a "flawed pattern of reasoning" that "closely resembles the flawed pattern of reasoning" in the stimulus, this is a Parallel Flaw question. Keep an eye out for common flaw types.

Step 2: Untangle the Stimulus
Analyze the essayist's argument. The conclusion, at the very end of the stimulus, is that the human mind is a type of computer. The evidence is that the human mind and computers share a similar trait: they both are able to do logic.

Step 3: Make a Prediction
Start by finding the argument's assumption. The essayist assumes that if two things (human minds and computers) have an attribute in common (they both do logic), then both must be the same kind of thing (human minds must be types of computers). This overlooks the possibility that two things can have a feature in common but be fundamentally different types of things. The correct answer will present a common characteristic in order to conclude that one item must be a type of the other item.

Step 4: Evaluate the Answer Choices
(C) matches the prediction. The author says both organisms and communities are interdependent and uses that fact to conclude that communities are types of organisms.

(A) fails to match the prediction. First, the common characteristic presented is the willingness to sacrifice, but that trait as described is not quite comparable: animals sacrifice lives for relatives, whereas humans sacrifice well-being for the community. Second, the argument does not conclude that humans are a type of animal or vice versa, but instead indicates that there may be a biological cause that explains the behavior in both groups. Finally, **(A)**'s conclusion is less certain than that of the stimulus due to the phrase "[i]t is probable."

(B) is Half-Right/Half-Wrong. The evidence matches the reasoning in the stimulus, but the conclusion does not suggest that poetry is a type of plastic art or that plastic arts

are a type of poetry. Rather, the conclusion of **(B)** asserts that one criterion is not sufficient to categorize the plastic arts.

(D) presents a rule about vitamins in general and then draws a conclusion about a specific vitamin. This choice neither introduces a common trait shared by two disparate entities nor concludes that one entity is therefore a type of the other entity. Additionally, the reasoning in **(D)** is sound and so cannot be the correct answer to a Parallel Flaw question.

(E) does not suggest that friendship is a type of cooperation or vice versa. The conclusion of **(E)** asserts that because two different things (cooperation and friendship) share a common trait (obligations), they can share another similar trait (the requirement to prioritize goals over self-interest).

24. (D) Assumption (Necessary)

Step 1: Identify the Question Type
The correct answer is an "assumption required by the argument," so this is a Necessary Assumption question. You can use the Denial Test to check your answer.

Step 2: Untangle the Stimulus
Refuting the popular belief in the first sentence, the conclusion comes in the second sentence. The author argues that if objective evaluation of poetry is possible, then a poem's meaning must be separate from the reader. The author's evidence, which follows the Evidence Keyword *for*, is that if the aesthetic value of a poem can be discussed, then it must be possible for at least two readers to agree on the poem's meaning.

Step 3: Make a Prediction
This argument is a little easier if you write out the evidence above the conclusion:

Evidence:

	discussion of aesthetic value possible	→	at least two readers can agree on meaning
If			

Conclusion:

	objective evaluation possible	→	~ meaning assigned by reader
If			

There are two different scope shifts here. First, there is the subtle shift as the author suggests that if the meaning isn't assigned by the reader, then at least two readers can agree on a poem's meaning. Second, the author assumes that objective evaluation and a discussion of aesthetic value are related. That second assumption is a more overt gap, and the correct answer will likely point out that connection between the mismatched concepts in the sufficient terms. So, the author must assume that objective evaluation requires a discussion of aesthetic value.

Step 4: Evaluate the Answer Choices

(D) matches the prediction. It connects the two mismatched concepts of "objective evaluation" and "aesthetic value."

If	poem can be objectively evaluated	→	aesthetic value can be discussed

(A) is a Distortion. It is incorrect because the argument concerns discussing aesthetic value, which isn't the same as simply determining that a poem has aesthetic value. Additionally, **(A)** contains only terms from the evidence, and none of the mismatched concepts from the conclusion.

(B) can be translated as this:

If	at least two readers can agree on meaning	→	objective evaluation possible

However, that is not a necessary assumption of the argument. An objective evaluation *requires* that the meaning is not decided by the reader (and thus, at least two readers agree on the meaning). However, that doesn't mean that if two readers agree on the meaning that is *sufficient* to make objective evaluation possible. So, **(B)** reverses the order of the Formal Logic terms. **(B)** also fails to make a connection to the mismatched concept from the evidence about discussing aesthetic value.

(C) is too general, referring to the discussion of a poem rather than a discussion of the poem's aesthetic value. It also fails to match the prediction because it does not include the conclusion's mismatched concept of objectively evaluating poetry.

(E) goes Out of Scope by introducing literature in general. Additionally, the stimulus discusses "*at least* two readers" rather than "*more than* two readers," as in **(E)**.

25. (B) Flaw

Step 1: Identify the Question Type

Because the correct answer describes the "grounds" on which the argument in the stimulus is "most vulnerable to criticism," this is a Flaw question.

Step 2: Untangle the Stimulus

The dean's conclusion in the last sentence is that the math department's request for sole responsibility for teaching a

social sciences stats course is unfounded. The dean's evidence is that the course covers only high school–level math. By way of an analogy, the dean says that the inclusion of math in a course is not enough to require a math professor to teach it.

Step 3: Make a Prediction

Start by finding the dean's assumption. Here, the dean's conclusion is that the math department's demands are unreasonable. The evidence removes one possible reason for the math department to own the course: the math involved is low level. However, the dean's argument overlooks any other possible reason why the math department should teach the stats class. In other words, the dean assumes that a high math level is the *only* reason the math department should have ownership over the course. However, just because one reason for the math department's request isn't valid doesn't mean that the request itself isn't valid. There may be other reasons why the stats class should be overseen by the math department.

Step 4: Evaluate the Answer Choices

(B) matches the prediction. The dean refutes a view (that the math department should teach the stats class) by showing that one possible reason for the view (that the stats class involves math) is insufficient (because the math isn't complicated).

(A) is a Distortion. The dean assumes that math expertise is unnecessary to teach this particular course, but does not make a connection between expertise and teaching ability in general. The dean may well think that a mathematics professor could teach the class wonderfully, but the dean just thinks a math professor is unnecessary.

(C) is an Irrelevant Comparison. While both history and math are mentioned in the stimulus, students' knowledge about the two subjects is not.

(D) is a Distortion much like the one in **(A)**. The dean doesn't argue that math professors shouldn't teach the course or are incapable of teaching the course, merely that the department's request is unsupported. Or, in other words, that math professors are not the only professors who could teach the stats class.

(E) is Extreme and a Distortion of the dean's analogy. The analogy indicates only that some courses that include a historical perspective (for example, music history or art history) don't need to be taught by history professors, so there could be some courses that include a mathematical perspective (social sciences stats, for example) that don't need to be taught by a math professor. The dean is not making the Extreme assertion that *any* policy that applies to history courses should also apply to math courses.

Section IV: Logic Games

Game 1: Trial Advocacy Teams

Q#	Question Type	Correct	Difficulty
1	Acceptability	D	★
2	"If" / Could Be True	C	★
3	Could Be True	A	★
4	"If" / How Many	B	★★
5	"If" / Must Be True	E	★
6	"If" / Could Be True	C	★★

Game 2: E-Mail Messages

Q#	Question Type	Correct	Difficulty
7	Acceptability	D	★
8	Maximum	C	★★★
9	"If" / Must Be True	A	★
10	Must Be False (CANNOT Be True)	E	★★
11	"If" / Must Be True	D	★★
12	"If" / Maximum	B	★★★

Game 3: Mercotek Productivity Rankings

Q#	Question Type	Correct	Difficulty
13	Acceptability	D	★
14	"If" / Could Be True	B	★
15	Must Be False (CANNOT Be True)	C	★
16	Completely Determine	C	★★
17	"If" / Could Be True	C	★★
18	Complete and Accurate List (Of What CANNOT)	E	★★

Game 4: Shuttle Van Stops

Q#	Question Type	Correct	Difficulty
19	Acceptability	E	★
20	"If" / Complete and Accurate List	D	★★
21	"If" / Partial Acceptability	D	★★
22	"If" / Must Be True	C	★★★
23	"If" / Must Be False	D	★★★★

Game 1: Trial Advocacy Teams

Step 1: Overview
Situation: Setting up trial teams in a law school class

Entities: Six students (Gambini, Little, Mitchum, Richardson, Saito, Veracruz); three teams (1, 2, 3)

Action: Distribution/Matching Hybrid. Split the six students up into the three teams and then decide which ones prepare opening arguments and which ones prepare final arguments.

Limitations: Each student is on only one team, and each team has exactly two students—one who prepares the opening argument and one who prepares the final argument.

Step 2: Sketch
List the students by initial. To assign the students to teams, set up a table with a column for each team. In each column, there should be two slots: one for the student preparing the opening argument and one for the student preparing the final argument. Make sure these slots are labeled and lined up across the chart:

GLMRSV

	1	2	3
Open	—	—	—
Final	—	—	—

Step 3: Rules
Rule 1 places Mitchum on the same team as either Gambini or Veracruz. Mitchum cannot be on the same team as both, because that would be three people on one team. Also, note that this rule does not indicate which student gives the opening argument and which one gives the final argument. So, there are two possible blocks:

M		G/V
G/V	OR	M

Rule 2 indicates that Little prepares an opening argument. However, it does not state what team Little is on, so simply place an L next to the "opening" row.

Rules 3 states that either Gambini or Richards prepares a final argument—but not both. Therefore, only one of them prepares a final argument. That means the other one must prepare an opening argument. So place a G/R next to each row. Note that this rule does not say whether they are on the same team or not. They could be, but they do not have to be.

Before making deductions, take note that Saito is never mentioned in any of the rules. Saito is the Floater of the game and is not directly restricted from any position. Place an asterisk above him in the roster of entities.

Step 4: Deductions
With most of the rules already drawn into the sketch, there will not be any major deductions. The only rule to consider is Rule 1. While it does present two possible blocks, neither one can be placed into the sketch for certain, so there is no benefit to Limited Options. Furthermore, Gambini is the only Duplication in the rules, but the rules aren't easily combined to make a solid deduction.

Instead, focus on what rules will be frequently tested in the questions. In this game, there are two questions to constantly consider: 1) Who's on the team with Mitchum; and 2) which arguments do Gambini and Richardson prepare? Also, take note that two opening argument positions are filled: one by L and one by G/R. That leaves only one opening position. Numbers can be critical to a game such as this one.

Also note that there are no team numbers mentioned in any of the rules, questions, or answer choices. Furthermore, Sequencing is not an issue here. So, students can be assigned to any team without affecting or violating any rules. Your final Master Sketch should look something like this:

GLMRŠV

	1	2	3	
Open	—	—	—	L, G/R
Final	—	—	—	G/R

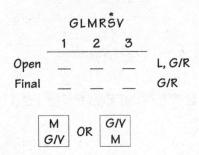

Step 5: Questions

1. (D) Acceptability
This is a typical Acceptability question. Go through the rules one at a time, and eliminate answers that violate those rules.

Rule 1 requires Mitchum to be on the same team as either Gambini or Veracruz. That eliminates **(C)**, which puts Mitchum on a team with Saito. Rule 2 requires Little to prepare an opening argument. That eliminates **(B)**. Rule 3 requires that either Gambini or Richardson (but not both) prepare a final argument. That eliminates **(A)**, in which both prepare a final argument, and **(E)**, in which neither one prepares a final argument. That leaves **(D)** as the correct answer.

2. (C) "If" / Could Be True
There are two New-"If"s for this question. First, Gambini is on the same team as Mitchum. Second, Gambini prepares a final argument, which means Gambini's teammate, Mitchum, will prepare an opening argument. Also, with Gambini preparing a

final argument, Richards must prepare an opening argument (Rule 3).

Thus, the other two teams will have opening arguments prepared by Richards and Little (by Rule 2). That means Saito and Veracruz will be split between those teams to prepare the final arguments. However, it cannot be determined who is teamed up with whom:

	1	2	3	
Open	M	__	__	L, R
Final	G	__	__	S, V

With that, only **(C)** is possible, making that the correct answer. Veracruz and Saito are preparing final arguments, so that eliminates **(A)**, **(B)**, and **(D)**. Furthermore, Saito and Veracruz have to be on different teams, which eliminates **(E)**.

3. (A) Could Be True

The correct answer will be the one that is possible. The four wrong answers all must be false.

The limitation set to Gambini and Richardson by Rule 3 is that one has to prepare an opening argument and one has to prepare a final argument. But nothing precludes them from being on the same team. That means **(A)** is possible and is, thus, the correct answer. For the record:

If Gambini and Veracruz were on a team together, then Mitchum couldn't be with either one of them. That violates Rule 1, making **(B)** false. If Gambini prepares an opening argument on a team with Little, Little would have to prepare the final argument. That violates Rule 2, making **(C)** false. Putting Little or Saito on a team with Mitchum would leave no room for Gambini or Veracruz to be with Mitchum. That would violate Rule 1, making **(D)** and **(E)** false.

4. (B) "If" / How Many

If Veracruz is on a team with Richardson, Veracruz cannot be on the same team as Mitchum. That means Mitchum must be on a team with Gambini (Rule 1). That leaves Little and Saito to be on the last team together.

By Rule 2, Little must prepare an opening argument, so Saito will have to prepare the final argument for their team. However, that's all that can be determined.

R/V	M/G	L/S

By Rule 3, Gambini or Richardson will prepare a final argument, but there's no indication which one here. Either one could still prepare the opening argument and either one could still prepare the final argument. So, their two teams are still undecided in terms of who prepares which argument.

That means Little and Saito are the only two students whose argument can be determined. That makes **(B)** the correct answer.

5. (E) "If" / Must Be True

For this question, Little is on the same team as Richardson. Little has to prepare an opening argument (Rule 2), so that means Richardson prepares a final argument. By Rule 3, Gambini must prepare an opening argument. That makes **(E)** the correct answer.

For the record: Mitchum could still be on a team with either Gambini or Veracruz. If Mitchum was on a team with Veracruz, Gambini would be on the last team with Saito. Furthermore, with Mitchum and Veracruz, either one could give the opening argument. In that case, **(A)**, **(B)**, **(C)**, and **(D)** could all be false.

6. (C) "If" / Could Be True

If Saito prepares an opening argument, that fills up the quota of opening arguments. One opening will be prepared by Saito, one by Little (Rule 2), and one by either Gambini or Richardson (Rule 3). That leaves Mitchum and Veracruz to prepare final arguments, along with either Gambini or Richardson.

	1	2	3	
Open	S	L	G/R	
Final	__	__	__	M, V, G/R

However, with Mitchum and Veracruz both preparing final arguments, they can't be on the same team as one another. By Rule 1, Mitchum must be on a team with Gambini. With Mitchum preparing the final argument, that means Gambini prepares the opening argument. By Rule 3, that means Richardson will prepare a final argument.

	1	2	3	
Open	S	L	G	
Final	__	__	M	V, R

The question is looking for two people who could be on a team together. Mitchum is teamed up with Gambini, which eliminates **(A)**, **(B)**, and **(D)**. And, because Richardson and Veracruz are both preparing final arguments, they cannot be together, which eliminates **(E)**. That leaves **(C)** as the only acceptable pair, and thus the correct answer.

Game 2: E-Mail Messages

Step 1: Overview

Situation: A worker checking e-mail while on vacation

Entities: Three associates (Hilary, Jerome, Lula)

Action: Strict Sequencing. Determine how many messages each associate sends, and on what day the messages were received. So this is Strict Sequencing—with a twist.

Limitations: This game is a little more complicated than ordinary Sequencing games. While Sukanya can receive only one message per day, there is no indication of how many messages she receives. However, she does receives at least one message from each associate (for a minimum of three), but no more than two from each associate (for a maximum of six).

Step 2: Sketch

With a lot of information yet to be determined, only set up what is known. List the three associates by initial, and set up slots for the three messages that must be received, leaving room to add more slots as needed. Also, make a shorthand notation of the limitation that each associate can only send two messages.

HJL (max 2 each)

$$\underline{} \quad \underline{} \quad \underline{} \quad \ldots \quad \ldots \quad \ldots$$
$$1 \quad\; 2 \quad\; 3$$

Step 3: Rules

Rule 1 limits the sender of the first email: It can't be Lula. That means it must be either Hilary or Jerome. Place H/J in the first slot.

Rule 2 indicates that the last sender must be the same as the first sender, who must be either Hilary or Jerome (by Rule 1). That means at least one person must send two messages. So, at the very least, there will be a fourth message. Add one slot to the sketch and place H/J in it. This still does not confirm how many messages there are in total, so there could still be extra slots between the third message and the final message. Finally, make a note in shorthand that the first and last message will be from the same associate:

$$\underline{\text{H/J}} \quad \underline{} \quad \underline{} \quad \ldots \quad \ldots \quad \underline{\text{H/J}}$$
$$1 \qquad 2 \qquad 3 \qquad\qquad\quad \text{Last}$$

First = Last

Rule 3 sets up a Block of Entities, with one of Jerome's messages being sent immediately after one of Hilary's. It's important to note that the rule stipulates this must occur exactly once:

$$\underline{\text{H}} \quad \underline{\text{J}} \quad \textit{once}$$

Rule 4 states that Jerome must send exactly one of the first three messages. Note this in shorthand:

J exactly one of 1, 2, 3

Step 4: Deductions

Hilary and Jerome are the core of each of the first three rules, and these rules can be combined (along with Rule 4, which also affects Jerome) to create some significant deductions.

Either Hilary or Jerome will send the first *and* last messages. Depending on whom it is, that will help determine where the block from Rule 3 can be placed. This calls for Limited Options.

In the first option, Hilary sends the first and last messages—and that's all (because nobody can send more than two messages). In that case, Jerome must send the second message, because Jerome has to send one message immediately after Hilary (Rule 3). The third message cannot be from Hilary (because that would then be the last message, with no message from Lula), and it cannot be from Jerome (because Jerome can only leave *one* of the first three messages by Rule 4). Thus, the third message must be from Lula. After that, Hilary will be the last message, but there could still be a second message from Jerome and/or Lula in between.

$$\text{I)} \quad \underline{\text{H}} \quad \underline{\text{J}} \quad \underline{\text{L}} \quad \ldots \quad \ldots \quad \underline{\text{H}}$$
$$\qquad\;\; 1 \quad\; 2 \quad\; 3 \qquad\qquad\quad \text{Last}$$

In the second option, Jerome will send the first and last messages—and that's all. In that case, for Jerome to send a message immediately after Hilary, Hilary will have to be the second-to-last message. Because Jerome can only leave *one* of the first three messages (Rule 4), the second message will be from Lula or Hilary (who can still send a second message). Then, depending on how many messages are sent, the last two messages will be, in order, Hilary then Jerome.

$$\text{II)} \quad \underline{\text{J}} \quad \underline{\text{H/L}} \quad \ldots \quad \ldots \quad \underline{\text{H}} \quad \underline{\text{J}}$$
$$\qquad\;\; 1 \qquad 2 \qquad\qquad\qquad \text{Last}$$

Keep track of Numbers as you work through the game.

Step 5: Questions

7. (D) Acceptability

Even with complex setups, Acceptability questions can be deftly handled by going through the rules and eliminating unacceptable answers.

Rule 1 states that Lula doesn't send the first message, so that eliminates **(A)**. Rule 2 states that the first and last messages are from the same person, which eliminates **(C)**. Rule 3 states that there must be one message from Jerome immediately after a message from Hilary. That eliminates **(B)**. Finally, Rule 4 states that exactly one of the first three messages must be from Jerome, which eliminates **(E)**. That leaves **(D)** as the correct answer.

8. (C) Maximum

Read the question carefully. This question asks for the maximum number of emails after Jerome's first message and before Hilary's first message. That means Jerome must send his first message before Hilary sends her first message, which places you in the second option. That means Jerome must send the very first message (by Rule 1), and he also must send the last message (Rule 2). Hilary would have to send the next-to-last message (Rule 3).

$$\underset{}{\underline{\text{J}}} \quad \dots \quad \underset{}{\underline{\text{H}}} \quad \underset{}{\underline{\text{J}}}$$

Each associate can only send two messages, so Jerome is done. Hilary could send a second message, but all that matters for this question is putting as many messages between Hilary's first message and Jerome's first. To do that, the only person who could send messages in between would be Lula—who can only send two messages. In that case, Lula would send the second and third messages. Hilary would then send the fourth message. If Hilary sends one message then that would be it, with Jerome sending the fifth and final message:

$$\underset{1}{\underline{\text{J}}} \quad \underset{2}{\underline{\text{L}}} \quad \underset{3}{\underline{\text{L}}} \quad \underset{4}{\underline{\text{H}}} \quad \underset{5}{\underline{\text{J}}}$$

If Hilary sends two messages, Hilary would send the fourth and fifth message, with Jerome sending the sixth:

$$\underset{1}{\underline{\text{J}}} \quad \underset{2}{\underline{\text{L}}} \quad \underset{3}{\underline{\text{L}}} \quad \underset{4}{\underline{\text{H}}} \quad \underset{5}{\underline{\text{H}}} \quad \underset{6}{\underline{\text{J}}}$$

In either case, there would be two messages between Jerome's and Hilary's first messages, making **(C)** the correct answer.

9. (A) "If" / Must Be True

For this question, there are only four messages. This could happen in either option. The first and fourth messages will be from the same person—either Hilary or Jerome. If Hilary sends the first and fourth messages, then Jerome sends the second message (Rule 3), which leaves Lula to send the third message. If Jerome sends the first and fourth messages, then

Hilary sends the third message (Rule 3), which leaves Lula to send the second message:

$$\text{I)} \quad \underset{1}{\underline{\text{H}}} \quad \underset{2}{\underline{\text{J}}} \quad \underset{3}{\underline{\text{L}}} \quad \underset{4}{\underline{\text{H}}}$$

$$\text{II)} \quad \underset{1}{\underline{\text{J}}} \quad \underset{2}{\underline{\text{L}}} \quad \underset{3}{\underline{\text{H}}} \quad \underset{4}{\underline{\text{J}}}$$

Because the question is asking for something that must be true, **(A)** is the correct answer. All of the four wrong answers are possible, but none of them *must* be true.

10. (E) Must Be False (CANNOT Be True)

The correct answer for this question will be a message that cannot be sent by Lula. The remaining answers all could be sent by Lula.

By Rule 1, Lula can't send the first message. So, by Rule 2, Lula also can't send the last message. The maximum number of messages is six. If there were six messages, Lula couldn't send the first or the sixth, but could send any one in between. So, Lula will never send the sixth message, making **(E)** the correct answer.

For the record, sketches for other questions in this game will verify that Lula can be in any of the other listed positions. The two sketches for the previous question show Lula sending the second or third message, which eliminates **(A)** and **(B)**. Furthermore, the sketches for the final question of the set show that Lula can send either the fourth or fifth message, which eliminates **(C)** and **(D)**.

11. (D) "If" / Must Be True

For this question, there are six messages, with Lula sending the fifth one. The first and sixth messages will both be from either Jerome or Hilary. However, if it were Jerome, that would violate Rule 3, because there would be no room for Hilary to send a message immediately before Jerome. So, the first and sixth messages must be from Hilary, which is the first option. As already determined from that option, to satisfy Rule 3, Jerome must send the second message. Finally, Jerome can only send one of the first three messages (by Rule 4), so Lula must send the third message, leaving Jerome to send the fourth:

$$\underset{1}{\underline{\text{H}}} \quad \underset{2}{\underline{\text{J}}} \quad \underset{3}{\underline{\text{L}}} \quad \underset{4}{\underline{\text{J}}} \quad \underset{5}{\underline{\text{L}}} \quad \underset{6}{\underline{\text{H}}}$$

The question is asking for something that must be true, making **(D)** the correct answer.

12. (B) "If" / Maximum

For this question, Lula will send two messages. The question asks for the maximum number of messages that could be sent between those two.

To start, Lula cannot send the first message (Rule 1). So, the earliest message Lula can send is the second message. However, even with the maximum of six messages, Lula couldn't send the sixth message (Rule 2). That already allows for only two messages, at most, between Lula's messages. That eliminates **(D)** and **(E)**.

However, there is still one more problem. The first and last message must be from the same associate (Jerome or Hilary). In either case, if Lula sends the second and fifth messages, there would never be a message from Jerome immediately after a message from Hilary. That would violate Rule 3. So, Lula cannot be the second and fifth messages. To separate Lula's messages at all, they would have to be second and fourth, or third and fifth. That eliminates **(C)**.

If Lula sends the second and fourth messages, Jerome would send the first and sixth messages, with Hilary sending the third and fifth messages.

$$\frac{J}{1} \quad \frac{L}{2} \quad \frac{H}{3} \quad \frac{L}{4} \quad \frac{H}{5} \quad \frac{J}{6}$$

If Lula sends the third and fifth messages, Hilary would send the first and sixth messages, with Jerome sending the second and fourth messages:

$$\frac{H}{1} \quad \frac{J}{2} \quad \frac{L}{3} \quad \frac{J}{4} \quad \frac{L}{5} \quad \frac{H}{6}$$

That means there's a maximum of one message between Lula's messages, making **(B)** the correct answer. (Note that, once two messages in between was ruled out, the sketch from the previous question could have been used to confirm the possibility of one message in between.)

Game 3: Mercotek Productivity Rankings

Step 1: Overview
Situation: A company carrying out a productivity study

Entities: Six crews (F, G, H, R, S, T)

Action: Loose Sequencing. Rank the six crews in order of productivity—a standard Sequencing game. A quick glance at the rules reveals that there are no rules about exact slots or distances between entities. All the rules contain the phrase "more productive" so this is a Loose Sequencing game. There may also appear to be a Matching component based on determining each crew's shift (day or night). However, a glance at the rules indicates that the game is primarily concerned with Sequencing, and the day-shift/night-shift issue is more of a limitation than a true action.

Limitations: There are no ties in the sequencing. There are exactly two night shifts in a given week, and those shifts will be either G and T or S and H.

Step 2: Sketch
Looking ahead to the rules, each one provides relative, nonfixed rankings. So this game is Loose Sequencing. Therefore, there's no need to draw slots. Simply list the entities for now, and build a Loose Sequencing sketch based on the rules.

Step 3: Rules
Rules 1–5 are all the same, setting up a relative relationship between two entities. F is more productive than G. R is more productive than S. R is more productive than T. S is more productive than H, and G is more productive than T. Simply notate these relationships in shorthand. You can either list out each rule separately and then combine them after or you can build the sketch combining the Duplications as you uncover them.

Step 4: Deductions
As with any Loose Sequencing game, the key to setting up a solid diagram is to combine the rules based on Duplications. R is the first entity duplicated. R has to be more productive than S (Rule 2) and T (Rule 3). The order of S and T cannot be determined, so place R at the top and draw two branches down—one to S and one to T. Then, H will be ranked lower than S (Rule 4). G will rank higher than T (Rule 5), but on a separate branch than R, because G and R are not connected. Finally, F will rank higher than G (Rule 1):

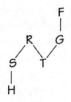

As always with Loose Sequencing, take a moment to determine what could be ranked first and what could be ranked last. Because F and R have no crews that have to be ranked more productive, either one of them could be ranked first. Similarly, because T and H have no crews that need to be ranked less productive, either one of them could be last.

Finally, make a note on the side that there are two night-shift crews—either G and T or S and H. Be ready to reference that quickly should a question ask.

$$\text{Night: } G\,\&\,T \quad or \quad S\,\&\,H$$

Step 5: Questions

13. (D) Acceptability
Four answers here will violate the rules, so test each rule individually, eliminating answers to find the one that's acceptable. Rule 1 states that F needs to be more productive than G, which eliminates **(C)**. Rule 2 states that R is more productive than S, but no answer violates that rule. Rule 3 states that R is more productive than T, which eliminates **(A)**. Rule 4 states that S is more productive than H, which eliminates **(B)**. Rule 5 states that G is more productive than T, which eliminates **(E)**. That leaves **(D)** as the correct answer.

14. (B) "If" / Could Be True
For this question, F is ranked third. G is less productive than F (Rule 1), and T must be less productive than G (Rule 5), so neither G nor T can be ranked first or second. That leaves R, S, and H—in that order. H has to be ranked lower than S (Rule 4), which has to be lower than R (Rule 2), so H can't be ranked first or second, either. That leaves R and S to be the first- and second-ranked crews, respectively. For ranks four through six, G will be ranked higher than T. H has no relation to G or T, so H can receive any of the three remaining rankings.

$$
\begin{array}{cccccc}
\underline{R} & \underline{S} & \underline{F} & \underline{} & \underline{} & \underline{} \\
1 & 2 & 3 & 4 & 5 & 6
\end{array}
$$

$$G \ldots T$$
$$H$$

Because H could receive any ranking from fourth through sixth, **(B)** is the only possible answer, and is thus correct. For the record: S is ranked second, which eliminates **(A)**, **(C)**, and **(D)**. With the first three rankings determined, T cannot be ranked fourth because it still has to be ranked lower than G. That eliminates **(E)**.

15. (C) Must Be False (CANNOT Be True)

The correct answer to this question will be the one entity that cannot be ranked fifth. The remaining four shifts all could be.

In this case, a crew that is fifth will only have one crew ranked below it. F and R each must rank higher than at least two crews (G and T have to be ranked lower than F, and S and H have to be ranked lower than R). Therefore, neither one could be ranked fifth. That makes **(C)** the correct answer.

16. (C) Completely Determine

This question is looking for a piece of information that will allow you to determine the ranking of all six entities. From Step 4 you know that either F or R is first and either H or T is last. First consider whether each answer, at minimum, provides enough information to guarantee which entities are in the first and last slots.

(A) states that F is ranked second. Because only F or R could be ranked first, that will make R the first-ranked crew. However, either H or T could still be ranked last, so the ranking cannot be fully determined.

(B) states that G ranks fifth. T has to be ranked lower than G, so T will be ranked sixth. However, either F or R could still be ranked first, so this does not help determine the full rankings, either.

(C) states that H is ranked third. R and S (in that order) need to be ranked higher than H, so R will have to be ranked first and S will be ranked second. That leaves F, G, and T—in that order. That fills out the rest of the sketch:

$$\frac{R}{1} \quad \frac{S}{2} \quad \frac{H}{3} \quad \frac{F}{4} \quad \frac{G}{5} \quad \frac{T}{6}$$

That makes **(C)** the correct answer. For the record:

(D) If R ranks third, that makes F ranked first. However, either H or T could still rank sixth, so that doesn't help complete the rankings.

(E) If S ranks third, either F or R could still be ranked first *and* either H or T could still be ranked last. This is certainly not enough to determine complete rankings.

17. (C) "If" / Could Be True

This the first question (and, as it turns out, the *only* question) that requires determining which crews worked the night shift. For this question, the two night-shift crews will be ranked fifth and sixth. The night-shift crews are either G and T or S and H. Draw both possible outcomes.

If G and T were fifth and sixth, G would have to be fifth and T would be sixth (Rule 5). That leaves R, S, and H— which must be ranked in that order— and F, which can receive any of the top four rankings (because it only has to be ranked higher than G, by Rule 1).

$$\frac{}{1} \quad \frac{}{2} \quad \frac{}{3} \quad \frac{}{4} \quad \frac{G}{5} \quad \frac{T}{6}$$

R...S...H
F

If S and H are the night-shift crews, S would have to be fifth and H would be sixth (Rule 4). T is ranked lower than all of the remaining crews, So T will be ranked fourth. R can receive any of the remaining three rankings, and F and G will fill out the other two—in that order.

$$\frac{}{1} \quad \frac{}{2} \quad \frac{}{3} \quad \frac{T}{4} \quad \frac{S}{5} \quad \frac{H}{6}$$

F...G
R

Because R can be ranked third in the second option, **(C)** is the only answer possible, and is thus the correct answer. For the record:

G can't be ranked fourth because it's ranked fifth in the first option and because T is ranked fourth in the second option. That eliminates **(A)**.

Neither H nor T can be ranked fifth because G and S are the entities ranked fifth in the two options. That eliminates **(B)** and **(E)**.

Finally, S can't be ranked fourth in the first option because it still has to be ranked higher than H, and it can't be fourth in the second option because it's already ranked fifth. That eliminates **(D)**.

18. (E) Complete and Accurate List (Of What CANNOT)

This question is asking for a complete and accurate list of entities that CANNOT be ranked third. There are two strategies that can make short work of this.

One strategy would be to use previous work to find crews that can be ranked third. The answer to the Acceptability question shows that G can be ranked third. That eliminates **(A)** and **(D)**. The New-"If" of the second question of the set has F ranked third, so that eliminates **(C)**. Finally, the correct answer to the previous question demonstrates that R could be ranked third. That eliminates **(B)**, which leaves **(E)** as the correct answer.

Another strategy would be to use the Master Sketch to determine which crew(s) can't be third: because it must have three entities before it or because it must have four entities after it. T has to be ranked lower than R (Rule 3), and it has to be ranked lower than G (Rule 5), which itself has to be ranked lower than F (Rule 1). That means T is guaranteed to have at least three entities before it, and the highest ranking it could receive is fourth. No other entity has to be ranked that far down, which also confirms **(E)** as the correct answer.

Game 4: Shuttle Van Stops

Step 1: Overview

Situation: A shuttle van dropping off four passengers at four locations

Entities: Four stops (Fundy, Los Altos, Mineola, Simcoe) and four passengers (Greg, Jasmine, Rosa, Vijay)

Action: Strict Sequencing (Two Sequences). Determine the order in which the van makes the four stops from first to fourth, and determine the order in which the passengers get off the shuttle van from first to fourth. Because each set of entities will be ordered, this is merely Sequencing on two levels. Some may want to label this game a Hybrid of Distribution (assign the stop to a passenger) and Sequencing (order the four passenger-stop combinations). Others may perceive it as a Hybrid of Sequencing (order the four stops) and Matching (assign each stop a passenger). Those are equally reasonable categorizations as well. Ultimately though, it's not significant how the game is classified, because in any of those scenarios the sketch should look the same: two rows of four dashes.

Limitations: For the first sequence, the van will stop at all four locations, one at a time. For the other sequence, each passenger gets off at only one stop, each one getting off at a different stop.

Step 2: Sketch

For each of the four stops, in order, you need to determine the location and the departing passenger. Both sequences can be tracked in a simple chart:

	1	2	3	4
Stop: FMLS	__	__	__	__
Pass: gjrv	__	__	__	__

Step 3: Rules

Rule 1 states that Los Altos will be the first or second stop. Note this in shorthand to the side or put an L with arrows to spots 1 and 2 in the stops row.

Rule 2 must be interpreted carefully. The rule states that Rosa is still on board when the van reaches Mineola. That doesn't mean that Rosa must get off *after* Mineola. Rosa could also get off *at* Mineola without violating the rule. What this rule really means is that Rosa can't get off *before* Mineola. The rule can be written negatively as it is stated:

$$\text{Never} \quad \overset{M}{\underset{r}{}}$$

... or it can be written positively:

$$\overset{M}{\underset{r}{}} \quad \text{or} \quad \overset{M}{\underset{r}{}}$$

Rule 3 states that Jasmine is on board longer than Vijay. That just means that Vijay gets off at a stop before Jasmine:

$$v \ldots j$$

You can also deduce that Vijay cannot get off at the last stop and Jasmine cannot get off at the first stop. Add "~v" and "~j" under the appropriate slots in the sketch.

Rule 4 is the longest and potentially most confusing rule of the game. Like Rule 2, it requires careful interpretation. This rule is actually broken up into two rules, both of which are complex in their Formal Logic.

The first part of the rule indicates what happens if Jasmine is still on board when the van reaches Fundy. That means if Jasmine gets off *at or* after Fundy — just not before. In that case, Greg is still on board when the van reaches Simcoe. Again, that means Greg gets off after at *or* after Simcoe—just not before.

$$\overset{F}{\underset{j}{}} \quad \text{or} \quad \overset{F}{\underset{j}{}} \quad \longrightarrow \quad \overset{S}{\underset{g}{}} \quad \text{or} \quad \overset{S}{\underset{g}{}}$$

By the contrapositive: If Greg gets off before Simcoe, then Jasmine gets off before Fundy:

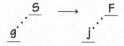

The second part of the rule tells us what happens otherwise, i.e., if Jasmine is *not* on board when the van reaches Fundy. In that case, Greg is not on board when the van reaches Simcoe. In other words, if Jasmine gets off before Fundy, then Greg must get off before Simcoe. Note that these rules are simply reversals of one another. So, if one condition happens—either (j ... F) or (g ... S)—so does the other. If one doesn't happen— (either j doesn't get off before F) or (g doesn't get off before S)—neither does the other. That makes the rule the same as if had been phrased as "if but only if." You can either write out the reverse of the rule and contrapose it or you can you alter the first part of the rule and its contrapositive by make the arrow a double arrow indicating that the sufficient condition is also necessary and that the necessary condition is also sufficient.

Step 4: Deductions

Given the complexity of this game, it's especially important to avoid making improper deductions. With Rule 2, some test takers will think that Rosa can't get off at the first stop. However, if the first stop is Mineola, then Rosa can certainly get off there, having been aboard the van until it reached Mineola. Similarly, Mineola can be the last stop, as long as Rosa stays aboard the van the rest of the time and gets off there, too. So, there are no deductions for that rule.

It may seem like Limited Options are warranted per Rule 1. However, placing Los Altos in either position leads to virtually no further deductions, making Limited Options unnecessary.

The last rule is entirely conditional and very open ended, so there are no major deductions. With few deductions you should expect several New-"If" questions, and indeed the question set is composed of one Acceptability question and four New-"If"s. Here's what the Master Sketch should look like:

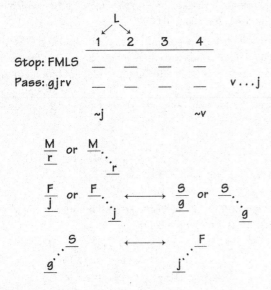

Step 5: Questions

19. (E) Acceptability

Carefully apply each rule to the answers, eliminating any answers that violate those rules. Rule 1 requires that Los Altos be the first or second stop. That eliminates **(B)**. By Rule 2, Rosa must be on board when the van reaches Mineola. However, she gets off before Mineola in **(D)**, so that can be eliminated. Rule 3 requires Jasmine to get off after Vijay, which eliminates **(C)**. In the remaining answers, Jasmine gets off at Fundy, which means that she was on board the van until it reached Fundy. By Rule 4, that means that Greg should have been on board until Simcoe. But Greg gets off at the first stop in **(A)**, long before the van ever reaches Simcoe (the last stop), so that answer can be eliminated. That leaves **(E)** as the only answer that doesn't violate any of the rules.

Note that **(E)** has Rosa getting off at Mineola. Remember that this does not violate Rule 2 because she was on the van the whole time until it reached Mineola.

20. (D) "If" / Complete and Accurate List

For this question, Mineola is the first stop. By Rule 1, that means Los Altos must be the second stop. The remaining stops can be Fundy or Simcoe in either order.

1	2	3	4
M	L	F/S	S/F
—	—	—	—

The correct answer will list everybody that could get off at the first stop. By Rule 3, Jasmine can never get off at the first stop, so that eliminates **(E)** immediately. By Rule 2, Rosa needs to be on board until the van reaches Mineola. Because Mineola is the first stop, Rosa is free to get off there or any stop afterwards. And there's no rule preventing either Vijay or Greg from getting off at the first stop or getting off at Mineola. That means, except for Jasmine, anybody could get off first, making **(D)** the correct answer.

While you wouldn't waste time drawing this all out on Test Day, here are two sketches to verify that Greg, Rosa, and Vijay can all get off first in this case:

1	2	3	4
M	L	F	S
r	v	j	g

1	2	3	4
M	L	S	F
g/v	v/g	j	r

21. (D) "If" / Partial Acceptability

For this question, Fundy is the first stop. By Rule 1, that makes Los Altos the second stop. Therefore, Mineola and Simcoe are the last two stops. According to Rule 2, Rosa has to stay on the van until Mineola, so Rosa can't get off at one of the first two stops. That eliminates **(B)** and **(E)**.

With Fundy being the first stop, Jasmine must still be on board when the van reaches it. By Rule 4, that means that Greg has to stay aboard until Simcoe. Because Simcoe is one of the last two stops, Greg can't get off at the first or second stop. That eliminates **(A)** and **(C)**.

Those deductions also mean Vijay and Jasmine, in that order (Rule 3), must get off at the first two stops:

1	2	3	4
F	L	M/S	S/M
v	j	g/r	r/g

That leaves **(D)** as the only possible listing, and thus the correct answer.

1	2	3	4
L	M	F	S
v	j	g	r

This sketch shows how **(E)** can be possible:

1	2	3	4
M	L	S	F
V	g	j	r

22. (C) "If" / Must Be True

This question provides a lot of information. First, it states that Greg is still on board when the van reaches Los Altos and Simcoe. Then, at the end, it states that Greg gets off second. That means Los Altos and Simcoe must be the first two stops, in either order. That leaves Fundy and Mineola to be the last two stops—in either order.

Regardless of the order of the first two stops, Greg is still on board when the van reaches Simcoe. By Rule 4, that means Jasmine cannot get off before Fundy. So Jasmine must get off at the third or fourth stop. Similarly, Rosa can't get off before Mineola (Rule 2), so Rosa will have to get off at the third or fourth stop, too. That leaves Vijay as the only passenger who can get off at the first stop:

1	2	3	4
L/S	S/L	F/M	M/F
v	g	j/r	r/j

Whenever Rosa gets off the van (third or fourth), it will have to be after the van stops at Simcoe (first or second). So, when the van reaches Simcoe, Rosa must still be on board, making **(C)** the correct answer. For the record:

Vijay is the first passenger to get off. That means he does not have to be on board when the bus reaches Los Altos or Simcoe—either of which could be the second stop. That eliminates **(A)** and **(B)**.

If Rosa gets off third at Mineola, then Fundy would be the last stop. Because Rosa doesn't have to be on board when the van reaches Fundy, that eliminates **(D)**.

If Jasmine gets off third at Fundy, then Mineola would be the last stop. Because Jasmine doesn't have to be on board when the van reaches Mineola, that eliminates **(E)**.

23. (D) "If" / Must Be False

For this question, Greg gets off the van before Simcoe. By Rule 4, that means that Jasmine must get off before Fundy. By Rule 3, Vijay must get off the van before Jasmine. Therefore, Vijay and Jasmine must both get off the van before it reaches Fundy:

$$
\begin{array}{c}
F \\
v \dots j
\end{array}
$$

That means **(D)** must be false, because Vijay couldn't possibly be on board the van when it reaches Fundy. For the record, the following sketch shows how **(A)**, **(B)**, and **(C)**, can all be possible:

PrepTest 56

The Inside Story

PrepTest 56 was administered in December 2008. It challenged 43,646 test takers. What made this test so hard? Here's a breakdown of what Kaplan students who were surveyed after taking the official exam considered PrepTest 56's most difficult section.

Hardest PrepTest 56 Section as Reported by Test Takers

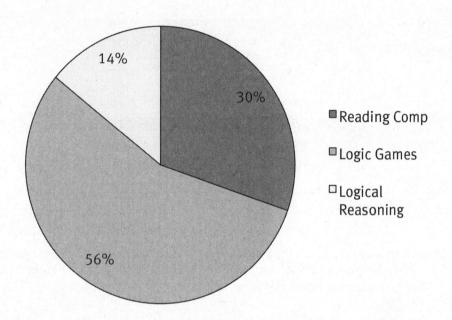

Based on these results, you might think that studying Logic Games is the key to LSAT success. Well, Logic Games is important, but test takers' perceptions don't tell the whole story. For that, you need to consider students' actual performance. The following chart shows the average number of students to miss each question in each of PrepTest 56's different sections.

Percentage Incorrect by PrepTest 56 Section Type

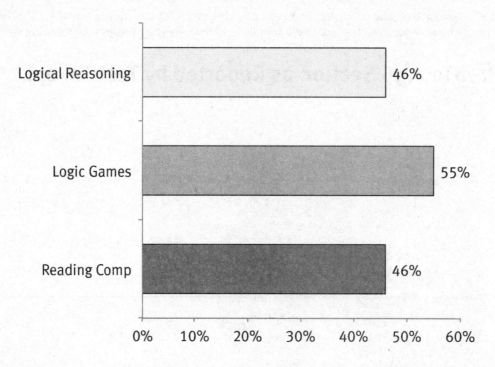

Actual student performance tells a somewhat different story. Although Logic Games was indeed higher in actual difficulty than Logical Reasoning and Reading Comprehension, because the Logic Games section has fewer questions than the other sections, students were missing about 12–13 questions in each individual section.

Maybe students overestimate the difficulty of the Logic Games section because it's so unusual, or maybe it's because a really hard Logic Game is so easy to remember after the test. But the truth is that the testmaker places hard questions throughout the test. Here were the locations of the 10 hardest (most missed) questions in the exam.

Location of 10 Most Difficult Questions in PrepTest 56

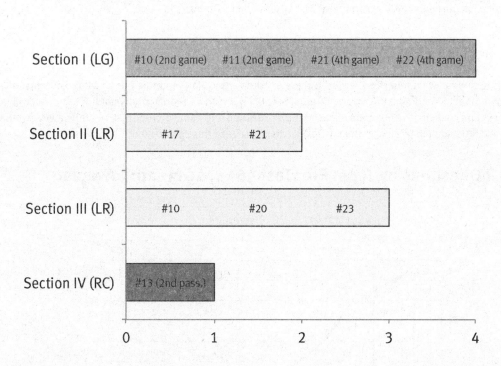

The takeaway from this data is that, to maximize your potential on the LSAT, you need to take a comprehensive approach. Test yourself rigorously, and review your performance on every section of the test. Kaplan's LSAT explanations provide the expertise and insight you need to fully understand your results. The explanations are written and edited by a team of LSAT experts, who have helped thousands of students improve their scores. Kaplan always provides data-driven analysis of the test, ranking the difficulty of every question based on actual student performance. The 10 hardest questions on every test are highlighted with a 4-star difficulty rating, the highest we give. The analysis breaks down the remaining questions into 1-, 2-, and 3-star ratings so that you can compare your performance to thousands of other test takers on all LSAC material.

Don't settle for wondering whether a question was really as hard as it seemed to you. Analyze the test with real data, and learn the secrets and strategies that help top scorers master the LSAT.

7 Can't-Miss Features of PrepTest 56

- Both Logical Reasoning sections began with a Flaw question. The only other PrepTests that have done that were PrepTest 19 (June 1996) and PrepTest 66 (June 2012).
- Multiple Matching games were common in the early days of the LSAT's current format (it happened three times from 1991–1993), but PrepTest 56 had two for just the third time since 1994.
- The first Matching game features the rare "if, but only if" Formal Logic structure. That structure first debuted in December 2004 (PT 45)—also in a Matching game.
- For the first time ever the Comparative Reading set of passages were the Law passage—although there was still a strong flavor of Social Science while discussing the definition of a "national minority."
- Historically (B), (C), and (D) have been ever so slightly more popular than (A) and (E) as answers. PrepTest 56 tried to even things up. Both (A) and (E) appeared at least 23 times and (B), (C), and (D) all appeared only 17 times.
- This was the first PrepTest administered following Barack Obama's election victory over John McCain.

- Section III, Question 24 talks about a radio station's "dismal ratings" and how it hasn't made any recent changes. Here's more bad news for the (fictional) radio station: PrepTest 56 was the first test students could prepare for while listening to Spotify, which launched a few days after PrepTest 55 was administered.

PrepTest 56 in Context

As much fun as it is to find out what makes a PrepTest unique or noteworthy, it's even more important to know just how representative it is of other LSAT administrations (and, thus, how likely it is to be representative of the exam you will face on Test Day). The following charts compare the numbers of each kind of question and game on PrepTest 56 to the average numbers seen on all officially released LSATs administered over the past five years (from 2013 through 2017).

Number of LR Questions by Type: PrepTest 56 vs. 2013–2017 Average

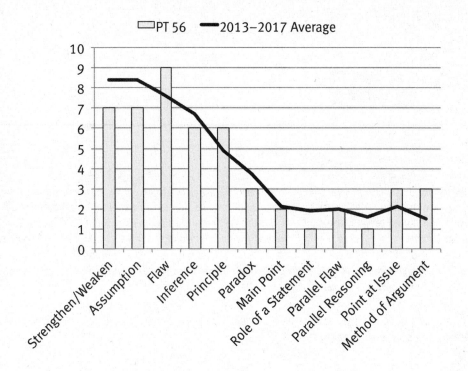

Number of LG Games by Type: PrepTest 56 vs. 2013–2017 Average

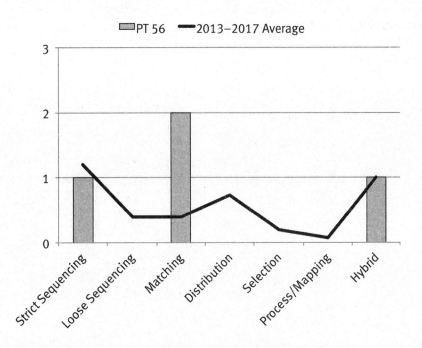

Number of RC Questions by Type: PrepTest 56 vs. 2013–2017 Average

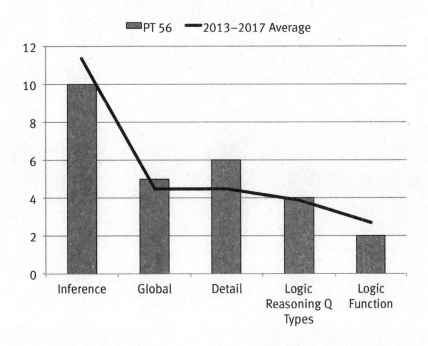

There isn't usually a huge difference in the distribution of questions from LSAT to LSAT, but if this test seems harder (or easier) to you than another you've taken, compare the number of questions of the types on which you, personally, are strongest and weakest. Then, explore within each section to see if your best or worst question types came earlier or later.

Students in Kaplan's comprehensive LSAT courses have access to every released LSAT and to a library of thousands of officially released questions arranged by question, game, and passage type. If you are studying on your own, you have to do a bit more work to identify your strengths and your areas of opportunity. Quantitative analysis (like that in the charts shown here) is an important tool for understanding how the test is constructed, and how you are performing on it.

Section I: Logic Games

Game 1: Saxophonist Auditions

Q#	Question Type	Correct	Difficulty
1	Acceptability	E	★
2	Must Be True	B	★★
3	Earliest	C	★★
4	Completely Determine	C	★★★
5	"If" / Could Be True	A	★★
6	Must Be True	E	★★★

Game 2: Furniture Moving

Q#	Question Type	Correct	Difficulty
7	Acceptability	A	★★
8	"If" / Must Be True	D	★★
9	"If" / Could Be True	B	★
10	Could Be True	B	★★★★
11	"If" / Could Be True	E	★★★★

Game 3: Parks and Trees

Q#	Question Type	Correct	Difficulty
12	Acceptability	D	★
13	Must Be True	C	★★★
14	"If" / Could Be True	A	★★
15	Must Be False	A	★
16	Could Be True	E	★★★

Game 4: Executive Site Visits at Manufacturing Plants

Q#	Question Type	Correct	Difficulty
17	Acceptability	A	★
18	"If" / Must Be True	A	★★
19	"If" / Could Be True	C	★★
20	Must Be False (CANNOT Be True)	D	★★★
21	"If" / Could Be True	E	★★★★
22	Must Be True	E	★★★★
23	"If" / Must Be True	B	★★★

Game 1: Saxophonist Auditions

Step 1: Overview

Situation: Six saxophonists auditioning, one at a time

Entities: Six saxophonists: Fujimura, Gabrieli, Herman, Jackson, King, Lauder

Action: Strict Sequencing. Your task is to decide in what order the saxophonists audition.

Limitations: Each saxophonist auditions exactly once. Each audition is scheduled to start every hour between the hours of 1 PM and 6 PM.

Step 2: Sketch

The setup makes clear that this game's action is Sequencing. Because there are rules (Rules 3 and 4, specifically) that determine the exact number of spaces between entities, use a Strict Sequencing sketch. Set up a row of six slots left to right and list the hours beneath them.

$$\frac{\text{F G H J K L}}{1 \quad 2 \quad 3 \quad 4 \quad 5 \quad 6}$$

Step 3: Rules

Rule 1 states that Jackson auditions earlier than Herman, but it doesn't tell you how much earlier. So, use an ellipsis between these two entities:

$$J \ldots H$$

Rule 2 is similar to Rule 1 but with different entities. It says that Gabrieli auditions earlier than King but doesn't indicate how much earlier. So, write it out the same way as Rule 1:

$$G \ldots K$$

Rule 3 creates a tighter Block of Entities than do Rules 1 and 2. Gabrieli will audition immediately before or immediately after Lauder. So, in any acceptable arrangement, you'll see this:

$$GL \text{ or } LG$$

Rule 4, like Rule 3, creates a tighter Block of Entities than Rules 1 and 2. Rule 4 states that Jackson and Lauder are separated by exactly one audition. Again, you don't know the order in which Jackson and Lauder appear, so have notation account for both possibilities.

$$J/L \_\_ L/J$$

Step 4: Deductions

As with any Strict Sequencing game, pay close attention to entities working together (Blocks of Entities) as well as entities that appear in more than one rule (Duplications).

Start with Rules 1 and 4 because both give information about Jackson. Rule 1's limitation can be incorporated with the two possibilities in Rule 4, so write down:

$$J \_\_ L$$
$$\therefore H$$
or
$$L \_\_ J \ldots H$$

Likewise, Rules 2 and 3 can be combined because both provide information about Gabrieli. When Rule 2's limitation is incorporated with the two possibilities in Rule 3, you can deduce the following:

$$GL \ldots K \text{ or } LG \ldots K$$

In Sequencing games, you should also consider which entities can go first and which can go last. Because Fujimura is not mentioned in any of the rules, Fujimura is not directly restricted from any position and is thus the Floater of the game.

So, Fujimura, Gabrieli, Jackson, and Lauder can go first, while Fujimura, Herman, and King can go last. Your Master Sketch should look roughly like this:

$$\frac{\text{F G H J K L}}{1 \quad 2 \quad 3 \quad 4 \quad 5 \quad 6}$$
$$GL \ldots K \text{ or } LG \ldots K$$
$$J \_\_ L$$
$$\therefore H$$
or
$$L \_\_ J \ldots H$$

Step 5: Questions

1. (E) Acceptability

For Acceptability questions, go through the rules one at a time, eliminating answers that violate the rules.

According to Rule 1, Jackson must audition before Herman. That eliminates **(D)**. Rule 2 states that Gabrieli must audition before King. That eliminates **(B)**. Rule 3 states that Gabrieli and Lauder must be immediately next to each other. **(A)** has Gabrieli and Lauder separated by three saxophonists, so eliminate that. Finally, for Rule 4, eliminate any answer choice that does not have Jackson and Lauder separated by exactly one saxophonist. **(C)** can be eliminated since it has two saxophonists between Jackson and Lauder. That leaves **(E)** as the only acceptable answer.

2. (B) Must Be True

The correct answer is the one that must be true in any acceptable arrangement. Take a brief look at your Master Sketch and note the key deductions. You know from combining Rules 2 and 3 that Lauder will always precede King. That leads directly to **(B)**.

You can also get to the correct answer by comparing each choice to the Master Sketch and eliminating those that could be false. Looking through the answer choices, only **(B)** must be true. For the record, **(A)** could be true as seen in the answer to the Acceptability question. **(C)** is incorrect because Jackson could audition at times besides 1 PM or 5 PM. For example, the sequence could be

F	J	G	L	H/K	K/H
1	2	3	4	5	6

(D) is proven incorrect based on that same sequence. **(E)** is also possible, but need not be true, as seen in a sequence such as

J	F/H	L	G	K	H/F
1	2	3	4	5	6

3. (C) Earliest

This question asks for the earliest possible audition for King. Based on initial deductions, the block of Gabrieli and Lauder must precede King, so that eliminates **(D)** and **(E)**. So, the earliest King can go without assessing the impact of Rules 1 and 4 is 3 PM. To confirm that this is possible, draw out a new sketch. Based on Rule 4, Jackson will have to occupy the 4 PM slot and Lauder will occupy the 2 PM slot. This puts Gabrieli in the 1 P.M. slot. The 5 PM and 6 PM slots can be occupied by Herman and Fujimura in either order. So the sketch looks like this:

G	L	K	J	H/F	F/H
1	2	3	4	5	6

Because no rules are violated by placing King in the 3 PM slot, **(C)** can be selected as the earliest time King's audition could be scheduled.

4. (C) Completely Determine

The correct answer here will allow for only one possible arrangement for all six entities. The wrong answer choices, on the other hand, will allow at least two of the entities to move among the spaces. When you need to test the choices one by one, do so strategically. The first choice relates to Herman, the next two to Jackson, and last two to Lauder. All three of these entities are restricted by the deduction linking Rules 1 and 4.

Of the three entities mentioned in the answers, Herman is the least restricted, since it just has to come later than Jackson. And indeed, testing **(A)** shows that it doesn't determine the order for all entities. With Herman in the 4 PM spot, Jackson and Lauder will take 1 PM and 3 PM, but they can do so in either order. Moreover, while this arrangement pushes Fujimura and King to the 5 and 6 PM spots, they too can swap order. Eliminate.

J/L	G	L/J	H	F/K	K/F
1	2	3	4	5	6

Now, note that **(B)** and **(D)** both involve the 1 PM spot. Whether you place Jackson or Lauder at 1 PM, the other entity takes the 3 PM spot. Either way, Herman is free to take any of the spots after Jackson. Wherever Herman goes, Fujimura (the Floater) is still free to move about too, so you know that neither of these answers determines the entire order. Eliminate both.

(C) is the next likely suspect. With Jackson scheduled for 5 PM, Herman must take the 6 PM spot and Lauder the 3 PM audition. Because Gabrieli must come sometime before King, Gabrieli cannot take the 4 PM slot and must therefore audition at 2 PM in order to fulfill Rule 3 and stay adjacent to Lauder. This, in turn, forces King into the 4 PM. slot. The only entity left is Fujimura, who, despite being the Floater, must occupy the 1 PM spot, the only audition time left. Thus, every saxophonist is assigned to one, and only one, audition time:

F	G	L	K	J	H
1	2	3	4	5	6

The condition in **(C)** completely determines the audition schedule, making **(C)** the correct answer choice. For the record:

According to **(E)**, Lauder auditions at 2 PM. That puts Jackson into the 4 PM audition. But, in this situation, Gabrieli can take the 1 PM or 3 PM auditions and still be okay under Rule 3. Eliminate **(E)**.

5. (A) "If" / Could Be True

This question states that Fujimura cannot audition at 1 PM So, this leaves two questions: (1) When can Fujimura audition? (2) Who else can audition at 1 PM?

Because Fujimura is a Floater, it remains unrestricted, so no huge deductions can be formed there. However, recall at the beginning the deduction that only Gabrieli, Jackson, and Lauder can go first in addition to Fujimura. At this point, it's worth drawing out the possible schedules for testing.

If Gabrieli is first, then Lauder must be second (Rule 3). That means Jackson must be fourth (Rule 4). Because Herman has to come after Jackson (Rule 1), the third audition can only be Fujimura or King. The remaining two auditions can be any of the remaining entities:

$$\frac{G}{1} \quad \frac{L}{2} \quad \frac{F/K}{3} \quad \frac{J}{4} \quad \frac{}{5} \quad \frac{}{6}$$

By this sketch alone, **(A)** is the only possible answer and can be confirmed by the following sketch:

$$\frac{G}{1} \quad \frac{L}{2} \quad \frac{F/K}{3} \quad \frac{J}{4} \quad \frac{K/F}{5} \quad \frac{H}{6}$$

For the record, the only other possible outcome would be Jackson or Lauder auditioning first, with the other saxophonist auditioning third (Rule 4). Depending on where Lauder auditions, Gabrieli can audition either second or fourth:

$$\frac{J/L}{1} \quad \frac{}{2} \quad \frac{L/J}{3} \quad \frac{}{4} \quad \frac{}{5} \quad \frac{}{6}$$

Once again, **(A)** is the only possible answer.

6. (E) Must Be True

When faced with a Must Be True question *without* a New-"If" clause, consider your initial deductions and previous sketches. The sketches for the previous two questions show Herman at 6 PM, so that eliminates **(C)**. Unfortunately, no other answers can be eliminated this way, and no other answers match initial deductions. So, be systematic and try testing the most limited entities first. Remember that you will eliminate any answer that can be false.

Because Gabrieli is mentioned in two rules, **(A)** is a good place to start. Consider if Gabrieli *must* audition before 5 PM. What if that were false and Gabrieli auditioned fifth? Then, King would audition sixth (Rule 2) and Lauder would be fourth (Rule 3). That would place Jackson second (Rule 4), leaving Herman the fourth audition (Rule 1). That leaves Fujimura as the only saxophonist who could audition first:

$$\frac{F}{1} \quad \frac{J}{2} \quad \frac{H}{3} \quad \frac{L}{4} \quad \frac{G}{5} \quad \frac{K}{6}$$

Because this is possible, Gabrieli doesn't *have* to be scheduled earlier than 5 PM, so that eliminates **(A)**. It also

eliminates **(D)** because King doesn't *have* to be scheduled earlier than 6 PM.

Of the remaining answers, **(E)** mentions Lauder, who is also limited by two rules. So this is next best choice to test. Once again, try to determine if this could be false. By the combination of Rules 2 and 3, Lauder cannot be last, so assign Lauder the 5 PM audition. This places Gabrieli at 4 PM and King at 6 PM. Jackson would have to be third (Rule 4). That would leave Fujimura and Herman for the first two auditions:

$$\frac{\cancel{H/F}}{1} \quad \frac{\cancel{F/H}}{2} \quad \frac{\cancel{J}}{3} \quad \frac{\cancel{G}}{4} \quad \frac{\cancel{L}}{5} \quad \frac{\cancel{K}}{6}$$

Unfortunately, this violates Rule 1. Thus, Lauder cannot be scheduled on or after 5 PM, so Lauder must always audition before 5 PM. That makes **(E)** the correct answer.

For the record, assigning Herman to the 2 PM audition would not violate any rules and would yield the following sketch:

$$\frac{J}{1} \quad \frac{H}{2} \quad \frac{L}{3} \quad \frac{G}{4} \quad \frac{K/F}{5} \quad \frac{F/K}{6}$$

That means Herman does not *have* to audition after 2 PM, eliminating **(B)**.

Game 2: Furniture Moving

Step 1: Overview

Situation: People helping move furniture

Entities: Four people (Grace, Heather, Josh, Maria) and three pieces of furniture (recliner, sofa, table)

Action: Matching. Assign pairs of people to move each piece of furniture. This is a straightforward Matching game because at least one entity will repeat.

Limitations: There will be six slots to fill: two slots for each piece of furniture. Each person will be matched up at least once. So, at least one person and at most two people will be assigned more than once.

Step 2: Sketch

With the numbers so definite, this game lends itself nicely to a column sketch. The sketch should be anchored around the three pieces of furniture, which will never change in number or kind. Two slots should then be drawn under each piece of furniture for each pair of movers. The initial sketch should look like so:

$$\begin{array}{c|c|c} \text{REC} & \text{SOF} & \text{TAB} \\ \hline \underline{} & \underline{} & \underline{} \\ \underline{} & \underline{} & \underline{} \end{array}$$

Step 3: Rules

Rule 1 is a Formal Logic statement that presents two rules in one. Statements with "if, but only if" (as well as "if, and only if") can be divided into two parts:

The first part requires that Grace move the sofa *if* Heather moves the recliner. Regardless of where *if* appears in a sentence, when it appears alone, it precedes a sufficient condition.

$$\frac{\text{REC}}{\text{H}} \longrightarrow \frac{\text{SOF}}{\text{G}}$$

The contrapositive prevents Heather from moving the recliner if Grace does not move the sofa. Write down this part of the rule like this:

$$\frac{\sim \text{SOF}}{\text{G}} \longrightarrow \frac{\sim \text{REC}}{\text{H}}$$

The second part of the rule requires that Grace move the sofa *only if* Heather moves the recliner. Recall that "only if" precedes the necessary result in a Formal Logic statement. The contrapositive prevents Grace from moving the sofa if Heather does not move the recliner. So, write down this part of the rule like this:

$$\frac{\text{SOF}}{\text{G}} \longrightarrow \frac{\text{REC}}{\text{H}}$$

$$\frac{\sim \text{REC}}{\text{H}} \longrightarrow \frac{\sim \text{SOF}}{\text{G}}$$

Before moving on, think about what these two rules mean in conjunction. If either Heather or Grace moves her respective piece of furniture, the other must as well. Conversely, if either one *doesn't*, the other won't either. In other words, either Heather and Grace will both move their respective pieces of furniture, or neither will.

Rule 2 is a simpler If/Then Formal Logic statement. Write out the original and contrapositive statement like so:

$$\frac{\text{TAB}}{\text{J}} \longrightarrow \frac{\text{REC}}{\text{M}}$$

$$\frac{\sim \text{REC}}{\text{M}} \longrightarrow \frac{\sim \text{TAB}}{\text{J}}$$

Rule 3 prohibits Grace and Josh from being paired up to move any piece of furniture. Note this as follows:

$$\text{NEVER}\ \boxed{\begin{array}{c}\text{G}\\\text{J}\end{array}}$$

Step 4: Deductions

When a majority of the rules are conditional statements, you need to ensure that you have correctly contraposed the statements. Keep an eye out for statements that can be combined. In this game, nothing definitively places any person with any piece of furniture. So be ready to let the new information in the questions lead to key deductions.

Step 5: Questions

7. (A) Acceptability

As always, running through the rules one at a time helps eliminate all the wrong answers. Because of the dense Formal Logic of the first rule, it's easier to start with simpler rules (like Rule 3) and work backward.

Rule 3 states that Grace and Josh can never move furniture together, so that eliminates **(B)**, which has them both moving the table. Rule 2 states that whenever Josh helps move the table, Maria must move the recliner. This eliminates **(C)** because Josh is moving the table without Maria moving the recliner. Finally, Rule 1, with its two rules in one, will likely eliminate the remaining two wrong answer choices. Remember, either Grace moves the sofa and Heather moves the recliner, or Grace doesn't move the sofa and Heather doesn't move the recliner. **(D)** can be eliminated because Heather is moving the recliner without Grace moving the sofa. Likewise, eliminate **(E)** because Grace is moving the sofa without Heather moving the recliner. That leaves **(A)** as the correct answer.

8. (D) "If" / Must Be True

If Josh and Maria move the recliner, the contrapositive for Rule 1 kicks in: Heather is not moving the recliner, which mandates that Grace not move the sofa. But Grace *must* move at least one piece of furniture, so she must move the table. A quick scan of the answer choices leads to **(D)**—a perfect match to the big deduction!

REC	SOF	TAB
J	—	G
M	—	—

(A) might be true but doesn't have to be. Heather could move the sofa, but she might only move the table. That would leave Josh and Maria to move the sofa, which is a perfectly valid sketch.

(B) might be true but doesn't have to be. Josh is already moving the recliner and doesn't have to move anything else.

(C) could be true but doesn't have to be. Maria is already moving the recliner and doesn't have to move anything else.

(E) could also be true but doesn't have to be. Heather could move the sofa instead, along with Josh or Maria, thereby leaving Maria to move the table with Grace.

9. (B) "If" / Could Be True

For this question, Heather is a repeating furniture mover—in fact she moves everything! That means the remaining three people will each move one piece of furniture. By Rule 1, because Heather is moving the recliner, Grace must move the sofa. That leaves Josh and Maria to help with the recliner and table, in either order:

REC	SOF	TAB
H	H	H
J/M	G	M/J

That leaves **(B)** as the only possible answer. **(A)**, **(C)**, **(D)**, and **(E)** all must be false based on the sketch.

10. (B) Could Be True

At first glance, it appears that trial and error is necessary. However, Rule 3 removes two answer choices immediately from consideration. Grace and Josh will never be paired up to move furniture, so **(A)** can be eliminated. Likewise, if Heather and Maria are paired up to move two pieces of furniture, that

will force Grace and Josh to move the third piece of furniture together. Eliminate **(D)**. After strategically narrowing down the answer choices, now you can try out the remaining contenders.

Incorporating **(B)** will force Heather and Josh to move the sofa together:

REC	SOF	TAB
G	H	G
M	J	M

This does not violate any of the rules, so **(B)** is the correct answer.

For the record, **(C)** will force Grace and Maria to move the sofa. The problem here stems from Rule 2. With Josh moving the table, Maria must move the recliner. Eliminate.

(E) will force both Grace and Heather to move only the sofa. This violates Rule 1's requirement that Heather moves the recliner whenever Grace moves the sofa. Eliminate.

11. (E) "If" / Could Be True

Assigning Josh and Maria to move the sofa will trigger Rule 1's contrapositive: Grace is not moving the sofa, which mandates that Heather not move the recliner. But Heather *must* move at least one piece of furniture, so she must move the table. Additionally, because Heather does not move the recliner, two of the three of Grace, Josh, and Maria must. Grace and Josh can never move furniture together, so the recliner will be moved by Maria and one of Grace or Josh:

REC	SOF	TAB
M	J	H
G/J	M	—

That is as far as you can deduce. The sketch eliminates **(A)** and **(B)**, which both have Heather moving the recliner. **(C)** and **(D)** are not possible because Heather is for sure one of the two people moving the table, not to mention in **(C)**, in light of Rule 3, Grace and Josh can never be paired up. That leaves only **(E)** as possible.

Game 3: Parks and Trees

Step 1: Overview
Situation: Planting varieties of trees in two public parks

Entities: Two public parks (Graystone and Landing) and four kinds of trees (maples, oaks, sycamores, tamaracks)

Action: Matching. You need to match each park with which of the four types of trees it has. A type of tree can be at more than one park, but doesn't *have* to be at any park.

You could also construe this as a double Selection game where you select which three of four types of tree each park has. Nonetheless, how you characterize the game is less important than being able to understand the rules and build them into a helpful Master Sketch.

Limitations: From the introduction, there are no numeric limitations. Each park can have any number of trees, and trees can appear in one park or both—or possibly neither! Don't assume all trees must be used. A quick glance at Rule 1 gives a definite assignment of the number of trees to each park, which will help in setting up the sketch. Going through the remaining rules, look for limitations on which trees can be planted in the same park together.

Step 2: Sketch
Use a standard Matching column sketch with the roster of entities above to yield the following:

M O S T

GRAY	LAND
—	—
—	—
—	—

If you had viewed the game as a double Selection game, you would set the sketch up by listing each of the two parks along with the potential roster of entities at each park. Then each type of tree would get circled or crossed out as with any typical Selection game:

Gray: M O S T
Land: M O S T

The remainder of the explanations will continue with just the Matching sketch.

Step 3: Rules
Rule 1 assigns *exactly* three trees per park. If you hadn't already built this into your sketch, now is the time. Also be sure to take note of how this limits the numbers. With a total of six spaces and only four types of trees, at least two tree

varieties will be duplicated, meaning at least two types of trees will appear in both parks.

Rule 2 suggests the possibility of Limited Options. Note this rule in shorthand for now and come back to it in Step 4.

At least one park: MS

Rule 3 provides a conditional statement, common to Selection games. Use your Formal Logic skills to translate and contrapose this statement as follows:

$$\text{If } O \longrightarrow T$$
$$\text{If } \sim T \longrightarrow \sim O$$

Rule 4 gives a definite assignment. Place an M under Graystone Park in your Master Sketch.

Step 4: Deductions
Revisit Rule 2 to see what can be gleaned from that information. Because there are only two parks, there are two possibilities: Either Graystone or Landing will have both maples and sycamores. This sets up Limited Options like so:

Option 1:

GRAY	LAND
M	—
S	—
—	—

Option 2:

GRAY	LAND
M	M
—	S
—	—

Note that each option also includes the possibility that *both* parks will boast maples and sycamores.

Now, think about Rule 3. In order for oaks to be planted in a park, there must also be tamaracks. That means if oaks are planted, two slots must be available. Because each park can only have three types of trees, the park that already has both maples and sycamores will *never* have oaks. So the third tree in that park will always have to be the only remaining variety: tamaracks.

Think through this a bit more. Every park that has oaks planted in it will also have tamaracks. Any park that *doesn't* have oaks planted in it will always have the remaining three varieties of trees—including tamaracks. So, it can be deduced that, no matter what, each park *must* have tamaracks planted in it. Adding in this information results in two solid options:

Option 1:

GRAY	LAND
M	—
S	—
T	T

Option 2:

GRAY	LAND
M	M
—	S
T	T

If O $\longrightarrow$ T
If ~T $\longrightarrow$ ~O

Step 5: Questions

12. (D) Acceptability

As with any Acceptability question, attack each of the rules eliminating any answers that violate one. Rule 1 requires that each park be planted with exactly three trees. No answer violates that rule. Rule 2 requires at least one park have both maples and sycamores. **(B)** has neither park with sycamores. Eliminate. Rule 3 requires that any park with oaks also have tamaracks. In **(A)**, Graystone and Landing have oaks but do not also have tamaracks. In **(C)**, Landing has oaks but no tamaracks. Eliminate **(A)** and **(C)**. Finally, Rule 4 indicates Graystone Park has maples. However, in **(E)** it does not. Eliminate. That leaves **(D)** as the correct answer.

13. (C) Must Be True

With Limited Options, remember the correct answer to a "Must Be True" question is definitely true in *both* options. Once again, keep in mind the major deduction of this game: both parks must have tamaracks. That immediately leads you to **(C)**. For the record:

(A) and **(B)** assign a tree variety that could be included but, according to the Limited Options sketches, doesn't need to be. On Must Be True questions, something that is merely possible is not enough.

(D) and **(E)** are numerically possible but, again, not necessarily true.

14. (A) "If" / Could Be True

For this question, both parks are planted with sycamores. This is possible in either option, so consider redrawing both options with the new information. Adding a sycamore to Landing in the first option leaves one more space in Landing,

which could be filled by either maples or oaks. Adding a sycamore to Graystone in the second option fills the sketch completely:

Option I:

GRAY	LAND
M	S
S	M/O
T	T

Option II:

GRAY	LAND
M	M
S	S
T	T

The correct answer only needs to be possible in one of the options. Eliminate the answer choices that are impossible in both options. **(A)** could be true in the first option, if the third variety under Landing is oaks. Then maples and oaks would each appear in exactly one park. Thus, **(A)** is possible and the correct answer.

For the record, because both parks will have sycamores in this scenario, it is impossible to have more maples than sycamores planted. This eliminates **(B)**. It is also impossible to have the same number of oaks as sycamores planted. If sycamores are in both parks, then oaks would need to be in both parks, which can't happen because at least one park will always have maples, sycamores, and tamaracks. This eliminates **(C)**. **(D)** is impossible because in both options Graystone has only the tree varieties of maples, sycamores, and tamaracks. Likewise, Landing only has the option of maples *or* oaks in the first option, never both, which eliminates **(E)**.

15. (A) Must Be False

With Limited Options, something that Must Be False has to be impossible in both options. If an answer is possible in either option, then it must be eliminated,

Looking at both options, maples, sycamores, and tamaracks will be the three trees planted in at least one of the parks. So, it is impossible for both parks to have oaks, as **(A)** says, in either option. Thus, **(A)** must be false and is the correct answer choice.

Even if you didn't get the Limited Options in the beginning, you can still use your deductive reasoning skills to answer this question quickly and efficiently by combining Rules 2 and

3. If at least one park is planted with sycamores and maples *and* any park planted with oaks must be planted with tamaracks, then it's impossible for the park planted with sycamores and maples to have oaks, too, as that would require a fourth tree: tamaracks. Thus, at least one park will never have oaks. **(A)** is impossible. **(B)**, **(D)**, and **(E)** all could be possible, according to your sketch, while **(C)** is your big deduction and must be *true*, not false.

16. (E) Could Be True

With Limited Options, the correct answer to a Could Be True merely needs to be possible in either option. Only eliminate answers that cannot happen in both options. Using previous work can also sometimes help verify the correct answer.

Because one park in each option contains maples, sycamores, and tamaracks, oaks are limited to one park. There will always be two parks with tamaracks, so it is impossible to have an equal number of parks with oaks and tamaracks. This eliminates **(A)**. Similarly, at least one park will always have sycamores planted in it. So, it's impossible for oaks to outnumber sycamores. Eliminate **(B)**.

From the earlier big deduction, both parks must have tamaracks. That eliminates **(C)** and **(D)**. That leaves **(E)** as the only possible answer choice. This can be verified by looking at the second sketch of the third question of the set.

Game 4: Executive Site Visits at Manufacturing Plants

Step 1: Overview
Situation: Executives visiting their company's three manufacturing plant sites on different days

Entities: Five executives (Quinn, Rodriguez, Sasada, Taylor, Vandercar) and three sites (Farmington, Homestead, Morningside)

Action: Distribution/Sequencing Hybrid. Each executive must visit a manufacturing plant on one of three days. The three sites will be sequenced, and the executives will be distributed into the three sites.

Limitations: Each executive will be assigned to exactly one site and each site will be assigned at least one executive. What is not known is exactly how many executives visit each site and in what order the sites are visited.

Step 2: Sketch
Keep track of your minimums and allow for the "outliers" to be incorporated into your sketch. As with any Hybrid game, your goal is always to incorporate both actions into a single sketch.

Anchor your sketch around the three days and then place two rows below each day: the top for the sites and the bottom for the visiting executives. Because each site must be visited by at least one executive, all three days will include at least one slot. However, because there are five executives and only three site visits, one or two of the visits will include *more* than one executive. Don't forget to keep track of the slots for the two additional executives:

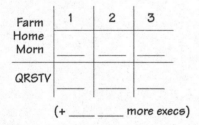

Step 3: Rules
Rule 1 affects the Sequencing action in the game, requiring that the Farmington site be visited before the Homestead site. Recall that Blocks of Entities can yield Limited Options, so you will want to refer back to this rule in Step 4. For now, note as such:

Farm . . . Home

Rule 2 is immensely helpful in narrowing down the numbers options. Knowing that one site—Farmington—will only have one visiting executive, you can deduce that the other two will either have two visiting executives each or one site will have

one visiting executive while the other has three. Come back to this once more information is gathered. For now, note as such:

Farm: Exactly 1 EXEC

Rule 3 affects both the Sequencing and Distribution actions in the game but should still be incorporated into one notation as such:

Note that even though three executives are listed in this sequence, they do not have to be assigned to three different days. While that would be possible, nothing in the rule prevents Rodriguez and Taylor from visiting a site on the same day. However, it's helpful to note in your sketch that Quinn cannot visit the site on day three, and Rodriguez and Taylor cannot visit the site on day one.

Rule 4 shouldn't be rushed, as it's easy to mistranslate. Although Sasada's visit cannot take place *after* Vandercar's site visit, that doesn't mean Sasada's visit *must* be before Vandercar's. While that is possible, nothing prevents Sasada from visiting the *same* site as Vandercar. Be sure to note both possibilities as such:

SV or S . . . V

Unlike in the previous rule, neither Sasada nor Vandercar can be excluded from any day's visit because they can each visit any site together, except Farmington (Rule 2).

Also note that every entity has a condition placed on it, so there are no Floaters.

Step 4: Deductions
As stated earlier, think about how the Block of Entities in Rule 1 can set up Limited Options. Farmington can never be last because Homestead must follow it. So, Farmington can be only the first or second site visited. This can be broken out into two options. In the first option, if Farmington is on day one, then the remaining two days will be Homestead and Morningside, in either order. In the second option, with Farmington on day two, Homestead must be on day three. That leaves Morningside for day one.

For both options, consider Rule 2's number breakdown. Close off Farmington in each option so that it only gets one slot, still being flexible with the two outlier entities. Finally, in the first option Vandercar cannot be the lone executive at Farmington (Rule 4). Vandercar must be with, or after, Sasada.

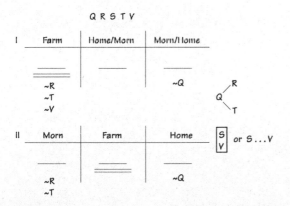

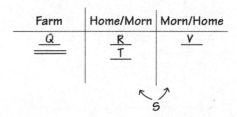

Step 5: Questions

17. (A) Acceptability

Even with a challenging Hybrid game, Acceptability questions can be deftly handled by going through the rules one at a time, eliminating answers that violate the rules.

Rule 1 is easy to test: Farmington must always be scheduled for a site visit before Homestead. Farmington is scheduled *after* Homestead in **(D)**, so eliminate that answer. Rule 2 requires that Farmington has only one visiting executive. **(E)** clearly violates that rule by scheduling both Rodriguez and Sasada for a visit to Farmington.

Continuing on, Quinn must visit a site *before* both Rodriguez and Taylor, but **(C)** has Quinn visiting a site after Rodriguez and with Taylor; eliminate that. In **(B)**, Sasada visits a site after Vandercar, which violates Rule 4. That answer can be eliminated. That leaves **(A)** as the only answer that doesn't violate any of the rules.

18. (A) "If" / Must Be True

There are two clues in the New-"If" clause for this question that should enable you to make some quick deductions. First, there are two executives—Rodriguez and Taylor—visiting the second site. Thus, the second site cannot be Farmington. This means Farmington must be the first site visited, which occurs only in the first option.

Second, Rodriguez and Taylor must follow Quinn's site visit, so that means Quinn will visit the first site, which is Farmington. That means Quinn will be alone. At this point, these deductions already lead to **(A)** as the correct answer.

If you had not already checked the answers for a "must be true" deduction, you could have continued making further deductions. Rule 4 prohibits Sasada from visiting a site after Vandercar. Coupled with the numbers requirement that at least one executive must visit each site, it can be deduced that Vandercar *must* visit day three's site, either with Sasada or without. Sasada will make a site visit on day two or day three:

For the record, either Homestead or Morningside could be the site Vandercar visits on day three, which makes **(B)** possible but not definite. Eliminate. Likewise, **(C)** is merely possible, since Sasada can visit either Homestead or Morningside. Eliminate. **(D)** gives only one of the two times when Sasada can visit a site, which means it's possible but not required. Eliminate. Finally, Sasada's maneuverability means the second of the three site visits could include exactly three of the executives or it could include just two—Rodriguez and Taylor. Eliminate **(E)**.

19. (C) "If" / Could Be True

The correct answer will be the only one possible. All the remaining answers will be false. Quinn must visit before Rodriguez and Taylor, while Sasada can never be preceded by Vandercar. Because none of the three other entities can come before both Quinn and Sasada, the pair must visit the site on day one.

Additionally, since the first option allows for only *one* executive on the first site visit, you must work with the second option. That means Quinn and Sasada visit Morningside.

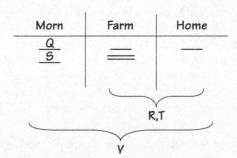

That eliminates **(A)** and **(B)** because the order in option two is Morningside, Farmington, and then Homestead. Because Farmington is second, the second site visit will include only one executive, which eliminates **(E)**. Sasada on day one eliminates **(D)**. That leaves only **(C)**.

(C) is possible if Vandercar is the executive who visits Farmington alone on day two. This would force Rodriguez and Taylor into day three in accordance with Rule 3:

Morn	Farm	Home
Q	V	R
S		T

Farm	Home	Morn
S	Q	R
═══	V	T

Farm	Home	Morn
Q	S	R
═══	T	V

Thus, **(C)** is the correct answer.

20. (D) Must Be False (CANNOT Be True)

For this question, the correct answer will be impossible in light of the rules. Because there are Limited Options, each answer choice has to be tested against *both* options before ruling it out. Furthermore, because there are few deductions about Homestead, it might be worth skipping this question at first to draw more possible outcomes. These can help eliminate answers that are, indeed, possible.

Even without skipping, you can use sketches from previous questions. The second question of the set's sketch shows two possible outcomes if Homestead is on day two: just Rodriguez and Taylor, which eliminates **(B)**, or Rodriguez and Taylor with Sasada, which eliminates **(E)**. If you temporarily skipped this question, you'd be rewarded with a sketch in the last question for this game that shows it is possible for Quinn and Vandercar to visit Homestead, which would eliminate **(A)**.

Whether you skipped or not, you can work efficiently by dealing with repeated restricted entities in the answers. **(A)** and **(D)** both include Quinn, who can never visit a site on day three because Rodriguez and Taylor must follow. Because Homestead can be visited only on the second or third days, that means Quinn can only visit Homestead on day two, which is possible only in the first option. That forces Rodriguez and Taylor into day three. That leaves Sasada or Vandercar for Farmington on the first day. However, Vandercar cannot precede Sasada, so it must be Sasada who goes to Farmington. Therefore, Quinn will never visit Homestead with Sasada. That means **(D)** is impossible and thus the correct answer.

You could verify **(A)** and **(C)** with additional sketches. However, once you've found something impossible, don't waste time on Test Day trying to prove every other answer is possible. That being said, for the record, here are sketches that verify **(A)** and **(C)** as possible:

21. (E) "If" / Could Be True

According to this question, Morningside will be visited by both Quinn and Vandercar. Quinn can only be scheduled for days one or two. Morningside can be day two in the first option and day one in the second option. The correct answer merely has to be possible in one of these options.

In the first option, Morningside will be scheduled for day two, visited by Quinn and Vandercar. Keep Rule 3 in mind, recalling that Rodriguez and Taylor must visit a site *after* Quinn, which will be Homestead in day three. That only leaves Sasada to visit Farmington on day one:

Opt. I

Farm	Morn	Home
S	Q	R
	V	T

A quick scan of the answer choices reveals no answer that is possible in this sketch. So, fill in the second option. Morningside will be visited first by Quinn and Vandercar. Pay close attention to Rule 4. Sasada can never visit a site after Vandercar. So, because Vandercar is visiting Morningside on day one, Sasada will have to visit Morningside on day one, as well. That leaves Rodriguez and Taylor to visit Farmington and Homestead on days two and three, in either order.

Opt. II

Morn	Farm	Home
Q	R/T	T/R
V	═══	
S		

(E) is the only possible answer, making it the correct answer. **(A)**, **(B)**, **(C)**, and **(D)** are all impossible based on the sketches.

22. (E) Must Be True

For an answer choice to be correct, it must be true in both options. Compare each one by one. You can also use your previous work to eliminate answers that could be false.

Option II allows for Farmington to be visited on day two, after Morningside and by only one executive. Eliminate **(A)** and **(D)**. This was also seen in the second sketch of the previous question.

Neither option suggests Vandercar must visit a site earlier than Rodriguez. Furthermore, the correct answer to the Acceptability question shows Vandercar visiting Morningside on day three *after* Rodriguez visits Homestead on day two. Eliminate **(B)**.

Remember that because of the way Rule 4 is phrased, Sasada could visit any site *with* Vandercar, including the one visited third. This is also verified by the sketch for the second question of the set, which shows Sasada can visit Morningside or Homestead on day three. Eliminate **(C)**.

That leaves **(E)** as the only possible correct answer choice. It's verified in both options. Farmingdale must be one of the first two sites visited, and it includes only one executive.

23. (B) "If" / Must Be True

The correct answer to this question must be true in both sketches, so you will need to draw both options out. This question schedules Sasada to visit Farmington, which can be true in either option. In addition to this new information, remember that Sasada cannot visit a site after Vandercar. Because only one executive can visit Farmington, Vandercar will have to visit a site after Sasada. Vandercar can visit either the second or third site in the first option, and must visit the third site in the second option.

In addition, Quinn can only visit a site on days one or two, in order to abide by Rule 3 and visit a site before Rodriguez and Taylor. So, in the first option, Quinn must visit the second site, with Rodriguez and Taylor visiting the third. In the second option, Quinn will visit the first site, again putting Rodriguez and Taylor on day three:

Opt. I

Farm	Home/Morn	Morn/Home
S	Q	R
===		T

Opt. II

Morn	Farm	Home
Q	S	R
	===	T
		V

In either option, Rodriguez and Taylor will always be scheduled to visit the third site. This leads to **(B)**.

For the record, **(A)** is required in the Option II, but only possible in Option I. Meanwhile, **(C)**, **(D)**, and **(E)** are possible only in Option I and therefore could be false.

Section II: Logical Reasoning

Q#	Question Type	Correct	Difficulty
1	Flaw	E	★
2	Point at Issue (Agree)	A	★
3	Weaken	B	★
4	Assumption (Necessary)	C	★
5	Flaw	E	★
6	Assumption (Necessary)	E	★
7	Parallel Flaw	C	★
8	Weaken	D	★★
9	Method of Argument	B	★★★
10	Assumption (Sufficient)	D	★
11	Method of Argument	B	★
12	Flaw	E	★
13	Paradox	A	★
14	Strengthen	D	★★
15	Flaw	B	★★
16	Principle (Identify/Strengthen)	D	★★
17	Point at Issue	E	★★★★
18	Principle (Parallel)	C	★
19	Inference	A	★★
20	Principle (Identify/Assumption)	E	★★★
21	Point at Issue	B	★★★★
22	Paradox	C	★★
23	Inference	E	★★★
24	Strengthen	A	★★★
25	Role of a Statement	B	★★★

1. (E) Flaw

Step 1: Identify the Question Type

The phrase "most vulnerable to criticism" is common language for a Flaw question. Look for the unwarranted assumption or the common LSAT flaw.

Step 2: Untangle the Stimulus

The author concludes swimming at night is not more dangerous than swimming during the day based on one piece of evidence: all recent regional shark attacks have occurred during the day, not at night. The author uses this to challenge the general preference—stated in the first sentence—of the region's swimmers to swim in the daytime.

Step 3: Make a Prediction

The problem here is the completeness of the author's evidence. More attacks may be occurring during the day, but that's simply because that's also the time most people are swimming. The author overlooks that an increase in night swimming could increase the likelihood of shark attacks at night. After all, if no one's currently in the water at night, the sharks have no one to attack. If the number of swimmers were equal at all times, then it's possible the number of attacks *would* show swimming at night is more dangerous.

Step 4: Evaluate the Answer Choices

(E) matches the prediction.

(A) might be true but is not a logical flaw in the argument. *Some* sharks may prefer to hunt at night, but that doesn't hurt the author's argument. *Most* sharks may prefer to hunt in the daytime. Therefore, the author's argument could still be correct.

(B) goes Outside the Scope because the source of the author's evidence is never identified.

(C) is Outside the Scope because the author is solely focused on the actual danger posed by shark attacks. People may feel more anxious because of the dark, but the author is not suggesting people should swim at night (if she was, this would be good reason why his recommendation is flawed); she's simply saying it's not more dangerous.

(D) also goes Outside the Scope by attacking the swimmers themselves, focusing on how knowledgeable they are. Granted, the author says popular opinion is wrong, but she is basing her conclusion on statistics, not the assumption that others are simply less knowledgeable and therefore incorrect. This stimulus does not include an ad hominem attack.

2. (A) Point at Issue (Agree)

Step 1: Identify the Question Type

The typical Point at Issue question asks for something about which two speakers disagree. But this question stem asks what Denise and Reshmi *agree* upon, so it is a variation on a regular Point at Issue question. Take a moment to characterize the answer choices. The correct answer will be a point of agreement. Thus, the four wrong answer choices will be points of disagreement or Outside the Scope of at least one speaker's argument.

Step 2: Untangle the Stimulus

First, summarize each speaker's argument. Denise begins by claiming that a reduction in crime requires punishment be both reliable and harsh enough to serve as a deterrent. Reshmi responds that crime can most effectively be reduced if everyone had access to educational opportunities, which would provide alternatives to a criminal lifestyle.

Step 3: Make a Prediction

Denise and Reshmi disagree about what methods would reduce crime. However, because they are bothering to discuss ways crime could be reduced, they must therefore both agree crime is reducible in the first place. Both arguments mention possible criminals making a conscious choice or decision not to commit a crime. They must therefore agree people can make such choices

Step 4: Evaluate the Answer Choices

(A) matches the prediction by suggesting that people have control over committing crimes and are not just acting out of some sort of overwhelming compulsion.

(B) is Extreme because neither Denise nor Reshmi says crime is the "most" important social issue.

(C) matches Denise's argument but fails to match Reshmi's.

(D) is Outside the Scope because it discusses economic need, which neither Denise nor Reshmi address. Arguably, Reshmi's mention of educational opportunities and a comfortable lifestyle indirectly touch on this, but Denise's argument does not.

(E) again, like **(C)**, matches Denise's argument but fails to match Reshmi's. That both choices are so similar indicates that both are wrong.

3. (B) Weaken

Step 1: Identify the Question Type

The phrase "most weakens the reasoning" indicates this is a Weaken question. Identify the conclusion, paraphrase the evidence, spot the assumption, and then look for an answer choice that would invalidate that assumption and make the conclusion less likely to be true.

Step 2: Untangle the Stimulus

The conclusion is the first sentence: unskilled workers have great advancement opportunities at Acme Corporation. As the Keyphrase "[a]s evidence" suggests, everything else that follows is evidence. The evidence is the single example of Ms. Garon, who rose from assembly line worker to Acme's president.

Step 3: Make a Prediction

"Unskilled workers," the group in the author's conclusion, is much broader than Ms. Garon, the specific example in the evidence. The author must therefore assume that Ms. Garon's experience is relevant to other unskilled workers. But look at the jump in terms: the conclusion discusses unskilled *workers*, whereas the evidence discusses unskilled *positions*. The weakener will likely suggest that Ms. Garon, while at one time holding an unskilled position, is unlike the average unskilled worker at Acme.

Step 4: Evaluate the Answer Choices

(B) gives a reason to believe that while Ms. Garon briefly worked as an assembly line worker, she may have actually been a top graduate from business school, destined to fill a management position. In other words, while she may have held an entry-level position, she wasn't actually an unskilled worker, and therefore her example is not valid evidence for the conclusion.

(A) is a 180. It actually strengthens the author's argument by providing an additional example of an entry-level worker who was able to rise to a position of status.

(C) is an Irrelevant Comparison. The author's argument isn't concerned with how often Acme promotes from the inside versus hires from the outside, but on whether good opportunities exist for unskilled workers. This comparison doesn't have the correct focus on unskilled workers. The author's focus, in contrast, is on whether or not the people promoted started as unskilled workers. If these in-house promotions are indeed from unskilled workers up to management, that would strengthen the argument, which would still be incorrect.

(D) goes Outside the Scope because how long Ms. Garon worked at Acme has nothing to do with how representative her success story is for the average unskilled worker at Acme.

(E) makes an Irrelevant Comparison focusing on what Acme pays entry-level employees compared to other businesses. This is irrelevant to how likely those employees are to advance at Acme.

4. (C) Assumption (Necessary)

Step 1: Identify the Question Type

Because the stem asks for the assumption the argument makes, this is an Assumption question. Additionally, because this assumption is definitely made, you are looking for a Necessary Assumption. Bracket the conclusion, paraphrase the evidence, and pinpoint the gap between the two.

Step 2: Untangle the Stimulus

The author opens with a lot of background information, but the Contrast Keyword [*h*]*owever* signals a shift to the argument. Yellow warblers' special molting song keeps other warblers out of their core territory. Also, during molting, they

can only fly short distances. Because of both of these facts, the author concludes that while molting, yellow warblers have no competition for food within their range of flight.

Step 3: Make a Prediction

The author makes two assumptions, one of which will be the correct answer. First, the evidence discusses warblers' restricted flying range, whereas the evidence mentions the core territory. The author assumes that the molting warblers' flying range does not exceed their core territory. Second, while the author's evidence demonstrates that yellow warblers don't mess with molting warblers' turf, that still leaves a lot of other animals that might compete for the food supply. In order for the author to be completely certain that yellow warblers have no competition for their food during molting, he needs to rule out the possibility than any other animal could be a competitor.

Step 4: Evaluate the Answer Choices

(C) rules out all the other birds from competition with the yellow warblers.

(A) goes Outside the Scope because it focuses on the amount of food, rather than the competition for it.

(B) goes Outside the Scope because it also fails to discuss the competition for food. Additionally, the author need not make an Extreme assumption that warblers are unique in how they lay claim to core areas.

(D) is a 180. While the "other kinds of birds" mentioned in this answer choice do not usually compete with warblers for food, the use of "often" implies that *sometimes* they do. Yet the author says warblers have *no* competition for food.

(E) goes Outside the Scope by focusing on the size of the feeding areas. Even if the areas are all different sizes the conclusion could still follow. The size of the area is immaterial; the focus of the argument is on competition *within* the area.

5. (E) Flaw

Step 1: Identify the Question Type

The question stem asks for the flaw Lana points out in Chinh's argument, so this is a Flaw question. Use Lana's comments to direct your evaluation of Chinh's argument. Keep an eye out for common flaw types.

Step 2: Untangle the Stimulus

Start by summarizing each argument. Chinh's conclusion is that TV producers should disregard the preferences of the viewers when making creative decisions. Chinh's evidence is that great painters don't think about what the public wants to see. Lana contradicts Chinh by introducing a new point about TV: it is made for the public. From there, Lana suggests that TV producers are more like CEOs than artists. This supports her recommendation that TV producers should consider the preferences of viewers.

Step 3: Make a Prediction

Both speakers use an analogy for their evidence. Chinh thinks TV producers are like great painters, whereas Lana thinks TV producers are like CEOs. Whenever an author uses an analogy for evidence, the author assumes the two things in the analogy are sufficiently alike to be comparable. So, Chinh's assumption is TV producers are sufficiently similar to great painters. Lana's assumption is TV producers and CEOs are sufficiently alike. Lana's disagreement with Chinh's argument is the choice of analogy; she essentially says TV producers and artists are not sufficiently alike for Chinh to use evidence about one to draw a conclusion about the other.

Step 4: Evaluate the Answer Choices

(E) is a short and sweet match to the prediction.

(A) describes a circular reasoning flaw, which is very rarely the correct answer to a Flaw question. Circular reasoning describes an argument that uses the same idea for both evidence and conclusion. Here, Lana doesn't argue Chinh's evidence is the same as Chinh's conclusion; instead she debates the relevance of the evidence.

(B) describes a representativeness flaw, which isn't occurring here. Both Lana and Chinh's arguments address the "viewing public" as a whole, which is a perfectly representative group of consumers. Lana doesn't critique Chinh's sample selection.

(C) says Chinh incorrectly infers that a causal relationship is intentional. However, Chinh's argument is a recommendation based on an analogy, not any sort of cause-and-effect relationship.

(D) may be a flaw that Chinh commits, but the question stem asks for how Lana addresses Chinh's argument. Lana suggests that Chinh is wrong about TV producers, not about painters. Lana doesn't think TV producers should be compared to painters at all, and therefore painters' objectives are irrelevant.

6. (E) Assumption (Necessary)

Step 1: Identify the Question Stem

Because the question asks for an assumption, this is an Assumption question. Additionally, because the assumption is *required*, the answer will be a necessary assumption, one without which the conclusion could not follow. Break down the argument into conclusion and evidence and look for the gap between the two. You can use the Denial Test to check or confirm answer choices.

Step 2: Untangle the Stimulus

The dietitian concludes that individuals who are more susceptible to heart disease as a result of high sodium intake

should eat fresh fruit and vegetables rather than canned or frozen fruit and vegetables. The dietician bases her conclusion on the single piece of evidence that potassium in plant foods—such as fruits and vegetables—helps prevent sodium's bad effects.

Step 3: Make a Prediction

Given that the dietitian recommends fresh produce over canned or frozen produce, there must be something preferable about fresh produce. In the evidence, the dietitian suggests potassium in plant foods is beneficial. The assumption will connect these ideas. So, the dietitian must be assuming fresh produce has more of the beneficial potassium than canned or frozen produce does.

Step 4: Evaluate the Answer Choices

(E) matches the prediction.

(A) is an Irrelevant Comparison. It wrongly compares the amount of potassium to sodium in all fruits and vegetables. Yet the argument in the stimulus compares just the amount of potassium in fresh versus canned or frozen vegetables.

(B) is Outside the Scope because it incorrectly focuses on sodium. The dietitian argues people should eat fresh produce as a way of maintaining heart health without *lowering* sodium consumption. Within the scope of this argument, she is unconcerned about *increasing* sodium consumption. Rather, her main evidence is about the intake of potassium. The dietitian is concerned about which type of produce has the most potassium, not the most sodium.

(C) is Extreme. The dietitian never says—or needs to say—potassium is the *only* way to protect against sodium, just that it is one way.

(D) is Outside the Scope and not required for the conclusion to follow. Even if the potassium in fruits and vegetables has zero or many negative side effects, the dietitian still may correctly argue eating fruits and vegetables would benefit people, if the positives outweigh the negatives. This argument is all about the good effects of potassium, not the bad.

7. (C) Parallel Flaw

Step 1: Identify the Question Type

The phrase "flawed pattern of reasoning most similar to" indicates this is a Parallel Flaw question. Approach the argument as you would a Flaw question. As you identify the conclusion and evidence and pinpoint the relevant gap between the two, keep common flaw types in mind. The correct answer choice will exhibit the same pattern of reasoning and the same flaw as the stimulus.

Step 2: Untangle the Stimulus

The author concludes Dana intentionally killed the plant. The author gives two pieces of evidence. First, Dana intentionally watered the plant every other day. Second, the frequent watering killed the plant.

Step 3: Make a Prediction

The author's argument assumes that just because Dana intentionally did some action (water the plant) and because that action had a given effect (killing the plant) that Dana intended for the effect to happen. In other words, the author overlooks the possibility that Dana had no idea that watering the plant would kill it. The correct answer will have the same overall structure—its assumption will be that some consequence had to be intentional, and it will overlook the alternative that though the *action* was intentional, the *consequence* might have been unintentional.

Step 4: Evaluate the Answer Choices

(C) matches. Because the restaurant owner intentionally did something that had a particular effect, the author concludes the restaurant owner intended for that particular effect to happen. In **(C)**, the author overlooks the possibility that the restaurant owner didn't know that removing the item from the menu would disappoint Jerry.

(A) leaves out the aspect of intent. In order for it to be parallel, the conclusion would have to say Jack intentionally made $100. While that may have been the result Jack desired, the answer choice doesn't go so far as to say Jack intended to do anything other than steal and bet.

(B) is wrong because the argument is logical; it has no flaw. Additionally, the conclusion of **(B)** is a recommendation, yet the conclusion in the stimulus is a judgment that an act's consequence was intentional.

(D) is also a logical argument. The heavy rain did not directly cause the flooding, but it did indirectly cause it. Additionally, **(D)** leaves out the aspect of intentionality. Clearly, the rain did not cause the fields to flood on purpose.

(E) is just like **(D)**. It's logical by indicating an indirect causation, and it never mentions intentionality.

8. (D) Weaken

Step 1: Identify the Question Type

The question stem asks for the answer that *undermines* the conclusion, so this is a Weaken question. Identify the conclusion, summarize the evidence, find the gap between the two, and then look for the answer choice that makes the conclusion less likely to be true. Oftentimes, the correct answer will undermine the author's assumption.

Step 2: Untangle Stimulus

The author concludes that a glacier probably deposited a volcanic boulder hundreds of miles from its birthplace. The evidence is the boulder doesn't match the area's sedimentary rock and glaciers moving south once covered the area in question.

Step 3: Make a Prediction

The author assumes there is no other way the boulder arrived in the area. Yet, if southward-moving glaciers moved the rock hundreds of miles, then two things must be true: the boulder originated north of its current location, and glaciers can move boulders at least hundreds of miles. To weaken this argument, the correct answer will indicate one of those is not the case. In other words, the correct answer will show that something besides the glacier must have brought the boulder to the area.

Step 4: Evaluate the Answer Choices

(D) weakens the argument by showing that the boulder did not likely come from north of the area. Therefore, the southward-moving glaciers probably didn't bring the boulder to the area.

(A) goes Outside the Scope by focusing on *most* boulders, rather than the argument's specific boulder. This choice says most boulders moved by glaciers haven't gone more than 100 miles, but that doesn't mean glaciers *can't* move boulders that far, so the argument is still valid.

(B) goes Outside the Scope by focusing too narrowly on the "closest source of volcanic rock." The conclusion suggests that the boulder is probably from hundreds of miles to the north, so it doesn't matter where the nearest source is. Even if the closest source is to the south, there could still be other sources to the north.

(C) goes Outside the Scope in the same way as **(B)**.

(E) goes Outside the Scope by focusing on other boulders, rather than the specific boulder in question. Just because the boulder is alone doesn't hurt the argument that glaciers brought it there.

9. (B) Method of Argument

Step 1: Identify the Question Stem

Because the question asks about the *function* of Craig's argument, the answer will focus on *how* Craig responds, rather than just *what* he says. This focus makes this a Method of Argument question. Look for the tactic Craig uses when he responds to Rifka.

Step 2: Untangle the Stimulus

Start by summarizing Rifka's argument. Rifka's conclusion is that stopping is unnecessary. Rifka's evidence includes a Formal Logic statement. The structure "not ... unless" is the clue. Translate this statement: if they need to stop for directions → they are lost. Craig concludes that they do need to stop based on the evidence that they are lost.

Step 3: Make a Prediction

Craig's response suggests that he has both a different conclusion and different evidence than does Rifka. Craig flips

Rifka's Formal Logic statement around: they are lost, so they need to ask for directions.

Step 4: Evaluate the Answer Choices

(B) captures how Craig rejects both Rifka's evidence and conclusion.

(A) is Half-Right/Half-Wrong. Craig does contradict Rifka's conclusion, but he also rejects Rifka's implicit evidence that they're not lost.

(C) similarly misses how Craig reverses Rifka's evidence. He can't, therefore, be accepting the truth of Rifka's evidence.

(D) goes Outside the Scope by suggesting that Craig has provided a counterexample. A counterexample would be a specific instance, but Craig's counterargument is no more specific than Rifka's argument.

(E) is a 180 because it wrongly suggests that Craig has no opinion about Rifka's conclusion. In actuality, Craig disagrees with Rifka's conclusion.

10. (D) Assumption (Sufficient)

Step 1: Identify the Question Type

The phrase "if which one of the following is assumed" indicates an Assumption question. Because the conclusion follows logically from the assumption, you are looking for a sufficient assumption. Identify the conclusion, paraphrase the relevant evidence, and pinpoint the gap between the two.

Step 2: Untangle the Stimulus

Search for Keywords that help unlock the author's argument. *Therefore*, at the bottom of the stimulus, introduces the conclusion: tragedy isn't satire or romance, and comedy isn't satire or romance. In the sentences preceding the conclusion, the author lays out the main difference: major characters in comedy and tragedy go through moral changes, whereas major characters in satire and romance have morals that mirror their world.

Step 3: Make a Prediction

In the conclusion, the author states there's no overlap between two different sets of genres (tragedy and comedy versus satire and romance). For there to be absolutely no overlap between the two sets, it must be true that their distinguishing features are mutually exclusive. Thus, the author assumes major characters in satire and romance do not go through moral changes, and major characters in tragedy and comedy don't reflect their worlds. Either one of these could be the right answer.

Step 4: Evaluate the Answer Choices

(D) directly matches the prediction.

(A) goes Outside the Scope of the argument by mentioning "[s]ome" characters. The critic is concerned only with major characters. Additionally, this choice discusses only the characteristics of romance and satire and doesn't address

tragedy and comedy (or their characteristics), which are included in the conclusion.

(B) goes Outside the Scope by focusing on changing visions of the world, rather than on changing moral qualities. Additionally, change is associated with tragedy and comedy in the stimulus, so this answer doesn't show the link (or lack thereof) with satire and romance.

(C) is a Distortion. Idealized worlds (and thus characters) are an aspect of romance literature, while debased worlds (and characters) are an aspect of satire. According to the stimulus, characters in tragedies change, but that doesn't mean they have to run the gamut from idealized to debased. This choice jumbles up all the vocabulary in the stimulus but ignores the central assumption: satire and romance are different than tragedy and comedy.

(E) introduces minor characters, who are Outside the Scope. The argument revolves around major characters only. Additionally, even if this choice was about major characters, it would simply restate a piece of the evidence. The correct answer in an Assumption question will never simply restate evidence.

11. (B) Method of Argument

Step 1: Identify the Question Type

Here, the tiny word *by* indicates the question type. Because the question asks *how* Frank argues against Lance, this is a Method of Argument question. Use Keywords to help focus on the general structure of Frank's response, rather than on the specific content of it.

Step 2: Untangle the Stimulus

Start by summarizing both arguments. First, Lance concludes that, based on experience, every rule has some exception. But Frank concludes, after "[t]herefore," that Lance's conclusion is wrong. Frank's evidence is that Lance has himself stated a general rule. By applying Lance's general rule about rules having exceptions to Lance's rule itself, Frank shows that Lance's conclusion must have at least one exception. If Lance's conclusion has at least one exception, then the conclusion itself isn't always accurate.

Step 3: Make a Prediction

Frank uses Lance's own conclusion to show that Lance's argument is paradoxical and therefore wrong.

Step 4: Evaluate the Answer Choices

(B) matches because Frank's argument is designed to demonstrate how Lance's own reasoning is contradictory.

(A) wrongly suggests that Lance's flaw is circular reasoning—evidence same as conclusion. While Lance's argument is barebones, he does suggest that experience is the evidence that teaches us about the general. Experience and general rules are not the same.

(C) goes Outside the Scope because Frank doesn't try to show that Lance is wrong about exceptions. He hypothetically accepts the idea that every general rule has an exception but then demonstrates how that reasoning is in itself contradictory. However, he concludes by saying Lance should withdraw his conclusion, not that Lance should conclude the opposite.

(D) goes Outside the Scope because Frank never mentions experience or responds to Lance's mention of experience. Frank begins his argument focusing on Lance's conclusion; he is unconcerned with Lance's evidence.

(E) goes Outside the Scope by focusing on real cases. Frank's point is that, even in purely hypothetical terms, Lance's argument fails to make logical sense.

12. (E) Flaw

Step 1: Identify the Question Type

The phrase "most vulnerable to criticism" is common language for a Flaw question. Look for the unwarranted assumption or the common LSAT flaw.

Step 2: Untangle the Stimulus

The author concludes the energy subsidy has not accomplished its goal. The evidence outlines what that goal is: to help rural residents gain access to electricity. The author thinks the subsidy has failed because many of the most isolated rural populations still have no electricity.

Step 3: Make a Prediction

The author incorrectly interprets the subsidy's goal to the extreme. According to the author himself, the subsidy was intended to *help* rural areas. That doesn't mean *all* rural areas would gain electricity. So it may be possible that even though the results of the subsidy (electricity access) haven't touched everyone (the most isolated rural populations), the subsidy has still helped residents of rural areas in general and has therefore arguably achieved its purpose. The author overlooks this possibility.

Step 4: Evaluate the Answer Choices

(E) raises the overlooked alternative by suggesting many people could have benefited from the subsidy, even if not everyone did.

(A) goes Outside the Scope by contemplating what might have happened without granting the subsidy. The author's argument is simply that the subsidy failed. The author doesn't go even further to say the subsidy's inexistence could have led to success.

(B) goes Outside the Scope by introducing a new criterion for failure. The author never suggests that the subsidy is a failure because it helps people besides those whom it was intended to help. Rather, the author suggests the subsidy is a failure because it didn't help all the intended people.

(C) goes Outside the Scope by introducing other people in the nation, when the author's argument is only about the subsidy directed toward the rural population.

(D) also goes Outside the Scope by discussing people who live in urban areas. While the author touches on urban populations earlier in the stimulus, he (correctly) doesn't include them in his discussion of the subsidy itself. This isn't a flaw in his argument.

13. (A) Paradox

Step 1: Identify the Question Type

The phrase "most helps to explain" is common language for a Paradox question. Additionally, the question stem reveals the paradoxical situation—unemployed retirees are more likely to have heart attacks on Mondays than on other days.

Step 2: Untangle the Stimulus

The question stem indicates the paradoxical fact—unemployed retirees are more likely to have heart attacks on Mondays. What makes this paradoxical is that *employed* people are more likely to have heart attacks because Monday is the first day of the workweek and therefore extra stressful. So, if unemployed retirees aren't going to work on Mondays, why do they still have more heart attacks on Mondays than on other days?

Step 3: Make a Prediction

The correct answer will suggest something about Mondays and stress that would lead unemployed retirees to have more attacks on that day.

Step 4: Evaluate the Answer Choices

(A) suggests that even though unemployed retirees don't go to work on Mondays, they still treat that day as the beginning of the "workweek" for their large projects. This could lead them to experience the same kind of heart attack–inducing stress on Mondays that employed people experience, thus resolving the paradox.

(B) goes Outside the Scope by discussing retired people who have part-time jobs. Having a part-time job may explain why these specific retired people are more likely to have heart attacks on Mondays, but the stimulus only mentions *unemployed* retired people.

(C) doesn't solve the paradox because it eliminates a possible explanation. Declining health habits might explain the risk to unemployed retirees, but if they remain unchanged from employment to retirement, then that possible reason disappears. Additionally, this answer choice fails to provide any new information as to why Mondays are special.

(D) may be true, but it doesn't explain why Mondays specifically are more dangerous to unemployed retired people than any other day.

(E) is a 180 because it strengthens the paradox. If *work-related* stress causes increased heart attacks on Mondays, then the fact that unemployed retired people are more at risk than employed people seems even more bizarre.

14. (D) Strengthen

Step 1: Identify the Question Type
Because the stem indicates that the correct answer will support the psychologist's conclusion, this is a Strengthen question. Break the argument down into conclusion and evidence and find the psychologist's assumption. Look for an answer choice that makes that assumption more likely to be true.

Step 2: Untangle the Stimulus
The conclusion is that very, very overconfident people are more likely to start a business. The evidence comes from a survey taken of entrepreneurs and business managers. In the survey, the entrepreneurs showed much more confidence than the business managers.

Step 3: Make a Prediction
The conclusion can be restated as a causal argument. The psychologist is really arguing that being super overconfident causes people to start businesses. The evidence is a correlation—people who started businesses (entrepreneurs) are more confident. The psychologist must then be assuming three things. First, the causality is not reversed (starting a business raised confidence); second, an outside thing didn't cause both the overconfidence and the entrepreneurship; and third, the two are not merely coincidentally correlated. The correct answer will strengthen the link between overconfidence and starting businesses.

Step 4: Evaluate the Answer Choices
(D) reinforces the connection between confidence and starting a business by adding the fact that the most overconfident business managers also tried to start businesses at one time.

(A) is Outside the Scope because the *types* of questions asked in the survey are irrelevant; rather, the confidence of the participants' responses matter. The psychologist might be able to determine how overconfident the survey respondents were no matter what kind of question was asked. If anything, this could weaken the argument because it could be the psychologist asked the wrong type of questions for this group of people.

(B) goes Outside the Scope by focusing on some entrepreneurs' preparation. The psychologist is concerned solely with confidence and bases his conclusion on that. That some entrepreneurs knew the accurate odds (rather than just the fact that they are enormous) doesn't factor in to his argument.

(C) goes Outside the Scope by introducing the idea of success in business. The argument is just concerned with the likelihood of *starting* a business, regardless of whether it eventually fails or succeeds. Also, this wouldn't help the psychologist prove there is a connection between confidence and entrepreneurship: the business managers (as managers) could be incredibly successful too.

(E) goes Outside the Scope by introducing business acumen and failing to mention likelihood of starting a business.

15. (B) Flaw

Step 1: Identify the Question Type
The phrase "reasoning is flawed" indicates this is a Flaw question. Break down the argument into conclusion and evidence and find the gap between the two. Identify where the author's reasoning goes wrong, keeping common flaw types in mind.

Step 2: Untangle the Stimulus
The conclusion is that the fourth-floor lab must be cleaned out. The stimulus presents three Formal Logic statements, signaled by the words "if" and "only," as evidence:

If	*Agnes's proposal is approved*	→	*the fourth floor lab must be cleaned out*
If	*Immanuel's proposal is approved*	→	*he will work in the second floor lab*
If	*a proposal is approved*	→	*director supports it*

Additionally, the author says the director will support both Agnes's and Immanuel's proposals.

Step 3: Make a Prediction
In a Flaw question, the word *only* is a huge clue to use Formal Logic and to consider overlooked alternatives. You know that the director will support both proposals. But that is a necessary consequence, rather than a trigger; nothing follows from the director supporting a proposal. The author mistakenly assumes that just because the author supports Agnes's and Immanuel's proposals that both will be approved. The correct answer could be phrased as a necessary versus sufficient flaw or as an overlooked alternative: it may be that despite the director's support, one or the other or both will be denied.

Step 4: Evaluate the Answer Choices

(B) matches the prediction. The author overlooks the chance that the director could support a proposal that still gets rejected.

(A) goes Outside the Scope by focusing on lab size rather than the gap in logic between the director supporting a proposal and the proposal being approved. The author doesn't have to justify that the fourth-floor lab is larger; accept the evidence, in Formal Logic form, as true.

(C) is an Irrelevant Comparison. The *level* of the director's support, or enthusiasm, is irrelevant. The stimulus introduces a yes/no situation: Does the director support a proposal or no? In addition, nothing in the stimulus indicates these proposals are in competition with each another.

(D) goes Outside the Scope by focusing on what Immanuel will want. Based on the Formal Logic, regardless of his desire, Immanuel will work on the second-floor lab. The author doesn't address his wants, but that isn't what is flawed with this argument.

(E), like **(A)** and **(D)**, also introduces something the author does not discuss in his evidence. But because the evidence on the LSAT is to be taken as true, the Formal Logic statements he presents are sufficient. The author doesn't need to prove that they are accurate or that there aren't other options. The correct answer choice needs to address the gap between the evidence and the conclusion, not attack the evidence itself.

16. (D) Principle (Identify/Strengthen)

Step 1: Identify the Question Type

The word *principles* clearly identifies this as a Principle question. In addition, the phrase "most helps to justify" indicates a task identical to that in Strengthen questions. So, approach this question the same way you would a Strengthen question: look for an answer that would make the conclusion more likely to follow from the evidence. The correct answer will be a principle that supports the argument's assumption. Remember, stating the assumption itself is always a valid strengthener.

Step 2: Untangle the Stimulus

The author concludes that Outdoor Sports Company's decision to provide incentives to existing customers who give their friends' email addresses to the company is unethical business practice. The evidence is that incentives encourage people to exploit their personal relationships for financial gain, which can possibly hurt the integrity of those relationships.

Step 3: Make a Prediction

Attack this question like a basic Strengthen question and start by finding the assumption. In the conclusion, the author makes the value judgment that the Outdoor Sports

Company's program is an unethical business practice. Notice that the focus is on "encouraging others" to exploit their relationships, not on the actual exploitation of relationships. The author is concerned with the business's practice, not the customers' acts. Look to the evidence for what the author means by "unethical." The new information in the evidence is that encouraging people to exploit friendships could be risky for the integrity of those relationships. Therefore, the author assumes that doing something that encourages other people to potentially risk the integrity of their relationships is unethical. The correct answer will make the assumption more likely to be true.

Step 4: Evaluate the Answer Choices

(D) states the author's assumption and so matches our prediction. Once the assumption is stated (becoming evidence), it is no longer merely assumed, and so the conclusion becomes valid.

(A) wrongly focuses on what it is unethical for people to do, rather than on what is unethical to encourage people to do. In other words, while many of the words in **(A)** are the same as those in the right answer, **(A)** fails to match the point of the author's conclusion (which, of course, is the most important part of the argument). Additionally, this answer choice turns evidence in the stimulus into a conditional clause—"*if* in doing so they risk damaging the integrity"—which is too weak in this situation.

(B) goes Outside the Scope by focusing on the way the information is gathered. **(B)** fails to link the conclusion to the evidence by not mentioning the idea of jeopardizing the integrity of personal relationships.

(C) is Extreme. While the author does judge the business's practice as unethical because of how it could *possibly* damage the integrity of people's relationships, the damage discussed in the stimulus is neither deliberate nor assured. Rather, the Outdoor Sports Company is deliberately trying to expand their advertising.

(E) goes Outside the Scope because it ignores what makes a business practice unethical. Additionally, "almost certainly damage" is Extreme. The stimulus merely says there is a risk of damage.

17. (E) Point at Issue

Step 1: Identify the Question Type

When the question stem indicates that the right answer is a *claim* that two speakers "disagree about," it is a Point at Issue question. First, summarize each speaker's argument. Then, use the Decision Tree to narrow down the correct answer choice. The speakers must each have an opinion on the correct answer choice, and those opinions must differ.

Step 2: Untangle the Stimulus

Glen argues the main thing law should do is make virtuous citizens. His evidence is that when the law emphasizes procedure, individuals become indifferent about society's welfare. In response, Sara argues that if the law's role were to create virtuous citizens, then the government would have to decide what is virtuous. Sara notes this would be a danger far worse than the government's overprotection of individual rights.

Step 3: Make a Prediction

Sara's rebuttal of Glen suggests that she disagrees with his main conclusion about the primary role for law. Scan for a choice that matches that prediction or use the Point at Issue Decision Tree. To use the Decision Tree, take an answer choice and ask these three questions: Does Glen have an opinion on this matter? Does Sara have an opinion on this matter? Do they disagree on this matter? The correct answer choice will answer all three of those questions in the affirmative.

Step 4: Evaluate the Answer Choices

(E) captures Glen's main point, with which Sara disagrees.

(A) is Outside the Scope because neither Glen nor Sara speaks to citizens' ability to make good choices. Additionally, while they disagree over government's role, neither of them discusses a situation where government doesn't interfere at all.

(B) seems close, but it ignores the role of law. It's possible both Sara and Glen agree with this statement. Sara simply doesn't think government—or law—should be the body concerned with promoting virtuousness. But she still may think virtuousness in general is more important than rights.

(C) is something Sara would agree with, but Glen's opinion on this is unclear. Sara introduces the idea that government would have to decide what is virtuous; Glen may think law can primarily focus on creating virtuous citizens without *government* having to decide what is virtuous.

(D) is unsupported. Glen would agree with this statement, but so might Sara. Sara isn't attacking Glen's opinion on what occurs when law's procedural side is emphasized; rather, she is concerned with what he thinks law's primary role should be.

18. (C) Principle (Parallel)

Step 1: Identify the Question Type

The word *principle* makes it clear that this is a Principle question. This particular Principle question mimics a Parallel Reasoning question, as evidenced by the phrase "most similar to." First, broaden the conclusion to identify the principle behind the argument in the stimulus. Then, search for the answer choice that follows the same reasoning and correctly applies that same principle.

Step 2: Untangle the Stimulus

The conclusion comes in the middle of the stimulus, marked by the word "but." The author concludes that even though skipping credit card payments is sometimes permitted, it's almost never good for the cardholder to do so. In other words, cardholders usually shouldn't skip payments. The evidence is that finance charges keep accumulating, and the cardholder ends up paying overall much more than she would have months earlier.

Step 3: Make a Prediction

The evidence is about how deferring payments leads to greater costs in the long run. The conclusion is about what is bad for the cardholder. Therefore, the author's assumption is that things that lead to greater costs in the long run are bad for cardholders. This assumption can be generalized to other situations besides cardholders. So, look for the answer choice that matches by showing a situation where greater costs in the long run are ultimately bad.

Step 4: Evaluate the Answer Choices

(C) matches the stimulus. Just like the offer in the stimulus, which carries heavy finance charges later on, the immediate benefit of using funds for new roads will result in greater maintenance costs in the long run.

(A) goes Outside the Scope by introducing the idea of finding other ways to achieve the same benefit. The author in the stimulus never states that cardholders should find other ways to achieve the same benefit (retaining money in the short term). Additionally, this answer choice ignores the concept of short term versus long term.

(B) isn't parallel because it makes a positive recommendation whereas the stimulus makes a negative one. The stimulus says people should *not* do something that is good in the short term but bad in the long term. But that doesn't mean the stimulus would agree that people *should* do something that is bad in the short term (increased payroll) but good in the long run (greater hiring power). Additionally, increased payroll could arguably be bad for a company in both the short and long term, which confounds the time aspect of the stimulus.

(D) is a 180. It recommends a plan (buying used equipment) that is good in the short term but will actually cost more in the long run. The stimulus recommends *against* a plan with that pattern.

(E) goes Outside the Scope by focusing on practicality rather than the costs associated with time.

19. (A) Inference

Step 1: Identify the Question Type

Because the right answer "follows logically" from the stimulus, it is a statement that must be true. This is an Inference question. The stimulus acts as evidence for the correct answer choice. Accept each sentence in the stimulus as true and find an answer choice that must be true on the basis of one or more of those sentences. Keep an eye out for Formal Logic, especially in Inference questions with a short stimulus like this one.

Step 2: Untangle the Stimulus
Here, the first statement of the stimulus is a Formal Logic statement. Recall that "No X is Y" means that the members of group X and the members of group Y are exclusive. So in this case, the first statement translates as:

If   *literature student*   →   *~ physics student*

Likewise, the contrapositive is:

If   *physics student*   →   *~ literature student*

In other words, no student can study both literature and physics. Skip the second statement for now and translate the third statement as

If   *rhetoric student*   →   *~ physics student*

With the contrapositive being:

If   *physics student*   →   *~ rhetoric student*

So, no student can study both physics and rhetoric. Now, turn your attention to the second statement: several physics students are taking art. On the LSAT, "several" means "some," which means "at least one."

Step 3: Make a Prediction
To make a prediction, combine the less concrete information (several students are taking physics and art) with the Formal Logic statements in the rest of the stimulus. So, some students are taking physics and art. Because these students are taking physics, it must be true they are not taking literature and are not taking rhetoric. Putting it all together, it must be true that there is at least one art student (who is also taking physics) who is not taking literature and is not taking rhetoric.

Step 4: Evaluate the Answer Choices
(A) matches the prediction.

(B) is Extreme because the stimulus does not directly connect literature and art students with a Formal Logic statement. The only connecting link between literature and art is physics. Art

students who are also taking physics will not be taking literature. But the Formal Logic in the stimulus doesn't restrict art students who aren't taking physics; they can take any other class they want.

(C) could be true but need not be. It is possible some students are taking rhetoric only, but it's also possible there are *not* students who are taking rhetoric but not literature. Perhaps all students in rhetoric are also enrolled in literature.

(D) is the more Extreme version of **(C)**. Again, it doesn't have to be true. Perhaps no rhetoric students are enrolled in literature, but it's equally possible some students are enrolled in both.

(E) could be true as long as these students are not taking physics. Like **(B)**, however, without this key piece of information (whether or not these students are in physics), **(E)** is not a "must be true" statement and therefore must be eliminated.

20. (E) Principle (Identify/Assumption)

Step 1: Identify the Question Type
This Principle question (indicated by the word *principles*) asks you to identify the broad principle that must be assumed for the psychologist's conclusion to be logical. Approach this question as you would an Assumption question. Look for the author's necessary assumption to be worded in general terms in the correct answer choice. You can use the Denial Test to check your answer.

Step 2: Untangle the Stimulus
The conclusion can be located after the Conclusion Keyphrase "[f]or this reason." The psychologist concludes psychotherapists should never provide psychotherapy on talk shows. The evidence is that the necessity to entertain is almost always incompatible with providing high-quality professional help to the guests on the talk shows.

Step 3: Make a Prediction
Predict the answer for this Principle question like you would for any other Assumption question. The evidence is that TV psychotherapy is unlikely to be high quality. The conclusion says psychotherapists should never do it. Therefore, the author assumes psychotherapy should only be provided in a manner likely to be of high quality.

Step 4: Evaluate the Answer Choices
(E) matches the prediction. To say that psychotherapy should only be done in a manner likely to be high quality is the same as saying psychotherapy that is unlikely to be high quality should not be provided.

(A) is Extreme. The appropriateness of psychotherapists' attempts to entertain a broad audience is inappropriate to providing high-quality psychological help. However, a psychotherapist may appropriately entertain an audience when not providing psychological help.

(B) makes an Irrelevant Comparison between context and the actual advice. The psychotherapist says context directly affects quality, regardless of the nature of the advice. The psychotherapist doesn't say one is more significant than the other.

(C) is Extreme. The psychologist's argument is about a situation in which there is a large chance therapy won't be high quality. Choice **(C)** says psychotherapy shouldn't be provided if there is "any chance" the therapy might be less than high quality. The psychotherapist might think it is acceptable to provide therapy when there is a medium or low chance of it being less than the best.

(D) goes Outside the Scope by focusing on the interests of the audience, rather than the quality of psychotherapy provided to the guest. Additionally, this isn't really an assumption: the psychologist actually states such shows are supposed to entertain broad audiences.

21. (B) Point at Issue

Step 1: Identify the Question Type
When the question indicates that the right answer is a *claim* two speakers "disagree about," it is a Point at Issue question. First, summarize each speaker's argument. Then, use the Decision Tree to narrow in on the correct answer choice. The speakers must each have an opinion on the correct answer choice, and those opinions must differ.

Step 2: Untangle the Stimulus
Tania points out that in order to give a truly unbiased opinion, a critic would have to be speaking about things of no interest to him. Therefore, she argues, art critics cannot give a (conventionally) fair critique because they cannot separate themselves from the emotional and passionate connections art requires. Monique, however, says the best art critics can still be fully engaged in the artwork, yet render an opinion after removing their biases and consulting general principles of aesthetics.

Step 3: Make a Prediction
Note that neither is arguing whether critics engage passionately with art. Tania and Monique are arguing over whether or not art critics can be unbiased. Tania says no, but Monique says yes. Once you've elicited out the issue, evaluate each answer choice for a match to the prediction. Don't hesitate to apply the Decision Tree to eliminate wrong answers.

Step 4: Evaluate the Answer Choices
(B) matches the prediction. Tania thinks a good art critic is incapable of being unbiased but Monique argues that a good art critic can be unbiased, after certain steps are taken.

(A) is incorrect because both of them may agree on it. Monique clearly says art is not simply a passion. Yet while Tania says art is a passion, she never says it is *only* a passion. She may agree that it is more.

(C) is a statement with which both Tania and Monique would disagree. Both Tania and Monique argue that art critics should feel emotion towards artworks.

(D) fails because there's no argument over what defines fairness. Tania provides a definition, but Monique doesn't comment on it. They are both simply arguing over whether art critics can present an unbiased critique or no.

(E) is Extreme. Neither Tania nor Monique determines what the "most important aspect" of art criticism is. Additionally, if anything, they both agree art critics should or must passionately engage with art.

22. (C) Paradox

Step 1: Identify the Question Type
The phrase "most helps to resolve the apparent discrepancy" indicates this is a Paradox question. Read the stimulus to identify the seemingly contradictory statements, and then evaluate the answers to find the one choice that helps to explain how the two statements may reasonably coexist. Watch out for answers that verify or strengthen the facts but don't resolve the mystery at hand.

Step 2: Untangle the Stimulus
The question stem includes no hint about what the paradoxical situation is, so the next task is to find it in the stimulus. On the one hand, judicial decisions are not usually written with high literary quality. On the other hand, high literary quality is sometimes found in dissenting judicial opinions. What accounts for the difference between judicial opinions in general and dissenting opinions?

Step 3: Make a Prediction
In talking about judicial decisions in general, the author mentions they tend not to be high literary quality because they are written to determine the law. So, if dissenting judicial opinions are not written to determine the law, then there is no reason to think they are typically not high literary quality.

Step 4: Evaluate the Answer Choices
(C) matches the prediction. Dissenting opinions don't determine the law. Therefore, they can be written in any manner.

(A) is Outside the Scope because it focuses on how many judges are involved in a dissenting opinion, rather than on its effect on the law or literary quality.

(B) is also Outside the Scope. It might conform to our expectations of reality but does nothing to resolve the paradox. The choice discusses the difference between judicial decisions and literary works but doesn't explain the difference between judicial decisions and dissenting opinions.

(D) makes an Irrelevant Comparison by focusing on what judges spend more time reading, rather than focusing on the quality of what they write. Further, it makes no distinction between judicial opinions in general and dissenting opinions.

(E) makes another Irrelevant Comparison. Which decisions are read more frequently has no impact on whether dissenting opinions determine the law or why they are more likely to contain writing of high literary quality.

23. (E) Inference

Step 1: Identify the Question Type
This is an Inference question because the right answer is "properly inferred" from the stimulus. Accept each sentence in the stimulus as true and find an answer choice that must be true on the basis of one or more of those sentences. Stick to the information given and beware of making faulty assumptions.

Step 2: Untangle the Stimulus
In the first sentence, the ecologist makes a Formal Logic statement: without conservationists' intervention, squirrel monkeys will become extinct. In other words, the conservationists' intervention is required for the squirrel monkeys' survival. This statement yields the following translation:

$$\text{If } \begin{array}{c}\textit{squirrel} \\ \textit{monkeys} \\ \textit{survive}\end{array} \rightarrow \begin{array}{c}\textit{conservationists} \\ \textit{intervene}\end{array}$$

Then the ecologist gives us a condition that will result in the squirrel monkeys' survival:

$$\text{If } \begin{array}{c}\textit{large tracts of} \\ \textit{habitat} \\ \textit{preserved}\end{array} \rightarrow \begin{array}{c}\textit{squirrel} \\ \textit{monkeys} \\ \textit{survive}\end{array}$$

These two statements can be combined to form one chain:

$$\text{If } \begin{array}{c}\textit{large} \\ \textit{tracts of} \\ \textit{habitat} \\ \textit{preserved}\end{array} \rightarrow \begin{array}{c}\textit{squirrel} \\ \textit{monkeys} \\ \textit{survive}\end{array} \rightarrow \begin{array}{c}\textit{conservationists} \\ \textit{intervene}\end{array}$$

The last sentence doesn't include any Formal Logic but simply provides a fact about squirrel monkeys: they do well in second-growth forests because of the food supply.

Step 3: Make a Prediction
Now that the statements have been combined to form one chain, that chain can also be contraposed like this:

$$\text{If } \begin{array}{c}\textit{conservationists} \\ \sim\textit{intervene}\end{array} \rightarrow \begin{array}{c}\textit{squirrel} \\ \textit{monkeys} \\ \sim\textit{survive} \\ \textit{(extinct)}\end{array} \rightarrow \begin{array}{c}\textit{large tracts} \\ \textit{of habitat} \\ \sim\textit{preserved}\end{array}$$

The right answer will follow from the original chain or its contrapositive.

Step 4: Evaluate the Answer Choices
(E) matches the prediction. Based on the contrapositive of the connected Formal Logic statements, it must be true that if no conservationists' intervention occurs, then no large tracts of habitat are preserved.

(A) goes Outside the Scope because the ecologist's statements are only about the second-growth forests, not other habitats.

(B) goes Outside the Scope by suggesting that at least one conservationist will actually be doing the work of preserving second-growth forest. We know that if those forests are preserved that the conservationists did *something*, but we don't know exactly what they did. There could be ways of intervening that resulted in *others* preserving the forest.

(C) is Extreme. The ecologist never states that the squirrel monkeys would die off without this food supply, just that they flourish when it is there. Even if their favorites disappear, squirrel monkeys could arguably eat something else.

(D) wrongly contraposes the Formal Logic in the stimulus. According to the first sentence, if the squirrel monkeys survive, it is because the conservationists have intervened. The ecologist never states that intervention alone will guarantee their existence. This answer choice incorrectly negates the Formal Logic without reversing.

24. (A) Strengthen

Step 1: Identify the Question Type
The word *strengthens* indicates a Strengthen question. Break down the argument into conclusion and evidence, predict the central assumption, and find an answer choice that validates the author's assumption.

Step 2: Untangle the Stimulus
The conclusion is in the last sentence, marked by "[t]hus." The author says there must have been many more Byzantine documents sealed with lead than there are lead seals remaining. The evidence is that because lead was relatively valuable, people would recycle the lead seals after opening the document that the seal was on.

Step 3: Make a Prediction

The evidence says a lead seal is recast into something else after its document is opened. The conclusion says the number of total documents sealed in the empire greatly outnumbered the number of remaining seals. Therefore, the author assumes that a significant number of seals were destroyed and thus must have been on documents that got opened. The correct answer will support this assumption.

Step 4: Evaluate the Answer Choices

(A) fills in the author's missing link. If the *majority* of seals were on documents that got opened, then those seals likely were recycled. That would support the notion that the number of documents sealed was well over 40,000.

(B) goes Outside the Scope by introducing the destruction of the documents, which is not in the stimulus. Whether or not the documents were destroyed doesn't affect the total number of original documents and how it stacks up against the number of seals.

(C) makes an Irrelevant Comparison. The amount of lead in the seals today as compared to their original amount of lead doesn't address the number of documents issue.

(D) would help explain why 40,000 lead seals remain, but it doesn't discuss the total number of documents. It's possible that there were at most 40,000 important documents and then only 2 unimportant documents. If anything, **(D)** would weaken the author's argument that the number of documents many times over outnumbered the number of seals.

(E) goes Outside the Scope by including "at any given time." The argument is about how many documents and seals there were *throughout* a given period rather than at any specific point in that period.

25. (B) Role of a Statement

Step 1: Identify the Question Type

The phrase "the role played ... by the proposition" indicates this is a Role of a Statement question. Using Keywords, determine whether the statement in question is evidence or conclusion, and then go back and refine your categorization as necessary.

Step 2: Untangle the Stimulus

In the absence of any Conclusion Keywords in the stimulus, the One-Sentence Test will help isolate the components of the farmer's argument. Right off the bat, the first sentence appears to be the farmer's opinion and main point: farmers' use of insecticides is counterproductive. The next sentence, starting with the Evidence Keyword [*b*]*ecause*, states why: insects' increasing resistance means increasing amounts of insecticides must be used.

Step 3: Make a Prediction

The question asks for how the farmer uses the statement "farmers have to use greater and greater amounts of costly insecticides to control insect pests." That statement came up as part of the evidence. Because it describes the *result* of increases in insects' resistance, it acts as a subsidiary conclusion.

Step 4: Evaluate the Answer Choices

(B) matches the prediction. The idea that insecticide uses causes insect resistance to increase is a causal explanation for why farmers have to use greater amounts of pesticide. This in turn is used to prove that using insecticide is counterproductive.

(A) is Half-Right/Half-Wrong. As the answer choice says, the statement isn't the only conclusion in the stimulus, but it wrongly states that the statement in question is the main conclusion.

(C) wrongly suggests that the statement in question is the only conclusion. First, there are two conclusions, and second, the statement in question is the subsidiary one.

(D) wrongly suggests that the statement is used to support an intermediary conclusion. In contrast, the claim is the intermediary conclusion that offers direct support for the author's main conclusion. The claim itself is supported by the information about insects' increasing resistance to insecticides.

(E) gets the conclusion wrong. While the statement in question does identify a phenomenon (increased use of insecticides), the farmer's main point isn't to explain what causes that phenomenon, but to use that phenomenon to support his argument that a course of action is counterproductive.

Section III: Logical Reasoning

Q#	Question Type	Correct	Difficulty
1	Flaw	C	★
2	Inference	E	★
3	Principle (Identify/Strengthen)	B	★
4	Flaw	A	★
5	Main Point	D	★
6	Method of Argument	D	★
7	Paradox	E	★
8	Strengthen	A	★
9	Assumption (Necessary)	A	★★
10	Flaw	C	★★★★
11	Inference	E	★
12	Principle (Identify/Strengthen)	A	★★
13	Strengthen	A	★
14	Parallel Flaw	B	★
15	Inference	D	★★
16	Assumption (Sufficient)	A	★★
17	Flaw	C	★★
18	Assumption (Necessary)	E	★★
19	Main Point	E	★★★
20	Weaken	D	★★★★
21	Flaw	D	★★★
22	Inference (Could Be True EXCEPT)	B	★★★
23	Principle (Apply/Inference)	E	★★★★
24	Parallel Reasoning	D	★★
25	Assumption (Necessary)	E	★★★

1. (C) Flaw

Step 1: Identify the Question Type

The phrase "most vulnerable to criticism" identifies this as a Flaw question. Break down William's argument into conclusion and evidence, and use them to determine why his assumption is unwarranted. Keep common flaw types in mind.

Step 2: Untangle the Stimulus

Anna starts off this discussion by presenting information about rainbows claimed by scholar Pliny the Elder. But William concludes Pliny the Elder's claim cannot be correct. William's evidence is that Pliny the Elder also made claims about the existence of headless people and curing headaches with snails—dubious claims to say the least.

Step 3: Make a Prediction

What William fails to consider with his *ad hominem* attack is that the truth, or lack thereof, of Pliny the Elder's dubious claims has no bearing on the veracity of the rainbow claim. Pliny the Elder may have been wrong about the headless people but still correct about rainbows. In other words, being wrong once (or even three times) doesn't make someone wrong all the time.

Step 4: Evaluate the Answer Choices

(C) is correct and points out William's error in suggesting that making invalid claims on one topic invalidates one's claims on another topic.

(A) is a Distortion. William doesn't make Anna's conclusion appear extreme; he merely suggests that it's wrong.

(B) is a Distortion. William doesn't argue Pliny the Elder was in bad faith when he reported about strange creatures but simply that he was wrong. Furthermore, that's not the problem with William's argument. William's error is assuming that Pliny the Elder's incorrect claims about unheard-of creatures (whether in bad faith or not) affects the accuracy of the scholar's assertion about rainbows.

(D) is a 180. William clearly seems to find Pliny the Elder's assertions to be absurd and invalid. This is actually what Anna does.

(E) is Out of Scope. The timing of Pliny the Elder's writing is irrelevant to the argument. Pliny the Elder could have written his claims about headless people last year and William would probably still make the same argument.

2. (E) Inference

Step 1: Identify the Question Type

The phrase "which of the following is most strongly supported" identifies this as an Inference question. Accept each sentence in the stimulus as true and find an answer choice that is supported on the basis of one or more of those

sentences. Also watch out for extreme language in the answer choices.

Step 2: Untangle the Stimulus

The shareholder has some concerns. Despite the success of the company's current operations, the company is looking to expand to the food service industry. However, that move comes with a high risk and the potential of siphoning off money needed by other operations. The shareholder finishes by pointing out that a second option for expansion—pharmaceuticals—would entail a lower risk.

Step 3: Make a Prediction

Accepting each statement as true, the argument suggests that expansion into pharmaceuticals would likely result in less chance of losing money than expansion into food services.

Step 4: Evaluate the Answer Choices

(E) is correct and matches your prediction.

(A) is a Distortion. Actually, the shareholder claims the current operations are successful. While the move into food services might steal needed funds from those operations, there's no indication of a *current* need for more funding.

(B) is a Distortion. The stimulus says only that expansion into pharmaceuticals would provide a lower risk than food services. While earlier in the argument the shareholder claims food services would siphon funds, that doesn't guarantee pharmaceuticals wouldn't.

(C) is Extreme. Note that the shareholder claims that the food services operation *may* siphon funds from other operations and comes with a high risk. That kind of wording suggests losing money is definitely a possibility, but not a certainty.

(D) is also Extreme. "Only if" suggests the company couldn't be profitable in any scenario other than expansion into pharmaceuticals. Translated into Formal Logic, this choice says, "If increased profits are possible, then the company must have expanded into pharmaceuticals." Yet, the shareholder argues that current operations are successful; they may continue to be so. Additionally, even a high-risk prospect can result in a profit, so the company might still make money in the food service industry.

3. (B) Principle (Identify/Strengthen)

Step 1: Identify the Question Type

The word *principles* clearly identifies this as a Principle question. In addition, the phrase "most helps to justify" indicates a task identical to that in Strengthen questions. So, approach this question the same way you would a Strengthen question: look for an answer that would make the conclusion more likely to follow from the evidence. The correct answer will be a principle that supports the argument's assumption. Also, when a question asks about one of two opinions in a stimulus, watch out for answers that validate the wrong opinion.

Step 2: Untangle the Stimulus
In this argument, Mariah concludes that Adam should not judge the essay contest. However, unlike Joanna (who suggests bias, which Mariah refutes due to the anonymity of the contestants), Mariah's reasoning is that Adam has no experience in critiquing essays.

Step 3: Make a Prediction
The principle, or broader rule, behind Mariah's argument is that a lack of experience constitutes a reason to be dismissed as a judge.

Step 4: Evaluate the Answer Choices
(B) is correct and matches your prediction. Mariah doesn't necessarily assume expertise has to be the "primary" prerequisite, but, if valid, this principle certainly would justify her argument.

(A) is a Distortion. This may be tempting because Mariah does reject Joanna's suggestion of bias. However, Mariah doesn't reject this reasoning because she feels that bias is insufficient grounds for dismissal. She rejects it because the essay authors are anonymous, which suggests that there wouldn't be bias in this case.

(C) is a 180. Mariah suggests expertise is the main factor for dismissing Adam as a judge, whereas Joanna would say objectivity is more important.

(D) is also a 180 and is almost identical to **(C)**. Two such similar answers suggest both are wrong. Again, Mariah suggests that Adam should be dismissed for lack of expertise, not because of fairness concerns.

(E) is Outside the Scope. This might be a principle that Joanna would use, but Mariah's argument is about expertise, not bias. As Mariah says, the essays' authors aren't identified, so bias is irrelevant.

4. (A) Flaw

Step 1: Identify the Question Type
The word *flawed* clearly identifies this as a Flaw question. Break down the author's argument, identifying conclusion and evidence and determining the assumption. Then, evaluate how the author's reasoning goes wrong. Remember to keep an eye out for common flaw types.

Step 2: Untangle the Stimulus
The argument states that NoSmoke is made up of two ingredients. A study showed one of those ingredients *by itself* did not decrease cigarette cravings. The author concludes that, if the same is true for the second ingredient, then NoSmoke as a whole would not decrease cravings.

Step 3: Make a Prediction
Notice that the author ignores the possibility that the two ingredients may decrease cravings when *combined*, even though each ingredient is ineffective by *itself*. More generally, confusing properties of a whole with the properties of its individual parts (or vice versa) is a classic flaw on the LSAT.

Step 4: Evaluate the Answer Choices
(A) nicely points out the author's assumption that whatever can't be done by the individual ingredients can't be done by the combined ingredients.

(B) is a 180. There is no correlation in the argument and the author is claiming a *lack* of causation.

(C) is Outside the Scope. The study used smokers, and the author's conclusion was about reducing cravings in smokers, so there is no reason to suspect the study is unrepresentative.

(D) is Outside the Scope. This argument is not concerned with quitting smoking or "ways" other than reducing cravings. It attacks only the claim that NoSmoke reduces cravings.

(E) is Outside the Scope. The author never states or implies any claim of bias. There is no element of an *ad hominem* attack in this argument.

5. (D) Main Point

Step 1: Identify the Question Type
The phrase "most accurately expresses the main conclusion" identifies this as a Main Point question. Focus on Keywords, look out for subsidiary conclusions, and expect to combine statements in the argument to paraphrase the author's main point. Also consider using the One-Sentence Test and remember that words of contrast frequently indicate the author's disagreement with previous statements and, by extension, the author's conclusion.

Step 2: Untangle the Stimulus
The gardener starts off by introducing a recommendation made by researchers: allow some weeds to grow in gardens to repel caterpillars. However, once the gardener starts the second sentence with the word "[w]hile," you get the sense that the gardener has a bone of contention with the researchers. Sure enough, the gardener calls the recommendation "premature." This surely seems like the gardener's main point. Following this claim are two other possible outcomes weeds' presence may engender: depleted soil and the attraction of other pests. In other words, they are evidence to back up the gardener's dissent.

Step 3: Make a Prediction
Simply put, the gardener's overall point is that researchers' recommendation to allow weeds to grow is premature.

Step 4: Evaluate the Answer Choices

(D) is correct and nicely summarizes the gardener's cautionary opinion.

(A) is incorrect because it summarizes the gardener's concession to the researchers, not his final conclusion. The gardener does claim that it's wise to avoid using pesticides, but this is not the primary concern at hand. The gardener is far more concerned about the recommendation to let weeds grow.

(B) is a Distortion. It incorrectly focuses on the gardener's evidence, not his conclusion. As support, he states in the last sentence that weeds may attract other kinds of damaging pests, but that doesn't mean he thinks there will necessarily be a net increase. The number of other pests may be less than the number of repelled caterpillars.

(C) is a 180. This summarizes the researchers' argument, not the gardener's. The gardener is not ready to accept this argument.

(E) is a Distortion. While the gardener *is* skeptical about the researchers' argument, his focus is not on how well growing weeds will achieve the intended effect (reducing caterpillars) but on what unconsidered, unwanted effects the weeds might cause.

6. (D) Method of Argument

Step 1: Identify the Question Type

The phrase "executive's reasoning does" indicates that the question is asking *how* the executive makes her argument and thus identifies this as a Method of Argument question. The correct answer will reflect, likely in abstract terms, the *way* in which the executive advances her main point. Note any Keywords and stay focused on the structure of the argument rather than the content.

Step 2: Untangle the Stimulus

In this argument, the executive provides two situations: ads were printed in a magazine and posted on that magazine's website. The executive then mentions that data on customer response was only available for one of the two mediums: online. Without having data from the print ads, the executive simply concludes that the results of the print ads probably mirrored the results of the online ads.

Step 3: Make a Prediction

Paraphrase the executive's reasoning in broad terms: lacking data about one situation, the executive makes a conclusion about that situation by using existing data from a second, similar situation.

Step 4: Evaluate the Answer Choices

(D) is correct and matches your prediction.

(A) is Outside the Scope. The executive's prediction of the intensity of response to the print ads is based on information from the online ads, not on any factor that caused the print ads.

(B) is a Distortion. The executive compares analogous, similarly particular situations. Both print and online ads are specific. She doesn't draw her conclusion from advertising in general.

(C) is Outside the Scope. The only specific instance the executive has information about is the online advertisement. The executive does not draw a statistical generalization on those ads; it is a qualitative generalization: "response to the ads on the website was much more limited than is typical." Additionally, the executive's main point was to use that generalization to draw a different generalization about the print ads.

(E) is Outside the Scope. This choice, with its reference to "comparable events," is close, but the executive's argument uses the current performance of online ads to draw a conclusion about the current performance of the print ads. The executive does not use the present performance to draw a conclusion about the future performance of those ads.

7. (E) Paradox

Step 1: Identify the Question Type

The phrase "most help explain" identifies this as a Paradox question. Read the stimulus to identify the seemingly contradictory statements, then evaluate the answers to find the one choice that helps to explain how the two statements may reasonably coexist. Watch out for answers that verify or strengthen the facts, but don't resolve the mystery at hand.

Step 2: Untangle the Stimulus

Something unusual has happened here. Coyotes have been removed from a small island because they were preying on wild cats and, more importantly, plover, which were dwindling in number. One would expect that removing the predators (the coyotes) would help the plover population rebound. Instead, once the coyotes were gone, the plover numbers plummeted, and they disappeared altogether.

Step 3: Make a Prediction

Why would the plover have disappeared after conservationists removed the coyotes? The key here is that the coyotes also preyed on wild cats (a piece of information that should not have gone unnoticed). Find an answer choice that explains why removing the coyotes resulted in the plover disappearance.

Step 4: Evaluate the Answer Choices

(E) is correct. The coyotes' removal would likely have resulted in an increase in wild cats. If the wild cats also prey on plover, the conservationists' action merely replaced one predator with another. This choice explains why the plover didn't survive and thus resolves the paradox.

(A) is a 180. This provides evidence as to why the coyotes preyed on plover. If the plover were that easy for the coyotes to kill, then it would be even stranger that the plover population collapsed after the coyotes were removed.

(B) is Outside the Scope. Without evidence stating what happened to the wild cat population after the coyotes were removed, this answer can't help explain the plover's situation. Furthermore, one would likely expect the wild cat population to *increase* after its predators, the coyotes, were gone. If the plover fluctuated along with the wild cats, one would expect them *both* to have increased.

(C) is Outside the Scope. Whether coyotes are susceptible to the same diseases is irrelevant to the disappearance of the plover. Because the disease is considered common to plover and therefore wouldn't result in population fluctuation, this wouldn't explain the dramatic turn of events as described in the stimulus.

(D) is an Irrelevant Comparison. Having lived on the island for an unspecified amount of time with coyotes as predators, it would certainly be understandable if the wild cat population wasn't as big as it used to be. However, this has no bearing on the plight of the plover.

8. (A) Strengthen

Step 1: Identify the Question Type
The phrase "most strengthens the economist's reasoning" identifies this as a Strengthen question. Break down the argument into conclusion and evidence, predict the central assumption, and find an answer choice that validates the economist's assumption.

Step 2: Untangle the Stimulus
The economist states there are two solutions to cutting personnel costs: lay off some employees or reduce wages across the board. Both hurt morale, with laying off employees being less damaging. The economist then concludes that companies are likely to lay off employees when they need to reduce personnel costs.

Step 3: Make a Prediction
Notice that the economist concludes companies are likely to lay off employees for the sole reason that layoffs are less damaging to morale—as if morale was the most important consideration in making the decision. The economist focuses on only one factor in making a decision and ignores other potentially more important factors. To strengthen the economist's view, find an answer that verifies his assumption that companies make personnel moves based on their effect on morale.

Step 4: Evaluate the Answer Choices
(A) is correct and strengthens the economist's conclusion that layoffs are likely when companies must reduce personnel

costs during recessions. If morale is the biggest deciding factor in such decisions, then layoffs make the most sense.

(B) is Outside the Scope. This choice talks about when companies would *increase* wages, whereas the argument only discusses when companies would decrease wages.

(C) is Outside the Scope. The argument is not about whether companies can make a profit but about how companies can reduce costs. That some companies can't make a profit doesn't help explain why the economist would think companies would choose laying off employees over reducing wages.

(D) is Outside the Scope. Although this choice may explain what would happen if companies chose to reduce wages, it does not strengthen the economist's point that layoffs are the likely route. Furthermore, if reduced wages *did* lead to resignations, one could argue (perhaps a little cynically) that companies would be more likely to choose this route instead, as it would lead to a potentially greater reduction in personnel costs. That would make this answer choice a 180.

(E) is a 180. This choice actually goes against the economist by providing a reason why companies would *not* want to lay off employees.

9. (A) Assumption (Necessary)

Step 1: Identify the Question Type
The word *assumption* identifies this as an Assumption question. Additionally, the word *relies* indicates you are looking for a Necessary Assumption, one without which the conclusion cannot be logically drawn from the evidence. You can use the Denial Test to check or eliminate answer choices.

Step 2: Untangle the Stimulus
The Keyword [*t*]*hus* identifies the author's conclusion: The success of chain bookstores is a detriment to book consumers. Why? The Keyword *for* identifies the author's main piece of evidence: this success has put a damper on the variety of available books.

Step 3: Make a Prediction
Bridging the mismatched terms in the evidence and conclusion can lead to solid predictions. Here, the author must assume that a lack of variety is a detriment to consumers.

Step 4: Evaluate the Answer Choices
(A) is correct and matches your prediction: consumers would be better off with more variety. If they were not better off with variety, then there would be no reason to claim that the success of chain bookstores has been to the detriment of consumers.

(B) is a 180. This choice points out a benefit of chain stores, making their success seem more positive and less detrimental. The author wouldn't assume good things about chain bookstores and then conclude they are bad for consumers.

(C) is an Irrelevant Comparison. The size of the average bookstore (which would factor in both chain and independent stores) today versus the size 20 years ago is irrelevant to the author's conclusion. In addition, if bookstores are now larger, that could weaken the argument by showing how consumers now have more books from which to choose.

(D) is also an Irrelevant Comparison. The author is not concerned about comparing the physical sizes of the average bookstore over time. He is concerned with the total number of independent versus chain bookstores.

(E) is Outside the Scope. Without evidence stating chain stores are more expensive, this answer doesn't factor into the author's argument. This choice also weakens the author's argument by suggesting that the variety of books is not as important to consumers as price.

10. (C) Flaw

Step 1: Identify the Question Type
The word *flawed* clearly identifies this as a Flaw question. Break down the concert promoter's argument, identifying his conclusion and evidence and determining his assumption. Then, evaluate how his reasoning goes wrong. If an argument has more than one possible flaw, beware of answers that distort one of those flaws or are extreme.

Step 2: Untangle the Stimulus
The concert promoter suggests critics are mistaken and a particular concert series *does* have popular appeal. His evidence is merely that sales of memorabilia are equal to those of comparable concert series.

Step 3: Make a Prediction
There are two issues with the concert promoter's argument. First, he must assume that the sale of memorabilia indicates popular appeal. Second, the promoter concludes that the one series has popular appeal because of its similarity to other series. However, he never explicitly states whether those other series have popular appeal; instead, he assumes they do. If those other series were unpopular, then having equivalent sales would probably indicate a lack of popularity in the promoter's series.

Step 4: Evaluate the Answer Choices
(C) is correct and matches your prediction. The promoter errs by assuming the popularity of the comparable series.

(A) is Outside the Scope. The sale figures cited by the concert promoter are facts, not emotional considerations.

(B) is Extreme. The promoter merely assumes that memorabilia sales are one indicator, not necessarily the *only* indicator of popular appeal. That word should have sent up a red flag.

(D) is a 180. The promoter states the other events are *comparable*, not dissimilar.

(E) is Outside the Scope. The argument does not have a classic parts-versus-the-whole flaw. Although the concert promoter does not make a distinction between the series and the individual concerts, this is not why his argument is flawed. The argument is entirely concerned with the quality of the series, not of the individual components of the series.

11. (E) Inference

Step 1: Identify the Question Type
The phrase "is best supported by the information above" identifies this as an Inference question. Accept each sentence in the stimulus as true and find an answer choice that follows on the basis of one or more of those sentences. Stick to the information given and beware of going outside the scope.

Step 2: Untangle the Stimulus
You are given a little bit of information about two types of solar UV radiation: UV-A causes wrinkles and UV-B causes sunburn. You are also told that sunscreens from before ten years ago protected users from UV-B and not UV-A.

Step 3: Make a Prediction
Combining the terms provided in the stimulus allows you to deduce that sunscreens from before ten years ago protected users from sunburn, but not from wrinkles.

Step 4: Evaluate the Answer Choices
(E) matches the prediction. Because sunscreens from earlier than ten years ago didn't protect against UV-A, then wrinkles were just as likely to appear on people who wore sunscreen as on those who didn't.

(A) is Outside the Scope. The stimulus only tells you about the change in sunscreen protection, not about how frequently the sunscreen was actually used.

(B) is Extreme. Because older sunscreen didn't protect people from wrinkles, there may be plenty of people who have premature wrinkles and *did* wear sunscreen. Also, people could still use new sunscreen and get premature wrinkles from something other than UV-A radiation. There is nothing in the stimulus that says "most" premature wrinkles are caused by UV-A radiation, just that UV-A radiation *can* cause them.

(C) is Outside the Scope. Just because the sunscreen didn't protect users from UV-A radiation does not mean the cause of premature wrinkling was unknown. Sunscreen makers simply may have been unable (or uncompelled) to create a sunscreen that protects users from UV-A radiation until 10 years ago.

(D) is a Distortion. The statements imply that newer sunscreen has UV-A protection. However, that does *not* mean that it no longer has UV-B protection (which protects against sunburn). Newer sunscreen may protect users from both types of UV radiation, meaning that users are still as protected from sunburn as they were in the past. This would be correct if sunburn and wrinkles were reversed.

12. (A) Principle (Identify/Strengthen)

Step 1: Identify the Question Type
The word *principles* identifies this as a Principle question. In addition, the phrase "most helps to justify the reasoning" indicates a task identical to that in Strengthen questions. So, approach this question the same way you would a Strengthen question: look for an answer that would make the conclusion more likely to follow from the evidence. The correct answer will be a principle that supports the argument's assumption.

Step 2: Untangle the Stimulus
The advice columnist presents data that show people suffering from major stress are more likely to be seriously injured playing competitive sports than people without stress. Because of this, the columnist goes one step further and suggests *no* sports activity should be used to combat stress.

Step 3: Make a Prediction
The columnist assumes that if people with stress should avoid one type of activity (in this case, competitive sports), then they should also avoid all types of activities in the same general category (in this case, sports in general). Find an answer choice that states this prediction in broad terms.

Step 4: Evaluate the Answer Choices
(A) is correct and matches your prediction perfectly.

(B) is Outside the Scope. The columnist's recommendation is about a method for coping with stress that *shouldn't* be used. The columnist says nothing about methods that *should* be used, and while the columnist uses some studies' results as evidence, the focus of this argument is not on the importance of scientific study.

(C) is Outside the Scope. Recommending one thing for a group of people does not mean recommending the opposite for the opposite group. So, just because the columnist recommends that stressed people avoid competitive sports does not mean the columnist thinks nonstressed people should compete in competitive sports. This answer choice is essentially an incorrect contrapositive of the columnist's argument.

(D) is a 180. If the columnist makes the jump from avoiding competitive sports to avoiding all sports, it would seem just as likely that the columnist would make the jump from avoiding competitive sports to avoiding any competitive activity. This principle is contrary to the columnist's reasoning.

(E) is Outside the Scope. It may be a good idea to avoid sports activities in this case, but the choice focuses too narrowly on

people with a history of sports injuries, whereas the columnist is concerned with anyone coping with stress—regardless of injury history.

13. (A) Strengthen

Step 1: Identify the Question Type
The phrase "adds the most support to the argument" identifies this as a Strengthen question. Break down the argument into conclusion and evidence, predict the central assumption, and find an answer choice that validates the assumption. Don't let scientific words throw you; paraphrase the argument in simple terms.

Step 2: Untangle the Stimulus
The conclusion of this argument uses the term *communal foraging*. Instead of rooting through your knowledge of ecology, you should see that the argument defines this for you quite neatly at the end. In basic terms, the argument concludes that tent caterpillars let their nest-mates know where food can be found. The evidence states that tent caterpillars leave behind a trail of chemicals when looking for food, and they leave stronger trails when they find food sources and weaker trails when they do not.

Step 3: Make a Prediction
Notice that the author assumes that trails left behind by tent caterpillars actually convey information to other tent caterpillars. To validate this, find something that would verify that the stronger trail is used for the purpose of giving information to other members of the nest.

Step 4: Evaluate the Answer Choices
(A) is correct and matches your prediction perfectly. If hungry caterpillars are more likely to follow heavier trails of chemicals, then that indicates they are using the strength of the trail to find a definite source of food rather than wasting time looking around. This strengthens the idea that the trails are left for "communal foraging," as defined in the argument.

(B) is a 180. If caterpillars cannot detect the concentration of pheromones, then strong and weak trails would seem identical. In that case, leaving a strong trail would not seem to help the nest-mates find food any faster.

(C) is Outside the Scope. This may provide some insight into how a caterpillar lives, but it does not connect the chemical trails to providing information to other caterpillars about food sources.

(D) is an Irrelevant Comparison. Knowing that the pheromones of tent caterpillars are different from pheromones left by other animals does not connect the different strengths of the trails to the concept of communal foraging.

(E) is Outside the Scope. It is important that tent caterpillars' nest-mates are able to detect the chemicals, in order to interpret information about food sources. However, knowing that *other* species of caterpillars can detect the chemicals is irrelevant.

14. (B) Parallel Flaw

Step 1: Identify the Question Type
The phrase "flawed reasoning … most similar to" identifies this as a Parallel Flaw question. Approach the argument as you would a standard Flaw question. Identify the evidence and conclusion and pinpoint the relevant gap between the two, keeping in mind common flaw types. The correct answer choice will exhibit the same pattern of reasoning and the same flaw as the stimulus.

Step 2: Untangle the Stimulus
The argument makes a subsidiary conclusion that because top actors have a loyal following, movies with top actors tend to do well. It then concludes that movies with unknown actors likely will not do well.

Step 3: Make a Prediction
This argument is a classic example of treating a characteristic of a group as if the characteristic were unique to that group. It's like saying, "Dogs have four legs; therefore, animals that are not dogs cannot have four legs." Recognizing this flaw, find the one answer that has the exact same flaw in logic. In Formal Logic terms, the stimulus says, "If a movie has a top actor, then it's likely to do well." The conclusion negates this statement without reversing: "if a movie does not have a top actor, then it's unlikely to do well." You want an answer choice whose conclusion simply negates the evidence.

Step 4: Evaluate the Answer Choices
(B) is correct. Here, you are told that gardens with bee balm often have the eventual characteristic of abundant crops. Then the argument concludes that gardens *without* bee balm will likely *not* have abundant crops. That is the same flaw as the original argument, making this the correct answer.

(A) is incorrect because it contains no flaw. This argument says animals need to devote most of their energy to finding food to maintain optimal energy levels. It then concludes that devoting energy elsewhere will result in less than optimal energy levels. The logic of this argument is sound.

(C) is flawed, but in a different way than the original argument. This argument states that keeping confidences is important to friendship because keeping confidences allows for openness. The argument then goes a little too far in claiming that openness is therefore *essential* to friendship. The conclusion of the stimulus includes the qualifier "unlikely," and nothing similar is present in the conclusion of **(C)**. Additionally, in the original argument, the main conclusion negates the subsidiary conclusion. In this answer choice, however, the main conclusion discusses a "high degree of openness," which is part of the evidence *for* the

subsidiary conclusion but not the subsidiary conclusion itself.

(D) is close but not quite right. Here, visual aids can help teach math skills. However, the conclusion doesn't say that *without* visual aids you likely *cannot* teach math skills. It just says that teaching math skills will be more difficult. This would be correct only if the original argument concluded that movies with unknown actors would have a harder time doing well.

(E) is incorrect because it contains a different flaw than does the original argument. This argument nicely illustrates the classic LSAT flaw of confusing necessity with sufficiency. The argument states that understanding rules of perspective is *necessary* for success but then concludes that understanding rules will lead to success. A necessary condition is not sufficient to guarantee a definite result.

15. (D) Inference

Step 1: Identify the Question Type
The phrase "statements above, if true, most strongly support" identifies this as an Inference question. Accept each sentence in the stimulus as true and find an answer choice that is supported by one or more of those sentences. Watch out for answers that use the exact words from the stimulus but distort the author's meaning.

Step 2: Untangle the Stimulus
This stimulus discusses a recent trend in history writing: an emphasis on historical trends is being replaced by an emphasis on details. As a result, the author states, historical trends are overlooked. As a further result, parallels between historic trends and current trends are also overlooked, and this lessens our ability to learn from the past.

Step 3: Make a Prediction
Combining all of this information shows the author is saying that the change from an emphasis on historical trends to an emphasis on details has resulted in a lessening of our ability to learn.

Step 4: Evaluate the Answer Choices
(D) is correct and matches your prediction.

(A) is a Distortion. *Studying* details is not the problem. The problem is emphasizing those details *in writing* such that historical trends become overlooked.

(B) is Extreme. The author says emphasis on details has replaced the emphasis on trends, with the latter being *often* overlooked. But that doesn't mean that the *only* time trends can be noticed is when details aren't emphasized. Nothing in the stimulus says the two can't occur together, just that they often haven't been.

(C) is Extreme. What lessens the ability to learn is overlooking the parallels between historical and current trends. Just looking at historical trends does not necessarily result in the "best" ability to learn. Also, this answer says people who look at historical trends and *not* details are "best" able to learn. Maybe the people who learn best are those who look at *both*. In short, because the statements just identify what lessens our ability to learn, you cannot truly infer what enhances our ability to learn the best.

(E) is Extreme because it is too specific. Studying trends and details does not have to be "equal." The author might go for this, but it is just as likely that the author would want a mixture of the two in something other than a 50/50 split. The author may even want a return to emphasizing only historical trends or mainly historical trends. The author never makes a clear indication, so this is not supported.

16. (A) Assumption (Sufficient)

Step 1: Identify the Question Type
The word *assumed* identifies this as an Assumption question. Additionally, the question stem states that the argument will be complete *if* the assumption is added, so you are looking for a sufficient assumption. Only one answer choice will provide an assumption that makes the therapist's conclusion follow inevitably from the evidence. Keep an eye out for Formal Logic in Sufficient Assumption questions.

Step 2: Untangle the Stimulus
The therapist starts off with a claim: trust is "essential" to happiness. Using Formal Logic, this translates to:

$$\textbf{If} \quad \textbf{happiness} \quad \rightarrow \quad \textbf{trust}$$

The evidence is a string of Formal Logic:

$$\textbf{If} \quad \sim \textbf{isolated} \quad \rightarrow \quad \begin{array}{c}\textbf{meaningful} \\ \textbf{emotional} \\ \textbf{connection}\end{array} \quad \rightarrow \quad \textbf{trust}$$

Step 3: Make a Prediction
Notice that the Formal Logic in the evidence and conclusion both end in "trust." The therapist never explicitly makes the jump from not being isolated in the evidence to happiness in the conclusion. Instead, she assumes that anyone who is happy is not isolated.

Step 4: Evaluate the Answer Choices
(A) is correct and matches your prediction perfectly. This translates to: if someone is isolated, then he isn't happy. Adding this to the evidence chain lets the conclusion be logically linked.

(B) goes backwards on the Formal Logic. The therapist claims a lack of trust results in no emotional connection, which then leads to isolation. It can be validly claimed, therefore, that

the therapist also assumes that anyone who has *no* emotional connections will be *unhappy*. However, that does not mean that anyone who *does* have emotional connections will be *happy*. That incorrectly negates the Formal Logic and does not help connect the evidence to the conclusion.

(C) is a Faulty Use of Detail. This is perfectly accurate based on the evidence. In fact, it's a restatement of one piece of the evidence. However, it fails to connect the evidence to the concept of happiness in the conclusion, so it does not work as an assumption. Remember that an assumption is an *unstated* piece of information that connects the evidence to the conclusion. This answer simply restates the evidence—a classic LSAT trap.

(D) is Outside the Scope. This may be true, but in order for the conclusion to follow, the assumption must make people who *do* feel isolated sufficient to guarantee happiness. Adding information about people who *do not* feel isolated is irrelevant to the argument.

(E) also goes backwards on the Formal Logic. This answer incorrectly reverses the Formal Logic in the evidence and does not connect the evidence to the concept of happiness in the conclusion.

17. (C) Flaw

Step 1: Identify the Question Type
The phrase "most vulnerable to criticism" identifies this as a Flaw question. Break down the author's argument, identifying his conclusion and evidence and determining his assumption. Then, evaluate how the author's reasoning goes wrong. Remember to keep an eye out for common flaw types.

Step 2: Untangle the Stimulus
The author presents you with two pieces of information: *Sirat Bani Hilal* is the only Arabic epic poem still performed today, and it is usually sung (unlike most other epics). It is an interesting correlation, but the author then makes the sudden leap that the singing factor is the primary reason for the epic's continued performance.

Step 3: Make a Prediction
This argument is a textbook example of an author implying causation based on a mere correlation. Just because two things occur together does not mean that one caused the other.

Step 4: Evaluate the Answer Choices
(C) is correct and points out this classic LSAT flaw.

(A) is Extreme. None of the evidence here seems impossible (or even that difficult) to corroborate.

(B) is Outside the Scope. The fact that the play is still performed and the fact that it is sung do not indicate biased information.

(D) is Outside the Scope. The only opinion offered in this argument is the author's. Without knowing what the popular opinion is, you cannot claim that the author is turning opinion into fact.

(E) is also Outside the Scope. The evidence is merely a collection of facts. There are no sufficient or necessary conditions for the author to confuse.

18. (E) Assumption (Necessary)

Step 1: Identify the Question Type

The word *assumption* identifies this as an Assumption question. Additionally, the word *depends* indicates you are looking for a necessary assumption, one without which the fund-raiser's conclusion cannot be logically drawn from the evidence. You can use the Denial Test to check or eliminate answer choices.

Step 2: Untangle the Stimulus

The fund-raiser states donors often don't have the right to vote on charities' policies. She argues this lack results in donors feeling less emotionally connected to their charity. The fundraiser then argues that giving donors the right to vote will increase the amount of money donated.

Step 3: Make a Prediction

By saying the lack of a vote decreases donors' emotional connection to a charity, the fund-raiser suggests having the right to vote would result in donors having a greater emotional connection to a charity. However, she makes an unsupported jump to the conclusion. There is a distinction between having an emotional connection and giving money for which the fund-raiser does not account. The fund-raiser must therefore assume a greater emotional connection will lead to larger monetary donations.

Step 4: Evaluate the Answer Choices

(E) is correct and captures the essence of that assumption.

(A) is Extreme. There are many problems with this answer, the most important of which is that it offers no connection as to why the author feels that a right to vote will lead to increased donations. Furthermore, a right to vote does not have to be the *most* effective way for donors to influence the charity's decisions. As long as it's *a* way, donors will probably feel more emotionally connected.

(B) is a Distortion. This choice is tempting but problematic because it only tells you about charities that have increased their donations. What about all of the charities that *have not* increased donations? The fund-raiser is trying to show that increasing emotional connections leads to increased donations. This answer too conveniently ignores the possibility that a lot of charities may also have increased emotional connections but *failed* to increase donations. By reversing the cause and effect, this answer distorts the assumption and is therefore incorrect. This answer choice

may strengthen the argument, but it is not a necessary assumption.

(C) is Extreme. It strengthens the evidence about increasing emotional connections but fails to connect that evidence to the concept of increased donations mentioned in the conclusion. **(C)** also would fail the Denial Test because even if it wasn't "every" charity that had this result, the conclusion that "most charities could probably increase the amount of money they raise" could still hold.

(D) is also Extreme. The fund-raiser may feel that reducing a donor's influence may lead to a decrease in donations. However, the fund-raiser never goes so far as to suggest that donors would stop giving *any* money to the charity. Furthermore, the right to vote is described as a direct influence on policies, but the fund-raiser never suggests what would happen if donors did not have "any influence" whatsoever. Lastly, the author would not need to assume that "[m]ost potential donors" would have this reaction. Even if it was less than half, it would not affect the force of the argument.

19. (E) Main Point

Step 1: Identify the Question Type

The phrase "most accurately expresses the main conclusion" identifies this as a Main Point question. Specifically, you must identify the conclusion of Leslie's argument. Focus on Keywords, look out for subsidiary conclusions, and expect to combine statements in the argument to paraphrase Leslie's main point.

Step 2: Untangle the Stimulus

From the very first sentence, Leslie's main conclusion is pretty clear: Erich's quest for the treasure is irrational. By saying, "I'll show you," Leslie indicates everything from that point forward will provide evidence to back up that point. Sure enough, by the time Leslie states, "I rest my case," her point has been made: the quest for the treasure is irrational.

Step 3: Make a Prediction

Find an answer choice that restates Leslie's conclusion that Erich's quest for treasure is irrational.

Step 4: Evaluate the Answer Choices

(E) correctly states the overall conclusion of Leslie's argument.

(A) is a Faulty Use of Detail. This is true. However, Leslie was just using that analogical example to prove the point about Erich's quest for the treasure. It is *a* point, but not the main point.

(B) is Extreme. Leslie clearly doesn't want Erich to risk his physical well-being for this particular treasure (which Leslie claims is less valuable than the world). But this answer says "regardless of the possible gains," which eliminates the possibility of Erich risking his physical well-being for things far more valuable than the treasure in question. Leslie never goes that far, so this answer does not work.

(C) is also Extreme. This choice is close, but Leslie does not claim the treasure has "no value"—just that it is less valuable than the world.

(D) is Outside the Scope. Leslie may hope that Erich is convinced, but Leslie's argument is directed at telling Erich that the quest is irrational. Use the last line to clarify this point. When Leslie says, "I rest my case," she means, "Your quest is irrational." It is not Leslie saying, "You can be *convinced* that your quest is irrational." This subtle distinction is what makes **(D)** incorrect. The evidence is about Erich's quest, not about Erich's susceptibility to persuasion.

20. (D) Weaken

Step 1: Identify the Question Type
The phrase "most weaken" identifies this as a Weaken question. Break down the argument into evidence and conclusion, determine the central assumption, and then look for an answer choice that attacks that assumption.

Step 2: Untangle the Stimulus
The article in question refers to a study showing that people who take vitamin C supplements tend to have a lower risk of heart disease. Based on this study, the article concludes that people who take vitamin C supplements are healthier than average.

Step 3: Make a Prediction
Notice that the argument makes a conclusion about one's overall health yet focuses its evidence solely on heart disease and vitamin C. But while people who take vitamin C have better heart health, they may be less healthy than the average in other ways. Therefore, the author assumes that high doses of vitamin C provide a net health benefit; in other words, that vitamin C has more positive than negative side effects. To weaken this argument, find an answer choice that suggests one could be negatively affected by vitamin C supplements.

Step 4: Evaluate the Answer Choices
(D) is correct and weakens the argument by showing how the supplements reduce one's resistance to infectious diseases. That would make it less likely that those who take vitamin C supplements are healthier overall.

(A) is an Irrelevant Comparison. The argument is about the health benefits of vitamin C supplements. The effects of vitamin C consumed outside of supplements have no bearing on the argument, especially because you're not told whether the effects are better or worse—just that they are different.

(B) is Outside the Scope. This answer states that other dietary changes would reduce heart disease just as well as vitamin C supplements, but that does not change the fact that vitamin C supplements still reduce heart disease. Therefore, this has no effect on the argument. Nor does it address the overall health level discussed in the article's conclusion.

(C) is Outside the Scope. This choice gives you a way to lower the risk of heart disease even more than taking vitamin C supplements alone, but it still does not change the fact that vitamin C reduces heart problems. It's possible that those who take vitamins C and E are even *healthier* than those who take vitamin C alone, but it still could be true that those who take vitamin C are healthier than average.

(E) is a 180. This choice actually strengthens the argument and is the opposite of what you want, as it provides yet another reason why vitamin C is good for one's health.

21. (D) Flaw

Step 1: Identify the Question Type
The phrase "most vulnerable to criticism" clearly identifies this as a Flaw question. Break down Boris's argument, identifying his conclusion and evidence, and look for something that he fails to do in his response to George.

Step 2: Untangle the Stimulus
George wants to know why people are now so interested in learning ballroom dancing when it was not very popular in the 1980s and early 1990s. Boris responds by saying that people started learning certain ballroom dances in 1995, and the popularity of ballroom dancing caught on from there.

Step 3: Make a Prediction
Referring again to the additional direction in the question stem, take a moment to consider what Boris failed to do. Notice that Boris explained why dances other than merengue and related dances exploded in popularity, but he never actually answered the big question: Why is there interest in dancing in the first place? To answer that, he would have needed to explain *why* many people learned merengue and related dances starting in 1995.

Step 4: Evaluate the Answer Choices
(D) is correct and points out the flaw in Boris's argument. He accounts for the subsequent popularity expansion but not the initial revival.

(A) is Outside the Scope. There is no need for the people learning specific dances in 1995 to be the same people learning other dances now. If this were the case, it could weaken Boris's answer because it limits the dancing population to those who started in 1995, but it is not a flaw inherent in his argument.

(B) is Outside the Scope. George does not want to know why it was *un*popular before 1995; he wants to know why it *is* popular now.

(C) is Outside the Scope. There is no need to connect a specific type of ballroom dancing to any other form of dancing—prevalent or not. The fact is ballroom dancing is of interest now, and other types of dancing are irrelevant to the question.

(E) is Extreme. Because George never asked about all types of ballroom dancing, just ballroom dancing in general, there was no need for Boris to account for all types.

22. (B) Inference (Could Be True EXCEPT)

Step 1: Identify the Question Type

The phrase "each of the following could be true EXCEPT" identifies this as an Inference EXCEPT question. Begin by taking a moment to characterize the answers in order to avoid choosing a wrong answer. The four incorrect answers to this question will be possible ("could be true"). The one correct answer will be the one that is the exception—the one that absolutely cannot be true (i.e., must be false) and directly contradicts the stimulus.

Step 2: Untangle the Stimulus

In this stimulus, the author presents some scientists' views on Neanderthals and Cro-Magnons: they should be considered distinct species. But the author disagrees, as indicated by "[y]et." You are told that both groups lived in different environments but had tools that were exactly alike. Next comes the most important phrase of the stimulus: "only if they faced the same daily challenges … would they have used such similar tools." The Formal Logic of this statement is this:

If	*similar tools*	→	*same challenges AND met challenges the same way*

Combined with what you know, this means the two groups of hominids lived in different environments but used the same types of tools, which therefore means they must have faced the same daily challenges. Finally, the last sentence tells you the two groups are probably members of the same species, with their morphological differences simply a result of their different environments.

Step 3: Make a Prediction

From here, move confidently into the answers to find something that is in complete contrast to what you know. Remember that the correct answer choice must be false and that incorrect choices could be true.

Step 4: Evaluate the Answer Choices

(B) contradicts the stimulus and is therefore correct. The stimulus discussed two groups of hominids who lived in different environments but, by the Formal Logic provided,

must have faced the same daily challenges (because their tools were similar). Two environments, same daily challenges. Stating daily challenges are unique to an environment is in complete contrast to the stimulus.

(A) is a 180. This choice must be true according to the last sentence. The two groups have morphological differences, yet the author suggests they *are* the same species.

(C) is an Irrelevant Comparison. The morphological differences between Neanderthals and Cro-Magnons are described in the statements as "minor." However, without any description of the differences between Cro-Magnons and modern humans, there is no way to say for sure whether those differences are greater or not. So, this could be true.

(D) is Extreme. The fact that Cro-Magnons and Neanderthals both used the same tools is evidence to suggest they are the same species. So, a general rule stating using similar tools is *required* for two groups to be of the same species could be at play. It does not *have* to be true, but it could be.

(E) also could be true. The stimulus states these two groups lived in different environments, so it is not a stretch to say that they could have been geographically isolated from each other.

23. (E) Principle (Apply/Inference)

Step 1: Identify the Question Type

The word *principles* clearly identifies this as a Principle question. Moreover, the phrase "[w]hich one … most closely conforms to the principles stated above" tells you that the correct answer must follow a principle in the stimulus. Treat this as you would an Inference question; take note of all key terms and Formal Logic provided in the stimulus and find an answer choice that must be true on the basis of one of the principles.

Step 2: Untangle the Stimulus

The stimulus provides two principles regarding summer weather. The first states that any summer day with intermittent winds and temperatures below 84 degrees all afternoon is "pleasant." The second states that any *humid* summer day with no wind or temperatures above 84 degrees all afternoon is "oppressive."

Step 3: Make a Prediction

Accept each principle as true and find the one answer that conforms to these definitions. Write out the Formal Logic to help you evaluate the answer choice:

If	*wind AND temperature below 84°*	→	*pleasant*

If	~ pleasant	→	~ wind OR temperature ~ below 84°
If	humid AND (temperature above 84° OR ~ wind)	→	oppressive
If	~ oppressive	→	~ humid OR (temperature ~ above 84° AND wind)

Step 4: Evaluate the Answer Choices

(E) is correct and must be true based on the second principle. It is a humid day with no wind. Regardless of the temperature, the lack of wind is sufficient for a humid summer day to qualify as "oppressive."

(A) is close. This choice satisfies the sufficient condition of staying below 84 degrees all afternoon. However, according to the Formal Logic, there are *two* sufficient conditions that need to be met for a summer day to be pleasant. This day had no wind, so it does not satisfy the conditions of the principle.

(B) is also close. With temperatures above 84 degrees all afternoon, this day certainly seems to meet the criteria for "oppressive." Unfortunately, the "oppressive" principle only applies to days with high humidity. Because this day had low humidity, the "oppressive" principle cannot be applied.

(C) is missing one piece. Here, the temperature remained at a constant 84 degrees all afternoon. Yet neither principle addresses what temperatures of exactly 84 degrees mean. Temperatures would have to be either below 84 degrees or above 84 degrees for one of the principles to apply. Had it been under 84 degrees, that along with the occasional periods of wind, would have made it "pleasant."

(D) is incorrect because the conditions to make a day "oppressive" are either temperatures above 84 degrees or no wind. This day never had temperatures above 84 and had intermittent winds. Hence, as per the principle, even though this day was humid, there is nothing else to justify calling it "oppressive."

24. (D) Parallel Reasoning

Step 1: Identify the Question Type

The phrase "reasoning ... most similar to" identifies this as a Parallel Reasoning question. Characterize the conclusion in

the argument and eliminate any answer choice with a different type of conclusion. Alternatively, analyze the argument and find an answer choice that matches the reasoning piece by piece.

Step 2: Untangle the Stimulus

Despite its length, the argument in the stimulus is pretty straightforward. The author concludes that the local radio station will not win first place this year in the regional ratings race. Why? The author claims that the radio station has never finished better than fifth place in the ratings and conditions haven't changed positively for the station.

Step 3: Make a Prediction

The author predicts something will not happen this year because it has not happened in the past. Find an answer choice that provides another argument that uses past performance to indicate a definite continuation of that trend in the next occurrence.

Step 4: Evaluate the Answer Choices

(D) is correct. Based on past performance (stock prices have always been lower on Mondays), the author predicts, with certainty, that the stock will be lower the next Monday. That perfectly matches the structure of the stimulus, even though the stimulus has a negative prediction: "will not win." That could also be viewed in the affirmative by saying that it will lose the ratings race. Likewise, **(D)** could be rewritten to say stock prices will not be the same or higher. So, positive/negative is not applicable here to determine whether the stimulus and **(D)** are parallel.

(A) is incorrect for a couple of reasons. Here, the past trend is that every swan the author has seen is white. To be parallel to the original argument, the author must claim that the next swan spotted will also be white. However, this argument concludes that *all* swans are therefore probably white. That is like saying the radio station in the original argument will probably *never* win the ratings race. That is not what the original argument says, so this is not exactly parallel. Additionally, the conclusion in the original argument is an unequivocal prediction, while this conclusion is an assertion of probable fact.

(B) is incorrect because of the level of certainty. The past trend here is the coin coming up heads. Like the original argument, the next toss is predicted to be heads. However, unlike in the original argument, the prediction is qualified: it says the next toss will *probably* be heads. The original argument has no such qualification, making these arguments unparallel.

(C) fails to provide any past trend that supports a prediction. Instead, it simply provides an assertion of fact stating all lions are mammals.

(E) also fails to support a conclusion about the future based on past trends. Rather, this choice uses a Formal Logic statement ("[o]nly trained swimmers are lifeguards") to predict that the next lifeguard will be a trained swimmer as well.

25. (E) Assumption (Necessary)

Step 1: Identify the Question Type

The word *assumption* identifies this as an Assumption question. Additionally, the word *required* indicates you are looking for a necessary assumption, one without which the chef's conclusion cannot be logically drawn from the evidence. You can use the Denial Test to check or eliminate answer choices.

Step 2: Untangle the Stimulus

The chef in this argument describes the first step in preparing mussels in a given recipe: sprinkle them with cornmeal. The point of that step, as the chef tells us, is to eject the sand from the mussel. However, the chef has decided to skip this step because mussels from seafood markets do not contain sand.

Step 3: Make a Prediction

The argument seems relatively straightforward, but notice that the chef never actually states that he purchased his mussels from a seafood market. The chef therefore assumes the mussels he is using come from a seafood market.

Step 4: Evaluate the Answer Choices

(E) is correct and matches your prediction. To confirm, try denying this answer. What if the chef *wasn't* using mussels from the seafood market? In that case, the mussels would not be guaranteed to be free of sand and there would be no apparent reason for the chef to skip the sand-removal step. Because denying this choice tears apart the chef's argument, it must be assumed for the argument to logically work.

(A) is Outside the Scope. Because farm-raised mussels don't contain sand, they don't need to be cleaned. It doesn't matter that cornmeal isn't used to clean them.

(B) is Outside the Scope. The only reason for cornmeal (as described by the chef) is to remove sand. Because sand has no known effect on other contaminants, this is not an issue. Maybe those contaminants are taken care of in step two.

(C) is Outside the Scope. It may seem tempting, but it is not necessary for the chef's argument. What if cornmeal *did* affect the taste? That might give the chef even more reason to skip that first step. So even if this answer were not true, the argument could still work. Therefore, it is not a required assumption.

(D) is Outside the Scope. It does not matter when the recipe was written. Even if it was written years after the availability of farm-raised mussels, the cornmeal step is still in there, and the chef would still probably skip it as long as he believes his mussels contain no sand.

Section IV: Reading Comprehension

Passage 1: Literary Works of Amos Tutuola

Q#	Question Type	Correct	Difficulty
1	Global	B	★
2	Inference	D	★★
3	Inference	A	★
4	Detail	D	★
5	Detail (EXCEPT)	E	★★
6	Logic Function	A	★
7	Global	C	★

Passage 2: Inclusive Fitness Theory of Kin Recognition

Q#	Question Type	Correct	Difficulty
8	Global	A	★★
9	Detail	C	★
10	Inference	D	★
11	Logic Function	A	★
12	Inference	A	★★★
13	Detail	B	★★★★
14	Inference	E	★★★
15	Logic Reasoning (Weaken)	C	★★★

Passage 3: Definition of National Minority

Q#	Question Type	Correct	Difficulty
16	Global	E	★★
17	Inference	C	★★
18	Detail (NOT)	D	★
19	Inference	E	★★
20	Logic Reasoning (Parallel Reasoning)	A	★★
21	Logic Reasoning (Principle)	B	★★★

Passage 4: Women's Education in France

Q#	Question Type	Correct	Difficulty
22	Inference	C	★
23	Global	E	★★
24	Logic Reasoning (Parallel Reasoning)	A	★★★
25	Detail	B	★
26	Inference	E	★★
27	Inference	C	★

Passage 1: Literary Works of Amos Tutuola

Step 1: Read the Passage Strategically
Sample Roadmap

line #	Keyword/phrase	¶ Margin notes
6	praised	
7	fresh, inventive	Fans praise inventive approach to novel
8	however, dismissed	
9	simple	
10	unwelcome	Critics dismissive; rehashing & taking liberties
11	However; properly	
13	essential	Au—T's works significant—can't classify as novel
14	too facilely	
19	are not	
20	not; but	
21	right	Au—T is not a true novelist
22	not strikingly	
23	but it is important	
24	whereas	
27	most useful	—T is teller of folktales
35		Characteristics of folk tale teller in African oral trad.
36	not	
37	but	
38	Thus	
40–41	in fact; most brilliant	
43	:	
44	for example	
51	most revealingly	How T uses the characteristics
53	for example	

Discussion

Paragraph 1 introduces you to the **Topic** of this passage, Amos Tutuola. Immediately, two contrasting opinions are provided about Tutuola's works: some critics praise his inventive approach to the novel, while others dismiss him for simply rehashing and taking liberties with well-known stories. The author's opinion appears with the Contrast Keyword [*however*]. The author doesn't obviously side with either group of literary critics, instead calling both groups out for assuming "too facilely" that Tutuola wrote novels. The author points out that true understanding of Tutuola's contribution to literature requires clearly defining the genre of Tutuola's works. The author thereby sets the stage for a discussion of the proper classification of Tutuola's works—and it probably won't be novels. This discussion of genre will serve as the **Scope** of the passage. In addition, the **Purpose** also seems pretty evident: illustrate how Tutuola's works can be better understood by classifying them under the proper genre. Notice how the author steers the discussion away from the conflict between groups of literary critics—whether Tutuola is a good writer or not is an idea the author introduces but is not the main focus. Additionally, the author remains quiet on his own view of the worth of Tutuola's works, focusing solely on the classification of them.

The first sentence of paragraph 2 finds the author claiming Tutuola's works won't satisfy the definition of "novel," no matter how loose the definition is. Therefore, Tutuola can't be a novelist. Instead, the author offers an alternative classification in a sentence that clearly lays out the **Main Idea** of the passage: "Tutuola is not a novelist but a teller of folktales." While agreeing with some of Tutuola's critics who say Tutuola isn't original, the author makes their criticism irrelevant by arguing they are using the wrong set of standards. Tutuola's not supposed to be original (like a novelist would be). Instead, Tutuola should be regarded as working in the African oral tradition of storytelling.

Paragraph 3 defines the characteristics of a folktale teller in this tradition. The stories are already known and shared by the community. The teller is praised not for the story itself but for the delivery and embellishments made to the tale for the sake of good storytelling. In fact, improvisation and modifications to the stories are expected and even valued.

Paragraph 4 shows how Tutuola utilizes these characteristics in his own works, thus solidifying the author's Main Point. The author provides multiple examples of Tutuola's adherence to the oral storytelling tradition (e.g., resetting stories in modern times, blending linguistic styles, and incorporating traditional folktale-telling techniques) as further evidence that Tutuola's works should be evaluated not as novels but as the literary equivalent of oral folktales.

1. (B) Global

Step 2: Identify the Question Type

Any question that asks you to determine the "main point" of the passage is a Global question.

Step 3: Research the Relevant Text

In most cases, the "relevant text" for a Global question is your own estimation of the Topic, Scope, Purpose, and Main Idea that you made during Step 1. But in this case, the author's unequivocal point of view appears in lines 20–21: "Tutuola is not a novelist but a teller of folktales."

Step 4: Make a Prediction

The claim from lines 20–21 serves as an efficient, concise paraphrase of the main point. Tutuola shouldn't be held to the novelist's standard of originality.

Step 5: Evaluate the Answer Choices

(B) accurately echoes this sentiment.

(A) is a Faulty Use of Detail. It contains nothing inaccurate. However, it merely regurgitates some minor facts from the first paragraph without touching on the overall theme of classifying Tutuola's works.

(C) sounds tempting but makes the mistake of suggesting Tutuola writes novels. That goes against everything the author says in the first sentence of paragraph 2.

(D) distorts the debate mentioned in the opening paragraph. The author does introduce two groups of critics, but their division is over the worth of Tutuola's works, not the classification of them. As the author implies, both groups of critics regard Tutuola's works as novels. Only the author suggests that Tutuola's works should be seen as folktales.

(E) makes folktales the center of attention, but that's not the focus of this passage. Amos Tutuola is not used in this passage as merely an example of the folktale genre, as this answer suggests. Instead, the folktale is introduced as the most applicable classification of Tutuola's works.

2. (D) Inference

Step 2: Identify the Question Type

This question asks you to apply Tutuola to a hypothetical modern-day Irish author. It resembles an Inference question because it looks for something that must be true about Tutuola applied to something not directly in the text. This could also potentially be construed as a Logic Reasoning (Parallel) question.

Step 3: Research the Relevant Text

You're looking to match Tutuola's writing approach to that of another author. Tutuola's approach was outlined by a few examples in the fourth paragraph: he embellishes familiar tales with personal interpretations or by transferring them to modern settings.

Step 4: Make a Prediction
The best strategy here is to compare the answers to the examples in the fourth paragraph of the passage to find the match.

Step 5: Evaluate the Answer Choices
(D) sounds exactly like the passage. In lines 46–47, Tutuola is described as transferring traditional tales to modern settings. That sounds exactly like a modern Irish author transplanting traditional Irish tales into contemporary settings. This is consistent and thus the correct answer.

(A) is a 180. Tutuola applied folktale conventions to his modern works, not the other way around. Tutuola was criticized specifically for *not* following the conventions of the modern novel.

(B) also is a 180. Tutuola took an oral form of storytelling and turned it into a literary style. This answer choice has the Irish author taking a literary style and turning it into an oral form.

(C) is a Distortion of the passage. Tutuola may have blended languages and linguistic constructs, but nothing in the passage suggests that he combined *characters* from different cultures in his storytelling.

(E) is Half-Right/Half-Wrong. It mentions the omniscient narrator that, according to lines 53–55, Tutuola used. However, that narrative voice is described as one that summarizes the story at the end. More importantly, though, this answer discusses original stories. Tutuola didn't tell original stories; he told well-known stories in an inventive manner.

3. (A) Inference

Step 2: Identify the Question Type
The question stem asks you to characterize the author's attitude toward something discussed in the passage. Thus, it belongs to a specific subset of Inference question.

Step 3: Research the Relevant Text
The author first mentions Tutuola's position in world literature in lines 10–15. The author wants to make sure Tutuola's genre is correctly classified, but you have to continue reading through paragraph 2 to find that classification. In lines 20–21, the author asserts Tutuola is a teller of folktales, not a novelist. The author goes on to say in lines 27–29 that classifying Tutuola's works as folktales in the African oral tradition is the "most useful approach."

Step 4: Make a Prediction
From this text, you can conclude the author feels Tutuola's place in world literature is defined by his being a teller of folktales.

Step 5: Evaluate the Answer Choices
(A) describes that feeling perfectly.

(B) is Outside the Scope. The author never discusses any renewed interest in the study of oral traditions.

(C) is a 180. The "[h]owever" in line 11, the "too facilely" in line 14, and the "but" in line 23 indicate the author is actually rather displeased by the literary critics' assumptions and oversights.

(D) suggests that some people feel translations are ruining the integrity of Tutuola's works. There's no suggestion in the passage that translations pose any problems (or that they even exist). Therefore, the author never expresses any attitude about this.

(E) is Outside the Scope. This passage is entirely devoted to Tutuola's works and does not discuss or suggest any future trends. You could have stopped reading at "optimistic." The author isn't "optimistic" about anything; he simply wants Tutuola's works to be properly characterized.

4. (D) Detail

Step 2: Identify the Question Type
The phrase "according to the passage" is a sure sign of a Detail question.

Step 3: Research the Relevant Text
The question stem directs you to find the criticism of Tutuola's works. This criticism is described in lines 8–11.

Step 4: Make a Prediction
Basically, the criticism is that Tutuola retells well-known stories and takes unwelcome liberties with the details.

Step 5: Evaluate the Answer Choices
(D) says exactly that.

(A) is a 180. The author is the one who claims Tutuola's works are based on African oral tradition, not the critics. According to lines 8–9, the critics dislike that Tutuola's stories are "simple retellings of local tales." They wouldn't want even *more* adherence to the oral folk-telling tradition.

(B) is also a 180. The passage says Tutuola mixes languages, but this is not cited as a source of complaint. In fact, the author mentions it in the same sentence that he introduces the critics who *praise* Tutuola's works.

(C) is Outside the Scope. The author suggests critics incorrectly classify Tutuola's works as novels, not as folktales, but the critics themselves don't weigh in on the fusion of styles. They don't seem to be aware such a fusion is happening.

(E) is yet another 180. Again, the author suggests that critics *do* actually see Tutuola's works as novels. Furthermore, there's nothing in the passage to imply that Tutuola himself characterizes his stories as novels. If anything, the first half of this answer choice is more along the lines of the author's point of view.

5. (E) Detail (EXCEPT)

Step 2: Identify the Question Type
The question stem asks what the author attributes (or, rather, doesn't attribute) to Tutuola. That makes this a Detail EXCEPT question. You need to find the one answer not mentioned in the passage.

Step 3: Research the Relevant Text
Because the author discusses Tutuola throughout the passage, one might expect this question to take a little more time than others. You may need to use your global understanding of the passage, coupled with some careful fact-checking of the answer choices, to get through this one. If you want to knock out wrong answers, however, a good place to start looking for attributes of Tutuola's works is in the fourth paragraph.

Step 4: Make a Prediction
There's a whole universe of details not mentioned in the passage, so predicting the outlier might be tough. However, you do know from the passage's Main Idea what the author wouldn't attribute to Tutuola, and that's anything having to do with being a novelist.

Step 5: Evaluate the Answer Choices
(E) discusses turning folktales into novels. Given the author's insistence that Tutuola didn't write novels, this seems like something the author would never have claimed. As it turns out, this is the exception and is therefore the correct answer.

(A), with the repetition of ideas for emphasis, is found in lines 43–45.

(B), with the relocation to modern settings, is found in lines 46–47.

(C), which mentions international recognition, can be found in the first sentence of the passage.

(D), with the omniscient narrator, can be found in lines 54–55.

6. (A) Logic Function

Step 2: Identify the Question Type
Because this question asks you to find what the author was attempting to do with a particular reference, it's a Logic Function question.

Step 3: Research the Relevant Text
Logic Function questions always have relevant text that goes beyond the lines referenced in the question stem. In this case, because the text in question is evidence, it's important to look back up to what the author is trying to prove. Here, start back at line 21. That's when the author talks about the critics who complain Tutuola's stories aren't original. After the "but" in line 23, the author makes the claim that original stories are characteristics of novels, whereas pulling from traditional lore is expected of folktales.

Step 4: Make a Prediction
The "corpus of traditional lore" is the collection of non-original material that characterizes folktales. This characterization is what the author uses to differentiate folktales from novels, which require originality and realism.

Step 5: Evaluate the Answer Choices
(A) matches your prediction nearly exactly.

(B) is Outside the Scope. While the author is discussing two literary genres here, he's doing it to explain differences in characterization, not to argue for their equal worth. The author isn't concerned with the value of the two genres. If anything, the author is more concerned with the value of Tutuola's works as folktales, not as novels.

(C) is a 180. The author here is trying to sharply differentiate between the two genres, not explain why they should be mixed. Additionally, the critics aren't against blending genres. In fact, according to the author, they don't even see Tutuola's works as a combination of genres—they see the works only as novels.

(D) is a Distortion. This section of text describes the characteristics of two dissimilar genres but does so in order to point out the difference, not to illuminate any direct counterparts between the two. The author's point is that novels and folktales are essentially mutually exclusive (novels require originality while folktales draw on traditions).

(E) is also a Distortion. The author might agree that the distinguishing characteristics of novels and folktales are poorly understood, but he doesn't want critics to analyze two genres. Instead, he wants them to analyze Tutuola's works within the confines of just one of the two.

7. (C) Global

Step 2: Identify the Question Type
Any question asking for the "primary purpose" of an entire passage is a Global question.

Step 3: Research the Relevant Text
The Purpose of the passage comes across pretty clearly in the author's use of the words "essential" in line 13 and "most useful approach" in line 27. Additionally, think back to the Topic, Scope, Purpose, and Main Idea that you outlined in Step 1.

Step 4: Make a Prediction
The author recommends reclassifying Tutuola's works in order to better understand them. The examples of Tutuola's works in the last paragraph help provide specific evidence to back up that recommendation. So, a good prediction of the author's Purpose would be "to use examples of Tutuola's works to show how those works should be alternatively classified as folktales for more proper evaluation."

Step 5: Evaluate the Answer Choices

(C) says basically that.

(A) is a Distortion. This passage predominantly narrows Tutuola's works to the realm of folktales and doesn't ascribe any further range.

(B) is too broad. This answer mischaracterizes the passage's focus, which isn't on the literary genre of folktales in general but on how Tutuola's works in particular fit that genre. Additionally, the passage doesn't present a challenge to folktales' validity, nor does it defend the genre. The author simply *defines* the genre.

(D) is also too broad. While the author does distinguish between the two genres, he has a purpose beyond just that. He differentiates the two in order to prove that Tutuola's works belong in the folktale category. Answers **(B)** and **(D)** misapply the focus of the passage as being on the genres of literature when the passage is really concerned about the works of Tutuola.

(E) is a Distortion. The author covers the critics' disagreement in the first paragraph, but there are two problems. First, the critics' disagreement isn't over Tutuola's place in world literature (the author introduces that idea), and second, their disagreement isn't anything more than a starting place for the author's main purpose: to prove Tutuola's works belong in the folktale category.

Passage 2: Inclusive Fitness Theory of Kin Recognition

Step 1: Read the Passage Strategically
Sample Roadmap

line #	Keyword/phrase	¶ Margin notes
2	regardless	Ways of Kin Recog. are common
5	turned	Bio: Why exist? Reason: IFT
6–7	One response	
11–12	not solely; but more generally; Whereas	goes beyond Nat. Sel. – not just offspring; all relatives
13	traditional view	
17	posits	
18	because	
20	helped	explains honeybee evol.
21	including	
25	also	IFT —> may explain cannibalism
26	usefully	
30–31	provide an illustration	Ex. spadefoot toad tadpoles
34	but	
39	Yet	They eat w/in species, but not own kin
42	suggests	
44	Interestingly	except when starving
48	But there may be other reasons	Other reasons
49	For example	Ex: Tiger salamander larvae
52	Furthermore	
53	especially	
54–55	The fact that	
57	suggests	avoid eating each other b/c it can kill them
60	simply as	
61	not as	save own life

Discussion

This passage starts off with a typical LSAT contrast. Scientific understanding of how an event occurs is improving, but there's still a big question about why that event occurs. In this passage, the event is kin recognition (the **Topic** of the passage). And, as in most Natural Sciences passages, you are introduced to one explanation. In this case, the offered explanation is the inclusive fitness theory (the **Scope** of the passage). The bulk of the first paragraph gives background information on the theory: Unlike traditional theories in which natural selection favors individuals with the most offspring, the inclusive fitness theory states that animals recognize family because natural selection favors organisms that nurture their relatives. The reason is that doing so aids the success of the total genetic makeup of an organism's family. The paragraph ends by showing how this theory has already been applied to help explain honeybees that don't reproduce but exist merely to nurture relatives.

Paragraph 2 offers another application of the inclusive fitness theory, this time to species that practice cannibalism. The theory again explains why animals would want to recognize their own kin. Eating kin would be detrimental to the success of one's genetic lineage. To illustrate this, the author provides an example of spadefoot toad tadpoles. In some cases, one tadpole will accidentally eat another (or something similar), which can trigger physical changes that lead the tadpole to feast frequently on fellow tadpoles. Inclusive fitness theory holds that it's adaptive for these cannibalistic tadpoles to recognize kin so as to avoid eating relatives, which would impair their families' genetic survival. While the theory seems to apply pretty well in general, an interesting note pops up at the end of the paragraph suggesting that in extreme circumstances (when tadpoles get very hungry), tadpoles may eat siblings in order to save themselves.

The "[b]ut" at the beginning of Paragraph 3 suggests exceptions to inclusive fitness theory's ability to account for cannibalism. Sure enough, the author provides the example of tiger salamander larvae. These larvae can also become cannibalistic. However, they are also plagued by a deadly bacterium. As it turns out, it's more deadly if the larvae get it from eating family than if they get it from another source. So, unlike the tadpoles, the salamander larvae don't avoid eating kin because of the desire to maintain genetic lineage; they avoid eating kin for personal reasons—they don't want to die.

There's a lot of scientific jargon, but the key to success here is to break things down into simple language. The **Purpose** of the passage is to discuss the inclusive fitness theory and show examples of when it explains kin recognition and when it can't. With no strong author opinion, the **Main Idea** is just that the inclusive theory suggests that kin recognition improves the overall survival of an animal's genetic makeup, and while the theory explains some instances of kin

recognition, other cases suggest that other explanations for kin recognition may be needed.

8. (A) Global

Step 2: Identify the Question Type
This is a typical Global question stem. The correct answer will state the author's overall "main point."

Step 3: Research the Relevant Text
There's no reason to reread the text for Global questions. You've summarized the author's Purpose and Main Idea as part of your strategic reading. Structural Keywords often provide a pretty accurate basis for answering Main Idea questions in passages like this one without a strong authorial opinion. The passage begins with an introduction of a theory that "posits" (line 17) that kin recognition developed to aid an organism's total genetic representation. The theory is then applied to honeybees (lines 20–24) and tadpoles (Paragraph 2). The "[b]ut" in line 48 really drives home the final point—the inclusive theory can't explain everything (particularly not the salamander larvae).

Step 4: Make a Prediction
The correct answer will match your Main Idea summary: inclusive fitness (the theory that adaptive behavior improves the survival of an organism's gene pool, not just itself) can explain the adaptive value of some, but not all, examples of kin recognition in the animal kingdom.

Step 5: Evaluate the Answer Choices
(A) is a perfect fit. This answer accurately describes the inclusive fitness theory, mentions the supporting examples, and (most importantly) mentions the fact that it doesn't necessarily explain everything.

(B) is Extreme and Outside the Scope. The passage isn't focused on the mechanisms used to recognize kin but rather on the reasons that kin recognition may be adaptive. Moreover, the passage doesn't suggest that there are as many mechanisms as there are purposes.

(C) is a 180. The salamander example more likely supports traditional evolutionary theory (as described in lines 13–16), which argues that natural selection favors the survival of individual organisms. Remember, by recognizing kin, the salamanders are looking out for themselves. The salamander research runs contrast to the inclusive fitness theory, which posits that natural section favors an organism's total genetic representation (including family).

(D) is a Faulty Use of Detail. This may be accurate, but it focuses too much on the salamander research and the traditional theory of natural selection. It completely ignores the inclusive fitness theory, which is the primary focus of the entire passage.

(E) is Extreme. The author concludes that inclusive fitness theory explains some, *but not all*, instances of kin recognition.

9. (C) Detail

Step 2: Identify the Question Type
The categorical nature of the phrase "[t]he passage states" indicates a Detail question.

Step 3: Research the Relevant Text
Spadefoot tadpoles are described throughout the second paragraph.

Step 4: Make a Prediction
There's a lot of information, so predicting the answer may not be feasible. Instead, let's go through the answers and research only the likely candidates. In heavily detailed passages, do not answer questions based on memory because wrong answers will usually include misapplied details.

Step 5: Evaluate the Answer Choices
(C) is mentioned in lines 35–39. The eating of another tadpole can change a tadpole's dietary habits (turning it carnivorous), which causes the tadpole to become larger. That detail about a change in body size makes this answer correct.

(A) is Outside the Scope. Lines 39–42 suggest that the tadpoles can differentiate between siblings and non-siblings, but there's nothing stated about recognizing other carnivores.

(B) is a Distortion and Extreme. Lines 37–39 describe how tadpoles can grow to become exclusively carnivorous, but there's nothing about the tadpoles being selective about what kind of animals they eat.

(D) is a 180. The behavior of the tadpoles is mentioned as direct support for the inclusive fitness theory.

(E) is a Distortion. The passage does not state that the carnivorousness develops to protect the evolutionary success of the species. The passage discusses the ability to recognize kin that develops to protect the species.

10. (D) Inference

Step 2: Identify the Question Type
Contrast the directness of the wording in the stem of the previous question with the looseness of the language here. You're asked to determine what the author "would be most likely to agree with" concerning something discussed in the passage. That makes this an Inference question.

Step 3: Research the Relevant Text
Look for where "evolutionary explanations of kin recognition" are discussed. According to the author, the inclusive fitness theory "has helped to explain" (line 20) and can be "applied usefully to" (lines 25–26) some instances of kin recognition.

"But" (line 48) there may be other explanations for kin recognition.

Step 4: Make a Prediction
You may not be able to predict verbatim what the correct answer will say, but look for the answer choice that must be true based on the information you gathered during Step 3.

Step 5: Evaluate the Answer Choices
(D) essentially paraphrases the passage.

(A) is a 180. According to the first paragraph, understanding of mechanisms has increased despite a lack of explanation for why kin recognition occurs.

(B) is yet another 180. Lines 12–19 directly show how the inclusive fitness theory runs in contrast to the traditional evolutionary theory.

(C) is Outside the Scope. There is no suggestion on the author's part that theories need to ignore any characteristics of any organisms.

(E) is Outside the Scope and a tad Extreme. The author doesn't mention any current theories outside of the inclusive fitness theory. However, by virtue of the last paragraph conflicting with the inclusive fitness theory, it's evident that the author does not find that theory to be entirely successful.

11. (A) Logic Function

Step 2: Identify the Question Type
This question stem asks for the function of a particular part of the passage, so it's a Logic Function question. Focus on what the author's *doing* as opposed to *saying*.

Step 3: Research the Relevant Text
To understand the function of the last sentence of the second paragraph, you need to remember the function of everything that came before it. The bulk of the second paragraph was about the tadpoles that avoided eating siblings in order to improve the survival of their genetic lineage. This example was provided in support of the inclusive fitness theory.

Step 4: Make a Prediction
However, the last sentence begins with "[i]nterestingly," suggesting that not all is as it seems. Sure enough, just as you're being led to believe that tadpoles would spare family members to protect the genes, you learn that some tadpoles will eat their siblings after all—so as not to die from hunger. So, the author uses this sentence to provide an instance that goes contrary to the other evidence, making the inclusive fitness theory seem inapplicable in certain cases.

Step 5: Evaluate the Answer Choices
(A) is a perfect match. Just as you were being lulled into believing that the inclusive fitness theory was a winner, along comes this fact that throws a monkey wrench into the system.

(B) is Outside the Scope. The fact in the last sentence is referring only to the spadefoot toad tadpoles and makes no comparison to other species.

(C) is a 180. The Keyword "[i]nterestingly" means that the last sentence will probably run contrary to everything that came before it.

(D) is Extreme. While the sentence in question may undermine the validity of the inclusive fitness theory, it doesn't necessarily make the tadpoles' behavior unexplainable. In fact, it is explained—they're very hungry and are more interested in saving themselves.

(E) is another 180. The information that precedes the last sentence is not less relevant. It's plenty relevant as support for why the inclusive fitness theory is plausible.

12. (A) Inference

Step 2: Identify the Question Type
Any question stem asking you to find what the passage "most strongly supports" is an Inference question.

Step 3: Research the Relevant Text
The mechanism of a tadpole for recognizing kin is described in lines 39–42. It involves nipping at other tadpoles to determine whether they are siblings or not.

Step 4: Make a Prediction
From this information, it's possible to determine several statements that must be true. However, only one such statement will be in the answer choices. Keep that in mind as you evaluate them.

Step 5: Evaluate the Answer Choices
(A) is definitely supported by the information in the passage. Nipping on other tadpoles is not a visual act, so the mechanism seems to be at least partially based on taste or touch.

(B) is Outside the Scope. You know this is the behavior of cannibalistic tadpoles, but you don't know what non-cannibalistic tadpoles do. For all you know, they may nip at other tadpoles, too. In fact, according to the passage, tadpoles can become cannibalistic after first accidentally eating another tadpole. So, it doesn't seem much of a stretch to consider that some non-carnivorous tadpoles might also nip other tadpoles.

(C) is also Outside the Scope. Based on the last sentence, you know that tadpoles will still eat siblings in extreme circumstances. However, that's not because the mechanism doesn't work—it's because of hunger. There's no support for this.

(D) is a 180. The tadpoles utilize this mechanism after changing physiologically and becoming carnivorous.

(E) is another 180. Lines 31–32 states that all of these tadpoles start life as omnivores. Furthermore, you don't have

any information about other species beyond the tadpoles, so you can't infer this.

13. (B) Detail

Step 2: Identify the Question Type
The phrase "[t]he passage states" indicates a Detail question.

Step 3: Research the Relevant Text
The question stem gives you another phrase ("the mechanisms that enable organisms to recognize … relatives"). "[M]echanisms" are mostly discussed early in the first paragraph.

Step 4: Make a Prediction
In fact, the answer to this question is clearly presented in lines 4–6: Improvements in understanding these mechanisms have led to questions about why they occur. Look for the correct answer to paraphrase this idea.

Step 5: Evaluate the Answer Choices
(B) is a clear match.

(A) is Outside the Scope and Extreme. The first sentence says that mechanisms exist throughout the animal kingdom, regardless of complexity. However, that doesn't mean that you should assume they have a similar purpose in *all* species. In fact, by the two examples in the second and third paragraph, you get the sense that mechanisms can serve multiple purposes.

(C) is a Distortion. Some people might be tempted by this because it uses "1960s" from the passage. However, the 1960s is only when the inclusive fitness theory was developed. For all you know, there were many other theories developed long before the 1960s.

(D) is Outside the Scope. While the passage may suggest that there is not a full explanation of their purpose, the author never states that this is because there is not more understanding of the mechanisms.

(E) is also Outside the Scope. While the passage may discuss different purposes for the mechanisms, there's no description of how similarly or differently the mechanisms operate.

14. (E) Inference

Step 2: Identify the Question Type
Because this question asks about what the passage suggests rather than what it directly states, it's an Inference question.

Step 3: Research the Relevant Text
The honeybees were mentioned at the end of the first paragraph.

Step 4: Make a Prediction
According to the paragraph, the honeybees' behavior of nurturing relatives was "previously mysterious," but the

inclusive fitness theory helped explain it. You want an answer choice that's consistent with this prediction.

Step 5: Evaluate the Answer Choices

(E) is the correct answer. The honeybees' behavior was mysterious under traditional theories, so some supplement (in this case, the inclusive fitness theory) was needed to dispel some of the mystery.

(A) is a Distortion. The behavior was known, it was just unexplained.

(B) is Outside the Scope. There's no discussion of this kind of reciprocal nurturing.

(C) is Extreme. While the new theory helps to explain this behavior, the behavior was simply described as previously mysterious. This suggests the behavior was merely an enigma and not necessarily a catalyst for fully rejecting the traditional theory.

(D) is a Distortion. The inclusive fitness theory (which helps explain the honeybees' behavior) still states that evolution proceeds by natural selection—just in a different way from what traditional theories state.

15. (C) Logic Reasoning (Weaken)

Step 2: Identify the Question Type

The language of this question stem is almost identical to that of a Weaken question in the Logical Reasoning section. The correct answer will be a fact that makes the author's conclusion less likely to follow from the evidence presented. The research clue here is clear: your task is to weaken the author's final statement.

Step 3: Research the Relevant Text

Classic ways of weakening arguments in Logical Reasoning will work equally effectively in Reading Comprehension Logic Reasoning questions. In the last sentence, the author concludes that kin recognition in tiger salamanders can be explained as a means for preserving their own lives and not as a means for aiding their relatives' survival. While the evidence regarding the deadly bacterium definitely supports kin recognition being used to preserve the individual, there is no evidence to say that kin recognition is not used to aid relatives' survival. The author overlooks the possibility that kin recognition may serve to protect oneself *and* one's relatives.

Step 4: Make a Prediction

To weaken the claim, the correct answer choice will show a way in which the tiger salamander's use of kin recognition protects an individual with which the predator salamander shares genetic material.

Step 5: Evaluate the Answer Choices

(C) gives a fact that would weaken the author's claim. If this were true, then kin recognition would provide a way for

salamanders to protect their offspring, making kin recognition valuable beyond survival of the individual. By protecting potential family, this weakens the author's claim that this case of kin recognition is exclusively self-serving. It's good to note for this question that the correct answer is the only one that focuses on kin recognition, the topic of the argument the question asks us to weaken.

(A) is Outside the Scope. What's relevant is not whether the disease affects cannibalistic or non-cannibalistic salamanders but whether or not it affects kin and kin recognition.

(B) is also Outside the Scope. It discusses what makes salamanders carnivorous or omnivorous, but it has no bearing on why salamanders recognize kin.

(D) is a Distortion. It misapplies some information from the first paragraph about the number of offspring (part of the traditional evolutionary view). However, once again, the number of offspring a salamander has is not directly relevant to the reason for being able to recognize kin.

(E) Is Outside the Scope. Even if this were true, according to the passage, the salamanders are still immune to the one deadly bacterium that's mentioned. The author uses this evidence because that particular bacterium is more deadly to the individual when consumed through kin. Greater immunity to *other* diseases isn't relevant to kin recognition.

Passage 3: Definition of National Minority

Step 1: Read the Passage Strategically
Sample Roadmap

line #	Keyword/phrase	¶ Margin notes
Passage A		
1	no	No univ. def for "nat'l min"
8	but	2 appl. of "nat'l min"
10–11	also vaguely	terms are vague
17	While; lack	
18	presents difficulties	
19	particularly problematic	Problem e.g., Roma
23	not even	
25	Instead	
Passage B		
28	four	Cap's def of min. 5 crit
33	one	
35	problematic	
38	thus	
39	Because; essentially	Problem e.g., Roma meet 4 of 5 crit
42	patently unfair	
44	However; easily	Au—Roma meet def of nat'l min
46	should, therefore	
53	For example	
57	rather than	

Discussion

The **Topic** of passage A is presented immediately in the first sentence: national minority. According to the author of passage A, there is no universally accepted definition for the term national minority. This lack of definition constitutes the **Scope** of passage A. The author offers two frequent applications of the term but further complains that other terms (e.g., nation and people) used in defining national minority are similarly vague. In the second paragraph, the author discusses how this lack of accepted definitions is potentially harmful, particularly to one group: the Roma. The author's **Purpose** is merely to describe this problem in general and how it affects the Roma in particular. The **Main Idea** of passage A is that the lack of an agreed upon definition of "national minority" (as well as "nation" and "people") has negative consequences for certain groups, including the Roma.

As would be expected, the **Topic** of passage B is also the definition of a minority. However, the author of passage B isn't concerned about the lack of a definition. The **Scope** of passage B is one specific definition of national minority: Capotorti's definition. Passage B starts off by laying out the five criteria for Capotorti's definition: four empirical ones and one legal. The author of passage B then discusses a problem with the legal criterion, particularly in respect to the Roma. Similar to passage A, one purpose of passage B is to describe how a national minority definition is problematic for the Roma. However, the second paragraph provides a more refined **Purpose**: show how the Roma should qualify as a national minority using the remaining, more objective criteria. The **Main Idea** of passage B is that the legal criterion of Capotorti's definition poses a problem to the Roma by denying them status as a national minority despite their fulfillment of the remaining objective criteria.

Before going to the questions, it's important to note the relationship between the two passages. Both are concerned with the definition of national minority—although one is concerned about the lack of a single accepted definition and one critiques one definition in particular. More notably, both passages are concerned with how these definitions cause problems for the Roma.

16. (E) Global

Step 2: Identify the Question Type
Even though this question asks for the main point of only one passage, it's still a Global question because it focuses on that passage as a whole.

Step 3: Research the Relevant Text
Look to your Roadmap and your broader understanding of the big picture (Topic, Scope, Purpose, and Main Idea) when predicting an answer for a Global question.

Step 4: Make a Prediction
The main point of passage A was laid out in a fairly straightforward manner: The lack of definition for "national minority" (as well as "nation" and "people") has led to problems for certain groups, particularly the Roma.

Step 5: Evaluate the Answer Choices
(E) says exactly that.

(A) is Outside the Scope. The author doesn't mention a conflict of definitions. The problem for the Roma is caused by the lack of one universally accepted definition.

(B) ignores the entire reason *why* the Roma are not considered a minority. It leaves out the discussion of vague definitions that constituted the entire first paragraph. Additionally, this is actually a detail from lines 38–39 of passage B.

(C) is a 180. This reverses the causality. It's the lack of an accepted definition that causes problems in applying terms to the Roma, not the other way around.

(D) is Extreme. The author complains that there's no universally accepted definition, but never goes so far as to say any definition will fail, even if it is applied to a group like the Roma.

17. (C) Inference

Step 2: Identify the Question Type
A question asking you to define a word from the passage(s) as it is used in context is an Inference question.

Step 3: Research the Relevant Text
The question stem clearly directs you to lines 19 and 35, but in order to properly predict the answer, you'll need to read at least the entire sentences containing those words so that you can derive context.

Step 4: Make a Prediction
In both passages, the word *problematic* is used to describe how the Roma are affected by the definition (or lack of definition) of national minority. In passage A, the vague definitions are too broad for the Roma and in passage B, the legal criterion of the definition is too narrow for the Roma. In both cases, "problematic" refers to causing problems.

Step 5: Evaluate the Answer Choices
(C) is synonymous with causing problems.

(A) is Outside the Scope. Neither passage discusses an intense debate arising over the definition or lack thereof.

(B) is Extreme. The lack of definition may be considered confusing and unclear to the author of passage A, but the definition is crystal clear in passage B—it just causes problems.

(D) is Outside the Scope. Solving the problem isn't a primary concern in either passage. Additionally, given that the author of passage B feels that the Roma satisfy all the criteria except for one, the problem doesn't seem all that difficult to solve. In fact, at the end of the first paragraph of passage B, the author even implies the easy solution: exclude the legal criterion.

(E) is Extreme. Again, there's nothing really incoherent about the definition provided in passage B. It just causes problems in its inapplicability to the Roma.

18. (D) Detail (NOT)

Step 2: Identify the Question Type

Because this question focuses on claims stated (or, in this case, NOT stated) in the passage, it's a Detail question. Four of the answers to this question will be found in passage A and one will not.

Step 3: Research the Relevant Text

The only part of passage A that discusses the Roma is paragraph 2.

Step 4: Make a Prediction

It's always hard to predict what the outlier will be. Check each choice against lines 17–27. There's also a good chance that the right answer will appear in passage B.

Step 5: Evaluate the Answer Choices

(D) isn't mentioned in passage A. In fact, this detail comes from lines 48–49 of passage B. This is the exception and is therefore the correct answer.

(A) pretty much rewords the last sentence of passage A.

(B) is directly mentioned in line 24 of passage A.

(C) is found in line 21, which tells you the Roma have no homeland.

(E) matches the claim that the Roma are worse off than other groups, a claim from lines 19–20.

19. (E) Inference

Step 2: Identify the Question Type

This is an Inference question because it asks you to crystallize the authors' points of view as they're presented in the passages.

Step 3: Research the Relevant Text

Passage A discusses the Roma in paragraph 2 and passage B in lines 34–60.

Step 4: Make a Prediction

You should characterize the correct answer to an Inference question whenever you can. In Comparative Reading specifically, recognizing the relationship between the two passages can lead to quick points. In both passages, the Roma are presented as a specific group that experiences problems due to issues with the international definitions of national minority. You want an answer choice that conveys this shared attitude.

Step 5: Evaluate the Answer Choices

(E) is correct. It's a perfect match that accurately expresses both authors' shared idea that the Roma illustrate relatively distinctive problems with national minority definitions.

(A) is a 180. It's the author of passage B who explicitly complains about the states' "arbitrary right to decide if the Roma constitute a minority" (lines 40–41).

(B) is also a 180. The author of passage A uses the Roma as a specific example of the difficulties caused by the lack of a universally accepted definition of "national minority" within international law. The author of passage B also uses the Roma as a noteworthy example, but Capotorti's definition is simply that: one possible definition. It is not necessarily an international law.

(C) is off because if anything, the author of passage A seems more inclined to argue that the Roma are an example of a group that doesn't constitute a nation. Passage B doesn't discuss the idea of "nation," therefore while the author may agree, this answer choice is not supported by the content of the passage.

(D) is also a 180. The author of passage A is concerned with the lack of an internationally approved definition of minority while the author of passage B bemoans states' "arbitrary" right to decide if the Roma are a minority or not. Neither one seems inclined to champion case-by-case decisions.

20. (A) Logic Reasoning (Parallel Reasoning)

Step 2: Identify the Question Type

Because this question stem asks you to find an answer choice containing the relationship "most analogous to" that between the passages, this resembles a Parallel Reasoning question from the Logical Reasoning section.

Step 3: Research the Relevant Text

Instead of researching specific lines from the passage, use your broader assessment of the passages' relationship to build your prediction.

Step 4: Make a Prediction

Both passages are concerned with how the Roma are affected by national minority definitions. However, while passage A was primarily concerned with how vague definitions affect the Roma, passage B was concerned with one particular definition and had the additional purpose of showing how the Roma mainly satisfy that definition. The right answer to this question should apply the same conceptual purposes to an entirely different situation.

Step 5: Evaluate the Answer Choices

(A) matches up nicely. Here, instead of a group of nomadic people, you have welders. Like passage A, the first article is concerned with a vague definition of a term (here, *technical*) that affects the group. And, like passage B, the second article argues that the group should satisfy the definition of that term under a particular set of criteria (here, the "union's criteria").

(B) distorts passage A. The author of passage A doesn't feel that there is an accepted definition of national minority. That doesn't match the first article's suggestion that there are accepted "current criteria." Additionally, the second document is too broad to match passage B. Passage B is concerned with one particular standard (not "any") and, further, how one group fits it.

(C) distorts passage B. Passage B is an argument that the Roma fit a certain definition as laid out earlier in the passage. The second article in **(C)** focuses too much on the descriptive aspect only, without a further point. Additionally, the first article doesn't quite match passage A. The author of passage A doesn't want a "*revised* definition"; instead the author shows the issues that arise from having *no* agreed upon definition.

(D) is Outside the Scope. The first article here attacks the people enforcing a set of laws (citing "disregard"), which the author of passage A never does. Additionally, the second article discusses essentially how to create criteria, not how one group matches already existing criteria.

(E) is also Outside the Scope. These two articles express two differing opinions on the relationship between two terms: professionalism and technical expertise. The original two passages are both only concerned primarily with one term: minority. Also, the second article has a negative slant ("Classified as *Neither*") that the author of passage B doesn't include.

21. (B) Logic Reasoning (Principle)

Step 2: Identify the Question Type
This question wants you to identify a principle underlying both passages. Because this resembles a Principle question from Logical Reasoning, you can classify it as such here too.

Step 3: Research the Relevant Text
As you examine your Roadmap for each passage, look for areas of overlap between the passages.

Step 4: Make a Prediction
Both passages are concerned with how the Roma are affected by issues concerning definitions of national minority. In both cases, the Roma are negatively affected because they aren't technically covered by current definitions. The correct answer choice will get across the idea that not being definitively covered by the rules can cause problems for some groups.

Step 5: Evaluate the Answer Choices
(B) fits both passages very well. Specifically, in both passages, the Roma aren't officially recognized as a national minority in some countries, and that has a detrimental effect on their interests. Thus, this choice is correct.

(A) works great for passage A, but the author of passage B doesn't have any concern about vague definitions.

(C) is a 180. Neither author would likely have problems with provisions that apply to minority groups. In fact, given both authors' concern for the Roma, they would both probably favor provisions that apply to minority groups.

(D) doesn't apply to both authors. The author of passage B mentions that the Roma have legal and court systems in their jurisdictions, but he introduces it to prove the Roma try to preserve their culture, not to argue that other governments should recognize those court systems. Additionally, the author of passage A doesn't mention this at all.

(E) is a Distortion. Neither author seems to mind that the Roma aren't considered citizens, and they do not discuss whether the Roma should be allowed dual citizenship. The problem is that the Roma are denied status as a national minority.

Passage 4: Women's Education in France

Step 1: Read the Passage Strategically
Sample Roadmap

line #	Keyword/phrase	¶ Margin notes
2		Trad. ed. of Fr. women in 19th C.
4	failure	
6–7	"missed opportunity"; in spite of	Critic: needed reform
10	would not be	
11	However	
13	two in particular	Au: 2 prop. Made
15	great extent	
16	first; endeavored	First prop:
18		—less religious emph.
19	More importantly	
20	because	—available to both sexes
22	should	
23	Thus	—taught by both sexes
24	essential	
28	limitation; however	—Problem
32	second; more comprehensive	Second prop:
33	advocated	
35	only	—coed
37		—radical
39	however	
42	neither	
44	neither	
45	bespeaks the immensity	Prop. failed b/c cult. & pol. obst.
46	obstacles	
47	Nevertheless	
48	was not entirely lost	late 19th C—reform began to take shape
54	needed	How obst. overcome

Discussion

The opening paragraph describes how the education of women in 19th-century France (the **Topic**) followed long-standing traditions. That's followed by a complaint by one observer that France missed an opportunity during the time after the Revolution to reform education and make it nondiscriminatory. But, once the author uses the Contrast Keyword "[h]owever" in line 11, it's clear the author has a bone to pick with that particular observation. In fact, the author points out that legislators did, in fact, try to reform education during that time. The author mentions two proposals in particular that tried to implement egalitarian ideals (the **Scope**).

These proposals are outlined in paragraph 2. The first proposal suggested that women's curricula be revised to have less religious emphasis, that instruction be available to people (and taught by people) of both sexes, and that public schools be established for both men and women. Another "however" in line 28 indicates the problem with this first proposal: Girls would be removed from school at the young age of 8 so that they could learn domestic skills at home. The second proposal was a little more radical and "comprehensive." Its main distinguishing aspect was that it was the "only" proposal that recommended coed schools (lines 35–36). Unfortunately, another "however" in line 39 details the problem with the second proposal: the proposal still defined women by their roles in the domestic sphere.

After comparing the two proposals (the first part of the passage's Purpose), paragraph 3 suggests that their failure showed the "immensity" of the obstacles that needed to be overcome at that time. However, their egalitarian ideals persisted (as indicated by the "nevertheless" in line 47). The rest of the paragraph explains how nearly a century later, the two proposals were used as justification for later reforms because by that time they were considered legitimate examples of historical tradition. So the overall **Purpose** was not only to compare the two proposals, but also to show how they eventually helped serve as the foundation for later reform. The **Main Idea** is that legislators didn't necessarily miss an opportunity for reforming women's education after the Revolution. They put forth proposals to reform education but weren't successful due to cultural obstacles that weren't overcome until nearly a century later.

22. (C) Inference

Step 2: Identify the Question Type

The words "can be inferred" in the question stem indicate an Inference question. You are to determine what must be true based on the passage.

Step 3: Research the Relevant Text

This question is looking for information about legislators who passed educational laws in the 1880s. That wording (especially the use of the date) leads you right to lines 48–57.

Step 4: Make a Prediction

In these lines, you learn that not only did the legislators establish secondary schools for women, but they also abolished education fees and made attendance mandatory for all students. Armed with that information, it's time to go through the answers. Don't stop until you find one that must be true.

Step 5: Evaluate the Answer Choices

(C) is a valid inference. By eliminating education fees, it certainly seems that the legislators had economic motives in addition to gender-related motives in their reforms. This is the correct answer.

(A) is unsupported. While one may assume that these legislators started to shy away from the idea that women were solely defined as domestic, that doesn't suggest a complete removal of domestic skills from education.

(B), if anything, is a 180. In the lines that end the passage, it seems that, on the contrary, legislators were well aware of past obstacles and even had to demonstrate that their reforms were rooted in tradition, in order to make sure they were accepted.

(D) is unsupported. Neither of the discussions about reforms—whether in the eighteenth or nineteenth century—discusses political compromise. While it is true that the earlier reforms failed because of cultural and political obstacles, that doesn't mean that the legislators in 1880 were more open to compromise. Perhaps the cultural and political obstacles were simply less significant at that time.

(E) seems to refer directly to the reduced religious emphasis as defined in the first proposal. However, because the legislators in the 1880s used that first proposal as part of the foundation of their reform, you can't infer that they were more inclined to allow a religious role in education. None of the reforms they passed have anything to do with religion.

23. (E) Global

Step 2: Identify the Question Type

Any question asking about the organization of a passage is a Global question because the question's scope is the entire passage. Remember, the correct answer choice will be complete and correctly ordered.

Step 3: Research the Relevant Text

A solid Roadmap pays off big dividends with Global questions about organization.

Step 4: Make a Prediction

Recall the structure of the passage. The author started by discussing the state of women's education in the nineteenth century, following the French Revolution. After presenting one complaint about this state (the government missed its chance to bring about educational change), the author counters by introducing two proposals of the time that aimed to reform that state. After discussing how these proposals' failures indicated major obstacles, the author concludes by showing the proposals' influence on eventual educational reform.

Step 5: Evaluate the Answer Choices

(E) captures just about everything, and all in the correct order.

(A) is correct for the first two clauses, but then fails on two accounts. First, the problems with the proposals are more pragmatic issues than they are inconsistencies. Second, this answer entirely ignores the last paragraph and the discussion of the eventual reform.

(B) falls apart almost immediately because the movement toward gender equality is not really a focus of the discussion in the first paragraph. Rather, the lack thereof is discussed. Furthermore, like **(A)**, this answer fails to address the reform mentioned in the last paragraph.

(C) is close, but the eventual change still required a break with tradition.

(D), like **(B)**, fails by refocusing the first paragraph on discussing the egalitarian aims in France. Furthermore, any aims mentioned are not modified at the end of the passage.

24. (A) Logic Reasoning (Parallel Reasoning)

Step 2: Identify the Question Type

The question stem asks you to analogize between content in the passage and content in the answer choices. Thus, it's similar to a Parallel Reasoning question from the Logical Reasoning section.

Step 3: Research the Relevant Text

The proposals were discussed in the second paragraph: the first in lines 16–27 and the second in lines 31–38.

Step 4: Make a Prediction

The first proposal suggested making education available to men and women. The second proposal suggested making education equal for everyone. You want a similar set of housing proposals that mimic the "something for everyone" and "everyone gets the same" concepts.

Step 5: Evaluate the Answer Choices

(A) is an instant winner.

(B) is a Half-Right/Half-Wrong with a Distortion. The first proposal is a perfect match, but the second proposal focuses on improving the quality in general rather than making it equal for everyone.

(C) is also Half-Right/Half-Wrong with a Distortion. The second proposal is a good match, but the first proposal offers a "those who can pay" qualification that isn't found in the first educational reform proposal.

(D) misses the point of the first education proposal. Again, the second proposal is a good match, but the first proposal focuses on improving the quality rather than improving access.

(E) is Outside the Scope. The second proposal focuses on uniform quality, rather than non-discrimination, and the first proposal focuses too narrowly on cost, which is something the first educational proposal never does.

25. (B) Detail

Step 2: Identify the Question Type

The phrase "according to the passage" indicates a Detail question.

Step 3: Research the Relevant Text

The second proposal is described in the second half of paragraph 2.

Step 4: Make a Prediction

The word *only* in line 35 is a good indication of a distinctive feature of that proposal. According to that line, the second proposal was the only proposal that called for coed schools.

Step 5: Evaluate the Answer Choices

(B) is a perfect match.

(A) is actually a feature of the first proposal (lines 21–23).

(C) is Outside the Scope. This choice is in contrast to the first proposal, which removes girls from school at the age of eight, and the author never states anything in the passage about the second proposal that would indicate a goal of "lifelong learning."

(D) is Extreme. While the author describes the coed schools recommended in the proposal as breaking with religious tradition, he never goes so far as to say the proposal looked to abolish religious schools.

(E) is pulling from the wrong part of the passage. The first proposal, not the second, called for both public schools and home learning for girls. The public schools to replace the predominantly religious education girls had previously received.

26. (E) Inference

Step 2: Identify the Question Type

The looser language of the question stem ("based on the passage" ... "most clearly suggests") indicates an Inference question.

Step 3: Research the Relevant Text

The proposals are first mentioned at the end of paragraph 1. Right before that, in lines 4–11, is the complaint of one observer about educational reform. The observer rued the lack of reform "in spite of the egalitarian" aims of the French Revolution.

Step 4: Make a Prediction

The author's "[h]owever" in line 11 suggests that the author believes the egalitarian aims of the French Revolution were not completely ignored. And the last sentence of the paragraph reinforces the idea that the two proposals were indeed egalitarian, as the observer would have wanted.

Step 5: Evaluate the Answer Choices

(E) captures the egalitarian nature of the proposals.

(A) is Outside the Scope. The passage doesn't discuss "excesses" of the new government.

(B) is also Outside the Scope. While it's true that the proposals may be rooted in a larger belief in the power of education, this answer choice ignores the more specific thrust of the passage: the egalitarian aspect of the proposals. The "power of education" concept is not discussed in the passage.

(C) is a 180 and Extreme. Because both proposals failed, it's hard to infer that they had "vast" popular support.

(D) is Outside the Scope. This answer brings up other reforms not discussed in the passage.

27. (C) Inference

Step 2: Identify the Question Type

Any question that asks you to project the author's opinion ("author would most likely describe") from the information in the passage is an Inference question.

Step 3: Research the Relevant Text

The author doesn't express much opinion in this passage, but your Roadmap should tell you that lines 27–31 and lines 39–42 describe the shortcomings of the two proposals, and the beginning of paragraph 3 continues that discussion.

Step 4: Make a Prediction

Most comments about the proposals were saved until the beginning of the last paragraph, in which the author says the failure of both proposals illustrates the tremendous obstacles faced by reformers. You need to look out for wrong answers that distort this point of view.

Step 5: Evaluate the Answer Choices

(C) is a valid inference. The largely egalitarian proposals were clearly well-meaning, and the fact that they failed due to the immense cultural and political obstacles to egalitarian education shows that they were as much as (if not more) than could be done at the time.

(A) is a 180. Given that the second proposal is described as "a bulwark against the traditional gender roles enforced by religious tradition" (lines 37–38), it's difficult to infer that the proposal was "modest."

(B) is unsupported. While the first proposal in particular may have had an incomplete view of equality, the author never suggests anything is unethical about either proposal.

(D) is a 180. The author presents an explanation of why they failed in the last paragraph, indicating that it's not necessarily difficult to understand the reasoning.

(E) doesn't agree with the last paragraph, which says that the proposals failed because of "cultural and political obstacles," not because they weren't comprehensive.

PrepTest 57

The Inside Story

PrepTest 57 was administered in June 2009. It challenged 32,595 test takers. What made this test so hard? Here's a breakdown of what Kaplan students who were surveyed after taking the official exam considered PrepTest 57's most difficult section.

Hardest PrepTest 57 Section as Reported by Test Takers

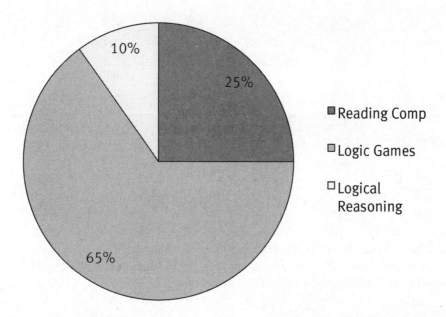

Based on these results, you might think that studying Logic Games is the key to LSAT success. Well, Logic Games is important, but test takers' perceptions don't tell the whole story. For that, you need to consider students' actual performance. The following chart shows the average number of students to miss each question in each of PrepTest 57's different sections.

Percentage Incorrect by PrepTest 57 Section Type

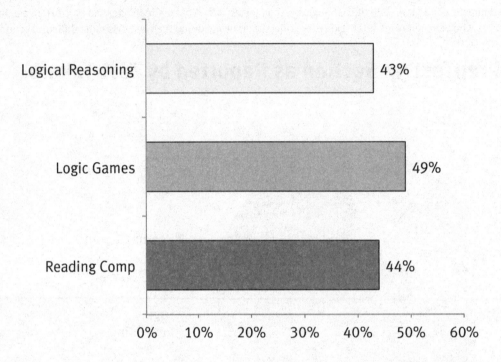

Actual student performance tells a somewhat different story. Although Logic Games was indeed higher in actual difficulty than Logical Reasoning and Reading Comprehension, because the Logic Games section has fewer questions than the other sections, students were missing about 11–12 questions in each individual section.

Maybe students overestimate the difficulty of the Logic Games section because it's so unusual, or maybe it's because a really hard Logic Game is so easy to remember after the test. But the truth is that the testmaker places hard questions throughout the test. Here were the locations of the 10 hardest (most missed) questions in the exam.

Location of 10 Most Difficult Questions in PrepTest 57

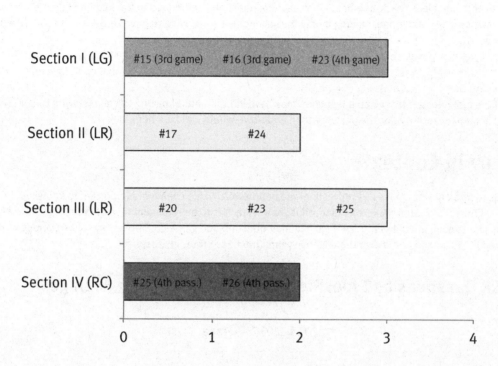

The takeaway from this data is that, to maximize your potential on the LSAT, you need to take a comprehensive approach. Test yourself rigorously, and review your performance on every section of the test. Kaplan's LSAT explanations provide the expertise and insight you need to fully understand your results. The explanations are written and edited by a team of LSAT experts, who have helped thousands of students improve their scores. Kaplan always provides data-driven analysis of the test, ranking the difficulty of every question based on actual student performance. The 10 hardest questions on every test are highlighted with a 4-star difficulty rating, the highest we give. The analysis breaks down the remaining questions into 1-, 2-, and 3-star ratings so that you can compare your performance to thousands of other test takers on all LSAC material.

Don't settle for wondering whether a question was really as hard as it seemed to you. Analyze the test with real data, and learn the secrets and strategies that help top scorers master the LSAT.

9 Can't-Miss Features of PrepTest 57

- PrepTest 57 had four Role of a Statement questions. That was the most since October 2004 (PrepTest 44).
- There's usually about three and a half Paradox questions per test. PrepTest 57 had three in the first seven questions of Section III. The only other PrepTests to have three in the first seven questions of a section were PrepTest 14 Section II (February 1995) and PrepTest 79 Section I (September 2016)—both of which had three in the first five questions.
- This test is probably most notorious for the Toy Dinosaur game. It is well-regarded as one of the toughest logic games of all time. The Explanations will show that the game can be approached with the same Logic Games Method as any other game. That said, a Matching/Selection Hybrid is quite rare. The only other one that has ever been released was on PrepTest B (February 1999).
- Although famous for the Toy Dinosaur game, the longer-lasting Logic Games innovation that debuted on this test was the Rule Substitution question that accompanies the first game, and now at least one appears on nearly every test.
- Less monumental than the two previous Logic Games tidbits was that Spatial Matching—which as only appeared three times since 2001—made its second appearance in that timeframe. The other times were PrepTest 46 (June 2005) and PrepTest 75 (June 2015).

- It only took seven released tests for Comparative Reading to appear in each of the different topic areas. PrepTest 57 marked the first time it was a Humanities passage.
- Most tests contain at least three of four Logic Reasoning questions embedded in the Reading Comprehension section. Not PrepTest 57 though—it had none, making it only the second test since 1992 to have zero. The other was PrepTest 35 (October 2001).
- Section III Question 11 was about creating vaccines to viral diseases. Test takers may have remembered that question after hearing that the World Health Organization declared the H1N1 virus—swine flu—a global pandemic on the Thursday following Test Day.
- This was the first released test when a test taker may have inquired about paying the test fee with Bitcoin (which was first released in January 2009). Alas, the answer—then and now—would still be a definitive *no*.

PrepTest 57 in Context

As much fun as it is to find out what makes a PrepTest unique or noteworthy, it's even more important to know just how representative it is of other LSAT administrations (and, thus, how likely it is to be representative of the exam you will face on Test Day). The following charts compare the numbers of each kind of question and game on PrepTest 57 to the average numbers seen on all officially released LSATs administered over the past five years (from 2013 through 2017).

Number of LR Questions by Type: PrepTest 57 vs. 2013–2017 Average

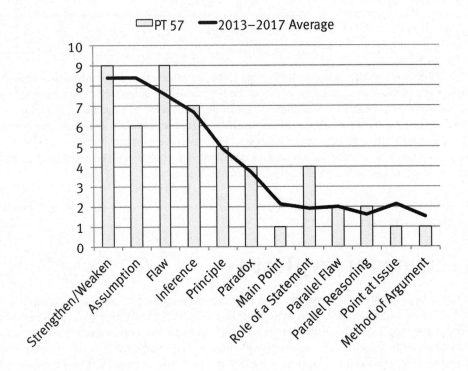

Number of LG Games by Type: PrepTest 57 vs. 2013–2017 Average

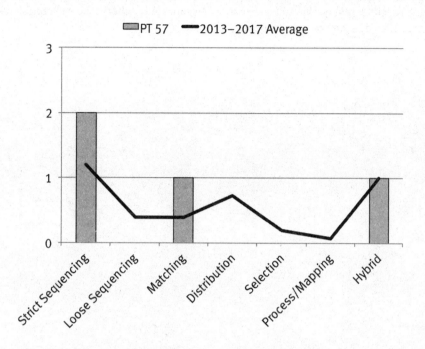

Number of RC Questions by Type: PrepTest 57 vs. 2013–2017 Average

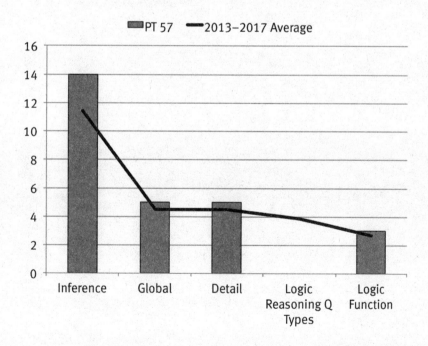

There isn't usually a huge difference in the distribution of questions from LSAT to LSAT, but if this test seems harder (or easier) to you than another you've taken, compare the number of questions of the types on which you, personally, are strongest and weakest. Then, explore within each section to see if your best or worst question types came earlier or later.

Students in Kaplan's comprehensive LSAT courses have access to every released LSAT and to a library of thousands of officially released questions arranged by question, game, and passage type. If you are studying on your own, you have to do a bit more work to identify your strengths and your areas of opportunity. Quantitative analysis (like that in the charts shown here) is an important tool for understanding how the test is constructed, and how you are performing on it.

Section I: Logic Games

Game 1: Student Activities

Q#	Question Type	Correct	Difficulty
1	Acceptability	D	★
2	Must Be False (CANNOT Be True)	B	★★
3	Must Be False (CANNOT Be True)	C	★
4	Must Be False (CANNOT Be True)	D	★
5	Rule Substitution	C	★★

Game 2: Actor Auditions

Q#	Question Type	Correct	Difficulty
6	Acceptability	B	★
7	"If" / Could Be True	B	★
8	Must Be False (CANNOT Be True)	E	★★
9	Must Be False (CANNOT Be True)	D	★★
10	Could Be True	C	★★
11	"If" / Could Be True	B	★★

Game 3: Toy Dinosaurs

Q#	Question Type	Correct	Difficulty
12	Partial Acceptability	B	★★
13	"If" / Must Be True EXCEPT	D	★★★
14	Could Be True	A	★★★
15	"If" / Must Be True	E	★★★★
16	"If" / Must Be True	A	★★★★
17	"If" / Could Be True	B	★★★

Game 4: Charitable Foundation Grants

Q#	Question Type	Correct	Difficulty
18	Acceptability	C	★
19	Must Be False (CANNOT Be True)	D	★★
20	"If" / Could Be True EXCEPT	E	★★★
21	"If" / Could Be True	B	★★★
22	Must Be False (CANNOT Be True)	D	★★★
23	Completely Determine	E	★★★★

Game 1: Student Activities

Step 1: Overview

Situation: A student performing activities

Entities: Six activities (G, H, J, K, L, M)

Action: Strict Sequencing. Determine the order in which the activities will be performed. A quick glance at the rules indicates that some entities must be immediately before or after other entities, so this is a Strict Sequencing game.

Limitations: Each activity will be performed once, one at a time. In other words, a standard 1–1 Sequencing game.

Step 2: Sketch

Simply draw out six numbered slots in a row, list your entities, and go to the rules.

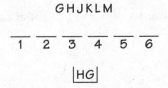

Step 3: Rules

Rule 1 provides a block: grocery shopping is immediately after hedge trimming.

K ... G
M ... L

Because of this ordering, grocery shopping cannot be first and hedge trimming cannot be sixth.

Rules 2 and 3 dictate two relative relationships: kitchen cleaning sometime before grocery shopping and motorbike servicing sometime before laundry.

JM or MJ

Based on these rules, neither kitchen cleaning nor motorbike servicing can be the last activity. Also, neither grocery shopping nor laundry can be the first activity.

Rule 4 provides another block. However, unlike the block from the first rule, the order of the entities in this block is undetermined. Motorcycle servicing can be immediately before *or* after jogging.

K ... HG

Step 4: Deductions

As with many Sequencing games, it's crucial to combine rules with duplicated entities. In this case, the first two rules both provide information about grocery shopping. It has to be performed after both hedge trimming and kitchen cleaning.

However, since hedge trimming must be *immediately* before, kitchen cleaning must be performed earlier than that entire block.

JM ... L or MJ ... L

Similarly, motorbike servicing is mentioned in both of the last two rules. It has to be performed before laundry. However, it also has to be part of a block with jogging. Thus, jogging and motorbike servicing will be performed consecutively, with laundry being performed sometime afterward:

GHJKLM

1	2	3	4	5	6
~H				~K	G/L
~G	~G				
~L	~L				

K ... HG
JM ... L
or
MJ ... L

Because these two combined rules share no entities, they cannot be combined further. However, this adds more limitations to when certain activities can be performed. Because kitchen cleaning needs to be performed before *two* activities, it cannot be sixth *or* fifth. Similarly, because laundry must be performed after two activities, it cannot be first or second. The block of hedge trimming and grocery shopping must be performed after kitchen cleaning, so hedge trimming cannot be first, which means grocery shopping cannot be second. Finally, the block of jogging and motorbike servicing must be performed before laundry, so neither jogging nor motorbike servicing can be last.

Based on all of these deductions, it's important to note that the last activity can only be grocery shopping or laundry. It is also important to notice that the game has two Blocks of Entities. These blocks will most likely be jockeying for positions and must be placed to allow for other entities to be placed. That will surely play a role in answering the questions. Simply seeing the blocks written to the side may be sufficient for you to notice for instance that H and G can't be first and K can't be fifth or sixth, without actually writing those negative deductions under the first, fifth, and sixth spots. It's personal preference and continual practice that will inform you as to whether or not writing all the negative deductions is helpful for you or whether it unnecessarily muddles the sketch.

Step 5: Questions

1. (D) Acceptability

To answer Acceptability questions efficiently, simply go through the rules one at a time and cross out each answer that violates the rules. According to Rule 1, grocery shopping must be immediately after hedge trimming. **(E)** has kitchen cleaning in between them, so that answer can be eliminated. Rule 2 states that kitchen cleaning must be earlier than grocery shopping, which is violated by **(B)**, eliminating that answer. Rule 3 states that motorbike servicing must be earlier than laundry, which is violated by **(C)**, eliminating that answer. Finally, Rule 4 states that motorbike servicing must be immediately next to jogging. **(A)** has too many activities in between, so that answer can be eliminated. That leaves **(D)** as the only answer that doesn't violate the rules.

2. (B) Must Be False (CANNOT Be True)

The correct answer to this question will be the activity that cannot be done third, no matter what. Start by thinking about which entities are most restricted. Those would be the ones involved in the two blocks. It's better to start with the hedge trimming/grocery shopping (HG) block because the order is predefined.

Placing that block will affect the motorbike servicing/jogging (MJ or JM) block. A little deductive reasoning shows that the HG block can't be in the third and fourth slots, respectively. If it were, K would have to be one of the first two activities (by Rule 2), thereby forcing MJ into the fifth and sixth slots—but that would leave no space for laundry. So, since HG can't be in the third and fourth slots, hedge trimming can't be third, making **(B)** the correct answer.

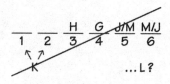

For the record, here are sample results to illustrate why the remaining answers are all acceptable:

$$(A) \quad \frac{K}{1} \quad \frac{H}{2} \quad \frac{G}{3} \quad \frac{J/M}{4} \quad \frac{M/J}{5} \quad \frac{L}{6}$$

$$(B) \quad \frac{K}{1} \quad \frac{M}{2} \quad \frac{J}{3} \quad \frac{}{4} \quad \frac{}{5} \quad \frac{}{6}$$

$$(D) \quad \frac{J/M}{1} \quad \frac{M/J}{2} \quad \frac{K}{3} \quad \frac{}{4} \quad \frac{}{5} \quad \frac{}{6}$$

$$(E) \quad \frac{K}{1} \quad \frac{J}{2} \quad \frac{M}{3} \quad \frac{}{4} \quad \frac{}{5} \quad \frac{}{6}$$

$$\left. \rule{0pt}{40pt} \right\} \boxed{HG}, L$$

3. (C) Must Be False (CANNOT Be True)

The correct answer to this question will be the one that cannot be true. Eliminate any answer that is possible.

With so little to work with, each answer will need to be checked one at a time. If you are running short on time, this is

a good question to hold off on as it will likely take some time or previous work to reference.

To test **(A)**, hedge trimming will be fourth. That makes grocery shopping fifth (by Rule 1). That leaves laundry to be sixth, since kitchen cleaning needs to be earlier than grocery shopping (Rule 2), and you need two consecutive spaces for motorbike servicing and jogging. The remaining entities can go in any order, as long as motorbike servicing and jogging are consecutive.

$$\frac{}{1} \quad \frac{}{2} \quad \frac{}{3} \quad \frac{H}{4} \quad \frac{G}{5} \quad \frac{L}{6}$$

$$\underbrace{\qquad} K, \boxed{J/M}$$

That eliminates **(A)**.

This also eliminates **(E)** because this sketch could be completed like so: K M J H G L. Even when the question calls for testing out each answer choice, look for ways to be strategic.

Testing **(B)**, if jogging is fourth, then motorbike servicing must be done fifth, with laundry sixth. The remaining three activities will take up the first three positions.

$$\frac{K}{1} \quad \frac{H}{2} \quad \frac{G}{3} \quad \frac{J}{4} \quad \frac{M}{5} \quad \frac{L}{6}$$

This is possible, which eliminates **(B)**.

Testing **(C)**, if kitchen cleaning is second, what could be first? It can't be any of the four activities in the blocks (grocery shopping, hedge trimming, jogging, and motorbike servicing). It also can't be laundry, since laundry has to be performed after motorbike servicing (Rule 3). That leaves no activity for the first position. Since that can't happen, **(C)** is the correct answer. This new deduction can be built into the Master Sketch.

For the record, **(D)** would work like so:

$$\frac{J/M}{1} \quad \frac{M/J}{2} \quad \frac{L}{3} \quad \frac{K}{4} \quad \frac{H}{5} \quad \frac{G}{6}$$

4. (D) Must Be False (CANNOT Be True)

The correct answer to this question will be the activity that cannot be done fifth, no matter what. Whatever is placed fifth will leave only one position after it to be the last activity, which can only be grocery shopping or laundry. If it were grocery shopping, then hedge trimming would be fifth (Rule 1), which eliminates **(B)**.

If laundry were sixth, then it could be preceded by either block. So, it could be hedge trimming fourth with grocery shopping fifth—eliminating **(A)**. Or the fourth and fifth activities could be jogging and motorbike servicing, in either order. That eliminates **(C)** and **(E)** and leaves **(D)** as the correct answer.

You could also recognize that laundry can't be fifth, because that would force both blocks to precede laundry, and kitchen cleaning would also need to precede the hedge trimming-grocery shopping block. That puts five entities in the first four slots, leaving nothing left for the sixth slot, which means laundry will never be fifth.

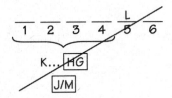

5. (C) Rule Substitution

For this question, Rule 3 will be removed from the game and replaced with another rule. The correct answer will be a new rule that resets the exact same limitations as Rule 3, without adding any new restrictions.

Rule 3 involves motorbike servicing being performed before laundry. However, removing this rule would alter not only the relationship between motorbike servicing and laundry, but also the relationship between jogging and laundry—because the block of jogging and motorbike servicing will be affected by any rule that affects either activity individually. Therefore, the new rule must reestablish that laundry must follow the block of motorbike servicing and jogging.

(C) does this perfectly. Since jogging has to be in a block with motorbike servicing, anything that comes after one of those activities would have to come after both. By making laundry later than jogging, this answer effectively makes laundry later than the block of jogging and motorbike servicing, which follows the relationship created by the original rules.

For the record, **(A)** doesn't work because it merely limits the placement of laundry. By not relating it to either motorbike servicing or jogging, that block can now be placed *after* laundry (L in the fourth slot, MJ in the fifth and sixth slots, respectively), which would change the effect of the original rules. **(B)** doesn't work because it now allows laundry to be *before* jogging, a condition that wasn't allowed in the original setup. That also eliminates **(E)**. **(D)** doesn't work because it not only fails to reestablish the relationship between laundry and the block of jogging and motorbike servicing, but it also creates a new relationship between laundry and hedge trimming that was never required in the original setup.

Game 2: Actor Auditions

Step 1: Overview
Situation: Actors going on auditions

Entities: Three actors (Gombrich, Otto, Raines); four days (Wednesday, Thursday, Friday, Saturday)

Action: Strict Sequencing. Determine the days on which the three actors audition. This requires sequencing each actor's first and second auditions on two distinct days between Wednesday and Saturday. Here, the twist on Strict Sequencing is that more than one actor can audition per day, i.e., more than one entity can go into a single slot of the sequence. This game could also be viewed as a Distribution game or Distribution/Sequencing Hybrid game, as the six auditions are distributed among the four days. Regardless of how the game is classified, the sketch would be the same, and the first rule, a Sequencing rule, is key.

Limitations: Each actor auditions twice on two different days. At least one actor auditions each day.

Step 2: Sketch
The easiest way to set this game up is a table with four columns—one for each day, Wednesday through Saturday. Since at least one actor has to audition each day, each column should include one slot with room to add up to two more.

Step 3: Rules
Rule 1 dictates that Otto's first audition is before Raines's first audition. Since this only refers to each actor's *first* audition, make sure that's clearly notated in your shorthand.

$$O_1 \ldots R_1$$

Based on this, Raines cannot audition on Wednesday. However, Otto *could* audition on Saturday, since Otto will audition a second time.

Rule 2 creates a Block of Entities. At least one day has to include Gombrich and Raines. Two important things to note: 1) Since each actor has two auditions, it can't be assumed that Gombrich and Raines will automatically be together each time one of them appears. After all, Gombrich can audition with Raines on one day and then audition solo (or with Otto) on another. 2) The rule says *at least* one day will include both actors. That suggests that the two actors could go on both of their auditions together.

Rule 3 dictates the audition schedule for at least one of the actors. At least one actor (which, again, suggests that maybe two actors can do this) will audition on Thursday and Saturday.

At least one actor: Thu. and Sat.

Step 4: Deductions
The rules don't offer a lot of concrete information to work with. While Raines can't audition on Wednesday, there are still three possible audition schedules for Raines: Thursday and Friday, Thursday and Saturday, and Friday and Saturday. Gombrich could be paired with Raines on any of those days. Furthermore, any of the three actors are capable of auditioning on Thursday and Saturday to satisfy the last rule.

It is possible to set up Limited Options based on Otto's first audition—which can only take place on Wednesday or Thursday. (Otto's first audition cannot be on Friday or Saturday, since it has to precede both of Raines's auditions.)

If Otto's first audition is on Wednesday, there's very little that can be deduced. Either Gombrich or Raines (or both) could audition on Thursday and Saturday to satisfy Rule 3. So, Otto's second audition could be on any of the remaining three days. Raines could audition on any two of the last three days. And Gombrich can audition on any pair of days—as long as at least one of them is shared with Raines.

However, if Otto's first audition is on Thursday, there's a lot to be deduced. First, Raines can't audition until Friday (Rule 1), which means Raines must audition on Friday and Saturday. That leaves Gombrich as the only actor left to audition on Wednesday. With that, Otto is the only actor who can audition on Thursday and Saturday, so Otto's second audition must be on Saturday (Rule 3). Finally, in order to satisfy Rule 2, Gombrich's second audition will have to coincide with one of Raines's auditions—either Friday or Saturday.

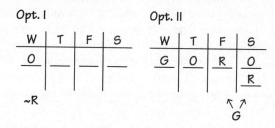

If spotted, there is certainly some value to setting up these options. However, Limited Options are usually more readily apparent than they are here. If these options were not recognized, the game can still be managed efficiently, as both of these sketches would have been developed for the fourth question of the set. In that case, the Master Sketch would simply be the initial sketch with Raines shut out of Wednesday and the three rules listed beneath.

Step 5: Questions

6. (B) Acceptability

As usual, running through the rules one at a time helps eliminate all of the wrong answers. Don't forget any limitations presented in the overview.

According to Rule 1, Otto's first audition must be before Raines's first audition. This eliminates **(C)**, which has Otto's first audition on Thursday and Raines's first audition on Wednesday. Rule 2 dictates that Gombrich and Raines must audition on the same day at least once. That never happens in **(E)**, making that a wrong answer. Rule 3 dictates that at least one actor auditions on Thursday and Saturday. None of the actors have that schedule in **(A)**, making that a wrong answer.

The remaining answers don't violate any of the three given rules. However, the overview provided the limitation that at least one actor auditions on each day. In **(D)**, none of the actors audition on Friday, which eliminates **(D)**. That leaves **(B)** as the only acceptable outcome.

7. (B) "If" / Could Be True

This question starts off by placing Otto's auditions on Thursday and Saturday—thus satisfying the requirement of Rule 3. This is fully set up in the second option. Even if you didn't set up Limited Options, the same logic used to develop the second option would have led to the exact same sketch for this question.

With that sketch, Gombrich's schedule must be either Wednesday and Friday or Wednesday and Saturday. **(B)** is the only answer to offer one of those possibilities.

8. (E) Must Be False (CANNOT Be True)

The correct answer will be the only one that must be false. The most limited entity of the game is Raines. Since Raines's first audition must be later than Otto's first audition, Raines's first audition can't be on Wednesday. That means the earliest Raines's first audition will be is Thursday, which in turn means that the earliest Raines's second audition will be is Friday. That immediately makes **(E)** stand out as the correct answer—since Raines's second audition can't be earlier than Friday.

For the record, whether or not you set up Limited Options, Gombrich only needs to audition with Raines once. Otherwise, Gombrich can audition on any of the days. So, Gombrich's second audition could be on Thursday or Friday

without violating any rules. That eliminates **(A)** and **(B)**. Otto's second audition was Saturday in the previous question, which eliminates **(C)**. If Raines's second audition was on Friday, then the first audition would be on Thursday. Otto's first audition would have to be on Wednesday (by Rule 1). Then Gombrich would be the actor who auditions on Thursday and Saturday. This is also acceptable, which eliminates **(D)**.

9. (D) Must Be False (CANNOT Be True)

If you set up Limited Options, these answers are easily tested against the two options. In the first option, with Otto's first audition on Wednesday, Otto's second audition can be on any of the remaining days. Therefore, **(A)**, **(B)**, and **(C)** are all possible and can be eliminated. In the second option, with Otto's first audition on Thursday, Otto's second audition must be on Saturday, which means Otto can't audition on Thursday and Friday. That makes **(D)** the correct answer.

If you didn't set up Limited Options, then this question is best handled by testing multiple answers at the same time. This can be done by setting up two sketches. The first would place Otto's first audition on Wednesday, which would enable you to test **(A)**, **(B)**, and **(C)** simultaneously. The second sketch would place Otto's first audition on Thursday, which would enable you to test **(D)** and **(E)** simultaneously. Note that this would set up the exact same sketches as the Limited Options. So, even if you didn't set up Limited Options ahead of time, you'd still have them set up here, which can help with the remaining questions.

10. (C) Could Be True

With Limited Options, **(C)** is clearly possible in the second option. However, even without Limited Options, some minor deductions can swiftly eliminate the remaining answers. Raines can't audition on Wednesday (Rule 1), which eliminates **(A)** and **(E)**. If all three actors auditioned on Friday, then none of them could have a Thursday/Saturday schedule, which would violate Rule 3. That eliminates **(B)**. Finally, if Otto's first audition was on Friday, then Raines's first audition would be on Saturday (Rule 1); but that leaves no day for Raines's second audition. That eliminates **(D)**.

11. (B) "If" / Could Be True

For this question, Gombrich auditions on Wednesday and Saturday. This is possible in either option, so two sketches will be needed. This would be the case even if you didn't set up Limited Options. With Gombrich on Wednesday and Saturday, that means only Otto or Raines could have a Thursday and Saturday schedule to satisfy Rule 3.

Otto could only audition on Thursday and Saturday in the second option. Even without Limited Options, having Otto's first audition on Thursday would automatically place Raines's auditions on Friday and Saturday (Rule 1).

W	T	F	S
G	O	R	G
			O
			R

If Raines auditioned on Thursday and Saturday, that could only happen in the first option. Even without Limited Options, Otto's first audition would have to be on Wednesday (Rule 1). Then, since somebody must audition on Friday, that will also have to be Otto.

W	T	F	S
G	R	O	G
O			R

Going through the answers, **(B)** is the only answer possible in either of the sketches for this question (specifically, the second sketch).

Game 3: Toy Dinosaurs

Step 1: Overview

Situation: A display of toy dinosaurs

Entities: Seven dinosaurs (I, L, P, S, T, U, V); four colors (green, mauve, red, yellow)

Action: Selection/Matching Hybrid. Determine which dinosaurs will be selected for the display, and determine the correct color of each selected dinosaur. A rare, but not unheard of, Hybrid of Selection and Matching.

Limitations: Exactly five of the seven dinosaurs are selected. Each dinosaur can only be one color. Two important notes: 1) There are only four colors for the five selected dinosaurs, so at least two dinosaurs must be the same color. 2) There is no limitation that each color must be used, so the display might include only two or three different colors—maybe even just one.

Step 2: Sketch

Selection games typically need only a list of the entities so that the entities selected can be circled and the entities not selected can be crossed out. The same can be done here with two minor adjustments. First, make a note that exactly five of the seven dinosaurs will be selected. Second, have some space under each dinosaur to match colors.

$$\text{I L P S T U V} \quad \text{Pick 5}$$
$$\text{g m r y}$$

Rule 1 states that exactly two of the dinosaurs will be mauve. Make a note of this to the side.

Rule 2 provides information for one of the five dinosaurs selected: it will be the stegosaur and it will be red. Place an r under the S in the entity list, and circle it to show it's selected.

Rule 3 must be translated properly. By the Formal Logic, if the iguanadon is one of the five dinosaurs selected, it must be green. That doesn't mean that the iguanadon is selected, but it can't be any other color. Similarly, this doesn't prevent any other dinosaur from being green. It's just that the iguanadon (if selected) must be. So, place a g under the I in the entity list, but don't circle it since it may not be selected.

Rule 4 is similar to Rule 3, setting up the same Formal Logic for the plateosaur being yellow. So, place a y under the P in the entity list, but don't circle it.

Rule 5 is more Formal Logic. In this case, in order to include the velociraptor, it must be that the ultrasaur is not included. In other words, if the ultrasaur is included, then the velociraptor can't be. In short, this means that the display can't include both the ultrasaur and the velociraptor.

$$\text{Never } ⓊⓋ$$

It's important to note that the display doesn't have to include one or the other. It just can't include both. Another way of representing this could be to change the list of entities to replace U and V with just one option of U/V.

Rule 6 puts a limitation on the coloring of the lambeosaur and the ultrasaur. Should they both be included in the display, they can't both be mauve. One of them can be—just not both.

$$\text{L \& U } \textit{not both mauve}$$

Like with the previous rule, this doesn't mean one of them has to be mauve. They just can't both be mauve. It also doesn't mean that both have to be selected. The display could include just one of them—and that one could be any color.

Step 4: Deductions

The Numbers are crucial to handling this game. For starters, only five of the seven dinosaurs are selected, and the display can't include both the ultrasaur and the velociraptor. That's a severe limitation on the selection. If one of them is selected, then that leaves only five dinosaurs from which to select the remaining four. If neither of them is selected, then the other five must be chosen.

Also, the selection requires two mauve dinosaurs. Those can't include the stegosaur (Rule 2), the iguanadon (Rule 3), or the plateosaur (Rule 4). That leaves just four dinosaurs: lambeosaur, tyrannosaur, ultrasaur, and velociraptor.

The tyrannosaur is a Floater, so it could be mauve with any of the other three dinosaurs. However, if the tyrannosaur isn't mauve, the two mauve dinosaurs couldn't be the ultrasaur and velociraptor (Rule 5), and they couldn't be the ultrasaur and the lambeosaur (Rule 6). In that case, the two mauve dinosaurs would be the lambeosaur and the velociraptor.

Even if you don't think of the specific combinations ahead of time, it's vital to consider the dinosaurs that could be mauve and keep track of the numbers throughout the game.

$$\text{I L P Ⓢ T U/V} \quad \text{Pick 5}$$
$$\text{g   y r} \qquad\qquad \text{g m r y}$$

$$\text{Exactly 2 mauve: TL, TU, TV, or LV}$$

Step 5: Questions

12. (B) Partial Acceptability

For Partial Acceptability questions, go through the rules one at a time and eliminate answer choices that directly violate the rules. Any rule that applies to information not listed in the answer choices should be saved for last. In this case, since colors aren't listed in the answer choices, start with any rules that don't focus primarily on colors.

Rule 2 requires the display to include a stegosaur. There's no stegosaur in **(D)**, so that can be eliminated. Rule 5 indicates that the display can't include both the ultrasaur and the velociraptor. That eliminates **(A)** and **(E)**. The remaining rules all focus on colors. So, test the remaining two answer choices by assigning colors based on the rules.

By Rule 1, two of the dinosaurs must be mauve, but that can't be determined yet. By Rule 2, the stegosaur in both remaining answers will be red. By Rules 3 and 4, the iguanadon in **(C)** will be green and the plateosaur in both answers will be yellow. With one red, one green, and one yellow dinosaur in **(C)**, the remaining dinosaurs (lambeosaur and ultrasaur) will have to be mauve to satisfy Rule 1. However, by Rule 6, those two dinosaurs can't both be mauve, so **(C)** is eliminated.

Therefore, **(B)** is the only answer that doesn't violate the rules, making it the correct answer.

For the record, the coloring could be as follows:

I L P S T U/V
g m y r m g

13. (D) "If" / Must Be True EXCEPT

For this question, the tyrannosaur is not selected. That leaves just six dinosaurs for the five spots, but the display cannot include both the velociraptor and the ultrasaur (Rule 5). So, one of those two has to be selected along with the remaining four dinosaurs—iguanadon, lambeosaur, plateosaur, and stegosaur.

The stegosaur will be red (Rule 2), the iguanadon will be green (Rule 3), and the plateosaur will be yellow (Rule 4). The remaining two dinosaurs must be mauve (Rule 1). The lambeosaur will be one of them. The second mauve dinosaur will be either the ultrasaur or the velociraptor.

However, by Rule 6, the two mauve can't be the lambeosaur and the ultrasaur. So, the second mauve dinosaur will have to be the velociraptor.

I L P S T U/V
g m y r m

Since the ultrasaur is not in the display, **(D)** is the correct answer.

14. (A) Could Be True

The correct answer to this question will list two dinosaurs that could be displayed together. The remaining four answers will list dinosaurs that can't be displayed together without violating the rules.

Since this question requires testing answers individually, it's worth skipping temporarily in favor of questions that require one sketch instead of potentially five. In fact, the next

question sets up the display with a yellow tyrannosaur. The resulting sketch can be used to quickly test **(B)**, **(D)**, and **(E)** for this question, leaving only two answers to be tested.

If this question isn't skipped, the answers must all be tested. To avoid testing each answer individually, look for a way to test multiple answers simultaneously. The first three answers all include a green lambeosaur. If that were included, the only dinosaurs left that could be mauve would be the tyrannosaur, the ultrasaur, and the velociraptor. However, the ultrasaur and the velociraptor can't both be selected. So, in order to have two mauve dinosaurs (Rule 1), one of the ultrasaur or velociraptor must be selected as mauve, and the second mauve dinosaur would be the tyrannosaur.

I L P S T U/V
g g y r m m

Because the second mauve dinosaur could be the velociraptor, **(A)** is the correct answer. For the record:

When the green lambeosaur is included, the tyrannosaur has to be mauve, which eliminates **(B)**. And if the ultrasaur is included, it too would have to be mauve, which eliminates **(C)**.

To verify that the last two answers are wrong, test what happens if the yellow tyrannosaur were selected. This is set up in the sketch for the next question:

I L P S T U/V
g m y r y m

Because the ultrasaur wouldn't be in the display, that eliminates **(D)**. And since the velociraptor would have to be mauve, that eliminates **(E)**.

15. (E) "If" / Must Be True

For this question, the tyrannosaur must be selected, and it must be yellow. That leaves the lambeosaur, the ultrasaur, and the velociraptor as the possible mauve dinosaurs. They can't be the ultrasaur and the lambeosaur (Rule 6) and they can't be the ultrasaur and the velociraptor (Rule 5), so they must be the lambeosaur and the velociraptor. That means the ultrasaur (by Rule 5) can't be in the display.

I L P S T U/V
g m y r y m

(E) is the only answer that is confirmed, making it the correct answer.

The fifth dinosaur could be the plateosaur, which means **(A)** and **(B)** could be false. The fifth dinosaur could also be the iguanadon (which would be green), leaving only one yellow dinosaur. That would make **(C)** false. And the lambeosaur has to be mauve in this case, making **(D)** false.

16. (A) "If" / Must Be True

For this question, the display must include the iguanadon, which must be green, and the ultrasaur. By including the ultrasaur, the velociraptor will not be selected (Rule 5). Once again, that leaves only three dinosaurs that could be mauve: lambeosaur, tyrannosaur, and ultrasaur. By Rule 6, the ultrasaur and lambeosaur can't both be mauve. So, one of them will be, which means the second mauve dinosaur must be the tyrannosaur. That makes **(A)** the correct answer.

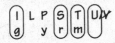

17. (B) "If" / Could Be True

If there are two green dinosaurs, that confirms the colors of all five dinosaurs: two mauve, two green, and one red (the stegosaur). Therefore, there are no yellow dinosaurs, which eliminates **(A)**.

Since none of the dinosaurs are yellow, the display can't include the plateosaur (Rule 4). That leaves six dinosaurs. However, the display can't include the ultrasaur and the velociraptor (Rule 5). So, one of those two has to be selected along with the remaining four dinosaurs: iguanadon, lambeosaur, stegosaur, and tyrannosaur.

The lambeosaur must be in the display, which eliminates **(C)**. The tyrannosaur must be in the display, which eliminates **(D)**. And the display has to have either the ultrasaur or the velociraptor, which eliminates **(E)**.

That leaves **(B)** as the only possible answer. In that case, the two mauve dinosaurs would be the lambeosaur and the velociraptor because it can't be the lambeosaur and ultrasaur (Rule 6).

Game 4: Charitable Foundation Grants

Step 1: Overview
Situation: A foundation awarding grants

Entities: Four areas of charity (medical services, theater arts, wildlife preservation, youth services)

Action: Matching. Determine which of four areas will receive a grant in each of four quarters of a year. The task is to match the grants to quarters. Because a grant can be awarded more than once, this game is classified as Matching rather than Distribution. This game also offers a twist—in Rule 3—regarding consecutive quarters, so some may view it as a Hybrid game of Sequencing and Matching. Whichever way this game is characterized, the sketch is based on the calendar year referred to in the opening paragraph.

Limitations: At least one grant is awarded every quarter. With four quarters, that means at least four grants are awarded. However, because the overview provides no information regarding how many grants are assigned to each area, it's possible that some areas will be awarded multiple grants while others go unawarded. Furthermore, if there were only one grant per quarter, that would total four grants. If any quarter includes more than one grant, there will automatically be more grants than areas—forcing at least one area to receive multiple grants. Expect duplication in this game.

Step 2: Sketch
Whenever a Logic Game offers a timeline, that's usually a good template for the setup. In this case, set up four columns, one for each quarter. In each column, start off with one slot to indicate the minimum of one grant that needs to be awarded each quarter. List the awards above.

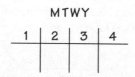

Step 3: Rules
Rule 1 stipulates that all four areas will be awarded a grant at least once. Make a note next to entities indicating that they all must be used.

Rule 2 sets a maximum for the total number of grants. Since there is already a minimum of one grant awarded each quarter, that's a total of four grants. So, this rule allows an additional two grants to be awarded. However, it should be noted that this rule merely sets a limit. It does not state that there must be six grants awarded. It is possible that the four grants in the setup will be the only four grants awarded. Still, make a note beneath the sketch indicating the limitation.

Rule 3 states that any area awarded multiple grants will receive those grants in different nonconsecutive years. Again, jot this information in shorthand to the side.

Rule 4 requires that medical services receives exactly two grants. Add a second M to the entity list. That raises the total number of grants to at least five. Only one more grant could be awarded. And since the rule states that medical services gets exactly two, any sixth grant will be awarded to one of the remaining three areas.

Rule 5 establishes a grant for quarter 2. Wildlife preservation can now be added to the sketch in the second column. Before moving on, it's important to note two things: this is not necessarily the only grant awarded in the second quarter, and wildlife preservation could still be awarded another grant in another quarter.

Step 4: Deductions
The rules offer minimal concrete information. Moreover, only two of the areas are specifically mentioned (medical services and wildlife preservation), and neither one relates to the other in any significant way. Therefore, deductions are going to be relatively sparse here. However, it still helps to note that, by Rule 3, wildlife preservation can't be awarded a grant in quarters 1 or 3. A simple "No W" notation in each column will suffice.

Without major deductions, it's important to focus on the two concepts that will most likely be tested in this game. First: the fact that no two areas can be awarded grants in the same or consecutive quarters, which is particularly important for medical services. Since medical services must be awarded two grants, there are three possible outcomes for when they can be awarded: quarters 1 and 3, 1 and 4, or 2 and 4. These outcomes will hold true should any other area get two grants.

Second: the number of grants awarded. The game already acknowledges at least five grants: two for medical services, one for each of the remaining three areas. If there's a sixth grant, it must be a second grant to one of the three areas other than medical services.

MTWY   (max 1 more – T, W, or Y)

1	2	3	4
—	W	—	—
~W		~W	

areas with 2 awards =
different non-consecutive quarters

Step 5: Questions

18. (C) Acceptability

This is a typical Acceptability question, best managed by going through the rules one at a time and eliminating answers that violate them.

All four areas are listed in each answer choice, so nothing violates Rule 1. Rule 2 limits the number of grants to six. There are seven grants awarded in **(E)**, eliminating that answer. Rule 3 states that any grants awarded to the same area must be in different nonconsecutive quarters. **(D)** awards grants to theater arts in consecutive quarters (first and second), so that can be eliminated. Rule 4 requires two grants be awarded to medical services. There's only one grant awarded to medical services in **(A)**, so that can be eliminated. Rule 5 requires a grant be awarded to wildlife services in the second quarter. That doesn't happen in **(B)**, eliminating that answer. That leaves **(C)** as the correct answer—the only one that doesn't violate any of the rules.

19. (D) Must Be False (CANNOT Be True)

The correct answer to this question must be false. The remaining four answers will all be possibly true, if not definitely true. Don't spend too much time testing each answer. Instead, consider the numeric limitations, move briskly past anything that looks remotely possible, and look for something that violates the restrictions.

(A) is possible. After all, if medical services was awarded a grant in quarters 1 and 3, then the theater arts and youth services could get grants in quarter 4, finishing the sketch.

(B) is possible. Then, medical services could be awarded grants in quarters 1 and 3, with youth services getting a grant in any quarter.

(C) is possible. Then, medical services could be awarded grants in quarters 2 and 4, with theater arts getting a grant in any quarter.

(D) violates the numbers. This would give two grants to wildlife preservation and two to youth services. Add to that the two that have to go to medical services and the one that has to go to theater arts, and that totals seven grants. That violates Rule 2, meaning this answer cannot be true and is thus the correct answer.

For the record, **(E)** is possible. If medical services received grants in quarters 1 and 3, then quarter 4 could feature grants awarded to theater arts, wildlife preservation, and youth services.

20. (E) "If" / Could Be True EXCEPT

For this question, wildlife preservation and youth services will each be awarded a grant in the same quarter. Wildlife preservation already receives a grant in the second quarter, so that's one possible quarter to give grants to both areas.

Since, by Rule 3, wildlife preservation can't receive a grant in the first or third quarters, the only other possibility is the fourth quarter.

Therefore, if one quarter includes a grant for wildlife preservation and youth services, it will be either the second or fourth quarter. In either case, by Rule 3, neither of those two areas will be able to receive a grant in the third quarter. That means **(E)** cannot be true, making it the correct answer.

If this wasn't readily apparent, you could draw out the two possibilities:

1	2	3	4		1	2	3	4
__	W	__	__	or	__	W	__	W
	Y							Y

In the first sketch, by Rule 3, youth services can't be awarded a grant in quarters 1 or 3. And in the second option, youth services can't be awarded a grant in quarter 3. No further deductions can be made.

(A) is possible in the first sketch, as long as medical services gets its second grant in the fourth quarter and theater arts gets grants in the first and third quarters.

1	2	3	4
T	W	T	M
	Y		
	M		

This also confirms **(B)** as possible.

(C) is also possible in the first sketch if grants for medical services are given in the first and third quarter and any other grant is given in the fourth quarter.

1	2	3	4
M	W	M	W/Y/T
	Y		
	T		

~M

(D) is possible in the second option. Here's one way it could work:

1	2	3	4
M	W	M	W
			Y

T

21. (B) "If" / Could Be True

If only one quarter has two grants being awarded, that means only five grants will be given (two in the quarter with two grants and one each in the remaining three quarters). That means, to satisfy Rules 1 and 4, two grants will be given to medical services and exactly one grant will be given to the remaining areas.

By those numbers, **(A)** must be false (since this would lead to a sixth grant being awarded) and **(C)** must be false (since wildlife services already receives its grant in the second quarter).

If **(B)** were true, that would mean theater arts gets a grant in the first quarter. Therefore, medical services would receive grants in the second and fourth quarter, leaving youth services to receive its grant in the third quarter.

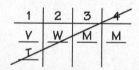

Since that could be true, **(B)** is the correct answer.

For the record, if youth services and theater arts both received grants in the first quarter, that would mean each other quarter could only include one grant. The second quarter already has wildlife preservation, so that would force medical services to receive its grants in the third and fourth quarters, violating Rule 3. So **(D)** cannot be true.

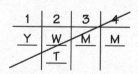

If theater arts were awarded a grant in the second quarter, that quarter would be the one with two grants: theater arts and wildlife preservation. If youth services received its grant in the first quarter, that would again force medical services to receive its grants in the third and fourth quarters, violating Rule 3. So **(E)** cannot be true.

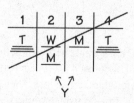

22. (D) Must Be False (CANNOT Be True)

The correct answer to this question will be definitely false, while the remaining four answers will all be possible. Again, the best approach is not to draw out any sketches

immediately. Instead, move swiftly through the answers, bypassing any choices that seem possible and looking for an answer that violates the numeric restrictions. If all five answers seem possible, then you'll need to start drawing sketches.

For **(A)**, this would mean that one quarter would include grants for theater arts, wildlife preservation, and youth services. That seems possible in the second quarter. On Test Day, that's a good sign to move on. If you had to test it out, it could work like so:

1	2	3	4
M	W	M	W/T/Y
	T		
	Y		

For **(B)**, this would leave one grant in each of the last two quarters for a total of six grants. That's within the requirements of Rule 2, so this seems possible. There are many ways this would work out, so if you had to test it out, one way would work like so:

1	2	3	4
M	W	M	T/Y
T/Y	Y/T		

(C), like **(B)**, would create a total of six grants. This is equally possible and one way it could look is like this:

1	2	3	4
M	W	M	W/Y/T
T/Y			Y/T

If **(D)** were true, then no other areas could receive grants in the first and fourth quarters. However, that would force medical services to receive its required two grants in the second and third quarters. That would violate Rule 3, which means this answer cannot be true.

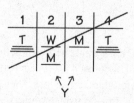

That makes **(D)** the correct answer.

For the record, **(E)** would be fine, as long as medical services receives its two grants in the first and third quarters and the remaining two areas each receive one grant in either the first or third quarter.

1	2	3	4
M	W	M	W
T/Y		Y/T	

23. (E) Completely Determine

The correct answer to this question will be a piece of information that, when added to the sketch, allows for only one possible outcome. Each answer choice will need to be tested individually, but you may want to focus on answers that establish significant entities into the sketch or further restrict numeric outcomes.

(A) suggests that two theater grants are awarded, which rounds out the numbers of the grants: two medical services, two theater grants, one wildlife preservation, and one youth services. However, there are too many possible arrangements of when those grants will be awarded. The medical services could be awarded in quarters 1 and 3, with the theater arts being awarded in 2 and 4. In that case, the youth services could be awarded in any of the four quarters. With too many possible outcomes, this choice can be eliminated.

(B) can be eliminated for the same reasons **(A)** can be eliminated. Again, the numbers would be figured out, but there would be too many possible outcomes of when the grants could be awarded.

(C) establishes three grants awarded in the first quarter. They would have to be medical services, theater arts, and youth services (since wildlife preservation receives a grant in the second quarter and a grant in the first quarter would violate Rule 3). However, in that case, the second grant for medical services could still be awarded in either the third or fourth quarter. Since the arrangement can't be completely determined for certain, this answer can be eliminated.

1	2	3	4
M	W	—	—
T			
Y		↖ ↗	
		M	

(D) establishes three grants awarded in the second quarter. One of them will be for wildlife services. However, the other two can't be determined for certain. They could be medical services and theater arts (which would mean youth services receives grants in the first and third quarters and medical services receives its second grant in the fourth quarter) or they could be medical services and youth services (which would mean theater arts receives grants in the first and third quarters and medical services receives its second grant in the

fourth quarter). There are other possible outcomes when the three grants in the second quarter are wildlife services, theater arts, and youth services, but just knowing that more than one possibility exists is enough to eliminate this answer.

(E) establishes three grants awarded in the third quarter. They would have to be awarded to medical services, theater arts, and youth services (since wildlife preservation receives a grant in the second quarter). That would mean medical services would have to receive its other grant in the first quarter. Then, the only grant that could be awarded in the fourth quarter would be wildlife preservation (to avoid violating Rule 3). The sketch would look like so:

1	2	3	4
M	W	M	W
		T	
		Y	

That accounts for every quarter, and it includes the maximum allowable number of grants by Rule 2. Because this is the one and only possible outcome, it makes **(E)** the correct answer.

Section II: Logical Reasoning

Q#	Question Type	Correct	Difficulty
1	Principle (Identify/Assumption)	A	★
2	Inference	A	★
3	Paradox	D	★
4	Flaw	D	★
5	Strengthen	E	★
6	Flaw	C	★
7	Assumption (Sufficient)	A	★
8	Parallel Flaw	E	★
9	Weaken	C	★
10	Principle (Identify/Inference)	B	★★
11	Point at Issue	C	★
12	Assumption (Sufficient)	D	★★★
13	Role of a Statement	C	★
14	Weaken	E	★
15	Flaw	A	★★
16	Role of a Statement	B	★★
17	Weaken	E	★★★★
18	Inference	D	★★★
19	Parallel Reasoning	C	★★
20	Weaken	D	★★★
21	Role of a Statement	E	★★★
22	Strengthen	A	★
23	Inference	B	★★
24	Assumption (Necessary)	E	★★★★
25	Inference	C	★★
26	Flaw	B	★

1. (A) Principle (Identify/Assumption)

Step 1: Identify the Question Type

Because the one right answer is a principle, this is a Principle question. Here, the correct answer matches the *reasoning* in the stimulus, so you are identifying the principle that underlies the author's argument.

Step 2: Untangle the Stimulus

Because the question stem uses the word *reasoning* in its description of the stimulus, the stimulus will contain an argument. Start untangling the stimulus by analyzing the argument into evidence and conclusion. The conclusion comes at the end of the stimulus, marked by the Conclusion Keyword [*s*]*o*. The author recommends that doctors never treat colds with antibiotics. The evidence comes after *however*, where the author tells us that antibiotics don't work on viruses and that viruses cause colds. Additionally, antibiotics might even cause bad side effects.

Step 3: Make a Prediction

Predict by generalizing the argument. In more general terms, the argument states that doctors should never give patients something that doesn't work and that could have bad side effects.

Step 4: Evaluate the Answer Choices

(A) matches the prediction.

(B) goes Out of Scope by introducing drugs that might have a positive effect. In the stimulus, antibiotics are described as having no effect on colds, and any possible positive effects are not discussed.

(C) goes Out of Scope in two ways. First, it defines when a drug should be prescribed. The argument, in contrast, defines when a drug should not be prescribed. Second, **(C)** alludes to drugs that can have a positive effect, but the stimulus is about drugs that have no intended effect.

(D) goes Out of Scope by introducing the doctor's uncertainty about the drug's beneficial effect. The stimulus makes it certain that antibiotics do not affect colds.

(E) goes Out of Scope by introducing patients' claims about medications' effectiveness. In the stimulus, we learn that patients ask for antibiotics, but there is no discussion of patients claiming that antibiotics are effective.

2. (A) Inference

Step 1: Identify the Question Type

Because the correct answer logically follows from the previous information in the stimulus, this is an Inference question. The one correct answer is a conclusion supported by information in the stimulus, which is the evidence of the argument.

Step 2: Untangle the Stimulus

Make an inventory of the information in the stimulus, paraphrasing the information as simply as you can. First, runners use two different types of thinking strategy. Associative strategies focus on sensations in the body. Dissociative strategies ignore sensations in the body. Another difference between the two strategies is that the associative ones demand so much attention that they cause mental exhaustion. Finally, it is important for runners going into races to be mentally fresh.

Step 3: Make a Prediction

Link together the connected information to predict what must be true. First of all, we know that runners should go into race day mentally fresh. We also know that associative strategies cause mental exhaustion. Thus, runners going into race day should not use associative strategies.

Step 4: Evaluate the Answer Choices

(A) matches the prediction.

(B) goes Out of Scope by focusing on what runners should do during the race, rather than prior to entering the race.

(C) goes Out of Scope by introducing alternating between the two strategies. Nothing in the stimulus discusses that idea.

(D), like **(B)**, focuses on the time "during races," rather than leading up to the race. Furthermore, nothing in the stimulus indicates the frequency that each strategy is used.

(E) is Extreme. While the stimulus gives us reason to think that there is one time (right before a race) when runners shouldn't use associative strategies, that is not strong enough to support the inference that dissociative strategies are "generally more effective." Further, **(E)**, like **(B)** and **(D)**, gets the relevant time period wrong. The stimulus is about entering a race, while **(E)** is about a day's training run.

3. (D) Paradox

Step 1: Identify the Question Type

This is a Paradox question because the one correct answer "helps to resolve the apparent discrepancy" in the stimulus.

Step 2: Untangle the Stimulus

Read strategically to figure out which two ideas don't seem to fit together. The Contrast Keyword [*n*]*onetheless* suggests that the information after it doesn't seem to fit with the information before it. So, the bank made loans and the recipients of the loans were supposed to increase their loan payments as more time passed. But as time passed, recipients actually decreased their average payment amount.

Step 3: Make a Prediction

The bank set up the loan schedule, but there's no guarantee that the loan recipients stuck to it. It could be that the recipients paid back more than they were required to early on or that they failed to make payments later on. If either were the case, then it would make perfect sense that the bank was receiving less money at the end of the time period.

Step 4: Evaluate the Answer Choices

(D) matches the prediction. If the three biggest borrowers paid off their loans early, then it makes sense that the bank received less money at the end of the time period.

(A) goes Out of Scope by focusing on companies besides the ten borrowers that the stimulus discusses.

(B) goes Out of Scope by introducing other banks.

(C) makes an Irrelevant Comparison. Like **(B)**, it fails to focus on MetroBank, the bank in the stimulus.

(E) goes Out of Scope by introducing a new type of loan—one with decreasing payments. The stimulus, by contrast, was only about ten loans that each had graduated payment plans.

4. (D) Flaw

Step 1: Identify the Question Type

Because the correct answer describes how the argument is flawed, this is a Flaw question.

Step 2: Untangle the Stimulus

The professor's conclusion is that universities don't support fair and tolerant debate. His evidence is the story about what happened at his university—two students taunted a speaker and others clapped for them.

Step 3: Make a Prediction

Predict the logical flaw by finding the professor's assumption. Here, the scope of the conclusion is broad—universities these days. But the scope of the evidence is narrow—the professor's university and this one event there with some students. The professor's assumption will close the scope shift between the evidence and conclusion. Thus, the professor is assuming that universities in general are similar to this one event at the professor's university. In making this assumption, the professor overlooks the alternative possibility that other universities are not similar to this one university and that they do not have similar incidents. The flaw is that the professor's evidence is just too small to support the general conclusion.

Step 4: Evaluate the Answer Choices

(D) matches the prediction. The professor uses narrow, unrepresentative evidence to make a broad conclusion.

(A) misses the mark. While both the conclusion and evidence reflect the author's opinion, neither is sufficient to draw a broad conclusion about all universities. Even if the majority of the students present had been surveyed for their opinion, they still couldn't have provided any statement based on the incident to draw such a general conclusion.

(B) mischaracterizes the conclusion in the stimulus because the professor advocates nothing.

(C), like **(A)**, fails to address the flaw. Even though the professor does offer his own opinion on the incident—"hurled vicious insults"—the flaw in reasoning is not the use of opinion, but the broad generalizing with a single incident that is not known to be representative. Also like **(B)**'s misuse of *advocating*, there is no "appeal" in the stimulus as **(C)** states.

(E) goes Out of Scope by differentiating between the students' behavior and their motives. Neither is central to the logical flaw of providing too little evidence to support a grand indictment.

5. (E) Strengthen

Step 1: Identify the Question Type

Because the correct answer strengthens the argument in the stimulus, this is a Strengthen question.

Step 2: Untangle the Stimulus

The conclusion is the last sentence—emphasizing the flavor of foods would be a better way of encouraging people to eat more healthfully. The evidence comes from studies—most people select food on the basis of flavor.

Step 3: Make a Prediction

The author is assuming that because people eat based on flavor, emphasizing the flavors can influence people's food choices. The correct answer will introduce new evidence that shows this is true.

Step 4: Evaluate the Answer Choices

(E) matches the prediction by showing that people are more likely to eat foods that they are told are flavorful.

(A) goes Out of Scope by focusing on what people currently believe, rather than on how their behavior might be altered by health experts.

(B) goes Out of Scope by contrasting tasty junk food and healthful bland food. The stimulus, in contrast, is about food that is both tasty and healthful.

(C) is a 180 if anything; it demonstrates that emphasizing the nutrition of food is "moderately successful" at leading people to eat healthful foods. However, it could still be the case that focusing on taste is more successful or less successful; therefore, this answer choice has no guaranteed effect on the argument.

(D) weakens the argument by suggesting that when people focus on flavor, they rate the least healthful foods as more flavorful than the nutritious foods.

6. (C) Flaw

Step 1: Identify the Question Type

Because the correct answer will describe why "the argument is flawed," this is a Flaw question.

Step 2: Untangle the Stimulus

The author's conclusion is that if business schools discourage their students from taking risks and encourage their students to want to be socially accepted, then they could cause future business people to be more ethical. The evidence starts with the studies at the beginning of the stimulus. First, people who are more likely to take risks tend to adhere to fewer ethical principles in business. Second, people who want to be socially accepted tend to have more ethical principles. Finally, people with more ethical principles tend to act more ethically.

Step 3: Make a Prediction

Start by finding the author's assumption. The conclusion is about how business schools could cause something to happen. The evidence is based on correlations—certain types of people are more likely to be a certain way. So, the assumption is that there is a causal factor to the correlations. In other words, the author assumes that the desire to be accepted socially causes people to act more ethically and that taking more risks causes people to act less ethically. The overlooked alternative is that there is no causal relationship between the desire to be accepted socially, the propensity for risk taking, and ethical behavior. In other words, the author has committed the logical flaw of confusing correlation with causation.

Step 4: Evaluate the Answer Choices

(C) matches the prediction.

(A) mischaracterizes the author's conclusion. The conclusion is not a claim about what is *always* true.

(B) makes an Irrelevant Comparison in importance of goals. The argument is about how one goal could be achieved, not about whether or not it is more important than some other goal.

(D) goes Out of Scope by mischaracterizing both the evidence and conclusion. **(D)** suggests that the evidence in the stimulus is about actions that most people believe are morally wrong. In contrast, the evidence was a correlation between types of people and number of ethical principles. **(D)** also suggests that the conclusion is that certain actions are morally wrong, when in fact the conclusion is really one way that business schools might achieve an outcome.

(E) incorrectly suggests that the conclusion simply restates the evidence—circular reasoning. The conclusion, however, adds the causal claim about how business schools can change their students' behavior, which was never presented in the evidence.

7. (A) Assumption (Sufficient)

Step 1: Identify the Question Type

The phrase "if assumed" indicates that this is a Sufficient Assumption question.

Step 2: Untangle the Stimulus

The conclusion is that Lessing's claim about literature is wrong. Lessing's claim is that the medium of an art form determines the kind of representation the art form must use. Therefore, what the essayist is really arguing for is that the medium of an art form does not determine the kind of representation that the art form must use. The essayist's evidence is the example of the imagists, whose poetry consists of assorted images put together.

Step 3: Make a Prediction

The essayists's conclusion goes against Lessing. Thus, look for the idea in the essayist's evidence that suggests where Lessing goes wrong. The evidence is about poetry that is made of assorted images. Lessing, in contrast, discusses poetry where events occur in sequence. Thus, for the essayist to argue against Lessing, the essayist must be assuming that there is a difference between poetry made of assorted images and poetry where events occur in sequence.

Step 4: Evaluate the Answer Choices

(A) matches the prediction.

(B) goes Out of Scope by introducing the idea of subject matter. The stimulus is about the kinds of representation that allow an art form to be legitimate, not the kinds of subject matter.

(C) goes Out of Scope by introducing Lessing's frame of reference. Whether or not Lessing knew about imagist poetry has nothing to do with the claim that Lessing made and the author's refutation of it.

(D) goes Out of Scope by suggesting that the imagists' poems do represent something. The author and Lessing might very well agree on this; where they disagree is about whether the poems represent events occurring in sequence.

(E) goes Out of Scope by failing to address anything about imagist poetry. If **(E)** suggested that art is either simultaneous or successive, but not both, *and* that imagist poetry was simultaneous, then it would be a sufficient assumption because it would show that imagist poetry was fundamentally different from Lessing's idea of literature. However, **(E)** doesn't reference imagist poetry or anything specific to it.

8. (E) Parallel Flaw

Step 1: Identify the Question Type

Because the correct answer "most closely parallels" the *questionable* reasoning in the argument, this is a Parallel Flaw question.

Step 2: Untangle the Stimulus

The conclusion comes before the evidentiary phrase "on the grounds that." The psychiatrist concludes that multiple personality disorder does not exist. Her evidence is that she's never encountered such a case in all her years of practicing psychiatry.

Step 3: Make a Prediction
There are two ways to predict a Parallel Flaw question. First, you can use the conclusion test. Second, you can predict the flaw as a whole. Either strategy is effective for this question. So, we can characterize the argument's conclusion as a very certain assertion that something does not exist. The flaw, on the other hand, needs to tie in the evidence. Here, the flaw is that the psychiatrist has made the unwarranted assumption that if she hasn't seen something, then it doesn't exist. It is also accurate to say that the psychiatrist has overlooked the possibility that multiple personality disorder patients are out there, just not in her practice.

Step 4: Evaluate the Answer Choices
(E) matches the prediction because the conclusion is a certain assertion that something doesn't exist. The flaw is that Jerod improperly assumes that if he hasn't seen it, then it isn't there.

(A) fails to match the stimulus because its conclusion isn't certain enough. The word *seldom* makes it too uncertain.

(B) fails to match the stimulus because its conclusion isn't certain enough. The word *probably* makes it too uncertain.

(C) fails to match the stimulus because its conclusion is a value judgment that some course of action isn't necessary. Additionally, the evidence in **(C)** doesn't match the conclusion because *rarely* makes it too uncertain. In the stimulus, the psychiatrist had "never" seen a multiple personality disorder case.

(D) fails to match the stimulus because its conclusion is an uncertain prediction ("would probably continue"), rather than a certain assertion that something doesn't exist.

9. (C) Weaken

Step 1: Identify the Question Type
The one correct answer "calls into question" the stimulus, so this is a Weaken question.

Step 2: Untangle the Stimulus
This stimulus is slightly unusual in that it is just a conclusory claim, without any evidence. Basically, the author suggests that it wouldn't have a big effect on world hunger if more people became vegetarians.

Step 3: Make a Prediction
The correct answer choice will suggest that if people became vegetarians, then it would have a big effect on world hunger.

Step 4: Evaluate the Answer Choices
(C) weakens the stimulus by showing that if people were vegetarians, then the land now used to produce meat could be used for grain that would potentially feed many more people.

(A) goes Out of Scope by focusing on what causes hunger, rather than on how a change in diet would affect hunger.

(B) goes Out of Scope by introducing the idea that herds and crops are similar in that they both get diseases and by failing to include how this fact relates to world hunger.

(D), like **(A)**, explains how people come to be hungry, but it doesn't show how diet change would affect their hunger.

(E) goes Out of Scope by focusing on the historical past. The stimulus is about what would happen in the future. Further, **(E)**, like **(A)** and **(D)**, merely explains how people get hungry.

10. (B) Principle (Identify/Inference)

Step 1: Identify the Question Type
Propositions on the LSAT means *principles*, so this is a Principle question. Here, the correct answer is the principle that matches the dairy farmer's statements.

Step 2: Untangle the Stimulus
Because the question describes the stimulus as *statements*, rather than as reasoning or an argument, read from the top down, paraphrasing each idea as you go like in an Inference question. First, the farmer cares about the environment where the cows live. Recently, the farm has tried to make the environment better. The changes are also supposed to increase blood to the cows' udders, which would increase milk production in the cows and profits for the farm.

Step 3: Make a Prediction
Although the farmer states that the farm cares about the conditions the cows live in, it looks like the farm also cares about increasing profits. Fortunately, they've found a way that helps cows to be more comfortable and helps the farm to make more money. The correct answer will show that looking out for a good environment can be compatible with making money.

Step 4: Evaluate the Answer Choices
(B) matches the prediction.

(A) is Extreme. The language "cannot ... unless" indicates Formal Logic. The stimulus is not built with Formal Logic statements. Additionally, **(A)** emphasizes the farmer's knowledge of physiology, which isn't an important idea in the stimulus.

(C) makes an Irrelevant Comparison between cows and other farm animals, none of which are mentioned in the stimulus.

(D), like **(A)**, uses Formal Logic ("only if") and is thus Extreme. Additionally, **(D)** goes Out of Scope by introducing the idea of "quality of the product," which is never discussed in the stimulus.

(E), like **(A)** and **(D)**, sets up a Formal Logic relationship. This time "the key to" is the Extreme phrase. Further, **(E)** is Extreme when it discusses "maximizing" profits. The farmer in the stimulus discussed "increasing" profits, but we can't assume that he increased them all the way to maximum.

11. (C) Point at Issue

Step 1: Identify the Question Type
Because the correct answer is the statement that Pat and Amar *disagree* about, this is a Point at Issue question.

Step 2: Untangle the Stimulus
Paraphrase each speaker's statements. Basically, Pat argues that email helps people reach a level of intimacy that would take much longer to achieve in person. Amar, on the other hand, argues that you need direct personal contact to have intimacy.

Step 3: Make a Prediction
There seems to be a direct disagreement between the speakers about what leads to intimacy. Pat thinks email leads to greater intimacy. Amar thinks that direct personal contact leads to intimacy. Look for the answer choice that matches their disagreement about what leads to intimacy, but also remember to use the Decision Tree to prove that you have found the correct answer.

Step 4: Evaluate the Answer Choices
(C) matches the prediction because both speakers have an opinion about whether intimacy can come about just by email. Pat thinks that email communication alone can lead to intimacy, but Amar thinks that email without direct personal contact will never lead to intimacy.

(A) goes Out of Scope because Amar states no opinion about the effect barriers to self-revelation have on intimacy.

(B) goes Out of Scope because neither Pat nor Amar state an opinion about the effect email could have on intimacy between friends. In fact, Pat specifically references the effect email could have on strangers, not on friends.

(D) goes Out of Scope because Pat states no opinion about social bonds. Further, **(D)** is Extreme. Amar suggests that if there are no social bonds, then there is no intimacy. In contrast, **(D)** says that if there are social bonds, then they always lead to intimacy.

(E) goes Out of Scope because Amar states no opinion about barriers to self-revelation.

12. (D) Assumption (Sufficient)

Step 1: Identify the Question Type
The stem indicates that the correct answer is the assumption that makes the criminologist's argument logical, thus this is a Sufficient Assumption question. Whenever a question stem includes both assumed and inferred, it is an Assumption question.

Step 2: Untangle the Stimulus
The conclusion is the prediction that criminal organizations will start to get involved with biotechnology and information technology. The evidence is that most criminal organizations intend to generate profits and that biotech and information could lead to big profits.

Step 3: Make a Prediction
The conclusion is very extreme, suggesting that criminal organizations will absolutely take some course of action. Whenever an author makes an extreme conclusion like this, the author overlooks many other possibilities. Here, for example, the author overlooks the possibility that criminal organizations could take other courses of action besides biotechnology and information technology. So, the assumption will make the argument logical by removing the overlooked possibilities. It will do this by connecting the evidence tightly to the conclusion. The evidence shows that criminal organizations intend to profit and that biotechnology and information technology promise to be profitable. The assumption will connect these ideas to the conclusion by stating that if some course of action could satisfy an organization's main purpose, then that organization will absolutely do it. If that link is added to the argument, then the argument is completely logical.

Step 4: Evaluate the Answer Choices
(D) provides the extreme words like *any* and *will* that make this answer choice sufficient to guarantee the conclusion. Thus, **(D)** is correct.

(A) reverses the logic in the stimulus. The correct answer needs to lead to the conclusion that organizations will undoubtedly get increasingly involved in promising areas. **(A)**, by contrast, starts from that premise.

(B) is too weak. While it is probably true that at least one criminal organization will become aware of promising biotech and infotech, that fact isn't enough to prove that criminal organizations will absolutely get involved in those areas. Remember, this is a sufficient Assumption question, where the correct answer needs to completely establish the logical validity of the conclusion. **(B)** would be a correct answer in a Necessary Assumption question.

(C) goes Out of Scope by focusing on what criminal organizations are already doing, rather than on what they will do in the future.

(E) goes Out of Scope by introducing the idea of legality. The stimulus never distinguishes whether or not promising biotech and infotech are legal or illegal.

13. (C) Role of a Statement

Step 1: Identify the Question Type

Because the stem asks about how a statement from the stimulus "figures in the argument," this is a Role of a Statement question.

Step 2: Untangle the Stimulus

Read the stimulus from the top down, describing the function of each statement as you go. So, the first sentence gives us the opinion of education administrators as well as their evidence for holding that opinion. The second sentence informs us that many teachers hold the opposite opinion (fearing rather than liking computers), but use the same evidence to reach their opinion. The third sentence, starting with the Contrast Keyword [b]*ut*, introduces the author's conclusion—the reason is wrong. The last sentence of the stimulus spells out the author's reason for disagreeing with both education administrators and teachers.

Step 3: Make a Prediction

The statement in question is about computers allowing school to offer more courses with fewer teachers. This is the education administrators' reason for liking computers as well teachers' reason for fearing computers. Finally, it is the reason that the author seeks to demonstrate is wrong.

Step 4: Evaluate the Answer Choices

(C) matches the prediction. The point of the author's argument is to show that the reason is wrong.

(A) mischaracterizes the way the statement fits into the author's argument. The author argues against the statement, rather than using the statement to explain an observation.

(B) mischaracterizes the author's conclusion as the solution to a problem. While the author does rebut the administrators and teachers, the author never offers a solution. Rather, the author suggests that the supposed problem (from the teachers' perspective) or advantage (from the administrators' perspective) was never really there in the first place.

(D) is a 180. The argument goes against the statement.

(E) is incorrect because the conclusion is not the statement in question. The conclusion is the sentence beginning with *But*.

14. (E) Weaken

Step 1: Identify the Question Type

Because the correct answer "most seriously weakens" the argument, this is a Weaken question.

Step 2: Untangle the Stimulus

The conclusion is that foraging causes the size of older bee brains to grow. The evidence, coming after *since* in the last sentence, is that foraging takes more brain power than caring for young bees.

Step 3: Make a Prediction

Start by finding the assumption. If you have identified the conclusion as a claim of causation, finding the assumption is easy. All claims of causation are based on the same assumptions—that nothing else is the cause, that causation is not reversed, and that it's not a coincidence. Weaken the argument by attacking these assumptions. So, here the most likely candidate for an assumption is that foraging and nothing else causes the growth in bee brains or that it's not big brains that lead to foraging (the reversal of the author's claim). Thus, the correct answer will show that something else causes bee brains to get bigger or that large brains lead to foraging.

Step 4: Evaluate the Answer Choices

(E) matches the prediction because if the bees that never forage have brains the same size as those that do forage, then it must be something else besides foraging that causes bee brains to get bigger.

(A) makes the Irrelevant Comparison between bees that have foraged for a long time and bees that have foraged for a shorter time. In contrast, the stimulus compares bees that have foraged with bees that have never foraged. Perhaps a single foraging experience is sufficient for brain growth.

(B) goes Out of Scope by introducing information about what happens to bees that used to forage but no longer do. The stimulus is about the effect the foraging has on any bee, whether they still forage or not.

(C) makes the Irrelevant Comparison between bees that forage far away and bees that forage close to home. The stimulus compares foragers to non-foragers, but does not mention foraging distance at all.

(D) goes Out of Scope by failing to mention foraging altogether. If the older bees have larger brains, even if just marginally, then the author's conclusion that foraging leads to larger brain size is not weakened.

15. (A) Flaw

Step 1: Identify the Question Type

The correct answer will explain why David's response is "vulnerable to criticism." Therefore, David's response is flawed, and this is a Flaw question.

Step 2: Untangle the Stimulus

Because the correct answer is about how David responds to Carla, we still need to understand both arguments. Summarize Carla's efficiently, then spend more time analyzing David's. Basically, Carla recommends that public university professors get some paid opportunities to do research without teaching. This research will improve human knowledge and improve the professors' teaching. David concedes to Carla's evidence that research causes good outcomes. But David still questions Carla's conclusion. In not so many words, it looks like David concludes that Carla is just wrong.

Step 3: Make a Prediction
David asks why professors should get time off from teaching, but Carla has already provided two good responses to this question. Thus, the flaw in David's response is that he has completely disregarded Carla's evidence.

Step 4: Evaluate the Answer Choices
(A) matches the prediction.

(B) mischaracterizes David's response because David does concede that professors conduct research. Thus, David does not think that teaching is the only function of professors.

(C) is Extreme by introducing the idea that *all* funding comes from "tax money." Neither Carla nor David explicitly mentions tax money, and we can't assume that just because the arguments are about public university professors that the only resources in question would be from taxes. Regardless of where the funds come from, David fails to consider the potential benefits Carla has cited.

(D) suggests that David believes that research is the only reason for professors to go on a leave of absence. Even if David fails to consider other reasons for a leave of absence, Carla's argument focuses on the benefits that spring from research done during a leave. So, David need not consider other potential benefits that Carla didn't bring up, but he does go astray in not even discussing the ones she did.

(E) goes Out of Scope by introducing vacations. While Carla and David both discuss paid leaves of absence, we cannot assume that paid leaves are the same as vacations. After all, as Carla describes and David concedes, professors do research while on leave.

16. (B) Role of a Statement

Step 1: Identify the Question Type
Because the correct answer "accurately describes the role played" in the argument of a specific statement, this is a Role of a Statement question.

Step 2: Untangle the Stimulus
Read the stimulus from the top down, describing the function of each statement as you go. The first sentence introduces the topic, dictation software, and tells us what it does. The second sentence tells us that dictation software was claimed to save labor, but the author thinks the claims are wrong. The third sentence gives the author's evidence. Basically, thinking and editing are what make writing laborious, not just the typing. Finally, the author describes a disadvantage of proofreading software.

Step 3: Make a Prediction
The statement in question came as the second half of the second sentence. The Opinion Keyword *fails* in the statement

shows that this is somebody's value judgment. Because no other person is identified as stating this opinion, it must be the author's. Thus, the statement in question is the author's conclusion.

Step 4: Evaluate the Answer Choices
(B) matches the prediction, because the statement is the author's conclusion and no other statement in the stimulus is a conclusion.

(A) suggests that the argument includes at least one subsidiary conclusion. Because a subsidiary conclusion would have its own evidence, and because neither of the pieces of evidence given by the author is supported by subsidiary evidence, there is no subsidiary conclusion.

(C) suggests that the statement in question is a subsidiary conclusion—a piece of evidence for the main conclusion, which also has supporting evidence for itself. Because the statement is actually the main conclusion, **(C)** is wrong.

(D) suggests that the statement is evidence. However, it is actually the conclusion.

(E) suggests that the statement is subsidiary evidence. However, there is no subsidiary conclusion in the argument, and the statement in question is the only conclusion.

17. (E) Weaken

Step 1: Identify the Question Type
Because the correct answer "most weakens" the argument, this is a Weaken question.

Step 2: Untangle the Stimulus
Signaled by *so*, the conclusion is that the unnamed magazine wouldn't have to depend so much on donations if it followed the practice of *The Brick Wall Review* and republished its poems in a separate anthology. The evidence, following the evidentiary Keywords "[a]fter all," is that the poems in the unnamed magazine are similar to those in *The Brick Wall Review*.

Step 3: Make a Prediction
Start by finding the assumption. Here, the conclusion is that the unnamed magazine could have the same results with its anthology as does *The Brick Wall*. The evidence is that the poems in each magazine are very similar. So, connecting these two ideas, the assumption is that if the magazines have the same poems, then they'll have the same kind of results from their anthologies. The author is overlooking the possibility that there could be some other difference between the two magazines, their poems, or their anthologies. Thus, the correct answer will weaken the argument by pointing out some difference between the unnamed magazine and *The Brick Wall*.

Step 4: Evaluate the Answer Choices

(C) weakens the argument by showing that *The Brick Wall*'s anthology publishes poems besides those originally published in its regular issues. This is not part of the plan that the patron proposes for the unnamed magazine. Thus, **(E)** points out a relevant difference between *The Brick Wall*'s anthology and the anthology project proposed for the unnamed magazine.

(A) points out a similarity between the unnamed magazine and *The Brick Wall*, rather than a difference. Additionally, **(A)** goes Out of Scope by focusing on the how the journals cover their operating expenses, rather than on the effect an anthology could have for the magazine's revenue.

(B) sounds like a strengthener if anything because it may imply that the unnamed magazine is more selective than *The Brick Wall*. Therefore, the anthology may also be of higher quality. However, **(B)** fails to describe how the poets that it mentions are related to any anthology project, so it is Out of Scope.

(C) goes Out of Scope by focusing on how the poets are compensated, rather than on the effect an anthology could have for the unnamed magazine.

(D) goes Out of Scope by focusing on how *The Brick Wall* pays for the operating expenses not covered by the sales of the anthology. The stimulus, by contrast, only discusses the portion of the operating expenses that are covered by the sales of the anthology.

18. (D) Inference

Step 1: Identify the Question Type

Because the correct answer completes the argument, it is a statement that must follow from the statements in the stimulus. Thus, this is an Inference question.

Step 2: Untangle the Stimulus

Make an inventory of the information in the stimulus, paraphrasing the information as simply as you can. First, one wouldn't trust the average person to treat someone with a serious medical condition. Next, the author tries to make an analogy by using the Keyword *similarly*. Good public servants care about the public, so they would do the right thing.

Step 3: Make a Prediction

The correct answer will complete the author's analogy, showing the proper course of action that public servants would take. So, think about what a public servant could do that would be similar to not trusting an average person to treat a medical patient. The correct answer will show that a public servant should not trust an average person to treat public problems.

Step 4: Evaluate the Answer Choices

(D) matches the prediction.

(A) goes Out of Scope by introducing surveys. Public opinion surveys did not factor into the statements about not trusting an average person to treat a medical patient.

(B) makes an Irrelevant Comparison by indicating who is more qualified to make public decisions. Note that the first sentence is about who should not treat a medical patient, rather than about who should treat the patient.

(C) goes Out of Scope by focusing on public servants' ignorance. The point of the stimulus is that we shouldn't trust the average person because of their ignorance. So long as public servants follow that rule, it doesn't matter how knowledgeable they are.

(E) makes another Irrelevant Comparison by providing a definition of what makes a good public servant. The stimulus is about whose recommendations a good public servant should ignore, rather than about what makes for a good public servant.

19. (C) Parallel Reasoning

Step 1: Identify the Question Type

The phrases "pattern of reasoning" and "most similar to" indicate that this is a Parallel Reasoning question.

Step 2: Untangle the Stimulus

The words *requires* and *if* indicate that this stimulus is built of Formal Logic statements. The best strategy is to translate them all into Formal Logic algebra. So, the first statement becomes "If X, then Y" when X stands for "winning" and Y stands for "willingness to cooperate." The second statement becomes "If Y, then Z." As we already determined, Y stands for "willingness to cooperate." Z will stand for "motivation." The team captain's conclusion can be translated into "If ~Z, then ~X." Remember, X stands for "winning," and Z stands for "motivation."

Step 3: Make a Prediction

The overall logical structure of the stimulus is:

$$\text{If} \quad X \quad \rightarrow \quad Y \quad \rightarrow \quad Z$$

$$\text{If} \quad \sim Z \quad \rightarrow \quad \sim X$$

The correct answer will share the same logical structure.

Step 4: Evaluate the Answer Choices

(C) matches the format of the Formal Logic. We can translate **(C)** into this:

$$\text{If} \quad \begin{array}{c} X \\ \text{(retain} \\ \text{its} \\ \text{status)} \end{array} \rightarrow \begin{array}{c} Y \\ \text{(raises} \\ \text{more} \\ \text{money)} \end{array} \rightarrow \begin{array}{c} Z \text{ (increased} \\ \text{campaigning)} \end{array}$$

$$\text{If} \quad \begin{array}{c} \sim Z \\ (\sim \text{ increased} \\ \text{campaigning}) \end{array} \rightarrow \begin{array}{c} \sim X \ (\sim \text{ retain} \\ \text{its status}) \end{array}$$

(A) fails to match the stimulus because it only involves two terms—being healthy (X) and exercise (Y). So, translating it into Formal Logic algebra would look like this: If X → Y, but Y could lead to ~X.

(B) translates into Formal Logic algebra like this:

$$\text{If} \quad \begin{array}{c} X \\ (\text{improve}) \end{array} \rightarrow \begin{array}{c} Y \\ (\text{learn}) \end{array} \rightarrow \begin{array}{c} Z \ (\text{make} \\ \text{some} \\ \text{mistakes}) \end{array}$$

$$\text{If} \quad \begin{array}{c} Z \ (\text{make some} \\ \text{mistakes}) \end{array} \rightarrow X \ (\text{improve})$$

So, **(B)** gets the evidence right but reverses the order in the conclusion. Note that **(B)**'s conclusion is an improper contrapositive of its evidence, while the conclusion in the stimulus is the proper contrapositive of its evidence. **(B)** would be parallel if it concluded with "If you never make mistakes, then you'll never improve."

(D) translates into Formal Logic algebra like this:

$$\text{If} \quad \begin{array}{c} X \\ (\text{repair} \\ \text{own}) \end{array} \rightarrow \begin{array}{c} Y \\ (\text{enthusiastic}) \end{array} \rightarrow \begin{array}{c} Z \\ (\text{mechanical} \\ \text{aptitude}) \end{array}$$

$$\text{If} \quad \begin{array}{c} \sim X \ (\sim \text{ repair} \\ \text{own}) \end{array} \rightarrow \begin{array}{c} \sim Z \\ (\sim \text{ mechanical} \\ \text{apptitude}) \end{array}$$

Like **(B)**, **(D)** gets the evidence correct but wrongly contraposes the evidence in the conclusion. Here, the error is negating both sides of the conditional, but not reversing them. **(D)** would be parallel if it concluded with "if you don't have mechanical aptitude, then you can't repair your own bike."

(E) translates into Formal Logic algebra like this:

$$\text{If} \quad \begin{array}{c} X \ (\text{get} \\ \text{ticket}) \end{array} \rightarrow \begin{array}{c} Y \ (\text{wait} \\ \text{in line}) \end{array} \rightarrow \begin{array}{c} Z \\ (\text{patience}) \end{array}$$

$$\text{If} \quad \begin{array}{c} \sim Y \ (\sim \text{ wait in} \\ \text{line}) \end{array} \rightarrow \begin{array}{c} \sim Z \\ (\sim \text{ patience}) \end{array}$$

So, **(E)** incorrectly contraposes the second half of the evidence. **(E)** would be parallel if it concluded with "if you are not patient, then you can't get a ticket."

20. (D) Weaken

Step 1: Identify the Question Type
Because the correct answer "most seriously weakens the argument," this is a Weaken question.

Step 2: Untangle the Stimulus
The conclusion is that setting the speed limit to 90 a decade ago has since reduced the highway accident rate. The evidence is that every year since the change, the rate of accidents has been at least 15 percent lower than it was a decade ago.

Step 3: Make a Prediction
The key to predicting the assumption, and then the weakener, is realizing that this is a causal argument. The author's whole argument is that it was changing the speed limit that caused the decrease in accidents. As with any causal argument, one assumption is that the thing identified as being the cause (here the speed limit change) is the only cause. So, the author is overlooking the possibility that something else happened a decade ago that might also be responsible for the decrease in accidents. The weakener will show that there was something else that could have caused the decrease in accidents.

Step 4: Evaluate the Answer Choices
(D) matches the prediction by introducing improvements in automobiles that help drivers control their cars more effectively. Those changes are other factors that would very likely lead to the decrease in accidents.

(A) goes Out of Scope by focusing on the years before the change in speed limit. The argument is only about what happened in the decade between when the speed limit was changed and now.

(B), like **(A)**, focuses on the wrong time frame. The argument is about what has happened over the last decade, not about how it was exactly 10 years ago.

(C) makes an Irrelevant Comparison between what the speed limit is and how fast people actually drive. Even if we assume that people driving faster leads to accidents, we can't tell if people slowed down after the speed limit changed (and yet still drove faster than the speed limit) or if everybody kept driving the same speed as before the change. Also, it says *most* people drive faster than the speed limit, but maybe there are *some* people who did opt to slow down with the limit. In short, **(C)** does not provide information that is concrete enough to actually affect the strength of the argument.

(E) goes Out of Scope by introducing equipment that helps to prevent harm to passengers. The stimulus is about whether or not cars get into accidents, not about how badly passengers get hurt in those accidents.

21. (E) Role of a Statement

Step 1: Identify the Question Type
The phrase "plays which one of the following roles" indicates that this is a Role of a Statement question.

Step 2: Untangle the Stimulus
Read the stimulus from the top down, describing the function of each statement as you go. The first sentence introduces the critics' point of view. The second sentence presents an assumption held by the critics as well as a further consequence of that assumption. The further consequence is critical, and in the third sentence the author suggests that the criticism in the second sentence is wrong. The author then presents evidence for why the criticism in the second sentence is wrong.

Step 3: Untangle the Stimulus
The statement in question comes after the author's conclusion and is introduced with the Evidence Keyword *for*. It must be a piece of evidence for the author's conclusion.

Step 4: Evaluate the Answer Choices
(E) matches the prediction because the statement in question is evidence for the author's conclusion, and the conclusion is an attempt to undermine the logic behind the critics' point of view.

(A) is backward. The statement in question supports the author's conclusion.

(B) goes Out of Scope because the author never suggests that the statement in question is misleading. The author thinks the critics are wrong, but not because they have been misled.

(C) is wrong because the conclusion is that the criticism is misplaced. The statement in question is evidence for that conclusion.

(D) fails to describe the statement in question. The false assumption in the stimulus is that there are greater difficulties involved in a space launch than in social problems. The author disagrees with *that* assumption, not with the statement in question.

22. (A) Strengthen

Step 1: Identify the Question Type
The phrase "would most strengthen" indicates that this is a Strengthen question.

Step 2: Untangle the Stimulus
The conclusion is that the Clovis point did not originate in North America. The evidence is that archeologists discovered some Clovis points in Siberia.

Step 3: Make a Prediction
Start by finding the assumption. Here, the assertion in the conclusion that the Clovis points weren't invented in North America needs some additional connection to the fact that archeologists discovered some Clovis points in Siberia. The author is overlooking the possibilities that the Clovis points discovered in Siberia weren't made there or that they were made later than Clovis points that have been discovered in North America. The assumption plugs up the holes in the argument by removing those overlooked possibilities. So, the author is assuming that the points discovered in Siberia *were* made in Siberia and *were* made earlier than the points that have been discovered in North America. The correct answer will reinforce at least one of these assumptions.

Step 4: Evaluate the Answer Choices
(A) matches the prediction by showing that the points discovered in Siberia are older than any of those discovered in North America. While **(A)** doesn't completely prove the argument (because the points found in Siberia could still have been made in North America), it doesn't need to prove the argument in order to strengthen it. A proper strengthener just makes the conclusion more likely to be true.

(B) does not strengthen the argument. If the land bridge disappeared before the first Clovis point was made, and yet Clovis points have appeared in both Siberia and North America, then it would be a mystery as to where they first appeared. But the timing of the bridge's disappearance would not strengthen the argument that the points were first invented somewhere other than North America.

(C) makes an Irrelevant Comparison between the effectiveness of Clovis points and earlier spear points.

(D) goes Out of Scope by failing to mention anything about Clovis points. Even if artifacts were found in Siberia after some of the groups left Siberia, that does not impact when or where the Clovis points were invented.

(E), like **(D)**, fails to mention anything about Clovis points. It does, however, make it possible that the Clovis point was invented in North America, and then brought to Siberia by paleohumans. This would explain why there is a cache of Clovis points there. So, if anything, **(E)** could weaken the argument.

23. (B) Inference

Step 1: Identify the Question Type
Because the stimulus gives evidence against the correct answer, this question features the classic downward-flowing logic of an Inference question. There's a twist, though, in that the correct answer is the one that must be false based on the stimulus, rather than the one that must be true. The four wrong answers are statements that could be true, meaning

the stimulus either gives evidence for them or they are Out of Scope.

Step 2: Untangle the Stimulus
While the stem has a twist, you can still treat the stimulus as you would any other Inference question. Proceed by making an inventory of the information in the stimulus, paraphrasing the information as simply as you can. The topic is taxi drivers. They are paid by their passengers, so it makes sense that they get to decide when to stop working in a given day. When they get the money they want for that day, they stop. Finally, the author suggests that because taxi drivers can stop when they want to, they would be more likely to stop earlier on a busier day.

Step 3: Make a Prediction
First and foremost, remember that the correct answer goes against the stimulus. The stimulus is about how taxi drivers get to choose when they stop working and that on busy days they choose to work less. The correct answer will contradict this idea.

Step 4: Evaluate the Answer Choices
(B) goes against the stimulus because it suggests that on busy days, when taxi drivers are able to take more fares, they would actually work longer hours, because they are making more money each hour.

(A) goes Out of Scope by introducing financial needs. The stimulus does include the fact about taxi drivers setting their daily targets, but we cannot assume that those daily targets would necessarily be based on financial needs.

(C) goes Out of Scope by suggesting that taxi drivers have traded their wage for freedom to set their schedule. Based on the stimulus, we do know that taxi drivers have such freedom, but we don't know how that freedom relates to their wage. In fact, the stimulus never mentions wage, focusing instead on daily income.

(D) goes Out of Scope by introducing standard of living. Like **(A)**, we know that taxi drivers set a target for daily income, but we don't know how that relates to standard of living.

(E) makes an Irrelevant Comparison between those paid by production and those paid by hourly wage. **(E)** compares the efficiency of the two groups, an idea which is not part of the stimulus.

24. (E) Assumption (Necessary)

Step 1: Identify the Question Type
The phrase "assumption on which the argument depends" indicates that this is a Necessary Assumption question.

Step 2: Untangle the Stimulus
The conclusion is signaled by *so*. Simply put, the author thinks that the meaning of a poem is not just what the writer wanted to say to the reader. The evidence is in two pieces,

one before and one after the conclusion. Put together, the evidence is that no writer of great poems wants to make contradictions, but that readers can find contradictions in great poems.

Step 3: Make a Prediction
The assumption bridges the gap between the evidence and conclusion. The best way to predict what would bridge the gap is to first identify the gap itself. So, look to the conclusion for new ideas, those not already connected to the evidence. The conclusion discusses "meaning," which is not an idea that the evidence discusses. Similarly, the evidence discusses readers of poems, which is not an idea that the conclusion discusses. Therefore, the correct answer will create some connection between the readers of poems and the meaning of poems. The assumption is that what the reader sees in a poem contributes to the meaning of the poem.

Step 4: Evaluate the Answer Choices
(E) matches the prediction by linking the reader's interpretation of the poem to the poem's meaning.

(A) goes Out of Scope by discussing the frequency that readers agree with the author on the meaning. Whether they disagree only sometimes or all of the time doesn't impact the conclusion.

(B) goes Out of Scope by indicating that the author intended one primary idea. Whether the author intended one or several ideas, **(B)** fails to connect the readers of the poem to the meaning of the poem.

(C) is in scope, mentioning both readers and meaning, but the logic is distorted. It disconnects the reader's interpretation of the poem from its true meaning by suggesting that reader's understanding of meaning is based on the author's intention.

(D) is Extreme. Remember that Extreme answers are usually wrong in necessary Assumption questions. By using the Denial Test on **(D)**, you'll get "Not everyone reading a great poem can discern every idea that the author intended." That statement would not destroy the conclusion as it should if it were the right answer. Also, **(D)** fails to appropriately connect the concepts of the reader and the meaning of the poem, as was predicted.

25. (C) Inference

Step 1: Identify the Question Type
Because the correct answer "must be true" based on the stimulus, this is an Inference question.

Step 2: Untangle the Stimulus
Make an inventory of the information in the stimulus, paraphrasing statements as simply as you can. First, we learn Weston's campaign contributions law. The law states that if

you make a contribution greater than $100 and you don't live in Weston and have never lived in Weston, then you must register with the city council. Next, we learn that Brimley complied with the law. The reason the author knows this is because all of the contributions to Brimley came from those who live in, or used to live in, Weston.

Step 3: Make a Prediction

Connect the statements in order to make a prediction. The first part of the stimulus is about the law. If you make certain types of contributions, then you have to register with the city council. In the second part of the stimulus, we learn that there were no such contributions to Brimley. If we put these two pieces together, we can see that those who contributed to Brimley weren't required by the law to register with the city council (because they all live in, or used to live in, Weston).

Step 4: Evaluate the Answer Choices

(C) matches the prediction.

(A) need not be true because nonresidents who used to live in Weston could have contributed more than $100 to Brimley and still not have been required to register their contributions.

(B) goes Out of Scope because the stimulus doesn't tell us if any contributors to Brimley's campaign actually registered with the city council. All we can be sure of is that the contributors were not required by law to register with the city council.

(D) goes Out of Scope because, like **(B)**, the stimulus doesn't tell us about any contributors who actually did register.

(E), like **(B)** and **(D)**, misses the distinction between what was required by law (none of the contributors needed to register) and what actually happened (some of the contributors might still have registered, even though it wasn't required of them).

26. (B) Flaw

Step 1: Identify the Question Type

The phrase "vulnerable to criticism" indicates that this is a Flaw question.

Step 2: Untangle the Stimulus

The phrase "as we can conclude from" indicates that what precedes it is the conclusion, and what follows it is the evidence. So, the conclusion is that Flavius was generally unpopular. The evidence is that many theatrical satires were written about him.

Step 3: Make a Prediction

Start by finding the assumption. Here, the conclusion is about Flavius' subjects in general—the average person, in other words. But the evidence is about plays. The assumption bridges that scope shift. So, the author is assuming that the plays represent the views of the average person. The author is overlooking the possibility that the plays do not represent the views of the average person. This is especially likely given the fact in the first sentence of the stimulus that Flavius cut funding from the arts.

Step 4: Evaluate the Answer Choices

(B) matches the prediction. The playwrights are not likely to represent the average person, given that they have a special reason to dislike Flavius.

(A) goes Out of Scope by introducing the plays not written about Flavius.

(C) mischaracterizes the argument's assumption, which is not about Flavius's attitudes, but is about the attitudes of his subjects toward him. Further, **(C)** neglects the fact that the stimulus provides direct evidence that Flavius was against the arts.

(D) goes Out of Scope because whether or not Flavius's attempts succeeded is not directly related to the author's argument about how Flavius's subjects disliked him.

(E) goes Out of Scope by focusing on virtues, rather than on the attitudes of Flavius's subjects toward him.

Section III: Logical Reasoning

Q#	Question Type	Correct	Difficulty
1	Paradox	A	★
2	Flaw	C	★
3	Main Point	A	★
4	Paradox	B	★
5	Method of Argument	A	★
6	Weaken	A	★★
7	Paradox	C	★
8	Flaw	C	★
9	Strengthen	D	★
10	Flaw	C	★★
11	Weaken	A	★★
12	Assumption (Necessary)	E	★★
13	Inference	D	★★★
14	Principle (Apply/Inference)	D	★★
15	Parallel Flaw	C	★★
16	Principle (Identify/Inference)	C	★★★
17	Assumption (Necessary)	D	★★★
18	Flaw	B	★
19	Principle (Identify/Strengthen)	D	★★★
20	Parallel Reasoning	E	★★★★
21	Role of a Statement	B	★★
22	Flaw	B	★★★
23	Inference	C	★★★★
24	Assumption (Sufficient)	C	★
25	Inference	E	★★★★

1. (A) Paradox

Step 1: Identify the Question Type
A question stem that directs you to *explain* something, such as the *findings* in this question, is a Paradox question requiring you to provide an explanation for seemingly contradictory or paradoxical situations.

Step 2: Untangle the Stimulus
The stimulus provides information on the activities of students that performed best and those that performed worst. The perplexing facts are that the best performers had part- or full-time jobs while the worst performers were not burdened with employment. Another less perplexing distinction between the two groups is that the best performers had limited social lives while the worst performers had very active social lives.

Step 3: Make a Prediction
For a Paradox question, focus on the contradictory facts. For example, in this stimulus both the best and worst performing students had their history classes early in the morning. Thus, this factor cannot explain why some performed better than others, but does suggest that both groups would need to be well rested. Anticipate that the correct answer must explain how the best performers overcame or maybe even benefited from spending more time at jobs than the worst performers, keeping in mind that there was also the distinction in the social lives of the two groups.

Step 4: Evaluate the Answer Choices
(A) fits the prediction by explaining that students with jobs made up for lost study time, but that those with active social lives did not.

(B) is a 180. If the best students worked late into the night, it would be even more puzzling that they were still able to perform better in those early morning history classes.

(C) is Out of Scope. The study found that both student groups attended class early in the morning.

(D) is an Irrelevant Comparison. The part-time versus full-time job distinction is never at issue. Rather, it's the job versus no job distinction that comes into play.

(E), like **(D)**, goes astray by distinguishing between part- and full-time jobs when the stimulus does not. According to this choice, having a part-time job is beneficial to academic performance and thus would resolve the paradox for the best performers with part-time jobs. However, because the choice also indicates that having a full-time job is detrimental to academic performance, the choice would deepen the mystery for those best performers with full-time jobs.

2. (C) Flaw

Step 1: Identify the Question Type
The question stem explicitly asks for a *flaw* in the politician's argument. Break the argument down, identifying the evidence, conclusion, and assumption. Keep the common LSAT flaws in mind.

Step 2: Untangle the Stimulus
The politician's opinion is that those at the meeting should not accept Kuyler's argument. The Keyword *for* indicates the evidence: Kuyler's hypocrisy in entering into government contracts despite implying it would be improper to do so.

Step 3: Make a Prediction
While one of the rarer of the common LSAT flaws, this stimulus presents an *ad hominem* attack; the author rejects the argument of another based on an attack against the speaker rather than the merits of the argument itself. On the LSAT, someone's hypocrisy is not valid evidence against her argument.

Step 4: Evaluate the Answer Choices
(C) is the *ad hominem* attack answer.

(A) does not accurately describe the argument. One common form of the correct Flaw answer is a description of the evidence and conclusion of the argument. **(A)**, while in that form, does not match the evidence in the stimulus, which states that *most* were not persuaded. This choice is Extreme, indicating that nobody was persuaded.

(B) is incorrect because it inaccurately describes the politician as relying on likely biased testimony. There is no indication that the politician is using biased testimony as evidence. The author's only evidence is the fact that Kuyler's company has had contracts with the government.

(D) also inaccurately describes the politician's argument. The politician ignores or, at least, does not mention, the grounds for Kuyler's argument, instead focusing on Kuyler's hypocrisy.

(E) is a Distortion of the argument's components. According to this choice, the fact that most people were not persuaded by Kuyler is the evidence the politician uses to support the politician's conclusion. While the politician's conclusion is in agreement with that majority view, the Evidence Keyword *for* indicates that the politician's "basis," or reason, is Kuyler's hypocrisy. Again, many Flaw answer choices will describe the author's argument, and the descriptions of the evidence and conclusion in the answer choices must match the components of the argument in the stimulus.

3. (A) Main Point

Step 1: Identify the Question Type
The question asks you to identify the conclusion of the argument, and is thus a Main Point question.

Step 2: Untangle the Stimulus

For a Main Point question, you only need to find the conclusion of the argument without worrying about the evidence or assumption. However, the Evidence Keywords *after all* indicate that the evidence follows and the conclusion precedes it. The contrast in the first sentence also indicates that it is the conclusion. Conclusions on the LSAT are often presented in contrast to the idea of another.

Step 3: Make a Prediction

The conclusion is clearly about countries specializing in trade. Pay attention to the Contrast Keyword [*a*]*lthough*, which refers to increasing productivity. So, the author is making a concession that specialization will increase productivity, but the point that she really wants to make is that "such specialization carries risk." The right answer may or may not refer to increased productivity, but it must focus on specialization in trade carrying risks.

Step 4: Evaluate the Answer Choices

(A) matches the prediction.

(B) focuses on the example used in the evidence and makes no mention of the author's overall main point.

(C) also refers to the evidence.

(D) also refers to the evidence.

(E) is a concession made by the author but does not include her main point about the risks of free trade.

4. (B) Paradox

Step 1: Identify the Question Type

Any question asking you to *explain* something is a Paradox question, which requires you to reconcile two apparently contradictory facts. This question stem provides additional guidance, directing you to reconcile the difference in the average rankings.

Step 2: Untangle the Stimulus

The group of storytellers, who were told that they would be given cash prizes, were ranked lower than the group of storytellers who were not told of the prizes. One might expect that those informed of the cash prizes would try harder and do better than those not informed of the prizes. Hence, there's a mystery requiring an explanation.

Step 3: Make a Prediction

Why would those with a greater incentive to do well receive lower rankings? You might be able to come up with a specific prediction, such as the potential for cash prizes causes stress, which in turn produces lapses in concentration. While such a specific prediction will likely help you recognize a similar means of reconciling the paradox, there are likely a multitude of potential specific explanations for the mystery. Thus, you usually should make a general prediction of what the right answer choice should do to resolve the paradox. For

example, here, the correct answer should provide some way that knowing there is the potential for prizes can actually hinder one's writing despite the extra incentive to do well.

Step 4: Evaluate the Answer Choices

(B) matches the prediction that the existence of prizes might impede writing in some way. Instead of the specific prediction that the pressure of prizes causes mistakes, this choice indicates that prizes cause cautiousness and thus hamper creativity.

(A) may very well explain why those aware of the prizes did not do better than those oblivious to the prizes. However, it provides no explanation for doing worse.

(C) fails to at all touch on the effect on the cash prizes on the rankings, the source of the mystery. For Paradox questions, it is vital to focus specifically on the contradictory facts in order to avoid picking an answer that relates to an irrelevant background detail.

(D) would only explain the discrepancy if it also provided that the group unaware of the prizes wrote the most realistic stories. In order to explain the discrepancy between the two groups, the correct answer must provide some factor that applies only, or with greater force, to one group over the other.

(E) is wrong for the same reason as **(D)**. If neither group knew the standards, then that can't account for a difference between the two groups' ratings.

5. (A) Method of Argument

Step 1: Identify the Question Type

A question that asks you how or in what way an author makes her point is a Method of Argument question. You must focus on the structures and general components of the arguments rather than the specific details. Notice the additional specific directions in the question stem: you are not just asked generally for Hernandez's method of argument, but more specifically how Hernandez responds to Green's objection.

Step 2: Untangle the Stimulus

Hernandez first makes a recommendation (to replace staff cars after four years not three) based on a generalization (that three-year-old cars are still in good condition) and a benefit (big savings). Green disagrees with the recommendation and provides specific counterexamples (salespeople with big territories wear out their cars in three years). In response, Hernandez indicates that she did not mean to include those specific extreme counterexamples (only normal use cars).

Step 3: Make a Prediction

The correct answer should indicate that Hernandez backtracks a bit on the generalization (that three-year-old cars are in good condition) by excluding the specific counterexamples raised by Green (the cars of salespeople with big territories).

Step 4: Evaluate the Answer Choices

(A) matches the prediction. But for Method of Argument questions for which you do not have a prediction make sure all the pieces of the answer, which will be phrased generally, match something in the stimulus. **(A)** states that Hernandez explicitly qualifies a premise used earlier. First, ask yourself, "What premise did Hernandez use earlier?" That matches up with either the generalization that "three-year-old cars are still in good condition" or the asserted "big savings." Next, ask yourself, "Does Hernandez qualify one of those premises in her response to Green?" Yes, Hernandez qualifies the generalization that three-year-old cars are in good condition by limiting it to those subjected to normal use.

(B) does not match. Hernandez simply does not criticize the salespeople.

(C) does not match because Hernandez does not dispute that salespeople with large territories wear out their cars in three years, but specifies she was only referring to "normal use."

(D) is inaccurate because Green, not Hernandez, raises the issue of the size of the sales territories.

(E) is incorrect because Hernandez does not refer to any of the phrases used by Green. The only phrase that Green raises is "big territories." Hernandez does not even disagree with Green that some salespeople have big territories, let alone indicate that "big territories" is somehow ambiguous.

6. (A) Weaken

Step 1: Identify the Question Type

The question stem explicitly directs you to weaken the argument.

Step 2: Untangle the Stimulus

The author concludes that raising the minimum wage will cause an increase in unemployment based on the premise that businesses will not be able to afford to employ as many workers at the higher rate.

Step 3: Make a Prediction

Weaken questions often turn on the author's ignored possibility; what the author has failed to consider in jumping to her conclusion. Make a general prediction that the answer should provide a way that more expensive workers will not cause employers to hire fewer workers.

Step 4: Evaluate the Answer Choices

(A) fits within the general prediction by providing a means by which businesses can absorb the cost of more expensive workers without reducing their labor force.

(B) has no effect on the amount of employment, only the balance between skilled and unskilled workers within that workforce. If you assume that skilled workers earn more, then

a higher percentage of skilled workers would mean a more expensive workforce. So, if this choice has any effect on the argument, it would be to strengthen the conclusion that a smaller workforce would be the result of a raise in the minimum wage.

(C) is Out of Scope because the acceptability of an increase in unemployment would not make it less likely to happen. This choice is again actually in line with the author's prediction of an increase in unemployment.

(D) does not undermine the reasoning because the author limits her analysis to "such jobs," i.e., minimum wage jobs. Notice if an author qualifies or lessens the scope of her argument because such modesty makes the argument less subject to attack. Similarly, the conclusion would still be wholly true if only one additional worker were unemployed as a result of the wage hike. This choice certainly allows for a number of workers to have their wage increased by a "significant" increase in the minimum wage, even if most workers make somewhat more than the current minimum wage. The author does not make any claim as to the extent of the increase in unemployment.

(E) does not definitively weaken the argument. While a Weaken answer need not disprove an argument and need only make the conclusion even a little less likely, it must do so unambiguously. An answer choice that could be cleverly spun as either a weakener or a strengthener will not cut it for either. While it could be asserted that a declining unemployment rate indicates a trend that could potentially counterbalance any effect on unemployment caused by a raise in the minimum wage, it could also be asserted that years of declining unemployment portend a greater susceptibility to an impending rise in the rate. This may be because of the cyclical nature of unemployment rates or because the rate is already below the "normal" level of unemployment.

7. (C) Paradox

Step 1: Identify the Question Type

A question that asks you to *explain* an unexpected result is a Paradox question.

Step 2: Untangle the Stimulus

Focus on the two apparently contradictory pieces of information. Removing the viruses was expected to increase the growth rate of plankton, but instead the population got smaller.

Step 3: Make a Prediction

For Paradox questions, generally paraphrase what the correct answer choice should do. Here, the correct answer should provide a negative consequence of removing viruses from the population or a way that the viruses were benefiting the plankton. Watch out for wrong answers that actually deepen the mystery. Choices that indicate that the viruses were harming the plankton would be 180s, a common wrong answer type for Paradox questions. It is often helpful to both think about what would resolve the mystery and what would deepen it.

Step 4: Evaluate the Answer Choices

(C) fits the prediction of a benefit the viruses were providing the plankton in the form of nutrients from other organisms killed by the viruses. Thus, removing the viruses deprives the plankton of a food source.

(A) is Out of Scope. The plankton are not currently near maximum levels; their population has decreased.

(B) is a 180. Removing the competing organism should benefit the plankton population, not decrease it.

(D) provides no direct indication that the bacteria that can result from the removal of the viruses have any effect on the plankton.

(E) would only explain why the removal of the viruses might not result in an increase in the plankton population, but it does not provide any explanation for why removing the viruses from the water would make the situation even worse for the infected plankton population.

8. (C) Flaw

Step 1: Identify the Question Type

The phrase "vulnerable to criticism" indicates a Flaw question.

Step 2: Untangle the Stimulus

The council member concludes that to avoid anarchy, the Senior Guild's request for a temporary parking exemption must be denied on the grounds that granting the exemption will inexorably lead to granting a multitude of exemptions to not just this particular ordinance but many others as well.

Step 3: Make a Prediction

If something seems silly or far-fetched in a Flaw question stimulus, latch onto it and predict how the flaw will relate to the question. Is it really likely that granting this one temporary parking exemption to seniors will necessarily result in "anarchy"? Also, as you assess Flaw question answer choices, ask yourself "does the author do this?" Only select an answer if you can match up each general term in it with something specific from the stimulus.

Step 4: Evaluate the Answer Choices

(C) relates to the somewhat absurd slippery slope assumption of the argument that granting one exemption will lead to all manner of exemptions; thus, it is correct. If a Flaw answer choice starts with the phrase "presumes without warrant," it is correct if it accurately states a necessary assumption of the argument. Here, the author does assume that "one event" (granting the single exemption) will lead to a

"particular causal sequence of events" (other exceptions, to the parking ordinance, to exemptions of other ordinances, to anarchy).

(A) is incorrect because the city council member never makes any mention of, let alone distorts, the Senior Guild's argument. In fact, the city council member acknowledges that the Senior Guild's case is convincing.

(B) is incorrect because the city council member does not urge the council to deny the Senior Guild's request based on the character or behavior of the Guild's members.

(D) is incorrect because the evidence the city council member uses is not contradictory, just unconvincing and unlikely.

(E) is a Distortion. Ask, "Does the author do this?" The answer is no. Rather than fail to make a distinction between deserved and undeserved exceptions, the author explicitly indicates that the Senior Guild's exemption is likely deserved and predicts that some future exemptions will be undeserved.

9. (D) Strengthen

Step 1: Identify the Question Type

The question stem directly asks you to strengthen the argument.

Step 2: Untangle the Stimulus

The physician concludes that her country suffers significantly fewer ulcers per capita than two other countries based upon the relative number of ulcer prescriptions.

Step 3: Make a Prediction

The physician makes a pretty large logical leap from evidence about the relative number of prescriptions for ulcers to the actual relative numbers of ulcers. This assumes that the number of prescriptions for ulcers is an accurate measure of the number of cases of ulcers and that no factors complicate the use of this surrogate measure for the number of actual ulcers. For example, if people in one country were more likely to use over-the-counter or herbal medications for ulcers, then the relative number of prescriptions in each country would not indicate the relative number of ulcers. Because you are asked to strengthen the argument, predict that the correct answer will explain why the number of prescriptions per actual cases of ulcers is consistent throughout the three countries. You may also eliminate a reason, such as the one previously mentioned, which would weaken the argument.

Step 4: Evaluate the Answer Choices

(D) hits the mark for a strengthener by indicating that an ulcer sufferer in one country is just as likely as an ulcer sufferer in the other countries to get a prescription for ulcer medication. This confirms that the number of prescriptions is a good surrogate measure for the number of ulcers, and it eliminates the possibility that some factor is distorting the numbers.

(A) is Out of Scope. This claim has no effect on the argument because it says nothing about the rates of our country in comparison.

(B) is a 180 that actually weakens the argument by indicating that the number of prescriptions is not a good indicator of the number of cases of ulcers.

(C) makes an Irrelevant Comparison. Other countries outside the study are irrelevant to the physician's conclusions about his country in comparison to the other two countries in the study.

(E) is another 180 that weakens the argument by indicating a factor which distorts the comparison and makes the surrogate measure of prescriptions an unreliable basis for comparison. This is complex because if you assume that "better" reporting means fuller reporting, then this would strengthen the conclusion that the physician's country has fewer ulcers. However, "better" really means more accurate. Systems that either under-count or over-count would be worse than a more accurate system. If the systems are worse in the other countries because they overestimate the number of prescriptions, then according to this answer those countries might be the ones with fewer ulcers. An answer that could either strengthen or weaken depending on how it is interpreted cannot be correct.

10. (C) Flaw

Step 1: Identify the Question Type
The question directly asks you to identify the flaw in the argument.

Step 2: Untangle the Stimulus
The columnist concludes that bicycles bear at least some responsibility for more than half of traffic accidents involving bicycles. The evidence is that more than a quarter of such accidents involve bicyclist failure to obey traffic regulations and another quarter or more of such accidents involve inadequate bicycle safety equipment.

Step 3: Make a Prediction
The author must be adding at least 25 percent of accidents involving bicyclist traffic regulation violations and at least 25 percent of accidents involving inadequate bicycle safety equipment to arrive at more than 50 percent of accidents caused in some part by the bicyclists. Clearly, percentages are involved but this is not the classic flaw of a shift from percentages or proportions to actual numbers. The evidence is about percentages and the author properly stays on track with a conclusion about percentages. However, despite the proper addition, the author is not considering that there could be an overlap between those two 25 percent groups. So, here it is very possible that bicyclists that do not bother to have proper safety equipment also do not bother to obey traffic regulations. So, both factors can be at play in a single

accident. In that case, you should not count this accident twice in determining the percentage of accidents that are at least partly the fault of the bicyclist. In fact, if it turns out that both factors are involved in every bicycle-related traffic accident, then the author could only definitely conclude that more than one-quarter of traffic accidents are partly the fault of the bicyclist. That general prediction should help you recognize the correct answer.

Step 4: Evaluate the Answer Choices
(C) matches the prediction because if both factors can be involved in the same accident, then that accident should not count twice in determining the percentage of accidents for which the bicyclist is at fault.

(A) is Out of Scope. Flaw answer choices that start with "presumes, without justification/warrant" must describe a necessary assumption of the argument. While motorists may potentially be another cause the columnist is overlooking, motorists are never mentioned in the argument. So they need not be involved in any necessary assumption for the argument to hold.

(B) does not work because it improperly describes the author's evidence as the existence of a correlation (and a subsequent jump to causation in the conclusion). The part of this choice that states "on the basis of a correlation" suggests that the evidence is a correlation. However, the evidence in the stimulus is explicitly premised on the existence of a causal relationship right from the start, not a mere correlation.

(D) is Out of Scope. Just because the columnist fails to cite sources does not mean the argument is logically flawed. In fact, it is a logical flaw to dismiss an argument based on an attack on its source, rather than an attack on the quality of the argument itself.

(E) is Out of Scope. The severity of injuries is unrelated to the cause of the accidents resulting in those injuries.

11. (A) Weaken

Step 1: Identify the Question Type
A question that directs you to *counter* a claim or argument is a Weaken question. Many Strengthen/Weaken question stems will direct you as to what to use as the conclusion. Here, it specifies that you should counter the "doctors' claim."

Step 2: Untangle the Stimulus
The clue in the question stem directs you to the very end of the stimulus for the conclusion that states "doctors claim they can produce a vaccine that will produce permanent immunity to that disease." So, the conclusion is that doctors can produce a vaccine yielding permanent immunity to hepatitis E. The evidence is that doctors have isolated a portion of the virus, which is the necessary first step in creating a vaccine that stimulates an antibody response.

Step 3: Make a Prediction

Ideally, to weaken an argument, identify the assumptions and play off of them. Here, a couple assumptions are predictable. First, the author assumes that just because the necessary first step has been accomplished, the rest of the process is achievable. So, the argument could be weakened by indicating that the next steps in creating a vaccine for hepatitis E might be more challenging than they had been in creating vaccines from the isolated viruses of other diseases for which immunity has been achieved. Second, there is a scope shift from evidence about an antibody response to a conclusion regarding permanent immunity. Concluding that the immunity will be *permanent* is extreme. So you could weaken this argument with a choice that indicates that even if a vaccine can trigger an immune response, it might not result in permanent immunity.

Step 4: Evaluate the Answer Choices

(A) weakens the argument because it indicates that the conclusion does go too far in asserting that immunity will be permanent. Exposure to the virus as a child did not produce permanent immunity, which undermines the claim that exposure to the vaccine will trigger a permanent immune response.

(B) is a 180 because it strengthens the argument. If anything, this might give the doctors reason to believe that they are on to something if exposure to one strain causes immunity to every strain.

(C) is another 180. It would strengthen the doctors' claim, not counter it. If a successful trial has already been done on another strain, then it can only increase the likelihood that the researchers can create a similar effect in others.

(D) is Out of Scope. It increases the need for the vaccine, but the number of people exposed does not speak directly to the vaccine's effectiveness.

(E) is another 180. It strengthens the doctors' claim that it's even possible to create permanent immunity to other viruses.

12. (E) Assumption (Necessary)

Step 1: Identify the Question Type

When the question stem calls for an assumption *required* by the argument, it is a Necessary Assumption question.

Step 2: Untangle the Stimulus

The author concludes that "international law" is not effective (defined as enforceable by police) because there is no international police force.

Step 3: Make a Prediction

To qualify as an effective law, a command must be backed up by an effective enforcement mechanism.

If	effective law	→	effective enforcement mechanism

The author then concludes that effective law is not possible because there is no international police force. Concluding that a goal is not obtainable because some factor is absent indicates that the factor is necessary for the goal. In this case, the logic would chain together like this:

If	effective law	→	effective enforcement mechanism	→	int'l police force

or its contrapositive:

If	~ int'l police force	→	~ effective enforcement mechanism	→	~ effective law

The necessary assumption will properly tie the international police force to the other components of the logical chain.

Step 4: Evaluate the Answer Choices

(E) maps out as "If effectively enforce law → international police force." That's a correct match to the prediction.

(B) maps out as "If international police force → effective law." That is backward from the logical chain.

(A) is a Faulty Use of Detail. It focuses on background information from the first sentence and does not relate to the essential judgment of the conclusion that international law is not effective. The concept of effectiveness has to be included in the correct scope shift answer.

(C) is Out of Scope. The differences between international law and that of an individual society are immaterial. For all we know, this could be just one of many differences.

(D) is Extreme. The author does not need to assume that this is the *primary* purpose of a police force. The police force can have other purposes and still fulfill its necessary duty of enforcing laws to make them effective.

13. (D) Inference

Step 1: Identify the Question Type

A question stem that asks you to use the statements above to *support* one of the following answers is an Inference question (while a Strengthen question would ask you to use an answer to *support* the conclusion or argument above).

Step 2: Untangle the Stimulus

For an Inference question, inventory the information in the stimulus, accepting everything as true. Especially note Formal Logic statements, concrete statements, emphasis, and big LSAT concepts, such as causation, necessity, paradoxes, etc. The stimulus contains forceful statements regarding still-life painting, such as "more than any other genre" lends itself to self-expression; the still-life painter "invariably chooses, modifies, and arranges objects to be painted"; and the still-life painter "has considerably more control over composition and subject."

Step 3: Make a Prediction

In summary, the bulk of the information suggests that still-life painting is superior in a number of respects to other genres, but it is not predictable which detail(s) the correct answer will focus upon. It is often necessary to research the Inference answer choices and ask, "Does this have to be true?" Start with the most modestly phrased answers.

Step 4: Evaluate the Answer Choices

(D) is a good place to start testing because "not always" is modest phrasing, and it relates to a way that still-life painting is superior to other genres. So, can you know that in other genres of painting, "the artist does not always choose, modify, and arrange the objects to be painted"? Well, still-life painters *invariably* do that, and that is what gives them more control and better self-expression than other genre artists.

(A) is Extreme. The only reference to the "reflection of a preexisting external reality" indicates that still-life paintings go beyond just that. While this suggests that other genres may merely reflect external reality, it does not support the inference that landscapes and portrait *most* naturally do so.

(B) is also Extreme. The stimulus suggests that choosing, modifying, and arranging the objects lend greater control over the composition and subject of a painting. However, this choice goes too far because it suggests that this is the *only* way to control the composition and subject of a painting.

(C) is Out of Scope. The art historian only discusses the genres of representational painting. Nonrepresentational painting is never mentioned.

(E) is also Out of Scope. We only know that the artist has considerably more control over the still-life painting subject matter than over the portrait subject matter. No mention is made of how frequently the artist attempts to exhibit any control within the portrait.

14. (D) Principle (Apply/Inference)

Step 1: Identify the Question Type

Reference to a rule or policy, or here *regulation*, indicates a Principle question. The stem specifies that the correct answer will *violate* this regulation.

Step 2: Untangle the Stimulus

The regulation restricts what can be labeled "nonfat." For a food that normally does not contain fat to be labeled "nonfat" requires that most people mistakenly believe it ordinarily contains fat. It also requires that the label state that the food ordinarily contains no fat.

If **food doesn't ordinarily contain fat AND labeled "nonfat"** → **most people mistakenly believe the food contains fat AND the label states food ordinarily contains no fat**

Step 3: Make a Prediction

The correct answer choice will present a situation that violates the food labeling regulation in the stimulus. The food regulation requires that the label "nonfat" only be applied to foods that ordinarily contain fat with one exception: if people mistakenly believe that the food ordinarily contains fat. In that case, the "nonfat" label must also indicate that the food ordinarily contains no fat. So, scan for an answer choice that erroneously contains a "nonfat" label in light of the regulation. The wrong answer choices will either be in compliance with the regulation or be Outside the Scope of the regulation.

Step 4: Evaluate the Answer Choices

(D) violates the regulation because the "nonfat" label is only warranted when the food ordinarily contains fat or people mistakenly believe it does. Because applesauce does not fall within either instance, the "nonfat" label is in violation of the regulation.

(A) is Outside the Scope of the regulation. Because the regulation only concerns the circumstances under which food can be labeled "nonfat," any food not labeled "nonfat" is Out of Scope.

(B), like **(A)**, is Outside the Scope of the regulation. Only foods that are labeled as "nonfat" are covered. **(B)** gives another example of a food that is *not* labeled "nonfat."

(C) is not in violation of the regulation because garlic baguettes ordinarily contain fat.

(E) falls squarely within the exception noted in the regulation because most people mistakenly believe that salsa contains fat, and the "nonfat" label indicates that salsa does not ordinarily contain fat.

15. (C) Parallel Flaw

Step 1: Identify the Question Type
A question stem asking you to match the reasoning in the stimulus with similar *flawed* reasoning in the answer choices is a Parallel Flaw question.

Step 2: Untangle the Stimulus
The conclusion is that it is "never acceptable to offer experimental treatments to patients" in the absence of extreme symptoms. That's because of the evidence that patients with extreme symptoms are best able to weigh risks and benefits of experimental treatments.

Step 3: Make a Prediction
The correct answer to a Parallel Reasoning and Parallel Flaw question should use the same type of evidence to reach the same type of conclusion. So, start by eliminating any answer that has a conclusion of a different type or level of certainty. The medical ethicist's conclusion that it is "never acceptable" to take a certain action is a definite recommendation against an action. The same type of conclusion could be phrased as it is "wrong" to do something or one "should not" do something. If that does not eliminate all the wrong answers, then match the flaw in the stimulus to the answer that commits the same flaw. The ethicist assumes that just because people without extreme symptoms are not as perfectly able to weigh the pros and cons of experimental treatments as those with extreme symptoms, they should *never* be offered experimental treatments. This assumes that the people without extreme symptoms cannot be sufficiently able to weigh the risks and benefits for themselves because they are not *best* able. It further assumes that the benefits of experimental treatments do not outweigh the downsides of giving the option to those not perfectly suited to judge the treatment. Select the answer that assumes that some group that is uniquely and best qualified to do something is the only group that should do something.

Step 4: Evaluate the Answer Choices
(C) indicates that someone "should not" take an action—forming judgments about living abroad. The evidence is that they have not done something another group has done—lived abroad and then returned. So, **(C)** commits the same flaw by assuming that *only* those exceptionally qualified to judge should form judgments.

(A) can be eliminated based on its conclusion that someone "should not *expect*" something to happen. The stimulus's conclusion indicates what is unacceptable, wrong, or ill-advised to do, not what can be expected to happen or not.

(B) can be eliminated solely based on the qualifier *likely*. It is also not the right type of conclusion. Level of certainty words, such as *likely* or *probably*, are very easy to spot and they are reasons to eliminate some answers.

(D) uses the qualifier *some*, which does not match the conclusion in the stimulus. This choice also does not recommend against an unacceptable action, but rather makes a conditional prediction.

(E) can also be eliminated based solely on its conclusion, which judges something as "not worthwhile" to do, rather than unacceptable. However, this is a closer call because there can be some subjectivity as to whether certain conclusions fit neatly into one of the common conclusion types. In a close call, go to the next strategy and pick or eliminate the choice based on whether its flaw is parallel to the flaw in the stimulus. In this instance, **(E)** does not indicate that one group should not receive something *only* because it is not in the *best* position to weigh costs and benefits. Thus, **(E)** is not parallel.

16. (C) Principle (Identify/Inference)

Step 1: Identify the Question Type
The phrase "conforms to" indicates a Principle question. A Principle question stem must be read carefully for any additional direction as to whether the stimulus contains an argument, statements, or a general rule. This question specifies that the stimulus consists of statements, so this is an Identify the Principle question that acts much like an Inference question.

Step 2: Untangle the Stimulus
Paraphrase the statements in the stimulus in general terms: the pace of technological advancements has created feelings of instability causing us to feel unable to achieve what we want.

Step 3: Make a Prediction
Find a general match for the paraphrase of the stimulus made in Step 2, and watch out for wrong answers that contain distortions or deviations.

Step 4: Evaluate the Answer Choices
(C) rearranged a bit indicates that technological changes can cause changes in people's feelings about life. The stimulus starts with changes in technology, which sets off a chain of events leading to changes in people's feelings about their ability to achieve what they want. This is a match without any deviations.

(A) is a Distortion. The stimulus does not indicate that it has become objectively difficult for people to obtain their goals, only that people now feel that they do not have enough time to achieve their goals. How people feel is not necessarily indicative of reality.

(B) is another Distortion because the stimulus never balances the pros and cons of technological advances.

(D) is a Faulty Use of Detail. The last phrase of the stimulus "or at least what we think we want" is reused in this answer choice. The stimulus indicates that people feel they don't have enough time to achieve what they think they want, *not* that the shortage of time actually creates difficulty for people to know what they want.

(E) flips the causal relationship in the stimulus, which indicates that technological advances cause changes in feelings, not vice versa.

17. (D) Assumption (Necessary)

Step 1: Identify the Question Type
A question that has an assumption than an argument *relies on* is a Necessary Assumption question.

Step 2: Untangle the Stimulus
The consumer concludes that she is entitled to a refund from the jewelry store because the watch she purchased stopped working the next day, and a department store would give a refund in that case.

Step 3: Make a Prediction
The consumer assumes that the jewelry store should follow the precedent of department stores. A rare Assumption answer type is one that indicates a piece of conditional evidence gets triggered. Notice that the argument starts with the conditional evidence that *if* you buy a watch at a department store and use it only as intended, then the department store will give a refund for a watch that stops working the next day. The rest of the argument proceeds from that starting point. So, the consumer must assume that the triggering conditions actually were met, i.e., that the watch was used only as intended.

Step 4: Evaluate the Answer Choices
(D), as predicted, contains the assumption that the watch was used only as intended.

(A) is Out of Scope because what constitutes a "saleable" item is never mentioned in the argument.

(B) makes an Irrelevant Comparison about the quality of watches at each of the two retailers. The scope of the argument, however, is limited to refunds for watches that stop working the next day.

(C) is Out of Scope. The purchaser's expectations are not discussed in the argument. To obtain the refund, the watch only need be used in the way it was intended to be, regardless of expected performance.

(E) is Out of Scope. No conditions were given on different policies between new watches and old watches, and thus old or new is irrelevant to the consumer's contentions.

18. (B) Flaw

Step 1: Identify the Question Type
The question stem directly asks you to identify the flaw.

Step 2: Untangle the Stimulus
The author concludes that the therapists practicing new forms of psychotherapy are more effective than the therapists practicing traditional forms, based on a study which showed that among those studied, the patients referred to experimental psychotherapy by their doctors made more progress than those referred to traditional psychotherapy.

Step 3: Make a Prediction
The scope shift here is that in the study patients did better in the experimental therapy, and the author concludes that those practicing experimental therapies are thus more effective. Nothing earth-shattering here—the assumption is that the therapists that got better results should be considered more effective. Any time there are two study groups and the author uses a comparison of the two to reach a judgment, the author must assume that all else is equal between the two groups. In this case, to judge the therapists using experimental therapy more effective, the author must assume all else was equal between the patients and care in the two groups. However, if the experimental therapy patients also received prescription medications while the traditional psychotherapy patients did not, then it would not be clear whether it was the psychotherapist that was more effective or the medication. But that specific of a prediction is not necessary because there could be a large number of potential confounding factors that could be raised by the correct answer. Be armed with a general understanding that the correct answer will likely explain that the difference between the two groups may include factors other than the therapist and choice of therapy: experimental or traditional. Finally, a further refinement to your prediction can come from noticing a potential difference between the two study groups suggested by the stimulus. Here, the two groups were not selected at random to receive experimental or traditional therapies but were selected based on doctor recommendations. It is possible that doctor recommendations might skew what types of patients get the experimental therapy and what types of patients get the traditional therapy.

Step 4: Evaluate the Answer Choices
(B) is correct because it identifies a difference between the two groups that throws off the comparison. If doctors referred patients with more readily treatable problems to the experimental therapies and patients with tougher to treat problems to the traditional therapies, then it is problematic to conclude that the therapists using experimental therapies are more effective just because they had better success at curing easier cases.

(A) is Out of Scope because the author doesn't ignore this possibility but rather implicitly assumes that training and techniques do not account for the difference in results between the two groups. If the two groups of therapists use the same techniques, and one group gets better results with their patients, then that would increase the validity of the findings and remove a potential flaw from the author's argument.

(C) is not an assumption of the argument. The argument focuses on the effectiveness of the therapist and the therapy actually used, not what forms the therapists are also trained in but did not use.

(D) is not a valid ignored possibility because if it were true that the experimental and traditional psychotherapists differed in a personality trait relevant to effective treatment then that may be cause for the author to conclude that those practicing experimental therapies indeed are more effective. Conversely, if it's a trait that would hurt effectiveness, then the psychotherapists using experimental therapies would have patients seeing better results despite their therapists lacking that personality trait. To be the correct answer to a Flaw question, the ignored possibility must unambiguously weaken the argument. Whether the psychotherapists are more effective because of, or despite a personality trait, they're still deemed more effective. So, although the author doesn't mention personality traits, it may still conform to his conclusion.

(E) is Extreme. It is not a necessary assumption of the argument. It is very important to pay close attention to the format of a Flaw answer choice. A choice, like **(E)**, that is presented as an unwarranted assumption must qualify as a necessary assumption of that author's argument. **(E)** is too extremely worded to qualify as a necessary assumption. You can use the Denial Test on a Flaw answer choice that is phrased as an unwarranted assumption to confirm whether or not it is a necessary assumption. If it were true that rapport has some influence on the effectiveness of treatment, it would not destroy the argument that the experimental therapy is more effective. So this is not a necessary assumption of the argument.

19. (D) Principle (Identify/Strengthen)

Step 1: Identify the Question Type
Be sure to glean all the necessary information out of any Principle question stem. First, according to the wording of the stem, the answer choices for this question will consist of a principle (generalization or rule). Second, the stimulus will contain reasoning, which should be broken down to evidence and conclusion. Finally, you must use the principle in the correct answer to justify the reasoning. So, this is an Identify the Principle question to be attacked primarily as a Strengthen question, but be aware that the answers will likely be worded more generally than the stimulus.

Step 2: Untangle the Stimulus
The conclusion recommends against supporting political systems that allow extreme freedom on the grounds that allowing extreme freedom could set off a chain of events that may lead to a preference for totalitarian regimes.

Step 3: Make a Prediction
The correct answer to an Identify the Principle question will frequently just describe the evidence and conclusion in general terms and you must match up the pieces, accepting a broadening of the terms but eliminating deviations. Here, the conclusion is to not support a political system that allows extreme freedom, and the evidence is that such a system might lead to a preference for totalitarian regimes.

Step 4: Evaluate the Answer Choices
(D) matches the prediction. Its pieces, while broader in some ways, match the pieces of the argument. **(D)** describes the conclusion as this: a recommendation to not support any political system. The evidence is that it could lead to a preference for totalitarian regimes. Clearly, the concern about leading to a preference for totalitarian regimes is a direct match to the stimulus's evidence. While you might initially have concerns that it is extreme to not support "any" political system that leads to a preference for totalitarianism, this broadness is generally not a problem for Principle questions acting as Strengthen questions. The situation in the stimulus (a system allowing extreme freedom) falls under the general rule regarding any political system leading to a preference for totalitarianism, so that rule supports the result in the stimulus. For example, if you want to argue that chimpanzees are smarter than poodles, a general rule that all primates are smarter than all canines would support your argument even though the terms of the rule are far broader.

(A) is a Distortion. The evidence is not limited to systems that will *inevitably* lead to the establishment of a totalitarian regime, but focuses on a system that *could* lead to a preference for totalitarianism. A rule against supporting the first kind of system (inevitable) is narrower and does not include a judgment to not support the second kind of system (could lead to).

(B) is another Distortion. The stimulus recommends against supporting a political system rather than making a conclusion about what people should expect. Also, the system at issue in the stimulus does not in the long run maximize freedom but instead leads to a potential preference for totalitarianism.

(C) is a 180. The conclusion recommends against a system of extreme freedom, which may allow for wise or unwise choices. Because **(C)** recommends supporting only systems that give people freedom to make wise choices, that still runs counter to the essayist's recommendation. Nothing indicates that the system *only* allows for wise choices.

(E) is another Distortion. It was the expectation of people to thrive when they have the opportunity to make unwise decisions that was unrealistic, *not* that the political system itself was based on unrealistic expectations.

20. (E) Parallel Reasoning

Step 1: Identify the Question Type
A question asking you to match the reasoning "most similar" in the stimulus and the answer choices is a Parallel Reasoning question.

Step 2: Untangle the Stimulus
Start by characterizing the conclusion and eliminating any answer choices that do not have the right type of conclusion. The conclusion that "some acts of securing mutual benefit are not moral actions" can be summarized as "some X are not Y." It should become quickly apparent that all the conclusions in the answer choice set are in that form. Thus, you must work with the entire argument and map out the Formal Logic.

Evidence:

If	moral action "X"	→	keeping an agreement "Y"

If	keeping an agreement "Y"	→	merely securing mutual benefit "Z"

Link Evidence:

If	moral action "X"	→	keeping an agreement "Y"	→	securing mutual benefit "Z"

Additional Evidence:

Some keeping an agreement (Some "Y") are not moral actions "X"

Conclusion:

Some acts of securing mutual benefit (Some "Z") are not moral actions "X"

Step 3: Make a Prediction
The correct answer should map out as follows:

Evidence:

If	"X"	→	"Y"	→	"Z"

Some "Y" are not "X"

Conclusion:

Some "Z" are not "X"

Step 4: Evaluate the Answer Choices
(E) maps out the same way:

Evidence:

If	books "X"	→	texts "Y"	→	documents "Z"

Some texts "Y" are not books "X"

Conclusion:

Some documents "Z" are not books "X"

(A) does not map out correctly:

Evidence:

If	calculators "X"	→	computers "Y"	→	automated reasoning devices "Z"

Some automated reasoning devices "Z" are not calculators "X"

Conclusion:

Some automated reasoning devices "Z" are not computers "Y"

(B) does not map out correctly:

Evidence:

If	exercise "X"	→	beneficial "Y"	→	promote health "Z"

Some beneficial things "Y" are not exercise "X"

Conclusion:

Some exercise "X" does not promote health "Z"

(C) does not map out correctly:

Evidence:

If	metaphors "X"	→	comparisons "Y"

Some comparisons "Y" are not surprising "Z"

$$If \quad metaphors \; "X" \quad \rightarrow \quad surprising \; "Z"$$

Conclusion:

Some comparisons "Y" are not metaphors "X"

(D) does not map out correctly:

Evidence:

$$If \quad \begin{array}{c} architecture \\ "X" \end{array} \quad \rightarrow \quad \begin{array}{c} design \\ "Y" \end{array} \quad \rightarrow \quad art \; "Z"$$

Some design "Y" is not architecture "X"

Conclusion:

Some art "Z" is not design "Y"

21. (B) Role of a Statement

Step 1: Identify the Question Type
The question asks you to identify the *role* played in the argument by a specific claim from that argument. Thus, this is a Role of a Statement question, and you should underline in the stimulus the statement identified in the question stem before breaking the argument down into its components of evidence and conclusion.

Step 2: Untangle the Stimulus
The author concludes in the first sentence that resistance to technology increases as a society becomes more technologically advanced. The statement at issue is the evidence that follows: the more technologically advanced, the more a society is aware of technology's drawbacks.

Step 3: Make a Prediction
The correct answer must indicate that the statement is a piece of evidence in support of the conclusion. It is common for multiple answer choices to indicate that the statement is a piece of evidence in support of a conclusion or claim. Then it becomes a matter of which choice correctly characterizes the conclusion.

Step 4: Evaluate the Answer Choices
(B) correctly indicates that the statement is a piece of evidence and further correctly describes the conclusion that it supports.

(A) incorrectly identifies the statement as a conclusion.

(C) is a Distortion. It correctly identifies the statement as a piece of evidence but then inaccurately indicates that the conclusion is about the quality of human relations in technologically advanced societies.

(D), like **(A)**, also incorrectly identifies it as a conclusion by describing it as a generalization based on another claim, rather than functioning as evidence supporting another claim.

(E) is a Distortion. It correctly identifies the statement as a piece of evidence but then inaccurately indicates that the conclusion is about how resistance to technological innovation affects the quality of human relations.

22. (B) Flaw

Step 1: Identify the Question Type
"[V]ulnerable to criticism" indicates a Flaw question, but also notice that the type of flaw is specified: an ignored possibility.

Step 2: Untangle the Stimulus
The conclusion is at the end: "this belief is false." However, that is vague and difficult to work with. Vague terms, such as "this belief," need to be defined. Also, any time the author concludes that somebody else's claim is false, translate the conclusion into the opposite of what the others claim. The belief referred to is "that these [nonwealthy] candidates will compromise their views to win support." If the author concludes that this belief is false, then the author's conclusion may be paraphrased as follows: nonwealthy candidates will *not* compromise their views to win support.

The evidence is that the wealthy are dispersed among the various political parties equally.

Step 3: Make a Prediction
The scope shift is from evidence regarding an equal distribution of wealthy donors among the political parties to a conclusion that nonwealthy candidates will not compromise their views to appeal to those donors. This equates the individual views of candidates with their political parties. In other words, it assumes that all candidates' views are in line with a political party. The question stem directs that the answers will be in the form of an ignored possibility. Thus, a solid prediction would be that the author ignores the possibility that candidates might hold views that differ from or go beyond the views of any individual political party's dogma.

Step 4: Evaluate the Answer Choices
(B) matches the prediction indicating that political parties might not encompass all the varied views of individual candidates. This ignored possibility would weaken the argument (as a Flaw answer phrased as an ignored possibility must in order to be correct) that candidates would not have to change their views to appeal to wealthy donors (who are dispersed among the political parties).

(A) is Out of Scope. What the primary function of political parties is does not weaken the argument regarding whether candidates would change their beliefs to appeal to wealthy donors. Thus, it is not a flaw the author commits.

(C) is Out of Scope. The stimulus is about democratic elections that are not fully subsidized, so it is irrelevant what happens in subsidized elections.

(D) makes an Irrelevant Comparison. Whether it is easier or harder for a wealthy or nonwealthy person to win an election does not impact whether when nonwealthy candidates would need to change their views to win support. It is also important to accept the evidence as true, which means accepting the fact that in unsubsidized elections, "non-wealthy candidates must be supported by wealthy patrons."

(E) is Out of Scope. What other flaws this type of democracy might have are irrelevant to whether candidates will change their views to get elected.

23. (C) Inference

Step 1: Identify the Question Type
A question that directs you to use information in the stimulus to support an answer (direction of support flowing downward from stimulus to an answer) is an Inference question.

Step 2: Untangle the Stimulus
Modern "brushless" car washes have mitters which are easier on most cars' finishes than the brushes that were once used. In light of the new cars today that have clear-coat finishes, this is very important as they are more easily scratched than cars with older finishes.

Step 3: Make a Prediction
Accept all statements as true in an Inference stimulus, and focus on the most concrete and emphasized facts. Notice that the author emphasizes that the finishes on old cars were less prone to scratches than the newer finishes.

Step 4: Evaluate the Answer Choices
(C) relates to the emphasized fact and is correct. If the mitters do not readily scratch the newer more sensitive finishes, then it can be deduced that they will not usually scratch the hardier older finishes.

(A) is not supportable because we don't know how the older car finishes responded to the brushes that were once used. Even if a higher percentage of older cars were scratched, there could have been far fewer cars overall on the road.

(B) is not supportable because we have no idea how or why the modern "brushless" cars came into existence. The causal relationship suggested by this answer fits the stimulus, but as with any causal relationship, it could be coincidence or the reverse.

(D) is Out of Scope. We do not know which one is *more effective*; rather, all we know is that mitters are easier on cars' finishes than the brushes.

(E) is not supportable because we do not know how many cars in use today are the new versions with clear-coat finishes and how many have older finishes. Do not interpret the *many* in the final sentence of the stimulus as *most*. On the LSAT, *many* like *some*, means "at least one."

24. (C) Assumption (Sufficient)

Step 1: Identify the Question Type
The question stem formulation "if assumed … conclusion follows logically/is properly drawn/properly inferred" indicates a Sufficient Assumption question.

Step 2: Untangle the Stimulus
The argument concludes that the contracting vessel in lancelets is a heart based on the facts that it resembles the heart of other sea animals and its contractions resemble the contractions of other animals' hearts.

Step 3: Make a Prediction
The scope shift is from something resembling a heart to that thing actually being heart. For a Sufficient Assumption question, that link has to be made absolutely in order to prove the conclusion true. So if anything that resembles a heart in the ways described is in fact a heart, then the conclusion that this vessel is a heart would be certainly true.

Step 4: Evaluate the Answer Choices
(C) matches the prediction and guarantees that the vessel, which resembles a heart, is in fact a heart. So, the conclusion follows.

(A) is wrong because it only indicates that any animal with a heart has to have a contracting vessel, but that does not mean that every animal with a contracting vessel has a heart. So, it does not establish that lancelets have a heart just because they have a contracting vessel.

(B) is Out of Scope. Primitive animals other than lancelets are irrelevant and can only support the idea that some primitive animals have a heart. But this can in no way prove that the lancelet's vessel is a heart.

(D) reverses the author's logic. **(D)** states that knowing that the contracting vessel is a heart requires that it undergo muscular contractions (If heart → muscular contractions), but this does not definitively support the contention that the lancelet's contracting vessel must be a heart. **(D)** attempts to go backward on the arrow.

(E) is wrong because it only indicates that any animal with a heart has to have an artery, but that does not guarantee that the lancelet has a heart to begin with.

25. (E) Inference

Step 1: Identify the Question Type
A question that asks you to use the statements to support an answer choice (direction of support is downward from stimulus to answers) is an Inference question.

Step 2: Untangle the Stimulus
The manager recommends that the company reconsider its decision to abandon the old software and replace it with the new software. The manager cites examples of several other companies in the region that have officially replaced the

existing software with the new software, yet many employees continue to use the old software even though they are familiar with how to use the new software.

Step 3: Make a Prediction

For Inference questions, accept all the statements as true and look for what else must be true based on those statements (or just like in a Necessary Assumption question, look for what the author must believe but did not explicitly state). Either way, give preference to a modestly phrased answer choice. It is implicit in the manager's statements that she believes that her company employees will not adapt well to the new software or will prefer the old software as the other company's employees have in the examples she cites. But she never says why.

Step 4: Evaluate the Answer Choices

(E) is on track with the prediction and is phrased very modestly (*many* just means "at least one").

(A) makes an Irrelevant Comparison. It is not known from the stimulus which software is more flexible. The only reference to flexibility is that the new software is advertised as more flexible, but there is no reason to know whether or not that is the case.

(B) makes an Irrelevant Comparison between the importance of familiarity versus flexibility. We only know that the new software is advertised as more flexible and it would be true that the employees are more familiar with the old software. However, there is no suggestion as to the real reason many prefer the old software. It is pure speculation to say that they are choosing the familiar over the more flexible, as the choice might be based on a completely different factor.

(C) is purely speculative. The manager never says why the other company's employees prefer the old software.

(D) contradicts the manager's statements to some extent because the manager says that the other company's employees can all use the new software and gives no indication that she believes some of her employees would not be able to.

Section IV: Reading Comprehension

Passage 1: FCC and UCC

Q#	Question Type	Correct	Difficulty
1	Global	A	★
2	Logic Function	A	★
3	Inference	D	★
4	Inference	C	★
5	Inference	E	★★

Passage 2: Science and the Humanities

Q#	Question Type	Correct	Difficulty
6	Global	E	★
7	Inference	C	★
8	Inference	D	★★★
9	Detail	B	★
10	Logic Function	D	★
11	Inference	C	★
12	Inference	B	★★★

Passage 3: Willa Cather

Q#	Question Type	Correct	Difficulty
13	Inference	E	★★★
14	Detail	C	★★
15	Inference	C	★★
16	Global	A	★★
17	Inference	E	★★
18	Inference	E	★★★
19	Global	B	★

Passage 4: Fractal Geometry

Q#	Question Type	Correct	Difficulty
20	Global	B	★
21	Inference	C	★★
22	Detail (EXCEPT)	D	★★
23	Logic Function	D	★★
24	Detail	E	★★
25	Detail (EXCEPT)	A	★★★★
26	Inference	E	★★★★
27	Inference	D	★★★

Passage 1: FCC and UCC

Step 1: Read the Passage Strategically
Sample Roadmap

line #	Keyword/phrase	¶ Margin notes
4	early; only	FCC–early only focused on broadcasters
5	chiefly	
7	not recognized	
8	merely; Unless	
10	did not	Citizens–no standing
11	Consequently	
14	landmark; changed	Change MS UCC case with FCC
20	charged	
21	advocated	
23	Arguing; lacked	
24	rejected	FCC said church lacked economic interest–no hearing needed
25	though; attempted to mollify	
27	Further; claimed; since	
30	However; :	
32	?; real reason	Issue standing for citizen groups?
33	more likely	
37	appealed	1st Appeal–FCC rejects church
38	granted	
40	little avail: ; dismissed	
41	granted	
42	appealed again	
43	unprecedented; revoking	2nd Appeal–Judge overrules
44	ruling	
46	legitimate	
47	should	
49	estblished; formidable	Case–strong ruling
51	Subsequent	More case support
58	because of	Public role expanded

Discussion

As usual, the Topic and Scope are revealed early on in paragraph 1 in this law passage. The **Topic** is the FCC. Specifically, the author's **Scope** is the FCC's concerns for the public when it comes to license renewal. The rest of the paragraph details "early history," which addressed "only" the broadcasters' interests while the public's rights "were not recognized." The paragraph wraps up by indicating that citizens had no standing "unless" they were directly involved in a licensing bid; "consequently," the FCC was in the industry's pocket.

Paragraph 2's initial Emphasis Keyword calls attention to a "landmark" 1964 Mississippi case that "changed the course of that history." In challenging a TV station's license renewal, the United Church of Christ "charged" that the station was racist. Lines 23–29 detail the FCC's response: "no hearing was necessary," "since" the FCC agreed that the UCC was right about the racist misconduct. This begs the question (signaled by the colon in line 30) of why the station's license was renewed if it was clearly misbehaving? The author's view ("the real reason ... was more likely") is that the higher-ups didn't want the community sticking its nose into the "closed worlds" of power.

The next steps, outlined in paragraph 3, were the "dismissed" UCC charge and "full renewal," followed by an "unprecedented" revocation. The judge becomes the hero of the tale (lines 42–48), ruling that community involvement, like that of the UCC, was in the public interest.

Paragraph 4's references to "formidable precedent" and "subsequent rulings" take you to the present day, where the public's right to weigh in on broadcast licenses has been well established, and their inquiries aren't just race-based anymore but a "range of other matters," all "because of" the UCC's heroism. The author's **Purpose** is to trace the history of the public's ability to influence broadcast licensure renewal, leading to the author's **Main Idea**—"A landmark case changed the course" of history, and a subsequent judicial ruling took the "unprecedented step" of allowing public involvement in licensing proceedings—a revolution that all dates back to a determined Jackson, Mississippi, church in 1964.

1. (A) Global

Step 2: Identify the Question Type

This is a Global question because it asks for the "main point" of the passage.

Step 3: Research the Relevant Text

Instead of rereading a specific part of the passage, your research will entail using the Big Picture concepts you identified during Step 1 (Topic, Scope, Purpose) to predict the Main Idea.

Step 4: Make a Prediction

The author's Main Idea is that thanks to the efforts of a church group in Jackson, Mississippi, in 1964, the public now has broader access to the broadcast licensing decisions made by the FCC.

Step 5: Evaluate the Answer Choices

(A) is the only answer that matches this prediction.

(B) blows up the "biased coverage" alleged by the church in lines 20–22 into a Main Point. Paragraph 4 makes clear that racial bias is now only one of many issues considered when licenses come up for renewal.

(C) is a bit Extreme (government agencies are now "forced" to listen to the public?). It is also too broad because this passage is solely about the FCC (not other agencies) and about the 1964 UCC case (not the complete history of the FCC).

(D) is a Distortion. To say that the FCC is now more responsive to the public (in terms of license renewals, anyway) doesn't mean that it's less so to the broadcasters—simply that the balance has been fixed.

(E) broadens to "citizens' groups" when the author focuses on just one Mississippi church group. Also, **(E)** distorts the author's Main Point. The significance of the UCC case isn't in the public merely having access to the hearings; it's in the recognition of their right to weigh in and potentially influence the FCC's licensing decisions.

2. (A) Logic Function

Step 2: Identify the Question Type

This is a Logic Function question because it asks why the author made a particular mention. The phrase "in order to" always signals this type of question.

Step 3: Research the Relevant Text

In a Logic Function question, context is always key. In addition to reading the lines referenced in the question stem, you must also consider how those lines fit into the paragraph as a whole.

Step 4: Make a Prediction

Paragraph 4 is an epilogue of sorts, explaining how the "formidable precedent" of the Mississippi case altered the course of licensing applications thereafter. Lines 54–59 show how the scope of topics up for debate has expanded—these widely ranging issues "are now discussed" in broadcast licensure hearings "because of" what the UCC did.

Step 5: Evaluate the Answer Choices

(A) matches perfectly.

(B) implies that the author is sounding a warning, when in fact the tone throughout (and certainly in paragraph 4) seems satisfied that the public's ability to weigh in is now pretty well protected.

(C) introduces the nonissue of the frequency of opportunities for citizens to express their views. But this would theoretically hinge on how often licenses are up for renewal, not on anything having to do with the expanded list of topics up for consideration since the UCC case.

(D) doesn't reflect the shift the author has made from the UCC case to its legacy. The author has ceased discussion of the particular station from 1964 by the time paragraph 4 comes along.

(E) also improperly focuses on the Mississippi station sued back in the 1960s—improperly because the scope of paragraph 4 is the present day. It's inferable that other stations' practices may well have fallen short of their civic duty, but the list of topics in lines 54–59 doesn't speak to that.

3. (D) Inference

Step 2: Identify the Question Type
This is an Inference question since it asks for what the passage "affirms."

Step 3: Research the Relevant Text
The question stem is devoid of any clues that will direct your research of the passage.

Step 4: Make a Prediction
Whenever the question stem fails to direct you to a specific part of the passage, the valid inference can come from anywhere in the text. So, instead of trying to predict every single thing that must logically follow from the passage, the best approach is to go straight to the answer choices, keeping in mind the author's point of view. Be prepared to look for textual support for any inference you intend to select.

Step 5: Evaluate the Answer Choices
(D) essentially paraphrases lines 8–11 and is therefore correct.

(A) is Outside the Scope. Broadcasters' economic goals are never mentioned. Moreover, (A)'s interest in marginalizing public input goes against the pro-citizen thrust of the passage.

(B) distorts lines 11–13. The author states that the FCC seemed to be exclusively in the service of the broadcasters. But that doesn't suggest that the industry dictated what actions the FCC chose to take. Rather, the FCC excluded citizen input because the public lacked standing.

(C) misrepresents the passage's scope, which is not whether the FCC was empowered to renew or cancel licenses, but whether citizens with no economic interest in a TV station could nonetheless be heard.

(E) is Extreme. It exaggerates the importance of the UCC's case. You can't infer from the passage that citizens' groups

had no previous success in influencing "government agencies" in general.

4. (C) Inference

Step 2: Identify the Question Type
The looser language of this question stem ("with which one … would the author be most likely to agree") indicates an Inference question.

Step 3: Research the Relevant Text
The question stem hasn't given you any clues as to a specific part of the passage to research, so any of the passage's 59 lines is fair game.

Step 4: Make a Prediction
If you can't make a prediction, then just attack the choices boldly, looking for the one choice that's been written to have no flaws. Remember that the correct answer is one that *must* be true (the hallmark of a valid LSAT Inference) and that is in line with the author's viewpoint.

Step 5: Evaluate the Answer Choices
(C) puts the lesson of the precise case described in the passage in abstract terms. When the UCC took to the courts, they were able to expand, and thus protect, the public's interest insofar as broadcasting licenses were concerned. This makes (C) correct.

(A) is unsupported. Although the UCC clearly brought the TV station's discriminatory and racist policies to the FCC's attention, there's no reason to infer that the agency would otherwise have never heard about them.

(B) is too broad and Extreme. This cynical indictment of private industry's prejudice ("by their very nature") against the public finds no support in the text.

(D) is Extreme. That the courts were needed to intervene in the 1964 Mississippi case doesn't necessarily mean that *no* government regulation can safeguard against business's acting against the public interest.

(E) is too pointed. The author is by no means committed to agree that the government "can't be trusted to favor" the public over industry. Indeed, it seems as if the FCC became more likely to do the right thing once the Mississippi case was decided. Furthermore, the court that eventually came down in favor of the UCC is also part of the government.]

5. (E) Inference

Step 2: Identify the Question Type
The phrase "the passage suggests" indicates an Inference question. The correct answer won't be directly stated in the text, but it must be true based on the text.

Step 3: Research the Relevant Text
Of course, paragraph 3 is relevant since it was mentioned in the question stem. But be prepared to dig into the following

paragraph, since the question asks for what the case in the third paragraph established.

Step 4: Make a Prediction
Paragraph 3 announces the resolution of the UCC suit upholding citizens' rights to "challenge the renewal" of a TV station's license, even though the UCC had no economic interest in the station's business. That plays right into paragraph 4, which explains that this "case established a formidable precedent." Now the public can question a station's practices when it comes up for renewal.

Step 5: Evaluate the Answer Choices
(E) speaks to the important establishment of balance in the process of renewing stations' licenses, as paragraph 4 implies. This is therefore a valid inference and the correct answer.

(A) is a Distortion, since the passage only discusses the rights of citizens at meetings held by the FCC, not by individual broadcasters. Furthermore, regular town-hall-style meetings, while surely a positive development, were not part of the UCC suit as far as we're told.

(B) is Outside the Scope. Licensure, not programming decisions, is the territory covered by the terms of the court's ruling in the UCC suit.

(C) is Extreme. Even in cases involving clear misconduct the FCC does not *need* public input. The court's holding specifies that the public has the right to challenge licensure due to legitimate concerns (lines 45–48). However, the court did not limit that right to only "cases involving clear misconduct."

(D) is a Distortion. It's not that the FCC *must* receive input from the public; it's that the FCC must allow for the public to challenge the agency's decisions. Lines 45–48 spell that out.

Passage 2: Science and the Humanities

Step 1: Read the Passage Strategically
Sample Roadmap

line #	Keyword/phrase	¶ Margin notes
1	should; dispel	
2	misunderstanding; prevent; much-needed	Auth: reconcile sci/hum
4	should not	
6	primarily; misunderstanding	Basically misunderstood
10	absurd	
11	feel; nothing more	Humanists—sci too reductive
14	caricature	
15	ignorant	Auth: they don't know real sci
17	For example; claimed	
19–20	also assert	
21	especially	Ex.
23	can never	
25	on the other hand	
26	nothing more	Scientists—hum. is just emotion—useless
29	useless because	
32	believe	
33	should; only a secondary	
35	Thus; misconceptions	Auth: correct the mis-understanding
36	alike; need of correction	
37	more acceptable	
40	Both	
43	but; :	Find common ground
45	in fact; does not depend	
46–47	exclusively; in fact	
50	uninformed; insist	
51	only	
52	only; fruitful	If views stay the same reconciliation unlikely
53	unlikely	
54	however; possible, even probable; if	
55	rather than	If note common obj. combination probable
56	only	

Discussion

The first sentence tells us clearly what the author thinks: we "should" (strong authorial recommendation) "dispel the misunderstandings" blocking a "much-needed" (strong Emphasis/Opinion Keyword) synthesis or amalgamation of science and the humanities. When the author's point of view is revealed early on in the passage, jump on it. That degree of openness gives you a tremendous handle on the gist of the passage before paragraph 1 is over. And as if it weren't enough that the **Topic** (science and the humanities) and **Scope** (the gap that separates them) are revealed so soon, lines 4–8 reveal the author's **Purpose**: to explain what the gap is "primarily the result of"—a misunderstanding of each side's underlying philosophy.

Unsurprisingly, one such misunderstanding occupies paragraph 2: Some humanists think scientists reduce everything to the mechanical laws of math, physics, and chemistry. But that's a "caricature" by those "ignorant of" what science really is, and line 17 provides an example, always welcome: to the ignorant humanists, science is clueless about basic human values because science can't appreciate the "irreducible spiritual element" of the artistic and moral human mind.

Yet "on the other hand," says paragraph 3, scientists have their blind spot as well. They caricature humanists as emotional, sentimental, and above all undisciplined, "useless because" what the humanists think about and produce can't help our species survive.

The author has had enough of this impasse that is "in need of correction," pointing to "a much more acceptable position"—and notice, even its name is a synthesis. "Scientific humanism" accepts that both people of science and people of the arts want to understand the world better. Science doesn't just rely on raw data (lines 45–46), nor are humanists utterly oblivious to "controlled evaluation" (i.e., measurement). Study the commonalities in the fields, the author advises (lines 53–56), and a reconciliation and "fruitful collaboration" become likely. There's your **Main Idea**, expressed as clearly at the end as Topic, Scope, and Purpose are revealed at the outset.

6. (E) Global

Step 2: Identify the Question Type

Any question that seeks the "main idea of the passage" is a Global question.

Step 3: Research the Relevant Text

The very nature of a Global question means that the entire passage is "relevant text."

Step 4: Make a Prediction

The Main Idea of the passage is the author's forceful recommendation that scientists and humanists correct their misunderstandings and synthesize the approaches of their fields.

Step 5: Evaluate the Answer Choices

(E) correctly reflects the author's conviction.

(A) puts the onus for the dilemma on scientists only, yet humanists too are guilty of a fundamental misunderstanding that prohibits the desired synthesis.

(B) suggests that the author is pleased with the current state of the science-humanism relationship. The passage isn't interested in the benefits each discipline has heretofore provided, but in ensuring that their reconciliation will benefit society even more.

(C) is a classic Extreme wrong answer. To say that a science-humanities synthesis is "much-needed" is not to say that in its absence, the sky will fall and technological development will cease. Indeed, our author is so confident about the possibility of reconciling the two fields that he spends no time discussing the consequences of failure.

(D) offers an Irrelevant Comparison. The author makes no mention of scientific-humanist cooperation that somehow we've lost sight of and need to return to. Lines 1–4 imply that the gap between the disciplines "still" exists as it always has.

7. (C) Inference

Step 2: Identify the Question Type

The phrase "most likely to characterize" indicates an Inference question. You'll need to use what the author says about humanists' misunderstanding of science to find the choice that must be true.

Step 3: Research the Relevant Text

Humanists' misconceptions are the subject of paragraph 2.

Step 4: Make a Prediction

Lines 10–14 summarize the misconception: humanists think of scientists as data pushers, soulless, and non-spiritual. The correct answer will be in line with this idea.

Step 5: Evaluate the Answer Choices

(C) both paraphrases the view that scientists "are interested in nothing more than" physical laws (lines 11–14) and picks up on the approved authorial view (lines 45–46) that "science in fact does not depend exclusively on measurable data."

(A) is a misuse of the charge in 22–24 (made by humanists and directed at scientists) that science can never "adequately explain" life's spiritual elements. So, if anything, this would be a 180 because it is a view held by the humanists, not a misunderstanding they have about science.

(B) is far too complimentary of science. Humanists reject the scientific mind-set precisely because they see it as exclusively focused on the practical.

(D), like **(B)**, mischaracterizes lines 22–24. To humanists, science turns its back on (not "recognizes") spirituality. Once again, this is a 180. The humanists believe there are aspects of the human mind, including those manifested in the arts, that are "inexplicable."

(E) is a Distortion. According to lines 40–41, humanists employ description as much as scientists do. This is not a point of difference, in the humanists' mind, between the two disciplines.

8. (D) Inference
Step 2: Identify the Question Type
Two parts of this question stem help you identify it as Inference: one obvious clue (the word "inferred") and one slightly less obvious but equally reliable phrase ("author would be most likely to agree with").

Step 3: Research the Relevant Text
The stem doesn't point you to a particular part of the passage, so you'll need to use the whole text as a basis for the correct answer. Luckily, this author has a very clear point of view throughout the passage.

Step 4: Make a Prediction
By way of prediction, remind yourself that the author finds both the scientist and the humanist guilty of mischaracterizing the other and that in many ways they're not so very far apart. The correct answer will be consistent with this.

Step 5: Evaluate the Answer Choices
(D) points to a commonality raised in lines 44–47: the humanities have in fact "profit[ed] from attempts at controlled evaluation," i.e., the scientific analysis of, and deduction from, concrete data. **(D)** is therefore correct.

(A) is a Distortion. The author asserts that both science and the humanities already "attempt to describe and explain" (lines 40–41), so he'd hardly agree that scientific humanism would extend the practice of description from one to the other.

(B) is a 180. Scientists do share the humanists' goal of "clearer understanding of people and their world" (lines 43–44).

(C) is also a 180. Controlled measures, says the author, very much do have a place in humanists' study (lines 46–47).

(E) is a Faulty Use of Detail. The author posits two conditional statements. **(E)** is tempting if you read lines 52–53 out of context; that is, ignoring the "if" clause beginning in line 50. Lines 53–56 present an alternate "if" clause where the author indicates a belief that this "fruitful combination … is … possible, even probable." The author's ultimate prediction is now known without knowing which "if" clause he expects to be triggered.

9. (B) Detail
Step 2: Identify the Question Type
Anytime you see the direct wording "according to the author," you're looking at a Detail question.

Step 3: Research the Relevant Text
The phrase "primary cause of … separation" is a clue leading you to paragraph 1, where the author discusses why science and the humanities have yet to synthesize.

Step 4: Make a Prediction
Lines 5–6 directly state that the science-humanities split is "primarily the result of" a basic misunderstanding of each discipline's theoretical underpinnings by the other. Since this is a Detail question, that's good enough for a solid prediction.

Step 5: Evaluate the Answer Choices
(B) is a perfect match. It even expressly mentions "misunderstanding" and "philosophical foundations."

(A) paints the scientists as the sole culprits, which is unfair, especially since the humanists' misreading of scientists' philosophical stance is the subject of paragraph 2.

(C) distorts the author's use of "reductionism," which is meant to refer to the "absurd" way in which humanists view scientists (as "reducers" of life to mere mechanical processes).

(D) distorts the same lines, 9–10. Moreover, both sides' prejudices are to blame, and **(D)** ignores that mutuality altogether.

(E) blames only the humanists, which is just as unfair as **(A)** blaming only the scientists.

10. (D) Logic Function
Step 2: Identify the Question Type
This is a Logic Function question because it asks for the function of a particular part of the passage. Here, you're asked to determine why the author wrote the last paragraph.

Step 3: Research the Relevant Text
The last paragraph is relevant here, as are the notes you jotted on that paragraph in your Roadmap.

Step 4: Make a Prediction
As your Roadmap notes, paragraph 4 offers "a much more acceptable position" that incorporates both disciplines' "common elements." So the author's purpose in this paragraph is to offer his case for synthesizing science and humanism.

Step 5: Evaluate the Answer Choices
(D) is a perfect match for this prediction. The "alternative" mentioned in **(D)** is the author's own position.

(A) is Extreme because the reconciliation between science and humanism, if that's to be considered a "proposal," isn't *implausible* based on the views presented in paragraphs 2 and 3. Rather, those paragraphs exist to show why the reconciliation hasn't happened yet, and in line 54, that author cites that under the right conditions the reconciliation is "probable."

(B) is Half-Right/Half-Wrong. Paragraph 4 certainly promises reconciliation. But since paragraphs 2 and 3 describe "misunderstandings," the views they present can't at all be deemed "correct."

(C) is a 180. Rather than support the views presented in either paragraphs 2 and 3, paragraph 4 offers "a much more acceptable position" to the views presented in those paragraphs.

(E) is wrong because paragraph 4 moves past the distinct views of paragraphs 2 and 3 to a common ground on which scientists and humanists can both stand. No "specific examples" of the views in paragraphs 2 and 3 are presented.

11. (C) Inference

Step 2: Identify the Question Type
The first three words of the question stem ("the passage suggests") automatically make this an Inference question.

Step 3: Research the Relevant Text
The words "author would recommend" point you to paragraph 4, where the author makes recommendations concerning the synthesis of science and humanism.

Step 4: Make a Prediction
The lines that deal directly with humanists' role in bridging the divide are 46–47, in which the author points out that humanists benefit from controlled evaluation, a philosophical approach they hang around the necks of scientists as a shortcoming. So, the author would likely suggest that humanists make room in their viewpoint for more "scientific" approaches to their discipline.

Step 5: Evaluate the Answer Choices
(C) directly follows from the prediction.

(A) draws a false distinction between two practices that, to the humanist, are both part of the scientists' playbook already.

(B) is a 180. The belief that science doesn't account for spirituality is part of the humanist's misconception (lines 19–24), not a modification that needs to be made.

(D) advocates for the correction of a fault that the author never ascribes to the humanists. The passage doesn't suggest that humanists are going around clamoring vociferously about the importance of art in people's lives.

(E) is not something the author indicates the humanists need to prove. Although the humanities may not support "practical survival," that does not mean that they are "useless" (line 29). The passage recommends that scientists walk in

humanists' shoes and vice versa, and **(E)** doesn't touch on this.

12. (B) Inference

Step 2: Identify the Question Type
The words "the author suggests" indicate an Inference question. Specifically, you're asked to find what the author suggests about scientists' views of humanists.

Step 3: Research the Relevant Text
Lines 27–28 are clearly relevant, since they're directly referenced in the question stem. But as always, context will play an important role in finding the correct answer here.

Step 4: Make a Prediction
Having just explained how scientists are wrongly caricatured as soulless stiffs, the author uses lines 27–28 to expose an equally egregious misrepresentation. But it's the following lines (29–31) that convey the widespread misconception that those vagrant, undisciplined fantasies are "useless" for "practical survival."

Step 5: Evaluate the Answer Choices
(B) matches the prediction.

(A) is tempting if you stop at the word "emotion" in line 26. Yes, some scientists find humanists too concerned with emotion and sentiment. But there's nothing about the phrase "vagrant fancies of an undisciplined mind" that connotes *wild* emotion.

(C) is unsupported. There's no evidence of intransigence—or stubbornness—in scientists' caricature of humanism.

(D) is also unsupported; optimism is not listed as a trait usually pinned on humanists.

(E) implies that the scientists charge humanists with simultaneously holding contradictory views. But nothing in the passage, and certainly not in paragraph 3 where the quotation arises, agrees with this. Indeed, scientists seem not to find humanists logical at all.

Passage 3: Willa Cather

Step 1: Read the Passage Strategically
Sample Roadmap

line #	Keyword/phrase	¶ Margin notes
Passage A		
1	high quality	
2	invariably	
3	Indeed	Cather followed Turg & Tolstoy
5	not	
6	but	Used Turg's method for char. emotions
11	must; but	
12	must; but only	
13	Similarly	
14	argued; must	
15	avoid	
16	instead	
19	anticipates; :	Turg's "secret" Cather's "not named"
23	both	
24	absolute importance	Cath & Turg both selective & simplified
25	both	
Passage B		
32	assert vehemently	Cather anticipated narratology
33	prefer	
34	anticipated; important	
35	:	
37	broadens	breaks earlier paradigms
38	simplifies	
39	:	
41	*not*	
42	:	
46	rather; exactly	
47	appropriate	
48	Indeed; severest critics; always questioned	Critics—Zabel Cather may be poor novelist
50	fail	
54	inconclusive	Critics—Edel
55	treat as failures	
56	:	Cather criticized for "narrative" elements
61	essential	

Discussion

As is the case here, you can anticipate that these paired passages have the same **Topic**—here, it's novelist Willa Cather—and that they will likely diverge with respect to Scope and Purpose. Because the task is Comparative Reading, you must also be alert to where the two passages are in sync and where they differ.

Passage A states that Cather "invariably" cited Tolstoy and Turgenev as examples of novel writing at its best; and "indeed" she followed in Turgenev's manner according to Edmund Wilson by not directly describing her characters' emotions. Turgenev occupies the rest of paragraph 1—his habit of describing characteristics without explanation, his being a "secret psychologist," his insistence on knowing his characters through and through. Yet all of this discussion of Turgenev is predictably meant to cast light on the real **Topic**, Cather.

Paragraph 2 links the two authors: Turgenev's "secret psychology" became Cather's "thing not named"—feelings and impressions left by the prose without being spelled out on the page. (Indeed, it's called an "impressionist aesthetic," line 18.) The rest of paragraph 2 explains what's true of "both writers": they selected and simplified, they fused the physical world with emotional reality, and they concentrated on mood.

The **Scope** of passage A is Cather's narrative technique. The **Purpose** of passage A is to describe the impressionistic technique Cather used in her work and its relationship to Turgenev's work. The **Main Idea** is that Cather shared with Turgenev a preference for "selection and simplification": depicting a character through his or her appearance and actions rather than direct description of his or her thoughts and emotions.

Passage B notes that Cather agreed with many of her critics that *Death Comes for the Archbishop* wasn't a novel at all; she herself preferred the word "narrative," a preference that passage B's author says presages the 1960s French critical phenomenon known as "narratology." That approach "broadens and simplifies" by ignoring such traditional aspects of the novel (lines 43–44) as realism, causality, and direct expression of character.

Cather's "severest critics" take most issue with her as a novelist. She was evidently not a purveyor of the above-named traditional aspects, so the likes of Zabel and Edel found her books fragmented and unstructured. We then see passage B's author agreeing with passage A's author in calling Cather's technique "impressionistic." Critics like Edel and Zabel seem inclined to pick on the very elements of her work (lines 56–60) that passage B's author—and presumably the French narratologists—most admire.

The **Scope** of passage B is Cather's focus on pure narrative as opposed to novelistic conventions. The **Purpose** of passage B

is to discuss the features of Cather's work that demonstrate that focus. The **Main Idea** is that Cather's work better exemplifies the features of what would later be referred to as "pure narrative" than the techniques imputed to "realistic" novelists.

13. (E) Inference

Step 2: Identify the Question Type

As with any other Reading Comprehension passage, the phrase "author ... would be most likely to agree with ... " indicates an Inference question. In this case, you're asked to identify a point of agreement between the authors of the two passages.

Step 3: Research the Relevant Text

Both passages are relevant here, so predict this answer using your global comparison of the passages from Step 1.

Step 4: Make a Prediction

Both passages esteem the impressionistic elements of Cather's writing, lauding its subtlest touches of carefully chosen detail that speaks to the reader without spelling everything out. The umbrella term "impressionism" covers passage A's evocation of Cather's "thing not named" as well as passage B's praise for her "preference for the bold, simple, and stylized." The correct answer will be consistent with this.

Step 5: Evaluate the Answer Choices

(E) is entirely consistent with the views of passage A. Lines 23–24 say that Cather believed in the importance of "selection and simplification" when presenting characters.

(A) is unsupported. In neither passage do we get any sense of Cather's seeing *Archbishop* as anomalous in her career.

(B), like **(A)**, focuses on a distinction between her novels when in fact it's the contrast between two kinds of novelistic technique that interests both passages.

(C) is a 180. Passage A's author praises that which narratology esteems—attributes like indirection and ambiguity. To be consistent with passage B's view, this answer should have said "novel rather than narrative" as opposed to vice versa.

(D) attempts to suggest that Cather actually embraced the techniques of the traditional novel, but that flies in the face of lines 40–47. Furthermore, nothing in passage A suggests that the impressionistic technique ascribed to Cather resembles the conventions of the realistic novel.

14. (C) Detail

Step 2: Identify the Question Type

The direct, categorical language of this question stem—"[p]assage B indicates"—is a sure sign of a Detail question.

Step 3: Research the Relevant Text
You can be certain that the correct answer will be stated somewhere in passage B. Beyond that, your research won't get any more specific.

Step 4: Make a Prediction
Because the question stem wasn't more specific, forming a prediction is difficult, if not impossible, since any of passage B's 33 lines can yield the correct answer. Instead, go straight to the choices, prepared to find your answer in passage B before you select it as correct.

Step 5: Evaluate the Answer Choices
(C) is spot-on. Cather preferred the word *narrative* to *novel* in describing her *Death Comes for the Archbishop* (lines 31–33), so that's the exception of which **(C)** speaks.

(A) is a Distortion. You might be able to surmise that the narratologists would be into Cather's work, but there's no indication in passage B that the narratologists ever read or dealt with it directly.

(B) isn't mentioned at all. Nothing in passage B cites Cather's view of any other novelists, pro or con.

(D) is a detail out of passage A, not passage B.

(E) is Extreme. Cather's severest critics took issue with her handling of traditional novelistic elements, but that doesn't necessarily mean they represented most contemporary critics.

15. (C) Inference

Step 2: Identify the Question Type
You know from the words "it can be inferred" that this is an Inference question. Specifically, you need to select the answer choice that would best exemplify Cather's technique as described in both passages.

Step 3: Research the Relevant Text
The question stem's mention of both passages is key. Find mentions of Cather's technique from both authors and incorporate both into your prediction.

Step 4: Make a Prediction
Passage A's author cites the indirect evocation (which she shared with Turgenev) of character through described behavior, while passage B's author praises boldness, simplicity, and stylization (lines 58–59) and an eschewing of "direct psychological characterization" (line 43). The answer choices present five ways of dealing with character, and you need to find the one that displays Cather's characteristic indirect technique.

Step 5: Evaluate the Answer Choices
(C) is correct. A clumsier novelist might say "Rodney was timid," but an artful one might say "Rodney entered the dining room, his martini slightly quivering in his hand" to give

the same impression. There you have it: behavior indirectly suggesting psychology.

(A)'s detailed list of elegant fixtures would directly assert that the character is wealthy. Sounds like the kind of "overloading ... with unnecessary detail" (lines 15–16) passage A decries.

(B) is a 180. Listing a character's "emotional scars" hardly qualifies as careful selection of a piece of behavior to convey emotion.

(D) is conventional and utterly explicit. This emphasis on causality and chronology is exactly the kind of technique Cather avoided (lines 56–57).

(E) deals with a "detailed narration" which is exactly what Turgenev suggests to avoid in line 16. **(E)**'s broad canvas that does not maintain a focus on individual psychology also runs afoul of Cather's technique. Furthermore, it focuses on the conveying of theme rather than Cather's preferred focus—the portrayal of character.

16. (A) Global

Step 2: Identify the Question Type
Even though it only asks about one of the two passages, this is still a Global question because it seeks the passage's "main point."

Step 3: Research the Relevant Text
The entirety of passage B is relevant here. Finding the Main Point is the same task for passage B as it is for any Reading Comp passage: Base your prediction on your Topic, Scope, Purpose, and Roadmap.

Step 4: Make a Prediction
Taken by itself, passage B concentrates on a single aspect of Cather's writing, the aspect that presaged the theory of narratology but that irked critics looking for traditional novelistic skill.

Step 5: Evaluate the Answer Choices
(A) aptly summarizes that essential conflict, which properly recognizes passage B's interest in the impressionistic, "non-novelistic" elements of Cather's work.

(B) is Extreme in alleging that "most commentators" found flaws in Cather's style. Those who did take her to task did so on the grounds of her "distinctive narrative techniques," but you can't say they were in the majority.

(C) is a Distortion. Cather's intentionality in her narrative technique is never mentioned, let alone is it broad enough to be correct in this Global question.

(D) presumes an awareness and appreciation of Cather by the 1960s French narratologists, which is not supported by the passage.

(E) is Half-Right/Half-Wrong. Cather certainly seems to have worked in opposition to traditional novelistic techniques. But both the traditional novelist and Cather sought to "sketch their [characters'] inner lives," though each chose different means of doing so.

17. (E) Inference

Step 2: Identify the Question Type

Once again, any question asking for what the author(s) would most likely agree with is an Inference question. Here, you're specifically seeking a point of agreement between the two authors.

Step 3: Research the Relevant Text

Both passages are relevant here, so you'll need to approach this question almost as if it were a Global question.

Step 4: Make a Prediction

Your Global understanding of the passages tells you that the correct answer will probably have something to do with Cather's technique, since that's territory both passages cover. Beyond that, you'll have to take each choice in turn and select the one supported by both passages.

Step 5: Evaluate the Answer Choices

(E) is correct. Passage A's author speaks of Turgenev's "impressionistic aesthetic that anticipates Cather's" (lines 18–19), while passage B's author points directly to "Cather's impressionistic technique" (line 56).

(A) uses a concept (stream of consciousness) that never shows up in either passage. Moreover, passage B contains just the tiniest hint of the techniques used by Cather's contemporaries.

(B) is supported only by passage B, which discusses how Cather intended her works to be classified (line 33). Only passage B touches on the distinction between novels and narratives.

(C) is only supported by passage B, and even then it is Extreme. Because passage A never mentions narratology, you can't infer that passage A's author would consider narratology an appropriate critical approach. Furthermore, passage A's author never says it is the "most appropriate" approach, just that looking at her works as narratives is more appropriate than looking at them as novels.

(D) is a Distortion. While there is a legitimate link between passage A's phrase "the thing not named" and techniques taken up in passage B, neither passage ever deals with Cather's influence on later writers.

18. (E) Inference

Step 2: Identify the Question Type

This is another question focusing on what the authors "would be likely to agree" with, so it's an Inference question. But pay attention; the "NOT" tells you that the correct answer will be

something neither author would identify as a characteristic of Cather's work

Step 3: Research the Relevant Text

The relevant text here is any text that describes features of Cather's work. In this case, the lines describing things Cather avoided in her work would be even more useful, since this is essentially an EXCEPT question.

Step 4: Make a Prediction

Passage A's author would say that Cather, like Turgenev, wouldn't be caught dead depicting or explaining characters' emotions directly (lines 5–6; 9–10), nor would she "overload the work with unnecessary detail" (lines 15–16). Passage B's author would be loath to say that Cather employed "direct psychological characterization" (line 43), causality, or strict logic (line 44).

Step 5: Evaluate the Answer Choices

(E) describes narration that way too directly tells the reader who the character is and what he wants and worries about. **(E)** is therefore correct since it's an unlikely element in Cather's writing, as portrayed in lines 4–8.

(A) shows the kind of selectivity both authors credit as Cather's style; one can even imagine figuring out just what kind of person would sit in that particular chair.

(B) could be found in Cather's work. Chronological time strictly followed is a traditional technique. The impressionistic Cather would surely drift back and forth in time in her narratives (lines 56–57).

(C) lists some of the things Cather would surely offer up to the reader, who would then infer the character's emotions from those selected details.

(D) is unsupported. Neither passage explicitly refers to the use of dialogue as either a Cather-like technique or a conventionally novelistic one. However, if what a character says can be considered "action," then it would be consistent with both passages if Cather did represent dialogue exactly as **(D)** describes, leaving us to figure out what emotions are conveyed by the spoken words.

19. (B) Global

Step 2: Identify the Question Type

The words "central purpose" indicate that this is a Global question.

Step 3: Research the Relevant Text

The entirety of both passages is relevant. Use your understanding of Purpose from Step 1 to predict your answer here.

Step 4: Make a Prediction

Hopefully you're starting to see just how much focusing on the similarities between the passages can pay off in the questions. Once again, both authors describe some of Cather's distinctive traits, often in similar terms.

Step 5: Evaluate the Answer Choices

(B) is a perfect match.

(A) is a Distortion in the case of passage A and flat-out untrue in the case of passage B. Passage B's author mentions no influences on Cather, and even passage A's author only goes so far as to credit Edmund Wilson with seeing Turgenev as an influence; Cather herself said that she found Turgenev and Tolstoy to be of high quality, but that's different from embracing either one as a direct influence.

(C) is hardly a "central purpose" of either passage. Passage A contains only a hint of Cather's contemporary critical reputation (Edmund Wilson's esteem of her). Passage B does address her critics' main complaint, but that's presumably only part of the critical reception she received (to say nothing of the fact that you don't know whether this reception came along during Cather's lifetime).

(D) never happens in passage A, which spends no time identifying the realistic novel's "archetypal form."

(E) is a Distortion. Neither passage pinpoints any European influence on Cather, and what European literary theory there is in passage B came along in the 1960s after Cather's death.

Passage 4: Fractal Geometry

Step 1: Read the Passage Strategically
Sample Roadmap

line #	Keyword/phrase	¶ Margin notes
2	Although	
4	:	Fractal def.
8	significant	
9	insight	Koch curve—how generated
10	begins	
23	Since	Each segment the same
27	Theoretically	
28	but	
31	However	
33	dramatically	
34	major attraction; :	Computer models simple process—complex pattern
35	incredibly	
37	captivated by	
38	astonishing	Computer images → public interest
39	enthusiastic	
42	anticipate	Some experts predict huge impact
43	significance will rival	
44	expect	
48	reservations	Others doubt value
48	preoccupation	
50	lack of interest	
52	while	
55	only	Very few new theorems proven w/fractal geo
57	According to	
59	only if	Needs theorems & proofs

Discussion

Perhaps the abstract nature of fractals seemed unfamiliar to you. Even the author admits (lines 3–4) that the math community can't agree on a definition. Fractal geometry is the **Topic**, the **Scope** being its utility. But first the author has to define fractals to some extent.

What's agreed upon is that fractals "commonly exhibit" self-similarity (circle the colon in line 4, which signals a much-needed definition). Paragraph 1 describes the "significant" Koch curve and how mathematicians generate it. This provides "insight" as an extended example of a pattern in which "each part ... looks basically like the object as a whole." That part-to-whole relationship will itself prove to be "significant" in the questions that follow. The words used in the Koch process tell most of the story: "At this stage ... the process is repeated ... then ... repeated indefinitely."

Paragraph 2 belabors the point: The same treatment is applied to each piece of the design such that the computer can get involved when the pieces get too tiny. This "illustrates" a "major attraction" of fractals: Their simple generation process leads to "incredibly complex patterns."

The resulting computer imagery, says paragraph 3, "captivates" and "astonishes" "enthusiastic" viewers, and some experts predict great impact right up there with geometry and calculus. It's not necessary to understand exactly how and why. The key turning point is line 47: Others doubt fractals' value because its purveyors "lack interest in theory." Math, say these purists, is about theorems and proofs, and to date fractals haven't come up with many proofs that couldn't be found by traditional means. Line 59 offers the always provocative "only if" signal of necessity: Fractal geometry needs precision, theorems, and proofs before it can join the pantheon of mathematical languages. By the end, if not before, the author's **Purpose** is clear: to describe the potential impact of fractal geometry, and the **Main Idea** is that it's going to take a while before fractals can realize their hoped-for potential.

20. (B) Global

Step 2: Identify the Question Type

Any question that asks for the "main point" of a passage is a Global question.

Step 3: Research the Relevant Text

In any Global question, the relevant text is the entire passage. Instead of researching specific lines, consult your Roadmap and your understanding of Topic, Scope, and Purpose.

Step 4: Make a Prediction

The passage's Main Idea is that although fractal geometry has some potentially exciting applications, its ultimate role in the math world is uncertain as long as fractal geometers are unable to sustain theorems and proofs with their discipline.

Step 5: Evaluate the Answer Choices

(B) is a match for this prediction.

(A) is Extreme because although much of the passage is devoted to what fractals are and how exciting their promise is, it ignores the author's warning that fractals aren't yet what they're cracked up to be (paragraph 3). **(A)** goes a step too far, indicating that fractals are "likely" to make pre-fractal mathematics "obsolete."

(C) is the main point of paragraph 1. But it leaves out the potential applications of fractals and, most of all, paragraph 3's warnings of the field's current weaknesses.

(D) is both incomplete and a Distortion. First, it only focuses on the Koch curve example. Second, fractal geometry isn't useful because it doesn't rely on theorems. It's useful *despite* not relying on theorems.

(E) confuses the author's central focus. The passage isn't about a contrast between simple and complex shapes. Indeed, if you draw out the Koch curve as far as line 16 says—a straight line with two sides of a triangle protruding from it—you see that a fractal can indeed describe an "ordinary shape."

21. (C) Inference

Step 2: Identify the Question Type

This is an Inference question because it asks you for the author's intended meaning of a term as it's used in the passage.

Step 3: Research the Relevant Text

The question stem directs you to lines 24–25, but as always, context is important, especially when trying to determine the meaning of a term in the passage.

Step 4: Make a Prediction

"Since" (line 23) the rules of fractal generation are "fully explicit and always the same," computers can step in and continue the process when the drawing gets too teeny. The phrase in quotes must mean to be completely spelled out.

Step 5: Evaluate the Answer Choices

(C) is the best match for this prediction.

(A) is unsupported. It's hard to imagine the rules for a Koch curve being illustrated by an example, or how that illustration would help the computer create such a curve.

(B) is a Distortion. The rules are detailed enough for a computer to follow, but that doesn't mean that they're simple. Computers can handle complexity, and simplicity wouldn't seem to be relevant to the generation of really complex images.

(D) is also a Distortion. Just because the rules for generating a Koch curve can be followed by a computer doesn't mean that they need to or that the process would be lengthy.

(E) is unsupported. "Explicit" carries no connotation of unanimity, and full agreement wouldn't necessarily contribute to fractal generation.

22. (D) Detail (EXCEPT)

Step 2: Identify the Question Type
The opening phrase ("according to the description in the passage") indicates a Detail question. And the "EXCEPT" indicates that you must find the answer choice that doesn't comport with the author's description of self-similarity.

Step 3: Research the Relevant Text
The concept of self-similarity is initially defined in lines 5–7.

Step 4: Make a Prediction
According to those lines, self-similarity involves an object in which each part resembles the whole. You don't know what the odd man out will say verbatim, but you do know that it will be a description of a system in which each part does not resemble the whole.

Step 5: Evaluate the Answer Choices
(D), in which each maple seed resembles the other maple seeds, is the odd man out. There's no mention here of a part-whole relationship. Furthermore, some of the seeds are a different size from others, which disagrees with the idea of self-similarity. (D) is therefore correct.

(A) agrees with the passage. The branch looks like the tree it's a part of.

(B) is also a match. Each part of the frost is similar to the entire frost pattern.

(C) sounds a lot like self-similarity. Each blood vessel pattern resembles the overall blood vessel pattern.

(E) is an example of self-similarity, since one floret is a dead ringer for the entire head of florets.

23. (D) Logic Function

Step 2: Identify the Question Type
The phrase "serves primarily to" indicates a Logic Function question, since you need to determine the purpose of the author's explanation of how to generate a Koch curve.

Step 3: Research the Relevant Text
The question stem refers to lines 10–20, but to know why the author wrote those lines, you may also need to read the sentences preceding them.

Step 4: Make a Prediction
From reading lines 8–10, you learn that the Koch curve is a significant fractal that provides insight into fractal geometry. So the Koch curve is a prime example of a fractal that the author describes in detail to show how fractals are structured.

Step 5: Evaluate the Answer Choices
(D) narrows it down to the principal feature of a fractal: the same self-similarity that we discussed in the previous question and that immediately precedes the introduction to the Koch curve. (D) is therefore the correct answer.

(A) mentions traditional geometry, which is discussed in line 47, far from where the Koch curve is discussed.

(B) is a 180. A *natural* form that fractals can potentially describe is a cloud (line 45). A Koch curve is manmade.

(C) is a Distortion. The author's discussion of the Koch curve is as precise as it gets, but that's so you the reader can understand it, not so the author can anticipate an objection to the field.

(E) is a 180. The Koch curve is an example of a fractal, but the author says in line 3 that there's no exact definition of fractals.

24. (E) Detail

Step 2: Identify the Question Type
This question asks about what the author presents, or states directly. It's therefore a Detail question.

Step 3: Research the Relevant Text
The phrase "characteristic of fractal geometry" leads you primarily to the first two paragraphs.

Step 4: Make a Prediction
Fractal geometry has several characteristics listed throughout paragraphs 1 and 2, so instead of pre-phrasing a bunch of them, go to the answer choices and check them against the lines that describe fractal geometry.

Step 5: Evaluate the Answer Choices
(E) is a straightforward paraphrase of lines 31–36 and is therefore correct.

(A) is a Distortion. Enthusiasts claim that fractal geometry will rival calculus (line 43), but even they don't say their field may supplant it.

(B) is also a Distortion. Fractal geometry is discussed alongside traditional math, not as a part of it. And computers are enabling smaller, more complex fractals. But their speed is never mentioned, nor is there a connection between that speed and fractal geometry's role in the mathematical community.

(C) isn't stated at all. No comparison to other fast-growing math fields is ever mentioned.

(D) conflates two things mentioned in the passage—computers and math proofs. But even if computers would be useful or even essential in generating proofs, (D) is still flawed in suggesting that there's something about fractal geometry that "encourages" using computers for that purpose.

25. (A) Detail (EXCEPT)

Step 2: Identify the Question Type

Since the question stem concerns statements made about a particular aspect of the passage, it's a Detail question. The "EXCEPT" indicates that you'll need to find the answer choice that isn't stated or supported by the passage.

Step 3: Research the Relevant Text

The Koch curve is described in lines 8–20 and discussed further in lines 27–36.

Step 4: Make a Prediction

It's nearly impossible to predict what's NOT stated in the passage about the Koch curve. But armed with the relevant lines from the text, you can go into the answer choices, ready to eliminate any that are corroborated by the author.

Step 5: Evaluate the Answer Choices

(A) runs contrary to the text. The total number of protrusions is potentially infinite (lines 27–28), although drawing a Koch curve is limited by how tiny each repeated segment becomes. But computers can take over where the manually constructed segments become too small to perceive. Therefore, **(A)** is correct.

(B) is stated in lines 11–13. The line segments keep getting shorter because each is the length of one-third of the segment from which it's taken. The same process repeated endlessly has to lead to smaller and smaller segments.

(C) just paraphrases lines 27–28 and line 31.

(D) comes from lines 14–16. With each stage, the protrusions are the same length as the part of the generating segment.

(E) is definitely true from lines 11–20. The initial protrusions are each one-third the length of the original segment. Each additional set of protrusions is one-third of *its* generating segment. So the length of each segment depends on what the length of the original line was.

26. (E) Inference

Step 2: Identify the Question Type

This is an Inference question because it asks for what someone in the passage "would be most likely to agree with." Here, it's not the author's view that matters, but that of the proponents of fractal geometry.

Step 3: Research the Relevant Text

The question stem contains a reference to lines 39–40. But the practitioners of fractal geometry are discussed through line 47. Read all these lines before making a prediction.

Step 4: Make a Prediction

Fractal geometers believe fractal geometry has the potential to be right up there with calculus, and that it could describe something as free-form and wispy as a cloud with

architect-like precision. The correct answer is the one that's logically consistent with this.

Step 5: Evaluate the Answer Choices

(E) can be inferred from combining what the author says in lines 39–47 with the fact that fractals are based on the self-similarity concept. According to fractal geometers, their discipline must be able to explain some sort of self-similarity within clouds, the only natural form described in the passage. Thus, **(E)** is correct.

(A) is unsupported. The Koch curve merits no distinction as "most important"; rather, it is simply a method that's useful for insight into fractal geometry (lines 8–10).

(B) is a Distortion. Fractal geometry is never cited as a replacement for the traditional kind, just as a brand new tool for brand new insights.

(C) is Extreme and unsupported. So far, computer imagery has helped to popularize fractals (lines 37–39), but given the utility of computers when fractals become too small to draw by hand, it's hard to imagine that publicity could ever be the *most* important use of computers in this field.

(D) is also Extreme. Studying self-similarity didn't necessarily have to wait for the advent of computer technology; you could have drawn a little Koch curve sample in your test booklets by hand to better visualize what paragraph 1 described, thus it was not *impossible*.

27. (D) Inference

Step 2: Identify the Question Type

The question stem asks for the answer choice that the passage "supports" rather than "states," so this is an Inference question.

Step 3: Research the Relevant Text

You don't get any clues here to focus your research, so the whole passage is fair game.

Step 4: Make a Prediction

Don't waste time trying to predict the countless valid inferences that could be drawn from the passage. Go straight to the choices, prepared to select the answer that *must* be true, and reject any choice that is outside the passage's scope, exaggerates views in the passage, or contradicts the information presented.

Step 5: Evaluate the Answer Choices

(D) must be true, since fractal geometry is a direct example of such a theory. It has proven applications (lines 39–47), but no one has been able to establish a precise definition of fractals (line 3). **(D)** is therefore correct.

(A) is clearly contradicted by the many people referenced in lines 37–39 who find fractal geometry interesting and "appealing" but couldn't know or care less about the underlying theorems and proofs.

(B) is a Distortion. Most of the advances in *fractal geometry* required computer imagery; but computers' role in other mathematical theories goes unmentioned.

(C) is Extreme. The author makes no claim that fractal geometry will supplant traditional geometry.

(E) is also Extreme. Many mathematicians are already enthusiastic supporters of fractal geometry despite the absence of a theorem-and-proofs system. Others are not, but clearly such a formal system is not a necessary condition for enthusiasm within the field.

PrepTest 58

The Inside Story

PrepTest 58 was administered in September 2009. It challenged 60,746 test takers. What made this test so hard? Here's a breakdown of what Kaplan students who were surveyed after taking the official exam considered PrepTest 58's most difficult section.

Hardest PrepTest 58 Section as Reported by Test Takers

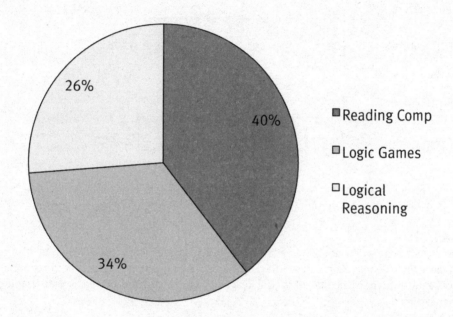

Based on these results, you might think that studying Reading Comprehension and Logic Games are the key to LSAT success. Well, those sections are important, but test takers' perceptions don't tell the whole story. For that, you need to consider students' actual performance. The following chart shows the average number of students to miss each question in each of PrepTest 58's different sections.

Percentage Incorrect by PrepTest 58 Section Type

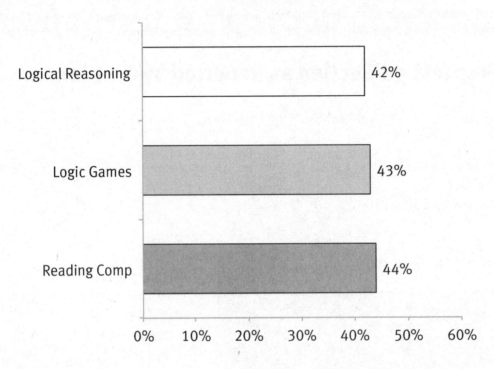

Actual student performance tells quite a different story. On average, students were almost equally likely to miss questions in all three of the different section types. While Reading Comp was indeed the hardest section on PrepTest 58, because of the number of questions in each section, a nearly identical number of Logical Reasoning questions were missed as were Reading Comprehension and Logic Games questions combined.

Maybe students overestimate the difficulty of the Logic Games section because it's so unusual, or maybe it's because a really hard Logic Game is so easy to remember after the test. But the truth is that the testmaker places hard questions throughout the test. Here were the locations of the 10 hardest (most missed) questions in the exam.

Location of 10 Most Difficult Questions in PrepTest 58

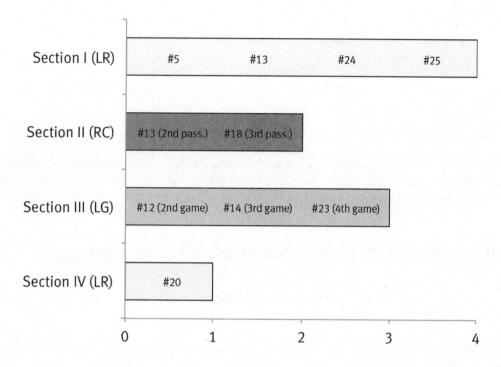

The takeaway from this data is that, to maximize your potential on the LSAT, you need to take a comprehensive approach. Test yourself rigorously, and review your performance on every section of the test. Kaplan's LSAT explanations provide the expertise and insight you need to fully understand your results. The explanations are written and edited by a team of LSAT experts, who have helped thousands of students improve their scores. Kaplan always provides data-driven analysis of the test, ranking the difficulty of every question based on actual student performance. The 10 hardest questions on every test are highlighted with a 4-star difficulty rating, the highest we give. The analysis breaks down the remaining questions into 1-, 2-, and 3-star ratings so that you can compare your performance to thousands of other test takers on all LSAC material.

Don't settle for wondering whether a question was really as hard as it seemed to you. Analyze the test with real data, and learn the secrets and strategies that help top scorers master the LSAT.

8 Can't-Miss Features of PrepTest 58

- PrepTest 58 has no Role of a Statement questions, no Point at Issue questions, and no Parallel Reasoning questions. It's not all that uncommon for a test to be missing a single LR question type, but this is the only test ever to be missing three!
- With all those Argument-Based question types missing, PrepTest 58 also set a record for the fewest Argument-Based questions on a single test. Two Main Point questions and three Method of Argument questions accounted for the only five Argument-Based questions on the test.
- For the second time in five tests, there were only six Strengthen/Weaken questions—tied for the fewest ever. PrepTest 58 joined PrepTest 32 (October 2000) and PrepTest 54 (June 2008) as the only tests that have ever had that few.
- So, with the dearth of Strengthen/Weaken and Argument-Based questions, what question types were more plentiful? 12 Assumption questions set the record for the most on a single test. To date, the only other test to have that many was PrepTest 76 (October 2015). Also, five Paradox questions was the most since PrepTest 43 (June 2004).
- The Logic Games section of PrepTest 58 has two Selection games. The only other test to ever do so was PrepTest 33 (December 2000).

- For the second test in a row, the Comparative Reading set was a seven-question Social Science set of passages. However, this was the first PrepTest where the Comparative Reading set was in the fourth position.
- The right answer in the Logic Games section was (B) for a record-tying eight times. The only other time that has happened was PrepTest 17 (December 1995), but that was on a 24-question Logic Games section. So, PrepTest 58 set the record by having (B) as the correct answer for nearly 35% of all LG questions.
- When many test takers walked out of the LSAT that Test Day in late September, knowing they had no more LSAT studying to do, they may have thought of the lyrics of the #1 Billboard song at the time: "I Gotta Feeling" by the Black Eyed Peas. Who knew the lyrics "I gotta feeling that tonight's gonna be a good night" were about satisfied LSAT test takers?

PrepTest 58 in Context

As much fun as it is to find out what makes a PrepTest unique or noteworthy, it's even more important to know just how representative it is of other LSAT administrations (and, thus, how likely it is to be representative of the exam you will face on Test Day). The following charts compare the numbers of each kind of question and game on PrepTest 58 to the average numbers seen on all officially released LSATs administered over the past five years (from 2013 through 2017).

Number of LR Questions by Type: PrepTest 58 vs. 2013–2017 Average

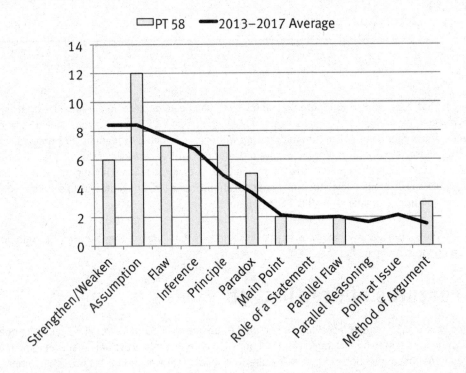

Number of LG Games by Type: PrepTest 58 vs. 2013–2017 Average

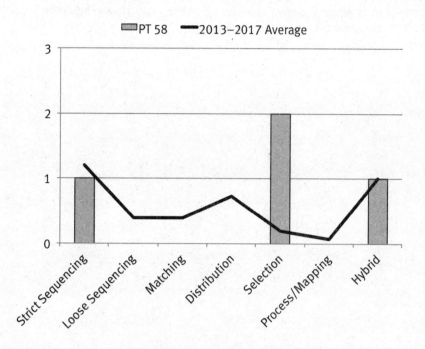

Number of RC Questions by Type: PrepTest 58 vs. 2013–2017 Average

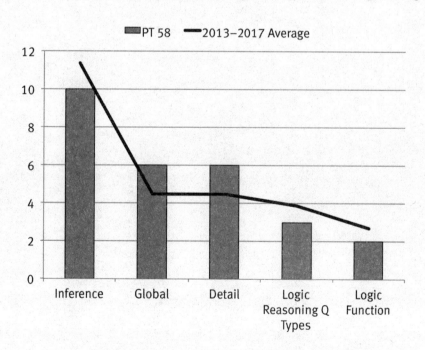

There isn't usually a huge difference in the distribution of questions from LSAT to LSAT, but if this test seems harder (or easier) to you than another you've taken, compare the number of questions of the types on which you, personally, are strongest and weakest. Then, explore within each section to see if your best or worst question types came earlier or later.

Students in Kaplan's comprehensive LSAT courses have access to every released LSAT and to a library of thousands of officially released questions arranged by question, game, and passage type. If you are studying on your own, you have to do a bit more work to identify your strengths and your areas of opportunity. Quantitative analysis (like that in the charts shown here) is an important tool for understanding how the test is constructed, and how you are performing on it.

Section I: Logical Reasoning

Q#	Question Type	Correct	Difficulty
1	Assumption (Necessary)	C	★
2	Principle (Parallel)	D	★
3	Strengthen	E	★★
4	Principle (Identify/Inference)	E	★
5	Weaken	A	★★★★
6	Method of Argument	A	★
7	Parallel Flaw	B	★
8	Paradox (EXCEPT)	E	★
9	Flaw	E	★★
10	Inference	B	★
11	Flaw	A	★★★
12	Assumption (Sufficient)	D	★★
13	Main Point	B	★★★★
14	Assumption (Necessary)	D	★
15	Inference	D	★★
16	Assumption (Necessary)	E	★
17	Paradox	B	★★
18	Flaw	C	★★
19	Assumption (Necessary)	D	★
20	Inference	E	★★
21	Principle (Apply/Inference)	C	★★
22	Assumption (Necessary)	C	★★★
23	Principle (Identify/Assumption)	C	★★
24	Weaken	E	★★★★
25	Assumption (Sufficient)	A	★★★★
26	Method of Argument	A	★★★

1. (C) Assumption (Necessary)

Step 1: Identify the Question Type

Because you're asked to find an assumption required by the argument, this is a Necessary Assumption question.

Step 2: Untangle the Stimulus

The commentator's conclusion is a prediction that we'll need to restrict water use sooner rather than later to meet the growing demand for freshwater. The evidence is the growing world population; while the current supply of freshwater meets our needs, those needs will soon dramatically increase because there will be many more humans over the next few decades.

Step 3: Make a Prediction

Of course, the commentator's conclusion isn't guaranteed to come true. She's relying on something else to be true. In order for us to need restrictions on water use, it must be true that no additional sources of freshwater will become available to us over the next few decades to help us keep pace with the growing population.

Step 4: Evaluate the Answer Choices

(C) matches the prediction. The Denial Test quickly confirms that **(C)** is the correct answer. If the freshwater supply *will* increase sufficiently to meet the increased needs of humankind, then restrictions might not be necessary, and the commentator's argument is in trouble.

(A) introduces other natural resources, which don't figure at all in the commentator's argument. The conclusion can still follow from the evidence no matter what we do with other natural resources.

(B) isn't necessary to the argument either. Even if the total supply of freshwater has held constant, the commentator is arguing that the current amount won't be enough to support the substantial increase in human population that's expected over the next few decades.

(D) doesn't hold up to the Denial Test. Even if attempts to synthesize water *do* actually increase the supply of freshwater available, there's no guarantee that additional freshwater will be enough to support the increased demand for freshwater resulting from population growth, and restrictions may still be necessary.

(E), like **(D)**, doesn't hold up to the Denial Test. Even if previous water conservation measures have increased the supply of freshwater available, there's no guarantee those measures will be enough to support the increased demand for freshwater resulting from population growth, and restrictions may still be necessary.

2. (D) Principle (Parallel)

Step 1: Identify the Question Type

The word *principle* in the stem indicates a Principle question, but always read Principle stems more closely to see what's asked. Here, both the psychologist's argument and the argument in the correct choice will be illustrative of the same broad principle. So it's a Parallel Principle question where you're asked to determine the principle and find its proper application in the choices.

Step 2: Untangle the Stimulus

The psychologist's advice for anyone trying in vain to recall a word or name is to think of something else, because focusing on recalling the word will only make it more difficult for one to do so.

Step 3: Make a Prediction

There's no way of knowing what subject matter will be present in the correct answer, but stop to make sure you have a good handle on the principle the psychologist is using. In short, the psychologist's principle is something like this: "To bring about a desired outcome, one should distract oneself from trying to make it happen, because concentrating on the outcome will make it less likely to happen." Now you just need to find the choice that applies this principle.

Step 4: Evaluate the Answer Choices

(D) says that the more intensely one concentrates on falling asleep, the less likely it is that one will fall asleep quickly. This is a perfect match to the principle illustrated by the stimulus.

(A) would be correct if it said that the best way to achieve happiness is to concentrate on pursuing things other than happiness, but by introducing wealth and fame, **(A)** makes a value judgment that has nothing to do with the principle.

(B) is off the mark because the psychologist's principle isn't about staying motivated or encouraged to achieve a goal; the principle is about the actions that will make a desired event more or less likely to happen.

(C) isn't a good match for the principle because it casts distraction in a bad light, and the principle advises seeking out distractions and diversions.

(E) advises turning one's attention to the hardship of others not because concentrating on one's own sorrow makes it unlikely to go away, but because one's sorrow will seem more manageable when compared to that of others. This isn't the same principle as the stimulus.

3. (E) Strengthen

Step 1: Identify the Question Type

Because the stem asks for something to "support a claim made," this is a Strengthen question.

Step 2: Untangle the Stimulus

The letter to the editor argues that the editorial is unjustified in its conclusion that the Planning Department spends five times as much money now as it did in 2001 to perform the same duties. The editorial's conclusion was apparently based on evidence that the Department's budget went from $100,000 in 2001 to $524,000 for this year.

Step 3: Make a Prediction

The only fact that you have is that the Planning Department's budget has indeed increased fivefold from 2001 to this year. However the editorial alleges that the Department is performing the same duties as before; it's just spending more money to do it. The letter to the editor claims that allegation is unjustified. To strengthen the letter writer's claim, find a choice that will support the idea that the editorial's conclusion is illogical. Because the editorial doesn't seem to allow for the possibility that the Planning Department took on more duties between 2001 and this year, you can probably exploit this vulnerability in order to shore up the letter writer's position.

Step 4: Evaluate the Answer Choices

(E) strengthens the letter writer's criticism of the editorial by stating that the Planning Department's duties have actually expanded since 2001.

(A) is irrelevant to the argument. No matter what other departments have done, the editorial's conclusion about the Planning Department's budget could still be justified.

(B) also doesn't help. Even if certain areas of the Planning Department's budget have been reduced, the overall budget has still increased fivefold, so without any information about the Department's duties, the editorial can still argue that the Department is spending more money to perform the same duties.

(C) is irrelevant. The editorial's argument hinges on a comparison between this year's budget and the budget in 2001. The fluctuations in the budget in the intervening years have no bearing on that comparison.

(D) doesn't provide enough information to help anyone's argument. It's unknown how the adjustment for inflation affected the figures. Besides, the figures provided by the letter writer are in line with the editorial's conclusion, so even if the editorial adjusted for inflation, that didn't seem to have too much of an impact on the editorial's conclusion.

4. (E) Principle (Identify/Inference)

Step 1: Identify the Question Type

This is a Principle question. Even though the stem doesn't use the word *principle*, it indicates that the right answer will be a general statement illustrated by the specific example in the stimulus.

Step 2: Untangle the Stimulus

The example describes how jury verdicts in mock trials compared with the trial judge's own opinions. When the judge instructed the jury in opaque technical language, jurors, taking cues from the judge's nonverbal behavior, returned a verdict that mirrored the judge's opinion. When the judge used clear, accessible language to instruct the jury, jurors were more likely to return verdicts that contradicted the judge's opinion.

Step 3: Make a Prediction

Try to determine a broad conclusion that can be drawn from this stimulus. The general rule that this example illustrates is that sometimes, the kind of language that a judge uses to instruct a jury could have an effect on the jury's verdict.

Step 4: Evaluate the Answer Choices

(E) matches the prediction. The example is a clear illustration of the possibility that the way a judge instructs a jury could affect the verdict.

(A) is a Distortion. The technical language used by the judges appears to have contained more legal jargon than the nontechnical language, but that doesn't necessarily mean that it was any more precise.

(B), as a rule, isn't consistent with the fact that sometimes juries returned verdicts at odds with the judge's opinion, despite the fact that the judge had a no less important status in the courtroom.

(C) is a 180. When judges issued instructions in technical jargon, jurors apparently took cues from the judges' nonverbal behavior, so it would appear that nonverbal behavior can communicate effectively.

(D) is an Irrelevant Comparison. Nothing in the stimulus indicates a flaw with respect to the use of mock trials in this example. Presumably the same results could have been reached if real trials had been used.

5. (A) Weaken

Step 1: Identify the Question Type

The stem's use of "most seriously weakens" indicates this is a Weaken question. Make sure to weaken the doctor's argument and not that of anyone else who might be mentioned in the stimulus.

Step 2: Untangle the Stimulus

The doctor concludes that medical practitioners should always be allowed to prescribe herbs as remedies, even though there's little evidence of their effectiveness. The evidence is that there's no chance of dangerous side effects and at least a small chance of benefit if a patient takes an herbal remedy.

Step 3: Make a Prediction

The doctor assumes that just because herbs are safe to consume and might help treat a patient's illness, that it will *always* be acceptable to prescribe them. In other words, the doctor assumes that there will never be a circumstance when prescribing herbs is not appropriate. To weaken this argument, identify a circumstance in which prescribing herbs would not be preferable.

Step 4: Evaluate the Answer Choices

(A) weakens the argument by suggesting that sometimes herbs are prescribed instead of medicines when the medicines would be more effective. This suggests that, contrary to the doctor's conclusion, prescribing herbs isn't always the way to go.

(B), if true, means that someone is guilty of false advertising when it comes to herbal remedies, but how the herbs are marketed is Out of Scope. Even if their effectiveness is unproven, the argument's assertion that the herbs might be effective is still logically sound.

(C) isn't a reason to disallow the prescription of herbal remedies specifically. Certain patients could presumably have allergic reactions to any medicines, herbal or otherwise.

(D) doesn't weaken the argument. Even if those who prescribe alternative medicines are motivated to do so by profit, that's not a reason to keep those medicines from being prescribed, as long as they are still beneficial to patients' health.

(E) is Out of Scope. The source of the benefit to the patient doesn't matter as long as there is a benefit in the first place.

6. (A) Method of Argument

Step 1: Identify the Question Type

Because this question is focused on what the argument *does*, rather than what the argument says, this is a Method of Argument question.

Step 2: Untangle the Stimulus

The author concludes that freedom of markets doesn't take away a government's right to regulate the withdrawal of money by lenders and investors in a climate of impending financial crisis. The support for this conclusion is the idea that freedom of speech doesn't take away a government's right to forbid someone from yelling "Fire!" in a crowded theater, because that could cause a dangerous stampede.

Step 3: Make a Prediction

To predict the answer to a Method of Argument question, focus not on the content of the argument (what it assumes, what would strengthen or weaken it, etc.) but on the structure; that is, *how* the author proceeds from evidence to conclusion. Here, the author supports the conclusion that free-market principles are not violated by the government's need to prevent total economic collapse by making an

analogy to a similar situation in which free-speech principles are not violated by the government's need to prevent dangerous stampedes in crowded places such as theaters.

Step 4: Evaluate the Answer Choices

(A) matches the prediction of the structure of the argument. In fact, **(A)** is the only choice that points out the author's use of an analogy.

(B) is Out of Scope. The author doesn't support the conclusion on the basis that the conclusion would best explain a set of observations. There is no set of observations offered in the argument.

(C) is also Out of Scope. No experimental results are offered to support the author's conclusion.

(D) is Out of Scope and a Distortion. No explanations for phenomena are discussed, and the author doesn't cite the analogy of the crowded theater as a specific instance of a nation on the brink of financial crisis. They're two totally different events that are analogous in a key respect.

(E) is incorrect because the author doesn't reach the conclusion by using an empirical generalization. A specific, analogous example (that of yelling "Fire!" in a crowded theater) is used to prove the author's point.

7. (B) Parallel Flaw

Step 1: Identify the Question Type

Because the flawed reasoning in one of the choices closely parallels that in the stimulus, this is a Parallel Flaw question.

Step 2: Untangle the Stimulus

According to the stimulus, negative ads, despite candidates' objections, actually benefit their targets. The evidence for this conclusion is that most elections have been won by candidates who were the targets of such ads.

Step 3: Make a Prediction

The main problem with this argument is that it confuses correlation with causation. In other words, it doesn't consider the very logical possibility that the candidates who win elections do so *despite* the negative ads aimed at them, and not because of those ads. Now, find the choice that argues that a perceived detriment is actually a benefit simply because most of those who have experienced the detriment went on to succeed.

Step 4: Evaluate the Answer Choices

(B) is a perfect match because, like the stimulus, **(B)** argues that a perceived detriment (harsh reviews) is actually a benefit because most people who experienced that detriment went on to succeed. Also, like the stimulus, **(B)** doesn't consider the possibility that the actors won awards despite their harsh reviews and not because of them.

(A) argues that an activity that many people dislike should nonetheless be undertaken because of its benefits. However, unlike the original stimulus, the evidence doesn't illustrate a correlation between most people experiencing the detriment and the suggested benefit.

(C) doesn't attempt to turn a negative thing into something positive. Studying doesn't have the same similarity to negative campaign ads that harsh reviews do. Also, studying is an action carried out by the students themselves in pursuit of a goal. In the stimulus, the politicians aren't running negative ads against themselves in pursuit of any goal.

(D) would be on the right track if it said that horror films are beneficial to film critics *despite* their dislike of such films. But saying that horror films are successful because other people enjoy them is another idea entirely.

(E) says that the sleepiness that many people dislike must be acceptable to those who experience it. But that's different from saying that the sleepiness actually benefits them.

8. (E) Paradox (EXCEPT)

Step 1: Identify the Question Type
This is a Paradox question because it asks for an answer that resolves a discrepancy in the stimulus. However, eliminate such answers in this case because this is an EXCEPT question. The right answer will be a fact that doesn't help resolve the paradox.

Step 2: Untangle the Stimulus
Despite the fact that, on average, Springfield residents live farther from their places of employment than Rorchester residents do from theirs, the demand for public transportation is not necessarily higher in Springfield, because Springfield has only half as many bus routes as does Rorchester.

Step 3: Make a Prediction
As the stimulus suggests, one would expect Springfield to have more bus lines. Find a reason why Springfield would have fewer. Any answer that shows why Springfield residents wouldn't need additional lines would do the trick. Before checking out the choices, characterize the choices. There will be four that will help resolve this discrepancy and one that will not. That odd man out will be the correct answer.

Step 4: Evaluate the Answer Choices
(E) does not help resolve the paradox. If Springfield's population were larger than Rorchester's, one would expect there to be higher demand for city services such as public transportation. So, **(E)** deepens the mystery rather than resolving it.

(A) resolves the paradox. If three-quarters of Springfield's residents are commuting to the same workplace every day, then they could all get to work on the same bus route, and Springfield wouldn't need nearly as many bus routes to make sure that everyone gets to work.

(B) resolves the paradox by suggesting that Springfield residents don't need public transportation because they can drive to work.

(C) resolves the paradox by suggesting that Springfield residents rely more heavily on their railway system than their bus system to get around town, thereby explaining the lower demand for bus lines.

(D) resolves the paradox by suggesting that the few bus routes that do exist in Springfield come more often and travel farther. So, Springfield's bus system could transport more people to locations that are farther away despite not having as many bus routes as Rorchester.

9. (E) Flaw

Step 1: Identify the Question Type
The phrase "vulnerable to criticism" indicates that this is a Flaw question, but read on to find a clue to the flaw: The argument fails to consider some possibility. So keep this in mind as you untangle the argument and predict the answer.

Step 2: Untangle the Stimulus
Fat substitutes such as N5 are often used by people who need to reduce their fat intake. But the argument concludes that these fat substitutes are useless. In studies cited as evidence, subjects who ate foods prepared with N5 ended up hungrier afterward than after eating foods prepared with real fat and ate more to quell that hunger, consuming more calories than they saved by eating N5 in the first place.

Step 3: Make a Prediction
Remember from the question stem that the argument fails to consider a possibility. The conclusion that N5 is useless is quite strong, and not necessarily proven by the evidence. After all, N5 isn't supposed to be a *calorie* substitute, just a *fat* substitute. So, what if the subjects in the study, after eating food prepared with N5, moved on to eat other food that contained more calories but didn't contain any fat? Then N5 has done its job as a fat substitute, and it isn't useless, as the argument alleges.

Step 4: Evaluate the Answer Choices
(E) is another way of phrasing the overlooked possibility predicted. Even if people's total caloric intake doesn't decrease, N5 can still be useful, as long as people's fat intake decreases.

(A) is irrelevant to the argument. Even if only one or two foods can be prepared with N5, that has no bearing on whether or not it's useful as a fat substitute.

(B) introduces side effects, which are Out of Scope. The author is only concerned with N5's effectiveness as a fat substitute.

(C) isn't a possibility that the author needs to consider. The argument here is that N5 doesn't actually reduce a person's fat intake because it could increase that person's overall caloric intake. Whether or not people who consume N5 pay attention to their caloric intake doesn't matter in the studies.

(D) might need to be considered if the author were trying to argue that people who want to reduce their fat intake should remain unaware that N5 is calorie-free. But for the purposes of this argument, whether or not they know that N5 contains no calories isn't relevant. The point is that people who consume N5 consume more calories later than they saved by eating the N5-prepared foods.

10. (B) Inference
Step 1: Identify the Question Type
The stem indicates that the stimulus is a set of statements, not an argument, and that those statements will support the right answer. Those are both strong indications that this is an Inference question.

Step 2: Untangle the Stimulus
The music historian points out that some critics think that the poverty of postwar recording studios was bad for bebop because it forced them to record short solos. But the historian believes that the concise nature of these recordings makes them superb artistic works and contributed to a conciseness in the musicians' live playing as well.

Step 3: Make a Prediction
There's no Formal Logic in these statements, and not very many connections can be made between the statements. So, proceed directly to the choices, keeping in mind that the correct answer is a statement that is strongly supported by the music historian's statements.

Step 4: Evaluate the Answer Choices
(B) is directly supported because it accurately summarizes the historian's main points. If, as a result of the impoverished postwar recording conditions, bebop musicians recorded solos that survive as superb artistic works and that brought a worthwhile conciseness to their live solos, then the bad conditions seem to have had some beneficial consequences.

(A) is unsupported because the historian doesn't suggest that representations of live solos have no artistic value at all; he merely suggests that they are not comparable to the recorded solos.

(C) is Extreme due to the word *always*. The historian indicates that the conciseness of these recorded solos is of value, but this isn't to say that short recordings are invariably better than longer ones. That's too broad a statement to be supported by this stimulus.

(D) similarly uses the misleading word *overall*. The live music of the generation immediately following bebop does lack the compactness of early bebop musicians' live music, but this is

just one factor contributing to the overall quality of these musicians' work.

(E) says that difficult recording conditions are necessary for the recording of short solos, an idea that is completely unsupported by the stimulus. The difficult conditions contributed to the shortness of the solos, but perhaps other conditions could have just as easily caused early bebop musicians to record short solos.

11. (A) Flaw
Step 1: Identify the Question Type
Any question stem asking for a "reasoning flaw" is a Flaw question.

Step 2: Untangle the Stimulus
The argument concludes that there's no causal connection between damage to human chromosome number six and adult schizophrenia. This conclusion is supported by a perceived lack of correlation between the two phenomena: Some people without damage to the chromosome still develop schizophrenia, and some people who do have chromosomal damage don't develop schizophrenia.

Step 3: Make a Prediction
At first, the argument might seem logically sound. But notice how broad and declarative the conclusion is. It's entirely possible for there to be a specific site on human chromosome number six that, if damaged, could lead to schizophrenia. Perhaps some people have damage on the chromosome that isn't on that specific site, and that's why they don't have schizophrenia. That could explain the findings cited in the argument while still leaving room for a causal connection between chromosomal damage and adult schizophrenia. So, the argument's flaw is that it isn't specific enough. It draws too broad a conclusion because it doesn't allow for the possibility of schizophrenia being causally linked to some types of chromosomal damage, but not others.

Step 4: Evaluate the Answer Choices
(A) matches this prediction perfectly.

(B) is Extreme. The argument never presumes that chromosomal damage is the *only* possible cause of schizophrenia. As a matter of fact, the author is trying to sever that causal link, so the argument wouldn't assume that there was such a link.

(C) is unsupported. There's nothing in the argument to suggest that the sample of people studied is unrepresentative of the general population.

(D) is also unsupported. The argument doesn't assert that schizophrenia causes damage to chromosome number six, nor does it assert that damage to chromosome number six causes schizophrenia. The argument doesn't acknowledge causes or effects at all.

(E) describes a flaw that the argument is trying to avoid. The argument works hard to show that there is no causation between schizophrenia and chromosomal damage despite the presence of correlation between the two.

12. (D) Assumption (Sufficient)

Step 1: Identify the Question Type
The stem says that one of the choices, if assumed, will make the conclusion follow from the evidence. That means this is a Sufficient Assumption question.

Step 2: Untangle the Stimulus
The councilperson's conclusion is that the edifice that the art commission wants to purchase qualifies as art. The evidence is that the edifice has caused experts to debate what constitutes art, and that causing such a debate is the purpose of art.

Step 3: Make a Prediction
Notice the Mismatched Concepts between the evidence and the conclusion of this argument. The evidence mentions that the edifice *fulfills the purpose* of art. But the conclusion suddenly asserts that the edifice *is actually* art. There's a difference here. The purpose of an umbrella is to shield me from the rain. A plastic sheet held over my head could fulfill that same purpose, but that doesn't automatically make a plastic sheet an umbrella. So, the councilperson assumes here that anything that fulfills art's purpose qualifies as art.

Step 4: Evaluate the Answer Choices
(D) is a clear match for the prediction.

(A) says that causing debate among experts is necessary for something to qualify as art. But to enable the conclusion to follow directly from the evidence, **(A)** would need to say that causing debate among experts is *sufficient* for something to qualify as art. Then the edifice would be art just by virtue of the debate it inspired, and nothing else.

(B), if assumed, would mean that no expert would be certain that the edifice qualifies as art. So, that would make it even more difficult to establish the councilperson's conclusion that the edifice does qualify as art.

(C) would enable the councilperson to conclude that no city resident should oppose the art commission's purchase of the edifice, because the edifice does actually fulfill the purpose of art. But the conclusion of the argument is that the edifice qualifies as art, and **(C)** alone doesn't establish that conclusion.

(E) doesn't help link the evidence to the conclusion because the conclusion itself is that the edifice qualifies as art. **(E)** doesn't help prove that because it's contingent upon the conclusion already being true.

13. (B) Main Point

Step 1: Identify the Question Type
Because the correct answer expresses the conclusion of the stimulus, this is a Main Point question.

Step 2: Untangle the Stimulus
The first sentence cites an established premise: To be intriguing, one has to continually stimulate the curiosity of others. The next sentence claims that one way to do that is to constantly broaden one's abilities and intellectual reach. The final sentence says that expanding one's mind makes it impossible to be totally understood, thereby maintaining one's aura of mystery.

Step 3: Make a Prediction
To predict the answer to a Main Point question, find the choice that fulfills the One-Sentence Test. In other words, if only one of these sentences could be used to express the author's main idea, which sentence would it be? The last sentence begins with [*f*]*or,* an Evidence Keyword, and it seems to be providing support for why expanding one's mind would stimulate curiosity in others. The first sentence begins with "it is a given that," which probably means that the first sentence is providing a commonly held belief that will be used as a jumping-off point for the conclusion. That leaves the middle sentence, which is the main point because it's the author's recommendation for how to inspire the perpetual curiosity of others.

Step 4: Evaluate the Answer Choices
(B) is an adequate paraphrase of the middle sentence and, thus, the correct answer.

(A) paraphrases the first sentence, which is provided as an already established fact. A fact that is already a given doesn't need to be proven in an argument, and therefore wouldn't be the main point of an author's reasoning.

(C) paraphrases the last sentence, which begins with an Evidence Keyword ([*f*]*or*) and which provides support to the middle sentence.

(D) is a Distortion of the middle sentence, which says that broadening one's abilities is sufficient to inspire the perpetual curiosity of others. **(D)** says that broadening one's abilities is necessary, which is a totally different idea.

(E) changes the idea of inspiring curiosity in others to inspiring curiosity in oneself, which is not a concern in this argument.

14. (D) Assumption (Necessary)

Step 1: Identify the Question Type
This is a Necessary Assumption question, because it calls for an "assumption required by the argument."

Step 2: Untangle the Stimulus

The conclusion is that film producers make films that theater managers will find attractive to younger audiences. The evidence for this is that film producers want their film to be shown as widely as possible, and the managers of the theaters that show the films will show only those films that they believe will turn a profit.

Step 3: Make a Prediction

Finding the central assumption in an argument is, at its most basic, a matter of bridging together Mismatched Concepts from evidence to conclusion. In the evidence, it's said that film producers only have a shot at getting their films shown at theaters if the managers are convinced that the films will turn a profit. In the conclusion, it says that film producers will therefore make films that theater managers are convinced will appeal to younger audiences. Connect the idea of profitable films to films directed at younger audiences. Therefore, the author must be assuming that theater managers consider films that attract younger audiences more profitable on the whole than other films.

Step 4: Evaluate the Answer Choices

(D) is a clear match for this prediction. It correctly bridges the Mismatched Concepts between the evidence and the conclusion.

(A) doesn't hold up to the Denial Test. Even if adults consume *more* of the foods and beverages sold at movie concession stands than do either children or adolescents, that doesn't necessarily mean that they'll be buying enough of those foods to yield a profit. Besides, food-and-beverage concession revenue is just a part of the profit, and not the primary focus of this argument.

(B) need not be true in order for the argument to work. The theater managers are only concerned with whether the films they show appeal to younger audiences. The films don't have to appeal *exclusively* to younger audiences, though; they could also appeal to older audiences, and the managers would surely just consider this icing on the cake.

(C) blows up a detail of the argument. Food- and-beverage concession revenue is mentioned as a part of the overall revenue, but in order for this argument to work, it doesn't need to be true that concession stands generate more revenue than ticket sales to the films themselves.

(E) is a Distortion. Films that appeal to older audiences don't have to be flops in order for this argument to work; it need only be true that films geared toward younger audiences are generally more profitable than other films, in a relative sense.

15. (D) Inference

Step 1: Identify the Question Type

The stem asks you to accept all the statements in the stimulus as true and then determine the choice that must be true on the basis of them. That makes this an Inference question.

Step 2: Untangle the Stimulus

Genetic research funding only comes from two sources: Government exclusively funds most research, and the rest is funded exclusively by corporations. Research can't proceed without funding from one of these two sources. Also, almost all advances in that research create ethical dilemmas.

Step 3: Make a Prediction

If an immediate pre-phrase of the correct answer doesn't come to mind, proceed directly to the choices, prepared to eliminate any choice that doesn't have to be true based on the stimulus.

Step 4: Evaluate the Answer Choices

(D) may seem obvious, but that's a good sign. Because government or corporate funding is necessary for genetic research, then any advances in genetic research (and the ethical dilemmas that arise from them) are made possible only with the help of that funding.

(A) is a Distortion. The stimulus says that government is the "exclusive source of most genetic research." The rest of the research is funded solely by corporations. However, it's unclear whether *advances* are more likely to come from government-funded or corporate-funded research.

(B) is a Distortion. Most genetic research is funded by the government, and most advances in genetic research give rise to ethical dilemmas, but that doesn't mean that *most* government-funded research leads to advances that give rise to ethical dilemmas.

(C) is unsupported. The stimulus indicates that funding can come from government or corporations. However, it's possible that all of the advances come from government research.

(E) doesn't have to be true, because the stimulus doesn't say that government funding is what is responsible for the ethical dilemmas in genetic research.

16. (E) Assumption (Necessary)

Step 1: Identify the Question Type

This is a Necessary Assumption question, because it asks for the "assumption required by the argument."

Step 2: Untangle the Stimulus

The conclusion is that sometimes, a business needs to become a different corporation to survive. The evidence indicates that businesses need to adapt to survive, and that sometimes, adaptation requires a change in a business's corporate philosophy.

Step 3: Make a Prediction

Connect the terms between the evidence and the conclusion to find the central assumption. The evidence says that survival requires adaptation, which sometimes requires changing the corporate philosophy of a business. The conclusion says that survival requires a business becoming a different corporation. The idea of changing corporate philosophy (from the evidence) needs to be connected to the idea of becoming a different corporation (from the conclusion), so the proper assumption here is that changing a business's corporate philosophy must necessarily change it into a different corporation.

Step 4: Evaluate the Answer Choices

(E) matches the unmatched terms in the argument and also matches the prediction of the central assumption.

(A) is a Distortion of the evidence, which says that sometimes, in order to adapt and survive, a business has to change its corporate philosophy. But **(A)** goes too far by saying that all businesses have to change their corporate philosophies in order to survive. Also, **(A)** doesn't incorporate the idea of becoming a different corporation, which was the new term in the conclusion.

(B) suffers from the same deficiency. It doesn't discuss a business becoming a different corporation, so there's no way to reach the conclusion from the evidence if we assume **(B)**.

(C) is on the right track, but it reverses the logic. To reach the conclusion, you need an assumption saying that changing a business's corporate philosophy necessarily means becoming a different corporation. **(C)** says that becoming a different corporation means changing the corporate philosophy. This reversal allows for the possibility of changing the corporate philosophy without necessarily changing the corporation.

(D) is at odds with the part of the argument that says that a business's survival sometimes depends on changing its corporate philosophy. Also, **(D)** has nothing to do with a business becoming a different corporation, so it doesn't allow the conclusion to be reached from the evidence.

17. (B) Paradox

Step 1: Identify the Question Type

Because there is an apparent conflict in the stimulus that needs to be resolved by the correct answer, this is a Paradox question.

Step 2: Untangle the Stimulus

The paradox concerns the results of two surveys given ten years apart to the residents of area L. In the first survey, residents reported satisfaction with their living conditions despite those conditions being below their country's average. In the second survey, even though area L's living conditions were now the same as the national average, residents reported dissatisfaction with those conditions.

Step 3: Make a Prediction

In a Paradox question, make sure you are clear on exactly what the paradox is so that you know when you've found the answer that resolves it. Here, find a choice that explains how residents of area L appeared more satisfied with their below-average living conditions than with living conditions that were on par with the rest of the country.

Step 4: Evaluate the Answer Choices

(B) resolves the paradox. If the average living conditions nationwide took a dip between the two surveys, then it's possible that the living conditions in area L (which now match that average) also took a dip. This would explain the dissatisfaction of area L residents during the second survey.

(A) would explain why the responses of area L might differ from those of another area with similar living conditions, but it doesn't explain why the responses of area L seem to have changed for the worse despite an apparent improvement in living conditions.

(C) has no bearing on the mystery at hand because it doesn't matter how the survey's designers define optimal living conditions.

(D) doesn't help resolve the paradox because the residents of area L appear to consider their situation in need of improvement even after a supposed improvement in living conditions.

(E) would explain why residents of area L appeared satisfied with below-average living conditions, but it doesn't explain why they would be dissatisfied with living conditions that match the national average.

18. (C) Flaw

Step 1: Identify the Question Type

This is a Flaw question because you're asked to identify a reason why the travel agent's reasoning is open to criticism.

Step 2: Untangle the Stimulus

The travel agent concludes that passengers are safer on a major airline than on a new low-fare airline. This is apparently because major airlines have been around long enough to have longstanding, reliable records indicating their degree of safety, and the newer airlines have not been around as long.

Step 3: Make a Prediction

Just because a major airline has more safety records doesn't mean that those records actually indicate a higher degree of safety. The longstanding, reliable records that the travel agent cites could actually be quite damning when it comes to a major airline's overall safety. So, it appears that the travel agent is overlooking the possibility that a major airline's longstanding, reliable records could point to a dangerously low level of safety. With that possibility taken into account, the argument is seriously impaired.

Step 4: Evaluate the Answer Choices

(C) matches the overlooked possibility at the heart of the travel agent's flawed argument.

(A), if considered as a possibility, would actually make the argument more persuasive. If major airlines have been around longer than most low-fare airlines but still have the same number of accidents, then it would stand to reason that the major airlines are safer on average than the newer low-fare airlines.

(B) is a 180. The stimulus does indicate that very few low-fare airlines have been around long enough to reliably establish a safety record. However, the stimulus also says that the major airlines have long-standing and reliable safety records. So, it is incorrect to say *each* are from "too brief a period."

(D) isn't assumed by the travel agent. In order for her argument to work, it needn't be true that the safest airlines have to have the most reliable records. It need only be true that having reliable records indicates that an airline is safer than an airline without reliable records. However, among airlines that do have reliable records, the safety rankings can vary.

(E) doesn't need to be considered by the travel agent. She isn't arguing that the major airlines are completely accident-free, but that the major airlines are comparatively safer than the newer low-fare airlines. This could still be proven even if the major airlines have had one or two accidents.

19. (D) Assumption (Necessary)

Step 1: Identify the Question Type

The stem asks for the "assumption required" by the argument, so this is a Necessary Assumption question.

Step 2: Untangle the Stimulus

The economist's conclusion (signaled by [*t*]*hus*) is that the economy would improve if the government were to lower income taxes. The evidence is that the current weak state of the economy is caused by reluctance on the part of consumers to spend their money. That reluctance has been made worse by the fact that the average income has lowered significantly over the past five years.

Step 3: Make a Prediction

When an argument concludes with a prediction, you can often find the assumption if you ask yourself, "what would have to happen in order for that prediction to come true?" In order for lowering income taxes to actually help the economy improve, it would have to be true that lower income taxes would alleviate the reluctance of consumers to spend their money. After all, it's that reluctance that's keeping the economy from improving. Apparently, the economist assumes that lowering the income tax will remove that impediment.

Step 4: Evaluate the Answer Choices

(D) matches the prediction perfectly. If you're unsure, use the Denial Test. Let's say that, contrary to **(D)**, consumers wouldn't be less reluctant to spend money even if their income taxes were lowered. If that's true, then there's no reason to lower the income tax because the cause of the weak economy would still be there. So because the argument can't work without **(D)**, it must be the central assumption.

(A) isn't necessary to the argument because it has nothing to do with income taxes, which are what the economist says will affect the economy.

(B) gets it backward. The argument says that lower average income is part of what's keeping consumers from spending their money. Reversing that causal relationship isn't necessary to make the argument work. In order to establish the economist's conclusion, it needs to be true that lowering income taxes will increase the average income enough to make consumers more willing to spend money and strengthen the economy.

(C) indicates that the problem of the weak economy may worsen if income taxes stay where they are, but this isn't the same as indicating that lowering income taxes is all the government needs to do to improve the economy (which is what the economist is arguing in the first place).

(E) discusses government spending, which doesn't figure in the argument at all. The economist is concerned with consumer spending.

20. (E) Inference

Step 1: Identify the Question Type

Any question asking for a choice that must be true is an Inference question.

Step 2: Untangle the Stimulus

A recent experiment put people with two different lipid profiles, type A and type B, on a low-fat diet. A type B lipid profile puts a person at a much greater risk of heart disease than does a type A profile. On the diet, the type B volunteers saw a drop in their cholesterol levels, but the type A volunteers saw no benefit, and some of the type A volunteers actually shifted to type B profiles after being on the diet.

Step 3: Make a Prediction

It may not be worth considering every possible pre-phrase to an Inference question, because many things must be true on the basis of a given set of facts. Instead, proceed directly to the choices, keeping in mind that you should proceed through the choices until finding one that *must* be true based on the stimulus.

Step 4: Evaluate the Answer Choices

(E) must be true. If people with type B lipid profiles have higher risk of heart disease than people with type A profiles, then it must be true that switching from a type A profile to a type B profile would indicate an increase in one's risk of heart disease. The stimulus confirms that this happened to some of the type A volunteers in the experiment after they were put on the low-fat diet.

(A) is certainly not a valid inference. As a matter of fact, 40 percent of the type A volunteers switched to type B profiles, which means that their risk of heart disease increased. And the type B volunteers kept the same profile, which suggests that all of them may have maintained the same level of risk.

(B) is a Distortion. The stimulus does say that a person with a type B profile is at greater risk of heart disease than a person with a type A profile, but this isn't necessarily because a type B person has a higher cholesterol level. And just because people with type B profiles experienced a drop in cholesterol levels doesn't mean they started at levels higher than people with type A profiles.

(C) is Out of Scope. Nothing can be inferred about the other changes that the volunteers in the experiment made to their lifestyles.

(D) is a Distortion. The only people in the study who changed their lipid profiles were type A volunteers, and there's nothing in the stimulus that indicates that their cholesterol levels went down; the stimulus only indicates that happened for the type B volunteers.

21. (C) Principle (Apply/Inference)

Step 1: Identify the Question Type
The word *principle* in the stem indicates a Principle question, but read more closely to find the exact task. Here, the broad, law-like principle will be in the stimulus, and you'll need to find the narrow choice that is the correct application of the principle. So, this is an Apply the Principle question.

Step 2: Untangle the Stimulus
The columnist's principle, in a nutshell, is that the presence of total freedom of thought and expression is no excuse to profit from exploiting depraved popular tastes.

Step 3: Make a Prediction
It's impossible to say with any certainty what form the correct answer will take. Just know that it will be an instance of the principle being applied in a more specific context.

Step 4: Evaluate the Answer Choices
(C), like the stimulus, is in favor of complete freedom of expression when it comes to publishing. Also, **(C)** says that this freedom does not give publishers *carte blanche* to attempt to profit from pandering to depraved tastes, which is exactly the qualification provided in the stimulus.

(A) cites a condition under which freedom of expression should not be guaranteed. The stimulus advocates unfettered

freedom of thought. Also, **(A)** contains no element of profit from exploiting depravity.

(B) also doesn't contain an element of profit or attempted profit, so it's missing a crucial part of the principle in the stimulus.

(D) leaves the door open for the government to intervene in the freedom of production of certain recordings, which flies in the face of the unconditional freedom of expression advocated by the columnist.

(E) merely cautions against criticism of statements that exhibit depravity. The columnist doesn't touch this issue; the stimulus says that freedom of thought doesn't necessarily relieve people of their moral responsibility to refrain from profiting from depravity.

22. (C) Assumption (Necessary)

Step 1: Identify the Question Type
The question stem asks for an assumption on which the argument depends, so this is a Necesary Assumption question.

Step 2: Untangle the Stimulus
The conclusion is signaled by the word [t]hus: The rate at which a society changes can be measured by monitoring the amount of deference that the young show to the old. The evidence indicates that the rate of change in a society is inversely proportional to the value that its younger members find in the advice of its older members.

Step 3: Make a Prediction
Whenever the conclusion of an argument introduces a new term not mentioned in the evidence, look for the central assumption to use that term. Here, the new term is *deference*. The evidence only discusses the value that young people find in the advice of older people. In order to make the argument work, the author must be assuming that there's some sort of connection between the two; in other words, the assumption is that the deference that young people show to their elders is a function of how much they value their elders' advice.

Step 4: Evaluate the Answer Choices
(C) is the clearest match for the prediction and is quite necessary in order for the argument to be logically cohesive.

(A) is a Distortion. The argument doesn't depend on the younger members of a society being conscious of the society's rate of change. Besides, **(A)** doesn't allow the author to reach a conclusion about deference.

(B) may be tempting, but it distorts the author's evidence. According the argument, young people don't value advice that they *think* is irrelevant to them. However, just because they think it's irrelevant doesn't mean that it actually is. The concept we need to connect to deference is the perceived value (or perceived usefulness), not the actual value (or actual usefulness).

(D) is all but stated in the evidence, so it isn't something the author really assumes implicitly. Also, **(D)** has nothing to do with deference, which is another reason to eliminate it.

(E) is Out of Scope. The stimulus does not distinguish between practical and impractical advice. Furthermore, **(E)** doesn't allow the author to reach a conclusion about deference, and can be eliminated on that basis alone.

23. (C) Principle (Identify/Assumption)

Step 1: Identify the Question Type
This stem uses the word *principles*, which makes this a Principle question. Because the question stem indicates there is a recommendation in the stimulus, the politician must use reasoning to reach that recommendation. Hence, the correct answer will be a principle assumed by the politician in reaching that recommendation.

Step 2: Untangle the Stimulus
The politician's recommendation is to impose a tariff to raise the price of imported fruit to more than that of domestic fruit. She defends this recommendation by discussing the consequences of inaction: Foreign growers will outcompete domestic growers, whose farmland will subsequently be converted to more lucrative uses. This will ultimately result in the disappearance of a unique way of life.

Step 3: Make a Prediction
Find a broad, law-like rule governing the politician's recommendation. Even though she admits that foreign growers can grow fruit that is both better in quality and cheaper to grow, she still recommends making it more expensive, presumably to spur people to buy more domestic fruit. Clearly, for this politician, the cost of not imposing a tariff (the loss of a unique way of life) is great enough that she wishes to encourage domestic farmers to continue growing fruit, despite the fact that they can't do it as cheaply as foreign growers. So the principle here should be something like, "Economic concerns are sometimes outweighed by societal concerns."

Step 4: Evaluate the Answer Choices
(C) is the only choice that properly encapsulates the rule guiding the politician's reasoning.

(A) is a 180. The politician isn't too worried about what's best for her country's economic interest, because she advocates that farmers continue growing fruit even though it's less economically efficient than just importing fruit.

(B) has two problems. The use of *always* indicates that the politician would apply this rule to every conceivable situation, which is a bit Extreme. Furthermore, it isn't just the interests

of producers that motivate the politician. She's trying to ensure that society at large still retains this one unique way of life.

(D) discusses the citizens of other countries, who don't figure too prominently in the politician's argument. She doesn't want a tariff because her country's citizens should come before the citizens of other countries; she wants a tariff because preserving a way of life in her country comes before making the most economically advantageous choices.

(E) is a 180 because the politician recommends using government intervention to continue an economically *inefficient* farming practice in her country.

24. (E) Weaken

Step 1: Identify the Question Type
Any question asking for something that *undermines* the argument is a Weaken question.

Step 2: Untangle the Stimulus
The argument concludes that the bear population in the Abbimac Valley will increase if the road through the Kiffer Forest Preserve is kept closed. The evidence for this is that during the eight years that the road has been closed, the bear population in the preserve, which houses most of the bears living in the Abbimac Valley, has nearly doubled.

Step 3: Make a Prediction
There's a subtle scope shift here that is the key to the entire argument. The conclusion is that the bear population in the valley as a whole will increase if the road is kept closed. This is based on evidence that the population in the preserve has increased after the road was closed. This argument assumes that the closing of the road contributed to an increase in the bear population of the entire valley, but all that's been demonstrated is that the preserve's population has increased. So, if you find a choice that says that the increase in the preserve's population doesn't necessarily translate to an increase in the population throughout the valley, then the prediction that ends the argument will be considerably weakened.

Step 4: Evaluate the Answer Choices
(E) undermines the argument because it suggests that the increase in the preserve population was due to migration from other parts of the valley rather than an actual increase in the overall number of bears. This impairs the author's ability to rely on the preserve population increase as an indicator that the valley's overall population will increase.

(A) is close, but it doesn't go far enough to weaken the argument. If the increase in the preserve's bear population was due to migration *from outside the valley*, then the argument isn't weakened at all.

(B) leaves the door open for a large part of the preserve's population increase to have been caused by migration from bears living outside the valley, or perhaps a reproductive boom within the preserve. Such a situation would actually strengthen the argument.

(C) doesn't hurt the argument. Even if a small fraction of the increase in the preserve's bear population is due to migration from outside the valley, then it's still entirely possible for the road to have encouraged that migration from outside, thereby increasing the overall population of the valley.

(D) is insufficient to weaken the argument. Without information on how much the population outside the preserve has decreased, **(D)** doesn't affect the argument. If the growth of the preserve population far outpaces the decline in the non-preserve population, then the overall population of the valley will still increase, and the argument is untouched.

25. (A) Assumption (Sufficient)

Step 1: Identify the Question Type
The stem asks for the choice that, if assumed, would make the conclusion follow from the evidence, so this is a Sufficient Assumption question.

Step 2: Untangle the Stimulus
The ultimate conclusion of the argument is that all made-to-measure wigs should be dry-cleaned. There are four key pieces of evidence. Wigs with handmade components are more expensive than those with none; made-to-measure wigs range in price from medium-priced to expensive; wigs that don't use human hair don't have handmade foundations; and wigs that do contain human hair should be dry-cleaned.

Step 3: Make a Prediction
Words like *if*, *any*, and *all* in the stimulus are clear signs that Formal Logic is present here. When you have many pieces of evidence with these Keywords, turn them into Formal Logic statements and try to string them together. This will help you see where the gap is. The four pieces of evidence as Formal Logic statements are:

If	handmade components	→	more expensive than without

If	made-to-measure	→	ranges from medium-priced to expensive

If	~ human hair used	→	~ handmade foundation

If	human hair used	→	should be dry-cleaned

The conclusion can be translated to:

If	made-to-measure	→	should be dry-cleaned

If you contrapose the third piece of evidence, you can connect that to the fourth piece:

If	handmade foundation	→	human hair used	→	should be dry-cleaned

If	made-to-measure	→	ranges from medium-priced to expensive	→	handmade foundation	→	human hair used	→	should be dry-cleaned

The assumption, therefore, is that all wigs ranging from medium-priced to expensive have handmade foundations. That, if true, will make it logically necessary for made-to-measure wigs to be dry-cleaned.

Step 4: Evaluate the Answer Choices
(A) is a direct match for the prediction.

(B) provides no connection to made-to-measure wigs, so it can't help establish the conclusion from the evidence.

(C) simply combines the Formal Logic of the evidence, but it still fails to connect made-to-measure wigs to the logic and therefore doesn't help establish the conclusion.

(D) comes close, but the evidence says that made-to-measure wigs are priced at least in the medium range. **(D)** would establish that wigs with handmade foundations are similarly priced, but this doesn't guarantee that made-to-measure wigs have handmade foundations. They could be two totally different types of wigs that just happen to be similarly priced.

(E) also doesn't properly establish a connection between made-to-measure wigs and handmade foundations.

26. (A) Method of Argument

Step 1: Identify the Question Type

The stem is less interested in the content of the philosopher's argument than the structure. Whenever a stem asks *how* the author's argument is structured, you're dealing with a Method of Argument question.

Step 2: Untangle the Stimulus

The philosopher argues against denying that animals have rights on the grounds that only humans can follow moral rules. To support this argument, he points to the fact that wolves, along with foxes and domesticated dogs, don't tolerate an attack by one wolf on another if the latter wolf has already demonstrated submission.

Step 3: Make a Prediction

Remember that Method of Argument questions are much more interested in the how of an argument than in the *what*. So focus on how the philosopher structures his argument. His conclusion is a challenge to a premise that's used to deny that animals have rights (that premise being that animals don't follow moral rules). He supports that challenge with a set of examples of animals who behave as though they do recognize moral rules.

Step 4: Evaluate the Answer Choices

(A) matches the prediction perfectly. The philosopher provides counterexamples (those of the wolves, dogs, and foxes) to refute the premise that only humans are capable of following moral rules.

(B) is off the mark. The philosopher isn't trying to prove that all animals possess morality. He just cites isolated examples of certain animals that may behave according to some sort of moral code.

(C) is a Distortion. The philosopher isn't trying to undermine morality as a basis for being worthy of rights. He's merely arguing that if it is a basis for being worthy of rights, then we can't count animals out, because they seem to behave as though they have some rudimentary sense of morality.

(D) is a misrepresentation. The philosopher isn't trying to establish a claim. He's trying to refute a claim. Also, there's no contradiction exposed in his argument.

(E) is a 180. If anything, the philosopher is trying to show that the concept of morality is applied too narrowly by introducing examples of animals that also seem to possess a moral sense.

Section II: Reading Comprehension
Passage 1: Archaeology of Textiles

Q#	Question Type	Correct	Difficulty
1	Global	B	★★★
2	Inference	E	★
3	Detail	E	★
4	Inference	D	★★
5	Global	C	★
6	Detail	E	★
7	Logic Function	A	★

Passage 2: Emeagwali's Computer Innovations

Q#	Question Type	Correct	Difficulty
8	Global	D	★★
9	Detail	C	★
10	Inference	A	★★
11	Logic Function	B	★★
12	Logic Reasoning (Strengthen)	A	★
13	Inference	E	★★★★

Passage 3: Tangible-Object Theory

Q#	Question Type	Correct	Difficulty
14	Global	B	★★
15	Detail	A	★★
16	Detail	B	★★★
17	Inference	A	★★
18	Inference	E	★★★★
19	Inference	C	★★★
20	Inference	D	★★★

Passage 4: Music's Effects and Emotions

Q#	Question Type	Correct	Difficulty
21	Detail	E	★★
22	Inference	C	★
23	Logic Reasoning (Parallel Reasoning)	B	★★★
24	Global	A	★★
25	Logic Reasoning (Weaken)	C	★
26	Global	B	★
27	Inference	D	★★★

Passage 1: Archaeology of Textiles

Step 1: Read the Passage Strategically
Sample Roadmap

line #	Keyword/phrase	¶ Margin notes
1	Traditional	Trad. arch. sources remains/text
4	however; little	Not useful for textile research
6	particularly unavailing	
7	thwarted	
9	until recently; discarded	
10	useless	Why
12	meanwhile	
13	moreover	
14	Yet despite	
15	obstacles; great deal	Still—researchers learned a lot
16	also	
20	much more	Tech. advances helped
21	especially	
22	Successful	
28	important	Arch. changed as a science
29–30	Once little more	
32	transformed	
34	fundamental precept	
35	even	Keep everything
36	Thus	Results
43	also advanced; :	Also learn about production
46	valuable	
47	For example	
49	in fact	
50	Similarly	Ex. Statue of Athena
54	Because	
56	assumed	
57	But	
59	in fact	

Discussion

Paragraph 1 introduces the **Topic** of the passage, the archaeology of textiles. Initially, the author discusses the *traditional* archaeological sources—remains and texts—which provide limited information for researchers. The remains are quite troubling for ancient textile production researchers due to the perishable nature of cloth. Now, the author starts to set up a current problem: These sources are not particularly useful for textile research, though researchers have been able to learn a lot about ancient textile production. At this point, a good strategic reader will anticipate that the author is going to address this problem in more depth or elaborate on the potential solution indicated by the Contrast Keywords "yet, despite …"

Sure enough, the first sentence of Paragraph 2 confirms the author's **Scope**: recent advances in the analysis of remains have yielded a great deal more information than researchers had before. Next, the author lists several modern methods of analysis that have proven successful. The author asserts that the field of archaeology has philosophically become more focused on itself as a science, even going so far as to preserve all objects regardless of noticeable value. The author finishes off the paragraph with an example of how researchers were able to find the oldest known complete garment from a heap of dirty linens preserved well before anyone began the study of ancient textile production. At this point, the author's **Purpose** should be clearer: to explain and illustrate how much archaeology now knows about ancient textile production.

Paragraph 3 continues with another example of how the study of ancient textile production has been aided by these recent research developments, but in a different way. Researchers can now recreate the processes of ancient textile production as a valuable way to test hypotheses. The two examples at the end of the paragraph—proper ID of looming weights that had long been disregarded and proper ID of production time for the Athena statue dress—serve to further reinforce the author's **Main Idea**—technological and philosophical changes in archaeology have made big gains in knowledge of ancient textile production.

1. (B) Global

Step 2: Identify the Question Type
The phrase "main point" identifies this question as a Global question. A quick review of the Roadmap and brief paraphrase of the author's main points is all that is needed to confidently ascertain the correct answer choice.

Step 3: Research the Relevant Text
Because Global questions do not point you to one part of the passage in particular, you'll need to call upon your Roadmap for a review of the passage in its entirety.

Step 4: Make a Prediction
Take a brief moment to take stock of what you just read. There is little evidence for archaeologists studying ancient textile production. However, by studying a variety of new advances, researchers have been able to gain much more knowledge about ancient textiles and how they were produced.

Step 5: Evaluate the Answer Choices
(B) echoes that sentiment.

(A) is Extreme. The author never goes so far as to credit the entire discipline of archaeology with advancements. Rather, the author stays focused on the advancements in research concerning the archaeology of textiles.

(C) is a Faulty Use of Detail. Although it's a great summary of the author's points in paragraph 3, this question calls for a statement that encompasses the entire passage, not just one paragraph.

(D), like **(A)** is Extreme. The author is focused on the advancements in research concerning the archaeology of textiles, but makes no claims of "sweeping changes."

(E) focuses too closely on one detail in the passage. It also goes too far in attributing "most significant findings" to the advancements in reconstruction techniques.

2. (E) Inference

Step 2: Identify the Question Type
In this Inference question, you'll need to glean the author's tone toward the history of ancient textile production from context within the passage.

Step 3: Research the Relevant Text
A brief review of the end of paragraph 1, along with the first sentences in paragraphs 2 and 3, clearly shows that the author believes advancements are being made in this field. Pay attention to the Emphasis Keywords the author uses: "researchers have learned a *great deal* about ancient textiles and those who made them" (lines 15–16); "technological advances in the analysis of archaeological remains provide *much more information than* was previously available" (lines 19–21); and "the history of textiles and of the craftswoman who produced them has *also advanced on a different front.*" (lines 43–44).

Step 4: Make a Prediction
The use of these Keywords indicates that the author feels that a great amount of progress is being made concerning the history of ancient textile production

Step 5: Evaluate the Answer Choices
(E) matches the prediction that the author believes that a number of advances are being made concerning the history of ancient textile production.

(A) can be eliminated because nothing in the passage suggests the author is *skeptical* of anything.

(B) can be eliminated because the word *doubtful* does not match the author's positive view of the advances.

(C) can be eliminated because nothing in the passage suggests the author is *impatient* about the pace of the research.

(D) is Out of Scope. It is not known to what extent the author thinks the advances will attract more researchers. Rather, the author focuses heavily on how the advances already made are aiding existing researchers in new discoveries.

3. (E) Detail

Step 2: Identify the Question Type
In this Detail question, "the passage indicates" tells you that the correct answer will be a close paraphrase, if not a direct quotation, from the passage.

Step 3: Research the Relevant Text
Pay close attention to the content clues in the question stem to guide your research. The question is directing you to the portion of the author's passage that discusses the "recreation of ancient techniques." From your Roadmap, recall that the author discussed this information in paragraph 3. Specifically, the author discusses the re-creation of the actual production of cloth in lines 45–51 and how that re-creation aided the determination of which two statutes of Athena was adorned with a particular dress.

Step 4: Make a Prediction
The correct answer will likely focus on the statues of Athena as a specific example of how the researchers used the re-creation techniques to determine which statue wore the garment.

Step 5: Evaluate the Answer Choices
(E) is the only choice that mentions Athena, and it matches the prediction quite closely.

(A) is a Faulty Use of Detail. Although "unrevealing terminology" (line 14) in ancient texts was mentioned, the re-creation of ancient techniques was not used to determine the meanings of those terms.

(B) is a Distortion. Tracing the sources of raw materials is mentioned in line 25, but it is done by isotope fingerprinting. It is not done by re-creation of ancient techniques.

(C) is Out of Scope. Museums are mentioned (line 31), but nothing about putting together displays is discussed.

(D) is a Faulty Use of Detail. The shirt is discussed in the second paragraph as an example of something that was preserved even though its value was not immediately known. However, implementing ancient techniques would not have verified the shirt's age.

4. (D) Inference

Step 2: Identify the Question Type
This Inference question requires you to ascertain how narrowly defined the author means the term "traditional sources" to be.

Step 3: Research the Relevant Text
The question refers to the first line, which defines "traditional sources" as "archaeological remains and surviving texts."

Step 4: Make a Prediction
The correct answer will be something that this definition *excludes*. So, four answers will describe actual remains or old texts. In essence, they will describe something one would physically find at an archaeological site or the writings of ancient people. The correct answer will not fit either category. There are too many things to predict that would not fit that description, so don't make a specific prediction. Instead, eliminate the four answers that surely do fit, or home in on the one stand-out exception.

Step 5: Evaluate the Answer Choices
(D) is correct. This is something created by modern scholars as the author discusses in paragraph 3, not an actual archaeological remain that they found.

(A) would be considered a traditional source of evidence. Even if the clay objects cannot be readily identified, they are still actual remains that were found.

(B) would be considered a traditional source of evidence, as it describes an actual remain found at an archaeological site.

(C) also describes an actual remain found at an archaeological site, so this would also be considered a traditional source of evidence.

(E) mentions "ancient accounts," which would fit under the category of "surviving texts."

5. (C) Global

Step 2: Identify the Question Type
This Global question asks for the author's purpose in writing the passage.

Step 3: Research the Relevant Text
Recall your Roadmap as well as the Topic, Scope, Purpose and Main Idea. The author's purpose is to explain and illustrate how much researchers within the field of archaeology concerning the history of ancient textile production now know in light of technological and philosophical advancements made by researchers. Also, worth noting is how these advancements have enabled researchers to cope with the scant "traditional sources" of evidence available to them.

Step 4: Make a Prediction
A brief review of your Roadmap gives you a great prediction in hand: The author has written this passage to show how advancements have enabled researchers to deal with the traditional lack of evidence available in the study of ancient textile production.

Step 5: Evaluate the Answer Choices
(C) is a match. The author gives an account of how researchers studying ancient textile production have been able to make successful discoveries using advances in technology in spite of the lack of evidence available.

(A) is Out of Scope. There is no suggestion that any of the methods discussed in the passage are controversial.

(B) is Out of Scope. The author never makes any recommendations for future researchers based on the information presented in the passage.

(D) is a Distortion. The author may suggest that traditional methodologies are insufficient. However, the author never rejects them, nor does the author reject—or even address—any views on those methodologies.

(E) is a Distortion. The author alludes to how these advancements can help researchers test and confirm their hypotheses. However, the author never mentions what those hypotheses are, let alone maintains it as a focus throughout the passage.

6. (E) Detail

Step 2: Identify the Question Type
In this Detail question, the phrase "according to the passage" indicates that the answer will be a close paraphrase, if not a direct quotation, of the text.

Step 3: Research the Relevant Text
Pay close attention to the content clues in the question stem. "An element in the transformation of archaeology in the past century" leads you to paragraph 2, specifically lines 31–33, which read "the field has transformed itself into a scientific pursuit of knowledge about past cultures." The next sentence starts, "as part of this process," which is a clear indication of an element in the transformation—exactly what the question is asking for.

Step 4: Make a Prediction
The concept described in lines 33–36 ("preserving all objects, even those that have no discernible value") is a perfect prephrase of the correct answer.

Step 5: Evaluate the Answer Choices
(E) is a great match for the prediction.

(A) is Out of Scope. The author never mentions any increase in interest regarding ancient crafts.

(B) is a Distortion. The archaeologists were said to adopt the precept (i.e., the principle) of preservation. However, there is

no mention of adopting any particular *technique* of preservation.

(C) is Out of Scope. The second and third paragraphs mention preservation and recreation of artifacts, but there's no mention of restoring broken ones.

(D) is a Faulty Use of Detail. The passage does mention the oldest known complete garment (the 5000-year-old shirt mentioned in line 38). However, the purpose of that detail is to exemplify the tenet of preserving items. The mere act of discovering the item in the first place was not exactly new or indicative of a transformation in the field of archaeology.

7. (A) Logic Function

Step 2: Identify the Question Type
In this Logic Function question, the correct answer will properly encompass the author's purpose for including the information discussed in paragraph 1.

Step 3: Research the Relevant Text
Review your Roadmap, paying close attention to your margin notes and Keywords. The author uses paragraph 1 to set the stage for the remainder of the passage. Specifically, the author describes how the traditional sources of evidence available to researchers studying ancient textile production proved problematic. However, in response to these obstacles, the advancements made in this field have been that much more important.

Step 4: Make a Prediction
The correct answer must show that the author presents the obstacles in order to emphasize how important the advances were to researchers studying ancient textile production.

Step 5: Evaluate the Answer Choices
(A) is a solid match to the prediction.

(B) is a Distortion on a few fronts. The author does mention shreds of textiles that were discarded, which perhaps qualifies as a body of evidence that was neglected. However, the author neither describes those shreds in detail nor uses such details to cast doubt on any views. Further, the following paragraphs outline modern methods, not views based on conventional sources.

(C) is a Faulty Use of Detail. New technologically based methods are described throughout the second and third paragraphs, not the first.

(D) is a Faulty Use of Detail and a Distortion. Recent research isn't described until the following paragraphs. Also, the passage is focused on studying textiles, not the role of women in ancient cultures.

(E) is a Distortion. While the first paragraph hints at the idea of new research methods, they're not really described until the following paragraphs. Moreover, the author never makes

any recommendations of what *should* be done by any branch
of archaeology, established or otherwise.

Passage 2: Emeagwali's Computer Innovations

Step 1: Read the Passage Strategically
Sample Roadmap

line #	Keyword/phrase	¶ Margin notes
1	success	PE—designs computers to solve real-world problems
4	fueled	
7	breakthroughs	Breakthrough parallel computers on task
8	Whereas	
11	pioneered	
14	most; difficult	
15	:	Ex. oil flow prediction 1989
17	Until	
18	but because	
19–20	too slow and inefficient	
22	requires	Why oil flow hard to calculate
29	In order to solve	
32–33	great difficulties	Hard to break up tasks on parallel computers
36	turned to	
42	demonstrated	PE—used tree analogy
45	enable	
49	breakthrough	1996—weather prediction
51	claims; powerful enough	
55	believes	Uses honeycomb analogy
58	shift; asserts	PE—predicts more nature analogies
60	thereby	

Discussion

The first sentence in paragraph 1 introduces the **Topic** of the passage, Philip Emeagwali's computer innovations. Initially, the author discusses the reason for Emeagwali's success with designing computers to solve real-world problems, namely that his pursuit of innovation in design draws heavily upon nature. This is a hint of the author's Scope, which is confirmed in paragraph 2. The author then narrows her discussion to the 1980s where Emeagwali had a breakthrough with successful parallel computer systems. After distinguishing parallel computer systems, the author gives an example of how the parallel computer systems were successful: oil flow prediction.

In paragraph 2, the author continues discussing oil flow prediction and begins by explaining why oil field flow is so difficult to calculate. Mid-paragraph, the author confirms her **Scope**: Natural processes showed Emeagwali how to design computers. Specifically, the author describes how Emeagwali referenced a tree-branching pattern as a model for how parallel computers could operate without interfering with the smaller separate computers' tasks. The paragraph ends by detailing Emeagwali's tree analogy. It is now clear that the author's **Purpose** for writing the passage is to explain how Emeagwali used natural processes to model parallel computer design.

Paragraph 3 focuses on another Emeagwali breakthrough. In 1996, Emeagwali proposed using the geometry of bees' honeycombs as a model for weather prediction. The author ends the passage by pointing out that Emeagwali predicts more and more computer scientists will look to nature for ways to solve complex problems. In sum, the author's **Main Idea** is that Emeagwali used analogies to natural processes to design massive parallel computer systems in order to solve real-world problems.

8. (D) Global

Step 2: Identify the Question Type
The correct answer to this Global question will reflect the Topic, Scope, Purpose, and Main Idea of the passage.

Step 3: Research the Relevant Text
A brief glance at the passage Roadmap shows that the correct answer should include references to Emeagwali's success with designing parallel computer systems. In addition, the correct answer should mention how the parallel computer systems are based on natural processes to solve many current problems.

Step 4: Make a Prediction
The Main Idea from the Roadmap should be sufficient to get the correct answer: Emeagwali used analogies to natural processes to design massive parallel computer systems in order to solve real-world problems.

Step 5: Evaluate the Answer Choices
(D) is correct, as it accurately reflects the author's sentiments in the passage as a whole.

(A) is a Distortion. Even though Emeagwali did enable parallel computer systems to solve the oil field flow prediction problem, that's not to say he solved a "wide array of problems that supercomputers cannot solve."

(B) is a Distortion. In addition to making no mention of Emeagwali's accomplishments or reference to natural processes, this answer goes too far by saying that Emeagwali blames the scientists for the lack of a solution. Also, the parallel computer system solutions have presented their own issues and are not without difficulty.

(C) is a Distortion. Although the systems described for oil flow and weather are based on mathematical principles, Emeagwali is not said to have discovered those principles. Emeagwali merely used those principles to fuel his idea for parallel computing.

(E) is too narrow. This paraphrases Emeagwali's opinions about the future in the last lines of paragraph 3, but it fails to address the focus of the passage as a whole: Emeagwali's own success in developing parallel computing systems in the first place.

9. (C) Detail

Step 2: Identify the Question Type
The correct answer to this Detail question will be a relevant detail or statement from the passage. Without a line reference or any content clues, you'll need to review each answer and cross-reference each against the passage text.

Step 3: Research the Relevant Text
Use the content clues in each answer choice to direct your research in the passage.

Step 4: Make a Prediction
Because this answer could be from anywhere in the passage, it's best to skip the prediction step and go right to the answers.

Step 5: Evaluate the Answer Choices
(C) is correct. According to lines 11–13, Emeagwali "pioneered the use of massively parallel computers" to predict the flow of oil.

(A) is a Distortion. While it's suggests that parallel systems will become more common, there is no indication anywhere in the passage that sequential computer systems will become *obsolete*.

(B) is Out of Scope. The author never discusses how Emeagwali's solution for the oil flow production dilemma came about. And there's no indication that solving the oil dilemma was his *first* breakthrough.

(D) is Extreme. While Emeagwali did use nature as a model, there is no indication that he was the *first* to do so.

(E) is Extreme. Emeagwali is said to have made breakthroughs in designing parallel systems, but there is no indication that he was the *first* to apply parallel processing to real-world problems.

10. (A) Inference

Step 2: Identify the Question Type
The correct answer to this Inference question will characterize Emeagwali's point of view.

Step 3: Research the Relevant Text
Without a strong content clue in the question stem, the answer can come from anywhere in the passage where the author discussed Emeagwali's point of view.

Step 4: Make a Prediction
Because there are many possible correct answers, go right to the answer choices, keeping in mind Emeagwali's point of view: Using processes from natural systems can provide solutions to real-world problems in computer science.

Step 5: Evaluate the Answer Choices
(A) is correct. Emeagwali's belief that analogies to natural systems' processes can provide solutions to tech problems faced by computer scientists is supportable throughout the passage, especially in paragraph 3.

(B) is a 180. The first sentence in paragraph 3 indicates that Emeagwali believes massively parallel computer systems will be powerful enough to predict global weather patterns a *century* in advance.

(C) is Extreme. While Emeagwali believes that computer scientists in the future will increasingly look to nature for elegant solutions to complex tech issues, it's not inferable that he believes *most* computer designs in the future will be inspired by natural systems.

(D) is Out of Scope. The author mentions in paragraph 3 that Emeagwali believes that computer scientists in the future will increasingly look to nature for elegant solutions to complex technical problems. But, that doesn't indicate whether Emeagwali believes that massively parallel computers will become useful in basic and everyday computing tasks as well.

(E) is Extreme. While the mathematical structure of branching tress is useful for designing computer systems to predict oil field flow, the author does not tell us that this is its *primary* usage above all other things.

11. (B) Logic Function

Step 2: Identify the Question Type
The correct answer to this Logic Function question will describe the purpose of the first two sentences (lines 22–29) in paragraph 2.

Step 3: Research the Relevant Text
Use the Keywords that bookend these sentences to evaluate the purpose of these statements. In the first sentence, the author lays out what the usage of computers to model oil field flow *requires*. At the beginning of the third sentence, the author writes "in order to solve this problem," which follows the two sentences in question.

Step 4: Make a Prediction
The Keywords indicate that the author is describing why oil flow is hard to calculate and thus presents a problem in light of the requirements for using computers (specifically, supercomputers mentioned in the first paragraph) to model oil flow production.

Step 5: Evaluate the Answer Choices
(B) is a perfect match to the prediction because the first two sentences explain the problem with using supercomputers to model oil field flow.

(A) is a 180. A problem faced by computer scientists in using supercomputers to model oil field flow is not a model that Emeagwali's work challenged.

(C) is a Distortion. The lines describe the simulations and calculations that need to be solved, not the network design that solves the calculations. That's described later in the paragraph.

(D) is a similar Distortion. Again, the lines describe what needs to be solved. The model Emegawali used to solve that problem is described later in the paragraph.

(E) is Faulty Use of Detail. How scientists will understand certain systems evolved by nature is irrelevant to the two sentences at issue.

12. (A) Logic Reasoning (Strengthen)

Step 2: Identify the Question Type
The correct answer to this Strengthen question will present a fact that makes Emeagwali's prediction in lines 56–59 more likely.

Step 3: Research the Relevant Text
Begin by paraphrasing Emeagwali's prediction. Emeagwali believes that computer scientists in the future will increasingly look to nature for elegant solutions to complex technical problems because the paradigm shift will allow for us to better understand the natural systems. In sum, because this information is now easier to understand, computer scientists will jump at the opportunity to use these systems in future computer design.

Step 4: Make a Prediction

The correct answer must be a fact that makes it more likely that just because the natural systems are easier to understand after the paradigm shift, then computer scientists will look to nature for solutions to tough problems.

Step 5: Evaluate the Answer Choices

(A) is correct. It makes Emeagwali's prediction more likely by showing that scientists didn't used to have this information available. Now that they do, they are more likely to use it.

(B) is irrelevant. Whether or not scientists have discovered more of the variables that affect global weather patterns does not further confirm that they will use natural systems to create solutions to problems.

(C) is irrelevant. Whether or not human activity affects the success of computer designs for the prediction of natural phenomena has no bearing on whether scientists will build these designs around natural system processes.

(D) is irrelevant. Whether or not Emeagwali's designs are supported by the same principles has no bearing on whether the computer scientist will look to these principles for future designs.

(E) is a 180. If many traditional tech designs were developed using mathematical principles of which the designers were unaware, then that makes it less likely that increased awareness now will spark future reliance on natural systems processes for computer designs.

13. (E) Inference

Step 2: Identify the Question Type

The correct answer to this Inference question will come directly from the information in the passage regarding Emeagwali's 1989 breakthrough of using massively parallel computers to predict the oil field flow.

Step 3: Research the Relevant Text

The author begins her discussion of Emeagwali's oil field flow prediction breakthrough in the first paragraph in line 11 and concludes the discussion through the entire second paragraph. Use your Roadmap and Keywords to narrow your search.

The author describes the breakthrough and why oil flow is difficult to calculate through line 30. Here, the author begins the next sentence with "One of the great difficulties of parallel computing is …" The correct answer will come from what follows.

Step 4: Make a Prediction

The passage states that parallel computing in general presents the issue of "dividing up tasks among the separate smaller computers so that they do not interfere with each other." The correct answer must be supportable based on this information.

Step 5: Evaluate the Answer Choices

(E) is the correct answer, which matches the prediction.

(A) is a 180. The end of paragraph 1 states that supercomputers were "too slow and inefficient to accurately predict" this kind of information.

(B) is Out of Scope. While Emeagwali may have been the first computer scientist to successfully use massively parallel computers to predict oil field flow, that doesn't mean he was the first to think of it.

(C) is Out of Scope. The public's awareness of the Internet or its capabilities is never discussed in the passage.

(D) is a 180 and Out of Scope. Clearly, Emeagwali would not have developed such a complex solution unless it served a valuable purpose. Also, whether oil companies might seem reasonable is not inferable since the role of oil companies as the impetus behind Emeagwali's discovery is never discussed.

Passage 3: Tangible-Object Theory

Step 1: Read the Passage Strategically
Sample Roadmap

line #	Keyword/phrase	¶ Margin notes
1	Proponents	Tangible-object theory
2	argue	
5	depends on the claim	
6	such as	You can "hold" it
7	also accepts; premise	
8	confers	
11–12	for example	Right to do whatever
16	thereby	Creator gets rights
17	But	
18–19	not necessarily; instead	Can retain some rights on transfer
22	for example	Common rules
26	argue	In IP, keep rights to copy perform.
33	for example	T.O. proponents: you can own idea
35	According	
36	chief advantage; justifies	
37	without recourse; widely accepted	
38	but problematic supposition	
39	But while	
40	seems plausible	
41–42	cannot accommodate	Auth: Problem—tangible form isn't the important part
44	More importantly	
46	more crucial; more valuable	
47	Suppose	
50	not	Poet analogy
51	but	
52	unless	

Discussion

Paragraph 1 starts off discussing proponents' view of the **Topic** of the passage, tangible-object theory of copyright. (As you continue to read, you should know to anticipate that the author will discuss the opponents' view or an alternative.) The basic tenet of this view is that "every copyrightable work can be manifested in some physical form" or that it can be held. In addition, the owner has several rights to do as she sees fit as long as those actions do not infringe upon another person's rights. Basically, the proponents feel that the owner has the right to do whatever she wants.

In paragraph 2, the author begins by discussing the rights of the owner as creator of the object. Although the owner can transfer ownership, the owner can still retain some rights after transfer, which is the notion of "retained rights." The author then discusses how retained rights are common within law and give us an example concerning the sale of land. But, the author goes back to discussing intellectual property and where retained rights fit into that area. In intellectual property, an owner who transfers ownership can still retain the right to copy the object for profit and to use it as a guide for the production of similar things like a performance.

So far, it would seem the author is focusing on the proponents of tangible-object theory, since she's just written a great analysis of their position. Paragraph 3 begins with the primary advantage proponents believe tangible-object theory has: You can own ideas. The author takes a turn immediately after, though, and begins detailing problems with the abstract, intangible nature associated with things such as ideas. The author's **Scope** is now confirmed: the tangible-object theory's proponents and its problems. In addition, the author's **Purpose** for writing the passage is to outline the position of those in favor of tangible-object theory and show problems with the logic of that view. The author concedes that their view is compatible with tangible objects. However, it's difficult to apply these same concepts to such "evanescent things" as ideas or broadcasts. The author ends with a poet analogy, explaining how a poet could dictate an entire poem to a friend, and if the friend writes it down, then the friend is the owner, unless the poet can show ownership of the ideas expressed in the poem.

In sum, the author's **Main Idea** is that tangible-object theory's emphasis on ownership going to the creator of a tangible form is problematic.

14. (B) Global

Step 2: Identify the Question Type

The correct answer to this Global question will encompass the key points made by the author regarding tangible-object theory.

Step 3: Research the Relevant Text

A brief review of the passage's key points helps isolate what the author views as important. She spends a great deal of time discussing the proponents' view of tangible-object theory and how it applies to things in physical form. However, the author's voice comes through loud and clear at the end of the passage, where she emphasizes how problematic this view is with intellectual property and other property that cannot be held.

Step 4: Make a Prediction

The correct answer will need to discuss how tangible object theory applies to copyright and intellectual property. In addition, it will also indicate problems with the application of tangible-object theory to copyright and intellectual property creations.

Step 5: Evaluate the Answer Choices

(B) encompasses these exact sentiments and matches the prediction.

(A) is too narrow. Although it is true that the notion of retained rights as applied to copyright and intellectual property can help clarify ownership, this is too neutral and does not characterize the author's critique in the final paragraph.

(C) is too narrow. While the author focuses heavily on retained rights, the author does not go so far as to say that retained rights is all there is to say about copyrighting.

(D) is Out of Scope. The circulation of ideas, free or not, is never discussed in the passage.

(E) is a 180. The author's critique in the third paragraph—especially the poet analogy—indicates that the application of tangible-object theory to ideas is not straightforward and problematic, at best.

15. (A) Detail

Step 2: Identify the Question Type

The correct answer to this Detail question will be a direct quote or a close paraphrase of the portion of the passage where the author discussed the basis for tangible-object theory—surely, to be applicable to copyright and intellectual property, that basis must still exist.

Step 3: Research the Relevant Text

Recall in paragraph 1 where the author discussed the basis for tangible-object theory. Specifically, the author mentioned that it "depends on the claim that every copyrightable work can be manifested in some physical form." It can be extended to anything that can be held.

Step 4: Make a Prediction

Likewise, the correct answer will need to state the basis that copyright and intellectual property are capable of being in physical form.

Step 5: Evaluate the Answer Choices

(A) is a close paraphrase of lines 5–7 and is a match to the prediction.

(B) is a 180. The proponents' of tangible-object theory acknowledge that the owner can transfer ownership and still retain some rights. In that instance, tangible-object theory would still be applicable.

(C) is a 180. In paragraph 3, the author explicitly states that tangible-object theory's application to copyright and intellectual property is problematic because "the work of conceiving ideas is more crucial and more valuable than that of putting them into tangible form."

(D) is irrelevant. Recognizing the right to own abstract, intangible things is not the appropriate basis for applying tangible-object theory to copyright and intellectual property. Also, this application would extend to more than a few cases.

(E) is a Distortion. The owner's right to destroy an item of intellectual property does not necessarily indicate that the item is in tangible form.

16. (B) Detail

Step 2: Identify the Question Type
The correct answer to this Detail question will characterize a question that was answered in the passage.

Step 3: Research the Relevant Text
Because there's no content clue or line reference in the question stem, it is best to go through each answer choice one by one. Cross-compare the content clues in the question stem to where that information was discussed, if at all, by the author.

Step 4: Make a Prediction
Rather than make a prediction, characterize the answer choices to know what you are looking for: If you can answer the question from information in the passage, then you have the correct answer. All four wrong answer choices will be outside the scope of the passage.

Step 5: Evaluate the Answer Choices
(B) is the correct answer. In addition to the sale of land, the proponents of tangible-object theory also hold that ownership of copyright and intellectual property—specifically a literary manuscript or a musical score—can involve retained rights (lines 25–32).

(A) is Out of Scope. Changes to existing laws related to copyright are never discussed in the passage.

(C) is Out of Scope. The effect of tangible-object theory on how cases involving intellectual property issues are decided is never discussed.

(D) is Out of Scope. Whether existing copyright law provides protection against unauthorized copying of items in which the creator has not yet applied for protection is never discussed.

(E) is Out of Scope. The standard procedures concerning the transfer of intellectual property are never discussed, let alone what about them is common to most legal systems.

17. (A) Inference

Step 2: Identify the Question Type
The correct answer to this Inference question will be a correct application of tangible-object theory to the example provided in the question stem.

Step 3: Research the Relevant Text
In the question stem, the inventor describes an innovative idea to an engineer who then drafts a prototype that the engineer then produces from his own materials. Recall the poet analogy at the end of paragraph 3 (lines 47–53). The author used the poet analogy to show that the form of the item does not clearly determine ownership.

In this example, the application of tangible-object theory would be problematic because the creator of the tangible object would be the engineer, not the inventor. In addition, there would seem to be no ground for the inventor to claim copyright unless the inventor can be said to already own the ideas expressed in the prototype.

Step 4: Make a Prediction
The correct answer will indicate that the engineer, and not the inventor, is entitled to claim ownership since it cannot be determined from the information whether the inventor already owned the ideas for the invention.

Step 5: Evaluate the Answer Choices
(A) is the correct answer because it properly indicates that only the engineer can claim ownership to the invention.

(B) is a 180. The inventor is not entitled to claim ownership to the invention.

(C) is a 180. The engineer and the inventor are not equally entitled to claim ownership to the invention.

(D) is a Distortion. The notion of retained rights is never discussed within the context of ideas and other intangible intellectual property.

(E) is a 180 and a Distortion. The inventor cannot claim ownership of the invention regardless of who retains any rights.

18. (E) Inference

Step 2: Identify the Question Type
The correct answer to this Inference question will correctly characterize the view of legal theorists who support the tangible-object theory of intellectual property.

Step 3: Research the Relevant Text
Research all references to the legal theorists who are the proponents of the tangible-object theory:

In paragraph 1, the author explains that the legal theorists believe copyright and similar intellectual property rights can be explained as a logical extension of the right to own concrete tangible objects (those that can be manifested in physical form).

In paragraph 3, the author states that the proponents see the primary advantage of tangible-object theory's application to intellectual property as a means to provide ownership to intangible/abstract things such as ideas.

Step 4: Make a Prediction
To be consistent with either of these viewpoints, the correct answer choices must be something the proponents of tangible-object theory must believe.

Step 5: Evaluate the Answer Choices
(E) is the correct answer choice, because the proponents of tangible-object theory must believe that the law need not invoke the notion of inventors' ownership of abstract ideas, which would likely give ownership to the creator if he is different from the inventor. Rather, the proponents of tangible-object theory would hold that the inventor is the owner because it was his idea.

(A) is Out of Scope. The proponents' view regarding what constitutes copyright protection of a literary work does not depend on the edition being produced by an established publisher.

(B) is Out of Scope and a 180. While it's unknown whether the proponents' feel legal systems rely on the tangible-object theory of intellectual property to avoid asserting ownership of abstract ideas, this view seems incompatible with the other information discussed by the author.

(C) is a Distortion. In paragraph 2, the author states that under the notion of retained rights, the original producer does retain the right to copy the object for profit. However, this is "among the rights typically retained by the original producer," not necessarily one of the only two rights the author mentions.

(D) is a 180. According to lines 4–6, the proponents of tangible-object theory believe that every copyrighted trademark can be manifested in physical form.

19. (C) Inference

Step 2: Identify the Question Type
The correct answer to this Inference question will correctly characterize the author's point of view in the passage.

Step 3: Research the Relevant Text
Because there's no content clue or line reference in the question stem, it is best to go through each answer choice one by one. Cross-compare the content clues in the answer choices to where that information was discussed, if at all, by the author.

Step 4: Make a Prediction
Rather than make a prediction, characterize the answer choices to know what you are looking for: If you can support the answer with information in the passage, then you have the correct answer. All four wrong answer choices will be outside the scope of the passage or too extreme to be supportable.

Step 5: Evaluate the Answer Choices
(C) is the correct answer and a proper inference based on information in the passage. The last sentence of paragraph 1 states that "one may also transfer ownership of [an object] to another." Now, think about context for the statement. As the author is defining what tangible-object theory of intellectual property is, the author ends with this statement.

(A) is Extreme. It is not necessarily in most transactions that rights are retained. Rather, it's only known that they can be in certain situations.

(B) is Extreme. While retained rights are applicable to areas of law that involve intellectual property, it is not for sure that only those areas of laws that do involve intellectual property have the notion of retained rights.

(D) is Extreme. There is no reason to believe that ownership of intellectual property is *sufficiently* protected as the law is currently written.

(E) is Out of Scope. Protection of computer programs under intellectual property law is never discussed. So, the author's opinion on this matter is unknown.

20. (D) Inference

Step 2: Identify the Question Type
The correct answer to this Inference question will correctly characterize the author's point of view in the passage.

Step 3: Research the Relevant Text
Because there's no content clue or line reference in the question stem, it is best to go through each answer choice one by one. Cross-compare the content clues in the answer choices to where that information was discussed, if at all, by the author.

Step 4: Make a Prediction
Rather than make a prediction, characterize the answer choices to know what you are looking for: If you can support the answer with information in the passage, then you have the correct answer. All four wrong answer choices will be outside the scope of the passage or too extreme to be supportable.

Step 5: Evaluate the Answer Choices
(D) is the correct answer and is supportable based on the information in paragraph 3. In order to have ownership under the existing law, the creator of the work would be assumed to

own the ideas contained within those works. Otherwise, the producer could claim ownership.

(A) is a Distortion. The author never attacks the notion of retained rights and why the proponents believe it applies to intellectual property. If anything, the author seems to go into great detail about why the proponents believe that retained rights applies to intellectual property.

(B) is a Distortion. Questioning the validity of the justification for intangible items to have copyright protection is more the opinion of the tangible-object theory proponents. However, the author's opinion is at issue.

(C) is a 180. The author would likely believe that creators of original tangible works do own those ideas upon which the work is based.

(E) is a 180. In paragraph 3, the author states that the belief that evanescent things such as live broadcasts of sporting events can be copyrighted is a "standard assumption."

Passage 4: Music's Effects and Emotions

Step 1: Read the Passage Strategically
Sample Roadmap

line #	Keyword/phrase	¶ Margin notes
Passage A		
2	positive	Music too simple—uninteresting
4	required	
6	however; overwhelming; prefer	too complex—overwhelming
11	whereas	like language—sequence needed
13	Likewise	
14–15	for example	
18	also	
20	possible explanation	continuous/rhythmic = relaxing
22	Thus	
25	Even	Not like danger sounds
27	for example	
Passage B		
34	key determinant	Musical emotion: expectation
38	The more	tension
39	the more	satisfaction
43	causes	Course—expectation mismatch = neg. emotion
44	results from	
47	result	
48	result	
51		Factors: complexity familiarity
55	minimal	
56	increases	too new = bad ↑ing famil. = good
57	decreases	too old = bad
60	As such	trained listeners = more complex

Discussion

The **Topic** of passage A is presented immediately in the first sentence: music's effects. According to the author of passage A, if a sound is too simple or too complex, then we find it uninteresting and overwhelming. Rather, like language, the sounds need coherence to connect the individual sounds and make them easier to understand. The **Scope** of passage A appears to be what's interesting and soothing about the effects of music. The author compares music to the human language in that a sequence is needed. The author also notes that a lack of sequence is not particularly moving for us or provides an opportunity for appreciation. Finally, the author discusses what's relaxing about music: its continuity and rhythm. Continuous noise indicates peace and a lack of disturbance. The author's **Purpose** is to delineate what makes music interesting and soothing as well as overwhelming. The **Main Idea** of passage A is that music can be interesting and overwhelming depending on complexity, while it can also be soothing because of its rhythmic quality.

As would be expected, the **Topic** of passage B also concerns music: specifically, the emotional aspect of music. The author of passage B isn't concerned with what gives us pleasure when we listen to music, but rather how these reactions are brought about. The author describes three certain elements that create expectations: expectation of the future course of the music, the buildup of tension, and the relaxation that follows the resolution of that tension. The **Scope** of passage B is how the expectations and familiarity determine the satisfaction when listening to music. The author of passage B then discusses how when expectations are mismatched, negative emotions result. Positive emotions result when expectations match the actual course of music. Similar to passage A, one purpose of passage B is to describe how complexity and familiarity determine satisfaction when listening to music. When music is too new or too old, we don't enjoy it. As familiarity with new music increases, though, we are more inclined to enjoy the music. A trained listener prefers more complex melodies. The **Purpose** of passage B is to examine the relationship between expectations of music and satisfaction. The **Main Idea** of passage B is that the degree of familiarity influences expectations of music and the emotions experienced.

Before going to the questions, it's important to note the relationship between the two passages. Both are concerned with the effect music has on the listener—although one is concerned with how the listener reacts and one is concerned with what brings about those reactions. More notably, both passages support the view that complexity and familiarity play a role in whether the listener enjoys the music.

21. (E) Detail

Step 2: Identify the Question Type

The correct answer to this Detail question will be a concept that both passages identified as a positive musical experience.

Step 3: Research the Relevant Text

In passage A, the author states that "a certain complexity can be expected to have a positive effect on the listener," (lines 1–2). In passage B, the author states that "a trained listener will have a greater preference for complex melodies …" (lines 61–62).

Step 4: Make a Prediction

Thus, both passages reference *complexity* as a concept that influences a positive musical experience.

Step 5: Evaluate the Answer Choices

(E) is the correct answer choice because it lists the concept of complexity.

(A) is only in passage A. The concept of continuous sound is linked to a positive musical experience in lines 20–30.

(B) is only referenced in passage B. The concept of tension is listed as an element that can lead to a positive listening experience (lines 37–42).

(C) is only referenced in passage A. The concept of language is mentioned as an analogous example of when sequence is needed to provide a positive listening experience (lines 10–18).

(D) is Out of Scope. The concept of improvisation is not discussed in either passage.

22. (C) Inference

Step 2: Identify the Question Type

The correct answer to this Inference question will correctly characterize something in common between the two passages that draws the attention of the reader.

Step 3: Research the Relevant Text

To determine what the passages have in common, go back to the Roadmap. Both passages discuss the emotional aspect behind music and what effect music has on the listener.

Step 4: Make a Prediction

The correct answer must reference the emotional aspect of music and how that affects the listener.

Step 5: Evaluate the Answer Choices

(C) is the correct answer because it references the impact music has on the emotions of the listener.

(A) is Out of Scope. The theory behind how music is composed is never discussed in either passage.

(B) references a concept discussed only in passage A.

(D) is Out of Scope. The most effective techniques for teaching novices to appreciate complex music are never discussed in either passage.

(E) is Out of Scope. While music is analogized to human language, the effect music has had on the development of spoken language is not discussed.

23. (B) Logic Reasoning (Parallel Reasoning)

Step 2: Identify the Question Type
The correct answer to this Parallel Reasoning question will have the same preference mentioned in the first paragraph of passage A.

Step 3: Research the Relevant Text
In the first paragraph of passage A, the author believes the listener prefers "some sort of coherence" that connects the various sounds and makes them comprehensible.

Step 4: Make a Prediction
The correct answer will need to show a preference for continuity within a work or a sense of coherence that drives the listener's enjoyment.

Step 5: Evaluate the Answer Choices
(B) is the correct answer. The simplicity of the plot and coherence makes it easy to follow, resulting in a positive viewing experience, which is analogous to the preference for coherence among music listeners.

(A) is a Faulty Use of Detail from passage A. Continuous sound is not discussed until the third paragraph.

(C) is Out of Scope. The length (or amount) of music is never discussed in either passage.

(D) is Out of Scope of the first paragraph in passage A. While melody is important, the speed or tempo of the music is never discussed in either passage.

(E) is Out of Scope. The preference of sweet to bitter is never discussed in either passage.

24. (A) Global

Step 2: Identify the Question Type
The correct answer for this Global question will encompass the entirety of passage B.

Step 3: Research the Relevant Text
A quick review of your Roadmap related to passage B indicates that the author of passage B wants the reader to come away knowing that the level of satisfaction of expectations for a listener determines what emotional experiences the listener endures.

Step 4: Make a Prediction
The correct answer will need to discuss the satisfaction of emotions as a relevant concept concerning a positive listening experience.

Step 5: Evaluate the Answer Choices
(A) correctly contains the author of passage B's sentiments because it characterizes the author's main point, which is that they type of emotion experienced is determined by whether the listener's expectations are satisfied.

(B) is too narrow and a Distortion. The distinction between trained and untrained listeners is only mentioned in the last paragraph. Further, the preferences of trained listeners are based on experience and familiarity, not emotional self-manipulation.

(C) is too narrow. While the author of passage B does discuss the negative emotions associated with the mismatch of the listener's expectations with the actual course of the music, that concept is not the primary focus of passage B.

(D) is too narrow. While this may be an accurate claim, it does not address the overall scope of the passage about the connection between expectations and satisfaction.

(E) is a Distortion. While relaxation eventually follows the buildup and release of tension, the author of passage B never addresses the likelihood that relaxing music usually produces this effect.

25. (C) Logic Reasoning (Weaken)

Step 2: Identify the Question Type
The correct answer choice will weaken the explanation provided in passage A for why some music has a relaxing effect on listeners.

Step 3: Research the Relevant Text
The first two sentences in the third paragraph of passage A warrant attention. The author of passage A explains that the continuous and rhythmic nature of music produces a relaxing effect.

Step 4: Make a Prediction
The correct answer choice will present a fact that makes it less likely or believable that the continuous and rhythmic nature of music produces a relaxing effect.

Step 5: Evaluate the Answer Choices
(C) is the correct answer. If people find the steady and rhythmic nature of a rocking chair to be stressful, then surely we could question whether the continuous sounds of music have a relaxing effect.

(A) is Out of Scope. The complexity of music is not offered in passage A as an explanation for why music has a relaxing effect.

(B) is irrelevant. How the rhythmic sound is produced has no effect on whether the rhythm itself is still a valid reason for why the listener finds the music relaxing.

(D) is Out of Scope. The effect of expectations on the listener's satisfaction and relaxation is a concept discussed in passage B.

(E) is irrelevant. Although passage A discusses the effect of simplicity on the listener, the amount of music that is written to be simpler now versus in the past is irrelevant to whether the listener experiences relaxation.

26. (B) Global

Step 2: Identify the Question Type
The correct answer to this Global question will target both passages' commonality.

Step 3: Research the Relevant Text
A quick review of your Roadmap indicates that both authors are focusing on the emotions experienced by the listeners as a result of various concepts related to how music is created and eventually heard.

Step 4: Make a Prediction
The correct answer's title must focus on the emotions associated with listening to music.

Step 5: Evaluate the Answer Choices
(B) is the correct answer because the title "The Psychology of Listener Response to Music" applies appropriately to the soothing and over whelming listener experience described in passage A as well as the satisfaction of emotional expectations described in passage B.

(A) is Out of Scope. The biology behind the emotions associated with listening to music are never discussed. Both authors focus purely on the psychological response.

(C) is Out of Scope. The differences between music and other art forms is never discussed in either passage.

(D) is Out of Scope. The cultural patterns associated with listeners' responses to music is never discussed in either passage.

(E) is Out of Scope. How the conductor conveys meaning to the listener is never discussed in either passage.

27. (D) Inference

Step 2: Identify the Question Type
The correct answer to this Inference question will indicate a point of agreement between both authors.

Step 3: Research the Relevant Text
The author of passage A indicates that having a continuous sound makes music enjoyable to the listener. It makes the music safer and more predictable. Likewise, the author of passage B indicates that having the music match the listener's expectations, along with the buildup and release of tension, causes music to have a relaxing effect.

Step 4: Make a Prediction
The correct answer will note this area of agreement between the authors, namely that the listener should know where the music is going or be able to predict its eventual course.

Step 5: Evaluate the Answer Choices
(D) is the correct answer because it must be true based on information in the passage. Since both authors agree that predictability of music's course is highly important to a satisfying listening experience, then it must be true that without it the listener is less likely to feel relaxed.

(A) is a 180 for the author of passage B. According to passage B's author, only "trained listeners" develop a preference for complex melodies, while naive listeners will prefer simpler, more familiar music.

(B) is a Distortion, improperly combining ideas unique to each passage. Only passage B, and not passage A, makes any distinction between knowledgeable and less knowledgeable listeners. And discontinuous and unpredictable sounds are only addressed in passage A, not passage B. If anything, passage B's author suggests that preference develops from familiarity and would thus be based on predictable sounds, not unpredictable ones.

(C) is Out of Scope. The artistic value of music is never discussed by either author. Rather, the passages focus on how and why those strong emotional responses from listeners are elicited.

(E) is Out of Scope. The volume of music—softness versus loudness—is never discussed in either passage.

Section III: Logic Games

Game 1: Construction of Monuments

Q#	Question Type	Correct	Difficulty
1	Acceptability	E	★
2	Latest	C	★
3	Completely Determine	E	★★
4	Must Be True	A	★★
5	Supply the If	E	★★★
6	"If" / Could Be True	C	★

Game 2: Day Care Volunteers

Q#	Question Type	Correct	Difficulty
7	Acceptability	C	★
8	"If" / Could Be True	B	★★
9	"If" / Must Be False (CANNOT Be True)	C	★
10	"If" / Could Be True	B	★
11	"If" / Must Be True	A	★★
12	Must Be True	B	★★★★

Game 3: Flyhigh & Getaway Airlines

Q#	Question Type	Correct	Difficulty
13	Partial Acceptability	D	★
14	How Many	D	★★★★
15	"If" / Must Be False	B	★
16	Must Be True	B	★
17	"If" / Could Be True EXCEPT	C	★★

Game 4: Summer School Courses

Q#	Question Type	Correct	Difficulty
18	Acceptability	C	★
19	Maximum	D	★★
20	"If" / Could Be True	B	★★★
21	"If" / Must Be True	E	★★★
22	Must Be True	B	★★★
23	Rule Substitution	B	★★★★

Game 1: Construction of Monuments

Step 1: Overview
Situation: Recording historical information

Entities: Six monuments—F, G, H, L, M, S; five years—601, 602, 603, 604, 605

Action: Strict Sequencing. Determine the order in which construction began for the monuments.

Limitations: There are six monuments, but only five possible years. That means at least one year saw construction start on at least two monuments. Also, nothing in the overview requires that each year must see the start of some monument's construction.

Step 2: Sketch
Start by setting up a list of the six monuments and a column for each of the five years. However, the rules will be needed to determine how many slots each column receives:

```
        F G H L M S
 601 | 602 | 603 | 604 | 605
_____|_____|_____|_____|_____
     |     |     |     |
```

Step 3: Rules
Rule 1 establishes the relative order for three of the monuments—G, L, and F—to start construction in three different years (but not necessarily consecutive years):

G . . . L . . . F

Rule 2 limits H's construction to either 604 or 605.

Rule 3 requires that M's construction began before 604. So, that means M's construction began in 601, 602, or 603.

Rule 4 confirms the numbers of the game. There will be two monuments in 601, and each of the remaining four monuments will begin in exactly one of the remaining years.

Step 4: Deductions
This game lacks major deductions. With H relegated to only two years, drawing out Limited Options may seem tempting. However, placing H's construction in 604 or 605 does not yield further deductions that would warrant Limited Options in this case.

The best that can be done here is to label which monuments can't be placed in certain columns (e.g., H wasn't begun in 601, 602, or 603, and M wasn't begun in 604 or 605).

Also worth noting is that only G, M, or S could be the two monuments constructed in 601, because H cannot have begun construction in 601, and L and F were each constructed in years following the construction of G.

Entering the questions, the Master Sketch should look something like this:

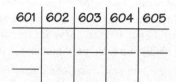

```
        F G H L M S
 601 | 602 | 603 | 604 | 605
_____|_____|_____|_____|_____
_____|_____|_____|_____|_____
     |     |     |     |
 No H  No H  No H  No M  No M
```

G . . . L . . . F

H = 604 or 605

G, M, or S = 2 constructed in 601

Step 5: Questions

1. (E) Acceptability
Rule 1 dictates the order G ... L ... F. That eliminates **(C)**. Rule 2 dictates that H wasn't begun earlier than 604. That eliminates **(B)**. Rule 3 dictates that M was begun earlier than 604. That eliminates **(D)**. Rule 4 dictates that two monuments were begun in 601. That eliminates **(A)**.

That leaves **(E)** as the correct answer—the only one that doesn't violate any of the rules.

2. (C) Latest
By Rule 1, L was begun earlier than F and later than G, so it can't have been begun in 605 or 601. That eliminates **(A)** and **(E)**.

Because the question asks for the latest year in which L could have been begun, it's a good idea to start testing out the choices from the bottom up, beginning with **(D)**. If L was begun in 604, then F was begun in 605. However, that would leave no room for H in 604 or 605, violating Rule 2. That eliminates **(D)**.

If L was begun in 603, then F was begun in 604 or 605. In either case, H was begun in the other year. That leaves G, M, and S as the monuments begun in 601 and 602. That doesn't violate any of the rules, so 603 is the latest year construction on L could have begun. **(C)** is the correct answer.

3. (E) Completely Determine
The correct answer will be a "new rule" that allows us to determine the exact year that each monument was constructed. Keep an eye on each of the first three rules as you work through the choices.

(A) If F was begun in 603, then G and L must have been begun in 601 and 602, respectively (to satisfy Rule 1). Because M cannot have been begun in 604 or 605 (to satisfy Rule 3), it must be the second monument constructed in 601. However, it is still unclear when H was begun, because H still could have been begun in 604 or 605 (with S begun in the other year). This doesn't completely determine the order. Eliminate.

(B) If G was begun in 602, then L was begun in 603. This also requires that M and S were the two monuments that began construction in 601. However, F could have been begun in 604 or 605 (with H begun in the other year). This doesn't completely determine the order. Eliminate.

(C) If H was begun in 605, then F could have been begun in 603 or 604. This doesn't completely determine the order. Eliminate.

(D) If M was begun in 602, then G was begun in 601 (with S) and L was begun in 603. However, F could have been begun in 604 or 605 (with H begun in the other year). This doesn't completely determine the order. Eliminate.

(E) If S was begun in 604, that means H was begun in 605 (to satisfy Rule 2). This requires that G, L, and F were begun in 601, 602, and 603, respectively (to satisfy Rule 1). Finally, that means M was the second monument begun in 601. That creates a complete sketch, making **(E)** the correct answer.

4. (A) Must Be True

Be sure to characterize the answer choices. For the purposes of answering this question, the correct answer "must be true" and the four wrong answers "could be or must be false."

To satisfy Rule 1, F cannot have been begun in 601 or 602. The earliest it could have been begun is 603. In that case, because M cannot have been begun in 604 or 605 (to satisfy Rule 3), M was begun in 601 or 602.

If F was begun in 604 or 605, M was begun in a prior year (because M can only have been begun in 601, 602, or 603). Therefore, no matter when F was begun, it must be true that it was begun in a later year than when M was begun. That makes **(A)** the correct answer. For the record:

(B) could be false if F was begun in 603 and S was begun in 604.

(C) could be false if H was begun in 604 and F was begun in 605.

(D) could be false if H was begun in 604 and S was begun in 605.

(E) could be false if M was begun in 601 and G was begun in 602.

5. (E) Supply the If

For the purposes of this question, the correct answer "must make L the monument begun in 602," and the four wrong answers "could or must make the construction of L begun in a

year other than 602." Keep this in mind as you test out the choices.

(A) If F's construction began in 605, H's construction was begun in 604 (to satisfy Rule 2). However, it is still possible for G's construction to have begun in 602 and L's construction to have begun in 603. Eliminate.

(B) If G's construction began in 601, then L's construction could have begun in 602 or 603. Eliminate

(C) If H's construction began in 604, then F's construction could have begun in 605. This allows for L's construction to have begun in 602 or 603. Eliminate.

(D) If M's construction began in 601, then L's construction could have begun in 602 or 603, because it's impossible to determine whether G's construction began in 601 or 602. Eliminate.

Thus, **(E)** must be the winner. If S's construction began in 603, then F's construction began in 604 or 605 (to satisfy Rule 1). Whichever year F was begun, H's construction began in the other (to satisfy Rule 2). That means G's construction began in 601 and L was begun in 602 (to satisfy Rule 1). Because L must be the monument begun in 602, this is the correct answer.

6. (C) "If" / Could Be True

If M's construction began in a later year than L (and, by default, G, to satisfy Rule 1), then M's construction must have begun in 603. After all, M's construction wasn't begun in 604 or 605 (to satisfy Rule 3).

Draw a new sketch that incorporates this deduction. With M's construction begun in 603, that means L's construction began in 602 and G's construction began in 601. F was then begun in 604 or 605, with H begun in the other year. That leaves S to be the second monument begun in 601:

601	602	603	604	605
G	L	M	F/H	H/F
S				

Based on that new sketch, **(C)** is the only answer that could be true and thus, the correct answer.

Game 2: Day Care Volunteers

Step 1: Overview
Situation: Organizing a day-care group

Entities: Seven employees—Felicia, Leah, Masatomo, Rochelle, Salman, Terry, Veena

Action: Selection. Determine who will be selected to volunteer for the volunteer group.

Limitations: Although there is no limit to the minimum size of the group, there is a maximum of seven employees from which to select volunteers.

Step 2: Sketch
Because the size of the group isn't determined, merely list the seven entities. As you go through the game, circle entities that are selected and cross out entities that are rejected.

F L M R S T V

Step 3: Rules
Rules 1 and 2 provide some straightforward Formal Logic. Be sure to translate the original rule for each and form its contrapositive.

$$R \rightarrow M$$
$$No\ M \rightarrow No\ R$$

$$M \rightarrow T$$
$$No\ T \rightarrow No\ M$$

Rules 3 and 4, taken together, provide a minimum number of volunteers—information that was previously unknown. First, the Formal Logic can be written out as presented:

$$No\ S \rightarrow V$$
$$No\ V \rightarrow S$$
$$and$$
$$No\ R \rightarrow L$$
$$No\ L \rightarrow R$$

However, what these rules are really saying is that if one of these two people in each pair do not volunteer, then the other one in the pair must volunteer. In other words, there will always be a minimum of **two volunteers**: at least one in each pair must volunteer—possibly both. So, these rules can be simply written as:

V or S (or both)
L or R (or both)

Rule 5 provides a complex Formal Logic statement. Remember that "neither X nor Y" means that you don't have X AND you don't have Y. So, properly translated, the rule reads:

$$T \rightarrow No\ F\ and\ No\ V$$
$$V\ or\ F \rightarrow No\ T$$

This rule can also be interpreted to say that Terry and Felicia can never volunteer together, nor can Terry and Veena:

Never TF
Never TV

Step 4: Deductions
Besides the alternative interpretations of the rules, this game lacks any major deductions. That's because all of the rules are conditional, which means that the rules will only be utilized under certain conditions—none of which have been provided yet.

The key to working through this game will be to look for information that will set off the conditional statements and following the logic until all conclusions can be made.

The Master Sketch is simply a listing of the entities and conditional rules.

F L M R S T V
$$R \rightarrow M$$
$$No\ M \rightarrow No\ R$$

$$M \rightarrow T$$
$$No\ T \rightarrow No\ M$$

V or S (or both)
L or R (or both)

Never TF
Never TV

Step 5: Questions

7. (C) Acceptability
Rule 1 dictates that Masatomo must volunteer if Rochelle does. That eliminates **(D)**. Rule 2 dictates that Terry must volunteer if Masatomo does. That eliminates **(B)**. Rule 3 is not violated by any of the remaining answers. Rule 4 dictates that either Rochelle or Leah volunteered. That eliminates **(A)**. Rule 5 dictates that Terry and Veena cannot volunteer together. That eliminates **(E)**.

That leaves **(C)** as the correct answer—the only one that doesn't violate any of the rules.

8. (B) "If" / Could Be True

As with any New-"If" condition, consider which rules are being invoked for the purposes of making deductions. In this particular instance, if Veena volunteers, Rule 5 dictates that Terr y cannot (Never TV). Eliminate **(D)** and **(E)**. According to Rule 2, that means Masatomo cannot volunteer (If No T → No M). Eliminate **(C)**. This in turn means that Rochelle cannot volunteer (by Rule 1's contrapositive "If No M → No R"). Eliminate **(A)**. With that, **(B)** is the only answer that could be true.

Note: By Rule 4, Leah must volunteer [L or R (or both)]. But, in this instance, any choices that contain Leah have been eliminated already.

For the record, the new sketch is:

F (L) M̶ R̶ S T̶ (V)

9. (C) "If" / Must Be False (CANNOT Be True)

Characterize the answer choices. For the purposes of this question, the correct answer "must be false" and the four wrong answers "could be or must be true."

Incorporate the New-"If" clause into the Master Sketch. If Terry does not volunteer, then Rule 2 dictates that Masatomo cannot volunteer, which in turn means that Rochelle cannot volunteer (by Rule 1):

F (L) M̶ R̶ S T̶ V

Thus, **(C)** cannot be true, making that the correct answer.

Note: By Rule 4, Leah must volunteer.

10. (B) "If" / Could Be True

If Masatomo volunteers, Rule 2 dictates that Terry must also volunteer (If M → T). By Rule 5, that means neither Felicia nor Veena volunteer (Never TF; Never TV). By Rule 3, Veena not volunteering means that Salman must volunteer [V or S (or both)]:

F̶ L (M) R (S) T V̶

Thus, **(A)**, **(C)**, **(D)**, and **(E)** are eliminated, leaving **(B)** as the only answer that could be true.

11. (A) "If" / Must Be True

For the purposes of this question, the correct answer "must be true," while the four wrong answers "could be or must be false."

If Felicia volunteers, then Rule 5 dictates that Terr y cannot (Never TF). According to Rule 2, that means Masatomo cannot volunteer (If No T → No M), which in turn means that Rochelle

cannot volunteer (If No M → No R). By Rule 4, that means that Leah must volunteer:

(F) (L) M̶ R̶ S T̶ V

With that, **(A)** is the only answer that must be true.

(B), **(C)**, **(D)**, and **(E)** all could be true, but need not be true. So, each could be false.

12. (B) Must Be True

For the purposes of this question, the correct answer must be "At least one of the people in the answer must always be selected," while the four wrong answers will show that "the selection can be made without including either person in the answer choice."

It makes sense to start with choices that contain one of the required pairs. So, start with **(B)**. Leah can volunteer. However, if Leah does not volunteer, then Rule 4 dictates that Rochelle must volunteer [L or R (or both)]. By Rule 1, that means Masatomo must also volunteer (If R → M). So, if Leah doesn't volunteer, Masatomo must volunteer. Thus, **(B)** is the correct answer.

You can also use previous sketches on this question to knock off wrong answer choices quickly.

For the record, the following acceptable groups show why the remaining answers are wrong:

(A) Eliminating Felicia or Terry from the order does not require that the other be selected. If Terry does not volunteer, then neither does Masatomo (Rule 2) or Rochelle (Rule 1). But, that still leaves Leah, Salman, and Veena as possible volunteers.

F̶ L M̶ R̶ S T̶ V

(C) Eliminating Leah or Veena from the order does not require that the other be selected. If Leah does not volunteer, then Rochelle must volunteer (Rule 4). And, if Veena does not volunteer, then Salman must volunteer (Rule 3). Felicia, Terry, and Masatomo can still be selected as volunteers.

F V̶ M (R) (S) T V̶

(D) Eliminating Rochelle and Salman from the order does not require that the other be selected. If Rochelle does not volunteer, then Leah must volunteer (Rule 4). If Salman does not volunteer, then Veena must volunteer (Rule 3). Thus, Terr y cannot be selected (Rule 5), which means Masatomo cannot be selected (Rule 2). Felicia can still be selected as a volunteer.

F (L) M̶ R̶ S̶ T̶ (V)

(E) Eliminating Salman and Terry from the order does not require that the other be selected. If Salman does not volunteer, then Veena must volunteer (Rule 3). If Terry does not volunteer, then neither Masatomo nor Rochelle can volunteer (Rules 1 and 2). If Rochelle is not selected, then Leah must volunteer (Rule 4). Felicia can still be selected as a volunteer. Same sketch as **(D)**.

Game 3: Flyhigh & Getaway Airlines

Step 1: Overview
Situation: Flights for two airlines

Entities: Five planes—P, Q, R, S, T

Action: Sequencing/Matching Hybrid. The overview provides little information other than the entities for the game. However, a quick glance at the first two rules provides the action: Determine the order in which the planes take off (Sequencing) and determine whether each flight is domestic or international (Matching).

Limitations: From the overview, the only limitation is that each plane will take off exactly once. The rules will provide further limitations.

Step 2: Sketch
After the overview, the best that can be done is to list the five entities, separated into their respective subgroups (Flyhigh Airlines and Getaway Airlines). Once the actions are established by the first two rules, the basic sketch for a Sequencing/Matching Hybrid game is to have two rows of five ordered spaces—one row for the five flights and one row for the type of flight:

```
Flyhigh:
P Q          1   2   3   4   5
Getaway:
r s t        __  __  __  __  __

dom/int      __  __  __  __  __
```

Step 3: Rules
Rule 1 establishes that the five flights will take off one at a time, confirming that the sequencing game action will be a strict 1:1 ratio.

Rule 2 adds the matching action to the game: Each flight must be categorized as either domestic or international—not both.

Rules 3 and 4 provide some concrete information that defines the flight categorization for P (international), Q (domestic), and R (domestic). For now, this information can be written off to the side in shorthand:

```
              Q
         ⋯ dom.
P ⋯
int.     ⋯ r
              dom.
```

Rule 5 states that all international flights must depart first, then the domestic flights:

All int. ... All dom.

Rule 6 requires that any Gateway flights that are domestic must depart before any Flyhigh flight that is domestic.

All *Gateway* dom. ... All Flyhigh dom.

Step 4: Deductions
The rules for this game are fairly direct and concrete. Therefore, it's important to consider how all of this information can be incorporated into the main sketch.

Rules 3, 4, and 5 provide the most helpful information immediately. By Rules 3 and 4, there are already ready one international flight and two domestic flights. Because all international flights must depart before all domestic flights (by Rule 5), at least the first flight must be international and at least the last two flights must be domestic.

The only international flight determined so far is P, but that doesn't have to be the first flight. If any other flights are international, those could be first.

Of the two domestic flights determined (Q and R), Q must go later because of Rule 6. However, Q is the only possible domestic Flyhigh flight (because the other Flyhigh flight, P, is international). Therefore, by Rule 6, there can't be any flights after Q. So, Q must be the fifth and final flight.

R does not have to be the fourth flight, because any of the other Getaway flights could also be domestic. Going into the questions, the Master Sketch should look something like this:

1	2	3	4	5
—	—	—	—	Q
int.	—	—	dom.	dom.

Step 5: Questions

13. (D) Partial Acceptability
Using the big deduction made during the game setup, Q must be the fifth and final flight. This eliminates **(A)**, **(B)**, and **(C)**. Rule 5 dictates that international flights must depart before domestic flights. Because P is international (by Rule 3) and R is domestic (by Rule 4), that eliminates **(E)**. Thus, **(D)** is the correct answer.

If you missed the big deduction early on, you can still use the rules to attack the answer choices. Rule 1 is not violated by any of the answer choices. Rules 2, 3, and 4 focus on the matching aspect of the game, which is not indicated in the answer choices. However, this information will be helpful in testing the later rules.

Rule 5 dictates that international flights must depart before domestic flights. Because P is international (by Rule 3) and R is domestic (by Rule 4), that eliminates **(E)**. Rule 6 dictates that any Gateway domestic flight must depart before Flyhigh's domestic flight. The only Flyhigh domestic flight is Q (by Rule 4), and R is a Gateway domestic flight (by Rule 4). That eliminates **(A)**, **(B)**, and **(C)**.

That leaves **(D)** as the correct answer—the only one that doesn't violate any of the rules.

14. (D) How Many

Using the big deduction made during the game setup, Q must be the fifth and final flight. So that leaves four flights that could depart second. If one of Gateway's flights is international, then it could depart first, allowing P to depart second. If all of Gateway's flights are domestic, then any one of them (R, S, or T) could be second. So, with four possible planes that can depart second, **(D)** is the correct answer.

15. (B) "If" / Must Be False

If S departs sometime before P (an international flight, according to Rule 3), then S must be an international flight (per Rule 5). At this point, the relative order of four of the flights can be determined. Because S and P (in that order) are international, they must depart before domestic flights R and Q (in that order, by Rule 6):

$$s \ldots P \ldots r \ldots Q$$

The only plane not in the sequence is T, which could depart at any time except for fifth (because it was deduced that Q is always fifth). Eliminate **(C)**, **(D)**, and **(E)**. Depending on when T takes off, the departing position of the remaining planes can be: S first or second; P second or third; R third or fourth; Q fifth.

Because S can only depart first or second, **(B)** is the only answer that must be false.

16. (B) Must Be True

For this particular question, the correct answer "must be true," and the four wrong answers "could be or must be false."

Based on the deductions made, Q must be the last plane to depart. That makes **(B)** the correct answer. For the record:

(A) is a clever trap, because some people may assume that P is the only international flight and therefore must depart first. However, if any Gateway flight is also international, then that flight can depart first.

(C), **(D)**, and **(E)** can all be eliminated using previous work. The answer to the Acceptability question shows that R, S, and T could all hold different departure positions than each answer choices indicates.

17. (C) "If" / Could Be True EXCEPT

For the purposes of this particular question, the correct answer "must be false," while the four wrong answers "could be true."

If S is the third flight to depart, there's no definite way of determining whether S is domestic or international.

If S were international, then the first three flights would have to be international (by Rule 5). With two domestic flights already determined (Gateway's r and Flyhigh's Q), the remaining planes would all be international (Flyhigh's P and Gateway's t and s). R and Q would have to depart in that order (by Rule 6) and P and T could depart in any order:

1	2	3	4	5
P/t	t/P	s	r	Q
int.	int.	int.	dom.	dom.

If S were domestic, then T could still be domestic or international, departing in any open position:

1	2	3	4	5
P	t/r	s	r/t	Q
int.	int./dom.	dom.	dom.	dom.

1	2	3	4	5
t	P	s	r	Q
int.	int.	dom.	dom.	dom.

Despite the many possibilities, **(C)** must be false because that would make R and T the two planes to depart fourth and fifth (in some order). However, Q must the fifth plane to depart, so that cannot happen. That makes **(C)** the correct answer.

Game 4: Summer School Courses

Step 1: Overview
Situation: Summer school sessions

Entities: Seven courses—history, linguistics, music, physics, statistics, theater, writing

Action: Selection. Select which of the seven courses the student takes.

Limitations: At least three courses must be selected, but there's no maximum.

Step 2: Sketch
Because the number of courses isn't completely determined, merely list the seven entities. As you go through the game, circle courses that are selected and cross out courses that are rejected.

H L M P S T W

Step 3: Rules
Rules 1, 2, and 3 all provide straightforward Formal Logic rules. Translate each statement and its contrapositive:

$$H \rightarrow \text{No S and No M}$$
$$S \text{ or } M \rightarrow \text{No H}$$

$$M \rightarrow \text{No P and No T}$$
$$P \text{ or } T \rightarrow \text{No M}$$

$$W \rightarrow \text{No P and No S}$$
$$P \text{ or } S \rightarrow \text{No W}$$

Rule 1 can also be interpreted to say that the student can't take history and statistics together; and the student can't take history and music together.

Never HS; Never HM

Rule 2 can be interpreted to say that the student can't take music and physics together; and the student can't take music and theater together.

Never MP; Never MT

Rule 3 can be interpreted to say that the student can't take writing and physics together; and the student can't take writing and statistics together.

Never WP; Never WS

Step 4: Deductions
When a game is entirely dependent on Formal Logic, as this game is, there usually aren't any major deductions to be made. That's because all of the rules are conditional, which

means that the rules will only be utilized under certain conditions—none of which have been provided yet.

However, it's important to keep a few things in mind for this game. First, the student must take a minimum of three courses. Because all of the rules prohibit certain courses from being offered together, you have to be careful about what courses are chosen to avoid eliminating too much from the schedule. Numbers are crucial to games such as this.

Second, linguistics is never mentioned in any of the rules. That means that linguistics can always be selected or rejected without affecting any of the other courses.

Finally, it should be noted that music is the most limiting course, because that would eliminate three courses (history by Rule 1 and physics and theater by Rule 2). That will play an important role in keeping track of the numbers.

The Master Sketch is simply a listing of the entities and conditional rules.

H L M P S T W

$$H \rightarrow \text{No S and No M}$$
$$S \text{ or } M \rightarrow \text{No H}$$

$$M \rightarrow \text{No P and No T}$$
$$P \text{ or } T \rightarrow \text{No M}$$

$$W \rightarrow \text{No P and No S}$$
$$P \text{ or } S \rightarrow \text{No W}$$

Never HS; Never HM
Never MP; Never MT
Never WP; Never WS

Step 5: Questions

18. (C) Acceptability
Rule 1 dictates that history and statistics can't be taken together, nor can history and music. That eliminates **(A)** and **(B)**. Rule 2 dictates that music and theater can't be taken together. That eliminates **(E)**. Rule 3 dictates that writing and physics can't be taken together. That eliminates **(D)**.

That leaves **(C)** as the correct answer—the only one that doesn't violate any of the rules.

19. (D) Maximum
Because of the restrictions placed on so many courses, the student certainly couldn't take all seven courses. That eliminates **(A)**.

Selecting music would eliminate three other courses, automatically dropping the number of courses to, at most, four. To maximize the number of courses, eliminate M. That leaves six courses. However, many of these courses (e.g., history and statistics) can't be together. So six courses can't be done. That eliminates **(B)**.

With music eliminated, writing and statistics become the most limiting entities. Writing would eliminate physics and statistics, leaving four courses at most. Statistics would eliminate history and writing, again leaving four courses at most. If you get rid of one, the other would still be around—reducing the course count to a maximum of four. So, to maximize the course load, eliminate both. However, that *still* leaves only four courses at most.

No matter what you do—if you keep writing or statistics, or get rid of them both—you can't select more than four courses. That eliminates **(C)**.

The final question is: Can four courses be selected? If you do eliminate writing and statistics, you'd be left with history, linguistics, physics, and theater. That selection doesn't violate any of the rules, therefore it is possible to take four courses. That means **(B)** is the correct answer.

Note: Now it is clear that the student will either select three courses (the minimum) or four courses (the maximum).

20. (B) "If" / Could Be True

For the purposes of this particular question, the correct answer will be two courses that the student could also not take, while the four wrong answer choices will contain courses that if selected will violate at least one of the rules.

If the student doesn't take physics and doesn't take writing, then that leaves five courses: history, linguistics, music, statistics, and theater.

At this point, history and music are the two most limiting courses. Each one would eliminate two of the remaining courses. That would leave three courses—the minimum that must be selected. So it makes sense to start with **(B)**.

(B) works because that would get rid of the two most restrictive entities. That would leave linguistics, statistics, and theater—an acceptable trio of courses. Thus, **(B)** is the correct answer. For the record:

(A) and **(C)** don't work because both answers would leave music and theater together, which violates Rule 2.

(D) doesn't work because it would leave history and statistics together, which violates Rule 1.

(E) doesn't work because it would leave history and music together, which also violates Rule 1.

21. (E) "If" / Must Be True

If music is taken, then that eliminates history (by Rule 1), physics (by Rule 2), and theater (also by Rule 2). That leaves linguistics, statistics, and writing. To satisfy the minimum of three courses, at least two of the remaining courses are

needed. However, Rule 3 prohibits statistics and writing to both be selected. So, to satisfy the minimum requirement, one of those must be selected along with linguistics.

Because linguistics has to be selected in either case, **(E)** is the correct answer.

22. (B) Must Be True

For the purposes of this particular question, the correct answer "must be true," while the four wrong answers "could be or must be false."

Once the courses are selected, that selection must include at least one of the courses in the correct answer. In other words, it would be unacceptable to select neither course in the correct answer choice.

To test the answers, determine what would happen if both courses were removed. If you can still select the minimum of three courses, then you have your answer. According to **(B)**, if linguistics and theater were removed from selection, that would leave history, music, physics, statistics, and writing. Taking music would eliminate history (by Rule 1) and physics (by Rule 2). That would leave writing and statistics as the remaining two courses. However, that would violate Rule 3.

If music were not taken, taking writing would eliminate physics and statistics (by Rule 3). However, that would leave only history. That wouldn't satisfy the minimum of three.

If music and writing weren't taken, that would leave history, physics, and statistics as the three courses. However, that violates Rule 1.

Therefore, in any case, it is impossible to select at least three courses when linguistics and theater are taken out of the picture. Therefore, the selection must include at least one of them, making **(B)** the correct answer.

*Y*ou can also use your previous sketches on this question to knock off wrong answer choices quickly. For the record:

(A), **(D)** A course load of linguistics, theater and writing shows why the selection doesn't have to include history, statistics, music, or physics.

(C) A course load of history, physics, and theater shows why the selection doesn't have to include linguistics, or writing.

(E) A course load of history, linguistics, and physics shows why the selection doesn't have to include theater or writing.

23. (B) Rule Substitution

For this question, Rule 2 is removed from the game and replaced with one of the answers. The correct answer will be the one replacement that will create the exact same scenario that Rule 2 created.

Specifically, by removing Rule 2, music can now be selected along with physics or theater. The correct answer will re-establish the limitations that music will be taken with neither physics nor theater.

The only other information known about music is that, by Rule 1, it can't be taken with history. If, as **(B)** says, music can only be selected with linguistics, statistics, and/or writing, then that means it can't be selected with history (Rule 1), physics, or theater. That brings back the same exact restrictions dictated by Rule 2 without adding anything new. That makes **(B)** the correct answer. For the record:

(A) adds two different restrictions to music that were never dictated by the original rules.

(C) reinstates the condition that physics and math can't be taken together. However, it doesn't reestablish that music and theater can't be taken together. It also puts restrictions on physics (e.g., physics cannot be taken with statistics) that the original rules never suggested.

(D) reinstates the condition that theater and math can't be taken together. However, it doesn't reestablish that music and physics can't be taken together. It also puts restrictions on theater (i.e., theater cannot be taken with physics) that the original rules never suggested.

(E) takes away the possibility of having physics, theater, and math all together, which partially replaces Rule 2. However, this answer eliminates math if physics *and* theater are taken. The problem is that it doesn't eliminate math if physics or theater alone is taken. Rule 2 would not have allowed that, so this rule doesn't completely serve the exact same function.

Section IV: Logical Reasoning

Q#	Question Type	Correct	Difficulty
1	Paradox	E	★
2	Weaken	C	★
3	Main Point	A	★
4	Principle (Parallel)	C	★
5	Flaw	A	★
6	Inference	D	★
7	Paradox	A	★★
8	Flaw	B	★
9	Inference	A	★★★
10	Weaken	D	★★
11	Assumption (Necessary)	E	★
12	Method of Argument	A	★
13	Inference	C	★
14	Flaw	D	★★
15	Inference	B	★★★
16	Principle (Identify/Inference)	B	★★★
17	Assumption (Necessary)	D	★
18	Flaw	E	★★★
19	Assumption (Sufficient)	B	★★
20	Paradox	E	★★★★
21	Assumption (Necessary)	D	★★
22	Parallel Flaw	C	★★★
23	Strengthen	B	★★★
24	Assumption (Sufficient)	B	★★★
25	Principle (Identify/Weaken)	A	★★

1. (E) Paradox

Step 1: Identify the Question Type

Because the question stem asks for a choice that best "explains the situation" in the stimulus, this is a Paradox question.

Step 2: Untangle the Stimulus

In the stimulus for a Paradox question, look for a word like [y]et to point you to the seeming contradiction. Here, even though automated flight technology is reliable for guiding aircraft, it's not a perfect safeguard against human error.

Step 3: Make a Prediction

It may be a stretch to predict the exact answer that will resolve this apparent discrepancy. However, you still need to characterize the right answer. The correct answer choice will explain how automated flight technology is susceptible to human error despite its reliability.

Step 4: Evaluate the Answer Choices

(E) resolves the paradox. If automated flight technology takes its cues from human commands, a bad judgment call from a human operator could cause problems for the automated flight technology, even if that technology is working properly.

(A) doesn't explain the paradox because the stimulus says that automated flight technology is sometimes subject to human error even when it *is* functioning correctly.

(B) would help explain the paradox if you could establish that the smaller aircraft not always having up-to-date automated flight technology is a direct result of human error. But because that is not established, **(B)** doesn't help.

(C) discusses what happens when automated flight technology fails, but this doesn't help explain why human error is still a factor when the technology doesn't malfunction.

(D) removes both human error and the automated flight technology from the picture, so even if **(D)** is true, the question of why automated flight technology is still subject to human error has not been answered.

2. (C) Weaken

Step 1: Identify the Question Type

This stem uses the word *weakens*, so this is a Weaken question.

Step 2: Untangle the Stimulus

The argument concludes with a recommendation. To keep our hands warm during the winter, gloves are unnecessary; we simply need to put on an extra layer of clothing. The evidence for this is that our hands can be kept warm as long as our vital organs are warm under that extra undershirt or sweater.

Step 3: Make a Prediction

Notice the author's extreme language in the argument: "one never needs gloves or mittens" … "one can *always* keep one's hands warm … by putting on an extra layer." Any time an author uses extreme language like that in an argument, jump on it. Here, in order to draw so strong a conclusion, the author assumes that the extra layer of clothing will always protect one's hands, or that there will never be an extreme circumstance in which it will be dangerous to have one's hands exposed, no matter how many layers one wears. Therefore, to weaken the argument, seek out an answer choice that gives such an extreme circumstance.

Step 4: Evaluate the Answer Choices

(C) provides that extreme circumstance. If at any point during the winter, temperatures dip low enough to cause frostbite, and the extra layer fails to keep one's hands warm, then the author's argument is in serious trouble, and gloves would certainly be necessary in some circumstances.

(A) is Out of Scope because the argument doesn't concern which body parts are more important to keep warm from a physiological standpoint. The author is merely recommending a surefire way to keep your hands warm during the winter, so the argument is unaffected whether or not **(A)** is true.

(B) makes a comparison between several layers of light garments and one or two heavy garments when it comes to keeping one's vital organs warm. But without a connection to keeping one's hands warm, that comparison is totally irrelevant.

(D) doesn't affect the argument because the author isn't trying to argue that putting on an extra layer of clothing is the *most* effective way to keep one's hands warm. As long as putting on an extra layer of clothing is effective at all, the author's argument is still sound.

(E) also goes too far. The author doesn't argue that putting on an extra layer of clothing warms one's hands by stimulating circulation through physical effort, so even if **(E)** is true, the author's argument remains untouched.

3. (A) Main Point

Step 1: Identify the Question Type

This is a Main Point question, because the stem simply asks for an answer choice that expresses the main conclusion of the argument.

Step 2: Untangle the Stimulus

In the first sentence, the author explains why we are drawn to music with a simple recurring rhythm. Such music reminds us of being in the womb. The support for this is given throughout the rest of the argument. At birth, a baby is deprived of the comforting sound of his/her mother's regular heartbeat. So when a person seeks out warmth and security, it makes sense to be drawn to simple recurring sounds that mimic the mother's heartbeat.

Step 3: Make a Prediction

When predicting the answer to a Main Point question, be careful about using Keywords. Here, the obvious Conclusion Keyword is [*t*]*hus*, but this Keyword, like many Conclusion Keywords in Main Point arguments, signals a subsidiary conclusion, not the main one. The author's main point isn't that it is natural for us to be strongly drawn to simple recurring rhythmic sounds. The author's main point is that we are strongly drawn to such sounds because those sounds remind us of the womb, which was the first place in which we encountered the comfort that sound could bring.

Step 4: Evaluate the Answer Choices

(A) matches the prediction of the author's main point. None of the other answer choices discusses music at all, which was the whole reason the author introduced any evidence relating to birth, the womb, or the mother's heartbeat.

(B) is a piece of information that is found in the second sentence of the argument, a sentence beginning with "after all," which is a key phrase that generally signals evidence. Besides, the author only brings up this point in an attempt to prove that the mother's heartbeat has a recurring rhythm not unlike the musical rhythms people find most comforting.

(C) is a piece of information that is only offered as part of a larger explanation for why we seek out music that has a simple recurring rhythm—because we have a primordial desire to replicate the sense of comfort we felt inside the womb.

(D) is close, but it doesn't incorporate the appeal of music with a simple recurring rhythm, which is the whole reason the author brings up the warmth and security of the womb in the first place.

(E) is a Distortion. The comforting sound of the mother's regular heartbeat may be why we are attracted to music with a simple recurring rhythmic sound, but the author's point isn't that the heartbeat itself is a simple recurring rhythmic sound.

4. (C) Principle (Parallel)

Step 1: Identify the Question Type

The presence of *principle* in the stem is a likely clue that this is a Principle question, but pay close attention to the rest of the stem. There will be a broad principle underlying the linguist's narrow statements, and that same broad principle will be illustrated by another narrow set of statements in the answer choices.

Step 2: Untangle the Stimulus

The linguist points out that despite the ability of most people to identify whether a sequence of words in their own dialect is grammatical, many of those same people can't specify the exact grammatical rules that apply to that particular sequence of words.

Step 3: Make a Prediction

You need not predict the subject matter of the right answer, but you can certainly extract the principle from the stimulus before applying it to the choices. The linguist appears to invoke the principle that sometimes people can know whether or not a thing meets certain criteria without knowing exactly what the criteria are. In other words, people may not be able to define a thing, but they can still know it when they see it. The correct answer choice will be a successful application of the same principle to a different situation.

Step 4: Evaluate the Answer Choices

(C) is a perfect match. Just as the linguist says that people can identify a grammatical sequence without knowing what makes a sequence grammatical, **(C)** says that people can identify a waltz without knowing what makes a piece of music a waltz.

(A) discusses how some people's writing ability doesn't translate from a journalistic style to a poetic style. But **(A)** is missing the key component of identification. No one in **(A)** is identifying whether a poem is emotionally moving or satisfying without knowing what makes a poem emotionally moving or satisfying, so it doesn't apply the principle.

(B), if it invokes a principle at all, invokes the principle that applying concepts to concrete tasks requires more knowledge that it does to discover the concepts in the first place. This doesn't match the principle.

(D) indicates that an experience can be enjoyable even if we're unable to describe it in vivid detail, which is a vastly different principle from the one in the stimulus. The linguist's statements have nothing to do with an experience or the description of that experience.

(E) would be correct if it said that people could identify a game as chess even without knowing the defining characteristics of chess, but **(E)** veers off track when it introduces the idea of playing ability.

5. (A) Flaw

Step 1: Identify the Question Type

Because you're asked to find why the company president's reasoning is "most vulnerable to criticism," this is a Flaw question.

Step 2: Untangle the Stimulus

The president declares that her company will interview applicants for the management consultant position only if those applicants have worked for firms from the top 1 percent of firms worldwide. She believes that this will ensure that the applicant selected for the job is one of the best consultants available.

Step 3: Make a Prediction

When analyzing an argument in a Flaw question, you should always ask yourself, "Why isn't the conclusion established by the evidence?" In this case, determine why the president's plan might not guarantee that her company will hire one of the best consultants. Of course, it's entirely possible that the company could hire someone who, despite working for a top firm, isn't one of the best consultants. Just because someone was employed by a top firm doesn't mean that he or she is automatically one of the best consultants. But this is something that the president erroneously assumes.

Step 4: Evaluate the Answer Choices

(A) states this flaw in a different way. When predicting the answer to a Flaw question, be sure to scan the answer choices for the issue you predicted, not the precise language of your pre-phrase.

(B) is irrelevant because no information is given on the size of the sample of management consulting firms worldwide. For all you know, the president could be taking into account every single management consulting firm existent across the globe.

(C) gets it backward. The president takes for granted that if a firm is recognized as one of the top 1 percent of firms worldwide, then all of its individual employees will be among the best consultants.

(D) is Out of Scope. The president's argument is concerned with selecting a top applicant. She hasn't predicted with any certainty that the applicant selected will accept the position once it is offered.

(E) isn't something the president presumes at all. The argument doesn't discuss whether the president believes the new hire will be competent at all tasks in the new job. The president is merely concerned with making sure her company hires one of the best consultants available.

6. (D) Inference

Step 1: Identify the Question Type

Because this stem indicates that the stimulus contains *information* that will support the correct answer, this is an Inference question. (If the correct answer *supports* the stimulus, you're likely looking at a Strengthen question.)

Step 2: Untangle the Stimulus

In an Inference question, untangling the stimulus involves accepting all the information as true, making any useful connections between statements, and translating Formal Logic whenever appropriate. Here, the stimulus makes a comparison between beginner and expert chess players. Beginners consider the consequences of a move before making it, while experts use pattern recognition, in which they consider the consequences of a move from a prior

occasion before making a similar move in the current situation.

Step 3: Make a Prediction

There isn't any Formal Logic in this stimulus, and not many connections can be made between the statements. So go straight to the answer choices, remembering that the answer must follow directly from the stimulus.

Step 4: Evaluate the Answer Choices

(D) is the only one that is strongly supported by the stimulus. If an expert player's pattern-recognition technique involves drawing upon similar experiences in past games in order to make a decision, then the successful use of that technique depends on the expert's memory. After all, the expert has to remember having been in a similar situation previously in order to use the technique in the first place.

(A) is a Distortion. Nothing in the stimulus supports the idea that beginners are *better* than experts at thinking through the consequences of chess moves. They just go about it in different ways.

(B) is another Distortion. The stimulus doesn't suggest that beginners should use pattern-recognition techniques when evaluating potential moves. As a matter of fact, beginners probably *can't* use pattern recognition because they have no prior experience to draw upon.

(C) is Extreme. Yes, experts use pattern-recognition techniques. But that doesn't mean that such techniques are necessary in order to improve one's chess game.

(E) is Out of Scope. There's nothing in the stimulus to suggest that pattern-recognition skills are universal enough to be able to translate from one type of game to another, and even if they were, that's no guarantee that pattern-recognition skills will improve one's chess-playing skills.

7. (A) Paradox

Step 1: Identify the Question Type

Any question stem asking you to "resolve an apparent discrepancy" is a Paradox question.

Step 2: Untangle the Stimulus

The farmer admits that the best way to ensure that corn kernels dry at the right speed is to sun-dry the corn while it is still in the field. However, the farmer doesn't follow this method. Instead, he dries the ears of corn on a screen in a warm, dry room.

Step 3: Make a Prediction

It's not necessary to know exactly why the farmer acts contrary to what he recognizes is the best method, but you need to know how to recognize the right answer when you see it. Here, find a reason why the farmer doesn't sun-dry his corn.

Step 4: Evaluate the Answer Choices

(A) indicates that circumstances prevent the farmer from being able to sun-dry his corn. At the time of year when the corn would ordinarily be drying in the sun, the region where the farmer grows his corn experiences a long, cloudy season. This is the correct answer because it explains why the farmer has to resort to drying the corn indoors.

(B) is Out of Scope because it deals with expense. If anything, **(B)** deepens the mystery because it confirms that the farmer's method of drying the corn is less effective *and* less cost-efficient than the preferred method.

(C) says that the preferred method of drying isn't the only method, but that doesn't explain why the farmer chooses to follow a method that he knows isn't preferable to drying the corn in the field.

(D) discusses what happens to kernels that aren't sufficiently dry. That doesn't explain why the farmer has chosen his particular method of drying.

(E) discusses what happens to kernels that are too dry. Like **(D)**, that doesn't explain why the farmer has chosen his particular method of drying.

8. (B) Flaw

Step 1: Identify the Question Type

You're asked to find why the factory manager's argument is flawed, so this is definitely a Flaw question.

Step 2: Untangle the Stimulus

The factory manager concludes that in order to survive, the factory's products must be more competitively priced, and the only way to do this is to completely refurbish the factory. The evidence for this is that if the factory were to be refurbished with new equipment, then the factory's products would be more competitively priced.

Step 3: Make a Prediction

Always keep classic flaws in mind as you untangle arguments in Flaw questions. One of the most common flaws is confusing necessity and sufficiency. In the evidence of this argument, the factory manager says that refurbishing the factory would be sufficient to make the products more competitively priced. But all of a sudden, the conclusion seems to treat refurbishment as necessary in order to lower prices and stay afloat. This unwarranted shift from sufficiency to necessity is always a logical flaw—after all, couldn't there conceivably be other ways to make the products more competitively priced? The evidence allows for such alternative solutions, but the conclusion doesn't.

Step 4: Evaluate the Answer Choices

(B) matches the predicted flaw. The manager improperly shifts from treating one solution to the price problem as the only solution.

(A) is not the flaw here. The factory manager actually does recognize that the price of auto parts can change over time; that's why the manager proposes a way to lower that price to make it more competitive.

(C) misrepresents the manager's argument. The manager does argue that outdated and inefficient equipment is one cause of the high price of the factory's auto parts, but it's not logical to reverse that cause and effect in this argument. Causal patterns do figure prominently in arguments throughout the LSAT; they just aren't the problem here.

(D) is untrue. The manager does consider causes of the problem; he explicitly states that one cause of the high price of the factory's auto parts is the factory's outdated, inefficient machinery.

(E) is also untrue; the manager does make a definite recommendation. He recommends completely refurbishing the factory as the only way to keep prices competitive.

9. (A) Inference

Step 1: Identify the Question Type

The words "properly inferred" are a clear indication that this is an Inference question.

Step 2: Untangle the Stimulus

Thanks to a major shipment from Africa, pythons have gotten much less expensive to own. But there's a catch. Many African pythons are afflicted with a liver disease that is difficult to detect early on but that is always fatal within six months of contraction. Some pythons hatched in North America also have the disease, but not nearly in the same proportion as those hatched in Africa.

Step 3: Make a Prediction

There's no Formal Logic present, and no immediate or obvious connections to make between the statements. Many different valid inferences can be made based on this information, so instead of trying to pre-phrase them all, go to the answer choices prepared to find the choice that is directly supported by information from the stimulus.

Step 4: Evaluate the Answer Choices

(A) must be true if the stimulus as true. If some North American pythons have the liver disease, then according to the stimulus, the disease will be undetectable in its early stages but will prove fatal within six months. In other words, the pythons will appear to be healthy but will die within six months of contracting the disease. Don't be afraid of **(A)** simply because it seems obvious. If it must be true, it's a correct inference.

(B) isn't a valid inference. Yes, the stimulus says that a higher proportion of African-hatched pythons has the liver disease, but that could simply be because there are far more pythons in Africa and therefore more of an opportunity for the disease to spread. There need not be a higher inherent susceptibility on the part of the African pythons.

(C) is Extreme. The disease does have a six-month incubation period, but what if a python catches the disease several months after hatching? In that case, it could live to be much older than six months despite ultimately contracting the disease.

(D) certainly doesn't have to be true. There could be a number of reasons why the pythons are inexpensive, one reason being the drop in demand due to the increase in the number of available pythons over the past two months.

(E) is Out of Scope; you can't properly infer anything about pythons that were hatched in neither Africa nor North America. If a stimulus tells you that all the tall kids wear red, that doesn't mean that the short kids don't wear red.

10. (D) Weaken

Step 1: Identify the Question Type
This stem uses the phrase "most seriously weakens," so this is clearly a Weaken question.

Step 2: Untangle the Stimulus
The argument concludes that most people need to take vitamin pills. The reason for this is that most people eat far fewer than the five servings of fruits and vegetables that nutritionists believe can meet a person's daily vitamin requirement.

Step 3: Make a Prediction
The most straightforward way to weaken an argument is to challenge its central assumption. The author sees vitamin pills as the only alternative to the five daily servings of fruits and vegetables that most people don't get. In reaching the conclusion, the author assumes that there's no other way to get those vitamins. So seek an answer choice that would provide a source other than vitamin pills that would allow people to get the vitamins they're not getting from fruits and vegetables.

Step 4: Evaluate the Answer Choices
(D) provides that source. If manufacturers of foods that aren't fruits and vegetables fortify those foods with vitamins, then the people who don't eat enough fruits and vegetables can still get their vitamins without taking pills.

(A) suggests that even people who eat the recommended number of servings of fruits and vegetables may not get enough vitamins from those servings. But this doesn't undermine the idea that they need to get their vitamins from pills. If anything, it strengthens the idea that they'll need to get their vitamins from alternative sources.

(B) is an Irrelevant Comparison. The strength or weakness of an argument urging people to take vitamin pills doesn't

depend on whether or not certain fruits and vegetables contain more nutrients than others.

(C), if true, might make it difficult to agree on a universal amount of fruits and vegetables that will constitute five daily servings. But that does nothing to support or undermine the idea that people will need to turn to vitamin pills to make up for the vitamins they aren't getting from produce.

(E) introduces fiber, which is Out of Scope. The author is only concerned with how people can get the vitamins in fruits and vegetables without eating five daily servings of them.

11. (E) Assumption (Necessary)

Step 1: Identify the Question Type
This is a Necessary Assumption question, because the stem asks for the assumption "required by the argument."

Step 2: Untangle the Stimulus
The researcher concludes that armadillos don't move rapidly into new territories. This conclusion is based on the results of an experiment in which the researcher tagged armadillos at a site during the spring, and then returned in the fall to find the vast majority of the tagged armadillos within a few hundred yards of where they had been tagged.

Step 3: Make a Prediction
Before going to the answer choices, think about what the researcher might be taking for granted (or ruling out, for that matter) in order to reach her conclusion. Because the researcher didn't keep constant watch over the armadillos from spring to fall, she must be assuming that between her two visits to the site, the armadillos didn't travel more than a hundred yards away from the site. That's the only way her conclusion is valid based on her evidence.

Step 4: Evaluate the Answer Choices
(E) is a great paraphrase of the prediction. Because **(E)** is phrased negatively, it may not seem obvious as the correct answer. But that negative phrasing makes it incredibly susceptible to the Denial Test. If you deny **(E)** and say that most of the recaptured armadillos *did* actually move to a new territory during the summer and return to the old territory in the fall, then the researcher's argument disintegrates. Thus, **(E)** is necessary for the argument to work and is therefore the correct answer.

(A) is irrelevant. It doesn't matter whether or not any armadillos living at or near the research site last spring were able to escape tagging. The researcher's argument only concerns those armadillos that were tagged and then recaptured.

(B) certainly need not be true for the argument to work. If the researcher only recaptured a small minority of the armadillos she tagged last spring, then it would actually be harder, not easier, for her to draw her conclusion.

(C) is Extreme. It doesn't need to be true that every single armadillo tagged in the spring survived to the fall.

(D) misses the point of the argument. The issue is not whether the tagged armadillos are identifiable, but where the armadillos were recaptured. Whether or not it's possible for the armadillos to remove their tags is a separate question that doesn't need to be answered in order for the argument to be valid.

12. (A) Method of Argument

Step 1: Identify the Question Type

This is about as short as Logical Reasoning question stems get. However, even from these few words (and a glance at the answer choices), the question is much more interested in what Rahima does to structure her argument rather than the particulars of what she says. That makes this a Method of Argument question.

Step 2: Untangle the Stimulus

Read Sahira's argument first for context. Sahira argues that governments are justified in subsidizing artists. Her justification for this is the idea that otherwise, great artists would pander to the tastes of the public instead of producing their best work simply because they'd be worried about making ends meet. Rahima responds by saying that Sahira's argument depends on the idea that artists have to produce work that isn't their best in order to capture popular acclaim. Rahima then goes on to say that this isn't necessarily true.

Step 3: Make a Prediction

Focus on Rahima's response to Sahira. You don't need to figure out her conclusion or evidence or assumption; you just need to determine *how* her argument works. First, Rahima points out an idea on which Sahira's argument depends, and then she challenges it. Always form your predictions in this general way, and use verbs if you can; this will help you see which answer choice most closely matches your prediction.

Step 4: Evaluate the Answer Choices

(A) is the best match for the prediction.

(B) is a 180, because Rahima challenges a crucial component of Sahira's argument, which is a far cry from supporting it.

(C) is incorrect because Rahima doesn't indicate whether or not she agrees with Sahira's conclusion. If anything, by disputing Sahira's assumption, it seems more likely that Rahima doesn't accept Sahira's conclusion.

(D) doesn't make sense because Rahima doesn't reach her own conclusion, and she actually challenges one of Sahira's implicit premises.

(E) is Out of Scope. Rahima doesn't mention any standard used by Sahira, and she certainly doesn't accuse Sahira of being self-contradictory.

13. (C) Inference

Step 1: Identify the Question Type

This is an Inference question because it asks for a conclusion in the answer choices that is supported by the information in the stimulus.

Step 2: Untangle the Stimulus

In the Yucatán peninsula, the north has an arid climate and the south has a wet climate. This is important for the survival of adult frogs, which are vulnerable to dehydration. Small adult frogs seem to be more vulnerable to dehydration than are large adult frogs, because the small frogs' low body-weight-to-skin-surface ratio makes survival in arid climates impossible for them. Large adult frogs don't seem to have this problem.

Step 3: Make a Prediction

The many pieces of information offered up in the stimulus could support a whole host of valid inferences, so don't waste your time listing them all. Instead, proceed to the answer choices, remembering not to stop until you've found the choice that follows from the stimulus.

Step 4: Evaluate the Answer Choices

(C) is a valid inference. If large adult frogs don't have the problem that keeps small adult frogs from being able to survive in arid climates, then large adult frogs can presumably live in both arid and wet climates, while small adult frogs can live only in wet climates. Thus, more of the peninsula can be home to the large adult frogs, and **(C)** must be true.

(A) is unsupported. There's nothing in the stimulus to suggest that large and small adult frogs can't coexist in the wet area of the peninsula. The stimulus merely discusses a difference between the two sizes of adult frog when it comes to survival in arid climates.

(B) is a 180. Presumably, because the wet areas can be home to small and large adult frogs, whereas the arid areas can only host large adult frogs, frogs living in wet areas should weigh less on average, not more, than frogs in arid areas.

(D) could be true, but certainly doesn't have to be. For all you know, the south could be home to more small adult frogs than large adult frogs because the south's wetter climate makes it the only place where small adult frogs can live.

(E) is an Irrelevant Comparison. The stimulus makes no indication that location makes any difference in the permeability of a small adult frog's skin. As a matter of fact, the stimulus seems to contradict the idea that small adult frogs can survive at all in the arid climate of the north.

14. (D) Flaw

Step 1: Identify the Question Type
Because you need to determine why the editorial's argument is "most vulnerable to criticism," this is a Flaw question.

Step 2: Untangle the Stimulus
The editorial concludes that the government must address the rising crime rate. The only support for this is a recent survey in which 77 percent of people feel the crime rate is increasing and 87 percent of people are in favor of tougher sentences for criminals.

Step 3: Make a Prediction
The conclusion is a recommendation that the government "firmly address the rising crime rate," but it hasn't even been established that the crime rate is on the rise. The only thing that's been established is that the majority of survey respondents *feel* that the crime rate is on the rise. But those people aren't necessarily correct. This editorial seems to place inappropriate reliance on people's perceptions of the crime rate, and this is definitely a logical flaw, because feelings aren't the same as facts.

Step 4: Evaluate the Answer Choices
(D) expresses the prediction in slightly different words, but it is nonetheless the correct answer.

(A) is a Distortion. The survey results aren't necessarily inconsistent. It's possible to believe that criminals should receive harsher sentences without believing that the crime rate is increasing.

(B) describes something the argument isn't doing. If the argument had concluded that the government should punish criminals more severely in order to lower the crime rate, then it would be presuming a connection between punishment and the crime rate. But there's no such recommendation in the editorial, so **(B)** is not the flaw here.

(C) is irrelevant because the editorial is only addressing the current state of affairs. The results of similar surveys administered in past years wouldn't do anything to bolster or undermine the reliability of the survey cited by the editorial.

(E) is Extreme. While the argument does mention that the majority of survey respondents feel that crime is becoming more frequent and that criminals aren't being punished harshly enough, that's a far cry from presuming that tougher sentences are the "most effective means" of lowering the crime rate. The editorial merely presses the government to solve the crime problem; it doesn't tell the government how to solve the problem.

15. (B) Inference

Step 1: Identify the Question Type
The stem says that the statements in the stimulus will support one of the answer choices, so that makes this an Inference question.

Step 2: Untangle the Stimulus
Computer-dependent proofs are less certain than proofs that don't require computers. This is because human cognition, which would be used to provide certainty, can't verify computer-dependent proofs. More certainty can be achieved with proofs that don't rely on computers because human calculation can often verify such proofs.

Step 3: Make a Prediction
On Inference questions, it's often inefficient to attempt to pre-phrase answers. However, always keep in mind that you're seeking the answer choice that follows directly from the stimulus. It's not good enough to find a choice that seems believable or reasonable; find the answer that is supported by the stimulus.

Step 4: Evaluate the Answer Choices
(B) is supported by the part of the stimulus that says that "human cognition alone cannot verify computer-dependent proofs." If this is true, then a computer-dependent proof could contain errors that humans can't detect, and we would never know, because our cognition alone wouldn't be able to verify the proofs.

(A) is Extreme. Computer-dependent proofs provide less certainty than those that don't depend on computers, but a computer-dependent proof could still provide *some* certainty. We don't have to completely remove the computer from the proof in order to achieve any degree of certainty.

(C) is Extreme. The stimulus indicates that on the whole, proofs that depend *primarily* on computers are less certain than those that don't. But a computer could potentially replace human calculation in one single instance in a proof without the overall certainty of the proof being reduced.

(D) distorts the stimulus by turning an issue of relative certainty into one of absolute certainty. Human calculation helps provide a greater degree of certainty to proofs that aren't dependent on computers, but this is not to say that human calculation automatically lends complete certainty to anything.

(E) is Extreme. The stimulus merely says that when verifying simple arithmetic, electronic calculators are used for convenience rather than as a supplement to human cognition. This still leaves the door open for technology to provide artificial devices to supplement the cognitive abilities of humans in other instances. When dealing with an Inference question, beware answer choices that use extreme language; such choices are rarely correct.

16. (B) Principle (Identify/Inference)

Step 1: Identify the Question Type
[*P*]*ropositions* is a word that the LSAT often uses in place of *principles*, so this is a Principle question. Also, note that the answer choices are broadly stated, law-like rules, one of which is illustrated by the specific, narrowly drawn situation in the stimulus. This is another hallmark of Principle questions.

Step 2: Untangle the Stimulus
Madden argues that the industrialist's typical approach to problems (simplification) can exacerbate problems when applied to farming. To prove this point, Madden cites the way industrialists deal with the problem of water retention and drainage. These industrialists don't reach adequate solutions because their overly simplistic viewpoint doesn't allow for the fact that retention and drainage can happen simultaneously in good soil.

Step 3: Make a Prediction
Madden is clearly against farming problems being solved by industrialists instead of farmers. His main point is that farmers should solve their own problems because industrialists are too often given to oversimplifying those problems. Take this main point and find the answer choice that states it broadly.

Step 4: Evaluate the Answer Choices
(B) is a principle that Madden can certainly get behind. If industrialists cause problems with their tendency to oversimplify, then Madden would advocate an approach to farming problems that views them in all their complexity.

(A) is Extreme. Madden never asserts or even intimates that good farming depends more on drainage and retention than on any other factor. Madden simply uses drainage and retention as an example of a problem that industrialists oversimplify.

(C) is also Extreme. Madden might argue that farmers are better at solving farming problems than are industrialists, but extending this to include anyone else goes too far.

(D) goes further than Madden's argument allows. Perhaps it's possible that Madden would advocate industrial solutions to farming problems as a last-ditch effort, so the principle that industrial solutions should never be sought isn't one that necessarily underlies Madden's reasoning.

(E) is a Distortion. The problem-solving approach of industrialists isn't necessarily flawed on a fundamental level—Madden just says that the approach is flawed when it comes to solving farming problems. Perhaps there are situations in which the simplistic approach of the industrialists would be useful.

17. (D) Assumption (Necessary)

Step 1: Identify the Question Type
The language in this stem ("assumption required by the argument") is standard language for a Necessary Assumption question.

Step 2: Untangle the Stimulus
The critic concludes that it is impossible for contemporary literary works to be tragedies. There are two pieces of evidence. that modern works can't be tragedies in the classical sense unless their protagonists are seen as possessing nobility; and that our current age is one in which no one believes that human endeavors are governed by fate.

Step 3: Make a Prediction
The words *cannot* and *unless* in the first sentence are a good indication that Formal Logic might be helpful. That sentence translates to: "If the protagonist is not seen as possessing nobility, then modern works cannot be tragedies." However, the author concludes that modern works are certainly not tragedies without establishing the condition that the protagonists are not seen as noble. Instead, the author claims that people don't believe in endeavors governed by fate. In order for the argument to work, the author must assume a connection between the concept of endeavors not being governed by fate and the condition that protagonists are not seen as noble.

Step 4: Evaluate the Answer Choices
(D) provides exactly the missing link predicted.

(A) is a 180. Clearly the critic thinks that classification of a work as a tragedy should depend on characteristics of its audience, because the critic invokes audience beliefs to declare that modern works can't be tragedies.

(B) is Extreme. It needn't be true that the belief that human endeavors are governed by fate is false; the evidence merely says that no one takes the belief seriously anymore. Furthermore, **(B)** provides no link between the evidence and conclusion.

(C) isn't necessary to the argument either. Even if all plays that were once classified as tragedies meet the author's criteria for classification as tragedies, the argument can still be made, because the critic is concerned with how to classify *contemporary* works of literature.

(E) is merely a contrapositive (and an impure one, at that) of the Formal Logic statement in the argument's first sentence. However, because the critic doesn't assert that all modern literature contains ignoble characters who persevere, **(E)** doesn't enable the critic to reach the conclusion from the evidence provided.

18. (E) Flaw

Step 1: Identify the Question Type
Anytime you see "vulnerable to criticism," you know you're dealing with a Flaw question.

Step 2: Untangle the Stimulus
The conclusion of the argument dissuades the university's grad students from unionizing, and it supports that position by stating that most of the grad students disapprove of a recent attempt by a small minority of students to unionize. The argument admits that most grad students were unaware of the attempt, but most of those who were aware don't believe that a union would effectively represent or pursue their interests.

Step 3: Make a Prediction
There's a big discrepancy in the argument. The first sentence says that most graduate students at the university are unaware of the minority who attempted to unionize. How can most of the grad students disapprove of the attempt at unionization, as the argument concludes, if most of them don't even know it happened? This author appears to be mistaking an absence of approval for compelling evidence of disapproval, which isn't logically sound because there's no proof that students wouldn't approve of the unionization attempt if they found out about it.

Step 4: Evaluate the Answer Choices
(E) puts this flaw in different words, but still matches the prediction.

(A) is Out of Scope. No long-standing practice is discussed in the argument.

(B) is Out of Scope. The point of the argument isn't to give reasons why some grad students disapprove; the point is that students shouldn't unionize simply because there is disapproval in the first place.

(C) is a Distortion. The argument doesn't conclude that the grad students shouldn't unionize because most of them were unaware of the previous attempt at unionization; it discourages unionization on the basis of the purported disapproval from the majority of grad students.

(D) is irrelevant. There might well be other possible reasons for unionizing, but they don't need to be considered in order for this argument to work. In order for this argument to be logically sound, the author needs proof that there is indeed the mass disapproval cited in the last sentence. That proof would make the conclusion follow from the evidence.

19. (B) Assumption (Sufficient)

Step 1: Identify the Question Type
The question stem indicates that one of the answer choices, if assumed, will make the conclusion follow from the evidence. That makes this a Sufficient Assumption question.

Step 2: Untangle the Stimulus
The conclusion of the argument is signaled by [*t*]*hus*. Griley does not believe in democracy. The evidence comes in two parts. Apparently, Griley believes that any popular artwork is probably not good. Also, the first sentence gives us a more general rule. Anyone who believes in democracy has a high regard for the wisdom of the masses.

Step 3: Make a Prediction
Rearrange the pieces of this argument so that you can clearly see the gap in the logic. The first sentence says something that's true of *anyone* who believes in democracy, so it can be translated into Formal Logic. "If one believes in democracy, then one has high regard for mass wisdom." Next, the conclusion says that Griley does not believe in democracy. This is your cue to contrapose the Formal Logic statement. "If one doesn't have high regard for mass wisdom, then one doesn't believe in democracy." The only other thing you know about Griley from the evidence is his belief that popular artwork isn't likely to be good. So if you can tie that belief to a disregard for the wisdom of the masses, then the contrapositive will be triggered and Griley will indeed not believe in democracy, which is the argument's conclusion. So pre-phrase the assumption as "if one believes that popular artwork is unlikely to be good, then one does not have high regard for the wisdom of the masses."

Step 4: Evaluate the Answer Choices
(B) matches this prediction perfectly.

(A) indicates that Griley's belief about popular artwork is enough to guarantee that he's an elitist, but that has no connection to the first statement about belief in democracy.

(C) gives a conditional statement based on Griley's not being an elitist. But the evidence confirms that Griley is an elitist, and besides, you need an answer choice that will tell you that Griley does *not* have a high regard for the wisdom of the masses. That's the only way to guarantee the argument's conclusion that he doesn't believe in democracy.

(D) gets the terms backward. To guarantee that the conclusion follows from the evidence, you need an answer choice that says that the belief that popular artwork isn't good is *sufficient* for a disregard for the wisdom of the masses, not *necessary*.

(E) merely mixes up the sufficient and necessary conditions of the first sentence of the argument. The first sentence of the argument says that a high regard for the wisdom of the masses is necessary for belief in democracy. **(E)** says the opposite. Without a connection to Griley's elitism or his belief that popular artwork is substandard, **(E)** can't properly bridge together the terms of the argument.

20. (E) Paradox

Step 1: Identify the Question Type
Because you're asked to find the answer choice that best helps explain the results of a study, this is a Paradox question.

Step 2: Untangle the Stimulus
The study took two groups of people and had one group lower its salt intake while the other group maintained high salt intake throughout the study. The group that cut its salt intake saw lower blood pressure, as expected, but the group that maintained high salt intake also had low blood pressure.

Step 3: Make a Prediction
It's often a waste of time to pre-phrase the exact answer to a Paradox question, but make sure to characterize the answer so that you know what you're looking for. Find an answer choice that explains how the high-salt group maintained low blood pressure despite confirmation that salt intake increases blood pressure.

Step 4: Evaluate the Answer Choices
(E) matches the prediction by reversing the causal mechanism between blood pressure and salt intake. If certain people have to increase their salt intake in response to a predisposition to abnormally low blood pressure, then that could explain why some people who consume a lot of salt nonetheless have low blood pressure.

(A) is in line with the idea that high salt intake leads to high blood pressure, so if anything, **(A)** further deepens the mystery—why, if **(A)** is true, did the high-salt group maintain low blood pressure?

(B) opens the door for other factors to contribute to high blood pressure, but it doesn't give us a reason why the group in question had remarkably low blood pressure.

(C) presents a fact about people with high blood pressure, but it does nothing to help explain how a group of people can have very low blood pressure despite very high salt intake.

(D), like **(C)**, focuses on some people that have high blood pressure. So, it doesn't do anything to help explain the mystery centered around people with very low blood pressure despite very high salt intake.

21. (D) Assumption (Necessary)

Step 1: Identify the Question Type
Because the stem asks for an "assumption on which the argument depends," this is a Necessary Assumption question.

Step 2: Untangle the Stimulus
The conclusion comes at the end of the argument. Thanks to the media's attention to lottery winners, people likely greatly overestimate the chances of their winning a jackpot. The main evidence for this is the disproportionate amount of attention the media pays to lottery winners relative to the very slim odds of winning a lottery jackpot, coupled with the fact that most people become at least marginally aware of events that receive such media attention.

Step 3: Make a Prediction
Pre-phrasing the central assumption in an LSAT argument is always a matter of filling in the missing link, the thing that must be true for the argument to work. Here, in order for people to greatly overestimate their chances of winning a jackpot due merely to media coverage, the author of the argument must be assuming that people's estimation of their chances of winning is affected by becoming aware of other people who have won a jackpot. This isn't necessarily mind-blowing, but it isn't stated directly in the argument, and it must be true in order for the argument to be logically sound.

Step 4: Evaluate the Answer Choices
(D) is the best match for this prediction. If you're ever unsure of your answer in a question asking for a necessary assumption, ask whether it must be true for the argument to hold. Here, if **(D)** were untrue, and becoming aware of people who have won a jackpot has no effect whatsoever on people's ability to estimate their chances of winning such a jackpot, then the argument crumbles. So **(D)** needs to be true and therefore must be the central assumption.

(A) goes too far into the reasons why media coverage contributes to people's overestimation of their chances of winning. In order for the argument to be logically sound, the media doesn't need to intentionally misrepresent the odds of winning in the specific way spelled out by **(A)**.

(B) veers off course by changing the focus of the argument to those who do and don't receive lots of media attention. Whether or not people other than jackpot winners receive media attention, the author can still make this argument about media coverage causing people to overestimate their odds of winning the lottery.

(C) gets too specific by discussing people who purchase lottery tickets. The author is simply arguing that many people overestimate their chances of winning the lottery. Whether or not these people actually buy lottery tickets is a separate issue.

(E) works against the argument by pointing to a group of people who are influenced by the media but who nonetheless do not overestimate their chances of winning a major jackpot. This certainly need not be true for the argument to work.

22. (C) Parallel Flaw

Step 1: Identify the Question Type
The stem indicates that the task is to find the answer choice with flawed reasoning parallel to the stimulus. So this is a Parallel Flaw question.

Step 2: Untangle the Stimulus

There is Formal Logic terminology in the stimulus, so the best approach is to abstract the stimulus into algebraic terms. The first sentence can be translated to this:

If X (well publicized) and Y (established writer) → Z (successful)

The stimulus goes on to say that because Julia is an established writer and had a successful book tour, the tour must have been well publicized. In algebraic terms:

If Y and Z → X

This is flawed because a necessary condition (in this case, a successful book tour) could potentially happen even without any of the sufficient conditions being satisfied.

Step 3: Make a Prediction

It's impossible to know exactly what the right answer will say. But you know from the analysis that it will have the following structure. If X and Y, then Z. Therefore, because Y and Z, X. In other words, the argument will present two sufficient conditions for a necessary result. It will then claim that the necessary condition coupled with one of the sufficient conditions is enough to conclude the other sufficient condition occurred.

Step 4: Evaluate the Answer Choices

(C) matches the flawed structure. The first sentence can be expressed as this:

If X (kept in the shade) and Y (watered more than twice weekly) → Z (die)

Then **(C)** goes on to say that because X and Z both happened, Y must have happened.

If X and Z → Y

This is the exact same flaw as the stimulus because **(C)**, like the stimulus, is attempting to claim that because the necessary condition occurred alongside one of the sufficient conditions, the other sufficient condition must have occurred.

(A) is not parallel because translating the first sentence shows there are two *necessary* conditions for a recipe to turn out—following it exactly *and* using high-quality ingredients. The stimulus has two *sufficient* conditions for a successful book tour. This alone is reason enough to eliminate **(A)**. Plus, the logic of **(A)** is not flawed, because the recipe's turning out did require the high-quality ingredients.

(B) has parallel evidence, but its conclusion differs from the stimulus. The first sentence translates to "If fastest microprocessor and most memory, then it will meet Aletha's needs" (in other terms, "If X and Y, then Z"). But then **(B)** goes on to say that because Z happened, X and Y happened. This is flawed, to be sure, but not in the same way as the stimulus.

(D) has reasoning that is actually correct. The first sentence translates to "If dry rot and poor drainage, then built near a high water table." Then it says that a certain house suffers from both dry rot and poor drainage. According to the first sentence then, it has been built near a high water table, which is exactly what **(D)** concludes.

(E) also has a valid argument because it is structured exactly like **(D)**. The first sentence translates to "If double vents and narrow lapels, then fashionably dressed." Because Joseph's suit met both sufficient conditions, it should follow that he was fashionably dressed, which is what **(E)** concludes.

23. (B) Strengthen

Step 1: Identify the Question Type

This question stem provides clear, categorical language indicating that this is a Strengthen question.

Step 2: Untangle the Stimulus

This argument, like many science-based arguments, attempts to provide an explanation for a phenomenon. Here, the phenomenon is a line of eight large craters of different ages. The two most plausible explanations for the formation of the craters are volcanic activity and meteorites. According to the author's conclusion, the craters' linearity and disparity of age points to their having been caused by volcanic activity and not by meteorites.

Step 3: Make a Prediction

Whenever an author argues that Y was caused by X and *not* by Z, you can strengthen the argument with additional evidence that either further supports X (volcanic events) or discredits Z (meteorites) as the likely cause. It's unknown exactly what form this evidence will take, but you can approach the answer choices having predicted the character of the correct answer.

Step 4: Evaluate the Answer Choices

(B) does exactly what you need by making it highly unlikely that meteorites were responsible. Of course, this doesn't prove that *volcanoes* were responsible, but **(B)** is correct because it eliminates a plausible alternative, which is a common way to strengthen arguments on the LSAT.

(A) does show that volcanoes can cause craters, but because the craters in **(A)** are all the same age, **(A)** has no effect on this argument, which concerns a line of craters that are of different ages.

(C) weakens this argument by undermining the idea that either volcanoes *or* meteorites are responsible for the formation of the craters.

(D) also weakens the argument by suggesting that there isn't any volcano strong enough to form the craters in question. Expect one or more weakeners among the answer choices for a Strengthen question, and vice versa.

(E) might appear to strengthen the author's arguments because it attacks the explanation (meteorites) that the author wishes to discredit. However, the author argues against meteorites in general, so even if, as **(E)** suggests, a single meteorite shower couldn't have formed the craters, there's still the possibility of craters being formed by a series of meteorite showers.

24. (B) Assumption (Sufficient)

Step 1: Identify the Question Type
This stem asks us to find the answer choice that, if assumed, makes the conclusion follow logically. This is classic language for a Sufficient Assumption question.

Step 2: Untangle the Stimulus
The argument concludes that genuine creative geniuses tend to anger the majority by virtue of their dissatisfaction with habitual assent to common beliefs. The evidence for this is that those who share that dissatisfaction seek out controversy and, by extension, the enjoyment that comes from debunking popular views.

Step 3: Make a Prediction
In Assumption questions, one of the most straightforward ways to predict the answer is to bridge unmatched terms or ideas between the evidence and conclusion. Here, the evidence shows that those dissatisfied with habitual assent enjoy demonstrating that popular views are false. And the conclusion asserts that same dissatisfaction causes creative geniuses to anger the majority. If those who enjoy debunking popular views also tend to anger the majority, then the argument's conclusion is all but proven.

Step 4: Evaluate the Answer Choices
(B) matches this prediction perfectly.

(A), if assumed, might help the author prove that creative geniuses are themselves angry, but it does nothing to help establish the conclusion that geniuses anger the majority.

(C) distorts the argument, which says that creative geniuses and others who are dissatisfied with habitual assent enjoy debunking popular beliefs. This tells us nothing about what these geniuses themselves believe.

(D) has all the right elements, but in the wrong order. If people who anger the majority enjoy demonstrating the falsehood of popular viewpoints, then those people have something in common with people who are dissatisfied with habitual assent and who seek out controversy, but this does not mean that these two groups of people are one and the same.

(E) merely reverses the terms of the conclusion, but without any connection to seeking controversy or enjoying demonstrating the falsehood of popular beliefs, **(E)** cannot logically complete the argument.

25. (A) Principle (Identify/Weaken)

Step 1: Identify the Question Type
This is a long stem, but if you read it closely, you'll see that you're being asked to find the principle underlying Larissa's critique of Claude's argument, so approach this as a Principle question.

Step 2: Untangle the Stimulus
Claude argues that candidates for a job who salt their food without first tasting it are less desirable because they are making a decision based on inadequate information. Larissa makes two analogies to criticize that policy. Even before setting foot into a supermarket, Larissa wears a sweater in anticipation of it being too cold inside. Also, before opening any credit card offer that comes in the mail, Larissa already knows it won't be worth her time.

Step 3: Make a Prediction
Find the principle underlying both of Larissa's analogies. The one thing they have in common is that in each case, Larissa has made a decision without having all the information, which would count against her in Claude's eyes. But Larissa's defense is that she already knows that supermarkets are invariably too cold for her and that credit card offers that arrive in the mail are invariably not worthwhile for her. Presumably, then, Larissa might argue that some of Claude's job candidates salt their food before tasting it not because they have poor judgment but because food is invariably too bland for them. So Larissa's principle, broadly stated, is that something that appears to be bad decision-making may just be an application of what is generally true in a given set of circumstances.

Step 4: Evaluate the Answer Choices
(A) is a bit long-winded, but it is a great match for the prediction.

(B) is not a valid principle to use in criticizing Claude's policy because Claude isn't using job-related behavior as a basis for his inferences—he's basing his inferences on whether job candidates salt their food.

(C) is Extreme, because Claude doesn't necessarily use his food-salting observations as exclusive indication of a candidate's job suitability. Besides, this principle has no relationship to either of the analogies Larissa uses in her rebuttal of Claude's reasoning.

(D) is Out of Scope. There's no indication of the generally expected social norms when it comes to salting one's food, much less any indication that the job candidates' behavior doesn't conform to those norms.

(E) is off the mark because Larissa doesn't use her supermarket/credit card analogies as examples of occasional lapses of rationality in an other wise reasonable pattern of decision-making.

PrepTest 59

The Inside Story

PrepTest 59 was administered in December 2009. It challenged 50,444 test takers. What made this test so hard? Here's a breakdown of what Kaplan students who were surveyed after taking the official exam considered PrepTest 59's most difficult section.

Hardest PrepTest 59 Section as Reported by Test Takers

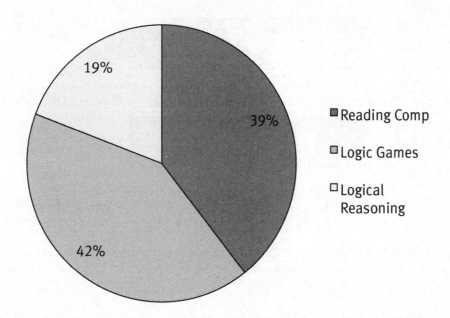

Based on these results, you might think that studying Logic Games is the key to LSAT success. Well, Logic Games is important, but test takers' perceptions don't tell the whole story. For that, you need to consider students' actual performance. The following chart shows the average number of students to miss each question in each of PrepTest 59's different sections.

Percentage Incorrect by PrepTest 59 Section Type

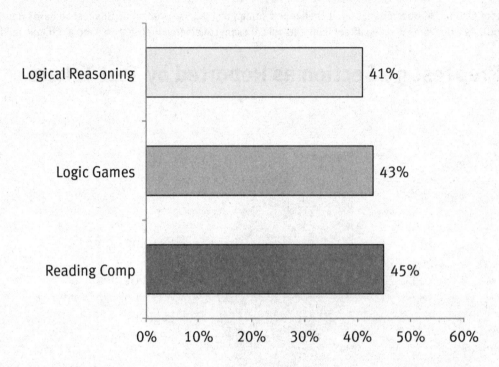

Actual student performance tells quite a different story. On average, students were almost equally likely to miss questions in all three of the different section types, and on PrepTest 59, Reading Comprehension was somewhat higher than Logic Games in actual difficulty.

Maybe students overestimate the difficulty of the Logic Games section because it's so unusual, or maybe it's because a really hard Logic Game is so easy to remember after the test. But the truth is that the testmaker places hard questions throughout the test. Here were the locations of the 10 hardest (most missed) questions in the exam.

Location of 10 Most Difficult Questions in PrepTest 59

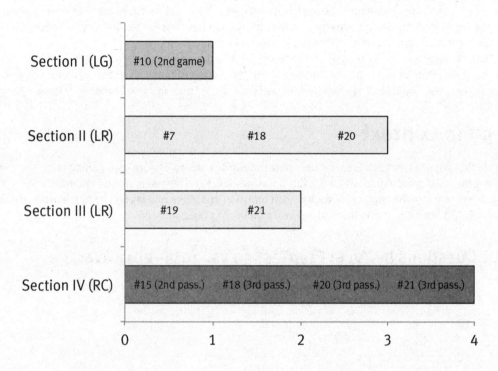

The takeaway from this data is that, to maximize your potential on the LSAT, you need to take a comprehensive approach. Test yourself rigorously, and review your performance on every section of the test. Kaplan's LSAT explanations provide the expertise and insight you need to fully understand your results. The explanations are written and edited by a team of LSAT experts, who have helped thousands of students improve their scores. Kaplan always provides data-driven analysis of the test, ranking the difficulty of every question based on actual student performance. The 10 hardest questions on every test are highlighted with a 4-star difficulty rating, the highest we give. The analysis breaks down the remaining questions into 1-, 2-, and 3-star ratings so that you can compare your performance to thousands of other test takers on all LSAC material.

Don't settle for wondering whether a question was really as hard as it seemed to you. Analyze the test with real data, and learn the secrets and strategies that help top scorers master the LSAT.

7 Can't-Miss Features of PrepTest 59

- PrepTest 59 had more room for error than many tests released around the same time. Only 90, 79, and 65 questions correct were needed for a 172, 164, and 156 respectively. Those were the lowest totals needed for those scores since December 2004 (PT 45).
- Section II had a Strengthen question for questions 1, 3, and 5. It's the only LR section ever to have three of its first five questions be Strengthen questions.
- Like PrepTest 54 (June 2008), PrepTest 58 has three Strict Sequencing games. As of its release it was just the third time that had ever happened. However it happened three more times shortly after: PrepTests 62 (December 2010), 63 (June 2011), and 69 (June 2013) all also had three Strict Sequencing games. However, it did not happen even once from 2012–2017.
- With the introduction of Rule Substitution questions on the LG section of PrepTest 57, PrepTest 59 appears to be the death knell for the previous king of difficult LG questions: the Rule Change question. No Rule Change question has appeared since it last appeared on this test, and PrepTest 59 remains the only test where both a Rule Substitution and Rule Change question appear together.

- This is the ninth test to feature Comparative Reading, so there weren't many *firsts* left to hit. However, this test crossed two off the list: it was the first time it appeared as the first passage of the section and the first time it included eight questions.
- Some students seek out the Humanities passage because they think it may be easier than the other passage types. However, the Isamu Noguchi Sculpture passage is the only Humanities passage to ever have an average difficulty over three stars—including three 4-Star questions as shown in the earlier graph.
- "Empire State of Mind" was the #1 song on the Billboard Hot 100 the day PrepTest 59 was administered. Was there anything about New York on this test? Well, oddly enough there was. Section II, Question 14 about doughnuts versus bagels was a real—but slightly edited—New York Times Letter to the Editor in 1997. Check the acknowledgements page!

PrepTest 59 in Context

As much fun as it is to find out what makes a PrepTest unique or noteworthy, it's even more important to know just how representative it is of other LSAT administrations (and, thus, how likely it is to be representative of the exam you will face on Test Day). The following charts compare the numbers of each kind of question and game on PrepTest 59 to the average numbers seen on all officially released LSATs administered over the past five years (from 2013 through 2017).

Number of LR Questions by Type: PrepTest 59 vs. 2013–2017 Average

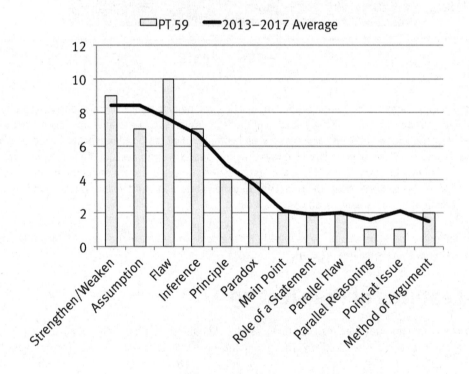

Number of LG Games by Type: PrepTest 59 vs. 2013–2017 Average

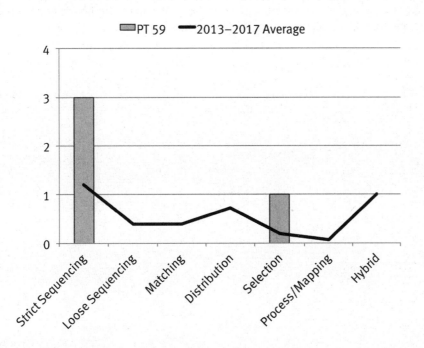

Number of RC Questions by Type: PrepTest 59 vs. 2013–2017 Average

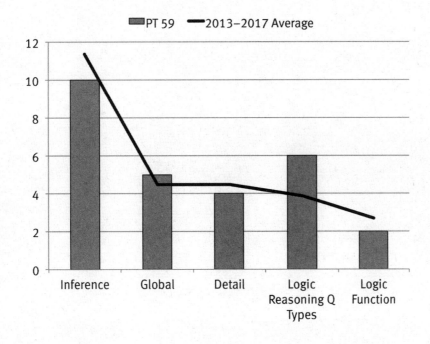

There isn't usually a huge difference in the distribution of questions from LSAT to LSAT, but if this test seems harder (or easier) to you than another you've taken, compare the number of questions of the types on which you, personally, are strongest and weakest. Then, explore within each section to see if your best or worst question types came earlier or later.

Students in Kaplan's comprehensive LSAT courses have access to every released LSAT and to a library of thousands of officially released questions arranged by question, game, and passage type. If you are studying on your own, you have to do a bit more work to identify your strengths and your areas of opportunity. Quantitative analysis (like that in the charts shown here) is an important tool for understanding how the test is constructed, and how you are performing on it.

Section I: Logic Games

Game 1: Law Firm Departments

Q#	Question Type	Correct	Difficulty
1	Acceptability	C	★
2	"If" / Could Be True	A	★
3	Must Be False (CANNOT Be True)	C	★★
4	"If" / Could Be True	D	★
5	"If" / Must Be True	C	★★

Game 2: Museum Photographs

Q#	Question Type	Correct	Difficulty
6	Acceptability	C	★
7	"If" / Could Be True	E	★
8	Completely Determine	D	★★
9	"If" / Must Be False (CANNOT Be True)	B	★
10	Rule Substitution	D	★★★★

Game 3: Alicia's Courses

Q#	Question Type	Correct	Difficulty
11	Acceptability	D	★
12	Partial Acceptability	E	★★★
13	Completely Determine	C	★★★
14	Supply the If	A	★★
15	"If" / Must Be True	D	★★★
16	Rule Change	A	★★★

Game 4: Annual Meetings in North American Cities

Q#	Question Type	Correct	Difficulty
17	Acceptability	A	★
18	Must Be True	E	★★
19	Completely Determine	D	★★★
20	Complete and Accurate List	E	★★★
21	"If" / Must Be False (CANNOT Be True)	E	★★
22	Could Be True	B	★★
23	Must Be False	B	★★

Game 1: Law Firm Departments

Step 1: Overview

Situation: A building housing a law firm

Entities: Seven departments (F, H, I, L, P, S, T)

Action: Strict Sequencing. Determine which departments are on each of the three floors. Because Rule 2 calls for one department to be immediately above another, the order matters, and that's why this game is classified as Sequencing. However, if you perceived the game as Distribution, it is likely your sketch would look exactly the same—you would just need to be mindful of the twist of spatially organizing the departments. Either characterization of the game would work; the important part will be building the rules into the sketch and making accurate deductions.

Limitations: Each department will be placed on exactly one floor. With only three floors for the seven departments, there will have to be at least one floor with multiple departments. However, each floor can house no more than four departments.

Step 2: Sketch

Step 1's Overview lends itself perfectly to a visual setup: three floors, top to bottom. Next to each floor, spaces will be added, as necessary, to house the seven departments. However, because the numbers haven't been dictated yet, leave each row empty for now. List the initials of each department and don't forget a note that no floor can house more than four departments.

F H I L P S T

Top:
Middle:
Bottom:

Max. 4 depts. /floor.

Step 3: Rules

Rule 1 creates a Block of Entities, as probate and tax law must be placed on the same floor.

| P T |

Rule 2 provides a vertical Block of Entities based on the word *immediately*. Therefore, whatever floor health law is on, injury law will be on the floor directly beneath it.

H
I

Rule 3 defines the layout of one of the three floors. It will contain just one department: labor law.

Step 4: Deductions

The last two rules provide information for all three floors: one will have labor law by itself, one will have health law, and one will have injury law. Because health law has to be directly above injury law, there are only two ways these three departments can be arranged: 1) health law on the top floor, injury law on the middle floor, and labor law on the bottom floor, or 2) labor law on the top floor, health law on the middle floor, and injury law on the bottom floor.

The Limited Options are worth drawing out. With the floor with labor law closed off, that leaves two floors that can house the remaining four departments. Remember, by Rule 1, probate and tax law must be together on one of those floors. However, that does not mean that the remaining two departments (finance law and securities—both Floaters in the game) must be together on the other floor. They can be, but they don't have to be.

F H I L P S T

Opt. 1   _Opt. 2_

Top: H   Top: L ||
Middle: I   Middle: H
Bottom: L || Bottom: I

| PT | max. 4 depts/floor

Step 5: Questions

1. (C) Acceptability

Rule 1 dictates that probate and tax law are on the same floor. That eliminates **(B)**. Rule 2 dictates that health law is immediately above injury law. That eliminates **(A)** and **(E)**. Rule 3 dictates that labor law occupies a floor by itself. That eliminates **(D)**.

That leaves **(C)** as the correct answer—the one that doesn't violate any of the rules.

2. (A) "If" / Could Be True

If injury and probate are both on the middle floor, then that fits the first option. That means health law is on the top floor (by Rule 2) and labor law is on the bottom floor because it has to be by itself (by Rule 3). With probate on the middle floor, that means tax law must be there, too (by Rule 1).

Top: H
Middle: I P T
Bottom: L ||

(B), **(C)**, and **(E)** are all false based on the placements of the departments in the sketch. **(D)** is also false because labor law must be by itself on the bottom floor. That leaves **(A)** as the only answer possible because family law is not limited by any of the rules.

3. (C) Must Be False (CANNOT Be True)

For this question, four of the answers will be an acceptable listing of departments for any one floor. The correct answer will be a listing that can never be found on any floor.

Based on the deductions for this game, each floor must have either health law, injury law, or labor law. **(C)** doesn't list any of those three departments, making it an impossible arrangement. That makes **(C)** the correct answer.

4. (D) "If" / Could Be True

If family law and securities are together, they must be on the same floor as either health law or injury law (because labor law must be by itself). The remaining two departments, probate and tax law, will be together (by Rule 1) but on a different floor. After all, if probate and tax law were on the same floor as family law and securities, they would all be on a floor with either health law or injury law, creating a floor with five departments. That would violate the information in the overview.

Opt. 1

Top: H [FS]/[PT]
Middle: I [PT]/[FS]
Bottom: L ||

Opt. 2

Top: L ||
Middle: H [FS]/[PT]
Bottom: I [PT]/[FS]

Therefore, family law and securities will be on one floor with either health law or injury law for a total of three departments. A second floor will have probate and tax law with either health law or injury law (whichever one is not on the same floor as family law and securities). That's also a total of three departments. The third floor will have just one department—labor law.

Based on those arrangements, **(B)**, **(C)**, and **(E)** are all false because no floor has exactly two or four departments. **(A)** is also false because that would place labor law on the middle floor, thus forcing health law and injury law to be separated by a floor and violating Rule 2. Therefore, **(D)** is the only answer possible, and it is the correct answer.

5. (C) "If" / Must Be True

If probate is on the middle floor with exactly two other departments, one of those departments must be tax law (by Rule 1). The other department must be either health law or injury law because labor law must be on a floor by itself. That finishes off the middle floor. The remaining departments

(family law and securities) will have to be placed on another floor together with either health law or injury law—whichever one is not on the floor with probate and tax law.

Making sure that health law is immediately above injury law and that labor law is by itself, there are only two possible layouts:

Opt. 1

Top: H F S
Middle: I P T
Bottom: L ||

Opt. 2

Top: L ||
Middle: H P T
Bottom: I F S

(A) and **(B)** are false in both options. **(D)** and **(E)** are possible, but they don't have to be true. **(C)** is the only answer that must be true no matter what, making it the correct answer.

Game 2: Museum Photographs

Step 1: Overview

Situation: Hanging photographs in a museum

Entities: Seven photographs (F, G, H, I, K, L, M)

Action: Strict Sequencing. Determine the order in which the paintings are hung.

Limitations: Each painting is in one of seven sequential positions, numbered 1–7, making this a basic one-to-one sequencing game.

Step 2: Sketch

All that's needed is a series of seven numbered slots and a list of the entities (by initial) to fill those slots.

FGHIKLM

$$\underline{\quad}_1 \quad \underline{\quad}_2 \quad \underline{\quad}_3 \quad \underline{\quad}_4 \quad \underline{\quad}_5 \quad \underline{\quad}_6 \quad \underline{\quad}_7$$

Step 3: Rules

Rule 1 provides a predefined order for two of the paintings. Wherever *Gardenias* is hung, *Katydid* will be hung in the very next spot.

G K

Rule 2 contains two pieces of information. First, *Hibiscus* will be in some position before *Katydid* but not necessarily immediately before.

H . . . K

This rule also tells us that *Hibiscus* will not be the first photograph. Simply mark "~H" under the first position in the sketch.

Rule 3, like Rule 1, dictates that two paintings be immediately next to one another—in this case, *Irises* and *Lotus*. However, unlike the first rule, the order is not predefined. So be sure to consider both orders as possible.

IL *or* LI

Rule 4 limits the placement of *Magnolia* to one of the first three paintings.

Rule 5 limits the placement of *Fence* to either the first or seventh position.

Step 4: Deductions

There's a lot of information in this game. There are two Blocks of Entities: GK and IL (or LI). By Rule 2, H must be somewhere before K. Therefore, H must come before the GK block. Because H can't be first, the earliest H could be is second.

However, the GK block could still take up any two of the remaining five positions. That's too many possibilities to sketch out.

Similarly, the IL (or LI) block is entirely unlimited by the remaining rules, so it can placed in any of the seven positions.

Rule 5 suggests the possibility of Limited Options. However, the placement of F does not significantly affect any of the other entities, so it's not worth setting up both options.

With no entities established, no real number issues, and only the one deduction to be made from duplicated entities (combining Rules 1 and 2), there are no further deductions to be made.

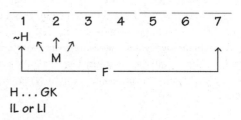

FGHIKLM

$$\underline{\quad}_1 \quad \underline{\quad}_2 \quad \underline{\quad}_3 \quad \underline{\quad}_4 \quad \underline{\quad}_5 \quad \underline{\quad}_6 \quad \underline{\quad}_7$$

H . . . GK
IL *or* LI

Step 5: Questions

6. (C) Acceptability

Rule 1 dictates that *Gardenias* be hung immediately before *Katydid*. That eliminates **(A)**. Rule 2 dictates that *Hibiscus* be hung somewhere before *Katydid* but not first. That eliminates **(B)**. Rule 3 dictates that *Irises* and *Lotus* be hung immediately next to one another. That eliminates **(D)**. Rule 4 is not violated by either of the remaining answers. Rule 5 dictates that *Fence* be hung either first or seventh. That eliminates **(E)**.

That leaves **(C)** as the correct answer—the one that doesn't violate any of the rules.

7. (E) "If" / Could Be True

If *Irises* is immediately before *Gardenias*, then that allows the two blocks in this game to be combined. By Rule 1, *Gardenias* will be immediately before *Katydid*. By Rule 3, *Lotus* will be immediately before *Irises* (because *Gardenias* is immediately after *Irises* for this question). The final order is as follows:

L I G K

By Rule 2, *Hibiscus* must be before this entire block. Because *Hibiscus* cannot be first (also by Rule 2), the earliest it could be is second. That leaves only two possible placements for the large block: third, fourth, fifth, and sixth or fourth, fifth, sixth, and seventh.

With the first placement, *Hibiscus* would have to be second. That would make *Magnolia* first (by Rule 4) and *Fence* seventh (by Rule 5).

The second placement would force *Fence* to be first (by Rule 5). Then *Hibiscus* could be second or third, as could *Magnolia*. Their order cannot be completely determined.

M	H	L	I	G	K	F
1	2	3	4	5	6	7

or

F	M/H	H/M	L	I	G	K
1	2	3	4	5	6	7

Based on those two options, **(E)** is the only answer that could be true.

8. (D) Completely Determine

The correct answer will be a "new rule" that allows the order of the seven paintings to be completely determined with nothing left uncertain. This would involve placing both blocks and determining the definite order of *Irises* and *Lotus*.

(A), **(B)**, and **(E)** all appear to be unlikely candidates because none of them will help determine whether *Irises* comes before or after *Lotus*. Even if all three of those answers were true at the same time, *Irises* and *Lotus* would be the sixth and seventh paintings in an indeterminable order, making *Fence* the first:

F	H	M	G	K	I/L	L/I
1	2	3	4	5	6	7

Without knowing the order of *Irises* and *Lotus*, none of these are sufficient for determining the complete order with certainty.

(C) places *Irises* second. However, *Lotus* could still be first or third. Whichever position it is, *Magnolia* would have to be the other position (by Rule 4). With the first position filled by either *Lotus* or *Magnolia*, *Fence* would have to be seventh (by Rule 5). The remaining three positions would be, in order, *Hibiscus*, *Gardenias*, and *Katydid*.

L	I	M	H	G	K	F
1	2	3	4	5	6	7

or

M	I	L	H	G	K	F
1	2	3	4	5	6	7

With two possible outcomes, this is not sufficient for determining the complete order with certainty.

(D), the only answer remaining, must be correct. If *Lotus* is first, then *Irises* would have to be second (by Rule 3), and *Fence* would have to be seventh (by Rule 5). That would leave only the third position for *Magnolias* (by Rule 4). The remaining three positions would have to be, in order, *Hibiscus*, *Gardenias*, and *Katydid* (by Rules 1 and 2).

L	I	M	H	G	K	F
1	2	3	4	5	6	7

Because that is the only possible outcome, with no uncertainty, **(D)** is the correct answer.

9. (B) "If" / Must Be False (CANNOT Be True)

If *Magnolia* is second, that limits the entities that could be first. None of the entities in the two blocks (*Gardenias*, *Katydid*, *Irises*, or *Lotus*) could fit there. Also, by Rule 2, *Hibiscus* can't be first. That leaves only one possibility: *Fence*.

In that case, *Hibiscus* could be third, which eliminates **(A)**. The remaining four positions would be filled by the two blocks, in either order:

F	M	H	G	K	I/L	L/I
1	2	3	4	5	6	7

or

F	M	H	I/L	L/I	G	K
1	2	3	4	5	6	7

So *Gardenias* could be either fourth, eliminating **(D)**, or sixth, eliminating **(E)**.

Alternately, *Hibiscus* could be fifth. That would make *Gardenias* and *Katydid* the last two paintings, leaving *Irises* and *Lotus* in the remaining two positions:

F	M	I/L	L/I	H	G	K
1	2	3	4	5	6	7

That eliminates **(C)**.

If *Hibiscus* were fourth, that would leave a single open position, third, between *Magnolia* and *Hibiscus*. With only two blocks left, there are no single photographs to take up that final position, making **(B)** impossible and, thus, the correct answer.

10. (D) Rule Substitution

For this question, Rule 2 is removed from the game and replaced with one of the answers. The correct answer will be the one replacement that creates the same scenario created by Rule 2.

Specifically, by removing Rule 2, *Hibiscus* no longer has to be hung before *Katydid* and is now free to be hung first. The correct answer will again force *Hibiscus* to be hung before

Katydid and prevent *Hibiscus* from being hung first—without adding any new limitations.

(A) adds a new limitation to *Hibiscus*, forcing it to be second when *Fence* is seventh. However, with the original rules, *Hibiscus* was never limited to any one position based on the placement of *Fence*. This answer doesn't work.

(B) is very tempting. By forcing *Hibiscus* to be before *Gardenia*, that reinstates the limitation that *Hibiscus* be before *Katydid* (because *Gardenia* and *Katydid* form a block by Rule 1). Also, limiting the first photograph to *Fence* or *Magnolia* reinstates the limitation that *Hibiscus* can't be first. Unfortunately, that also prevents *Irises* or *Lotus* from being first, a limitation that was not established with the original rules. By creating new limitations, this answer doesn't work.

(C) works in keeping *Hibiscus* out of the first position. However, it does nothing to re-establish the condition that it has to be hung before *Katydid*. With this rule, *Hibiscus* could be fifth, and the *Gardenia-Katydid* block could be third and fourth. This answer doesn't work.

(D) needs to be translated carefully. According to the rule, if *Hibiscus* is not second, then it must be between *Magnolia* and *Gardenias*. That means there's no way it could be first. Furthermore, by being before *Gardenias*, it would have to be before *Katydid*, too (because of the block created by Rule 1). And if *Hibiscus is* second, it would still have to be before *Katydid*, because there would only be one space before *Hibiscus* and *Katydid* has to be part of a block with *Gardenias*. Therefore, this rule reestablishes all of the limitations from the replaced rule.

The only other consideration is that this rule forces *Hibiscus* to come after *Magnolia* if *Hibiscus* is not second. However, because of the limited placement of *Magnolia* by Rule 4, *Hibiscus* would always have been after *Magnolia* in any position other than second. So this rule re-establishes all of the replaced conditions and adds no new limitations. That makes **(D)** the correct answer.

For the record, **(E)** re-establishes the condition that *Hibiscus* be before *Katydid*, but it adds a limitation to *Fence* that would force *Fence* to be first. This was never a limitation in the original sketch, making this a wrong answer.

Game 3: Alicia's Courses

Step 1: Overview

Situation: Figuring out a course schedule

Entities: Seven courses (G, J, M, P, R, S, W); S can be at 9 AM and 3 PM.

Action: Selection. Determine which courses Alicia takes in a semester.

Limitations: Exactly four of the courses will be selected, and they must be four different courses. Furthermore, one of the courses, Statistics, has two times: 9 AM and 3 PM. It should be noted that, despite there being two time options, Statistics is still one course. So, because Alicia can only take any given course once per semester, she cannot select both the 9 AM and the 3 PM options.

Step 2: Sketch

For this sketch, simply set up four spaces for the four courses that will be selected. When listing the entities, create two separate entities for the Statistics options, because that will most likely be a vital distinction.

$$G \; J \; M \; P \; R \; S_9 \; S_3 \; W$$

Step 3: Rules

Rule 1 provides the first piece of Formal Logic. Because the *if* of this Formal Logic rule is in the middle, be sure to translate it carefully. Rushing through a Formal Logic rule can easily lead to missed points.

According to this rule, if Alicia does not take Russian, she must take Japanese. By the contrapositive, if she doesn't take Japanese, then she must take Russian.

$$\text{No } R \rightarrow J$$
$$\text{No } J \rightarrow R$$

It can help to translate a rule like this even further. Basically, it's saying that if Alicia doesn't take one of those two courses, then she must take the other one. In other words, Alicia must take at least either Japanese or Russian—possibly both.

$$J \text{ or } R \text{ (or both)}$$

This can be noted in the sketch by filling in one space with J/R and noting that JR is also possible.

Rule 2 provides a similar Formal Logic construction. Again, with the *if* located in the middle of the rule, don't rush the translation. In this case, if Alicia takes Macroeconomics, then she can't take Japanese. By the contrapositive, if she takes Japanese, she can't take Macroeconomics.

$$M \rightarrow \text{No } J$$
$$J \rightarrow \text{No } M$$

This rule can also be translated further. In this case, if Alicia takes either one of those two courses, then she can't take the other. In other words, Alicia can't take them both.

$$\text{Never } JM$$

It should be noted that she doesn't *have* to take either one—she just can't take them both.

Rule 3 can be translated into Formal Logic similarly to the previous rule:

$$S_9 \rightarrow \text{No } W$$
$$W \rightarrow \text{No } S_9$$

It can also be translated that Alicia can't take both of those courses:

$$\text{Never } S_9W$$

Rule 4 is properly translated into Formal Logic as, if Alicia takes Psychology, then she must take Statistics at 9 AM. By the contrapositive, if she doesn't take the 9 AM Statistics course, she can't take Psychology.

$$P \rightarrow S_9$$
$$\text{No } S_9 \rightarrow \text{No } P$$

Rule 5 dictates one of the courses Alicia takes. It must be either Geography or World History but not both. Fill in one of the spaces with G/W and make a note that she can't take both.

$$\text{Never } GW$$

Step 4: Deductions

Besides the alternative interpretations of the rules, this game lacks any major deductions. That's because all of the rules are conditional, which means that rules will only be utilized under certain conditions—none of which have been provided yet.

It seems plausible to set up Limited Options using either Rule 1 or Rule 4. With Rule 1, selecting Russian or Japanese would have minimal impact on the rest of the rules (with the exception that taking Japanese would remove Macroeconomics, by Rule 2).

Rule 5 is a little more promising. If Alicia takes Geography and not World History, there are no further deductions. However, if she takes World History and not Geography, then a few things can be determined. First, taking World History means the 9 AM Statistics course is out (by Rule 3). That would then eliminate Psychology (by Rule 4). That leaves just four courses (Japanese, Macroeconomics, Russian, and 3 PM Statistics) for the remaining three slots. However, by Rule 2, Alicia can't take Japanese and Macroeconomics. So she would have to take just one of those and the remaining two courses (Russian and 3 PM Statistics):

$$W\ R\ S_3\ J/M$$

That provides two possible outcomes. Any other schedule would have to include Geography and not World History. While potentially helpful, it's not vital to have this deduction to succeed at this game.

$$G\ J\ M\ P\ R\ S_9\ \ S_3\ W$$

$$G/W\ J/R\ \underline{\qquad}\ \ \underline{\qquad}\ \ \text{(Can have JR)}$$

Never JM; Never S_9W; Never GW
$P \rightarrow S_9$
No $S_9 \rightarrow$ No P

Step 5: Questions

11. (D) Acceptability
Rule 1 dictates that Alicia must take Japanese if she doesn't take Russian. That eliminates **(B)**. Rule 2 dictates that she can't take Japanese if she takes Macroeconomics. That eliminates **(C)**. Rule 3 is not violated by any of the answers. Rule 4 dictates that she must take Statistics (at 9 AM, which is irrelevant to this question) if she takes Psychology. That eliminates **(A)**. Rule 5 dictates that she must take either Geography or World History. That eliminates **(E)**.

That leaves **(D)** as the correct answer—the one that doesn't violate any of the rules.

12. (E) Partial Acceptability
Rule 1 dictates that Alicia must take Japanese if she doesn't take Russian. While **(A)** doesn't have Russian, it could be the fourth course that's not listed. Therefore, **(A)** can't be eliminated just yet. Rule 2 dictates that she can't take Japanese if she takes Macroeconomics. That eliminates **(B)**. Rule 3 dictates that she can't take World History if she takes Statistics at 9 AM. However, you can't eliminate **(A)** or **(E)**, because the time isn't listed and those answers could refer to the 3 PM Statistics course.

By Rule 4, if she takes Psychology, she must take Statistics at 9 AM. That would make the 9 AM Statistics course the fourth option in **(C)** and **(D)**. However, because both of those answers contain World History, that would then violate Rule 3. Therefore, **(C)** and **(D)** can both be eliminated.

Finally, by Rule 5, she can't take both Geography and World History. That eliminates **(A)**.

That leaves **(E)** as the correct answer—the one that doesn't violate any of the rules.

13. (C) Completely Determine
For this question, Alicia will take Russian. The correct answer will be an additional "new rule" that will allow the selection of the remaining three courses to be completely determined with nothing uncertain.

For **(A)**, World History does supply a lot of information. If Alicia takes World History, then she can't take Geography (by Rule 5) or the 9 AM Statistics course (by Rule 3). That would then eliminate Psychology (by Rule 4). That leaves just three courses (Japanese, Macroeconomics, and 3 PM Statistics) for the remaining two slots. By Rule 2, Alicia can't take Japanese and Macroeconomics, so she would have to take just one of those and 3 PM Statistics:

$$W\ R\ S_3\ J/M$$

However, because the fourth course can't be completely confirmed, this answer doesn't work.

For **(B)**, Statistics would be helpful if it were the 9 AM course. That would eliminate World History, forcing Alicia to take Geography. However, the fourth course could still be Japanese, Macroeconomics, or Psychology. And this still doesn't consider the possibilities that would arise if she took the 3 PM Statistics course. Therefore, this answer doesn't work.

For **(C)**, taking Psychology gives us a lot of information. By Rule 4, that means she also takes Statistics at 9 AM. By Rule 3, that means she can't take World History. So by Rule 5, she must take Geography. Finally, for this question, Russian is also taken. That provides the full course load:

$$G\ P\ R\ S_9$$

By completely filling out the schedule, **(C)** is the correct answer. For the record:

For **(D)**, taking Macroeconomics eliminates Japanese by Rule 2. That leaves Russian, by Rule 1 (which was already given for this question anyway). However, it still can't be determined if Alicia takes Geography or World History. This answer doesn't work.

For **(E)**, taking Japanese eliminates Macroeconomics by Rule 2. However, it still can't be determined if Alicia takes Geography or World History. This answer doesn't work.

14. (A) Supply the If

For this question, the correct answer would make it possible for Alicia to take Statistics at either time. The four wrong answers will either make it impossible to take Statistics or limit Alicia to only one of the two available times.

It helps to look at the two rules that affect Statistics. By Rule 3, if she takes World History, then she cannot take the 9 AM Statistics class. That would set an improper limitation for this question, eliminating **(C)** and **(E)**. By Rule 4, if she takes Psychology, then she must take the 9 AM Statistics course, preventing her from taking the 3 PM course. That also sets an improper limitation for this question, eliminating **(B)** and **(D)**.

That leaves **(A)** as the correct answer. For the record, if Alicia did take Geography and Japanese, then she wouldn't take Macroeconomics (by Rule 2) or World History (by Rule 5). The remaining two courses could be Psychology, Russian, or either of the two Statistics courses.

15. (D) "If" / Must Be True

For this question, Alicia will take the 3 PM Statistics course. That means she can't take the 9 AM Statistics class. By Rule 4, that means she doesn't take Psychology. For this question, she also takes Geography. That means she can't take World History (by Rule 5).

That leaves only three options for the remaining two courses: Japanese, Macroeconomics, and Russian. However, she can't take both Japanese and Macroeconomics (by Rule 2). So she can only take one of those, which would leave Russian as the fourth course:

$$G\ R\ S_3\ J/M$$

Because Alicia must take Russian, **(D)** is the correct answer.

16. (A) Rule Change

For this question, Rule 4 is modified so that Alicia is no longer limited to the 9 AM Statistics course if she takes Psychology. She still has to take Statistics, but it could be at either time. Outside of that, the question is nothing more than a standard Acceptability question. As usual, just go through the rules one at a time (keeping in mind the change for this question) and eliminate any answers with violations.

Rule 1 dictates that Alicia must take Japanese if she doesn't take Russian. That eliminates **(B)**. Rule 2 is not violated by any of the answers. Rule 3 dictates that she can't take World History if she takes Statistics at 9 AM. However, without being given the times, no answer can be eliminated. The newly modified Rule 4 dictates that she must take Statistics (at any time) if she takes Psychology. That eliminates **(C)** and **(D)**. Rule 5 dictates that she can't take both Geography and World History. That eliminates **(E)**.

That leaves **(A)** as the correct answer—the one that doesn't violate any of the rules. (Note that with the new rule in this question, the Statistics course in **(A)** can now be the 3 PM course, which wouldn't affect Alicia's taking the World History course.)

Game 4: Annual Meetings in North American Cities

Step 1: Overview

Situation: An organization determining where to hold six annual meetings

Entities: Six cities (L, M, N, T, V, W)

Action: Strict Sequencing. Determine the order in which the six cities will be used for meetings.

Limitations: Each city will be used exactly once, making this straightforward one-to-one sequencing.

Step 2: Sketch

Simply list the six cities (by initial) and set up six slots to determine the order.

L M N T V W

1	2	3	4	5	6

Step 3: Rules

Rule 1 sets up a relative order for two cities: Los Angeles after Toronto.

T . . . L

Rule 2 sets up two entities in consecutive years: Vancouver and Washington, in either order.

VW or WV

Rules 3 and 4 split up two pairs of cities (Toronto & Montreal, and Vancouver & Los Angeles) in the same way. In both cases, the two cities will have another pair of cities between them. Also, the order is not predetermined in either case.

T/M ___ ___ M/T
V/L ___ ___ L/V

Step 4: Deductions

The first thing to do is recognize that, by Rule 1, Toronto cannot be sixth and Los Angeles cannot be first. This can be noted in the sketch.

With so many blocks, these entities are going to be very limited in their placement. The two blocks in Rules 3 and 4 will take up a lot of space. It would be wise to consider where the remaining two entities (New York and Washington) could go.

If either block (e.g., T/M ___ ___ M/T) were in 1 & 4, then the second block (V/L ___ ___ L/V) could be in 2 & 5 (putting New York and Washington in 3 & 6) or 3 & 6 (putting New York and Washington in 2 & 5). If either block is placed in 2 & 5, then

the second block could go in 1 & 4 (putting New York and Washington in 3 & 6) or 3 & 6 (putting New York and Washington in 1 & 4). Finally, if either block is placed in 3 & 6, then the second block could go in 1 & 4 (putting New York and Washington in 2 & 5) or 2 & 5 (putting New York and Washington in 1 & 4). Playing around a little leads to a great deduction. No matter how the two blocks from Rules 3 and 4 are arranged, New York and Washington will be forced into two positions that are also separated by two cities:

N/W ____ ____ W/N

If you don't come up with that deduction, the game can still be handled effectively. The game is based on your confidence with the rules and holds no other major deductions.

The finalized Master Sketch should look something like this.

L M N T V W

1	2	3	4	5	6
~L					~T

T . . . L
VW or WV

T/M ___ ___ M/T
V/L ___ ___ L/V
N/W ___ ___ W/N

Step 5: Questions

17. (A) Acceptability

Rule 1 dictates that Los Angeles must be after Toronto. That eliminates **(B)**. Rule 2 dictates that Vancouver and Washington be in consecutive years. That eliminates **(D)**. Rule 3 dictates that Toronto and Montreal be separated by exactly two other cities. That eliminates **(E)**. Rule 4 dictates that Vancouver and Los Angeles be separated by exactly two other cities. That eliminates **(C)**.

That leaves **(A)** as the correct answer—the one that doesn't violate any of the rules.

18. (E) Must Be True

The correct answer to this question will be definitely true. The four wrong answers will be possibly or definitely false.

If you made the major deduction in this game (that New York and Washington must be separated by exactly two cities), then **(E)** stands out as the correct answer.

If you didn't, there are two ways to work through this question. First, work through other questions, developing sketches that will verify certain answers as possibly false. This is probably the most efficient use of time if you didn't make the major deduction. Otherwise, you could test answer choices individually to see if they could be false.

For the record, the complete sketch for the third question of the set illustrates how **(A)**, **(B)**, and **(D)** could all be false:

V	W	T	L	N	M
1	2	3	4	5	6

And either sketch for the fifth question of the set illustrates how **(C)** could be false:

M	V	W	T	L	N
1	2	3	4	5	6

19. (D) Completely Determine

The correct answer will be a "new rule" that allows the order of the six cities to be completely determined with nothing uncertain. This would involve placing all blocks and determining the definite order of the cities within each block.

For **(A)**, if Los Angeles is fifth, then Vancouver would be second (by Rule 4). By Rule 2, Washington would have to be either first or third. Depending on where it goes, the Toronto-Montreal block could be first and fourth or third and sixth. Too many possibilities. This answer doesn't work.

For **(B)**, if Montreal is sixth, then Toronto would be third (by Rule 3). However, the Los Angeles–Vancouver block could still be either first and fourth or second and fifth. Too many possibilities. This answer doesn't work.

For **(C)**, if New York is fifth, then the third and sixth cities could still be either the Toronto-Montreal block or the Los Angeles–Vancouver block. Too many possibilities. This answer doesn't work.

For **(D)**, if Vancouver is first, then Los Angeles would be fourth (by Rule 4). By Rule 2, Washington would have to be second. The only possible positions for the Toronto-Montreal block would then be third and sixth. That would leave New York fifth. And, by Rule 2, Toronto has to be before Los Angeles. So Toronto would have to be third, making Montreal sixth.

V	W	T	L	N	M
1	2	3	4	5	6

Because the order is completely determined, **(D)** is the correct answer.

For the record, if Washington were in the second year, as **(E)** states, then the first and fourth cities could still be either the Toronto-Montreal block or the Los Angeles–Vancouver block. Too many possibilities. That answer doesn't work.

20. (E) Complete and Accurate List

For this question, the correct answer will include all possible positions for Washington without leaving any possibilities out and without including any positions that Washington could not fill. The best way to handle this question is to use sketches from other questions to determine what positions Washington can fill. Eliminate answers that omit those possibilities and test any positions in the remaining answers.

The correct answer for the Acceptability question (T V W M L N) places Washington third. That eliminates **(D)**. The sketch for the third question of the set (V W T L N M) places Washington second. That eliminates **(A)**.

Unfortunately, sketches in the remaining questions don't add any new information. Now it's time to test the remaining positions.

If Washington were first, then Vancouver would have to be second (by Rule 2). That would make Los Angeles fifth (by Rule 4). The Toronto-Montreal block would have to be third and sixth, with Toronto third and Montreal sixth (because Toronto has to be before Los Angeles by Rule 1). That leaves New York fourth.

W	V	T	N	L	M
1	2	3	4	5	6

Because Washington can be first, that eliminates **(B)** and **(C)**.

That leaves **(E)** as the correct answer. For the record, here are sketches to show that W could also be fourth, fifth, or sixth:

N	T	V	W	M	L
T	N	L	M	W	V
T	L	N	M	V	W
1	2	3	4	5	6

21. (E) "If" / Must Be False (CANNOT Be True)

If Montreal is first, then Toronto is fourth (by Rule 3). Because Toronto must be before Los Angeles, that means Los Angeles must be fifth or six. If it were fifth, then Vancouver would be second (by Rule 4). If it were sixth, then Vancouver would be third. Wherever Vancouver is placed, Washington must be immediately next to it (by Rule 2), leaving New York for the one remaining position.

M	V	W	T	L	N
1	2	3	4	5	6

or

M	W	V	T	N	L
1	2	3	4	5	6

(A), **(B)**, and **(D)** are all possible. **(C)** must be true. **(E)** is the only answer that is never true, making it the correct answer.

22. (B) Could Be True

Four of the answers to this question will be definitely false. The correct answer will be one that is possible or must be true.

(A) and **(E)** must be false because they would violate Rule 1, requiring Toronto to be before Los Angeles. If, as **(C)** says, Montreal were third, that would make Toronto sixth (by Rule 3). However, that would violate Rule 1. Eliminate. If, as **(D)** says, Vancouver were fourth, that would make Los Angeles first (by Rule 4). However, that would also violate Rule 1. Eliminate. That leaves **(B)** as the only possible answer. For the record, here is how that could work:

T	N	L	M	W	V
1	2	3	4	5	6

If you made the deduction that Washington and New York are separated by two cities, you also could have combined that information with the answer to the fourth question of the set. Knowing that Washington could be in any position, you would also know that New York could be in any position. That would make **(B)** possible.

Furthermore, if you tested locations for Washington in the fourth question of the set, you may have tested if Washington could be fifth. In that case, the sketch (seen here) would have shown New York second, confirming **(B)** as the correct answer.

23. (B) Must Be False

Four of the answers to this question will be true or possibly true. The correct answer will definitely be false.

For a question like this, it's good to look for entities that are very limited. For this game, Vancouver is limited by being in two blocks. By Rule 2, it must be immediately next to Washington. By Rule 4, it must be separated from Los Angeles by two other cities.

By combining those two rules, Los Angeles and Washington must be separated by either one city or three. They cannot be next to each other. That makes **(B)** the correct answer.

For the record, here are examples of how the remaining four answers could be true:

M	W	V	T	N	L
1	2	3	4	5	6

This sketch from the fifth question of the set shows how **(A)**, **(C)**, and **(D)** are all possible.

M	V	W	T	L	N
1	2	3	4	5	6

This sketch, also from the fifth question of the set, shows how **(E)** is possible.

Section II: Logical Reasoning

Q#	Question Type	Correct	Difficulty
1	Strengthen	A	★
2	Point at Issue	D	★
3	Strengthen	A	★
4	Flaw	E	★
5	Strengthen	E	★
6	Flaw	C	★
7	Role of a Statement	E	★★★★
8	Flaw	B	★
9	Parallel Flaw	C	★
10	Main Point	D	★
11	Paradox	B	★
12	Inference	C	★
13	Principle (Identify/Strengthen)	C	★★
14	Assumption (Necessary)	D	★★
15	Flaw	A	★★★
16	Parallel Reasoning	E	★★★
17	Assumption (Sufficient)	E	★
18	Role of a Statement	D	★★★★
19	Inference	C	★★★
20	Flaw	D	★★★★
21	Weaken	C	★★
22	Strengthen	A	★★★
23	Principle (Identify/Inference)	D	★★
24	Inference	B	★★
25	Weaken	B	★★★
26	Assumption (Sufficient)	B	★★★

1. (A) Strengthen

Step 1: Identify the Question Type
Because the question asks for something that will strengthen the researcher's reasoning, this is a Strengthen question.

Step 2: Untangle the Stimulus
The researcher argues that eating the three fruits mentioned causes atypical Parkinson's disease. The evidence comes from a sample of 100 people. The 35 people who have the disease all ate the three fruits regularly. Of the 65 people who don't have the disease, only 10 ate the fruits regularly.

Step 3: Make a Prediction
This is a classic case of correlation versus causation. The researcher has found a correlation between eating the fruit and having Parkinson's. However, that's not enough to conclude that one must have caused the other. After all, there could be other factors that cause Parkinson's, or the correlation might be just a coincidence. To strengthen the argument, a stronger connection must be made between the fruit and Parkinson's.

Step 4: Evaluate the Answer Choices
(A) does the job perfectly. By showing that symptoms disappear when people stop eating the fruit, it lessens the possibility of mere coincidence and makes it more likely that the fruit does indeed play a factor in the presence of Parkinson's.

(B) suggests that the healthy adults do eat the fruit sporadically. However, that does nothing to strengthen the connection between the fruit and Parkinson's. In fact, this would raise questions as to why those people don't at least show some symptoms of atypical Parkinson's if the fruit supposedly causes the disease.

(C) suggests that there may be other causes of Parkinson's. While it doesn't necessarily disprove the researcher's hypothesis, it does nothing to further it.

(D) goes against the researcher. If the fruit causes Parkinson's, then people who eat more of the fruit would be more likely to have the disease.

(E) mentions a component of the three fruits—vitamins. However, without a connection between vitamins and Parkinson's, this adds no value to the researcher's argument.

2. (D) Point at Issue

Step 1: Identify the Question Type
With the question asking about what two speakers are committed to disagreeing about, this is a Point at Issue question.

Step 2: Untangle the Stimulus
Price starts off by claiming that a corporation's primary responsibility is to its shareholders, because the shareholders are taking the greatest risk. Albrecht counters Price by suggesting that shareholders can invest their money in more than one corporation. Instead, Albrecht says that a corporation's primary responsibility is to its employees, because employees' livelihoods depend on the success of that one corporation.

Step 3: Make a Prediction
The Keyword in both speakers' arguments is *primary*. While neither of them rejects one group (shareholders or employees) as unimportant, the real point at issue is regarding which group should be the higher priority.

Step 4: Evaluate the Answer Choices
(D) correctly focuses on which group should get the most attention. Price would definitely agree with this statement, while Albrecht would disagree, saying that employees have the most at stake.

(A), with which Price would certainly agree, is never argued against by Albrecht. While Albrecht may feel that employees have more at stake in the company, he doesn't necessarily believe that corporations have no responsibility toward their shareholders.

(B), similarly, is never argued against by Price. While Price may feel that shareholders have more at stake in the company, he doesn't necessarily believe that corporations have no responsibility toward their employees.

(C) is consistent with Price's opinion. However, Albrecht's focus is on the employees, not the investors. Therefore, providing a means for investors to recoup their investment is not at issue between the two.

(E) is also consistent with Price's opinion. However, Albrecht is again more concerned with employees. And while he does say that shareholders *typically* have diversified portfolios, that doesn't rule out the possibility of *some* shareholders depending on one company's success. Therefore, the two speakers could potentially agree on this statement.

3. (A) Strengthen

Step 1: Identify the Question Type
Because the question asks for something that will support a given claim, this is a Strengthen question.

Step 2: Untangle the Stimulus
The author claims that a bank's internal auditing system will usually discover an accidental credit of a large sum of money, despite having to keep track of a tremendous number of transactions.

Step 3: Make a Prediction
Of all the errors that could happen at a bank, the author mentions just one that the bank's auditors would notice—an accidental large credit. To strengthen this claim, it would be helpful to have some evidence that shows why large credits would be detected.

Step 4: Evaluate the Answer Choices

(A) would strengthen the author's assertion. Flagging and using a separate system to double-check transactions involving large sums of money would increase the chances of detecting errors in such cases.

(B) would help prevent people from taking out or depositing someone else's money, but it doesn't address accidental credits to a person's account.

(C) would increase the likelihood of a *customer* spotting such an error, but wouldn't have an effect on the bank's internal system.

(D) suggests an increase in auditing staff relative to the number of accounts. However, the passage says that banks now face a huge number of transactions. We don't know if the increased ratio of auditors to transactions is sufficient to make errors "extremely unlikely" given the volume of transactions. Also, this doesn't directly address why large-sum transactions would be particularly detectable.

(E) would explain how banks could reduce the number of accidental credits by hackers. However, there is no reason to believe that most accidental credits are due to hackers.

4. (E) Flaw

Step 1: Identify the Question Type

"[V]ulnerable to criticism" is classic language used to indicate that the argument is inherently flawed, making this a Flaw question.

Step 2: Untangle the Stimulus

The scientist has discovered a correlation: severe atmospheric pollution coincided with high global temperatures. The scientist uses this evidence to conclude that the pollution must have caused the higher temperatures.

Step 3: Make a Prediction

Two events that just happen to coincide are used to claim that one must have caused the other. Mistaking mere correlation for causation is one of the most common flaws on the LSAT, and it is a perfect prediction for this question.

Step 4: Evaluate the Answer Choices

(E) clearly describes this archetypal LSAT flaw.

(A) brings in the concept of harm, which is not part of the scientist's argument in any way.

(B) is correct in that the author uses a potentially unrepresentative sample. However, the scientist only concludes that the causation occurred "in this case" and, therefore, doesn't use the sample to make a generalization.

(C) also goes awry because the scientist draws a conclusion about what happened "in this case" and, therefore, does not make the error of generalizing.

(D) indicates a potential assumption. However, there is nothing wrong with a scientist assuming the methods are reliable. If the scientist doubted the reliability of the methods, then what would be the point of the study? While this points out a valid assumption, it's not a flaw in the reasoning.

5. (E) Strengthen

Step 1: Identify the Question Type

Because the question asks for something that will strengthen Sabina's argument, this is a Strengthen question. However, this doesn't mean to ignore Gilbert's argument. Gilbert's argument may provide information that will give context to Sabina's claims.

Step 2: Untangle the Stimulus

Gilbert is complaining about a cookie's food label. Although the label claims that all of the ingredients are natural, one of the ingredients, alphahydroxy acids, is actually created synthetically at the company's plant. Sabina defends the label by stating that alphahydroxy acids can be found naturally—in sugarcane.

Step 3: Make a Prediction

The problem with Sabina's argument is that she ignores the fact that the acids in the cookies aren't taken from sugarcane. The acids are created at the plant. For her argument to work, Sabina must assume that the source of the acids is irrelevant. In other words, she's assuming that the acids can be considered natural because they *can* be found in nature, even through the actual acids used aren't. Anything that validates this assumption will strengthen her position.

Step 4: Evaluate the Answer Choices

(E) provides exactly the kind of loophole that Sabina's argument could use. By using such a loose definition of *natural*, the label can call synthesized ingredients natural as long as those ingredients could also be found naturally.

(A) doesn't help because it speaks to a recent change in the cookies. Any new labels may not list the alphahydroxy acids, but that has no effect on the correctness of the labels that *do* list those acids and, thus, no bearing on the label Gilbert is complaining about.

(B) says that other chemicals are used to create the cookies that don't end up in the cookies. That doesn't address Sabina's argument regarding the naturalness of alphahydroxy acids.

(C) is tempting, but it changes the situation. In fact, it can even help out Gilbert instead of Sabina. If the labels were printed before the switch to synthesized acids, then it suggests that the definition of *natural* may have been meant to include only ingredients taken from nature. In that case, the switch to synthesized acids would indeed invalidate the label, making it mistaken.

(D) brings up an Irrelevant Comparison to other products. Just because other products do the same thing, that doesn't mean their labels are any more or less mistaken. If their labels are also considered mistaken, then that weakens Sabina's argument.

6. (C) Flaw

Step 1: Identify the Question Type
Because the question asks why the reasoning is flawed, this is a Flaw question.

Step 2: Untangle the Stimulus
In this argument, an historian named Jaaks argues that a new book by a certain writer, Yancey, is factually inaccurate. The author of this argument disagrees, suggesting that Yancey's books are plenty accurate. The evidence for this is that Yancey's books (including the new one) use the same research methods and are all very popular.

Step 3: Make a Prediction
There is a tremendous scope shift in this author's argument. The author uses evidence of an historian's *popularity* to draw a conclusion about the *accuracy* of the information used in that historian's books. While the historian uses the same research methods in all her books, those methods could still be inaccurate, regardless of the books' popularity. The correct answer should expose the gap between accuracy and popularity.

Step 4: Evaluate the Answer Choices
(C) exactly points out the author's faulty connection of accuracy and popularity.

(A) suggests that the author invokes the opinion of a scholar, which never happens in this argument.

(B) suggests an ad hominem attack against Jaaks. However, the author does address Jaaks's claim and doesn't make any unnecessary attack on Jaaks herself.

(D) gets the reasoning backward. The author uses a general sample (of Yancey's previous books) to make a conclusion about one specific book.

(E) is Extreme. While the author assumes Yancey's methods are accurate, there is no assumption that those are the *only* accurate methods.

7. (E) Role of a Statement

Step 1: Identify the Question Type
This question provides a claim taken from the stimulus and then asks for the role played by that claim. That makes this a Role of a Statement question.

Step 2: Untangle the Stimulus
This argument starts out with an observation—the observation the question is asking about: seeing music performances live is a richer experience than listening to recorded music. Then comes one possible explanation for that: people don't actually see performers when listening to recorded music. However, the columnist rejects this explanation, offering an analogy of being read stories and suggesting that seeing a person is irrelevant to the experience of hearing them.

Step 3: Make a Prediction
As the question suggests, the claim being asked about is merely an observation—a fact that is not being disputed. The columnist describes one opinion that explains that observation and then rejects that opinion. So a good prediction of the role of that opening statement would be this: provide an observation for which some people offer an explanation that the columnist refutes.

Step 4: Evaluate the Answer Choices
(E) gets it absolutely right. The columnist is definitely trying to undermine an opinion, and the observation in question is what that opinion is trying to explain.

(A) is off because the opening observation is accepted. The columnist isn't arguing for or against that observation. Instead, the columnist is arguing against some people's explanation for that observation.

(B) reverses the logic. The observation in question is the claim, and the reasoning for that claim is what the columnist is arguing against.

(C) adds information the columnist never provides. The columnist rejects one explanation but never actually offers her own explanation.

(D) is off because the opening observation is accepted. Again, the columnist isn't arguing for or against that observation but instead is arguing against the explanation provided for that observation.

8. (B) Flaw

Step 1: Identify the Question Type
The classic language of "vulnerable to criticism" indicates that the argument is inherently flawed, making this a Flaw question.

Step 2: Untangle the Stimulus
The author presents two coinciding statistics as evidence. During the same 10 year period, sales of ice cream (which provides calcium) are reported to have dropped dramatically while sales of cheddar cheese doubled. The author concludes that people are switching from ice cream to cheddar cheese for their calcium needs.

Step 3: Make a Prediction

Unfortunately, the evidence provided is purely numbers. No information is given about why people are suddenly buying less ice cream and more cheddar cheese. By concentrating on only one factor (calcium), the author is overlooking alternative explanations for the figures.

Step 4: Evaluate the Answer Choices

(B) correctly exposes the author's failure to consider alternative explanations.

(A) is accurate in that there is no confirmation of the farmers' claims. However, the accuracy of their claims is irrelevant to the author's lapse in reasoning regarding the explanation for those claims.

(C) is only partially correct at best. While the claim about ice cream does come from dairy farmers, there is no source given for the figures on cheddar cheese. Also, as with **(A)**, this choice does not address the author's reasoning about the claims.

(D) adds an opinion that the author never suggests. The author makes no assumption about which food has more calcium. The author is only concerned about what foods people are eating and why.

(E) is a Distortion of the author's argument. The author never suggests (or assumes) that nobody eats both cheddar cheese and ice cream. Instead, he merely says that more people choose one over the other. That still allows for some people who eat both.

9. (C) Parallel Flaw

Step 1: Identify the Question Type

Because the question is looking for an argument with a similar pattern of reasoning and the reasoning will contain a flaw, which must also be parallel, this is a Parallel Flaw question.

Step 2: Untangle the Stimulus

This argument starts off with a limitation: no member of a particular theater group can be both a performer and an administrator. The author then presents two members who are not administrators. The author concludes that they must be performers.

Step 3: Make a Prediction

As the question suggests, this argument is inherently flawed. The limitation provided prevents certain members of a group (the theater group) from possessing two characteristics (performer and administrator) simultaneously. However, that doesn't mean that each member of that group must possess one of those two characteristics. It's possible that a given member possesses neither one. Nonetheless, based on the information that two specific people fail to possess one characteristic (administrator), the author faultily claims they

must possess the second (performer). While it's impossible to predict the scenario of the correct response, it will contain the same type of limitation (i.e., members of a group can't have two characteristics) and the same faulty application of that limitation (treating a lack of one characteristic as evidence of having the other).

Step 4: Evaluate the Answer Choices

(C) starts off with the same kind of limitation—members of a group (companies) can't have two characteristics (headquarters in Canada and Mexico) simultaneously. As does the stimulus, the argument provides two examples of members who lack one characteristic (they don't have headquarters in Mexico) and then faultily concludes that they must have the second characteristic (headquarters in Canada). This is a perfect match.

(A) doesn't provide a similar limitation on all members of a group. Instead, it only says that some people in one group fail to meet one characteristic. Furthermore, the logic of **(A)** is sound, not flawed.

(B) starts off with exactly the same kind of limitation—employees can't be both an accountant and an attorney. However, **(B)** presents a person who *is* both and correctly concludes that the person can't be a member of the group.

(D) starts off with the right kind of limitation. However, this argument presents a member who *does* possess one characteristic and correctly concludes that member can't possess the second.

(E) presents the same kind of limitation in slightly different wording. However, the rest of the argument revolves around numbers, which the original argument does not. In addition, the reasoning is sound, not flawed.

10. (D) Main Point

Step 1: Identify the Question Type

Because this question is looking for the main conclusion, that makes this a Main Point question.

Step 2: Untangle the Stimulus

The argument starts off with an accepted claim: chemical fertilizers are potentially hazardous and kill beneficial earthworms. The author uses this fact to conclude that chemical fertilizers shouldn't be used. The rest of the argument is merely more detailed evidence of earthworms' beneficial effects.

Step 3: Make a Prediction

While the word *thus* in the last sentence suggests a conclusion, it's not the main point of the entire argument. Keywords such as *thus* and *therefore* are usually reliable Conclusion Keywords, but in Main Point questions, they may not signal the *final* conclusion of the argument. The final sentence is merely a subsidiary conclusion about how earthworms are good for gardens. Because earthworms make a garden more fertile and chemical fertilizers kill earthworms, the author comes to the main conclusion that we shouldn't use chemical fertilizers, and this conclusion is your prediction.

Step 4: Evaluate the Answer Choices

(D) is the author's main conclusion, for which everything else is provided as support.

(A) is evidence for why the author feels earthworms shouldn't be harmed.

(B) is evidence for why the author feels chemical fertilizers shouldn't be used.

(C) is evidence for why the author feels earthworms are beneficial.

(E) is a point the author makes at the end of the argument. However, this point is used as evidence for a further point. As in **(C)**, it is evidence for why the author feels earthworms are beneficial—it is merely a subsidiary conclusion and not the main point.

11. (B) Paradox

Step 1: Identify the Question Type

Because this question is looking for something that will resolve a conflict between two statements, this is a Paradox question.

Step 2: Untangle the Stimulus

According to the author, medical research shows the Beta Diet to be healthier than other diets. However, the results seem to contradict that, because followers of the Beta Diet are more likely to be in poor health.

Step 3: Make a Prediction

The question is looking for an explanation as to why people following a healthier diet are in poorer health. While it may not be possible to come up with an exact prediction, it helps to recognize the scope shift from information about the diet itself to information about the people on the diet. That distinction is likely to be key in resolving the paradox.

Step 4: Evaluate the Answer Choices

(B) sheds some helpful light on the situation. While the Beta Diet itself may be very healthy, the people who use the Beta Diet have a condition that automatically makes their health poor. That explains the paradoxical results.

(A) only makes matters worse. If people on the supposedly healthier diet also have better health habits, then that makes it even more mysterious why they would be in poorer health.

(C) again makes matters worse. If people who switch to the Beta Diet experience a dramatic increase in health, that doesn't explain why people on the Beta Diet are in poorer health than others. In fact, this seems to say something entirely opposite.

(D) may explain why some people on the Beta Diet are in worse health than others on the Beta Diet. However, this says that they all gain some benefits, so it doesn't explain why they have poorer health than people on a conventional diet.

(E) says that there's a diet that's healthier than the Beta Diet. However, the stimulus compares the Beta Diet to conventional diets. The Beta Diet is described as healthier than conventional diets. If the diet proposed here is healthier than the Beta Diet, then it can't be considered one of those less healthy conventional diets. Therefore, it would be irrelevant in explaining why Beta Diet followers are in poorer health than the people on the conventional diets.

12. (C) Inference

Step 1: Identify the Question Type

This question is looking for something to fill in the blank at the end of an argument. That means the correct answer will be something that follows directly from the given information. Because it looks for something that is directly supported by given information, this is an Inference question.

Step 2: Untangle the Stimulus

The author starts off by talking about the benefits of a theoretical framework and then suggests that historians find a theoretical framework best for historical analysis. However, the author clearly sees a problem with that: the past is too complex, so a theoretical framework won't capture all the past's main trends.

Step 3: Make a Prediction

While the author recognizes the benefits of a theoretical framework, there seems to be a definite downside: it can't be used for everything. The author's conclusion (which is what this question is asking for) will articulate this limitation without going outside of the scope of the argument.

Step 4: Evaluate the Answers

(C) encapsulates the author's point perfectly. Because of the complexity of the past, the author directly claims that a theoretical framework will inevitably leave out some major trends.

(A) is Extreme. While the author definitely sees some limitations to the theoretical framework, that doesn't mean there's *no* benefit. In fact, the first sentence outlines two great benefits.

(B) makes an Irrelevant Comparison of history to other fields. The author never discusses other fields.

(D) discusses extending research, which is Out of Scope. Furthermore, this statement ignores the limitations of theoretical frameworks that are the author's main concern.

(E) contradicts the information in the first sentence. While the author feels that a theoretical framework has its limitations, that doesn't mean it brings *nothing* different to historical analysis

13. (C) Principle (Identify/Strengthen)

Step 1: Identify the Question Type

Because this question is asking for a principle, this is a Principle question. For this question, the principle will justify a specific argument. So the correct answer will be a broad principle that will effectively strengthen the argument.

Step 2: Untangle the Stimulus

According to Bethany, psychologists have found a way to help adults who suffer from nightmares. She concludes that this method should be taught to children who suffer from nightmares, because children who suffer from nightmares tend to continue suffering from nightmares as adults.

Step 3: Make a Prediction

Bethany clearly likes the idea of helping people alleviate the suffering of nightmares. However, helping adults when they're adults doesn't seem to be enough. Instead she also wants to tackle the problem before people become adults. So as a general principle, Bethany feels that psychologists should try to help those suffering from nightmares whenever possible—not just wait until those suffering are adults.

Step 4: Evaluate the Answer Choices

(C) gets to the heart of Bethany's desire to help adults out at any stage of life.

(A) is Out of Scope. It shifts the focus away from helping the situation to learning more about the cause of the situation. This is beyond Bethany's concern.

(B) gets the logic backwards. Bethany presents a technique that works on adults that she wants to teach to children, not the other way around.

(D) brings up the difficulty of identifying nightmare sufferers, which is not mentioned as a concern by Bethany.

(E) discusses a subset of children (those who are *unlikely* to suffer from nightmares as adults) that Bethany is not directly concerned with. In fact, she might be in favor of helping them, too, just in case they would develop nightmares.

14. (D) Assumption (Necessary)

Step 1: Identify the Question Type

Because this question is asking for what the author is assuming, it is an Assumption question. Additionally, because the argument *depends* on the assumption it is a Necessary Assumption question. You can use the Denial Test to check your work.

Step 2: Untangle the Stimulus

The author is arguing that the typical doughnut eater consumes about as many calories as the typical bagel eater. This is based on a few numbers: the doughnut eater will eat

four doughnuts that contain a total of 680 calories. The bagel eater will eat one bagel, which alone contains 500 calories but will approach 680 calories when spreads are added.

Step 3: Make a Prediction

The main problem with this argument is the disparity in how the numbers are calculated. The caloric value of the doughnuts is based on the doughnuts alone. The caloric value of the bagel is based on the bagel *plus* additional toppings. For this argument to work, the author must assume this is how the typical eater consumes these foods: doughnuts with no toppings and bagels with toppings. Any difference would change the numbers and invalidate the author's conclusion.

Step 4: Evaluate the Answer Choices

(D) addresses exactly what the author forgets to mention. It confirms that the typical doughnut eater is not adding anything that would further boost the caloric intake. The Denial Test confirms that this must be true: if the typical doughnut eater *did* add substances that increased the caloric intake, then the bagel eater would definitely take in fewer calories, spread or no spread.

(A) discusses the health impact of calories and fat, which is irrelevant. The argument is based solely on numbers, not impact.

(B) mentions how aware bagel eaters are of the calories. However, even if they *were* aware of the calorie content of a bagel, that wouldn't change the number of calories they take in.

(C) also brings up health benefits, which is irrelevant. Again, the argument is based solely on numbers, not the health impact of the foods involved.

(E) brings up the idea that doughnut eaters don't eat bagels. However, the argument is concerned with what these people eat in one sitting. Whether a typical doughnut eater eats bagels at other times has no effect on the argument.

15. (A) Flaw

Step 1: Identify the Question Type

The classic language of "vulnerable to criticism" indicates that the argument is inherently flawed, making this a Flaw question.

Step 2: Untangle the Stimulus

Bowers argues that we should pay no attention to any social philosophy that espouses anarchy. This is because Bowers feels that social philosophy must promote peace and order.

Step 3: Make a Prediction

Unfortunately, Bowers never says that anarchy is antipeace until the conclusion. Until the conclusion, anarchy is merely described as "the absence of government." While Bowers's evidence describes anarchy in objective terms, Bowers suddenly shifts to an alternative definition of anarchy—*chaos*—in the conclusion, which is unwarranted. Note that the LSAT may use the technical term *equivocation* to refer to this flaw as well.

Step 4: Evaluate the Answer Choices

(A) points out Bowers's flawed equivocation. Bowers starts off with a straightforward definition of *anarchy* ("absence of government"), and by the end of the argument, changes the definition to *chaos*.

(B) distorts the use of laissez-faire capitalism in the argument. The author is against anarchy, a described *extreme* form of laissez-faire, not laissez-faire in general.

(C) discusses the number of people who accept a viewpoint. However, Bowers never mentions how many people accept any viewpoint in the argument, so this is not a problem.

(D) brings up an assumption that Bowers never suggests. While Bowers clearly feels that peace is necessary for a social philosophy to be acceptable, there is no indication that Bowers feels peace will guarantee a flourishing society.

(E) suggests that Bowers rejects anarchy solely based on the opinion of the one writer who calls it *extreme* laissez-faire. However, Bowers rejects anarchy for other flawed reasoning. In fact, that *extreme* description appears to be irrelevant to Bowers's ultimate argument against anarchy.

16. (E) Parallel Reasoning

Step 1: Identify the Question Type

Because this question is looking for an answer with reasoning similar to the stimulus, this is a Parallel Reasoning question.

Step 2: Untangle the Stimulus

This argument is strongly based on Formal Logic. According to the argument, all lyrical composers are poets, and all poets have wit. There is one possible exception: poets who write only epigrams, who may or may not have wit. The argument then brings up a lyrical composer, Azriel. By the logic, Azriel must be a poet, which means he must have wit—unless he writes only epigrams. However, Azriel does not have that exceptional quality. So the argument correctly concludes that he has wit.

Step 3: Make a Prediction

While it's impossible to predict exactly what terms the correct answer will contain, it will follow the same flow of logic as the stimulus. Rules will state that something with one characteristic (lyrical composer—"X") will have a second characteristic (poet—"Y"), which will lead to a third (wit—"Z"), as long as that something doesn't fit an exceptional condition (epigrams—"Q"):

$$\text{If} \quad X \quad \rightarrow \quad Y$$

$$\text{If} \quad Y \quad \rightarrow \quad Z \text{ (as long as no Q)}$$

Then the argument will present an item "X" that has the first characteristic "Y" and isn't exceptional "~Q" and conclude that the item has the third characteristic "Z."

Step 4: Evaluate the Answer Choices

(E) gets everything right. One thing (townhouse) must have a second characteristic (residential), which will lead to a third (original code), as long as that something doesn't fit an exceptional condition (built last year). Then, the argument presents Bloom House, which has the first characteristic and isn't exceptional, and correctly concludes that it has the third characteristic.

(A) starts off perfectly, stating that something with one characteristic (squeeze toys) will have another characteristic (safety), with one exception (for cats). However, instead of creating a string of logic, the second statement presents an additional characteristic (prewrapped) that follows from the first. In addition, this argument reverses the Formal Logic in a flawed manner.

(B) also provides two characteristics (being a lawyer and having a website) that stem from one characteristic (being a politician). That's not the same.

(C) gets some of the logic right. There is a string of logic (visit permits are visas, which in turn are assigned by the office) and an exception (diplomatic channels). However, the argument illogically concludes that a certain visit permit is an exception without providing any reasoning.

(D) reverses the logic. The argument states that all winter garments are on sale. Then it concludes that a sale item must be a winter garment, ignoring the possibility that other items might also be on sale. Also, the second sentence of the argument ("None of the shirts in this store are designer clothes.") is negative and doesn't have a counterpart in the stimulus.

17. (E) Assumption (Sufficient)

Step 1: Identify the Question Type

Because this question is looking for something the author assumes, this is an Assumption question. Also, because the stem indicates that the conclusion is properly drawn *if* the answer is assumed, that means it is a Sufficient Assumption question. The author doesn't need the assumption for the argument to work, but the correct answer will be one possible way the conclusion is sure to be reached.

Step 2: Untangle the Stimulus

The author argues that teachers should never pretend to know an answer to a question. This is because teachers should never do anything that will make students lose respect for them. However, the evidence is merely a claim that, should a teacher merely pretend to know something, students would sense the ruse.

Step 3: Make a Prediction
While the author claims that students would sense a problem, she never goes so far as to say that would cause the students to lose respect for the teacher—the ultimate issue that teachers should avoid. Thus, the author is assuming that students will lose respect for the teacher if they sense the teacher is trying to hide ignorance.

Step 4: Evaluate the Answer Choices
(E) is exactly the assumption the author is making about students' thought processes.

(A) might explain why respect is so important to good teaching, but it doesn't explain why pretending to know an answer would lead to loss of respect.

(B) is tempting. However, even if students respect honesty above everything else, they can still respect a teacher for other reasons—just not as much. They wouldn't necessarily lose respect for the teacher altogether.

(C) is contrary to the author's reasoning. After all, if students' respect for a teacher was independent of how they perceived the teacher's knowledge, then the teacher could be seen as knowing very little without affecting the students' respect for that teacher.

(D) is irrelevant. Even if teachers can tell when students respect them, that doesn't make the connection between students' sensing a teacher's ignorance and losing respect for that teacher.

18. (D) Role of a Statement

Step 1: Identify the Question Type
Because this question asks for the role a particular statement plays in the argument, this is a Role of a Statement question.

Step 2: Untangle the Stimulus
The author starts by presenting a current state of affairs: food-producing capability has outpaced population growth. This goes contrary to arguments made by somebody named Malthus. However, because of agriculture's compromise of biological diversity, the author feels that this will all change. Food-producing capability will eventually erode, which will then match Malthus's prediction.

Step 3: Make a Prediction
The statement in question is the claim provided at the beginning of the argument, the claim that goes "contrary to Malthus's arguments." However, based on the subsequent evidence, the author says that in the future, things will change. In that case, the state of affairs presented in the statement will eventually reverse themselves.

Step 4: Evaluate the Answer Choices
(D) correctly characterizes that opening statement as a general fact that will eventually change, based on the given evidence.

(A) is actually the opposite of what's being said. Presently, the statement is true. It's in the future the claim will turn false.

(B) seems correct, because the statement is evidence against the view of Malthus. However, the author's conclusion is that the situation will change and Malthus will ultimately be correct, not misguided.

(C) is a Distortion. The statement in question actually undermines Malthus. It's the impending change in circumstances that will eventually support Malthus.

(E) is off base because the statement is not presented as a hypothesis; it's presented as factual information. Additionally, the author never questions the adequacy of the evidence backing up that claim.

19. (C) Inference

Step 1: Identify the Question Type
Because this question asks for something that must be true based on the given information, this is an Inference question.

Step 2: Untangle the Stimulus
According to this stimulus, there is a gathering with three groups of people: bankers, athletes, and lawyers. There is also some information about how the groups can and can't overlap: all of the bankers are athletes, and none of the lawyers are bankers.

Step 3: Make a Prediction
To find the one answer that must be true, it's vital to see how these groups definitely overlap. The ones we know the most about are the bankers. They're all athletes, but none of them are lawyers. So every banker is an athlete who's not a lawyer. The remaining people can overlap, but they don't have to.

Step 4: Evaluate the Answer Choices
(C) is definitely true. All bankers match this description: athletes who are not lawyers. Because the stimulus states that bankers are present, then there must be athletes who are not lawyers present.

(A) tries to reverse the given logic. However, just because all of the bankers are athletes, that doesn't mean that some additional athletes aren't bankers.

(B) is off base because we only know that lawyers are not bankers. For all we know, they could all be athletes.

(D) is absolutely false. The stimulus says that none of the lawyers are bankers. So there can't possibly be a banker who is also a lawyer.

(E) is possible but not confirmed. All that's known about lawyers is that they're not bankers. However, that doesn't prevent them from being athletes.

20. (D) Flaw

Step 1: Identify the Question Type
Because this question is asking for what makes the reasoning flawed, this is a Flaw question.

Step 2: Untangle the Stimulus
The investigator is claiming that a supplier is violating a contract that stipulates the rate of defective products to be less than 5 percent. This is based on a series of inspections done on samples sent by field inspectors from various locations. The testing revealed that 20 percent of the samples were defective.

Step 3: Make a Prediction
The numbers seem to speak volumes. A 20 percent defective rate is far above the stipulated 5 percent rate of the contract. And the samples were sent from various locations, eliminating any representation issues. The only wild card is the field inspectors who sent the samples to be tested. If inspectors choose which samples to send back to the lab, then the selection of samples would not be purely random.

Step 4: Evaluate the Answer Choices
(D) catches the weak link in the logic. If the field inspectors are choosing items that look defective rather than just pulling samples at random, then that could artificially inflate the numbers, making the rate of defects look abnormally high.

(A) can't be argued. While it's possible that the sample is unrepresentative because of what the inspectors choose, the *number* of samples chosen could be more than adequate.

(B) gets the numbers wrong. The investigator wouldn't expect the field inspectors to have an equal chance (50%) of picking a defective item as picking a nondefective item. The contract would suggest the odds of finding a defective item should be 1 in 20 (5%), and the investigator feels that the actual odds are 1 in 5 (20%).

(C) is irrelevant. Even if most of the defective items are from a few select sites, the overall defective rate is still 20 percent, far higher than the contract stipulates.

(E) brings up an unnecessary assumption. The number of visits to which manufacturing sites is not relevant to the samples selected and is not part of the investigator's argument.

21. (C) Weaken

Step 1: Identify the Question Type
Because this question asks for something that will weaken the argument, this is a Weaken question.

Step 2: Untangle the Stimulus
The essayist discusses the extinction of certain animals in a given area within 2,000 years of the arrival of humans. The essayist rejects the idea that hunting caused the extinctions merely due to implausibility. Instead, the essayist brings up another possibility: disease-causing microorganisms. With no absolute evidence, the essayist concludes that the microorganisms are the primary cause of the extinctions.

Step 3: Make a Prediction
Without any hard evidence, it's hard to accept the essayist's conclusion. Because the essayist is merely choosing the microorganism hypothesis over the hunting hypothesis, a good weakener would make it less likely that microorganisms would be the cause or more likely that hunting (or something else) was the cause.

Step 4: Evaluate the Answer Choices
(C) gives some strong evidence that hunting, not microorganisms, may have had a role in the extinction of species. According to this, among the species that were *not* hunted, very few went extinct—despite the extinction of "many species of animals." This suggests that hunting played a strong role in the extinctions, undermining the essayist's argument.

(A) actually strengthens the essayist's argument by suggesting that microorganisms were the root cause of the extinctions, effectively making the species vulnerable to hunters and predators.

(B) is irrelevant. It doesn't matter if humans are immune to certain diseases; it only matters what killed off the now extinct animal species.

(D) is also irrelevant. While it's great that some animals and humans can carry the microorganism without being affected, it's still possible that the animals that went extinct weren't among that fortunate group and were vulnerable to the microorganism.

(E) is Out of Scope. The essayist's argument only concerns the species that went extinct within 2,000 years.

22. (A) Strengthen

Step 1: Identify the Question Type
Because this question asks for something that will strengthen the argument, this is a Strengthen question.

Step 2: Untangle the Stimulus
The author cites data from a study. Workers at one plant were given a free nutritious breakfast, and they became more productive. Workers at a second plant were not given a free breakfast, and they did not become more productive. The author concludes that this study confirms that nutritious breakfasts lead to increased productivity.

Step 3: Make a Prediction

There's one major problem with the study. It states that the workers at Plant B weren't given a free nutritious breakfast. However, that doesn't mean they didn't buy one or make one. For this argument to work, the author must assume that the workers at Plant B didn't get a nutritious breakfast on their own. Anything that validates this assumption will strengthen the argument.

Step 4: Evaluate the Answer Choices

(A) confirms the author's assumption by showing that, generally, the workers at Plant B didn't get a nutritious breakfast some other way. That makes the correlation between breakfast and productivity tighter and helps the author's argument.

(B) brings up the start time to the workday. However, the time of day isn't relevant to whether or not the workers had a good breakfast.

(C) may seem tempting. However, even if the productivity levels were markedly different, the workers at Plant A increased productivity and the workers at Plant B didn't. Starting productivity levels are not important; it's the change in productivity that is attributed to nutritious breakfasts.

(D) potentially weakens the argument by bringing in another factor that could explain the greater productivity at Plant A.

(E) may also seem tempting, but the argument is about increasing productivity, not levels of productivity. Even if the workers at Plant B were overall more productive, they still didn't increase productivity over the month. It's possible that they could have been even more productive if they had eaten nutritious breakfasts.

23. (D) Principle (Identify/Inference)

Step 1: Identify the Question Type

Because this question asks for a generalization, this is a Principle question. The stimulus will provide a specific circumstance, and the correct answer will present that circumstance in a broader context.

Step 2: Untangle the Stimulus

The stimulus presents the circumstance surrounding the town of Hollyville. It helps to organize the information provided in chronological order. A few years ago, an earthquake hit another town, and Hollyville sent some aid. Last year, Hollyville was hit by a tornado and received aid from other people. This year, another town suffered a flood. In reaction, Hollyville sent a significantly greater amount of aid than it had to the earthquake-stricken town.

Step 3: Make a Prediction

Why the large increase in providing aid? It seems that empathy played a big role. After all, the dramatic increase in aid was given after Hollyville itself suffered from a disaster.

The general rule appears to be that people are more likely to give aid to disaster sufferers once they've have to endure their own disasters.

Step 4: Evaluate the Answer Choices

(D) perfectly captures the situation. Once Hollyville was struck by a disaster (tornado), the aid it provided to others in need was much greater than the aid it had provided to others before the tornado.

(A) doesn't work because the stimulus never discussed whether or not the inhabitants of Hollyville knew people in either the flooded town or the town that experienced an earthquake.

(B) starts off perfectly, but it digresses into the idea of supporting government relief programs—a concept never discussed in this stimulus.

(C) isn't good because there's no indication of whether or not the flooded river town was publicized. It's possible that Hollyville knew about the flooding because of the publicity, making the publicity at least partially responsible for the outpouring of aid, not entirely *unrelated*.

(E) doesn't work because neither town that Hollyville gave aid to experienced a similar hardship. Those towns experienced a flood and an earthquake, while Hollyville experienced a tornado.

24. (B) Inference

Step 1: Identify the Question Type

This question is looking for something to fill in the blank at the end of an argument. That means the correct answer will be something that follows directly from the given information. Because it looks for something that is directly supported by given information, this is an Inference question.

Step 2: Untangle the Stimulus

The author starts off by discussing consumers' use of credit cards. Fifty-nine percent of them anticipate paying off balances in full, incurring no interest charges. Then the author mentions that credit card companies try to win over customers with services that appeal to the customers' desires.

Step 3: Make a Prediction

Based on the research statistics, most customers would seem to be unconcerned with interest rates because they intend to pay off everything before interest is accrued. If credit card companies are only interested in what appeals to customers, then it's unlikely that interest rates are high on their list of selling points. The correct answer will most likely offer some variation on that idea.

Step 4: Evaluate the Answer Choices

(B) is a solid match. If credit card companies want to concentrate on consumer concerns and consumers aren't concerned about interest rates, then credit card companies will not concentrate on interest rates.

(A) is a Distortion. While consumers would be indifferent with regard to interest rates, there may be other factors that would be of great interest to them (e.g., bigger spending limits or increased time to pay off balances).

(C) brings up a comparison that is unwarranted by any of the information in the stimulus. The stimulus doesn't discuss consumers' opinions about borrowing money from banks.

(D) isn't supported because consumers merely are described as wanting to pay off balances in full before interest accrues. In fact, if the card offered a longer period to pay before interest accrues, that might be very attractive to consumers.

(E) is plausible, but the author never provides any evidence that number of locations is a concern for consumers, let alone the credit card companies. We need an answer that proceeds from the *therefore* that begins the last sentence, not an answer that introduces an entirely new idea.

25. (B) Weaken

Step 1: Identify the Question Type
Because this question asks for something that will weaken the argument, this is a Weaken question.

Step 2: Untangle the Stimulus
The author concludes that the level of carbon dioxide in the atmosphere today is significantly less than it was 3 billion years ago. The evidence is a potentially confusing mass of science. However, break it down into simple terms. Three billion years ago, the sun was dimmer. A dimmer sun would freeze oceans today, but back then, the oceans were water, not ice. To prevent freezing, Earth would have needed more greenhouse gases than we have today.

Step 3: Make a Prediction
Clearly, the author would be correct in suggesting that Earth had a higher level of greenhouse gases 3 billion years ago. After all, that's the only way the oceans would stay liquid. However, the author concludes that liquid oceans were due to a higher level of carbon dioxide, which is merely one such greenhouse gas. In fact, the author even mentions a second possible greenhouse gas, methane, in the evidence. By choosing carbon dioxide, the author ignores alternative greenhouse gases that could have fit the bill. Bringing up any alternative to carbon dioxide would effectively weaken the author's argument.

Step 4: Evaluate the Answer Choices
(B) brings up exactly the alternative that the author should have considered: methane. Because methane is also a greenhouse gas, then that could have been what helped keep the oceans from freezing 3 billion years ago—not carbon dioxide.

(A) would strengthen the author's argument by discarding an alternative explanation. Eliminating volcanic activity as a possible cause for the liquid oceans makes carbon dioxide a more likely candidate.

(C) also strengthens the author's argument by discarding an alternative explanation. If the minerals wouldn't prevent the oceans from freezing, then it must have been something else—possibly the carbon dioxide.

(D) introduces a correlation between the Sun's luminosity and complexity of life forms. However, that doesn't address the oceans, making it irrelevant to the argument at hand.

(E) is at best irrelevant and at worst potentially strengthens the argument. If less radiation reached Earth 3 billion years ago, then it would seem even more likely that the oceans would have frozen. So something must have prevented the water from freezing—maybe more carbon dioxide.

26. (B) Assumption (Sufficient)

Step 1: Identify the Question Type
Because this question asks for something that is assumed, this is an Assumption question. The language "follows logically if … assumed" indicates a Sufficient Assumption question.

Step 2: Untangle the Stimulus
The commentator starts by presenting a necessary condition for the proper functioning of a free market: the ability to contact sellers and compare their selling prices with the product's actual worth. The commentator then concludes that the auto repair industry doesn't meet this condition, even though consumers can find selling prices and get estimates from the individual businesses.

Step 3: Make a Prediction
The commentator mentions that the auto industry provides two of the necessary components of a free market. It provides written estimates from individual businesses (so consumers can contact sellers) and advertises prices (so consumers can obtain selling prices). The only thing missing is the actual worth of the product, which the commentator never mentions for the auto repair industry. To claim that the auto repair industry isn't satisfying all of the conditions, the commentator must be assuming that consumers can't access the final piece of the puzzle: the worth of the product.

Step 4: Evaluate the Answer Choices
(B) addresses the missing link: the inability to determine the worth of the product. Without that, the auto repair industry doesn't meet all of the necessary criteria, and the commentator's conclusion is validated.

(A) has no effect on the commentator's argument. If people don't choose to take advantage of a free market, that doesn't mean it doesn't exist.

(C) may be tempting, but the commentator claims that buyers only need to be able to contact a "large number" of sellers. Because the evidence states that estimates are available from *many* businesses, that could be good enough to satisfy the criteria. The commentator need not assume that all auto repair shops give written estimates.

(D) brings up the worth but only states that the prices are greater than the worth. That may be good enough to qualify as a comparison of selling price to worth, in which case the auto repair industry *does* meet all of the criteria—contrary to what the commentator is suggesting.

(E) is irrelevant because standardized prices are not mentioned by the commentator as a required component of a free market.

Section III: Logical Reasoning

Q#	Question Type	Correct	Difficulty
1	Paradox	A	★
2	Weaken	A	★
3	Inference	C	★
4	Paradox	C	★
5	Flaw	C	★
6	Principle (Parallel)	B	★
7	Inference	A	★
8	Flaw	B	★★
9	Main Point	D	★
10	Assumption (Sufficient)	E	★★
11	Strengthen	B	★
12	Assumption (Necessary)	A	★★
13	Weaken	D	★★
14	Method of Argument	C	★
15	Parallel Flaw	C	★
16	Assumption (Necessary)	E	★★★
17	Paradox (EXCEPT)	A	★★
18	Principle (Identify/Assumption)	D	★★
19	Inference	E	★★★★
20	Flaw	D	★★★
21	Inference	E	★★★★
22	Flaw	D	★★
23	Method of Argument	B	★★★
24	Flaw	E	★★★
25	Assumption (Necessary)	B	★★

KAPLAN

1. (A) Paradox

Step 1: Identify the Question Type
Because the question asks for something that will explain a seemingly contradictory situation, this is a Paradox question.

Step 2: Untangle the Stimulus
According to the stimulus, life-extending and pain-reducing technologies require a lot of money to research and are unlikely to provide financial return. Yet people continue to invest in those technologies.

Step 3: Make a Prediction
Why would somebody invest in something that is unlikely to provide financial return? A reasonable prediction would be an answer that discusses what investors receive if it *does* provide financial return; it should be significant enough to warrant the risk. Another prediction might be that such an investment provides a reward other than financial return.

Step 4: Evaluate the Answer Choices
(A) explains why people would take the risk: the potential for much greater returns than with ordinary investments.

(B) explains that a lot of great technologies have already been developed. However, that doesn't mean they turned a profit or provided any financial return.

(C) brings up other risky investments but still doesn't explain why people would invest in them.

(D) would make matters worse. If some promising investments fail, then why would people invest in risky ones?

(E) also makes matters worse. If failed research offers no greater understanding of the world, then investments in those would fail in two ways: no monetary return and no benefit to science. This provides another reason to *not* invest.

2. (A) Weaken

Step 1: Identify the Question Type
Because the question asks for something that will weaken the department chair's argument, this is a Weaken question.

Step 2: Untangle the Stimulus
The department chair is getting defensive about the new textbook she selected. She claims the textbook was selected for academic reasons, not for the textbook company's generous donation—which wouldn't have been given if the department chair had chosen another textbook. As evidence, she points to her department's textbook committee, which gave the textbook the highest ratings.

Step 3: Make a Prediction
The department chair is claiming that the book was chosen for academic reasons because she based her decision on the ratings of her textbook committee. To make this claim, she must be assuming that the textbook committee made the decision academically. If the committee members were aware

of the potential donation, they may have been swayed to inflate the ratings. Anything that questions whether this book was selected academically would undermine the department chair's assumption and weaken the argument.

Step 4: Evaluate the Answer Choices
(A) gets to the root of the problem. While the department chair didn't use the donation as a deciding factor, the committee did. That undermines the idea that the textbook was chosen solely for academic reasons.

(B) potentially strengthens the argument by describing an academic policy that has always been in place: always choose the textbook with the highest ratings.

(C) doesn't weaken the argument if the introductory textbook was also chosen for academic purposes.

(D) may be tempting. However, even if this were the case, there would still be other members of the committee making the decision who could use academic reasons to override the chair's potential bias.

(E) provides information about the behavior of the textbook company, but this has no impact on the reasoning for the department's decision.

3. (C) Inference

Step 1: Identify the Question Type
Because the question asks for something that is strongly supported by the given information, this is an Inference question.

Step 2: Untangle the Stimulus
This stimulus gives us information about a substance, hemoglobin, that carries oxygen through the body. It starts in the lungs and can carry up to four molecules of oxygen. Every time it adds an oxygen molecule, it changes shape and becomes more open to receiving oxygen. As a result, it becomes more effective at grabbing additional oxygen molecules.

Step 3: Make a Prediction
While it may not be possible to predict the wording of the correct answer, it will be consistent with the process described. It helps to paraphrase the process to understand it without getting caught up in the scientific terms. If a hemoglobin molecule has one oxygen molecule, it could add a second. It would then change shape, become more open, and be able to add a third more effectively than it did the second. If it grabs a third, it will open up more and be able to grab a fourth one more effectively. If it does grab a fourth, it will change shape, but that's it—it has reached maximum capacity and will accept no more.

Step 4: Evaluate the Answer Choices
(C) is a match. With each additional oxygen molecule it picks up, the hemoglobin molecule becomes more effective. So

hemoglobin that has picked up three oxygen molecules will definitely be more effective than hemoglobin that has picked up only one.

(A) is not for certain. With three oxygen molecules, the hemoglobin molecule will be very open to receiving a fourth, but other factors may be at play. Perhaps it only needs to carry three molecules, or perhaps a fourth molecule isn't available.

(B) is Extreme. While the open shape makes the hemoglobin molecule more effective, there's nothing to say that the open shape is the *only* factor in determining effectiveness.

(D) seems contrary to the information given. According to the argument, the hemoglobin molecule changes shape with each oxygen molecule; nothing in the stimulus suggests that it reverts back to its original shape upon taking on four molecules.

(E) may be tempting. However, it's possible that each hemoglobin molecule has one oxygen molecule to begin with. In that case, it doesn't need to pick up any more, even though it could.

4. (C) Paradox

Step 1: Identify the Question Type
Because the question asks for something that will explain a seemingly contradictory pair of facts, this is a Paradox question.

Step 2: Untangle the Stimulus
The stimulus presents two scenarios for drivers: short trips and long trips. On short trips, a driver is more likely to get into an accident when there's a passenger. The opposite is the case on long trips—drivers are less likely to get into an accident when there's a passenger.

Step 3: Make a Prediction
The stimulus suggests why passengers can create problems on short trips—they can be distracting. So why are they better for long trips? While it may not be worth coming up with an absolute prediction, know that the correct answer will provide a reason why passengers are an asset on long trips.

Step 4: Evaluate the Answer Choices
(C) provides an acceptable explanation. Passengers help on longer trips because they keep drivers alert.

(A) provides information on when people are more likely to drive alone, but it doesn't explain why they're safer on long trips with passengers.

(B) distinguishes good and bad drivers but ignores why passengers would be a factor.

(D) is irrelevant. The stimulus only differentiates between having passengers and not.

(E) is also irrelevant. Actual numbers don't necessarily have an effect on the proportions. Also, this doesn't address the primary issue of whether the drivers have passengers.

5. (C) Flaw

Step 1: Identify the Question Type
Because the question is asking why an argument is flawed, this is a Flaw question. Make sure to read both speakers' arguments for context, but the correct answer will be a flaw in the mayor's argument.

Step 2: Untangle the Stimulus
The challenger has a problem with the mayor. The mayor promised to increase employment opportunities and claims to have done so by citing an 8 percent increase in jobs. However, the challenger argues that those jobs were merely due to a relocated office that brought along staff from outside the city. The mayor defends herself by stating that the 8 percent increase in jobs is higher than that under previous mayors.

Step 3: Make a Prediction
The mayor tries an interesting distraction technique by pointing to the inferior performance of her predecessors. However, that still ignores the challenger's contention that the new jobs were already filled by people who came from *outside* the city. The mayor created no new jobs for the unemployed people already living *in* the city.

Step 4: Evaluate the Answer Choices
(C) explains exactly what the mayor did wrong: ignored the fact that people already living in the city didn't get any new job opportunities.

(A) would be a good assumption for the mayor to have—you would expect her to assume that job availability is important to the city's citizens. However, her flaw is in thinking she lived up to their expectations when the facts suggest otherwise.

(B) brings up irrelevant numbers. The problem is that the mayor failed to bring in jobs for the city's citizens. It doesn't matter how many people in the city are unemployed—the mayor still failed to provide jobs for any of them.

(D) attributes to the challenger claims about how the newcomers affected population size and priorities. However, the challenger never makes such claims.

(E) suggests that the mayor is putting words in the challenger's mouth, which she's not. She's merely stating her own flawed defense.

6. (B) Principle (Parallel)

Step 1: Identify the Question Type
Because the question is looking for a situation that conforms to a principle, this is a Principle question. However, the principle isn't merely given. The principle will apply to the

stimulus and then needs to be reapplied to a different circumstance in the correct answer (similar to Parallel Reasoning).

Step 2: Untangle the Stimulus
The author defends psychologists, who are criticized for not attempting to determine the way a particular function of the brain works, by claiming that technology currently makes it impossible for them to do so.

Step 3: Make a Prediction
The author is applying a pretty reasonable principle: if it's not possible to do something, then somebody should not be criticized for failing to do it. The correct answer will reapply this principle to a new situation.

Step 4: Evaluate the Answer Choices
(B) applies the same principle as the stimulus. It's not possible for the utility companies to do something (use nuclear fusion to provide the nation with electricity), so they shouldn't be criticized for not doing it.

(A) defends a group based on a different principle: it looks like they're trying to cut corners, but technology has allowed them to do the job more efficiently.

(C) defends a group based on a different principle: the action being criticized leads to an unconsidered benefit.

(D) also defends a group based on a different principle: the action people are complaining isn't being done would result in negative consequences if it were done.

(E) also defends a group based on a different principle: the CEOs don't have to perform a certain action because that action is irrelevant to what they're doing.

7. (A) Inference

Step 1: Identify the Question Type
Because the question is asking for information that is "strongly support[ed]" by the stimulus, this is an Inference question. Furthermore, the question asks us for something the stimulus implies about people who are most successful at ending their bad habits.

Step 2: Untangle the Stimulus
This stimulus discusses the difficulty of breaking bad habits. The reasoning described is that stopping the bad habits has immediate effects that are painful, while long-term benefits of kicking the habit are not immediately felt and therefore are not perceived strongly.

Step 3: Make a Prediction
This question is looking for something that can be inferred about people who *are* successful at ending their bad habits. If the hard part is getting through the painful immediate effects so that one can get to the long-term benefit, the people who succeed would seem to be those who can let their immediate pains be outweighed by the long-term gains.

Step 4: Evaluate the Answer Choices
(A) describes just such a personality—someone who can envision that far-off benefit vividly.

(B) is a 180. If people could imagine their current, vivid pain lasting a long time, they would be more likely to stop whatever's causing that pain. So they would be more likely to go back to the bad habit.

(C) is plausible but not supported by the information given. The stimulus doesn't suggest that the number of previous attempts (successful or otherwise) has any effect on the success of subsequently ending a habit.

(D) discusses one's awareness of behavioral characteristics, a concept that is not discussed or implied in the stimulus.

(E) sounds possible, but it brings up the pain of the habit itself. The stimulus only brings up the immediate pain of stopping the habit. If the immediate pain of quitting the habit is even worse than the pain from the habit itself, people would probably revert to the habit so that the pain would be relatively less.

8. (B) Flaw

Step 1: Identify the Question Type
The classic language of "vulnerable to criticism" indicates that the argument is inherently flawed, making this a Flaw question.

Step 2: Untangle the Stimulus
The author claims that modern archaeologists are learning more about the Mayans' achievements. One of those achievements, the author concludes, was a strong grasp of mathematics. The author provides evidence of high-level math found in the writings of Mayan religious scribes.

Step 3: Make a Prediction
The problem here is that author makes a conclusion about the general population of Mayans ("people in general") based on the writings of one group: religious scribes. It's possible the religious scribes had a strong grasp of mathematics while the general population didn't.

Step 4: Evaluate the Answer Choices
(B) points out this flaw of representation. The evidence comes from a group that may not represent the abilities of the general population.

(A) discusses the author's failure to define *intellectual achievement*. However, the author doesn't need a precise definition to make her point. The use of the phrase *intellectual achievement* can be adequately understood in context of the argument.

(C) brings up the achievements of other civilizations. However, the author is not comparing the Mayans to other civilizations, so this is irrelevant.

(D) refers to the author's use of the word *scientific*. However, the word is used just once and in only one sense.

(E) presents a classic LSAT flaw, but the author never claims causality in this argument.

9. (D) Main Point

Step 1: Identify the Question Type
Because the question is looking for the main conclusion of the argument, this is a Main Point question.

Step 2: Untangle the Stimulus
The manager starts off with a strong claim: there is no reason for creativity to be a goal of employee training. The rest of the argument is reasoning to support that claim: many jobs don't require creativity, creativity can be disruptive, and creativity probably can't be taught anyway.

Step 3: Make a Prediction
All of the negative information about creativity is merely provided as evidence for the initial claim. Because that initial claim (creativity should not be a goal of employee training) is supported by everything else, the claim is the main point.

Step 4: Evaluate the Answer Choices
(D) accurately expresses that initial claim—the main point of the argument.

(A) is evidence to support the claim in the first sentence. After all, the main conclusion (creativity is not a proper goal of training) can be claimed *because* creativity can be disruptive.

(B), although it is in the last sentence, is not the conclusion. Again, it is merely evidence that can be used (by putting the word *because* before it) to support the main conclusion in the first sentence.

(C) is also evidence because it's information used to support the claim in the first sentence.

(E) states that creativity is in demand, which the manager never admits.

10. (E) Assumption (Sufficient)

Step 1: Identify the Question Type
Because the question is looking for something that *if* assumed would make the conclusion true, this is a Sufficient Assumption question. Don't let the word *inferred* fool you—the producer's conclusion is inferred based on the assumption the question is looking for.

Step 2: Untangle the Stimulus
The producer suggests that a public boycott of advertisers, although not a direct act of government censorship, would still constitute censorship. The reasoning behind that claim is that boycotts lead to canceled ads, which eventually lead to canceled shows, resulting in a limited number of shows for people to watch.

Step 3: Make a Prediction
The producer makes a valid point that boycotting ads can ultimately lead to a reduced number of shows that people could watch. The producer's overall conclusion will follow if a boycott-induced reduction in programming automatically constitutes censorship.

Step 4: Evaluate the Answer Choices
(E) provides a loose enough definition of *censorship* to justify the producer's reasoning. If any action that restricts programming is censorship, then the reduction caused by boycotts would qualify.

(A) brings up an irrelevant hypothetical. The author is concerned about whether boycotting *does* constitute censorship, not whether shows would be unrestricted without boycotts.

(B) suggests that boycotts would cause potentially acceptable shows to be cancelled. However, that still may not fit the definition of *censorship*. Thus, it does not necessarily lead to the author's conclusion.

(C) brings up the potential audience for violent shows. However, the issue is not whether anyone wants to watch the shows but whether cancelling those shows constitutes censorship.

(D) still fails to discuss what constitutes censorship—whether or not there is broad agreement about which shows "erode values."

11. (B) Strengthen

Step 1: Identify the Question Type
Because the question is looking for something that will strengthen an argument, this is a Strengthen question.

Step 2: Untangle the Stimulus
The author is arguing that printed books probably won't be replaced by electronic books, as some predict. The evidence is that, while electronic formats may be more convenient for research, bookstores and public libraries will continue stocking nonelectronic (i.e., print) books.

Step 3: Make a Prediction
Any argument that's based on a prediction hinges on an assumption that circumstances surrounding the prediction won't change. In this case, the author is assuming that nothing will change that will prevent the bookstore and libraries from providing printed materials. Any answer that shows things won't change will help the author's cause.

Step 4: Evaluate the Answer Choices
(B) verifies that printed books will still be provided to the outlets that offer them, thus lending credence to the author's prediction.

(A) doesn't help the author. If scientists prefer the electronic books, then that just supports the idea that printed books could be replaced by electronic books for their needs.

(C) also doesn't help. This shows why some people would stop using public libraries—a place that offers printed books. If some people stop using the public libraries, the libraries may be less inclined to carry printed books.

(D) hurts the author by stating that electronic books are becoming more popular. That suggests that electronic books may eventually take over after all.

(E) also goes against the author by suggesting that some people may give up printed books for electronic ones.

12. (A) Assumption (Necessary)

Step 1: Identify the Question Type
Because the question is looking for an assumption the argument *depends* on, this is a Necessary Assumption question. You can use the Denial Test to check your work.

Step 2: Untangle the Stimulus
The author discusses a school that modified its air-conditioning system. That resulted in an 18 percent decrease in humidity. Twenty-four hours later, the school nurse experienced a 25 percent increase in visitors. The author uses this correlation to conclude that the humidity caused illnesses.

Step 3: Make a Prediction
This argument looks like a classic LSAT case of causation versus correlation. A correlation is provided (humidity decreased, and nurse visits increased within 24 hours of each other), and the author then implies causality. While a number of assumptions are involved in correlation-causation arguments, there's a more pressing issue here. The author concludes that decreased humidity makes people sick. However, the evidence only mentions people visiting the nurse. There's nothing to suggest that these visitors were actually sick. For this argument to work in any way, the author first has to assume that people visiting the nurse were actually sick.

Step 4: Evaluate the Answer Choices
(A) picks up on the main assumption. If nobody was sick (maybe people visited to pick up some forms), then the connection between humidity and illness is broken. The author must assume that at least some of the visitors were ill.

(B) is Extreme. The 25 percent increase could still result in only a minority of students affected.

(C) might help, but the question is looking for a required assumption. It's not necessary that the symptoms take 24 hours to appear. It could take much less time (e.g., 6 hours), but people could wait until the symptoms get worse before visiting the nurse.

(D) may be tempting because it uses the same numbers as the author. However, the 25 percent increase refers to visits to the nurse, not an individual's probability of becoming ill.

(E) discusses the cost-effectiveness of the modified system but ignores the author's conclusion, the argument about whether the modification made people ill.

13. (D) Weaken

Step 1: Identify the Question Type
Because the question is asking for something that will weaken an argument, this is a Weaken question.

Step 2: Untangle the Stimulus
The author provides some statistics from a recent study of people in car accidents. Of the people who were driving large vehicles, a small percentage were injured. Of the people driving small vehicles, a large percentage were injured. The author uses this data to conclude that people who drive larger cars are less likely to be injured in an accident than people who drive smaller cars.

Step 3: Make a Prediction
Whenever a conclusion is based on a study or survey, it's important to consider factors that may affect the practicality of the results. In this case, the statistics provide the percentage of people injured in each vehicle type. However, it doesn't provide information about how many accidents each vehicle is in. If large vehicles are involved in a significantly greater number of accidents, then even a lower percentage can translate into greater numbers—undermining the author's conclusion.

Step 4: Evaluate the Answer Choices
(D) uses numbers to contradict the author. For example, say that during a given time period, 5,000 people drove large cars and the 5,000 drove small cars. This answer choices says that a large car is more likely to be involved in an accident, so say 5 percent of large cars are in accidents and only 1 percent of small cars. Then even if 60 percent of the people in small cars were injured and only 20 percent of the people in large cars were injured, that would be 30 and 50 injuries, respectively, making large cars much less safe.

(A) discusses the location of accidents, which is irrelevant to an argument regarding vehicle size.

(B) says that some people drive both types of cars, but the author never assumes that people can only drive one type of car. When a person is in an automobile accident, that individual is driving just one car.

(C) discusses medium-sized cars. However, the argument is a comparison between large and small cars, so medium-sized cars are irrelevant.

(E) discusses overall percentages of injuries but ignores the disparity between large and small cars.

14. (C) Method of Argument

Step 1: Identify the Question Type

Because the question is asking for the argumentative technique being used, this is a Method of Argument question.

Step 2: Untangle the Stimulus

The economist starts off by stating that a trade deficit can indicate a weak economy but it doesn't cause the weakness. Because of that, the economist suggests (via a comparison to sticking a thermometer in cold water to reduce a fever) that restricting imports to reduce a trade deficit would not lead to the intended results.

Step 3: Make a Prediction

The comparison of restricting imports to dunking thermometers is definitely an analogy. And the point of the analogy is to show that certain actions (in this case, reducing the trade deficit) will not lead to intended results.

Step 4: Evaluate the Answer Choices

(C) completely describes the economist's actions: using an analogy to show that a course of action will be futile.

(A) is off base because the author never attacks an assumption and never claims that anything contains a falsehood.

(B) may be tempting because it brings up the analogy the economist employs. However, the economist doesn't show that the analogy is faulty; in fact, the economist uses that analogy to make a point.

(D) is incorrect because the economist never attacks or even mentions anyone who made a claim.

(E) is Extreme. The economist suggests that a course of action won't lead to the intended results but never suggests that the actual results would be *disastrous*. Placing a thermometer in a glass of water won't cure a fever, but it won't make the patient worse, either.

15. (C) Parallel Flaw

Step 1: Identify the Question Type

The question is looking for an argument with similar reasoning to the stimulus, and the stimulus and the correct answer will both be flawed in the same way. Hence, this is a Parallel Flaw question.

Step 2: Untangle the Stimulus

The author provides two separate instances that can be acceptable on their own: making threats and asking for money or a favor. The author then concludes that it can be acceptable to do both at the same time: ask for money or a favor while making threats.

Step 3: Make a Prediction

While the two actions may each be acceptable under certain circumstances, the author erroneously suggests that they would be acceptable when performed together. After all, asking for money or favors while making threats would be extortion. While it isn't be possible to predict the scenario of the correct answer, it will make the same mistake: say that two things are okay by themselves and conclude that it's okay to combine them.

Step 4: Evaluate the Answer Choices

(C) is a perfect match. Two things are okay by themselves (taking drug A for a headache or taking drug B for a headache), but the author faultily concludes that it's okay to combine them (taking both drugs together for a headache).

(A) is flawed, but for different reasons than the stimulus. In this case, something is acceptable in two circumstances, and the author concludes that it must be unacceptable in other circumstances. While the reasoning is flawed in that it ignores alternative acceptable circumstances, this is not the same flaw as in the stimulus.

(B) is also flawed for different reasons. The author suggests something is easy to do under certain circumstances, then concludes that it's usually easy to do. This is not like the stimulus.

(D) may be flawed in that it draws an unqualified conclusion ("*cannot* be operated safely") from qualified evidence ("ability … *can* be impaired by *certain* prescription drugs"), but this is not the same flaw as in the stimulus.

(E) offers two results (treacherous roads and full streams) from one cause (rain), then faultily concludes that the presence of those results certainly indicates the cause. While this reversal of logic is surely flawed, this is not the same flaw as in the original stimulus.

16. (E) Assumption (Necessary)

Step 1: Identify the Question Type

Because the question is looking for an assumption the argument *requires*, this is a Necessary Assumption question.

Step 2: Untangle the Stimulus

The author states that a genetic mutation can reduce levels of a certain enzyme (cathepsin C). That in turn can increase one's chance of getting periodontitis (i.e., gum disease). However, the author describes a possible solution: doctors are trying to find ways to increase levels of cathepsin C back to normal. This, the author concludes, will prevent people from getting periodontitis.

Step 3: Make a Prediction

This is a classic case of an author eliminating one possible cause of a result and concluding that the result will never happen. While lower levels of cathepsin C can lead to gum disease, that doesn't mean it's the only thing that can cause gum disease. If that one cause is eliminated, there may be other causes that the author is overlooking. For this argument to work, the author must be assuming that low levels of cathepsin C are the only cause of periodontitis and that resolving that issue will eliminate the disease.

Step 4: Evaluate the Answer Choices

(E) gets right to the author's assumption: getting rid of the problem of low cathepsin C levels will remove the problem of periodontitis altogether. The Denial Test is useful for seeing why this assumption is required. If a person with normal cathepsin C levels *can* suffer from periodontitis, then that suggests there are other causes not addressed. That would kill the author's argument on the spot.

(A) may be very tempting. However, while the author assumes that cathepsin C is the only root cause of periodontitis, there may be other solutions. For example, scientists might come up with a way to destroy diseased cells that cathepsin C would normally destroy. That would potentially eliminate gum disease without having to raise cathepsin C levels.

(B) is ultimately irrelevant. It doesn't matter what causes the low levels of cathepsin C. The point is that scientists are working on restoring the levels—no matter what causes the levels to drop in the first place.

(C) isn't required. The author's conclusion is based on whenever scientists solve the problem of low cathepsin C levels ("Once that happens …"), whether it's next week or next century.

(D) may tempt you. However, even if people without the genetic mutation get gum disease, they could still get the gum disease due to low levels of cathepsin C—just brought about for some nongenetic reason. Therefore, even if this were false, the author's argument could still work. That means this is not required for the argument.

17. (A) Paradox (EXCEPT)

Step 1: Identify the Question Type

Because the question is looking for something that will explain a discrepancy, this is a Paradox question. However, the *EXCEPT* indicates that the four wrong answers will all resolve the paradox and the one correct answer will not.

Step 2: Untangle the Stimulus

The author presents two facts that seem to be at odds with one another. Most new movies have plots that are similar to plots from old movies. However, people still enjoy seeing new movies every year.

Step 3: Make a Prediction

If the plots aren't really new, why do people enjoy seeing new movies? Because four of the answers provide explanations, it's not worth making four predictions. Instead, eliminate anything that explains why people enjoy seeing new movies and select the one that fails to do so.

Step 4: Evaluate the Answer Choices

(A) might explain why studios *make* movies based on old plots. However, it doesn't explain why people would want to *see* those movies. Therefore, this is the correct answer.

(B) explains why people would see the new movies. Even though the plots are borrowed, people *think* the plots are different due to slightly different details.

(C) also explains why people would see new movies. There are too many movies to see all of them, so people can choose which movies they see—potentially avoiding movies that have plots they've already seen.

(D) also provides a reason why people would see new movies with similar plots. There's a certain pleasure in seeing familiar stories told in different ways.

(E) also explains why people would be okay with the new movies using old plots. If the old plots are from over 50 years ago, they would be unfamiliar to younger viewers or people who have seen many movies since and may not remember the specific plot points.

18. (D) Principle (Identify/Assumption)

Step 1: Identify the Question Type

Because the question asks for a principle that *underlies* an argument, this is an Identify the Principle question, specifically one that seeks a principle that the author assumes.

Step 2: Untangle the Stimulus

The author is arguing that, despite what some people claim, government should still provide resources for space exploration. The reasoning is that, while space exploration doesn't directly affect most people, unexpected indirect benefits may not be realized otherwise.

Step 3: Make a Prediction

The correct answer will take the author's reasoning for defending space exploration and generalize it to apply to other circumstances. In this case, the general rule is a fairly reasonable one: if something (in this case, space exploration) provides benefits—even if those benefits are unexpected and have an indirect effect—then governments should continue to support it.

Step 4: Evaluate the Answer Choices

(D) is just the kind of general rule that the author applies to space exploration. Space exploration produced unintended benefits in the past, so the author suggests that governments should continue to support it.

(A) is accurate in that space exploration's intended consequences don't directly affect most people. However, this ignores the author's essential reason for continuing the funding—the *un*intended benefits.

(B) may be something the author would espouse elsewhere. However, it doesn't concentrate on the argument at hand, which is about whether or not government funding should be used for such projects.

(C) creates a relationship (between practicality of goals and unexpectedness of consequences) that is unsupported by the mere one example of the argument.

(E) may be tempting because the author advocated the continued funding of space exploration. However, this principle misses the reasoning behind that suggestion—the potential for unexpected benefits—instead referring more generally to "advanc[ing] the welfare of society."

19. (E) Inference

Step 1: Identify the Question Type
Because this question asks for something that directly follows the given information, this is an Inference question.

Step 2: Untangle the Stimulus
The stimulus starts off with some rather convoluted Formal Logic. If understanding a word requires knowing the dictionary definition, then it also requires understanding each word of that definition. The stimulus then mentions that some people (including all babies) don't know the dictionary definitions of the words they say.

Step 3: Make a Prediction
Untangling this stimulus must be done very carefully. It's important to note that the first sentence is conditional. The author doesn't confirm that understanding a word requires knowing its definition. However, *if* that's the case, then it also requires understanding the words in the definition:

If	**need to know definition**	→	**need to know words in definition**

By the contrapositive:

If	**~ need to know words in definition**	→	**~ need to know the definition**

The last claim states that all babies (and potentially some other people) don't know the dictionary definition of their words but that doesn't mean they don't understand those words. That would be true *if* knowing the definition is not necessary to understanding. It's not worth predicting an answer in this case. Instead, check each answer to find one that must be true.

Step 4: Evaluate the Answer Choices
(E) is correct. Babies don't know the definitions of any of their words, so if some of them understand their words anyway, then (as this answer suggests) knowing the definition isn't necessary for understanding.

(A) takes the argument in the opposite direction from where the author is going. The author might well concede that some babies don't understand some of the words they utter. However, this is not a conclusion regarding understanding a word and knowing its dictionary definition, the author's concern.

(B) is possible, but it presents a conclusion without linking it logically to the preceding evidence (about babies). We are looking for a statement that "follows logically from the statements above."

(C) doesn't quite work. The first half suggests that even if one is unaware of a word's definition (as babies are), the words *can* be understood. However, that doesn't mean (as the second half says) that the babies *will* understand them. Maybe only adults can understand words in this way.

(D) provides an improper negation of the Formal Logic of the first statement. The Formal Logic in the stimulus states that if you *do* need to know the definition of a word, then you must understand the words in the definition. However, it doesn't say anything about what would be the case if you *don't* need to know the definition.

20. (D) Flaw

Step 1: Identify the Question Type
Because the question is looking for a flaw in the reasoning, this is a Flaw question.

Step 2: Untangle the Stimulus
The argument concerns the peppered moth, which can blend into its background to avoid predators. Looking at the history of the moth, the author says that the lightest peppered moths contrasted too much with the background and, thus, were easily spotted and eaten. The author concludes that the darkest moths blended in the best.

Step 3: Make a Prediction
The author makes the classic error of drawing a conclusion that is too extreme. The lightest moths may have contrasted with the background too much, suggesting that a darker shade may be been better for survival. However, the author makes a leap to saying the darkest moths had the greatest advantage. However, while the lightest moths may have been too light, the author fails to consider that the darkest moths may have been too dark. Perhaps the moths that blended best were the ones that weren't too light or weren't too dark (or, as Goldilocks would say, the one's that were just right).

Step 4: Evaluate the Answer Choices

(D) brings up the middle ground that the author overlooks.

(A) brings up an Irrelevant Comparison regarding the number of predators. Regardless of which moths had more predators, better blending in would make them less visible—to any number of predators.

(B) is not an assumption the author makes. If the moths could control how well they blend into the environment, then the naturally lighter and darker moths should be equally able to adapt and avoid detection.

(C) isn't necessary for the author's argument. Even if individual moths with similar coloring had a different likelihood of being seen, the group of moths of that color as a whole could still be more susceptible to predators than moths of a darker or lighter color.

(E) brings up another unnecessary assumption. The moths could have other defense mechanisms. Blending in may simply be the one that most affects their chances of survival.

21. (E) Inference

Step 1: Identify the Question Type

Because the question asks for something "strongly supported" by the given information, this is an Inference question.

Step 2: Untangle the Stimulus

The historian mentions that the standard configuration of letters on a keyboard was designed to slow people down. The reason was that old technology would jam if people typed too fast. While research shows that other configurations can be more efficient and require less effort, it would be too costly and inconvenient to make a widespread switch.

Step 3: Make a Prediction

There's not much to predict here. The best that can be done is have a basic understanding of the information provided and avoid any answer that is not entirely backed up by that information.

Step 4: Evaluate the Answer Choices

(E) is supported. After all, the keyboard was designed to slow people down in order to prevent jamming. Computers don't jam. So if the keyboard were designed for something that didn't jam, the need for a slower typing speed would be removed.

(A) is plausible because research has shown that those keyboards can be more efficient. However, there's no evidence about any people (let alone "most people") who actually use them. Furthermore, the argument states that other keyboards *can* double typing speed. That doesn't mean that people (or, again, even most people) absolutely will type faster. Perhaps they need significant experience with the new keyboard before experiencing benefits.

(B) compares early typewriters to later ones, but the stimulus gives us no information about more recent typewriters. Perhaps typewriters of all vintages suffered from jammed keys.

(C) is tempting. However, even if designers did predict the eventual arrival of nonjamming technology, they still had to create a keyboard layout for the typewriters that *did* jam.

(D) is contrary to the information given. The historian states that the extra cost is preventing the switch, suggesting that the cost factor is overriding the potential benefit—not the other way around.

22. (D) Flaw

Step 1: Identify the Question Type

Because the question asks for the flaws in the argument's reasoning, this is a Flaw question. It's important to note that the question is looking for multiple flaws—not just one.

Step 2: Untangle the Stimulus

The author presents a general rule: if one agrees to do something, one has an obligation to do so. From that, the author concludes that an obligation to do something implies that one agreed to do it. The author then goes on to equate having a legal obligation with merely having an obligation.

Step 3: Make a Prediction

The first mistake the author makes is a classic reversal of Formal Logic. According to the first piece of evidence, agreeing to do something is sufficient to conclude that one has an obligation to do it. However, the author faultily concludes that being obligated to do something means one *must* have agreed to do it (making agreement a necessary condition). In fact, one might be obligated to do something for some other reason. Furthermore, the author then suggests (for no given reason) that being required to do something in general is the same as having a legal obligation—as if there can't be obligations other than legal ones.

Step 4: Evaluate the Answer Choices

(D) discusses both flaws: treating a sufficient condition (agreeing to do something) as if it were necessary and assuming that obligations can't be anything other than legal obligations.

(A) brings up a failed distinction between being obligated to do something and the action having good consequences. However, consequences are not discussed or relevant to the argument.

(B) is a 180. It states that the author assumes there can be obligations that don't involve agreements. However, that's exactly the opposite of what the author first concludes—an obligation *does* imply an agreement.

(C) is incorrect because the author's first conclusion is *not* logically equivalent to the opening premise—it's an improper reversal. Furthermore, the author doesn't talk about what actions people should or shouldn't agree to.

(E) incorrectly implies that the author uses the word *action* inconsistently. Furthermore, whether or not people are willing to perform certain actions is not the same as whether or not they're obligated to do so. Thus, that's irrelevant to the argument.

23. (B) Method of Argument

Step 1: Identify the Question Type

Because the question asks for a technique being used in the argument, this is a Method of Argument question.

Step 2: Untangle the Stimulus

The author starts off by suggesting something that's needed to predict an invention: a conception of how that device will work and what will happen when it's used. However, the author then finds a problem with this notion. Inventing something means developing a conception. If predicting means developing a conception, then that automatically implies inventing—so one would be predicting the occurrence of something that is already happening.

Step 3: Make a Prediction

The paradox described here may be difficult to grasp. The good news is the correct answer doesn't require a complete understanding of the content. Instead, it's important to predict *how* the author makes her point. In this case, the author feels there's a self-contradiction to the idea of predicting an invention (i.e., it can't really be done). That self-contradiction comes from a clash between the accepted meanings of *predicting* and *inventing*.

Step 4: Evaluate the Answer Choices

(B) summarizes the author's technique: appealing to definitions (of *inventing* and *predicting*) to suggest something is impossible (can't predict an invention).

(A) doesn't work because, while the author feels you can't predict an invention, she never offers a counterexample—just a reasoned explanation using the definitions of *inventing* and *predicting*.

(C) goes astray because the author doesn't believe there are any implications to predicting an invention. She feels it can't be done in the first place.

(D) brings up the idea that predicting an invention is considered scientific—an idea that is not mentioned in the stimulus.

(E) goes too far, saying that predicting *any* event implies the event is already taking place. The author only suggests this is true of predicting inventions.

24. (E) Flaw

Step 1: Identify the Question Type

The classic language of "vulnerable to criticism" suggests the argument is inherently flawed, making this a Flaw question.

Step 2: Untangle the Stimulus

The author starts out by mentioning the theory of 18th-century European aesthetics, which provided an understanding of all art—even early abstract art. Then in the 1960s, artists rebelled and intentionally created works outside the bounds of European aesthetics. The author concludes that a complete theory of aesthetics can never exist.

Step 3: Make a Prediction

The author can logically argue that modern art has made 18th-century European aesthetics incomplete. However, the author goes too far in saying that there can't be *any* complete theory. Just because one formerly complete theory is now incomplete doesn't mean a new, now-complete theory can't come along.

Step 4: Evaluate the Answer Choices

(E) expresses the author's flawed assumption: that no other theory could be as complete as 18th-century European aesthetics was.

(A) describes an assumption about what's more important to a complete theory. A complete aesthetic theory would, by definition, provide "an understanding of all art." Furthermore, the author actually suggests the opposite—that a theory is incomplete unless it accounts for the beauty of rebellious art.

(B) is a 180. The author argues that the 1960s artists *consciously* rebelled, suggesting they *were* guided by their knowledge of 18th-century European aesthetics. They were guided to go against it.

(C) also runs counter to the author's ideas. According to the stimulus, 18th-century European aesthetics did apply to *all* art until the 1960s—that includes any art from any part of the world.

(D) is Extreme. While 1960s art may have been the first to break from 18th-century European aesthetics, other, more recent art may also not be encompassed by the old theory. The author does not discuss other recent art.

25. (B) Assumption (Necessary)

Step 1: Identify the Question Type

Because the question asks for an assumption the argument requires, this is a Necessary Assumption question.

Step 2: Untangle the Stimulus

The science writer states that all scientists have beliefs that can bias their writings. However, the science writer defends scientific papers by saying that multiple scientists review the papers before publication. Because reviewers would remove anything they disagree with, the science writer concludes that these papers will be free of bias.

Step 3: Make a Prediction

The problem with this argument is that, according to the science writer, reviewers will only remove a bias that *they don't share*. However, if the reviewers share the bias, that bias won't be removed and will stay in the paper. For this argument to work, the author must assume that the reviewers will have enough different beliefs to eliminate all biases.

Step 4: Evaluate the Answer Choices

(B) identifies the assumption perfectly. The author must assume that no biases are shared by all scientists. After all, if any of them were shared by all scientists, they'd probably be left in the published papers.

(A) contradicts the science writer, who says in the first line that "all scientists" have some bias.

(C) brings up the scientific value of the papers, which is not in question in this argument.

(D) is not a necessary assumption. Even if other components had bias, the review process should get rid of those biases as well—as long as they're not shared by all reviewers.

(E) is also not necessary. Even if there were other ways to prevent bias, that doesn't affect whether or not this particular process works.

Section IV: Reading Comprehension

Passage 1: Parallel Computing

Q#	Question Type	Correct	Difficulty
1	Global	C	★
2	Logic Reasoning (Parallel Reasoning)	C	★★
3	Inference	E	★★
4	Logic Function	B	★
5	Logic Reasoning (Method of Argument)	C	★
6	Global	B	★★
7	Inference	A	★
8	Inference	E	★

Passage 2: Statutory Legal Education

Q#	Question Type	Correct	Difficulty
9	Global	C	★
10	Detail	E	★
11	Logic Reasoning (Weaken)	B	★
12	Logic Function	A	★
13	Detail	E	★★★
14	Inference	B	★★
15	Inference (EXCEPT)	A	★★★★

Passage 3: Isamu Noguchi Sculpture

Q#	Question Type	Correct	Difficulty
16	Detail	C	★★★
17	Detail	D	★★★
18	Inference	D	★★★★
19	Logic Reasoning (Parallel Reasoning)	C	★★
20	Inference	E	★★★★
21	Inference	B	★★★★
22	Logic Reasoning (Weaken)	A	★★

Passage 4: Ultimatum Game

Q#	Question Type	Correct	Difficulty
23	Global	B	★★
24	Inference	D	★★★
25	Global	D	★
26	Inference	C	★★
27	Logic Reasoning (Strengthen)	D	★★

Passage 1: Parallel Computing

Step 1: Read the Passage Strategically
Sample Roadmap

line #	Keyword/phrase	¶ Margin notes
Passage A		
4	remarkable; But	Comp models can accurately simulate climate but variable concerns
6	Because even	
7	significant	
8	important	
11	Since	
12–13	no alternative	
15	requires	To get it right need lots of calculations
16–17	For example	
20–21	completely inadequate	Indiv. computers can't do it
22	However	Can do it w/combined indiv. computers on internet
30	successful, although only when	Public interest impt
Passage B		
35		"Parallel" problems — many natural probs can be solved at same time b/c function together
41	but	
43	example	Thomas — Ex. ants akin to a computer
46	But	
49	more complex	
53	great paradigm shift	Big shift from sequential to parallel
58	Since	
59	inherently	
60	only makes sense	Auth – parallel computing is best
61	exploits	
63	will perform best	
64	in contrast	

Discussion

Paragraph 1 of passage A begins speaking of the promise of computer simulations for predicting the motions of the ocean and the atmosphere. This provides a general **Topic**, computers, and **Scope**, their use in predictions. The Keyword *but* at the beginning of the second sentence signals a potential complication. Such systems have many variables with large ranges, and even small variability can have a big impact. Paragraph 2 discusses these complications a bit more. The only way to account for these variables is with massive numbers of calculations. The last sentence is the key, indicating that current computers are not able to handle the task. Paragraph 3 provides a clear **Purpose** of this passage: proposing a possible solution to the problem. That solution is the **Main Idea:** by linking networks of individual computers, large problems can be solved much more quickly. The last sentence says that, while this is possible, it will only become widespread when it captures the public's attention. This type of causal clause at the end of the passage should be noted for a potential question.

Passage B begins by explaining that many systems in nature are parallel. It then defines parallel systems, the passage's **Topic**, as being made up of many similar items moving simply individually but together moving as a complicated whole. This is a relatively abstract paragraph. The abstraction is made more specific in Paragraph 2, which starts with an example, ants. Ants are simple creatures that work together to create a complicated system. The paragraph ends with a comparison between ants and computers, calling an ant colony a type of live computer. A comparison is a red flag for a potential question later. More importantly, this finally sets up a relationship between both passages—they both talk about computers. Paragraph 3 finally delves into the concept of parallelism in terms of computers, the **Scope**. The **Purpose** is merely to explain what the author calls a "paradigm shift in the field of computing." The **Main Idea** is that there is a shift from using one computer at a time to using many computers at once for computation-intensive problems. This is similar to the Purpose in passage A, and this similarity should be noted. Passage B even goes so far as to say that this mimics natural systems, so it is a natural progression.

1. (C) Global

Step 2: Identify the Question Type
The words *main point* identify this as a Global question.

Step 3: Research the Relevant Text
The question asks specifically for the main point of passage B, so ignore passage A for the time being.

Step 4: Make a Prediction
Passage B brings up parallel computing specifically to discuss how the computing world is changing. The third paragraph is really what the entire passage was leading up to, so the main point is likely a paraphrase of this major change.

Step 5: Evaluate the Answer Choices
(C) correctly identifies the paradigm shift currently taking place as the main point of passage B.

(A) This may be true, but it is only a point that helps to explain why the paradigm shift is taking place.

(B) is Extreme. While sequential computing may not be the best way to solve computation-intensive problems, that does not mean that it is a completely useless paradigm.

(D) This discusses what kind of simulations computers will be undertaking in the future. Passage B only talks about how future calculations may be undertaken, not which projects they'll be used for.

(E) This references computers modeled after the human mind. This is far from the main point of the passage, though it might catch an unaware test taker as an emotionally attractive thought.

2. (C) Logic Reasoning (Parallel Reasoning)

Step 2: Identify the Question Type
The question uses the word *analogous* to relate parts of the two passages. That means that the piece of each passage must be parallel to the corresponding part of the other in its reasoning.

Step 3: Research the Relevant Text
First, the section of passage A that discusses large-scale climate trends is located at the end of the first paragraph and the beginning of the second paragraph. Secondly, look for specific examples in passage B. The second paragraph of passage B should attract your attention, as it is an entire paragraph based around a specific example.

Step 4: Make a Prediction
The large-scale climate trends in passage A were an example of a highly complex, computationally intensive problem. Passage B only has one such example: an ant colony.

Step 5: Evaluate the Answer Choices
(C) matches the prediction.

(A) This is what you would need to predict the trends, according to both passages.

(B) This is the opposite of what you would need. You need to compare a complex system to a complex system, not to one element of that system.

(D) While passage B does discuss a paradigm shift, this is certainly not analogous to a climate simulation.

(E) This refers to the old paradigm of sequential computing. Again, this is discussed in passage B but is far from analogous to climate simulation.

3. (E) Inference

Step 2: Identify the Question Type

This is an Inference question by virtue of using the word *inferred* in the question stem. This question asks you to infer something about both authors' opinions.

Step 3: Research the Relevant Text

There is no clear location reference in this question, so utilize your Topic, Scope, Purpose, and Main Idea to help locate support for the correct inference.

Step 4: Make a Prediction

The authors both talk about computer systems from different starting points and come at the subject from different angles, but you do know that both authors believe that parallel computer systems will help to deal with large computations. Look for a paraphrase of this in the answer choices.

Step 5: Evaluate the Answer Choices

(E) fits the prediction well and is the answer.

(A) is a Distortion. The entire reason for parallel systems is that they can handle the number of calculations required for the brute force approach.

(B) is not supported anywhere in either passage. In fact, considering both authors' confidence in parallel systems, this may well be contrary to their opinions.

(C) addresses a point raised in passage A but doesn't even get that right. Passage A said they will become truly useful once the public accepts them, not that they are not feasible. Passage B doesn't even address this issue.

(D) talks about simple simulations, something that is Out of Scope. The passage only discusses complex simulations, so nothing can be inferred about simple simulations.

4. (B) Logic Function

Step 2: Identify the Question Type

The phrase *in order to* brands this question as a Logic Function question.

Step 3: Research the Relevant Text

The question provides a passage and a line reference (lines 30–32) in which to look for the detail. Remember, however, that a Logic Function question has to do with the "why" and not the "what," so also look at your Roadmap to understand where the detail falls in the flow of the passage.

Step 4: Make a Prediction

The last paragraph of passage A discusses a possible solution to the large simulation problem and a potential drawback. The potential drawback is the public participation. Therefore, the "why" of the author bringing this fact up is to discuss a potential drawback or limiting factor to the proposed solution.

Step 5: Evaluate the Answer Choices

(B) is a paraphrase of the prediction and the correct answer.

(A) might well be what the author would hope to do in the future, but it is not the reason the author made the statement in this passage.

(C) is completely off-topic. Public support is what is needed to make this a success, not government support.

(D) is a Distortion. The author plainly states that more support is needed to make this approach a success.

(E) is another Distortion. While forces beyond the designer's control would affect this model, that does not make this model infeasible.

5. (C) Logic Reasoning (Method of Argument)

Step 2: Identify the Question Type

The words *relates to* indicate that this is a Method of Argument question. It asks for the relationship of one passage's purpose to the other.

Step 3: Research the Relevant Text

Refer to the Topic, Scope, Purpose, and Main Idea to make sure that you have a proper understanding of the main ideas in each passage. You can only relate one passage to another with a strong understanding of the big picture.

Step 4: Make a Prediction

Passage A brought up the fact that a particular type of computer system might help to solve large-scale computation problems and simulations. Passage B goes through a rather long explanation of how one of these systems works. So by describing such a system, passage B provides a reason to consider the proposed solution of passage A.

Step 5: Evaluate the Answer Choices

(C) uses wording that is a little loftier, but it matches the prediction and is correct.

(A) is a silly answer choice given the purpose of Comparative Reading on the test. One thing that is for sure is that the paired passages will have at least a passing similarity to each other.

(B) errs by giving passage B the power to cast judgment on passage A's solution. The only time the feasibility of passage A is mentioned is in passage A.

(D) The need for the "brute force" approach is fairly well spelled out in passage A, not passage B.

(E) is factually incorrect, as the two passages agree on the limitations of individual computers.

6. (B) Global

Step 2: Identify the Question Type

This is a primary purpose question that asks you to meld the two passages.

Step 3: Research the Relevant Text
Check the Purpose for each passage to find the answer to this question.

Step 4: Make a Prediction
The common theme of both passages is that parallel computing systems will help with computing calculation-heavy problems and simulations, so that should be your prediction.

Step 5: Evaluate the Answer Choices
(B) matches the prediction.

(A) is a Distortion of the facts and makes the answer Extreme. While the traditional paradigm is not great for computationally heavy problems, there is no information about other types of problems and thus you can't conclude that traditional computing doesn't work well for these.

(C) Remember that the authors are concerned with parallel systems, which may or may not be made up of desktop computers. Either way, this is not the main point, as it does not address solving large-scale problems.

(D) goes too far in saying that the new paradigm has already taken over. Neither author would agree with that.

(E) gives you a lot to think about. The purpose of the passages is not to describe problems but rather solutions. Also, you have no time frame to work with, so you can't be too sure of the use of the word *recently* in this choice.

7. (A) Inference

Step 2: Identify the Question Type
You are being asked to look at a particular statement made by the author and extrapolate meaning from that statement. Using a statement to support a further supposition is the task on this Inference question.

Step 3: Research the Relevant Text
The line reference (lines 51–52) asks you to evaluate the comparison of an ant colony to a computer. Refer to your Roadmap and read the sentence within that context.

Step 4: Make a Prediction
Because this comparison is essentially a segue to the next paragraph about computers, the comparison really should be a summation of the meaning of the example. The example in the second paragraph of passage B is used to show how simple elements can gather together to create a more complex system, and that should be your prediction.

Step 5: Evaluate the Answer Choices
(A) matches well and is the correct answer.

(B) While this may be true, explaining what inspired the paradigm shift in computing is not why the author compares ants and computers.

(C) simply reverses the comparison without adding any meaning.

(D) is not only worded strongly but is also well off-topic. Passage B never discusses what problems parallel computing might solve with any specificity

(E) is a Distortion and Out of Scope. The understanding of the behavior of units within a system has led to parallel computing systems but not the *same* specific rules. We don't have a lot of computer systems building anthills!

8. (E) Inference

Step 2: Identify the Question Type
This is an Inference question. The words that help identify this question are *would be most likely to agree*, denoting the need to go a step beyond the passage yet with strong support from the actual text.

Step 3: Research the Relevant Text
The question asks you to infer author B's reaction to the last paragraph of passage A. Refer to the last paragraph of passage A and your Topic, Scope, Purpose, and Main Idea for passage B.

Step 4: Make a Prediction
The type of system proposed in the last paragraph of passage A is what the author of passage B would refer to as a parallel system. You know that author B would believe a few things: that these systems are faster than traditional sequential computing, that they are similar to many natural systems, and that a paradigm shift is currently underway. The inference should be one of these facts or some combination of them.

Step 5: Evaluate the Answer Choices
(E) hits the nail right on the head. It might seem obvious after you make a prediction, but this can be a hard one to find otherwise.

(A) is a Distortion of the facts. An ant colony is described as a kind of live computer. A computer system is simply a computer system—no need for *live*.

(B) is Extreme and also 180 from the correct answer. This type of system could potentially simulate climate systems.

(C) would only occur in the old sequential computing paradigm, the wrong one for this question.

(D) makes a prediction for which you have no evidence. Author B might hope for that, but you can't say he'd agree with any degree of certainty

Passage 2: Statutory Legal Education

Step 1: Read the Passage Strategically
Sample Roadmap

line #	Keyword/phrase	¶ Margin notes
3	vital	
4	but; too little	Too little attn to statutory law in law school
8		
12	however	
13	does not depend	
15	For example	Ex. lawyer and shop owner
22	But	Statutes not always so cut and dry – must learn to interpret them
24	that is one reason	
25	essential	
26	Another	Must learn statutory synthesis
29	but	
31	In contrast	Seeing coherent whole is beneficial
37	especially important because	b/c of specialization
40	One possible argument against	Dissent – regional variation prevents general application
44–45	usually not; some truth to this objection	
47	but	
49	inappropriate	
50	But	Auth – still OK for nat'lly oriented schools b/c skills are the value, not the specific statutory knowledge
54	important; even	

Discussion

Paragraph 1 begins with a sentence with multiple functions. It provides a working definition of the term *statute* and the opinion that most law schools do not teach much in the way of statutory law. This sets up a potential discussion of both the current system and how statutory law fits into that system. This provides the **Topic**, legal education, and the **Scope**, the role of statutory law within legal education. The paragraph then states that the current system uses judicial decisions and analysis of cases. The words "too little attention" in lines 4–5 also shout the author's point of view: get more of this statutory education into the legal education system. This hints at the purpose of the passage and allows you to take a guess as to outline of the passage. You might want to know why statutes are so important, why they aren't present in the system now, and maybe how the author hopes to integrate them. Actively predicting what lies ahead, even if you turn out to be off-track and need to adjust, will keep you thinking in a profitable way on the LSAT.

Paragraph 2 takes a while to get there, but it begins to explain why statutes are so important. It begins by explaining how the current system does not necessarily correlate to the actual practice of law. After a detailed example, it reiterates that the ability to understand and apply statutes is a valuable legal skill.

Paragraph 3 begins with "Another skill that teaching statutory law would improve ..." This implies that the above paragraph described at least one skill provided by this type of teaching (in case you had missed that). It names this new skill "synthesis." This means that by studying all of the particular laws of an area, a student not only learns the statutes but gains an idea of how all of those laws function together to create a coherent system.

So far the author has discussed a lot about why statutory law is good, but paragraph 4 comes back in to discuss one possible reason against it. Statutes vary so much from region to region that a student's knowledge would become obsolete if the student changed geographic areas. Reading critically, however, notice that after announcing this problem, the author switches direction. In line 50, the author uses the word *but* to signal a contrast. He then continues to attempt to overcome this objection by saying the specific knowledge might be obsolete but the synthesis will still create benefits. This solidifies the author's **Purpose** of discussing the benefits of including statutory education in law school. Likewise the author's **Main Idea** is that law schools should provide training in statutory law because the benefits of such training outweigh any objections.

9. (C) Global

Step 2: Identify the Question Type

The words *main point* signal that this is a Global question.

Step 3: Research the Relevant Text

Refer to your Topic, Scope, Purpose, and Main Idea.

Step 4: Make a Prediction

The author is clearly in favor of introducing more statutory law education into the legal system. He believes his argument is strong enough even to introduce an objection and overcome it. The main idea needs to include both the author's point of view as well as that point of view's strength.

Step 5: Evaluate the Answer Choices

(C) matches this prediction. It says that despite a potential objection, statutory law should be introduced because it yields a benefit. The answer choice even uses the word *synthesize*, which is the major benefit named by the author.

(A) has good intentions but veers of course in several places. You don't know exactly what the overall needs of law students are, so you can't be sure that removing something to add statutory law would yield a net benefit, only that there is benefit to statutory law education. Also, the author never suggests that any added curricula need to be standardized.

(B) introduces a common problem, the relative scale. The author never measures these two against each other; he only points out the lack of one and the overabundance of another. You have no idea if the author would agree with a 180 shift.

(D) while this statement might be true, it is certainly not vital enough to the passage to be the main point. The scope of this choice is much too narrow.

(E) is Extreme. The author believes there isn't enough statutory law education in many places, but that doesn't mean that law schools are generally deficient. Also, this deficiency, if you accept it, certainly does not mean that students do not learn how to analyze the law. In fact, in paragraph 1, case law, the opposing force to statutory law in this passage, is described using the word *analysis*.

10. (E) Detail

Step 2: Identify the Question Type

This question asks for an answer that is *cited* in the passage. If an answer is explicitly contained in the passage, the question is a Detail question.

Step 3: Research the Relevant Text

Using your Roadmap, you can pinpoint paragraph 4 as the one that discusses arguments against including statutory law in legal education.

Step 4: Make a Prediction
The major stated objection is that laws are different in different geographic regions. Look for something that paraphrases this objection.

Step 5: Evaluate the Answer Choices
(E) hits the prediction right on the nose and is correct.

(A) poses a potential real-life concern that is not addressed at all in the passage. It also introduces a value scale about which skill is more important that you cannot evaluate.

(B) is factually inaccurate.

(C) might be true and even sounds a bit snarky, but it is not the objection mentioned by the author.

(D) is Extreme in its use of the word *irrelevant* as well as not being relevant itself.

11. (B) Logic Reasoning (Weaken)

Step 2: Identify the Question Type
The word *weaken* indicates that this is a Weaken question, just like the type in the Logical Reasoning section.

Step 3: Research the Relevant Text
Look at the author's main argument here because the question asks about the passage in general. Use your Topic, Scope, Purpose, and Main Idea for this.

Step 4: Make a Prediction
The author spends the entire passage arguing for more inclusion of statutory law in the current legal education system. He argues that this will aid lawyers by giving them a skill they do not gain currently. Any reason why teaching this skill in school will yield less of a net benefit would weaken the author's argument.

Step 5: Evaluate the Answer Choices
(B) essentially negates the need to teach the subject in law schools, because a newly minted lawyer will learn these lessons quickly and easily in actual practice. This matches the prediction and is the correct answer.

(A) would be read as a strengthener, if anything, and is thus a 180.

(C) might help to strengthen the objection found in paragraph 4, but the author acknowledges this issue and overcomes the objection by sidestepping it. He says an advantage is gained by learning how the laws fit together, even if the specific laws become useless due to geographic relocation. The manner in which the author overcomes the objection means that strengthening that objection would not weaken the author's argument.

(D) merely states a fact suggested by the passage and would not undermine the author at all.

(E) states an irrelevant fact. Even if this were true, it is not necessarily a bad thing, as the author notes that most lawyers specialize.

12. (A) Logic Function

Step 2: Identify the Question Type
The question is asking for the intent of the author when including a detail. Logic Function questions deal with the *why* of a part of the passage. The words *in order to* are a great tip-off to this question type.

Step 3: Research the Relevant Text
Immediately refer to your Roadmap to help find an answer to a Logic Function question.

Step 4: Make a Prediction
The question is asking for the reason the author included the term *synthesis* in paragraph 3. The main idea of paragraph 3 is to provide a potential benefit of adding statutory law to current curricula. The best reason for the inclusion of a detail or term in this paragraph would be to further the main end of this paragraph.

Step 5: Evaluate the Answer Choices
(A) is a perfect match to the prediction and the right answer.

(B) would be a better fit if the question asked about a detail in the beginning of paragraph 4, but it doesn't apply to the current question.

(C) is tempting, but there is a relative value scale here. You know that the author thinks statutory law education should be included, but you don't know that he finds it more important than case analysis.

(D) is a Distortion. This is a skill gained by the study of statutory law, not a skill necessary for it.

(E) mentions an example provided in paragraph 2, not paragraph 3.

13. (E) Detail

Step 2: Identify the Question Type
When a question is asking you to find information within the passage to help answer a question in the choices, you must find explicit information. While it might seem convoluted, if you have to find an explicit detail, you are involved in a Detail question.

Step 3: Research the Relevant Text
There is not a lot to work with in this question stem. Use your Roadmap to locate where details mentioned in the answer choices will be spelled out.

Step 4: Make a Prediction
Just as the location of the text is hard to judge from the question stem, it is hard to make a prediction on a question

as broad as this. However, a solid understanding of the big picture will help you zero in on specifics quickly as needed.

Step 5: Evaluate the Answer Choices

(E) is correct. The author mentions quickly in paragraph 1 that schools focus too little on statutory law and mostly use case law. Because you can find direct support in the passage, this is the correct answer choice.

(A) is a Distortion. It mixes synthesis, a skill learned by study of statutes, with case analysis.

(B) asks about particular branches of legal practice, an area not addressed by the passage.

(C) asks what skills are common to both legal education styles. All you know from the passage is that they are on the opposite ends of the spectrum, not that they have any shared qualities.

(D) may be a tempting choice. However, the only stated objection to not including statutory education was directed towards national programs, not regional ones.

14. (B) Inference

Step 2: Identify the Question Type

The question asks for something that the author would agree with. Because the only thing about the author that you know is what has been stated, you must take those statements and extrapolate a step further. Anytime you have to do this, the question is an Inference question.

Step 3: Research the Relevant Text

The question is fairly open-ended, asking for an inference about training in statutory law, which is mentioned in all of the paragraphs.

Step 4: Make a Prediction

It is hard to make a firm prediction because many things are said about training in statutory law. However, you do know that the author is in favor of such training. You also know that he believes synthesis (or understanding of the overall system) gained by this training is a major benefit. Lastly, you know that his initial reason for including this type of training is the example listed in paragraph 2. Keep these in mind as you check the answer choices.

Step 5: Evaluate the Answer Choices

(B) is an accurate assessment of the example given by the author in paragraph 2.

(A) is Half-Right/Half-Wrong. According to the author, regional schools are potentially deficient in statutory law training, not case analysis.

(C) might well be in line with the author's opinion. It might, however, not be. The point is that the passage provides no support either way, making this invalid as an inference.

(D) is factually inaccurate. Synthesis means the geography of the study is unimportant.

(E) mentions specialization and a value scale about how much training is needed, neither of which has support in the passage. In fact, specialization is specifically mentioned as benefiting from statutory law.

15. (A) Inference (EXCEPT)

Step 2: Identify the Question Type

The question asks what the author would expect to come about as a result of his proposed change. A complication is the use of the word *EXCEPT*. This means that four of the answers will be valid inferences and one will not be valid. The invalid inference is the correct answer.

Step 3: Research the Relevant Text

This is an open-ended question, though answers may tend to focus on the benefits provided in the last three paragraphs.

Step 4: Make a Prediction

You do not know exactly what the answer will be for this question, but you do know a few things about the author's feelings towards this course of action, and this will help you weed out the proper inferences (wrong answers). You know that the author believes synthesis will be a major benefit to training in statutory law.

Step 5: Evaluate the Answer Choices

(A) is completely off the beaten track here and thus is the answer. While knowledge of the statute makes sense, training in statutory law will not result in the ability to research court decisions, which relate to case law.

(B) is essentially an example of synthesis and, therefore, a valid inference.

(C) Knowledge of how statutes are formulated would be a result of training in statutory law.

(D) Familiarity with specific statutes would be a result of training in statutory law.

(E) Understanding the formation of a system of laws would lead to an understanding of the problems associated with drafting it.

Passage 3: Isamu Noguchi Sculpture

Step 1: Read the Passage Strategically
Sample Roadmap

line #	Keyword/phrase	¶ Margin notes
3	deeply original	
5	but; instead	Noguchi – innovative and unconventional artist
9	one particular	One piece is illustrative
10	typifies	
12	such exquisite	
13	deft	
18	never	Became stonecutter for Brancusi
25	because	Sculptors use shadows – "negative light"
26		Only gold gave off positive light
28	wanted	Noguchi wanted purely reflective sculpture – Fuller portrait
29	purely	
33	suggested	Chrome-nickel
35	just	
36	first time	Brand new and cheap
37	finally	
39	did not	
40	merely	
41	What he saw	Noguchi found that completely refl. surfaces had "invisibility" of surface
43	fundamental	
46		Ex. seaplane pilots
49	conceived	Viewer 1st sees reflected surroundings then sculpture and dimensional relationships
51	only	
55	only secondarily	
56	stunning	Noguchi continued to innovate
59	genius	

Discussion

Paragraph 1 introduces the **Topic** of the passage, Isamu Noguchi. The first sentence even hints at the **Scope** of the passage as well, his desire to ask and attempt to answer deep questions. The author mentions that Noguchi might have become a scientist but instead became an artist, drawing a potential comparison between the two disciplines. The last sentence of the paragraph is a strong foreshadowing of the purpose of the passage. If the author states that one particular example typifies the concepts brought up earlier in the introduction, it's a fairly safe bet that the rest of the passage will involve discussing how and why that example supports this statement. Here, the author gives you the **Purpose**, explaining that the story behind one of Noguchi's sculptures will typify his "scientific" approach to his "art."

As the second paragraph begins with "By his early twenties," this paragraph will give background on Noguchi as part of the story behind this example sculpture. As the paragraph continues, you learn how Noguchi came to ponder a single unusual fact: sculptors could not create a purely reflective sculpture with current materials. The author explains why this was so, mentioning that all current materials (other than the prohibitively expensive gold) could not be relied upon to remain reflective. Note that this comparison singles out gold from all other metals. This might come up in the question set. Also note that Constantin Brancusi and Italy are mentioned in this paragraph. These are potential context clues for a Detail question. Notice, also, that potential confusion about the term *negative light* (line 24) is minimized by tying its meaning to "shadows." For your purposes in this passage—getting more questions right—this relationship will suffice. Avoid getting bogged down in the minutiae of technical terms whenever possible.

Paragraph 3 begins by stating Noguchi's desire to create the type of sculpture he noted did not yet exist in the last paragraph. After returning to the United States, Noguchi met R. Buckminster Fuller. Noting the change of location and the second proper name may again yield points later. Fuller's main contribution in this paragraph is that he brings together Noguchi with his ideas and a new material, chrome-nickel steel. Noguchi and his creative, often unusual, scientifically artistic mind then put his ideas together with the metal for a potential solution. This leads directly into paragraph 4, which you should predict might be a natural point for the passage to discuss the sculpture at hand.

Indeed, paragraph 4 begins with a discussion of the actual creation of the sculpture of Fuller (whose name is not used again). Further critical attention to the paragraph shows a continued explanation of what this sculpture meant to Noguchi and how his mind conceived of this new iteration of a classic art form. He compares this sculpture to that of perfectly still water. This should be a big red flag for a potential question. If the sculpture that plays such a large role in this passage is used in an analogy or comparison, it's very likely that there will be a question about that comparison.

The last paragraph returns to the original Topic and Scope. While the author discussed the example sculpture for three paragraphs, this discussion was merely to exemplify Noguchi's unusual mind. Paragraph 5 returns to this concept, mentioning that even when Noguchi received acclaim for his works, he simply moved onto the next deep question and challenge. Noguchi was not a one-trick pony, as it were. While this paragraph does not tell if he was successful in those endeavors, it does categorically let you know that Noguchi had future endeavors. Ultimately the author's **Main Idea** is that Noguchi's effort to create a purely reflective sculpture was indicative of his unconventional and creative approach as an artist.

16. (C) Detail

Step 2: Identify the Question Type

While not the clearest of question stems, a few words point towards this question being a Detail type. By beginning with "In saying that …" and ending with "the author draws a distinction between," the stem is letting you know that the author actually stated a fact that will answer this question. Questions looking for stated facts fall into the Detail category.

Step 3: Research the Relevant Text

This question helps you greatly by providing not only a direct quote but also a line reference. It should be noted that this line reference places the quote in paragraph 2, when Noguchi first gains the background to launch his innovative idea.

Step 4: Make a Prediction

The question is asking for a distinction. This means that the correct answer will contain two parts, both of which must be correct. After reading the text in context, the first part should be something that has to do with traditional sculpture materials, such as brass and bronze, and the second should be a metal that has a different characteristic. "Nonoxidizing gold" is given as an example of the second metal, one that does not lose its reflective nature while the other two do. Therefore, the answer should be a distinction between metals that lose their luster and metals that can be relied upon not to lose their luster.

Step 5: Evaluate the Answer Choices

(C) is an almost perfect match.

(A) goes wrong in a few places. The term *moderately reflective* introduces a gray area to the reflective scale that you are ill equipped to judge from the passage. You are only given highly reflective and non–highly reflective, not a middle ground. The second part talks about metals that can be made highly reflective but only in certain applications. The only application you know anything about is sculpture.

(B) mentions a highly reflective metal that is "technically suited" to sculpture, using a term not found in the passage. The passage also compares highly reflective to non–highly reflective, not two types of highly reflective metals, as this choice presents.

(D) brings in nonmetallic materials, which is completely Out of Scope for the passage.

(E) again compares differing types of highly reflective metals, which does not match the prediction.

17. (D) Detail

Step 2: Identify the Question Type
A question that asks you to answer a question based on information in the passage will require the passage actually to answer that question. That may seem a semantic point, but the answer to the question will be a fact that must be stated in the passage. When you are searching for actual statements, you have a Detail question on your hands.

Step 3: Research the Relevant Text
This question has the potential to consume a lot of time. There is no line reference or even a clear subject matter location reference. Take the answer choices one at a time and refer to your Roadmap to locate your detail.

Step 4: Make a Prediction
While this one would be hard to nail down due to the sparse information provided in the question's stem, you should keep the points of view and relationships you noted through your reading in mind as you approach each answer choice.

Step 5: Evaluate the Answer Choices
(D) is correct here. Lines 58–60 clearly state that Noguchi did indeed receive acclaim just before he moved onto other ventures.

(A) is not answered by the passage because while you know Noguchi had the skills to cut and polish stone, you are left unaware of how he came by these skills. Knowing that he had these skills is very different than knowing how he came by them.

(B) poses a question which may well have an answer that is yes, after all the passage focused on his sculpture. Even the last sentence that implies he moved on cannot be read to mean he moved onto other art forms. This question can be tempting because the answer may be yes in real life, but the passage does not give a solid fact to support this opinion. Because you need a fact from the passage, this answer choice is not correct.

(C) asks about materials other than metal used by Noguchi post-Brancusi. The only nonmetallic material mentioned in the passage (stone) is used while Noguchi was with Brancusi,

so you have no idea what, if any, nonmetallic materials Noguchi used after this association ended.

(E) is so vague that it is almost immediately recognizable as incorrect. "At any time in his career" is very broad language, and the passage was concerned with a specific period of time. This answer choice could be tempting, however, if a test taker were still unclear as to the meaning of *negative light* and other technical terms. Translucent or internally lighted sculptures are not even mentioned, let alone supported.

18. (D) Inference

Step 2: Identify the Question Type
The words *the author would agree* denote an Inference question. If the author would agree with the answer choice, then it must be consistent with his stated opinions but be one step further than his explicit statements. Such a question is always seeking an inference on the LSAT.

Step 3: Research the Relevant Text
Like the previous question, this question stem does not give much information to help you locate the correct answer. Keep in mind that questions like this will require you to take each choice in turn and research them one by one. This can take time, so this may be a good question to come back to at the end of the passage.

Step 4: Make a Prediction
A completely non-location-specific inference can be a hard question for which to make a prediction. A very quick survey shows that all five answer choices contain Noguchi's name and four of them start with *Noguchi*. You do know that the author found Noguchi to be innovative, questioning, and experimental in his approach, having a markedly atypical mind for the art world. The answer may hit on this point, but it's just a prediction. If you do not find this, check each answer choice as it comes.

Step 5: Evaluate the Answer Choices
(D) can be reached using a very loose interpretation of the prediction. One who is interested in innovation and experiments would be less concerned with maintaining consistency than achieving interesting results. Even had you not found this choice by paraphrasing your prediction, however, none of the other choices will suffice.

(A) can be eliminated for more than one reason. Firstly, Noguchi's work did not necessarily embody the solution to a problem as much as it explored new means of expression. More glaringly, there is absolutely no evidence in the passage to support the idea that Brancusi had ever even thought of creating a statue like Noguchi's

(B) addresses Noguchi's "scientific" mind. It veers off course, however, when it says that Noguchi had no formal training. This is an extreme statement and is not backed up in the slightest by the passage.

(C) introduces a scale of relative importance, claiming that one of Noguchi's influences was more important than the other. However, as the passage presents the argument, both influences were needed, and neither was markedly more important. In short, the passage does not supply information to be able to decide more or less between these two.

(E) can be eliminated in simplest terms by looking at the second half of the answer choice. While an argument can be made that the passage talks about scientific thinking in art, how artistic thinking would affect science is never mentioned.

19. (C) Logic Reasoning (Parallel Reasoning)

Step 2: Identify the Question Type

This question asks you to find an answer that is analogous in reasoning to something discussed in the passage. Analogous reasoning is the hallmark of Parallel Reasoning questions in Logical Reasoning.

Step 3: Research the Relevant Text

The passage does not give a line reference, but it does give a contextual location by referring to Ford. Either a quick scan for that name or, better yet, a glance at your Roadmap will place Ford in paragraph 3.

Step 4: Make a Prediction

In this passage, Henry Ford is mentioned only as a way of introducing the new metal that will help Noguchi create his interesting new statue. Noguchi used this material, made for cars, to create a positive-light sculpture. The correct answer choice will have something to do with a person taking a new substance and using it for a purpose other than what was originally intended.

Step 5: Evaluate the Answer Choices

(C) is the clearest example of the prediction.

(A) talks about a new type of material, but it's being used for its intended purpose after a celebrity endorsement. This does not match the prediction.

(B) involves a material being experimented with but still within the realm of its original intended use.

(D) begins by mentioning a new product but then veers offtrack by mentioning research, an evaluation process, and a decision to use another product.

(E) again mentions the use of a new material but again moves past the mark by mentioning several other new materials.

20. (E) Inference

Step 2: Identify the Question Type

This question stem is easily identifiable by the use of the word *inferences*. Other words, like *strongly supports*, also indicate this is an Inference question.

Step 3: Research the Relevant Text

Much like some of the other questions in this question set, this is an open-ended Inference question. There is a complete lack of information about what or where to research to find the right answer. Take each answer choice in turn and research it.

Step 4: Make a Prediction

With so little information in the stem, it is impossible to come up with a true prediction. Keep in mind the points of view and ideas noted in your Roadmap, however. Look at each answer choice and attempt to find the problem with four of them.

Step 5: Evaluate the Answer Choices

(E) is the correct answer. This is discussed partially at the end of the second paragraph and partially in the fourth paragraph. A negative-light sculpture, discussed in paragraph 2, is the type of sculpture that existed before Noguchi. Remember from before that the only thing that negative light was really tied to was the word *shadow*. Positive light, discussed in paragraph 4, is the type of sculpture that requires the reflection of surrounding objects.

(A) mentions Fuller before he met Noguchi. While you know Fuller existed before, the passage gives zero information on which to base any conclusion about his actions before their meeting.

(B) introduces the term *commercially viable*. Not only is this not supported, but it also says "more" commercially viable, introducing a value scale that you are not given a way to evaluate.

(C) is a subtle Distortion. Noguchi's sculptures would rely on the shape of surrounding materials, and only a distortion of those shapes would be discernable. The answer choice implies that the sculpture would take the surrounding materials' shape. Taking on an exact shape is not the same as relying on the distortion of another shape, and that makes this answer choice incorrect.

(D) is not at all confirmable from the answer passage. In fact, the passage seems to imply that if a positive-light sculpture were coated with an oxidizable substance, then it would turn into a negative-light sculpture. That transformation might or might not affect the clarity of the image depicted, and you are not given any information either way to support or reject this claim. Therefore, this is not a valid inference.

21. (B) Inference

Step 2: Identify the Question Type

Here is another easily typed question in which the stem comes right out and asks which of the following *inferences* is supported by the passage.

Step 3: Research the Relevant Text
This question at least narrows down your search slightly. It asks about the "portrait of Fuller," which is the new positive-light sculpture produced by Noguchi. This places the bulk of the answer somewhere in paragraph 4.

Step 4: Make a Prediction
You know that Noguchi created this sculpture after conceiving of the idea of a positive-light sculpture in Italy and returning to the United States to be introduced to the new material. You can apply this knowledge to the answer choices to find the correct one.

Step 5: Evaluate the Answer Choices
(B) is the correct choice, but with a twist. It refers to sculptures that Noguchi made prior to the time reference of 1927. This means you have to research 1927, which appears just at the start of the second paragraph. The year 1927 is when Noguchi travelled to Europe, after winning an award for his capture of the human form in his early sculptures. Now it becomes clear that this choice is indeed correct. His sculpture of Fuller depicted Fuller's human form, and thus his later sculpture was at least similar to his early sculpture in their depiction of the human form.

(A) introduces the use of chrome-nickel steel by other sculptors, something that simply isn't mentioned in the passage.

(C) is a direct contradiction of the passage. Noguchi's entire purpose in his sculpture of Fuller was to create something new and inventive.

(D) may or may not be true, but without specific support in the passage, it cannot be a valid inference.

(E) is again a contradiction of the passage itself. Noguchi is the first to create a positive-light sculpture and thus the first to escape the negative-light (shadow-reliant) method.

22. (A) Logic Reasoning (Weaken)

Step 2: Identify the Question Type
The word *weaken* indicates that this is a Weaken question. Use the same strategy as you would for Weaken questions in the Logical Reasoning section.

Step 3: Research the Relevant Text
While you have a Weaken question, you don't have much to go on regarding research. The only thing that is mentioned is the author's position, which appears in many places in the passage.

Step 4: Make a Prediction
While you may not be able to make a solid and unshakeable prediction without any research, you can make some headway. The author's main idea is that Noguchi was incredibly inventive and atypical. If you are trying to weaken

that conclusion, anything that shows Noguchi to be derivative or ordinary has the potential to be the correct answer.

Step 5: Evaluate the Answer Choices
(A) comes right out and says that Noguchi had access to positive-light sculptures by Brancusi while he was employed by him in Europe. This would mean that positive-light sculptures were not entirely Noguchi's idea, thus weakening the author's main idea.

(B) might be true, according to the last paragraph. If the statement might reflect how things actually played out, based on the passage, then it doesn't contradict or weaken the author's position.

(C) has the same problem as **(B)**. This might be true, so it doesn't weaken the author's position. This choice has the added mistake of being wildly irrelevant as well, so even if it were true, it wouldn't come close to addressing the author's main position.

(D) is Out of Scope. You don't know anything about Noguchi's other sculptures other than that some of some of them detailed the human form. However, what Noguchi did with other sculptures has little bearing with how his single sculpture of Fuller impacts the author's position.

(E) speaks to Noguchi's internal thought process. This entire topic is never mentioned and would not affect the result of Noguchi's innovation even if it were true, meaning it could not weaken the author's position.

Passage 4: Ultimatum Game

Step 1: Read the Passage Strategically
Sample Roadmap

line #	Keyword/phrase	¶ Margin notes
1		Experiment
3	:	Proposer
6		Responder
9	but; neither	
11		Ultimatum Game
14	instinctively	
15	because	Many offer 50% as fair
16	therefore likely	
18		4/100 offer less than 20% – risky
20	quite risky; most; reject	
21	:	
22	?	But why reject? – otherwise 0
23	so	
25–26	primarily; one would expect; any	
28	explain	Ancestors needed group members
31	depended	
33	counterproductive	
35	But	Explains offer amount, but not rejections
36	at best explains	
37	not	
38	more compelling explanation	Better explanation
41	therefore	More than 1 to 1 interactions – reputation
46	But	If accept low offer get more low offers
48	Consequently	
49	should have favored	If reject get higher offers
51	Because	
54	Therefore	Maintaining self-esteem gives better reputation in future negotiations
56	because	
59	beneficial	

Discussion

Paragraph 1 begins by referring to an experiment. A quick skim shows that the rest of the paragraph is simply gives factual information regarding the physical steps of the experiment. This tells you that the **Topic** of this passage will involve this experiment.

As you move onto the second paragraph, the experiment is named: "Ultimatum Game." The rest of the paragraph speaks of the statistical results of the game over its many trials with a wide variety of subjects. After moving past many of the details about the statistical numbers, notice the structure of the paragraph. In line 21, the author refers to a "puzzle" and asks a rhetorical question. The question is about the puzzling results of the experiment, which is the **Scope** of the passage. If people behaved according to rational self-interest, they would presumably act differently than the results of the game show. This question goes unanswered by the end of the paragraph, hinting at what might come in the next paragraph. Thus, the **Purpose** of the passage will be to discuss and potentially explain these puzzling results.

Paragraph 3 confirms what was coming down the pipe. It beings with "Some theorists explain," introducing at least one potential explanation for the puzzling results. A quick skim shows that the explanation has something to do with the evolutionary benefits of the bonds among small groups of hunter-gatherers. We do not want to outcompete our group members into oblivion. However, the end of paragraph mentions that this theory only addressed one side of the issue: why people offer fair amounts. It does not address why people reject small offers. This distinction should be noted, as it may show up in a question later on in the question set.

Paragraph 4 begins with a bombshell. If the author offers "a more compelling explanation," the author is really handing you his point of view. Whatever is coming in this paragraph is going to be what the author believes to be the stronger explanation. Reading further highlights the distinction in the second explanation, that emotions tie us to our small groups. Here the author's **Main Idea** is revealed: The results of the Ultimatum Game can be explained by these emotions that are built over time and are not designed for one-time anonymous transactions, so they get in the way of exercising self-interest in such transactions. This fixes the problem left by the first explanation, as it explains why people reject unfair amounts. Oddly, the passage hints that this explanation would also explain why people offer fair amounts, though it never says so directly. This absence should be noted as fodder for a potential question later on. An authorial point of view will almost certainly be represented in the question set, so this distinction is important to find.

23. (B) Global

Step 2: Identify the Question Type
The words *main idea* identify this question as a Global, or big-picture, question.

Step 3: Research the Relevant Text
When answering a Global question, you must refer to the Topic, Scope, Purpose, and Main Idea found during your review of the passage.

Step 4: Make a Prediction
The overall picture of the passage contains an experiment, its puzzling results, and potential solutions to the puzzle. You need to find an answer that summarizes this. A quick glance at the answer choices shows that they all mention specific details, so you may have to take the general idea and make it more specific. The experiment led to a problem where people behaved contrary to logical self-interest, and two explanations try to show how we evolved to allow this to happen. This is a solid prediction to move ahead with.

Step 5: Evaluate the Answer Choices
(B) matches the prediction fairly closely and is the correct answer.

(A) While this statement might be partially true, based on the results of the experiment, this answer choice is too narrow. You are looking for the main idea of the passage, not something that is true but only sets the stage for the main idea of the passage.

(C) has the same problem as **(A)**; it is too narrow. This answer choice is the main idea of paragraph 4, not the main idea of the passage as a whole.

(D) again refers mainly to paragraph 4 and is thus too narrow in scope to be the correct answer.

(E) is factually inaccurate. This answer choice is the opposite of what is claimed in paragraph 3.

24. (D) Inference

Step 2: Identify the Question Type
The question asks what the passage *implies*, which signals an Inference question.

Step 3: Research the Relevant Text
The question stem only refers to the Ultimatum Game, a concept spoken of in all four paragraphs. This makes research difficult.

Step 4: Make a Prediction
While it is hard to research this question, you do know a few things about this topic. Referring to your Roadmap, you know that the experiment is outlined in paragraph 1, the results are detailed in paragraph 2, and the odd results are most likely explained (according to the author) in paragraph 4. This may help you as you work through the answer choices.

Step 5: Evaluate the Answer Choices

(D) is the only proper inference in the answer choices. Paragraph 4 talks of an explanation for the puzzling results of the experiment dealing with emotions. It says that we aren't built to make one-shot anonymous interactions and, thus, we react oddly to the Ultimatum Game.

(A) says that two strangers develop trust in each other. While the explanations may deal with people trusting, the game by no means requires this connection.

(B) is Extreme. While the experiment is certainly a challenge to a basic assumption of theoretical economics, it is far from responsible for its being overturned.

(C) is a subtly wrong answer. While the Ultimatum Game does end up with results different from those expected, the statistics in the second paragraph specifically show that these odd results are indeed predictable.

(E) The concept of this choice is on the right track, but the first word of the choice, *proof*, is much too strong to be supported by the passage.

25. (D) Global

Step 2: Identify the Question Type

This is a Global question, specifically a primary purpose question.

Step 3: Research the Relevant Text

For a Global question that asks for the primary purpose, you should look directly to your developed Topic, Scope, Purpose, and Main Idea. The prediction should be a paraphrase of the Purpose.

Step 4: Make a Prediction

The Purpose noted from Step 1 is "to offer an explanation for the puzzling results of the Ultimatum Game." Look for this in the answer choices.

Step 5: Evaluate the Answer Choices

(D) matches the prediction almost word for word and is correct.

(A) uses the word *survey*. Because the author takes a position on which explanation is more likely, the author is doing more than surveying, a neutral action.

(B) introduces two theories but says they complement each other. In fact, one theory was a partial explanation, while the second, in the author's opinion, was a full explanation.

(C) says that the author's primary purpose was to argue for the validity of the results. The validity of the results are assumed, however, in paragraph 2 to set the stage for the explanations described in paragraphs 3 and 4.

(E) begins with the word *defend*, which is not what the author is doing. Secondarily, the experiments' methodology is not in question.

26. (C) Inference

Step 2: Identify the Question Type

The question is asking you to find a sentence to tack on to the end of the passage. When you must take the stated material and find an answer that goes a step further based on that, you have an Inference question.

Step 3: Research the Relevant Text

Look at the final paragraph in terms of the overall passage.

Step 4: Make a Prediction

You already know that the explanation in paragraph 4 was the author's pick as the most compelling. It explicitly mentions why people would reject a low offer, though the paragraph inexplicably does not mention how the theory would explain people making fair offers to begin with. Because that is missing and you are asked to add something that seems to be implied, this is a workable prediction to begin matching to the answer choices.

Step 5: Evaluate the Answer Choices

(C) addresses this missing piece of implied information, making it the correct answer.

(A) is Extreme. Even if this were true for this one experiment, this choice implies that it is a consistent fact. That is far too strong to be supported.

(B) is Out of Scope. The focus is on the behavior of the "responder" not on the frequency that such hypothetical anonymous interactions actually occur.

(D) also goes beyond the scope of the passage. This statement would introduce whole new topics and require support that is not found in the passage.

(E) might indeed be true, but it does not follow the path of paragraph 4 or the overall progression of the passage. Remember, just because an answer might be a true fact doesn't mean it has to be true for the question at hand.

27. (D) Logic Reasoning (Strengthen)

Step 2: Identify the Question Type

The question is asking what would make the author change his mind. This means that you need to know what the author's point of view is, what the original idea is, and take that opinion one step further by strengthening the explanation in the third paragraph.

Step 3: Research the Relevant Text

The question is clearly rooted in paragraph 3. However, because you are also using the author's point of view, you must take some of the rest of the passage into account—specifically paragraph 4, where the author's point of view shows up.

Step 4: Make a Prediction

The author suggests that the solution in paragraph 4 is a better explanation than the one offered in paragraph 3 because it accounts for why people would reject a low offer. Because that is the author's main stated problem with the explanation in paragraph 3, fixing that problem would be the surest way to make the author change his mind on the subject.

Step 5: Evaluate the Answer Choices

(D) uses the specifics of the explanation to match the general prediction. Therefore, **(D)** is the answer.

(A) is attempting to increase the size of the groups. While this might change the classification of the group size, it would have little to do with fixing the author's problem with the explanation in paragraph 3.

(B) is Out of Scope, adding irrelevant information to the mix. Remember, an inference must be just a step beyond the explicitly stated details; it cannot add wild details that are only marginally related to the topic.

(C) cannot find support within the passage and is thus not a valid inference. Large social groups are Out of Scope.

(E) again talks about social groups that you know nothing about and gives information that would not help to allay the author's objection to paragraph 3's explanation.

PrepTest 60

The Inside Story

PrepTest 60 was administered in June 2010. It challenged 32,973 test takers. What made this test so hard? Here's a breakdown of what Kaplan students who were surveyed after taking the official exam considered PrepTest 60's most difficult section.

Hardest PrepTest 60 Section as Reported by Test Takers

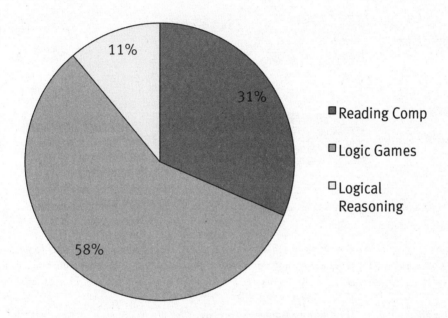

Based on these results, you might think that studying Logic Games is the key to LSAT success. Well, Logic Games is important, but test takers' perceptions don't tell the whole story. For that, you need to consider students' actual performance. The following chart shows the average number of students to miss each question in each of PrepTest 60's different sections.

Percentage Incorrect by PrepTest 60 Section Type

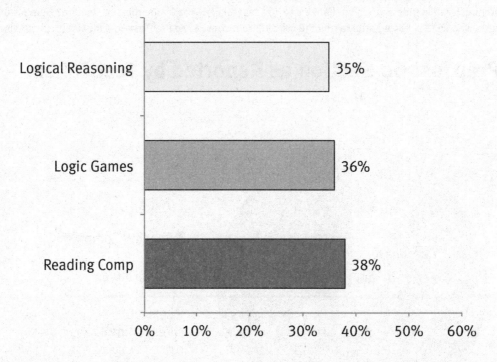

Actual student performance tells quite a different story. On average, students were almost equally likely to miss questions in all three of the different section types, and on PrepTest 60, Reading Comprehension was somewhat higher than Logic Games in actual difficulty.

Maybe students overestimate the difficulty of the Logic Games section because it's so unusual, or maybe it's because a really hard Logic Game is so easy to remember after the test. But the truth is that the testmaker places hard questions throughout the test. Here were the locations of the 10 hardest (most missed) questions in the exam.

Location of 10 Most Difficult Questions in PrepTest 60

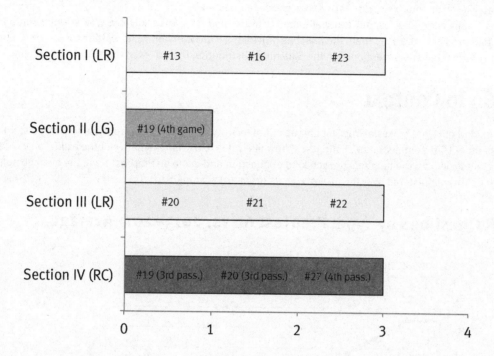

The takeaway from this data is that, to maximize your potential on the LSAT, you need to take a comprehensive approach. Test yourself rigorously, and review your performance on every section of the test. Kaplan's LSAT explanations provide the expertise and insight you need to fully understand your results. The explanations are written and edited by a team of LSAT experts, who have helped thousands of students improve their scores. Kaplan always provides data-driven analysis of the test, ranking the difficulty of every question based on actual student performance. The 10 hardest questions on every test are highlighted with a 4-star difficulty rating, the highest we give. The analysis breaks down the remaining questions into 1-, 2-, and 3-star ratings so that you can compare your performance to thousands of other test takers on all LSAC material.

Don't settle for wondering whether a question was really as hard as it seemed to you. Analyze the test with real data, and learn the secrets and strategies that help top scorers master the LSAT.

7 Can't-Miss Features of PrepTest 60

- Question 19, from the first Logical Reasoning section, was removed from scoring. It was the fourth LR question to ever be removed, and no test has had an LR question removed since then.
- Rule Substitution questions debuted on PrepTest 57 and were on every test from PrepTest 57–66, except PrepTest 60.
- The Logic Games section ended with a Matching/Distribution Hybrid. Although there was also one a bit earlier on PrepTest 55 (October 2008), there have only been four ever—the others were on PrepTest A (February 1996) and PrepTest 25 (June 1998).
- There are many variations on Strict Sequencing games. However, the Landscaper with Mulch and Stone game was truly unique. It has some interesting mechanics and is the only Strict Sequencing ever to feature just two entities. It's also one of only three games ever to have only two rules.
- The answer choice distribution for PrepTest 60 is unusual. In Logical Reasoning, (A), (B), and (E) are each correct only seven times, but (C) and (D) are each correct 14 times. (C) and (D) are also the most frequently occurring right answers in Reading Comprehension. For the whole test (C) and (D) are each correct 25 or more times, and (A), (B), and (E) are each correct 16 times or fewer.

- Most tests have at least a few EXCEPT or LEAST questions in Logical Reasoning or Reading Comprehension, but PrepTest 60 features no such questions. It is only the second test since 1995 with that characteristic. A lack of such questions is more common lately though: four tests 2012–2017 also lack such questions.
- For the soccer fans out there, Test Day was well-timed to avoid distractions. Luckily, the World Cup in South Africa didn't start until four days after the test. Then, the matches provided a nice diversion while waiting for scores. Coincidentally Spain—one of the three areas mentioned in the Matching/Distribution Hybrid—won the World Cup that July.

PrepTest 60 in Context

As much fun as it is to find out what makes a PrepTest unique or noteworthy, it's even more important to know just how representative it is of other LSAT administrations (and, thus, how likely it is to be representative of the exam you will face on Test Day). The following charts compare the numbers of each kind of question and game on PrepTest 60 to the average numbers seen on all officially released LSATs administered over the past five years (from 2013 through 2017).

Number of LR Questions by Type: PrepTest 60 vs. 2013–2017 Average

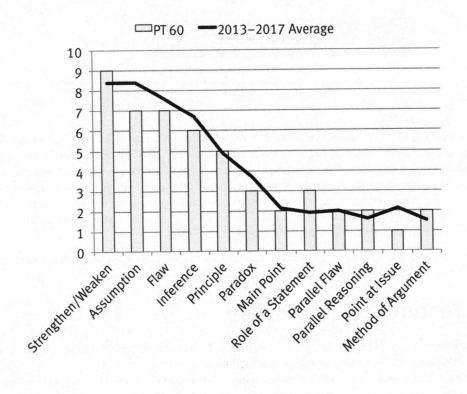

Number of LG Games by Type: PrepTest 60 vs. 2013–2017 Average

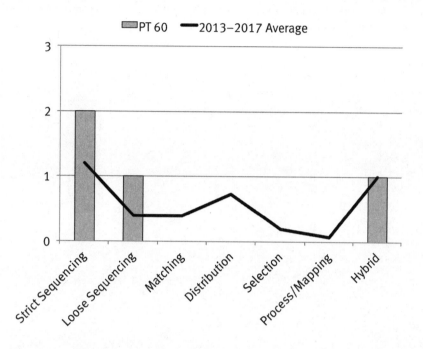

Number of RC Questions by Type: PrepTest 60 vs. 2013–2017 Average

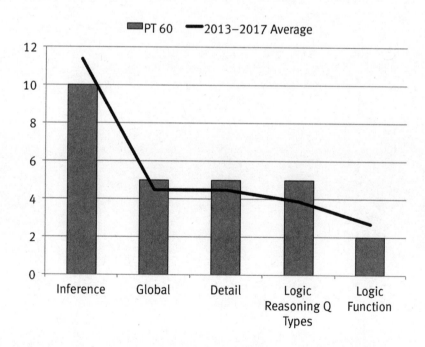

There isn't usually a huge difference in the distribution of questions from LSAT to LSAT, but if this test seems harder (or easier) to you than another you've taken, compare the number of questions of the types on which you, personally, are strongest and weakest. Then, explore within each section to see if your best or worst question types came earlier or later.

Students in Kaplan's comprehensive LSAT courses have access to every released LSAT and to a library of thousands of officially released questions arranged by question, game, and passage type. If you are studying on your own, you have to do a bit more work to identify your strengths and your areas of opportunity. Quantitative analysis (like that in the charts shown here) is an important tool for understanding how the test is constructed, and how you are performing on it.

Section I: Logical Reasoning

Q#	Question Type	Correct	Difficulty
1	Flaw	D	★
2	Method of Argument	E	★
3	Inference	B	★
4	Role of a Statement	D	★
5	Paradox	C	★
6	Weaken	B	★
7	Assumption (Necessary)	C	★
8	Main Point	E	★
9	Paradox	D	★★
10	Flaw	D	★★
11	Strengthen	C	★
12	Flaw	A	★★
13	Weaken	C	★★★★
14	Assumption (Necessary)	D	★
15	Flaw	B	★★
16	Weaken	C	★★★★
17	Parallel Reasoning	A	★★★
18	Principle (Identify/Strengthen)	E	★★★
19	Item Removed from scoring		
20	Assumption (Necessary)	D	★★★
21	Parallel Flaw	B	★★★
22	Assumption (Sufficient)	A	★★★
23	Principle (Identify/Strengthen)	E	★★★★
24	Inference	C	★★
25	Method of Argument	C	★

1. (D) Flaw

Step 1: Identify the Question Type
The phrase "reasoning is questionable" identifies this as a Flaw question. Note that the question stem also indicates one of the classic LSAT flaws, namely an overlooked possibility, so think about alternate possibilities as you analyze the argument.

Step 2: Untangle the Stimulus
Jim concludes that the sample does contain iron. His reasons for thinking so are that magnets attract iron and that this particular substance attached to the magnet.

Step 3: Make a Prediction
What possibility has Jim overlooked? Although magnets do attract iron, they may also attract other substances, so the sample in question may not contain iron but rather some other component that attached to the magnet. Jim's questionable reasoning relies on the faulty assumption that magnets attract *only* iron.

Step 4: Evaluate the Answer Choices
(D) provides exactly that overlooked possibility and is the correct answer.

(A) contradicts the evidence rather than identifying a flaw in Jim's reasoning. Your task when identifying a flaw is *not* to question the evidence provided but rather to determine why the given evidence does not support the author's conclusion.

(B) gets the relationship backwards; the flaw is that magnets may attract elements other than iron. What other substances iron may attract is irrelevant.

(C)'s mention of the orientation of the magnet lies outside the scope of the argument, so it cannot be the flaw here.

(E) introduces an irrelevant comparison between the relative strengths of magnets.

2. (E) Method of Argument

Step 1: Identify the Question Type
The phrase "method of reasoning" is synonymous with Method of Argument, so your task is to untangle the structure of the author's argument.

Step 2: Untangle the Stimulus
The author's conclusion appears in the last sentence; the book Horatio wants must be either misplaced or stolen. To arrive at this conclusion, the author eliminates several reasons why Horatio might not be able to find the book (improper catalog information, use by another library patron, awaiting shelving, or part of a special display).

Step 3: Make a Prediction
Here the author eliminates possible reasons why the book might not be in its proper location on the shelf before putting forth the remaining possibilities (misplaced or stolen).

Step 4: Evaluate the Answer Choices
(E) precisely matches the predicted argumentative structure. If you have difficulty interpreting an answer choice in a Method of Argument question, tie the generic language back to the specifics of the argument. Here the "other possible explanations" are the ones identified in Step 2, and the "observed fact" is that the book is not in its expected location.

(A) fails because in the stimulus, the conclusion and evidence refer to the same object rather than shifting scope to make a generalization about similar objects.

(B) is Out of Scope. The argument does not mention any deficiency in the library's system.

(C) should be eliminated because no conclusion is rebutted.

(D) cannot be the correct answer because the argument does not reject a generalization.

3. (B) Inference

Step 1: Identify the Question Type
This question stem uses standard Inference question language ("properly inferred"), so accept each statement as true and seek out logical connections as you read.

Step 2: Untangle the Stimulus
The stimulus states a fact in the first sentence, that the level of atmospheric sulfur dioxide is higher than it was ten years ago. Then it announces this increase is *troubling* since it occurred despite stricter regulations on emissions that were imposed ten years ago. The final sentence provides a related if/then statement. This conditional statement provides a useful starting place.

Step 3: Make a Prediction
The final sentence states that

If	regulations followed	→	sulfur dioxide levels decrease

The contrapositive is

If	sulfur dioxide levels don't decrease	→	regulations were not followed

Because the first sentence states that sulfur dioxide levels have, in fact, *increased*, it must be true that at least some of the coal-burning power plants did not follow the new regulations.

Step 4: Evaluate the Answer Choices

(B) directly states that the regulations have been violated, something that must be true based on the facts provided.

(A) is wrong because the stimulus does not provide enough information to state definitively what will happen to sulfur dioxide levels in the future, regardless of whether current regulations are followed.

(C) goes awry in the same as way **(A)** by making an unsupported claim about future results.

(D) is incorrect because the relative amount of pollution contributed by coal-burning power plants lies outside the scope of the given information.

(E) is Extreme. The assertion that regulations will *never* reduce atmospheric sulfur dioxide levels is not supported by the one example in the stimulus.

4. (D) Role of a Statement

Step 1: Identify the Question Type

This question stem uses classic Role of a Statement language. As you untangle the stimulus, find the claim that there will be a crisis in landfill availability and determine what part it plays in the argument.

Step 2: Untangle the Stimulus

The second sentence contains the claim about a crisis in landfill availability, a claim maintained by "some people." In both Logical Reasoning and Reading Comprehension, the phrase *some people* generally introduces a viewpoint with which the author disagrees. As expected, the next sentence begins with the Contrast Keyword [*h*]*owever*, which introduces the author's opposing conclusion.

Step 3: Make a Prediction

In this stimulus, the author introduces the claim in question in order to refute it by pointing out the faulty assumption upon which the *unsound* conclusion rests.

Step 4: Evaluate the Answer Choices

(D) matches the prediction and describes the structure of the argument perfectly. The author's argument is designed to weaken or "cast doubt" on the inevitability of a crisis in landfill availability.

(A) is incorrect because the first sentence of the argument merely provides background information about landfill design.

(B) is a Distortion. "Some people" would put forth this claim as a conclusion, but not the author of this argument.

(C) is a 180. The claim contradicts the author's conclusion rather than supports it.

(E) is incorrect because the claim is not made by the author and so cannot be the author's intermediate conclusion.

5. (C) Paradox

Step 1: Identify the Question Type

The phrase "resolve the apparent discrepancy" identifies this as a Paradox question.

Step 2: Untangle the Stimulus

Identify the paradox while you untangle the stimulus. On the one hand, Country X has a low incidence of disease P. The Contrast Keyword [*n*]*evertheless* points out the seeming discrepancy; residents of Country X who have the disease are much more likely to die from it.

Step 3: Make a Prediction

Although the specific details may be hard to predict, look for an answer choice that explains why disease P affects fewer residents of Country X but does so much more virulently.

Step 4: Evaluate the Answer Choices

(C) is the correct answer. If Country X counts only the most severe cases of disease P, it follows that those cases, though fewer in number, would more likely end fatally.

(A) is Out of Scope. It shifts from how fatal the disease is to how contagious it is.

(B) contradicts the facts in the stimulus, so it cannot explain the paradox.

(D) is Out of Scope because the yearly fluctuations are irrelevant to the paradox at hand.

(E) is Out of Scope because the stimulus does not mention diseases other than disease P.

6. (B) Weaken

Step 1: Identify the Question Type

The phrases "potential challenges" and "calls into question" signal that this is a Weaken question. However, notice that you are asked to weaken the *evidence* rather than the *conclusion*. Start by finding the conclusion and evidence as usual.

Step 2: Untangle the Stimulus

The Evidence Keyword *since* appears in the second sentence and points you to the conclusion that immediately precedes it; the author claims that the effort to rehabilitate the otters was not worthwhile. His evidence cites figures of affected otters and the low numbers that were saved, then goes on to state that the actual proportion of rehabilitated otters is even lower than these studies show, because many dead otters have never been found.

Step 3: Make a Prediction

The argument provides some evidence in the form of the number of otters that were actually observed and counted, so those facts cannot be challenged. However, the last sentence introduces an unknown factor: How can researchers know how many otters were killed immediately if not all of the dead otters were found? This is the problematic piece of evidence. If the number of dead otters that were not found cannot be accurately determined, then the rehabilitation efforts may actually have been more successful than the argument asserts.

Step 4: Evaluate the Answer Choices

(B) raises the very question about the evidence that seemed suspect: How can there be an estimate of a count of what has not been found? This matches the predicted concern and is the correct answer.

(A) is Out of Scope because the argument is not concerned with other species of sea otters or with otters that live outside the spill zone.

(C) is Out of Scope because the argument pertains only to the rehabilitation of otters that were affected by the oil spill.

(D) is also Out of Scope because the rehabilitation effort described does not concern animals other than sea otters.

(E) is Out of Scope because the argument concerns the effectiveness of the rehabilitation efforts, not their cost.

7. (C) Assumption (Necessary)

Step 1: Identify the Question Type

The question uses standard language for a Necessary Assumption question. Untangle the stimulus by finding the psychologist's conclusion and evidence.

Step 2: Untangle the Stimulus

The Conclusion Keyword [*s*]*o* signals the psychologist's conclusion that cancer-patient support groups may indeed have genuine therapeutic value. What reason does the psychologist give for this belief? Such groups reduce participants' stress levels. Also, research shows that a weakened immune system increases vulnerability to cancer.

Step 3: Make a Prediction

Both the evidence and the conclusion mention support groups. However, the evidence mentions reduced stress levels, while the conclusion refers to genuine therapeutic value. The psychologist must assume that reductions in stress level can have genuine therapeutic value.

Step 4: Evaluate the Answer Choices

(C) provides a specific therapeutic benefit of stress reduction. If stress weakens the immune system, then a reduction in stress would mitigate this effect, thereby making the patients less vulnerable to cancer. **(C)** is the correct answer.

(A) fails to mention the support groups or their effect, so it does nothing to bridge the gap between evidence and conclusion.

(B) is Extreme in its assertion that no disease is a biochemical phenomenon.

(D) explains how participation in a support group might reduce stress but not how that turns into a therapeutic benefit to cancer patients. Thus, it falls short of providing the necessary link between the evidence and conclusion.

(E)'s statement that stress is a *symptom* of a weakened immune system also fails to bridge the critical gap between support groups and therapeutic benefit to cancer patients. To be correct, the answer must show that alleviating stress will strengthen the immune system.

8. (E) Main Point

Step 1: Identify the Question Type

The phrase "main conclusion" identifies a Main Point question. Use Conclusion Keywords and the One Sentence Test to find the main conclusion of the argument.

Step 2: Untangle the Stimulus

The value judgment on adobe in the first sentence strongly suggests that this sentence is the main conclusion. As expected, the rest of the argument provides details to convince the reader that adobe is an ideal material for building in desert environments.

Step 3: Make a Prediction

Don't get bogged down in the details in the stimulus; focus instead on the structure of the argument. Here the author establishes that adobe is an ideal material for building in the desert. The characteristics of adobe that follow only serve to provide support for the author's claim.

Step 4: Evaluate the Answer Choices

(E) is correct. The phrase "especially suitable material" closely matches the author's judgment that adobe is an "ideal material."

(A) is Out of Scope. Its emphasis on adobe as a substitute for other materials in structures where heat-conduction properties are important is broader in scope than the author's conclusion, which focuses only on desert environments.

(B) restates evidence that the author uses, but the question asks for the conclusion.

(C) also mentions facts from the evidence, not the conclusion. Furthermore, the word *constant* distorts the details provided.

(D) is a Distortion. the word [*I*]*deally* may be tempting at first glance, but reading the entire choice reveals an ideal quality of desert *buildings* rather than ideal *material* for building them.

9. (D) Paradox

Step 1: Identify the Question Type

The phrase "resolve the apparent discrepancy" identifies a Paradox question. Determine the apparent discrepancy as you untangle the stimulus.

Step 2: Untangle the Stimulus

The stimulus describes two studies that show large discrepancies between the percentages of plants that have patterned stems. How could one study yield 70 percent with patterned stems while the other yielded only 40 percent?

Step 3: Make a Prediction

The stimulus does not provide much information about the study other than that the two studies covered approximately the same geographical area. The different results could easily be explained by something else that was not constant between the two studies.

Step 4: Evaluate the Answer Choices

(D) provides a key difference between the two studies. If the first study used a broader definition of *patterned*, then it would probably find a higher percentage of plants with patterned stems.

(A) may be tempting, but it does not state that the second study was conducted at a different time of year. Thus, it does nothing to explain the difference in the studies.

(B) does identify a difference between the two studies; however, including other plants in the first study would not affect the percentage of plants of the variety discussed that have patterned stems.

(C) is Out of Scope. Because the studies are comparing the *percentage* of plants with patterned stems, the actual *number* of plants studied is irrelevant.

(E) does identify a difference between the two studies; however, the fact that collecting information about patterned stems was merely a secondary goal of one of the studies does nothing to explain the discrepant findings.

10. (D) Flaw

Step 1: Identify the Question Type

The phrase "reasoning flaw" is standard language in a Flaw question. Because the question asks for a *description* of the flawed reasoning, expect the answer choices to use generic language.

Step 2: Untangle the Stimulus

The Contrast Keyword [*h*]*owever* signals the letter writer's conclusion that the proposed solution for the disposal of the contaminated dredge spoils would damage commercial fishing operations. The letter writer's sole piece of evidence follows the key phrase "[o]ne indication of this is that" and states more than 20,000 people have signed petitions opposing the proposal.

Step 3: Make a Prediction

The letter writer provides no information about the 20,000 petitioners but bases his conclusion on their opinions. Thus, he must assume these 20,000 people know what they are talking about. This flawed assumption can be described as an

inappropriate appeal to authority, a flaw pattern that recurs on the LSAT.

Step 4: Evaluate the Answer Choices

(D) questions the petitioners' expertise and is the correct answer.

(A) fails because the letter writer does not even present the editor's view, let alone distort it.

(B) fails to address the hole in the logic. Although the letter writer does not establish that the use of sand-capped pits is a viable solution, that omission is not a flaw in gap between the evidence and conclusion.

(C) fails because the letter writer does not indicate any vested personal interest in a particular solution to the problem of waste disposal.

(E) fails because the potential existence of a third solution has no bearing on the conclusion that the editor's proposed solution would damage commercial fishing.

11. (C) Strengthen

Step 1: Identify the Question Type

This question uses standard language for a Strengthen question. Determine how to make the conclusion more believable by reinforcing the assumption.

Step 2: Untangle the Stimulus

The author's main point is the first sentence: most universities today offer students a more in-depth and comprehensive education than ever before. The Illustration Keywords "for example" in the second sentence signal the beginning of the evidence, which states that history courses at most universities now require the reading of textbooks that include fuller histories of Africa and Asia and of the Americas' indigenous cultures.

Step 3: Make a Prediction

For the author to claim that universities now offer a more in-depth and cosmopolitan education, she must assume a link exists between such education and history courses that require the type of reading described. This argument will be strengthened by an assertion that confirms that reading about the histories of diverse cultures leads to an in-depth and cosmopolitan education.

Step 4: Evaluate the Answer Choices

(C) directly states the central assumption, so it definitely strengthens the argument.

(A) is Out of Scope of the argument because students' interest levels do not affect the conclusion.

(B) introduces study-abroad programs, which may or may not offer a more in-depth and comprehensive education. Be skeptical of choices that introduce new terms rather than connecting the evidence provided to the disconnected term in the conclusion.

(D) has no impact on the argument because the author relies only on history courses to establish the conclusion. Other courses are irrelevant to this argument on its own terms.

(E) negates without reversing. The assumption is that students who study diverse cultures will get a cosmopolitan education. This is not the same as saying that students who do *not* study diverse cultures will *not* get a cosmopolitan education. This distortion is similar to the Formal Logic flaw of mistaking a sufficient condition for a necessary one.

12. (A) Flaw

Step 1: Identify the Question Type
The phrase "most vulnerable to criticism" is common language for a Flaw question, Look for the unwarranted assumption or the common LSAT flaw.

Step 2: Untangle the Stimulus
The author's conclusion is signaled by the Contrast Keyword [*h*]*owever*. He claims that the disclosure of statistics about each airline's number of near collisions and its fines for safety violations will not achieve the goal of making the public more informed about airline safety. The single piece of evidence (following *because*) is that the airlines will likely not give complete reports if the information is provided to the public.

Step 3: Make a Prediction
The author assumes that incomplete reports from the airlines cannot make the public more informed about airline safety. However, the author has overlooked the possibility that some information may be better than no information.

Step 4: Evaluate the Answer Choices
(A) matches the prediction exactly and is the correct answer.

(B) is Extreme in stating that the public has a right to *all* information about matters of public safety. The author does not make this assertion.

(C) is Extreme in its assertion that information about airline safety is *impossible* to find without government disclosure. Furthermore, the argument addresses the shortcomings of a plan that relies on government disclosure of such information.

(D) is Out of Scope. Who has responsibility for reporting accurate information has no bearing on whether the public would be better informed about airline safety. Also, notice the shift in language from *incomplete* in the argument to *inaccurate* in this answer choice. **(D)** fails on both counts.

(E) can be eliminated because the airlines' revenues lie outside the scope of the argument.

13. (C) Weaken

Step 1: Identify the Question Type
This question uses standard language for a Weaken question. Make the conclusion less believable by undermining the assumption.

Step 2: Untangle the Stimulus
When you see a phrase like "Many economists claim," you should expect that the author will disagree with the position he attributes explicitly to others. The Keywords "this shows that" indicate that the evidence has just been presented and that the conclusion is coming up. The author's contrasting conclusion is that the economists overestimate the degree to which people are motivated by "financial rewards" in their job choices. The single piece of evidence is that most people surveyed do not name salary as the most desirable feature of a job.

Step 3: Make a Prediction
The assumption is that salary is the only relevant financial reward associated with job selection. A weakener will invalidate that assumption, likely by presenting another financial reward that motivates peoples' job choices.

Step 4: Evaluate the Answer Choices
(C) matches the prediction and invalidates the author's assumption. If jobs that pay a particular salary vary considerably in their other financial benefits, then contrary to the author's view, it is less likely that financial reward is an unimportant consideration in job selection.

(A) is Out of Scope. The purchasing power of one's salary is not relevant to motivating factors in job choice.

(B) demonstrates that higher salary may be a desirable factor in choosing between identical jobs, but that commonsense fact does nothing to this stimulus. If there was an observed relationship between higher salaries and different jobs, that information might help evaluate this argument, but as it is, **(B)** has no effect.

(D) identifies the desirability of having effort appreciated when one successfully completes a challenging task, but it fails to comment in any way on the relative desirability of salary.

(E) fails to address whether the people who are unaware of the demands of a high-salary job would still desire the high salary even if they were better informed.

14. (D) Assumption (Necessary)

Step 1: Identify the Question Type
This question uses standard language for an Assumption question. Notice that the question asks about the *researchers'* argument.

Step 2: Untangle the Stimulus
The researchers conclude that students do not become more engaged in the learning process when class sizes are smaller and teachers devote more time to each student. Their evidence is that students' grades remained unchanged when class sizes were smaller and teachers devoted more time to each student. Notice the shift in scope from grades in the evidence to the degree of engagement in the learning process in the conclusion. The assumption must bridge this gap.

Step 3: Make a Prediction
In drawing a conclusion about the students' engagement in the learning process from a study that considered students' grades, the researchers assume that grades are an indicator of engagement in the learning process.

Step 4: Evaluate the Answer Choices
(D) matches the prediction exactly and is the correct answer.

(A) is Out of Scope because the researchers are concerned with the size of classes rather than the size of schools.

(B) fails to address how an increase in individual attention by a teacher affects students' engagement in the learning process. The proportion of attention given to each student is not at issue here.

(C) is irrelevant to the argument because the researchers are concerned with smaller class size rather than with fewer teachers.

(E) is Out of Scope because parental support for the proposed law has no impact on the results obtained by enacting the law.

15. (B) Flaw

Step 1: Identify the Question Type
The phrase "reasoning ... is questionable" signals a Flaw question. Notice that the question indicates a flaw in *Rebecca's* argument. You should still read Camille's argument but focus on the flaw in Rebecca's. Finally, determine what Rebecca takes for granted.

Step 2: Untangle the Stimulus
Rebecca concludes that the manufacturers do not exaggerate claims about the amount of money that can be saved by using a water-saving faucet. Her evidence is that her water bills have gone down since she installed the water-saving faucet. She assumes that the savings on her water bills are consistent with the manufacturers' claims.

Step 3: Make a Prediction
Rebecca takes for granted that she saves as much money as the manufacturers claimed she would, without knowing how much that is.

Step 4: Evaluate the Answer Choices
(B) matches the prediction precisely and is the correct answer.

(A) is a Distortion. The manufacturers make a claim about the cost of water bills rather than the cost of installing the faucet, so **(A)** cannot be the flaw in the argument.

(C) does not address Rebecca's error in reasoning. She still does not know what the manufacturers claim. Consistency among their claims is not at issue.

(D) is Out of Scope because Rebecca's argument concerns cost savings rather than satisfaction with performance.

(E) does not compare Rebecca's savings to those claimed by the manufacturers.

16. (C) Weaken

Step 1: Identify the Question Type
This question uses standard language for a Weaken question.

Step 2: Untangle the Stimulus
The Conclusion Keyword [*clearly*] prefaces the spokesperson's conclusion that the company will reduce air pollution more by buying the old cars than by redesigning the plants. The evidence is that old cars of the type the company plans to dispose of account for a higher percentage of air pollution than do the plants.

Step 3: Make a Prediction
Though the spokesperson's use of air pollution figures seems convincing, he may have overlooked something about the old cars that would explain how the disposal plan might not result in an overall reduction of pollution. Look for the correct answer to provide a reason this plan won't have the intended effect.

Step 4: Evaluate the Answer Choices
(C) explains how the spokesperson's plan may not work. If the purchased cars were not actually running, then they were not contributing to air pollution. So the company would have reduced air pollution more by redesigning the plants.

(A) does not weaken the argument because even a small number of old cars could cause more pollution than the plants.

(B) is Out of Scope because the spokesperson is concerned with the effectiveness of the plan rather than cost.

(D) suggests that the company might reduce pollution even more by purchasing newer cars, but it fails to show that the purchase of the old cars will not reduce pollution by the desired amount.

(E) fails because complaints from citizen groups are irrelevant to the effectiveness of the plan.

17. (A) Parallel Reasoning

Step 1: Identify the Question Type

The phrase "most similar in its reasoning" identifies a Parallel Reasoning question. Focus on the structure of the conclusion and evidence rather than on the content.

Step 2: Untangle the Stimulus

The conclusion appears at the end of the argument: "our ancestors were at least partially altruistic." Characterize this conclusion as a qualified, positive value judgment. The chain of evidence is as follows: humankind has survived; the survival of humankind required occasional self-sacrifice by our ancestors; such sacrifice requires some degree of altruism.

Step 3: Make a Prediction

The parallel argument will have a qualified, positive value judgment as its conclusion. Compare the evidence if more than one answer remains after eliminating every choice with a different type of conclusion.

Step 4: Evaluate the Answer Choices

(A) is the correct answer. The conclusion that "some students manage their time well" is a qualified, positive value judgment. The use of evidence also matches that of the original argument. Something has definitely happened (students raise grades). This event requires a certain characteristic (increased study time). This characteristic requires another condition (good time management). Therefore, at least some of the first thing has the third condition as well (some students have good time management).

(B) can be eliminated by its conclusion type. It concludes "plants that consume insects must be incapable of photosynthesis." That's an unqualified assertion of fact.

(C) has a very different type of conclusion, an If/Then statement that makes a prediction. This is not at all parallel in structure.

(D) can be eliminated because the conclusion is a definite prediction.

(E) contains an "either...or" in its conclusion that is not matched by the stimulus.

18. (E) Principle (Identify/Strengthen)

Step 1: Identify the Question Type

This question is a Principle question. The phrase "most helps to justify the reasoning" indicates the correct answer will identify a principle that strengthens the bus driver's argument.

Step 2: Untangle the Stimulus

The bus driver's conclusion is that he should not be reprimanded for the accident. His evidence is that even though he might have avoided the collision by reacting more

quickly, he was abiding by all traffic regulations while the garbage truck driver was not.

Step 3: Make a Prediction

The assumption here is that his failure to respond more quickly should not reprimanded, given that his actions lay within the boundaries of the law. Predict that the principle will be right in line with this assumption.

Step 4: Evaluate the Answer Choices

(E) matches the prediction closely and makes the driver's claim of blamelessness stronger.

(A) does not apply to the situation because it fails to mention the reprimand (or lack thereof) to the second driver.

(B) does not apply to the situation because the police report confirmed that the bus driver did not violate any traffic regulations, not that the garbage truck driver was solely responsible for the collision.

(C) does not apply to the situation because the bus driver did not violate a traffic regulation.

(D) does not strengthen the bus driver's argument because the driver concedes that she might have been able to avoid the accident.

19. Item Removed from Scoring

This question was removed from scoring and was not published when the test was released.

20. (D) Assumption (Necessary)

Step 1: Identify the Question Type

This question uses standard language for a Necessary Assumption question. Untangle the stimulus by finding the historian's conclusion and evidence.

Step 2: Untangle the Stimulus

The historian provides evidence before arriving at the conclusion that today's generation of television viewers exercise their imaginations less frequently than did the previous generations of radio listeners. The key pieces of evidence are that radio listeners regularly exercised their imaginations and that they had to visualize for themselves such dramatic elements as characters' physical appearances and spatial relationships. Notice the scope shift from radio listeners to television viewers.

Step 3: Make a Prediction

The historian suggests that television viewing does not require the same exercise of the imagination as does radio listening because television presents the visual images of the characters' physical appearances and spatial relationships. But in order to conclude that the current generation exercises its imagination less frequently, the historian assumes that the current generation is not involved in some other activity that would exercise the imagination.

Step 4: Evaluate the Answer Choices

(D) matches the prediction precisely and is the correct answer. The Denial Test works well to confirm that this is a required assumption. If something other than radio did fill the gap as a medium for exercising the imagination, then the historian's conclusion makes no sense. Because the negation of **(D)** causes the historian's argument to fall apart, it must be the correct answer.

(A) fails to address why television watchers do not exercise their imaginations from some other activity. People today could spend as much time watching television and yet still have time to engage in other activities that exercise the imagination.

(B) is Out of Scope because the historian does not consider the effect of familiarity with the entertainment medium.

(C) introduces the issue of creativity, which may or may not be related to the exercise of the imagination.

(E) is irrelevant because the distinction the historian draws is that television viewers actually see the images and do not imagine them; whether television viewers think about the images is not at issue.

21. (B) Parallel Flaw

Step 1: Identify the Question Type

The phrase "pattern of flawed reasoning ... is most similar" identifies a Parallel Flaw question.

Step 2: Untangle the Stimulus

The conclusion is that most of the mayoral candidates have the skills necessary to be a good mayor. Characterize the conclusion as a value judgment about most people. Words such as *most*, *each*, and *no* identify Formal Logic, so summarize the evidence as well. Each mayoral candidate is a small-business owner. Most small-business owners are competent managers. No competent business manager lacks the skills necessary to be a good mayor.

Step 3: Make a Prediction

A scan of the answer choices reveals that only **(C)** can be eliminated by conclusion type alone. Because this argument relies on Formal Logic, symbolize the logic of the argument in order to make its pattern of reasoning more apparent.

If	mayoral candidate	→	small business owner

Most small business owners are competent managers

If	competent manager	→	possess mayoral skills

Therefore, most mayoral candidates possess mayoral skills.

The author falsely assumes that most of this year's candidates come from the majority of small-business owners who possess these skills.

Step 4: Evaluate the Answer Choices

(B) is the correct answer because the pattern of logic exactly matches that of the argument in the stimulus.

(A) contains a somewhat similar logical chain, but it is *not* flawed. Most managers have worked in sales; that ensures a minimum of at least a year of service and comes with an understanding of marketing. Thus, most managers meet the conditions to be certain they understand marketing.

(C) can be eliminated immediately because it has a different type of conclusion than the stimulus.

(D) contains a different flaw, a scope shift. The conclusion is about *most* films at this year's festival, while the evidence concerns avant-garde films and films under an hour long. There's no way to know this describes the majority of the films at the festival.

(E) is also flawless and, therefore, incorrect. All of the helmets at the store contain plastic. Most contain rubber, and all of those must contain plastic as well. Thus, it is true that most of the helmets in the store (all of which contain plastic) also contain rubber.

22. (A) Assumption (Sufficient)

Step 1: Identify the Question Type

The phrase "if which one of the following is assumed" identifies a Sufficient Assumption question.

Step 2: Untangle the Stimulus

The Keyword [*h*]*enc*e signals the conclusion that the invention of money probably occurred independently in more than one society. The key piece of evidence is that money is an artificial human invention and is not rooted in an innate human ability.

Step 3: Make a Prediction

The claim that an invention that is not rooted in an innate human ability must have occurred independently in different societies rests upon the assumption that there is no other way for an invention to become so widespread.

Step 4: Evaluate the Answer Choices

(A) confirms the assumption by noting that some societies have been so isolated that money must have been invented independently by at least some groups. The Denial Test shows that **(A)** is, in fact, the correct answer. If no societies have been geographically isolated enough not to have been influenced by any other society, then every society has been influenced by at least one other society. That detracts from the conclusion by providing a way that this artificial human invention could have been spread without independent creation.

(B) is irrelevant because the argument is about money, not language.

(C) distorts information in the stimulus. Furthermore, such a binary classification would not lead to the conclusion that money probably occurred independently in more than one society.

(D) is a Faulty Use of Detail because it does little more than restate the evidence.

(E) is irrelevant to whether the invention of money occurred independently.

23. (E) Principle (Identify/Strengthen)

Step 1: Identify the Question Type
This question is a Principle question; the correct answer will identify a principle that strengthens the argument.

Step 2: Untangle the Stimulus
The conclusion is that strong laws against libel can make it impossible for anyone in the public eye to have a good reputation. The Keyword *for* signals the reason for this claim, namely that no one will say anything bad about public figures.

Step 3: Make a Prediction
The assumption must connect the lack of negative comments with the impossibility of earning a good reputation. The predicted principle is that a public figure cannot have a good reputation unless some people are willing to say bad things about public figures.

Step 4: Evaluate the Answer Choices
(E) matches the substance of the prediction perfectly.

(A) does not apply to the situation because the argument concerns countries that do have strong laws against libel.

(B) does not justify the conclusion because it fails to mention the good reputations. Some public figures having bad reputations does not imply that some have good reputations.

(C) is Out of Scope; belief in one's statements does not apply here, nor is the argument concerned with determining which statements constitute libel.

(D) contradicts the evidence, which says that no one will make negative comments about public figures, so it cannot be a principle that would justify the reasoning in the argument.

24. (C) Inference

Step 1: Identify the Question Type
The phrase "most strongly supported by the information above" identifies this as an Inference question. Do not mistake this for a Strengthen question, in which the answer choices would support the argument above.

Step 2: Untangle the Stimulus
This dense stimulus contains a lot of factual information, so knowing where to start can be difficult, if not impossible. Inventory the information and note connections between the statements, but do not bog down in the technical jargon. Some mushrooms use cellulose to make beta-glucans, which can slow, reverse, or prevent cancer in mammals. The degree of antitumor activity is directly related to the degree of branching. Beta-glucans do not kill cancer cells directly; instead, they increase immune-cell activity.

Step 3: Make a Prediction
No one statement stands out as the most definite, and there is no chain of logic to make deductions from. Instead of trying to predict, evaluate the choices to determine which one follows from the facts provided. Be wary of answer choices that contain extreme statements that cannot be supported by the stimulus.

Step 4: Evaluate the Answer Choices
(C) is the correct answer, supported by the final two sentences of the stimulus. Because a greater degree of branching increases antitumor activity and because antitumor activity stimulates immune-cell activity in mammals, it must be the case that greater branching leads to greater immune-cell activity.

(A) is Extreme. Mammals may be able to obtain some benefit from eating cellulose even though they cannot directly obtain glucose from the cellulose.

(B) distorts the stimulus, which implies that if a mushroom is capable of producing beta-glucans, then extracts from that mushroom can slow, reverse, or prevent the growth of cancerous tumors in mammals. **(B)** reverses the relationship by stating that mushrooms that contain cancer-fighting agents must be able to turn cellulose into beta-glucans.

(D) distorts the last sentence of the stimulus. The beta-glucan extracts do not kill cancer cells directly, but the stimulated immune cells may, in turn, kill the cancer cells.

(E) is Extreme. The stimulus states that some organisms capable of obtaining glucose from wood can use cellulose to make beta-glucans, but **(E)** exaggerates that statement to apply it to all such organisms.

25. (C) Method of Argument

Step 1: Identify the Question Type
This question is a variant of a Method of Argument question because it asks about *how* the argument is constructed. The question stem indicates a comparison is present in the argument, and then asks for which specific comparison is made.

Step 2: Untangle the Stimulus

The conclusion of the argument is the first sentence, that a law is successful primarily because the behavior it prescribes has attained the status of custom. The Keywords "[j]ust as" signal a comparison. Just as manners are followed out of custom, so too are laws obeyed.

Step 3: Make a Prediction

The argument compares the reason that manners are followed to the reason that laws are obeyed.

Step 4: Evaluate the Answer Choices

(C) matches this analysis and is the correct answer.

(A) is Out of Scope because the argument says nothing about how manners and laws vary from society to society.

(B) fails because the argument states that laws are followed through custom, not that custom *determines* laws.

(D) is Out of Scope because ethical requirements are irrelevant in this stimulus.

(E) fails because the argument does not draw any comparison between penalties for violating manners and laws.

Section II: Logic Games

Game 1: Arts and Crafts Workshops

Q#	Question Type	Correct	Difficulty
1	Acceptability	B	★
2	Must Be False (CANNOT Be True)	D	★
3	Must Be False (CANNOT Be True)	A	★
4	"If" / Could Be True	A	★★
5	"If" / Must Be False (CANNOT Be True)	E	★★
6	How Many	C	★★

Game 2: TV Actors in Opening Credits

Q#	Question Type	Correct	Difficulty
7	Acceptability	E	★
8	Must Be False (CANNOT Be True)	C	★
9	How Many	D	★
10	"If" / Partial Acceptability	A	★★
11	"If" / Must Be True	C	★★
12	"If" / Must Be True	C	★★

Game 3: Landscaper with Mulch and Stone

Q#	Question Type	Correct	Difficulty
13	Could Be True	E	★★
14	Must Be True	D	★★
15	"If" / Must Be True	E	★★
16	"If" / Must Be True	A	★★
17	"If" / Could Be True	B	★★★

Game 4: Travel Magazine Interns

Q#	Question Type	Correct	Difficulty
18	Partial Acceptability	A	★★
19	"If" / Must Be True	B	★★★★
20	"If" / Could Be True	B	★★★
21	"If" / Could Be True	D	★★★
22	"If" / Could Be True	E	★★★
23	Must Be False (CANNOT Be True)	C	★★★

Game 1: Arts and Crafts Workshops

Step 1: Overview

Situation: Arts and crafts workshops at a community center

Entities: Six workshops—J, K, N, Q, R, S

Action: Strict Sequencing. Schedule the workshops according to when they are given.

Limitations: Exactly two workshops will be given per day, one in the morning and one in the afternoon.

Step 2: Sketch

A horizontal framework (similar to a calendar) will work well. Because this is Strict Sequencing, create a double row of dashes to indicate morning (a.m.) and afternoon (p.m.) slots in the schedule.

```
        Wed  Thu  Fri
a.m.    ___  ___  ___

p.m.    ___  ___  ___
```

Step 3: Rules

Rule 1 says Jewelry Making is a morning workshop given with either Kite Making or Quilting. Visualize this framework and sketch it accordingly.

$$\frac{J}{K} \text{ or } \frac{J}{Q}$$

Rule 2 says Rug Making is an afternoon workshop given with either Needlepoint or Scrapbooking:

$$\frac{N}{R} \text{ or } \frac{S}{R}$$

Rule 3 says Quilting has to be on an earlier day than both Kite Making and Needlepoint. This means that Quilting can't be on the last day (Friday) and that Kite Making and Needlepoint can't be on the first day (Wednesday). Build those negative deductions into your sketch and write the precise rule in shorthand nearby.

```
        Wed  Thu  Fri
a.m.    ___  ___  ___        K
                         Q <
p.m.    ___  ___  ___        N
        ~K        ~Q
        ~N
```

Step 4: Deductions

There are no major deductions to gather from combining the rules. Blocks of Entities are important in strict sequencing, but there are no defined blocks here. You might have drawn a sketch in which Jewelry Making is paired with Kite Making and

one in which Jewelry Making is paired with Quilting; however, neither of these pairings would let you definitively place the other workshops. So, there's no benefit to drawing each separately. There are Duplications (Quilting appears in both Rule 1 and Rule 3, for example), but they don't lead anywhere. Pay attention to Quilting though, as a key entity that likely will surface during the questions. Your final Master Sketch should look something like this:

```
        Wed  Thu  Fri
a.m.    ___  ___  ___            K
                           Q <
p.m.    ___  ___  ___            N
        ~K        ~Q
        ~N
```

$$\boxed{\frac{J}{K}} \text{ or } \boxed{\frac{J}{Q}} \qquad \boxed{\frac{N}{R}} \text{ or } \boxed{\frac{S}{R}}$$

Step 5: Questions

1. (B) Acceptability

Rule 1 requires Jewelry Making to be in the morning, so eliminate **(E)**. Rule 2 says Rug Making must be scheduled in the afternoon; this eliminates **(D)**. Rule 3 requires Quilting to be on an earlier day than both Kite Making and Needlepoint; this eliminates **(A)**, with Kite Making before Quilting, and **(C)** with Quilting on the same day as Needlepoint.

(B) is the only acceptable schedule.

2. (D) Must Be False (CANNOT Be True)

Here, you must determine which workshop can't be given on Thursday morning. Without many deductions so far, you must try each choice. Instead, attempt this question late in the process, after you've finished the Acceptability question and have drawn sketches for other questions. In the New-"If" question that placed Kite Making on Friday morning, you learned that Scrapbooking, Needlepoint, or Jewelry Making could be given on Thursday morning, so **(A)**, **(C)**, and **(E)** can be eliminated. This leaves Kite Making and Quilting. If Kite Making goes on Thursday morning, then Jewelry Making has to be paired with Quilting on Wednesday (so that Quilting can come before Kite Making).

```
        Wed  Thu  Fri
a.m.     J    K   ___

p.m.     Q   ___  ___
```

This forces Rug Making to Friday afternoon with either Scrapbooking or Needlepoint, which doesn't violate any rules; **(B)** must be eliminated also. That leaves **(D)** as the correct answer. If Quilting is on Thursday morning, then Jewelry Making must be paired with Kite Making on Friday to satisfy Rules 2 and 3.

	Wed	Thu	Fri
a.m.	__	Q	J
p.m.	__	__	K

But Quilting must also be given on an earlier day than Needlepoint. The sketch doesn't accommodate this situation, so Quilting on Thursday morning is impossible.

3. (A) Must Be False (CANNOT Be True)

Knowing what cannot happen is just as valuable as knowing what must happen. Always make deductions with this in mind. You already deduced that, because Quilting has to be given on an earlier day than both Kite Making and Needlepoint, neither Kite Making nor Needlepoint can be given on Wednesday. This immediately makes **(A)** false and, therefore, the correct answer.

4. (A) "If" / Could Be True

If Kite Making is given on Friday morning, then it can no longer be given on the same day as Jewelry Making. Then based on Rule 1, Jewelry Making must be given in the morning with Quilting given on the afternoon of the same day. This creates a block that can either be placed on Wednesday or Thursday.

	Wed	Thu	Fri
a.m.	J	__	K
p.m.	Q	__	__

	Wed	Thu	Fri
a.m.	__	J	K
p.m.	__	Q	__

Rug Making has to be in the afternoon on the same day as Needlepoint or Scrapbooking, so incorporate that into each sketch. Further, because Quilting has to come before both Kite Making and Needlepoint, Needlepoint has to go on Friday in the second sketch:

	Wed	Thu	Fri
a.m.	J	S/N	K
p.m.	Q	R	S/N

	Wed	Thu	Fri
a.m.	S	J	K
p.m.	R	Q	N

Considering both these sketches, only **(A)** is possible and is therefore the correct answer.

5. (E) "If" / Must Be False (CANNOT Be True)

If Quilting is given in the morning, then Jewelry Making has to be on the same day as Kite Making. But this isn't the only block created by the New-"If." Because Rug Making can never be on the same day as Quilting (Rule 2), and because Quilting has to be on an earlier day than Needlepoint (Rule 3), Quilting must be on the same day as Scrapbooking. This means that Rug Making and Needlepoint must be on the same day. Thus, the three blocks are.

J	Q	N
K	S	R

Quilting must be given on an earlier day than both Kite Making and Needlepoint, so the Quilting-Scrapbooking block must go on Wednesday, leaving each of the other blocks free to occupy either Thursday or Friday.

	Wed	Thu	Fri
a.m.	Q	J/N	N/J
p.m.	S	K/R	R/K

Thus, the only choice that must be false is **(E)**.

6. (C) How Many

This question asks how many workshops could be scheduled for Wednesday morning. You already know that of the six workshops, Kite Making and Needlepoint can't be given anytime on Wednesday. That leaves four workshops. Rug Making has to be given in the afternoon, so now only three workshops—Jewelry Making, Quilting, and Scrapbooking—are eligible to be given on Wednesday morning. This makes **(C)** correct.

If you were unsure about **(C)**, consult your previous work—in this case, question 3. In this question, **(A)** is correct, meaning that each of the remaining choices can be the schedule for Wednesday. These choices have Jewelry Making, Quilting, and Scrapbooking all as possibilities for Wednesday morning. This confirms that three workshops could be scheduled in that slot.

Game 2: TV Actors in Opening Credits

Step 1: Overview
Situation: Actors appearing in opening credits

Entities: Six actors—G, H, J, L, M, P

Action: Loose Sequencing. Sequence the actors according to when they appear in the credits. A quick glance at the rules indicates that the first three rules all indicate relative relationships so this is Loose Sequencing rather than Strict.

Limitations: The actors appear one after another, so no two actors will appear simultaneously.

Step 2: Sketch
Most of the rules provide relative order relationships between entities. Even though the final rule indicates an entity that can't fall in a certain slot, it is unlikely you'll need a series of numbered dashes as a framework. If there are questions about entities in fixed positions, then a Strict Sequencing style sketch can be drawn for those questions, but for now just work on building the loose sequence.

Step 3: Rules
Rule 1 places Lin and Mitchell before Henson.

$$\begin{array}{c} L \\ {\searrow} \\ M \quad H \end{array}$$

Rule 2 places Lin and Paredes before Jhalani; add this to your loose sequence.

$$\begin{array}{c} P \\ L \\ M \end{array} \begin{array}{c} J \\ H \end{array}$$

Rule 3 is in If/Then form, so translate and contrapose carefully.

$$\text{If } M...P \rightarrow H...G$$
$$\text{If } G...H \rightarrow P...M$$

Rule 4 is very concrete: Geyer isn't last. Even though this cannot be built directly into the loose sequence, it should still be written to the side. Do not simply try to remember rules.

Step 4: Deductions
In any Sequencing game, consider negative deductions about where entities cannot be placed. Those deductions will be valuable here, especially because there aren't any strictly defined Blocks of Entities. To determine the earliest position for an actor, count the number of actors who must come before. Jhalani must be preceded by both Paredes and Lin, so the earliest Jhalani can appear is third. The same is true for Henson, who must appear after both Lin and Mitchell. To determine an actor's latest possible position, count the number who must come after. For example, Lin must be followed by both Jhalani and Henson, so the latest Lin can appear is fourth. Because Lin, Mitchell, and Paredes all must have at least one actor after them, and because Geyer can't be last (Rule 4), the only actors that can be last are either Henson or Jhalani.

Then there's Rule 3. Expect to use this rule and its contrapositive more than once during the questions. Entering Step 5, your Master Sketch should look akin to this:

$$\begin{array}{c} P \\ L \\ M \end{array} \begin{array}{c} J \\ H \end{array}$$

$$\text{If } M...P \rightarrow H...G \qquad \text{If } G...H \rightarrow P...M$$

Step 5: Questions

7. (E) Acceptability
Rule 1 says Lin and Mitchell must both appear before Henson; this eliminates **(C)**. Rule 2 says Lin and Paredes both must precede Jhalani; this eliminates **(A)**. Rule 4 says Geyer doesn't appear last, so **(D)** is wrong. Finally, Rule 3 says that if Mitchell is earlier than Paredes, Henson must appear earlier than Geyer; **(B)** must be eliminated because it fulfills the sufficient condition but not the necessary one.

Only **(E)** remains as an acceptable answer.

8. (C) Must Be False (CANNOT Be True)
This question doesn't add any new information, so use your Master Sketch to answer it. Lin cannot appear fifth because Lin must precede both Henson and Jhalani. **(C)** must be false; therefore, it is the correct answer.

9. (D) How Many
Negative deductions are useful with this type of question. Here, there are three actors that don't have to appear before other actors—Geyer, Henson, and Jhalani. Geyer can't appear last because of Rule 4, which leaves only Henson and Jhalani. This makes **(D)** correct.

10. (A) "If" / Partial Acceptability
Redraw the loose sequence, incorporating the new information.

$$\begin{array}{c} G \\ P \quad / \quad \backslash \\ {>}J—M—H \\ L \end{array}$$

With Jhalani earlier than Mitchell, the only actor who can appear last is Henson, making **(A)** the correct answer.

11. (C) "If" / Must Be True

This New-"If" has Lin appearing right before Geyer, so redraw.

Also, because Geyer now appears before Henson, the contrapositive of Rule 3 is triggered, and Paredes must appear before Mitchell.

Now Lin must appear before at least three other actors (Geyer, Jhalani, and Henson), so the latest Lin can appear is third. Therefore, **(C)** must be true. Each of the other choices could be false.

(A) could be false because Geyer could appear fourth. Geyer only needs to appear before Jhalani and Henson.

(B) could be false because Jhalani could appear last.

(D) could be false because Mitchell could appear after Geyer—as long as Mitchell is before Henson.

(E) could be false because Lin could also appear first; no one must be before Lin.

12. (C) "If" / Must Be True

If Mitchell appears first, then Mitchell certainly appears before Paredes, which means Henson must appear before Geyer (Rule 3). If Henson can no longer appear last, then Jhalani appears sixth.

That's already enough to identify **(C)** as the correct answer. Each of the other choices could be false.

Geyer only has to be preceded by Mitchell, Lin, and Henson, so Geyer could appear fourth, which eliminates **(A)**.

(B) could be false because Henson could appear as late as fourth without violating any rules (if Geyer appears fifth and Jhalani appears sixth).

(D) could be false because Lin could appear third, followed by Henson, Geyer, and Jhalani.

Jhalani is the only actor who must appear after Paredes, so Paredes could appear fifth, which means **(E)** could be false.

Game 3: Landscaper with Mulch and Stone

Step 1: Overview

Situation: A truck hauling seven loads of either just mulch or just stone

Entities: Seven loads of material—three are mulch and four are stone, but beyond that, they're indistinguishable

Action: Strict Sequencing. Determine the order of the loads.

Limitations: The cargo bed must be cleaned before switching to a different type of material. Expect that limitation to resurface in the rules and questions.

Step 2: Sketch

Because the numerical order of the loads is referenced in the game, a series of seven numbered dashes is a useful framework. Also, when listing these entities, write three Ms and four Ss to keep track of them.

M M M S S S S

___ ___ ___ ___ ___ ___ ___
 1   2   3   4   5   6   7

Step 3: Rules

Rule 1 states the cargo bed can be cleaned a maximum of three times. Take this rule out of the abstract and turn it into something you can see in the sketch. Anytime you see S-M or M-S in the sequence, the cargo bed needs to be cleaned. This means that the sequence can switch from mulch to stone (or vice versa) up to three times in the sequence.

| S M | or | M S | → cleaning

Max 3 cleanings

Rule 2 is the more concrete of the two rules: the fifth load must be mulch. Fill that in immediately.

M̸ M M S S S S

___ ___ ___ ___ M ___ ___
 1   2   3   4   5   6   7

Step 4: Deductions

You only have three mulch loads in the sequence, one of which must be the fifth load. If you separate two mulch loads with at least one stone load, the cargo bed will have to be cleaned twice—once to switch from mulch to stone, and again to switch back to mulch. The same is true in the reverse. If you switch from stone to mulch and then back to stone, the cargo bed will have to be cleaned twice. It's impossible to have all three mulch loads separated because that would require at

least four cleanings. Thus, any acceptable order would require at least two consecutive mulch loads (all three together would work as well). Similarly, it's impossible to have all four stone loads separated. In fact, the stone must be hauled in no more than two groups of consecutive loads, that is, two pairs of consecutive loads or a single load and a series of three consecutive loads. Four consecutive loads of stone would be fine, too. Build those deductions into the Master Sketch:

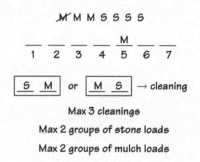

M̸ M M S S S S

___ ___ ___ ___ M ___ ___
 1   2   3   4   5   6   7

| S M | or | M S | → cleaning

Max 3 cleanings

Max 2 groups of stone loads

Max 2 groups of mulch loads

Don't be nervous about attempting questions with so little deduced. With only two rules, you won't be able to gather a lot of information in advance. Three of the five questions have New-"If" conditions, so you'll make more deductions using the information added by those questions. Consider trying those New-"If" questions first.

Step 5: Questions

13. (E) Could Be True

You don't have many exact deductions, but your deductions about the groupings of loads will be useful as you eliminate any choice that must be false.

(A) is false because you know there must be at least two consecutive mulch loads.

(B) is also false. If the second, third, and fifth loads are mulch, then the stone loads will be split into three groups.

S	M	M	S	M	S	S
1	2	3	4	5	6	7

↑ clean   ↑ clean   ↑ clean   ↑ clean

This goes against your initial deductions and violates the rule requiring a maximum of three cleanings.

(C) is false because it would also split the stone loads into three groups.

S	M	S	S	M	M	S
1	2	3	4	5	6	7

↑ clean   ↑ clean   ↑ clean   ↑ clean

(D) also creates three groups of stone loads and, therefore, must be false.

$$\begin{array}{ccccccc} \underline{S} & \underline{S} & \underline{M} & \underline{S} & \underline{M} & \underline{M} & \underline{S} \\ 1 & 2 & 3 & 4 & 5 & 6 & 7 \\ \uparrow & \uparrow & \uparrow & & \uparrow & & \\ \text{clean} & \text{clean} & \text{clean} & & \text{clean} & & \end{array}$$

(E) would only require two cleanings of the cargo bed and, therefore, is acceptable.

$$\begin{array}{ccccccc} \underline{S} & \underline{S} & \underline{S} & \underline{M} & \underline{M} & \underline{M} & \underline{S} \\ 1 & 2 & 3 & 4 & 5 & 6 & 7 \\ & & & \uparrow & & & \uparrow \\ & & & \text{clean} & & & \text{clean} \end{array}$$

14. (D) Must Be True

When you've made at least one major deduction, look for a "must be true" question to reward you with a point. Here, **(D)** states a deduction you already made.

(A) The second load could be mulch, so this choice doesn't have to be true as in the following sequence.

$$\begin{array}{ccccccc} \underline{M} & \underline{M} & \underline{S} & \underline{S} & \underline{M} & \underline{S} & \underline{S} \\ 1 & 2 & 3 & 4 & 5 & 6 & 7 \\ & & \uparrow & & \uparrow & \uparrow & \\ & & \text{clean} & & \text{clean} & \text{clean} & \end{array}$$

(B) The first two loads could be different materials.

$$\begin{array}{ccccccc} \underline{M} & \underline{S} & \underline{S} & \underline{S} & \underline{M} & \underline{M} & \underline{S} \\ 1 & 2 & 3 & 4 & 5 & 6 & 7 \\ \uparrow & & & & \uparrow & & \uparrow \\ \text{clean} & & & & \text{clean} & & \text{clean} \end{array}$$

(C) The sketch drawn for **(B)** shows that this could be false and, therefore, is incorrect.

(E) The sketch drawn for **(A)** shows that the four loads of stone could be hauled in pairs of two.

15. (E) "If" / Must Be True

If the third load is mulch, then there's only one more load of mulch to place in the sequence. Even if you're not sure where it must go, you are sure that it cannot go first or seventh because either of those placements would prevent any consecutive loads of mulch. If the first and seventh loads can't be mulch, they must both be stone.

$$\begin{array}{ccccccc} \underline{S} & \underline{} & \underline{M} & \underline{} & \underline{M} & \underline{} & \underline{S} \\ 1 & 2 & 3 & 4 & 5 & 6 & 7 \end{array}$$

Thus **(E)** must be true.

16. (A) "If" / Must Be True

If the cargo bed is only cleaned twice, that means you must see exactly two M-S or S-M blocks. There are only two ways to

accomplish this given that the fifth load is mulch. The mulch loads can be third, fourth, and fifth, or they can be fourth, fifth, and sixth.

$$\begin{array}{ccccccc} \underline{S} & \underline{S} & \underline{M} & \underline{M} & \underline{M} & \underline{S} & \underline{S} \\ 1 & 2 & 3 & 4 & 5 & 6 & 7 \\ & & \uparrow & & & \uparrow & \\ & & \text{clean} & & & \text{clean} & \end{array}$$

$$\begin{array}{ccccccc} \underline{S} & \underline{S} & \underline{S} & \underline{M} & \underline{M} & \underline{M} & \underline{S} \\ 1 & 2 & 3 & 4 & 5 & 6 & 7 \\ & & & \uparrow & & & \uparrow \\ & & & \text{clean} & & & \text{clean} \end{array}$$

In both cases, **(A)** is the only answer choice that is always true. Each of the other choices is false in at least one of the two sketches here.

17. (B) "If" / Could Be True

For this question, no more than two loads can be hauled simultaneously. But you already know that at least two loads of each material must be hauled simultaneously. This creates the following blocks, which must alternate: S-S, S-S, M-M, and M.

Given that mulch must be the fifth load, there are only two possible sequences.

$$\begin{array}{ccccccc} \underline{M} & \underline{M} & \underline{S} & \underline{S} & \underline{M} & \underline{S} & \underline{S} \\ 1 & 2 & 3 & 4 & 5 & 6 & 7 \end{array}$$

$$\begin{array}{ccccccc} \underline{M} & \underline{S} & \underline{S} & \underline{M} & \underline{M} & \underline{S} & \underline{S} \\ 1 & 2 & 3 & 4 & 5 & 6 & 7 \end{array}$$

Considering both these possibilities, only **(B)** could be true. Every other choice must be false.

Game 4: Travel Magazine Interns

Step 1: Overview

Situation: Assigning interns for a travel magazine

Entities: Six interns—F, G, H, J, K, L

Action: Distribution/Matching Hybrid. Determine the assignment of interns to two fields—three photographer's assistants and three writer's assistants—to each of three countries.

Limitations: Exactly two interns will be assigned to each country—one photographer's assistant and one writer's assistant.

Step 2: Sketch

Try to incorporate both the Matching and Distribution into your Master Sketch. A table works best.

F G H J K L

	Rom	Sp	Tus
photog's asst ___ ___ ___			
writer's asst ___ ___ ___			

Step 3: Rules

Rule 1 states Gombarick and Lha are trained in the same field (writing or photography), meaning they will both appear in the same row of your sketch.

G and L—always same row

Rule 2 states Farber and Kanze are in different fields and, therefore, in different rows of the sketch. Push this rule further: this means that of F and K, one will appear in the "writer's assistant" row and one will appear in the "photographer's assistant" row. Fill that in along with the next three rules, all of which are Master-Sketch-friendly.

Rules 3, 4, and 5 all provide information that can be built right into the Master Sketch. Hall is a photographer's assistant (Rule 3); Jackson is assigned to Tuscany (Rule 4); Kanze can't be assigned to Spain (Rule 5).

F G H J K L

	Rom	Sp	Tus
photog's asst H F/K			
writer's asst K/F			
		~K	J↑

Step 4: Deductions

In games involving Distribution, always look for Blocks of Entities (or pairs that can never be blocks). Chances are that those blocks will only fit into the sketch in one or two ways. In this case, because Farber and Kanze must be in different fields, and because Hall is already a photographer's assistant, there's only one field for Gombarick and Lha: writer's assistant. This leaves the only open slot in the photographer's assistant row for Jackson. Now you know that Jackson is the photographer's assistant assigned to Tuscany.

The Numbers are already worked out in the opening paragraph—two interns per country, three interns per field. Whenever you're matching or distributing a set of entities, make sure you have the number possibilities as fully determined as you can before you do the questions. Your final Master Sketch should look something like this:

F G H J K L

	Rom	Sp	Tus
photog's asst H F/K J			J
writer's asst K/F G L			
		~K	J↑

Because you have a lot of solid deductions and because the interns are nearly completely distributed to their fields, the non New-"If" questions can be handled quickly. If you didn't make those deductions however, the New-"If" questions would be best to do first (after you've handled the Acceptability question).

Step 5: Questions

18. (A) Partial Acceptability

Rule 1 requires Gombarick and Lha to be in the same field; this eliminates **(B)**. Rule 3 says Hall must be a photographer's assistant; this eliminates **(D)**. Rule 5 prohibits Kanze from being assigned to Spain; this eliminates **(E)**. Finally, Rule 2 says Farber and Kanze must be in different fields, so you must see exactly one of them in each field; this eliminates **(C)**.

Only **(A)** remains and must therefore be correct.

19. (B) "If" / Must Be True

For this question, eliminate any choice that could be false. The New-"If" doesn't restrict Farber's field, so consider both possibilities. If Farber is the photographer's assistant in Romania, then Kanze is a writer's assistant, and Hall is assigned to Spain.

F G H J K L

	Rom	Sp	Tus
photog's asst H F J	F	H	J
writer's asst K G L		G/L	

~K   J↑

If Farber is the writer's assistant in Romania, then Kanze is a photographer's assistant assigned to Romania, meaning Hall is still assigned to Spain.

F G H J K L

	Rom	Sp	Tus
photog's asst H K J	K	H	J
writer's asst F G L	F	G/L	L/G

~K   J↑

This makes **(B)** your answer.

20. (B) "If" / Could Be True
If Farber and Hall are assigned to the same story, then Farber must be a writer's assistant, which makes Kanze a photographer's assistant, as in the previous question. Because Kanze can't be in Spain, assign Kanze to Romania and Hall to Spain (along with Farber).

F G H J K L

	Rom	Sp	Tus
photog's asst H K J	K	H	J
writer's asst F G L	G/L	F	L/G

~K   J↑

In this case, only **(B)** could be true. Every other choice must be false.

21. (D) "If" / Could Be True
If Farber is a writer's assistant, then Kanze is a photographer's assistant who must now be assigned to Romania (Kanze can't go to Spain and Jackson is in Tuscany). This forces Hall to go to Spain.

F G H J K L

	Rom	Sp	Tus
photog's asst H K J	K	H	J
writer's asst F G L			

~K   J↑

Therefore, eliminate **(A)**, **(B)**, and **(E)**. Also eliminate **(C)** because Kanze can't be paired with Hall on the same story. **(D)**, however, could be true because Lha could fill the writer's assistant slot in Romania. Note that this question could also be answered using the sketch from the previous question.

22. (E) "If" / Could Be True
Because Gombarick is a writer's assistant, the only way for Gombarick and Kanze to be assigned to the same story is if Kanze is a photographer's assistant. This makes Farber a writer's assistant. Thus, the only available slot for Kanze is in Romania. Due to this New-"If," Gombarick must go to Romania also, leaving Farber and Lha to go to either Spain or Tuscany.

F G H J K L

	Rom	Sp	Tus
photog's asst H K J	K	H	J
writer's asst F G L	G	F/L	L/F

~K   J↑

With this sketch, only **(E)** could be true.

23. (C) Must Be False (CANNOT Be True)
Here you must eliminate any choice that can be assigned to Tuscany. In the Master Sketch, the writer's assistant row is virtually unrestricted, so any of Farber, Kanze, Gombarick, and Lha could be the writer's assistant in Tuscany; eliminate **(A)**, **(B)**, **(D)**, and **(E)**, leaving **(C)** as the correct answer. Hall is a photographer's assistant (Rule 3). Because Jackson already is the photographer's assistant for Tuscany, Hall cannot be assigned there.

Section III: Logical Reasoning

Q#	Question Type	Correct	Difficulty
1	Paradox	A	★
2	Strengthen	B	★
3	Assumption (Sufficient)	A	★
4	Weaken	B	★
5	Role of a Statement	D	★
6	Parallel Reasoning	D	★
7	Role of a Statement	C	★
8	Flaw	C	★
9	Principle (Identify/Strengthen)	C	★
10	Inference	C	★
11	Assumption (Necessary)	D	★★
12	Inference	E	★
13	Weaken	D	★★
14	Inference	D	★
15	Main Point	D	★★
16	Flaw	E	★★
17	Inference	D	★★★
18	Principle (Apply/Inference)	C	★★
19	Flaw	D	★★★
20	Strengthen	A	★★★★
21	Strengthen	E	★★★★
22	Assumption (Necessary)	A	★★★★
23	Parallel Flaw	C	★★★
24	Principle (Identify/Strengthen)	B	★★★
25	Point at Issue	C	★

1. (A) Paradox

Step 1: Identify the Question Type

This Paradox question is identified by the phrase "explain the discrepancy." This stem is especially helpful as it points out where this discrepancy will arise; the correct answer will explain the difference between the intended versus the actual results of the highway improvements.

Step 2: Untangle the Stimulus

Paraphrase the discrepancy. The purpose of making the highway improvements is to reduce traffic jams and delays. However, once these improvements are made, the traffic jams and delays actually increase.

Step 3: Make a Prediction

The correct answer will describe a way these improvements exacerbate the problem that they were intended to fix. Because this could be a number of things, evaluate the answer choices boldly. Eliminate any answer choices that do not resolve the issue.

Step 4: Evaluate the Answer Choices

(A) provides something about these highway improvements that makes matters worse: Such improvements bring in more traffic than before. That helps resolve the paradox, certainly.

(B) does not resolve the issue. Whether these improvements are undertaken when the population is in an upswing, downswing, or has leveled off does not explain why there are more delays and traffic congestion than before the improvements are made.

(C) deepens the mystery. If the rate of accidents were to decrease with these improvements, one might expect to see fewer delays rather than an increase in congestion. This choice serves to make the actual results that much more inexplicable.

(D) is Out of Scope. The author is concerned with traffic Issues in general, not the types of vehicles on the roads.

(E) is an Irrelevant Comparison. The comparison between the rates of traffic in urban areas versus rural/suburban areas has no effect on the discrepancy.

2. (B) Strengthen

Step 1: Identify the Question Type

For this Strengthen question, the answer choice will make the conclusion more likely to be true by confirming the author's central assumption.

Step 2: Untangle the Stimulus

Apparently signals the author's conclusion: the ads that come over the supermarket's audio system are effective. The support given states that customers who completed their purchases within 40 minutes of these ads being played were significantly more likely to purchase the products advertised than customers who checked out prior to the airing.

Step 3: Make a Prediction

Here, the author assumes that the advertisements *caused* people to purchase these items. To support this argument, look for a fact that confirms the causal link.

Step 4: Evaluate the Answer Choices

(B) strengthens the stimulus by eliminating a potential weakener: consumers did not go to the store intending to buy the product. If that's the case, it stands to reason that something that happened in the store—inferably the ads played on the audio system—caused them to buy the product.

(A) can be eliminated because it is irrelevant how many people went through the checkout lines before or after the ad was aired. What matters is how many bought the product before or after the ad was aired.

(C) goes wrong in two ways. Firstly, it does not clarify which consumers reported buying the advertised products (were they the ones who heard the ads or not?) In addition, it works against the author's argument by claiming that many consumers buy some of the advertised products on a regular basis regardless of ads played in the store.

(D) has no effect on the argument. If consumers don't recall hearing the ad, then it might or might not have affected their buying decision. Perhaps they responded to it subliminally, perhaps not.

(E) works against the argument. If many consumers already buy these products on occasion, it's less likely the ads influenced their purchase decisions.

3. (A) Assumption (Sufficient)

Step 1: Identify the Question Type

The question stem asks for a sufficient assumption. The correct answer will provide a missing link between the evidence and conclusion that will allow the conclusion to be logically drawn.

Step 2: Untangle the Stimulus

The conclusion follows the Keyword *so* and states that the new library will not be completed on schedule. Note the Formal Logic word [*u*]*nless* in the first sentence. The author provides two conditions that guarantee the conclusion: failure to obtain the building permit by February 1, or failure to complete other work on the library construction plan ahead of schedule. Finally, the author reveals that the building permit will not be obtained by February 1.

Step 3: Make a Prediction

Consider all of the evidence given to identify the gap in an author's logic.

The author has ruled out one of the ways to meet the planned construction schedule and thus concludes that the library will not be completed on time. To be certain of this, he must have assumed the other sufficient condition will not be met (i.e.

that none of the other activities required for construction can be completed ahead of schedule).

Step 4: Evaluate the Answer Choices

(A) matches the prediction perfectly: nothing will be completed early. That's enough to ensure the author's conclusion follows logically.

(B) is irrelevant. Whether or not the officials admit, deny, or refuse to comment on the status of completion has no effect on the author's argument.

(C) merely confirms a portion of the author's evidence (the building permit will not be obtained on time), but it doesn't provide any new information about the other possible way to hit the scheduled deadline.

(D) is irrelevant. Initial rejection and subsequent resubmission of the building permit application is immaterial. You know that it will not be obtained by February 1; the reason for this doesn't matter.

(E) eliminates a potential workaround, confirming that, indeed, construction cannot start until the permit is received. It does not address the other way the building could be completed on time.

4. (B) Weaken

Step 1: Identify the Question Type

This is a clearly worded Weaken question. The correct answer choice will be the only one to present a fact that makes the author's assumption less likely to be true.

Step 2: Untangle the Stimulus

The argument's conclusion appears at the end of the stimulus, signaled by "this study shows that." The author concludes that the smell of peppermint worsens insomnia. The evidentiary basis for this is that participants in a sleep clinic study inhaled peppermint or bitter orange scents and those who smelled peppermint had more trouble falling asleep. You're also told that bitter orange does not help people fall asleep more easily.

Step 3: Make a Prediction

The author's assumption is quite broad here; he assumes there's no reason other than the smell of peppermint for those participants to have more trouble falling asleep than those who smelled bitter orange. A weakener will show that assumption to be invalid, likely by providing an alternate explanation for this phenomenon.

Step 4: Evaluate the Answer Choices

(B) provides that reason: the peppermint participants had worse cases of insomnia to begin with. If that's true, then it's less likely that peppermint exacerbated their cases of insomnia.

(A) is Out of Scope. The argument never addresses people who do not suffer from insomnia.

(C) is irrelevant. Whether or not the people knew that what they were inhaling was part of a study would not necessarily have any effect on the physiological effects of the scents.

(D) is Out of Scope. This study focused on patients' abilities to fall asleep in the first place, not whether they have difficulty staying asleep.

(E) has no definitive effect on the force of the argument. First, the stimulus makes no mention of whether either the peppermint or the bitter orange scent qualifies as *pleasant*. In addition, the nature of the "dramatic effect" is unknown: Is it a positive or negative effect? Without these pieces of information, this choice does nothing to weaken the author's conclusion.

5. (D) Role of a Statement

Step 1: Identify the Question Type

You're asked to determine how a particular claim "figures in the argument." That phrasing identifies this as a Role of a Statement question. Untangle the stimulus as usual and determine whether the claim in question is part of the evidence or the conclusion; refine from there if necessary.

Step 2: Untangle the Stimulus

The claim that "[d]ogs learn best when they are trained using both voice commands and hand signals" appears as the first sentence in the argument. Pay attention to the Keywords that follow that sentence. "After all" indicates that what follows is support for the claim that precedes it.

Step 3: Make a Prediction

The claim mentioned in the question stem is the author's conclusion. The author uses the results of the study cited in the remainder of the stimulus to support the contention that dogs learn best when they are trained a certain way.

Step 4: Evaluate the Answer Choices

(D) correctly identifies the role of the statement in question.

(A) is incorrect because the statement is not a premise (evidence); it's the main conclusion.

(B) is incorrect because the claim is directly stated in the stimulus; it's not an implicit (unstated) assumption.

(C) is incorrect because the statement is the conclusion, not background information.

(E) is incorrect because this argument has just one conclusion, in the first sentence. The study used as evidence is the only other part of the stimulus, and even it contains no intermediate conclusion(s).

6. (D) Parallel Reasoning

Step 1: Identify the Question Type

This question asks you to identify the answer choice with reasoning "most similar" to that found in the stimulus. This is typical Parallel Reasoning language, so the correct answer must contain the same type of conclusion, supported by the same type of evidence, as the argument given.

Step 2: Untangle the Stimulus
The stimulus is short, so paraphrase the entire argument in a single statement: It is *unlikely* that a test pilot will have trouble operating a plane tomorrow, because many other test pilots have not experienced difficulty operating that plane.

Step 3: Make a Prediction
Decide whether it will be simpler to characterize and compare individual components of the argument or to abstract the entire structure before you begin to evaluate each answer choice.

Now, characterize the conclusion and evidence within the argument: it is unlikely that a certain member of a group (a test pilot) will experience something (difficulty operating the plane) because *many* other members of that group have not had such an experience. Note the qualification of *unlikely* in the conclusion and *many* in the evidence. Such qualifications must also be present in the correct answer choice.

Step 4: Evaluate the Answer Choices
(D) mimics that same reasoning: It is *unlikely* that a certain member of a group (a reviewer) will experience something (enjoy the book) because *many* other members of that group have not had such an experience. It's a perfect match.

(A) is incorrect because it says the experience is *likely*, not *unlikely*. In addition, it uses different terms in the conclusion and evidence ("book reviewers" versus "average reader", "well written" versus "enjoy").

(B) is incorrect because it uses different terms in the conclusion and evidence ("book reviewers" versus "people," "very entertaining" versus "boring").

(C) is incorrect because it says "neither of the two" rather than *many* reviewers in the evidence. Also, it states these two are reviewers who *enjoyed* the novel, but in the conclusion it refers to an upcoming review without indicating whether that review's author enjoyed the novel.

(E) fails to demonstrate parallel structure both because it contains a more extreme conclusion (*anyone*) and it references different groups in the conclusion and evidence ("reviewers" versus "general public").

7. (C) Role of a Statement

Step 1: Identify the Question Type
This is a slightly different wording than is typical for a Role of a Statement question. The question stem is asking for the *point*, or purpose/role, of the scientist's mention of astrology in the argument. A quick glance at the answer choices indicates it is an example of something. Keep that in mind.

Step 2: Untangle the Stimulus
The author establishes that in order for a theory to be taken seriously, it must impact how we see the world. The author then affirms that such impact is necessary, but not sufficient, for theories to be taken seriously. To emphasize this latter point, the author refers to the example of astrology.

Step 3: Make a Prediction
Use clues given to you in the question stem and answer choices to predict efficiently.

Astrology is used as an example of a theory that has the ability to affect how we see the world yet need not be taken seriously.

Step 4: Evaluate the Answer Choices
(C) matches the prediction.

(A) is incorrect because astrology is used as an example of a theory that does indeed affect our perception of the world. It is unknown why it should still not be taken seriously.

(B) is Out of Scope. This stimulus speaks only to theories and whether they should be taken seriously. The question of whether an idea should be considered a theory at all is not discussed.

(D) is incorrect because astrology is used as an example of a theory that should *not* be taken seriously.

(E) is a 180. Astrology is used as an example of a theory that should *not* be taken seriously, even though it does affect our perception of the world.

8. (C) Flaw

Step 1: Identify the Question Type
Using the typical "most vulnerable to criticism" wording, this Flaw question asks for a problem with Clark's reasoning. A brief glance at the answer choices indicates that the correct answer choice will cite the type of flaw, as well as how that flaw is characterized in the argument.

Step 2: Untangle the Stimulus
Clark contends that his neighbor Michaela must be a critically acclaimed playwright because the theater performing her new play cites critical acclaim as a main factor in its selection process.

Step 3: Make a Prediction
The correct answer to an LSAT Flaw question should describe (often in general terms) why the evidence fails to provide sufficient support for the conclusion.

The problem with Clark's logic is that he's mistaking something that is one factor in the selection process as a required characteristic of any play performed by the theater. The stimulus never states that critical acclaim is either sufficient or necessary for selection.

Step 4: Evaluate the Answer Choices

(C) matches the prediction; it correctly identifies the flaw in the author's reasoning.

(A) is the wrong flaw because critical acclaim is neither sufficient nor necessary for performance by the theater. The author is falsely assuming it's a necessary condition, but that doesn't match the flaw described here.

(B) is the wrong flaw because the author does not rely on a cause-and-effect relationship in the argument. Rather, the author cites only one factor for consideration and claims the play must meet that condition.

(D) questions the reliability of the source that provided the evidence, but its reliability is not in question.

(E)'s mention of whether the playwright's critical acclaim preceded or resulted from the selection of her play as a featured performance is irrelevant.

9. (C) Principle (Identify/Strengthen)

Step 1: Identify the Question Type

This Principle question asks you to identify the broad principle underlying the legal theorist's argument. Look for the author's central assumption to be worded in general terms in the correct answer choice.

Step 2: Untangle the Stimulus

The legal theorist's conclusion is the first sentence: governments should not be permitted to use an individual's personal diaries as a source of incriminating evidence against that individual. The evidence follows: diaries are described as being silent conversations with the writer and, as such, no different from personal thoughts.

Step 3: Make a Prediction

Only the conclusion mentions incriminating evidence, while the support the legal theorist provides does nothing more than outline similarities between a diary and an individual's thoughts. Here, the theorist must assume that one's private thoughts ought to be kept off the record, regardless of how those thoughts are expressed (aloud, written, or kept to oneself). The key issue here is intent. If the thoughts were intended to be private, they should not be used in criminal prosecution.

Step 4: Evaluate the Answer Choices

(C) correctly outlines the principle underlying the theorist's reasoning with its mention of the intent behind individuals' remarks.

(A) is Out of Scope. Neither corporations nor interoffice memos are ever discussed in the theorist's argument.

(B) is Out of Scope. The legal theorist never gives the precondition of severe crime as a reason to reevaluate the restrictions on evidence admissibility.

(D) is too broad. The theorist never contends that the government should never confiscate personal correspondence as a general rule; instead he confines his assessment to the content of personal diaries.

(E) is Extreme and goes against the argument presented by the legal theorist, who maintains that there ought to be limits on how far governments can exercise power to prosecute suspected criminals.

10. (C) Inference

Step 1: Identify the Question Type

In typical Inference question style, you're asked to identify the choice that is supported by the statements above. Accept each statement as true, seek out Formal Logic, and pay careful attention to the level of certainty exhibited by the language in the stimulus. The correct answer choice is the one that is supported by the stimulus, provided the given theories are correct.

Step 2: Untangle the Stimulus

Evaluate the stimulus, statement by statement. A flickering gas ring orbits a black hole. In addition, the rate of flickering could be attributable to the size of its radius. Lastly, a conditional statement: the black hole must be spinning for the gas ring to maintain an orbit with this radius.

Step 3: Make a Prediction

When a question stem provides you with extra information, use that to your advantage.

When Formal Logic is present in a stimulus, expect the test maker to assess your understanding of what must be true on the basis of these statements. Given that the physical theories relating the rate of flickering and orbit size are correct, it must be true that the black hole is spinning.

Step 4: Evaluate the Answer Choices

(C) matches the prediction precisely. That means the wrong answer choices are either merely possible or contradictory.

(A) is merely possible. Only a condition requiring spinning black holes is mentioned. What is true of stationary black holes is never discussed.

(B) is merely possible. What must be true about gas rings emitting flickering X-rays is not discussed.

(D) is merely possible. Why the black holes are spinning is never discussed.

(E) is merely possible. What is true of stationary black holes is never discussed; this is the same reason **(A)** was discarded.

11. (D) Assumption (Necessary)

Step 1: Identify the Question Type
For this Assumption question, the correct answer choice will provide a missing piece of evidence that is necessary for the conclusion to be valid.

Step 2: Untangle the Stimulus
First, identify the conclusion, which is signaled by the Keyword [*t*]*herefore*: the black water phenomenon that struck the bay last year is the worst it ever could have been in the past 200 years. The author's evidence is the fact that this phenomenon wiped out five species of coral, some of which were over 200 years old.

Step 3: Make a Prediction
The evidence unequivocally states that last year's black water phenomenon wiped out five species of coral that had survived for over two centuries, but that does not necessarily relate to the intensity of the phenomenon experienced last year. What's missing is some assurance that nothing other than the most intense black water could have destroyed these coral species.

Step 4: Evaluate the Answer Choices
(D) gets it right by eliminating the possibility of a preexisting condition (something else besides the black water phenomenon) that contributed to the coral loss. Because this question asks for a necessary assumption, you can check with the Denial Test: if it were true that the mounds of coral were especially fragile, then it might not be true that the intensity of last year's event was markedly worse.

(A) has no effect on the author's conclusion. The frequency, or infrequency, of the black water phenomenon does not relate to the severity of any one occurrence.

(B) is too broad to be something required in order for the conclusion to be true. It need not be true that every species of coral in the bay was seriously harmed from last year's event. Rather, the correct answer need only confirm that the five species of coral in question were wiped out due to the devastating severity of last year's event—the worst in 200 years.

(C) is Out of Scope. The effect (or lack thereof) of the black water on species that utilize coral Is not at issue and thus cannot confirm the author's conclusion about the intensity of the phenomenon; if anything, the lack of damage to these organisms would imply the phenomenon was not exceptionally intense.

(E) is an Irrelevant Comparison. The distinction between older versus younger coral specimens is immaterial to the author's conclusion.

12. (E) Inference

Step 1: Identify the Question Type
This is clearly worded Inference question, so the correct answer choice to must be true in light of the statements presented in the stimulus. Accept each statement as true, seek out Formal Logic, and pay careful attention to the level of certainty of the language in the stimulus.

Step 2: Untangle the Stimulus
Paraphrase the stimulus piece by piece. The term "miniature," although used by many nurseries to label fruit trees, is not used in the same way by all nurseries. Take, for example, the Stark Sweet Melody nectarine tree. Some nurseries label it exclusively as miniature, while others do not. What is certain, though, is the Formal Logic relationship in the final statement:

	a fruit tree variety is not suitable for growing in a tub or a pot	→	**not correctly labeled "miniature"**
If			

Step 3: Make a Prediction
The contrapositive of the Formal Logic here reads as follows:

	correctly labeled "miniature"	→	**suitable for growing in a tub or pot**
If			

Survey the answer choices to find the one that must be true.

Step 4: Evaluate the Answer Choices
(E) provides a correct translation of the Formal Logic statement (recall that *unless* translates as "if not.") So, if the Stark Sweet Melody tree is not suitable for growing in a tub or a pot, then some nurseries mislabel it as miniature. From the example in the stimulus, you already know that some nurseries label these trees as miniature. Thus, **(E)** must be true.

(A) is too broad. There's no way to know what [*m*]*ost* nurseries do, given the stimulus speaks only to "[m]any nurseries." Further, only the Stark Sweet Melody variety of nectarine trees is addressed here, not fruit trees in general.

(B) reverses the relationship with its use of *unsuitable*. That directly contradicts the assertion in the stimulus that the labeling is correct only if the trees are *suitable* for growing in a tub or pot.

(C) is Extreme. Miniature trees are only mislabeled if they are not suitable for growing in a tub or a pot. It is unknown that *every* Stark Sweet Melody tree is unsuitable in this way.

(D) is possible but not necessarily true. It could be true that at least one nectarine tree is indeed miniature but is not labeled as such. However, that is not a known fact based on this stimulus.

13. (D) Weaken

Step 1: Identify the Question Type
For this Weaken question, the correct answer will provide additional information that would make the assumption less likely to be true.

Step 2: Untangle the Stimulus
The psychologist's conclusion (signaled by [*t*]*hus*) is that many of our tendencies are genetic, rather than influenced by our environment (nature, not nurture). The psychologist's evidence is that identical twins (with the same genetic makeup) separated at birth still develop the same ethical beliefs, manner of dress, and career paths.

Step 3: Make a Prediction
The author's underlying assumption is that the similarities are solely due to the twins' genetic makeup, because they grew up in different environments. The correct answer choice will present a fact that contradicts that assumption. Perhaps something else accounted for these similarities, or maybe other identical twins do not grow up to have such similar tendencies.

Step 4: Evaluate the Answer Choices
(D) provides such a fact. If it's true that identical twins that grow up together develop different tendencies, than it's likely that something besides genetics gives rise to their tendencies.

(A) has no effect on the psychologist's argument. The issue is whether nature or nurture gives rise to certain lifestyle decisions, not when they occur or how radical the changes are.

(B) does not hurt the psychologist's argument. Notice that the psychologist qualifies that genetics is the reason for "many of our inclinations," not all. So this allows for a "few differences."

(C) has no effect on the psychologist's argument. The issue is whether genetics in general gives rise to particular behavioral patterns. No judgment is made as to which genes cause certain tendencies.

(E) is Out of Scope. Nonidentical twins are never discussed.

14. (D) Inference

Step 1: Identify the Question Type
The correct answer to this Inference question will provide a statement that logically completes the last sentence by connecting information presented in the stimulus.

Step 2: Untangle the Stimulus
Evaluate each statement in the stimulus. Note the Formal Logic present. The first statement's translation and contrapositive are:

If	humans happy	→	love and friendship primary motives
If	love and friendship are not primary motives	→	humans not happy

However, economic needs can be met in the absence of love or friendship to motivate actions. The author points to the example of a merchant society, which merely requires that economic utility motivates action.

Step 3: Make a Prediction
Note how these statements can be connected. Economic needs can be met without love or friendship to motivate actions, but if that's the case, then it must be true that humans are not living happily in that society.

Step 4: Evaluate the Answer Choices
(D) makes that connection between the first and second statements, thus providing an inferable conclusion to fill in the blank at the end of the stimulus.

(A) is Extreme. It need not be true that economic utility and love/friendship are mutually exclusive motivators within any given society. Perhaps all three could be simultaneous motivators.

(B) contradicts the stimulus. If economic needs can be met in the absence of happiness, then happiness does not require that economic needs are met.

(C) is Out of Scope. How economic needs are satisfied is never discussed.

(E) contradicts the stimulus. If economic needs can be met in the absence of factors required for happiness, then happiness cannot be required.

15. (D) Main Point

Step 1: Identify the Question Type
For the purposes of this Main Point question, use Keywords and context to determine the author's conclusion. Anticipate connecting terms within different statements to formulate the correct answer.

Step 2: Untangle the Stimulus

Pay attention to the Contrast Keywords. These Keywords are often associated with the author's point of view. This argument is no exception. The Keyword [*h*]*owever* signals the author's conclusion: This infrastructure is likely to appear and grow rapidly.

Step 3: Make a Prediction

Connect the statements in the stimulus to complete the prediction of the main point: The fuel-distribution infrastructure needed for cars that burn hydrogen is likely to appear and grow rapidly.

Step 4: Evaluate the Answer Choices

(D) is a perfect match.

(A) is incorrect because it restates background Information used to support the main point. The author's conclusion is that the Infrastructure of fuel stations to support these vehicles is likely to be put in place soon, not that the technology already exists.

(B) goes wrong in the same way as **(A)**. It's true that the fuel-distribution infrastructure still needs to be created, but the author's contention is that the infrastructure will be put into place soon.

(C) is too broad. The argument speaks to the likelihood of the infrastructure development due to specific technology (that associated with hydrogen-fueled cars), not a new kind of technology.

(E)'s mention of similarities in consumer demand is never addressed in the argument.

16. (E) Flaw

Step 1: Identify the Question Type

This Flaw question uses the characteristic "most vulnerable to criticism" language in the question stem. A brief look at the answer choices tells you that the correct answer will include the type of flaw, as well as how it's demonstrated in the context of the argument.

Step 2: Untangle the Stimulus

The author recommends that experts not interfere with the natural habitats in the wild. The recommendation is based on the belief that changing an environment to help preserve endangered species is always detrimental to the nonendangered species within that environment.

Step 3: Make a Prediction

As you read the evidence, you ought to have raised an eyebrow at the discussion concerning endangered versus nonendangered species. The importance of that distinction is never made clear. That's the missing link: the author assumes that the survival of endangered species is no more important than the survival of nonendangered species.

Step 4: Evaluate the Answer Choices

(E) highlights that faulty assumption. If the preservation of the endangered species is paramount, then the conclusion does not follow from the author's evidence.

(A) is not a flaw present in the argument. If anything, the author is worried that wildlife management experts will succeed at their efforts to help the endangered species but thereby harm the nonendangered species in some way.

(B) is not a flaw present in the argument. In fact, the author's concern seems to be that a nonendangered species could become endangered.

(C) is Out of Scope and, thus, not the flaw here. The preservation of the overall diversity of species is never addressed in the argument.

(D) is not a flaw in the argument. The health of the environment is outside the scope of the argument.

17. (D) Inference

Step 1: Identify the Question Type

The correct answer to this Inference question is a statement that must be true on the basis of the information provided in the stimulus. The four wrong answer choices are simply possible or contradict the stimulus in some way.

Step 2: Untangle the Stimulus

Any signals Formal Logic. However, the first sentence contains a qualifier ("can contain") rather than certainty. The next statement provides something concrete:

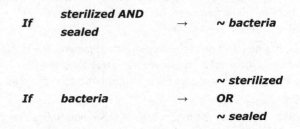

Then the author goes on to discuss how various food preservation techniques involve 1) sterilizing food, 2) sealing off food, or 3) slowing the growth of bacteria. Finally, at least one of these techniques *may* also destroy natural food enzymes that cause spoilation or discoloration. (Note the lack of certainty in that last statement.)

Step 3: Make a Prediction

Here, there are too many possible valid inferences to try to predict the correct answer. Note that the Formal Logic statement is the most concrete piece of information and head to the answer choices. Eliminate any that need not be true.

Step 4: Evaluate the Answer Choices

(D) must be true. Because only sterilized *and* sealed techniques guarantee the elimination of bacteria, it's possible that any other technique could contain bacteria. (Note the tentative language that's easy to support here, "can contain" bacteria)

(A) is Extreme, and it contradicts a portion of the stimulus. In fact, one acceptable food-preservation technique--slowing the growth of disease-causing bacteria--does not necessarily produce food free of disease-causing bacteria.

(B) is not supported by the stimulus. The last sentence states that at least one preservation method may *also* destroy enzymes in addition to sterilizing, sealing, or slowing the growth of bacteria in food. This answer could be false.

(C) is Out of Scope. The rate of discoloration that results from various preservation methods is never discussed.

(E) is Extreme. The absence of bacteria in food does not require that the food was preserved at all; at least the stimulus never explicitly makes this claim.

18. (C) Principle (Apply/Inference)

Step 1: Identify the Question Type
The correct answer choice to this Principle question will correctly apply the principle in the stimulus to an appropriate situation. Look for Formal Logic to be present in the stimulus.

Step 2: Untangle the Stimulus
Note the "if and only if" Formal Logic language. That means that the terms discussed are both necessary and sufficient for the other to occur. Essentially, the arrow works both ways, so the principle can be translated and contraposed as:

If	*risking life is acceptable*	↔	*risk bearer gains a benefit or volunteers*
If	*the risk bearer gains no benefit and does not volunteer*	↔	*risking life is not acceptable.*

Step 3: Make a Prediction
Because there are so many possibilities, it is best to go through each answer choice and apply the principle as translated. Look for either term to be present. Then, assess whether the other term is also present.

Step 4: Evaluate the Answer Choices
(C) correctly applies the principle. Because the motorcyclist bore the risk voluntarily, the risk of fatal injury is acceptable.

(A) is incorrect because it is not clear that the activity poses a risk to life. Thus, the principle does not apply.

(B) violates the principle. The risks are not acceptable because neither is there a benefit gained from the risk nor did the people volunteer to bear the risk of secondhand smoke.

(D) is incorrect because it is not clear that the benefit of inexpensive, convenient travel cannot be had without health risks.

(E) is incorrect because the principle given applies only to a scenario that involves risk to life, and this answer choice does not.

19. (D) Flaw

Step 1: Identify the Question Type
The correct answer choice to this Flaw question will describe the type of flaw present in the stimulus.

Step 2: Untangle the Stimulus
The ecologist presents two theories for why sea butterflies avoid predation: (1) their appearance and (2) the chemical compounds they produce. Because a recent study found that predators ate food pellets containing one of the compounds, regardless of which one was present in the pellet, the ecologist concludes that the compounds are not the reason predators avoid sea butterflies.

Step 3: Make a Prediction
To draw his conclusion (it's not the chemicals), the ecologist assumes that because no individual compound is repellent to predators, the explanation for the ability to avoid predation does not lie with the compounds sea butterflies produce. This should remind you of the Group versus Member type of LSAT flaw. Here, the author assumes that no combination of individual components produces the observed result.

Step 4: Evaluate the Answer Choices
(D) correctly characterizes the flaw in the ecologist's argument.

(A) is not a flaw in the argument. The compatibility of the theories cited in the argument is immaterial to the author's overall conclusion.

(B) is not a flaw in the argument. The author draws a conclusion on the basis of a study. Statistical correlation is never discussed.

(C) is not a flaw in the argument. Although one theory contends that chemical compounds *may* be sufficient to avoid predation, the author does not then conclude that they're the only cause. In fact, the author concludes that they are not a factor at all.

(E) is not a flaw in the argument. The conclusion is otherwise never presented in the stimulus.

20. (A) Strengthen

Step 1: Identify the Question Type

This Strengthen question, signaled by the word *justified*, is a bit unorthodox. But the task remains the same: Find an additional piece of evidence that supports the application of the principle in the stimulus.

Step 2: Untangle the Stimulus

Note the Formal Logic phrase "only if" in the principle. It translates and contrapose as follows:

If	criticism of another okay	→	~ serious harm AND intent to benefit another

If	serious harm OR ~ intent to benefit another	→	criticism of another ~ okay

Now, evaluate the application of the principle to determine what additional information is needed. Jarrett's criticism of Ostertag's essay is deemed unacceptable. The reason given is that there was no benefit to anyone.

Step 3: Make a Prediction

There are two sufficient conditions given that would deem Jarrett's criticisms unacceptable, and neither deals with whether the criticism is actually beneficial—only *intent* is discussed. To support the application of this principle, the correct answer must say that either the criticism caused serious harm or it was not intended to benefit someone besides Jarrett.

Step 4: Evaluate the Answer Choices

(A) provides a condition sufficient to deem Jarrett's criticism unacceptable: Jarrett knew that the criticism would not benefit anyone.

(B) is incorrect because it does not clarify Jarrett's intent. Whether or not the criticism actually conveyed a benefit is outside the scope.

(C) is Out of Scope. Whether or not the criticism might antagonize Ostertag is immaterial.

(D) is not inconsistent with the principle. It is not clear that any prestige Jarrett might gain is incompatible with intent to benefit someone other than himself.

(E) is incorrect because Jarrett need only have intent to benefit others, not necessarily Ostertag.

21. (E) Strengthen

Step 1: Identify the Question Type

The correct answer for this Strengthen question will provide a fact that makes the safety consultant's assumption more likely to be true.

Step 2: Untangle the Stimulus

The safety consultant attributes the minivans favorable safety record to the fact that they are primarily driven by low-risk drivers, not to the fact that they are made to be safer. The consultant's reasoning is based on the results of crash tests, which reveal that minivans are not any better at protecting their passengers than are other similar types of vehicles.

Step 3: Make a Prediction

The author assumes there is no likely explanation for the low number of injuries per minivan other than the safe nature of their drivers. A strengthener will confirm this assumption in some way, perhaps by ruling out an alternate possibility.

Step 4: Evaluate the Answer Choices

(E) presents a fact helpful to the consultant's argument. This does not prove that the low-risk drivers are absolutely the reason, but it does eliminate the possibility that the minivans are inherently safer. That is all that is needed.

(A) does not necessarily have a favorable effect on the argument. How the low-risk drivers come to own minivans is immaterial. In fact, it suggests that low-risk drivers choose vehicles other than minivans.

(B) does not necessarily have a favorable effect on the argument. The comparison still allows for minivans to be as safe as the other vehicles. More importantly, it does not provide a reason for that safety record.

(C) does not affect the argument. The passenger capacity for minivans is immaterial.

(D) would harm the consultant's argument by providing an alternative reason (size) for the safety of the vehicle.

22. (A) Assumption (Necessary)

Step 1: Identify the Question Type

The correct answer for this Assumption question will provide a necessary piece of evidence that must be true in order for the consumer advocate's conclusion to follow. Because this question asks for a necessary assumption, it's a good candidate for the Denial Test.

Step 2: Untangle the Stimulus

The consumer advocate blames the government for the increased cost of gasoline. The advocate establishes an indirect relationship: the government's policies have increased fuel demand, which has led to a steady increase in the price of gas.

Step 3: Make a Prediction
In order for the government to be culpable, it must be responsible for the anything that results from its action--both direct and indirect.

Step 4: Evaluate the Answer Choices
(A) picks up on this assumption. Use the Denial Test: If it's true that the government cannot bear responsibility for that which it indirectly causes, then it cannot be responsible for the indirect results of fuel prices rising. Then the consumer advocate's conclusion cannot stand.

(B) is Out of Scope. The issue is whether the government can be responsible for indirect results of its actions. The foreseeabilty of those consequences is not in issue.

(C) is Out of Scope. Rising gas prices need not be a necessary result of rising consumer demand. It just so happened that in this instance, prices did rise.

(D) is Out of Scope. The obligations of the government regarding fuel demand are immaterial to the advocate's argument.

(E) is also Out of Scope. Government policies that do not affect demand have no bearing on the advocate's argument, which only discusses what happens when policies increase demand.

23. (C) Parallel Flaw

Step 1: Identify the Question Type
For this Parallel Flaw question, the correct answer choice will contain the same kind of conclusion, evidence, and flawed logic as the stimulus.

Step 2: Untangle the Stimulus
A glance at the stimulus flags Formal Logic indicators: "will develop" and "only if." When Formal Logic is present, translate the entire stimulus. First, it's noted that a species with rapid mutations leads to new evolutionary adaptations in each generation. This is translated as follows:

If rapid mutations → new evolutionary adaptations

Second, species that survive dramatic environmental changes must develop new evolutionary adaptations in each generation. This is translated as follows:

If survive dramatic changes → new evolutionary adaptations

Finally, the argument's conclusion: a species with rapid mutations will survive dramatic environmental changes. This is translated as follows:

If rapid mutations → survive dramatic changes

Step 3: Make a Prediction
Now, put the argument in abstract terms. If "rapid mutations" is term X, "new evolutionary adaptations" is term Y, and "survive dramatic changes" is term Z, then you have this:

Evidence:

If X → Y

If Z → Y

Conclusion:

If X → Z

Note that the author is assuming that just because two conditions lead to the same result, then It must be true that one condition leads to the other. Translate each answer choice to its abstract form and find the same flawed pattern of reasoning.

Step 4: Evaluate the Answer Choices
(C) matches the flawed pattern of reasoning as follows:
Evidence:

If X (perfect honest) → Y (always tell the truth)

If Z (morally upright) → Y (always tell the truth)

Conclusion:

If X (perfect honest) → Z (morally upright)

(A) has a different logical relationship than does the stimulus. The first piece of evidence is a match. But the second piece of evidence provides a condition to lead to term A rather than term B.

(B) only has two terms, not three. Plays performed in front of different audiences always get different reactions, and because all plays are always performed in front of different audiences, all plays always get different reactions.

(D) does not contain flawed logic. The chain follows:

Evidence:

| If | X (productive herb garden) | → | Y (soil is well drained) |

| If | Y (soil is well drained) | → | Z (good soil) |

Conclusion:

| If | X (productive herb garden) | → | Z (good soil) |

(E) introduces a fourth term in the conclusion. A healthful diet and a healthy person are different terms.

24. (B) Principle (Identify/Strengthen)

Step 1: Identify the Question Type

In this Principle question, the correct answer choice will identify a broad principle that strengthens the music critic's argument.

Step 2: Untangle the Stimulus

The conclusion appears first; the music critic argues that selling a lot of records does not constitute success for an underground rock group. Selling a lot of records could be due to the music being too trendy to be underground; in fact, many underground musicians actually consider it desirable for their records to not sell well. On the other hand, bad sales could also be due to incompetence.

Step 3: Make a Prediction

The disconnected term is *success*, which appears only in the conclusion. The music critic must assume that success as an underground rock group necessitates that the music not be too trendy to be authentic to the genre and that the group demonstrates competence.

Step 4: Evaluate the Answer Choices

(B) is a principle that helps firm up the critic's assumption, and thereby strengthens the reasoning.

(A) doesn't support the reasoning. A group's sales is "no mark" of success; thus, there is no reason they must be mediocre.

(C) distorts the argument. The argument does not address all the criteria underground musicians may have for considering a recording successful; it only says that *many* underground musicians don't favor high sales.

(D) doesn't go far enough to support the conclusion. Competence is required, but the music also must be

authentic to ensure success. Poor sales do not guarantee authenticity.

(E) weakens the music critic's argument by claiming those factors necessary for success are in fact *not* marks of success.

25. (C) Point at Issue

Step 1: Identify the Question Type

The question asks for the point of disagreement between the two speakers, a characteristic Point at Issue question stem. Summarize Graham and Adelaide's arguments independently. Then, use the Decision Tree to reveal the correct answer.

Step 2: Untangle the Stimulus

Graham argues that the ability of a computer to defeat the world's chess champion (inferably human) is evidence that any type of human intellect governed by fixed principles can be mastered by that computer. Thus, the creation of a truly intelligent machine is a sure thing.

Adelaide disagrees. She argues that the computer in Graham's argument is merely an extension of the humans who created it. Therefore, it's their intellect that enabled them to use a computer to defeat a chess champion.

Step 3: Make a Prediction

In this instance, a prediction may seem apparent: Graham and Adelaide are arguing over who should be congratulated for defeating the chess champion: The computer? Or the humans who built it?

If that prediction does not come to mind, use the Decision Tree to find the correct answer choice. Once you find the answer choice that contains something discussed by Graham and Adelaide, as well as a point of disagreement, then you have the answer.

Step 4: Evaluate the Answer Choices

(C) highlights the issue of contention between Graham and Adelaide. Graham argues that it should be attributed to the computer, while Adelaide directly disagrees and says it should instead be credited to the programmers who built it.

(A) is incorrect because neither speaker discusses whether chess is the best example of this kind of human activity, only that it is an example.

(B) is incorrect because neither speaker discusses whether chess is a characteristic human activity.

(D) is incorrect because neither disagrees as to whether intelligence can be demonstrated in such a way.

(E) is incorrect because neither speaker discusses tools in general, only computers.

Section IV: Reading Comprehension

Passage 1: New Urbanists

Q#	Question Type	Correct	Difficulty
1	Global	D	★
2	Detail	C	★
3	Inference	D	★★★
4	Inference	B	★
5	Logic Reasoning (Weaken)	D	★★
6	Inference	E	★★
7	Logic Reasoning (Assumption)	A	★★★

Passage 2: Honeybee Communication

Q#	Question Type	Correct	Difficulty
8	Global	C	★
9	Global	A	★
10	Inference	D	★★
11	Inference	D	★★
12	Logic Reasoning (Method of Argument)	C	★

Passage 3: Luis Valdez and *Actos*

Q#	Question Type	Correct	Difficulty
13	Global	C	★★
14	Logic Function	E	★★★
15	Logic Function	A	★
16	Detail	D	★
17	Inference	D	★
18	Inference	C	★★
19	Inference	C	★★★★
20	Inference	B	★★★★

Passage 4: Contingency Fees in Western Australia

Q#	Question Type	Correct	Difficulty
21	Logic Reasoning (Parallel Reasoning)	B	★★
22	Detail	A	★★★
23	Global	E	★★
24	Detail	C	★★
25	Inference	B	★★★
26	Detail	D	★★★
27	Logic Reasoning (Weaken)	B	★★★★

Passage 1: New Urbanists

Step 1: Read the Passage Strategically
Sample Roadmap

line #	Keyword/phrase	¶ Margin notes
4	phenomenon	Suburban sprawl
7	contend	New Urbanists: sprawl hurts civil life
8	contributes to the decline	
10	note	
13	robs	
14	as difficult	Analogy
16–17	contend, as it is	
20–21	add; not only; but also; resulting in	More problems
25	certain to be ill prepared	Economic segregation
26	Moreover, because	
28	only	More driving → Less social
29	forced	
34	instead	
37	advocate	New Urb. solution: mixed $ urban-type neighborhoods
43	believe	Benefits
45	thus	
46	Opponents; claim	Critics: people enjoy cars + mobility
48	legitimate desire	
50	However	New Urb. response
51	do not	
52	instead; suggest; should	
53	more critical view	
55	fundamentally concerned	Long-term social costs most important
57	attitude	
58	should be valued absolutely, regardless	

Discussion

This passage begins with the views of some new thinkers on a subject. Here, the subject is "suburban sprawl," and the thinkers are representatives of a school known as New Urbanism. As a predictive reader, key questions to consider are whether the author agrees or disagrees with the new thinkers, whether he offers a competitive view (either his own or someone else's), and whether he participates in or merely referees the debate that follows. In this passage, the debate takes a long time to develop. And while the author considers New Urbanists to be "prominent town planners," he offers little commentary or opinion of his own; instead, he devotes most of the passage to describing New Urbanists' views with just a sentence allotted to the opposition. Thus, you should have anticipated several questions about New Urbanists' values and recommendations.

The **Topic** is identified as suburban sprawl by the end of the first sentence. The **Scope**—the New Urbanist critique—begins to take shape in the next few lines. The bulk of the paragraph one outlines the New Urbanists' argument: "[S]uburban sprawl contributes to the decline of civic life and civility" (lines 8–9). It does so because of traffic patterns and zoning ordinances that separate homes from stores, schools, and other communal spaces. This, in turn, robs residents of opportunities for interaction and active community membership. Strong predictive readers will anticipate two avenues along which paragraph two might develop; either it will offer more detail and support for the New Urbanist critique, or it will introduce their proposed solution.

In fact, paragraph two does both. It opens with two further criticisms that New Urbanists level against suburban sprawl. First, the similarity among suburban houses produces an unhealthy lack of diversity (especially economic diversity) among the residents. Second, the necessity of driving everywhere turns "community members" into "motorists," a status New Urbanists consider inherently antisocial. The author introduces the New Urbanists' proposed solution at line 36. They suggest town planning based on early twentieth-century urban neighborhoods; smaller streets, differently priced housing options, and nearby stores and schools would encourage the diversity, pedestrianism, and above all, interactivity lacking in areas of suburban sprawl. As a test taker, you should wonder where this argument is going.

In paragraph three, the expected conflict emerges. The author offers a single sentence to those who disagree with New Urbanists. The counterargument is simple: suburbs grow because people choose the enjoyment and mobility that come with the automobile-based lifestyle. The Keyword [*h*]*owever* at line 50 signals the author's shift back to articulating the New Urbanist point of view. New Urbanists don't want to deny anyone choices, but they want a more critical view of suburban sprawl to emerge. The author

introduces a note of frustration in the passage's final lines by characterizing the opposing view as valuing mobility, consumption, and wealth "absolutely." Still, the author's Purpose falls short of an explicit endorsement. The **Purpose** is to *explain* or *outline* New Urbanists' critique of suburban sprawl and their proposed solution. The **Main Idea** develops the Purpose: the New Urbanists claim that suburban sprawl harms civic life and suggests planning modeled on early twentieth-century urban neighborhoods."

1. (D) Global

Step 2: Identify the Question Type

The phrase "main point of the passage" identifies this as a Global question.

Step 3: Research the Relevant Text

For straightforward Global questions, review your Purpose and Main Idea summaries. Avoid rereading large portions of the text or researching details.

Step 4: Make a Prediction

The summaries here reflected the author's basic neutrality. He presented the New Urbanists' critique of suburban sprawl and their proposed solution. And, the Main Idea summary paraphrased those: the New Urbanists claim that suburban sprawl harms civic life and suggest planning modeled on early 20th-century urban neighborhoods. The correct answer's language may differ slightly, but its meaning will be quite close to that prediction.

Step 5: Evaluate the Answer Choices

(D) fits the Main Idea summary almost perfectly. It's broad enough in scope to fit the passage as a whole, and it reflects the author's neutral tone.

(A) is too narrow. This accurately summarizes the point of view of those who criticize New Urbanists, but these critics are given just one sentence in the third paragraph. Their opinions certainly aren't the author's main point.

(B) is a classic Distortion—a wrong answer designed to catch test takers who read only the first half of the choice. New Urbanists do decry the lack of social interaction in suburban sprawl areas, but their proposed reform is to build along the lines of small urban communities, not "specific reforms of zoning laws," as the second half of the answer choice states.

(C) is too narrow to constitute the main point of the passage and contains nothing about the problems with the suburbs that New Urbanists detail. It also focuses on vocabulary word—gratifying—that the author quotes, but the answer as a whole doesn't match your summary of the passage's Main Idea.

(E) is also too narrow to fit a global question stem. New Urbanists cite traffic flow as one of the factors contributing to the problems of suburban environments, but both their critique and proposed solution include much more.

2. (C) Detail

Step 2: Identify the Question Type
The opening phrase—"According to the passage"—lets you know that the correct answer will be a detail explicitly stated in the passage. Here, the research clue points you to the part of the passage that defines why New Urbanists find the necessity of driving in the suburbs problematic.

Step 3: Research the Relevant Text
Look to the middle of paragraph two, lines 28 to 35 specifically, for the answer. You should have a margin note that summarizes this important point as well.

Step 4: Make a Prediction
Using margin notes and passage text, find that the New Urbanists' argument is simple: driving a lot is bad for the community because motorists act more antisocial than pedestrians (line 35). The correct answer should make this exact point.

Step 5: Evaluate the Answer Choices
(C) matches the point made in the passage almost exactly.

(A) is Out of Scope. The financial impact of suburban driving is never mentioned in this passage.

(B) is a Distortion. According to New Urbanists, driving time takes people away from healthy interaction with other *people*, not away from work.

(D) is Out of Scope and can distract those who bring an outside agenda to their reading of an LSAT passage. Air pollution from driving is a valid environmental concern, but it's not an issue addressed in the passage.

(E), like **(D)**, may be true, but is Out of Scope for this passage. Children are mentioned only in paragraph two, where the New Urbanists are concerned that growing up in the suburbs will insufficiently prepare children for life in a diverse society. There's no mention of parents interacting with their children.

3. (D) Inference

Step 2: Identify the Question Type
The phrase "most strongly suggests" identifies this as an Inference question, so the correct answer must be true based on the text. While you're told that the correct answer will reflect the New Urbanists' point of view, your research isn't narrowed much by this stem. Nearly the entire passage is given over to the New Urbanists' arguments.

Step 3: Research the Relevant Text
When a question stem fails to narrow your research to a specific paragraph or portion of text—a failure common to inference questions—base your prediction on a scan of your Roadmap and your understanding of the Topic, Scope, Purpose and Main Idea of the passage.

Step 4: Make a Prediction
Before reading the answer choices, refresh your memory of the passage's Main Idea and review your margin notes. The main problems with suburban environments, according to New Urbanists, are that they are spread out, reducing interactivity; they are uniform, reducing diversity; and they require a lot of driving, increasing antisocial behavior. The proposed solution would create more compact, urban environments to reduce these problems. Paragraph three states that New Urbanists don't want to deny people choices but hope that a more critical attitude will balance the purely personal considerations that have led to suburban sprawl. An overview like that one shouldn't take more than a few seconds and offers the information you need to identify the correct answer.

Step 5: Evaluate the Answer Choices
(D) is correct. Although this answer is written in generic language, it makes a point that New Urbanists are sure to agree with. The "spatial configuration of suburban neighborhoods" means they are spread out, with schools and shops located too far from residences. According to New Urbanists, the policies that promote this sprawl reflect the values of suburban dwellers and result in people being less civic-minded and more antisocial. Infer that New Urbanists would agree that suburban sprawl both "influences and is influenced by" residents' attitudes.

(A) is an Extreme Distortion. The passage claims that New Urbanists are concerned about the mode of transportation—driving versus walking—not the amount of time spent traveling. Further, there is no indication of which factor, this one or any other, is the *primary* one affecting the maintenance of civility.

(B) is Out of Scope. Paragraph three mentions zoning policies because they appear to reflect the personal preferences of those who choose suburban life. However, the passage says nothing about residents' opportunities to impact zoning plans, and the distinction between the private and public sectors is likewise irrelevant.

(C) is another Out of Scope choice. The passage doesn't indicate the New Urbanists' opinion of suburban residents finding suburban jobs. If anything, New Urbanists would expect suburban residents to have longer commutes—to where, you're simply not told.

(E) is Extreme. In the third paragraph, the New Urbanists acknowledge personal choices but hope for a more critical attitude to be brought to town planning. However, that's not to say that personal values should not have any effect at all on planning.

4. (B) Inference

Step 2: Identify the Question Type

Vocabulary-in-context questions like this one fall under the heading of Inference questions because they ask what the author meant by using a certain word or phrase in the passage. This question asks about two separate uses of the same word. Because the test makers are interested in your comprehension (not your memory), they tell you where to locate each instance.

Step 3: Research the Relevant Text

In the first sentence, the author uses *communities* in the sense of physical places where people live. In the final sentence of paragraph one, the author uses an analogy to relate concepts of *community* and *family*, thus distinguishing both from the physical locales that house them.

Step 4: Make a Prediction

Keep your paraphrase close to the meaning of the passage. In the first instance, "communities" refers to collections of residences and the infrastructure that supports them. In the second, "community" refers to the sense of belonging or civic identity shared by those who belong to the same physical "community."

Step 5: Evaluate the Answer Choices

(B) matches the prediction and the author's usage. This answer choice substitutes the term "dwellings" for "residences" or "buildings" and the phrase "sense of belonging together" for "civic identity," but it reflects the passage precisely.

(A) is a 180. The author uses "community" differently in each instance.

(C) is a Distortion on both counts. The first instance misses the literal, physical sense of community intended by the passage. By distorting the meaning in the first instance, the answer makes the distinction drawn in the second instance—"have something else in common"—meaningless.

(D) is a Distortion of both uses of the term "community." In neither case does the author focus on people who share "professional or political ties," and it is the first use of the term, not the second, that implies physical "proximity."

(E) is again a Distortion of both meanings. In the first instance called for by the question stem, the author refers to physical "communities," not to loose associations of people. And for the second instance, the author used the concept of "community" to convey the sense of belonging among residents, not similarities in background or lifestyles.

5. (D) Logic Reasoning (Weaken)

Step 2: Identify the Question Type

The phrase "would most weaken" identifies this question as a Weaken question. This stem requires you to weaken the position taken by the critics of New Urbanists. Thus, the correct answer must strengthen the New Urbanists' position by questioning the exact criticism directed against them in the passage.

Step 3: Research the Relevant Text

The critics' position is easy to find using your Roadmap; their main point is that suburban residents choose to live as such because they enjoy the mobility their cars provide.

Step 4: Make a Prediction

The critics' argument is a causal one; they want to tell you *why* people choose the suburbs. Expect the answer to weaken this argument by offering an alternative cause. If residents chose the suburbs for something other than automobile-enabled mobility and pleasure, the critics' position is diminished.

Step 5: Evaluate the Answer Choices

(D) is correct. This answer suggests an alternate cause, that is, economics. If the driving force behind suburban living is cost, it's less likely that a preference for driving and mobility was the motivation.

(A) is a 180. This choice is designed to catch those who attempt to weaken the New Urbanists' position and not that of their critics. The critics would welcome this fact because it contributes to their argument that people choose suburban life for its convenience and mobility.

(B) is an Irrelevant Comparison. The critics make no distinction based on distance traveled and certainly none among urban, suburban, and rural travel patterns.

(C) is irrelevant. Ease of access to shopping and entertainment are not synonymous with "enjoyment and personal mobility." Besides, if most people with easy access to shopping and entertainment do *not* live in the suburbs, it's still possible that the people who *do* live in the suburbs choose to do so to secure enjoyment and personal mobility. In that case, the critics' argument still stands.

(E) is a Faulty Use of Detail. In paragraph three, the author writes that zoning plans reflect the values of suburban residents, but the critics' position in no way depends on whether candidates' positions on zoning influence those votes.

6. (E) Inference

Step 2: Identify the Question Type

This is an Inference question because of the phrase "most strongly suggests," which should help you to understand the research clue. The correct answer will be based in the portion of the passage that discusses the practical results—that is, what would occur—of the New Urbanists' proposal.

Step 3: Research the Relevant Text
A scan of your margin notes will lead you to the final third of paragraph two for the New Urbanists' proposition. To find out what it means to plan towns in the manner of early twentieth-century urban neighborhoods, read lines 40 to 42, following the Illustration Keyword *includes*.

Step 4: Make a Prediction
Your targeted research makes the correct answer unambiguous. It must reflect "narrow, tree-lined streets, parks, corner grocery stores, cafes, small neighborhood schools, all within walking distance."

Step 5: Evaluate the Answer Choices
(E) is correct. In order to have "corner grocery stores" and "small neighborhood schools … within walking distance," more grocery stores and schools are needed. This is an Inference question, so the passage doesn't *say* more are needed. But, that conclusion is unavoidable based on the passage. Notice that the wrong answers stray far from the relevant passage text.

(A) is a Faulty Use of Detail. The author mentions heavy traffic caused by the proliferation of "collector roads," but the only zoning policies discussed (in paragraph three) reference how suburban sprawl reflects individual values, not traffic patterns.

(B) is a 180, at worst. Currently, suburbs contain uniform housing. Because New Urbanists advocate mixed housing, the number of multifamily dwellings would likely increase, not decrease.

(C) is Out of Scope. The passage doesn't make any claim that supports a conclusion about the amount of time it would take to travel to and from the city center or how often suburban residents would do so if suburbs were redesigned along the lines suggested by New Urbanists.

(D) is also Out of Scope. Coordination of zoning policies between various government agencies is never addressed in the passage.

7. (A) Logic Reasoning (Assumption)

Step 2: Identify the Question Type
This stem is a gold mine for the strategic reader. The correct answer is an inference that can be drawn from paragraph two; that much is clear from the outset. It's the second half of the question stem that tells you how to proceed. Because the correct answer will be one of the New Urbanists' assumptions, look for one of their arguments and, more precisely, for a gap between one of their conclusions and the evidence provided.

Step 3: Research the Relevant Text
Paragraph two opens with two arguments made by New Urbanists, both of which critique suburban sprawl. The first

(lines 19–26) concludes that the suburbs lack diversity because the houses are all the same price. The second (lines 26–36) concludes that suburban residents have less positive social interaction because the layout of suburban roads requires much driving and because driving is more antisocial than walking. Of the two, the first (causal) argument is more clearly missing a necessary premise.

Step 4: Make a Prediction
In order for the conclusion that suburban residents are economically similar to follow from the evidence that they live in similarly priced houses, New Urbanists must assume that people of different economic status don't buy similarly priced homes. If people of different economic classes will spend the same amount for a home, their argument is seriously damaged.

Step 5: Evaluate the Answer Choices
(A) fills the gap in the argument; it uses a negative paraphrase of something you may have stated affirmatively in your prediction. If those who buy similarly priced homes come from similar economic circumstances, than those from high statuses don't buy inexpensive homes.

(B) wouldn't be an assumption of New Urbanists because they believe that the suburbs continue to be economically uniform. If zoning could introduce diversity, they might choose it as a solution instead of proposing new town plans.

(C) doesn't fill the gap in the New Urbanists' arguments either. Those hostile toward motorists are out of scope of the passage.

(D) is unfounded. The health benefits of walking aren't discussed. Remember that Reading Comprehension questions are always passage based. Don't consider outside knowledge.

(E) is a Faulty Use of Detail. The author mentions that suburban houses are often identical (lines 20–21), but this is just an aside to the argument. The relevant evidence concerns price parity, and so too must the assumption.

Passage 2: Honeybee Communication

Step 1: Read the Passage Strategically
Sample Roadmap

line #	Keyword/phrase	¶ Margin notes
Passage A		
4	but	Honeybee dance
8	discovered; observed	Dance pattern = comm. food location
9–10	deciphered; thereby deduced	
11	Yet	?s remain
13	discovered	Wing vibration sounds
16	reasoned	Theory: use sound to communicate
17	might explain	
18	But	
19	mistakenly believed	
20	so	
21	unresolved; subsequently proposed	new theory: smell-based comm.
22	rather than; key	
23	hypothesized	
24	not from; but from	
26	Yet	Refute smell theory
28–29	not be possible if; in fact necessary; Finally	
31	showed	Sound = important factor
32	do indeed; essential	
Passage B		
35	All	
37	But	Some animals use symbolic communication
38	for example	
40	found	Ex. vervet monkey alarm calls
47	suggest	
49	first to crack the code	Honeybee dance symbolic
53	believed; rely on	
55	but	
56	While	Bees don't follow all dance info
57	do not	
61	found	
62	ignored	
63	presumably because	Ex. bees don't follow b/c no flowers

Discussion

The paired selections used in the comparative reading passages are always similar enough to one another in Scope that test makers can ask questions that reward you for accurately comparing and contrasting them. Here, passage A took a narrative approach, chronologically outlining developments in the research of honeybee communications. Passage B attempts a bigger task, illustrating what is known about animals that communicate symbolically. Still, the bulk of passage B supports itself with the same research on honeybees that passage A covered. In these two comparative reading passages, nothing suggests that the authors would disagree. Both offer much the same about honeybee dance researchers, but while passage A's author is content simply to convey the narrative, passage B's author wants to relate it to a bigger scientific question.

Passage A's three short paragraphs are arranged in chronological order. The passage is anchored throughout by Sequence Keywords and phrases: "In ancient Greece" (line 1), "In the 1940s" (line 7), "In the 1960s" (line 13), *subsequently* (line 21), and [*f*]*inally* (line 29). Once you realize that the passage is telling a story, ask what the story is about. The **Topic** is clearly the honeybee's communicative dances. The **Scope** is revealed as the history of developments in the research of the honeybee dance. Because each period mentioned corresponds to the work of a particular researcher or research team, the Keywords you've circled and your margin notes should paraphrase the story beside the text: Aristotle observed the bees' dance and associated it with the discovery of food; von Frisch decoded the dance's message but failed to determine the mechanism by which the information was relayed to the other bees in the hive; Wenner thought the mechanism might be sound, but during his time, honeybees were thought to be deaf, so he switched his hypothesis to smell; Gould disproved the olfactory hypothesis; and finally, Kirchner and Michelsen showed that sound (from bees' wings) is central to the dance's message. The author's **Purpose** simply is to tell, or to outline, this history, and the **Main Idea** can be stated: over time, scientists have shown that sound is essential to honeybees' ability to communicate information about food through their dances.

As mentioned earlier, passage B's **Topic**, at least initially, is broader: animal communication. Don't be alarmed. Comparative reading passages are always related. Indeed, the **Scope** quickly narrows to animals that engage in symbolic communication, and the first species cited is bees. Nonetheless, there is a detour through another example—vervet monkeys that have different alarm sounds for different types of predators—in the remainder of paragraph one. In paragraph two, however, you're back on familiar ground. Here, you find the familiar von Frisch and Wenner, whom the first author introduced early in passage A.

Passage B's author is explicit here that honeybee dances are an example of symbolic communication he's interested in. In paragraph three, the author shows that honeybees do not simply accept any information communicated by dancing hive mates. To illustrate, he cites Gould (another researcher mentioned in passage A), who showed that bees wouldn't respond to a dance that correctly identified a food source where other bees had no reason to think flowers would be growing. The author's **Purpose** is to illustrate, or to give examples of, the science of symbolic communication among animals. The **Main Idea** adds more description: studies show that vervet monkey alarm calls and honeybee food dances are examples of symbolic communication in animal species.

The most important relationship to note between the two passages is that the subject—honeybee dances—that dominates passage A is used as illustration of symbolic communication in passage B. Because the authors have no argument or point at issue between them, this difference in focus is likely to be what test makers focus on in order to ask compare-and-contrast questions that accompany comparative reading passages.

8. (C) Global

Step 2: Identify the Question Type
Occasionally, familiar question types will be worded differently in the comparative reading context. Such is the case here, where you're asked for one of the common *aims* of the two passages. Because aim is just another word for purpose, the strategic reader shouldn't feel uncomfortable.

Step 3: Research the Relevant Text
There's no need to research within the text for such a high-level question. Instead, refresh your memory with the two passages' Purposes and Main Ideas. Passage A's was to show that, over time, scientists demonstrated the importance of sound to honeybee communicative dances. Passage's B's Main Idea was to illustrate scientific research showing that certain species use symbolic communication.

Step 4: Make a Prediction
The two passages share their interest in the science of animal communication. Passage A focused entirely on the honeybee, while passage B added the example of vervet monkey alarms.

Step 5: Evaluate the Answer Choices
(C) matches the prediction. Each passage describes several scientific studies. In some cases, they even mention the same ones.

(A) is Out of Scope. Neither passage goes so far as to say that animals, even those that communicate symbolically, have "human-like intelligence."

(B) is Out of Scope for passage A. Only passage B mentions primates. Passage A is focused entirely on the honeybee's dance.

(D) is a Distortion. There is no indication of *controversy* among the scientists who've studied animal communication.

(E) if Out of Scope. While passage B mentions that von Frisch considered the honeybee dance a "language" (at line 50), passage A doesn't even raise the question. Besides, neither author focused on the conditions required for a system of communication to be considered a language.

9. (A) Global

Step 2: Identify the Question Type
This question is the counterpart to the first question in the set. The phrase "characterizes a difference" tells you that the choices won't be details or statements of facts from the passages. When stems lack targeted research clues, consult your Purpose and Main Idea summaries.

Step 3: Research the Relevant Text
Having identified this as a comparative reading twist on the Global question, confine your research to your Purpose and Main Idea summaries. Here, look for the differences between the two.

Step 4: Make a Prediction
Both passages covered scientific research on animal communication. While passage A focused exclusively on historical developments in the study of the honeybee dance, passage B used both the honeybee dance and the vervet monkey alarm cries to illustrate symbolic communication. This summary should help to discriminate between the correct choice and the four wrong ones.

Step 5: Evaluate the Answer Choices
(A) is an accurate characterization of the main difference between the two passages. Passage B included discussion of other animals because of its author's broader interest in symbolic communication.

(B) is Half-Right/Half-Wrong. The description of passage A is acceptable, but the description of passage B is a 180. Passage B does provide supporting evidence including Gould's experiment with the boat of flowers and the research on vervet alarm calls.

(C) is a 180. Passage B's mention of vervet monkey alarm calls immediately rejects the idea that it's "entirely about" honeybee communication.

(D) is a Distortion for passage B and Out of Scope for passage A. Passage B focuses on symbolic communication, not the difference between symbolic and non-symbolic communication. And passage A never mentions this distinction and thus cannot be said to be making use of it.

(E) is Out of Scope immediately, as passage B never discusses human communication.

10. (D) Inference

Step 2: Identify the Question Type
Don't confuse this question stem with that of a logic reasoning (strengthen) question. Here, you're asked to use Gould's research to support the correct answer, making this an Inference question. The reference to Gould's research is a helpful clue to guide your research.

Step 3: Research the Relevant Text
Gould's research is mentioned in each passage's paragraph three. In passage A, Gould disproved Wenner's olfactory hypothesis by showing that bees could direct their hive mates to food sites they hadn't visited themselves. Passage B reports Gould's experiment, showing that bees ignore information from dances telling them to go to food that actually exists at a location where none should be found.

Step 4: Make a Prediction
It may seem hard to predict the wording of the correct answer for an Inference question like this one, but you have strong paraphrases of both of Gould's experiments described in the passages. The correct answer will not stray from what the author wrote about them.

Step 5: Evaluate the Answer Choices
(D) accurately summarizes Gould's experiments. Passage A reported the experiment in which the dance sent other bees to the site the dancer hadn't visited, while passage B reported the one in which the other bees ignored instructions to go to the site that the dancer had been to. This choice follows directly from the information in both passages and is the correct answer.

(A) is a Distortion. According to passage A, Gould's research showed that olfactory information was irrelevant to the honeybee dances. While passage B talked about bees ignoring dance information, nothing in either passage suggested that bees would visit sites of their own choosing.

(B) is a Distortion of the information about Gould's experiment recounted in passage B. The bees' knowledge of where flowers grew allowed them to ignore the reporting bee's dance; you're never told it is related to instinct. Further, nothing prevented the forager from reporting the flowers he'd found in their unlikely locale.

(C) is Out of Scope. Neither passage mentions the foraging bee's level of experience as relevant to its success in finding food.

(E) is Out of Scope. The notion of bees communicating by "leaving a trail" is not associated with Gould's research in either passage.

11. (D) Inference

Step 2: Identify the Question Type

Here is a model comparative reading question—a familiar type requiring the test taker to research in both passages. The stem tells you explicitly that this is an Inference question. The correct answer will be a statement of fact with which *both* authors would agree.

Step 3: Research the Relevant Text

It may seem that the question stem gave you no research help, so check your margin notes for statements on which both authors might have an opinion. Passage A does not comment on symbolic communication or vervet monkeys. Passage B will say nothing about Aristotle, Kirchner, or Michelsen. The statement in the correct answer likely will be about the work of von Frisch, Wenner, or Gould.

Step 4: Make a Prediction

This question gives you a manageable range of predictions without zeroing in on a specific sentence or quote. Poor test takers abandon the strategic approach when a question stem lacks a line reference or quoted excerpt; great test takers predict the scope of the correct answer as well as they can and then determine the wrong answers in light of the prediction.

Step 5: Evaluate the Answer Choices

(D) is correct. Both authors consider von Frisch's work to be among the seminal studies of honeybee dances, and both credit him with being the first "to decipher," or "to crack the code," of the dances.

(A) is Out of Scope for passage A and a Distortion for passage B. Only passage B mentioned bees ignoring their hive mate's signals, and they did so because the dance was sending them to a location unlikely to have pollinating flowers, not because the dance lacked the proper smells.

(B) is a 180. Passage A says that Wenner considered sound as a possible mechanism for the dance information but abandoned the hypothesis because most researchers in his time thought honeybees deaf. Passage B cites Werner as having proposed the now discredited olfactory hypothesis.

(C) is Out of Scope for passage A and Extreme for passage B. Passage A is only about honeybees, while passage B merely claims that *some* species communicate symbolically, not necessarily *most*.

(E) is Out of Scope. Experience levels among forager bees play no role in either passage.

12. (C) Logic Reasoning (Method of Argument)

Step 2: Identify the Question Type

Here, you have a question stem asking for the relationship between the two passages. Because this type of question has answers that speak abstractly about *how* each passage is structured, this is akin to a Method of Argument question.

Step 3: Research the Relevant Text

The question stem—"describes a relationship between the two passages"—gives you no reason to anticipate doing any targeted text research. Once again, rely on your understanding of the Purpose and Main Idea of each passage.

Step 4: Make a Prediction

These passages have a common interest in the scientific studies of honeybee communication. Passage A confines itself entirely to the history of this subject, while passage B uses it alongside the study of vervet monkeys to illustrate symbolic communication in animals. The correct answer will fall within the scope of these summaries.

Step 5: Evaluate the Answer Choices

(C) is a succinct, if general, statement of the relationship you summarized. The "phenomenon" in question is the honeybees' food dance; this is the correct answer.

(A) misstates the relationship by suggesting that there was some element of conflict between the two authors. Nothing in either passage suggested that the authors see things differently.

(B) is a Distortion that reverses the roles of the passages. Passage A discusses the honeybee dance but doesn't use it as an example of any broader concept, while passage B had two examples of symbolic communication.

(D), like **(A)**, implies a conflict between the passages. None was present. In fact, both passages suggest that the mechanism by which honeybees communicate is now fairly well understood.

(E) is likely the most tempting of the wrong answers, but it distorts the relationship of the passages beyond recognition. Passage A features a historical account of honeybee research but it is only one example of passage B's "primary concern," which is symbolic communication.

Passage 3: Luis Valdez and *Actos*

Step 1: Read the Passage Strategically
Sample Roadmap

line #	Keyword/phrase	¶ Margin notes
1		Chávez union efforts → '60s political activism
7		Ex: UFW grape boycott
9	also	Valdez used theater to organize workers
13	generally credited	Birth of Chicano theater movement
23	delighted	Farm worker improvisations
24	ridicule	
25	guided	Created "actos"
27		Definition
32	quintessential	Expanded
33	According to; should	Goals of actos
35	and	
36	should	
37	Because	
41	rightly criticizes	Y B-G: Valdez given too much credit (Auth agrees)
43	as if	
46		Actos linked to carpas
52	no doubt	Auth: carpas influential;
55	in fact	collective accomplishment;
56	still	Valdez crucial
57	crucial ; neither	
58	nor	
59	but; distinctive	Blend of genres

Discussion

This passage's most welcome feature, at least for the LSAT test taker, is the clear conclusion at the end of the final paragraph. It concisely states the author's overall position and summarizes the Purpose and Main Idea. Most LSAT passages don't include such a premade conclusion; when one does, use it for all it's worth. It provides a prediction for any global questions that accompany the passage and helps to eliminate answers that contradict the author or stray too far from the point of view.

Paragraph one opens with some historical context. In fact, the paragraph is full of Sequence/Chronology Keywords. You're told first about Cesar Chavez and the birth of the Chicano political movement in the early 1960s. But, this is really just background to the passage's **Topic**—Valdez and the birth of Chicano theater—introduced at line 9. Noting how the dates dovetail. By 1965, Chavez and his United Farm Workers Union had made an international political impact. At this point, Chicano theater is just starting, spearheaded by Valdez's Teatro Campesino. The strategic reader will also see that the author is subtly distanced ("are generally credited by scholars") from those who laud Valdez as the founder of the Chicano theater movement. This is the first hint at the passage's **Scope**, which will turn out to include not only the story of Valdez and the Teatro Campesino, but also a debate over how much credit Valdez should receive for creating Chicano theater.

Paragraph two goes into detail about the founding of the Teatro Campesino. Its first fifteen lines are narrative, and your margin notes should briefly summarize the high points: Valdez got farm workers to improvise situations they faced at work and in life and then shaped them into sketches he labeled *actos*. The troupe first performed for farm workers and grew popular as they continued. The narrative becomes more complicated in the final third of the paragraph. First, from lines 33 to 38, you learn Valdez's goal for the *actos*: they should comically depict farm workers' problems, offer a solution, lampoon management, and inspire social action. The author positively evaluates Valdez's goal at the end of the paragraph. *Actos* had "palpable immediacy" (lines 38–39) because they came from real life situations.

To this point, there have been only hints and feints at the true Scope and Purpose of the passage, but paragraph three introduces a debate that leads to the author's conclusion. Yolanda Broyles-Gonzalez has criticized those who "credit Valdez individually" as the inventor of *actos*. She wants the farm workers who improvised scenes for him to get more credit. Broyles-Gonzalez supports this position with the example of *carpas*, a working-class theater genre from earlier in the century. The author concurs that many of the farm workers would have known *carpas* and must have adapted their style and conventions. Using Broyles-Gonzalez as a foil,

the passage's author is now ready to summarize. The long final sentence, which serves as the author's **Main Idea**, makes three points: 1) Teatro Campesino was a "collective accomplishment," 2) Valdez was "crucial" to the creation of *actos*, and 3) *actos* blend *carpas* and European theater. In light of this summary, the author's **Purpose** is best described as to both portray the development of actos and evaluate the extent of Valdez's influence.

13. (C) Global

Step 2: Identify the Question Type
This is a typical Global question stem, identified by the phrase "main point of the passage."

Step 3: Research the Relevant Text
For strategic readers who have summarized the Purpose and Main Idea, Global questions usually involve no research within the text. A passage like this one, where the author's conclusion is so clearly stated might constitute the exception.

Step 4: Make a Prediction
At the end of the passage, the author concluded that the creation of Teatro Campesino and its *actos* was a collective effort, but noted that Valdez deserved special credit for bringing his artistic vision and training to the process. Be careful as you evaluate the answer choices to seek out the one that correctly matches the *meaning* of the author's Main Idea. Wrong answers here are certain to include terms or concepts from the passage but will distort or misstate them.

Step 5: Evaluate the Answer Choices
(C) paraphrases the passage's final sentence and matches your prediction in meaning and scope.

(A) is a 180. The new challenger, Broyles-Gonzalez, questions Valdez's individual impact by citing the earlier historical forms his actors must have known.

(B) distorts the connections among several passage details. In the paragraph one, you learned that Valdez approached Chavez about using theater to organize farm labor, but the extent of Chavez's influence isn't of interest to the author or the critics she cites.

(D) takes a point made by Broyles-Gonzalez and attempts to inflate it to the Main Idea of the passage. The author acknowledges the value of the point made here, but it's too minor to constitute the Main Idea.

(E) is Half-Right/Half-Wrong. It starts convincingly enough, but the author never claims that Valdez leveraged political or academic creations to make his theater group successful.

14. (E) Logic Function

Step 2: Identify the Question Type
Logic Function questions center on *how* the author uses a paragraph, a detail, an example, or, in questions like this

one, a single word. In this vocabulary-in-context variant, the word will always be one that has multiple meanings. Your task is to research the text and define the word in question with your own paraphrase.

Step 3: Research the Relevant Text

The word at issue here was associated with an Emphasis Keyword —*palpable*—and comes from a sentence that also contains an Evidence Keyword—[*b*]*ecause*—to explain the author's use of *immediacy* to describe *actos*. Here, the author claims that their immediacy came from the real life situations they depicted.

Step 4: Make a Prediction

Wrong answers will contain other possible meanings of the word referred to in the question stem. Don't bring in your outside knowledge. The correct answer will describe a performance that appears true because of its similarity to the actors' real life circumstances. That's just what the author was describing in the text.

Step 5: Evaluate the Answer Choices

(E) is correct. The author credits the *actos* with "palpable immediacy" because they told of the actors' personal experiences.

(A) distorts the passage's earlier references to outgoing audience members and field side performances. You never read that the audiences and actors were in close physical proximity.

(B) is Out of Scope. It may be true that the informal, improvisational nature of *actos* led to actors "breaking the fourth wall," but you haven't learned that from the passage, so it cannot be the correct answer.

(C) distorts the author's praise of the *actos* performances by focusing on the "ease" with which they were created. The author never says that the work these actors did was easy.

(D) is a Faulty Use of Detail, referring to details earlier in the paragraph about Valdez and his troupe creating *actos*. The "palpable immediacy" here refers instead to the troupe's performances of the *actos* and the effect they had on audiences.

15. (A) Logic Function

Step 2: Identify the Question Type

Like the preceding question, this one asks *how* the author uses an element in the text. This time, the reference is to a sentence, specifically the second sentence in the passage. Logic Function questions will always provide precise research clues.

Step 3: Research the Relevant Text

The second sentence is in the short background portion at the start of the passage. It tells you how influential Chavez and

the United Farm Workers were when Valdez started putting together a theater group for farm workers.

Step 4: Make a Prediction

A common mistake made by poorly trained test takers is to look for an answer that says what the reference in a Logic Function question was *about*, rather than what the author was doing with it. Here, the author is helping the reader to understand where Valdez's Chicano theater came from, socially and politically. The right answer will paraphrase the author's rhetorical purpose for including the reference.

Step 5: Evaluate the Answer Choices

(A) accurately describes the role of the portion of paragraph one about Chavez and the United Farm Workers. In the following sentence, the author tells you that Valdez created the Teatro Campesino to organize farm workers, and paragraph two goes into detail about Valdez's own background and his political goals for the *actos* his group performed.

(B) is a 180. Chavez and his union apparently paved the way for a robust Chicano theater.

(C) is a Distortion. The passage does not dispute that the *actos* were effective as political performances, so countering such a claim is not the author's reason for mentioning the accomplishments of the United Farm Workers. Moreover, the accomplishments cited in the second sentence had already happened at the time of the Teatro Campesino's founding, so they would be Out of Scope with respect to how effective the theater group's work was.

(D) misses the scope of the passage altogether. The author makes no claim that scholars have excluded Chicano theater from their studies. Indeed, the main dispute later in the passage is among scholars of that movement's history.

(E) is a classic Faulty Use of Detail. The argument over the extent of Valdez's influence comes much later in the passage. The author includes the second sentence to provide background for introducing Valdez and for telling how and why he formed his group, not for the scholarly debate over how much credit he should receive.

16. (D) Detail

Step 2: Identify the Question Type

The stem's opening phrase—"The passage indicates"—tells you that the correct answer will be found explicitly in the text. Your task is to find where the author told you what *actos* and *carpas* had in common.

Step 3: Research the Relevant Text

The author introduced *carpas* in paragraph three, following the Emphasis Keyword *especially*, which highlights how central they were to Broyles-Gonzalez's thesis. The remainder of that sentence describes the similarities between *carpas* and *actos*; both were informal, satirical, and staged for working-class audiences.

Step 4: Make a Prediction

One or more of the three similarities you identified in your research will almost certainly be found in the correct answer.

Step 5: Evaluate the Answer Choices

(D) is correct. The author noted the satirical nature of both *actos* and *carpas* and mentioned satire in the sentence comparing the two genres.

(A) is Half-Right/Half-Wrong. The author cites European theater as an element in *actos* (lines 58–59) but does not associate this with *carpas* at any point.

(B) is a Faulty use of Detail; Valdez was a former member of the San Francisco mime troupe (lines 29–30), but this fact is in no way associated with *carpas* in the passage.

(C) is a Distortion. While the passage states that *carpas* were "performed in tents to mainly working-class audiences" (lines 48–49), there's no support for the claim that they were performed on farms.

(E) is Out of Scope. Although paragraph one indicates that Valdez was motivated to create a theater that would organize farm workers, nothing in the passage associates *carpas* with the labor movement. Indeed, the implication is that *carpas* were performed in an era preceding the organization of farm workers.

17. (D) Inference

Step 2: Identify the Question Type

The question type is signaled clearly by the word "inferred." Somewhat subtler is the referent-reading clue in this stem. While the entire passage is about Valdez, his views are likely to surface in paragraph two, where the author detailed the creation of the Teatro Campesino and Valdez's goals for *actos*.

Step 3: Research the Relevant Text

It's tempting to reread large portions of text to extract all of the possible opinions that might be associated with Valdez; that likely would waste time. Instead, review your margin notes from paragraph two to get the outline of Valdez's program and agenda. He got farm workers to improvise for him, guided their performances into short skits, and wanted the skits to be satirical and inspire social action.

Step 4: Make a Prediction

Use the crucial information you've extracted to your margin notes to identify the correct answer and to eliminate the clearly wrong ones. A good Roadmap will tell you what you need to know about Valdez's views.

Step 5: Evaluate the Answer Choices

(D) is correct. From what you learned of him in the passage, Valdez would give an emphatic "yes" if asked whether

untrained actors could be successful. After all, he used farm workers to create the Teatro Campesino.

(A) is not supported. Nothing in the passage indicates that Valdez himself had any opinion of, or even knowledge of, *carpas*.

(B) is not supported. All you know of Valdez's relationship with Chavez is that Valdez approached him about organizing farm workers through the theater. Nothing in the passage reveals whether Valdez was dissatisfied with Chavez's support.

(C) is not suppoerted. The passage tells you that Valdez was a trained student of the theater, and includes that background among his influences. There's nothing to indicate that he disdained that tradition in his work with the Teatro Campesino.

(E) is a 180, at worst. Valdez's goal was to create theater that had a social impact and that could help organize labor.

18. (C) Inference

Step 2: Identify the Question Type

The first clue that this is an Inference question is the opening phrase—"Based on the passage ..." in the stem. The next part of the stem—"it can be concluded that"—reminds you that the correct answer to an inference question must be true based on information in the passage. Note that your task in this question is similar to one you might find in comparative reading. The correct answer must be something that both the author and Broyles-Gonzalez would agree with, which is a research clue as well.

Step 3: Research the Relevant Text

Information about Broyles-Gonzalez is found only in paragraph three. She believes that critics have overemphasized Valdez's individual role in creating *actos*. Her primary evidence is the likelihood that the performers he used would have been influenced by the earlier *carpas* genre. The author follows with the opinion that the development of *actos* was a collective endeavor and that *actos* are a mixture of the *carpas* and European theater influences. It's worth noting, too, that the author uses the Opinion Keyword *rightly* (line 41) when describing Broyles-Gonzalez's criticism of theater historians.

Step 4: Make a Prediction

When test makers ask you to find a point of agreement between two people, research both opinions. At least some of the wrong answers are likely to contain points of view that only one of the two parties would agree with. Here, the author appears to be convinced by Broyles-Gonzalez's assertion that *carpas* did inform the development of Valdez's *actos*, although the author maintains that Valdez deserves a great deal of credit for the latter.

Step 5: Evaluate the Answer Choices

(C) is correct. The main point on which the author seems to agree with Broyles-Gonzalez is that *actos* reflect the influence of the earlier *carpas* genre.

(A) is Out of Scope. Nothing is said about from where either the author or Broyles-Gonzalez thinks that *carpas* came.

(B) is a Distortion. Broyles-Gonzalez, so far as you know from the passage, ascribes no motive to the scholars who have praised Valdez. You know only that she thinks their conclusions have exaggerated his importance.

(D) is a Distortion. Broyles-Gonzalez bases her critique, which the author appears to agree with it, not on whether or how much Valdez knew about *carpas*, but rather on the likelihood that his performers did.

(E) is Out of Scope. Broyles-Gonzalez's opinion on the extent of European influence on *actos* is not reported in the passage.

19. (C) Inference

Step 2: Identify the Question Type

This is an Inference question because you're asked to select the answer choice that "the statements in the passage most strongly support". Here, you have a research clue; the correct answer will be something that can be deduced about Valdez's theater troupe, the Teatro Campesino.

Step 3: Research the Relevant Text

Facts about the Teatro Campesino are scattered throughout the passage. It grew out of Valdez's 1965 efforts to create a theater that would help the farm labor movement (lines 8–13); many credit it with initiating Chicano theater (lines 13–15); it consisted of farm workers who were likely familiar with *carpas* (lines 51–54).

Step 4: Make a Prediction

Most of the places where the passage mentions the Teatro Campesino have already been used in other questions; that's typical. Don't reject predictions or correct answers because they refer you back to the same section of text tested in a previous question. Test makers' attention focuses around Keywords; that's what makes the accompanying text so crucial for you. Here, you can't predict which of the references to Teatro Campesino will be rewarded in the correct answer, so use your Roadmap to help you eliminate wrong answers and zero on the credited response.

Step 5: Evaluate the Answer Choices

(C) must be true based on the passage. This answer choice rewards you for combining the facts from the second and third sentences. If Chavez and the United Farm Workers had already received international attention by the time Valdez first considered founding a theater group, then the theater group must not have played a role in the labor union's earliest efforts to achieve such recognition.

(A) is Out of Scope of the passage, which never mentions the response of farm owners to the Teatro Campesino.

(B) is a Distortion. Valdez is the only person who you know was part of the San Francisco Mime Troupe.

(D) is Out of Scope. Presumably theater for Mexican Americans was performed in Spanish, but this is not stated in the passage, nor is any reference to later performances in English. It's never enough for inference answers to be reasonable; they must have clear support in the passage text.

(E) also strays beyond the passage text. While you learned in paragraph one that Chavez's labor efforts had an impact in Mexico and in the United States, you never learn the nationality of critics who praised the Teatro Campesino.

20. (B) Inference

Step 2: Identify the Question Type

This is the fourth Inference question associated with this passage. Test makers richly reward test takers' ability to determine what must follow from the explicit language of the passage. There's no research clue in this stem, so you'll start your analysis at a fairly high level.

Step 3: Research the Relevant Text

When Inference questions lack research clues, use your summaries of Topic, Scope, Purpose, and Main Idea to prepare yourself to evaluate the choices. Here, the passage's long, final sentence provided the author's main point and, by the time you get to this question, your familiarity with the Roadmap should allow you to make quick work of evaluating the choices.

Step 4: Make a Prediction

Use your complete understanding to eliminate the clearly wrong answers. If necessary, you can use the remaining choices as research clues to ensure your certainty with the correct choice.

Step 5: Evaluate the Answer Choices

(B) is the correct answer and rewards you for combining statements from the passage. You know from the first two paragraphs, that the *actos* of the Teatro Campesino were the most influential form of Chicano theater in the 1960s. You know, from lines 35 to 36, that *actos* were satiric and comical. Together, these statements ensure that **(B)** is true based on the passage.

(A) is Extreme. Broyles-Gonzalez used *carpas* to support her thesis that the Teatro Campesino was a collective accomplishment, but the passage does not discuss the extent to which others have studied the genre.

(C) is a Distortion. This answer could trap a hurried student who doesn't read the entire choice. According to paragraph two, Valdez took pains to ensure that the *actos* reflected the real life experiences of farm workers. The passage does not support the statement that he tried to recreate *carpas*.

(D) reverses the roles of Valdez and the performers in the creation of the *actos*. The farm workers actually improvised scenes first, and Valdez molded them into the scenes that they performed (lines 24–28).

(E) is Out of Scope. The only reference the author makes to the 1970s (line 16) notes that this is when the Chicano theater movement reached its high point. The passage is silent on what, if anything, Valdez did later in his career.

Passage 4: Contingency Fees in Western Australia

Step 1: Read the Passage Strategically
Sample Roadmap

line #	Keyword/phrase	¶ Margin notes
2		LRCWA report
4–5	important recommendations	Recs about contingency fees
7	only if	
8	Because	Paid only if case won; usually higher $ than regular fees
11	Although	
12	recommended	One rec. type "uplift"
13	only one	
15	require	
17	intended; prevent	
18	gaining disproportionately	Goal: prevent unjust lawyer fees
19	thus; ensure	
20	not eroded; further	
21	recommendation	
22	should be permitted only	2 conditions
23	two; : first	
24	must; only	1) Last resort
26	second	
27	must	2) Client can't pay
30	Unfortunately	Auth: problem–lawyers must research client finances & costs
32	forced; not only	
33–34	but also	
36–37	onerous; not least	Costs hard to predict
41	In addition; burdensome	
44–45	unfair; unjustly limit	Auth: unfair to clients w/o liquid assets
46	inaccessible	
49	More importantly; primary	
50	all	
51	First	3 reasons to use contingency fees
52	Second	
55	Finally	
58	reasonable	

Discussion

This passage introduces its **Topic**—the Law Reform Commission of Western Australia's (LRCWA's) recommendations for contingency fees—immediately. Paragraph one defines contingency fee agreements—that is, the lawyer is paid if successful—and tells you a potential issue—fees are usually high. The Scope is found in the following paragraph, but a good strategic reader will anticipate that the author opinion (or a debate among other scholars) is coming.

Paragraph two further defines LRCWA's recommendations. Its report likes only "uplift" fee agreements, which pay the successful lawyer the normal fee plus an agreed-upon percentage. The report recommends uplift arrangements in order to prevent unreasonable profiteering by attorneys, who might claim fees so high the plaintiff's recovery may be inadequate. Moreover, the report recommends that uplift agreements be used when 1) all other fee agreements fail, and 2) the client could not otherwise afford to pursue the case. Note that you still haven't read the author's opinion at this point.

The first word of paragraph three is an Opinion Keyword. It gives you the author's point of view on the recommendations and introduces the **Scope**, that is, problems with the report's recommendations. The first problem, according to paragraph three, is that it's difficult for lawyers to assess their client's financial situation and to anticipate the costs of a given trial. After all, the cost of a case changes and grows depending on the other side's strategy.

Paragraph four reveals the author's second concern about the report's limitations: it would make contingency fee agreements available only to the poorest clients. The author finds this unfair to others and notes that even wealthy clients might not be able to pursue their cases if they lack access to cash. Finally, at line 49 with the emphasis phrase "[m]ore importantly," the author lists three reasons why contingency arrangements should be accessible to everyone. You need not memorize all three, but certainly read and understand them. They indicate that contingency fees: finance legal actions, shift the risk of losing to the lawyer, and make lawyers work harder. A Roadmap will facilitate your research on these three reasons. At the end, you can see that the author's **Purpose**—to critique the report's recommendations—dovetails neatly with the passage's Scope. A summary of the **Main Idea** would be: LRCWA recommendations on contingency fees are flawed because they burden lawyers and treat some clients unfairly.

21. (B) Logic Reasoning (Parallel Reasoning)

Step 2: Identify the Question Type

Of the several types of logical reasoning questions test makers will repurpose for reading comprehension, Parallel Reasoning is most popular. Here, the correct answer will be analogous to the LRCWA report's definition of uplift fee agreements. Research the report's definition and abstract its key features. The correct answer may have nothing to do with legal actions, but it will mirror the uplift fee model exactly.

Step 3: Research the Relevant Text

The passage defined uplift fee agreements at the beginning of paragraph two. Under the uplift arrangement, the lawyer is paid only if the case is won at which time he receives a fee plus an agreed-upon percentage of the recovery.

Step 4: Make a Prediction

The correct answer will describe a fee arrangement in which the party doing the work is paid only if successful. If successful, an agreed-upon fee that is higher than the basic rate is paid.

Step 5: Evaluate the Answer Choices

(B) is correct. Here, the consultants are paid only if they help the company. Don't be distracted by the fact that they receive double instead of a percentage. The fact that they earn more than their basic fee is the key to making this choice's scenario similar to uplift agreements.

(A) is more like a class action lawsuit than an uplift agreement between one plaintiff and his lawyer. Here, the initial costs are absorbed by a big group whose members promise to divide the proceeds if successful.

(C) is a 180. As paragraph three makes clear, the point of contingency agreements is to shift the risk of loss to the attorney, not to apportion it.

(D) describes a possible way to make an arrangement with your lawyer, with the rate determined by risk and overhead. But that's not how the report describes uplift agreements.

(E) is closer to a lawyer asking for a retainer from a client who may not be able to pay than it is to the uplift agreement described in the passage.

22. (A) Detail

Step 2: Identify the Question Type

This is a Detail question. The phrase "The passage states" indicates the correct answer will be something explicitly stated as fact in the text. Don't be dismayed by the lack of a research clue in this stem. The correct answer should be associated with a Keyword and contained in a crucial piece of the text highlighted in your Roadmap.

Step 3: Research the Relevant Text

The stem is unhelpful, so use the answer choices as research clues. Confirm or disconfirm each choice with reference to the text.

Step 4: Make a Prediction

While the question stem gave you nothing concrete with which to research, portions of the passage should stand out as likely places to find the correct answer. Test makers will reward you for understanding definitions and points of support, not memorization. Check the answer choices, and expect test makers to offer something crucial to the argument.

Step 5: Evaluate the Answer Choices

(A) is correct. This was one of the reasons the author cited for making contingency agreements available to clients. It follows the Sequence Keyword [*s*]*econd* at line 52.

(B) is a 180. At the end of paragraph one, the author states that contingency agreements produce fees higher than usual.

(C) is Out of Scope. The passage never assesses the likelihood that the report's recommendations will be implemented.

(D) is a 180. It contradicts the author's final point in support of contingency agreements (see lines 57–59).

(E) is Extreme. This is consistent with the definition of the uplift agreements, which is the only type of contingency-fee agreement recommended by the LRCWA. However, that does not mean this is how contingency agreements *usually* work in actuality.

23. (E) Global

Step 2: Identify the Question Type

Almost all LSAT passages contain a straightforward Global question like this one. It's a little unusual to find it in the middle of the question set, but a quick scan of the question stems reveals the phrase "author's main purpose." With its straightforward task and short answers, this is a good question to attempt first, while the big picture of the passage is still fresh in your mind.

Step 3: Research the Relevant Text

Global questions shouldn't require textual research if you've Roadmapped appropriately. Your Purpose summary should begin with something like "to critique" or "to evaluate." The correct answer has to reflect that tone. This author was not a neutral reporter.

Step 4: Make a Prediction

Because the correct answer to a main-purpose question like this one summarizes what the author was trying to accomplish, the verb(s) it uses must accurately reflect the author's goal. That will help to evaluate the choices quickly.

But, don't let it make you a careless reader. As this question illustrates, test makers disguise wrong answers.

Step 5: Evaluate the Answer Choices

(E) is correct. If you read only the first verb here—"explain"—you may prematurely eliminate the answer. The passage does, in fact, explain uplift agreements in paragraph two. This choice is unequivocally correct because it's the only one to include "critically evaluate," which is the author's primary goal.

(A) is a 180. The author is the critic here, not the defender.

(B) is a Distortion. This reflects the goals of LRCWA's report, not those of the author, who focuses solely on evaluating the report's recommendation.

(C) is a Distortion. First, the author doesn't attempt to "support" anyone else's view. Second, the author's criticism is that it would be burdensome to attorneys and unfair to many clients, but that's not to say it would make situations worse.

(D) is Out of Scope. The author never opines on the possible significance of the enactment of LRCWA's recommendations, although the passage implies that restrictions would limit the use of contingency agreements for many clients and would make the business of running a law practice harder.

24. (C) Detail

Step 2: Identify the Question Type

There's no attempt to disguise the question. The correct answer will be something "given by the passage." But, contrast this question with question 22. Here, you're told exactly where to research the text. This will allow for a nearly exact prediction of the correct answer.

Step 3: Research the Relevant Text

In paragraph three, the author discusses the difficulties facing attorneys assessing clients' qualifications to enter uplift agreements under LRCWA's proposed standards. He gives two such difficulties. First, it would be onerous for lawyers to investigate their clients' financial situations; second, it's hard to assess costs because they tend to change as cases unfold.

Step 4: Make a Prediction

Your research shows that the correct answer must say one of two things, either that the lawyer must investigate a potential client's finances or estimate the probable cost of litigation. Note that the author emphasized the second of the two reasons with the Keywords "not the least of which is," making the changing costs of cases the most likely suspect as the right answer here.

Step 5: Evaluate the Answer Choices

(C) matches the prediction. The wording of the choice is simply a paraphrase of what followed the emphasis signal "not the least of which is" in the passage.

(A) is a Distortion; it was the cost of cases, not the length of trials, that was cited in the passage. Do not bring in outside information, however reasonable, to justify an answer choice. The length of a potential trial is definitely one of the costs associated with conducting a legal case but far from the only one, and it was never mentioned as a detail in the passage.

(B) is Out of Scope. While perhaps a reasonable point, this is not mentioned in the passage.

(D) is a Distortion. This choice accurately states one of LRCWA's proposed restrictions. It's the resulting investigative burdens, however, that the author says would make it difficult for lawyers to assess which clients qualify.

(E) is a Distortion. The author does, indeed, say that lawyers would have to spend time investigating both the legal issues of the case and their clients' financial situations, but he doesn't state that the latter takes time away from the former.

25. (B) Inference

Step 2: Identify the Question Type

This question gives you an unmistakable research clue: it quotes a portion of the text and cites the lines in which it appears. Find the choice that matches the author's intended meaning for the phrase in its context in the passage. When test makers pose this kind of question, the quoted language itself will be open to multiple interpretations if considered apart from the passage. But, the author's intended meaning will be clear from the way in which the word or phrase is used in the passage text.

Step 3: Research the Relevant Text

Lines 18 to 19 refer to the heart of paragraph two. The sentence in which the quoted phrase tells you what LRCWA's recommendations intend to prevent immediately follows; the author adds "and thus ensure just compensation to plaintiffs is not eroded."

Step 4: Make a Prediction

The author tells you that the intent is to ensure "just compensation" and uses the phrase quoted in the question stem to imply *un*just compensation. Look for the answer that means the lawyer gets an unfair portion of the damages reward.

Step 5: Evaluate the Answer Choices

(B) is verbose, but its meaning matches the prediction and the author's intent. For the attorney to get "a higher portion ... than is reasonable" given the work and risks would, indeed, be unjust.

(A) doesn't indicate that the amount is unfair or unjustified. It's unlikely that LRCWA wants to prevent lawyers from making a profit for their work; the commission is merely trying to avoid outrageous, unreasonable percentages of the reward.

(C) confuses the clients' perception of unfairness with unfairness in fact. For all you know, the client might think the lawyer deserves more or deserves nothing. That's beside the point of the phrase as it's used in the passage.

(D) is a blatant 180. In any contingency agreement, the lawyer's pay rests on success with the case. The quote specifically references those cases in which contingency agreements result in unfair, unreasonable proportions for the lawyer.

(E) isn't supported by the passage either. There's nothing in the passage to suggest that the judge or the jury knows the details of the fee agreement or that either considers the lawyer's fee.

26. (D) Detail

Step 2: Identify the Question Type

There are a lot of details in this passage, related both to LRCWA's report and the author's criticisms of them. Not surprisingly, test makers will reward you for noting of the most important ones. Signaled by the opening phrase—"According to the passage"—this is the third detail question in this set. This question's research clue guides you to paragraph two.

Step 3: Research the Relevant Text

The report's recommendations are all found in paragraph two. There, you're told that LRCWA wants only uplift fee arrangements to be used and wants even those used only as a last resort, when no other agreement works and the client can finance the case in no other way.

Step 4: Make a Prediction

Even when test makers call for an answer that was stated in the passage, they're unlikely to mimic its phraseology. In fact, they may well use words from the passage in wrong answers. To prepare yourself to evaluate Detail-question answer choices, paraphrase the text and know the meaning and intent of the language used. Here, the right answer may not use phrases like "last resort" or "financially unable to pay," but it certainly will match the meaning of the relevant portion of the passage.

Step 5: Evaluate the Answer Choices

(D) is correct, paraphrasing LRCWA's first restriction, that contingency arrangements be used only as a "last resort." If a noncontingency fee arrangement were "practicable," the LRCWA plan would require the client and attorney to use it instead.

(A) is a Faulty Use of Detail, conflating one of the author's criticisms with the report recommendations. Near the end of paragraph four, the author cited attorney diligence as one reason that clients might prefer to use contingency agreements, but LRCWA's recommendations don't address lawyers' increasing commitment to their cases.

(B) is a Distortion. LRCWA is concerned with lawyers receiving an unfair portion of a damages award, not with the award's overall size.

(C) may be possible, as there may be cases in which the client could not afford to pay constitute cases of "last resort" as defined by LRCWA. However, the passage doesn't directly say that. In Detail questions, wait for the answer that was stated outright in the passage.

(E) is a Distortion. Even if the lawyer were reasonably sure the expenses would be covered, LRCWA's recommendations would favor another fee arrangement. The opening phrase of this answer choice—"Not to be used except"—could tempt a student who didn't read the entire answer choice. But the remainder of the choice details an exception not found in the passage.

27. (B) Logic Reasoning (Weaken)

Step 2: Identify the Question Type
In this question stem, test makers borrowed typical Weaken question language—"most seriously undermines"—straight from the Logical Reasoning section. Treat the relevant portion of the passage as you would a Logical Reasoning stimulus, and look for the answer that makes it less likely that the author's conclusion follows from his evidence.

Step 3: Research the Relevant Text
The author has two criticisms of LRCWA's proposal. The first, from paragraph three, is that the report's recommendations would burden lawyers who would be forced to assess their clients' financial situations and case costs. The second, from paragraph four, is that the proposal would be unfair to clients who could afford other fee arrangements but might prefer to enter into a contingency agreement.

Step 4: Make a Prediction
Whether you prefer the Logical Reasoning section or the Reading Comprehension section, allow your strengths from one to help you with the other. Here, you're asked to make an argument's conclusion less likely; by the final question in the set, you should understand the arguments well. To weaken the first, the answer suggests the burdens imposed by assessing client finances and case costs is less onerous than the author assumes. To weaken the second, the answer must present a fact that makes it less likely that LRCWA's recommendations are unfair to clients of certain socioeconomic levels.

Step 5: Evaluate the Answer Choices
(B) weakens the author's first criticism. If lawyers routinely engaged in the assessment of their prospective clients' finances as described, it would be less likely that LRCWA's recommendations increase burdens, thus weakening the author's criticism.

(A) is irrelevant. While higher proportions of uplift fee arrangement lawsuits filed by low-income litigants speaks to the fact that contingency fee agreements may make legal representation more accessible to some, this fact wouldn't affect the weight of the criticisms contained in the text.

(C) is irrelevant. The likelihood of the recommendations being implemented has no bearing on the author's argument against them. Moreover, LRCWA's recommendations are, ostensibly at least, intended to benefit clients, not lawyers; this answer choice contradicts itself.

(D) is irrelevant. If the facts in this choice are true, the need for the report's recommendation is less necessary and its intended benefits are less important. But, they have no impact on the author's criticisms, which focus on the investigative burden placed on lawyers and the potential unfairness to well-off clients.

(E) is Out of Scope of the author's criticisms. The fee arrangements actually used in most jurisdictions are irrelevant to his concerns about the restrictions on the use of uplift agreements. If anything, this choice strengthens the author's overall argument through an additional objection to the recommendations, though it doesn't strengthen or weaken the arguments he makes in the passage. He might argue that learning a new fee arrangement is another burden placed upon lawyers.

PrepTest 61

The Inside Story

PrepTest 61 was administered in October 2010. It challenged 54,345 test takers. What made this test so hard? Here's a breakdown of what Kaplan students who were surveyed after taking the official exam considered PrepTest 61's most difficult section.

Hardest PrepTest 61 Section as Reported by Test Takers

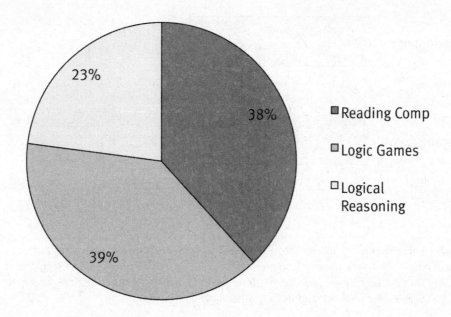

Based on these results, you might think that studying Reading Comprehension and Logic Games are the key to LSAT success. Well, those sections are important, but test takers' perceptions don't tell the whole story. For that, you need to consider students' actual performance. The following chart shows the average number of students to miss each question in each of PrepTest 61's different sections.

Percentage Incorrect by PrepTest 61 Section Type

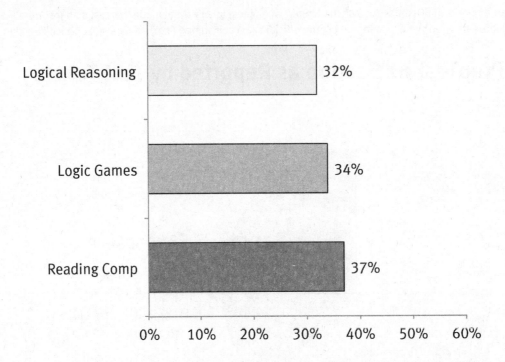

Actual student performance tells a somewhat different story. On average, students were almost equally likely to miss questions in all three of the different section types. Although Reading Comprehension and Logic Games were somewhat higher in actual difficulty than Logical Reasoning, because the Logic Games section has fewer questions than the other sections, that means there were fewer incorrect answers from the Logic Games section than from any other individual section.

Maybe students overestimate the difficulty of the Reading Comp or Logic Games sections because a really hard passage or Logic Game is so easy to remember after the test. But the truth is that the testmaker places hard questions throughout the test. Here were the locations of the 10 hardest (most missed) questions in the exam.

Location of 10 Most Difficult Questions in PrepTest 61

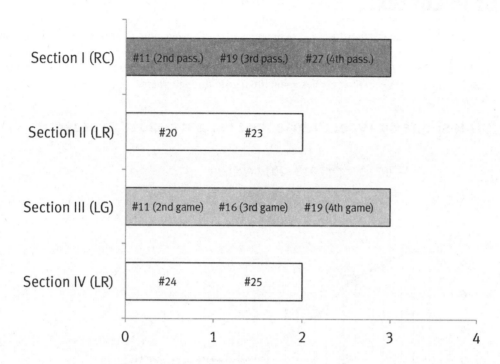

The takeaway from this data is that, to maximize your potential on the LSAT, you need to take a comprehensive approach. Test yourself rigorously, and review your performance on every section of the test. Kaplan's LSAT explanations provide the expertise and insight you need to fully understand your results. The explanations are written and edited by a team of LSAT experts, who have helped thousands of students improve their scores. Kaplan always provides data-driven analysis of the test, ranking the difficulty of every question based on actual student performance. The 10 hardest questions on every test are highlighted with a 4-star difficulty rating, the highest we give. The analysis breaks down the remaining questions into 1-, 2-, and 3-star ratings so that you can compare your performance to thousands of other test takers on all LSAC material.

Don't settle for wondering whether a question was really as hard as it seemed to you. Analyze the test with real data, and learn the secrets and strategies that help top scorers master the LSAT.

6 Can't-Miss Features of PrepTest 61

- Nearly every test has some interesting features, but PrepTest 61 is unusually mundane. To begin with, the number of questions needed for a certain score are all within one of the all-time averages, e.g. for all released PrepTests the average number of correct answers for a 151 is 57.97, and on PrepTest 61, 58 correct answers are needed for a 151.
- All Logical Reasoning questions are within two of their all-time averages.
- The Logic Games section contains two Sequencing games (albeit one Strict and one Loose), one Distribution game, and one Hybrid game. That's a pretty standard construction—10 tests from 2007–2017 have also had two Sequencing games, one Matching/Distribution game, and one Hybrid.
- In Reading Comprehension, the Comparative Reading set of passages are Natural Science for the sixth time in 11 tests. Additionally, the number of questions on the four passages are 6-6-7-8—the most popular construction.
- One small anomaly is that (E) is correct in the Logic Games section only twice. That's not even the record for the fewest number of times though, but it may have meant test takers had to do a bit less answer choice testing on many questions.
- The #1 film the weekend PrepTest 61 was administered was *The Social Network*. That reminds us, follow us on Facebook for more information about your LSAT preparation!

PrepTest 61 in Context

As much fun as it is to find out what makes a PrepTest unique or noteworthy, it's even more important to know just how representative it is of other LSAT administrations (and, thus, how likely it is to be representative of the exam you will face on Test Day). The following charts compare the numbers of each kind of question and game on PrepTest 61 to the average numbers seen on all officially released LSATs administered over the past five years (from 2013 through 2017).

Number of LR Questions by Type: PrepTest 61 vs. 2013–2017 Average

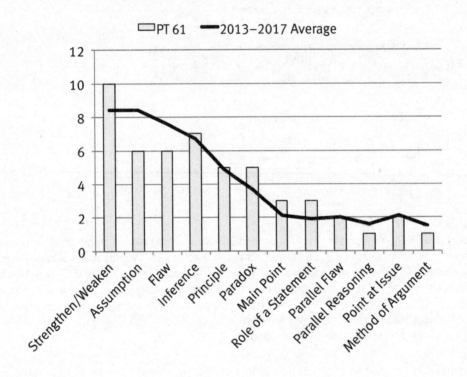

Number of LG Games by Type: PrepTest 61 vs. 2013–2017 Average

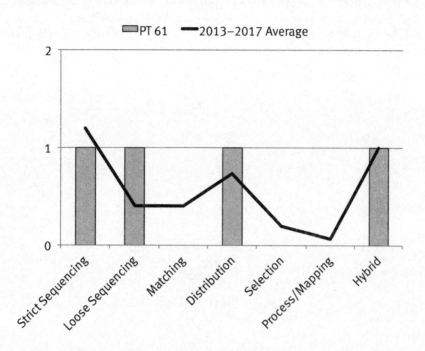

Number of RC Questions by Type: PrepTest 61 vs. 2013–2017 Average

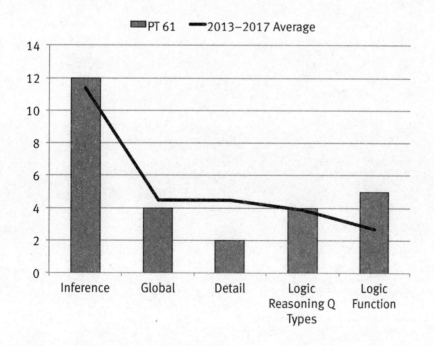

There isn't usually a huge difference in the distribution of questions from LSAT to LSAT, but if this test seems harder (or easier) to you than another you've taken, compare the number of questions of the types on which you, personally, are strongest and weakest. Then, explore within each section to see if your best or worst question types came earlier or later.

Students in Kaplan's comprehensive LSAT courses have access to every released LSAT and to a library of thousands of officially released questions arranged by question, game, and passage type. If you are studying on your own, you have to do a bit more work to identify your strengths and your areas of opportunity. Quantitative analysis (like that in the charts shown here) is an important tool for understanding how the test is constructed, and how you are performing on it.

Section I: Reading Comprehension

Passage 1: Universal Declaration of Human Rights

Q#	Question Type	Correct	Difficulty
1	Logic Function	D	★
2	Logic Function	B	★★
3	Inference	B	★
4	Detail (EXCEPT)	D	★
5	Inference	E	★
6	Inference	A	★★

Passage 2: The Value of Forgeries

Q#	Question Type	Correct	Difficulty
7	Global	C	★
8	Inference	A	★★
9	Logic Function	E	★
10	Logic Reasoning (Parallel Reasoning)	C	★★
11	Inference	B	★★★★
12	Inference	E	★★★
13	Logic Reasoning (Strengthen)	B	★

Passage 3: Can Animals Lie?

Q#	Question Type	Correct	Difficulty
14	Global	B	★★★
15	Logic Function	A	★★
16	Inference	D	★★★
17	Logic Reasoning (Strengthen)	D	★★
18	Logic Reasoning (Point at Issue)	C	★★
19	Global	B	★★★★

Passage 4: African American Historiography

Q#	Question Type	Correct	Difficulty
20	Global	D	★
21	Inference	E	★★
22	Inference	A	★★★
23	Inference	E	★★★
24	Detail	E	★★
25	Inference	B	★★★
26	Logic Function	A	★★
27	Logic Reasoning (Parallel Reasoning)	B	★★★★

Passage 1: Universal Declaration of Human Rights

Step 1: Read the Passage Strategically
Sample Roadmap

line #	Keyword/phrase	¶ Margin notes
3	first	UDHR – 1st int'l treaty to affirm HR
4	expressly affirm	
6	Although	
14	felt	Same language in UN charter, but not strong enough
15	not strong enough	
16	did not go far enough	
17–18	lobbied vigorously	
19	proposed	
20	required	
22	implied an obligation	
24	Ultimately	
25	instead	UDHR adopted instead of strengthening Art. 1
32		Drafting process
35	argued passionately	Debate
37	essential	Final language
41	also asserted	
45	While; progressive	
46–47	weaknesses; most regrettable	Progressive but not binding
50	Nevertheless; has led, even in	
52	clearly deserves recognition	Auth – pro UDHR b/c it has been gateway to HR laws

Discussion

This passage dives right into its **Topic**—the Universal Declaration of Human Rights (UDHR)—in the first sentence. The author seems especially interested in the UDHR's timing and its status as a formative document in the development of international human rights law. Even here, at the beginning of the passage, the author's use of the Sequence Keywords "the first" alerts the strategic reader to pay attention to the UDHR's origins and its importance as a seminal treaty, which inform the **Scope** of the passage throughout.

Before delving further into the story of the UDHR, the author spends the bulk of paragraph one discussing the treaty's predecessor, Article 1 of the UN Charter. Article 1 addressed the subject of human rights, but many parties to the UN Charter felt that it "did not go far enough" and pushed for more robust provisions that would require signatories to take action to secure universal human rights. The author sums up the paragraph with another Sequence Keyword: [*u*]*ltimately*, Article 1 was not adopted. "[I]nstead," work on the UDHR was initiated.

Anticipate that the next paragraph will focus on that work.Indeed, paragraph two outlines the "elaborate … drafting process" that resulted in the UDHR. The author's language is increasingly emphatic here. Parties debated the UDHR "passionately." The result was a document with the "essential principles of freedom and equality" and an assertion of "fundamental human rights." The author lists those principles and rights between lines 39 and 44, things that should be noted in the margin next to the passage text.

What's missing thus far in the passage? The author's evaluation or critique. Although the testmakers will occasionally include purely expository passages, these are rare. Expect to find the author's voice and point of view at the end of a passage like this one. That's exactly what paragraph three delivers. Using a series of Contrast Keywords—[*w*]*hile* (line 45), "For all its …" (lines 47–48), [*n*]*evertheless* (line 50)—the author offers what he sees as the pros and cons of the UDHR. The treaty was "progressive," with "strong language and high ideals," but was, ultimately, "purely programmatic," a reference to its lack of enforcement, something the author finds "most regrettable." In the end, though, the author returns to the UDHR's status as the first document of its kind and considers it praiseworthy for the influence it's had on advancing the cause of international human rights. The author closes with three specific reasons that the UDHR "clearly deserves recognition." Don't try to memorize or even to paraphrase all three in the margin notes. Instead just make a note of their mention in the passage in case a question requires you to return to the list.

The final paragraph reveals the author's **Purpose** of evaluating the strengths and weaknesses of the UDHR as a formative human rights document. A proper summary of the

Main Idea should reflect both sides of the author's take: although UDHR's lack of legal enforcement was a regrettable weakness, it's important as the first articulation of international human rights and for its influence on subsequent human rights efforts.

1. (D) Logic Function

Step 2: Identify the Question Type

The question asks why the description "purely programmatic" was included in paragraph three. The phrase is contained in the question stem, along with the line reference (line 49). When presented with a Logic Function question like this one, locate the referenced text. *What* the passage said will not be nearly as important as *how* the author used the specific vocabulary.

Step 3: Research the Relevant Text

Here, research is a snap. Follow the clues in the question stem to the beginning of paragraph three. There, the Keywords and margin notes indicate that the author is discussing the UDHR's weaknesses, the most prominent of which is its lack of enforceability.

Step 4: Make a Prediction

Use your research to predict the correct answer to this question. Given the context of the referenced text, the author must be using the phrase "purely programmatic" to emphasize the lack of enforcement mechanisms in the UDHR. The treaty has "strong language and high ideals," but it is not legally binding.

Step 5: Evaluate the Answer Choices

(D) matches your prediction with a succinct paraphrase of the author's criticism of the UDHR. This states what the author is emphasizing and so is the correct answer.

All four of the wrong answers misidentify the purpose of this portion of the passage.

(A) distorts the criteria that the author believes make the UDHR praiseworthy; in lines 50 to 56, the author writes of how the UDHR has already inspired the creation of human rights conventions. The author used the description "purely programmatic" to criticize, not praise, the UDHR for its unenforceability.

(B), too, cites a positive aspect of the UDHR. That alone is enough to eliminate this answer choice. The author isn't talking about how the drafters translated ideals into standards here at all.

(C) discusses the drafting process, which was the subject of paragraph two, not three. The answer choice distorts even that. Nowhere in the passage does the author emphasize compromises that were made to ensure passage of the UDHR.

(E) introduces an ideal found nowhere in the passage. The only reference to the UN hierarchy comes near the beginning of paragraph two (line 33), where the author mentions how elaborate the UDHR's drafting process was.

2. (B) Logic Function

Step 2: Identify the Question Type

Question stems that ask *why* or *how* the author uses certain references in the text signal Logic Function questions. The testmakers offer clear research clues, making it easy to find the relevant details within the passage. Use your Roadmap to determine the *function*—the rhetorical purpose—in the author's use of the details. This question stem is a little unusual in that it has two citations; you're asked why the author "quotes directly from both." Expect that the two quotations either clearly contrast with one another or that one reinforces or explains the other. (It's not uncommon, by the way, to see questions similar to this one associated with paired Comparative Reading passages.)

Step 3: Research the Relevant Text

Check the references and note that both are in paragraph one, bookending the discussion of failed Article 1 of the UN Charter. Between the two, Keywords and margin notes show that the primary response to Article 1 was the complaint that it wasn't strong enough. The proposed language quoted at lines 20–22 was intended to make the charter's human rights provisions more robust.

Step 4: Make a Prediction

As your research made clear, the author's purpose in quoting the two documents was to contrast their relative strength. That should be enough to distinguish the correct answer easily.

Step 5: Evaluate the Answer Choices

(B) matches the prediction. The author's purpose was to highlight the difference in the language of the two documents, the first criticized for being too weak and the second offering a proposed remedy.

(A) is a Distortion. Nothing in the passage suggests that the definition of human rights had changed, only the strength of the language seeking to guarantee human rights.

(C) is a 180. The author's purpose was to reveal differences, not commonalities, between the two documents.

(D) also distorts the author's intention—not an attempt to point out important provisions, but to show how the second document attempted to strengthen the provisions of the first.

(E) misses the boat entirely. Nothing in paragraph one (indeed, nothing in the passage) is intended to comment on prose styles.

3. (B) Inference

Step 2: Identify the Question Type

Questions that ask for the author's attitude, or in this case *stance*, toward a topic are a variety of Inference question. Although it's unlikely that the author will say, "I feel such and such," the correct answer must follow from the attitudes and opinions that the author stated explicitly in the passage. In this question, you're asked for the author's attitude about the UDHR, the Topic of the passage as a whole.

Step 3: Research the Relevant Text

The author's point of view, his evaluation, came out in paragraph three. That paragraph was, in fact, dominated by Contrast and Opinion Keywords. The author began with a criticism of the UDHR but concluded that it "Nevertheless ... clearly deserves recognition."

Step 4: Make a Prediction

The author gives the UDHR "qualified praise" or "applauds it but also points out its limitations." Whether you chose the language in which the correct answer is written is beside the point. Your research should have led you to a nearly perfect prediction. As long as your paraphrase accurately reflects the author's opinion, the correct answer will be undeniable.

Step 5: Evaluate the Answer Choices

(B) is the one with the right tenor. The author qualifies his clear approval of the UDHR with comment on its drawbacks, chiefly its lack of enforceability.

(A) is Extreme. The opening sentences of paragraph three show that the author's approval is not "unbridled."

(C) mischaracterizes the author's tone. The word "absolute" should raise a red flag. By noting the UDHR's flaws first, but saying that it "clearly deserves recognition" in spite of them, the author comes down on the positive side of the fence.

(D) has the same qualified strength as the correct answer, but the author simply isn't negative about the UDHR.

(E) is a 180 and Extreme. This author is not at all hostile toward the UDHR.

4. (D) Detail (EXCEPT)

Step 2: Identify the Question Type

The opening phrase—"According to the passage"—identifies this as a Detail question. In addition, "EXCEPT" in the question stem indicates that the correct answer choice will be something contradictory to or never mentioned in the passage. Here there are two challenges: First, it is the wrong answer choices that are details from the passage, and second, the clue is the UDHR itself, which appears numerous times throughout the passage.

Step 3: Research the Relevant Text

It's tough to research something that's ubiquitous in a passage, but the margin notes provide a good starting point.

The opening paragraph states that the UDHR was the first international human rights treaty and that it followed the unsuccessful Article 1. Paragraph two covers the debates during its drafting. That paragraph also contains the list of UDHR's provisions, which seem particularly likely to be included in a Detail EXCEPT question like this one. Paragraph three consists of the author's opinions and evaluations of the UDHR, ending with his list of the UDHR's contributions to later human rights efforts.

Step 4: Make a Prediction
You cannot predict what the passage didn't say, but the key pieces of text that you noted in your survey of the margin notes serve as a prediction, of sorts, for what the wrong answers will contain. As you characterize the answer choices, remember that the correct answer could be either outside the scope of the passage or could directly contradict what the author said in the passage.

Step 5: Evaluate the Answer Choices
There's no better way to attack a question like this than to move through the answer choices from top to bottom. Strike through any that you know are mentioned in the passage. If you encounter one you're not sure about, skip it. If a clear winner doesn't surface, then you can research the skipped choice in the passage.

(D) turns out to be the right answer here. It contradicts the very end of the passage. The author says the UDHR "has led … to the creation of legally binding human rights conventions" (lines 50–52). By saying that the UDHR had "no *practical* consequences," the testmakers distort the author's critique of the UDHR's enforceability. That's quite different, though, from asserting that it had no real impact.

(A) is found at lines 43–44 of the passage, where the author lists the UDHR's provisions.

(B) comes from paragraph one, specifically from lines 24–26, where the author describes how the state obligation proposal failed, giving rise to the UDHR.

(C) comes from the beginning of paragraph two, where the author wrote that the "mandate for producing the document was given to the UN Commission on Human Rights." The fact that paragraph two was about the drafting of the UDHR signaled that this was a good place to check whether this answer's statement was included in the text.

(E) nearly quotes lines 3–4 in paragraph one, just swapping in "explicitly" for "expressly."

5. (E) Inference

Step 2: Identify the Question Type
This is a straightforward Inference question stem asking what the author would agree with. That means the correct answer must be true based on the author's point of view as

presented in the passage. The challenge here is that the question stem lacks any research clues.

Step 3: Research the Relevant Text
When you face an Inference question that doesn't refer to a specific detail or portion of text, use your Purpose and Main Idea summaries as a starting point. Here, note that the author's Purpose was to present the background to the UDHR and evaluate its strengths and weaknesses. The passage's Main Idea centered on the facts that the UDHR was the first document of its kind, was the product of strong debate, and is praiseworthy despite its lack of enforceability.

Step 4: Make a Prediction
It is clear what sparks the author's interest in the UDHR. The bulk of the passage addresses the issue of the UDHR's strength. Expect those subjects to be included in the choices (albeit with the author's point of view distorted or contradicted in the wrong answers).

Step 5: Evaluate the Answer Choices
(E) contains a statement with which the author would agree. It combines statements from paragraph one (groups pushing for the UDHR wanted it to require states to take action to protect human rights) and paragraph three (the UDHR wound up being "purely programmatic"). Thus, its staunchest supporters would have welcomed enforcement provisions.

(A) is both Extreme and a Distortion of the author's point in paragraph one. The author doesn't suggest that ambiguity was the problem with Article 1; rather, it was criticized for being too weak. Moreover, because Article 1 was never adopted, it would be bizarre for the author to have opined on how effectual it was.

(B) contradicts the author's opinion as it's expressed in paragraph three. There, the author argues that the UDHR "clearly deserves recognition" despite some regrettable shortcomings.

(C) contradicts the author's tone in paragraph two, where the author focused on the UDHR's drafting process. Far from easy, the drafters went through an "elaborate" process (line 31) and debated "passionately" (line 35) before "finally" approving (line 37) the document.

(D) doesn't contradict the passage, but there's nothing in the text to suggest that the author would affirmatively agree with this choice either. The author calls the principles of the UDHR "essential" (line 37) and the rights it enumerates "fundamental" (line 42). There is no way to determine whether the author feels any important rights have been omitted.

6. (A) Inference

Step 2: Identify the Question Type

This long question stem offers a hypothetical, modern-day case and asks you to apply to it the point of view of the UN delegates mentioned in paragraph one. It's an Inference question, because the answer will follow from what's stated in the passage. Be patient whenever you encounter a long question stem. Getting the correct answer depends on making a quality prediction, which can only be formed from a clear understanding of what the stem is calling for. If you misunderstand the question, any subsequent work is wasted time.

Step 3: Research the Relevant Text

The delegates mentioned in lines 11–14 felt that Article 1 wasn't strong enough. Shortly afterward (lines 17–22), the author says the drafters pushed strenuously for enforcement provisions that would require states to act in response to human rights violations.

Step 4: Make a Prediction

The correct answer here will mirror the response of those early human rights advocates. It will call for states to act to secure human rights on behalf of those who have been abused.

Step 5: Evaluate the Answer Choices

(A) models that prediction. It calls for strong action to be taken to remedy the human rights violations.

(B) is Out of Scope. The passage never says that the staunch human rights proponents called for unanimous approval by UN member states.

(C) is too weak to satisfy those who are like the early human rights advocates mentioned in the passage. Indeed, they were critical of conventions that called only for censure and instead pushed for a document that would require action and enforcement.

(D) would have upset the human rights advocates even more than **(C)**. Leaving the offending state to its own devices flies in the face of their concern that member states act to prevent and remedy such abuses.

(E) distorts the human rights advocates' view of who should be required to take action. They pushed for a requirement that *states* take action. It's possible that they would welcome the participation of nongovernmental agencies, but that doesn't follow from the passage.

Passage 2: The Value of Forgeries

Step 1: Read the Passage Strategically
Sample Roadmap

line #	Keyword/phrase	¶ Margin notes
1	commonly assumed; even if	Common view – forgery never equal to original
3	Yet even	
4	duped	
6	For instance	but even experts get fooled
12–13	great embarrassment	Ex. HvM not Vermeer
14	Astonishingly	
17	initial enthusiasm	
18	argue	
20	would have justified	
21	thus; difficult	Forgery success leads to difficult questions
23	?	
26	?	
27	convincing	Auth – pro Lessing's answers
29	indeed inferior	
30	argues; but not because	
32	For example	
35	argues instead	Lessing – forgery is not less b/c of technique but b/c of intangibles
39	but	Ex. originality/vision
40	as opposed to	
41	Thus	
47	Even if	
52	Whereas	
56	nothing	Auth – even if great technique, forgers still don't provide works of hist. signif.
57	therefore	
58	lacks	

Discussion

The passage opens with "is commonly assumed," an excellent indication to the strategic reader that the author will soon introduce a counterpoint. Although he does, be careful; his point turns out to be much more subtle than a simple statement that the common assumption is wrong. He'll wind up spending the bulk of the passage unpacking the implications of the assumption and building his argument for how it should be treated. The **Topic**, introduced in the first sentence, is artistic forgeries. The common assumption is that no matter how aesthetically pleasing a forgery might be, it never has the aesthetic merit of an original work. The author's response is a cautionary tale: "even the most prominent art specialists can be duped." He provides the example of a 1937 forgery by Han van Meegeren, who signed the painting as Jan Vermeer, a Dutch master from the seventeenth century. The painting fooled so many that it hung in a museum, as a Vermeer, for several years. When van Meegeren confessed that the painting was a forgery, the art critics were so embarrassed that one even clung to the belief that the painting had to be an original Vermeer.

Although the author goes into great detail about the van Meegeren forgery (and discusses it throughout the passage), that painting itself isn't the Scope of the passage. The Scope develops in paragraph two, where the author asks a series of questions prompted by van Meegeren's success in tricking even art experts. Having witnessed the art world's initial response to the forged Vermeer, some philosophers challenged the common assumption that opened the passage: the forgery must have aesthetic merit sufficient to warrant the praise the critics gave when they thought it was an original. For the author, the philosophers' response raises two questions. First, are forgeries inherently inferior to originals? Second, are we justified in thinking less of a painting when we find out it's a forgery, and if so, why? The passage's **Scope** is finally revealed in the final sentence of paragraph two. It's the answers that a philosopher of art—Lessing—gives to those two questions, answers that the author finds "convincing."

As a strategic reader, anticipate that the passage's final two paragraphs will develop and embrace Lessing's answers.Lessing's answer, the author says at the opening of paragraph three, is that forgeries *are* inferior, but not because of what's visible. The author illustrates with the example of van Meegeren's forged Vermeer. There, the composition, technique, and use of color are "flawless." For Lessing, the forgery's inferiority stems from its "intangible qualities," its lack of originality and vision. Lessing distinguishes these qualities from the technical, aesthetic qualities visible on a work's surface. The author applies these "intangible" qualities to Vermeer, giving him credit for pioneering a "new way of seeing" and new artistic techniques in the

seventeenth century. The margin notes should reflect the differences between the two criteria that Lessing (and thus, the author) uses to judge artistic merit.

In the final paragraph, the author applies Lessing's criteria to the van Meegeren forgery. Grant him all the technical plaudits you like, says the author; the forgery shows "undoubted mastery" of Vermeer's techniques. But there's the rub: Vermeer's work is "historic" and "truly impressive" because he invented these novel techniques. Van Meegeren's work, technically brilliant though it may be, is inferior because it adds "nothing new or creative to the world of art."

In the end, the author winds up agreeing with the common assumption that opened the passage: forgeries are inferior. The author's **Purpose** is not to contradict that assumption but actually to explain why it's true. The **Main Idea** simply summarizes Lessing's analysis: forgeries are inferior because they lack the intangible originality and vision of originals, not due to any technical deficiency.

7. (C) Global

Step 2: Identify the Question Type
This is a typically worded Global question. Summarizing the author's Purpose and Main Idea at the end of the passage Roadmap will support a great prediction of the correct answer.

Step 3: Research the Relevant Text
No need to consult the passage at all. Use the Purpose and Main Idea summaries as paraphrases of what the correct answer must contain.

Step 4: Make a Prediction
The correct answer here will paraphrase the author's summary of Lessing's criteria for judging the artistic value of forgeries. Forgeries, he says, may be technically or aesthetically superior works, but they're inferior artistically because they lack originality and vision.

Step 5: Evaluate the Answer Choices
(C) accurately paraphrases the main point. Just as Lessing would have it, forgeries are deficient in originality and vision.

(A) is Half-Right/Half-Wrong. Although the author would agree that van Meegeren's work was "artistically" inferior, he attributes that to its lack of originality. Aesthetically, the author called van Meegeren's work "flawless" (line 34).

(B) mangles the terminology of the passage. The work's "aesthetic value" is entirely a function of its visible characteristics. Its "artistic value" is what encompasses the "intangible qualities" introduced in paragraph three.

(D) cites a fact from the passage but misses the passage's main point. The author didn't write the passage for the purpose of showing that art critics can be deceived, but rather to articulate Lessing's criteria for assessing their artistic worth.

(E), much like **(D)**, distorts the passage's Main Idea by focusing on the fact that art critics can be deceived but eliding the criteria for assessing a forgery's artistic merit.

8. (A) Inference

Step 2: Identify the Question Type
The correct answer to this inference question will be a statement with which Lessing must agree. Because the author appears to embrace Lessing's argument wholeheartedly, the correct answer will echo the author's points in paragraphs three or four as well.

Step 3: Research the Relevant Text
Lessing's answers to the troubling questions raised by "successful" forgeries are given in paragraph three. There, the author explains that Lessing judges art on both its technical and aesthetic qualities (those "perceptible on the picture's surface") and its intangible qualities, such as originality and vision. Lessing considers these independent; thus, an aesthetically superior work may be inferior as art because of deficiencies in its intangible qualities.

Step 4: Make a Prediction
The correct answer will follow from what your research revealed. Find the answer in which a painting is simultaneously aesthetically superior and artistically lacking.

Step 5: Evaluate the Answer Choices
(A) captures the prediction perfectly. In the passage, the author explains that, using Lessing's criteria, one can acknowledge van Meegeren's *aesthetic* excellence even while questioning his work's artistic value.

(B) is Out of Scope. Neither Lessing nor the author ever mentions an artwork's *financial* value.

(C) is Extreme and Out of Scope. The author uses the fact that museums and critics were fooled by van Meegeren's erstwhile Vermeer as background to the troubling questions of a forgery's artistic merit. Lessing, as far as you know from the passage, doesn't offer art museums advice of any kind.

(D) is a Distortion. The passage provides adequate information to draw a conclusion about how Lessing would compare van Meegeren's forgery to an original Vermeer. It doesn't address how he would rank the van Meegeren work in relation to any other pieces of art.

(E) distorts Lessing's criteria by reversing the terms. From the passage, Lessing judges some aesthetically superior works (the van Meegeren forgery, for example) to be artistically inferior because they lack originality and vision. Nothing is said of how Lessing would assess aesthetically inferior works. Notice the Formal Logic at work here. The passage indicates that Lessing does not consider aesthetic merit sufficient for

great art. He may, however, still regard it as necessary. That can't be determined from the information given.

9. (E) Logic Function

Step 2: Identify the Question Type
Here is a Logic Function question with a clear content clue to guide your research. The key to effectively handling a question like this is to predict the answer that explains *why* the author employed the referenced detail and avoid answers that simply repeat what the passage said about the detail.

Step 3: Research the Relevant Text
The content clue in the stem—the "critic's persistence in believing van Meegeren's forgery to be a genuine Vermeer"—is found at the end of paragraph one. At this point, the author has yet to introduce Lessing and his criteria for judging artistic merit. For now, the author is still emphasizing (note the Keyword [*a*]*stonishingly* at the beginning of the sentence) just how deceptive a well-executed forgery can be.

Step 4: Make a Prediction
Make sure your prediction is responsive to the call of the question, which asks for the author's purpose for including the detail. Notice that each of the answer choices begins with a verb that corresponds to the author's purpose. In this case, then, the right answer will say something along the lines of "give an example of a forgery that fooled even experts" or "emphasize just how difficult it can be to spot a good forgery."

Step 5: Evaluate the Answer Choices
(E) gets it right. The verb *illustrate* corresponds perfectly with the author's use of the consternated critic. The critic's response underlines the point of the paragraph: good forgeries can fool even experts.

(A) is a Distortion. It's true that the art critic wouldn't budge from his assessment of the work as an original Vermeer, but the author doesn't use the critic to characterize other art critics as intransigent. He uses the example to underline just how deceptive forgeries can be.

(B) imputes a position to the author that he doesn't take in the passage. Nothing suggests that he doubts the critic's qualifications. On the contrary, it's the fact that even these highly qualified experts were fooled that makes the question of a forgery's merit so compelling.

(C) would please the duped critic, but not the author. The author uses this example because the forgery was so good that even after the question of its origin was laid to rest, one critic couldn't bring himself to admit he'd been fooled.

(D) distorts not only the use of this example but of the passage as a whole. The author makes no claim that there is any confusion over the concept of what a forgery is. The open question is over its value and why we are or aren't justified in treating forgeries as inferior works.

10. (C) Logic Reasoning (Parallel Reasoning)

Step 2: Identify the Question Type

This question stem indicates a Parallel Reasoning question. The correct answer will reflect a situation with the same reasoning or reaction as that cited in the passage, although it's likely to involve an entirely different situation.

Step 3: Research the Relevant Text

A quick check of the line reference reveals that this question is asking about the critics who were embarrassed to discover that the purported Vermeer was actually a forgery. Just above this reference, the author told you the critics had praised the work profusely until learning it wasn't authentic.

Step 4: Make a Prediction

The answer choices in Parallel Reasoning questions are likely to use several different subject matter areas. The prediction must help you find the answer choice with the same reasoning or response to that in the passage, regardless of what the answer choice is about. Here then, the correct answer choice must involve people who claimed to appreciate something until they discovered its origin or its creator was not what they expected.

Step 5: Evaluate the Answer Choices

(C) is exactly what the question is asking for. The diners appeared to be satisfied with their meals until it was revealed that the food had been prepared by someone other than the famous restaurant's master chef. This response is parallel to that of the embarrassed critics.

(A) is a different type of response because, in this example, it's known from the beginning that the works are "cover" versions. This answer would correspond to a situation in which art critics rejected from the start a new work "in the style of Vermeer."

(B) is inapplicable because it appears to involve only original artwork. It's not the year in which van Meegeren painted that flummoxed the art critics, but the fact that he passed his work off as that of a more famous artist. Don't confuse this example with Lessing's criticisms later in the passage. There, Vermeer was given credit as the originator of a style and of new artistic techniques. The year in which he painted wasn't important, but rather the fact that no one had previously painted in this way.

(D) distorts the point of the van Meergeren example, and of the entire passage. Nowhere in the selection does the author address political motives behind the responses of art critics.

(E) distorts the author's purpose for including the detail. It was not to show that the art critics liked the work because Vermeer is one of their favorite painters. Rather, the author's

purpose for including the detail was to show how the critics revised their opinions upon learning the forger's true identity.

11. (B) Inference

Step 2: Identify the Question Type

This is an Inference question because the right answer must be true based on the passage. The research clue—"Lessing"—makes the research relatively straightforward here.

Step 3: Research the Relevant Text

Lessing's views were laid out in paragraph three. The author says that Lessing judges artworks on both their aesthetic or technical ("surface") merit and on their intangible qualities (such as "originality of vision"). Thus, work that shows innovation and thereby adds something new to art is more valuable than a comparably executed work that does not.

Step 4: Make a Prediction

Use your research to find the answer containing a view that corresponds to the author's description of Lessing's thesis. The correct answer will follow directly from Lessing's criteria and judgments as they are presented in the passage.

Step 5: Evaluate the Answer Choices

(B) may not have been worded as expected, but it is the clear winner. Lessing has to take the historical circumstances surrounding a work's creation into account because he considers originality and innovation to be some of the fundamental criteria for judging a work's artistic merit.

(A) is Out of Scope. There's nothing to indicate how common Lessing considers forgeries to be or how often they've "fooled" museum curators.

(C) distorts Lessing's praise of originality. From what you learn of Lessing in the passage, he believes innovative technique, not whether later artists recognize and follow the innovations, makes a work important.

(D) is also Out of Scope. There's no historical survey of attitudes toward forgery here and certainly none of attitudes associated with Lessing's analysis.

(E) is a fairly subtle Distortion, but its language is too rigid to be supported by the passage. Lessing and the author appear to value innovation in artistic technique as one way an artist can be original. But the passage makes clear they also value new "vision" and new ways of "seeing." It's possible that they would consider "innovative" an artist who employs only known techniques but whose work expresses a new vision. Notice the Formal Logic here. Lessing may consider new techniques sufficient, but not necessary, to establish an artist as "innovative."

12. (E) Inference

Step 2: Identify the Question Type

This is an open-ended Inference question. The correct answer follows from the passage and *must be true* based on it. But, there's no research clue in this stem. The correct answer may come from anywhere in the passage.

Step 3: Research the Relevant Text

Given the lack of a specific reference in the question stem, it's impossible to target any portion of the text. In questions like this one, turn instead to the Scope, Purpose, and Main Idea summaries. Use what is presented in the passage as a whole to eliminate answers that conflict with, distort, or fall outside the scope of the passage.

Step 4: Make a Prediction

Follow the guidelines laid out under Step 3. If you're unable to eliminate all four wrong answers or to spot the one with a valid inference based on the passage, use those remaining choices as research clues and consult the corresponding portions of the passage text.

Step 5: Evaluate the Answer Choices

(E) is the correct answer. The main example, used throughout the passage, is van Meegeren's forged Vermeer. The author considers this work a forgery because van Meegeren signed Vermeer's name to it, not because it was a copy of another painting by Vermeer.

(A) is Out of Scope. The author doesn't tell you anything about how forgeries have been assessed at different points in history.

(B) is Extreme. Forgery, as discussed and exemplified in the passage, seems to be a matter of intentional deception. Nothing here suggests that either the author or Lessing would call someone who uses another artist's technique a forger.

(C) distorts and misuses terms from the passage. Work with a new artistic vision is indicative of an artist who merits praise in Lessing's view. No criteria for a "successful forger" are offered in the passage.

(D) contains an Irrelevant Comparison. Nothing in the passage suggests that artists are more or less creative early in their careers.

13. (B) Logic Reasoning (Strengthen)

Step 2: Identify the Question Type

This question stem adapts the Strengthen question type from Logical Reasoning to the Reading Comprehension context. It's useful to note that the question stem simply contains the conclusion that the correct answer will support.

Step 3: Research the Relevant Text

Lessing's views are laid out in paragraph three. There, the author states that aesthetic quality isn't sufficient for artistic merit. For a work to qualify as artistically outstanding, Lessing requires it to display originality or vision as well.

Step 4: Make a Prediction

The correct answer will simply provide a fact that makes it more likely that an artist, like van Meegeren with his Vermeer forgery, can produce an aesthetically excellent work that lacks the originality or vision to be artistically great.

Step 5: Evaluate the Answer Choices

(B) provides an example that supports Lessing's judgment. The training pieces described in the answer choice are aesthetically successful ("beautiful"), but they aren't great art, presumably because of their status as "[r]eproductions."

(A) is Out of Scope. The passage doesn't address the question of whether forgers can carry on dual careers as original artists or what impact doing so would have on the assessment of their work.

(C) is reminiscent of the author's discussion of van Meegeren's success in fooling art critics with his faux Vermeer. But this example has no impact on Lessing's conclusions about what constitutes artistic merit.

(D) might assist in determining the criteria for "successful" forgery, but it neither strengthens nor weakens Lessing's argument about the relationship between aesthetic excellence and artistic merit.

(E) is reminiscent of wrong answers **(D)** from the fifth question of the set and **(A)** from the sixth question of the set. The passage makes no mention of how attitudes toward forgeries changed over time, yet this is the third answer choice to suggest that something about this issue can be determined from the text.

Passage 3: Can Animals Lie?

Step 1: Read the Passage Strategically
Sample Roadmap

line #	Keyword/phrase	¶ Margin notes
Passage A		
2		Language used to change behavior – humans "read" others
5	most common	
8–9	in contrast; because	Animals don't
10	possible exception	
11	cannot	
13–14	but; no evidence	Ex. male frog doesn't know influence
18	marked contrast	Ex. primates don't use perception of others-Macaques
20	for example	
22	yet; no evidence	
24	but	
25	similarly; do not	-Chimps
29	not as purposeful	
Passage B		
30		Human comm. – creative; Animal comm. – rigid
32	whereas	
36	Obviously; :	Animals communicate w/o intention
39	explains	Grice on intention
43	But	
45	widely believed; uniquely	
47	exemplifies	Maritain – Ex. bees
48	Although	
50	asserts	
51	:	
52	but	
53	But	Auth – scientists use flawed circular reasoning
56	In fact	
60	calls into question not only	Recent info suggests animals may speak with intent
62	but also	

Discussion

In the short first paragraph of passage A, the author introduces the **Topic**: using language to influence the behavior of others. Then he states that humans commonly do this by reading the listener's mental state.

Right off the bat, you can see that the long second paragraph will shift the **Scope** to animal communications and that the author's **Purpose** is to show that animals can't use communication to influence others the same way humans can. In contrast to humans, the author writes, an animal (excepting maybe chimpanzees) can't perceive its counterpart's mental state. So, although an animal's vocalization may benefit it by causing others to alter their behaviors, it cannot be said to be intentional on the part of the "speaker." The author supports this contention with three examples (all three should be represented in the margin notes or, at a minimum, indicate where and what the examples are). There's a male frog whose calls attract females and drive off other males, but no evidence that the frog is aware his call is having this effect. Macaques give alarm calls, but it doesn't seem that they give them as a result of knowing that other macaques are unaware of the danger. Even chimps don't change their calls when other chimps are in need of information. The last sentence is a nice statement of the author's **Main Idea**: he concludes that a lot of animal communication isn't as goal oriented or purposeful as it seems.

Passage B is a little longer. As always with Comparative Reading, it shares the first passage's **Topic** but comes at it with a slightly different Scope and Purpose. From the short, one-sentence first paragraph, it's clear passage B's author intends to take issue with those who, like passage A's author, believe that when communicating, animals aren't so purposeful and creative. This author isn't explicit about this disagreement at first. But the fact that she opens by saying "[m]any scientists distinguish animal communication systems from human language" hints at her **Scope** and **Purpose**: she will attempt to weaken that distinction in her passage.

In paragraph two, the author outlines the arguments her opponents make. She focuses on a statement they "commonly" make, that animals can't lie. Then she outlines the test for when an individual is lying. It requires knowing the speaker's intentions; indeed, it must be clear that the individual wants his false utterance to be believed. Her opponents hold the "widely believed" view that intention is "uniquely human." She illustrates their view with the example of Maritain's discussion of the honeybee dance. Maritain concluded that honeybee communication is "merely a conditioned reflex" and lacks "conscious intention." What's still missing is the counterargument from passage B's author, which should be anticipated in paragraph three.

In the final paragraph, passage B's author takes on her opponents with two distinctly LSAT lines of attack. first, she points out a logical flaw in their argument, and second, she introduces a fact that weakens their assumption. Specifically, she accuses them of circular reasoning. They start from the premise that animals cannot have intention in order to prove that animal communication is different from that of humans because animals lack intention. The author then introduces recent research that "calls into question" her opponents' reasoning. She doesn't go into any detail, but merely asserts that such research exists. Her discussion of the evidence provides a good summation of passage B's **Main Idea**: the assumption that animal communication is mere reflex isn't as sound as is commonly believed.

Although there's nothing to indicate that passage B was written in response to passage A, these two passages take opposites sides on the issue of animal communications. Passage A is the more expository of the two. Its author asserts his point and supports it with three examples from the animal kingdom. He makes no mention of opposing views, though he certainly has a position to assert and support. Passage B, on the other hand, is written to address an opposing view. The author of the second passage characterizes her opponents and illustrates their position. Then she attacks their reasoning. She mentions the existence of evidence to support her view, but doesn't cite it specifically.

14. (B) Global

Step 2: Identify the Question Type
This is standard language for a Global question accompanying Comparative Reading passages. It asks for a primary concern common to both authors. The answer choices will be in the form of a question that both passages seek to answer.

Step 3: Research the Relevant Text
No need to research within the passage. Use the summaries of the Purpose and Main Idea of each passage to predict the correct answer. Passage A sets out to show or demonstrate that animals lack the intention to influence others' behaviors when they communicate. Passage B attempts to show that those who believe animals cannot intend to deceive their hearers are making logical errors and overlooking evidence to the contrary.

Step 4: Make a Prediction
The correct answer will focus on the key point at issue between the two passages: whether animals have intentions toward the behavior of others when they communicate.

Step 5: Evaluate the Answer Choices
(B) matches the prediction perfectly. It's the only answer that gets at the fundamental question underlying both passages: To what degree, if any, are animals consciously intending to

influence their hearers' behavior? The wrong answer choices each present points addressed in only one passage or neither passage.

(A) is the question that passage B's author uses to characterize her opponent's point of view (lines 34–35). Although this may be of interest to passage A's author, he never mentions it explicitly in his passage.

(C) is another question somewhere in the periphery of each author's concerns. Both authors might be interested in research on this question, but neither wrote their passage for the purpose of answering it.

(D) is too specific. Although both passages mention nonhuman primates (chimpanzees), the passages aren't intended to contrast them with other animals. Rather, the mention of primates is used as evidence to support the main points made in each of the passages.

(E) is not of primary concern to both passages. The two passages, taken together, provide evidence that there is not, in fact, scientific consensus about animal communication. Be careful, though—the correct answer choice needs to be a question that each author was seeking to answer. Neither author wrote for the purpose of determining whether consensus exists.

15. (A) Logic Function

Step 2: Identify the Question Type
Here's a standard Logic Function question stem that asks the author's purpose in employing a certain detail. Make sure your prediction is responsive to the question stem. The testmakers aren't asking you what's true of Maritain; they're asking why the author of passage B is referencing him. Note, too, that this is the only question in the set that does not require you to consider both passages. The answer comes from paragraph two of passage B alone.

Step 3: Research the Relevant Text
Passage B's author referenced Maritain—specifically his discussion of the honeybee dance—near the end of paragraph two (lines 45–52). To understand why the author talked about Maritain, look no further than the Illustration Keyword *exemplifies*. What's Maritain an example of? Look right before the referenced text. His discussion of the honeybees exemplifies the view that intention is exclusively a human trait.

Step 4: Make a Prediction
Solid research forms a solid prediction of the correct answer. The author of passage B cites Maritain's conclusions to illustrate the view of those who think animals cannot have intentions when they communicate. It's worth noting, too, that the author considers that view fundamentally flawed. She'll spend paragraph three explaining why she thinks so.

Step 5: Evaluate the Answer Choices
(A) gives the author's reason for including Maritain's views—they describe an interpretation of animal communication—and correctly identifies them as views with which the author disagrees.

(B) is a 180. Maritain stands for the view that animals lack intention.

(C) is another 180. It's the author's position that animals may be spontaneous and creative. Maritain argued the opposite.

(D) accurately describes Maritain's view, but it doesn't address why he's referenced in passage B. The author isn't trying to maintain that animal communication is mere conditioned reflex. In fact, she finds that view flawed and vulnerable to recent findings that it may not be true.

(E) is Out of Scope. Whether the author of passage B respects Maritain is beside the point and certainly doesn't address why the author included the reference to him. His work illustrates the views of the passage A author, nothing more.

16. (D) Inference

Step 2: Identify the Question Type
This is an Inference question tailored to the Comparative Reading format. The correct answer will follow from the passage B author's point of view, but it will comment on passage A's position.

Step 3: Research the Relevant Text
As noted earlier, passage B wasn't written in direct response to passage A, but it is clear that the author of passage B would consider the author of passage A to be one of her opponents. No need to re-read any specific pieces of text. The Roadmap contains all the necessary information to answer the question correctly. Passage B's author considers the views of those who deny intention to animal communication as logically flawed, resting on circular reasoning. She also thinks that recent research may suggest that they're wrong.

Step 4: Make a Prediction
Paraphrase passage B's criticisms—found in paragraph three—as the basis for what the correct answer to this question must contain. It may cite the logical flaw, the recent counterevidence, or a combination of the two.

Step 5: Evaluate the Answer Choices
(D), which offers a brief summary of the criticisms in paragraph three of passage B is correct. The author finds her opponents' assumptions to be flawed and suggests that there is research-based evidence that they're not taking into account.

(A) is Out of Scope for both passages. All parties apparently agree that humans are able to judge their listeners' mental states. Whether they sometimes communicate without doing so is irrelevant.

(B) is Out of Scope for each passage. Passage B's author never questions her adversaries' qualifications. She's engaged in an academic debate with them and, you can tell from the passage, considers them peers who happen to be wrong.

(C) is Extreme. The author claims recent research suggests there's less of a gap between human and animal communication than was previously assumed. That's a far cry from "well-known evidence" that animals lie.

(E) distorts both short passages. It's likely that all of the scientists involved in the debate appreciate that communication systems confer evolutionary advantages. That's certainly not the basis of the passage B author's criticism of her opponents.

17. (D) Logic Reasoning (Strengthen)

Step 2: Identify the Question Type

This is another question in which the testmakers have adapted a common question type to work in the Comparative Reading context. The main task here is to strengthen Maritain's argument. But to do so, you must provide an assertion mentioned in passage A, so there's an element of Detail question here as well. To predict the correct answer to this question, research passage B to determine Maritain's view. Then research passage A to find the assertion that supports it.

Step 3: Research the Relevant Text

The margin notes lead to the end of passage B, paragraph two. Maritain's view comes in the paragraph's final sentence (lines 48–53). He asserted that the honeybee dance was mere reflex, not conscious, intentional communication.

To support that, look for an assertion in passage A suggesting that, even lacking a conscious intention to do so, animals can communicate in ways that influence their counterparts. Of the three examples cited by the author of passage A, the activity of the male *Physalaemus* frog is the most relevant. His calls attract females and deter other males although, according to the author of passage A, nothing suggests that the calling male is aware that he's having this effect.

Step 4: Make a Prediction

Look for an answer that discusses the male *Physalaemus* frog with reference to his apparent lack of intention. If passage A is right about the frog's behavior, it would give Maritain an example from another species parallel to his interpretation of the honeybee. He could say, in essence, "Here's another species where communication is effective in changing behavior despite being a mere conditioned reflex."

Step 5: Evaluate the Answer Choices

(D) matches the prediction squarely. It cites the expected example from passage A for the relevant reason.

(A) distorts Maritain's view. Maritain doesn't claim that other honeybees have any thoughts at all, let alone contradictory ones that are changed by seeing the communicating bee's dance.

(B) is Out of Scope. Neither author (nor, as far as you can see, Maritain) doubts that communication evolved because it benefits the communicator. Maritain's point is that the animal's communication is unintentional.

(C) has no direct effect on Maritain's view, good or bad. If the chimps are considered analogous to honeybees, then the fact that they can sense their hearers' mental states undermines the argument that animals lack intention. If the chimps, being higher primates, are distinguished from honeybees, then they're simply irrelevant. Either way, this assertion doesn't strengthen Maritain's view.

(E) mentions only the circumstances that trigger macaque calls. Because it doesn't address the macaques' intention or lack thereof in making their calls, this answer can't help or hurt Maritain's argument about the honeybees.

18. (C) Logic Reasoning (Point at Issue)

Step 2: Identify the Question Type

The language "most likely to disagree over" indicates the correct answer choice must contain a statement on which the two authors would *disagree*. This resembles the Point at Issue questions that appear in the Logical Reasoning section. The correct answer choice will be something about which the two authors have opposing opinions.

Step 3: Research the Relevant Text

There are no research clues in this question stem. Use the summaries of each author's Purpose and Main Idea to evaluate the choices.

Step 4: Make a Prediction

The main split between the two authors is on the question of intention in animal communication. Passage A's author thinks animals lack the ability to attribute mental states to others, rendering their communication less purposeful than it appears. Passage B's author isn't so sure. She thinks recent research may indicate that human and animal communication is more similar than has been assumed. Use that prediction to determine the correct answer or to eliminate the four wrong ones.

Step 5: Evaluate the Answer Choices

(C) is correct. The wording of the answer echoes line 62 in passage B. The two authors are committed to disagreeing over whether there is a qualitative distinction between human and animal communication. Passage A's author finds animal communication to lack intention, while passage B's author challenges that assertion.

(A) is incorrect because there's not enough information in the passage to know whether the authors disagree on this. It's possible that they are in complete agreement regarding the extent to which human communication is based on our perceptions of our listeners' mental states.

(B) is likely something that the authors *agree* on. Both appear to be interested in the question and committed to getting at the truth on this subject. Both authors have an opinion on this question, and those opinions are not opposite.

(D) contains subtle wording. It's possible that the two authors would agree that chimpanzees have some ability to judge the mental states of other chimps. The author of passage A admits that chimps may be an exception to the general rule that animals' influences on others are inadvertent (line 10). Passage B's author cites research suggesting that chimps and other animals might communicate in ways similar to that of humans (lines 59–61).

(E) is yet another on which the authors may agree. Both accept that animal communication influences other animals in ways that benefit the "speaker." What they don't see eye to eye on is whether such communications are *intentional*.

19. (B) Global

Step 2: Identify the Question Type
Prepare for this question by taking a few moments to compare and contrast the tone and method of argument of each passage. The question is high-level enough to fall under the Global question category. Almost every Comparative Reading selection has at least one question like this, making it worthwhile to catalog briefly the differences between the two passages.

Step 3: Research the Relevant Text
There are no research clues that focus your attention on particular parts of either passage. Use Scope, Purpose, and Main Idea summaries in conjunction with an overview of differences between the two passages as the basis for your evaluation of the answer choices.

Step 4: Make a Prediction
Although a word-for-word prediction is unlikely here, take a moment to recall the differences between the passages. Passage A was not written to address an explicit opposing view; it used concrete examples to advance a thesis. Passage B was written in direct opposition to an opposing view: it characterized the arguments that the author's opponents make and referred to outside research without citing specific examples in detail.

Step 5: Evaluate the Answer Choices
(B) is correct. It hits upon the fact that passage B was written to refute arguments made by specific scientists while passage A simply advanced its point without acknowledging any

opposing views. By taking note of these differences in style and structure, you prepared yourself to get this point handily.

(A) doesn't answer the call of the question stem. The passages show no difference in how optimistic or pessimistic their authors are regarding the prospects for ultimately resolving the questions of animal communication.

(C) is moot in distinguishing the passages. If anything, passage B is the one that challenges opposing viewpoints. Although there's nothing to suggest that passage B's author is closed to other opinions, passage A's author doesn't even mention other views.

(D) suggests no difference between the two authors professionally. Both authors appear to be scientists or science writers, supportive of good research that advances the field of study.

(E) is a 180. Passage B's author is anything but circumspect in her critique of opponents. She challenges both their reasoning and evidence.

Passage 4: African American Historiography

Step 1: Read the Passage Strategically
Sample Roadmap

line #	Keyword/phrase	¶ Margin notes
1	contrast	Afr Am historians adopted transnat'l view of history
6	not the least	Why?
7	necessity	
10	First; problem	① Citizenship
14	not; resolved; Because	
15	central issue	
16	critical	
18–19	enormous; While some; insisted	Debate over emigration
20	others	
22	certainly not	
23	but	
24	profound pessimism	
25	begun to question	
29	dominant	② Nationalism
36	troubled; argued	Afr Am intellectuals troubled by nat'lism – leads to imperialism
43	Yet; distrust	
45	Deliberately or not	Auth – despite distrust of US nat'lism, Afr Am historians also built their own "nat'l" myth
47	glorious	
48	overturning	
50	Thus, one might argue	
58	Hence	

Discussion

From its opening Keywords ("In contrast to the mainstream"), it is clear that this passage will focus on a contrast. The **Topic** is African American historians at the opening of the twentieth century. The **Scope** will involve what distinguishes them from their mainstream contemporaries. The attributes of the African American historians that the author finds most distinctive will give the Scope a little more detail.

In paragraph one, the author identifies a "transnational perspective" as the main feature that made African American historians different from their mainstream colleagues. The paragraph also provides a golden opportunity for anticipatory reading when the author asserts that there are "several reasons" for the African Americans' transnational point of view. Expect the subsequent paragraphs to explain these reasons in some detail.

Paragraph two doesn't disappoint. The reason for the difference in perspective was the problem of citizenship for African Americans of the time. Without explaining why, the author asserts that the Fourteenth Amendment did not "genuinely resolve" the question of citizenship for African Americans. The result, according to the author, was a debate over emigration out of the United States, an issue with "enormous" historical implications. The black community was divided, with some leaders calling for a right to full citizenship and others encouraging emigration to an African homeland. There was no consensus, but some African Americans were at a point of "profound pessimism" regarding their allegiances.

As expected, paragraph three outlines another reason for the distinctive transnational focus of African American historiography at the time. Mainstream historians were strongly nationalist in their "glorification" of the United States The author says this prompted a kind of myth making about national temperament and destiny on the part of mainstream historians. Their African American counterparts were "troubled" by this. They saw nationalism as leading to imperialism and colonization.The Contrast Keyword that kicks off paragraph four ([*y*]*et*) may come as something of a surprise. But trained test takers know that an LSAT passage in which the author outlines two opposing views often ends with a critique or evaluation. In this instance, the author asserts that the turn-of-the-century African American historians were, in a sense, acting similarly to the nationalist mainstream historians they criticized. The Contrast Keywords "for all their ..." (line 43) signals that the author will cite what he considers to be an inconsistency in their work. The author makes clear (in line 45) that this may not have been deliberate. Nonetheless, he says, the African American historians who so distrusted the mainstream's "glorification" (line 28) of the American nation were themselves "reconstructing a glorious African past." The language that follows is dense, so use the

Keywords to stay focused on the author's purpose. The reason that the African American historians glorified the African past of black Americans was to overturn negative depictions and establish a shared identity. "Thus," the author says, their work was a kind of nationalism for a diasporic community who saw themselves as having a shared culture, of being a "'nation' without a homeland." The final sentence in the paragraph summarizes the author's interpretation of the African American historians: they took it as their task to write the history of a scattered African people.

By the end of the passage, the author's **Purpose** is clear. He wants to *explain* why turn-of-the-century African American historians took a transnational perspective and to *evaluate* the goals of their work in light of these reasons. An appropriate **Main Idea** summary needs to include both the explanation and the critique: African American historians took a transnational view in response to the profound nationalist focus of mainstream historiography, but this view led African American historians to create a kind of African nationalism for their diaspora community. That's a long summary, but this is a complex passage in which the author has two goals. Although it's important always to make your summaries and paraphrases as succinct as possible, solid predictions for Global questions will remain out of grasp if your Main Idea summary ignores key parts of the passage. Additionally, with eight right answers at stake, a solid Roadmap is that much more important. Nearly 30 percent of the questions in the section are associated with this passage.

20. (D) Global

Step 2: Identify the Question Type
This is a generic Global question stem. It calls for the "main idea of the passage," something a strategic reader is eminently prepared to give.

Step 3: Research the Relevant Text
There's no need to reread or research any of the text here. Simply recall the Main Idea summary.

Step 4: Make a Prediction
The Main Idea summary is fairly lengthy here, so it's no surprise that the answer choices are too. The Main Idea summary included both of the author's goals: explain why the African American historians took a transnational perspective (their distrust of mainstream nationalism) and reveal their own "nationalism" in writing about a glorious African past. The correct answer must include both of those crucial parts of the passage.

Step 5: Evaluate the Answer Choices
(D) gives the complete and accurate description of the passage as a whole. It summarizes both the African American historians' response to mainstream nationalism and the

author's argument that they produced a kind of nationalist history themselves.

(A) is Out of Scope. The author says nothing about what historians "now recogniz[e]."

(B) seizes on one side of a relatively minor point in the passage and attempts to elevate it to the Main Idea. There was indeed a debate over emigration that influenced the work of the African American historians, but the author doesn't claim that advancing the pro-emigration camp was a goal of the historians, let alone their "primary" one.

(C) is a classic Distortion. The African American historians discussed in the passage and their mainstream contemporaries certainly had different, and sometimes opposing, goals and perspectives. But it is not the purpose of the passage to characterize the state of historiography at the turn of the twentieth century. The author is interested in explaining why the African American historians wrote and worked as they did. By misstating the author's Purpose in the passage, **(C)** is a demonstrably wrong answer choice.

(E) distorts the passage beyond recognition. The author doesn't opine on which perspective—that of the mainstream or that of the African American historians—prevailed.

21. (E) Inference

Step 2: Identify the Question Type
Relatively rare, these Vocabulary-in-Context questions fall under the heading of Inference questions, because the correct answer is based on, rather than stated in, the passage text. The question stem will always indicate where the word or phrase in question is located in the passage. Simply refer to the context to see *how* the author used it.

Step 3: Research the Relevant Text
The reference to line 47 reveals that the author used "reconstructing" in reference to the African American historians efforts to formulate a collective identity for black Americans. It refers to their work in writing a history that began in Africa, one that establishes a common culture for African Americans.

Step 4: Make a Prediction
The correct answer will give an accurate paraphrase of the meaning of "reconstructing" as it's used in the passage. Anticipate the answer to say something along the lines of "formulating a concept" or "establishing an identity."

Step 5: Evaluate the Answer Choices
(E) is a match for the prediction. This is the only answer that could apply to the work of the African American historians as it's described in paragraph four. If substituted into the sentence for "reconstructing"—"shaping a conception of a glorious African past"—the meaning of the sentence is unchanged.

All the wrong answer choices change or distort the author's intended meaning of the word "reconstructuring" in line 47.

(A) turns the sentence into nonsense. Although the African American historians set out to "overturn[ ] degrading representations," these historians were attempting to establish a glorious African past, not correct misconceptions about it.

(B) distorts the sentence beyond recognition. The historians were never said to be in the business of establishing a chronology of events in the African past.

(C) implies that the "glorious African past" was already well established. Such a reading would conflict with the word "formation" earlier in the same sentence.

(D) distorts the author's intentions in the original sentence. Using this phrase would suggest that the historians were somehow writing to support the agenda of other actors, something that the author makes no mention of.

22. (A) Inference

Step 2: Identify the Question Type
This is an open-ended Inference question stem. It contains no research clues or other guidance. Thus, the best approach is to use the Scope, Purpose, and Main Idea summaries to eliminate wrong answers. If more than one candidate seems likely, you can use the answer choices as research clues and consult the passage. If the clearly correct answer choice surfaces as you're evaluating the choices initially, so much the better.

Step 3: Research the Relevant Text
With no research clues in the question stem, don't conduct any passage-based research unless one of the answer choices calls for it. Before evaluating the choices, simply refresh your memory of the author's Scope, Purpose, and Main Idea.

Step 4: Make a Prediction
The author has two goals in the passage: to explain that the African American historians worked in reaction to the nationalist mainstream historian, and to show how they wound up creating, perhaps inadvertently, a form of nationalism themselves. Remember that in any LSAT Inference question, the correct answer *must be true* based on what's in the passage.

Step 5: Evaluate the Answer Choices
(A) turns out to be the correct answer. In paragraph two, the author says that emigrationism was a central issue because of the Fourteenth Amendment's failure fully to resolve citizenship issues. If that's right, emigrationism would have received less attention if the Fourteenth Amendment had completely settled citizenship questions.

(B) is unsupported by the passage. The author doesn't tell you what the historians of diaspora groups generally do.

(C) is Extreme. The author characterizes neither the mainstream historian's American nationalism nor the African American historian's African nationalism as exaggerating the glories of their respective subjects. The word [*m*]*ost* at the beginning of this answer choice should put you on alert that the choice may be too extreme to follow from the passage.

(D) is both Extreme ("must ignore") and Out of Scope ("the ways in which one nation's foreign policy decisions affected other nations"). Nationalism, as used in the passage, has more to do with glorifying the country that one is writing about than it does with the particular aspects of politics and diplomacy one's work covers.

(E) wildly distorts the author's discussion of nationalism, almost to the point of making this choice a 180. The African American historians discussed in the passage largely rejected mainstream nationalism. The fact that they, perhaps inadvertently, created a type of diasporic, nation-in-exile "nationalism" hardly qualifies as embracing the inevitable dominance of the nation-state.

23. (E) Inference

Step 2: Identify the Question Type
Here's another Inference question. Determine which answer best represents the African American historian's approach as it is described in the passage. Target your research effectively using the content clue from this stem.

Step 3: Research the Relevant Text
The approach taken by the turn-of-the-century African American historians is described most fully in paragraph three. They were seeking to give a cultural identity to black Americans and to establish the existence of an African American past.

Step 4: Make a Prediction
Research provides a nearly ideal prediction: the correct answer will be a study that shows how African American culture is rooted in Africa. It will serve to give an identity to its subjects while taking a transnational approach.

Step 5: Evaluate the Answer Choices
(E) fits the prediction perfectly. The study described in this answer choice attempts to show that there is a unified African American culture rooted in African traditions.

(A) is Out of Scope. Neither the mainstream historians nor their African American counterparts are described as having an interest in the conflicts among the national mythologies of various Western nations.

(B) hints at a subject that may have interested the early African American historians. They worked, in part, to correct negative images of blackness. But this choice goes too far by

using a study that attempts to establish the character of the United States and European nations based on their treatment of minorities. Moreover, the author said that the threat of imperialist ambitions was one of the reasons that the African American historians distrusted the mainstream's nationalism (lines 36–42). This doesn't seem like something their studies would have ignored in order to focus on the treatment of minorities within the country.

(C) suggests a subject that might have interested either the mainstream or African American historians mentioned in the passage, though the two groups would have undoubtedly taken different approaches to the subject. The answer fails, however, to provide anything that suggests a transnational approach or an interest in establishing black Americans' African heritage, the distinctive characteristics of the African American historians as they're depicted in the passage.

(D), like **(C)**, offers a topic of interest to the early African American historians without suggesting anything indicative of their approach, which is what the question stem calls for. Emigration was a hot-button issue among African Americans during the period addressed in the passage, but nothing in **(D)** suggests a transnational approach or an attempt to define African American cultural heritage.

24. (E) Detail

Step 2: Identify the Question Type
Although the answer choices are phrased as questions, this stem actually poses a routine Detail question task. The correct answer will be a question that can be answered by something explicitly stated in the passage.

Step 3: Research the Relevant Text
There's nothing in the stem to guide your research. Use the answer choices as research clues.

Step 4: Make a Prediction
Beyond characterizing the right (a question answered by a detail from the passage) and wrong (a question whose answer is not mentioned in the passage) answer choices, take each answer choice in turn. If it's outside the scope or if it distorts or contradicts the passage, eliminate it. You may find it necessary to research two or three of the choices in the passage in order to determine finally which one is the correct answer choice.

Step 5: Evaluate the Answer Choices
(E) turns out to be the right answer. The latter part of paragraph two (lines 18–21, in particular) discusses the split among African American leaders, some of whom called for full U.S. citizenship and others who called for emigration from the country.

(A)'s answer simply doesn't surface in the passage. Not one African nation is named by the author in any context.

(B)'s question, like **(A)**'s appears nowhere in the passage. No African languages are mentioned.

(C)'s answer isn't to be found in the passage. This (along with the preceding two choices) is the type of answer that can tempt you to pull in outside knowledge. A familiarity with U.S. history, such as knowing what territories were controlled by the United States in the early twentieth century, might make it seem as though you read them in the passage. Remember that LSAT Reading Comprehension questions are always based entirely and exclusively on the passage text.

(D) is never discussed in the passage. Although paragraph two (see lines 11–13) said that the Fourteenth Amendment failed to resolve all citizenship issues, it never claimed that "textual ambiguities" in the amendment were or were not to blame.

25. (B) Inference

Step 2: Identify the Question Type
Here's another Inference question ("The author ... would most likely agree") lacking any research or context clues. Once again, use the Scope, Purpose, and Main Idea summaries to evaluate the choices. Eliminate all those that conflict with, distort, or fall outside the scope of the author's point of view. If more than one choice remains, research the passage, using the answer choices as your clues.

Step 3: Research the Relevant Text
No research is possible initially. Instead, turn to the Scope, Purpose, and Main Idea summaries to get a handle on what to look for.

Step 4: Make a Prediction
The correct answer will be one with which the author must agree given what he's said in the passage. This author holds that the early African American historians took a transnational view, in part because of their dislike of mainstream historians' strong nationalist focus. In addition, he feels that the African American historians wound up creating a brand of nationalism through their efforts to reconstruct a shared African past for their subjects, who saw themselves as a diaspora "'nation' without a homeland."

Step 5: Evaluate the Answer Choices
(B) is something with which the author would unequivocally agree. The efforts of the African American historians that he characterizes as "a sort of nation building" (lines 44–45) were taken on behalf of people who lacked a homeland or sovereign territory.

(A) is a Distortion. The example from the passage—African Americans—is of a diasporic community seeking to establish a common *continent* as its cultural homeland. Nothing in the passage suggests that the author feels all members of diasporic communities need share the same country of origin.

(C) is a 180. Indeed, at line 55, the author uses the word "mythical" to describe the African American historians' depiction of a single, shared African origin for African American culture.

(D)'s phrase "*most prominent* African American historians" is unsupportable. Indeed, the author never distinguishes any of the historians about whom he writes based on their prominence. There's simply nothing in the passage that suggests that the author would agree with this statement.

(E) is Extreme. The offending language is "entirely different." In the passage, the mainstream historians and their African American counterparts had different approaches and goals, but nothing suggests that they covered exclusive subject matter. Almost certainly, both would have written about the Civil War, Reconstruction, and changes to the U.S. Constitution, although they likely would have had different interpretations of those events.

26. (A) Logic Function

Step 2: Identify the Question Type
This is a Logic Function question asking for the author's purpose in writing paragraph two. Answer this question based on the margin notes beside that paragraph. Remember to predict an answer that explains *why* the author included the paragraph, not what the paragraph said.

Step 3: Research the Relevant Text
Research the margin notes beside the paragraph. They should reveal, especially within the context of the passage as a whole, the author's purpose in writing the paragraph. As you review the passage, recall that even before reading paragraph two, you anticipated that it would detail one of the reasons (alluded to in paragraph one) for the African American historians' transnational focus. Indeed, paragraph two discussed the first such reason: problems with citizenship.

Step 4: Make a Prediction
Keeping your prediction focused on why the author wrote paragraph two, expect the correct answer to say something along the lines of "to show one reason that the African American historians took a transnational approach."

Step 5: Evaluate the Answer Choices
(A) matches the prediction. This answer responds directly to the call of this Logic Function question.

(B) states an implication of the fact that the Fourteenth Amendment didn't clear up all of the citizenship issues, but proving that wasn't the author's reason for writing the paragraph.

(C) is a Faulty Use of Detail. The African American intellectuals who took issue with American imperialism are discussed in paragraph three of the passage.

(D) cites a fact from paragraph three (see lines 20–21), but, like **(B)**, it misses the author's purpose. Paragraph two was written to explain one reason why the African American historians took the position they did. The debate over emigration was part of the background to their interest in transnational issues.

(E) goes wrong by making the Fourteenth Amendment central to the purpose of the paragraph. Paragraph two sets out to explain a motivation of the African American historians, not to evaluate of the Fourteenth Amendment.

27. (B) Logic Reasoning (Parallel Reasoning)

Step 2: Identify the Question Type
When there are two schools of thought or practice discussed in a passage, it's typical for the testmakers to reward understanding of what each held or believed. Be careful, though, with this Parallel Reasoning question. The correct answer will show a similar way of thinking to that taken by the mainstream historians, but its subject matter need not have anything to do with history.

Step 3: Research the Relevant Text
The mainstream historians' work was described at the beginning of paragraph three. They were "firmly rooted" in nationalism, and their dominant theme was the "glorification of the nation." This led them to create new genealogies and myths about America and her destiny.

Step 4: Make a Prediction
There's no way to anticipate the subject matter of the answers in Parallel Reasoning questions. It's irrelevant, anyway. Your prediction should focus on what the example in the correct answer needs to do. Here, it needs to show someone writing in a way that glorifies the subject, or that creates a myth proclaiming the subject's superiority or destiny.

Step 5: Evaluate the Answer Choices
(B) is correct. The biographer in the answer choice is glorifying his subject, creating a story of inevitable success. This is similar to the ways in which you're told the mainstream historians treated their subject, the United States.

(A) gives an example that is a recommendation to continue a course of action. Nothing in the passage describes the mainstream historians as suggesting that past policies should continue; indeed, nothing in the passage describes them as offering recommendations of any kind.

(C) describes a value judgment (this is the best medication) based on original intention (this is what the medicine was designed to do). The passage doesn't mention the mainstream historians' judgments or suggest that they prefer the use of products designed for a particular task.

(D)'s example features an exposé. The author says nothing that makes the mainstream historians comparable to investigative journalists.

(E) strains to compare the mainstream historians to a scientist who reaches a conclusion based on observing the same results as an experiment is repeated. There's nothing in the passage to suggest that the mainstream historians' confidence in their conclusions increased as they saw the same events unfold several times or that they conducted experiments of any sort. It's difficult to imagine historians working in this way, given what they study.

Section II: Logical Reasoning

Q#	Question Type	Correct	Difficulty
1	Flaw	D	★
2	Principle (Parallel)	E	★
3	Inference	C	★
4	Method of Argument	D	★
5	Principle (Identify/Strengthen)	A	★
6	Strengthen	C	★
7	Point at Issue	D	★
8	Flaw	A	★★
9	Main Point	E	★★
10	Inference	A	★★
11	Weaken	A	★★★
12	Paradox	A	★
13	Assumption (Sufficient)	B	★★
14	Weaken	D	★★
15	Inference	B	★★
16	Assumption (Necessary)	C	★★
17	Role of a Statement	A	★★
18	Flaw	A	★
19	Paradox (EXCEPT)	D	★★
20	Weaken	C	★★★★
21	Principle (Identify/Strengthen)	E	★★★
22	Strengthen (EXCEPT)	C	★★
23	Parallel Flaw	D	★★★★
24	Assumption (Sufficient)	B	★★★
25	Paradox	D	★

1. (D) Flaw

Step 1: Identify the Question Type
Because the question stem states that Mary's argument is "vulnerable to criticism," this is a Flaw question. Find the way in which Mary's evidence fails to establish her conclusion.

Step 2: Untangle the Stimulus
Mary's entire argument is a response to Jamal. Her conclusion is that Jamal's statements taken together are inconsistent. The statements are that Mary has a legal right to sell her business because she owns it, yet she has no right to sell it because doing so would harm her loyal employees.

Step 3: Make a Prediction
Mary is committing the classic flaw of equivocation—confusing the meaning of a key term in the argument. Jamal claims that Mary has the *legal* right to sell her business. But when he says that she has no right to sell her business and harm her loyal employees, he's more likely referring to her *moral* or *ethical* right, which is quite different. But Mary doesn't recognize that difference, and her rebuttal of Jamal's argument is therefore flawed.

Step 4: Evaluate the Answer Choices
(D) matches this prediction perfectly and is thus the correct answer.

(A) isn't important to the argument. Whether Jamal is arguing that Mary doesn't have a right to sell her business now or at any time is not the problem with Mary's reasoning.

(B) is a possibility that's Out of Scope. She isn't arguing about the issue of her employees' rights. She's arguing about the consistency of Jamal's statements.

(C) isn't the flaw because Mary doesn't actually claim that she has a right to sell the business. She's just attempting to show an inconsistency in Jamal's argument.

(E) isn't the problem with Mary's argument. She doesn't make any attacks against Jamal or his character.

2. (E) Principle (Parallel)

Step 1: Identify the Question Type
For this Principle question, you'll first need to identify the broad principle illustrated by the specific situation in the stimulus. Then, search for a different specific scenario that conforms to the same principle among the answer choices.

Step 2: Untangle the Stimulus
According to the argument, having an organ that continues to function after all the other organs have stopped working would provide animals with no survival value. Therefore, it's efficient that animals generally don't have one organ that outlasts all the others.

Step 3: Make a Prediction
In general, the author is suggesting it's efficient for all parts of an entity to last about the same length of time, because there would be no value to having one thing last after everything else has broken down. The correct answer will apply this general rule to a new scenario.

Step 4: Evaluate the Answer Choices
(E) matches the principle exactly, favoring the efficiency of all car parts lasting the same amount of time because one longer-lasting part would add no value to the car.

(A) fails to indicate any one item that does or does not outlast all other comparable items.

(B) fails to indicate any one item that does or does not outlast all other comparable items. It's also important to note the classic LSAT trap of providing an answer with the same topic as the stimulus (animal organs) but failing to match the structure.

(C) goes against the principle by showing that one car outlasting all other cars can actually be valuable.

(D) fails to indicate any one item that does or does not outlast all other comparable items.

3. (C) Inference

Step 1: Identify the Question Type
Because this question asks for something that must be true based on the stimulus, the answer will be an Inference. "Must be true" Inference questions often involve Formal Logic, so be ready for it.

Step 2: Untangle the Stimulus
Right off the bat, the first statement provides Formal Logic:

If	economic success AND success with liberties	→	overall success

The next statement is less certain. If an administration protects liberties but doesn't care for the environment, it *may* still succeed overall. The last claim is that the current administration protects liberties but doesn't care for the environment.

Step 3: Make a Prediction
Because the current administration protects liberties but not the environment, the second sentence supports the statement that the current administration still *may* be an overall success, or it may not be. However, because the administration does protect liberties, if it's also economically successful, then the first sentence *would* support the inference that it does have overall success. The correct answer will conform to this logic.

Step 4: Evaluate the Answer Choices

(C) matches the logic perfectly. Knowing that the current administration protects liberties, if it is also economically successful, confirms that the administration would be an overall success.

(A) gets the logic backwards. Even if the current administration were an overall success, economic success is merely one possible explanation, not a certainty.

(B) is not certain because the logic implies that, even without concern for the environment, the administration may be an overall success.

(D) distorts the logic because there's no absolute connection between economic success and caring for the environment.

(E) distorts the logic. While an administration can still succeed *without* environmental protection, that's not to say that *providing* environmental protection would guarantee overall success.

4. (D) Method of Argument

Step 1: Identify the Question Type

The phrase "proceeds by" in the stem indicates a Method of Argument question. Additionally, this stem is asking for a summary of the argument's evidence, so pay close attention to how the author supports her contention.

Step 2: Untangle the Stimulus

The conclusion is the second sentence: the bill to prohibit fishing in Eagle Bay should be enacted. What follows is the support for this view. The bay is incredibly polluted, and a study has shown that 80 percent of the bay's fish have high toxin levels. So, the author says, continuing to allow fishing would cause problems for public health.

Step 3: Make a Prediction

Notice "thus" in the last sentence. This isn't signaling the conclusion of the argument but rather a capper on the author's evidence, which the question is asking about. The only reason the author brought up this evidence was to cite the negative effect on public health that would occur if the ban weren't enacted.

Step 4: Evaluate the Answer Choices

(D) matches this prediction and is therefore correct.

(A) distorts the claim in the second sentence of the stimulus. It introduces the economy, which the author never cites in order to support her endorsement of the fishing ban.

(B) brings in morality, which is Out of Scope. It would be too great a leap to say that the author's invoking public health has anything to do with a moral principle.

(C) brings in an Irrelevant Comparison regarding the ban's positive and negative effects, which the author does not do. Nor does she accuse the ban's opponents of not having done

so. She only mentions negative public health effects to lend credence to her support of the ban.

(E) introduces a prediction that is Out of Scope. The only effects the author predicts are those that would occur if the legislature *didn't* enact the ban.

5. (A) Principle (Identify/Strengthen)

Step 1: Identify the Question Type

This Principle question asks for a broad rule that helps *justify* Simpson's response. That makes this akin to a Strengthen question, which means using argument-based skills to untangle the stimulus.

Step 2: Untangle the Stimulus

Vandenberg argues that the art museum is not doing what it's supposed to because of the lesser weight given to contemporary art. Simpson counters that the smaller amount of contemporary art is acceptable because there are few high-quality pieces of contemporary art.

Step 3: Make a Prediction

Even if there were a shortage of quality contemporary pieces, the museum could still provide a more balanced representation of art by collecting more contemporary artwork, even if it's of lesser quality. In order to justify calling the smaller contemporary collection appropriate, Simpson must be acting on the principle that lesser-quality pieces are unacceptable for the museum.

Step 4: Evaluate the Answer Choices

(A) solidly presents the principle behind Simpson's argument. If the museum should only collect high-quality art, that would make the small contemporary section appropriate.

(B) is Extreme and somewhat contrary to Simpson, because she finds the comparatively smaller contemporary section acceptable, despite the founders' intention to provide equal representation.

(C) is Extreme and doesn't work, because even if the museum didn't have to collect every style from every period, it may still need to provide a better balance, making the small contemporary section unacceptable.

(D) is Out of Scope because Simpson never mentions the curators' belief about the museum's purpose; only their opinion of contemporary art is discussed.

(E) is also Out of Scope because there's no mention of the curators' intentions—only their judgment about the quality of contemporary art.

6. (C) Strengthen

Step 1: Identify the Question Type

The stem asks for what "most strengthens the reasoning," so the correct answer choice will contain a fact that will make the conclusion more likely to follow from the evidence.

Step 2: Untangle the Stimulus

The conclusion in the last sentence says that large corporations' actions have influenced the government's decisions to curtail funding for major alternative-energy initiatives over the last five years. The evidence describes those actions: large companies actively discourage alternative-energy projects.

Step 3: Make a Prediction

One way to strengthen the argument is to validate its central assumption. The argument assumes that there is a link between what large corporations do and what the government does. Any answer choice that reinforces this link will strengthen the argument.

Step 4: Evaluate the Answer Choices

(C) strengthens the argument. If *all* projects whose funding has been curtailed by the government have also been discouraged by large corporations, then that bolsters the link between the government's and the corporations' actions.

(A) has no effect on the argument. The lack of funding might be unfortunate for the alternative-energy projects in general, but it doesn't strengthen the idea that the government has been influenced by large corporations.

(B) is a 180 because it could actually weaken the argument by suggesting that any change made to the government's funding of a project was going to happen anyway, with or without the influence of large corporations.

(D) is also a 180. If the government is curtailing funding for projects left and right with little consideration given to whether those projects are encouraged by large corporations, then that works against the author's contention that the corporations are influencing the government's decisions.

(E) is Out of Scope. Discouraging certain forms of research might impugn large corporations, but it doesn't do anything to suggest that they're influencing the government's actions.

7. (D) Point at Issue

Step 1: Identify the Question Type

This stem asks for what Talbert and Sklar disagree on, so it's a Point at Issue question. Predict the Point at Issue while reading the arguments, if possible, but be prepared to use the Decision Tree.

Step 2: Untangle the Stimulus

Talbert argues that chess is good for school-age children and then provides a laundry list of benefits. Sklar objects to teaching chess to school-age children because it doesn't have societal value and distracts their attention from subjects that do have societal value.

Step 3: Make a Prediction

Fortunately, Talbert and Sklar come right out at the beginning of their respective arguments and state the Point at Issue.

Talbert endorses the idea of teaching chess to school-age children; Sklar objects to it. That's what they disagree on.

Step 4: Evaluate the Answer Choices

(D) matches this prediction, and it also passes the Decision Tree test. Talbert would give **(D)** an emphatic "yes," whereas Sklar would say "no." If both speakers have contradictory opinions about an answer choice, then that choice is the Point at Issue between them.

(A) is something Talbert clearly agrees with, but there's no evidence of Sklar's opinion on this.

(B) isn't covered by either speaker. Neither Talbert nor Sklar compares chess to other activities regarding their ability to promote mental maturity.

(C) is something Sklar disagrees with, but it isn't the Point at Issue because Talbert has no opinion on science.

(E) Talbert says that chess promotes mental maturity, but that's a far cry from saying that playing chess and studying science are necessary for mental maturity. Also, once again, the issue of mental maturity isn't on Sklar's radar.

8. (A) Flaw

Step 1: Identify the Question Type

"[V]ulnerable to criticism" in the question stem indicates a Flaw question. In order to find the flaw in Theodora's argument, you'll still need to read Marcia's argument for context.

Step 2: Untangle the Stimulus

Marcia concludes that vegetarian diets don't always lead to nutritional deficiencies because vegetarians can have fully nutritious diets without eating animal products. Theodora replies that if most people became vegetarians, then those who work in meat-based industries would lose their jobs, and that their resultant poverty would keep them from affording a nutritionally sound diet. Because of this, she says Marcia is wrong to claim that vegetarian diets don't lead to nutritional issues.

Step 3: Make a Prediction

As soon as Theodora says that Marcia is wrong to claim that vegetarianism cannot lead to nutritional deficiencies, the flaw has already been committed. Marcia *didn't* claim that vegetarianism can't lead to nutrition problems; she just claimed that not all vegetarian diets do. Theodora doesn't even address Marcia's argument, and therein lies the flaw.

Step 4: Evaluate the Answer Choices

(A) correctly states this flaw. Theodora's rebuttal fails because it aims to refute a claim Marcia never made.

(B) is not a flaw in Theodora's argument. She doesn't ignore the results of the research Marcia cites. She just uses her own evidence, which would be fine if she were arguing against what Marcia actually said.

(C) distorts one of Theodora's claims. She doesn't assume that a major shift to vegetarianism is necessary for the collapse of meat-based industries; she states that such a shift is *sufficient* for those industries to collapse.

(D) describes another type of flaw, equivocation, which isn't present here. Both Marcia and Theodora use the term "diet" in the same sense.

(E) is incorrect because Theodora doesn't assume that people would become vegetarians after losing their jobs. She claims that these people would end up with nutritionally deficient diets because of poverty.

9. (E) Main Point

Step 1: Identify the Question Type

This question simply asks for the "main conclusion," aka the Main Point, of the argument. Look for Conclusion Keywords to aid your search.

Step 2: Untangle the Stimulus

The musicologist defines the criterion by which to classify musical instruments: the action they use to produce music. While a piano's strings make the sounds, it's the action of hammers striking the strings that produces the sound. Thus, the musicologist concludes, the piano is rightfully classified as a percussion instrument—not a string instrument.

Step 3: Make a Prediction

While the argument ends with the information about hammers striking the piano's strings, that's merely evidence to back up the main point, which is that the piano is not really a string instrument—it's a percussion instrument. The correct answer will express this main point (as indicated in the stimulus by the Keyword [s]o).

Step 4: Evaluate the Answer Choices

(E) accurately expresses the main point about the piano's classification.

(A) distorts the first sentence, taking a given fact (how instruments *are* classified) and turning it into a recommendation (how they *should* be classified).

(B) is Out of Scope. Musicians are not discussed in the argument.

(C) is Out of Scope because it suggests that some people classify the piano as a string instrument, which is not directly mentioned—let alone the main point.

(D) is a 180 and thus the complete opposite of the musicologist's main point.

10. (A) Inference

Step 1: Identify the Question Type

This question is asking for a proper inference of what must be true given the information in the stimulus.

Step 2: Untangle the Stimulus

The first half of the stimulus provides a string of information: agricultural runoff poured out of a large river, which caused increased phosphorous in a particular ocean region, leading to more plankton near the ocean surface. The second half discusses the consequences: when the plankton decay, they fall to the floor and get eaten by bacteria, which wind up taking in oxygen at the same time. This leads to less oxygen, which affects what fish can live in the area.

Step 3: Make a Prediction

Seeing how all of this information connects, the correct answer should simply stay consistent with the flow of logic without making any unwarranted claims or using extreme language.

Step 4: Evaluate the Answer Choices

(A) is exactly what the first few sentences express: the runoff caused the increase in phosphorous, ultimately contributing to the increase in plankton.

(B) is Extreme. While the information does suggest that more fish could live in the area prior to the phosphorous increase, it doesn't state that *most* fish could.

(C) makes an unwarranted connection between the runoff and the bacteria. The runoff affected the growth of plankton, not the bacteria.

(D) suggests that the increase in runoff had to be exactly proportional to phosphorous levels. However, this is never stated, so it's possible that even a small increase in runoff could have led to such a drastic increase in phosphorous.

(E) goes Extreme by taking the results of this particular ocean region and generalizing it to any body of water.

11. (A) Weaken

Step 1: Identify the Question Type

The question stem asks for what "weakens the reasoning," so find the answer that makes the conclusion less likely to follow from the evidence.

Step 2: Untangle the Stimulus

The argument concludes that drivers are possessive of their parking spaces even when leaving them and that they get more possessive when they sense that someone else wants the parking space. This conclusion is based on psychologists' observations that drivers took the least amount of time leaving a space when no one was waiting, more time when someone was waiting quietly, and even more time than that when another driver honked impatiently.

Step 3: Make a Prediction

The argument, for all its detail, is essentially causal. Psychologists noticed a correlation between the amount of time it took drivers to leave a parking space and the presence and aggression of another driver waiting for the space. The argument imputes causality to this correlation, though, and presumes that drivers took longer *because* another driver was present. Any answer choice that provides another explanation for drivers' delays in leaving their spaces will therefore weaken this argument.

Step 4: Evaluate the Answer Choices

(A) is a valid weakener because it suggests that drivers aren't taking longer out of a sense of possessiveness, but because they feel pressure from other drivers to vacate their spaces.

(B) doesn't affect the argument because it discusses the amount of time drivers spend *entering* a space, not leaving it.

(C) seems to bring up an alternative explanation for the long times: the nearness of other vehicles. However, the argument never states that the waiting cars were "nearby." If all of the waiting cars in the study were far enough away, then proximity wouldn't be a factor, leaving possessiveness as a valid explanation.

(D) Even if people are more likely to have cars waiting to take their parking spaces in shopping mall lots, the psychologists' findings can still show that possessiveness is the reason why people take longer to leave their spaces.

(E), if anything, strengthens the argument by suggesting that an emotional response to impatience from another driver leads to delays in leaving the parking spaces. Possessiveness might therefore be a legitimate factor.

12. (A) Paradox

Step 1: Identify the Question Type

Because the question asks for something that resolves a paradox, this is a Paradox question.

Step 2: Untangle the Stimulus

The stimulus states that shark teeth are extremely common, relative to other vertebrate fossils. However, the mystery is that shark skeletons are relatively *un*common.

Step 3: Make a Prediction

To resolve this paradox, the correct answer will provide a reason why shark skeletons are less common than other vertebrate skeletons, despite the prevalence of shark teeth.

Step 4: Evaluate the Answer Choices

(A) helps explain this discrepancy. The equal likelihood of bone and tooth fossilization explains why shark teeth are so common, while the lesser likelihood of cartilage fossilization explains why shark skeletons are rare compared to those of other vertebrates.

(B) separates the locations where teeth and skeletons are found, but it doesn't explain why that makes shark skeletons so rare compared to those of other vertebrates.

(C) discusses the difficulty of identifying shark teeth, but it does nothing to explain their commonness or the lack of the skeletons.

(D) is Out of Scope. Sharks alive today are irrelevant. Moreover, the paradox is about shark fossils compared to other vertebrate fossils, not about the commonness of shark teeth in general.

(E) makes matters worse. If the tooth and skeleton fossilization processes are the same, one would expect teeth and skeletons to be equally common.

13. (B) Assumption (Sufficient)

Step 1: Identify the Question Type

The stem says that one of the answers, if assumed, makes the conclusion "properly drawn." Find the gap between the evidence and the conclusion.

Step 2: Untangle the Stimulus

"Thus" in the last sentence signals the conclusion: photographs are interpretations of reality. The evidence is that photographers invariably express their own worldviews in their photographs, no matter how realistic those photographs might be.

Step 3: Make a Prediction

Connect unmatched terms between the evidence and the conclusion to find the missing link. The conclusion says that photographs interpret reality. The evidence says that photographs express the worldview of their photographers. Therefore the conclusion will follow from the evidence, if it were true, that expressing a worldview involves interpreting reality.

Step 4: Evaluate the Answer Choices

(B) is a perfect match for this prediction.

(A) makes a shift to interpreting "a subject" rather than reality, which distorts the scope of the argument in an unhelpful way.

(C) broadens the idea of expressing a worldview to include all visual art. But without making a connection between expressing a worldview and interpreting reality, **(C)** can't make the conclusion follow.

(D), in Formal Logic terms, is saying that if something interprets reality, then it expresses a worldview. But that doesn't guarantee that photographs are interpretations of reality just because they express a worldview. That's getting the logic backwards.

(E) likens nonrealistic photographs to realistic photographs, but that similarity doesn't have anything to do with interpreting reality, so **(E)** doesn't help establish the conclusion of the argument.

14. (D) Weaken

Step 1: Identify the Question Type
The stem is very straightforward: find the choice that weakens the argument, or that widens the gap between evidence and conclusion.

Step 2: Untangle the Stimulus
The argument concludes that marks found in a piece of sandstone were caused by geological processes rather than by worms, even though the marks resemble worm tracks. The evidence for this is that the marks were made long before worms were known to have existed.

Step 3: Make a Prediction
Yet another causal argument—the supposed cause of the marks is "geological processes." The rejected cause is worm movement. Therefore, there are two ways to weaken this argument: show that geological processes are not likely to be the cause, or show that worms could have made the marks after all.

Step 4: Evaluate the Answer Choices
(D) directly attacks the author's supposed cause for the marks and is therefore the correct weakener for the argument.

(A) might be tempting, but the age of the sandstone isn't important. What matters is the age of the *marks* in the sandstone.

(B) strengthens the argument by making it more plausible that geological processes could have been responsible for the marks in question.

(C) brings up a third possible source of the marks: other animals. This certainly doesn't help the author. However, without stating if these animals existed at the time or the location of the sandstone, it doesn't provide enough to weaken the conclusion of the author, who was more concerned with debating geological processes versus worms, anyway.

(E) doesn't affect the argument. Even if worms are the earliest known multicellular animal life on earth, that doesn't change the fact that the marks predate all multicellular animal life by more than half a billion years.

15. (B) Inference

Step 1: Identify the Question Type
When a question asks for something that fills in the blank at the end of a passage, it's looking for an inference that follows directly from the statements preceding that blank.

Step 2: Untangle the Stimulus
According to the stimulus, certain organs (e.g., eyes or wings) often develop because they provide the only way to accomplish certain tasks. The author then suggests that, if certain animals are unrelated, it would make sense that these organs evolved at different times. However, the reasoning

then suggests that, regardless of different backgrounds and locations, animals basically need to accomplish the same things.

Step 3: Make a Prediction
The correct answer will complete this train of thought. If animals need to accomplish similar tasks and certain organs often provide the only means of accomplishing those tasks, it would logically follow that these animals would often develop similar organs to accomplish those similar tasks.

Step 4: Evaluate the Answer Choices
(B) perfectly combines the given information, expressing the inference that animals with similar needs will develop similar organs.

(A) is unsupported as the stimulus discusses organ development, not living environments.

(C) may be tempting, but it doesn't incorporate the idea that animals with similar needs will develop *similar* organs. Also, the answer is Extreme because the original claim states that organs are *often* the only way to accomplish certain tasks—which doesn't allow the conclusion that animals with similar needs *will* develop those adaptations.

(D) is unsupported because similar organs will develop to accomplish similar needs, but that doesn't mean animals with *different* needs will look alike.

(E) misuses "eyes and wings," which are merely examples of shared adaptations, and not ones the author suggests that all animals with similar needs will develop.

16. (C) Assumption (Necessary)

Step 1: Identify the Question Type
The stem asks you to identify "an assumption on which the engineer's argument depends." So find what must be true in order for the evidence to lead to the conclusion.

Step 2: Untangle the Stimulus
The engineer concludes with a solution to the heat (and money) wasted by steel plants: feed that heat into thermophotovoltaic generators, which can convert that heat into electricity. This conversion, says the engineer, will save the plants money by reducing their electric bills.

Step 3: Make a Prediction
Notice, though, that the engineer is essentially recommending trading one expense (higher electric bills) for another expense (the thermophotovoltaic generators). Therefore, in order for the generators to be worth it and actually save money, the engineer has to assume that the generators cost less than the amount that would be saved on the electric bills. If they don't cost less than that amount, there would be no point in installing them. Even without such a prediction, be prepared to apply the Denial Test to eliminate

those choices that don't have to be true for the argument to be valid.

Step 4: Evaluate the Answer Choices

(C) is a great match for this prediction.

(A) is a common Distortion for this type of question because it misrepresents what the engineer is arguing. His conclusion is simply that the generators will save money, not that they'll save more money than any other alternative systems. So **(A)** doesn't have to be true to make the argument work.

(B) also misrepresents the argument. It need not be true that the steel plants have a way of feeding heat into the generators using *current technology*. The engineer is just saying that if the plants could figure that out, they could save money.

(D) doesn't work because electricity doesn't have to be the primary source of energy for steel plants. The argument isn't about how much or how little the plants rely on different energy sources. It's about whether or not the generators would save money for the plants.

(E) makes the heat-electricity conversion process necessary for reducing steel plants' energy bills, but the engineer is just putting forth the generators as a *sufficient* means of achieving this, so **(E)** doesn't have to be true in this argument.

17. (A) Role of a Statement

Step 1: Identify the Question Type

Unlike traditional Role of a Statement questions, this unique variation doesn't provide a claim and ask for the role that claim plays. Instead, it provides the role (something corresponds to "standard antibiotic" in the given analogy) and asks for the phrase that performs that role.

Step 2: Untangle the Stimulus

The herbalist begins by discussing two types of medicine: standard antibiotics, which have one ingredient, and herbal remedies, which have multiple ingredients. Because of this, the herbalist argues that herbal remedies are more effective against bacteria. To illustrate the challenge bacteria face, the herbalist compares bacteria to cooks. As a bacterium would have a harder time trying to combat a remedy with multiple ingredients, a cook would have a harder time trying to please a group of guests with multiple tastes.

Step 3: Make a Prediction

A great way to make sense of all this is to generalize the analogy and see how all of the pieces match up. In both cases, some entity (bacteria or cooks) faces a challenge. With a simpler case (a standard antibiotic or a single guest), the entity has fewer obstacles to deal with (one active ingredient or one taste). The more complex case (herbal remedy or multiple guests) provides a greater challenge (multiple ingredients or multiple tastes). From that, it's quick to see

that "standard antibiotic" shares the same role as "a single guest" in the analogy.

Step 4: Evaluate the Answer Choices

(A), the single guest, is the part of the cook analogy that corresponds to the standard antibiotic.

(B) is off because multiple guests correspond to the herbal remedy, not the standard antibiotic.

(C) is off because the pleasure experienced by the single guest corresponds to the single ingredient in the antibiotic, not the antibiotic itself.

(D) is off because the cook corresponds with the strain of bacteria.

(E) is Out of Scope because the analogy never mentions the cook's ingredients.

18. (A) Flaw

Step 1: Identify the Question Type

Again, the key phrase "vulnerable to … criticism(s)" indicates a Flaw question. Look for the scientists' argument and identify the gap between the evidence and conclusion.

Step 2: Untangle the Stimulus

The scientists' argument comes at the end of the stimulus: the barn owl locates sound through some auditory scheme and not through vision. The evidence of this hypothesis (naturally) is an experiment. Even without the distorting lenses, mature owls still behaved as though they misjudged the location of the sources of sounds.

Step 3: Make a Prediction

There's a big problem with the scientists' interpretation of their results. They put the distorting lenses on the owls when the owls were young and left them on until the owls matured. So it's possible that the owls' sense of vision was warped irreparably by having the distorted lenses on during their physical development. In that very possible case, the owls could still be using their (warped) sense of vision to locate sounds, and the argument no longer works.

Step 4: Evaluate the Answer Choices

(A) also describes this overlooked possibility (the most common of LSAT flaws) and is therefore correct.

(B) is far too broad to be something assumed by this argument. The scientists aren't taking for granted in their experiment that *all* owls have equally good vision.

(C) is off base because there's no indication in the argument that the scientists considered the owls' behavior to be at all similar to human reasoning processes.

(D) isn't something the scientists needed to consider at all. They can draw conclusions about barn owls without having to take other bird species into account.

(E) is wrong because the experimental results were very relevant to the scientists' hypothesis. The scientists just failed to consider an alternative hypothesis to explain those same experimental results.

19. (D) Paradox (EXCEPT)

Step 1: Identify the Question Type
This question asks for something that will *explain* a trend in journalism. Explaining something indicates a Paradox question, and the *EXCEPT* indicates that four answers will resolve the paradox and the credited answer will not.

Step 2: Untangle the Stimulus
According to the author, journalists continue to use quotes to publish false and unsupported claims. However, despite this continued reporting of false claims, other journalists are challenging those claims less and less.

Step 3: Make a Prediction
With Paradox questions, it's not necessary to predict exactly what the correct answer is. Instead, it's enough to know that four of the answers will explain why other journalists won't contest the claims they print, despite the questionable nature of those claims. The correct answer will do nothing to resolve the issue—or possibly make the situation even more inexplicable.

Step 4: Evaluate the Answer Choices
(D) is correct, because it makes matters even more mysterious. If the principle of journalism is that debate draws attention, it wouldn't make sense that journalists are doing less debating.

(A) explains the trend, because the potential to lose customers would discourage journalists from disputing quotes.

(B) explains the trend, because journalists wouldn't have the specialized knowledge to challenge the unsupported claims.

(C) explains the trend, because the journalists would be more likely to sympathize with (and thus less likely to argue against) the people making the unsupported claims.

(E) explains the trend, because challenging the claims would be damaging to journalists' reputations.

20. (C) Weaken

Step 1: Identify the Question Type
The stem asks for the choice that "most weakens the argument." So find the answer that makes the conclusion less likely to follow from the evidence.

Step 2: Untangle the Stimulus
The argument concludes that computers, not humans, should interpret EKG data. The evidence is a study: a cardiologist was pitted against a computer program that analyzes EKG data. The computer program correctly identified more of the cases that later turned out to be heart attacks than did the cardiologist.

Step 3: Make a Prediction
But what if the computer were just indiscriminately diagnosing everything as a heart attack? Then it's totally reasonable to believe that the computer would beat the cardiologist at diagnosing the positive heart attack cases. But in order to go along with the author's conclusion, more evidence is needed that the computer was better at diagnosing the negatives too—that is, cases when there *weren't* heart attacks.

Step 4: Evaluate the Answer Choices
(C) correctly exploits that vulnerability in the argument. If the cardiologist was better than the computer program at diagnosing the negative cases, then it's essentially a draw, and the author can't wholeheartedly endorse computer programs to do all EKG interpretation.

(A) doesn't hurt the argument. The cardiologist could have made only subtle mistakes in interpreting the EKG data and still not be as well suited to the analysis as a computer program.

(B) doesn't affect the argument because there's no evidence given that interpreting EKGs involves making subjective judgments.

(D) distorts the scope of the argument. The argument isn't about whether EKGs always provide enough of a picture to make an accurate diagnosis. The argument is about whether a computer program or a cardiologist is better suited to interpret EKGs.

(E) doesn't provide enough information to be a proper weakener. Perhaps the cardiologist was much *more* skilled and experienced than most other cardiologists. In that case, the computer looks even better as an interpreter of EKGs, because it would have bested one of the best, so to speak.

21. (E) Principle (Identify/Strengthen)

Step 1: Identify the Question Type
This Principle question asks for a broad rule that helps *justify* the author's reasoning. That makes this similar to a Strengthen question, which means using argument-based skills to untangle the stimulus.

Step 2: Untangle the Stimulus
The author recommends that the national speed limit for straight, high-speed highways be set to 120 kph (75 mph). The evidence is that 120 kph (75 mph) is the average speed on straight, high-speed highways, and a study shows that raising the speed limit to the average speed would reduce the accident rate.

Step 3: Make a Prediction
Because the recommendation is based on an idea that it would reduce accidents, the author must be acting on the principle that reducing accidents is a good enough reason to recommend a course of action.

Step 4: Evaluate the Answer Choices
(E) clearly expresses the principle guiding the author's recommendation of raising the speed limit.

(A) is Extreme, because the author never suggests that speed limits should *only* apply to high-speed highways. While this argument only discusses high-speed highways, the author never indicates that other highways should be exempt from having national speed limits.

(B) distorts the author's argument. While the author does want to make the speed limit uniform across the nation, this entirely ignores the reasoning behind that recommendation: reducing the accident rate.

(C) brings up the need for all high-speed roadways to have roughly the same average speed. However, the author merely discusses a national average and makes no mention of the range of individual roadways.

(D) mentions laws that are widely violated—a concept that is never discussed in the argument.

22. (C) Strengthen (EXCEPT)

Step 1: Identify the Question Type
This question stem seeks the answer that doesn't strengthen the argument. So find the answer that either weakens the argument or has no effect on it.

Step 2: Untangle the Stimulus
The psychiatrist concludes that first-year students who spend a lot on recreation could afford to reduce that spending without their anxiety or depression increasing. The evidence for this is that first-year students who spend the most on recreation don't score any lower on tests for anxiety and depression than those who spend the least.

Step 3: Make a Prediction
Don't try to predict the four strengtheners that will be the wrong answer choices here. Instead, just go to the answer choices and prepare to eliminate any choice showing that first-year students may indeed stabilize or even decrease levels of anxiety and depression even while reducing spending on recreation.

Step 4: Evaluate the Answer Choices
(C) shifts from first-year university students to adults age 40 to 60, which is likely a very different population. Therefore, **(C)** doesn't help the argument and is the correct answer. Furthermore, **(C)** draws a strong correlation between decreased anxiety and depression and increased spending.

The psychiatrist's whole point is that first-year students can manage their anxiety and depression even if they spend less.

(A) doesn't prove the argument to be valid, but it does corroborate the psychiatrist's evidence by saying that similar evidence is reported at other universities. So **(A)** is a strengthener.

(B) strengthens the argument by suggesting that students with the highest levels of spending can actually *decrease* their anxiety and depression by lowering their spending to more moderate levels.

(D) makes the psychiatrist's tests more reliable, which in turn supports the conclusion she bases on them.

(E) shows that the psychiatrist's prediction has already come true, so that certainly strengthens the idea that the psychiatrist's prediction is valid.

23. (D) Parallel Flaw

Step 1: Identify the Question Type
Because the question is looking for an analogy that demonstrates the same flawed reasoning as the original stimulus, this is a Parallel Flaw question.

Step 2: Untangle the Stimulus
The argument starts off with information about all brick houses on River Street: they have front yards. The argument then discusses the houses on River Street with front yards: most of them have two stories. The conclusion is about brick houses on River Street: most of them have two stories.

Step 3: Make a Prediction
With Parallel Flaw questions, start by recognizing the flaw in the argument. While the brick houses all have front lawns, it's not clear which houses with front lawns have the two stories. It's possible that there are 10 brick houses, many with one story, while there are 20 two-story wood houses with front lawns. Because there is no absolute connection between brick houses and number of stories, the conclusion is unwarranted. To assist in testing the answer choices, notice the structure: a group of entities (brick houses) *all* have a particular property (front lawns). *Most* things with that property have a second property (two stories). The argument concludes that *most* entities in the original group have the second property.

Step 4: Evaluate the Answer Choices
(D) matches the stimulus in both structure and flaw. A group of entities (legislators) all have a property (public servants), and most things with that property have a second property (never run). The argument faultily concludes that most entities in the original group have the second property—ignoring the possibility that while a lot of legislators do run for office, even more public servants never run.

(A) distorts the reasoning because both pieces of evidence are about the same group (legislators) and the conclusion is about a different group (politicians)—which are merely a subset of the original group.

(B) is off because the evidence discusses the properties of *most* legislators and *most* politicians, with no group *all* having the same property.

(C) doesn't match the conclusion because it discusses "not every public servant" instead of "most" members of a group. Additionally, the evidence provides information about "some" public servants instead of "most."

(E) is off because the evidence discusses the properties of *most* public servants and *most* legislators, with no group *all* having the same property.

24. (B) Assumption (Sufficient)

Step 1: Identify the Question Type
The phrase "if which one of the following is assumed" indicates that this is a Sufficient Assumption question. Find the connection between the evidence and conclusion.

Step 2: Untangle the Stimulus
The historian's conclusion is at the end of the argument: the more history one knows, the less likely one is to see history as the working out of moral themes. There are two main pieces of evidence: 1) holding clear moral beliefs is necessary for seeing history as the working out of moral themes and 2) as one learns more about history, one is less likely to morally judge human behavior.

Step 3: Make a Prediction
Formal Logic is useful here. The conclusion can be translated to this:

| If | you know more about history | → | unlikely to see history as moral themes |

The first piece of evidence can be translated to

| If | likely to see history as moral themes | → | hold clear moral beliefs |

The second piece can be translated to

| If | you know more about history | → | less likely to judge behavior |

To make the first piece of evidence line up with the conclusion, contrapose it:

Evidence:

| If | ~ hold clear moral beliefs | → | ~ likely to see history as moral themes |

| If | you know more about history | → | less likely to judge behavior |

Conclusion:

| If | you know more about history | → | ~ likely to see history as moral themes |

To make the conclusion logically follow, connect "less likely to judge behavior" to "don't hold clear moral beliefs." So the proper assumption is this:

| If | less likely to judge behavior | → | ~ hold clear moral beliefs |

Step 4: Evaluate the Answer Choices
(B) matches this perfectly.

(A) introduces the concept of moral disapproval, which doesn't appear anywhere in the argument and therefore can't be used to connect the pieces of the argument.

(C) introduces the new concept of understanding history, which also doesn't appear in the argument.

(D) just reverses the first Formal Logic statement in the evidence, but that doesn't help it connect to any other statements in the argument.

(E) discusses objectivity as it relates to increasing knowledge, but objectivity isn't within the scope of the argument. Stick closely to the terms and concepts already discussed in the argument to find what will connect them.

25. (D) Paradox

Step 1: Identify the Question Type
Because the question is asking for something that accounts for a discrepancy, it's asking for a resolution to a paradox.

Step 2: Untangle the Stimulus
As usual with a Paradox stimulus, something is amiss. Most students at a particular school would prefer a president with

a lot of experience. However, given a list of candidates, most students chose one with no experience.

Step 3: Make a Prediction

The question becomes: Why would students choose a candidate with no experience when they expressed a preference for a candidate with experience? Two explanations seem likely: either the students had no idea their choice was inexperienced, or the list of candidates didn't include any experienced presidents.

Step 4: Evaluate the Answer Choices

(D) is right in line with the explanation that students were unaware of their choice's lack of experience.

(A) fails to explain why the students chose an inexperienced candidate when there were experienced candidates available. Even if it was hard to differentiate the experienced candidates, it doesn't explain why students abandoned their preference and went with one of the inexperienced candidates.

(B) deepens the mystery, because such a list would have given students ample opportunity to choose someone who satisfied their preference.

(C) is off because, even if the list was incomplete, it still could have included experienced candidates. It offers no real reason why the students chose someone with no experience.

(E) is tempting because it *might* explain why someone would choose a candidate with *little* experience. However, it doesn't provide a reason why students chose a candidate with *no* experience.

Section III: Logic Games

Game 1: Business Convention Car Trip

Q#	Question Type	Correct	Difficulty
1	Acceptability	A	★
2	Must Be False (CANNOT Be True)	E	★★
3	"If" / Could Be True	A	★
4	"If" / Must Be True	C	★★★
5	Must Be False (CANNOT Be True)	D	★★★

Game 2: Ancient Artifacts

Q#	Question Type	Correct	Difficulty
6	Acceptability	A	★
7	How Many	C	★
8	Must Be False (CANNOT Be True)	A	★
9	"If" / Must Be True	C	★
10	"If" / How Many	B	★
11	Rule Substitution	D	★★★★

Game 3: Track Team

Q#	Question Type	Correct	Difficulty
12	Acceptability	D	★
13	Must Be True	D	★★★
14	Completely Determine	B	★
15	Must Be False (CANNOT Be True)	A	★★★
16	"If" / Must Be True	E	★★★★
17	"If" / How Many	B	★★★

Game 4: Nurses' Information Sessions

Q#	Question Type	Correct	Difficulty
18	Acceptability	D	★
19	Must Be False (CANNOT Be True)	C	★★★★
20	"If" / Could Be True	D	★★★
21	"If" / Could Be True	B	★★
22	"If" / Must Be True	B	★★★
23	Could Be True	A	★

Game 1: Business Convention Car Trip

Step 1: Overview

Situation: Workers travel to a business convention in two cars

Entities: Six workers—F, G, H, J, K, L—and two cars—Cars 1 and 2

Action: Distribution. Assign each worker exactly once between the two cars. There is also the added twist of determining who drives each car.

Limitations: At least two workers must ride in each car. So the distribution could be two in one car and four in the other, or three in one car and three in the other. Exactly one worker in each car is assigned as the driver, while the rest are passengers.

Step 2: Sketch

A standard Distribution column sketch serves the purpose here; create two columns and label them 1 and 2. Although it's unknown exactly how many passengers are assigned to each car (anywhere from two to four), there are at least two in each car. So place two slots in each column in the Master Sketch to start:

F G H J K L

1	2
__	__
__	__

In addition, don't forget to make a note of distinction for whichever passenger drives the car. Circling this passenger (as that information becomes known) is sufficient.

Step 3: Rules

Rule 1 states that either Faith or Gus drives the car that Hannah rides in. You don't know which car this is, so notate the rule as it will appear in the sketch:

Rule 2 is essentially the same restriction as Rule 1, but with different entities. Either Faith or Kenneth drives the car in which Juan is a passenger, so notate the rule similarly:

Rule 3 is the most concrete; it pairs up Gus and Lisa together in a car. Notate how this Block of Entities will appear in the sketch:

Step 4: Deductions

Gus and Lisa are the only workers who must ride together in either Car 1 or Car 2, thereby forming the only Block of Entities in the game.

No individual rule explicitly sets up Limited Options in this game. Nor does any rule restrict a worker to Car 1 or Car 2, exclusively. So, there are no Established Entities in this game.

After working through the rule, the Numbers restrictions remain: either two workers in one car and four workers in the other, or three workers in each car.

Finally, note which entities appear in more than one rule. In addition to Rule 3, Gus is also mentioned in Rule 1. However, this Duplication doesn't lead to a solid deduction because Faith could also drive the car in which Hannah is riding.

Take a moment to combine the rules to yield any additional deductions. While no single rule defines two options for this game, take a look back at Rule 3. Notice that there is no difference between Car 1 and Car 2; all that really matters is the groups of passengers that are created, not to which car each passenger is assigned. If Gus and Lisa ride together, they either ride without Juan or in the same car as Juan. Juan is worth noting because he must ride in the car that either Faith or Kenneth is driving—which would then max out that car to four passengers (Gus, Lisa, Juan, and either Faith or Kenneth). So if Gus and Lisa ride in the same car as Juan, then Faith or Kenneth must drive.

Rule 1 nails down who must drive—Faith or Kenneth. Faith or Gus must drive Hannah's car. Thus, Hannah would need to be added to the car. But, that's too many passengers (five) in one car, leaving only one passenger for the other car. Thus, Kenneth must drive the car that holds Gus, Lisa and Juan. Faith must drive Hannah in the other car. That's one option:

Option I:

1	2
Ⓚ	Ⓕ
G	H
L	
J	

Another option rests on the case of Gus and Lisa taking a different car than Juan. Then, Faith or Kenneth must drive Juan's car. Hannah can then be assigned to either, as long as it's driven by Gus or Faith:

Option II:

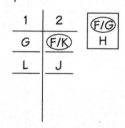

Remember, it's not important *which* car (1 or 2) the passengers are assigned to. So the assignment of passengers in each option can work for either car.

The finalized Master Sketch should look something like this.

F G H J K L

Option I: Option II:

Step 5: Questions

1. (A) Acceptability

For Acceptability questions, eliminate any answer choices that violate one or more of the rules:

Rule 1 requires that Hannah ride in a car driven by Faith or Gus. This eliminates **(D)**.

Rule 2 requires Juan ride in a car driven by Faith or Kenneth, which eliminates **(B)** and **(E)**.

Rule 3 requires that Gus and Lisa ride together, which eliminates **(C)**.

This leaves **(A)** as the correct answer because it doesn't violate any of the rules.

2. (E) Must Be False (CANNOT Be True)

The correct answer will contain a pair of workers who *cannot* be the two drivers. The wrong answer choices all contain possible pairs of drivers. In each option in the Master Sketch, either Faith or Gus (or both) must drive. Here's where that thorough setup work pays off. Only **(E)** is missing either Faith or Gus, so it cannot be an acceptable pair of drivers. Therefore, **(E)** is correct.

Trial and error (in case you missed the options in the setup) arrives at the same conclusion. Kenneth and Lisa *cannot* be the two drivers, because Faith or Gus must drive Hannah's

car; if Kenneth and Lisa are the only drivers, there is no car available for Hannah.

All the remaining answer choices are acceptable pairs of workers who could be the two drivers. **(B)** is possible in Option I. **(A)**, **(C)**, and **(D)** are all possible in Option II. **(A)** is possible if Gus drives Hannah and Lisa in one car and Faith drives Juan and Kenneth in the other car. **(C)** is possible if Lisa drives Gus in one car and Faith drives Kenneth, Juan, and Hannah in another car. **(D)** is possible if Gus drives Hannah and Lisa in one car and Kenneth drives Juan in another car, with Faith riding in either car.

3. (A) "If" / Could Be True

When faced with a New-"If" question, always draw a mini-sketch. In this case, recopy one of your options (or both) in accordance with the new information in the question stem. The New-"If" states that Lisa drives one of the cars, so resketch Option II with this adjustment. Recall that either Faith or Gus (or both) must drive. Because Lisa will drive the car Gus rides in (Rule 3), Faith must drive Hannah (Rule 1) and Juan (Rule 2) in the other car. This leaves Kenneth with the option to ride in either car:

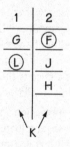

The correct answer will be possible in the new mini-sketch, while the wrong answer choices will be impossible. Because Kenneth can travel in either car, **(A)** is correct.

All the wrong answer choices contain pairs of workers who are prohibited from riding in the same car in the new mini-sketch. **(B)** is incorrect because Faith and Lisa travel in separate cars. **(C)** is incorrect because Gus and Hannah are in separate cars. **(D)** is incorrect because Gus and Juan are in separate cars, and **(E)** is incorrect because Hannah and Lisa cannot be in the same car.

4. (C) "If" / Must Be True

Recopy one of your options (or both) in accordance with the new information in the question stem. The New-"If" states that Faith travels with two other workers in Car 1 and is not the driver of the car. This only works in Option II. Recall that either Faith or Gus (or both) must drive in any sketch. So if Faith is not a driver, Gus and Kenneth must be the drivers in Option II. Gus must drive Lisa (Rule 3) and Hannah (Rule 1) in Car 2. Faith can't ride in Car 2 with Gus, Lisa, and Hannah because that violates the new condition that Faith rides with only two other workers. So in Car 1, Kenneth must drive Juan (Rule 2) and Faith.

The correct answer choice must be true in the new mini-sketch. Because all workers are assigned to a specific car, the four wrong answer choices will all be impossible in the new mini-sketch. **(C)** is correct because Juan is the other person in Faith's car besides the driver, Kenneth.

Gus is not in Faith's car, making **(A)** incorrect. Similarly, Hannah is in a different car than Faith; thus **(B)** is incorrect. Kenneth is the driver in the car with Faith, not the other passenger, so **(D)** is incorrect. Finally, **(E)** is incorrect because Lisa is not in Car 1 with Faith.

5. (D) Must Be False (CANNOT Be True)
When Limited Options are warranted in a game, use them to characterize the answer choices. The correct answer choice will be impossible in either option; the four wrong answer choices will be possible in either one or both options. Compare each answer choice to the options and eliminate any answer choices that could work in either option.

(D) doesn't work in either option and is correct. In Option I, Kenneth drives Gus, Lisa, and Juan; thus, he is not the only person other than the driver. In Option II, Kenneth would have to be driving Juan in one car, with Gus, Lisa, Faith, and Hannah in the other car. Thus, Kenneth cannot be the only person other than the driver in one of the cars.

All the other answer choices are possible in at least one option. **(A)** is possible in Option II if Gus and Lisa travel in one car and Faith drives Hannah, Juan, and Kenneth in the other car. **(B)** is possible in Option I. **(C)** could occur in Option II if either Faith or Kenneth drives Juan in one car and Gus drives everyone else in the other. **(E)** is possible in Option II if Gus drives Lisa in one car and either Faith or Kenneth drives everyone else in the other car.

Game 2: Ancient Artifacts

Step 1: Overview

Situation: An archaeologist dates artifacts

Entities: Six artifacts—F, H, J, N, P, T

Action: Loose Sequencing. Determine the order of the ages of the artifacts. A quick glance uncovers that all the rules place entities in relation to each other; there are no specified distance restrictions between entities, nor is any entity restricted to one or two dates.

Limitations: No two artifacts are the same age (no ties).

Step 2: Sketch

As with any Loose Sequencing game, build a tree of entities, placing each entity in relation to others as you move through the rules.

Note that first is the oldest and the sixth is the most recent. Label the top of the sketch as oldest and the bottom as most recent to avoid confusion.

Step 3: Rules

Rule 1 indicates that the figurine is older than both the jar and headdress.

Rule 2 dates the necklace and the jar sometime before the tureen.

Rule 3 gives two possibilities: either the headdress and necklace are both dated after (above) the plaque

or both the headdress and necklace are dated before (below) the plaque.

Step 4: Deductions

Once you've incorporated all your Blocks of Entities established by each rule into one sketch, any necessary deductions will appear.

The first two rules are easy to combine based on the Duplication of the jar.

The either/or language and subsequent options in Rule 3 create Limited Options. Draw two sketches based on the two possibilities for how the plaque is dated in relation to the headdress and the necklace.

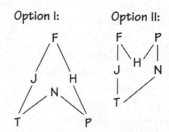

In this game, there are no Established Entities nor any significant Number restrictions to be aware of.

The finalized Master Sketch should look something like this.

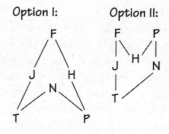

Quickly identify which entities can be ordered first and which can be ordered last in any Loose Sequencing game before moving on to the questions. In Option I, the figurine or the necklace could be first, and the tureen or the plaque could be last. In Option II, the figurine or the plaque could be first, and the tureen or the headdress could be last. There are no Floaters.

Step 5: Questions

6. (A) Acceptability

For Acceptability questions, eliminate any answer choices that violate one or more of the rules:

Rule 1 requires that the figurine appears before the jar and headdress in the list; this eliminates **(D)**.

Rule 2 requires the tureen come after the necklace and the jar, which eliminates **(B)** and **(E)**.

Rule 3 indicates that the plaque must be either before both the headdress and necklace or after both the headdress and necklace—it cannot be in the middle of the two. This eliminates **(C)**.

(A) is the only answer choice left and must be correct.

7. (C) How Many

Noting which artifacts could be the oldest in either option makes short work of this question. Because three artifacts—the figurine (Options I or II), the necklace (Option I), or the plaque (Option II)—could each be first, **(C)** is correct.

All the wrong answer choices either list too few [**(A)** and **(B)**] or too many [**(D)** and **(E)**] artifacts that could be first.

8. (A) Must Be False (CANNOT Be True)

When Limited Options are warranted in a game, use them to characterize the answer choices. The correct answer choice will be an artifact that cannot be fourth in either option; the four wrong answer choices will each list an artifact that could be fourth in at least one option. The figurine, **(A)**, cannot be fourth, because in either sketch there are at least three artifacts that must be discovered after the figurine (the jar, tureen, headdress, and plaque in Option I; the jar, tureen, and headdress in Option II). Thus, the latest the figurine can be placed is third.

All the wrong answer choices list artifacts that could be fourth in at least one option. The headdress, **(B)**, could be discovered fourth in Option II, sometime after the figurine and plaque. The jar, **(C)**, could be fourth in Option II if the necklace is fifth and the tureen is sixth. The necklace, **(D)**, could be fourth in Option I, with the tureen and plaque fifth and sixth. And the plaque, **(E)**, could be fourth in Option I if the jar is fifth and the tureen is sixth.

9. (C) "If" / Must Be True

Recopy one of your options (or both) in accordance with the new information in the question stem. Here, the figurine can only be third in Option II. For the figurine to be dated third, the plaque and necklace must be first and second, respectively. Thus the necklace, **(C)**, is the correct answer.

All the wrong answer choices need not be true (could be possible or are impossible) in the new mini-sketch for this question. The headdress, **(A)**, and the jar, **(B)**, come after the figurine, so they must be later than third and cannot be second. The plaque, **(D)**, must be first. And the tureen, **(E)**, can only be fifth or sixth.

10. (B) "If" / How Many

For this question, recopy one of your options (or both) in accordance with the new information in the question stem. This New-"If" question asks how many artifacts could be second if the plaque is first. The plaque can only be first in Option II, so start there.

If the plaque is first, then only two artifacts (the figurine or the necklace) could be second; each of the other artifacts must be after more than just the plaque. Thus, **(B)** is the correct answer.

All the wrong answer choices either list too few [**(A)**] or too many [**(C)**, **(D)**, and **(E)**] artifacts that could be first.

11. (D) Rule Substitution

The correct answer to this question is a piece of information that yields the same Final Sketch if substituted for Rule 2—that is, another rule that would result in the necklace and jar both being older than the tureen as shown below:

If you choose not to skip this question, the best strategy is trial and error through each answer choice until you uncover the statement that would yield the intended result.

(D) does this by stating that the tureen is more recent than everything but the headdress and plaque. If this is the case, the tureen is more recent than the figurine, the jar, and the necklace, and the sketch is re-created.

All the wrong answer choices lead to a different final setup than the existing rules allow. **(A)** incorrectly places the tureen as older than the headdress. **(B)** places the tureen below the figurine and necklace, but does not correctly place it below the jar. **(C)** states that the jar and necklace both go above the tureen or below the tureen, but they both must be above the tureen. Finally, **(E)** is incorrect because it indicates that the plaque goes either above or below both the necklace and the tureen, but the plaque's age is never determined based on Rule 2.

Game 3: Track Team

Step 1: Overview

Situation: A coach assigns runners in a track meet

Entities: Five runners—Q, R, S, T, U

Action: Selection/Sequencing Hybrid. Determine which four of the five runners will run in the meet, and then place these four runners in order.

Limitations: Exactly four of five runners will run in the track meet. Each runner chosen will run exactly one of the races in the track meet.

Step 2: Sketch

As with any Hybrid game, determine which action will anchor the sketch. Usually, any present Sequencing action is dominant. This game yields itself nicely to a Strict Sequencing setup—a row of numbered slots. In addition, add a slot to the side for the runner who is left out of the meet.

$$\begin{array}{cccc|c} Q & R & S & T & U & \quad out \\ \underline{} & \underline{} & \underline{} & \underline{} & \underline{} \\ 1 & 2 & 3 & 4 \end{array}$$

Step 3: Rules

Rule 1 uses Formal Logic: if Quinn runs in the meet, Terrell must be immediately after. Draw out the Formal Logic statement:

$$Q_{in} \rightarrow \boxed{QT}$$

Don't forget the contrapositive: if Terrell doesn't come right after Quinn, then Quinn must be out of the meet.

$$\sim\boxed{QT} \rightarrow Q_{out}$$

Rule 2 is not conditional—it always applies. This rule can be added to the sketch: indicate under positions 2 and 4 that Smith cannot run there.

$$\begin{array}{cccc|c} Q & R & S & T & U & \quad out \\ \underline{} & \underline{} & \underline{} & \underline{} & \underline{} \\ 1 & 2 & 3 & 4 \\ & \sim S & & \sim S \end{array}$$

Rule 3 is another Formal Logic rule. If Uzoma is out, Ramirez is second. And the contrapositive is that if Ramirez is not second, Uzoma is in the meet.

$$U_{out} \rightarrow R_2$$
$$\sim R_2 \rightarrow U_{in}$$

Rule 4 is similar. If Ramirez is second, then Uzoma is out, and if Uzoma is in, Ramirez is not second.

$$R_2 \rightarrow U_{out}$$
$$U_{in} \rightarrow \sim R_2$$

Step 4: Deductions

Usually, conditional rules don't yield many deductions that can be incorporated directly into the final sketch. However, Rule 1 is an exception. Quinn cannot run the fourth race, because this would violate Rule 1; add this to the sketch.

However, the big deduction in this game results from the duplication of the same entities in Rules 3 and 4. Rules 3 and 4 can be combined into a single rule: Uzoma is out if, and only if, Ramirez runs the second race. This means that either Uzoma is out of the meet and Ramirez runs the second race, or Uzoma is in the meet and Ramirez does not run the second race. Use this deduction to set up Limited Options. Draw Option I with Uzoma out of the meet and Ramirez running the second race:

Option I:

$$\begin{array}{cccc|c} & R & & & \quad out \\ & & & & \quad U \\ \underline{} & \underline{} & \underline{} & \underline{} & \underline{} \\ 1 & 2 & 3 & 4 \\ \sim Q & \sim S & & \sim S \\ & & & \sim Q \end{array}$$

Then, draw Option II with Uzoma selected as one of the four runners and Ramirez forbidden from running the second race:

Option II:

$$\begin{array}{cccc|c} & & & & \quad out \\ \underline{} & \underline{} & \underline{} & \underline{} & \underline{} \\ 1 & 2 & 3 & 4 & \quad \sim U \\ & \sim S & & \sim S \\ & \sim R & & \sim Q \end{array}$$

In Option I, because Uzoma is out, the remaining four runners must participate in the meet. Because Quinn must be running, the only races Quinn and Terrell can run are third and fourth, respectively, leaving Smith to run the first race. Notice that Smith can only run the first or third races if she runs in the meet.

Your finalized Master Sketch should look something like this.

Option I:

$$\underset{1}{S} \quad \underset{2}{R} \quad \underset{3}{Q} \quad \underset{4}{T} \quad \Big| \quad \overset{out}{U}$$

Option II:

$$\underset{1}{\underline{}} \quad \underset{\substack{2 \\ \sim S \\ \sim R}}{\underline{}} \quad \underset{3}{\underline{}} \quad \underset{\substack{4 \\ \sim S \\ \sim Q}}{\underline{}} \quad \Big| \quad \overset{out}{\sim U}$$

Step 5: Questions

12. (D) Acceptability

For Acceptability questions, eliminate any answer choices that violate one or more of the rules:

Rule 1 requires that Quinn's race is immediately followed by Terrell's race. **(C)** violates this rule.

Rule 2 prohibits Smith from running the second or the fourth races; this eliminates **(B)**.

Rule 3 requires that Ramirez run the second race of any meet that does *not* include Uzoma. **(E)** violates this rule.

Rule 4 forbids Ramirez from running the second race in any meet that includes Uzoma; **(A)** does this and is eliminated.

Thus, **(D)** is left as the correct answer.

13. (D) Must Be True

This question asks you for a runner who must always be selected to run in the meet. Recall that Q can never run in the meet without Terrell running the race immediately after. So, not selecting Terrell forbids Quinn from running in the meet also. That would leave only three runners to run in the meet, not the required four runners. Therefore, Terrell must always run in the race—whether or not Quinn runs in the meet. Thus, **(D)** is correct.

All the wrong answer choices are runners who could possibly not run in the meet. **(A)** is incorrect, because Quinn could be left out. Ramirez, **(B)**, can also be left out and the runners selected could be Quinn, Terrell, Smith, and Uzoma. **(C)** is incorrect because Smith could be left out and the runners selected could be Quinn, Terrell, Ramirez, and Uzoma. Finally, **(E)** is incorrect because Uzoma could be left out, as in Option I.

14. (B) Completely Determine

This question is a good one to save for the last in the set, because you'll have to go through each answer choice individually. It asks for a piece of information that determines exactly who runs in the meet (and the one runner who does not), as well as which races the four selected runners run. **(B)** is correct. If Ramirez runs the second race, Uzoma must be

out of the meet. Thus, Smith, Quinn, and Terrell must run second, third, and fourth respectively. This is also Option I.

$$\underset{1}{S} \quad \underset{2}{R} \quad \underset{3}{Q} \quad \underset{4}{T} \quad \Big| \quad U$$

All the wrong answer choices leave some information unknown (e.g., which runner is not selected for the meet or which race someone runs). **(A)**, **(C)**, and **(D)** are incorrect (and only possible in Option II) because all that must be true from each answer choice is that Uzoma and Terrell are selected to run in the meet. Nothing more is known about Smith or Quinn. **(E)** is incorrect because even if Ramirez is out (in Option II), thereby selecting Smith, Quinn, Terrell, and Uzuoma to run in the meet, it's still not known which race each runner *must* run; there are multiple race options for each runner.

15. (A) Must Be False (CANNOT Be True)

The correct answer will be false or impossible in both options; the four wrong answer choices will be possible in at least one option. **(A)** is correct. If Ramirez runs immediately before Smith, the only race Smith can run is the third, requiring that Ramirez run the second. If Ramirez runs the second, Uzoma is out—which is only possible in Option I. However, no room is left for Quinn and Terrell; Smith must run first in Option I.

$$\boxed{QT}$$
$$\underset{1}{\underline{}} \quad \underset{2}{R} \quad \underset{3}{S} \quad \underset{4}{\underline{}} \quad \Big| \quad U$$

All the four wrong answer choices are possible in both options. **(B)** is possible in Option II; the meet could be Smith, Quinn, Terrill, and Uzoma in that order, with Ramirez out. **(C)** is possible in Option II; the meet could be Smith, Terrell, Ramirez, and Uzoma in that order, with Quinn out. **(D)** is possible in Option II; the meet could run Uzoma, Quinn, Terrell, and Ramirez in that order, with Smith out. Finally, **(E)** is possible in Option II, with Uzoma, Terrell, Smith, and Ramirez running the meet in that order, and Quinn out.

16. (E) "If" / Must Be True

If Uzoma runs in the first race, Option II must be the relevant option. Also, if Uzoma runs in the first race, neither Ramirez (Rule 4's contrapositive) nor Smith (Rule 2) can run in the second race. This leaves only Terrell or Quinn to run in the second race. Sketch both possibilities. If Terrell runs in the second race, then Quinn must be out of the race entirely, and Smith must run the third race, and Ramirez must run the fourth race. If Quinn runs the second race, Terrell must run in the third race, leaving Smith out of the race entirely and leaving Ramirez to run the fourth race.

$$\frac{U}{1} \quad \frac{T}{2} \quad \frac{S}{3} \quad \frac{R}{4} \quad \Bigg| \quad \frac{Q}{}$$

$$\frac{U}{1} \quad \frac{Q}{2} \quad \frac{T}{3} \quad \frac{R}{4} \quad \Bigg| \quad \frac{S}{}$$

The correct answer choice must be true in either mini-sketch. Before tackling the answer choices, take a moment to notice the only thing both options have in common: Ramirez is running the fourth race. Thus, **(E)** is correct.

All the four wrong answer choices are either possible or impossible in at least one option. **(A)** and **(C)** are incorrect because both of these possibilities exist for Quinn. **(B)** is incorrect because Smith could also run in the third race. **(D)** is incorrect because there are multiple options for Terrell (she runs the second or third race and may, but need not, run in the second race).

17. (B) "If" / How Many

If both Quinn and Smith run in the race, remember that Quinn's race must be immediately followed by Terrell's race (Rule 1). So either Ramirez or Uzoma will be the runner left out of the race. Smith can run the first or third race (Rule 2). Draw out both options. If Smith runs the third race, then Quinn and Terrell must run the first and second races, respectively.

$$\frac{S}{1} \quad \frac{}{2} \quad \frac{}{3} \quad \frac{}{4} \quad \Bigg| \quad \underline{\quad}$$

$$\frac{Q}{1} \quad \frac{T}{2} \quad \frac{S}{3} \quad \frac{}{4} \quad \Bigg| \quad \underline{\quad}$$

The correct answer lists the number of runners who could run the first race in light of the new condition in the question stem. Thus, there are only two runners—Smith and Quinn—who can run the first race. **(B)** is correct; the four wrong answer choices give an inaccurate number of runners who could run the first race.

Game 4: Nurses' Information Sessions

Step 1: Overview

Situation: Nurses conducting information sessions at a community center

Entities: Seven nurses—F, G, H, J, K, L, M

Action: Strict Sequencing. Determine the order of the nurses' sessions.

Limitations: Each session is on a different day; each nurse conducts one session.

Step 2: Sketch

The sketch for this game is a standard Strict Sequencing framework of numbered dashes with the roster of entities nearby.

```
      F G H J K L M
      __ __ __ __ __ __ __
      1   2   3   4   5   6   7
```

Step 3: Rules

Rule 1 indicates that there are at least two sessions between Heany's session and Moreau's session. Be careful—this doesn't tell you whether Heany's or Moreau's session comes first. Indicate both possibilities:

```
      H__ __ ... M
           or
      M__ __ ... H
```

Rule 2 creates a Block of Entities: Griseldi and Khan. It should be indicated as

```
      GK
```

Rules 3 and 4 create two loose Blocks of Entities. Juarez conducts a session sometime after Moreau's session, and Lightfoot conducts a session sometime before Farnham's session, which is sometime before Khan's session.

```
      M . . . J
      L . . . F . . . K
```

Rule 5 is the most concrete; it states that Lightfoot cannot conduct a session on the second day. Some test takers prefer to always start with the most concrete rules—those restrictions that can be built directly into the Master Sketch. Whenever you tackled Rule 5, it can be indicated under position 2.

```
      F G H J K L M
      __ __ __ __ __ __ __
      1   2   3   4   5   6   7
         ~L
```

Step 4: Deductions

Combine the blocks created in Rules 2 and 4 because they both include Khan's session. This duplication yields a larger Loose Sequencing block:

```
      L . . . F . . . GK
```

Combine Rules 1 and 3, both of which contain Moreau's session:

```
      H__ __ . . . M . . . J   or

           J
      M:__ __ . . . H
```

Stop to think about where each entity can go. Farnham cannot conduct a session on the first, sixth, or seventh day. Griseldi cannot conduct a session on the first, second, or seventh day. Juarez cannot conduct a session on the first day. Khan cannot conduct a session on the first, second, or third day. Lightfoot cannot conduct a session on the second, fifth, sixth, or seventh day. Finally, Moreau cannot conduct a session on the seventh day. Turning negatives into positives, this means Heany, Lightfoot, or Moreau must conduct the session on the first day and Heany, Juarez, or Khan must conduct the session on the last day.

Your finalized Master Sketch should look something like this.

```
      F G H J K L M
```

H/L/M						H/J/K
1	2	3	4	5	6	7
~F	~L	~K		~L	~F	~F
~G	~G				~L	~G
~J	~K					~L
~K						~M

```
      L . . . F . . . GK

      H__ __ . . . M . . . J   or

           J
      M:__ __ . . . H
```

Step 5: Questions

18. (D) Acceptability

For Acceptability questions, eliminate any answer choices that violate one or more of the rules:

Rule 1 requires that Heany and Moreau's sessions be separated by at least two or more sessions; this eliminates **(E)**.

Rule 2 indicates Griseldi's session is immediately before Khan's session. All of the answer choices satisfy this rule.

Based on Rule 3, Juarez's session must be somewhere after Moreau's session, which eliminates **(C)**.

According to Rule 4, Lightfoot's session must come before Farnham's session, which must be before Khan's session; **(A)** breaks this rule.

Finally, Rule 5 eliminates **(B)** because it places Lightfoot's session on the second day.

Thus, **(D)** is left as the correct answer.

19. (C) Must Be False (CANNOT Be True)

The correct answer will be a day upon which Juarez's session cannot be scheduled; incorrect answer choices are possible days on which Juarez's session could be scheduled. During the setup, it was noted that Juarez cannot conduct the first session, but that is not an answer choice here. If the answer to a "Must Be" question is not clear from the Master Sketch, skip to other questions in the set. Then come back to this question if you have time and use previous work to eliminate incorrect answers.

(C) is correct. Placing Juarez's session on the fifth day would force Griseldi's session and Khan's session to be on the sixth and seventh days, respectively (Rule 2). Any other placement of the Griseldi-Khan block makes it impossible for there to be enough days to schedule Moreau's session before Juarez's session (Rule 3) *and* Lightfoot's and Farnham's sessions before the Griseldi-Khan block (Rule 4). However, now there is not enough room to separate Heany and Moreau's sessions as required (Rule 1). This arrangement puts Heany and Moreau's sessions on days 1 and 4, leaving only day 2 for Lightfoot's session to appear earlier than Farnham's session. That violates Rule 5.

H/M	L	F	M/H	J	G	K
1	2	3	4	5	6	7

~L

All the four wrong answer choices are possible placements for Juarez without violating any rules. **(A)** could work in this way:

M	J	L	H	F	G	K
1	2	3	4	5	6	7

(B) is possible as well.

L	M	J	F	G	K	H
1	2	3	4	5	6	7

Juarez's session could be scheduled for the sixth day. Thus, **(D)** is possible:

L	F	M	G	K	J	H
1	2	3	4	5	6	7

Finally, **(E)** is possible.

L	F	M	G	K	H	J
1	2	3	4	5	6	7

Note that this would be a great question to save until the end of the set. You could use your previous work to eliminate any answer choices that contain days on which Juarez could conduct his session and narrow down the answer choices.

20. (D) "If" / Could Be True

If Juarez's session is scheduled on day 3, then Moreau's session must be on day 1 or day 2 (Rule 3). If Moreau's session is on day 1, Lightfoot's session must go on day 4 (Rule 5), followed immediately by Farnham's session because they both must be scheduled prior to the Griseldi-Khan block (Rule 4). However, this arrangement forces Heany's session to be on day 2, violating Rule 1. Thus, Moreau's session must be on day 2, and Lightfoot's session must be on day 1. Only Farnham's session may be on day 4. Day 5 must be Griseldi's or Heany's sessions, day 6 could be Griseldi's or Khan's session (but not Heany's session, as that would separate the Griseldi-Khan block), and day 7 must be Khan's or Heany's session.

L	M	J	F	G/H	G/K	K/H
1	2	3	4	5	6	7

Thus, Griseldi's session could be on day 5, and **(D)** is correct.

(A) is impossible; day 1 must be Lightfoot's session. **(B)** is false; Khan's session cannot be on day 5. **(C)** is likewise impossible; only Griseldi or Khan could schedule a session on day 6. Finally, **(E)** is incorrect because Farnham must schedule a session on day 4, not day 2.

21. (B) "If" / Could Be True

If Khan's session is scheduled before Moreau's session, Rule 3 ties in with the block created by Rules 2 and 4.

L . . . F . . . $\boxed{GK}$ . . . M . . . J

Heany, the only entity not placed in this loose sequence, must schedule his session before Moreau's session. Otherwise, there's not enough room after Moreau for the proper spacing. In fact, Heany's session must be scheduled before Griseldi's session so that there are at least two sessions between Moreau's and Heany's sessions (Rule 1). Thus, Moreau must schedule a session right after Khan's session, and Juarez's session must be scheduled right after Moreau's session (Rule 3). Finally, Lightfoot cannot schedule a session on the second day, so he must be scheduled on the first day.

$$\frac{L}{1} \quad \frac{F/H}{2} \quad \frac{H/F}{3} \quad \frac{G}{4} \quad \frac{K}{5} \quad \frac{M}{6} \quad \frac{J}{7}$$

Heany's session could be scheduled on the third day; thus, **(B)** is correct.

All the four wrong answer choices list days on which certain nurses could not schedule their sessions. Griseldi cannot be scheduled on the third day, as she must be scheduled on the fourth day; thus, **(A)** is incorrect. Juarez must be scheduled for the last day; thus, **(C)** is impossible. Lightfoot is scheduled for the first day, so **(D)** is impossible, and Moreau's session is scheduled for the sixth day, eliminating **(E)**.

22. (B) "If" / Must Be True

If Griseldi's session is scheduled on the fifth day, Khan's session must be scheduled on the sixth day (Rule 2). Thus, Farnham's and Lightfoot's sessions must be scheduled sometime before Khan's session (Rule 4), with Farnham's session after Lightfoot's session, and Lightfoot's session scheduled either on the first or third day only (Rule 5). Finally, Heany's and Moreau's sessions must be separated by the required number of days (Rule 1), so one of them must have a session scheduled on day 7. This can only be Heany's session because Moreau's session must always be on an earlier day than Juarez's session (Rule 3). So Moreau and Juarez both must have sessions scheduled sometime between days 1 and 4.

```
              F
        ┌──────────┐
  L/M  ___  ___  ___   G    K    H
   1    2    3    4    5    6    7
        ~L        ~L
  └──────────────┘
        M . . . J
```

Looking at the new mini-sketch, the only *new* deduction (the Must be True answer to the call of the question) is that Heany's session is scheduled on the seventh day. Thus, **(B)** must be true.

All the four wrong answer choices are merely possible in light of the new mini-sketch. **(A)** is incorrect because Farnham's session could be scheduled on the second, third, or fourth days. **(C)** fails because Juarez could, but need not, schedule a session on the fourth day. **(D)** is similarly incorrect; Lightfoot's session could be scheduled on the first or third day. Finally, Moreau's session could be scheduled on the second day, but it doesn't have to be, making **(E)** incorrect.

23. (A) Could Be True

The correct answer is possible in your Master Sketch; the four incorrect answer choices Must Be False. From the Master Sketch, **(C)**, **(D)**, and **(E)** can all be eliminated because Lightfoot can never schedule a session later than day 4. So only **(A)** and **(B)** need to be tested.

Lightfoot's session could be on day 3, making **(A)** possible and thus correct. If you did all the other questions in the set before this one, the last question's sketch permits **(A)**:

$$\frac{M}{1} \quad \frac{J}{2} \quad \frac{L}{3} \quad \frac{F}{4} \quad \frac{G}{5} \quad \frac{K}{6} \quad \frac{H}{7}$$

All the four wrong answer choices are days on which Lightfoot could never schedule his session. Lightfoot cannot schedule a session on day 4 because then Farnham's, Griseldi's, and Khan's sessions would occupy days 5 through 7, leaving no room for Moreau's and Heany's sessions to be scheduled by the required number of days. Thus, **(B)** is incorrect. **(C)**, **(D)**, and **(E)** are all incorrect because if Lightfoot schedules a session later than day 4, there would not be enough room for the three additional nurses (Farnham, Griseldi, and Khan, respectively) to schedule their sessions after him.

Section IV: Logical Reasoning

Q#	Question Type	Correct	Difficulty
1	Principle (Identify/Inference)	E	★
2	Strengthen/Weaken (Evaluate the Argument)	B	★
3	Inference (EXCEPT)	A	★
4	Strengthen	D	★
5	Inference	C	★
6	Main Point	C	★
7	Inference	E	★
8	Weaken	E	★
9	Parallel Reasoning	D	★
10	Inference	A	★★
11	Flaw	A	★★
12	Paradox	C	★
13	Assumption (Sufficient)	A	★★
14	Paradox	A	★★
15	Flaw	B	★★
16	Main Point	C	★
17	Role of a Statement	D	★★
18	Point at Issue	A	★
19	Strengthen	E	★★★
20	Assumption (Necessary)	A	★★★
21	Weaken	C	★★
22	Role of a Statement	C	★★
23	Principle (Identify/Strengthen)	D	★★★
24	Flaw	E	★★★★
25	Assumption (Sufficient)	B	★★★★
26	Parallel Flaw	B	★★★

1. (E) Principle (Identify/Inference)

Step 1: Identify the Question Type

A *generalization* is merely a broad rule (i.e., a principle). The stimulus will contain a specific circumstance, and the correct answer will provide the same situation in broader terms.

Step 2: Untangle the Stimulus

The stimulus discusses a species of guppy. Some males of this species have large spots that help attract mates, while others have small spots and have less chance of mating. However, the tables are turned when predators are around, in which case the ones with large spots are more susceptible to detection and are thus less likely to survive.

Step 3: Make a Prediction

The correct answer will take the guppies' situation and broaden it to apply to other situations. So, in general, it appears that animals can have a characteristic that's helpful in one circumstance and problematic in another.

Step 4: Evaluate the Answer Choices

(E) matches exactly, because the male guppies have a trait (large spots) that helps with procreation yet hinders them in certain environments (locations with predators).

(A) starts off perfectly by discussing a trait that helps attract mates, but then it distorts the information by comparing the danger for one sex and the other when the stimulus only discusses the males.

(B) discusses a correlation between attraction and number of offspring, which is never mentioned in the stimulus.

(C), at worst, is contrary to the stimulus, because the organism that survives the longest (males with small spots) is *less* likely to procreate.

(D) makes the danger of the trait dependent on the sex of the species, but the stimulus only discusses the effect on males.

2. (B) Strengthen/Weaken (Evaluate the Argument)

Step 1: Identify the Question Type

If a question stem asks for the answer that would help evaluate an argument, it's essentially a Strengthen/Weaken question. The right answer will be an issue that, once clarified, will make the executive's argument stronger or weaker.

Step 2: Untangle the Stimulus

The programmer argues that the pay difference between programmers and technical writers is unfair and that programmers should receive a raise to correct this difference. The Mytheco executive explains the salary difference by pointing to seniority. He replies that many technical writers at the company have worked there longer than many of the programmers.

Step 3: Make a Prediction

But there's vagueness in the Mytheco executive's response surrounding the word "many." While there may be *many* technical writers who have greater seniority than *many* of the programmers, that doesn't say anything about the average writer or the average programmer. It's a representation issue, suggesting that the seniority of many writers represents the seniority of writers as a whole. However, if there are also many newly hired technical writers, those writers could balance out the long-term writers—possibly to the same average as the programmers. So it would be helpful to know how the average programmer compares to the average technical writer with respect to seniority.

Step 4: Evaluate the Answer Choices

(B) is the best match for this prediction.

(A) doesn't help evaluate the argument. Whether the technical writers have prior experience as programmers doesn't influence the validity of a pay structure based on seniority.

(C) brings up an inconsequential issue. The debate between the executive and the programmer centers on whether the difference in benefits and salary is justified, not whether benefits are linked to salary.

(D) doesn't affect the argument. Even if the executive had once worked as a technical writer, his argument justifying the technical writers' higher pay could still be valid.

(E) doesn't need to be clarified, because the executive's own salary isn't relevant to his assessment of the salary difference between programmers and technical writers.

3. (A) Inference (EXCEPT)

Step 1: Identify the Question Type

Because the statements in the stimulus will support the answer choices, the answers will be inferences—with one exception. That exception is what the question is asking for.

Step 2: Untangle the Stimulus

The stimulus provides a laundry list of advantages that cable stations have over broadcast networks: the ability to target specific audiences, lower ad rates due to subsidization from subscriber fees, and worldwide exposure. These advantages allow them to attract more advertisers.

Step 3: Make a Prediction

Four answers will follow the idea that cable stations have these advantages and advertisers are attracted to those advantages. The correct answer, the exception, will most likely present an advantage of broadcast networks or a reason why advertisers prefer broadcast networks.

Step 4: Evaluate the Answer Choices

(A) goes against the ideas presented in the stimulus because the stimulus expresses exposure to several countries as an advantage cable stations have over broadcast networks.

(B) is supported because the use of subscriber fees is an advantage ascribed to cable stations, not broadcast networks.

(C) is supported because low ad rates are described as an advantage that helps cable stations attract advertisers.

(D) is supported because a worldwide audience is described as an advantage that helps cable stations attract advertisers.

(E) is supported because the ability to target 24-hour news audiences is described as an advantage that helps cable stations attract advertisers.

4. (D) Strengthen

Step 1: Identify the Question Type

The stem asks for the answer that "most strengthens the reasoning." Find the choice that makes the conclusion more likely to follow from the evidence.

Step 2: Untangle the Stimulus

The last sentence of the argument is the conclusion: air pollution probably eliminated black spot and tar spot from plant populations. The evidence is that these diseases disappeared during the Industrial Revolution in English cities that became polluted by industrial activities.

Step 3: Make a Prediction

This argument is causal. A cause (air pollution) is held responsible for an effect (elimination of plant diseases). The correct Strengthener will reinforce this cause-effect relationship.

Step 4: Evaluate the Answer Choices

(D) reinforces the causal relationship. If the diseases returned once pollution subsided, then it's more likely that the pollution was actually responsible for the disappearance of the diseases.

(A) doesn't address whether or not the air pollution was responsible for getting rid of the plant diseases, so it doesn't help the argument.

(B) mentions the difficulty of eliminating infection, but even so, it doesn't help settle the issue of whether air pollution eliminated the infections that afflicted the plants.

(C) certainly doesn't support the idea that air pollution eliminated the plant diseases, because it suggests that the effects of air pollution aren't easily determinable.

(E) suggests that there's something special about black spot and tar spot, but that doesn't necessarily mean that these diseases were influenced at all by air pollution, so **(E)** doesn't affect the argument.

5. (C) Inference

Step 1: Identify the Question Type

Because the statements in the stimulus will support the correct answer, the correct answer will be an inference.

Step 2: Untangle the Stimulus

According to the author, there's a question about who created the abridgment of Shakespeare's *Hamlet*. Two pieces of evidence are presented to help answer that question. First, the person didn't have a personal copy of *Hamlet*. Second, only one character's speeches in the abridgment are truly accurate.

Step 3: Make a Prediction

With those two pieces of evidence, it appears that the author of the abridgment is somebody who didn't own the original play but was intimately familiar with one character's part. The correct answer will most likely identify the author as someone who fits that description.

Step 4: Evaluate the Answer Choices

(C) suggests someone who matches the description. An actor who performed in the play wouldn't have a personal copy (more likely would have been loaned one for the production) and would be really familiar with his character's lines (which he would have memorized).

(A) doesn't work because it seems unlikely that Shakespeare wouldn't possess a copy of his own work.

(B) is off because creating an easy production would seem harder with slipshod handling of certain parts.

(D) fits the first half of the description, because a spectator most likely wouldn't have a personal copy. However, there's no support for the idea that a spectator would have one character's lines down pat and a faulty memory of the others' lines.

(E) may be tempting because it discusses an actor. However, if the actor never performed in the play, there probably wouldn't be just one accurate set of speeches. Moreover, slipshod handling doesn't indicate someone trying to improve the play.

6. (C) Main Point

Step 1: Identify the Question Type

As straightforward as the LSAT gets, this question outright asks for the main point of the argument.

Step 2: Untangle the Stimulus

The musicologist starts by explaining a common complaint about Handel's arias: a poor balance of music and text. However, the word "Yet "indicates some dissent from the musicologist. Sure enough, the musicologist states that the criticism is refuted and provides a reason why the music is more prominent.

Step 3: Make a Prediction
When the author refutes a group of critics, that contention is typically the author's main point. That's certainly the case here, in which the musicologist's main point is that the critics' complaint is unwarranted. The information about the importance of the music is merely supporting evidence for why the critics are misguided.

Step 4: Evaluate the Answer Choices
(C) accurately expresses the main point, which is that the criticism about the lack of balance is undeserved.

(A) is an accurate fact, but it's the not the opinion the musicologist is trying to express.

(B) discusses the accessibility of the arias, which is never mentioned in the stimulus.

(D) goes contrary to the musicologist, who claims that the repetition is vital, not unnecessary.

(E) is Extreme because the musicologist refutes one criticism, not *most* criticisms.

7. (E) Inference
Step 1: Identify the Question Type
Because the statements in the stimulus will support the correct answer, the correct answer will be an inference.

Step 2: Untangle the Stimulus
The stimulus discusses a large design company, Baxe Interiors, which provides services to almost the entire corporate market. This is despite the fact that Baxe has won no awards for its works while other, smaller design companies have. However, corporate managers don't want to do business with companies that may go bankrupt, and they feel that only large companies are likely to avoid bankruptcy.

Step 3: Make a Prediction
It appears that, despite their award-winning work, smaller design companies still face a major obstacle—corporate managers see them as susceptible to bankruptcy. And because corporate managers don't want to do business with such companies, it seems that small companies will continue to lose business to larger companies—such as non-award-winning Baxe Interiors. The correct answer will likely express this unfortunate circumstance that small companies face.

Step 4: Evaluate the Answer Choices
(E) fits the scenario presented. Even though some smaller companies provide superior, award-winning work, corporate managers insist on choosing the large firm. That means the smaller companies' awards won't have an effect on Baxe's dominance.

(A) presents the possibility of other large design companies, but there's no evidence in the stimulus regarding the quality of other large companies' designs.

(B) brings up noncorporate designs, a concept that was never discussed and so is Out of Scope.

(C) is Extreme, because the statements only suggest that *several* design companies have provided award-winning designs. This is not enough to warrant that *most* designs from small companies are superior.

(D) is Out of Scope, because the managers' decisions are said to be based on a company's potential for bankruptcy, not the quality of its designs. The managers may be fully aware of the different levels of quality.

8. (E) Weaken
Step 1: Identify the Question Type
This stem is straightforward. It asks for the choice that most weakens the argument. So predict an answer that would undermine the relationship between the evidence and the conclusion.

Step 2: Untangle the Stimulus
The argument attempts to undo a causal relationship. It concludes that an asteroid strike in Mexico was not responsible for most of the dinosaur extinctions that happened around the same time. The evidence is that events such as the asteroid strike in question probably don't have any effects outside the region of the impact.

Step 3: Make a Prediction
But it hasn't been established that the dinosaur species that went extinct were spread out all over the world. The argument assumes that the dinosaurs weren't concentrated in the area of the impact. If they were, then the asteroid strike could be responsible for all the extinctions, and the author's argument would be severely weakened.

Step 4: Evaluate the Answer Choices
(E) provides that weakener and is therefore correct.

(A), if anything, strengthens the argument by suggesting that something other than the Chicxulub asteroid was responsible for the dinosaur extinctions.

(B) goes into the factors that determine the size of the asteroid crater, but that has nothing to do with whether or not the asteroid was responsible for mass dinosaur extinctions.

(C) doesn't weaken the argument because the author isn't arguing that the asteroid didn't kill *any* dinosaurs, just that it wasn't responsible for *most* of the dinosaur extinctions. So even if the asteroid was conclusively proven to have killed some dinosaurs, the argument is unaffected.

(D) Even if no other asteroid struck Earth at the same time as the one in question, the asteroid in question doesn't have to be responsible for the dinosaur extinctions, and the argument is therefore not weakened.

9. (D) Parallel Reasoning

Step 1: Identify the Question Type
Because the question is asking for an argument with similar reasoning to the argument in the stimulus, this is a Parallel Reasoning question.

Step 2: Untangle the Stimulus
The argument describes two even samples taken from two separate lots of peanuts. Fifty peanuts from the first sample had a particular infection, while 200 peanuts from the second sample had the same infection. The author then concludes, based on the sample batches, that the infection is more common in the entire second lot than in the entire first lot.

Step 3: Make a Prediction
The correct answer will follow the same, fairly straightforward construct: an equal-sized sample (1,000 peanuts) is taken from each of two groups (Lot A; Lot B). The sample from one group (Lot B) contains more instances of a particular trait (infection). The conclusion is that the trait is more prevalent in the entire group from which that sample was taken (Lot B).

Step 4: Evaluate the Answer Choices
(D) matches perfectly. An equal-sized sample (1,500 members) is taken from each of two groups (Liberals; Conservatives). One group's (Liberals) sample contains more instances of a particular trait (favoring Pollack). The conclusion is that the trait is more prevalent in the entire group from which that sample was taken (Liberals).

(A) does not have samples taken from two different groups. Its conclusion is a prediction rather than a comparison like that of the stimulus.

(B) also does not have samples taken from two different groups. Its conclusion is an if/then rather than a comparison. Also it has a lower level of certainty than the stimulus based on the word *likely*.

(C) theoretically does involve two groups (coffee plants pre-fungicide application and post-fungicide application). However, it's not a parallel situation because they are the exact same groups just at different time frames; they're not a sampling from two larger groups. Also, **(C)** has an assertion of a causal argument as its conclusion rather than a comparison, like the stimulus does.

(E) also can be eliminated based on its conclusion. It does not make a comparison based on samples taken from two different groups. Its conclusion is an assertion of fact.

10. (A) Inference

Step 1: Identify the Question Type
Because the economist's statements will support the correct answer, the correct answer will be an inference.

Step 2: Untangle the Stimulus
The economist starts out with a little Formal Logic: if there were widespread belief that losing one's job is a product of societal instead of personal issues, then society would demand government control of the economy. However, the economist claims at the end that government control of the economy could be disastrous.

Step 3: Make a Prediction
The author claims that job loss *is* in fact a condition of society, not personal shortcomings. However, the Formal Logic is about what would happen if that fact were widely believed. Combine the information provided: if the truth about job loss did become a widespread belief, the result would be greater demand for government control, which the economist says would be a disaster. The correct answer will stay consistent with that flow of logic.

Step 4: Evaluate the Answer Choices
(A) is consistent with the economist's claims. If people figured out the truth about what causes job loss, the results could be disastrous.

(B) distorts the information given. While job loss is described as a result of societal forces as opposed to personal shortcomings, there's no suggestion that confidence in one's abilities offers protection from society, let alone that belief in one's abilities is the *only* way to gain protection.

(C) also distorts the economist's statements. While the economist certainly sees government control of the economy as potentially dangerous, there's no warning against mere involvement of government in economic issues.

(D) restates what would happen *if* the belief about what causes job loss were to become widespread. However, even though the economist states that job loss *is* a result of social forces, there's no indication that this is a widespread belief yet.

(E) makes an unsupported comparison between people's responsibility for economic disasters and military invasions. While both situations are discussed, there is no indication of which one people should feel more responsible for.

11. (A) Flaw

Step 1: Identify the Question Type
The stem states that the reasoning in the argument is *flawed*, so identify the disconnect between evidence and conclusion.

Step 2: Untangle the Stimulus
The argument concludes that the Dalton airport probably won't be built. In the evidence, the author says that the airport will be built if a majority of Dalton residents favor it. But noise problems will probably prevent most Dalton residents from favoring the proposal to build the airport.

Step 3: Make a Prediction

If a majority of Dalton's residents favor the proposal to build the airport, then the airport will be built. In other words, the approval of those residents is sufficient to get the airport built. However, the author concludes that the airport won't be built simply because residents aren't likely to approve it. So the author takes a sufficient condition in the evidence and then makes it necessary in the conclusion. This is common LSAT flaw and quite common when "if-then" statements appear in the stimulus.

Step 4: Evaluate the Answer Choices

(A) is the only choice that accurately describes the flaw, and it is therefore correct.

(B) distorts the author's level of certainty. The argument's actual conclusion isn't that definite and isn't based on people believing in the truth of it.

(C) is wrong because the author actually concludes that the construction of the airport is unlikely. He doesn't use that unlikelihood to establish an even stronger conclusion.

(D) describes something that it would be *nice* for the author to consider, but it isn't something he would have to consider. He could make a perfectly sound argument for or against the possibility of the airport's construction without taking into account the opinions of the residents nearby.

(E) isn't a possibility that the author needs to consider. The airport may have plenty of potential benefits, but none of them needs to be considered in order for the author to predict whether or not it will be built. The problem here is that he takes something that would guarantee the airport's construction and then acts as though that thing is essential for it.

12. (C) Paradox

Step 1: Identify the Question Type

Asking for an explanation of something is a sure sign of a Paradox question. In this case, the stimulus will provide some discrepancy regarding travel times.

Step 2: Untangle the Stimulus

The author states that the speed limit on a particular road was reduced significantly. While one might expect that slower driving would result in longer car rides, the opposite effect occurred during rush hour; travel times dropped by 15 percent.

Step 3: Make a Prediction

While there's no need to predict exactly what caused this turn of events, it helps to know that the correct answer will explain how people spent less time driving when they were told to drive more slowly.

Step 4: Evaluate the Answer Choices

(C) provides a perfect explanation. Faster speeds led to more accidents, which caused lengthy delays. By slowing down, drivers had fewer accidents and thus caused fewer delays, resulting in overall shorter drives.

(A) mistakenly compares speeds during rush hour to speeds during other times of the day. However, it still offers no explanation as to why people spent less time driving during rush hour.

(B) discusses the lack of change during other times of the day, but it still offers no explanation why driving times went down during rush hour.

(D) only serves to make the mystery deeper. If the speed limits were as equally enforced at either 50 mph or 70 mph, then drivers would be driving more slowly. That should have resulted in longer drives, not shorter drives.

(E) brings up the number of drivers on the road. However, the number of drivers on the road doesn't impact the speed of the drivers. Even if it did, the number of drivers didn't change—which would further raise the question of why the drive times changed contrary to expectations.

13. (A) Assumption (Sufficient)

Step 1: Identify the Question Type

The question asks what, if assumed, would allow the conclusion to be properly drawn. That *if* makes this a Sufficient Assumption question.

Step 2: Untangle the Stimulus

The argument concludes that the artistic merit of a work of art can depend on its critics as well as its creator. The evidence is that a critic can affect, either through praise or ridicule, the amount of pleasure that one takes in the art.

Step 3: Make a Prediction

To predict an argument's central assumption, look for terms and ideas only mentioned in one part of the argument and connect them. The conclusion is the only place where artistic merit is mentioned, while the evidence discusses the amount of pleasure one takes in an artwork. So to make the argument cohesive, those two ideas should be linked—the amount of pleasure an artwork causes determines its merit. If that's true, then the conclusion follows.

Step 4: Evaluate the Answer Choices

(A) matches this prediction.

(B) could help establish the conclusion that critics can have an effect on the amount of enjoyment one gets from a work of art. However, that isn't the author's conclusion. **(B)** doesn't provide any link to the key concept of artistic merit.

(C) brings the artists themselves into the equation, but comparing their understanding of artistic merit to that of the critics doesn't help establish the conclusion either.

(D) would help establish a link between critical evaluation of an artwork and the viewer's experience of that artwork, but the link that properly connects the evidence to the conclusion has to bring artistic merit into the fold.

(E) also does not incorporate artistic merit and, like **(D)**, focuses instead on the connection between the critic's response and the viewer's response.

14. (A) Paradox

Step 1: Identify the Question Type
The question asks for something that will *explain* the given facts. That's a sign that the stimulus will contain a paradox to be resolved.

Step 2: Untangle the Stimulus
The author cites two facts from the past five years: automobile thefts have gone down, and people who steal cars are more likely to be convicted.

Step 3: Make a Prediction
Although not as mystifying as a typical Paradox question, the statements still need some explanation. While difficult to predict exactly, know that the correct answer will explain why thefts have decreased while convictions have increased.

Step 4: Evaluate the Answer Choices
(A) provides a good reason for both issues. Fewer car thieves would explain fewer thefts. And because thieves are less likely to abandon the cars by the time the owners notice, they're probably still driving the cars when the theft is reported—making them more likely to be caught.

(B) only half works. While the increase in car alarms could explain the decrease in thefts, the propensity for people to ignore those alarms would suggest that it's easier to get away with stealing the car.

(C) doesn't explain why automobile theft has gone down. And if the police are expending more energy on home burglaries, it doesn't explain why car thieves are getting convicted more often.

(D) adds mystery to the situation. If the market for car parts is lucrative, one would expect *more* thefts. And if stolen cars are quickly disassembled, there wouldn't seem to be enough time to catch as many thieves.

(E) doesn't help on either account. Just saying there are more thieves—regardless of age—makes it odder that the *number of* thefts has declined. And the leniency in punishing offenders does nothing to explain the number of convictions.

15. (B) Flaw

Step 1: Identify the Question Type
"[V]ulnerable to criticism" in the question stem is a sure sign of a Flaw question. So determine why the evidence doesn't necessarily establish the conclusion.

Step 2: Untangle the Stimulus
The legislator concludes that her constituents would support her bill to reduce the corporate income tax. Her evidence is that an overwhelming majority of her constituents who were surveyed said that they didn't favor high taxes.

Step 3: Make a Prediction
Many logical flaws occur when authors make unwarranted assumptions. In order for the survey results to justify the legislator's prediction, she has to assume that her constituents would recognize the corporate income tax as a high tax. But she provides no information on how high the tax currently is. If the constituents don't think of the corporate income tax as particularly high, then the survey results don't necessarily show that the bill will receive support.

Step 4: Evaluate the Answer Choices
(B) summarizes this overlooked possibility.

(A) isn't valid here because the legislator doesn't draw any conclusions about the opinions of the country's entire population. Therefore, the polled constituents don't have to represent anything.

(C) fails because the legislator doesn't base her conclusion on an absence of evidence that the constituents oppose the bill. The conclusion is based on the *presence* of evidence that the constituents oppose high taxes.

(D) describes circular reasoning, a flaw in which the evidence and conclusion of an argument are the same. But here the evidence and conclusion are quite different. The evidence is a poll. The conclusion is a prediction based on the poll.

(E) would be relevant if it were shown that the poll results are consistent with public support for the bill. But without knowing whether the corporate income tax is seen as high, **(E)** doesn't adequately describe what's wrong with the argument.

16. (C) Main Point

Step 1: Identify the Question Type
The question asks for the conclusion of the argument, so this is a Main Point question.

Step 2: Untangle the Stimulus
The author starts by recommending the ban on pets in nursing homes be lifted. The rest of the argument provides some benefits to pets in the nursing home: reduced stress and a more rewarding experience.

Step 3: Make a Prediction
When a recommendation is made, that is frequently the main point of an argument, with everything else serving as evidence to back up the recommendation. That is certainly the case here, with the main point being the author's recommendation to lift the ban on pets in nursing homes.

Step 4: Evaluate the Answer Choices

(C) accurately expresses the author's recommendation to allow pets in nursing homes.

(A) mentions the fact that a rewarding experience is important, but that's merely evidence to back up the author's recommendation to lift the ban.

(B) brings up the idea that nursing home residents should have the same rewards as everyone else, a sentiment never declared in the argument.

(D) mentions the fact that pets reduce stress, but that's merely evidence to back up the author's recommendation to lift the ban.

(E) is an idea that author would probably agree with, but it would still only serve as evidence to support the author's recommendation to lift the ban.

17. (D) Role of a Statement

Step 1: Identify the Question Type

The question mentions a claim from the stimulus and asks what role it plays in the argument. This is standard Role of a Statement wording.

Step 2: Untangle the Stimulus

According to the author, rainwater runoff results in more pollution in lakes and rivers than industrial discharge does, because the runoff gathers pollutants as it washes over buildings and pavements. This information is used to back up the peculiar conclusion that water itself is greatly responsible for water pollution.

Step 3: Make a Prediction

The claim in question is the first sentence of the argument, regarding the greater number of pollutants provided by rainwater runoff. That claim is merely evidence to support the conclusion in the last line: that water itself plays a big role in water pollution. The correct answer will identify the evidential nature of the opening claim.

Step 4: Evaluate the Answer Choices

(D) gets it right. It's merely evidence to support the conclusion in the last sentence.

(A) reverses the argument.

(B) is correct in that the claim is evidence, but the argument is not about which pollution is a more serious problem.

(C) distorts the information given. The opening sentence isn't a general rule based on the runoff information. Instead, it's more a statistic that is explained by the runoff information.

(E) is off because the author isn't concerned about other kinds of city pollution.

18. (A) Point at Issue

Step 1: Identify the Question Type

Because the question stem asks what Wong and Tate disagree over, this is a Point at Issue question. Either predict the Point at Issue or use the Decision Tree to evaluate the answer choices.

Step 2: Untangle the Stimulus

Wong argues that a transitional autocracy is sometimes needed to help a country become a democracy, which all countries would do well to become. Tate concedes that democracies provide valuable freedoms but argues that those freedoms are trumped by simpler material needs, which some countries can better serve as autocracies.

Step 3: Make a Prediction

Wong explicitly says that all countries are better off as democracies, while Tate says that some countries can better meet their citizens' needs with an autocratic form of government. Therefore, the two disagree on the question of whether a democratic government is always better for a country than an autocratic one.

Step 4: Evaluate the Answer Choices

(A) matches the prediction. However, even without predicting the answer, you can successfully apply the Decision Tree to **(A)**. Both Wong and Tate have opinions on **(A)**, and those opinions are in conflict. Therefore, this is the correct answer.

(B) isn't at issue between Wong and Tate because Wong never discusses the freedom and autonomy provided by a democracy.

(C) is Out of Scope for both speakers' arguments. Neither discusses conditions under which a country can or cannot become a democracy.

(D) is something Tate states directly, but it's impossible to say definitively what Wong's opinion is on this. As a matter of fact, Wong may agree, because he says all countries are better off as democracies.

(E) isn't discussed by Wong at all, and it distorts Tate's view that autocracies are sometimes comparatively better than democracies at meeting the material needs of people.

19. (E) Strengthen

Step 1: Identify the Question Type

Because the stem asks for the choice that *justifies* the application of the principle, this is a Strengthen question.

Step 2: Untangle the Stimulus

The principle says Arvue should hire the candidate who would be most productive in a new position in the event that no fully qualified candidate currently works for the company. The application of the principle says Arvue shouldn't hire Krall for a certain position because Delacruz is a fully qualified candidate.

Step 3: Make a Prediction

But in order to be sure that the application follows the principle, two issues need to be settled. First, ensure that none of the fully qualified candidates works for the company. Second, ensure that Delacruz would be the most productive in the new position (or at least more productive than Krall). Then Arvue would be justified in not hiring Krall.

Step 4: Evaluate the Answer Choices

(E) settles the aforementioned issues and is therefore correct.

(A) doesn't add any new information about Krall or Delacruz, so it doesn't justify passing over Krall in favor of Delacruz.

(B) establishes that Delacruz would be the most productive of the candidates who *don't* already work for the company, but if there are applicants for the position who *do* already work for the company, then Arvue wouldn't necessarily be justified in hiring Delacruz.

(C) Arvue should hire the most productive candidate if none of the fully qualified candidates already works for Arvue. But if Krall does work for Arvue, all bets are off and the Krall/Delacruz situation wouldn't necessarily be a valid application of the principle.

(D) again introduces candidates who already work for Arvue, making the principle impossible to apply in the given scenario.

20. (A) Assumption (Necessary)

Step 1: Identify the Question Type

The stem asks for an assumption required by the argument, so look for what must be true in order for the evidence to lead to the conclusion. Apply the Denial Test to the answer choices if necessary.

Step 2: Untangle the Stimulus

The argument concludes that development of important medicines can occur only if tropical rain forests are preserved. This is because the rain forests are the only place where several medicinally important plants can be found, and the forests still contain many species that haven't been studied but that would likely be medically important too.

Step 3: Make a Prediction

In order for preservation of the rain forests to be necessary for further development of important medicines, it would have to be true that the plants yet to be studied contain unique substance or ingredients—ingredients not available from the already studied plants. Otherwise, scientists would have gotten all the substances that the rain forests had to offer.

Step 4: Evaluate the Answer Choices

(A) matches this prediction and is therefore correct. **(A)** also withstands the Denial Test. If none of the yet-to-be-studied plants contains any yet-to-be-discovered substances, then rain forest preservation may not be necessary.

(B) actually undermines the argument by suggesting that scientists can develop important medicines even if the rain forests aren't preserved.

(C) doesn't have to be true because the argument doesn't depend on a certain proportion of tropical rain forest plants containing medicinally valuable substances. Even if only a small fraction of those plants contain such substances, the argument can still stand.

(D) doesn't have to be true. Even if scientists don't discover every single medicinally valuable substance in the rain forest plants, the argument can still be made that without preserving the rain forests, important medicines won't be developed.

(E) distorts the argument. The author isn't making recommendations when it comes to preserving the rain forest. The author's simply making a prediction that if the rain forests aren't preserved, important medicines won't be developed. Whether or not the forests *should* be preserved isn't a part of that argument.

21. (C) Weaken

Step 1: Identify the Question Type

The stem asks for the answer choice that most weakens the argument. So find the choice that threatens the link between evidence and conclusion.

Step 2: Untangle the Stimulus

The argument concludes that prehistoric ichthyosaurs were deep divers. The evidence is the porosity of the outer shell of ichthyosaurs' bones. This feature is shared by modern deep-diving marine mammals such as whales. In those modern mammals, having bones with porous outer shells aids in deep diving.

Step 3: Make a Prediction

To make this argument work, the author assumes that having bones with a porous outer shell guarantees that an animal was a deep diver. In other words, the author assumes that there would be no reason other than deep diving for a marine animal to have bones with porous outer shells.

Step 4: Evaluate the Answer Choices

(C) challenges the idea that animals with porous outer shells in their bones were automatically deep divers. If **(C)** is true, then the ichthyosaurs may not have been deep divers just because they had porous bones.

(A) suggests that porous bones aren't necessary for a marine mammal to surface after deep dives, but that isn't the issue in the argument. The real issue in the argument is whether porous bones are enough to establish that a marine mammal is a deep diver in the first place.

(B) broadens to marine mammal species in general. As long as there is a connection between porous bones and deep diving, the argument remains intact.

(D) doesn't hurt the argument because whales and ichthyosaurs don't have to have shared *all* the characteristics of deep divers in order for ichthyosaurs to have been deep divers.

(E) fails because the question isn't whether ichthyosaurs required porous bones to surface from deep dives. The argument concerns the question of whether ichthyosaurs' porous bones are enough to establish that they were deep divers.

22. (C) Role of a Statement

Step 1: Identify the Question Type
The question mentions a claim from the stimulus and asks what role it plays in the argument. This is standard Role of a Statement wording.

Step 2: Untangle the Stimulus
The librarian presents an opinion held by *some* people: that a grant should be used to restore the original town charter. Their stance is based on the imminent deterioration of the charter. However, the librarian refutes their argument, claiming that the charter has no scholarly value. As such, the librarian instead recommends using the grant to preserve documents with more significant scholarly value.

Step 3: Make a Prediction
The claim in question is about the looming deterioration of the town charter. This is presented as evidence for why some people feel the charter should be restored—an opinion refuted by the librarian.

Step 4: Evaluate the Answer Choices
(C) correctly recognizes the claim as evidence for the point refuted by the librarian.

(A) suggests that the librarian argues the charter *won't* deteriorate beyond repair. That's not the case. It will, but the librarian claims it doesn't matter because the charter has no scholarly value.

(B) mistakes evidence for conclusion. The conclusion the librarian rejects is about using the grant money to restore the document. The librarian doesn't reject the fact that the document will deteriorate.

(D) assigns the evidence to the wrong argument. The claim supports what *some* people argue, which is actually contrary to the librarian's argument.

(E) is off because the deterioration is actually irrelevant to the librarian. All that matters is its lack of scholarly value.

23. (D) Principle (Identify/Strengthen)

Step 1: Identify the Question Type
This Principle question asks for a broad rule that helps *justify* the columnist's argument. That makes this similar to a Strengthen question, which means using argument-based skills to untangle the stimulus.

Step 2: Untangle the Stimulus
The columnist starts by observing our continued ignorance about the relationships among various animal species. This leads to the recommendation that, if we want to protect any species, we should try to protect as many as possible. The reason for this is that allowing one species to die off could affect the lives of other species.

Step 3: Make a Prediction
The prospect of saving as many species as possible, even ones we're not really interested in, is recommended because any species's extinction could affect the species we *are* interested in preserving. The columnist assumes that if there's anything that could affect the species we do care about, we should do as much as possible to make sure that doesn't happen. The correct answer should be a broader presentation of that idea.

Step 4: Evaluate the Answer Choices
(D) presents the principle perfectly, albeit with some convoluted wording. In essence, this answer claims that if a change may jeopardize something important to us, we shouldn't let that change happen.

(A) isn't strong enough because only preserving "certain" species doesn't encapsulate the columnist's recommendation of preserving as many species as possible.

(B) suggests that we may be able to stop taking action once we learn everything about animals, a sentiment not implied by the columnist.

(C) is Out of Scope. The flourishing of human populations is a concept irrelevant to this argument.

(E) brings up actions that have the best consequences in the immediate future. However, the author doesn't differentiate between immediate and long-term goals.

24. (E) Flaw

Step 1: Identify the Question Type
The stem uses straightforward language (*flawed*), so this is definitely a Flaw question. Determine why the evidence doesn't necessarily establish the conclusion.

Step 2: Untangle the Stimulus
The argument concludes that long-term friends are probably the same age. There are two pieces of evidence for this: most long-term friendships start because someone felt comfortable approaching a stranger, and people are likely to feel

comfortable approaching strangers if those strangers are of their own age.

Step 3: Make a Prediction

Those pieces of evidence, though, don't establish that long-term friends are the same age. The author doesn't say that one feels comfortable approaching a stranger *only if* the stranger is one's own age. For all we know, many more things may also cause people to become comfortable approaching strangers. So in order for the author's conclusion to be established, the argument would need to show not only that people are comfortable approaching strangers their own age, but also that they're *not* comfortable approaching strangers that *aren't* of their own age.

Step 4: Evaluate the Answer Choices

(E) describes this same deficiency in the argument and is therefore correct.

(A) distorts the argument. The author doesn't assume that one will feel uncomfortable approaching a *person* only if that person is a *stranger*. The author assumes that one will feel uncomfortable approaching a *stranger* if that stranger isn't one's own age.

(B) isn't true because the argument doesn't say that long-term friends are the same approximate age because people in relationships similar to long-term friendships are also the same age.

(C), like **(A)**, makes a distinction between people who are strangers and those who aren't. That distinction is Out of Scope, though, because the argument only concerns one's comfort level when one is approaching strangers.

(D) accuses the author of assuming that people only approach strangers when they feel comfortable doing so. Not only is this something the author doesn't assume, but it doesn't touch on the age issue at all, and that's where the argument's problem lies.

25. (B) Assumption (Sufficient)

Step 1: Identify the Question Type

Because the question asks for the answer choice that, if assumed, makes the conclusion follow logically, this is a Sufficient Assumption question. Predict what will close the gap between evidence and conclusion.

Step 2: Untangle the Stimulus

The conclusion is the very first statement, which is that there can be no individual freedom without the rule of law. There are two pieces of evidence: individual freedom can't be attained without social integrity, and the pursuit of the good life is impossible without social integrity.

Step 3: Make a Prediction

The conclusion says, there can't be individual freedom without the rule of law. So, the rule of law is necessary for individual freedom. Translate this to

| If | individual freedom | → | rule of law |

The evidence says that social integrity is necessary for both individual freedom and the pursuit of the good life. Translate these as well.

| If | individual freedom | → | social integrity |

| If | pursuing good life | → | social integrity |

Start with the first piece of evidence, because it already has one term in common with the conclusion ("individual freedom") and will therefore be easier to connect. Focus on the terms that these statements don't have in common—"social integrity" in the evidence and "rule of law" in the conclusion. These are the terms that need to be connected by the assumption, which can be thought of as another "if-then" statement:

| If | social integrity | → | rule of law |

That will make the conclusion follow.

Step 4: Evaluate the Answer Choices

(B) says that social integrity depends on the rule of law. This is a great match for your prediction. **(B)** is therefore correct.

(A) names one more thing (the rule of law) that depends on social integrity, but combined with the evidence, it won't establish the conclusion that individual freedom depends on the rule of law.

(C), if combined with the evidence, would establish that pursuit of the good life depends on two things: social integrity and the rule of law. However, it still doesn't allow a connection between *individual freedom* and the rule of law.

(D) reverses the sufficient and necessary terms of the first piece of evidence, but without involving rule of law, **(D)** doesn't allow the conclusion to be inferred.

(E) merely reverses the sufficient and necessary terms of the conclusion, but that does nothing to link it to the evidence.

26. (B) Parallel Flaw

Step 1: Identify the Question Type

Because the question is asking for "flawed reasoning ... similar to" the economist's argument, this is a Parallel Flaw question.

Step 2: Untangle the Stimulus

The economist describes a characteristic of two different types of countries. Those with uneducated populations are economically and politically weak. Those with educated populations have a serious commitment to education. The economist then concludes that a nation with a strong commitment to education will not be economically or politically weak.

Step 3: Make a Prediction

The problem here is a confusion of necessity and sufficiency. While nations with uneducated populations are described as economically and politically weak, that's no indication that they're the *only* nations with that condition. Similarly, nations with educated populations having a commitment to education don't exclude other nations from having that commitment. So, when the author makes a conclusion about nations with a commitment to education, it doesn't have to refer to just those with educated populations. And even if it did, there's no guarantee those nations are economically and politically strong. The correct answer will make the same mistake, using the same structure: one group (uneducated nations) has a trait (weakness), while another group (educated nations) has a second trait (commitment); the author faultily concludes that *any* group with the second trait lacks the first trait.

Step 4: Evaluate the Answer Choices

(B) lines up on all accounts. One group (no empathy) has a trait (bad candidate), while another group (empathy) has a second trait (manipulation); the author faultily concludes that *anyone* with the second trait lacks the first trait. While empathetic people can manipulate others, they may not be the *only* people who can do that. Even if they were, there's no guarantee that they'd make good candidates.

(A) presents two groups with two different traits. However, there is no flawed conclusion drawn about animals that possess one of those traits.

(C) is certainly flawed. However, the flaw is that it presents one group that lacks a particular trait and concludes that a contrasting group must have that trait. It's not the same flaw, because it doesn't make a conclusion about people in general who have that trait.

(D) is a little more logical. The first claim is that high-quality poets have studied poetry. The next claim is that those who haven't studied poetry are more likely to be shocking, which makes them lower in quality. Without the stark flaw of the original, this answer doesn't work.

(E) fails to discuss two groups of people with two different traits. Therefore, it doesn't follow the same structure as the original argument.

Glossary

Logical Reasoning

Logical Reasoning Question Types

Argument-Based Questions

Main Point Question

A question that asks for an argument's conclusion or an author's main point. Typical question stems:

> Which one the following most accurately expresses the conclusion of the argument as a whole?

> Which one of the following sentences best expresses the main point of the scientist's argument?

Role of a Statement Question

A question that asks how a specific sentence, statement, or idea functions within an argument. Typical question stems:

> Which one of the following most accurately describes the role played in the argument by the statement that automation within the steel industry allowed steel mills to produce more steel with fewer workers?

> The claim that governmental transparency is a nation's primary defense against public-sector corruption figures in the argument in which one of the following ways?

Point at Issue Question

A question that asks you to identify the specific claim, statement, or recommendation about which two speakers/authors disagree (or, rarely, about which they agree). Typical question stems:

> A point at issue between Tom and Jerry is

> The dialogue most strongly supports the claim that Marilyn and Billy disagree with each other about which one of the following?

Method of Argument Question

A question that asks you to describe an author's argumentative strategy. In other words, the correct answer describes *how* the author argues (not necessarily what the author says). Typical question stems:

> Which one of the following most accurately describes the technique of reasoning employed by the argument?

> Julian's argument proceeds by

> In the dialogue, Alexander responds to Abigail in which one of the following ways?

Parallel Reasoning Question

A question that asks you to identify the answer choice containing an argument that has the same logical structure and reaches the same type of conclusion as the argument in the stimulus does. Typical question stems:

> The pattern of reasoning in which one of the following arguments is most parallel to that in the argument above?

> The pattern of reasoning in which one of the following arguments is most similar to the pattern of reasoning in the argument above?

Assumption-Family Questions

Assumption Question

A question that asks you to identify one of the unstated premises in an author's argument. Assumption questions come in two varieties.

Necessary Assumption questions ask you to identify an unstated premise required for an argument's conclusion to follow logically from its evidence. Typical question stems:

> Which one of the following is an assumption on which the argument depends?

> Which one of the following is an assumption that the argument requires in order for its conclusion to be properly drawn?

Sufficient Assumption questions ask you to identify an unstated premise sufficient to establish the argument's conclusion on the basis of its evidence. Typical question stems:

> The conclusion follows logically if which one of the following is assumed?

> Which one of the following, if assumed, enables the conclusion above to be properly inferred?

Strengthen/Weaken Question

A question that asks you to identify a fact that, if true, would make the argument's conclusion more likely (Strengthen) or less likely (Weaken) to follow from its evidence. Typical question stems:

Strengthen

> Which one of the following, if true, most strengthens the argument above?

> Which one the following, if true, most strongly supports the claim above?

Weaken

Which one of the following, if true, would most weaken the argument above?

Which one of the following, if true, most calls into question the claim above?

Flaw Question

A question that asks you to describe the reasoning error that the author has made in an argument. Typical question stems:

The argument's reasoning is most vulnerable to criticism on the grounds that the argument

Which of the following identifies a reasoning error in the argument?

The reasoning in the correspondent's argument is questionable because the argument

Parallel Flaw Question

A question that asks you to identify the argument that contains the same error(s) in reasoning that the argument in the stimulus contains. Typical question stems:

The pattern of flawed reasoning exhibited by the argument above is most similar to that exhibited in which one of the following?

Which one of the following most closely parallels the questionable reasoning cited above?

Evaluate the Argument Question

A question that asks you to identify an issue or consideration relevant to the validity of an argument. Think of Evaluate questions as "Strengthen or Weaken" questions. The correct answer, if true, will strengthen the argument, and if false, will weaken the argument, or vice versa. Evaluate questions are very rare. Typical question stems:

Which one of the following would be most useful to know in order to evaluate the legitimacy of the professor's argument?

It would be most important to determine which one of the following in evaluating the argument?

Non-Argument Questions

Inference Question

A question that asks you to identify a statement that follows from the statements in the stimulus. It is very important to note the characteristics of the one correct and the four incorrect answers before evaluating the choices in Inference questions. Depending on the wording of the question stem,

the correct answer to an Inference question may be the one that

- *must be true* if the statements in the stimulus are true

- is *most strongly supported* by the statements in the stimulus

- *must be false* if the statements in the stimulus are true

Typical question stems:

If all of the statements above are true, then which one of the following must also be true?

Which one of the following can be properly inferred from the information above?

If the statements above are true, then each of the following could be true EXCEPT:

Which one of the following is most strongly supported by the information above?

The statements above, if true, most support which one of the following?

The facts described above provide the strongest evidence against which one of the following?

Paradox Question

A question that asks you to identify a fact that, if true, most helps to explain, resolve, or reconcile an apparent contradiction. Typical question stems:

Which one of the following, if true, most helps to explain how both studies' findings could be accurate?

Which one the following, if true, most helps to resolve the apparent conflict in the spokesperson's statements?

Each one of the following, if true, would contribute to an explanation of the apparent discrepancy in the information above EXCEPT:

Principle Questions

Principle Question

A question that asks you to identify corresponding cases and principles. Some Principle questions provide a principle in the stimulus and call for the answer choice describing a case that corresponds to the principle. Others provide a specific case in the stimulus and call for the answer containing a principle to which that case corresponds.

On the LSAT, Principle questions almost always mirror the skills rewarded by other Logical Reasoning question types. After each of the following Principle question stems, we note the question type it resembles. Typical question stems:

Which one of the following principles, if valid, most helps to justify the reasoning above? (**Strengthen**)

Which one of the following most accurately expresses the principle underlying the reasoning above? (**Assumption**)

The situation described above most closely conforms to which of the following generalizations? (**Inference**)

Which one of the following situations conforms most closely to the principle described above? (**Inference**)

Which one of the following principles, if valid, most helps to reconcile the apparent conflict among the prosecutor's claims? (**Paradox**)

Parallel Principle Question

A question that asks you to identify a specific case that illustrates the same principle that is illustrated by the case described in the stimulus. Typical question stem:

Of the following, which one illustrates a principle that is most similar to the principle illustrated by the passage?

Untangling the Stimulus

Conclusion Types

The conclusions in arguments found in the Logical Reasoning section of the LSAT tend to fall into one of six categories:

1) Value Judgment (an evaluative statement; e.g., Action X is unethical, or Y's recital was poorly sung)

2) "If"/Then (a conditional prediction, recommendation, or assertion; e.g., If X is true, then so is Y, or If you an M, then you should do N)

3) Prediction (X *will* or *will not* happen in the future)

4) Comparison (X is taller/shorter/more common/less common, etc. than Y)

5) Assertion of Fact (X is true or X is false)

6) Recommendation (we *should* or *should not* do X)

One-Sentence Test

A tactic used to identify the author's conclusion in an argument. Consider which sentence in the argument is the one the author would keep if asked to get rid of everything except her main point.

Subsidiary Conclusion

A conclusion following from one piece of evidence and then used by the author to support his overall conclusion or main point. Consider the following argument:

The pharmaceutical company's new experimental treatment did not succeed in clinical trials. As a result, the new treatment will not reach the market this year. Thus, the company will fall short of its revenue forecasts for the year.

Here, the sentence "As a result, the new treatment will not reach the market this year" is a subsidiary conclusion. It follows from the evidence that the new treatment failed in clinical trials, and it provides evidence for the overall conclusion that the company will not meet its revenue projections.

Keyword(s) in Logical Reasoning

A word or phrase that helps you untangle a question's stimulus by indicating the logical structure of the argument or the author's point. Here are three categories of Keywords to which LSAT experts pay special attention in Logical Reasoning:

Conclusion words; e.g., *therefore, thus, so, as a result, it follows that, consequently,* [evidence] *is evidence that* [conclusion]

Evidence word; e.g, *because, since, after all, for,* [evidence] *is evidence that* [conclusion]

Contrast words; e.g., *but, however, while, despite, in spite of, on the other hand* (These are especially useful in Paradox and Inference questions.)

Experts use Keywords even more extensively in Reading Comprehension. Learn the Keywords associated with the Reading Comprehension section, and apply them to Logical Reasoning when they are helpful.

Mismatched Concepts

One of two patterns to which authors' assumptions conform in LSAT arguments. Mismatched Concepts describes the assumption in arguments in which terms or concepts in the conclusion are different *in kind* from those in the evidence. The author assumes that there is a logical relationship between the different terms. For example:

Bobby is a **championship swimmer**. Therefore, he **trains every day**.

Here, the words "trains every day" appear only in the conclusion, and the words "championship swimmer" appear only in the evidence. For the author to reach this conclusion from this evidence, he assumes that championship swimmers train every day.

Another example:

Susan does **not eat her vegetables**. Thus, she will **not grow big and strong**.

In this argument, not growing big and strong is found only in the conclusion while not eating vegetables is found only in the evidence. For the author to reach this conclusion from this evidence, she must assume that eating one's vegetables is necessary for one to grow big and strong.

See also Overlooked Possibilities.

Overlooked Possibilities

One of two patterns to which authors' assumptions conform in LSAT arguments. Overlooked Possibilities describes the assumption in arguments in which terms or concepts in the conclusion are different *in degree, scale, or level of certainty* from those in the evidence. The author assumes that there is no factor or explanation for the conclusion other than the one(s) offered in the evidence. For example:

> Samson does not have a ticket stub for this movie showing. Thus, Samson must have sneaked into the movie without paying.

The author assumes that there is no other explanation for Samson's lack of a ticket stub. The author overlooks several possibilities: e.g., Samson had a special pass for this showing of the movie; Samson dropped his ticket stub by accident or threw it away after entering the theater; someone else in Samson's party has all of the party members' ticket stubs in her pocket or handbag.

Another example:

> Jonah's marketing plan will save the company money. Therefore, the company should adopt Jonah's plan.

Here, the author makes a recommendation based on one advantage. The author assumes that the advantage is the company's only concern or that there are no disadvantages that could outweigh it, e.g., Jonah's plan might save money on marketing but not generate any new leads or customers; Jonah's plan might damage the company's image or reputation; Jonah's plan might include illegal false advertising. Whenever the author of an LSAT argument concludes with a recommendation or a prediction based on just a single fact in the evidence, that author is always overlooking many other possibilities.

See also Mismatched Concepts.

Causal Argument

An argument in which the author concludes or assumes that one thing causes another. The most common pattern on the LSAT is for the author to conclude that A causes B from evidence that A and B are correlated. For example:

> I notice that whenever the store has a poor sales month, employee tardiness is also higher that month. Therefore, it must be that employee tardiness causes the store to lose sales.

The author assumes that the correlation in the evidence indicates a causal relationship. These arguments are vulnerable to three types of overlooked possibilities:

1) There could be **another causal factor**. In the previous example, maybe the months in question are those in which the manager takes vacation, causing the store to lose sales and permitting employees to arrive late without fear of the boss's reprimands.

2) Causation could be **reversed**. Maybe in months when sales are down, employee morale suffers and tardiness increases as a result.

3) The correlation could be **coincidental**. Maybe the correlation between tardiness and the dip in sales is pure coincidence.

See also Flaw Types: Correlation versus Causation.

Another pattern in causal arguments (less frequent on the LSAT) involves the assumption that a particular causal mechanism is or is not involved in a causal relationship. For example:

> The airport has rerouted takeoffs and landings so that they will not create noise over the Sunnyside neighborhood. Thus, the recent drop in Sunnyside's property values cannot be explained by the neighborhood's proximity to the airport.

Here, the author assumes that the only way that the airport could be the cause of dropping property values is through noise pollution. The author overlooks any other possible mechanism (e.g., frequent traffic jams and congestion) through which proximity to the airport could be cause of Sunnyside's woes.

Principle

A broad, law-like rule, definition, or generalization that covers a variety of specific cases with defined attributes. To see how principles are treated on the LSAT, consider the following principle:

> It is immoral for a person for his own gain to mislead another person.

That principle would cover a specific case, such as a seller who lies about the quality of construction to get a higher price for his house. It would also correspond to the case of a teenager who, wishing to spend a night out on the town, tells his mom "I'm going over to Randy's house." He knows that his mom believes that he will be staying at Randy's house, when in fact, he and Randy will go out together.

That principle does not, however, cover cases in which someone lies solely for the purpose of making the other person feel better or in which one person inadvertently misleads the other through a mistake of fact.

Be careful not to apply your personal ethics or morals when analyzing the principles articulated on the test.

Flaw Types

Necessary versus Sufficient

This flaw occurs when a speaker or author concludes that one event is necessary for a second event from evidence that the first event is sufficient to bring about the second event, or vice versa. Example:

> If more than 25,000 users attempt to access the new app at the same time, the server will crash. Last night, at 11:15 PM, the server crashed, so it must be case that more than 25,000 users were attempting to use the new app at that time.

In making this argument, the author assumes that the only thing that will cause the server to crash is the usage level (i.e., high usage is *necessary* for the server to crash). The evidence, however, says that high usage is one thing that will cause the server to crash (i.e., that high usage is *sufficient* to crash the server).

Correlation versus Causation

This flaw occurs when a speaker or author draws a conclusion that one thing causes another from evidence that the two things are correlated. Example:

> Over the past half century, global sugar consumption has tripled. That same time period has seen a surge in the rate of technological advancement worldwide. It follows that the increase in sugar consumption has caused the acceleration in technological advancement.

In any argument with this structure, the author is making three unwarranted assumptions. First, he assumes that there is no alternate cause, i.e., there is nothing else that has contributed to rapid technological advancement. Second, he assumes that the causation is not reversed, i.e., technological advancement has not contributed to the increase in sugar consumption, perhaps by making it easier to grow, refine, or transport sugar. And, third, he assumes that the two phenomena are not merely coincidental, i.e., that it is not just happenstance that global sugar consumption is up at the same time that the pace of technological advancement has accelerated.

Unrepresentative Sample

This flaw occurs when a speaker or author draws a conclusion about a group from evidence in which the sample cannot represent that group because the sample is too small or too selective, or is biased in some way. Example:

> Moviegoers in our town prefer action films and romantic comedies over other film genres. Last Friday, we sent reporters to survey moviegoers at several theaters in town, and nearly 90 percent of those surveyed were going to watch either an action film or a romantic comedy.

The author assumes that the survey was representative of the town's moviegoers, but there are several reasons to question that assumption. First, we don't know how many people were actually surveyed. Even if the number of people surveyed was adequate, we don't know how many other types of movies were playing. Finally, the author doesn't limit her conclusion to moviegoers on Friday nights. If the survey had been conducted at Sunday matinees, maybe most moviegoers would have been heading out to see an animated family film or a historical drama. Who knows?

Scope Shift/Unwarranted Assumption

This flaw occurs when a speaker's or author's evidence has a scope or has terms different enough from the scope or terms in his conclusion that it is doubtful that the evidence can support the conclusion. Example:

> A very small percentage of working adults in this country can correctly define collateralized debt obligation securities. Thus, sad to say, the majority of the nation's working adults cannot make prudent choices about how to invest their savings.

This speaker assumes that prudent investing requires the ability to accurately define a somewhat obscure financial term. But prudence is not the same thing as expertise, and the speaker does not offer any evidence that this knowledge of this particular term is related to wise investing.

Percent versus Number/Rate versus Number

This flaw occurs when a speaker or author draws a conclusion about real quantities from evidence about rates or percentages, or vice versa. Example:

> At the end of last season, Camp SunnyDay laid off half of their senior counselors and a quarter of their junior counselors. Thus, Camp SunnyDay must have more senior counselors than junior counselors.

The problem, of course, is that we don't know how many senior and junior counselors were on staff before the layoffs. If there were a total of 4 senior counselors and 20 junior counselors, then the camp would have laid off only 2 senior counselors while dismissing 5 junior counselors.

Equivocation

This flaw occurs when a speaker or author uses the same word in two different and incompatible ways. Example:

> Our opponent in the race has accused our candidate's staff members of behaving unprofessionally. But that's not

fair. Our staff is made up entirely of volunteers, not paid campaign workers.

The speaker interprets the opponent's use of the word *professional* to mean "paid," but the opponent likely meant something more along the lines of "mature, competent, and businesslike."

Ad Hominem

This flaw occurs when a speaker or author concludes that another person's claim or argument is invalid because that other person has a personal flaw or shortcoming. One common pattern is for the speaker or author to claim the other person acts hypocritically or that the other person's claim is made from self-interest. Example:

> Mrs. Smithers testified before the city council, stating that the speed limits on the residential streets near her home are dangerously high. But why should we give her claim any credence? The way she eats and exercises, she's not even looking out for her own health.

The author attempts to undermine Mrs. Smithers's testimony by attacking her character and habits. He doesn't offer any evidence that is relevant to her claim about speed limits.

Part versus Whole

This flaw occurs when a speaker or author concludes that a part or individual has a certain characteristic because the whole or the larger group has that characteristic, or vice versa. Example:

> Patient: I should have no problems taking the three drugs prescribed to me by my doctors. I looked them up, and none of the three is listed as having any major side effects.

Here, the patient is assuming that what is true of each of the drugs individually will be true of them when taken together. The patient's flaw is overlooking possible interactions that could cause problems not present when the drugs are taken separately.

Circular Reasoning

This flaw occurs when a speaker or author tries to prove a conclusion with evidence that is logically equivalent to the conclusion. Example:

> All those who run for office are prevaricators. To   see this, just consider politicians: they all prevaricate.

Perhaps the author has tried to disguise the circular reasoning in this argument by exchanging the words "those who run for office" in the conclusion for "politicians" in the evidence, but all this argument amounts to is "Politicians prevaricate; therefore, politicians prevaricate." On the LSAT, circular

reasoning is very rarely the correct answer to a Flaw question, although it is regularly described in one of the wrong answers.

Question Strategies

Denial Test

A tactic for identifying the assumption *necessary* to an argument. When you negate an assumption necessary to an argument, the argument will fall apart. Negating an assumption that is not necessary to the argument will not invalidate the argument. Consider the following argument:

> Only high schools which produced a state champion athlete during the school year will be represented at the Governor's awards banquet. Therefore, McMurtry High School will be represented at the Governor's awards banquet.

Which one of the following is an assumption necessary to that argument?

> (1) McMurtry High School produced more state champion athletes than any other high school during the school year.

> (2) McMurtry High School produced at least one state champion athlete during the school year.

If you are at all confused about which of those two statements reflects the *necessary* assumption, negate them both.

> (1) McMurtry High School **did not produce more** state champion athletes than any other high school during the school year.

That does not invalidate the argument. McMurtry could still be represented at the Governor's banquet.

> (2) McMurtry High School **did not produce any** state champion athletes during the school year.

Here, negating the statement causes the argument to fall apart. Statement (2) is an assumption *necessary* to the argument.

Point at Issue "Decision Tree"

A tactic for evaluating the answer choices in Point at Issue questions. The correct answer is the only answer choice to which you can answer "Yes" to all three questions in the following diagram.

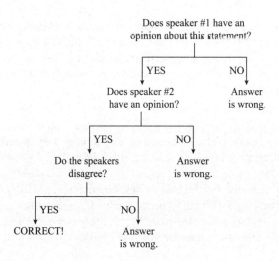

Common Methods of Argument

These methods of argument or argumentative strategies are common on the LSAT:

- Analogy, in which an author draws parallels between two unrelated (but purportedly similar) situations
- Example, in which an author cites a specific case or cases to justify a generalization
- Counterexample, in which an author seeks to discredit an opponent's argument by citing a specific case or cases that appear to invalidate the opponent's generalization
- Appeal to authority, in which an author cites an expert's claim or opinion as support for her conclusion
- Ad hominem attack, in which an author attacks her opponent's personal credibility rather than attacking the substance of her opponent's argument
- Elimination of alternatives, in which an author lists possibilities and discredits or rules out all but one
- Means/requirements, in which the author argues that something is needed to achieve a desired result

Wrong Answer Types in LR

Outside the Scope (Out of Scope; Beyond the Scope)

An answer choice containing a statement that is too broad, too narrow, or beyond the purview of the stimulus, making the statement in the choice irrelevant

180

An answer choice that directly contradicts what the correct answer must say (for example, a choice that strengthens the argument in a Weaken question)

Extreme

An answer choice containing language too emphatic to be supported by the stimulus; often (although not always) characterized by words such as *all*, *never*, *every*, *only*, or *most*

Distortion

An answer choice that mentions details from the stimulus but mangles or misstates what the author said about those details

Irrelevant Comparison

An answer choice that compares two items or attributes in a way not germane to the author's argument or statements

Half-Right/Half-Wrong

An answer choice that begins correctly, but then contradicts or distorts the passage in its second part; this wrong answer type is more common in Reading Comprehension than it is in Logical Reasoning

Faulty Use of Detail

An answer choice that accurately states something from the stimulus, but does so in a manner that answers the question incorrectly; this wrong answer type is more common in Reading Comprehension than it is in Logical Reasoning

Logic Games

Game Types

Strict Sequencing Game

A game that asks you to arrange entities into numbered positions or into a set schedule (usually hours or days). Strict Sequencing is, by far, the most common game type on the LSAT. In the typical Strict Sequencing game, there is a one-to-one matchup of entities and positions, e.g., seven entities to be placed in seven positions, one per position, or six entities to be placed over six consecutive days, one entity per day.

From time to time, the LSAT will offer Strict Sequencing with more entities than positions (e.g., seven entities to be arranged over five days, with some days to receive more than one entity) or more positions than entities (e.g., six entities to be scheduled over seven days, with at least one day to receive no entities).

Other, less common variations on Strict Sequencing include:

Double Sequencing, in which each entity is placed or scheduled two times (there have been rare occurrences of Triple or Quadruple Sequencing). Alternatively, a Double Sequencing game may involve two different sets of entities each sequenced once.

Circular Sequencing, in which entities are arranged around a table or in a circular arrangement (NOTE: When the positions in a Circular Sequencing game are numbered, the first and last positions are adjacent.)

Vertical Sequencing, in which the positions are numbered from top to bottom or from bottom to top (as in the floors of a building)

Loose Sequencing Game

A game that asks you to arrange or schedule entities in order but provides no numbering or naming of the positions. The rules in Loose Sequencing give only the relative positions (earlier or later, higher or lower) between two entities or among three entities. Loose Sequencing games almost always provide that there will be no ties between entities in the rank, order, or position they take.

Circular Sequencing Game

See Strict Sequencing Game.

Selection Game

A game that asks you to choose or include some entities from the initial list of entities and to reject or exclude others. Some Selection games provide overall limitations on the number of entities to be selected (e.g., "choose exactly four of seven students" or "choose at least two of six entrees") while others provide little or no restriction on the number selected ("choose at least one type of flower" or "select from among seven board members").

Distribution Game

A game that asks you to break up the initial list of entities into two, three, or (very rarely) four groups or teams. In the vast majority of Distribution games, each entity is assigned to one and only one group or team. A relatively common variation on Distribution games will provide a subdivided list of entities (e.g., eight students—four men and four women—will form three study groups) and will then require representatives from those subdivisions on each team (e.g., each study group will have at least one of the men on it).

Matching Game

A game that asks you to match one or more members of one set of entities to specific members of another set of entities, or that asks you to match attributes or objects to a set of entities. Unlike Distribution games, in which each entity is placed in exactly one group or team, Matching games usually permit you to assign the same attribute or object to more than one entity.

In some cases, there are overall limitations on the number of entities that can be matched (e.g., "In a school's wood shop, there are four workstations—numbered 1 through 4—and each workstation has at least one and at most three of the following tools—band saw, dremmel tool, electric sander, and power drill"). In almost all Matching games, further restrictions on the number of entities that can be matched to a particular person or place will be found in the rules (e.g., Workstation 4 will have more tools than Workstation 2 has).

Hybrid Game

A game that asks you to do two (or rarely, three) of the standard actions (Sequencing, Selection, Distribution, and Matching) to a set of entities.

The most common Hybrid is Sequencing-Matching. A typical Sequencing-Matching Hybrid game might ask you to schedule six speakers at a conference to six one-hour speaking slots (from 9 AM to 2 PM), and then assign each speaker one of two subjects (economic development or trade policy).

Nearly as common as Sequencing-Matching is Distribution-Sequencing. A typical game of this type might ask you to divide six people in a talent competition into either a Dance category or a Singing category, and then rank the competitors in each category.

It is most common to see one Hybrid game in each Logic Games section, although there have been tests with two Hybrid games and tests with none. To determine the type of Hybrid you are faced with, identify the game's action in Step 1 of the Logic Games Method. For example, a game asking you to choose four of six runners, and then assign the four chosen runners to lanes numbered 1 through 4 on a track, would be a Selection-Sequencing Hybrid game.

Mapping Game

A game that provides you with a description of geographical locations and, typically, of the connections among them. Mapping games often ask you to determine the shortest possible routes between two locations or to account for the number of connections required to travel from one location to another. This game type is extremely rare, and as of February 2017, a Mapping game was last seen on PrepTest 40 administered in June 2003.

Process Game

A game that opens with an initial arrangement of entities (e.g., a starting sequence or grouping) and provides rules that describe the processes through which that arrangement can be altered. The questions typically ask you for acceptable arrangements or placements of particular entities after one, two, or three stages in the process. Occasionally, a Process game question might provide information about the arrangement after one, two, or three stages in the process and ask you what must have happened in the earlier stages. This game type is extremely rare, and as of November 2016, a Process game was last seen on PrepTest 16 administered in September 1995. However, there was a Process game on PrepTest 80, administered in December 2016, thus ending a 20-year hiatus.

Game Setups and Deductions

Floater

An entity that is not restricted by any rule or limitation in the game

Blocks of Entities

Two or more entities that are required by rule to be adjacent or separated by a set number of spaces (Sequencing games), to be placed together in the same group (Distribution games), to be matched to the same entity (Matching games), or to be selected or rejected together (Selection games)

Limited Options

Rules or restrictions that force all of a game's acceptable arrangements into two (or occasionally three) patterns

Established Entities

An entity required by rule to be placed in one space or assigned to one particular group throughout the entire game

Number Restrictions

Rules or limitations affecting the number of entities that may be placed into a group or space throughout the game

Duplications

Two or more rules that restrict a common entity. Usually, these rules can be combined to reach additional deductions. For example, if you know that B is placed earlier than A in a sequence and that C is placed earlier than B in that sequence, you can deduce that C is placed earlier than A in the sequence

and that there is at least one space (the space occupied by B) between C and A.

Master Sketch

The final sketch derived from the game's setup, rules, and deductions. LSAT experts preserve the Master Sketch for reference as they work through the questions. The Master Sketch does not include any conditions from New-"If" question stems.

Logic Games Question Types

Acceptability Question

A question in which the correct answer is an acceptable arrangement of all the entities relative to the spaces, groups, or selection criteria in the game. Answer these by using the rules to eliminate answer choices that violate the rules.

Partial Acceptability Question

A question in which the correct answer is an acceptable arrangement of some of the entities relative to some of the spaces, groups, or selection criteria in the game, and in which the arrangement of entities not included in the answer choices could be acceptable to the spaces, groups, or selection criteria not explicitly shown in the answer choices. Answer these the same way you would answer Acceptability questions, by using the rules to eliminate answer choices that explicitly or implicitly violate the rules.

Must Be True/False; Could Be True/False Question

A question in which the correct answer must be true, could be true, could be false, or must be false (depending on the question stem), and in which no additional rules or conditions are provided by the question stem

New-"If" Question

A question in which the stem provides an additional rule, condition, or restriction (applicable only to that question), and then asks what must/could be true/false as a result. LSAT experts typically handle New-"If" questions by copying the Master Sketch, adding the new restriction to the copy, and working out any additional deductions available as a result of the new restriction before evaluating the answer choices.

Rule Substitution Question

A question in which the correct answer is a rule that would have an impact identical to one of the game's original rules on the entities in the game

Rule Change Question

A question in which the stem alters one of the original rules in the game, and then asks what must/could be true/false as a result. LSAT experts typically handle Rule Change questions by reconstructing the game's sketch, but now accounting for the changed rule in place of the original. These questions are rare on recent tests.

Rule Suspension Question

A question in which the stem indicates that you should ignore one of the original rules in the game, and then asks what must/could be true/false as a result. LSAT experts typically handle Rule Suspension questions by reconstructing the game's sketch, but now accounting for the absent rule. These questions are very rare.

Complete and Accurate List Question

A question in which the correct answer is a list of any and all entities that could acceptably appear in a particular space or group, or a list of any and all spaces or groups in which a particular entity could appear

Completely Determine Question

A question in which the correct answer is a condition that would result in exactly one acceptable arrangement for all of the entities in the game

Supply the "If" Question

A question in which the correct answer is a condition that would guarantee a particular result stipulated in the question stem

Minimum/Maximum Question

A question in which the correct answer is the number corresponding to the fewest or greatest number of entities that could be selected (Selection), placed into a particular group (Distribution), or matched to a particular entity (Matching). Often, Minimum/Maximum questions begin with New-"If" conditions.

Earliest/Latest Question

A question in which the correct answer is the earliest or latest position in which an entity may acceptably be placed. Often, Earliest/Latest questions begin with New-"If" conditions.

"How Many" Question

A question in which the correct answer is the exact number of entities that may acceptably be placed into a particular group

or space. Often, "How Many" questions begin with New-"If" conditions.

Reading Comprehension

Strategic Reading

Roadmap

The test taker's markup of the passage text in Step 1 (Read the Passage Strategically) of the Reading Comprehension Method. To create helpful Roadmaps, LSAT experts circle or underline Keywords in the passage text and jot down brief, helpful notes or paragraph summaries in the margin of their test booklets.

Keyword(s) in Reading Comprehension

Words in the passage text that reveal the passage structure or the author's point of view and thus help test takers anticipate and research the questions that accompany the passage. LSAT experts pay attention to six categories of Keywords in Reading Comprehension:

Emphasis/Opinion—words that signal that the author finds a detail noteworthy or that the author has positive or negative opinion about a detail; any subjective or evaluative language on the author's part (e.g., *especially, crucial, unfortunately, disappointing, I suggest, it seems likely*)

Contrast—words indicating that the author finds two details or ideas incompatible or that the two details illustrate conflicting points (e.g., *but, yet, despite, on the other hand*)

Logic—words that indicate an argument, either the author's or someone else's; these include both Evidence and Conclusion Keywords (e.g., *thus, therefore, because, it follows that*)

Illustration—words indicating an example offered to clarify or support another point (e.g., *for example, this shows, to illustrate*)

Sequence/Chronology—words showing steps in a process or developments over time (e.g., *traditionally, in the past, today, first, second, finally, earlier, subsequent*)

Continuation—words indicating that a subsequent example or detail supports the same point or illustrates the same idea as the previous example (e.g., *moreover, in addition, also, further, along the same lines*)

Margin Notes

The brief notes or paragraph summaries that the test taker jots down next to the passage in the margin of the test booklet

Big Picture Summaries: Topic/Scope/Purpose/Main Idea

A test taker's mental summary of the passage as a whole made during Step 1 (Read the Passage Strategically) of the Reading Comprehension Method. LSAT experts account for four aspects of the passage in their big picture summaries:

Topic—the overall subject of the passage

Scope—the particular aspect of the Topic that the author focuses on

Purpose—the author's reason or motive for writing the passage (express this as a verb; e.g., *to refute, to outline, to evaluate, to critique*)

Main Idea—the author's conclusion or overall takeaway; if the passage does not contain an explicit conclusion or thesis, you can combine the author's Scope and Purpose to get a good sense of the Main Idea.

Passage Types

Kaplan categorizes Reading Comprehension passages in two ways, by subject matter and by passage structure.

Subject matter categories

In the majority of LSAT Reading Comprehension sections, there is one passage from each of the following subject matter categories:

Humanities—topics from art, music, literature, philosophy, etc.

Natural Science—topics from biology, astronomy, paleontology, physics, etc.

Social Science—topics from anthropology, history, sociology, psychology, etc.

Law—topics from constitutional law, international law, legal education, jurisprudence, etc.

Passage structure categories

The majority of LSAT Reading Comprehension passages correspond to one of the following descriptions. The first categories—Theory/Perspective and Event/Phenomenon—have been the most common on recent LSATs.

Theory/Perspective—The passage focuses on a thinker's theory or perspective on some aspect of the Topic; typically (though not always), the author disagrees and critiques the thinker's perspective and/or defends his own perspective.

Event/Phenomenon—The passage focuses on an event, a breakthrough development, or a problem that has recently arisen; when a solution to the problem is proposed, the author most often agrees with the solution (and that represents the passage's Main Idea).

Biography—The passage discusses something about a notable person; the aspect of the person's life emphasized by the author reflects the Scope of the passage.

Debate—The passage outlines two opposing positions (neither of which is the author's) on some aspect of the Topic; the author may side with one of the positions, may remain neutral, or may critique both. (This structure has been relatively rare on recent LSATs.)

Comparative Reading

A pair of passages (labeled Passage A and Passage B) that stand in place of the typical single passage exactly one time in each Reading Comprehension section administered since June 2007. The paired Comparative Reading passages share the same Topic, but may have different Scopes and Purposes. On most LSAT tests, a majority of the questions accompanying Comparative Reading passages require the test taker to compare or contrast ideas or details from both passages.

Question Strategies

Research Clues

A reference in a Reading Comprehension question stem to a word, phrase, or detail in the passage text, or to a particular line number or paragraph in the passage. LSAT experts recognize five kinds of research clues:

Line Reference—An LSAT expert researches around the referenced lines, looking for Keywords that indicate why the referenced details were included or how they were used by the author.

Paragraph Reference—An LSAT expert consults her passage Roadmap to see the paragraph's Scope and Purpose.

Quoted Text (often accompanied by a line reference)—An LSAT expert checks the context of the quoted term or phrase, asking what the author meant by it in the passage.

Proper Nouns—An LSAT expert checks the context of the person, place, or thing in the passage, asking whether the author made a positive, negative, or neutral evaluation of it and why the author included it in the passage.

Content Clues—These are terms, concepts, or ideas from the passage mentioned in the question stem but not as direct quotes and not accompanied by line references. An LSAT expert knows that content clues almost always refer to something that the author emphasized or about which the author expressed an opinion.

Reading Comp Question Types

Global Question

A question that asks for the Main Idea of the passage or for the author's primary Purpose in writing the passage. Typical question stems:

Which one of the following most accurately expresses the main point of the passage?

The primary purpose of the passage is to

Detail Question

A question that asks what the passage explicitly states about a detail. Typical question stems:

According to the passage, some critics have criticized Gilliam's films on the grounds that

The passage states that one role of a municipality's comptroller in budget decisions by the city council is to

The author identifies which one of the following as a commonly held but false preconception?

The passage contains sufficient information to answer which of the following questions?

Occasionally, the test will ask for a correct answer that contains a detail *not* stated in the passage:

The author attributes each of the following positions to the Federalists EXCEPT:

Inference Question

A question that asks for a statement that follows from or is based on the passage but that is not necessarily stated explicitly in the passage. Some Inference questions contain research clues. The following are typical Inference question stems containing research clues:

Based on the passage, the author would be most likely to agree with which one of the following statements about unified field theory?

The passage suggests which one of the following about the behavior of migratory water fowl?

Given the information in the passage, to which one of the following would radiocarbon dating techniques likely be applicable?

Other Inference questions lack research clues in the question stem. They may be evaluated using the test taker's Big Picture Summaries, or the answer choices may make it clear that the test taker should research a particular part of the passage text. The following are typical Inference question stems containing research clues:

It can be inferred from the passage that the author would be most likely to agree that

Which one of the following statements is most strongly supported by the passage?

Other Reading Comprehension question types categorized as Inference questions are Author's Attitude questions and Vocabulary-in-Context questions.

Logic Function Question

A question that asks why the author included a particular detail or reference in the passage or how the author used a particular detail or reference. Typical question stems:

The author of the passage mentions declining inner-city populations in the paragraph most likely in order to

The author's discussion of Rimbaud's travels in the Mediterranean (lines 23–28) functions primarily to

Which one of the following best expresses the function of the third paragraph in the passage?

Logic Reasoning Question

A question that asks the test taker to apply Logical Reasoning skills in relation to a Reading Comprehension passage. Logic Reasoning questions often mirror Strengthen or Parallel Reasoning questions, and occasionally mirror Method of Argument or Principle questions. Typical question stems:

Which one of the following, if true, would most strengthen the claim made by the author in the last sentence of the passage (lines 51–55)?

Which one of the following pairs of proposals is most closely analogous to the pair of studies discussed in the passage?

Author's Attitude Question

A question that asks for the author's opinion or point of view on the subject discussed in the passage or on a detail mentioned in the passage. Since the correct answer may follow from the passage without being explicitly stated in it, some Author's Attitude questions are characterized as a subset of Inference questions. Typical question stems:

The author's attitude toward the use of DNA evidence in the appeals by convicted felons is most accurately described as

The author's stance regarding monetarist economic theories can most accurately be described as one of

Vocabulary-in-Context Question

A question that asks how the author uses a word or phrase within the context of the passage. The word or phrase in question is always one with multiple meanings. Since the correct answer follows from its use in the passage, Vocabulary-in-Context questions are characterized as a subset of Inference questions. Typical question stems:

Which one of the following is closest in meaning to the word "citation" as it used in the second paragraph of the passage (line 18)?

In context, the word "enlightenment" (line 24) refers to

Wrong Answer Types in RC

Outside the Scope (Out of Scope; Beyond the Scope)

An answer choice containing a statement that is too broad, too narrow, or beyond the purview of the passage

180

An answer choice that directly contradicts what the correct answer must say

Extreme

An answer choice containing language too emphatic (e.g., *all*, *never*, *every*, *none*) to be supported by the passage

Distortion

An answer choice that mentions details or ideas from the passage but mangles or misstates what the author said about those details or ideas

Faulty Use of Detail

An answer choice that accurately states something from the passage but in a manner that incorrectly answers the question

Half-Right/Half-Wrong

An answer choice in which one clause follows from the passage while another clause contradicts or deviates from the passage

Formal Logic Terms

Conditional Statement ("If"-Then Statement)

A statement containing a sufficient clause and a necessary clause. Conditional statements can be described in Formal Logic shorthand as:

If [*sufficient clause*]   → [*necessary clause*]

In some explanations, the LSAT expert may refer to the sufficient clause as the statement's "trigger" and to the necessary clause as the statement's result.

For more on how to interpret, describe, and use conditional statements on the LSAT, please refer to "A Note About Formal Logic on the LSAT" in this book's introduction.

Contrapositive

The conditional statement logically equivalent to another conditional statement formed by reversing the order of and negating the terms in the original conditional statement. For example, reversing and negating the terms in this statement:

If   A   →   B

results in its contrapositive:

If   ~B   →   ~A

To form the contrapositive of conditional statements in which either the sufficient clause or the necessary clause has more than one term, you must also change the conjunction *and* to *or*, or vice versa. For example, reversing and negating the terms and changing *and* to *or* in this statement:

If   M   →   O AND P

results in its contrapositive:

If   ~O OR ~P   →   ~M